THE MYRIAD FACES OF WAR

King George V

THE MYRIAD FACES OF WAR

Britain and the Great War, 1914–1918

TREVOR WILSON

POLITY PRESS

© Trevor Wilson 1986

First published 1986

Reprinted in paperback 1988 by
Polity Press, Cambridge, in association with Basil Blackwell, Oxford.

Editorial Office: Polity Press, Dales Brewery, Gwydir Street, Cambridge CB1 2LJ, UK.

Basil Blackwell Inc.
432 Park Avenue South, Suite 1505, New York, NY 100016, USA.

Basil Blackwell Ltd
108, Cowley Road, Oxford OX4 1JF, UK.

Library of Congress Cataloguing in Publication Data

Wilson, Trevor, 1928–
  The myriad faces of war.

  Includes index.
  1. World War, 1914–1918—Great Britain. 2. World
War, 1914–1918—Campaigns. 3. Great Britain—History—
George V, 1910–1936. I. Title.
D546.W52   1985   940.3'41   84–26439
ISBN 0-7456-0093-X
ISBN 0-7456-0645-8 Pbk

British Library Cataloguing in Publication Data

Wilson, Trevor
The myriad faces of war: Britain and the Great War 1914–1918.
1. World War, 1914–1918——Great Britain
1. Title
940.3'41 D546

ISBN 0-7456-0093-X
ISBN 0-7456-0645-8(Pbk)

Phototypeset by Gecko Limited, Bicester, Oxon.
Printed in Great Britain by TJ Press, Padstow

A man might rave against war; but war, from among its myriad faces, could always turn towards him one, which was his own.

F. E. Manning, The Middle Parts of Fortune *(London: Peter Davies, 1977), p. 182.*

For

Jane, Jenny, and Sara
and also for
Guy, Sean, Heidi, Oliver, and Mark

good companions

CONTENTS

Lord Kitchener, the secretary of state for war

Sir John French

Sir Douglas Haig

Successive commanders of the BEF

Sir John Jellicoe

Sir David Beatty

Successive commanders of the Grand Fleet

LIST OF MAPS

Sir Herbert Plumer

Sir William Birdwood

Sir Julian Byng

Sir Edmund Allenby

Four army commanders

PREFACE

During the writing of this book, I have been the occupant of an academic position at the University of Adelaide. Only that institution's commitment to the ideal of a community of scholars that knows no local or national boundaries has made this production possible. For the university's provision of study leave, research facilities, and – in an anxious period – relief from teaching responsibilities, I am indeed grateful. I should also like to acknowledge my particular debt, for both their encouragement and their patience, to my colleagues in the History department and especially to the successive occupants of the onerous post of departmental chairman.

In three periods of leave, including one of a whole year, I have received the hospitality of St John's College, Cambridge. Belonging to its fellowship has been an experience of the greatest value. I also wish to thank, for the periods of a term each during which I was their guest, the Research School of the Australian National University and the London School of Economics.

In preparing this book I have incurred a particular personal debt. Robin Prior has read all of this work, in many versions and on many occasions. In the course of so doing he has supplied me with more items of information than I have managed to acknowledge in the footnotes, and has brought to bear on the military and naval sections his unrivalled knowledge of the course and components of Great War battles on land and sea. His advice has saved this work from many defects and provided it with much wisdom.

For reading, and commenting upon, all or parts of this book I also thank with pleasure both John Grigg and F. B. Smith.

Among archivists and institutions which have aided this undertaking I must particularly acknowledge the assistance of Roderick Suddaby and the devoted staff of the Imperial War Museum, who both know the contents and value of the documents they hold and are eager to place their expertise at the service of scholars; the National Army Museum; the Bodleian Library; the Cambridge University Library; the Royal Artillery Institution Library, Woolwich; and the archive of Churchill College, Cambridge (particularly when it was presided over by Stephen Roskill). I also wish to acknowledge the assistance, in increasingly adverse financial circumstances, of the Barr Smith Library at the University of Adelaide.

There are many individuals who have aided me in this undertaking. Some of them (regretfully) I am bound to overlook, so many have been the years over which this work has been gestating. I am indebted (like so many of my Adelaide colleagues) to the resource, scholarly rigour, and academic versatility of the department's research assistant in London, Irene Cassidy. I should also like to thank the late Arthur Marder and the late Stephen Roskill for their advice on naval matters; Theo Barker and Ian McLean for seeking to guide me among the pitfalls of economic, and Bernard Waites of social, history; Henry Pelling for his discussions on issues political; Michael Howard for opening to me his command of the whole area of warfare; and John Terraine and Shelford Bidwell for offering enlightenment on intricate matters regarding guns and ammunition. And at the participant level my mother Beulah Wilson provided apt recollections of her girlhood in an Essex village during the Great War.

Finally I wish to thank Sara Wilson, who first counted the number of words; Oliver Daniel (Blaubell), who helped to sort the pages; and those other uplifters of my sometimes flagging spirits who figure in the dedication.

ACKNOWLEDGEMENTS

A version of chapter 17 of this book, 'Committee of inquiry', first appeared as an article in the *Journal of Contemporary History*, Vol.14, No.3, July 1979. I am grateful to the editor for permission to republish it here.

The following individuals and institutions have very kindly granted me permission to quote from documents and publications of which they hold the copyright. (I regret that in a few instances I have been unable to identify, or anyway establish contact with, copyright holders.)

Mr Francis Ashmead-Bartlett (correspondence of Ellis Ashmead-Bartlett).
Mr D. N. Allfree (memoirs of E.C. Allfree).
Mr Arthur Banks (maps from *A Military Atlas of the First World War* and *Douglas Haig: The Educated Soldier*).
Professor Quentin Bell (correspondence of Vanessa Bell).
Dr Alison Mackenzie, Mr David Oberlin-Harris (*per* Dr James Munson), and The Bodleian library (papers of the Reverend Andrew Clark).
The Honorable Mark Bonham Carter (correspondence of H. H. Asquith).
Mr Victor Bonham-Carter (papers of General Sir Charles Bonham-Carter).
C. & T. Publications and Mr Martin Gilbert (correspondence of Winston Churchill).
Lieutenant Colonel J. W. Chitty (papers of Geoffrey Coleridge Harper).
The Master, Fellows and Scholars of Churchill College in the University of Cambridge (papers of Lord Hankey).
J. M. Dent & Sons Ltd (excerpts from *Everyman At War* edited by C. B. Purdom).
Faber and Faber Publishers (excerpts from *Collected Poems 1909–1962* by T. S. Eliot, and *There's a Devil in the Drum* by John Lucy).
Bill Gammage (excerpts from his book *The Broken Years*).
Mr Martin Gilbert and George Weidenfeld and Nicholson Ltd (maps taken from *Recent History Atlas* and *First World War History Atlas*).
Harcourt Brace Jovanovich Inc (excerpts from *Collected Poems 1909–1962* by T. S. Eliot).
William Heinemann Ltd (excerpts from *The Middle Parts of Fortune* by F. E. Manning and *Sagittarius Rising* by Cecil Lewis both of which were first published by Peter Davies Ltd and reprinted by permission of William Heinemann Ltd).
David Higham Associates Ltd (excerpts from the *Collected Poems* of Herbert Read).
Major G. B. Horridge (papers of J. L. Horridge).
The Imperial War Museum (excerpts from *With a Machine-Gun to Cambrai* by George Coppard and quotations from the diary of Field-Marshal Sir Henry Wilson).
Lord Kennet (papers of his parents, E. Hilton Young, first Lord Kennet, and Lady Kathleen Scott).

Mr Peter Newbolt (extracts from 'Vitai Lampada' by Sir Henry Newbolt).

Wilfred Owen, Cecil Day Lewis and Chatto and Windus (excerpts from the poetry of Wilfred Owen).

Mr M. A. F. Rawlinson (papers of Lord Rawlinson of Trent).

Edgell Rickword and Carcanet Press Ltd (excerpts from *Behind the Eyes*, © the estate of Edgell Rickword).

George Sassoon (excerpts from the poetry of Siegfried Sassoon).

Mr Bertram J. Saunders (papers of Robert Saunders).

Mrs Anne Surfleet and Mrs Philippa Earp (memoirs of Arthur Surfleet).

Professor Albert E. Taylor (letters of Edgar Taylor).

Mr Michael Vyvyan (writings of R. H. Tawney).

Major Louis Yearsley (memoirs of P. M. Yearsley).

A note concerning the illustrations

All the illustrations in this book have been prepared for publication by Mr J. D. Tomlinson of the Advisory Centre at the University of Adelaide. His signal contribution to this undertaking is gratefully acknowledged.

The illustrations (apart from that on page 738, which reproduces the cover of a wartime pamphlet) are drawn from two sources.

i The caricatures of leading British figures on pages ii, x and xii are the work of the South Australian cartoonist John Chinner. They are here published for the first time, and are reproduced by kind permission of Mr Ken Chinner and Mrs Joan James.

ii The illustrations in the text are drawn from *The 'Manchester Guardian' History of the War* published in 9 volumes between 1915 and 1920. This invaluable source was drawn to my attention by Dr Frank Sear.

INTRODUCTION

This book seeks to describe Britain's experience in the war of 1914–18. In one sense its scope is limited. It sees the conflict from the standpoint of only one participating nation. So it pays meagre attention to the achievements and travails of Britain's allies. And it betrays little enthusiasm for the ambitions and doctrines of Germany's ruling elite.

In extenuation it may be said that this war – anyway in its major aspect – was a struggle between separate nations with their sometimes distinct systems of values. It is legitimate, therefore, to consider the war as an episode in one nation's history, as long as it is recognized that this is not seeing the war as a whole. More wide-ranging historians, certainly, will wish to present the war as a European (if not a world) experience. Even so, their accounts will in good measure constitute a blending and transmuting of various national histories.

In another sense the present work may be judged too wide-ranging. For an attempt is made to touch upon all major (and some pretty minor) aspects of Britain's involvement in the struggle. Is such an undertaking possible? Has not the discipline of history become so fractured into specialisms, employing distinct techniques of inquiry and exotic forms of language, that no place remains for the generalizer and the co-ordinator?

Often enough in preparing this work the writer has been tempted just to take the specialist historians at their word. Yet in the outcome he believes that he understands what he is saying, and has reached his judgements by considering the evidence and weighing the arguments. Hence this book rejects the notion that history is now the exclusive property of highly trained particularists. Rather, it reflects two convictions. One is that historians can still internalize the insights and evidence of colleagues well outside their own fields of specialization. The other is that historians are still able to transmit what they have learned to readers who are not trained historians; and to transmit it in the sense of informing, explaining, and convincing.

Whether in the present instance the endeavour has succeeded must be decided by others. If it has not, let it be hoped that this failure will be seen as springing from the shortcomings of the author, not from the hopelessness of the undertaking. For historians should not lightly abandon what have been two of the most beneficent aspects of their calling. One is that they practise a craft whose specialized discoveries are accessible to the whole profession. The other is that what they have to say is capable of being conveyed to responsive readers quite outside the ranks of qualified academics.

Is this book written from a particular standpoint? The answer may be more evident to the reader than the writer. For the latter has come to feel like a trench soldier under constant bombardment: not certain why he ever embarked on this matter, and

1

persisting in it only because, having got so far, it would be humiliating to give up before the end.

Yet some of the writer's attitudes remain discernible even to himself. One should be stated at the outset. In his view, Britain's involvement in the Great War was not some deplorable accident. Nor was it a malevolent deed clandestinely accomplished by home-grown plutocrats and diplomats. (This is not to say that such plutocrats and diplomats did not exist.) By the same token, the devoted prosecution of the war by vast numbers of Britons does not reveal them as deluded, irrational, and manipulated.

The outbreak of the war, in the judgement of this book, raised issues central to the life of the nation. The conflict was about preserving Britain as a major, and even as an independent, power, and about vindicating its liberal parliamentary system against the challenge of military autocracy. Certainly, British history in these years contains many manifestations of squalor, greed, and folly. Britain was fighting as a nation-state, and the unlovely face of nationalism often asserted itself among the populace. This provided rich openings for cheapjack politicians and sensation-loving press barons, who would have out-Kaisered the Kaiser if circumstances had given them half a chance. But other and worthier things, like national self-government and the viability of parliamentary democracy, were the central issues at stake in Britain's contest with Germany; and the world would have been a poorer place had these failed to surmount the challenge. Whether its impoverishment would have been so great as to justify the terrible losses sustained in preventing their overthrow is, of course, another matter. But that verdict must be left to the judgement of the reader.

Another aspect of this work deserves mention. Although human beings occupy the centre of its stage, their position is decidedly ambiguous. Quite often they appear to be less prime movers than helpless victims.

The Great War was in a large sense a contest of resources. Human beings, of course, constituted one important resource, in such forms as combatants, administrators, managers, labourers, and technicians. But their role in the contest sometimes seemed much less substantial than that of such other resources as technology, raw materials, the productive capacity of machines, and the killing power of weapons. The war of 1914–1918, particularly as it affected Britain and Germany, was the world's first conflict between advanced industrial states. It provided a graphic demonstration of the terrible powers for mutual destruction that industrialism had bestowed upon European man. That was one reason why the war proved so bewildering. Men like Lord Kitchener felt that they should be able to determine events on the battlefield. They found that war would be made in the forms that technology required. Kitchener's lament that this was not war, and that he did not know what to do about it, was but one expression of a general bafflement.

We become most aware of man as victim when we witness an event like the massacre of the British infantry on 1 July 1916. Nothing that human qualities such as valour or training or 'national character' might bring to bear could offset the terrible fury of high-explosive shells and machine-gun bullets. But if human helplessness appears particularly evident on such occasions, the argument offered here is that the situation was not all that different for those placed in positions of control. Shakespeare's words apply almost equally to the nation's leaders as to the 'poor bloody infantry':

> As flies to wanton boys, are we to the gods;
> They kill us for their sport.

Politicians and generals rarely recognized how limited were their powers of control. They denounced each other for trying to lose the war, or devised new courses by which it might be won. Yet the more the new men proposed different ways of proceeding, the more the war appeared determined to remain *la même chose*. Some historians, admittedly, reject this view. They believe the war could have been terminated swiftly and not too bloodily but for the stupidity of generals and the fecklessness of politicians. But this is to miss the essential tragedy of the war. Incompetent commanders and inconstant politicians there certainly were. But the difference they made was limited by the paucity of choices available to them.

The war did not drag on so long and so bloodily just because neither side managed to produce a Napoleon – that is, a decisive figure capable of transforming the military and political situation. For all we know, a Napoleon may have been there all along. But if so, he was a Napoleon in the Tolstoyan view of the first of that tribe: he did not command events but pursued the course which history had determined for him. The wealth that industrialism had made available for war-making, together with the stage reached by military technology, laid down that no masterstroke of strategy or weaponry would swiftly terminate this struggle. Only the grinding down of armies and peoples would eventually accomplish a conclusion.

Nevertheless, if the Great War seems to reduce humanity to ciphers, this book does not doubt that its proper subject is man – or, rather, men and women, in high estate and low, in handfuls and large masses, in political and social and military groupings. It seeks to avoid lapsing into Tolstoy's brand of determinism by discovering what contribution to shaping events could be made by exceptional individuals in high places, as well as by substantial groups drawn in to serve the common cause. It relates how vast military campaigns, whose course could scarcely be perceived by those commanding them, appeared to humble occupants of the firing line. It tries to see how the war impinged on particular classes and a particular sex and how it affected lives: extinguishing some, touching others scarcely at all, radically altering still others, and affecting most pretty nearly – at least for the duration and often for a good deal longer.

Plate 1   *Removing the emblems of Germany from the former German embassy in London.*

PART ONE

Going to War
August–December 1914

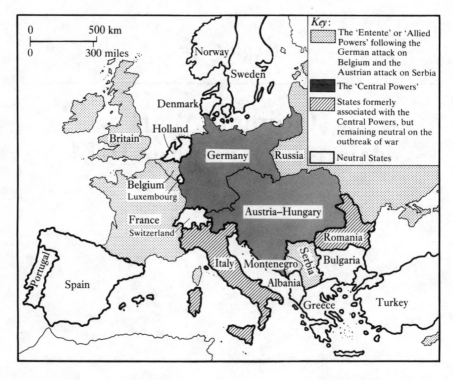

Map 1   *The European powers on 4 August 1914.* Source: *Martin Gilbert*, First World War Atlas *(London: Weidenfeld & Nicolson, 1970), p. 12.*

1

THE LIMITS OF ISOLATION

We are part of the community of Europe, and we must do our duty as such.

W. E. Gladstone, 10 April 1888

So long as no treaty obligation or true British interest is involved I am of your opinion that we should remain neutral. Balkan quarrels are no vital concern of ours . . . . But the march of events is sinister. The extension of the conflict by a German attack upon Franch or Belgium would raise other issues than those which now exist, and it would be wrong at this moment to pronounce finally one way or the other as to our duty or our interests.

Winston Churchill to Arthur Ponsonby, 31 July 1914

This war is life and death.

G. M. Trevelyan to Charles Trevelyan, c. August 1914

I

During the first six months of 1914 a group of high-minded Englishmen were making plans to celebrate, in the following year, an important centenary: 18 June 1915 would be the hundredth anniversary of the Battle of Waterloo. Yet what those people intended to honour was not that victory but the absence of a successor. By 1915 it would be 100 years since a British army had drawn blood in Western Europe. The object of celebration was the approaching century of peace.

British foreign policy in the years 1900 to 1914 has many interesting aspects: the treaty with Japan, relations with Turkey, intervention in Persia. But all are over-shadowed by one great problem. Why did that celebration never take place? Why did a nation that for so long had managed to remain seemingly detached from the affairs of Europe now decide to participate in a great and terrible European war?

This question can be answered on many levels. Some of them overlap and illuminate each other; others are not only unrelated but mutually exclusive. One type of answer looks for a solution not in the conscious decisions of statesmen and diplomats but in what are seen as those vital forces within a society that carry politicians and administrators before them. In the view of Barbara Tuchman: 'The diplomatic origins, so-called, of the Great War are only the fever chart of the patient; they do not tell us what caused the fever. To probe for underlying causes and deeper forces one must operate within the framework of a whole society and try to discover what moved the people in it.'[1]

One such account of 'underlying causes and deeper forces' is the Marxist-Leninist view that Britain was forced to war with Germany by the logic of capitalism. Industrial capitalism, of which Britain was the pioneer but no longer the unchallenged leader, contained internal contradictions that doomed it to destruction. In an attempt to escape

[1] Barbara Tuchman, *The Proud Tower* (London: Hamish Hamilton, 1966), Foreword.

7

these contradictions Britain was obliged to expand into, and exploit, the undeveloped parts of the world. These 'colonial' areas were not merely useful adjuncts to the system; they were the vital safety valves whereby the intolerable pressures within society were exported overseas. But such safety valves could not be available for ever. Other developing capitalist countries, such as Germany, equally required their outlets, and the number of these was limited. As the rivalry to acquire them grew more frenzied and deadly, an international explosion became inescapable. The nature of British capitalism, in short, was the reason why Britain went to war. The rulers of the country may have believed otherwise. They may have thought that they were acting to preserve the sanctity of treaties or the balance of power. The truth was that they were the instruments of profound and irresistible drives within the economic system.

Profound and irresistible drives are the basis of another sort of explanation for Britain's plunge into war. This view sees the war as springing from a malaise of the human spirit, from a breakdown of established modes of thought about relations within and between communities. In Britain this breakdown manifested itself in violent conduct by a number of sections that hitherto had advocated their causes, and endured their setbacks, in an orderly fashion. The acceptance of class-war doctrines by part of the labour movement, the subversive utterances of prominent Conservatives over the application of Home Rule to Ulster, and – most startling (as coming from so unexpected a quarter) – the conduct of the suffragettes in both committing acts of violence and courting violent retaliation, all provide evidence of this malaise. In the fields of culture and the arts Britain was not able to match the Continent, where really alarming assaults were being made upon established forms of harmony, expression, and pictorial representation. But if Britain had no Schönberg, Picasso, or Diaghilev, it may be claimed that the same retreat from settled values and known ways was reflected in the disturbing opening section of Gustav Holst's *Planets Suite*, in the profound questioning of liberal values encountered in E. M. Forster's *Howards End*, and even in the attack upon accepted modes of speech delivered in Bernard Shaw's play *Pygmalion*. Is it fanciful to observe that within weeks of the expression 'not bloody likely' first being uttered as part of the script by a reputable playwright in a respectable London theatre, Englishmen up and down the country were leaping to arms?

For anyone who has become surfeited with studying the diplomatic origins of Britain's involvement in the war, views such as the foregoing seem altogether more profound and satisfying. They take us beneath the surface minutiae into the broader context within which diplomats functioned. In the traditional terminology, they replace short-term by long-term explanations.

But there is a problem with long-term or 'depth' explanations: that of deciding what is their precise relationship with the events they are supposedly accounting for. What confidence have we that they are not mythical constructs emanating from the mind of the historian? For example, in the case of the Marxist-Leninist version of events there seem few compelling reasons for regarding Britain's overseas contests with Germany as the key that unlocks the door to the puzzle. It is plain that these contests harmed Anglo-German relations. But it would seem that imperial rivalry did much more damage to Britain's relations with Russia (hardly a country in the most advanced state of capitalism) and also with France, until it was decided that mutual concession was more profitable than confrontation. If appearances are anything to go by, Britain in 1914 was capable of ironing out its colonial differences with Germany as long as these were the only cause of contention between them. The Marxist case cannot depend on weighing the importance of the imperialist issue against other factors imperilling Anglo-German relations. It can only express the conviction that the British economy represented capitalism at its highest stage and that therefore its imperialist drives must be out of hand. Such an analysis is capable of no certain demonstration by reference either to what people believed at the time or to what has happened since.

There is a further difficulty. What is the supposed relation, in this case, between what Barbara Tuchman describes as the fever chart (diplomacy) and the fever (underlying causes)? How did the hypothetical crisis state of British capitalism transmit itself to the actions of statesmen like Sir Edward Grey and diplomats like Sir Eyre Crowe, who appeared to be ignorant of what was causing their actions? Are we to regard Grey, if not as a puppet on a string, then as the mercury in the thermometer, rising and falling in accord with the condition of the patient and finally bursting forth through the top of the glass? Or should we see him as a family physician who had contracted his patient's malady, so that though still capable of delivering a coherent – albeit erroneous – diagnosis, he was actually demented? These are not frivolous questions. At some point the connection must be established between the underlying causes that are being hypothesized and the actual conduct of diplomats and politicians. In the case of the Marxist hypothesis, this has yet to be accomplished.

Similar difficulties are encountered with the other explanation that has been put forward: that foreign policy is vitally connected with such phenomena as protest movements in politics and society and the rejection of accepted norms in the fields of art and music. The historian has no grounds for assuming that discord in musical harmony, improper language in the theatre, the fracturing of the image by painters, and the querying of liberal values by novelists are evidence of a society in dissolution. They may be evidence of a creative response to new challenges and opportunities. The historian is not sure, for that matter, whether these events have much at all to do with the mainstream of community life – let alone its attitudes to foreign powers. Certainly, we must take note that these interesting events were occurring. But we must also admit that if the creative or destructive (even if we knew which) agonies of artists have a connection with the conduct of governments in international crises, they have not been established.

Much the same must be said regarding the possible connection between disturbances within British society in the years 1910 to 1914 and the fact that Britain went to war in the latter year. If we did not know that such a war broke out, it would not be outrageous to argue that British society was equipped to withstand the shocks of female agitators, intransigent trade unionists, and even Curragh mutineers, without seeking salvation in international conflict. There were even perceptive observers who thought that a war, which was expected to produce economic dislocation and mass unemployment, would exacerbate rather than solve the country's internal difficulties. And again we must insist on knowing the direct relation between the fever and the fever chart. What is such an hypothesis telling us about the actual conduct and motivation of Britain's leaders? Asquith, Grey, and some other members of the Liberal Government have been strongly criticized for their conduct of foreign affairs. Yet no one has managed to picture them as surveying the disturbed state of Ireland and the reckless actions of the Conservative leaders and deciding that a war with Germany was the only solution. The furthest any historian has gone is to hint that, subconsciously, Asquith may have been guided by Britain's internal troubles towards welcoming an international conflict. Such hints (apart from their total want of supporting evidence) leave a great deal unexplained: for example, the apparent lack of any connection between Asquith's supposed unconscious inclination towards war and the train of events on the Continent, whereby armies were being mobilized and frontiers violated.

Anyway, before trying to assess such insubstantial notions it is worth noting one point. All the forms of upheaval that were reputedly racking British society in 1914 had developed in the previous five or six years. Yet Grey's approach to foreign affairs changed not one whit during the years 1905 to 1914 – except that he seemed more prepared to sit down with Germany at the conference table after the Moroccan crisis of 1911 than before it. His response to the crisis of 1914 was no more bellicose that his reaction to the crisis of 1905. The considerations that moved him in the one case moved him equally in the other. Given so even and so regular a reading of the temperature chart, what need have we to postulate that in 1914, unlike 1905, there was a fever raging beneath?[2]

II

This is not to say that the types of explanation looked at so far may be wholly set aside, on the grounds that they do not offer watertight accounts of why Britain entered the war. With all their shortcomings, they do remind us that in trying to provide such an account we must keep in mind the wider context. The diplomatic documents will give an incomplete picture, not only of what was in the mind of the public at large but even of what was in the minds of the diplomats. For they will omit what James Joll calls 'the unspoken assumptions'.[3] These were convictions and attitudes that, though they may have passed from our frame of reference, were so much part of the thinking of an earlier time that they 'went without saying'.

It is here that the actions of suffragettes and Ulstermen are illuminating. For they reveal the readiness of some protagonists of the women's vote and some enemies of Home Rule to disregard legality and instead resort to force. In these circumstances it is necessary to ask how British statesmen, and the British people, felt about the use of force generally. Today war, particularly against a major power, is widely regarded as a thoroughly undesirable proceeding, to be employed only as a last resort when mere survival is at stake. Was this the attitude of Englishmen before 1914? Or did they see war as something of a mixed blessing, involving some social distress and individual unhappiness but providing distinct benefits also: such as enhanced national security, territorial aggrandizement, a strengthening of the social fabric, a renewed pride in the nation and its institutions, an entrenching of the traditional order?

Clearly, the attitude of Englishmen to war before 1914 could not be the same as that after it. Some prior to the conflict may have speculated on the horrors of war between industrialized communities. But that is not the same thing as experiencing the carnage of the Somme, undergoing a foretaste of aerial bombardment on civilians, and learning how disappointing may be the fruits of a dearly bought victory. All this knowledge has not prevented individuals and even Governments in modern Britain from seeing war as an acceptable proceeding – witness the Suez crisis of 1956 and the Falklands campaign of 1982. Without such knowledge war was bound to be considered more widely then than now a tolerable means of safeguarding, and even of advancing, a country's international concerns.

Sometimes war was spoken of as if it constituted a positive good. 'I *adore* War', wrote the young Julian Grenfell in October 1914. 'It is like a big picnic without the objectlessness of a picnic.'[4] And a poet-member of his generation, welcoming the conflict, thanked God, who had 'matched us with His hour, And caught our youth, and

---

[2] There was, it may be remarked, a decided difference in the conduct of one key member of the Liberal Government in the crisis of 1914 as against the crisis of 1911. In 1914 David Lloyd George paid no visit to the Mansion House and came under no attack as a war-monger.

[3] James Joll, *1914: The Unspoken Assumptions* (London: Weidenfeld & Nicolson, 1968).

[4] Quoted in Bernard Bergonzi, *Heroes' Twilight* (London: Constable, 1965), p. 47.

wakened us from sleeping' and had rescued the poet from 'a world grown old and cold and weary'.[5] This enthusiasm for war immediately after its outbreak had its counterparts in the pre-war mind. A statement in 1908 by the Conservative leader in the Upper House (and former Foreign Secretary), Lord Lansdowne, has a particular interest because of the effect that two years of actual war were soon to have on him. Lansdowne was speaking in the debate on the first old-age pensions legislation, a measure providing pensions of 5 shillings a week to persons aged 70 years and over, as long as their total income did not exceed £21 per year. He deplored the measure on the grounds that it would cost as much as a great war and would be without a war's advantages, since 'a war has at any rate the effect of raising the moral fibre of the nation, whereas this measure, I am much afraid, will weaken the moral fibre of the nation and diminish the self-respect of the people.'[6] That this remark, with its wild miscalculations regarding the financial and personal consequences of a war, could be offered in all seriousness shows that grave misapprehensions were current about the nature of modern wars.

For Lansdowne was not alone in his delusions. His audience in the House of Lords would respond readily to the view that conflict enhanced 'moral fibre'. It was part of the Darwinian ethos of the age, expressed by the imperialist Lord Milner when he stated that 'competition between nations' was 'the law of human progress', 'the Divine Order of the World'.[7] Even more, it was part of the inherent dogma of the great public schools that Lansdowne's audience would have attended in their youth. In those repositories of Spartan living, unquestioned hierarchy, competitive games, and organized bullying, what was understood by moral fibre was a combination of qualities that reached their apotheosis on the field of battle. These were not the qualities of sensitivity and piety, or a readiness to challenge established authority and accepted standards, or an aspiration to uplift the downtrodden and to bring together separated nations. Rather, they were such attitudes as obedience to authority, devotion to king and country, certitude in the superiority of one's class and nation, fortitude in the face of hardship, responsibility to those under one's direction, and concern for 'manliness':

> The sand of the desert is sodden red –
> Red with the wreck of a square that broke; –
> The Gatling's jammed and the Colonel dead,
> And the regiment blind with dust and smoke,
> The river of death has brimmed his banks,
> And England's far, and Honour a name,
> But the voice of the schoolboy rallies the ranks:
> 'Play up! play up! and play the game!'[8]

Such attitudes were not the monopoly of those who had been educated at the great public schools. In a less concentrated form they constituted much of the nation's feeling about personal and international conduct. The more educated could express them in the rolling periods of Lord Rosebery, the Liberal imperialist who for a time had actually headed the Liberal Party and who said in 1893, regarding the acquisition of further territories: 'We have to consider not what we want now but what we shall want in the future . . . . we have to remember that it is part of our responsibility and heritage to take care that the world, so far as it can be moulded by us, shall receive an

---

[5] Rupert Brooke, *Peace*, quoted in ibid., p. 42.
[6] Quoted in E. T. Raymond, *Mr. Lloyd George* (London: Collins, 1922), p. 108. Raymond's comment on this utterance – 'How Lord Lansdowne's own moral fibre was raised by war is a matter of history' – is unjust. It required great courage for a man in Lansdowne's position to withstand in 1917 the doctrine of war *à outrance*.
[7] Quoted in Joll, *1914: The Unspoken Assumptions*, p. 19.
[8] Henry Newbolt, 'Vitaï Lampada' (The Torch of Life).

English-speaking complexion, and not that of other nations.' Englishmen, he went on, must consider 'the future of the race, of which we are at present the trustees'.[9]

For the less educated, the same views could more easily be expressed in popular novels, such as Erskine Childers's *Riddle of the Sands*; or in stirring songs like 'Rule Britannia' and 'Land of Hope and Glory', the latter with its rousing finale:

> Wider still and wider shall thy bounds be set;
> God who made thee mighty, make thee mightier yet.

Among popular writers and speakers and songsters of the time all these convictions – about national superiority, about competition between nations as the divine order of the world, about war as the breeder of moral fibre and the weeder-out of the morally inferior – existed in a jumbled mish-mash whose emotional power was not lessened by its frequent lack of coherence.

Yet after all this has been said, two large questions remain unanswered. Granted that national egoism, popularized Darwinism, and the cult of 'moral fibre' were noteworthy forces in English thinking before 1914, were they so powerful as to drive Englishmen into war when the survival of themselves and their values was not in jeopardy? And had the contrary forces within the country, those convictions that regarded war as undesirable and even disreputable, been so overcome that a British Government would rush to arms in the absence of any compelling external challenge?

The first of these questions focuses attention on a consideration that historians forget at their peril. The answer they arrive at to any historical problem will be determined in part by the question they ask. So far we have been considering proposed solutions to the problem: Why did Britain go to war in 1914? It is a standard question, and yet in a sense it is quite unwarranted. For it has never been shown that Britain in 1914 was like a hunter in quest of a prey, seeking war without much regard to the identity of the antagonist. The only question that can properly be asked is: Why did Britain go to war *with Germany* in 1914? And once the problem has been so restricted, it becomes difficult to concentrate attention on suffragette outrage and Ulster intransigence, or even on national egoism and social Darwinism, as forces in English life. As dynamos for driving Britain into war against France or the USA, against Italy or even Austria–Hungary, they seem too feeble to merit consideration. And it is difficult to believe that they would not have remained so in the case of every power, had not one power presented a most tangible menace – in the forms of a hostile fleet and a potentially vanquished Western Europe.

This brings us to the second question: Had those forces within Britain working against war become so enfeebled that the nation would leap to arms even when its survival was subject to no external challenge? This is a question rarely asked, and for an obvious reason. It is difficult, in seeking to explain why a country went to war, to do justice to those forces guiding it in the opposite direction. Yet an historian who did not know what happened after 31 July 1914 could adduce powerful reasons for concluding that Britain was unlikely to have entered a Russo-German war. For one thing, the voice of national egoism and imperial grandeur did not sound an unfaltering note. Even the prime poet of empire, Rudyard Kipling, was moved on the occasion of the Diamond Jubilee celebrations in 1897 to recall that he also owed some allegiance to the gospel of the Prince of Peace:

> The tumult and the shouting dies;
> The Captains and the Kings depart:
> Still stands Thine ancient sacrifice,

---

[9] Quoted in Max Beloff, *Britain's Liberal Empire 1897–1921* (London: Methuen and Co., 1969), p. 40.

> An humble and a contrite heart . . . .
> Far-called our navies melt away;
> On dune and headland sinks the fire:
> Lo, all our pomp of yesterday
> Is one with Nineveh and Tyre![10]

As R. B. McCallum aptly says of this poem: 'Even if it be considered as the most grotesque and shallow essay in humility that literary records disclose, the fact remains that it was written; it is to be found in hymn-books even now.' (He was writing in 1951.)[11]

Britain was not a military or, more important, a militaristic power. It saw its strength as resting in its navy. The population neither felt veneration for a military caste nor regarded its army leaders as entitled to a weighty voice in internal or international policy. This point was powerfully made in a First World War pamphlet called *The Truth About England* written by the educationist (and later Foreign Office official) J. W. Headlam. Its author, in common with most wartime pamphleteers, was more interested in some aspects of the truth about England than in others. Yet his portrait, if overdrawn, highlights facts of English life that ought not to be omitted from any discussion of war origins. Of the years immediately preceding 1914 he wrote:

> To us in England militarism was a completely unknown thing. It is not so much that it was disliked or dreaded, but it was non-existent . . . . To this the education of the people, in religion and politics alike, had contributed; England is at heart still Puritan and their Puritanism has taken from its founders all except the army which Cromwell built up. Among the quiet, sober working classes living a life in many ways so aloof, so self-centred, this you would always have found in the past that parents, father and mother alike, would never willingly allow a son to enter the army. The religious communities which provide so much of their intellectual as well as their spiritual nurture . . . were sternly opposed to the practice of war and to the profession of arms. And on the political side their whole energies and ideas have been directed towards the struggle to win for themselves better conditions of life.

The army, in Headlam's view,

> has belonged, as it were, to certain social classes; the rich, the aristocratic, the professional and the very poor; the great middle class and the well-to-do among the working men (and under modern conditions it is between these that the centre of gravity of the community lies) have had little part in it; to them the army has been something unknown; they had no interest in its life and traditions.[12]

One may be tempted to ask what qualifications the author of these words (son of a canon of the Established Church, educated at Eton and Cambridge and Berlin, and a professor of Greek by the age of 30) possessed to describe the attitudes of 'the quiet, sober working classes' towards the army. Nevertheless, there is much evidence in support of his view. Thus when William Robertson – the distinguished 'Wully' Robertson who was to work his way up from private soldier to Chief of the Imperial General Staff – at the age of 19 informed his parents, who were poor but respectable village tailors, that he intended to join the army, they were appalled. 'I would rather bury you than see you in a red coat,' was the response of his mother.

Much in Britain's history had caused it to be firmly anti-militarist. Geography had

---

[10] Rudyard Kipling, 'Recessional'.

[11] E. Halévy, *A History of the English People in the Nineteenth Century*, with a supplementary section by R. B. McCallum (London: Ernest Benn, 1961) vol. 4, p. 428.

[12] J. W. Headlam, *The Truth About England Exposed in a Letter to a Neutral* (London: Thomas Nelson, 1915). Headlam in 1918 adopted the name Headlam-Morley. Before the war he was an academic and then an inspector of schools. After 1914 he became an important figure in the British Foreign Office.

decided that, as long as its navy controlled the English Channel, the country could not be subject to a lightning military assault. It lived under a political system which stemmed from the sixteenth- and seventeenth-century struggles against an authoritarian Church and an absolute monarchy, the latter an institution whose last resort had proved to be a standing army. It viewed with unconcealed pride the peculiar features of British society that had emerged from those venerated struggles: liberty of the individual; representative institutions; decentralization of authority; toleration of dissent; adherence to a religious faith founded not on ecclesiastical authority but on the translucent certainties of Holy Scripture; and, in more mundane but still uplifting fields, commercial enterprise, limited taxation, and unparalleled industrial innovation and expansion.

These features of English life helped to shape not only the country's internal development but also its role in international affairs. For a good part of the nineteenth century Britain had pretensions to being the greatest power in the world. Its supremacy at sea, its burgeoning overseas empire, and its awesome industrial, commerical, and financial growth gave it the opportunity to become, like Louis XIV's France or Kaiser Wilhelm's Germany, an international menace, demanding the obeisance of other European powers and so driving them to unite against it. Nothing of the sort happened. If historians do not ask why, that is because they are functioning within the same frame of reference as the people they are writing about. They find it difficult to imagine what useful purpose could be served by requiring the humiliation of other powers and so courting their enmity. In terms of a people taking its satisfaction from the sanctity of liberal values and boundless economic development, the answer is none. But not all countries, or anyway their rulers, have found such qualities to be satisfaction enough – or, sometimes, to be satisfying at all.

The absence of a militarist tradition and the presence of a strong devotion to liberal, Protestant values had not saved Britain from periodic phases of international recklessness. 'Send a gunboat', 'We don't want to fight, but, by jingo if we do . . . .', the Crimea, Afghanistan, Khartoum, and Mafeking are sufficient reminders of that. Yet – for a major power in the time of its greatest potential for provoking international confrontations – the record of conflicts avoided, of arbitration agreed to, and of crises that never came to a showdown remains impressive. The failure of nineteenth-century Britain to call into being against itself an effective coalition of hostile European powers is a major historical event.

Nor is it true that in the first decade and a half of the twentieth century the voices speaking against war had fallen silent or were going unheeded. In 1909 a newspaper manager and journalist (who had in his time been a rancher and prospector in the western part of the USA) published a book called *Europe's Optical Illusion*. His name was Norman Angell. The book reappeared a year later under a title that speedily became famous: *The Great Illusion*. Angell's work was a tract against war. Its novelty lay in the fact that it grounded the anti-war case not on morality but on profitability. Angell claimed that the opponents of war let the side down by conceding that war was sometimes lucrative, while condemning it as an affront against morality. War, he asserted, yielded and could yield no profit. In times past, when rulers possessed a certain amount of portable wealth, it may have been possible for a successful invader to annex it. The growth of an economy based on commerce and industry had changed all that. Wealth had become individual and international, not national. Consequently, one nation could not annex the property of another because it possessed none. The development of industrial capitalism, far from contributing to the necessity for war, had removed its prime objective: the acquisition of loot. Yet, Angell insisted, this blinding truth was passing unrecognized, and so the menace of war was not receding. Governments and peoples were still held in the thrall of the great illusion, which was that wars could be waged to material advantage.

The validity of Angell's thesis need not detain us. What is important is its enormous popularity. Angell could proudly inform the readers of *Who's Who* that his work had appeared throughout Europe, America, and Asia, and had been translated into (among other languages) Hindi, Bengali, Urdu, Marathi, and Tamil. His readership in Britain was extensive. J. W. Headlam, in the wartime pamphlet cited earlier, wrote:

> Had you gone during the winter of 1913 to some quiet country town, some working-man's club, you would have found them forming groups to consider and discuss [Norman Angell's] teaching. They had always believed that war was wrong, and now they were told it was foolish; they drew the conclusion that it was impossible. It ceased to interest them, it was no longer important. A nation which deliberately went to war would be committing not only a crime but a blunder, and who could believe that in the twentieth century this was possible?

This passage would be more convincing if its author had admitted that these same working men probably provided part of the readership of the *Daily Mail*, with its constant raging against the menace of Germany, and of sensationalist novels retailing the invasion of Britain by an unnamed north European power. Yet it is important to recognize that the *Daily Mail* and the scare story were not for such people the only sources of information and opinion; that on war's eve they were responding to a powerful force of argument and conviction which was directing the public mind not towards war but away from it.

III

The object of the discussion so far has been to inquire whether we can account for Britain's involvement in war in 1914 simply by reference to internal factors; whether, that is, the pressure of economic or psychological or political forces within the country drove it to seek release by engaging in conflict overseas. No such case has been established. It may be true that delusions current in 1914 about the nature of war and its supposed ennobling qualities help to explain why the British Government, in considering the issue of involvement, did not have to ponder whether Englishmen would refuse to go to war whatever the circumstances. Ministers were confident (as, arguably, in the 1930s they could not be) that the people of Britain would accept and even embrace war when the grounds for it seemed sufficient. But – and this needs to be stressed – it does not follow that such delusions about the nature of war inspired either Government or people to embark on war when no sufficient grounds were offering. Rupert Brooke and Julian Grenfell wrote their words in response to the rape of Belgium, and Lansdowne's pre-war utterance was primarily concerned not with battle but with old-age pensions.

The conclusion seems irresistible that, whatever part internal factors may have played in causing the British government to prove less averse to the prospect of war in 1914 than it would in 1938 – when, in the somewhat crude expression of the time, Britain's Prime Minister turned all four cheeks to the enemy – we must look beyond Britain to understand why such a prospect existed.[13]

---

[13] Even the contrast between the response to war in 1914 and that in 1938 is suggestive only. Englishmen in 1914 were not much more enthusiastic about being embroiled in a conflict that started in Eastern Europe *and could be kept there* than was the case in the 1930s. If May 1940 be thought the truer parallel to August 1914, then of course there is no contrast in Englishmen's response that needs accounting for. Certainly, historians have not felt it necessary to hypothesize the existence of a psychological malaise in order to explain Britain's involvement in the second Battle of France. And the deplorable machinations of British capitalism in 1938 seem to lie not in its enthusiasm for war but in its refusal to engage in one.

For this purpose, it is essential to comprehend the nature of Britain's relationship with the continent of Europe before and during the century of peace. What those relations were in the nineteenth century has been somewhat concealed by the seeming devotion of British statesmen to the acquisition and retention of an empire, not a concern for events in Europe. This appearance is misleading. The empire bestowed great benefits, economic and emotional, on Englishmen. Yet Englishmen were pretty grudging in the efforts they were prepared to make on its behalf. They were imperialists on the cheap – vastly pleased to possess an empire as long as it did not prove an expense or an embarrassment, but little anxious to maintain it when it began to drain their resources or lower their international standing. The opinion of the imperialist W. S. Blunt in 1913 could be applied to almost any phase of Britain's imperial greatness: 'No country in Europe is less inclined than ours to the sacrifice demanded by the needs of an overgrown Empire. . . . The English nation is already overburdened with its dependencies and though everyone talks the language of Imperialism, the will to defend the Empire is altogether lacking.'[14] From this point of view, as Max Beloff suggests, the most prophetic of Kipling's poems of empire was not 'Recessional' but one that had appeared three years earlier in *The Jungle Book*:

> Here we sit in a branchy row,
> Thinking of beautiful things we know;
> Dreaming of deeds that we mean to do,
> All complete in a minute or two –
> Something noble and grand and good,
> Won by merely wishing we could.[15]

Britain's response to challenges from Western Europe was made of sterner stuff than this. For the simple fact was that its concerns in Europe were altogether more permanent and profound. Even had Britain possessed no material interests in the Continent (and as a market for British goods European nations – Germany not least among them – provided a considerable interest), Englishmen could not ignore what happened there. For although events outside Europe might affect Englishmen's pride or pockets, only from Western Europe could come a threat to Britain's very survival. As Kenneth Bourne points out, Britain's island position sheltered her from the Continent, but it did no more than that; it did not *isolate* her.

> The consolidation of Europe under one potentially hostile régime was rightly considered fatal to Britain's political, economic, and strategic security. In that event she would risk being shut out of one of her richest markets, faced with an antagonistic political system, and menaced simultaneously from an overwhelming number of offensive bases. To counter this awful possibility it was essential for Britain to have an auxiliary on the mainland to complement the offshore strength of the Royal Navy.[16]

English statesmen in the age of splendid isolation were not unaware of their country's vulnerability. What was lacking was any actual threat. In the mid-nineteenth century there simply was no power capable of bringing Western Europe under its sway, thereby depriving Britain of its markets on the Continent, facing it with a hostile political system, and menacing it with an overwhelming number of offensive bases. After 1815 France was in decline, Germany divided and economically under-developed, Russia remote and incompetently governed. Continental Europe had developed an internal balance of power that did not require Britain's weight in either scale to keep the balance even and hold a potentially dominant nation in check. It was

---

[14] Quoted in Max Beloff, *Britain's Liberal Empire*, p. 142.
[15] Ibid., p. 22.
[16] Kenneth Bourne, *The Foreign Policy of Victorian England 1830–1902* (Oxford: Clarendon Press, 1970), pp. 7–8.

in this unusual situation that Britain could indulge in the luxury of appearing to stand aloof from the affairs of the Continent.

After 1870 this situation ceased to obtain. The emergence of a united Germany, directed by the ruler of Prussia, welded together by the terrifying efficiency of the Prussian army, and accomplished by the peremptory defeats of two supposedly considerable military powers (Austria and France), critically upset the balance within Europe. The fact was recognized in Britain as early as 1875. In that year the French Government became convinced that Germany was planning a punitive attack that would permanently remove France from the ranks of the major powers. Both the British and the Russian Government indicated firmly to Germany that such a course would be unacceptable to them. Thus within five years of German unification the essential power alignment of 1914 had begun to manifest itself.

Yet there was no unbroken line from 1875 to 1914. At the former date Britain still stood aside from any recognized power grouping, and in the next two or three decades it was more often aligned against Russia and even France, on account of imperial matters, than with them. By 1914 this was no longer true. Britain was clearly associated with those countries that regarded Germany with fear or envy. Yet the difference may be explained by developments which confirmed and exaggerated the Continental imbalance that the German triumphs of 1866 to 1871 had demonstrated: the great expansion of German population and heavy industry that so markedly widened the gap between its own military capacity and that of its neighbours; the waywardness and unpredictability of the directors of German foreign policy following the removal of Bismarck; and, as a very weighty bundle of straw thrust upon the isolationist camel's back, the decision of Germany's rulers to make their country a considerable naval power. The navy was Britain's only bastion of defence (and, to repeat Kenneth Bourne's point, in most circumstances an inadequate one). Should it cease to function as a bastion, then overnight Britain would pass from the ranks of the major, or even independent, powers. If Britain lost command of the sea for any length of time, its economy would collapse and it would suffer starvation.

This last point needs to be stressed. For a great power Britain was, quite simply, absurdly vulnerable. This had not been true in the past. In Napoleon's day defeat at sea would not have constituted instant ruin, for Britain could still feed itself. But the vast expansion in its population since then had not been matched by a corresponding rise in home-produced foodstuffs. It was imported food, and the ability to pay for it by international trade, that enabled Britain not only to survive but to flourish. When Germany chose to challenge Britain's command of the North Sea, it threatened its most basic capacity to stay alive.

No country could remain unmoved by such a development. Certainly, it was possible to opt for doing nothing, but this would be a very positive response. Britain would be electing to abandon its great-power status. Henceforth it would be a client state either of the nation that menaced it or of other nations prepared (if able) to protect it.

If the rulers of Britain would not accept so dramatic a decline in status, then they must return to the direct involvement in European affairs which a similar Continental imbalance had called forth in the reigns of Philip II, Louis XIV, and Napoleon. Such involvement could be total: the creation of binding alliances with other countries hostile to Germany; the expansion of Britain's navy, regardless of cost or social consequences, on a scale that would outrun any German challenge; and the calling forth of the country's military energies by the diversion of manufacturing resources to military purposes and by the introduction of compulsory military service.[17] Yet much

---

[17] Diversion of industrial resources would necessarily have involved the creation of a wide range of industries of military significance, such as aniline dyes and optical lenses, in which Britain was deficient and depended on German imports.

within the British tradition worked against so Draconian a response. Even had a Liberal Government not been in power from 1905, it is difficult to envisage the country's rulers going so far. The implications in terms of taxation, apart from anything else, would probably have stopped short a Conservative Government.

Anyway, with the Liberals in office it was virtually certain that the British response would be a series of half-measures. That is, there would be associations with friendly powers but not alliances; arrangements with them for joint military action in hypothetical circumstances but no binding commitments to go to war; extension of Britain's naval power to a point providing adequate, but not lavish, security; and little, if any, expansion of military resources (apart from increased efficiency for an army whose size rendered it appropriate for the pre-Bismarckian, if not pre-Napoleonic, era). Moreover, there would at the same time be periodic attempts to persuade the menacing power to seek a *modus vivendi* so as to render such counter-measures unnecessary. This would appear to be as far as a liberal Britain could bring itself to go in acknowledging the passing of an age during which no threat had emanated from the continent of Europe.

The early years of the twentieth century spelled out the reality of the changed international situation. Until 1905 Britain's main concern overseas apparently remained imperial. The alliance with Japan in 1902 was directed against Russia, which threatened Britain not in Europe but in the Far East, India, and the Persian Gulf. But from 1905 the focus of attention shifted to the maintenance of the balance of power in Europe and to the threat that Germany posed to it. The change of emphasis coincided with a change of Government in Britain. Sir Edward Grey, the Liberal Foreign Secretary, was more convinced than his Conservative predecessor that the main objective of policy must be containment of Germany. And he was upheld in this view by changes of personnel among the officials of the Foreign Office that strengthened the anti-German element therein. Yet it is questionable whether these were crucial events in stimulating the redirection of British policy. More important was the fact that by 1905 the main elements in the German problem – naval building, diplomatic unpredictability, establishment of an imposing industrial-military complex – were becoming too evident to ignore. And with the Franco-German crisis over Morocco in 1905–6 British statesmen were obliged, for the first time since 1875, to ask themselves the fundamental question: Was a conflict in Western Europe from which Germany might well emerge the conqueror of France compatible with the survival of Britain?

IV

Something of the inwardness of relations between Britain and Germany in these years is revealed in an exchange of articles that took place in 1912 between A. J. Balfour and Prince Karl Max Lichnowsky. The second Moroccan crisis of the previous year had witnessed a serious deterioration in Anglo-German relations, and the German liberal newspaper *Nord und Sud* had sought the opinion of prominent individuals in both countries about what was at the base of these misunderstandings. Balfour and Lichnowsky were among the contributors.[18]

Balfour was a former Conservative Prime Minister, and it was during his Government (1902–5) that the entente with France had been formed. But the object of the entente had been primarily to settle outstanding colonial problems between France and Britain, and Balfour himself was no committed Germanophobe – indeed, in 1901 he had favoured an alliance with Germany.[19] In his *Nord und Sud* article, he stated as his

---

[18] The articles are reprinted in *England and Germany* (London: Williams & Norgate, 1912).

[19] It was for long believed that the military conversations between the British and French general staffs began

aim the presentation to German readers of 'the English point of view' – for 'I believe that in this matter there is only one English point of view.' He did not mean this in the sense that all his statements would be accepted equally by all Englishmen, but 'in a very real sense the deep uneasiness with which the people of this country contemplate possible developments of German policy, throws its shadow across the whole country, irrespective of party or of creed.'

The cause of this uneasiness, wrote Balfour, was not to be found in history. For Englishmen were conscious that they and the German nation had made common cause in past wars, and were not unmindful of 'their share in the great debt which all the world owes to German genius and German learning'. The explanation lay in the interpretation which Englishmen felt obliged to place upon 'a series of facts or supposed facts ... which taken together can neither be lightly treated nor calmly ignored.'

The first of Balfour's 'facts' ('the first, at least, to be realized') was the German Navy Bill and its results. He felt that German readers might not fully understand British opinion on this point. If Englishmen could be sure that a German fleet was going to be used only for defence, they would not care how large it was. To them aggression by Britain against Germany was unthinkable. 'There are, I am told, many Germans who would strongly dissent from this statement.' He asked German readers to consider the following. Putting aside the moral factor, Britain was a commercial nation, and war, whatever its outcome, would be ruinous to commerce. (The influence of Norman Angell, or rather of the powerful current of thought to which Angell had given expression, is plain here.) Secondly, Britain was a political nation, and an unprovoked war would shatter the most powerful Government and the most united party. And, thirdly, Britain was an insular nation, dependent on sea-borne supplies, lacking any great army, and therefore playing for quite unequal stakes 'should Germany be our opponent in the hazardous game of war'. Balfour placed great emphasis on this last point. If Germany should gain mastery of the sea, Britain could forthwith be conquered or starved into submission. British mastery at sea, on the other hand, gave it no power to conquer or starve Germany. 'Without a superior fleet, Britain would no longer count as a Power. Without any fleet at all, Germany would remain the greatest Power in Europe.'

Balfour then went on to ask: Could Englishmen believe that Germany required her navy only for purposes of defence? He answered:

> The external facts of the situation appear to be as follows: the greatest military Power and the second greatest naval Power in the world is adding both to her army and to her navy. She is increasing the strategic railways which lead to frontier States – not merely to frontier States which themselves possess powerful armies, but to small States which can have no desire but to remain neutral .... She is in like manner modifying her naval arrangements so as to make her naval strength instantly effective.

Perhaps it was the case that Germany was doing all this only for defence.

> Unfortunately, no mere analysis of the German preparations for war will show for what purposes they are designed.

Balfour then proceeded to the 'most difficult and delicate part' of his task. He insisted that ordinary Englishmen, and certainly he himself, did not believe that the great body of Germans, or their government, wished to attack their neighbours. 'The danger lies elsewhere': namely in the coexistence of 'that marvellous instrument of warfare', the German army and navy, 'with the assiduous, I had almost said the organized, advocacy of a policy which it seems impossible to reconcile with the peace of

---

during his premiership. But recent research shows that they did not start until after his Government had given way to the Liberals. See G. Monger, *The End of Isolation* (London: Nelson, 1963), ch. 9.

the world or the rights of nations.' This policy involved redrawing the map of Europe in harmony with what its advocates conceived as the present distribution of the German race, making Germany the heir of the Holy Roman Empire and acquiring ('at the cost of other nations') an overseas empire proportionate to Germany's greatness in Europe. 'All countries which hinder, though it be only in self-defence, the realization of this ideal, are regarded as hostile; and war, or the threat of war, is deemed the natural and fitting method by which the ideal itself is to be accomplished.' Of such aims Britain could not approve. 'We have had too bitter an experience of the ills which flow from the endeavour of any single State to dominate Europe; we are too surely convinced of the perils which such a policy, were it successful, would bring upon ourselves as well as upon others, to treat them as negligible.'

Balfour claimed himself unwilling to believe that war between Britain and Germany was inevitable, widely held though this view was. 'Germany has taught Europe much; she can teach it yet more': namely, 'that organized military power may be used in the interests of peace as effectually as in those of war; that the appetite for domination belongs to an outworn phase of patriotism; that the furtherance of civilization, for which she has so greatly laboured, must be the joint work of many peoples, and that the task for none of them is lightened by the tremendous burden of modern armaments, or the perpetual pre-occupation of national self-defence.'

But Balfour could not bring himself to end on this half-conciliatory note. If Germany was prepared to give a lead on the foregoing lines, he wrote, she would find a world already prepared to follow. 'But if there be signs that her desires point to other objects, and that her policy will be determined by national ambitions of a different type, can it be a matter of surprise that other countries watch the steady growth of her powers of aggression with undisguised alarm, and anxiously consider schemes for meeting what they are driven to regard as a common danger?'

Balfour received a firm reply from Prince Karl Max Lichnowsky, an hereditary member of the Prussian Upper House who had spent his career in the German diplomatic service. (The article under discussion gains a particular interest from the fact that, soon after its appearance, Lichnowsky was appointed the Kaiser's last Ambassador to London. In 1914 he was to be moved to despair by the blundering conduct of the German Government, and in 1916 wrote an apologia called *My London Mission* which fiercely criticized his country's part in bringing about the war. Its illicit publication early in 1918, by an 'idealist' member of the German General Staff, caused acute embarrassment to the German Government –not to mention Lichnowsky himself.)

Unlike Balfour's article, Lichnowsky's contribution to the *Nord und Sud* debate suffered from severe convolution in expression – or unusually tortured translation. Hence to paraphrase it is hazardous. Yet his main points emerge, if only with a struggle.

The essence of Lichnowsky's position was that a measure of hostility between Britain and Germany was part of the nature of things. Opposition between them, he wrote, was founded 'on development and division of power, on the whole array of political factors, which evade the influence of each' and could not be avoided without the sacrifice of vital interests. But he insisted that this opposition need not lead to war. A *modus vivendi* that 'shuts out war as an encroachment on essential aims and purposes' could be found.

Lichnowsky was not impressed by the tributes being paid by English writers to Germany's contributions to philosophy and the arts and to the bonds that these created between the two countries: 'Such considerations are effective enough in an after-dinner speech.' He insisted: 'friendship and alliance between nations rests rather on community of interests, and especially [community] of antagonisms.' A glance at the map of Europe, and at the existing balance of power, would make it clear why Britain was directing its attention, and possibly its warlike preparations, against Germany. As for the British navy, it was the instrument ('quite within the rights of the English') whereby Britain backed its diplomacy 'on every suitable opportunity' and, on occasion, threatened. 'Our duty is not to remain defenceless against this.'

Lichnowsky argued that international rivalry (which 'will always exist, unless the Utopian brotherhood of nations and confederation of States is established') was for Britain centred in German nationality. He did not seem to resent this rivalry, for he proceeded to offer a piece of outright Darwinism:

'The general good of the whole human race' is furthered by the 'survival of the fittest,' by the elevation of the most capable human beings, and, in my opinion, the roots of political ethics are to be found in that consideration. Men can only be 'freed from and lifted above nationality, faith, and colour' in the spiritual results of this struggle, of this international contest.

But Lichnowsky did not doubt that, in seeking a contestant in this 'peaceful match', Britain would pit itself against Germany. France, which in this effort 'must find protection or assistance against us', had already found full support in Britain.

From the standpoint of British policy it may appear justifiable to protect the weak against the strong, to oppose every new continental or colonial development of power, in whatever form it presents itself in the course of history; but it gives us food for thought when we find England always on the side of our enemies.

A war arising from the crises in Bosnia or Morocco, Lichnowsky claimed, would have found Britain fighting Germany 'on questions that only slightly affected British interests, and we know that it will be so in the future'. The British Government 'regards us as its most important and dangerous rival in international politics and economics'; he quoted the right-wing *Morning Post* as saying during the second Moroccan crisis that if Germany had attacked France, Britain would have had to use all her resources alongside the French.

At no point did Lichnowsky come to grips with the question of whether a German assault on France, whatever its origin, was really a question 'that only slightly affected British interests'. Nor did he concede Balfour's argument that the British navy constituted no major threat to Germany. On the contrary, he asserted that a strong German army (which – rather oddly – he observed had driven France into the arms of Britain and had forced Russia to divert its attention from Asia to the west) was no more of a threat to Britain than was the British navy to Germany. For the British navy, in the event of war and in the absence of a German fleet, would be 'more quickly in a position to cut off commerce on the sea and to force its will upon us in a Continental war'. Germany's navy existed, he continued, in order that 'we may not be defenceless on the water, and so as not to fall into dependence'. Balfour might reply, 'Give up the expansion of your sea-power and we will undertake nothing that can cause you uneasiness.' Lichnowsky's answer was: 'Eunuchs are admitted to the harem, the means is simple but not painless; we neither desire to enter a harem nor to lose our manhood.'

The conclusion he reached was much like his beginning: 'misunderstanding that rests on division of power and on the direction of progress' cannot wholly be removed. But as long as it did not leave the path of peaceful endeavour and moderate armaments, 'competition between Briton and German may be for the good of world civilization.' He ended on a heavily flippant note:

now that British customs, fashions, sport, and play have conquered the world, and are imitated by us as by others, there is no ground why the English example should not hold with regard to the fleet. Why should we only learn about lawn-tennis and polo, racing and regattas from our English friends, and not also the love of a fleet? I see no reason for any such limitation of our far-reaching Anglomania!

When the laughter from this parting jest had died away, the uncomfortable reality remained. Between the positions of these two respected and influential individuals no meeting place existed. After they had presented their views with as much moderation as they could muster, the gulf between them proved unbridgeable. In the name of progress and wholesome competition, Lichnowsky claimed for Germany the right to assume a role in European affairs that, however tastefully exercised, would reduce Britain to a subservient position. Balfour, notwithstanding his great debt to German philosophy, was prepared to utter to Germany's rulers a firm thus-far-and-no-further; and, should the need arise, to act on it.[20]

V

Controversy over Britain's role in the coming of war began even before 1914, as the diplomatic alignments became apparent. It has continued ever since. From 1905 Grey, as Foreign Secretary, was single-minded in associating his country's policy with that of France – and ultimately with that of Russia as well – in order to maintain a power bloc capable of deterring or withstanding Germany. As Grey wrote in June 1906, 'The Germans do not realize that England has always drifted or deliberately gone into opposition to any Power which establishes a hegemony in Europe.'[21]

In order to hold at bay the danger of such an hegemony, Grey put the maintenance of the entente at the forefront of his policy. For example, during the first Moroccan crisis he adopted a less accommodating position towards Germany than he personally favoured because it might place him at variance with the French. At the same time he was persuading a reluctant Prime Minister to authorize staff talks between the military authorities of Britain and France. Recognizing that these talks would be ill-received by a section of the Liberal Cabinet, he withheld from his colleagues the information that they were taking place. Thereafter he was usually uneasy about efforts to secure a rapprochement with Germany lest they should impair France's trust in British friendship. In 1911, as in 1905, Grey was quick to interpret German actions in Morocco as an attempt to shatter the entente – ignoring the measure of French provocation in both instances – and to close ranks with France in requiring a German climb-down. He then allowed naval staff talks to start with Russia, so that the military arrangements of the three entente countries, two of whom were formal allies, were becoming closely intertwined. When the crisis came in 1914, though he sought to bring

---

[20] Two years in London were to bring about a great change in Lichnowsky's attitude. In *My London Mission*, composed in 1916, he wrote: 'Is it not comprehensible that our enemies declare that they will not rest until a system which constitutes a permanent menace to our neighbours is destroyed? . . . Have not those proved to be right who divined that the German people was dominated by the spirit of Treitschke and of Bernhardi, which glorifies war as an end in itself and does not loathe it as an evil; that with us the feudal knight and Junker, the warrior caste, still rules and shapes ideals and values, and not the civilian gentleman; that the love of the duel which animates our academic youth still persists in those who guide the destinies of the nation?' Considering how close he had now come to the position earlier expressed by Balfour, it may be noted that in the same document Lichnowsky classed Balfour, along with militarists like Lord Roberts and pressmen like Lord Northcliffe and J. L. Garvin, among the 'pessimists' who during his time in London spoke of war with Germany as inevitable. The 'optimists' who believed that an understanding would be achieved included, in his account, Asquith, Grey, Haldane, 'most of the ministers in the Radical Cabinet', and the leading Liberal newspapers.

[21] Quoted in Monger, *The End of Isolation*, p. 300.

the powers to the conference table, he exercised no restraining hand on France or, particularly, on Russia.

If it be thought that nothing was at stake in 1914, that no country willed war but all stumbled into it, and that it did not really matter who won and who lost, then it is legitimate strongly to deplore Grey's direction of foreign policy. The role of Britain should not have been one of increasing participation in the European power balance, but rather that of an independent peacemaker seeking to break the vicious circle of suspicion and misunderstanding, of preparation and counter-preparation, that was driving all powers equally over the abyss.

Yet how warranted are the assumptions that underlie this argument? Was Grey entitled simply to ignore the powerful evidence suggesting that Germany was seeking a European hegemony incompatible with Britain's independence, and to construct no safeguards against it? Admittedly, as Balfour said in the article quoted above, Grey could not be certain of the purpose to which the Germans intended to put their military might, expanding navy, and strategic railways; possibly these were intended only for defence (possibly the German Government had no idea either). But no British Foreign Minister could afford to ignore Germany's great offensive capability. Historians have not dealt kindly with the statesmen of twenty or so years later who, in like circumstances, decided to gamble on German good will. That Grey should be condemned for not indulging in such a gamble may suggest that, at least as far as posterity is concerned, he occupied a situation in which he could not win.

In considering this matter, it is not necessary to become immersed in the argument as to whether the outbreak of war was the product of Germany's 'will to power' or of a series of diplomatic blunders that began in Berlin but did not end there. The situation with which Grey had to deal in August 1914 was this: Germany's rulers had initiated, and refused to withdraw from, a course of action that they recognized was likely to produce a war in Eastern Europe. The immediate consequence of this war, if all went according to German plans, would be the irreversible conquest of Belgium and France by Germany. Whether such a victory, and the September-type programme of German annexations emanating from it, would be the product of the German 'will to power' or of bungling by the rulers in Berlin could scarcely be Grey's concern. The consequences would not be different.[22]

Certainly, there are very serious criticisms to be made of Grey's conduct of foreign affairs. His attitude was often too simplistic. He was reluctant to recognize that it might be possible both to maintain the entente and to explore avenues of reconciliation with Germany. In the last days of peace he seemed to feel that he had a duty to try to restrain the recklessness of Germany and Austria-Hungary, but not to discourage the precipitate counter-measures of Russia and France. And it is difficult to excuse his action in concealing from the British Cabinet, as he did from 1905 to 1911, the existence of staff talks between French and British military authorities.

But it does not follow that these aspects of Grey's conduct really mattered. It is necessary to ask whether the course of European affairs, and Britain's involvement therein, would much have differed if some other Liberal Minister had occupied Grey's place. Any reply must rest on speculation, yet there are good grounds for suggesting that the answer is no. There were in the Liberal Government very important figures, like Haldane and (sometimes) Lloyd George, who genuinely wanted to direct British

---

[22] For the 'September programme', drawn up by Germany's civilian rulers in September 1914 while still confident of speedy victory in the West, see Fritz Fischer, *Germany's Aims in the First World War* (London: Chatto & Windus, 1967).

policy towards a *via media* between France and Germany. The unilateral slowing down of naval building by the Liberals immediately upon coming into office, their rigid refusal to introduce conscription or to convert industry to military purposes, the overtures made by Haldane to Germany after the first Morocco crisis and his active mission to Germany after the second, all showed that this element in the Government was not powerless. Yet their efforts came to nothing. The reason was the intransigence not of Grey but of the Kaiser.

What these efforts towards *rapprochement* revealed was that the role of independent arbiter, acting to break the vicious circle that was spiralling Europe to disaster, did not exist. There was no *via media*. The German Government had no use for an uncommitted Britain. What it required as the price of any scaling-down of naval building was a pledge of British neutrality in the event of any future European conflict. This, far from leaving Britain uncommitted, would have constituted a far-reaching and most formidable commitment (to Germany) – and one that would hardly have helped to break the vicious circle of fear and mistrust. That Britain remained within the French orbit may be accounted for, quite apart from the prejudices and shortsighted-ness of its Foreign Ministry, by the logic of Germany's actions and demands.

Given these circumstances, the decision to concert Britain's military preparations with those of France for the eventuality of a war in which they might be jointly involved hardly seems remarkable. Grey's secrecy in accomplishing it must certainly be criticized. But as long as Britain's rulers were determined (for the best of liberal reasons) to keep its army negligible in size, then some association with the only country that might make good its military deficiencies seemed inescapable. The problem was that Britain could not assure itself of French aid without appearing to give some reciprocal undertakings. Yet these 'moral obligations' had little or no substance. The suggestion that, thanks to the military 'conversations', Britain was bound to stand by France against Germany in any circumstances is specious (and no French Government thought otherwise). There was never any question that Britain would support a French aggression against Germany. And there was scant likelihood that a Liberal Cabinet would back up the French should they declare war upon Germany as a result of a conflict breaking out in Eastern Europe that caused Russia to invoke the terms of the Dual Alliance.

Thus the only circumstance in which the question of Britain's 'moral obligations' was likely to arise was that in which Germany, from motives of aggression or supposed strategic necessity, launched an attack on France. And the members of the Govern-ment who then argued that Britain had 'moral obligations' to France were precisely those who, obligations or no, believed passionately that, in the interest of Britain's survival, it must take France's side. Those Ministers (like Lord Morley and John Burns) who deplored Britain's supposed secret commitments to France also believed that on moral grounds Britain ought not to participate.

The conflict that racked the Liberal Cabinet in the first days of August 1914 had little to do with supposed British obligations to France arising out of prior military arrangements. From one point of view, firmly held by Grey among others, Britain's survival was at stake in any German assault upon France. Grey's attitude has been misunderstood because of his alleged confidence that the war would be over by Christmas, with Germany crushed between the *élan* of the French cavalry and the irresistible force of the Russian steamroller. No doubt Grey hoped that this would be the course of events. But his actions were based on the recognition that it might not. Had he been convinced of a swift and happy outcome to the opening compaigns, he could have halted British involvement at the point where it was made clear to Germany that its fleet would not be allowed to enter the Channel.

But there were powerful reasons for doubting whether France and Russia would prove a match for Germany and Austria-Hungary. The overwhelming defeat of Napoleon III in 1870, when Germany's strength *vis-à-vis* France was considerably less than it had since become, and the lamentable military record of Russia since 1815, culminating in the débâcle against Japan only ten years before, provided ample cause for doubt. The Foreign Secretary who warned the House of Commons on 3 August of 'what may happen to France from our failure to support France' and of the possibility of 'the whole of the West of Europe opposite to us . . . falling under the domination of a single Power', and who gloomily observed in private that the lamps were going out all over Europe and would not be relit in his time, was not being swept along by a flood of misplaced optimism. It was the menace, not the hope, of the situation that moved him.

What, then, of the members of the Government who doubted the merits of intervention? They too perceived the danger of a German triumph in the West; that is why their position throughout the crisis was so unstable. Yet much about the situation gave them pause. If fears of a German victory should prove unfounded, then British intervention might assist in the establishment of a tsarist, not a Hohenzollern, hegemony in Europe. Even if Germany did triumph, was it likely that a nation of such civilized attainments would ruthlessly exploit a military victory? Again, whatever the unpleasant consequences of a war from which Britain stood aside, could they be more horrible than war itself? And, after all, ought Britain to become involved in a quarrel between great powers over a Balkan matter of no intrinsic importance and in which neither side possessed the moral advantage?

The importance of the Belgian issue was that, except for a few intransigents, it swept aside the doubts of interventionists and abstainers alike. There might be grounds for questioning whether the survival of an independent France was a vital British interest. There was no doubt concerning an independent Belgium. Britain had not guaranteed that country's untrammelled status in 1839, and reaffirmed its guarantee at subsequent moments of crisis, because of excessive benevolence towards little nations. It had done so from compelling motives of self-interest. Every British concern about the balance of power on the Continent and trading relations with Western Europe and naval security in the North Sea and the English Channel was involved there. The Kaiser's assault upon so crucial and so oft-asserted an area of British anxiety defined, with even more fearful clarity than did his Navy Laws, the attitude of Germany's rulers to Britain's position in the world.

But there was another respect in which the German onslaught on Belgium affected Britain nearly. Particularly it affected those considerable sections – both within the ruling Liberal Party, and in the Labour and Irish parties that helped to keep Asquith in office – loath to enter a war. The Belgian issue – or what a Liberal journalist, H. W. Massingham (who until that moment had opposed intervention), called the 'stupefying panorama of German arrogance' – defined the nature of the struggle. Up to this point it had been possible to regard the developing conflict on the Continent as a squabble between great powers in which no worthy issue was involved. Now that appearance had vanished. The conflict had taken on the appearance of German militarism run mad. An autocratic, anti-liberal power was bent on trampling down the liberties and independence of the democratic countries of Western Europe, large and small. Such action, it was swiftly concluded among Liberals, Labour, and the Irish Nationalists, must be stopped at all costs – even at the cost of involvement in a terrible war.

VI

If it be thought that the object of the foregoing discussion has been to provide justification for the actions of the British Government and people in going to war, then it should be said that this has not been the intention. Rather, the purpose has been to lay bare the range of choices that actually confronted the makers of British foreign policy in the years 1905–14. Having done so, it is still possible to subject the decisions of Grey and his associates to profound criticism.

Had Britain stood aside from all international engagements in these years, there seems little doubt about what would have happened. Liberal democracy would have been crushed in Western Europe, and Britain would by stages have become dependent on the sufferance of the rulers of Germany. These would have been lamentable events. It does not follow that they would have been worse than the alternative: the bloodletting of the Somme and Passchendaele, the 'passing bells for those who die as cattle', the destruction of stable orders in Russia and Germany, the subsequent establishment under Stalin and Hitler of regimes whose capacity for atrocity outran the imaginings of civilized men in 1914, and the reduction of Western Europe to a minor force in world affairs. The slogan much used by proponents of nuclear disarmament in the 1950s, 'Better red than dead' – by which they meant better an unresisting acceptance of subjection to Russia than nuclear resistance to it – is *Realpolitik* of a high order. It embraces the one meaningful charge to be delivered against British intervention in the war of 1914. Supporters of that course did view as unthinkable a line of action that many people since their day have had reason to think about very seriously – namely, the refusal to engage in war whatever the provocation and however dire the likely consequences of abstention. Against such a charge no defence can be made for the directors of Britain's foreign policy in 1914. Sir Edward Grey did assume that, in the event of what appeared a German assault on fundamental British interests, the only appropriate response was armed resistance.

Yet the same charge must be levelled against not only those who endorsed Grey's policy but all but a tiny minority of those who opposed it. Doubtless there was a handful of pacifists who, while refusing to resist aggression, recognized that thereby they were choosing to fall under the heel of a ruthless conqueror. The majority of Grey's critics stopped far short of such realism. They evaded, rather than confronted, the implications of Germany's impending conquest of Western Europe. They argued that no vital British interest was being attacked, or that the war was the product of international capitalism, or that the real danger of the situation was not a German hegemony in Europe but a Russian hegemony, or that what people ought to be looking at was not the German hordes sweeping across Belgium but the 'diplomatic errors' which had got them there.

In such statements there was no hard-headed critique of the attitudes that were taking Britain into war. *Realpolitik* of the 'Better red than dead' variety was absent from the thinking of men like Bertrand Russell and Ramsay MacDonald and John Morley when they opposed entry into the war. Certainly, they deserve honour for possessing the personal courage and independence of mind to withstand the tide of feeling that was sweeping conformists and time-servers into the interventionist camp. But we should not fall into the error of overestimating their independence of mind. It was not of the calibre that enabled them to reject the values and ideals of their community. Nor should we ignore the fact that, for a great many other individuals of like courage and equal independence, these values and ideals made involvement in the war seem the only appropriate course of action.

VII

As the war went on, with its fearful casualties and unending stalemate, and with squalid episodes like the bribery of Italy and the violation of Greek neutrality (even if the latter, like the servant girl's excuse for her illegitimate baby, was 'only a little one'), doubts about the issue of involvement reasserted themselves in some quarters. But then the menace of August 1914 returned to the battlefield, and doubts vanished once more.

Between March and July 1918 the Germans made their last great bid for victory in the West. Employing large reinforcements from the now defunct Eastern Front, they threw themselves against the Allied line in France and drove the defenders back in confusion. For the first time in three and a half years, the war of movement had returned to the Western Front and the military power of Germany was on the march again.

In these circumstances, so reminiscent of the first weeks of the war, Massingham's radical periodical, the *Nation*, paused to take stock. In the years since the outbreak of war when, on account of the issue of Belgium, it had swung from opposing to supporting British intervention, this journal had not lost the habit of independence. It had resisted many of the 'total war' measures, such as conscription, that had been implemented by both Liberal and Coalition Governments. It had welcomed suggestions for seeking an end to the war by negotiation – suggestions that the country's rulers had rejected with derision. And during 1917 it had got so far out of line that the Government had for some months actually banned its overseas circulation. The judgement on the war of a journal so capable of preserving its balance in the heat of conflict is deserving of attention.

On 30 March 1918, confronting the military crisis in the West, the *Nation* wrote:

> In the full brunt of the German assault on France, the true character of the war stands revealed. Vain projects of Imperialism obscured it, and vainer diversions of strategy. Both have disappeared . . . . The war emerges from these mists, not as a war of adventure but morally and physically as a war of defence . . . . The war was not for colonies, Imperial ambitions, or a balance of power. It was to teach militarism a lesson of restraint. . . .

Perhaps this is not how posterity chooses to view Britain's involvement in the Great War. But it is the duty of posterity to take note that in the eyes of some men of good conscience and independent judgement this was how it appeared at the time.

2

The Dilemma of 2 August

There is a strong party [in the Cabinet] . . . against any kind of intervention in any event.

Asquith to Venetia Stanley, 2 August 1914

Oh Agadir, Agadir, and your courage then!

J. L. Garvin to Lloyd George, 2 August 1914

I

The second of August 1914 found the Asquith Cabinet facing the gravest crisis in its already much disturbed existence. Anyone wishing to believe that Asquith deliberately – or even unconsciously – chose war as a way out of his Government's domestic trials would do well to observe the troubles he was facing on that day. The fact of war was producing a chasm within his Cabinet that it lay beyond his powers to close.

The problems of the Liberal Cabinet on 2 August 1914 existed in the context of its parliamentary following – Labour and Irish Nationalists as well as Liberals. On this day, a Sunday, Labour was holding a mass anti-war rally in Trafalgar Square, and it was evident that many Liberal and Irish back-benchers were of the same persuasion. 'I suppose,' Asquith wrote to his confidante Venetia Stanley that day, 'a good ¾ of our own party in the H. of Commons are for absolute non-interference at any price. It will be a shocking thing if at such a moment we break up – with no one to take our place' (by which he presumably meant no one tolerable to himself as an alternative Government).[1]

If Asquith was using the expression 'absolute non-interference at any price' in its literal sense, then he was plainly misrepresenting the attitudes of his parliamentary followers. With negligible exceptions, they all believed in war for certain vital interests. For example, they would rather fight than tolerate a German war plan that, however benevolently, involved a military occupation of British territory or a naval occupation of the Channel. The problem – and, despite his hyperbole, Asquith doubtless recognized this – was the magnitude of the price that non-interference in war would exact. If it were sufficiently low, involving expansion of German influence in the Balkans but not elsewhere, then Asquith could hold his party and Government together in refusing to be drawn in. Churchill, for example, was happy to offer assurances that Balkan quarrels were no business of Britain's. Alternatively, if the price were sufficiently high, such as the Channel's being turned into a German lake, then again Asquith's task would be easy. Only a negligible group among his followers would resist going to war in such circumstances. The problem was what would happen if the issue were not so

---

[1] *H. H. Asquith: Letters to Venetia Stanley*, selected and edited by Michael and Eleanor Brock (Oxford: Oxford University Press, 1982), p. 146.

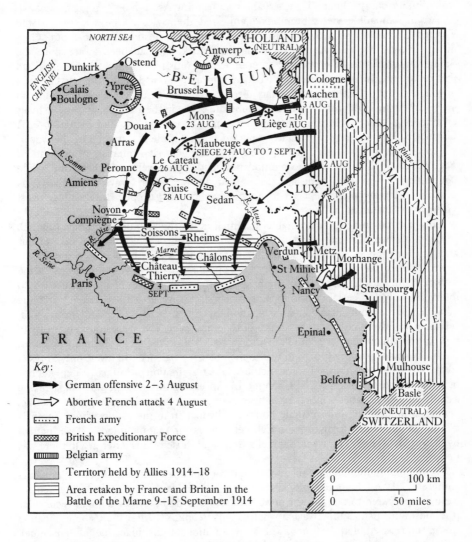

NORTH SEA

ENGLISH CHANNEL

Dunkirk
●Ostend
Calais
●Boulogne
Ypres

Antwerp
9 OCT

HOLLAND
(NEUTRAL)

B E L G I U M
Brussels

Cologne●
Aachen
3 AUG

Douai
Mons
23 AUG
Liège AUG
7–16

●Arras
Maubeuge
SIEGE 24 AUG TO 7 SEPT.

Peronne
Le Cateau
26 AUG

2 AUG

R. Somme

Amiens
Guise
28 AUG
Sedan
LUX

GERMANY

R. Rhine
R. Moselle
R. Meuse

Noyon●
Compiègne

R. Oise

Soissons
Rheims

Châlons

Verdun●
Metz
Morhange

LORRAINE

R. Seine
R. Marne

Château-
Thierry
4
SEPT

●St Mihiel

Paris

Nancy

Strasbourg●

FRANCE

Epinal●

ALSACE

Key:

➤ German offensive 2–3 August

⇨ Abortive French attack 4 August

French army

British Expeditionary Force

Belgian army

Territory held by Allies 1914–18

Area retaken by France and Britain in the
Battle of the Marne 9–15 September 1914

Mulhouse
Belfort●

Basle

(NEUTRAL)
SWITZERLAND

0   100 km

0   50 miles

Map 2 *The Western Front, 1914.* Source: *Martin Gilbert,* Recent History Atlas
(London: Weidenfeld & Nicolson, 1966), p. 25.

clear-cut: if the war were not confined to Eastern and South-Eastern Europe but spread to Western Europe as well, and yet still did not involve vital British concerns with blinding clarity. That was the situation confronting Asquith on 2 August.

Two incompatible views promptly manifested themselves. One was that of the Foreign Secretary, Sir Edward Grey. As a number of testimonies bear out, Grey during these days was in a profound state of shock. He had been aware since the Sarajevo murders that Europe had entered a dangerous phase. He had also imagined that he knew how it would be resolved: by Germany's and Britain's imposition of a negotiated settlement on the Balkan disputants. The discovery that the German Government had no intention of maintaining the peace in the Balkans, and was actively encouraging Austria-Hungary into war at whatever risk, shook him to the core. A Cabinet colleague, Herbert Samuel, reported of Grey: 'He is outraged by the way in which Germany and Austria have played with the most vital interests of civilisation, have put aside all attempts at accommodation made by himself and others, and, while continuing to negotiate, have marched steadily to war.'[2] For Grey the corollary was plain. If Germany was prepared to impose war on all Europe, Britain must resist German expansion in the West.

This attitude proved 'unacceptable' to a majority of the Cabinet, including Samuel. In his view, 'we were not entitled to carry England into the war for the sake of our goodwill for France, or for the sake of maintaining the strength of France and Russia against that of Germany and Austria. This opinion is shared by the majority of the Cabinet with various degrees of emphasis on the several parts of it.' Samuel would intervene only for certain specific reasons: first, to preserve the Channel and the Channel ports from attack and occupation by the German fleet and army; and, secondly, to maintain the independence of Belgium, 'which we were bound by treaty to protect and which again we could not afford to see subordinated to Germany'. That is, Samuel was not prepared to go to war to maintain the balance of power, only to resist so glaring a manifestation of its destruction as the termination of Belgian independence or a German domination of the Channel. In expressing this view he was not speaking as one of the Cabinet's more extreme anti-war members. Asquith placed Samuel among 'a moderating intermediate body', as distinct from the group whose intransigence was most likely to disrupt the Cabinet – the group that included, if it was not led by, Lloyd George. Yet between Samuel's views and those of this latter group there was no essential difference.

Shortly before the Cabinet met on the morning of 2 August, a number of Ministers gathered at Lloyd George's official residence. Their conclusion was: 'all agreed we were not prepared to go into war now, but that in certain events we might reconsider [the] position, such as the invasion wholesale of Belgium.'[3] After the Cabinet meeting this group reassembled for lunch, with a few additional individuals, including Samuel. The latter found 'general agreement' with his views. During the rest of the day, which included another Cabinet meeting, 'we remained solid.' His conclusion last thing at night was that if the question of war and peace had come to an issue during the day, all but a handful of the Cabinet would have been against war.

It is usual to portray Asquith as handling his colleagues with consummate mastery at this juncture. To prevent a rupture, he allowed decisions to be made only on those aspects of the situation concerning which there was general agreement. For example, there was near-unanimity that the German navy should not be allowed to use the

---

[2] Samuel to his wife, 2 August 1914, quoted in Cameron Hazlehurst, *Politicians at War July 1914 to May 1915* (London: Jonathon Cape, 1971), pp. 93 *et seq.*

[3] Diary of J. A. Pease, 2 August 1914, quoted in Hazlehurst, *Politicians at War*, p. 66.

Channel to wage war against the French. On the crucial issue of Britain's involvement in a Franco-German war on land he forestalled discussion until he was ready to carry an undivided Cabinet into the struggle.

This is a glamorized view. Certainly, Asquith avoided a decision and played for time. But this was all he could do if he was to escape a situation in which his Cabinet would fall apart at a time when his own position was hopelessly self-contradictory. For Asquith occupied no coherent place at this point. By common consent, he meant to stand by Grey if the intransigence of the Cabinet caused the Foreign Secretary to resign. Yet in the several accounts Asquith gave of how he viewed the actual issues he came down not with Grey but with Samuel – and so, essentially, with Lloyd George. When he claimed that he was prepared to leave office along with Grey, it was in opposition to those, among whom he included Lloyd George, who opposed intervention 'in any event'. This was an obtuse statement. Lloyd George was not against intervention 'in any event'. And Grey was prepared to resign for reasons with which Asquith apparently did not concur.

Writing privately on 2 August, Asquith said that he was quite clear in his mind about the right and wrong of the situation. Britain had a long-standing friendship with France and an interest to prevent it from losing its great-power status. But Britain was under no obligation to aid France or Russia militarily or navally. In so far as he chose between these positions, it was by concluding that there was no question at that moment of Britain's dispatching a military force to France. There was only one obligation requiring British military action. This was with regard to Belgium, which must not be 'utilized and absorbed by Germany'. In so saying Asquith was adopting virtually Samuel's position.

What course, then, lay open to the Prime Minister on 2 August? He could not lead his party into the war that was threatening on that day because there seemed no likelihood that it would consent. Nor, in terms of his reiterated position, did he have any grounds for resigning along with Grey and forming a war Government that had shed most Liberal Ministers. Well might he play for time, avoid decision, and hope that events would somehow clarify the issue one way or the other.

II

It must be said that the argument of the last few pages is not universally accepted. For some historians the dilemma of this day had no substance. In their view all the heart searching, the foregathering, and the firm stands taken for various positions were only play-acting or, at best, exercises in self-deception. The whole Cabinet recognized on 2 August that the solution of its dilemma was at hand. Hence when members consulted their consciences or talked of resigning for reasons of principle, they knew full well that they would never have to pay the price of principle or see the Government dissolve.

The basis of this view is as follows. It was general knowledge that the first consequence of war's breaking out in Western Europe would be a German invasion of Belgium. Hence as long as the Ministers who claimed to oppose British intervention kept the Belgian issue in reserve as a possible ground for changing their minds, they were not really espousing non-intervention. Their anguished conclaves before and after Cabinet meetings, like the impassioned notes flung across the table while those meetings proceeded, were all parts of a façade. So already by 2 August the Liberal Cabinet was in reality a war Cabinet, and Lloyd George – to take the most eminent example among many – was already a war Minister. When he suggested otherwise he was 'shamming' (to quote one historian), 'concealing his intentions without actually lying', and 'reaping the benefit of neutralist noisemaking' while not really intending to remain neutral.[4] For Lloyd George and others like him, the Belgian issue was 'a pretext for an otherwise humiliating *volte-face*' and an excuse for staying in a Government they had never intended to leave.

What is to be said about this? It may be admitted that there existed some ambivalence in the position of the non-interventionists. In the first place, any of them might succumb to a gust of jingoism at a crucial moment. Lloyd George's Mansion House speech during the Agadir crisis of 1911 bore witness to that. (Equally, any super-patriot might of a sudden perceive that the war would be an horrific event, which the nation should go to great lengths to avoid.) Secondly, opponents of intervention could rarely be unaware that a struggle between Germany and France was a matter of great moment to British Liberals. The values upheld by the progressive forces in Britain, both Liberal and Labour, would suffer a stunning blow if France were crushed by Germany as in 1870–1. For Conservatives the preservation of the balance of power against German expansionism did not necessarily have ideological overtones. But for those on the left of politics the maintenance of that balance seemed intimately involved with the survival of their political ideals.[5]

The situation of Labour on this matter was identical with that of the Liberals. Hence it overlooks a vital element in the situation to assert that, when the crisis came, 'Labour's war resisters soon melted into the precincts of Westminster, preferring patriotic anonymity to the notoriety of untimely pacifism' and so abandoning 'the principles of international socialism'.[6] The cause of 'international socialism' could hardly be reconciled with 'pacifism' in the circumstances of August 1914. If the Kaiser's forces overran Western Europe and showed no inclination to depart, then international socialism – along with parliamentary liberalism – was unlikely ever to recover.

Lloyd George, for one, was not unconscious of such ideological considerations. As long ago as 1898 he had, with rare insight, given expression to them. At that point it seemed that Britain and France would make war against each other following the clash of their imperialisms at Fashoda. Lloyd George deplored such a conflict, not on pacifist or anti-imperialist grounds but because of the harm it would do to democracy in Europe. In any war against France, he said, he did not doubt that Britain would be victorious. But what would be the result?

If we defeat France, we shall be defeating the only power on the Continent with a democratic Constitution. Emperors, Kings and aristocratic rulers will mock at the whole thing – two great democratic Powers at each other's throats, the only countries where you

---

[4] Hazlehurst, *Politicians at War*, pp. 14, 68, 69, 108.

[5] The point is sometimes made that no question of ideology was at stake in 1914 because the liberal states of Western Europe, although aligned against the autocracies of the Central Powers, were themselves associated with the reactionary Government of Russia. This point is not conclusive. The threat posed to Western democracy by Germany lay not simply in its system of government but rather in its combination of autocracy with geographical proximity and extreme military efficiency. Russia, although autocratic, was neither efficient militarily nor geographically proximate, and so it constituted no threat to Western liberalism. It was, on the other hand (because of its geographical position and its rivalry with both Austria-Hungary and Germany), a counter-balancing force to the Central Powers. Democratic countries, when facing a major danger, are not usually in a position to be choosy in accepting assistance. Churchill's act in welcoming Russia as an ally against Germany in 1941 is a case in point. He had not overcome his repugnance for the Communist regime but was happy to embrace any assistance against the prime menace of Nazi Germany. ('If Hitler invaded Hell, I would make at least a favourable reference to the Devil in the House of Commons.') The change in Britain's attitude to Russia after 1900, following the emergence of Germany as a major land and sea threat, is of a similar order.

[6] Hazlehurst, *Politicians at War*, p. 40.

have perfect civil and religious liberty in Europe quarrelling with each other to make sport for the titled and throned Philistines of Europe.[7]

In 1914 there was no question of the 'two great democratic Powers' being at each other's throats. And as long as France could withstand Germany, then there might be excellent reasons why British Liberals should preserve their peace-keeping role. But what if Germany were about to smash France with the relative ease of 1870–1? Where did the principles enunciated by Lloyd George in 1898 place him then? It might appear that the same liberal and democratic grounds that had demanded peace with France in 1898 required British intervention on France's side in 1914.

So if, in truth, there was some ambiguity in the position of war resisters, both Liberal and Labour, on 2 August, that ambiguity was the necessary product of the terrifying alternatives confronting them. They simply could not know what would happen to liberal principles, or democratic practices, or socialist ideals, if Britain stood aside from a war initiated by Germany against France. And their problem was made no easier by the dual manner in which they so often perceived Germany itself. In one sense Liberals could find much in Germany to admire. It was a major contributor to European civilization: the land of Luther and Beethoven and Goethe and town planning and scientific innovation. In another and ever more pressing sense it was a major impediment to the advance of civilization as they understood it: the land of blood and iron, of the Zabern incident, of the most powerful and loud-mouthed and dangerous of 'titled and throned Philistines'. Their problem was knowing how to act until they were certain which Germany they were really observing.

In the circumstances it is remarkable how steadfast the majority of the Cabinet were on 2 August in refusing to take France's side against Germany. Nor is the point met by saying that they were play-acting, knowing all along that the Belgian issue would resolve their difficulties. There are many occasions when a body of men can know something on the level of the intellect and yet, because of its grossly unpalatable nature, refuse to entertain it as part of their calculations. (At the present time there is obviously a vast gulf between what we 'know' concerning the preparations of the major powers for nuclear war, with all the frightful consequences it can produce, and what we actually consider to be the limits of conduct open to those countries within the international sphere.) Thus it was possible for the Liberal Cabinet to 'know' that Germany's military necessity, and military planning, pointed to action against Belgium, and still to balk at the belief that any civilized European country would annihilate Belgian independence as and when its military convenience required. To embrace such knowledge meant accepting something atrocious about the world in which they lived which Liberal statesmen proved reluctant to do.

Anyway, it is an over-simplification to claim that the Liberal Cabinet knew in advance how Germany proposed to treat Belgium. The most devoted anti-German in British military circles did not know that. In 1911 General Sir Henry Wilson, then Director of Military Operations and an architect of Anglo-French pre-war military arrangements, wrote a discourse on military prospects. He concluded that if Germany were to make an effective attack upon France, it must send its forces through Belgium. But he feared that Germany's action would not constitute so severe a violation of Belgian neutrality as to provoke that country either to resist or to appeal for outside aid. By an accident of geography, Wilson wrote, Belgium was a country divided into two unequal parts, of which the larger (some two-thirds of the whole) lay north of the river Meuse and the smaller lay south of it. There seemed good reason for the Germans to

---

[7] Quoted in John Grigg, *The Young Lloyd George* (London: Eyre Methuen, 1973), p. 223.

confine their passage through Belgium to the southern sector. Wilson deeply feared that the Belgian Government would accept this degree of intrusion and not regard it as cause for war. (The conclusion he drew is of passing interest. The British Government, he insisted, must forthwith tell the Belgian authorities that it would not tolerate such a cowardly response, would regard Britain's own military guarantee to Belgium as operative, and would require of the Belgians full resistance to German forces on their territory. The Liberal Government in 1911 failed to endorse Wilson's proposal.)

Thus even to British observers who expected the worst of Germany, it was not plain in 1914 that German military planning proposed the destruction of Belgian independence. It might involve only a limited territorial transgression that would not arouse Belgian resistance.

Clearly the difference between these two courses mattered to Liberal Ministers, even if they were unacquainted with Henry Wilson's paper. In virtually every observation they made on 2 August about Belgium as a possible cause for reconsidering their position, they introduced a significant qualification. The reference to Belgium is extended to mean more than a limited intrusion. Ministers speak of an invasion 'wholesale', of a 'substantial' violation, of Belgium being 'absorbed' and 'subordinated' by Germany. There is no warrant for assuming that Cabinet members resisting intervention in the fast-approaching war between Germany and France had already decided to change their minds the moment Germany intruded into Belgium, should such intrusion not threaten the Channel ports or produce a cry for help from the Belgian people.[8]

In keeping the issue of Belgium in reserve on 2 August, while not spelling out how they comprehended it, Ministers like Lloyd George were not necessarily 'shamming'. Rather, they were acknowledging that at this moment, as at every point since Germany had emerged as a mighty military-industrial power and had then embarked on a programme of naval building, the ultimate course of British foreign policy lay beyond British control – even the control of a British Government made up broadly of Liberal war resisters. Any German Government henceforth possessed the wherewithal to commit atrocious deeds. And even the most benevolent Liberal Minister could have no certainty, only hope, that such deeds would not be committed. The problem of 2 August was that hope was being largely, but not entirely, dashed. If, while attacking France, the Germans kept their navy out of the Channel (as they were proving ready to do), and if they moderated any incursion into Belgium, it was a nice point whether hope should yet be abandoned. And while this remained unsettled, the survival of the Liberal Cabinet was in grave peril. The dilemma was real enough.

---

[8] The importance of the distinction between a partial and a total German invasion of Belgium was apparent to more than Cabinet Ministers and military planners. As late as the evening of 3 August the anti-war Liberal MP Philip Morrell, striving to the last to keep Britain out of the conflict, stated in Parliament that he was 'not prepared to support a Government which goes to war. . . because there may be a few German regiments in a corner of Belgian territory'.

3

THE DISPOSITION OF ARMIES

Personally, I trembled at the reckless way Sir J. French spoke about 'the advantages' of the B.E.F. operating from Antwerp against the powerful and still intact German Army! So when it came to my turn to speak I formulated a number of questions to bring out the risk we would run of 'defeat in detail' if we separated from the French at the outset of the Campaign.

Diary of Sir Douglas Haig relating meeting of the War Council, 5 August 1914

I

In Britain, during August 1914, the troop trains ran on time. For once in the nation's history the decision to go to war produced prompt and efficient action. Late in 1912, in the aftermath of the second Moroccan crisis, the Government had established the Railways Executive Committee (REC) to plan the management of the railways in the event of war. One of its tasks was to arrange for the collection and dispatch of the British Expeditionary Force (BEF) – not only men but also horses, vehicles, guns, bicycles, stores. The members of the REC were supplied with a codeword to indicate the inception of a precautionary period. One member, receiving it by telephone on 31 July 1914, began asking his caller, 'What on earth are you talking about?' Then he realized.

II

The actions of Germany on 3 and 4 August had brought the Liberal Cabinet's indecision abruptly to an end. Confronted with the cynical brutality of the German ultimatum to Belgium, the precipitate movement of massed German troops towards the Liège forts holding the Meuse, and the deeply felt plea for aid from the Belgian monarch, the British Cabinet ceased to have doubts about the nature of this war. On the evening of 3 August the Cabinet agreed, with negligible dissent, to demand an assurance that Germany would respect Belgian neutrality. This message, dispatched the next morning, did not contain the time limit that Grey argued for. To Ministers as important as Asquith and Lloyd George it could be viewed as a last bid for British neutrality. Nor should it be dismissed as such. It is not pointless to speculate what would have happened if the German Government, preferring military reality to 'military necessity', had conformed to the British demand.

At noon on 4 August the Cabinet was informed of the massive German invasion of Belgium. It was then decided to send a second message to Germany, this time an ultimatum with a time limit to expire by midnight (11 p.m. British time). That afternoon Asquith informed the House of Commons of what was happening. When he read the terms of the German demands on Belgium, which justified invasion on the grounds that French troops had already entered Belgian territory, 'there was an outburst of incredulous laughter.'[1] The mood of Parliament, according to *The Times's* correspondent, had moved since Grey addressed it the day before from 'a slightly hesitant uncertainty . . . to a grim and all but unanimous determination'. And it is certainly the case that, whereas on 3 August back-bench Liberal and Labour voices had been raised against intervention, now they were silent. Asquith's announcement of the British ultimatum (although he did not use that word) brought forth 'an answering roll of cheers from every quarter of the Chamber'.

Plate 2   *A British troopship arriving at a French harbour.*

On 5 August, with war now a fact, Government leaders and their principal military advisers – acting as an ad hoc War Council – considered the use to be made of the BEF. Only one strategy had been prepared in the pre-war years: that which the British and French military staffs had developed with loving care ever since 1905. In accordance with it, the seven divisions of the BEF would move immediately to France and take up position on the left wing of the French army – which numbered some 70 divisions. On 5 August the newly created War Council pondered whether to adhere to this scheme. A voice as authoritative as that of Grey argued for delay, while the recently appointed commander of the Expeditionary Force, Sir John French, proposed that his troops be sent to Antwerp in northern Belgium. But the majority agreed that the BEF should go to France. Doubtless they were influenced by the fact that well-laid plans existed for this course and that no plans existed for any other. But it is questionable

---

[1] *The Times*, 5 August 1914.

whether (as is so often claimed) this was a major force behind their decision. The logic of the situation pointed irresistibly in this direction. After all, the immediate purpose for which the nation was going to war was to defend Belgium. Yet how could Britain accomplish this? Its first great act of war, and the only one of which it was capable in 1914, was the dispatch of the fleet to the north of Scotland. This may have been of immense long-term significance, but it seemed to have little direct bearing on Belgium and its needs. For Britain's ultimatum to Germany to be anything more than an empty gesture, its immediate implementation would have to rest on the French. They alone possessed the necessary army. The least Britain could do was to send them the BEF as a token contribution.

This proposal went to the full Cabinet for confirmation the next day, 6 August. Thereupon the newly appointed Secretary of State for War intervened. In the long term he saw the war as a protracted affair in which Britain would have to be a major military as well as naval participant. But as regards the immediate situation, he could not deem the country to be secure from invasion. In addition to the BEF, Britain had a Territorial Army raised for home defence, but the new War Minister chose to ignore it. At his instance it was decided that, for the moment, two of the BEF's seven divisions would be left behind.

Perhaps only a Secretary of State for War who was also a Field Marshal and Britain's most acclaimed soldier could have thus amended the military staff's carefully devised plans.

III

The decision having been taken, the trains proceeded to run. In the course of five days, 1,800 special trains were employed in various parts of the country. The docks and sidings of Southampton, in particular, were stretched to capacity as trains brought the troops in from the depots and the ships carried them off to secret destinations. The whole operation proceeded with admirable smoothness.

The men who went to France were all regular soldiers; that is, they were all in the army because they chose to be there. Of course, choice in such a matter was often a relative term. For officers and men alike, social position and economic opportunities and personal capabilities (or the lack of these) had usually set severe limits to the type of occupation that they might enter. Many officers chose to join the army because only there could they enjoy the lifestyle which they felt appropriate to their background and breeding. Many common soldiers entered the ranks because this was their only means of escape from slum life, sweated labour, tyrannical employers, or total want of employment. (It might also provide escape from importunate females or the approaching arm of the law.) Appropriately, the first infantry brigade to withstand the German onslaught at Mons, the Royal Fusiliers, was composed almost entirely of Cockneys. Since the transportation of criminals had ended in the mid-nineteen century, the British Government had offered few other opportunities for overseas travel to men from this social stratum.

To say that the BEF consisted of men who chose to be in the army is not to say that they chose to be there at this particular moment. When an individual joined the regular army, he signed up for a minimum of seven years in the service, followed by five years in the reserve – that is, five years during which, although returned to civilian life, he could be required to rejoin the ranks. As many regulars in August 1914 were serving in the outposts of Empire, or were not sufficiently trained to be fit for service anywhere, the need to call out the reservists was pressing. A good half of the men who crossed the

Channel in August 1914 belonged in this category. Some had established themselves in domestic life after their army service, and were rudely shaken by the letter or telegram ordering them back to the colours. Others had been convinced by renewed experience as civilians that the army was still the best of available evils. But for both sorts of reservist, as indeed for many regulars who had not served outside the army depots of Britain, the events of the ensuing days proved a taxing experience. Clad in rough khaki uniforms that felt like sandpaper, and shod in newly issued boots which had to be broken in on the cobbled roads of France, they were soon obliged to march prodigious distances in what, by North European standards, was a most creditable version of summer.

IV

As the BEF disembarked in France, its tiny numbers were sucked inexorably into the military planning of the great Continental powers.

In 1870–1 Germany had won a decisive victory over France and had deprived her of two of her provinces. Thereafter it was always possible that the struggle would be renewed, as France sought for revenge or as Germany chose to remove the menace of France for good. Given Germany's growing alignment with Austria-Hungary, as well as its own expanding influence in Turkey and the Near East, it became increasingly likely that in any future conflict Germany would have to contend against Russia as well as against France. For Moltke the elder, who had masterminded the victory in 1870, this threat of a war on two fronts admitted of no easy solution. Nevertheless, he did perceive a hopeful course of action. He was under no delusion that either France or Russia could be eliminated speedily. As far as France was concerned, that had not happened in the fortunate circumstances of 1870. But he believed that Germany was in a position to defeat the armies of its potential opponents piecemeal. The obvious action that a French army would take against Germany would be to cast itself into the lost provinces of Alsace and Lorraine. Moltke planned to make the French forces pay dearly both as they crossed the frontier and as they penetrated into the disputed territory. Then they would be smashed beyond recall by a German army held ready behind the rivers Rhine and Main. Only after that would the Germans take the offensive into French territory.

Moltke's prescription for the Russians was similar. The vast superiority of German road and rail communications behind the lines meant that, at whatever points the Russian armies chose to attack, German forces could move to await them and crush them one by one. If this did not produce a total Russian collapse, it would in time drive the Tsar to seek a settlement.

Moltke's post-1870 strategy deserves to be recalled with honour. For one thing, his plans were largely vindicated by the events of August 1914. In that month the French launched an assault into Lorraine, and the Russians invaded East Prussia. Both suffered crushing defeats, even though the German forces were making their main effort elsewhere. Secondly, Moltke's plans eliminated any *military* need for Germany to adopt an offensive posture in advance of a European war and, in particular, at the moment when a European crisis flared up. Finally, he did not commit Germany to a war against both France and Russia should the opportunity for a war against only one of them happen to offer itself.

It must be left to other historians to ponder why Moltke's plans disappeared with him. Was it simply folly on the part of his successors, or some deep expansionist craving within the psyche of Germany (or of the German ruling class)? Whatever the cause, Germany after 1900 became committed to a strategy opposed in every vital respect to Moltke's. This change is associated with Count von Schlieffen, who was Chief of the German General Staff from 1891 to 1906 and whose plans dominated German military thinking even after his retirement and death. Schlieffen accepted not just the likelihood but the inevitability of a two-front war. But he affected to believe that one of the two great powers that lay alongside Germany could be eliminated before its partner became effective – as long as Germany seized the initiative from the outset. As against the flexible strategy of the elder Moltke, which consisted of a response to the military initiatives of France or Russia or both, Schlieffen developed a strategy of terrifying inflexibility. He proposed to move on to the offensive instantaneously, in such a way that France would be crushed before Russia (against whom Germany would initially conduct a holding operation) could make itself felt.

The speedy elimination of France might seem a tall order. France had resisted for a long time even after all had seemed lost in 1870–1. And since that date its defensive capacity had much increased. It had constructed a string of fortifications along the Franco-German frontier, and a complex railway system that would enable it to move forces behind the lines to any threatened area. Schlieffen proposed to counter these difficulties by outflanking the French defences and the French army as a whole. He would place the great weight of his forces on his right wing in the north, drive through Belgium, and enter France across the largely undefended Franco-Belgian frontier. While the French would be pressing ahead into Alsace-Lorraine in the south, the Germans would descend from the north on both sides of Paris, isolate the capital, cut the French army's communications, and drive it into the Rhine or over the Swiss frontier. In six weeks the war in the West would all be over.

Schlieffen's scheme, into the application of which there went a vast amount of staff planning, was implemented in its essentials in July–August 1914. However, his successor, Moltke the younger, did introduce certain modifications. This was fortunate for Schlieffen's posthumous reputation, for since then attention has been concentrated on the modifications made to Schlieffen's plan rather than on the scheme's inherent defects. Yet it is the latter that deserve comment. Schlieffen's answer to the problem of France's speedy elimination was at best only partial. Yet in this situation an incomplete answer was no answer at all. First, his plan depended on the co-operation of his enemies – that is, on the French making no response to the threat of encirclement. His plan in no way removed the *capacity* of the French to halt their own advance and move laterally from south to north to meet the invader before they could be outflanked. Secondly, Schlieffen's plan presented an enormous problem of practicability. Was it possible for a German army, without motorized transport or (after it had left German territory) certain rail communications, to advance across Belgium, continue into France, swing south beyond Paris, and still be in a fit condition and with adequate supplies to sever the French lines of communication? As long as the French retained an army in the centre – and, according to their known plans, they would at least have one in Paris, the strongest fortress in Europe – which lines of communication were more likely to be cut, the French or the German? Schlieffen, not his fainthearted disciples, had failed to answer these questions.

V

If German military planning had moved, between the 1870s and 1914, from a cold appraisal of defensive capabilities into an offensive Cloud-Cuckoo-Land, the same had happened in France. As mentioned above, a line of fortresses had been constructed along the Franco-German border in order to prevent a repetition of the devastating attack that the Germans had launched in 1870. The French had also provided, in the centre, a gap between these fortresses. Into it, they had hoped, the German army might plunge to its destruction. But by 1914 this essentially defensive strategy had been abandoned. French military planners were sharing the belief of their German opposite numbers that a speedy decision could be achieved by a lightning offensive.

If anything, the French Commander-in-Chief, Joseph Joffre, and his associates accepted the logic of offensive doctrine more completely than did the Germans – and so suffered its unhappy consequences earlier and more thoroughly. As soon as their political masters allowed them, French headquarters responded to the German declaration of war by launching their armies, in mid-August 1914, first into the lost province of Lorraine in the south, then into the Ardennes in the centre. Obsessed by the belief that offensive *élan* on the part of the individual soldier was the determinant of victory, Joffre's advisers had neither acquainted their forces with the terrain over which they were to advance nor equipped them with ample heavy artillery. (Reliance was placed on light artillery, which could keep pace with a swiftly moving attack.) Further, they lacked accurate knowledge of the size of the German forces to be assailed – which proved to be much larger than expected. These omissions in French military planning produced offensives quite unlike those intended. Instead of headlong dashes, the French operations into Lorraine and the Ardennes in August 1914 took the form of cautious gropings forward into unfamiliar territory against uncalculated adversaries. They were repulsed with heavy loss.

Neither of Joffre's offensives seemed particularly related to the onrush of German forces through Belgium that was occurring at the same time. In truth, neither was related to it. Joffre was convinced that the German mass was concentrated opposite the French centre, and that he would catch the enemy in a deadly embrace. At the same time as this embrace was being rudely shrugged off, Joffre was finding himself obliged to take notice of the alarming events in the north. He had believed that the German attack on Belgium was limited in scope and could be held up by the rivers, fortresses, and armed forces of that country, with a minimum of Allied military aid. By the third week in August it was becoming plain that he was wrong. The impressive Belgian defences were being swept aside. A mighty German force, comprising at least two Armies, was about to descend on his Fifth Army on the far left of the French line. Should it not be checked, a substantial sector of the French fighting force would be in danger of envelopment.

On 25 August Joffre issued his second general order of battle. With it his great thrust into the lost provinces, and thence to the Rhine, and thence to Berlin, was over. His main concern now was to deploy troops from south to centre, so as to create behind his endangered left wing – and in front of Paris – a force capable in time of stemming the German advance.

4

WAR OF MOVEMENT

And those Nobodies of Mons, the Marne, and the Aisne, what were they? The 'hungry squad,' the men shut outside the factory gates, the useless surplus of the labour market.... Yet the Nobodies stood to it at Mons.

H. M. Tomlinson, Waiting for Daylight *(London: Cassell & Coy, 1929), pp. 136–7.*

The losses in the Guards are terrible.

Lord Stamfordham to Lord Crewe, 8 November 1914

I

If by late August 1914 the left wing of the French army was in danger, then so was the British Expeditionary Force. The BEF had taken up position alongside the French at Maubeuge, an industrial town bearing an uncomfortable resemblance to Stoke-on-Trent. Between Maubeuge and the sea, a distance of some 50 miles, there was almost no military force. In technical language, the British left flank hung in the air. So although the BEF was but a small component of the Allied forces, it was now involved in events of considerable magnitude.

The German sweep westwards through Belgium, on which depended the success of the Schlieffen plan, was being executed by its crack First and Second Armies. On 20 August the commander of this force made a momentous decision. He concluded that the furthest extension of his enemy's line lay directly to his south. If he brought his two Armies down upon it in parallel lines, he would fully engage the French with part of his force and outflank them with the rest. His plan involved a crucial miscalculation. He believed the BEF to be still disembarking on the coast. In fact, having taken up position alongside the French, it was now advancing into Belgium. The German First Army, instead of finding its way clear, crashed into the BEF at Mons. In rough figures the Germans at this point numbered 200,000, the British 75,000.

The battle of Mons on 23 August 1914, like so many aspects of the First World War, was a paradoxical event. There was the obvious paradox. The British were driven into retirement; their attempts to liberate Belgium ended before they had begun. Yet by thwarting the Germans' outflanking movement they achieved a considerable success.

But the contradiction goes deeper. The encounter at Mons, in terms of its setting and many of its features, seemed an entirely fitting way of introducing the British to twentieth-century warfare. This was the first battle in history fought in an urbanized industrial area. The district around Mons was an unlovely collection of pitheads,

41

factories, slagheaps, and shabby workers' dwellings. Again, this was the first occasion in which aircraft participated directly in a clash of arms: the Germans used them to spot the fall of shell. Further, the number of shells descending upon the British positions, if small enough by the standards of later battles, seemed so vast as to herald a new form of war – one in which heavy industry was threatening to render obsolete the skills and valour and endurance of individual fighting men.

Plate 3   *The battle of Mons: a photograph taken immediately before the commencement of fighting.*

Yet this was not how the battle of Mons appeared to contemporaries in Britain. Their vision of it found expression in the widespread belief – at however superficial a level of believing – that during the struggle, at a moment when all seemed lost, angelic hosts appeared on the battlefield to hold back the German hordes. No doubt the legend of the Angels of Mons was only an early manifestation of wartime credulity. Even so, superstition on this occasion expressed itself in seemingly inappropriate form. For it is not usual to associate supernatural warriors with a struggle conducted among slagheaps and factories. That is, to contemporaries the essence of the battle of Mons did not lie in its geographical setting or in the technological innovations that found expression there.

Even to those who discounted the angels, Mons seemed not a curtain-raiser to a new kind of war but a battle in the best traditional manner. David withstood, even if he did not quell, Goliath. The established virtues of individual courage and discipline and self-sacrifice and team spirit held firm against the worst that unbridled aggression and new-style efficiency could cast against them.

The real paradox of Mons lay in the BEF itself. The German armies, numbering well over a million men on the Western Front alone, embodied the concept of the nation in arms. Britain had rejected this concept. The 75,000 troops who held the line at Mons constituted a substantial part of the entire army which, at that moment, Britain could put in the field. No country had done more than Britain to create a mass industrial society; yet none had done less – if we are prepared to except the navy, which is a pretty big exception – to transmit the features of industrial massness to the sphere of war. Now war was imposing its own inexorable demands.

While Britain was discovering this fact, its regular army was obliged to hold the ring against superior forces by a series of painful delaying actions in the old manner, wherein speed and accuracy of rifle fire played a considerable part. In this sense Mons is not a curtain-raiser to later First World War battles like Loos, the Somme, and Amiens. It belongs in a nineteenth-century volume relating deeds of heroism and adventure: the heir of Khartoum and Mafeking.

> The river of death has brimmed his banks,
>   And England's far, and Honour a name,
> But the voice of the schoolboy rallies the ranks....

II

By the end of the day's fighting at Mons the commander of the BEF was making the painful discovery that his French allies were not – as he saw it – playing the game. Under pressure of the German onslaught the French Fifth Army on the British right was withdrawing. No attempt had been made to concert this action with the BEF. Thus the British forces, already with one flank vacant, were in danger of finding themselves alone on the other flank as well. Clearly, it was time to be going.

So began the long struggle back to safety known as the Great Retreat. For several days the BEF remained in the crucial position on the Allied left, which the German pursuit had to overwhelm so as to roll up the Allied line. On 26 August the British II Corps, which had borne most of the fighting at Mons, found itself so hard-pressed that it was obliged to stand and fight. This encounter at Le Cateau was a costly matter, owing to German superiority in numbers and artillery. But after it the BEF managed to disengage from the enemy, and was not again in serious danger of being caught.

On 29 August the French Fifth Army also stood and repelled the pursuers with great effect. Sir Douglas Haig, commander of I Corps of the BEF, wanted to participate in this action. His force had seen little fighting so far and, at this point, was nearer to the French on his right than to the British II Corps on his left. But the BEF's Commander-in-Chief, Sir John French, interposed a firm veto. The terms in which he did so indicated considerable pique against his French ally. Given the treatment he had received from the Fifth Army commander at Mons, he was entitled to feel some resentment. Whether he was entitled to let it influence his conduct in battle is another matter.

Sir John French's command, not least in these early weeks of the war, was full of issues of moment. He was in charge of almost the only army that Britain could put in the field. By accident, that army was straightway involved in events crucial to the safety of the Allied line. But it was not only Sir John's military skill that was early put to the test. He was the military leader of one party to an alliance in which the other partner possessed much the superior force. In this alliance Britain had a real but uncertain role to play. At the same time he was the principal link between the civil and military authorities of Great Britain, a particularly taxing post in a country where the civil arm had always guarded jealously its authority over the military. This last aspect of French's task was made no easier by the fact that since 6 August the Secretary of State for War, the occupant of the chief civilian post concerned with war direction, had been Lord Kitchener. Fifteen years before Kitchener had been French's own commanding officer in South Africa. He was a man with little cause to appreciate either the duties of a civil office or the legitimate point at which government authority ceased and military direction took over.

French had little experience to aid him in his multiplicity of tasks. He had won popular acclaim, and the admiration of his peers, as a cavalry commander in the Boer War. Britain had not seen his equal, it was said, since Oliver Cromwell. But this was inadequate training for the roles which awaited him after 1900: first that of staff officer in peacetime, then commander in a European war which was to offer few openings for cavalry action. In the interval between the war in South Africa and the war in Europe, French had held a variety of staff positions, culminating in that of Chief of the Imperial General Staff (CIGS). According to Lord Esher, who had done much to further his career, French during that time had developed a grasp of tactical problems and a strategic insight not previously suspected of him. Others, including the King, took more note of his volatile disposition and marked proneness to irascibility, and wondered in 1914 if he was really cut out for a task that was partly one of command and partly one of intermediary. Already in Britain's pre-war fracas between the Government and the military – the Curragh incident of March 1914 – French, among others, had so mishandled the situation that he had been obliged to resign as CIGS.

His appointment to head the BEF upon the outbreak of war provided him with the opportunity to redeem a jeopardized career. But in the ensuing weeks he hardly surmounted the multiple challenges of the post. He managed to lose touch with events on the battlefield at crucial stages: the actions at Mons and Le Cateau took place almost without his being aware of them. And his conduct during the Great Retreat shook the confidence of both Joffre and the British Government. For French went further than refusing to allow Haig's corps to aid his ally in the holding action of 29 August: he then proposed to withdraw from the Allied line altogether and remove the BEF to the far side of Paris. The effect that this might have on the Allied position as a whole seems not to have occurred to him.

This proposal startled not only the French Commander-in-Chief but also the British Cabinet. Certainly, when it sent Sir John to France it had stressed that he was in charge of an independent army, for whose survival he was responsible. But the Cabinet had said this in a particular context: namely, that he was not to engage in offensives unsupported by the main Allied force. In general he had been told that the special motive of his army was to assist the French in repelling the German invasion of Belgium and France. Confronted with his proposal to abandon his ally in the midst of a retreat, the Cabinet found it necessary to spell out its intentions. He was directed to remain in the fighting line 'conforming to the movements of the French Army': 'please consider [this] an instruction.' That the person delegated to deliver this directive was Kitchener, who arrived in Paris in the full panoply of a Field Marshal, made the experience doubly galling for French. But Kitchener spoke for the Cabinet as a whole.

These events did not as yet place Sir John's command in serious danger. And to offset them he enjoyed considerable respect among the rank and file of his army. He was not, admittedly, held in high regard by either of his corps commanders, Haig and Sir Horace Smith-Dorrien, or by his deputy Chief of Staff, Sir Henry Wilson. ('Sir John as usual not understanding the situation in the least' was Wilson's view on 3 September, during the last stages of the Great Retreat; 'a nice old man but absolutely no brains'.)[1] But French did, as far as can be judged, stand high in the regard of the general soldier. His bluff manner, martial bearing, and ability to convey to his troops a sense of concern for their well-being made him look and seem the right man to command the BEF. Whether such sentiments would survive the continuing wastage in numbers among the regular soldiers, and would offset incipient doubts in high places

---

[1] These quotations are from Sir Henry Wilson's diaries. A microfilm copy of the original diary is to be found in the Imperial War Museum.

about his capacity, must depend on whether in the ensuing months he could avoid repeating the misjudgements of August.

III

For thirteen days the retreat continued. On average, foot soldiers managed four hours' sleep every 24 hours, cavalrymen three hours'. The distance covered was some 200 miles. The summer heat was intense.

A corporal in the 1st Royal Berkshire Regiment, B. J. Denore, tells how he spent the last three days of the retreat.[2] On the tenth day, 3 September 1914:

> I was rounding up stragglers most of the night until 1 a.m., and at 3 a.m. we moved off again.
>
> The first four or five hours we did without a single halt or rest, as we had to cross a bridge over the Aisne before the R.E.'s [Royal Engineers] blew it up. It was the most terrible march I have ever done. Men were falling down like nine-pins. They would fall flat on their faces on the road, while the rest of us staggered round them, as we couldn't lift our feet high enough to step over them, and, as for picking them up, that was impossible, as to bend meant to fall. What happened to them, God only knows. An aeroplane was following us most of the time dropping iron darts; we fired at it a couple of times, but soon lost the strength required for that. About 9 a.m. we halted by a river, and immediately two fellows threw themselves into it. Nobody, from sheer fatigue, was able to save them, although one sergeant made an attempt, and was nearly drowned himself. I, like a fool, took my boots off, and found my feet were covered with blood....
>
> As I couldn't get my boots on again I cut the sides away, and when we started marching again, my feet hurt like hell.

They marched until 3 p.m. – 'nothing else, just march, march, march'. At last at 8 p.m.:

Plate 4   *British troops in retreat on 28 August 1914, five days after the battle of Mons.*

---

[2] Denore's account is in C. B. Purdom (ed.), *Everyman at War* (London: J. M. Dent, 1930), pp. 7–9.

we bivouacked in a field and slept till dawn. Ye gods! what a relief.

The next morning Denore was sent with six men on outpost duty:

> I had not posted the sentries more than half an hour, before an officer found two of them asleep. The poor fellows were afterwards tried by courts martial and shot.

The long retreat resumed about 3 p.m.:

> All through the night we marched, rocking about on our feet from the want of sleep, and falling fast asleep even if the halt lasted only a minute. Towards dawn we turned into a farm, and for about two hours I slept in a pigsty.

The next day, 5 September, they were joined by reinforcements from England, whose 'plump, clean, tidy, and very wide-awake' appearance contrasted markedly with the 'filthy, thin, and haggard' countenances of those who had marched from Mons. At a place called Chaumes, 'crowded with staff officers', they learned that they were about to change direction:

> an order [was] read to us that the men who had kept their overcoats were to dump them, as we were to advance at any moment. Strangely, a considerable amount of cheering took place then.

His company, Denore discovered, had covered 251 miles since Mons.

IV

By now the British were across the river Marne south-east of Paris. They had found a new security, for they were no longer in the precarious position on the far left of the Anglo-French line. To their left there now stood the new army that Joffre had set about forming on the outskirts of Paris. Nor was its importance confined to the aid it rendered the BEF. Its existence was fraught with profound strategic consequences.

In terms of arrows on maps, all was going for the Germans according to Schlieffen's plan. But the crucial factor in that plan, the envelopment of the French left, was missing. Despite the withdrawal from Belgium, the French and British still held a continuous line opposite the Germans. In the light of this situation the German Commander-in-Chief amended Schlieffen's plan so that his extreme right wing, instead of carrying on east beyond Paris, turned south before reaching it and so increased the weight that could be brought to bear against the French Fifth Army. Much speculation has been offered as to what would have happened if Schlieffen's original course around Paris had been preserved. The most likely consequence is clear enough. The communications of the German right wing were now dangerously stretched, and a new French force had been created capable of striking north and severing them. So it is probable that the German First Army would have suffered just such a calamity as had overtaken the Russians at Tannenberg.

As it was, the German right wing's revised line of advance to the south laid it open to a flank attack by the French from the direction of Paris. On 5 September this attack was launched. Simultaneously the Great Retreat ended, and the Allied forces rounded on their pursuers. In the resulting battle of the Marne the Germans found themselves seriously outmanoeuvred. Their First Army was forced to deploy to the west to meet the attack from Paris. Their Second Army was fully engaged by the French attacking from the south. A gap opened between the German forces, directly ahead of the BEF. Into it stumbled the British. Their advance revealed less drive and direction than the great opportunity called for. 'Sir John babbling about strategy instead of commanding his little force and pushing like the devil in pursuit,' fumed Henry Wilson. Nevertheless, the strategic consequences were enormous. The German First Army was in danger of being caught in a pincer: to escape it there was no alternative to retreat. On 9 September the German right, on which hinged all plans of a quick decision, began to fall back. The thrust to early victory was over.

It was still the general notion that one side or the other must be winning. As the Germans were doing so no longer, the belief momentarily gripped British and French headquarters that they were now marching towards triumph. Disillusionment was swift. The Germans fell back across the river Aisne and dug in on the commanding heights above it. With great difficulty British and French forces pushed across the river, but there they were checked. Attacks and counter-attacks against entrenched positions availed nothing. Wilson's diary reveals the import of these events. On 13 September, as the British were struggling across the Aisne, he was still in the grip of optimism and speculating that the Allies would be in Germany within four weeks. On the 17 September the tone changed: 'We were fairly quiet but we are in a stalemate'. Two days later the situation was not quiet and he was making preparations lest the BEF should be driven back across the river. The worst did not happen – 'A lot of shelling going on and I Corps [were] attacked several times but they repulsed all attacks' – but his conclusion for the day was ominous: 'Our men are behaving very well, but are not doing much more than holding their own.'

In expressions like 'stalemate' and 'not doing much more than holding their own' the grim pattern of the First World War in the West was beginning to assert itself.

V

Between the Aisne and the sea stretched an open line of 170 miles. The French moved to the left to outflank the Germans, but the Germans moved right to meet them. A similar attempt, still further north, produced the same result. Next the Germans sought to outflank the French, with equal lack of success. These movements, known as the Race to the Sea, were more truly a race for the flank, with neither side winning. But as the race proceeded throughout September, the gap between the contestants and the sea gradually closed. At this point Falkenhayn, the newly appointed German Commander-in-Chief, made a major decision. No immediate prospect of a complete victory in the West remained, but he could still hope for a strategic success there. By employing the new forces becoming available to him, he could mount a substantial attack through Belgium and northern France and seize the Channel ports as far down the coast as Calais.

Sir John French was also making an important decision. He was not happy about his position, stuck dead in the middle of France. He urged on Joffre that the BEF should be moved from there and should take up its old place on the Allied left, in that part of Belgium which remained out of German hands. Joffre was agreeable to the move, although not to the speed with which it was executed. Nevertheless, it was a minor triumph of staff work that, over a series of nights, the BEF was spirited away from under the Germans' noses and replaced by French forces. From the Aisne the BEF was entrained to Boulogne, on the coast of France, and thence to the district of Belgium around Ypres.

There were sound reasons for this redeployment. The move from the Aisne to Belgium shortened the lines of communication between the BEF and its home base, from which it drew its reinforcements, ammunition, medical supplies, and much of its food, and to which it sent its wounded. But Sir John French, ex-cavalry officer and hero of the dash to Kimberley, had another reason for the move. He wanted to escape the static, heavily defended positions on the Aisne. On the thinly held plains of Flanders he hoped to manoeuvre his mounted forces. As he told Joffre on 29 September: 'I feel sure the freedom of action which we shall thus gain will increase the value of our troops and enable the cavalry to assert their superiority by wide flanking movements on the flank.'

This was to prove just one of the Great War's many examples of the gulf between expectations and reality, between what men planned and what actually occurred. It is often asked why military commanders 'chose' trench warfare when this proved to be such as unimaginative way of conducting a war. The First Battle of Ypres in October and November 1914 seems a particularly frightful example of a trench contest. Yet neither commander chose it. Falkenhayn was seeking a swift move to Calais, Sir John a wide flanking movement and the assertion of cavalry superiority. Events were to dictate that the Germans never saw Calais and that the British discovered no 'freedom of action' and no 'wide flanking movements' – indeed, no flank at all.

For the best part of a month the BEF around Ypres, aided by the Belgians on their left and growing numbers of French on their right, withstood this latest German onslaught aimed at securing a strategic victory. Initially the Germans attacked on a wide front, employing a large proportion of inexperienced troops who had escaped military service in peacetime but had rushed to join up on the outbreak of war. As the assault continued, it became concentrated more and more on the British-held sector of the line, employing experienced German forces drawn from quiescent parts of the front and utilizing all available supplies of high-explosive shell. The British were outnumbered by a margin of between four to one and seven to one, and by vastly superior artillery. Their trenches were sketchy and usually waterlogged. German attacks followed the same pattern: mass waves of infantry in the wake of a furious artillery bombardment. On 24 October: 'The I Corps really took tea with the Germans .... These Germans attacked 5 times in close formations singing 'Die Wacht am Rhein' and the place became a shambles. They must have had 6000 or 7000 casualties.' (Henry Wilson). Gradually the British-held sector around Ypres contracted. One ridge after another was lost, usually after changing hands several times. But the BEF and its allies never conceded more than a local advance. The price paid by the attackers was always too great to allow of exploitation. By mid-November the Germans could support this cost no longer. The attempted break-through to Calais was abandoned.

It has earlier been suggested that, for the British, the battle of Mons belongs in one of those old-style books relating tales of heroism and adventure. If so, then the first battle of Ypres constitutes that volume's positively last chapter. The British regular army no longer had the capacity to fight a major battle. Of the force that had set off at the beginning of August, about one-third were dead and many more would never fight again. Battalions that had numbered about 1,000 men at the outset retained of their original force some 30 men and a single officer. Nor was it only the divisions that had trudged from Belgium to the Marne and back again that had lost so heavily. The British 7th division arrived on the Continent only on 7 October. It consisted entirely of regular soldiers, brought back from stations overseas. With no reservists among them, it was the most professional body employed by Britain during the entire campaign. This was reflected in its skill with the rifle. So fast and accurate was its fire that German troops advancing against it believed it to be equipped almost exclusively with machine-guns. But three weeks of continuous battle at Ypres practically destroyed the

7th division as a fighting force. When it was withdrawn from the line on 7 November, a month after arriving in France, its 12,000 men and 400 officers had been reduced to fewer than 2,500 men and 50 officers. Sir Henry Newbolt's river of death had not merely brimmed but had broken its banks.

VI

Britain's military involvement in the first five months of the war gains drama from the fact that the BEF seemed repeatedly to be engaged in the crucial area of fighting. Yet too much should not be made of this. The whole front in France and Belgium was crucial. German military leaders were not so wedded to their strategic preconceptions that, once war began, they would have passed up the opportunity of seizing victory at some unanticipated point if one had offered itself.

It was the exertions of the major Allied armies – the French and the Russians, not the British – that prevented the Germans from substituting some new strategy for their vain efforts against the Anglo-French left. The large-scale movements that the Russians mounted into Upper Silesia and the Carpathians between September and November 1914, notwithstanding their earlier disaster at Tannenberg, denied the German High Command a solution to the riddle posed by the Eastern Front. Russia remained for Germany a threat to the security and even survival of Germany's main ally, Austria-Hungary; and an opportunity for Germany to accomplish the major – yet perhaps not really decisive – victory that was eluding it in France.

Even more, German strategy in the West continued to be directed against the Allied left because nowhere else on that front did a real opportunity present itself. Along the Franco-German border the French line held firm. The French armies had paid dearly for their ill-judged offensives there during August; yet when the Germans sought to capitalize on this by themselves driving into France, they were held and thrown back. The battle of the Marne in early September, which is seen as a turning-point in military history, would have counted for little if meanwhile the French armies in the south and centre had not been withstanding relentless German assaults. Like the elder Moltke, the French strategists who after 1871 had developed a defensive policy and had made preparations accordingly were now being amply vindicated.

This is not to detract from the BEF's achievements. Doubtless if they had not checked the Germans at Mons or held the line at Ypres, the French would have managed to construct other defensive positions – but not without substantial losses of manpower and strategic territory. The German casualties at Ypres were such as to evoke an expression of dismay from the German Chancellor, Bethmann-Hollweg; and to the Kaiser's Adjutant-General the action was 'a first-class moral defeat'. And even greater than the BEF's accomplishments was what they portended for the war as a whole. Falkenhayn justified his decision to make a bid for Calais, rather than follow up successes against Russia, on two grounds. The first was that a victory over the Russian forces would not be final. The other was that 'our most dangerous enemy is not the one in the East, but rather England, with whom the conspiracy against Germany stands or falls.'

5

AN IRISH REGULAR I: TO THE AISNE

I

Among the regular soldiers who saw action at Mons, on the Aisne, and at Ypres was a southern Roman Catholic Irishman named John F. Lucy. He was 20 years of age.[1]

If the pre-war soldier was asked why he had enlisted, Lucy records, he would answer in one of two ways. When in inventive mood he would explain that he had spilled sugar on the grand piano while his mother was entertaining some members of the peerage, 'and of course one could not expect [one's] mother to put up with that kind of conduct'. If he was not feeling inventive, the soldier would answer more truthfully: 'I 'listed for me pound.' The pound was weight, not money. It referred to the soldier's daily ration of bread. Unemployment and the need for food were what usually drove men to join the colours. 'So it was with most of us who marched to Mons.'

There were some exceptions, among them 'a taciturn sergeant from Waterford who was conversant with the intricacies of higher mathematics, and who was very smart and dignified and shunned company', 'an ex-divinity student with literary tastes, who drank much beer and affected an obvious pretence to gentle birth', 'a national school teacher', 'a man who had absconded from a colonial bank', 'a few decent sons of farmers', and a remnant consisting of 'scallawags' and 'very minor adventurers'.

John Lucy belonged among the very minor adventurers. At the beginning of 1912 he and Denis, his younger, more daredevil brother, were just out of school, unsettled by the death of their mother, at odds with their father, a bit wild, unimpressed by a brief acquaintanceship with a newspaper office, and out of favour with their landlady (whose residence they had accidentally set on fire).

> We were tired of landladies and mocked the meaning of the word. We were tired of fathers, of advice from relations, of bottled coffee essence, of school, and of newspaper offices. The soft accents and slow movements of the small farmers who swarmed in the streets of our dull southern Irish town, the cattle, fowl, eggs, butter, bacon, and the talk of politics filled us with loathing. Blow the lot.
>
> As a matter of fact we were full of life and the spirit of adventure, and wanted to spread our wings.
>
> We got adventure. We enlisted.

When the Lucy brothers joined up they were too young to shave, still wore school caps (which earned them much mockery on their first appearance in barracks, particularly as they doffed them to the corporal), and spoke with rural Cork accents, which were despised by Dubliner and Belfast-man alike. Given the state of Anglo-Irish politics, they found swearing the oath of allegiance to the crown a cause of some natural qualms of conscience. To allay their uneasiness they chose to join an Irish

---

[1] All the quotations that follow are taken from Lucy's account of his experiences as a regular soldier before and during the First World War: John F. Lucy, *There's a Devil in the Drum* (London: Faber & Faber, 1938).

regiment. However, prudence suggested that it should be one stationed as far from home as possible, which meant Ulster. This did not run them into great sectarian difficulties. In the army the enmities which divided Catholic from Protestant in Ireland were submerged by the shared misfortunes and expectations that had brought men to this occupation.

John Lucy's chief expectation, adventure, was soon dashed. The military authorities did not regard the human material at their disposal as capable of exercising initiative, nor did they view independence of mind as a desirable quality in a new recruit. What they looked for was a high degree of physical fitness, great skill in the performance of certain basic tasks, a well turned-out appearance on the parade ground (a requirement that they carried to the point of mania), and the utmost obedience to orders and regulations. Gruelling punishments were invariably on hand for those who fell short of these requirements.

Lucy recounts his early months of military life:

> We drilled, and drilled, and drilled; the bugle bullying us on to parade after parade. Our weak muscles were wrenched at physical exercises at which everything for a solid hour was executed on the tips of our toes. This was our worst experience. We sprinted from one kind of torture to another while our mouths went dry, our bodies clammy and stale, and our limbs trembled.
> . . . It was a rotten life, and we were very, very sorry for having enlisted.

Many men broke under the strain. Some sought escape by going bad deliberately: in broad daylight they stole or smashed windows or attacked the police, 'and so got imprisonment and freedom'.

> Some developed an insolent obstinacy, became dirty and disobedient, and experienced the whole gamut of military punishment from simple confinement to barracks to imprisonment with hard labour, passing, still incorrigible, through the hands of hard-hearted and bitter provost sergeants and prison warders. . . . Others failed physically, their underfed bodies and weak muscles being unsuitable to produce the swiftness of limb and coordination of action required in the British infantry, and they were released labelled 'medically unfit', or 'not likely to become an efficient soldier'.

The unending round of punishment awaiting the persistent delinquents – those chronically untidy or late on parade – could be utterly demoralizing.

> I have seen a case-hardened defaulter – a reckless fellow of cheerful temperament – sob like a tormented child at the treatment meted out to him by the provost sergeant.

For the ordinary recruit, it was the NCOs – lance-corporals, corporals, and above all sergeants – who ruled their lives. The officers proper were aloof folk who had little to do with them.

In addition to training its recruits, the army sought to educate them. One hour in every day (except Saturday) was spent on schooling. For John Lucy, who was already well educated by army standards, this was unrelieved tedium. He had to spend 18 months in acquiring a first-class certificate for which he was qualified at the outset. And when he got it, it made him seem a freak to his less well qualified comrades and earned him the resentment of some NCOs.

During the opening spell of his army career ('the worst six months of my life') Lucy's existence was an unending round of

> military vocabulary, minor tactics, knowledge of parts of the rifle, route marches, fatigues, semaphore, judging distance, shooting, lectures on '*esprit de corps*', and on the history of our regiment, spit and polish, saluting, drill, physical training, and other, forgotten

subjects.... We became insensitive, bored, and revolted, and talked seriously of deserting after three months of the life. We spent our meagre pay on food.

But in due course, as the older recruits were drafted to the battalion's home station in England, the Lucy brothers found themselves starting to match up to the army's requirements. They became members of the depot's crack squad.

> In time we effaced ourselves. Our bodies developed and our backs straightened according to plan. We marched instead of walking, and we forced on ourselves that rigidity of limb and poker face that marks the professional soldier. Pride of arms possessed us, and we discovered that our regiment was a regiment, and then some.
>
> Romance revived, despite our queer way of attaining manhood, and [despite] the fact that we had become mere mechanical numbers of an infantry unit.

By the end of six months they were trained recruits. Their bodies, 'thanks to the hated physical training', were superbly fit and their spirits high.

> Our movements on parade synchronized to perfection, we drilled as one man, and at attention were as immobile as a row of iron railings.

Soon they too were drafted to the home-service battalion in England, on their way securing their first sight of London and finding, to their disappointment, that Londoners 'looked grim and walked about with set faces', not sparing a glance for the soldiers who were their protectors. Arrival at their battalion station provided a further let-down. Once more John and Denis Lucy found themselves regarded as newcomers, not greeted with open arms but subjected to further drudgery in the gymnasium and on the barrack square by yet more ferocious instructors. But, once they had settled in, life in a battalion proved acceptable. Consisting of 700 to 800 men and some 30 officers, the battalion seemed to Lucy like a little town, with many of the same attractions. Further, they were not wholly engaged in preparing for war. Working hours were not long, and holidays were numerous. And, once their training was completed, there were specialized jobs that could be learned, like machine-gunnery and signalling, and sundry occupations that could be mastered: those of cook, waiter, valet, clerk, butcher, armourer, storekeeper.

By the spring of 1914 John Lucy and his brother were beginning to take the business of soldiering quite seriously. ('On long country walks we found ourselves again, and planned to make the best of the army.') They decided to work for promotion, even though it would mean losing caste with their friends and earning the scorn of the ordinary, professional, long-service privates. So they set about devouring regulations, textbooks, and standing orders, and soon qualified as lance-corporals. Then came the uncomfortable discovery that, at least initially, the lance-corporal was the unhappiest man in the army: isolated from his old companions, watched by his seniors for the slightest shortcoming, and paralysed by the responsibility that his single stripe conferred. It was a situation that only time and experience could render tolerable, and many did not last it out. They threw up their stripes, disgusted with a system that demanded of them more than could possibly be accomplished in the time available and yet admitted no excuses. The Lucy brothers sweated it out, and John soon advanced to the rank of corporal.

The summer of 1914 passed peacefully.

> We two brothers, both now N.C.O.s, had quite settled down, and were satisfactorily taking our minor parts in the organization and running of our regiment.

International affairs were not the concern of professional soldiers. When war clouds gathered, they were delighted at the prospect of combat and glory, and willing to fight any foreigner.

Our state of mind was peculiar to our task. We despised all foreigners, and only wanted them at the end, the business end, of our snappy little Lee-Enfields.[2] We had great *élan* and great hopes.

They neither knew nor cared which Continental country they were to fight.

A dose of that rapid fire of ours, followed by an Irish bayonet charge[,] would soon fix things.

Then they learned that the enemy was Germany and received books with coloured illustrations of German uniforms and weapons.

The field-grey, rather baggy uniforms, comic boots, and helmets amused us. Anything strange or foreign was inferior, to the mind of the common soldier.

Preparations for war began. They disposed of review uniforms and mufti clothing and boots. In their stead came ammunition, iron rations, jack-knives, identity discs – and reinforcements.

Our reservists came streaming in to make up our war strength; cheerful, careless fellows of all types, some in bowler hats and smart suitings, others in descending scale down to the garb of tramps. Soon, like us, they were uniformed and equipped with field kits, and the change was remarkable. Smart sergeants and corporals and beribboned veterans of the South African war hatched out of that crowd of nondescript civilians, and took their place and duties as if they had never left the army.

The mobilization scheme of the British army ran like a well oiled machine, and by 13 August Lucy had said farewell to peace and to Britain.

Going to war seemed a light-hearted business. . . .
My brother and I left England as section commanders. We each had eight men. I was twenty years old and a full corporal. He was only nineteen. I was the small, dark, nervous Gaelic type, very proud and anxious to work well. He was bigger, golden-haired, careless, and easy, and a very good mixer with the men.

The battalion enjoyed an ecstatic reception from the French populace, both when they disembarked at Rouen next day, and during the train journey north-east to the Belgian frontier. They spent a night in a small village in Picardy, amidst attractive countryside, a warm kindly people, and nature at its most beautiful. Remembering the event after two decades, Lucy wrote:

the small number of us of the old Regiment who still live may recall that blissful period with tenderness and gratitude, unclouded by the vexed memories of the great events that followed.

II

On 22 August 1914, billeted in a small village south of Mons, the Irish battalion was informed that it would soon be encountering the enemy.

Keen as mustard, we overhauled our fighting gear, cleaning and recleaning our rifles and recently sharpened bayonets, easing up our cartridge clips, and looking forward eagerly to action.

That evening one company was sent ahead to act as outpost ('the first warlike act of the battalion'), and during the night Lucy and his squad of eight men were told to take forward the battalions' four ammunition carts. Next morning, Sunday 23 August, the

---

[2] The highly efficient standard army rifle.

tempo of events increased. First Lucy's squad encountered a group of wounded British cavalrymen, leading riderless horses that had belonged to fallen comrades. Then the rest of the Irish battalion came up, having first dug trenches as a defensive measure and then been ordered forward towards Mons, 'now visible through the slag heaps of many mines'.

> This dirty-looking factory town had no particular interest just then for us, until suddenly above the sound of the tread of our marching feet we heard the booming of field-guns.

They decided this must be the French artillery knocking hell out of the enemy, and pressed forward lest they miss the grand assault that would drive the Germans off the field.

Their progress was halted by a perspiring staff officer who rode up from behind with an order that the battalion should return to the trenches it had left that morning. This was not well received – the motto of the battalion was 'Attack, or counter-attack' – but the troops were not untrained for employing trenches when temporarily forced on to the defensive. Those that they had dug were of the 'kneeling' variety, some three feet deep, 'this being considered good enough for temporary occupation'. Lucy recounts:

> With many jokes the men settled into their defences and cheerfully waited for the enemy, presenting in his direction a line of first-class riflemen, each trained to fire fifteen well-applied shots a minute. Our two machine-guns poked their squat muzzles in support from their emplacements.

Close at hand was a young subaltern acting as observation officer for a battery of field guns situated on a back slope 300 yards to the rear.

> All then was ready, as far as we were concerned, for the battle of Mons.

At 3.30 p.m. the German artillery gave Lucy and his companions their 'first moment under shell-fire'. Initially the shells passed overhead and were greeted with hilarity.

> Then the enemy gunners shortened, and the shells exploded above our trenches, and the men, already taken in hand for exposing themselves, crouched low

– all except the commanding officer and his adjutant, who remained in the open throughout the bombardment, sending messages to the entrenched companies. Lucy experienced his first near-miss:

> One shrapnel bullet hit my pack, and I instinctively moved a little farther along the ditch to a burly sergeant, who laughed at me when I handed him the still hot ball for his inspection. I was too young to discern nervousness in the laugh.

Then the shelling stopped, and the defenders heard

> conch-like sounds – strange bugle calls. The German infantry, which had approached during the shelling, was in sight, and about to attack us.

Up to this point the only fire from the British side had come from the 18-pounder field guns. Now the officers' whistles sounded, and the riflemen opened fire.

> A great roar of musketry rent the air. . . . The satisfactory sharp blasts of the directing whistles showed that our machinery of defence was working like the drill book, and that the recent shelling had caused no disorganization. The clatter of our machine-guns added to the din.

The battle took the form of 'well-ordered, rapid rifle-fire at close range, as the field-grey human targets appeared, or were struck down' – to be replaced by further waves of German infantry who shared the same fate.

Our rapid fire was appalling even to us. . . . Such tactics [of massed assault] amazed us, and after the first shock of seeing men slowly and helplessly falling down as they were hit, gave us a great sense of power and pleasure. It was all so easy.

At last the surviving Germans began to retreat, their attack 'an utter failure'.

Soon all that remained was the long line of the dead heaped before us, motionless except for the limb movements of some of the wounded.

Casualties on the British side had been few – 'the least we had in any battle in the war'. One machine-gunner had been killed by a shell burst, and a lance-corporal who took his place was immediately wounded in the arm. The lance-corporal insisted on continuing to fire 'but he rather puzzled those near him by weeping at intervals, either with pain or fright'. The commanding officer and his adjutant, although exposed throughout, had escaped injury.

With night beginning to close in, Lucy's squad was sent to secure fresh stocks of ammunition. It was midnight before he rediscovered his company, and by that time they were engaged in evacuating their positions. The movement proceeded with a minimum of display:

All was very still and peaceful. Quiet words of command were passed along. . . . And off we went stealthily, in columns of fours from the battlefield of Mons.
In the morning the entire British Army was marching south in retreat.

III

Next morning, as they retreated, the battalion was ordered to cast off its packs and greatcoats. They resented doing this, as they also resented retreating. They believed that they had beaten off their assailants and should be in hot pursuit. The company commander assembled the NCOs to explain that, well though they had fought, they were in danger of being outflanked on the left by a much stronger enemy force: 'That sounded all right, but we wondered where the French army was.'

Two mornings later the battalion participated in II Corps's stand at Le Cateau. This time the enemy did not fling its infantry against the British riflemen.

The Germans had already learned their lesson from Mons, and had become cautious. Instead of men they sent shells in a steady and intense bombardment of the town [Caudry] behind us. . . . The streets nearer us began to melt away . . . . blinding flashes of concentrated explosions licked all about our single gallant field battery, which had been quickly marked down by the enemy, and which gradually slackened fire until it was ultimately smashed to silence.[3]

A hail of bullets and shells revealed that the infantry also had been discovered. Lying flat, Lucy's section took out their entrenching tools and dug as best they could until they were under cover at least from rifle and machine-gun bullets:

Lord, how we appreciated those entrenching tools, which we had hated so much during peace-time training.

Forced back again, Lucy lost two of his eight men to shelling, one killed and one wounded. But the Irishmen fought an orderly retreat, which was more than could be

---

[3] At Le Cateau the British artillery did not act on one of the major lessons learned from the Boer War: that to survive the artillery needed to be placed well to the rear of the infantry. (However the subsequent disappearance of the artillery from the view of the infantrymen did greatly increase the sense among rank-and-file soldiers that their fate was being determined by impersonal monsters, not by creatures of flesh and blood.)

said for a battalion of English soldiers on their right. These had panicked and were streaming down the road behind them.

A staff officer, his face hot with the shame of it, diverted the fleeing men into a side street in the first village we came to, shouting frantically at them: 'For God's sake men, be British soldiers.'

For Lucy, this was 'an unforgettable and disgraceful scene'.

I thought with pride of our Irishmen, extended and controlled, falling back steadily at the trail across country behind us, protecting that lousy mob, some of whom had even chucked away their weapons.

On 28 August the battalion entered the first billets to give them a complete night's rest for a week. The commander of II Corps, General Smith-Dorrien, inspected them.

He did not wear the hard and sometimes haughty look of other generals, and we liked him for it. Calm and kindly-eyed, he gazed from horseback on soldiers weary of marching and fighting. . . . General Smith-Dorrien knew that he viewed a body of men aching in every limb, to whom the smallest action, even that of moving rifles to attention, was an added minor torture, and he excused us [from marching to attention] – the good old stick. He was our man.

This was not the end of the marching, however. Rather, it proved their last good sleep in many days. The retreat resumed next morning and continuued without proper rest for day upon day, so that the men 'marched on in a trance, or rather in some idiot nightmare wherein images jostled material things, while the enemy relentlessly pursued us'.

Our minds and bodies shrieked for sleep. In a short time our singing army was stricken dumb. Every cell in our bodies craved rest, and that one thought was the most persistent in the vague minds of the marching men. . . . Men slept while they marched, and they dreamed as they walked. They talked of their homes, of their wives and mothers, of their simple ambitions, of beer in cosy pubs, and they talked of fantasies. Commonplace sensible remarks turned to inane jibberings. The brains of the soldiers became clouded, while their feet moved automatically.

Among the talkers was a sergeant who 'kept up a long dirge for hours on end about his lost pack,' although he was the only member of his platoon still wearing it; and a man who 'talked confidently and in a fresh voice of being a policeman in Paris, a city whose signboards became more ominously numerous as we went ever south'. The men's faces and hair grew steadily dirtier, and lice began to breed rapidly in their underclothing. A few men – but very few, and usually those of big stature – dropped out, and gazed with 'pained look in [their] troubled eyes' as their companions went past. John Lucy became anxious for his younger brother, and sought him out.

His usually bright face was bony with fatigue and begrimed with perspiration and dirt, but he was cheerful and contented. . . .
    I did not like seeing him look so tired, and I made a habit of paying him short visits like this during the march.
    One day he alarmed me, after a long period of silence, by remarking casually: 'One more turn to the left now, at the top of Tawney's Hill, and we're home, my lad.' As he spoke a halt was called, and he bumped helplessly into the man in front and woke up. He stoutly denied having spoken, and then I knew that he had been asleep on the march, and had been enthralled by the prospect of rest and refreshment in a farmhouse of our childhood days, where as little boys we had built forts in summer meadows and practised mimic war in the role of Irish chieftains dealing death and destruction to the Sassenach. My heart became sore with longing for the warmth and shelter of the large farm kitchen in Ireland.

In time even the officers begain to feel the strain. One captain turned his company about and marched towards the enemy. The commanding officer (who was on horseback, it being the task of the senior officers to ride up and down the line encouraging the men) galloped after him. The captain announced that he was tired of retreating; it was bad for morale, and he preferred to fight and, if need be, perish. He was relieved of his command, and his 'gallantly docile company' was brought back to the column under a junior officer.

The marching men crossed the river Oise, and then the Aisne, and then the Marne – being the last to get across before the sappers blew up the bridge. Finally, on 5 September, they passed over the Grand Morin. Here the retreat ended, and the men went into bivouac: 'We washed and changed our clothes, and slept, and fed, and slept again.' They 'noticed with satisfaction' that the soles of their feet were calloused with a 'thick, hard, healthy skin'. The battalion received reinforcements that more than made good its casualties (about 100 out of a total of 800 men). They took pleasure in telling the newcomers 'in an affected casual manner' about the realities of war – although they found themselves restrained by the realization that 'the killing of men cannot be loosely talked about'. They learned that the French on their right had already turned on their pursuers and were driving them back, and that on the following day 'we too would turn back facing north again, and start chasing Germans for a change. Now that was to our liking, and we felt braced about it.'

IV

Lucy's battalion was in reserve through most of the battle of the Marne and so saw little action. As it advanced, it encountered for the first time large numbers of German prisoners and 'many encouraging sights of an army in rapid retreat': 'The British army was certainly getting its own back.' The matter uppermost in their minds was: When would they see action again?

> The thought of another battle did not discourage us. We wanted a dig at the enemy, and smarted at the recollection of his having chased us. Our tails were up now, and we were different men – veterans in a way.

This thirst for renewed battle was soon to be satisfied. But its outcome was not what the Irish riflemen were expecting.

> On the evening of 13th September, a British aeroplane, one of the few the British Army possessed, approached us from the German side, and, wheeling around, alighted in a field to the right of our marching columns. The flying-officer climbed slowly out of his machine, and, coming stumbling towards us in his heavy kit, did not wait to find an officer, but shouted to us all: 'There they are, waiting for you up there, thousands of them.' And he waved his right arm towards the wooded heights, across the river Aisne, some three miles away.

Next morning the Irishmen were directed to cross the Aisne.

> The tone of the orders given us, the close inspection of our ammunition, and our rapid fall-in showed that there was immediate work ahead.

As they moved forward, British guns were bombarding the dominating heights on the far bank. Lucy experienced a succession of contrasting emotions. To begin with:

> It was a fine fresh morning, and we moved on exhilarated by a feeling of the unexpected. . . .

Then:

> We gripped our rifles hard. We felt on the edge of a fresh battlefield, with the curtain
> about to go up, and looked all about our front for the direction of the first threat of danger.

A burst of shrapnel that 'whipped and cracked above us' produced a third sensation:

> A curse or two expressed the nausea which every man with a stomach experiences when he
> feels helpless under a rain of slivers of steel and bullets hurled at him by an enemy two
> miles or so out of rifle shot.

The company found itself making for a railway bridge that had been blown up by the
enemy. All that existed to facilitate their crossing of the Aisne was a 'line of single
planks'. This sagged in the middle and had been 'hastily and precariously rigged
against what was left of the iron supports of the railway bridge'. Under heavy fire they
'blondined' across it (the expression pays homage to the famous tightrope walker).
They sustained few casualties themselves, but were aware that those following were
proving less fortunate. However, 'We did not turn to see.' The commanding officer,
'with his usual bravery', remained exposed during the whole period of the crossing.

Once over the Aisne, the British troops had to press on up the hill in the face of
heavy resistance. A shrapnel bullet penetrated Lucy's haversack and 'tore into the
middle of a folded towel inside it. I felt startled and angry at the tug it gave, and at my
narrow escape, and pushed on with the others.'

As they approached the crest the shelling gave way to rifle fire at close quarters.

> We cursed them, and relying on the luck of soldiers, we bowed our heads a little, shut our
> jaws, and went stubbornly on. Quicker we went, on to our toes, and crouching lower. In
> for a penny, in for a pound, quicker and quicker to get it over. Their rifles cracked sharply
> now, and the whistle and whine of bullets passing wide changed to the startling bangs of
> bullets just missing one.

Aided by British artillery fire, the Irish riflemen reached the edge of the plateau, where
they dug in. Only then did they become aware of numerous gaps in their ranks, which
they attributed to shelling – 'On the whole the enemy riflemen had been rotten shots.'
For the first time British infantry were beginning to encounter what would become for
them the war's dominating feature: its human cost. Resting in reserve while German
counter-attacks tried vainly to drive the British back down the hill, Lucy was plagued
by a soldier who 'morbidly occupied himself by passing in the names of the latest dead
and wounded. I did not want to hear them. . . . Each fresh name bludgeoned my brain.'

He sought solace from his brother, who was in a neighbouring platoon. Denis Lucy's
'absolutely calm' bearing restored his ease, and the casualties, on reflection, seemed
less terrible than he had supposed.

The day introduced him to one of war's necessary adaptations, a meal being served
to men in the battle line: 'hot tea, tepid meat, and broken loaves of bread'.

> This food was carried daily for miles, often through heavy fire, by our company colour-
> sergeants and their devoted ration parties. Its arrival broke the strain of fighting, and
> cheered us all up. In a short time we developed the habit of eating under any conditions,
> even the most appalling.

Lucy's section spent the night in one of a number of 'conveniently situated large
caves'. Although they remained in war gear, they proved not to be needed to beat back
an abortive night attack. In the morning the cry went out that the enemy was falling
back, and they readied themselves to resume the pursuit. For a brief moment longer,
they were able to remain confident that this was how the war would proceed. Yet they
were also becoming aware of a growing admiration for the Germans as a fighting force.

As Lucy's company was returning to the edge of the plateau where it had established a position the day before, the commanding officer of a company on their left came striding towards them, 'a tall gaunt captain with the light of battle in his eye', a 'very religious man he was too, always talking about duty, and a great Bible reader'. This officer was 'looking for blood'. He announced 'jubilantly and with certainty' that all the Germans had gone, except for one platoon which he had located in a wood on the left front. He was going to attack it with his company through the wood, and he needed volunteers from the troops on his right to 'move across the open' in support.

> I suppose he knew very well that the native pride of Irish troops could be depended on. Anyway the whole of 'A' Company immediately volunteered to assist. The officer selected the two nearest platoons, which happened to be mine and my brother's.

As his brother's platoon went first into the attack, John Lucy saw that Denis was almost abreast of the officer leading it, with his rifle held threateningly at high port. He made 'a good picture of the young leader going into battle', but was too conspicuous for his own safety. Dismayed, John Lucy raised himself high over the parapet of the cliff and shouted out 'Take care of yourself.' Denis looked back over his shoulder and gave a reassuring wink. ('The beggar would wink.')

Then the lieutenant of John Lucy's platoon drew his sword to signal the charge.

> We rose from cover and doubled forward over the grass to the right of my brother's platoon. There was an uncanny silence. . . . With a sinking heart I realized that our extended line made an excellent target, as we topped a slight rise, and went on fully exposed across flat country without the slightest cover.

The anticipation proved warranted. As they cleared the crest

> a murderous hail of missiles raked us from an invisible enemy. The line staggered under this ferocious smash of machine-gun, rifle- and shell-fire. . . .

A good half of the platoon fell.

> Some turned over on to their backs, and others churned about convulsively.

The survivors pressed on, but more fell as small-arms fire hit their legs.

> A bullet ripped through the sole of my right boot. . . . This low fire was a bloody business, and most efficient – the kind of stuff we were taught ourselves. I believe I was now beginning to get really afraid of these Germans.

With no officer left, a sergeant shouted to the platoon to lie prone. Thereupon

> a machine-gun raked the whole line, a weak and feeble line now, and shot accurately home into it. Some of the lying men flapped about, others, shot through the head, jerked their faces forward rapidly and lay still. I trembled with fear and horror.
> This was a holocaust. . . . The Catholic soldiers blessed themselves in a final act of resignation.

But the curve of the machine-gun's fire came short in Lucy's section. Dirt kicked in their faces and bullets ricocheted about their heads, 'but it was better than being hit direct'. Then, by luck or instinct, he spotted the machine-gun, and for a moment all the skill and training of the British regular soldier found an opportunity to assert itself.

> There it was, mounted daringly on the roof of a cottage, close to the left side of a chimney, about six hundred yards away, and directly to my front. With all my strength I shrieked the range, described the target, and ordered five rounds rapid fire. There was a heartening response as we opened fire at the first and only target we had seen in this terrible attack.
> In about four seconds some thirty bullets were whistling about that dark spot near the

chimney as we slammed in our rapid fire, glad to have work to do, and gloriously, insanely, and incredibly the German gun stopped firing, and then it disappeared as it was quickly withdrawn behind the roof.

Lucy shouted an order to fire three feet below the ridge of the roof: 'I ordered exultantly, and I could have whooped for joy. I was now commanding effectively.' Without the machine-gun the enemy fire lost a good deal of its venom.

Now thoroughly exercising his authority, Lucy looked about to see that all his section were firing. The man immediately on his right, a newcomer, was not, and when Lucy shouted at him he turned his head 'to show a grinning face' and then began to laugh.

He laughed and laughed and dug his face back in the grass. . . . The man was hysterical with fear. I did not know hysteria, and could not understand him.

Lucy moved to his right, swearing at the 'scrim-shanker', and struck him in the ribs with his rifle butt.

That steadied him, though his grin turned to a look of terror. I threatened him with a court-martial, and told him to pull his socks up. This sounded damn silly in the circumstances, even to myself, so I crept back to my central position to supervise the actions of more useful men.

The stress of battle produced other peculiarities of conduct. One man, wounded in the top of the head, came seeking the platoon sergeant to obtain permission to retire. Lucy told him to depart without delay, but the man insisted on proceeding down 'that awful line, under heavy fire, spurred by a most soldierly but ridiculous conscience to ask permission to fall out'. Somehow this stickler for duty accomplished his object and retired without further injury. (The head wound did not prove fatal.)

Lucy realized that his section was lying by chance against a tiny ridge, too insignificant to notice when they were standing but just enough to provide the cover that saved their lives.

On the left my brother's platoon was suffering badly. Nearly all the men had been hit, and only a few were returning fire. The shell-fire too was much heavier over them.

By this time all the officers of the two companies had been knocked out – two killed and seven wounded. The flashes from the swords that they had been waving as they led the attack had attracted the fire of the enemy gunners.

From this date swords went out of fashion. . . . Without officers, and sorely stricken, we still held on, until a sergeant waved us back, so we rose and returned to where we had started, exhausted and disappointed.

The attack had been a fiasco. And the roll-call after the action was a grim matter, reminding Lucy of 'Butler's picture of the Crimean roll-call'. The orderly-room clerk, to whom he went seeking news of his brother, would not divulge the total casualties – 'He had been forbidden to speak about them.' (They proved to be some 150, 'more than half the strength of the two unfortunate companies.') But the clerk did say, what Lucy had been told already by another soldier, that Denis Lucy had survived with only an arm wound.

It was not only the Irishmen who had suffered. The company on the left whose commander had initiated the attack had also lost heavily: 'Their wood was now a shambles of wrecked trees and human bodies.' Their only success had been to enter an enemy trench and bring back some prisoners. The sight of the Germans' field-grey uniforms aroused bitter feelings;

but as we continued to look at them, cold reason told us that they were only troops like ourselves, and not so straight-backed either. They looked pale and scared. The warlike commander of the left company, bleeding from several wounds in various parts of his body, and looking more fanatical than ever, would not have any of his hurts dressed until he had interrogated his prisoners. He questioned them in German, and was removed from them [only] with difficulty, and made to lie on a stretcher.

It was some days later that John Lucy learned that the news about his brother had been false.

Actually my brother was lying dead out in front, about three hundred yards away, all this time. . . . Only one man of his section had come back alive.

6

An Irish Regular II: Flanders Fields

I

The abortive attack on the Aisne on 15 September and the week of ferocious German assaults that followed were a melancholy time for Lucy and his companions. They were baffled by their failure on the 15th, which had dashed their expectation that from now on the enemy would retreat continuously. 'We had all thought we were pretty well invincible in attack, but we did not know what to think now.' They still mocked the Germans for their baggy trousers and poor marksmanship with the rifle. But they recognized that the enemy possessed real fighting qualities and that, when equipped with large quantities of artillery and machine-guns, the Germans could stop any British advance.

Further, the Irish riflemen had lost heavily in officers, including Lucy's gallant commander and adjutant (both wounded, the former seriously). The rank and file were coming to conclude that, although it was considered the acme of good leadership for officers to expose themselves, such an example was not needed, was indeed rather insulting, and that its effect was to deprive them of experienced leaders they could not afford to lose. (Not only those killed were permanently lost to them. Wounded officers were placed on the staff, or sent to England to train recruits.) Yet these infantrymen did not at all see themselves as a broken force. Certainly, they were delighted when, on 22 September, they were finally withdrawn from the Aisne fighting. But 'in spite of all, and though we had suffered heavy losses and felt a bit battered, our old spirit lived.'

John Lucy was bearing an added burden: the loss of his brother. His grief led him to take strange actions. On one occasion in October he encountered the sole survivor of Denis Lucy's section and – as he later recalled to his shame – berated the man. He told him that if he had done his duty and stuck with his commander, he also would be dead.

> That sounds nonsense now, but then I was beside myself with grief at the loss of my brave young brother. I dreamed of him at night, and once he appeared to visit me, laying a hand on each of my shoulders and telling me he was all right. I felt relieved after this curious dream.

But he still had to face the problem of going home on leave, aware that his father held him, as the older brother, responsible for Denis's action in joining up in the first place.

Leave, however, was no imminent problem. By mid-October, only three weeks after quitting the Aisne, the Irishmen were back in Flanders, advancing towards the sound of gunfire. They did so with less eagerness than they had felt when approaching Mons less than two months before: 'Did they feel,' Lucy wondered, 'as I did in my bones, that we were heading for the last round-up?' Yet to begin with, against a sketchy force of enemy, they made good progress, and by 17 October were advancing up Aubers Ridge. But five days later they were ordered back to Neuve Chapelle, allegedly to straighten the line. Large events were plainly imminent.

For some days sappers had been digging trenches to the east of this town, and these the three companies of Lucy's battalion occupied.

Our trenches, engineer-planned, were good, and clean cut in straight bays and traverses, some of which had been revetted with sandbags. We mentally thanked the sappers for their work.

The job had not quite been completed, however. There was a gap of 20 yards on the left where the trenches did not join up. And there were only the beginnings of a communication trench to the rear. According to Lucy, the construction of communication trenches always got left to last. Yet these facilitated such vital matters as the passage forward of rations and ammunition, the evacuation of wounded, and the movement of runners – as well as providing front-line troops with the reassuring knowledge that, if the worst happened, they had a way of escape.

The Irish battalion engaged in a host of activities in anticipation of the coming battle. Patrols were sent forward to provide advance warning, sentries posted, digging parties set to work, ration and ammunition parties dispatched to the rear, and runners sent off to learn the locations of the various headquarters. NCOs like Lucy, whose responsibilities were increasing as officers became fewer and less experienced, busied themselves seeing that latrines were made, fire bays improved, cubby holes dug to store ammunition, and duty rosters drawn up. With good cover and a splendid field of fire, they viewed their coming ordeal with confidence.

> All we wanted now was a little time for final improvements to finish off the good work of the sappers, and we would smash anything that came at us. We would give them 'gyp', as the troops said. But we got no time. The following morning the Germans came at us.
>
> It was the beginning of the end for us, for we had now arrived at the place of our destruction, and our fine battalion, still about seven hundred strong, perished here, almost completely, in the following five days.

II

The next morning, 23 October 1914, the Irish riflemen stood to, ready for a dawn attack. Patrols informed them that none was coming, and they settled down to routine activities. But the respite proved short.

> A tearing sound, increasing in force, caused us to raise our eyebrows, and petrified us all into watchful stillness. . . . It was the loudest shell we had heard in transit to date. . . . Would it never come down? It took an unbelievably long time. Then every man in the front line ducked as the thing shrieked raspingly louder and louder down on us. There was a terrific thump which shook the ground, and quite a pause, then a rending crash, so shatteringly loud that each of us believed it to be in his own section of trench. A perceptible wall of air set up by a giant explosion struck our faces. The monster shell had burst well behind us in amongst the houses of the village.

To blast their way through the British line, the Germans were employing the mighty howitzers that had demolished the Belgian forts. Lucy learned this only later, but he and his company had no doubt that they were to bear the brunt of a ferocious assault.

All that day the heavy shells kept coming, 'making the earth rock as in an earthquake', with field guns and smaller howitzers joining in, as well as 'the nasty stinging crash of five-nines'. As the German artillery established the range, the rate of fire speeded up:

> we crouched wretchedly, shaken by the blastings, under a lasting hail of metal and displaced earth and sods, half-blinded and half-choked by poisonous vapours, waiting for the enemy infantry, while our overworked stretcher-bearers busied themselves with new dead and wounded.

Time seemed to stand still. The infantrymen smoked nervously, passing cigarettes with trembling fingers. They felt hunger but had no desire to eat. Their mouths were parched, yet they were obliged to drink sparingly, not knowing when their bottles would be refilled. They lacked the consolation of a vigorous counter-bombardment, for ammunition was rationed for the British guns. In any lull Lucy ordered the stand-to. And to satsify himself, without unnecessary risk, that no attack was coming, he removed his cap and tilted his head back as he looked over the parapet, thus providing the smallest possible target for snipers. The Germans began interspersing their salvos of high explosive with bursts of shrapnel. The former were supposed to drive the British out of their trenches, the latter to kill them in the open. Their efforts were in vain; 'the troops held.'

Towards evening the sentries warned that the enemy were coming.

> At the same moment the earth hushed. The guns stopped. Thank Christ. Thank Christ. The relief was unspeakable. We stood up, stretching wide and loose, men once more and no longer cannon fodder.

The German infantry came marching, diagonally, across the British front in small squads, their attack aslant and badly directed, 'their men not yet extended in lines'.

> What tactics! A complete give-away. Marching about like that in 'columns of lumps' within two hundred yards of us. . . .
> We let them have it. We blasted and blew them to death. They fell in scores, in hundreds, the marching column wilting under our rapid fire. The groups melted away, and no man was able to stand in our sight within five minutes. The few survivors panicked, and tried to keep their feet in retreat. We shot them down through the back. A red five minutes. . . .
> We had cancelled out our shell-tortured day with a vengeance.

The German artillery, as if infuriated, resumed shelling until the dark. At some time in the night a patrol rushed in to say that an attack was coming, and the Irishmen fired round upon round at an unseen enemy, hearing groans and labouring sounds as the attack was stopped in its tracks.

The Germans, it became plain, were all out to capture Neuve Chapelle, 'and our unfortunate batallion, now rapidly diminishing in strength, was their main obstacle'. During the next three days, 24–6 October, the shelling continued with even greater intensity. Movement to the rear in daylight became impossible, so that the wounded had to wait for the dark before they could be evacuated. German shelling of the rear positions threw out the rations supply, and one night nothing came through. The numbers of the unwounded dwindled: Lucy's section, seven strong when they went into the line (among whom were six of the eight who had set out with him for France), contracted to three. Their condition grew more miserable.

> We were by now all very tired, cold, dirty, and ill-nourished. We were living on our nerves. Men detailed to rest gasped and groaned in broken sleep and jumped awake nervously when touched on the shoulder to be detailed for look-out.

The sequence of events – of day attacks and night attacks – became jumbled in their minds as dreams mingled with reality, but the proof of their endeavours was plain to see.

> The field [in front] was now simply covered with German bodies, the nearest only a few yards from the parapet and inside our single strand of wire.

Twice German troops penetrated the trenches to their left, and on the second occasion some of them managed to get behind the British front line.

On 26 October the two forward companies received a short respite. They were taken out of the front line to rest behind Neuve Chapelle, and in the evening were reinforced by 100 men fresh from Ireland, led by an inexperienced and easily flustered captain. But they were given no time to recuperate. That same day, in their absence, their trenches were overrun and Neuve Chapelle captured. The *château* which the commanding officer had been occupying was blown up, and the command of the battalion now devolved upon a captain. (Lucy discovered that he was now one of only four surviving corporals out of the 32 with which the battalion had gone to war.) The British counter-attacked before the Germans could consolidate, and by the morning of the 27th Neuve Chapelle was recaptured and Lucy was back in his front-line position. But this recovery proved short-lived. The trenches were barely recognizable, and soon the dreaded bombardment was upon them once more.

> Dumbly we suffered it. We seemed born for nothing else. And dumbly we saw again our comrades being maimed and massacred.
>
> Once more lines of German infantry, apparently inexhaustible, came over the field of dead, and again those of us still sound stood up to stave them off, but our strong ranks of riflemen were gone, and our weak fire caused alarmingly few casualties. . . . We shot and shot, and we stopped them once more on our company front, but they got in again on the left, and to some purpose.

Soon the left flank (which the new arrivals had been sent in to strengthen) was gone, and Lucy's sector was surrounded. Then came the added misery of being shelled by their own artillery. Somehow battalion headquarters got a message through telling them to retire, but this was no easy matter. The communication trench to the rear still ran for only a few yards. Its exit was covered by a German machine-gun. Singly the Irishmen crept down the trench, then dashed into the open, hoping to gain the next piece of cover before the machine-gun got them. Lucy noticed that the gun was following men as they dashed from shell hole to shell hole. So he waited until he heard the gun start to fire and then made a break for it, tumbling into cover with the gunburst just behind him. By a series of dashes he reached the ruined village, where he and a small company of survivors assembled. He now had one man under his command; another joined later. During a halt by a roadside the roll of the battalion was called. Only 46 men answered their names. Two officers survived. 'We had lost Neuve Chapelle for the second time.'

III

To all intents and purposes, Lucy's battalion had been wiped out. But its four dozen survivors had not seen the end of this year's fighting. The leavening that their experience could provide among untested soldiers was too precious. And, close at hand, the German thrust towards the township of Ypres itself was approaching its finale.

For Lucy and his fellow survivors, recovery from the blood-letting before Neuve Chapelle came quickly but was not complete. They regained their appetites and ate like hogs. They revelled in good sleeping. And although for a few days they over-reacted to the sounds of approaching shells, it was not long before one of the two survivors from his platoon announced that life was grand. But John Lucy could not wholly share this feeling. He was lonely for missing friends – 'Cheerful faces now gone, and the memory of deeds of rough kindness haunted me' – and dogged by a 'certain loss of interest'. His morale was further lowered by a military reorganization that merged the band of survivors with some 200 new arrivals.

We did not know most of them, and we were not greatly interested. They were a mixture of Special Reserve and Militia men, with one or two of our own old wounded sent back cured.

Lucy was separated from the two remaining members of his original section, and had to build again with four new men.

These had not the smartness of the Regulars, and I could not take them rapidly to my heart. Their habits were unsoldierly, and repellent to me.

In a 'brief fit of renunciation and despair' he burned his diary (the keeping of which nevertheless was greatly to aid him in later years in recalling the events of these weeks).

The fighting quality of the 250 men of the new unit ('it could hardly be called a battalion') was soon put to the test. On 1 November, only five days after the fall of Neuve Chapelle, they were marched to the north-east of Ypres and thence up the Menin road to Hooge. Their task was to relieve a battalion that had lost half its numbers to German fire ('The old story. . . . And we, with new, inexperienced, and untried men'). For three days the new unit occupied trenches that contained a lot of water and were poorly dug. Then they went into local reserve, and under constant shelling stood ready to retake any sections of trench overrun by the Germans.

We were all in the fight, and the country behind was empty of troops, as far as we could see. The dwindling Regular battalions faced assault after assault. . . . Practically every unit had lost three-quarters of its fighting strength. . . .

The German attacks continued without ceasing; 'and more and more enemy batteries thickened the circle of guns threatening Ypres'.

The health of those in the field since August began to fail. Many of us could not now digest bully beef and hard biscuits. Snow fell, and our lower limbs half froze while we slept out in the severest winter for many years.

On 10 November Lucy returned to the front line and next morning, in wet shell holes and crumbling trenches, his unit endured the thunder and blasting of his worst bombardment so far. He felt keenly the responsibilities of a junior NCO: pinned to the one section of trench, 'always under the close scrutiny of the men he was supposed to lead and encourage' and now dealing with raw soldiers some of whom 'could not even fire a rifle properly'. Under the bombardment a 'few of our fellows broke':

one poor chap entirely lost his head and ran back out of his trench. He had not a chance in the open. The earth was vomiting all round us and he tumbled over in a few yards.

No trained soldier would have done that.

But the security that the trench provided was entirely relative. The shelling took its grim toll.

A corporal, a burly fellow, fell near me, with a shrapnel bullet in his head. He lay unconscious all the day, nodding his holed head as if suffering only from some slight irritation, and did not become still until evening. . . .
Another soldier had his belly ripped open, and sat supporting his back against the trench, while he gazed with fascinated eyes at large coils of his own guts, which he held in both hands. . . .[1]
Maimed men passed crouching and crawling behind me, leaving trails of blood on the ground, on their way to a ditch which led back into the woods behind.

Some of the newcomers, Lucy noted, made too much noise when wounded, 'unlike our old men'. One young militia man in particular came along roaring on account of a

---

[1] Astonishingly, this man's entrails had not been penetrated, and he survived.

broken arm, until told to put a sock in it by a lance-corporal who said that if he had really been badly wounded he would not have breath with which to howl. 'That stopped his hysterics.'

Heavy shrapnel burst immediately above the trench, blotting out the sky, and flinging Lucy to the ground.

> My whole body sang and trembled. One ear was perforated by the concussion, and I could hardly hear.

The order went out to stand to, as the enemy were about to attack. The man on Lucy's left did not respond.

> I grasped his arm and shook him savagely: 'For Christ's sake, get up, you bloody fool. The Germans are coming.'

The man fell sideways, exposing a pack covered with blood.

> He was dead, and my eyes came off him to my shoulder, which was spattered with his brains and tiny slivers of iridescent bone.

Yet the bombardment had not accomplished its object. The British line held.

> Six German army corps were marshalled in the open, advancing like a parade on the weak British Army.
> The magnificent Prussian Guards made a review of it. They executed their famous goose-step in the sight of their foe, and the field-grey waves came on. . . .
> The left of the Prussian Guard attack caught us. Farther to our left the line broke, mended, broke and mended again. A counter-attacking English regiment went through a temporarily victorious enemy like a knife through butter, and recaptured a lost village with great dash.
> We stopped the Germans on our front, and they were the finest troops of Germany, led by the flower of her noblest houses.

During the next two days they beat off weaker attacks without difficulty. Then they went into reserve. Lucy's experience of fighting in 1914 was almost over.

While in reserve Lucy underwent an experience that, although to him a sign of frailty, serves as evidence of the extraordinary toughness and resilience of these regular soldiers. He was suffering, in addition to a perforated ear and sundry cuts and bruises, from haemorrhoids that were bleeding rather badly. So 'in a weak moment' he thought of going sick. He and a sergeant of like intent set off for a field ambulance, hoping not to return. But the 'weak moment' passed. While sheltering behind a house during a bombardment, 'we answered some call we could not resist, and returned feeling ashamed to our reserve trench.' (They took with them a frightened young lance-corporal who also was in the process of absenting himself. He later became the most distinguished soldier in the regiment, four times decorated for valour.)

On 19 November Lucy's unit returned to the line, relieving a battalion in a condition even more parlous than their own; but that night their place was taken by a London Territorial regiment, 'fresh and strong'. (Regular soldiers, says Lucy, 'got just a bit bored' by the way the newspapers played up the deeds of the Territorials. Still, he was quick to praise the achievements of these 'supposed Saturday-night soldiers'.) So at last the Irish riflemen departed for good from the battles of 1914. They were a sadly depleted body.

> This time only forty men of my regiment were able to march away. The rest were killed or wounded.
> Forty – forty left out of two hundred and fifty, and only about three weeks ago there were only forty-six left out of an entire battalion. I searched my mind for total figures and

roughly reckoned that in three months ninety-six men out of every hundred had been killed or wounded. I was too weary to appreciate my own luck.

While his companions were moving out, John Lucy lingered in the front line, talking to one of the Territorials ('a cultured man in the uniform of a private soldier', eager to hear praise for his regiment from a corporal in the regulars). Lucy looked out upon the battlefield at men he would not see again.

My eyes weakened, wandered, and rested on the half-hidden corpses of men and youths. Near and far they looked calm, and even handsome, in death. Their strong young bodies thickly garlanded the edge of a wood in rear, a wood called Sanctuary. A dead sentry, at his post, leaned back in a standing position, against a blasted tree, keeping watch over them.

He reflected on the unity that comradeship in arms imposed on his divided fellow countrymen.

Proudly and sorrowfully I looked at them, the Macs and the O's, and the hardy Ulster boys joined together in death on a foreign field. My dead chums.

Then he moved off south with the handful of survivors:

in a dazed way we inspected each other's faces, because every survivor was a phenomenon in himself. We exchanged half-smiles of appreciation and silent congratulation.

South of Hooge they found the Menin road stiff with French cavalry, ready to check the Germans if the British line broke: 'They were not wanted.'

7

OVER FOR CHRISTMAS

I have heard from a relative at the front of the courteous behaviour of a Saxon officer in command at Xmas.

A. Hopkinson to Lord Bryce, 2 February 1915

I

On 25 December 1914 the guns fell silent along much of the British front, and soldiers of both sides ambled freely around No-Man's-Land. The event was a mocking reminder of the belief, so often expressed a short time before, that the war would be over by the year's end.

By now the heat of August lay far behind. Even as the Allies began their advance from the Marne, the rain had started to fall. On the Aisne: 'All our men are tired and wet. Torrents of rain fell tonight' (Henry Wilson). During the transit from the Aisne to Ypres the weather seemed to improve, but then the rain began to descend once more. In the low-lying plain of Flanders the precarious security provided by trenches was offset by the miseries of water and cold. In November, as the German attacks slackened, the downpour did not. Major Charles Bonham-Carter, a company commander in the Ypres district, wrote in his diary just before Christmas:[1]

> Under the best conditions the trenches are muddy and unless actually standing on a board or straw, one sinks up to one's ankles, and when their condition is bad, it is easy to become badly bogged. Many instances have occurred of men having to be dragged out by their comrades, after losing all power of helping themselves. The continual standing on wet ground, the wearing of wet boots for several days without a change, and of wet clothes has a very bad effect on the men, who in some case[s] can scarcely move when they leave the trenches.

The consequence, for large numbers, was 'swollen feet, frost bite, and rheumatism'. The only answer, according to Bonham-Carter, was to keep the men working and not to allow them to 'sit or stand in the trenches and do nothing'. A few days later he wrote:

> Especially now that the men are employed in the trenches only, it is of supreme importance to prevent men from remaining dirty, and losing power of rousing themselves and lessening their self-respect. In the trenches I found that if not forced to work some men stood or sat in the mud, and got more and more miserable, until they lost all power of movement as all circulation in their legs and feet came to an end.

But on Christmas eve the weather briefly improved. 'A lovely day with bright sunshine and no rain,' Bonham-Carter noted. 'This is the first day without rain for a long time.' The change in the weather set the scene for one of the best-remembered episodes of

---

[1] The papers of Major Charles Bonham-Carter are in Churchill College, Cambridge.

the war on the British sector of the Western Front. Late in the evening of the 24th (it was approaching midnight, German time) lighted Christmas trees began appearing in German trenches. Soldiers on both sides started to sing carols to tunes that crossed national barriers even if the language used did not. Christmas day dawned clear and frosty. Neither side began firing. Then troops moved into No-Man's-Land, sometimes preceded by couriers bearing white flags to ensure that there would be no misunderstanding. A sort of fraternization commenced, as the soldiers of the two nations gazed at each other, swapped gifts, joined in burying their dead, spoke such pleasantries as the barriers of language would permit, and allowed themselves to be photographed alongside one another. At some places the truce continued for several days. Often it was only after visits from indignant superior officers that the shooting began again, and then after unofficial warnings – and apologies – had been transmitted across the lines.

Plate 5   *A section of a British trench, complete with firing recesses to prevent the men from being enfiladed in case of assault. The caps and legs of the trench occupants are just visible in the three nearest recesses.*

What did this event signify? In that the high command deplored it, the Christmas truce may be seen as an assertion of a community of interest by the sufferers in the trenches on both sides as against remote army commanders and even remoter bellicose civilians. Yet the importance of the event must not be exaggerated. When they participated in the Christmas truce, the rank-and-file soldiers and junior officers were not issuing a directive to their superiors that the killing had to stop. At most they were deciding that, at a time of year when it was customary for animosities to be suppressed – often on the understanding that they would be revived in due course – it seemed appropriate to apply this custom to war. But this constituted no determined dereliction of duty, especially as for the moment campaigning had come to a halt anyway, so that killing served no tangible purpose. (On various parts of the French front, where major operations were being conducted by Joffre even though it was mid-winter, there was certainly no truce this Christmas Day.) But the attitudes and convictions that had brought British soldiers to the fighting line remained. The unspoken assumption accompanying the Christmas Day pleasantries in No-Man's-Land was that, in due season, the struggle – and the slaughter – would be resumed.

II

Nowhere among Englishmen, in the army or out of it, did the birthday of the Prince of Peace produce widespread heartsearching about the continuation of Britain's involvement in the war. This may seem surprising, in view of the evident gulf between what had been said in August about the likely duration of the war and the actual situation in December. In part, this want of reappraisal suggests that anticipations of a short war had not been totally quelled. At the end of November Major Bonham-Carter wrote: 'Everyone here is extraordinarily optimistic about the end of the war coming quite soon, and even General Smith-Dorrien said he thought March would see the end of it.' Yet only a month before Smith-Dorrien, whose II Corps had been involved in every major action since Mons, had been warning the commander of the BEF that his soldiers were cracking under the German onslaught at Ypres. If he could so speedily recover his conviction that the war would soon be over, it is not surprising that other military leaders felt no need to call in question Britain's decision to participate.

But the matter must be taken further. From the start not everyone had believed that the war would be a short one. Kitchener is the best-known exception, but he was not alone. 'Make no mistake, gentlemen, we are in for a long and bitter war', the commander of the Second Cavalry Brigade had warned his officers early on. Indeed, it seems plain that although most people believed that the conflict would be brief, their belief fell short of total conviction.

It is true that the only aspects of war ever arousing great interest were those that were supposedly decisive – battles such as Blenheim and Waterloo. That is a principal reason why Napoleon's career exercised so great a fascination: he fought many seemingly decisive battles. It was easy to conclude that the armies of the powers would meet in a bloody, cataclysmic encounter, from which one would emerge victorious and the other vanquished. All recent major wars had apparently been swift, conclusive affairs: the Austro-Prussian, Franco-Prussian, and Russo-Japanese wars. And if there was a notable exception, that between the Northern and Southern States of the USA, it could be set aside as a civil war.

Yet, despite these precedents, people in Britain – in high places and in low – were not acting as if they expected this war to end quickly. At the first wartime meeting of the Cabinet it was decided to ask the House of Commons for an army of 500,000 men and credits of £100 millions. Parliament, and the public, agreed with alacrity. The call for recruits was swiftly answered. Yet it was evident that not one of the men now enlisting would appear on the field of battle until well into 1915. It requires more than Kitchener's commanding authority to explain why leaders and led consented, with such unanimity, to raise and train a great military force that could not possibly participate in the war unless it continued well beyond Christmas 1914.

Hope, delusion, and a misreading of the 'lessons of history' might all point to a short war. But once having decided to enter it, the nation started behaving as if it were involved in a different sort of conflict. Underlying this seeming inconsistency rested a dominant fact: that the decision to go to war in no way depended on calculations about its probable duration. As 1914 came to a close, this fact continued to dominate. For all but the wilfully deluded, the war was plainly far from over, and something of its horrific nature was already becoming apparent. Yet this was not seen as cause for reconsidering the decision of 4 August. Whatever the meaning of the Christmas truce, it constituted no first stage in a reappraisal of Britain's involvement in the war.

PART TWO

Ruling the Waves
1914–1915

Plate 6   *A British warship patrolling the North Sea.*

8

WAR OF JUDGEMENT: THE EXERCISE OF COMMAND OF THE SEA

The maritime domination of the North Sea, upon which our whole policy must be based. . . .

British Naval War Plan, July 1914

German Ocean [the name assigned to the North Sea].

Karl Baedeker, London and Its Environs:
Handbook for Travellers *(English language edition), Leipzig, 1911*

I

The silence (over Christmas) of the guns on the Western Front was noteworthy because it was unusual. But in another area of the war – and that, for Britain, the most crucial – such absence of gunfire did not excite comment. For the most striking thing about the war in the North Sea was the want of large actions and heavy death tolls.

Something of the apparent quiescence of the naval war may be gauged from the experience of Edward Hilton Young.[1] He joined the Grand Fleet in August 1914 as a lieutenant in the Royal Naval Volunteer Reserve. After serving briefly in HMS *Cyclops* he transferred to the *Iron Duke*, the flagship of the Grand Fleet and the nerve centre of Britain's most important arm of defence. 'I am at sea on Jellicoe's flagship,' he wrote proudly to his brother on 29 September 1914, 'which is really rather wonderful.' But in the ensuing weeks the wonder departed. In late October he wrote:

> The battle is further off, I believe, than ever. We have had a quiet time of late, I mean quiet for us. So much so that we have had time for diversions, an entertainment last night for the Admiral's benefit, with a very captivating can-can executed by gun-room stars: today, cutter races along the sunlit waters: with jokes.

Such frivolity did not satisfy Young for long. 'I like the life here', he wrote to his brother in mid-February 1915, 'but chafe much agst the innocupation of the work. . . . Here we go round & round.' 'Idleness in solitude', he admitted a fortnight after, '[has] got on my nerves.'

Young secured release from idleness in September 1915, when he joined a naval mission in Serbia intended to assist in thwarting an Austrian crossing of the Danube. In the course of it, he related in October:

---

[1] The papers of Hilton Young, first Lord Kennet, are in the University Library, Cambridge.

I went for a night journey up the river. . . to prospect a channel; an Austrian sentry shot his rifle off at us across the water, and after a year of war that was the first shot I had heard fired in anger.

He had needed to go a long way from the flagship of the British Grand Fleet to hear that shot fired.

II

In mid-July 1914 the principal part of the British fleet was holding a review off the south coast of England. According to Churchill, then First Lord of the Admiralty, it was the 'greatest assemblage of naval power ever witnessed in the history of the world'. Yet it had not been brought together in the hope of overawing Germany in the threatening international crisis, which was proceeding almost unnoticed in Britain. Rather, it was a matter of economy. A test mobilization happened to be cheaper than the usual summer manoeuvres. Yet the timing of the event proved felicitous. Britain's naval squadrons were gathered in home waters on a near-war footing just as the international situation began to deteriorate. Whatever their deficiencies, the nation's forces at sea, as on land, were by that country's standards surprisingly well prepared for war at its outset. The difference was that the issue of preparedness at sea mattered so much more.

Why was the naval issue so important to Britain? Even at the risk of some repetition, the matter is of such moment that it requires to be spelled out. The navy was Britain's pre-eminent means of survival in a world in which, in relation to other powers, it was not well equipped to survive. Such was the measure of its vulnerability that, without command of the North Sea, Britain was certain to lose not only its great-power status but also its fundamental independence – and this without necessarily becoming involved in a war at all.

Britain's dependence on sea power was occasioned by two things. First, although the nation possessed the manpower and the industry to become of consequence militarily, it was anything but that in 1914. Its Territorial Army was sufficient to repel the sort of minor invading force that alone could slip past its naval defences. But without its navy the country could be subjected to a full-scale military attack, and it was not remotely equipped to withstand one.

Secondly, should Britain's navy go to the bottom, its adversary would not need to invade it. Even if its whole male population and heavy industry were geared for war, Britain could still be crushed in a matter of months. Two-thirds of its food supply came from overseas, and its economy was centred upon the import of raw materials and the export of manufactured goods. The stocks of food and raw materials held in the country were usually sufficient for a month or six weeks. Britain under blockade would slide speedily into starvation and economic collapse.

This situation set the prime tasks of the British navy in 1914. Britannia did not, and could not, rule the waves of the world. It would have bankrupted itself if it had continued to try. The naval power of the USA in the Atlantic and the Pacific, of Japan in the Far East, and of Austria-Hungary and Italy (two-thirds of the Triple Alliance) in the Mediterranean could threaten Britain's trade routes in distant parts. But there seemed no likelihood that the USA or Japan would adopt a hostile stance or that Italy would make common cause with Austria-Hungary. So the only actual naval challenge came from Germany, and the German navy was constructed to operate only in the North Sea and the trade routes immediately surrounding Britain: that is, it could serve no purpose but to threaten Britain's survival.

Britain's naval-building policy was a response to this fact, and had been so at least from the moment that the dynamic – and sometimes demonic – Sir John Fisher became First Sea Lord. (He held the post from 1904 until 1910.) Previously Britain had built to a two-power standard: that is, it had at least matched the combined forces of whichever two countries possessed the largest navies after its own. In 1901 this honour had been enjoyed by France and Russia, the partners to the Dual Alliance. Hence, according to the then First Lord of the Admiralty, a naval war with the French and the Russians was 'less improbable than any other naval war which we can foresee'. By 1914 Britain had abandoned the two-power standard. It was concerning itself only with the naval construction of Germany, which it was seeking to outbuild to the tune of 60 per cent.

In support of this policy 'Jackie' Fisher and his successors instituted a number of operational changes. They scrapped many minor vessels that 'showed the flag' in distant waters but contributed nothing to the containment of Germany. As far as Fisher was concerned, these ships absorbed crews needed at home, and so they must go. He was determined that Britain should have on hand not only ships but also the sailors to man them. In 1911 it was decided to withdraw to the North Sea most of Britain's naval force in the Mediterranean, leaving France as the principal Entente power there. This was an expression less of Anglo-French solidarity than of Britain's resolution to concentrate all its efforts on the foremost problem, trusting that other regions would take care of themselves. In the following years preparations were made to move the main home stations of the British fleet from ports on the south coast of England, which had ceased to be appropriate now that France was no longer the principal danger, to bases further north. Here they would be ready to pounce on any sortie from Germany.

This, then, was the quintessential task of the British fleet in August 1914: to retain command of the North Sea and so withstand the menace of a totally destructive blockade. There was another task that the navy might perform, of great import but altogether secondary. This was the blockade of Germany. As a Continental power, Germany was not vulnerable to naval blockade to the same extent as an island nation like Britain. Nevertheless, Germany's economy had prospered with the aid of its merchant fleet and its considerable overseas trade. And in a long war it would suffer if it were denied access to rare metals and supports for its agriculture from outside Europe. So the British navy could serve as one among many forces in grinding Germany to defeat. But such a blockade must never take precedence over the navy's primary task of safeguarding Britain; that is, the blockade of Germany must not be conducted in a way which would place the British fleet at risk.

The most effective way in which to pursue both these tasks – to protect Britain, and to attack Germany by denying it access to the outside world – would be to destroy the German fleet. But in the existing state of naval technology the British had no way of forcing the Germans to give battle except by running unacceptable risks. Churchill, admittedly, did state in September 1914 that if the German navy would not come out and fight then 'it would be dug out like rats from a hole'. This constituted strategic lunacy. British battleships sailing into the narrow waters and closely protected harbours where the German navy sheltered would be exposing themselves to frightful losses before getting even within range of their opponents. It followed that the British navy could dispose of the German fleet only if the latter agreed to fight on the high seas. Otherwise Britannia might rule the North Sea, but she must accept as a distasteful fact of life the continued threat posed by an inactive but inaccessible German navy.

At the start of the war it was widely assumed in Britain that the German fleet would obligingly sail out to a naval Armageddon, notwithstanding its own numerical inferiority. This was the view, for example, of Lord Esher, who from a back-room position had played a considerable part in British defence preparations. No doubt this expectation was naive. It failed to recognize that, once the Germans found themselves at war with Britain, their mere possession of a navy would aid them to a limited degree. The very existence of German battleships, even though confined to harbour, prevented the British fleet from supporting an attack in some other important area (assuming there was one), or from mounting an amphibious operation against the German coast (if this should be practicable), or from sending supplies to Russia through the Baltic (should such supplies ever become available), or from severing Germany's iron-ore trade with Sweden.

Even so, there was a certain logic to Esher's expectations. The German navy would serve these relatively minor functions only if Britain and Germany were at war. Had the German authorities not constructed so menacing a fleet, there is no certainty that Britain would ever have aligned itself against them. Men such as Esher were assuming that a navy built at so high a cost would attempt, at whatever risk to itself, to accomplish a truly great objective – which could only be the destruction of the British fleet. The rulers of Germany – who were also the guardians of the German navy – would prove, unimpressed by this logic.

III

How substantial was Britain's naval position *vis-à-vis* that of Germany in 1914? Churchill subsequently described what would have been the ideal situation. The navy needed to be 'ready; not to be taken unawares: to be concentrated; not to be caught divided: to have the strongest Fleet possible in the best stations under the best conditions, and in good time, and then if the battle came one could await its result with a steady heart'.[2]

In one important respect, clearly, this ideal state had not been attained in August 1914. If the Grand Fleet was immediately dispatched to 'the best stations . . . in good time', it was hardly under 'the best conditions'. Britain's naval planners had taken long to decide where to relocate the main fleet bases once it had become apparent that their established positions on the south coast had ceased to be appropriate. Eventually, but very late in the day, their decision had come to rest on a position so far north that it was not on the mainland of Britain at all. This was Scapa Flow, in the Orkney Islands. Despite the atrocious climate of this latitude for much of the year, Scapa Flow was ideally placed geographically to face Germany's naval stations. It also possessed a superb natural harbour. But it was far removed from all the back-up facilities that a great navy requires; and at the outbreak of war it had still not been equipped with elementary defences against submarines and night raiders.

This omission kept the navy on tenterhooks during the early months of the war. Indeed, twice in 1914 suspected sightings of submarines caused the main British battle fleet to rush helter-skelter into the open sea. On the second occasion it did not come to rest until it had reached the coast of Ireland, where it was secure from attack but far from where it could have intercepted a German raid on cross-Channel communications. And the lack of naval facilities ashore meant that a host of support ships were needed at Scapa Flow to service the fleet. One sailor noted in November 1914 that, although the navy supposedly consisted of battleships, cruisers, destroyers, and submarines, by far the largest component of the fleet in Scapa Flow was the great body of auxiliaries:

---

[2] Winston S. Churchill, *The World Crisis 1911–1918*, vol. 1 (London: Odhams Press, n.d.), p. 132.

Looking round Scapa Flow today one sees Hospital Ships, Colliers, Patrol Yachts, Motor Boats, Store Ships, Ammunition Ships, Supply Ships, Tugs, Water Tankers, Oil Tankers, Repair Ships, Drifters acting as Tenders, Minesweeping Trawlers, Patrol Trawlers etc. etc. There are simply hundreds of these things – all sorts and conditions of floating craft.

He concluded:

it is extraordinary what a fleet of Auxiliaries is to be found when a fleet like ours makes a base where there is no dockyard.[3]

If the navy passed through great anxiety while Churchill's 'best station under the best conditions' was being converted from rhetoric to reality, in other respects his description was near enough to the facts. In the all-important combination of size of fleet and technological innovation, Britain had preserved a dominance over the Germans that enabled it to enter – as, indeed, it was to leave – the war without being effectively challenged.

Britain had started the century with a great numerical superiority. Had the nature of battleships not changed, there would have been scant chance of another country's overtaking it. The problem was that advances in technology could rapidly render an established navy obsolete and so decisively shift the balance of power towards the innovator. For a country so dependent on this single arm, safety for Britain could lie only in setting the pace of change itself, even at the cost of wiping out its existing lead. This was precisely what happend. In 1906 Britain launched the battleship *Dreadnought*. It drew on developments like the turbine engine, designed to produce greatly increased speed, and on a host of advances in naval gunnery (including smokeless powder and range-finders) intended to increase gun range. Its combination of big guns and engine power meant that it could outrun and outshoot any ship afloat.

The apparent loser from this innovation was Britain itself, as the greatest possessor of earlier battleships. But it was also the case that Britain had no monopoly of the know-how and industrial capacity to produce Dreadnoughts. The result was para-doxical. Britain had wiped out its own existing lead, but it had begun to establish a new margin of superiority before other countries could get in ahead of it. A refusal to secure the benefits of the second part of the paradox, because of the burden of accepting the first part, could well have been calamitous.

From 1906 all calculations of the necessary rate of naval building were governed by the number and size and speed of Dreadnoughts. When war broke out Britain's lead in this area was substantial. If we include in the calculation ships being built in British yards for other countries, which by the terms of contract could be requisitioned in the event of war (with money refunded), Britain soon after the outbreak had 24 Dreadnoughts as against Germany's 13, with another 13 laid down as against Germany's 10. Among those under construction were five in the super-Dreadnought (Queen Elizabeth) class, possessing a speed and gun range exceeding those of any vessels being built elsewhere.

But if this margin seems substantial, it was not to prove excessive. In October 1914 one of Britain's foremost battleships, the *Audacious*, sank after striking a mine. At that time four other Dreadnoughts were requiring repairs and two, which were on the point of completion, had not quite come into service, so that the number Britain could actually put to sea was 17. The total number of battleships possessed by Germany had now reached 15. No doubt not every German battleship was at that moment ready for

---

[3] From the diary of Geoffrey Coleridge Harper in Churchill College, Cambridge. For Harper's career during the war, see Chapter 61 below, 'The Supposed Inactivity of the Grand Fleet'.

action, any more than was the case in Britain; nevertheless, October 1914 revealed that Britain's pre-war margin of 60 per cent over Germany was anything but grandiose.

Nor was Britain's superiority as great as mere numbers of ships and estimates of fire power would suggest. The Germans possessed some of the advantages of being late starters. Their dockyards had been built more recently, and hence allowed for the construction of vessels of wider beam. This gave their ships greater watertight bulkhead capacity, reducing the likelihood that they would sink following damage during an action. British ships, by contrast, had to be designed to accord with existing dockyards, for pre-war Governments had jibbed at the expense of constructing new ones.

Again, in various areas of technology the Germans had a lead over Britain that enhanced the effectiveness of their battleships. Their shells were better designed; they were more likely to penetrate a ship before exploding, especially when striking at an oblique angle, thereby inflicting damage to the vitals rather than to the exterior. And their range-finding equipment was superior. Both these factors increased their strike capacity, while their larger bulkhead space and more substantial armour plating made them better equipped to survive the shells of their opponents. Indeed, it was arguable that for ships of equal size, gunnery, and speed a German vessel was superior to its British counterpart.

Yet this equation was in large measure academic. Except in the anxious weeks following the loss of the *Audacious* – of which the Germans knew nothing – Britain throughout the war possessed a superiority in numbers of ships, as well as in their size, speed, and weight of guns, that more than cancelled out any advantages accruing to the Germans through superior quality of shell, range-finding, and armour plating. Britain also possessed other major, if much less calculable, advantages over its rivals: those of seamanship and morale. The British fleet consisted of volunteer crews who had made the navy their lives, who had no doubt that they belonged to the dominant power, and who had the will and capacity to spend long periods at sea under all conditions. Only thus was Britain able to maintain its unrelenting blockade in most inhospitable waters. By contrast, German sailors were largely short-term conscripts who possessed neither great sea-going experience nor the sense of superiority enjoyed by their opponents.

Further, as the established naval power Britain held the strategic initiative. Much has been written about the lack of creative strategic thinking in the British fleet during the Fisher era, and about the reigning obsession with size and numbers of ships rather than the use to be made of them. This is instanced in various ways: for example, the absence of planning for combined naval and military operations. Yet the point can be over-stressed. The prime strategic task of the navy was too plain to require any inspired weighing of alternatives. Britain dominated the North Sea, and the German fleet must never be allowed to break free of that domination. It followed that Britain could not permit itself to be drawn into other naval activities which, however desirable in themselves, might imperil its command in the vital area.

IV

The man who was placed in command of Britain's Grand Fleet in August 1914 was Sir John Jellicoe. His powerful intellect and his exceptional capacity as a gunnery officer had early brought him to the attention of Fisher. As First Sea Lord, Fisher had employed Jellicoe as a major instrument in ensuring that Britain preserved her lead in naval design and construction. Well before 1914 Jellicoe had been singled out to take command of the fleet should war break out.

During his early career, in distant stations, Jellicoe had seen a deal of adventure – for example, in Egypt in 1882 and in China in 1900. Yet he was a cautious man, and his perception of the naval situation did not lessen his caution. He was quite aware that, ship for ship, British vessels might not be superior, or even equal, to German vessels. But probably what dominated his thinking was a recognition of the terrible vulnerability of battleships *per se*, whatever nation they belonged to. Recent developments in technology had produced trivial objects of sea warfare, such as the mine and the torpedo, capable of sinking great battleships without even the engagement of the main enemy fleet. As the *Audacious* episode had revealed, this made infinitely more difficult the preservation of that margin of naval superiority on which Britain depended for survival.

Jellicoe, in Churchill's oft-quoted expression, was the only man on either side who could lose the war in an afternoon. He could not, be it noted, win the war, for even the annihilation of the German navy would not achieve that. But if he led his own fleet to destruction, he would be sealing his country's doom. Jellicoe was determined never to place his force in a position where even the possibility of such a calamity might arise. He epitomized his attitude in a well-known memorandum of October 1914. He made the point that the invention of mines, torpedoes, and submarines had quite changed the circumstances in which capital ships could operate against an enemy. It had been accepted naval practice that if a British squadron encountered an inferior enemy force which then fled, the British must give chase. Failure to do so rendered a naval commander liable to court martial. Jellicoe insisted that this procedure was inapplicable in a situation where the new weapons might be brought to bear: a superior British force could rapidly be rendered inferior if it charged into a trap of torpedoes and mines. And, given that his primary task was to maintain his superiority, not to attack the enemy in any circumstance, he intended to assume – until convinced to the contrary – that if he encountered an enemy force which then fled, it was seeking to entrap him. Therefore, he would take up the pursuit only in such a way that he could be certain his path was clear. This might cause him to lose the opportunity to inflict a defeat on the enemy. He preferred to do this rather than risk incurring unacceptable losses himself.

Jellicoe's view was endorsed by the Admiralty. There was no disagreement among the directors of the navy either that his primary task was to maintain Britain's naval superiority or that the conduct of the navy must take account of the existence of weapons which could destroy capital ships without requiring capital ships to deliver them.

Jellicoe's concern for the safety of his fleet led him to adopt a strategy that has generally been called defensive. And his defensive posture has sometimes been compared unfavourably with that of more daredevil spirits, particularly Sir David Beatty, the commander of the battle-cruiser squadron. Such a judgement should be accepted only with reservation.

Any description of Jellicoe's strategy is in some measure a matter of definition. Apparently there were three types of strategy open to him. The first may be called, if somewhat tendentiously, a death-or-glory strategy. The British fleet could certainly bring the Germans to action. It could invade their naval bases, or it could send a temptingly small portion of its battleships towards the enemy coast (whereupon the whole German fleet would be happy to risk battle with it). Just possibly such conduct might bring about a British success. German mines, shells, and torpedoes might fail to find their targets. British gunfire might secure a large number of victims. But the chances that anything of the sort would happen were utterly remote. And the probability that Britain would suffer a fatal reverse was very great indeed. Only a desperate situation, or an extremely reckless commander, would permit such actions to take place. Jellicoe's position was not desperate, and he was not that kind of commander.

Apart from death-or-glory, two other forms of strategy were open to him. Either he could stand on the alert, ready to pounce on part or all of the German navy whenever it put to sea; or he could shelter in harbour, refusing to respond to German fleet movements unless they actively threatened cross-channel communications or the main approaches to Britain. If the former strategy be considered offensive, and the latter defensive, then there is no doubt which Jellicoe adopted. His posture was plainly one of offence. This was true not only during the first six months of the war, when there were a number of minor fleet actions, but also during 1915, when there was virtually none. Following the action at the Dogger Bank in January 1915, the German fleet became so cautious that it left harbour on only five occasions during the year. Each time Jellicoe's force moved out of its bases in an effort to intercept the Germans. As the latter hardly ventured beyond the fortified islands of Heligoland and Borkum before returning to harbour, Jellicoe never got the chance of bringing them to action. But action was plainly what he was seeking.

What may, indeed, be argued is that if Jellicoe's strategy was offensive, his tactics were not. Though he might seek battle, he would conduct it only in a way that did not endanger his margin of superiority. He would not allow his battleship force to become dispersed during an action and so give the enemy the chance to concentrate against part of it. He maintained a rigidly centralized command over all his units. He would not engage in night fighting: something, it is true, in which the fleet was utterly untrained but also something in which he felt no need to train it. And, as already mentioned, he would not hotly pursue an enemy unless assured that his path was clear. This meant that, against an adversary determined to disengage, he had little chance of conducting a prolonged action producing spectacular results.

Such tactical considerations were not, however, the prerogative of Jellicoe. The action at the Dogger bank on 23 January 1915 is a case in point. The main protagonists were the five battle cruisers commanded by Beatty and a German force, under Hipper, of four battle cruisers. (Among the latter was the *Blücher*, a vessel of inferior speed and firepower.) The Germans had not intended this encounter, which was a nicely laid British trap, and on sighting Beatty's force they headed for home. Beatty in the *Lion* led the pursuit. The *Blücher* was soon damaged beyond chance of escape. But the gunfire of the other German vessels wrought considerable damage on the *Lion*, silencing its radio and forcing it to drop out of line.

As the rest of the British force swept past him, Beatty sent three signals by flag that had the effect of rendering the action abortive. The first was an order to change direction because of a suspected sighting of submarines. The second enjoined a further change of direction in order to avoid mines that the Germans might be leaving in their wake. The third was a superbly ambiguous message that was intended to urge that the pursuit of the enemy be maintained but produced the opposite effect. Taken with the message immediately preceding it, it seemed to mean that the attack should be directed away from the leading German ships and towards the disabled *Blücher*. The outcome was that, while the *Blücher* was decisively disposed of, the three principal German cruisers escaped.

Many things are interesting about this episode, but what is noteworthy here is the significance of Beatty's two signals ordering changes of course. The first was a response to the threat of submarines, the second to the threat of mines. Yet there were no submarines in the vicinity, and the retreating Germans were not covering their tracks with mines. It was the danger, not the reality, to which Beatty was responding, and this inaugurated the confusion that enabled the Germans to escape. On this crucial matter of tactics there was no difference between 'Balaclava Beatty' (as Fisher disparagingly referred to him) and Jellicoe. Neither was prepared to do or die.

V

The same considerations that determined Britain's conduct of the naval war also dictated the manner of the British blockade of Germany. Indeed, there is little reason to doubt that the blockade would soon have been abandoned if its application had seriously threatened the defence of Britain. It is noteworthy that the navy never did attempt to cut off the iron-ore trade between Germany and Sweden, for all the importance of such an operation, because of the risks involved.

If conducted in the traditional manner, a blockade of the North Sea coast of Germany would have spread British vessels along 150 miles of sea in close proximity to the enemy shores. This would have laid individual battleships open to the sort of piecemeal attack and destruction that Jellicoe would not countenance even in the heat of battle. Yet in the years before the war Britain's naval advisers had proved reluctant to recognize that a traditional blockade was inconsistent with the country's safety. When at last they bowed to the dictates of technology, they contemplated instituting an observational blockade. This would have placed most, but not all, of the blockading force at a greater distance from the German coast but would have spread it over 300 miles of ocean. It is a nice question whether this would have marginally increased or decreased its peril. Whatever the answer, the risk could not be run.

Shortly before the outbreak of war the Admiralty came to the realization that, in order to blockade Germany, the main part of the British fleet need do no more than occupy precisely those positions from which it would be standing guard over Germany's naval challenge. The fleet based on Scapa Flow, awaiting the emergence of the German navy, also denied to neutral ships access to Germany.

The British Isles, as has been vividly remarked, lay in 1914 like a breakwater across the sea approaches to Germany. There were two gaps in this breakwater. One was the English Channel, only 20 miles across and easily rendered impassable by a quite small naval detachment. A minefield reduced the gap to a few miles, and no potential blockade runner could attempt the passage through the minefield without undergoing inspection by British ships. The other gap lay in the north, between the Shetland Islands and the coast of Norway, and was much wider. But it was here that the naval might of Britain was concentrated. A patrolling force functioning in this area was thus the auxiliary of a fleet of tremendous power. That did not relieve it of an intensely onerous task. The blockading squadron had to patrol ceaselessly the bleak waters between northern Scotland and Scandinavia, apprehending hundreds of neutral merchant ships, sending boarding parties to inspect their cargoes, and shepherding many of them to British harbours for closer investigation. But if this was tedious and uncomfortable work, the main dangers encountered were from the elements and from random action by enemy submarines and mines. With the main British fleet so close to hand, there was no danger that the Germans would send a substantial naval force to try to eliminate the cruisers and destroyers making up the spearhead of the British blockade.

VI

The achievements of British naval power in the first six months of the war were considerable – which is to say no more than that, having preserved naval superiority,

Britain was able to enjoy its benefits. Among these benefits, the German merchant marine was banished from the seas. Most German merchant ships overseas in August 1914 preferred internment in foreign ports to risking capture while trying to run the British gauntlet back to Germany. Yet more important, Britain's trade with the outside world was able to continue uninterrupted. The converted German passenger liners intended to harry Allied merchant shipping made only a small dent in it before being apprehended. And the German Far East fleet under Admiral Spee, after a briefly spectacular career against British shipping in the Pacific, was sent to the bottom.

Spee's triumphs had not been scored only over merchant ships. On 1 November 1914, at Coronel off the west coast of South America, he had destroyed the major part of a British squadron sent to apprehend him. But a German force could not operate indefinitely so far from its sources of supply, and Germany's overseas bases had been speedily overrun. Spee's triumph at Coronel spelt out his dilemma. In accomplishing this success he had expended half of his ammunition. The only way in which he could secure fresh stocks was by effecting a return to Germany, so abandoning his career as an overseas raider. As it happened, he failed to accomplish this object. He was caught and destroyed by a British force, under Sir Doveton Sturdee, off the Falkland Islands on 8 December 1914.

Despite the drama that has always been associated with these actions at Coronel and the Falkland Islands, each was in reality a grimly unequal contest. In both instances the victor had a decided superiority over his adversary, in terms not only of speed but also of weight and range of fire power. First Spee at Coronel and then Sturdee at the Falklands used that superiority to keep out of harm's way while undertaking the extinction of their opponents.

What these opening months of the war demonstrated was that the British navy was able to keep its superiority intact, retain command of the North Sea, bottle up the German fleet, and hold open Britain's trading links with the outside world. At the same time it was establishing, if hardly a moment too soon, a secure base in an advantageous position. The threat from mines was real enough, as was shown by the loss of the *Audacious*. But such mishaps were infrequent and haphazard, and so gave the Germans no opportunity to attempt a direct challenge. The threat from submarines was real too, and it severely inhibited the navy's freedom of action. The most spectacular submarine success occurred on 22 September 1914, when a single U-boat sank three elderly British cruisers patrolling in an exposed position. But the ineptitude on the British side that assisted this setback was not repeated. And although the menace of submarines to capital ships remained real, it could be contained, as events thereafter made clear. After the *Audacious* not a single Dreadnought-class battleship fell victim to submarine or mine during the rest of the war.

The navy had done better than this. On each occasion that the Germans ventured into the North Sea between August 1914 and January 1915, they found themselves in danger of being trapped by a superior British force. Sometimes they managed to elude it, as following a raid by German cruisers on British coastal towns on the night of 15–16 December. Sometimes they did not, as in the Heligoland Bight action in August 1914 and at the Dogger Bank in January 1915. But the important thing was the danger in which the Germans found themselves on every one of these occasions. Its pressure hemmed them in, reducing the German fleet to virtual immobility during 1915.

The development of wireless telegraphy was a major force in ensuring the Grand Fleet's capacity so to confine its adversaries. The British navy was blessed with a first-rate cryptographic section for deciphering German messages, and with a chain of wireless stations for pinpointing the whereabouts of German ships using their radios while at sea. Two fortuitous circumstances assisted the Grand Fleet in this aspect of its operations. First, late in August 1914 the Russians salvaged copies of the German naval codes from a wrecked German cruiser and passed these on to their ally. The event was no secret among the rank and file at Scapa Flow. The arrival on a British ship of two Russian officers who were straightway spirited off to the Admiralty was noted, and a sailor who had been on their vessel passed on the news that they were carrying confidential books and papers rescued from the wrecked German cruiser.[4] But the Germans never got wind of this. Secondly, the value of these codes was enhanced by the fact that German naval headquarters made excessive use of radio in communicating with its vessels, not only when they were at sea but even when they were docked in port. Nor did the Germans desist from this carelessness when faced with mounting evidence that the British were in some way – and there could really be only one way – securing advance knowledge of their naval movements.

Perhaps this aspect of the naval war is worth bearing in mind when one considers the claim often made that the war at sea proved Britain to be technologically much inferior to Germany – an argument that has provided the basis for large generalizations about the merits and demerits of the two countries' educational systems. The fact of technological inferiority in some respects is indisputable – for example, the poor quality of British mines and torpedoes. Yet it may be wondered if great truths can be discerned by comparing items of equipment in the two fleets. For despite their apparently identical nature, the navies of Britain and Germany were in fact very differently circumstanced. The former was constantly straining to preserve superiority in numbers, size, and speed and to take the offensive in battle and blockade. The latter was choosing passivity on all but a handful of occasions, and acting then only within severely constricted intentions. The difference in role and expectations of two such forces was likely to produce a difference in priorities that would reveal itself in particular areas of performance.

Wherever the balance lies in this argument, one point seems plain enough. In their use of wireless telegraphy, the British did not reveal a marked inferiority to their adversaries.

VII

Yet whatever the achievements of the British navy in the early months of the war, its performance was not regarded with undiluted satisfaction, either inside its ranks or outside. In part this was because it had sustained a number of minor setbacks. Reference has already been made to the destruction of a British force off Coronel, to the loss of the three elderly cruisers to a single U-boat, and to the successful return to Germany of the enemy squadron that bombarded British coastal towns. In addition, early in the war the navy had sustained a reverse in the Mediterranean.

When war broke out the Germans had on station in the Mediterranean a battle cruiser and a light cruiser, the *Goeben* and *Breslau*. It was expected that a British cruiser squadron would apprehend them. But thanks to a failure of initiative by the commander on the spot and ambiguous instructions from the British Admiralty, the German vessels managed to speed off in a direction no one had anticipated – Turkey (at that time adopting a posture of unfriendly neutrality towards Britain). The Turks allowed the *Goeben* and *Breslau* to pass through the Dardanelles and then converted them, nominally, into units of the Turkish fleet. The event strengthened (though only

---

[4] Diary of G. C. Harper, 24 October 1914.

marginally) the hand of that section of the Turkish Government that wanted to enter the war on the German side.[5]

None of these setbacks did great credit either to the commanders involved or to the British Admiralty. Even the major North Sea action of the first six months of the war, the contest already mentioned between the battle cruisers at the Dogger Bank, was a mixed accomplishment. The British navy pulled off a considerable coup in forcing the action at all, and it disposed of one German cruiser. But poor signalling, a failure of initiative by Beatty's second-in-command, and a pretty lamentable standard of gunnery, all helped to deprive the British cruisers of a more substantial achievement.

Yet discontent with the navy's performance was not fully to be explained in terms of setbacks sustained or opportunities insufficiently exploited. Rather, it was the product of expectations unfulfilled. It had been assumed that after six months of war Britain's dominance in the North Sea would be not only unchallenged but unchallengeable – because there would be no German fleet left to inhibit it. Naval history was seen primarily as a matter of climactic sea battles. Trafalgar was what gripped the imagination; not the fact that, if the French had never come out to be defeated, the result of the naval war against France would have been the same. The British public and the navy and the First Lord of the Admiralty could only wait anxiously for the moment when the naval challenge from Germany reached a similar culmination. And until it did, the sense of disquiet would continue.

It was probably as well for Britain that this feeling of unease never caused the men in responsible positions to embark on foolhardy action. Churchill might speak of digging the Germans like rats out of their holes; rank-and-file sailors might crave to sail into Kiel Canal and have it out with the German navy one way or the other;[6] voices might be raised among the press and public inquiring what the navy was doing and implying that it should be doing more. The directors of the navy, even when they happened to be the very people who uttered these sentiments, never allowed their frustration to translate itself into action. They did not lose sight of the crucial distinction between exercising maritime supremacy and engaging in the sort of conduct that, although intended to assert it, might have the effect of bringing Britain's naval dominance brutally to an end.

---

[5] It should be noted that some historians argue that, had the British squadron actually caught up with the *Goeben* and *Breslau*, it would not necessarily have had the better of the encounter. That was not a view held generally at the time.

[6] Diary of G. C. Harper, 22 October 1914.

9

THE OTHER BLOCKADE

The really serious danger that this country has to guard against in war is not invasion,
but interruption of trade and destruction of our merchant marine.
Admiralty memorandum of 1910

I

Unlike the first six months of the war, Britain's battle fleet rarely occupied the newspaper headlines in 1915. This is no cause for wonder. For after the Dogger Bank encounter in January 1915 there were not even minor fleet actions to attract the public's attention. Again, it should be stressed that this absence of stirring encounters is not to be attributed primarily to an obsession with defence among Britain's naval commanders. The ever-tightening blockade of the Central Powers constituted a decidedly offensive form of activity. But the German fleet made no attempt to counter it. Here lay the key to the British navy's seeming quiescence.

Such was the immobility of Germany's High Seas Fleet in 1915 that two of its principal auxiliaries, its airships and submarines, were diverted to independent operations. The German navy's powerful force of Zeppelins, potentially a valuable instrument for scouting in a fleet action, was sent off to bomb English cities. And the U-boat force, which had been designed to reduce the number of British battleships and thus to open the way for a fleet battle on approximately equal terms, was diverted to a campaign against merchant shipping. Neither activity could rescue the German fleet from its confinement.

Nevertheless, whereas the Zeppelin raids on Britain posed no great threat to that country, the submarine assault upon its commerce rapidly developed into a serious menace. The U-boat was proving much less of a danger to battleships than had been anticipated. But it soon showed itself able to pick off merchant vessels in large numbers and at little risk to itself. This presented the combatants with a quite extraordinary prospect. If Germany could create a large enough force of submarines, and Britain proved unable to devise a counter, then there arose the possibility that each adversary might establish a maritime blockade of the other. Such a development had hardly been feasible in any previous war.

Given Britain's extreme vulnerability to commercial strangulation, the rulers of Germany were presented with a most tempting opportunity. Yet in order to avail themselves of it, a number of serious obstacles had to be surmounted. A U-boat blockade did not mean that Germany would be able to close the sea lanes around Britain. Merchant ships approaching and leaving the British Isles would have to be eliminated one by one. This was a tall order, requiring a much greater force of submarines than Germany at that time possessed. Further, the manner in which U-boats could most effectively make their kills raised all sorts of difficulties.

87

Plates 7a and 7b   *Cause and effect: two stages in the sinking of the British liner* Falaba, *torpedoed on 28 March 1915.*

7a   *This photograph (which has suffered some water damage, the photographer having spent an hour in the sea before being rescued) shows the German U-boat which delivered the Falaba's death-blow.*

7b   *This photograph shows passengers clinging to an upturned lifeboat. (The destruction of this vessel, with the loss of some American lives, was the subject of a protest by President Wilson.)*

It should be observed that, except for big prizes, U-boats at this time did not usually attack from underwater. A submarine's speed was much reduced when travelling submerged, which gave its quarry a better chance of escape. And its supply of torpedoes was small. Hence most U-boats attacked on the surface, employing gunfire. (It follows that the crucial advantage enjoyed by the undersea vessel over the surface raider in 1915 was less its ability to attack unseen than its capacity to evade British patrols.) Nevertheless, the method by which a submarine disposed of a merchant ship usually violated the accepted modes of waging war on non-combatants. A U-boat could not capture an apprehended vessel; it could only sink it. And it could not provide the accommodation for passengers and crew to which, according to international convention, they were entitled. The most that it could do to safeguard their lives was, before delivering the *coup de grâce*, to give them time to abandon ship. But this might oblige the U-boat to remain on the surface for 20 or 30 minutes, a risky business in waters patrolled by the British.

It followed that if submarines were to make the maximum number of kills at the least hazard to themselves – and it was precisely on this question of numbers that the success of the U-boat blockade would stand or fall – their best course was to strike down each victim as swiftly as possible. That meant disregarding the safety of those on board, failing to ascertain whether the vessel contained war materials, and perhaps ignoring the possibility that the vessel belonged not to one of Germany's enemies but to a neutral nation. To pursue this course – destroying merchant and passenger ships, killing non-combatant seamen and civilians, imperilling neutrals, and so obliterating a major distinction between the individuals and commodities upon whom it was and was not deemed legitimate to wage war – would be to introduce a large new element of 'frightfulness' into twentieth-century warfare.

II

If it seems difficult to appreciate that such a development really could arouse profound indignation, then it is worth noting the following anecdote. It comes from the Edwardian childhood of Claud Cockburn, a product of a well-to-do English family.[1] (Like a number of others in such circumstances, he became a prominant recruit to the Communist Party between the wars.) The tale concerns his Uncle Philip, a former army officer who had retired on half-pay following an accident sustained – appropriately – at polo. Uncle Philip spent much of his time engaged in war games in a large outhouse on the Cockburn property. On one occasion, while pitting his talents against a Japanese admiral, he was convinced he had caught his adversary cheating. The Japanese team had captured a British troopship with one of their cruisers; at the next move the Admiral advanced the cruiser the full number of squares that had come up on the dice. Uncle Philip demurred. His adversary should have deducted from the value of the throw the time needed to transfer and accommodate the British soldiers aboard the Japanese vessel. With the aid of *Jane's Fighting Ships* he was able to show that this would have been a lengthy business.

The Japanese admiral was unimpressed. 'But we threw the prisoners overboard,' he explained. And he refused to retract the move. Uncle Philip was overcome with rage. He hurled the dice box through the window and stormed from the outhouse. In the nursery the youngsters could hear his bloodcurdling account of the massacre. 'Sea full of sharks, of course. Our men absolutely helpless. Pushed over the side at the point of

---

[1] Claud Cockburn, *In Time of Trouble* (London: Rupert Hart-Davis, 1956), p. 10.

the bayonet. Damned cruiser forging ahead through water thickening with blood as the sharks got them.' He never trusted the Japanese thereafter, even when they took the British side in the First World War.

What is noteworthy about this incident is that the victims of the ostensible Japanese ruthlessness were not civilian passengers or merchant seamen, but combatants who had become an encumbrance to their opponents. Yet Uncle Philip held passionately that even fighting men might not simply be sent to the bottom because it served the military ends of an adversary. It is easy to surmise his reaction a few years later when, as a move not in a game but in a real war, the Germans began drowning passengers and merchant seamen in order not to win a naval battle but to prosecute a blockade.

Certainly, in British naval circles generally the notion that submarines might be used indiscriminately against merchant shipping had been dismissed out of hand before the war. Fisher, admittedly, had warned that Germany might employ such methods, but his view had not been taken seriously. (Nor had been his own proposal some years earlier that, to resolve the problem posed by German naval expansion, Britain should 'Copenhagen' the German fleet before it became a serious menace.) In July 1914 the *Strand* magazine published a short story by Conan Doyle describing how an imaginary small power might reduce Britain to its knees by unleashing a submarine campaign against merchant shipping. The editor of the magazine asked some prominent naval figures to comment on the tale. With one accord they dismissed it as fantasy. Admiral W. H. Henderson, for example, refused to believe that in any real war 'territorial waters will be violated, or neutral vessels sunk. Such will be absolutely prohibited, and will only recoil on the heads of the perpetrators. No nation would permit it, and the officer who did it would be shot.'[2]

No doubt naval opinion was helped to adopt this high moral stand by the fact that it suited Britain's convenience to inhibit the permitted uses of submarines. For it was possible to dispose of Germany's merchant fleet employing 'humane' methods. Yet this was not the whole explanation. Admiral Henderson's views were all of a piece with Uncle Philip's outburst against his Japanese visitor, and with the Admiralty's refusal to countenance Jackie Fisher's proposal for a preventive strike against the German fleet. They spoke for an age which still believed that war should be conducted according to certain decencies and within defined limits, among which the preservation of the distinction between combatants and non-combatants occupied an honoured position.

Such sentiments were not absent from the mind of German ruling circles also - notwithstanding their calculated acts of terrorism in Belgium. The Kaiser, for example, baulked at countenancing the aerial bombing of London; he agreed only on receiving the assurance that attacks would be confined to naval and military installations. But, apart from their moral misgivings, there was a major practical reason why Germany's rulers should hesitate before abandoning approved methods of conducting a blockade at sea. One powerful neutral was demanding that these methods be observed.

III

The USA was the only major country of European origin and orientation not so far involved in the war. Few elements in America seemed anxious to enter the conflict, but many sections possessed a powerful preference for one side as against the other. Some ethnic groups, particularly those of Irish and German origin, had no love for the Allies.

---

[2] Quoted in I. F. Clarke, *Voices Prophesying War 1763–1984* (London: Oxford University Press, 1966), p. 105.

But the weight of sympathy in America plainly rested with the Entente. Arguably, this orientation stemmed from the USA's origin as an English-speaking, liberal, non-militaristic nation.

Commericial considerations served to underpin this pro-British inclination. Admittedly, the increasing stringency with which Britain interpreted its right to blockade Germany sometimes produced diplomatic tension with the USA. But, even so, the most signal effect of Britain's blockade of the Central Powers was to reinforce America's inclination towards the Allies. The blockade severed virtually all commercial links between the USA and Germany. At the same time, the war was witnessing a prodigious increase in economic relations between the USA and the Allies. For one thing, Britain was often prepared to assuage the indignation of American exporters denied access to Germany by itself purchasing their entire stocks. And, much more important, the war was converting the Allies into a vast market for the primary products, manufactured goods, and financial reserves of the USA. American producers, exporters, and bankers could avail themselves fully of these opportunities for enrichment, confident that – as long as disaster did not befall the Allied cause – Britain's own resources of finance and merchant shipping would render all such transactions secure.

Thus Germany could have no hope of securing the USA as an ally. Ideology, history, and economic relations all ruled that out. The best that the German authorities could hope for was that America would retreat into a rigid neutrality, refusing to do business with either side. The worst that might happen for Germany was that America would assume an ever more benevolent stance towards the Allies, culminating in active involvement on their behalf. Clearly, nothing was more likely to stimulate the latter process than an unrestricted submarine campaign against merchant shipping. It would involve a further assault upon non-combatants, thus confirming Germany's image as a militaristic, illiberal power. And its execution would endanger American lives and even American ships, and so invade the jealously guarded rights of the most powerful neutral.

It was a nice question whether the likely benefits to Germany of attempting a submarine blockade were sufficient to outweigh this menace. On the other hand, the matter was being decided by men who, a few months before, had authorized the invasion of Belgium without regard to the reactions of another powerful, and potentially neutral, nation.

IV

In February 1915 the German Government, in what appeared a parting of the ways, declared the waters around Britain a war zone. All merchant shipping therein was liable to attack. A warning was issued that, while all attempts would be made to safeguard the lives of passengers and crews, there could be no guarantee of their safety. The ensuing months would test three things: the effectiveness of the submarine weapon in its new role: the resourcefulness of the British navy in countering it; and the strength of America's response when it found some of its citizens the victims of German actions.

The force of the U-boat weapon soon established itself. Prior to February 1915 only 10 British merchant ships had fallen victims to submarines, as against 14 to mines and 51 to surface raiders. In the following months this balance was sharply reversed. In the first three months of the campaign the rise in sinkings was not dramatic – 39 ships all told. But Germany had a mere 22 operational submarines when the campaign began, only four of which could put to sea immediately. As the number of U-boats in commission rose, so did the total of their victims. In August 1915 42 merchant ships went to the bottom, a rate of loss greater than the capacity of British shipyards to provide replacements.

After August the U-boats' toll began to diminish (and did not regain that month's peak until the holocaust of 1917). But this was not because Britain's counter-measures were getting the upper hand. Some of them, at least for a time, did prove effective. Nets, to which were attached mines or buoys that lit up on contact, were spread across the Straits of Dover. These caused U-boats to forego using the short Channel route in order to reach the Atlantic approaches to Britain, and to take instead the longer route round the north of Scotland – so reducing the time they could spend at sea hunting their prey. Again, the gradual arming of British merchant ships limited the enthusiasm of submarine commanders for attacking on the surface. So did the introduction of deception craft like the Q-boats – old tramp steamers fitted out with concealed armament, which looked like sitting ducks for a surface attack until a U-boat got too close. (Like many of the war's novelties, the Q-boats were highly successful to begin with but soon lost their effectiveness.) Any measures that inclined U-boats to attack undersea using torpedoes, rather than on the surface with guns, reduced their striking power.

But the main British strategy to beat the U-boat blockade was misconceived and doomed to failure. It constituted what was thought of as an offensive strategy. That is, naval patrols were organized to go hunting for submarines. The greater the number of submarines, the more numerous became the patrols. Certainly, the odd submarine fell victim to these methods. But given the U-boat's capacity for concealment and the absence of effective underwater detection devices, there could be no significant success for these search-and-destroy operations. Indeed, by patrolling the lanes most used by merchant ships, the British were guiding the U-boats to the whereabouts of potential victims. What they were not doing was providing a shield for those victims. The essential point, that the way to counter submarines was not by going in search of them but by standing between them and their quarry, escaped Britain's naval strategists throughout 1915 – and for a good while after that.

What brought the submarine menace under control in late 1915 was not the actions of the British fleet but the response of that neutral power whom both sides were watching so carefully as they sought to blockade each other. The American Government would not admit that Germany was entitled to declare a blockade of British waters when it lacked command of the sea, nor to pursue its blockading activities by means that jeopardized American lives. In May 1915 the great British passenger liner *Lusitania* was attacked without warning by a submerged U-boat; in August another British passenger liner, the *Arabic*, suffered a similar fate. The *Lusitania* sank in twenty minutes, the *Arabic* in ten. The loss in civilian lives, particularly in the first instance, was severe, and on each occasion some Americans were among the victims. These actions escalated the U-boat war with a vengeance. They were acts not just against cargo ships and merchant seamen but against passenger ships with their large complements of women and children. And the manner of the attacks minimized the chances of survival. Little now seemed to remain of Admiral Henderson's firm conviction in July 1914 that no nation would permit such behaviour and that 'the officer who did it would be shot'. As Colonel House, President Wilson's special adviser, grimly observed when he heard of the fate of the *Lusitania*: 'America has come to the parting of the ways, when she must determine whether she stands for civilized or uncivilized warfare.' Woodrow Wilson in his turn informed the German Government that the issue at stake was not just the rights of property or commerce, but 'nothing less high and sacred than the rights of humanity'.

The indignation to which the *Lusitania* and *Arabic* incidents gave rise seems difficult to appreciate in retrospect. Given that modern war was proving itself a conflict between entire peoples, in which economic resource and civilian morale would play a part in the final decision, how valid was the distinction between combatants and non-combatants, between civilized and uncivilized warfare? Clearly, Britain did not intend to relax its own blockade of Germany if, on account of the longevity of the struggle, it began to deprive German civilians of the necessities of life. And even in the case of the *Lusitania* the British authorities were not necessarily abiding by their own rules. For there is reason to suppose that surreptitiously they were using the ship to convey a consignment of explosives, whose presence on board imperilled the lives of passengers and probably contributed to the speed with which the *Lusitania* sank.

Yet if the outcry against this assault on merchant ships, and especially on passenger vessels, now seems mystifying, that may indicate the sorry path down which Western man has travelled since Claud Cockburn's Uncle Philip flung away his dice box and severed relations with his Japanese visitor. The distinction between what does and does not constitute a legitimate target in war will always prove difficult to establish – and even more difficult to maintain once the conflict has departed radically from its anticipated course. Yet even the Kaiser was momentarily paying homage to the distinction between honourable and dishonourable war when he baulked at the bombing of London, though in logic there might appear little difference between London and Louvain. To decide that such distinctions and decencies had no place in war was to open a Pandora's box of mindless slaughter and gratuitously imposed suffering.

Here indeed may lie the explanation of a good part of the indignation aroused on both sides of the Atlantic by the *Lusitania's* death plunge: in the awareness that this deed served little, if any, military purpose yet thrust Europe a further stage along a retreat from humane standards to which there could be no assured end point. In this respect it needs to be recalled that the *Lusitania* was not done away with because, in addition to its considerable human cargo, it perhaps carried a quantity of explosives. On this matter the U-boat commander who fired the fatal torpedo could have no knowledge. Nor did his Government require that he should. The *Lusitania* was destroyed because the German authorities had decided to treat every vessel in those waters as a target for attack, whatever its cargo and without regard to the welfare of those on board. That this extension of the categories of humanity which war was deemed to embrace should have aroused feelings of revulsion might seem, to present-day observers, a cause for envy rather than incomprehension.

V

In August 1915, with the sinking of the *Arabic* and the loss of more American lives, President Wilson moved from protest to ultimatum. Germany must cease actions endangering American citizens or face the consequences. The German Government, having in February appeared to cross the Rubicon, now retraced its steps. In October U-boats were ordered 'to cease all forms of submarine warfare on the west coast of Great Britain and in the Channel'. (Nevertheless, the submarine campaign went on – with considerable effect – in the Mediterranean, where there was less danger that Americans would figure among the victims.)

What had this first U-boat offensive against British trade accomplished? At no time had it managed to threaten Britain with blockade. Germany's supply of submarines was never sufficient for that. Yet during the year they had destroyed 750,000 tons of shipping.[3] At the same time the submarine threat was contributing to growing congestion in British ports, thus impairing the country's shipping situation more severely than was revealed by the figures of ships sunk.

Equally ominously, the Admiralty's attempts to counter the submarine were proving dangerously inadequate. Some of the measures adopted had reduced its effectiveness, and 20 U-boats had been sunk during the course of 1915. But meanwhile Germany had added 61 new submarines to its fleet. Hence it had 58 operational at the beginning of 1916, as against little more than 20 a year earlier. What caused the respite from the offensive was nothing the Admiralty had managed to devise, but Germany's own second thoughts about provoking American intervention. Yet Britain's naval chiefs failed to recognize this. They believed that they had got the measure of the new weapon. Consequently, they were not planning anxiously against the day when Germany, in sufficiently desperate circumstances and with its submarine force much increased, might decide to assail Britain's lifelines and hang the consequences.

---

[3] An additional 75,000 tons were sunk by mines and 30,000 by surface raiders.

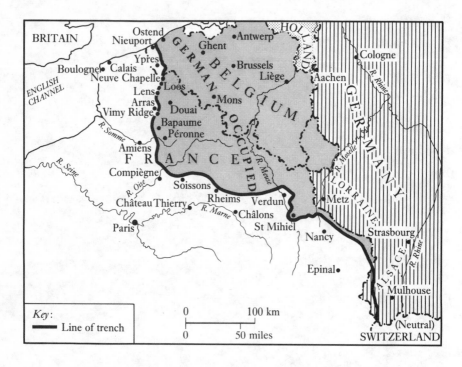

Map 3   *The Western Front, 1915*. Source: *Gilbert*, Recent History Atlas, *p. 27.*

PART THREE

Battlefronts
January–June 1915

10

STOCKTAKING

People in London are depressed. Both Russia's & France's capacities are obscure quantities.

Lord Bryce to H. A. L. Fisher, 15 October 1914

I don't know what is to be done . . . this isn't war.

Kitchener on trench warfare, in conversation with Sir Edward Grey

I

The winter of 1914–15, and particularly the turning of the year, was a time for taking stock among the civil and military leaders of every combatant power.

In some respects the directors of Britain's war effort had cause to be satisfied with what they saw. The nation had accomplished the transition from peace to war without civil disturbance, without a ministerial upheaval, and without the formation of a devoted anti-war party. The handsome response of the nation's young manhood to the call for recruits was confirmation of the country's commitment to the struggle, irrespective of its severity or duration. Equally, in some respects the conflict was not shaping badly. The Grand Fleet controlled the sea approaches to Britain and to the Continent. And the French army was holding its own, so that Western Europe was not in imminent danger of conquest.

In minor respects also there was cause for reassurance. The threat posed at the outset by Germany's naval bases in the north and south Pacific, with a strong naval squadron centred on Kiaochow on the China coast, existed no longer. Japan had declared war on Germany late in August 1914 and had swiftly overrun Kiaochow. And the German naval squadron, after its hour of glory, had vanished beneath the waves.

Another threat to the effectiveness of Britain's naval power had been swiftly dealt with: that posed by a belligerent Turkey. Conflict with Turkey was delayed for three months but could not be avoided indefinitely, given that country's long-standing feud with Russia and the role that Germany now played in its internal (particularly military) affairs. Certainly, it was unfortunate that in August 1914 British shipyards were constructing two battleships for the Turks. Anglo-Turk relations were not made easier when the British Admiralty requisitioned them – with compensation promised – for its own needs. But as it is now plain that the Turkish Government had arranged, as soon as the first vessel was completed, to send it direct to Germany, it is hard to believe that the Admiralty's action did anything to hasten the rupture of relations.

A hostile Turkey posed a possible threat to Britain's control of the Suez Canal, to the loyalty of its Muslim subjects, and to its supplies of Persian oil – the last an increasingly vital commodity since the Royal Navy had begun converting from coal to oil. But Britain's Muslim subjects did not respond to the Sultan's call for a Holy War,

99

thus dooming in advance the expedition that the Turks launched in January 1915 across the inhospitable Sinai Desert in an attempt to seize the Suez Canal. Meanwhile, Britain had moved swiftly to safeguard its oil supply. From southern Persia, a pipeline 140 miles in length conveyed oil for the navy to a refinery at Abadan, at the head of the Persian Gulf and precariously close to Turkish-ruled Mesopotamia. Even though there was no likelihood of early action by the Turks in this area, the British Government did not wait for a threat to develop. In October 1914 a division from India was landed at Bahrain (where Britain had treaty rights). And prompt upon the severance of relations with Turkey in November this force seized Turkish territory opposite Abadan and pushed north to occupy the port of Basra, situated at the confluence of the Tigris and the Euphrates.

In the long run it may have proved a misfortune for Britain that these first actions against the Turks seemed so easy. But for the moment the country's oil supplies were safe, its communications with the Far East remained open, and it had been shown that Britain did not automatically lose its power in distant parts when it was threatened nearer home.

Indeed, these opening stages of the war were entirely reassuring with respect to the strength of the bonds of Empire. No protest was raised in the English-speaking dominions when Britain declared war against Germany on their behalf. In Australia and Canada and New Zealand there was an immediate rush to the recruiting stations. Only in South Africa did disaffection assert itself, and then it was crushed by forces under Botha and Smuts, who had fought against Britain a decade and a half earlier. As for India, its internal situation was deemed sufficiently stable, and its frontiers secure enough, for the Viceroy readily to allocate three divisions for service overseas.

II

Nevertheless, as 1915 opened the rulers of Britain could not look at the circumstances of the war with great contentment. Some of Britain's coastal towns had been bombarded by enemy warships and its cities attacked from the air. The damage had been inconsiderable. But the events had caused anger, especially as the attackers had escaped scot-free.

But the cause for heartsearching went deeper. It was anything but clear how the war should be prosecuted to victory. The naval blockade, even when rendered more effective, showed little prospect of bringing Germany to its knees. Meanwhile Belgium remained under the heel of the invader. It was a nice question how the act of liberation, which was Britain's first object in the war, was to be accomplished.

What strategic alternatives confronted Britain as 1915 dawned? Some historians would argue none. They hold that Britain's rulers, prior to August 1914, had committed its military forces to act in conjunction with the French. Consequently, from then on British troops were obliged to conform to the strategy of the French high command.

This argument is unwarranted. All that had been committed in August 1914 was the original expeditionary force – a prudent decision, given that the BEF was too small to act on its own and that the soldiers of France were doing most of Britain's fighting for it. The great army that Britain was now training had not been contemplated before the war and certainly was not committed to any sphere of action. The British authorities had both the opportunity and the positive duty to consider its best employment.

Admittedly, there were strong reasons for sending Britain's new armies to the same

locality as the old. The obvious way to liberate Belgium and end the threat to the
Channel ports was to drive the invaders back the way they had come. And the French
army would remain, for no small while yet, the main military force of the Allies, and so
seemed entitled to whatever help Britain could give.

But the case was not open and shut. Before embarking on another campaign on the
Western Front, Britain's military planners must ponder the failure of the great French
and German offensives there in 1914. And, in so doing, they were bound to take into
account the awesome phenomenon that had appeared in the war's opening months:
trench warfare.[1]

III

The emergence of trench warfare in September 1914 was not in itself a cause for
surprise. British infantrymen carried spades along with their rifles and bayonets, for
the spade could serve as a vital weapon of defence. Soldiers seeking to ward off attack
or to hold newly won ground against a counter-attack must take advantage of whatever
cover man or nature provided. Trenches had proved themselves a highly effective form
of cover. Unlike buildings or trees, they were difficult to destroy by artillery
bombardment. They could usually be rendered continuous and hence difficult for an
attacking force to penetrate. And for soldiers on the defensive, with a brief period of
calm in which to choose their situation, trenches could be sited wherever it seemed
most advantageous to take a stand. All this is obvious. And yet the employment of
trenches in this war has often been seen as a prime example of military obtuseness, as if
troops under attack should have accepted a reduced chance of survival so as to retain
the unspecified benefits of remaining in the open.

But trenches were intended only to provide a breathing space: for an army forced to
fall back in haste from an unsound position, as with the German right wing at the
Marne, or for an army suddenly confronted with an overwhelmingly superior
adversary, as with the BEF at Mons and at Ypres. On each occasion the entrenched
force intended, at the first favourable opportunity, to leave its defences and resume the
advance. But here was the rub. Immediately, the adversary took appropriate defensive
measures, including the construction of trenches. This threatened to turn the struggle
in France into a stalemate, unless one of two things proved to be the case. Either one
side must be able to mount an offensive more quickly than the other could entrench
against it, or a form of frontal assault must be devised that could overwhelm a trench
system.

The mounting of an offensive in an area not yet subject to entrenchment depended
on two elements: speed and space. There must be transport facilities available whereby
the side determined to advance could move its forces to an unguarded area faster than
its adversary could both get there and entrench. So the attacker would turn the flank of
the defender. But could such an unguarded area be found? And, if so, could it be
exploited in time? In this respect, the Race for the Sea in September and October 1914
was an event of great moment for the development of the war in the West. When the
German right wing pulled back from the Marne, the whole German force came to rest,
from the Aisne south-east to the Swiss border, on the line that Schlieffen had
designated should be its position on Day 31 of the offensive. But it was to be a Day 31

---

[1] One of the most perceptive discussions of the topic of trench warfare is by John Keegan in issue no. 21 of
Purnell's History of the First World War, an illustrated history published in 128 weekly parts (London: Purnell &
Sons, 1969–71).

with no Day 32. For along the whole of this sector the Germans were digging in so as to render it not a springboard for a renewed advance but a bastion that would obviate the need for further retreat. Behind this bastion the German command was thinning out its forces and moving troops north, so that a renewed advance could be made on their right: that is, in the area between the Aisne and the sea. For there, it seemed, space (in the form of unentrenched territory) existed in abundance.

But if the space was there, which side could summon up superior speed to take advantage of it? The answer depended on the means of transport available. And this boiled down to which side had the better north-south railway system. For against a force being transported by rail, troops having to move on foot would be too slow, and adequate motorized transport did not exist. But in the event each side had a railway system at its disposal. Hence neither was able to entrain its forces first to the north, then sideways (by means of cross-country lines running east–west), before the other got in the way. That is, the Race to the Sea was in effect a series of parallel entrainments northwards, punctuated by sharp exchanges at places where the two sets of north–south railway lines were intersected by others running east–west. By the time the race was run there was no space to be had.

Of course, space would still have been available if, in the course of their dash north, one of the contestants had been forced to leave a tract of territory unoccupied. In other words, want of manpower might have left space within the line even while it was being eliminated on the flank. But this did not occur. The whole of the Western Front, from the coast to Switzerland, ran for only 475 miles, and much of that was quite unsuitable territory in which to launch a large-scale offensive. The armies available to each side for guarding this line ran into millions of men. And, thanks to the complex railway systems of France, Belgium, and Germany, reinforcements could be brought by either side to any threatened place. Hence neither contestant needed to leave a sensitive part unguarded. Rather, it was a matter of cramming into a restricted area vast numbers of men and industrial products.

If neither side could mount an offensive on the Western Front where it would not run up against a trench barrier, then there was only one alternative to stalemate. That was for one side to devise a form of assault that would smother its opponents' trenches long enough to render them pregnable. Yet already it was becoming plain that, in the wake of recent developments in military technology, trenches were not easy to render ineffective. They could not be got at quickly. Barbed wire entanglements, rapid-firing rifles, machine-guns, and shrapnel had together made it purposeless to launch cavalry against an unbreached trench system. First the infantry must clear a way. Yet if the soldier on foot was better equipped to find a passage across disputed territory and through barbed wire than the soldier on horseback, the advantage was rarely decisive. Certainly, in the absence of ample support from artillery employing high-explosive shell, infantry attacks on well defended trenches were also doomed.

By the end of 1914 all of the contestants on the Western Front had expended their supplies of high-explosive shell. The winter would have to pass as fresh stocks were being accumulated. But meanwhile British, French, and German forces in the West were being kept occupied in improving their trench systems: constructing shell-proof dug-outs, staking out barbed wire, preparing further lines of trenches at intervals behind the first line, joining the front and rear lines by communication trenches running at zig zag so that reliefs and reinforcements could make the hazardous journey to the front without venturing into the open, and laying telephone wires so that gunners out of sight of No-Man's-Land could be directed to rain down shells on an attacking force.

These sophistications in trench defences could not be accomplished overnight. But generally it proved to be the case that those seeking to end the dominance established on the battlefield by the combination of trenches and defensive weapons were facing a developing conundrum. As the supply of missiles with which to smother a trench system grew, so did the strength and complexity of the obstacles that an attacking force would have to overcome – that is, if the open warfare for which each side craved were ever to be re-established.

IV

Confronted by these ominous circumstances, three noteworthy members of Britain's governing circles were, by the end of 1914, putting forward schemes to circumvent the trench barrier in Flanders. Two of them, Churchill and Lloyd George, were members of the War Council. The third, Sir Maurice Hankey, was its secretary. Each believed that Britain, with its potential for combining sea power, man power, and heavy industry, was uniquely fitted to exercise a strategic initiative.

These three were men of recognized ability. Churchill was a descendant of the first Duke of Marlborough and the son of a one-time rising star in the Conservative Party. His own colourful adventures in the Sudan and South Africa had secured him national prominence and a place in Conservative politics. Then in 1904 he had taken a firm stand for free trade and had transferred his allegiance to the Liberal Party. With the Liberals soon thereafter in power, his own advance had been rapid. In office he was identified first with measures of social reform, then, as First Lord of the Admiralty, with safeguarding Britain's naval lead over Germany. His brilliance was widely acknowledged, though many deemed him self-absorbed and unreliable.

Lloyd George, Churchill's senior in years and standing, also aroused feelings of admiration and distrust. His background was quite unlike Churchill's. Reared in a small Welsh village amid strong Baptist influences (which, personally if not politically, he had soon come to reject), he proved an intensely political animal. He entered Parliament as a Liberal and a proponent of Welsh nationalism, but his opposition to the Boer War made him a national figure (if at the price of great unpopularity). His 'pro-Boer' sympathies led some to regard him as a pacifist – an unfounded judgement, as became evident when he sharply rebuked Germany during the Moroccan crisis of 1911. Certainly, as a Chancellor of the Exchequer seeking money for social reform, he begrudged expenditure on armaments up to August 1914. But once Britain became engaged in what he deemed a just war, his commitment to the struggle was unrelenting.

Hankey was not a public figure. The product of a middle-class family and a public school, he had joined the Royal Marines and attracted the attention of Admiral Fisher. From an involvement in naval intelligence he became secretary of the Committee of Imperial Defence; and with the formation of the War Council in November 1914 he was appointed its secretary. His upright character, complete discretion, and tireless devotion to his job won him the full trust of Asquith – as, subsequently, they would that of his successor.

How, in the first winter of the war, did these men propose to resolve the strategic dilemma?

Lloyd George was the only one of the three who appeared to contemplate actually pulling the BEF out of France and Belgium, leaving the French to hold the line in the West except in an emergency. He favoured operations in two areas: a landing in Syria to strike at Turks operating against Egypt, and a landing on Greek soil, in Salonika, to rally the Balkan states against Austria-Hungary. The latter operation was clearly the one that engaged his enthusiasm, and to it he was prepared to devote a substantial force. Lloyd George argued that there was no prospect of breaching 'the carefully prepared German lines in the west'; that it was desirable to make the enemy extend his line and fight in the open; that it was necessary to win 'a definite victory somewhere' so as to rally opinion at home and to attract wavering neutrals; and that his proposals 'would have the common purpose of bringing Germany down by the process of knocking the props under her'.[2] In the War Council on 7 January 1915 Lloyd George deplored the possibility that Britain's new armies might be thrown away on hopeless operations in France. Was it impossible, he asked, 'to get at the enemy from some other direction, and to strike a blow that would end the war once and for all'?

Hankey and Churchill also wrote papers on the strategic riddle. Hankey too referred to the 'remarkable deadlock' on the Western Front. And, like Lloyd George, he regarded it as axiomatic that the neutral Balkan states would enter the war on the Allied side as soon as they were confident that Britain was committing a substantial force to their region. The course he favoured was a decisive blow against Turkey, although he did not specify where. It was to be carried out by three army corps from Britain acting jointly with forces supplied by Greece and Bulgaria – two countries that happened to be neutral and in a state of mutual enmity.

As for Churchill, in the course of a letter to the Prime Minister pressing him for a greater measure of guidance and decision, he coined an unforgettable phrase. He urged that Britain's new armies should not be sent to 'chew barbed wire in Flanders'.

The conjunction of these three expositions, especially when linked with Churchill's subsequent identification with the Dardanelles operation, has given rise to one of the most powerful myths of the First World War. It holds that there existed two clear-cut strategies confronting Britain at the beginning of 1915, a Western strategy and an Eastern strategy, and that the trinity of Lloyd George, Hankey, and Churchill were at one in espousing the latter alternative. The truth is otherwise. There was no single Eastern strategy. And apart from being at one in deploring the pursuance of victory through frontal assaults upon existing German trenches, the three powerful minds were anything but united.

What Hankey was advocating was not at all the course that Lloyd George espoused. Hankey's proposed operation against Turkey had the great advantage that it was directed against an adversary which could not be succoured by Germany. But it envisaged the employment of troops not at Britain's disposal, in a region he had failed to specify. And, even if completely successful, an assault upon Turkey would fall far short of Lloyd George's 'blow that would end the war once and for all'.

In the Balkans the stakes were higher. Lloyd George was hoping to eliminate Germany's principal ally, something the rulers in Berlin would make great efforts to prevent. But the difficulties of mounting a campaign against Austria-Hungary were imposing and not easily calculable: problems of transportation by sea and land; problems of relations with Balkan states across whose territory (in the case of Greece) or in dangerous proximity to whose armed forces (in the case of Bulgaria) Allied troops and supplies must pass; and problems of estimating the extent of the hostile forces to be encountered at the other end. What counter-moves, to put the matter in a nutshell, would Germany make? Lloyd George recognized the existence of some of these hazards, for he wrote in his memorandum of 1 January 1915:

> The ground therefore has not been surveyed. It would take some time to collect the necessary intelligence as to the country, so as to decide where to land the Army and what

---

[2] Memorandum of 1 January 1915, quoted in *War Memoirs of David Lloyd George*, 2-volume ed. (London: Odhams Press, 1938), vol. 1. pp. 219–26.

shall be the line of attack. Transport would have to be carefully and secretly gathered. Large forces might have to be accumulated in the Mediterranean. . . . Military arrangements would have to be made with Roumania, Serbia, Greece and, perhaps, Italy. All this must take time. Expeditions decided upon and organised with insufficient care and preparation generally end disastrously.

These remarks are full of wisdom. But they raise a question about Lloyd George's place among the 'Easterners'. In one sense he seemed to be advocating not a Balkans operation but a feasibility study of a Balkans operation. To this extent he was not – or anyway not yet – a committed Easterner. Yet at some points he appeared to be prejudging the outcome of such a study and affirming that an operation against Austria-Hungary would certainly succeed as long as preparations were adequate. This ambiguity deserves to be noted, for it considerably limits the importance of Lloyd George's Balkans proposal of January 1915. In so far as that document was more than a *cri de coeur* against further offensives in the West, it lacked the detailed exposition that alone would make it the embodiment of an alternative strategy. Rather, it constituted an inspired piece of kite flying, expressed in compelling but sometimes dangerously misleading language. (To refer to Austria-Hungary and Turkey as 'props' whose removal would have the effect of 'bringing Germany down' may have been a telling piece of imagery, but it was not related to reality. Indeed, it constituted little more than sleight of hand with a wall map – upon which these countries appear 'below' Germany.)

How did Churchill view the rival attractions of Turkey and the Balkans as scenes for Britain's major effort in 1915? Even at his most cordial, he appears to have had only transitory sympathy for a Balkan expedition. He was inclined much more towards an operation against Turkey. But, as settings for Britain's principal action, he favoured neither. As he wrote to the First Sea Lord, Fisher, on 4 January 1915:

> I wd not grudge 100,000 men [against Turkey] because of the great political effects in the Balkan peninsula: but Germany is the foe, & it is bad war to seek cheaper victories & easier antagonists.[3]

Certainly, he deplored proposals to impale Britain's new armies upon the barbed wire of Flanders. But what he wanted to do was to strike against Germany further north, first by employing Britain's naval and military power to seize the island of Borkum, 6 miles off the German coast, and establish it as a forward base. 'Borkum is the key to all Northern possibilities,' he wrote to Fisher in the same letter. A week later, following a discussion in the War Council regarding a communication from Sir John French advocating continued action on the Western Front, Churchill wrote to French:

> I argued in the War Council strongly against deserting the decisive theatre & the most formidable antagonist to win cheaper laurels in easier fields. The only circs in wh such a policy cd be justified wd be after every other fruitful alternative had been found impossible. . . .
> I favour remaining in the N[orthern] theatre, but endeavouring, as our numbers and resources increase, [to] lengthen the G[erman] line and compel him to expose new surfaces to the waste of war.[4]

It is not wonderful that the opponents of a Western Front strategy failed to carry the day in the War Council meetings of January 1915. Action against Turkey (like that proposed by Hankey against German colonies in Africa) ran up against Churchill's objection that this would mean 'deserting the decisive theatre' so as to win 'cheaper

---

[3] Martin Gilbert, *Winston S. Churchill*, Companion Volume 3, pt 1, (London: Heinemann, 1972), p. 371.
[4] Ibid., pp. 401–2.

laurels in easier fields'. Action against Austria-Hungary presented awe-inspiring problems of communications, would depend on the dubious allegiance of Balkan powers, and promised at the end 'cheaper laurels' not easily come by. As for Churchill's scheme – which he favoured, in Lloyd George's hostile view, because it would bring more glory to himself – it suffered from a general objection and a particular. The general objection was that it involved placing a section of the Grand Fleet close to the German coast and hence at great risk. The particular objection (expressed by Jellicoe) was that, if it were possible for the British to capture a well fortified island 240 miles off the British coast, then the Germans should be able to recapture the same island, now with its fortifications smashed up, when it lay only 6 miles off their coast.

Furthermore, although there was broad agreement as to the undesirability of returning to the offensive in Flanders – Kitchener, Balfour, and well-nigh everyone else joined in the chorus of dismay at the prospect – the matter was not quite open-and-shut. Sir John French, in what Asquith called a very able statement of the case against action outside France, denied that the German lines were impenetrable. He claimed that it was largely a matter of ammunition, particularly supplies of high-explosive shells. 'Until the impossibility of breaking through on this side was proved, there could be no question of making an attempt elsewhere.'[5] Sir John was not just being obtuse. In one sense his assessment may have been correct. German trench defences, as they existed at the end of 1914, probably were not immune to an assault preceded by a heavy bombardment. What sort of defences would confront the British forces by the time they were actually able to lay down such a bombardment was, of course, another matter.

Sir John offered a further powerful reason why Britain must reinforce the Western Front. 'In the western theatre a German victory would be decisive.' A 'crushing defeat' of the French 'would be very dangerous and embarrassing to our own safety, and must be made impossible'.[6] There were really two points being made here, however murkily Sir John perceived them. First, Britain must assist in averting defeat in the West if the objects for which the nation had gone to war were not utterly to be thwarted. Western Europe therefore was the theatre from which Britain could not divert the major part of its attention, however tempting the alternatives elsewhere. The other point was Britain's continued dependence on the military power of France. A British effort anywhere else, whatever rewards it might bring, would be counter-productive if it caused the French to doubt their ally and so reduced their willingness to continue making the fearful sacrifices that must still be required of them.

Lloyd George, for one, railed against such restrictions on a British strategic initiative. 'Are we really bound', he asked Churchill on 29 January 1915, 'to hand over the ordering of our troops to France as if we were her vassal?'[7] And early in February, when discussing Joffre's objections to operations in the Balkans, Lloyd George asked: 'Are we to allow things to become impossible simply because one man chooses to dictate what our policy is to be?'[8]

Given that the man in question happened to be commander of the only military force capable at that moment of preserving a vital British interest – that of preventing the

---

[5] Gilbert, *Winston S. Churchill*, Companion Volume 3, pt 1, p. 392.

[6] Oddly enough, Sir John did not think that an Allied triumph in the West would be decisive. For the Allies, he argued, ultimate victory must come on the Russian front.

[7] Gilbert, *Winston S. Churchill*, Companion Volume 3, pt 1, p. 472.

[8] A. J. P. Taylor (ed.), *Lloyd George: A Diary by Frances Stevenson* (London: Hutchinson, 1971), pp. 29–30.

Germans from overrunning Western Europe – it might be thought that the one possible answer to Lloyd George's question was an affirmative.

V

The outcome of this stocktaking in the British Cabinet at the beginning of 1915 was somewhat, although not very, equivocal. Basically (even though it was not quite put this way), the War Council decided on 13 January to persevere with operations in France. But it did so negatively. It resolved that if by the spring of 1915 a stalemate had plainly developed there, then British forces would go elsewhere.

This at least showed that Britain was not conforming to French strategy because it had agreed to do so before the outbreak of the war. But it was also evidence that, notwithstanding deep misgivings about renewed operations on the Western Front, Britain's leaders could not turn decisively from it. Instead they found comfort in the rider that a sub-committee of the War Council should start seeking out 'another theatre and objective' in anticipation of deadlock being confirmed in the West.

The War Council, at the same meeting of 13 January, also found comfort in two projects that the Admiralty was directed to put in hand. One was to undertake some form of naval action in the Adriatic 'with a view (*inter alia*) of bringing pressure on Italy'. This scheme was not heard of again. The other was to prepare for 'a naval expedition in February to bombard and take the Gallipoli peninsula, with Constantinople as its objective'. Very much more was to be heard of this.

11

GENESIS OF A SIDESHOW

> If the Fleet gets through [the Narrows], Constantinople will fall of itself. . . .
>
> *Kitchener, speaking to Sir Ian Hamilton, 13 March 1915*

I

Modern studies of the Gallipoli operation sometimes carry a quotation from Napoleon. It is rendered variously: 'Who is to have Constantinople? That is always the crux of the problem'; or 'Essentially the great question remains. Who will hold Constantinople?' In whatever version, it is misleading as an epitome of the Gallipoli campaign of 1915. Certainly, Kitchener told Sir Ian Hamilton, when he dispatched him to command a military force in the Eastern Mediterranean, that if Constantinople fell, 'you will have won, not a battle but the war'.[1] But such hyperbole is common in times of great endeavour. It should not be regarded as a considered judgement.

What is certain (as has been suggested already) is that the leaders of Britain did not decide in January 1915 that a breakthrough to Constantinople was 'the crux of the problem'. Even those looking to operations in the Eastern Mediterranean agreed that the 'great question' was the maintenance of the Allied line in France and of British dominance in the North Sea. Hence the margin of superiority of the Grand Fleet must in no wise be hazarded in operations elsewhere. And if Kitchener said, as he did in the War Council more than once in January, that no troops could be spared for an offensive in the Eastern Mediterranean because he was not certain that the line in France was secure, then there was no appeal against this judgement. That was not just because Kitchener was the person who delivered it. Rather it was because a decision made on these grounds was incontestable.

II

If the attempt to subdue Constantinople early in 1915 had really sprung from a belief that this was the 'great question', then the manner in which Britain's leaders set about it would defy comprehension. We can better understand their conduct if we see their decision as the product of quite different assumptions: for example, Lloyd George's notion that Britain needed a victory 'somewhere', Churchill's premise that adversaries other than Germans were 'easier', and Kitchener's belief that a naval attack on the Dardanelles could be abandoned with no harm done if it did not prosper. Each of these assumptions begged a multitude of questions. But so long as the questions were not asked, then it apparently did not matter that such an operation was being instituted

---

[1] Sir Ian Hamilton, *Gallipoli Diary* (London: Edward Arnold, 1920), vol. I, p. 16.

without an exhaustive staff appreciation of the obstacles to be surmounted and the resources needed to overcome them. The obstacles would be less than they appeared, given the adversary involved. And the risks were worth taking seeing that the damage consequent upon a miscalculation would be nil.

Plate 8   *Reading the proclamation of war against Turkey from the steps of the Royal Exchange, London, on 6 November 1914.*

What was Churchill's part in these events? From the moment Turkey entered the lists against the Allies, he hankered for action against it. Indeed, he ordered a naval bombardment of the Dardanelles forts on 3 November 1914, prior to a formal declaration of war. This is not to say that Churchill had an *idée fixe* about the Dardanelles, giving an operation there precedence in his mind over all other lines of action. As has been pointed out, his principal inspiration was a blow against the major adversary, Germany, in the northern theatre. But his hankering after subsidiary action at Gallipoli came together in January with other events and attitudes. There was an appeal by the Russians for a 'demonstration' against the Turks. There was Kitchener's conviction that the one hopeful place for operations outside the Western Front was not Salonika, as argued by Lloyd George, but Gallipoli – even though he had no troops available for it. There was the general dismay caused in the Cabinet by the prospect of another attempt at a forward move in France, at a time when some sort of forward move seemed urgently called for. And, not least, there was the fragility of Churchill's own position.

Many things had contributed to this last element in the situation. As an individual Churchill did not inspire confidence on either side of Parliament, even if it is not always easy to divine why he aroused such mistrust; that is, many people of importance were agreeable to seeing him taken down a peg. Again, Churchill had suffered (not always justly) a number of personal humiliations since the outbreak of war, particularly his abortive attempt to preserve Antwerp as an Allied-held enclave in German-occupied Belgium. The navy also had incurred humiliations, some of which reflected no credit on the Admiralty. Further, there was a growing determination among members of the Government, particularly (but not exclusively) the Secretary of State for War, to curtail Churchill's frequent visits to France, where he was supposedly meddling in military affairs and exacerbating the ill-feeling between Kitchener and Sir John French. (Churchill could well have imagined that he was struggling to keep the peace between them.)

Following some minor setbacks at sea, in circumstances 'not creditable to the officers of the Navy' and 'far from glorious to the Navy', Asquith – without holding Churchill to blame – told him that it was 'time that he bagged something, & broke some crockery'.[2] This was early in November. The defeat of Spee at the Falkland Islands on 8 December seems not to have met Asquith's requirements, for on Christmas Eve he wrote that Churchill was 'meditating fearsome plans of a highly aggressive kind to replace the present policy of masterly inactivity'.[3] But Churchill's plans, as they concerned northern Europe, ran up against serious objections from his naval advisers. Hence by the New Year it was not certain that Churchill would be able to avoid a prolongation of 'masterly inactivity', notwithstanding its repugnance to his combative nature and the threat to his position that it entailed. To escape this situation he must find an operation of some moment that would not endanger Dreadnoughts or require the employment of troops. This was a tall order. But the forcing of the Dardanelles was, by Kitchener's word as well as his own, an operation of moment. Admittedly, Churchill was on record as saying that it could not be accomplished without a strong military contingent. But in a situation where the choice lay apparently between a purely naval attack there (employing pre-Dreadnought battleships) and doing nothing at all, he seemed to have cause to revise that judgement.

Responsibility for the abortive naval attack on the Dardanelles rests with many people. The Board of the Admiralty was sometimes a willing, if more often a reluctant, collaborator. Asquith (inexcusably) misrepresented the navy's conduct during the opening months of the war as 'masterly inactivity', and he pressed Churchill to be up and doing without establishing the wisdom – in naval terms – of such a course. Kitchener, Lloyd George, and most other members of the War Council felt free to indulge in bewildering changes of attitude towards the desirability or viability of an operation at the Dardanelles. No one among them asked the searching questions that the undertaking seemed to demand, or probed the known (if usually unexpressed) objections of the First Sea Lord, Admiral Fisher. (Fisher had been recalled to his former post in October 1914.)

Yet Churchill had a special responsibility for the coming calamity at the Dardanelles. The operation could never have been launched against his wishes or, indeed, without his vigorous initiative. Yet he was acting not on a rigorous appraisal of the feasibility of a naval forcing of the Dardanelles but on a succession of events pressing him to do something ('break some crockery') yet leaving him with only this one thing to do. So he drove on in the face of the growing, if variable, misgivings of his naval advisers until he found that he had brought them to a point where, at a critical moment, they would be driven no further.[4] Yet at the same time he was barely able to conceal from his

[2] Martin Gilbert, *Winston S. Churchill*, Companion Volume 3, pt 1 (London: Heinemann, 1972), pp. 250–3; Asquith in letters to Venetia Stanley and to King George V, 4 November 1914.

[3] Gilbert, *Winston S. Churchill*, Companion Volume 3, pt 1, p. 333; Asquith to Venetia Stanley, 24 December 1914.

[4] On 23 March 1915, when the Admiral in charge at the Dardanelles proposed calling off the naval attack to await a military landing, Churchill wanted to order him to go on. His leading naval advisers would not agree.

colleagues his own mounting desperation at the prospect of a naval attack lacking military support. ('The naval operations may at any moment become intimately dependent on military assistance,' he wrote urgently to Asquith on 11 March.)[5] And it is doubtful whether he even attempted to conceal his desperation from Sir Ian Hamilton, when he spoke to him shortly before Hamilton set out as commander of a putative Eastern Mediterranean force.

As First Lord of the Admiralty during the opening months of the war, Churchill deserves great credit for his personal courage, patriotism, and whole-hearted application to the business of making war. (Three days before the fateful War Council meeting that resolved to attempt a naval forcing of the Dardanelles, Churchill said to Margot Asquith, 'Why I would not be out of this glorious delicious war for anything the world could give me' – but he was then somewhat embarrassed by his use of the word 'delicious'.)[6] Yet, with all these positive qualities, it is difficult to overlook the profound irresponsibility of his conduct in this matter.

III

A word about geography is required here. What are the Dardanelles? The name refers to the narrow stretch of turbulent water that alone gives naval access to the Sea of Marmora and thence to the Turkish capital. This waterway is 41 miles long and very constricted: only 4 miles across at its widest point and three-quarters of a mile at its narrowest. On one side lies the Gallipoli peninsula, on the other the Asiatic shore of Turkey.

The Turkish defences of the Dardanelles in early 1915 were not without substance. On both the peninsula and the Asiatic shore stood forts manned by heavy guns. These were supplemented by groupings of mobile howitzers, which might change position from day to day. And in the waters of the Dardanelles lay a succession of minefields, themselves protected by shore batteries not visible from the waterline. The question was whether any force of battleships, let alone the pre-Dreadnoughts that were all Britain had available for this region, could vanquish these obstacles and effect a safe passage up the waterway.

By January 1915 there was already a British naval squadron standing guard over the entrance to the Dardanelles, just in case the *Goeben* and the *Breslau* should seek to return to the Mediterranean. Commanding the squadron was Vice-Admiral Carden, who in Great War parlance was something of a dug-out. In the last months of peace he had occupied the post of Admiral Superintendent of the Malta Dockyard, a familiar stepping-stone to retirement. (Despite his being the father of a young baby – whom he was reluctant to be seen carrying when the servants were handy – Carden was 57 years of age.) Only the outbreak of war had brought him to more active employment.

Churchill, it has to be said, did not regard Carden highly. On 23 December 1914 he wrote to Fisher: 'As for Carden – he has never even commanded a cruiser Sqn. & I am not aware of anything that he has done wh is in any way remarkable.'[7] This makes it all the more noteworthy that the First Lord would soon be offering Carden's sketchy replies to his own leading questions as if they were the weighty judgements of a well regarded authority.

On 3 January 1915 Churchill initiated the process by which a British naval force, without military assistance, sought to force a passage through the Dardanelles and to

---

[5] Gilbert, *Winston S. Churchill*, Volume 3, p. 338.
[6] Gilbert, *Winston S. Churchill*, Companion Volume 3, pt 1, p. 400.
[7] Ibid., p. 327.

overawe Constantinople. He sent Carden a somewhat tendentious telegram, whose key sentences read: 'Do you consider the forcing of the Dardanelles by ships alone a practicable operation? . . . Importance of results would justify severe loss.' Only a naval commander of great self-confidence, or considerable timidity, could have met this inquiry with a flat negative. Carden fell into neither category. Nevertheless, his reply was hardly enthusiastic: 'I do not consider Dardanelles can be rushed', Carden telegraphed on 5 January. 'They might be forced by extended operations with large numbers of ships.' This seemed to be a firm negative followed by a qualified affirmative, in which the word 'might' cried out to be probed. Yet no probing took place. Rather, some important figures at the Admiralty began warming to the prospect of a purely naval attack on the Dardanelles. This provided Churchill with the opening he required to take the proposal to the War Council.

That body, on the day Carden's telegram arrived, was engaged in discussing the merits of military action in Flanders, or northern Germany, or the Balkans. Lloyd George advocated the last of these, and Kitchener countered that the only promising sphere of action outside France was at Gallipoli. Churchill thereupon informed them of Carden's telegram. This happened to conflict with no one's favoured scheme – since it required no military force – and so met with no opposition. Churchill replied to Carden on 6 January: 'Your view is agreed with by high authorities here' (thus begging the question as to what Carden's view was). 'Please telegraph in detail what you think could be done by extended operations, what force would be needed and how you consider it should be used.' Yet on the following day Churchill persuaded his colleagues in the War Council to let him prepare plans for an operation against northern Germany. This, if launched, would leave no vessels available for action at the Dardanelles.

If Gallipoli had a really enthusiastic supporter at this time, it remained Kitchener, not Churchill. Again on 8 January Kitchener told the War Council of the likely merits of an operation there. Yet it was not a naval assault he meant but 'an attack . . . made in co-operation with the Fleet' by a military force – and this for the moment remained unavailable. He thought 150,000 men might be sufficient to capture the Gallipoli peninsula. Lloyd George expressed surprise at the modesty of the figure.[8]

On 12 January the Admiralty received Carden's plan of operation. It specified the size of the naval force he required. And it outlined the stages by which, beginning at the entrance to the Dardanelles and then proceeding forward, the guns of these ships would, with the aid of aerial spotting, crush the Turkish forts. After that the minefields would be swept. This plan made no attempt to explore the age-old question of whether naval guns really could subdue land defences – and not just temporarily but during what promised to be a lengthy and sporadic operation. ('Gales now frequent. Might do it all in a month about' was Carden's uncertain timetable.) Also lacking was an elaboration of the more recent problem presented by minefields, which must be cleared ahead of the fleet by light vessels vulnerable to gunfire and operating in a confined and turbulent waterway. Yet these apparent inadequacies did not dismay the Admiralty War Group, which responded with real enthusiasm to the scheme. In fact Admiral Fisher – in one of his rare moments of support for the undertaking –proposed to include in the bombarding force the mighty new battleship *Queen Elizabeth*, which

---

[8] To his credit Lloyd George did not fall into the trap of underrating Turkish soldiers as a fighting force. He had noted their devoted resistance in the last phase of the Balkan War of 1912, when Constantinople was in danger. See John Grigg, *Lloyd George: From Peace to War 1912–1916* (London: Methuen, 1985), p. 211. Yet Lloyd George's insight was only partial. He managed to subscribe to the view that a British fleet appearing off Constantinople would, by itself or with minimal military assistance, bring about the capitulation of the Turkish Empire.

possessed guns much heavier than anything Carden had asked for. (The *Queen Elizabeth*, be it noted, was not intended to do more than bombard. It would not proceed up the Dardanelles, for no undue risk could be taken with so precious a vessel.)

Next day, 13 January, Carden's plan went to the War Council. It was from this meeting that the Admiralty received its commission to 'prepare for a naval expedition in February to bombard and take the Gallipoli peninsula, with Constantinople as its objective'. This was an extraordinarily sloppy form of wording (and would in time become a subject of derision.) For how does a naval force 'take' a pensinula? And what was meant by its having Constantinople 'as its objective'? The reason for such imprecision is not far to seek. The War Council that day was not largely concerned with the Gallipoli proposal. The lion's share of its attention went to a scheme for launching a joint military and naval operation against the German forces holding the Belgian coast. Churchill was a strong advocate of this scheme. According to Sir John French, who had seen him the night before, Churchill 'thought the time was not yet ripe to consider a diversion of our troops to other more distant theatres'.[9]

Only towards the end of the War Council meeting did the proposed naval operation against the Dardanelles come up for consideration. If received with enthusiasm, it secured only cursory attention. According to the Council's minutes, the sole comments came from Lloyd George, who 'liked the plan', and from Kitchener, who 'thought it was worth trying. We could leave off the bombardment if it did not prove effective.' It was less than a week since these two had wrangled about whether a contingent of 150,000 troops in support of a naval force would be sufficient to 'take' the Gallipoli peninsula.

IV

On 5 February the Admiralty sent Carden his Dardanelles Operations Orders. They exhorted him not to use 'a large quantity of [the *Queen Elizabeth*'s] valuable ammunition', and warned him that 'wasteful expenditure of ammunition' by his other vessels 'may result in the operations having to be abandoned before a successful conclusion is arrived at'. These observations can hardly have been reassuring. Even more, the orders included this pregnant sentence: 'It is not expected or desired that the operations should be hurried to the extent of *taking large risks and courting heavy losses*' (emphasis added). So disappeared one of the major premises on which Carden had been persuaded to give his halting support for the naval assault on the Dardanelles: that, as Churchill assured him when first broaching the matter, the importance of the operation would justify 'severe loss'.

On 24 February 1915 Kitchener told the War Council: 'if the fleet would not get through the Straits unaided, the army ought to see the business through. The effect of a defeat in the Orient would be very serious. There could be no going back.' This statement demolished one of the principal arguments offered to the War Council in support of the naval operation – that (as Kitchener had told that body on 13 January and again on 28 January) 'if satisfactory progress was not made, the attack could be broken off.'

In short, almost before a shot had been fired the Dardanelles operation had begun to go awry. Second thoughts among the Admiralty Board were causing temporary enthusiasm to give way to profound misgiving. By 10 February every naval officer in the Admiralty, from Fisher downwards (so Hankey wrote to Balfour),[10] believed that

---

[9] Gilbert, *Winston S. Churchill*, Companion Volume 3, pt 1, p. 407.
[10] See A. J. Marder, *From the Dardanelles to Oran* (London: Oxford University Press, 1974), p. 2.

the navy could not force the Dardanelles without troops. A variety of grounds for doubt were being advanced, particularly from Fisher (whose opposition Churchill had no chance of allaying, because as the First Lord sought to meet one objection Fisher shifted to another). But underlying them all was the fact that only when it came to issuing Carden with his orders were some of the fundamental questions asked. How great was the efficacy of naval guns against land defences? How 'severe' were the losses that the naval expedition might sustain while still remaining effective? How much ammunition could the attacking vessels expend and yet constitute a viable force once through the Dardanelles? As his naval advisers began to grapple with these primary problems, Churchill (who 'still professes to believe that they can do it with ships')[11] found himself increasingly isolated.

Moreover as the country's naval authorities began to contemplate what they had undertaken, events in Europe were calling in question the War Council's casual endorsement of this operation. It was becoming plain what course the Germans had resolved on for this year. While maintaining a powerful defensive in the West, their offensive action would be designed to aid Austria-Hungary. This was not a clear-cut choice between East and West. Over half of Germany's divisions remained on the Western Front, so keenly was the menace of a French breakthrough felt by the German high command: hence the Germans did not have the forces available for a truly decisive blow in the East. But it was there that they chose to exercise their initiative, beginning in February 1915 with a strike against the Russians that produced a spectacular tactical, if not strategic, victory.

It was possible, if not quite certain, that the Central Powers' next move would be in the Balkans. That is, the Serbs might soon be in grave danger, especially as one Balkan state, Bulgaria, would almost certainly throw in its lot with Serbia's enemies once they began appearing in force.

So Britain's leaders were under considerable pressure to do 'something' in the region vaguely delineated as 'the East'. But did this mean more action, or less, at the Dardanelles? Initially it was taken to require military action in the Balkans. On 9 February Kitchener persuaded the War Council to send the important 29th division – the last of the regular divisions and hitherto meant for France – to Salonika, in the hope of securing the military allegiance of Greece and Romania and paralysing the hostile intentions of Bulgaria. These grandiose calculations were stopped short by the decision of the Greek monarch to decline the offer of British troops on his soil. His action laid bare both the insubstantial nature of Lloyd George's Balkan strategy and the fragility of Britain's authority in this region – an authority resting largely on a combination of naval power and prestige, and so offering a poor counter to the military might of the Hohenzollerns. Britain's leaders were thus confronted with a problem: Was this the moment to embark on a display of naval force against the Turks when that display was based on the premise that it might be abandoned in short order?

The belated opening of the naval bombardment of the Dardanelles on 19 February drove home the promise and peril of such an undertaking. Carden's initial broadsides sent a momentary shock wave through the Balkans, causing hostile neutrals to temper their enmity and friendly neutrals to appear more genial. Yet the bombardment itself was a considerable failure. And its effects in the Balkans could hardly be other than short-lived. For as the limited nature of Britain's commitment to the operation – which had been a prime justification for launching it – became evident, neutral enthusiasm for the Allied cause was bound to wane. In any case, the doubtful effectiveness of this

---

[11] Marder, *From the Dardanelles to Oran*; Hankey to Balfour, 10 February 1915.

form of assault rapidly became apparent. As Lloyd George observed a few weeks later, 'the reason why Greece did not intervene was not the personal opposition of the King, but the fact that by the most competent military judges in Greece Germany was still expected to win.'[12]

So, by the beginning of March 1915 the operation at the Dardanelles had become not an interesting optional extra but the only form of action open to Britain in a region where action seemed imperative – that is, if the Western Allies were not to look on with folded arms should the Germans turn their attentions to the Balkans. It was in these circumstances that the decision to make available a military force for the Dardanelles was taken.

On 10 March Kitchener informed the War Council that he could now release the 29th division – destined first for the Western Front, then for Salonika, then for the Western Front again – for the Dardanelles. Given the timing of the decision, this contingent would arrive in the Near East only after the expected naval forcing of the Dardanelles. If the naval effort prospered, then the military force might move in to eliminate such resistance as remained at Gallipoli, or it might come home again. If the naval effort bogged down, then an amphibious operation would take its place. Yet underlying this second stage of the inception of the Gallipoli operation there remained the primary assumption referred to at the outset: that the centre of Britain's military and naval endeavours must lie elsewhere. So what would go to the Near East would not be such a body of ships and soldiers as was deemed adequate for the proposed undertaking; it would be whatever could be spared from the sectors of Britain's primary commitment. A simple statistic makes this evident. For his putative military endeavour at Gallipoli Kitchener was assembling the 29th division, the Anzacs (presently stationed in Egypt), and a French contingent. All told, these numbered 75,000 men. That was half of the force of 150,000 that, a few weeks before, he had told the War Council would be necessary.

V

While the military force for the Eastern Mediterranean was being assembled and transported, the naval assault on the Dardanelles was failing to progress. Unfriendly weather hampered it. And Carden's assumption, which had gone unchallenged at the Admiralty, that heavy artillery at sea could indeed eliminate guns on land, and not just silence them for a time, was now in serious doubt. Further, notice was having to be taken of the fact that Carden had more to contend with than the Turkish forts. The navy's passage up the Dardanelles was being contested by the groups of mobile howitzers and by the succession of minefields. The latter were protected by shore batteries, concealed from the fleet's view. These batteries rendered it impossible for the motley collection of fishing trawlers that Carden had deemed adequate for the role of minesweepers to clear a path through the minefields ahead of the battleships. Carden tried by one means after another to solve the problems of minesweeping: attempts were made by day and by night, by stealth and by *force majeure*, and by placing the fishermen crews under the command of naval volunteers. Always the results were the same. The minesweepers could not function under enemy fire. The navy could not silence the enemy's guns. The path up the Dardanelles remained closed. In the face of this conundrum, Carden collapsed.

The command of the naval expedition passed to his second-in-command, John de Robeck. He set himself to apply Carden's next scheme for mastering the minefields.

---

[12] Trevor Wilson (ed.), *The Political Diaries of C. P. Scott 1911–1928* (London: Collins, 1970), p. 120.

Stinting no ammunition, he launched 16 of his 18 battleships in a massed daylight attack against the forts, intending so to smother the defenders with gunfire that the minesweepers could perform their task. This operation began on the morning of 18 March. It did not prosper. By the time it was called off in the late afternoon the attacking force had lost six battleships: three were sunk, including the French vessel *Bouvet*, which went down with almost all hands, and three were so severely mauled that they could not continue. These were heavy casualties: more than one-third of the bombarding force sunk or out of action. The main cause of the losses was a string of mines in an area thought to be free of them. However Turkish gunfire had shared responsibility in disabling two of the vessels, and it was not certain what had caused the calamity to the *Bouvet*. But in a sense the losses were not the worst of it. For this had been primarily a minesweeping operation, yet the minesweepers had never reached the minefields proper, let alone swept them. And the actual destruction of Turkish guns had proved derisory. There was but one positive accomplishment to set against this melancholy tale. The Turks had seriously depleted, though by no means exhausted, their stocks of heavy ammunition.

Strange things have been written about the action of 18 March and about the decision that followed it to abandon the naval assault on the Dardanelles. It has even been said (by Barrie Pitt) that the naval operation was called off 'at the moment it had succeeded'.[13] This seems an odd way to describe a minesweeping operation that, at severe cost in capital ships, had swept not a single mine. The attribution of success to the attack is based on an assumption that the Turks had entirely exhausted their stocks of heavy ammunition. Consequently, it is argued, had the British vessels returned the following day, they could have proceeded without difficulty.

This argument is quite without substance. Although definite statistics regarding Turkish ammunition remain elusive, it is clear that the forts had shells for at least two more attacks, and that both the howitzers and minefield defences (which were rendering minesweeping, and hence the passage of the fleet, impossible) were nowhere near the end of their resources. Anyway, there was no question of the naval attack's being resumed the next day. Even Roger Keyes, the Ritchie Hook[14] of the naval expedition, was not advocating that. The losses in vessels sustained on 18 March had to be made good if there was to be any prospect of de Robeck's force struggling through to the Sea of Marmora in anything but trivial numbers. And the fact had to be faced that, in a situation where, without efficient minesweeping, the Sea of Marmora would not be reached at all, de Robeck was without vessels that deserved the name of minesweeper. In this respect at least the naval operation was back at the starting point. Only now was some of the essential staff work about to be done.

Had the position at this point been the same as that of the previous January – that is, it must be a naval operation or nothing – then the naval attack might have been resumed. Keyes was preparing to throw himself into the task of converting destroyers into minesweepers.[15] With their superior speed they would not be so harassed by fire from the shore as the fishing trawlers. And where the latter had to proceed upstream against the Dardanelles current until they were above the minefields, and only on the return journey might dislodge the mines, the destroyers could cut loose the mines on the way up. Within a fortnight Keyes would have a small force of destroyers-turned-

---

[13] *Purnell's History of the First World War*, issue no. 28, introduction.

[14] A character in Evelyn Waugh's *Men at Arms* trilogy, who believed that the way to overcome the enemy was to 'biff, biff, biff' them without ceasing.

[15] See Marder, *From the Dardanelles to Oran*, pp. 24–5.

minesweepers in readiness; within a month, thanks to reinforcements from the Grand Fleet and elsewhere, he would have a considerable force.

None of this made the success of the operation certain. No one could tell what would be happening to the Turkish defences in the meanwhile. Nor could it be known, until tested, whether this new form of minesweeping would achieve all that much more than the old. Anyway, even if the minefields could be vanquished, great unknowables lay beyond. How many losses of capital ships would de Robeck sustain while pressing through the Dardanelles, and what would be the state of his ammunition supply by the time he reached Constantinople? And was it really to be believed that the Turkish capital – and, by implication, the Turkish empire – would fall prostrate before a British naval force isolated in the Sea of Marmora, with the shores of the Dardanelles in hostile hands and with its lines of communication perilously insecure?

Nevertheless, if it had remained a case of a purely naval attack or no attack at all, the risk might have appeared worth taking. But by the time of the 18 March débâcle, it had already ceased to be a matter of a naval attack or nothing. There now obtained precisely those circumstances that at one time virtually every person in authority had agreed were essential for a successful operation at the Dardanelles – and that growing numbers of them were, between 13 January and 18 March, again coming to regard as essential. An army was on its way to the Eastern Mediterranean to participate, if required, in the attempt to force the Dardanelles. Its commander was already on the spot, watching the events of 18 March with growing alarm. 'This has been a very bad day for us,' Ian Hamilton informed Kitchener; '. . . . it looks at present as if the Fleet would not be able to carry on at this rate, and, if so, the soldiers will have to do the trick.'[16]

Given that Hamilton, the military commander, thought like this and that de Robeck, the naval commander, viewed 18 March as 'a disastrous day', it is not surprising that they concluded that the naval operation should be suspended until the army was ready to be landed. Nor is it to be wondered at that even Keyes, if with pangs of regret, endorsed this change of plan. For that matter, it is hardly remarkable that the same view was taken (even before the change was decided upon) by the one-time man-on-the-spot who had initiated the naval operation. From hospital at Malta Carden wrote to de Robeck on hearing of the events of 18 March: 'Hope you had a satisfactory meeting with Hamilton, and that they will send a proper sized force[,] certainly 150,000 better if 200,000 I should think, and make a job of it.'[17] It may be thought regrettable that, two and a half months before, Carden had not urged Churchill to wait until they could secure 'a proper sized force . . . and make a job of it'.

VI

What was lost by the failure to press the naval assault through to victory? Given that the operation ended with victory nowhere in sight, this question may seem so speculative as to be not worth asking. But it has been asked, and answered, many times.

Plainly, a major success against Turkey, however accomplished, would have provided a welcome boost to Allied morale. And it would probably have reopened year-round trade between Russia and the outside world, enabling the Russians to sell their bottled-up grain harvest and so secure much needed foreign exchange. But the stakes are often stated to have been considerably higher than this. The naval forcing of the

---

[16] Quoted in Gilbert, *Winston S. Churchill*, vol. 3, p. 354.
[17] The de Robeck papers are in Churchill College, Cambridge.

Dardanelles, it has been proposed, could have facilitated the dismemberment of Turkey, transformed the situation in the Balkans, and preserved Russia as an active participant for the duration of the conflict. (This would have had the incidental effect of obviating the Rusian Revolution.)

Some of these points are manifestly absurd. The reopening of the Mediterranean route to Russia would not have enabled the Western Allies to pour weapons and ammunition into the hands of their ailing ally. The shipping was simply not available. Nor could Britain and France meet their own requirements of ammunition, let alone anyone else's. No large supplies of war material would have been available for Russia before 1917, and by that time nothing Britain could do would have counteracted the many forces bringing about the collapse of the Tsarist regime.[18]

It is almost as questionable whether the success of de Robeck's undertaking would have produced a momentous change in the attitude of the Balkan neutrals (i.e. Greece and Romania, which inclined towards the Allies, and Bulgaria, which favoured the Central Powers). Greece was at most interested only in entering the war against Turkey, upon whom it had territorial designs – the most important of which ran directly counter to the territorial designs of Russia. But if the naval operation knocked Turkey out of the war, Greek aid in that quarter would be neither needed nor welcome. As for the notion that Turkey's humiliation by a British fleet would cause Greece and Romania to pick a fight with the Central Powers, this was a plain *non sequitur*. If the navy's success enabled Britain to avoid military involvement in the Near East, then no Balkan state would want to provoke the Germans and Austrians into sending armed forces down upon them – least of all at a time when Russia's troops were in no position to help. (Only the presence of large numbers of Allied troops on its territory drove Greece to enter the war in 1917. And only the great Russian advance into the Carpathians in the second half of 1916 inspired Romania to join the Allied cause.)

Further, it was not likely that, if the appearance of a British fleet in the Sea of Marmora did send the Balkan dominoes tumbling, the Germans would witness this process unmoved. There was little they could do if the only consequence of the naval operation was that the pro-German Government of Turkey was overthrown and a neutralist Government took its place. But should Greece and Romania be inspired by this event to make war on the Central Powers, there was much the Germans could do. As it happened, six months were to elapse between Germany's initial successes over Russia in February 1915 and its strike against Serbia. But the German high command would hardly have adhered to this timetable had a British naval success over Turkey produced such extraordinary consequences in the Balkans.

Is it even the case that the appearance of de Robeck's force off Constantinople would have ended Turkey's involvement in the war? Underlying the hopes placed in this naval operation were two assumptions. The first was that, as the passage of the *Goeben* and *Breslau* through the Dardanelles had supposedly spelt victory for the pro-German forces in Turkey, so the passage of de Robeck's fleet would spell their overthrow. That is, a *coup d'état* in Constantinople would bring into office a neutralist regime and take Turkey out of the war. The second assumption was on a different plane altogether. Because Constantinople could be shelled from the sea (assuming de Robeck's vessels had ammunition left for the purpose), and because Turkey's main armament works were situated there, it was somehow thought that Turkey was totally vulnerable to a naval attack. From this it apparently followed that, as de Robeck

---

[18] Cf. Norman Stone, *The Eastern Front 1914–1917* (London: Hodder & Stoughton, 1975), where it is argued that lack of military equipment was not one of Russia's problems at the time of the revolution in March 1917.

approached the Sultan's capital, the Allies could begin dismembering the Turkish Empire to their hearts' content.

No attempt was made to sketch the scenario leading from the first assumption to the second – to explain how a neutralist Government in Constantinople would be persuaded, on de Robeck's say so, to preside over the demolition of the Turkish Empire. Discussions in the War Council played easily upon both the first assumption and the second. They never filled in the missing stage.[19] So Grey told the War Council on 26 February: 'what we really relied on to open the Straits was a *coup d'état* in Constantinople.' Churchill, while not dissenting from this view, nevertheless seemed not to recognize that the success of the naval attack 'relied on' the co-operation of elements in Turkey. His vision lay beyond the waters of the Dardanelles and the sea of Marmora. 'All [of Turkey in Europe] must pass into our hands,' he told the War Council on 3 March, 'and we ought to accept nothing less.' 'Constantinople,' he told the same meeting, 'was only a step towards the Balkans. If we granted Turkey an armistice [sic!] it should be on the condition of the military surrender of Turkey in Europe. We might, however, permit Turkey temporarily to hold on to Turkey in Asia.'

Writing to Jellicoe six days later, Churchill extended his horizons yet further: 'Constantinople is only a means to an end, and that end is the marching against Austria of the five re-united Balkan States.' Such grand designs were not peculiar to the First Lord of the Admiralty. The War Council on 10 January agreed to accept Russia's claim to both Constantinople and the Dardanelles, provided that (so Asquith told Venetia Stanley) 'both we & France should get a substantial share of the carcase of the Turk'. Even the setback of 18 March did not inspire the War Council to adopt more modest aspirations. A meeting the next day heard a discouraging report of that operation. ('Mr Lloyd George asked if any success had been achieved to counter-balance the losses. Sir Arthur Wilson [naval adviser] said . . . the forts had only been temporarily silenced.') Yet the War Council still felt free to ponder what it would do 'after the Straits had been forced, and Constantinople had passed into the hands of the Allies'.

In short, no one in the War Council seems to have asked the obvious question: Could there ever be a *coup d'état* in Turkey bringing to power a Government prepared to part with all of European Turkey in return for temporary retention of 'Turkey in Asia'? Nor did anyone inquire what a British fleet – possibly a good deal battered and short of supplies – would do if a neutralist Turkish Government refused to surrender on these terms. Presumably it would shell Constantinople's armaments works. But would it then have either the ammunition or the want of scruple to flatten the city? Perhaps these omissions should not seem surprising, seeing that the War Council remained bemused about what a fleet could accomplish against land positions. As at the first it had imagined that the naval expedition could 'take' the Gallipoli peninsula, so at the last – with the abandonment of the naval operation only days away – it believed that a force of ships could receive Constantinople into its hands.

VII

It is not enough just to set down the conduct of Britain's leaders in respect to the Dardanelles between January and March 1915. An attempt must be made to explain their conduct. It would be easy to say that the nation's rulers were incompetent. It would be charitable to say that they were utterly inexperienced in great affairs of this

---

[19] Quotations are from Gilbert, *Winston S. Churchill*, vol. 3, and Companion Volume 3, pt 1.

kind. Neither of these points quite accounts for the high degree of half-sense, not to say downright nonsense, that they are recorded as uttering in private conclave.[20]

The key to the puzzle may be thought to lie in a matter that is not to the discredit of Britain's rulers. They knew, if sometimes they were loath to acknowledge, the limited nature of Britain's power. The seemingly imminent collapse of Russia, the perilous situation of Serbia, the hostility of Turkey, and the disregard for Britain's authority revealed by the Balkan states, were all serious matters and appeared to require powerful action. Britain lacked the resources for such action. To intervene forcefully at any one of these points, the country would have had to denude those areas nearer home that were crucial to its safety. Whatever their shortcomings, Britain's leaders did not contemplate embarking on such a course.

So they fell instead into a different, if decidedly lesser, trap, and one that is not uncommon in war: that of concluding that the means available would be sufficient to accomplish whatever ends were required. First it was hoped that the naval forcing of the Dardanelles would bring about a change of Government in Constantinople that would take Turkey out of the war. Then, as the perils on the Eastern Front and in the Balkans manifested themselves, the initiators of the naval operation started believing that it could accomplish much more. It would at a stroke win over the military support of the Balkan neutrals and so safeguard Serbia, and it would rekindle the fighting resolve of Russia by holding out the prize of Constantinople. Two points went unnoticed. The first was that 'victory' (which is not an absolute term) over the Turks by naval means would be an altogether lesser affair than the type of victory likely to inspire Greece and Romania to make war against Germany. The second was that, however precarious Turkey's situation, no Turkish Government conceivable in 1915 would make peace on the terms now being demanded; so that the task of the naval expedition was being made more difficult, and the prospect of offering comfort to Russia correspondingly less probable.

The naval attack on the Dardanelles was a valid undertaking only on two conditions: first, that its objectives remained commensurate with the limited force being committed to it; and, second, that Britain either was so secure in this region or had so little at stake there that nothing would be lost if the operation were abandoned. Neither premise was warranted. From the time Turkey joined the enemy's ranks, Britain began committing itself to the cession of Constantinople to Russia. Thereby it embroiled

---

[20] Two examples of how good sense and its opposite could sit cheek by jowl in the War Cabinet's deliberations deserve mention.

(1) The following exchange occurred during a long discussion on the Dardanelles on 26 February 1915:

Lord Haldane said that, without a success in Russia, the Balkan States would not come in.

Sir Edward Grey agreed. The Russian situation overhung everything.

Mr. Lloyd George said that this made it more important than ever to bring the Balkan States in.

(2) A. J. Balfour wrote a highly perceptive memorandum on 24 February 1915 pointing out that two distinct objectives were under consideration concerning the Dardanelles. The first was to force a way through the Bosphorus to Russia. The second was to bring the Balkan states into the war. Both required a military commitment, but the latter would involve a much larger force than the former, and without such a force it would be positively dangerous, especially given the circumstances of Russia, to persuade a country like Romania to enter the fray. (Balfour even expressed doubt about whether any force that the Western Allies could provide would turn the scale in the Balkans.)

Concerning the first objective, the reopening of the sea route to Russia through the Dardanelles, Balfour wrote that Britain was committed to it and '*must* send as many troops as may be required' to make it a success.

All this seems eminently sensible. Yet at the War Council two days later Balfour seemed unconvinced of the need to provide any troops to accomplish his first objective. While Churchill was pleading for the 29th division to be sent to the Dardanelles, Balfour foresaw a sweeping victory over Turkey 'if the purely naval operation were carried out'.

itself in the pursuit not of a negotiated settlement with the Turks but of a total victory over them, such as only a military force could accomplish. No doubt the agonies of Russia made so handsome a reward seem warranted. But the reward invalidated the naval operation with its proposed termination in a change of Government in Turkey.

Equally, it was never the case that Britain's position in the Near East was so well founded or, alternatively, was of so little importance that it could afford to court a naval rebuff from the Turks. Allied authority in the area was precarious from the outset; and it should not have required the German successes over Russia in February to establish the truth that it was preferable to embark on no undertaking in the region than an undertaking that stood a good chance of failure. The most optimistic among scholarly studies of the naval operation[21] believes that it would have stood a 50–50 chance of success if the minesweeping force had been totally reorganized during the month following 18 March. It may be doubted whether Britain and its allies were ever so happily placed in the Eastern Mediterranean that they could afford to launch an operation with a one-in-two chance of failure.

That Britain in the early months of 1915, if it chose to disregard its naval and military responsibilities nearer home, possessed the resources to attack Gallipoli with a real chance of success can hardly be doubted. What was in doubt was whether the country could mount a successful campaign there without courting calamity in France and the North Sea. As long as these doubts remained, Gallipoli must go short – of ships and shells, of men and maps, above all of the dispassionate weighing of the ends to be attained and the means whereby they might be secured. These commodities were not to spare during the gestation of the Dardanelles operation. Consequently, success became dependent on an extraordinary run of good luck. In its absence, the way lay open to calamity.

VIII

In the light of the 18 March setback, the War Council informed de Robeck 'that he could continue the operations against the Dardanelles if he thought fit'. De Robeck speedily concluded that he did not think fit. The undertaking was too hazardous while the Gallipoli peninsula remained in enemy hands. No military or naval figure on the spot doubted this conclusion. But as soon as this decision reached London several members of the War Council, notwithstanding the communication they had just sent to de Robeck, wanted to urge him to go on. Churchill, temporarily shrugging off his anxiety to get troops involved, was most vocal in this respect. But the three senior naval advisers at the Admiralty, one of whom was Fisher, dug in their heels against this attempt to pressure the man on the spot. Churchill was in no position to act without them. So de Robeck's decision held the day.

For a month the fleet withdrew from the Dardanelles. When it returned it was no longer the shock force of the assault; it was the communication and artillery support of an infantry attack. The sideshow proper was about to begin.

---

[21] That by Marder, *From the Dardanelles to Oran*, ch. 1.

12

MOVES FORWARDS AND BACK: NEUVE CHAPELLE AND SECOND YPRES

I preface the few remarks that I am going to make [about the Dardanelles] by this assertion. We (French and English) have now reached a stage when to break the German line is not only an operation of war, but a certain operation of war, given sufficient troops and sufficient ammunition. At this particular moment we engage in operations in the Dardanelles.

Sir Henry Wilson to his wife (for transmission to Bonar Law), 17 March 1915

There is no chance of heavily defeating [the Germans].

Sir John French in discussion with Lord Esher, 20 March 1915

I

While British naval shells were pummelling the fortifications of Gallipoli, British military shells were falling in Flanders. The command of the BEF had decided on a forward move.

There were good reasons for this decision. The Germans, it was now becoming plain, were in some measure reversing their Schlieffen strategy. While leaving large forces in the West to hold the line there, they were preparing to strike heavy blows against Russia. It would be hazardous for the Western Allies to take advantage of this breathing space by calling a temporary halt to operations. Certainly, they needed time to lick their wounds, train their recruits, accumulate stocks of ammunition, and ponder the strategic alternatives. But Russia's resolve might weaken if faced by a seeming readiness on the part of its allies to fight to the last drop of Russian blood.

Plainly, only France in early 1915 was capable of launching a large-scale offensive on the Western Front that might take some of the pressure off Russia. But a British operation in Flanders would at least be an earnest of Britain's resolve for the future, and might have the incidental effect of spurring on the French.

II

The first fruit of this reasoning was the battle of Neuve Chapelle, 10–12 March 1915. The action was to prove a considerable achievement of British arms. With good reason, it excited the admiration of the French Commander-in-Chief.

Britain's military leaders introduced into the Neuve Chapelle operation several features that became thereafter a part of any well conducted artillery-cum-infantry attack. In this respect it was a striking demonstration of how quickly the military leaders of an unmilitaristic people could adapt to the particular demands of this conflict. For the commanders of the BEF did not try to ignore the central problem of accomplishing a forward move on the Western Front: the defensive capacity of earthwork, rapid-fire weapons, and barbed wire. Rather, they sought to master it by a combination of meticulous preparation, concealment of intent, and (above all) concentration – the concentration of an overwhelming force of soldiers, guns, and shells against a chosen sector of enemy front.

The area chosen for this endeavour by French and Haig was on the front of General Rawlinson's IV Corps (which was one of the three corps making up Haig's First Army). As long as an attack was to be made from some part of the British sector, there was much to recommend this choice. Opposite IV Corps's position lay the town of Neuve Chapelle, where earlier John Lucy's battalion had stood so devotedly. Beyond it lay Aubers Ridge. And beyond that lay the major rail centre of Lille.

Originally it had been intended that this British operation would coincide with a French offensive a bit further south, designed to take Vimy Ridge, thus much enhancing the Allied threat to Lille. But arrangements between the two commanders had proved difficult. And Joffre had become attracted by the prospects offering in a quite different part of the line, namely Champagne in the central section of the Western Front. (Here also, if only the Germans could be dislodged from the high ground, their communications would be placed in jeopardy.) So, in the northern sector, the British attack went ahead on its own.

What the British command was endeavouring to do was to refine the conduct of an offensive to the point where it would deprive the defenders of their balance of advantage. First, in recognition of the extent to which this was becoming an artilleryman's war, they assembled some 340 guns. For the limited sector under bombardment this provided a concentration of artillery without precedent in war. Secondly, they collected in the same area an overwhelming superiority in infantry. Thirdly, with the aid of aerial photography – itself a novelty for the BEF – both troops and artillery were made thoroughly familiar with the area to be attacked. The assault infantry were taken out of the front line and trained intensively to deal with the particular terrain and obstacles foreseen in the coming operation. And the artillery batteries, instead of firing at targets of their own detection and selection, were orchestrated so that each battery had its delineated targets, which it was to bombard according to a timetable: first the enemy barbed wire and front line of defence, then the rear lines, then Neuve Chapelle itself so as to bar the progress of German reinforcements. Fourthly, Haig was not only concerned with 'methodical preparation'; he was determined to retain 'the element of surprise'.[1] By elaborate preparation the attackers managed to conceal the extent of their build-up of guns and men. And Haig insisted that what had been proposed as a three-day preparatory bombardment be reduced to three hours (and he subsequently had it confined to a whirlwind 35 minutes), on the reckoning that the amplitude of guns would more than compensate for the brevity of their employment.

The opening phase of the operation on the morning of 10 March seemed to prove the validity of each of the presumptions underlying this attack. By both what it did, and did not, achieve the artillery demonstrated its importance. At one place in the line two British batteries had arrived too late to be properly registered, and so fired well off target. Here the initial assault was held up – a salutary reminder that Western Front battles were not contests between infantrymen to which the artillery contributed only sound and fury. Apart from this and one area on the right (where the attacking troops

---

[1] Quoted in John Terraine, *Douglas Haig: The Educated Soldier* (London: Hutchinson, 1963), pp. 139–40.

lost direction), the combination of severity and brevity in the opening bombardment tore gaps in the German wire and kept most of the front-line defenders under cover while the first assault-wave crossed No-Man's-Land. Further, the German command was not given the sort of warning that would cause it to start moving in reinforcements in advance of the infantry assault. The result was a striking initial success for the British. Rawlinson, in immediate command of the operation, wrote six days later: 'The programme which I had very carefully worked out before hand went like clockwork. The attack was a complete surprise to the enemy and the first rush of our gallant fellows was completely successful except on the extreme left. . . .'[2]

In this first rush British forces advanced against 2,000 yards of enemy line to a depth of 1,200 yards and captured Neuve Chapelle village. Haig promptly began preparing for an advance by the whole of the First Army, including a cavalry brigade to exploit the breakthrough. This large movement was to begin as soon as Rawlinson's corps had pressed on through Neuve Chapelle and taken Aubers Ridge.

But in the outcome Haig did not order forward the rest of his army. Nor did any of his cavalry crest Aubers Ridge. The rewards for such a methodically prepared attack proved, after all, to be disappointingly meagre. If this operation showed that the British command could rise to the challenge of a new style of war, it carried another, more ominous, message. It raised serious doubts as to whether, however much skill was employed, early success could produce a large-scale advance into enemy territory.

Rawlinson was, in fact, exaggerating when he wrote that the operation had gone 'like clockwork.' Real success was confined to the first couple of hours. After that the offensive bogged down. Partly it was Rawlinson's own fault. He had allowed his second wave of troops, whose task it was to exploit the capture of the German front line, to get mixed up with those making the initial attack. Hence there was a lamentable delay while the support troops were being gathered together and sent forward. (Also rather lamentably, Rawlinson tried to cast responsibility for this lapse upon one of his subordinates. When found out, he was very nearly sacked by Sir John French – rather ironically, in the light of French's own conduct toward Haig six months later.) Rawlinson took comfort over this mishandling of his forces by reflecting, 'we are learning the tactics which this trench warfare teaches, and on each occasion we shall improve on our methods.' His opponents, regrettably for him, were doing the same.

But it is unlikely that, had Rawlinson conducted things better, the operation would have achieved much more. Fastidious ground work had enabled the attack to prosper by combining two elements usually irreconcilable: preparation and surprise. Once the operation was in train, each proved a diminishing factor. The artillery was now having to seek out pockets of resistance in accordance with the development of the struggle. For this it lacked the preliminary registration that it needed to fire accurately and also adequate information about the situation at the front. (Communications from the battlefield consisted of telephone lines and human runners, both highly vulnerable to enemy action.) And headquarters, seeking to initiate fresh operations in accordance with the state of the conflict, sometimes failed to get their orders forward to front-line troops until after zero hour had passed.

Further, as preparation gave way to improvisation, so the element of surprise dwindled. At the commencement of the operation the German second line of defence was sketchy. By the next morning, when the British were in a position to assault it, the enemy had dug trenches and placed troops in readiness. Against these new obstacles

[2] Rawlinson to Major Clive Wigram, 16 March 1915, Rawlinson papers, National Army Museum. (Wigram was assistant private secretary to King George V.)

the assault forces flung themselves in vain, and the British artillery – so commanding at the outset, so inadequate in a fluid situation – was unable to help. The second and third days of the battle of Neuve Chapelle degenerated into a series of attacks and counter-attacks, all fruitless, all costly to the side taking the initiative. On the evening of 12 March Haig called off the operation. The village of Neuve Chapelle, acquired so dramatically at the outset, remained in British hands. But the path up Aubers Ridge and on to Lille remained barred.

<h1 style="text-align:center">III</h1>

On the day before this operation was launched Sir John French had talked concernedly about its likely human cost. He told Lord Esher that he anticipated 5,000 killed and wounded by the following night, and found it a solemn thought that at his command 'all those fine fellows' were going to their deaths. Sir John's estimate proved pretty accurate. The British suffered 13,000 casualties in the three days of fighting. (German losses, though calculated to be a good deal higher by British authorities, were about 1,000 fewer.)

In one quarter at least the outcome was viewed with approval: among the French. According to John Charteris, Haig's chief of intelligence, the initial success in 'ousting the Germans from an entrenched position' had greatly impressed the French Commander-in-Chief.[3] And Esher, after a lengthy discussion with a French general, wrote: 'The fact is that Neuve Chapelle was an immense tonic; the morale of both Armies is up 50%. It has been to us what the relief of Kimberley was in 1900.' Kimberley, it will be remembered, was Sir John French's great exploit of the Boer War, and its supposed repetition had (according to Esher) made him 'a heroic figure'.[4]

Elsewhere, however, feelings were mixed. Charteris admitted as much when he wrote that Joffre's approval was 'sufficient answer to the complaints in the Press about our losses'. (Ominously, he added that England would have to accustom itself to 'far greater losses than those of Neuve Chapelle before we finally crush the German army'.) Major Bonham-Carter, from his fairly modest position on the staff, managed only a muted note of praise. He called the action 'on the whole' a great success; briefly it had promised to be much more and had looked as if it might involve a big German retirement, but he believed the commanders were satisfied. At a more exalted level, Sir John himself was yet more guarded. For some extraordinary reason he was now expecting the war to end in June, but not because he scented victory. The Germans, he opined, would institute *pourparlers*. 'There is no chance of heavily defeating them. The War Office have sent out drawings of pontoons for crossing the Rhine; these were received with hilarity by the General Staff.'[5]

The person who divined most clearly the negative message of this operation was Rawlinson. Late in March he wrote:

> The experience of Neuve Chapelle has taught us all a great deal. . . . The losses are the feature most to be deplored – The great majority occurred on the 2nd & 3rd days in attacking the enemy's defended pivots & houses – These might all have been avoided if we had been content with the capture of the village itself instead of persisting in pressing on in order to get the cavalry through. I confess that this idea does not appeal to me – The cavalry will I fear do no good when they do get through for they are certain to be held up by wire & trenches in whatever direction they may attempt to go.[6]

[3] Quoted in Terraine, *Douglas Haig*, p. 145.
[4] Esher diary, 24 March 1915. The Esher papers are in Churchill College, Cambridge.
[5] Esher diary, 20 March 1915.
[6] Rawlinson to Wigram, 25 March 1915.

Rawlinson advocated a 'bite and hold' policy: bite off a piece of the enemy's line, such as Neuve Chapelle, which could be done without excessive loss, and force the enemy at much heavier cost to try to recapture it.

Rawlinson did not go on to speculate how long the war would last if the military chose so to prosecute it. Nor did he ask whether, if the generals favoured proceeding at this deliberate pace, they would escape the wrath of the army's masters – that is, of the Government, parliamentarians, controllers of the media, and the general public. It was still early days in the war, and hopes of a speedy decision remained widespread.

Anyway, not everyone in the military hierarchy embraced Rawlinson's wisdom. Significantly, one whose star was plainly on the rise did not. Sir Douglas Haig was disinclined to learn what (according to Rawlinson) 'experience has taught us' about the futility of seeking 'to get the cavalry through'. In his diary for 11 April Haig recounted being told that the commander of the Cavalry Corps, General Allenby, together with Allenby's chief staff officer, 'seem to be despondent regarding the possibilities of cavalry action in future'. They were prepared to dispense with cavalry as such: 'In their opinion, the war will continue and end in "trenches".' Haig was not of this view. He held that 'we cannot hope to reap the fruits of victory without a large force of mounted troops.'[7]

Haig's riposte, in the kindest view, was desperately illogical. It was no answer to Allenby's doubts about the 'possibilities' of cavalry action to say that such action must be feasible because nothing else would be. Yet within so flimsy a line of argument lay the authorization for further yet more costly, and even less productive, Neuve Chapelles.

IV

Before Sir John French could mount his next operation, the Germans struck against the BEF at Ypres. This had not been bargained for.

Despite the clear orientation of Germany's offensive activities towards the Eastern Front, there were good reasons why the German command should launch a local action against the Allies in Belgium. It would help to divert attention from the movement of their reserves to Galicia. And if they succeeded in overrunning the Ypres salient, this would shorten the German line, wrest the last particle of Belgium from the Allies, and soften the recollection of the first battle of Ypres with its thwarted ambitions and squandered German youth. Yet none of this, probably, would have inspired the Germans to action in Belgium had they not possessed a new weapon that promised them a limited success on the cheap. The weapon was poison gas.

The gas attack at Ypres on 22 April 1915 was not the first occasion on which the Germans employed 'noxious vapours' during this war. Using shells as the means of delivery, they had already done so at places on both the Eastern and the Western Fronts, but with so little success that the attempts had gone virtually unnoticed. The French also had projected gas by means of grenades. When delivered in this way it functioned only as an irritant, but larger French designs were probably in train.

Nevertheless, the Allied commanders in the northern part of the Western Front ignored gathering indications that a gas attack was at hand. Even the testimony of a German deserter equipped with a respirator failed to alert them. What caused this oversight? One contributory factor was the absence of the tell-tale signs associated with an offensive. The Germans did not dare accumulate reinforcements to exploit a

---

[7] Robert Blake (ed.), *The Private Papers of Douglas Haig 1914–1919* (London: Eyre & Spottiswoode, 1952), p. 90. All quotations from Haig's diaries hereafter are drawn from Blake's edition, unless otherwise indicated.

success lest they attract an Allied bombardment. For, owing to a shortage of shells, they intended to release the gas from cylinders, and this they could only do when the wind happened to be favourable. These cylinders would prove highly vulnerable should the Allies, ignorant of the presence of the gas weapon but alerted by the accumulation of reserves to a coming attack, begin shelling the German positions.

Yet it is probable that the main cause of the Allied command's failure to appreciate the imminence of a gas attack was simply disbelief. The employment of a dense cloud of gas to suffocate an adversary was something that they did not anticipate from their worst enemy. Correspondingly, when the Germans did indeed employ poison gas in this way, the sense of outrage felt among Britons, both combatants and civilians, was intense. Hankey received a letter from a staff officer in France saying that Canadian forces, who were early victims of the gas weapon, 'were so indignant at [the] use of poisonous gas that they killed their prisoners'.[8]

This response may well be difficult to comprehend. If death by poison gas was indeed atrocious, as readers of Wilfred Owen are vividly aware, the same was often enough true of death by conventional weapons. As C.R.M.F. Cruttwell grimly remarks: 'The extent to which a human body can be mangled by the splinters of a bomb or shell, without being deprived of consciousness, must be seen to be believed.'[9] Doubtless, Allied rage at the introduction of the gas weapon reflected envy of German ingenuity as much as anger at German ruthlessness. Any novel means of waging war was likely to

Plate 9 *'Respirator parade': an officer inspects the rudimentary gas masks which appeared promptly upon the introduction of poison gas to the battlefield.*

[8] Diary of Sir Maurice Hankey, 5 May 1915. The Hankey papers are in Churchill College, Cambridge. All but a small fraction of the Hankey diaries have been published for the war period, in Hankey's own *The Supreme Command 1914–1918*, 2 vols. (London: Allen & Unwin, 1961), and Stephen Roskill, *Hankey: Man of secrets*, vol. 1 (London: Collins, 1970). Quotations from the diaries in the present book have been checked against the original manuscript.

[9] C.R.M.F. Cruttwell, *A History of the Great War 1914–1918* (Oxford: Clarendon Press, 1934), p. 153.

appear devilish to its victims and so seem evidence that those who first used it were instruments of the devil. Nevertheless, as Cruttwell also points out, poison gas, when it took this form, was bound to be peculiarly repugnant. For the use of cloud gas appeared to be taking war yet another stage from its supposed role as a 'manly' activity – that is, an activity in which the qualities of valour, resourcefulness, endurance, and 'grit' would decide which adversary carried the day and which individuals survived the combat. None of the martial virtues signified when death was born on the very air which men breathed, so that the most elementary act for sustaining life served to extinguish it.

Before long it became apparent that this was a misjudgement. The speedy development of gas masks meant that the responsible, resourceful, alert soldier had an opportunity to ward off a gas attack that he did not have to escape an exploding shell. Yet the gas weapon remained repugnant. It never offered a quick, 'clean' way to die. And it hastened the conversion of war into a science-fiction nightmare. For to thwart it, combatants must don face coverings (gas masks) that transformed particular human countenances into the visages of indistinguishable ogres.

V

The British section of the Western Front, although well on the left of the Allied line, did not stretch quite to the sea. On the coast itself were Belgian troops, and next to them two French divisions. After these came the BEF.

It was said that Joffre kept his two divisions where they were so as to hinder the Belgians and the British from jointly concocting strategic movements at odds with those he was devising. It was also said that, mindful of Sir John French's proposed withdrawal from the Allied line during the Great Retreat, Joffre preferred to keep the British commander away from the coast – lest he should contemplate a yet more thorough withdrawal. Whatever the truth of these speculations, Joffre's two divisions (positioned on the left of the Ypres salient) served him ill at this juncture. One was a Territorial division, not the most renowned of French troops. The other was a Colonial division, including many black Algerians.

At 1700 hours on 22 April, after a long wait for a suitable wind, the Germans released a cloud of chlorine gas upon the French Colonials. The latter turned and fled, pulling back the French Territorials. A gap of 5 miles opened on the left of the Ypres salient. The task of plugging it fell to the Canadian division, immediately on the right of the French, and to three other divisions of Smith-Dorrien's Second Army. In the ensuing days these forces were subjected to intense pressure both from gas and – more deadly – from the massed German artillery that overlooked the Allied position. Inadequately supported by his allies, Smith-Dorrien – at his C.-in-C.'s insistence – flung his forces into one hopeless counter-attack after another.

Yet the Allied position in the Ypres salient did not collapse. One reason for this has already been mentioned. The Germans, in order to secure the precious advantage of surprise (a *sine qua non*, given the vulnerability of their gas cylinders), had not accumulated reinforcements to exploit the opening created by the gas. And once the novelty of the new weapon had passed, its effectiveness diminished. A major gas attack on 1 May failed to take a yard of ground, despite the only rudimentary gas masks available to the defenders. Ultimately, sheer weight of artillery fire forced the British to evacuate the bulge that had been exposed by the initial German success. But Ypres itself, and a reduced salient, remained in Allied hands.

It would have been a mercy to British forces had the Ypres salient been abandoned, late in 1914, in favour of a less exposed position. But the British authorities had proved unwilling to relinquish the last patch of Belgian territory in Allied hands, especially when so many British lives had been expended on its retention. The revised position after this second battle of Ypres in 1915 was yet more vulnerable to German bombardment and consequently (in terms of casualties to be endured) an even greater liability to the British. But this further heroic struggle to retain Ypres had only strengthened the case against its abandonment.

Between the first gas attack (22 April) and the end of May, the defence of Ypres cost the BEF 60,000 men killed and wounded and the French 10,000 men. German casualties were only 35,000. This favourable reckoning for the attacker, if uncommon in the Great War, was not surprising on this occasion. The Germans enjoyed first use of the gas weapon, overwhelming artillery superiority, and advantageous terrain from which to attack, to bombard, and to repel counter-attacks.

The British C.-in-C. had not come well out of this episode. As already mentioned, he had been caught napping with respect to the introduction of poison gas, and had instigated costly counter-attacks that stood no chance of success. Furthermore, midway through the struggle he had sacked Smith-Dorrien, allegedly for succumbing to undue pessimism, although many believed that personal pique had been a stronger motive. He had then manifested great pessimism himself. And he had handled his French allies ineptly. Clearly, he would need to do better in future.

13

FORWARD MOVES: GALLIPOLI

How lucky they are to escape Flanders & the trenches and be sent to the 'gorgeous East'.

Asquith (with respect to the Royal Naval Division) to Venetia Stanley, 26 February 1915

[L]ife and death has not the same significance it once had.

Corporal George Mitchell, Australian Imperial Force, in his diary for 11 June 1915

I

Three days after the Germans made their surprise gas attack at Ypres, Allied forces (British, Commonwealth, and French) launched their well heralded assault upon the Gallipoli peninsula.

Every phase of the operation to master Gallipoli, from first naval bombardment to last infantry thrust, has been the subject of intense historical scrutiny. Not infrequently, implicit questions underlie these studies. What went wrong? Why did well founded hopes go unfulfilled? Who blundered? Arguably, these questions are misleading. A different assumption may be much nearer the truth: that at no phase was the Gallipoli operation, even if blessed with reasonable military competence and a good measure of luck, assured of success. Rather, the odds against victory were, in whatever circumstances, ominously high.

Certainly, it is possible to agree that ill fortune and human fallibility bedevilled certain phases: the undetected line of mines that terminated the naval operation on 18 March; the failure clearly to define the infantry's objectives on 25 April; the confusion of purpose at Suvla Bay in August; and, simultaneous with Suvla Bay, the heroic but thwarted bid for Chunuk Bair at Anzac. But it does not follow that, had fate been kinder and had military shortcomings been less in evidence, the course of the British operations would largely have been different. Beyond the line of mines that 'changed the course of history' on 18 March lay other mines which the naval force at that moment lacked the capacity to remove. Similarly, beyond the high peaks that British forces must occupy lay other peaks, equally commanding, equally barring the road to the Narrows. In every case the success of an initial effort was no guarantee that subsequent undertakings would succeed.

When the Gallipoli operation is scrutinized without the prior assumption that it was entirely feasible, the 'great ifs' do not accumulate; they recede. Only 'little ifs' remain.

II

An amphibious operation against the Gallipoli peninsula, to have a good prospect of success, required two things: intense preparation and surprise. The two were rarely

Plate 10 *The landing beach at Cape Helles, immediately after British troops had established themselves.*

compatible in this war, as students of the Western Front are aware – although they do not always carry over this insight to their considerations of Gallipoli. Most of all were preparation and surprise difficult to reconcile in the case of an amphibious operation occurring far from the home base of the assaulting power. Even if the attempted naval forcing of the Dardanelles had not alerted the Turks to the coming military assault, they could hardly have remained unconscious of it. Warning enough was provided by the necessary accumulation in the Eastern Mediterranean of British troops, ships, stores, medical services, and landing craft. So one of the pre-conditions for a hopeful attack, surprise, was almost bound to be absent. But the operation launched on 25 April had the unhappy distinction of managing to forego much of the other precondition, preparation, as well.

The manner in which, on 12 March 1915, Kitchener informed Sir Ian Hamilton that he was being appointed to command the proposed Gallipoli expedition left no doubt that haste rather than deliberation was now the War Secretary's concern. Hamilton was given 24 hours in which to hand over his existing job, receive such scanty instructions as Kitchener could provide, select a staff, and make his departure. By 5 p.m. the next day he was off, taking with him the (somewhat bewildered) nucleus of a staff. His 75,000 troops (including a French division), their supplies, and most of the expert administrators needed for such an operation would follow later. Other necessary items overlooked in this helter-skelter departure never did catch up with him, because he did not know of their existence and had been denied the time in which to seek them out. He received no adequate maps or charts of tides. He learned too late that proper landing craft were in the process of construction for another (never-to-be-launched) operation. He did not know that the possibilities and pitfalls of an assault upon Gallipoli had been the subject of intense staff appreciations before the war. There was no escaping such oversights once it had been decided to rush into an undertaking for whose accomplishment time, even though it might also assist the enemy, was a commodity with which the British could not afford to dispense.[1]

Thanks to the speed of his dispatch, Hamilton reached the Dardanelles soon enough to witness the naval setback on 18 March. He concluded that the navy would not succeed by itself. It seemed to him to follow that he must take on the task of opening the Straits. This was not a considered judgement concerning his army's capability to overwhelm the Gallipoli defences. It was a judgement only about the navy's incapacity, which in terms of Kitchener's brief meant that a military attempt must be made. This imposed a heavy task upon him. The troops made available for the operation now had to be assembled and trained. The supplies that were arriving from Britain – thrown together without rhyme or reason for an operation that might not even take place – had to be re-sorted and re-packed. The coast of the Gallipoli peninsula must be reconnoitred for possible landing places.

That Hamilton managed, only six weeks after his arrival and (as it happened) on virtually the first day that the weather permitted, to put a force ashore on Gallipoli was a considerable accomplishment. Certainly, as has often been said, this display of professional competence and capacity for improvisation would have been more appropriate to a small-scale operation. Gallipoli was of a size that required a large professional staff rather than a leader and a small body of advisers. Hamilton and his handful of aides were making decisions in areas – such as the supply of essential stores and the provision of medical services – where specialist administrators were required and were becoming available. The operation was to pay dearly for his failure to employ them thoroughly. Yet his conduct was in keeping with the manner in which this campaign came into being: as an optional extra, as a rushed undertaking hit upon by single individuals in key posts, who first thought a naval operation worth a try and then resorted to an amphibious attack not because it looked a winner but because the naval assault looked the reverse. As the nature of the undertaking escalated, the scale and sophistication of the command structure directing it would always lag a large stage behind.

III

Hamilton had the responsibility of deciding where to land his forces. Surveying the shores of Gallipoli from the sea can hardly have been reassuring. Despite its lengthy coastline, the Gallipoli peninsula, at least in terms of 1915 technology, was a defender's dream. It presented the invader with a succession of steep hills running parallel or at right angles to the coastline. There were but a few beaches on which a large invading force could be accommodated, and these were overlooked by protective hills that were bound to aid the defence.

Hamilton noted four areas worthy of consideration: Bulair in the north (the neck of the peninsula); Suvla Bay half-way down; Gaba Tepe to the south of Suvla; and Cape Helles at the southernmost point. He decided against the first two. He ruled out Bulair because, being such an obvious place to attack, it was powerfully defended. Moreover, the shallowness of the water made it particularly inhospitable for a landing under fire,

---

[1] Commentators on the Gallipoli operation often quote, as if in approval, the post-war statement by Liman von Sanders (commander of the Turkish defences) that the 'British gave me four full weeks before their great landing' in which to prepare the resistance, and that 'the time was just sufficient to complete the essential arrangements.' It needs to be stressed that the British did not 'give' Sanders anything. They lacked the capacity, *in any circumstances*, to mount an invasion that would not provide the Turks with considerable warning.

and any force getting ashore there would face resistance on two fronts. He ruled out Suvla Bay on three grounds. Although landing there seemed straightforward, a ring of hills overlooking the bay was ideal for the defence. Further, the bay was too far up the peninsula for the purpose he was setting himself, that of neutralizing the forts at the Narrows. And, finally, at this part the Gallipoli peninsula was at its widest, and his forces were not sufficient to get to the far side without leaving their lines of communication exposed.

So Hamilton decided to attack at the third and fourth of his possible landing places. The Australian and New Zealand forces would go ashore just north of Gaba Tepe, where the peninsula was at its narrowest, and seize the high ground, so cutting off the line of retreat of the Turkish forces in the south. The principal assault, delivered by the British 29th division, was to be made at the southern tip of the peninsula. Its first object was to occupy the hill of Achi Baba, 'the capture of which as an observation post is a key to operations between ships and troops'; its ultimate objective was Khilid Bahr plateau, commanding the forts at the Narrows. Hamilton planned to land the 29th division, along with a Royal Marine Brigade, on five beaches at the southern and south-western end of the peninsula, 'with Achi Baba as the first objective, which it is hoped to capture before night-fall'. The artillery support for this phase would be provided by 'the Navy's guns only'.

Hamilton, perforce or by oversight, was leaving many matters unexplored. His assumption that possession of Achi Baba would provide some sort of command of the Turkish forts at the Narrows was at best a guess. As it happened, it was an incorrect guess – although the point was to prove academic, as Achi Baba did not fall to the British on the first or any subsequent day. Again, it may not be surprising that Hamilton considered beaches the obvious places on which to set down his force. Yet the beaches were by their nature exposed ground, and the hills backing them provided ideal cover from which the Turks might inflict heavy blows upon the invaders. As a naval lieutenant wrote in his diary two days before the attack: 'why do they decide to effect the landing on exposed beaches, covered with entanglements and open to enfilading fire from two directions, when there are nice steep cliffs quite easily climbed just to the side of the beaches affording nearly complete protection?'[2]

But more serious were the shortcomings that were none of Hamilton's doing. A landing at the best available beach, Suvla Bay, was ruled out because, among other things, he lacked the troops to bisect the peninsula at this point. That is, there was a disparity between the size of the force available to him and the task it might be expected to accomplish. Nor was that his only deficiency. Hamilton's point that 'the Navy's guns only' would provide artillery support for the 29th division's landing and assault on Achi Baba raised an interesting question that no one seemed to be asking. What relation did the fire power of these ships bear to the artillery needs of Hamilton's troops as they landed in the open against an entrenched enemy equipped with barbed wire, rifles, and machine-guns? All the experience of the Western Front had demonstrated that a great weight of shell was required just to subdue this sort of trench system long enough for the attacking infantry to get to grips with it. Yet the naval force at the Dardanelles had never been compiled with such a task in mind. It would be a remarkable coincidence if its guns happened to be adequate to the infantry's needs.

One thing plainly emerged from Hamilton's plan (as from Kitchener's instructions to him). His was not a scheme for a military occupation of the Gallipoli peninsula, followed by a march on Constantinople. The most Hamilton's force was supposed to

---

[2] Quoted in Eric Bush, *Gallipoli* (London: Allen & Unwin, 1975), p. 92.

do was to suppress the Gallipoli forts so as to facilitate the passage of the fleet through the Dardanelles. De Robeck had virtually ceased all offensive action during the six weeks of preparing for the landing, and would for the moment be fully occupied serving the artillery and transport needs of the army. Yet it was still taken for granted that he, not Hamilton, would deliver the blow that would knock Turkey out of the war. The great question, namely what reception would await his by no means grandiose body of ships when it appeared off Constantinople, continued to be begged.

IV

The events of 25 April 1915 bore witness to what an invading force must suffer when surprise is lacking, improvisation has been substituted for preparation, and no calculation has been made of its needs in manpower and fire power. Most of all, 'Sunday's battle' exposed the error of launching an amphibious operation not because it has been deemed feasible but because a quite distinct naval operation has proved ill-conceived.

The first to go ashore that day were the Anzacs. For reasons not finally established, they were put ashore at the wrong place: on a beach that, instead of being a mile in length, amounted to only a few hundred yards, and that opened not on to a sandbank but on to almost sheer scrub-bestrewn cliffs. The covering force that landed just before dawn – and, so as to facilitate surprise, without artillery support – pushed inland with great initiative. But the nature of the terrain broke up the attackers into small pockets of men incapable of consistent advance and hampered their rate of progress decisively. So although the Turks assigned to defend this area were not well placed, their faulty disposition was more than counter-balanced by the hindrances that geography presented to the invaders. And as the day wore on, no adequate support of men or material was reaching the Anzac covering force. Thousands of fresh troops were being ferried into the cramped space on which the landing had been made, but none knew where they were, where they ought to be, or what was occurring beyond the beach-head. By the time a forward move was being organized, the advance guard were either falling back to avoid being outflanked or were being forced back by mounting Turkish pressure. Such high points as the Anzacs had captured were gradually wrested from them, and they found themselves being driven towards the sea.

By nightfall the situation at 'Anzac Cove', as the place where fate or ill-fortune had landed them was henceforth to be known, seemed perilous. The divisional commanders were seriously contemplating evacuation, and prevailed on a reluctant Birdwood (commander of the Anzac Corps) to seek consent for this course from the Commander-in-Chief. Hamilton rejected the proposal: 'there is nothing for it,' he replied, 'but to dig yourselves right in and stick it out.' In a postscript he reaffirmed: 'You have got through the difficult business, now you have only to dig, dig, dig, until you are safe.'

By the time this reply reached its destination, commanders and troops alike had also concluded that digging, not evacuating, was the course required both by courage and by prudence. Yet that an invading force, which was supposed by that time to have bisected the Gallipoli peninsula, should be entrenching on a tiny beach-head packed with wounded and dying men was ominous indeed. Hamilton's exhortation, 'dig yourselves right in and stick it out', was worthy of the first battle of Ypres six months before. But this was an uncomfortable recollection. Once more an Allied force was settling willy-nilly into a position where it held none of the high ground, could maintain itself only at cost, and could not advance at all. By the end of the first day at Anzac, the promise of supplanting the stalemated trench fighting of France with open warfare and strategic *coup de main* was already proving illusory.

The fortunes of the invaders on the beaches further south were mixed, but overall they confirmed the ominous message of Anzac. At two beaches (code-named Y and S), where small landings had been added to the plan as an after-thought, Turkish resistance proved slight or non-existent. Hence the landings were effected with relative ease. But the S beach landing was intended only to protect the right flank of the main attack; and once ashore the force there dug in and did not try to advance. Y beach was meant to serve a similar function – to protect the left flank of the main landing. However, the force disembarked there was also supposed to link up with the next beach, X, on its right. This was prevented by the existence of a long, deep, and well defended ravine barely noticed by the inadequate British maps. So the troops contented themselves with digging in on the top of the cliffs above Y beach. There, as the day went on, they came under increasingly fierce Turkish attacks.

The heart of the operation lay in the three beaches (X, W, and V) at the south-western and southern end of the peninsula. The landing at X beach went well, aided by the intelligent use of naval guns. At other beaches the bombardment ceased as the boats carrying the invaders moved towards the shore, so giving the defence time to recover. At X beach, by contrast, the bombardment was continued while the troops were landing. This, along with the tiny number of defenders, enabled the cliffs overlooking the beach to be speedily seized. (For his display of initiative the captain of the bombarding vessel was rebuked by de Robeck. In time the rebuke was withdrawn.)

It was a different story at W beach. The naval bombardment, although punishing, had not submerged the defence. The Turkish forces were few in number and poorly equipped, but they had good trenches, skill with the rifle, and a powerful network of barbed wire between themselves and the invaders. They also had the discipline to hold their fire until the first landing boats were touching the shore and then to mow down the attackers as they floundered among the barbed wire. Yet as the day went on the Turks were driven back up the cliffs, and the British managed to establish a beach-head.

It was at V beach, which was intended to be the main thrust of the invasion, that the Gallipoli expedition made least progress and paid the heaviest cost. Despite limited resources and subjection to a heavy naval bombardment, the Turks managed to pour down a devastating rifle and machine-gun fire on the British troops as they came ashore. This completely pinned down the attack. Had Hunter-Weston, who com-manded the assault on the five southern beaches, kept himself informed of what was happening on V beach, or had Hamilton, the overall commander of the operation, been prepared to thrust the information down Hunter-Weston's throat, then the incoming troops destined for the holocaust of V beach might have been diverted to one of the more hospitable landings. But Hunter-Weston could not take his eyes off W beach, where things were bad enough. And Hamilton was prepared only to nudge, not direct, him. So fresh troops kept being pushed ashore at V beach, to find such precarious cover as they could or to join the wounded and the dead; until, in the spell between nightfall and moonrise, they were able to land reinforcements and to manage a limited advance in the dark.

What did the events of this day amount to? There are nations for whom 25 April 1915 is of great import. For Australia and New Zealand it is a day of national heroism, almost of national birth, whose essence lies in countless tales of individual valour. For Turkey it belongs with 18 March 1915 in a process of national regeneration, laying to rest the notion of the Turk as a worthless fighting man. But in the context of Britain and the First World War 25 April 1915 cannot have these large connotations. Certainly, for the British also there were many tales of heroism and sacrifice in daunting circumstances (as well as some instances of want of initiative and wasted opportunities). And there was the setting, which gave this operation a quality lacking in Western Front battles: the romantic aura of the Eastern Mediterranean; the flotilla of small boats bearing infantrymen towards a hostile shore in near-darkness or the first rays of dawn, wrapped in a silence so powerful that some occupants yearned for the enemy to start firing and others concluded, 'We shall land unopposed'; and then the terrible swarm of bullets thudding upon unprotected bodies, and the sea off Cape Helles crimson with blood, and (as one new arrival recorded) 'the long sad rows of eternally silent figures, their drenched and blood-stained khaki drying in the sun'.[3]

Yet 25 April 1915 demonstrated only what had become evident already in far-off Flanders and France: the formidable power of the defensive against assault by infantry and artillery – even an undermanned and undergunned defending force when it possessed a marked geographical advantage and when its assailants had failed to synchronize their artillery bombardment and infantry movements with the utmost deliberation. Cape Helles, notwithstanding its exotic setting and classical associations, had no lesson for the British army that had not become evident from Sir John French's futile counter-attacks at Second Ypres and his brief triumph at Neuve Chappelle.

V

At Anzac, in the days immediately following 25 April, the most the Commonwealth forces could do was to hold on against ferocious Turkish attempts to drive them into the sea. The Anzacs stood their ground and inflicted fearful losses on their adversaries. For the rest they continued to dig themselves into their absurdly cramped pocket on the peninsula. They began creating a base there, despite unremitting (if not overly heavy) shellfire. And they gradually overcame the menace of snipers.

What they could not do was to advance. They confronted terrain that presented a host of obstacles. They lacked numerical superiority, which they had effectually lost by the third day. And they were without artillery support that could get at the Turks under cover (whatever it could do to them in the open). In these circumstances the Anzacs had no recourse which would facilitate a break-out from their salient. After Birdwood, their commander, had launched a major attack on the night of 2–3 May that, at terrible cost to his troops, neither achieved anything nor looked like doing so, Hamilton seriously considered evacuating Anzac. By allowing himself to be dissuaded, he continued to tie up valuable resources in an operation that, as it then stood, served no purpose which Britain could afford to pursue.

At this stage Hamilton was still regarding the capture of Achi Baba as the crucial next step forward. So Cape Helles, not Anzac, remained the focal point of his endeavours. But for two days following 25 April the British forces there (and the French who now took over their right wing) were so exhausted, and the problems of ship-to-shore supply so formidable, that an immediate advance could not be organized. Indeed, on the morning of 26 April the troops at Y beach, having been studiously ignored by Hunter-Weston for over 24 hours, managed to encompass their own evacuation, so lessening the prospect of progress on the left. Only on 28 April could a major attack from Helles be mounted, and by then the Turks in the area, even though

---

[3] Quoted in Robert Rhodes James, *Gallipoli* (London: Batsford, 1965), p. 120.

badly battered and desperately in need of reinforcement, had managed to organize defensive positions. Hamilton's attempt on 28 April to complete the unfinished agenda of three days before failed decisively.

With this setback the fate of the Gallipoli campaign was settled. The notion that the Turkish defence, after an initial spirited resistance, would collapse utterly had vanished. Maybe it would still be possible for the Allies to win at Gallipoli. But they would never win on the cheap, by invoking the chimeras of 'surprise' and 'sea power' and 'the lesser adversary'. Victory at Gallipoli must mean a step-by-step operation, involving heavy casualties and a large expenditure of war material (as well as a further depletion of shipping resources). That is, the operation would require reinforcements of soldiers and supplies that could be obtained only at the expense of the Western Front – 'men and munitions that we can ill spare from France', as Kitchener wrote to Hamilton.

Yet no decision-making body in Britain had solemnly concluded that this was a proper order of priorities: that the country's still very limited resources could be better employed in weakening the Turkish army than the German army and in seizing territory on Gallipoli rather than in Belgium. Nor was any group doing so now. On 8 May 1915, while Allied forces at Helles were making another bid for Achi Baba (every bit as costly and as unrewarding as its predecessor), Hamilton received a reply from the War Office to an appeal he had made for more ammunition. It stated: 'The ammunition supply for your force was never calculated on the basis of a prolonged occupation of the Peninsula. It is important to push on.' So total a *non sequitur* deserves a place alongside the nonsense uttered in the War Council three months earlier, when its members had been discussing alternative strategies.

VI

Another war was being fought on Gallipoli. This was the war of ordinary soldiers.

There will always be a dichotomy between how military actions appear when they are judged by their contribution (or lack thereof) to strategy and when they are seen in terms of the conduct and experiences of the participants. In the case of Gallipoli this dichotomy was to prove particularly marked. And never was it more so than on the first day. The landing at Anzac Cove on 25 April 1915 was, in terms of strategy, a clear failure. And in so far as it was not an unrelieved failure, this was the more cause for regret. For the partial success of the landing – the getting ashore but then the failure to advance – was to produce a campaign far more costly, for no gain, than if the Anzacs had failed to remain on the peninsula at all. Yet the men who stormed ashore and lived to consider the matter saw their deeds as heroic, and so they were described by those (like the English newspaper columnist E. Ashmead-Bartlett) who recorded their actions. In view of what they accomplished in landing at an unprepared position upon a hostile and staunchly defended shore, and in thrusting forward into uninviting terrain, the judgement is not surprising.

This dichotomy persisted throughout the course of the Gallipoli campaign. From a sufficiently exalted position it is possible to pass over most of the ensuing attempts to advance as foregone failures. Yet from an elevation nearer the ground Gallipoli unfolds a tale of unrelenting drama. An historian has written of 'the unique and unforgettable atmosphere of Anzac'. The 'scenes behind the front lines, in the unbelievably restricted area captured by the Anzacs, astounded all new arrivals', who landed under a hail of shrapnel fire 'to discover a small but active ramshackle town perched on beach and cliff.[4] One observer likened it to 'the cave dwellings of a large and prosperous tribe of savages who live on the extremely steep slopes of broken sandy bluffs covered with scrub'.[5] An Australian colonel, nearing 50 years old and in action for the first time, wrote home that he would have to discontinue his regular letters until he resided

> in some more civilised place than these mountains in which we are existing in the most primitive fashion, living in dug-outs and trenches, and feeding on bully-beef, biscuits, bacon and tea. I am writing within a hundred yards of the firing line and the rattle of musketry and the boom of cannon is incessant.

Soon afterwards he related:

> We have been amusing ourselves by trying to discover the longest period of absolute quiet. We have been fighting now continuously for 22 days, all day and all night, and most of us think that absolutely the longest period during which there was absolutely no sound of gun or rifle fire throughout the whole of that time was 10 seconds. One man says he was able on one occasion to count fourteen but nobody believes him. We are all of us certain that we shall no longer be able to sleep amid perfect quiet, and the only way to induce sleep will be to get someone to rattle an empty tin outside one's bedroom door.[6]

The men who fought at Anzac, and to a lesser degree at Cape Helles, were henceforth set apart from other mortals by their involvement in this experience. To have survived there, even for a while, marked a person off as possessing several well regarded qualities: a high degree of courage, a capacity for improvisation, and an ability to adapt to a new lifestyle and to new expectations. For one thing, not only those in the front line but all who set foot on Gallipoli were in some danger. Birdwood had a narrow escape from death when a bullet grazed his head; and on another occasion, when bathing in the sea, he was admonished as shrapnel began bursting, 'Duck, you silly old dill' – and did so. By the same token, men in the front line found themselves called on to perform exhausting tasks usually kept for those in reserve – like carrying water (most precious of Anzac commodities) and supplies, and burying the dead. Again, rank-and-file soldiers at Anzac became engaged in manufacturing rudimentary hand bombs, which were the weapons most needed for their type of trench warfare but were in desperately short supply. And one of their number devised a weapon as simple yet sophisticated – and, at the key point called Quinn's Post, as essential to survival – as the telescope rifle.

Men did not come to terms with Gallipoli without making painful adjustments. The early days of fighting shattered many illusions: about war (especially in exotic climes) being an adventure; about valour as a quality that could overcome all obstacles; about the craven character and contemptible fighting ability of Middle Eastern 'races' (indeed, of any non-British 'race'); and about death in action for one's own side as being straightforward, dignified, and rare. A private at Anzac, wounded on 25 April, wrote: 'Sunday's battle and the horrors of the trenches Sunday night . . . have unnerved me completely.' He and his associates had set out, he said, 'to death and "Glory". What fools we are, men mad. . . . Where are the rest of my 13 mates?'[7]

New arrivals at Cape Helles early in May were taken aback by the desolate expressions on the faces of men who had gone forth so confidently only a week before. They soon found reason for the transformation. One man who landed at V beach later

---

[4] James, *Gallipoli*, pp. 171,174.

[5] Orlo Williams, chief cipher officer on Hamilton's staff, quoted in James, *Gallipoli*, p. 174.

[6] Colonel John Monash writing to his wife, quoted in A. J. Smithers, *Sir John Monash* (Sydney: Angus & Robertson, 1973), pp. 87–8, 101.

[7] Quoted in Bill Gammage, *The Broken Years* (Ringwood, Victoria: Penguin Books Australia, 1975), p. 59.

that month was a member of the regular army, having joined up shortly before the outbreak of war to escape the degradation of life as a Suffolk farm labourer:

> I want to say this simply as a fact, that village people in Suffolk in my day were worked to death. It literally happened. It is not a figure of speech. I was worked mercilessly.

Many years later he recalled his initial experience of actual war, on the peninsula. One of the first things he saw on stepping ashore was 'a big marquee'.

> It didn't make me think of the military but of the village fêtes. Other people must have thought like this because I remember how we all rushed up to it, like boys getting into a circus, and then found it all laced up. We unlaced it and rushed in. It was full of corpses. Dead Englishmen, lines and lines of them, with their eyes wide open. We all stopped talking. I'd never seen a dead man before and here I was looking at two or three hundred of them. It was our first fear. Nobody had mentioned this. I was very shocked. I thought of Suffolk and it seemed a happy place for the first time.[8]

That men should have experienced dismay in such circumstances is no cause for wonder. Perhaps more surprisingly, by and large it was short-lived. Some illusions, certainly, did not return: particularly the notion that victory would be a formality. But it gave way to a fierce determination that Allied goals would be attained however formidable the opposition. Certain Anzacs, evacuated from Gallipoli on account of wounds and at first dreading a return to the fighting zone, soon began agitating to get back. Some even stowed away on ships bound for the peninsula. One Australian who had expected the landing to be in the nature of a sporting activity, and whose expectation had been rudely shattered on 25 April, nevertheless was writing by June: 'Now that things are peaceful I am longing to scrap again. After the sternest days of fighting I had a keen desire to return home in safety, but now I do not give it a thought . . . . life and death has not the same significance it once had.'[9]

VII

While British infantrymen died in their thousands on Gallipoli, the naval force continued its less onerous role of ferrying in supplies and reinforcements and bombarding the enemy. This comparative lack of peril, in contrast to the terrible experience of the soldiers, bore hard on gallant sailors on whose behalf the land operation was proceeding. Particularly did it oppress the fiery spirit of Roger Keyes, de Robeck's Chief of Staff.[10]

Back in February, while the naval attack was in preparation, Keyes had 'never felt so "buoyant and confident" about anything in my life before. We are going to have a splendid affair.' By 8 March he was coming to realise that the naval forcing of the Dardanelles was 'a much bigger thing than the Admiralty or anyone out here realised'; nevertheless, 'We *are* going to get through.' The experience of 18 March gave even more cause for reflection: 'a very trying day . . . . It is very obvious that all the defences are run by Germans[,] their system of fire is wonderfully good.' Still, he remained 'one of the very few who were not [downhearted] that evening'. Indeed, he was eager to set about creating a new minesweeping force able to attack the minefields. 'We must thoroughly train them first, and then: – !'

But the succession of setbacks had rendered Keyes amenable to a change of plan. A few days later the principal naval officers, including Keyes, visited Hamilton and other

---

[8] Ronald Blythe, *Akenfield* (Harmondsworth: Penguin Books, 1973), pp. 41–3.
[9] Quoted in Gammage, *The Broken Years*, p. 60.
[10] The quotations that follow are from Keyes's letters to his wife, which are in Churchill College, Cambridge.

leaders of the military force to 'find out what they would be prepared to do'. Keyes recorded: 'their proposals were just what we had urged for several weeks and entirely satisfactory. . . . I can't help feeling that check [on 18 March] was in a way providential – galling as it was.' On 13 April, in the midst of conferences with the army leaders, he wrote: 'This *is* going to be such a splendid show!!! But [it] is an awful business working out all the details of this gigantic co-operation.' Then came the landings of 25 April: 'rather a desperate day and I fear between 3000 and 4000 casualties. But there never was a gallanter enterprise in History. . . . The op[p]osition was awful in places.' Three days later at Cape Helles came the first battle of Krithia: 'Today was disappointing[,] the men are dead dog tired – and have been fighting hard for 3 days.' On 30 April Keyes wrote: "Our losses really are awful – the Dublins lost nearly all their officers and over 600 men.'

There followed the second battle of Krithia, which raged from 6 to 8 May. This was too much for Keyes. The day before it began he had written that the 6th 'might well be the day we take ACHI BABA'. Instead it proved 'rather a desperate day'; he was galled by having to lie off shore, watching the army attacking and being unable to use all of the navy's great power. On the 10th he summed up second Krithia as a most desperate fight which had made very little progress. And he added: 'Personally I have come to the most momentous conclusion.'

Keyes's conclusion was that the naval action to force the Dardanelles must be resumed. He was becoming gripped by a conviction that was to obsess him for the rest of his days: that the Turks had been a beaten foe by the end of the naval attack on 18 March; that he, cruising in the Straits in pitch darkness at the end of that day, had known them to be beaten; and that de Robeck, despite his calm composure, had been shattered by the loss of ships and had seized on Hamilton's proposal for a military landing in order to escape having to resume the naval assault.

Keyes pressed on de Robeck and the other admirals his proposal for a renewal of the naval operation. They were not impressed. The most that de Robeck would do was to inform London that he would resume the naval attack if ordered to do so. But de Robeck also had come to a 'momentous conclusion', and one that struck at the heart of Keyes's scheme and a good deal more. He informed London: 'From the vigour of the enemy's resistance it is improbable that the passage of the Fleet into the Marmara will be decisive.' He repeated the point a few sentences later: 'The temper of the Turkish Army in the Peninsula indicates that the forcing of the Dardanelles and subsequent appearance of the Fleet off Constantinople will not, of itself, prove decisive.' It will be remembered that the military operation then under way at Gallipoli was intended only to open the Dardanelles for the fleet. Yet here was the commander of the naval force repudiating the fundamental notion on which first the naval attack and then the combined operation were based – that if the fleet, unaided or with military assistance, could get past the Narrows forts, its mere appearance off Constantinople would elicit Turkey's capitulation.

Neither Keyes's anxiety for action nor de Robeck's challenge to basic assumptions produced the soul-searching in London that they seemed to demand. But the impasse at Gallipoli, merging with other currents both military and political, helped to set in motion a train of events that had large consequences.

14

FORWARD MOVES: AUBERS RIDGE AND FESTUBERT

[T]he result of our attacks the day before yesterday have not been satisfactory . . . . we stand to-day just where we did three days ago except that we have lost some 10,000 officers and men in the First Army and expended a very large amount of Arty Ammunt.
Rawlinson, commander of IV Corps of First Army, to Major Wigram, 11 May 1915

We don't seem able to 'mount' an attack.
Henry Wilson's diary, 16 June 1915

I

In mid-March 1915, immediately following Neuve Chapelle and with the naval attack on the Dardanelles floundering, another forward move in Flanders was being contemplated. Haig, commander of Britain's First Army, was proposing a further attempt on Aubers Ridge. But a problem had arisen. It concerned ammunition. Haig wrote in his diary for 16 March:

> I went to Hazebrouck about 10.00 a.m. and saw Sir John French. He approved of my plan of operations but *there was no ammunition at present, as the expedition to the Dardanelles had to be supplied* [Haig's emphasis].
> It would be necessary to wait for a fortnight. Sir Ian Hamilton has gone to command [the] expedition against Constantinople. This lack of ammunition seems serious. It effectually prevents us from profiting by our recent success and pressing the enemy before he can reorganise and strengthen his position.

At the same time Major Bonham-Carter was telling his family: 'We have now got to wait for some time I fear owing to the ammunition difficulty – thanks to the despatch of the Dardanelles force and to strikes.' In London also the rate at which the war was swallowing up ammunition was causing much comment. Kitchener criticized Sir John French for his prodigious expenditure at Neuve Chapelle. Lord Esher blamed the War Office for not following the lead of the French in munitions production, as he had urged them to do four months earlier – 'but they would not listen'. And many people in authority deplored the recalcitrant attitude of the workforce to the need for increased output of guns and shells.

But there was as yet no coherent thinking about the extent of the ammunition shortage, let alone about how it should affect military planning. The diary entry by Haig just quoted, in which he reports his Commander-in-Chief as saying *'there was no ammunition at present'*, follows this with the baffling observation: 'It would be necessary to wait for a fortnight.' This hardly suggests a conviction that the matter constituted a major crisis. Again, by the beginning of April Kitchener was 'more hopeful as regards ammunition'.[1] And early in May, with his next forward move only a few days hence, French assured Kitchener: 'The ammunition will be all right.'[2] So whatever the munitions difficulties of the British, the military authorities did not see them as cause for abstaining from participation in the next assault on the Western Front.

II

Meanwhile, Joffre was preparing a major offensive for May in the northern part of his line, in the Artois region. His prime objective was the key observation position of Vimy Ridge. The British immediately on his left, Haig's First Army, were to assist him by again attempting what they had not accomplished when acting independently in March – the capture of Aubers Ridge. If the British contribution (which would be a minor part of the undertaking) achieved nothing else, it seemed certain to pin down German forces that could otherwise be sent against the French. But should success be achieved on both sectors and the two 'ridges' (of most unequal height) fall into Allied hands, the German position in the northern sector of the Western Front would be jeopardized.

Haig's plan for the May attack shows that he had not misread one lesson of Neuve Chapelle. The partial success there had been achieved by a brief but heavy preliminary bombardment. Contrary to a general opinion, Haig had not been so mesmerized by the weight of shell then employed that he had overlooked the contribution of brevity. Again at Aubers Ridge he hoped by a short but concentrated bombardment both to breach the German defences and to send forward his infantry before the enemy could bring up reinforcements. Whether on this occasion his ammunition supplies were adequate for a repeat performance is questionable. But that was not his only problem. For the enemy also had read the message of Neuve Chapelle. Haig was now to learn what the Germans further north were simultaneously discovering from the waning impact of poison gas: a method of attack that produced impressive results when first employed might yield sharply diminishing returns thereafter.

The British assault on Aubers Ridge on 9 May failed utterly. The infantry found themselves advancing against uncut wire into withering machine-gun fire, and fell in their thousands. These losses were not offset by even the minimum benefit expected of the operation. By the afternoon of that day the German command – so little did it feel threatened by the British action – had begun moving reserves away from the British sector to stem the attack by the French. The following morning Haig closed down the operation.

It is possible to enumerate several reasons for this setback, but less easy to discover which among them were decisive. There were clear shortcomings in the British bombardment. Accurate registration had not been obtained, despite aerial spotting. Many of the guns proved to be too worn to fire on target. Much of the inadequate supply of ammunition was faulty. Further, a large proportion of available shells were shrapnel, which was effective against men in the open but not against trenches, and against barbed wire only if employed in large quantities. Nevertheless, it is quite possible that a longer, better fired, and better supplied bombardment would not have removed the enemy obstacles. The Germans were accepting with considerable thoroughness the logic of their decision to stand on the defensive in the West. This was

---

[1] So Hankey told Haig: Haig's diary for 3 April 1915.
[2] Sir George Arthur, *Life of Lord Kitchener* (London: Macmillan, 1920), vol. 3, p. 236.

evident from their extensive use of barbed wire, their sound construction above ground (rather than below, owing to the high water level in Flanders) of trenches that were coming to resemble minor fortifications, and their skilful siting and protection of machine-gun posts – which could scarcely be put out of action by less than a direct hit. It was the last of these that took such pitiless toll of the attacking forces. If one element in the foregoing catalogue, the shortage of ammunition, was speedily seized on in some British quarters as the prime cause of the débâcle, it is far from certain that without it the attack would greatly have prospered.

III

The British assault on Aubers Ridge was called off early on its second day. The French operation that it was designed to support was not. The principal element in the French offensive, the attack on Vimy Ridge, enjoyed a striking early success. Briefly, a body of French troops occupied the crest of the ridge. They were too few in number (owing to heavy losses) and their reinforcements too far away (owing to poor generalship) for the position to be held. But it would require many weeks of further endeavour before the French commanders reluctantly concluded that, anyway this time, the prize was going to elude them. In these circumstances further British assistance seemed called for.

Haig's next attack, known as the battle of Festubert, was directed to a part of the line somewhat south of Aubers Ridge (against which no one seemed keen to strike a third time). The failure of 9 May had shaken his confidence both in the whirlwind bombardment as a suitable prelude and in the broad front as a suitable objective. Aubers Ridge, he concluded, 'showed that we are confronted by a carefully prepared position, which is held by a most determined enemy, with numerous machine guns'. These obstacles required an 'accurate and so fairly long' bombardment, with careful observation of '*each shot*' to ensure that the enemy's strong points had been eliminated 'before the Infantry is launched'.[3] The six days that elapsed before the next British endeavour hardly allowed for a full application of these methods, especially as Haig had no single artillery commander in a position to direct his whole bombardment. Even so, the artillery preparation of 36 hours did manage to cut the enemy wire with some efficiency.

In keeping with the decision to attack on a narrow front with limited objectives, the infantry assault opened with the first British night attack of the war – this being a type of action requiring meticulous preparation and modest goals. Thirty minutes before midnight on 15–16 May 10,000 men of Haig's 2nd division moved forward in the dark. Of the three brigades engaged, one achieved the hoped-for surprise and overran the enemy's front trench. The others, caught in the open by star shells and searchlights, were decimated by machine-gun fire. A bit further south, at dawn, the 7th division under General Gough also made a small amount of progress; and a renewed effort after a quite destructive bombardment on 17 May did even better. Briefly, it seemed as if the enemy were really succumbing to demoralization, with small numbers of German troops surrendering even before the infantry began their advance. But then enemy reinforcements (not taken from the French sector) appeared; their line stabilized; and further efforts against it proved fruitless. The fighting did not peter out until 25 May,

---

[3] Diary entries for 10 May 1915, quoted in John Terraine, *Douglas Haig: The Educated Soldier* (London: Hutchinson, 1963), pp. 148–9.

by which time ammunition supplies right along the British front had been expended. But any hope of a real success had departed a week earlier.

The attacks by the French continued, with ever-diminishing prospects of success, until a last effort in mid-June convinced them that the cause was lost. In these closing weeks the British contribution was restricted: first, to taking over an additional 5 miles of line from the French (the British now occupied 75 miles of the 475 mile front); and, secondly, to two diversionary attacks near their ally's left flank coinciding with the last French push. Despite some painstaking preparation, especially by General Allenby in command of V Corps, these efforts again failed, thanks to the equally competent preparations of their adversaries. Rawlinson wrote of the effort by his IV Corps:

> The artillery bombardment was very accurate, and in ordinary circumstances would, no doubt, have shaken the Germans sufficiently for our infantry to succeed; but in this case the Germans have deep dug-outs at the bottom of their trenches, into which they retired during the bombardment. In these they were safe from the heavy shell, so that, when our infantry advanced, the Germans simply lined the parapets and shot our men down as soon as they started the assault.[4]

How little the enemy's defences had been crushed by the bombardment was vividly brought home to a Scottish division about to attempt the crossing of 150 yards of No-Man's-Land. German voices were heard calling out: 'Come on, Jocks, we are waiting for you.'

For the rest, June 1915 on the British front was a relatively quiet month. As so often in this war, soldiers who had been through an intense experience, in which endeavour mingled with suffering, then found themselves undergoing a long spell of routine activity. This more secure life could soon become tedious. A member of an artillery brigade heavily engaged in the attacks of early May noted the contrast with June, 'where a whole month was spent without firing a round'.

> Time hung very heavily for officers and men alike. Books and newspapers were in great demand, and the arrival of the mail from home was the outstanding event of the day. The captain sketched, the subalterns loafed and read, and the gunners played 'house' all day . . . . [with] the droning, unceasing chant: 'Clicketty Click, Number Seven, Kelly's Eye, Legs Eleven, Number Nine, Top o' the House'. . . .[5]

IV

The British part in these Western Front offensives of May and June 1915 was decidedly the minor one, as casualty figures indicate. The one day's fighting at Aubers Ridge cost Britain 9,500 casualties, the 10 days of Festubert 16,500. By contrast, French casualties for the whole six weeks exceeded 100,000.[6] Yet in Britain the First Army's losses did not pass without criticism. They seemed to have been suffered to no purpose, since the army had neither taken ground nor made easier the path of the French. And they formed part of a seemingly unrelieved tale of woe. There were the

---

[4] Rawlinson to Lord Derby, 21 June 1915, quoted in Major-General Sir Frederick Maurice, *The Life of General Lord Rawlinson of Trent* (London: Cassell, 1928), p. 134. It should be noted that Maurice's transliterations of Rawlinson's documents are not always faithful to the original. Except in this and two other instances (on pages 309 and 319), all quotations from Rawlinson in this book are from the original documents.

[5] 'Mark Severn' (Major Franklin Lushington), *The Gambardier* (London: Ernest Benn, 1930), pp. 53–4.

[6] German casualties against both attacking forces were significantly lower: possibly only 33 per cent of British casualties and 60 per cent of French.

much heavier British losses being sustained in the defence of Ypres, and a further accession of casualties for meagre gains at Gallipoli. There was the failure of Joffre's great offensives in the Champagne and Artois. And, most ominous of all, at Gorlice early in May the Russians had sustained a crushing defeat at the hands of the Germans. Too plainly, this was only the beginning of a series of misfortunes for Britain's Eastern ally – misfortunes that the Franco-British actions on the Western Front were apparently doing nothing to mitigate.

Moreover, Britons had not yet reached the stage of accepting these blood-lettings in France as an inherent part of their quest for victory. It was still assumed that culpably wrong decisions had been made, that some individual or group was to blame, and that a rolling of heads was in order.

PART FOUR

Home Front
1914–1915

15

HOME AFFAIRS

I

A discussion of the war on the home front embraces, basically, two topics. One is the way in which the events of war impinged on civilian lives. The other is how people not in uniform (including those eligible to don it) responded to the conflict. But the two aspects intertwine. An air raid, for example, was a fact of war that directly affected civilian life. But it also influenced the way in which civilians viewed the enemy and hence the war as a whole.

The war was expected to have large, and distressing, effects on the home economy. In the House of Commons the radical MP Josiah Wedgwood – soon to be engaged on the battlefields of Flanders and Gallipoli – foresaw disruption of trade and industry, with consequent social upheaval. Ramsay MacDonald, the principal Labour opponent of Britain's involvement in war, warned that 'there are places like West Ham, where the whole population will encamp on the doorstep of the workhouse before the month is over.'[1] To meet this anticipated distress, relief committees were set up and large sums donated by the public.

The distress, by and large, never eventuated. There was some hardship among dependents of men entering the services. This applied early on to the wives (especially *de facto* wives) and children of recruits, in that separation allowances were slow in arriving. It applied over a longer period to other dependents of servicemen, such as elderly parents, widowed mothers, and infirm relatives, for whom until late in 1915 no state provision was introduced. In addition, to begin with there was some incidence of unemployment, especially in the cotton industry and among luxury trades.

But no social unrest resulted or seemed likely to. For one thing, the workers most affected by unemployment were women – the least militant element in the labour force. And anyway within a few months there was a positive outcry for workers, including females. Indeed, some parts of the country enjoyed prosperity from the start of the war. Districts such as Leicester, the focus of the boot and shoe industry, and Leeds, a major clothing producer, as well as the great centres of engineering and shipbuilding, were all subject to heavy military and naval demand. Boot manufacturers were soon reported to be opening their mail with dread, for fear it contained further orders. And towards the end of 1914 the Leicester Boot and Shoe Operatives Union noted that, for the first time in its history, not a man was receiving unemployment benefit. That city had appointed a strong committee of 54 to deal with distress arising from the war. In December it received a mere 10 applications. In the country generally, most of the large sums raised to meet cases of war-induced hardship went to other causes, particularly the Red Cross.

---

[1] Quoted in F. P. Armitage, *Leicester 1914–1918: The War-Story of a Midland Town* (Leicester: Edgar Backus, 1933), p. 16.

Equally, there proved to be no insupportable shortages caused by the war. Immediately on the outbreak, there was panic buying of food. In this the affluent, if only because they possessed money and vehicles, were conspicuous participants. But it soon transpired that, thanks to Britain's command of the sea, there was no desperate threat to supplies. The Government acted swiftly to command new sources of sugar, two-thirds of which had hitherto come from the Central Powers. But wheat supplies did fall short, owing to a poor world harvest and the tying up of Russian grain following the closure of the Dardanelles. And the quantity of meat available to civilians decreased as a result of the fairly generous way in which the army fed its recruits. But these reductions were not of an order to cause serious distress.

Plate 11a   *Men waiting to enlist outside the Central London Recruiting Depot.*

What did offset some of the benefits of full employment was a rise in prices. In February 1915 the General Federation of Trade Unions (GFTU) issued a pamphlet on the matter.[2] It agreed that there had been less unemployment than anticipated. But it argued that wages were being reduced by the climbing cost of food. This applied especially to the primary necessities, wheat and meat. (According to a government document on retail prices of this time, 'in the average working-class budget [bread and flour] represent about one-fifth of the total family expenditure.') Compared with average prices for 1914, stated the GFTU pamphlet, wheat had risen by 72 per cent, barley by 40 per cent, and oats by 34 per cent. As for meat, there had been no actual failure of supply –

> but prices have literally rushed up, particularly in respect of the poorer cuts. London street markets supply hundreds of thousands of the poorest with their main food supplies, and usually prices are low enough to enable the wife of the employed labourer or poorly-paid artisan to provide a sufficiency of rough food. To-day she must pass to a lower grade of sustenance. . . . Neck of mutton usually fetches from 2½d. to 3d. per lb.; the poorest and

---

[2] Documents quoted in this and the following paragraph were consulted in the Crewe papers in the University Library, Cambridge.

dirtiest samples, colloquially known as scrag of mutton, are now fetching from 4½d. to 6d. per lb. Pallid and unappetising bits of pickled brisket, usually 4½d. to 5d. per lb., are now on the stall of the street market ticketed at 8½d. and 9d. per lb.

As for fish, 'if it is more than three degrees from the manure stage', it had become so expensive that the Archbishop of Westminster was allowing his flock to eat cheaper flesh substitutes on fast days. The situation, admitted this document, was not yet desperate, but it was serious and would become more so unless the Government moved quickly.

At the same time a Board of Trade paper was referring to the 'recent sharp rise in coal prices', the causes of which were 'at present obscure'. Probably in part it resulted from the dislocation of rail traffic as a result of military requirements. But there was also an actual diminution in supply, as a consequence of recruiting. By December 1914 nearly 14 per cent of those employed in the mines six months earlier had joined up, and these were probably from among the more efficient workers. Their places had been filled to the extent of only 3.4 per cent (and, it may be speculated, these substitutes were unlikely to be as efficient). This combination of dislocated deliveries and diminished supply led both to shortages – in Bristol some elementary schools closed in January 1915 on account of the lack of fuel – and to a general rise in prices. By 1 February 1915 the cost of best Derbyshire coal on the London market had risen by roughly 20 per cent on the 1914 average. Other types of coal had gone up similarly.

Price rises exercised the attention of Government and legislators repeatedly in 1914 and 1915. In the first weeks of the war the Government took powers to requisition foodstuffs being withheld 'unreasonably' (that is, so as to force up prices). In mid-1915 it turned its attention to coal. In June agreement was reached with the coal merchants to limit profits. And the following month, the colliery owners having proved less amenable, the authorities took powers to limit the price at the pithead. Then in September the President of the Board of Trade announced that the Government had also acted to check the advance in meat prices. It had successfully resisted the rates proposed by the American beef companies and the shippers.

These actions would not eliminate price increases, only limit them. But in two major respects the increases actually halted. One concerned the price of bread, which (as already noted) was a crucial element in the working-class budget. Owing to a bumper harvest, and despite the continued closure of the Dardanelles, wheat prices fell steadily from the spring of 1915. The other respect was house rents, which again affected working people closely. In November 1915, after much agitation, the Government – in one of the most drastic pieces of wartime legislation – pegged the rents of working-class dwellings at their pre-war levels.

The effects of price rises on families and individuals depended not only on class but also on particular circumstances within a class. Members of the middle classes engaged in buying and selling might find ample opportunities for profit-making – not to say profiteering. Those who depended on savings and fixed incomes were suffering a drop in living standards. Among the working classes the same sort of distinction might be observed. For a family with several members who were able to take work, the combination of full employment, rising wages, ample overtime, and new job opportunities meant higher real income. For a family with only one breadwinner and several small children, price rises meant grievous times. Sylvia Pankhurst, struggling to serve the slum dwellers of the East End of London, encountered many in the latter condition. She relates:

Even the women who had received the full separation allowances promised, were in sad case. The wife of a Territorial, with two young children and expecting a third, got 1s. 5d. a day from the War Office. Having moved into London when her husband was called up she got no London allowance. Her rent was 6s. a week. She wept with despair at finding herself with only 3s. 11d. a week for food, fuel, light, and all the needs of her family! . . .

The high cost of food accentuated all hardship. Under the pressure of want, sickness went unattended. Many of the mothers who came to us had children due to attend some hospital as out-patients; but the mother could no longer afford either the fare to take them there, or the small charge for medicine. . . . One poor soul, supporting a bedridden husband and five children, had 10s. weekly from the [Poor Law] Guardians. Her rent was 7s. weekly and the Relieving Officer had forbidden her to take a lodger, on the ground that her rooms were only sufficient to accommodate her family. Her hungry little children were refused school meals because their mother was getting Poor Law relief.[3]

Plate 11b *A large party of German reservists, arrested while endeavouring to leave Britain, marching through Folkestone on their way to a detention camp.*

Yet overall it appears that more people in the labouring sector benefited than suffered from the trends of the early war economy. This is certainly the judgement of the historian of wartime Leicester. In the hosiery trade earnings were reported to have risen in one month by 14.5 per cent. And not all the vigorous demand for footwear emanated from the army. There was an abnormal demand for children's shoes – a clear sign of family prosperity. On the whole, it was concluded, children were 'better fed and better clothed than ever before.'[4]

Apart from these basic questions of wages and prices, there were various ways in which the war began to affect the lives of ordinary people. Early in the conflict the government empowered licensing authorities to impose early closing. Not all of them responded positively: no action was taken in Nottingham and Derby. But in Bristol (where a large body of Scottish troops was billeted) and in Leicester drinking establishments were closed at 9 p.m. Consequently: 'Letters in praise and blame of ale poured into the newspaper offices: it was a mere beverage, a tonic, a stimulant, a

---

[3] E. Sylvia Pankhurst, *The Home Front* (London: Hutchinson, 1932), p. 28.
[4] Armitage, *Leicester 1914–1918*, p. 104.

poison.'[5] For the committed drinker worse was to follow. The authorities took seriously the many complaints being made about over-imbibing among troops, soldiers' wives and above all munitions workers. Grandiose plans for the state to take over the drink trade, advocated by Lloyd George in March and April, came to nothing. But piecemeal restrictions followed one upon another. And even when designed for particular sectors of the community, the restrictions usually spread further. For example, 'treating' (that is, the purchase of a drink for another person) was prohibited, it being held that much drunkenness among soldiers was caused by the generosity of misguided patriots. The application of this ban became general. A man might be prosecuted (and this did happen) for buying a drink for his own wife. Again, the alcoholic content of beverages was in various ways reduced. And licensing hours became further constricted, first in munitions areas but then quite generally. So in Bristol in August 1915, and in London late in November, hours of opening were drastically confined to between noon and 2.30 p.m. and between 6.30 and 9.30 p.m. Off-licence sales were restricted to the former period. Some spokesmen for the working class complained that these constraints were an insult to the labour force. In other quarters the decline in drunkenness was considered most gratifying.

Various precautions were taken against air raids, even before the attacks commenced. At night street lights were dimmed, shop lighting was restricted, trains had to travel with drawn blinds, and cars might have lamps pointing only in the direction in which they were travelling. Against daytime raids warning systems were developed, though some were unlikely to be very effective: in Bermondsey policemen were delegated to travel about on bicycles with notices proclaiming 'Take Cover'.

In a great many other ways the duties of the police were extended. One was keeping a watch on aliens, both enemy and neutral. All foreigners had to register with the constabulary and must keep indoors between the hours of 9 p.m. and 5 a.m. unless furnished with a police permit. Those on the move were kept under particular surveillance. They were banned from sensitive areas, especially near the coast. And hotels and boarding houses, under threat of heavy penalties, were required to register full details of alien residents.

This form of supervision imposed a considerable burden on the police, especially early in the war while a register was being compiled. It was particularly onerous in those parts of London that contained large numbers of Russian Jews who had fled the Tsar's persecution. Such refugees were not necessarily enthusiastic about a war in which Britain was aligned with so devoted an autocrat and anti-Semite. The chronicler of one London district in wartime comments somewhat opaquely: 'We had many aliens in Bermondsey, some of whom gave considerable trouble.'[6]

In numerous other ways the police had to act against possible saboteurs. Amateur wireless stations were dismantled. Guards were set over the country's water supply – although they sometimes consisted of no force more ferocious than a troop of boy scouts. A register was taken of all keepers of homing pigeons – there were 1,000 such persons in Leicester alone – lest these feathered friends should be used to convey information to the enemy. Other forms of activity burdened the police. They were responsible for rounding up absentees and deserters from the armed forces. They found themselves helping the dependents of servicemen to fill in forms for separation allowances and pensions. And they had to deal with the problems posed by the threat of air raids: by enforcing lighting restrictions, warning people about patent fire extin-

---

[5] Ibid., p. 100.
[6] Henry F. Morriss, *Bermondsey's 'Bit' in the Greatest War* (London: Clifton Publishing House and Richard J. James, n.d.), p. 216.

guishers that would prove useless against incendiary bombs, and advising the proprietors of cinemas and music halls about preventing panic in the event of raids.

From early in the war the police had the assistance of a force of special constables. These were private citizens, usually above military age or in some essential occupation, who volunteered their services for a few hours a week. The force in Leeds was formed late in 1914, with a few hundred members; in the course of the war some 3,250 citizens would be enrolled there, although there was a fair rate of wastage. This body drew its members from the classes devoted to law and order: magistrates, bankers, solicitors, artisans, clerks. Indeed, in Leeds it sprang almost fully made from a pre-war organization called the Citizen's League, formed by 'ardent and loyal men . . . to fight local disorder' (that is, to deal with suffragettes and active trade unionists). Hitherto the League had been viewed by the authorities as an amateur and 'perhaps a little fussy' organization. Now its services proved acceptable.[7]

The hours of duty of the special constables were not all that exacting. They were usually on the job for four hours at a stretch, in some areas on two nights a week, in others only once a fortnight. But often enough the individuals who made up this force were already fully occupied during the day. So the experience of drilling, of standing guard over reservoirs or pumping stations or electricity works, of patrolling the streets and demanding the suppression of unguarded lights, proved endeavour enough. Nights when air raids threatened were the most demanding; and so it was in the areas prone to attack that their duties proved heaviest – but also took on their most evident purpose. In Leeds the threat of a raid caused special constables to be summoned immediately to their local police stations, extinguishing street lights on the way. From a look-out point on the Town Hall dome telephone messages went out to police stations concerning buildings from which lights were showing. Word was then passed to the patrols. It is recorded that only 10 minutes would elapse between a light's being detected and its extinction.

II

The activities of the special constables were one indication among many that the nation was taking the war seriously. Overall the people of Britain responded to the conflict with a convincing display of unity. On 3 August 1914 John Redmond, leader of the Irish Nationalists, firmly announced his party's support for Britain's cause. His speech made 'a profound sensation' and caused one Anglican bishop to proclaim: 'The great reconciliation is achieved. A new era in English history is dawned.'[8] A month later, on the day Parliament was prorogued, a Labour MP led the House of Commons in singing the national anthem. Between these two events the legislators – acting, it seems plain, in accord with public opinion – speedily endorsed the extreme demands made by the Government. These included a huge war credit, the appointment of a press censor, and the passage of the Defence of the Realm Act (DORA for short). This last measure was directed initially against espionage. But its sphere of reference was soon extended, until it gave the authorities power to suspend a great range of civil liberties.

Outside the House of Commons the suffragettes called off their campaign of violence and turned to patriotic endeavours. They were soon demanding that the

[7] W. H. Scott, *Leeds in the Great War 1914–1918* (Leeds: Libraries and Arts Committee, 1923), pp. 158–62. (This section was contributed by an ex-officer of the special constables.)

[8] *Annual Register for 1914* (London: Longman Green, 1915), p. 172; Albert Marrin, *The Last Crusade* (Durham, North Carolina: Duke University Press, 1974), p. 81.

authorities give women a fuller opportunity to serve the country. As for the male sex, men of all classes and conditions hastened to the recruiting offices. On a single day in September 30,000 joined up. The city of Leeds alone, between August and December 1914, provided 15,000 volunteers, including one of the best-remembered 'Pals' battalions. Edward Thomas, both poet and observer, roamed from Swindon to Newcastle-upon-Tyne in late August and early September 1914.[9] He wrote of the men enlisting:

> There was really no monotony of type among these recruits, though the great majority wore dark clothes and caps, had pale faces tending to leanness, and stood somewhere about five foot seven. . . . Clean and dirty – some of them, that is, straight from the factory – of all ages and features, they were pouring in. Some might be loafers, far more were workers. I heard that of one batch of two hundred and fifty at Newcastle, not one was leaving less than two pounds a week.[10]

Some men enlisted in response to external compulsion. Thomas writes:

> Wherever I went I was told that employers – 'the best firms' – were dismissing men, the younger unmarried men, in order to drive them to enlist. 'Not exactly to drive them,' said one, 'but to encourage.'

Yet he also tells of men who, rejected as unfit, returned to recruiting offices time and again until they were accepted. And other sources speak of youngsters under 18 and men over 40 who deliberately misrepresented their ages so as to qualify for enlistment. Moreover, it is difficult to believe that any sort of pressure from employers would have influenced the 30,000 South Wales coal miners who joined up in 1914 and 1915.

A few dissenting voices spoke out against Britain's involvement in the war. Two Cabinet Ministers, John Burns and Lord Morley, resigned office, but they slipped unnoticed from the political scene. A junior Minister, Charles Trevelyan, also left the Government, and Ramsay MacDonald gave up the chairmanship of the Labour Party when it decided to support intervention. But thereafter they both devoted themselves to a campaign to determine how foreign policy should be conducted in the future, and did not agitate for withdrawal from the war. The groups that resisted participation on religious or ideological grounds, such as the Jehovah's Witnesses and the Independent Labour Party, found themselves isolated and largely without influence beyond the confines of their sects.

For Keir Hardie, the man most closely identified with the formation of the Independent Labour Party, the onset of war was a personal tragedy. He had striven for an international socialist movement capable of pre-empting such a conflict. At the test it had collapsed. In the House of Commons on 3 August, following Grey's speech, Hardie threatened the Government with united resistance by the workers. It was a threat that he was not able to implement. Three days later, at a peace meeting in his own Welsh constituency, he was howled down after uttering a few sentences, and the gathering broke up in disorder. Subsequently, working-class audiences in Manchester and elsewhere proved scarcely more friendly.

Under such stress Hardie's position became barely coherent. He proclaimed that the nation must be united when its existence was at stake, and that the lads who had gone forth to fight their country's battles 'must not be disheartened by any discordant note at home'. He also said that before the war could be ended 'the German troops must be thrown back across their own frontier.'[11] Yet, soon after, he himself was

---

[9] *English Review*, October 1914, vol. XVIII, pp. 349–60.

[10] Two pounds a week was a good wage in August 1914. In the building industry at the time weekly wages ranged from 26/11d. for labourers at the bottom to 40/7d. for bricklayers at the top.

[11] Kenneth O. Morgan, *Keir Hardie* (London: Weidenfeld & Nicolson, 1975), pp. 266–7.

sounding many discordant notes. He again denounced the outbreak of the war, asserting that Germany had offered a reasonable compromise over Belgium which Grey had rejected. And he claimed that Russian militarism was a far more dangerous threat to humanity than the might of Germany.

Confronted by the crushing defeat of all he had striven for, and the evident endorsement by the labour rank and file of the Government's actions, Hardie's health, and then his mind, crumbled. He died in September 1915, aged only 59. His passing is referred to with delight in many diaries and letters of the time. In the ensuing by-election for his Welsh constituency the Labour candidate was heavily defeated. The seat went to a working-class jingo ('a Welsh Mussolini who turned as naturally to the advocacy of world war as of class war')[12] who stood without official support. It was a striking (if also rather squalid) demonstration of how deeply founded was the country's support for the struggle.

National unity centred on the person of Lord Kitchener, hero of the Sudan and South Africa. By a master stroke – at least in the short run – he was prevailed upon to accept the post of Secretary of State for War. His imposing figure and proven record in combat rendered him symbolic of the nation's determination to fight.

Yet in truth the nation did not require a figurehead. Its unity was ensured by the circumstances in which the war had broken out, and was reinforced by the events of the ensuing weeks. It goes without saying that some elements in Britain would readily have entered a European war however it had come about. But there were considerable sections of which this was not true. They would have resisted involvement for any but a 'righteous' cause. This the actions of Germany, from beginning to end of August 1914, provided. For the outrage aroused by the invasion of Belgium was powerfully reinforced by the nature of the German assault: the deliberate destruction of towns and cities, and the cold-blooded execution of civilian hostages. During the last weeks of 1914 the *Daily Chronicle* – not one of the more irresponsible journals – published a large illustrated booklet called *In the Trail of the German Army*. It consisted principally of photographs of the destruction wrought in Belgium. The captions throbbed with indignation, but the photographs were real – and eloquent enough. The text consisted of three pages dealing with German violations of the laws and usages of war and four pages devoted to a report by the Belgian Government on German outrages. Again, the tone was one of unsparing condemnation. But there were no inventions. (Many invented stories, alleging outrages against women and children, were certainly in circulation. They would in time secure official endorsement.)

As an atrocity publication *In the Trail of the German Army* seems tame today. And probably, had it recorded events in some 'backward' country, Britons in 1914 would not have waxed too indignant. For the violation of treaties and the destruction of property were not always deemed reprehensible when dealt out by 'civilized' Europeans to the 'uncivilized' members of other races. The point was that Belgium was considered part of the civilized world, with whom the generality of Britons felt identity. Looking at the photographs, it was a straightforward matter to imagine such events occurring at home. It seemed plain that an aggressive power that would inflict these injuries on a small and unoffending neighbour would, at its convenience, do the same to Britain. Here was the mainspring of the wide-ranging revulsion against Germany.

Nor was it long before the war began exacting its toll on British civilians, if only on a trifling scale. The threat from the air took longer to develop than expected. But in December 1914 raiding German cruisers shelled three East Coast towns, causing 700

---

[12] Morgan, *Keir Hardie*, p. 265.

casualties. Churchill epitomized the national indignation when he dubbed the raiders 'baby-killers'. Thereafter the menace from Zeppelins developed gradually. Various places near the coast were bombed in January and April 1915. Then, at the end of May, London received its first raid, with seven killed and 35 injured. The bombs fell in the East End, and next morning well dressed visitors flocked to these poverty-stricken parts of the city to view the damage. (For many it was a first visit. According to Sylvia Pankhurst, impatient passengers on the tops of buses were asking, even before they had passed Bishopsgate: 'Is this the East End?')[13] Between June and October 1915, whereafter the onset of winter caused the raids to cease, German airships visited the country on a further nine occasions. They killed 127 people and injured 352. These night attacks caused much anxiety, as well as the inconvenience of increasingly darkened streets. And, despite the diversion of gunnery and aeroplanes to anti-aircraft activities, there was not the compensation of the destruction of a single Zeppelin over Britain. Yet the infrequency of the raids and the comparative unimportance of the results ensured that they did little or nothing to damage British morale. What they did do was to confirm the popular image of the enemy as an unscrupulous murderer of civilians, to be resisted at all costs.

Plate 12   *A house wrecked at King's Lynn, on the east coast of England, by a Zeppelin raid on 19 January 1915. The raid killed 2 people, injured 30–40, and damaged about 150 homes.*

III

Citizens responded in a variety of ways to the challenge of war. Some of these responses may be deemed worthwhile and even sacrificial; others ranged from the trivial to the contemptible.

The obvious worthwhile response, voluntary enlistment, was open only to men of

---

[13] Pankhurst, *The Home Front*, p. 193.

military age and tolerably good health. Nevertheless, many wives, offspring, parents, and sweethearts were intimately involved in their decision. Sometimes they encouraged or even demanded the enlistment of their menfolk. Sometimes they did the reverse. Sir George Young had a youthful chauffeur whose parents forbade him to enlist, while his lady love threatened him with rejection unless he did so. The departure of men to the front, and to danger, caused intense suffering to many wives and parents and loved ones. But there were also some women, experiencing a measure of freedom and an assured income for the first time, who remarked that they did not mind if their husbands never came back.

Many people not eligible for the forces, including large numbers of females, found creative ways of responding to the war. Thousands of women enrolled for training as Voluntary Aids Detachments under the Red Cross. Others, less adventurous or less independently positioned, knitted and sewed for the troops. (According to a wartime song, 'Sister Susie's sewing shirts for soldiers.') Before long women were finding whole new areas of employment open to them: in munitions factories, in the public services, in government offices. Thus women hitherto familiar only with the domestic round, whether in the homes of parents and husbands or as servants in the houses of others, had a chance to 'do their bit'. Many thereby secured a measure of independence formerly outside their experience. But it would be misleading to glamourize the wearisome, and sometimes dangerous, employment through which, often enough, they gained it. Sylvia Pankhurst recalls:

> Sometimes a woman wrote to me, broken down in health by overwork, complaining of long walks over sodden, impromptu tracks, ankle-deep in mud, to newly-erected factories; of night shifts spent without even the possibility of getting a drink of water; of workers obliged to take their meals amid the dust and fumes of the workshop.

And she quotes a Government committee that reported on the health of munitions workers:

> Family life is impossible. Mothers and grown children make munitions, younger ones suffer neglect at home. In the lodgings of munition workers beds are never empty, rooms are never aired, as day and night shifts prevent this.[14]

A large burden was taken on by those, of both sexes, who set about organizing assistance or providing homes for the 200,000 Belgian refugees who flooded into the country in the first months of the war. Other organizations arranged financial assistance for the dependents of servicemen – not only wives and children awaiting separation allowances but also elderly parents and other dependents for whom, as has been mentioned, no official provision was made until late in 1915.

These activities, and a great many others dealing with war-induced needs, called heavily on private donations of money and goods. In mid-1915 C.F.G. Masterman, an acute social observer and not long since a Liberal Cabinet Minister, discussed this aspect in a survey of 'The Temper of the People'.[15] Quoting 'an observer who has most power of judging', Masterman said that in the opening 10 months of the war some £25 million, in money or in kind, had been donated; 'and this in face of (what no other belligerent nation has ventured to attempt) an immense increase in taxation – the doubling of the income-tax and a huge advance in the Beer and Tea Duties'. (The increase would not look all that immense as the war proceeded. The third war Budget, only two months later, increased income tax another 40 per cent, established an excess

---

[14] Pankhurst, *The Home Front*, p. 278.
[15] *Contemporary Review*, July 1915, vol. 108, pp. 1–11.

profits tax, and raised the duties on a whole range of consumer goods.) These donations, according to Masterman, came from all classes: 'with regular subscriptions by the weekly wage-earners – in Birmingham alone (for example) 20,000 of such wage-earners contributing their weekly pence; in Northumberland and Durham the trade unionists voting a weekly levy on wages for the trade unionists of Belgium'. On the Clyde and in Glasgow also, according to his informant, nothing was more remarkable than 'the regularity and the amounts paid by the workers themselves towards one or other of these national purposes'.

This spirit of service did not flag as the protracted nature of the struggle became apparent. Some change in attitude, certainly, did occur. Many offers of private accommodation for Belgian refugees were withdrawn once it became evident that this might prove a long and costly business. And many middle-class young women, having embarked on voluntary charitable work, were driven by changing economic circumstances to seek paid employment. But overall the community met the challenge of war-induced needs. In mid-1915 accounts began reaching Britain of the parlous conditions of many prisoners of war in Germany. Thenceforth, to the war's end, local committees acting through the Red Cross devotedly sent parcels to POWs on the basis of three parcels, each weighing 10 lbs, per man per fortnight. There were also comforts for troops at the front. The Christmas of 1915, it has been said, was the greatest parcel-sending time of the war. Unofficial committees came to the aid of families not familiar with such matters as the proper wrapping and addressing of gifts for serving soldiers. Even more important, these bodies collected money so as to ensure that every soldier from a district, however friendless or bereft of family, would receive at least one parcel at Christmas.

Another activity that involved members of the community in the expenditure of time and sometimes money was recruiting. Some individuals bore the cost of raising and equipping a battalion, as did the lord mayor of Leeds in the case of that city's 'Pals' Battalion. And a great many prominent people threw themselves into the task of addressing meetings and organizing recruiting activities. MPs of differing parties sank their animosities to the extent of appearing jointly on platforms arranged by the Parliamentary Recruiting Committee. Local identities appealed to their communities in their own languages – sometimes quite literally, as when Brigadier General Owen Thomas inaugurated in North Wales a campaign in the vernacular that had fortuitous results. In the same area the chairman of the Denbighshire recruiting committee early in the spring of 1915 set about establishing a register of every man in the county aged between 18 and 41. (He graded them according to age, employment, and physical defects, and starred those in essential industries.) He also compiled a register of women capable of serving on the land, in hospitals, or in munitions factories.[16] This proceeding, which was referred to Downing Street, foreshadowed – and may well have influenced – the introduction of the National Register and the Derby recruiting scheme in the later part of 1915.

The recruiting meeting served a dual purpose. It helped to replenish the ranks of the forces once the early rush to the colours had ebbed. And it stimulated enthusiasm for the struggle among rank-and-file citizens. Many recruiters, certainly, had little but their zeal to recommend them. Their utterances were shallow and cheaply emotive. And the endeavours of some hardly deserve to be classified as responses to the war except in the most self-regarding sense. They were less patriots than demagogues –

---

[16] See Ivor Nicholson and Trevor Lloyd-Williams (eds.), *Wales: Its Part in the War* (London: Hodder and Stoughton, n.d.), pp. 30–2.

and even money-grubbers – on the make. The journalist, political aspirant, bankrupt, and embezzler Horatio Bottomley was only the most extreme instance of a man who used the recruiting meeting as a vehicle for both self-advertisement and the acquisition of hard cash.

In more ways than this the patriotic spirit sometimes manifested itself in actions that were vicious or futile. One may instance the mania about spies, egged on by crude journalism like 'The Kaiser's Eyes' in the *Daily Express* for 29 September 1914; or the campaign against persons, places, and even commodities bearing German names; or the vendettas against members of the Government suspected, on pitiful grounds, of harbouring pro-German sympathies; or the ban introduced in some musical quarters on the performance of German compositions.

In truth, war gave believers in the doctrine of national superiority unusual opportunities to indulge in the practice of national hate. In October the devoted First Sea Lord, Prince Louis of Battenberg (whose misfortune it was to have been born in Austria and to be the son of a German prince), was forced to resign by a public outcry. Some weeks earlier his younger son, then aged 14 and a naval cadet at Osborne, had written home:

> What d'you think the latest rumour that got in here from outside is? That Papa has turned out to be a German spy & has been discreetly marched off to the tower, where he is guarded by beefeaters. . . . I got rather a rotten time of it for about three days as little fools . . . insisted on calling me German Spy & kept on heckling me & trying to make things unpleasant for me. . . .[17]

Such xenophobic outbursts were evident at all social levels. In early May 1915, following the sinking of the *Lusitania*, several Stock Exchanges decided to expel members of German birth, even when they were naturalized British subjects. And in the poorer quarters of London crowds rampaged against people of German and Austrian origin. These were ugly events. Shops were looted and wrecked. And the victims, according to the *Annual Register for 1915*, were in 'considerable danger'. In fact, for a day or more afterwards there was a bread famine in east and south London, owing to the large number of bakers among this persecuted group. These outbursts forced the Government to act – but against the recipients of violence not its instigators. Sir Maurice Hankey noted in his diary: 'Govt. decided to intern alien enemies owing to riots – as I had urged months before.' (However, Asquith's ministry did refuse, unless on grounds shown, to do the same to those who had taken out British naturalization.)

The Government's action did not, at least immediately, end such disorders. There were further vicious scenes in the East End of London following an air raid of 31 May in which seven died, and in Hull following a raid on 5 June which claimed no casualties. Sylvia Pankhurst witnessed incidents in the Hoxton district of London, the dreariest and most violent part of the East End in her considerable experience. ('In Hoxton Street I have more than once seen women fighting – a thing I have never witnessed in any other part of the East End.') She saw a yelling crowd dragging along 'a big, stout man, stumbling and resisting . . . , his clothes whitened by flour, his mouth dripping blood'. A woman was knocked to the ground and kicked by the crowd, and when Sylvia Pankhurst appealed to an army officer in a motor vehicle to intervene she was told 'I don't think we can; we are on military business.' (Fortunately, when it was realized that the woman was unconscious, the wrath of her attackers subsided.) Another man, also in flour-covered clothing, was being baited by a mob, who wrenched and jerked at his collar, thumped him on the back, and kicked him from the rear. '"All

---

[17] Richard Hough, *Louis and Victoria* (London: Hutchinson, 1974), p. 300.

Plate 13 *Anti-German rioting in London. A crowd breaking in the windows of a German-owned shop.*

right, Gov'ner; all right," he articulated between the blows, in humble and reasoning Cockney-tones.' Miss Pankhurst – who, it should be noted, utterly disapproved of the war – concluded sadly: 'Alas, poor Patriotism, what foolish cruelties are committed in thy name!'[18]

If xenophobia was one of the war's least healthy products, credulity was another. It was not just that people circulated, and even believed, the tale that late in August 1914 large numbers of Russian troops passed through Britain on their way to the Western Front. The story was upheld by a great many professed eye-witnesses, who supported it with graphic details. Sir George Young was converted to belief in the tale by no less a person than Sir Courtenay Ilbert, clerk of the House of Commons, who found the accounts too circumstantial to reject. Equally, the story of the angels who saved the British line at Mons was embraced tenaciously by people who omitted to ask why these angels were failing to make a badly needed second appearance. A clergyman who wrote to a religious periodical casting doubt on the probability of this tale was accused of revealing infirmity of faith.

Possibly these outbursts prove only that xenophobia and credulity lie close to the surface of affairs at any time. War legitimizes manifestations that would not normally be acceptable. But, plainly, this war was doing more than that. It was placing upon people a sort of pressure that caused them readily to lapse into superstition. And it was spurring them to action in circumstances that sometimes provided no opportunities for worthwhile deeds. Hence they resorted to behaviour which was purposeless and even cruel.

IV

If the war had established a large measure of national unity, that unity overlay, but did not suppress, standing forces of internal division. Anti-feminists drew strength from a

---

[18] Pankhurst, *The Home Front*, pp. 193–5.

situation in which only the male of the species could make a full contribution. One Anglo-Catholic cleric (writes Stuart Mews) came 'close to suggesting that the war itself was a divine retribution for the increasing rejection by women of their traditional role'.[19] And from early in the war such people were jumping to the conclusion that not all females were mending their ways. Much was said about sexual laxity among young women living near army camps, with a consequential crop of 'war babies' – an outcry soon dampened by the discovery that there had been no dramatic increase in ex-nuptial births. And complaints were raised about the manner in which soldiers' wives were drinking to excess – thanks, according to Canon E. A. Burroughs, to 'heedlessly liberal' separation allowances. In the view of this cleric, eighteen shillings a week and no husband were 'heaven' to women who, once 'industrious and poor', were now 'wealthy and idle'. 'And "heaven" for such people is too often hard by the public-house; largely because the latter is the normal receptacle of spare cash and they have few other ideas of spending.' (It is a fair guess that such spokesmen knew precious little about the drinking habits of working-class women in peacetime. A report by the National Society for the Prevention of Cruelty to Children in January 1915, based on information supplied by its inspectors, concluded that female drunkenness had declined since August 1914 and that the charges against soldiers' wives were 'a great slander'.)

If attitudes towards the sexes remained unchanged, and the war provided fresh opportunities to harp on old themes, the same was true regarding antipathies between social groups. Among the middle and upper classes there was much readiness to believe in, and deplore, a supposed lack of enthusiasm for the national cause among the working classes. From this were drawn appropriate class conclusions, as when (according to Masterman) the headmaster of a great public school attributed 'the "prevailing apathy" of the lower classes in this war to the fact that they have not received that training in character which the public schools alone can give'. The reverse side of this particular coin was the eager acceptance by workers of tales about widespread profiteering. Masterman wrote in July 1915: 'the workman has been told, and undoubtedly believes, up and down the country, that some employers and traders are making vast profits out of his necessities. The facts may be true or false; the belief in the facts is indisputable.'[20]

In politics also traditional antipathies persisted into wartime. By the outbreak of the war the Home Rule Bill, having passed the House of Commons on three occasions, was free of the shackles of the Upper House and required only the royal assent to make it law. The Government decided to place the measure on the statute book but to suspend its operation. It also promised safeguards for Ulster. This seemed meagre enough return for the Irish Nationalists' gesture of support. But it looked otherwise to the opponents of Home Rule. The Conservative leader was moved to a paroxysm of wrath and led his followers in a walk-out from Parliament.

The Government attempted something similar for the measure disestablishing and disendowing the Anglican Church in Wales. This too was to become law but was not to come into effect until six months after the war. On this occasion it was the supposed beneficiaries, the Welsh Nonconformists, who were outraged. They believed that the delay might constitute a fatal concession. The only prominent Welshman in the Government, Lloyd George, felt the strength of their wrath. It may have encouraged him into some ill-judged actions.

---

[19] Stuart Mews, 'Urban Problems and Rural Solutions: Drink and Disestablishment in the First World War', in Derek Baker (ed.), *The Church in Town and Countryside* (Oxford: Oxford University Press, 1979), pp. 452–3. The quotations in this paragraph are drawn from Dr Mews's article.
[20] Masterman, 'The Temper of the People'.

A month before this issue arose Lloyd George, speaking at Bangor, had deplored the effects of excessive drinking on the workmanship and time-keeping of the labour force. But it was only when confronting the anger of his Welsh followers on the disestablishment issue that he came out not just for admonition but for bold action on that other question dear to their hearts: liquor. On 29 March, the day before a crucial meeting of Welsh MPs, he announced: 'We are fighting Germans, Austrians and Drink, and so far as I can see the greatest of these deadly foes is Drink.' To defeat it, he proposed state purchase and control of the entire drink traffic. (It cannot be said that Lloyd George was single-minded in his views. A month later, in private conversation, he attributed the shortages of ships and shells principally to Government mismanagement. 'The idea that slackness and drink, which some people talk so much about, are the chief causes of delays, is mostly fudge.')[21]

Lloyd George's bold move was not a success. He did prevail upon the King to foreswear alcohol for the duration. This did not actually mean that George V gave up all drinking; 'under doctor's orders' he imbibed a certain amount, but only in private – a restriction he felt keenly.[22] But neither MPs nor bishops were inclined to follow this ostensible lead. The Bishop of Durham noted soon after: 'We drank champagne in spite of the King's example.' As for the idea of launching the state into the purchase and administration of the liquor industry, if it pleased some temperance advocates, it appalled others. And it certainly found no favour in 'the trade' or among orthodox economists. Nor did suspicion of Lloyd George and the Government abate among Welsh members. So the scheme for state purchase lapsed. And the offending measure to suspend unduly the disestablishment of the Welsh Church had to be withdrawn.

The persistence of these divisive issues and attitudes does not bespeak disunity on the central issue: the nation's involvement in war. But, at least in some respects, such controversies reflect the ethos of 'business as usual'. One part of the nation, the fighting part, would be totally involved in the waging of war. The other part might make a contribution, as in caring for refugees and donating to war charities; but for non-combatants generally life was expected to go on much as before. Even more, the new fact of war proved capable of being pressed into the service of old principles, beliefs, and prejudices: about class, or religion, or politics, or the roles of the sexes. The war would have to go on a good deal longer before its pressures would cause these things – and then only some of them – to change even a little.

'The truth is', wrote R. H. Gretton a decade after the end of the conflict, 'that through all the first period of the war to the early summer of 1915 the view of the British public was that the fighting part of the war, so to speak, was a professional business, and that the national part was backing up.' Britain, he concluded, was 'not a nation at war, but a nation supporting and encouraging part of itself at war'.[23] The contrast between the two parts is brought out in a letter of October 1914 written by Holcombe Ingleby, a Conservative MP,[24] to his son, a lieutenant in the Royal Naval Volunteer Reserve, at the time interned in Holland. Ingleby makes it clear that the family was doing all that could be expected of non-combatants: 'Our Belgians are rather nice & give no sort of trouble. Your mother is busy all day & every day with the Soldiers & Sailors' Assn. & is rapidly becoming a sort of Mrs Jellaby!' Nevertheless, he was aware of the limitations of the civilian contribution: 'I feel rather ashamed of myself to be doing so much partridge shooting at this critical time. But really, when you

---

[21] Christopher Addison, *Four and a Half Years* (London: Hutchinson, 1934), vol. 1, p. 73.
[22] Mews, 'Urban Problems and Rural Solutions', p. 476.
[23] R. H. Gretton, *A Modern History of the English People 1880–1922* (London: Martin Secker, 1930), p. 935.
[24] Ingleby's letters are in the Imperial War Museum.

are over 60, you are apt to be off the active list. Of course I address meetings & discourse eloquently on one's duty to one's country but it doesn't amount to much!'

In other words, more than business was continuing as usual well into 1915. The hunt after partridges went on: 'the shooting has been extraordinarily good this year,' Ingleby wrote 12 months after the above-quoted letter. Other forms of sport persisted: if not county cricket, then certainly racing and football. Some objection, admittedly, was raised to this last activity, on account of its attraction for working-class males who, it was considered, ought to have been in uniform. *Punch* in January 1915 dubbed football results 'The Shirkers' War News'. And Sir George Young wrote to his son Hilton, serving in the navy: 'The scandal of professional football, with the huge "gates" of loafing lads as spectators, is beginning to raise an outcry. How slow we English are!' The complaint, he added, was not against the educated and leisured classes; 'but among the poor and ignorant, the uprising of the proper spirit is slow work'.[25]

Yet football went on. So, with fewer public complaints, did many of the diversions of the leisured wealthy. In addition to partridge shooting and horse-racing, there was much good eating, lavish dressing, and gossiping. Hankey records in his diary for 27 April 1915 that he lunched at Ciro's Club, the 'latest fashion freak restaurant'. In the company were Mrs George Keppel, Reginald McKenna and his wife, and Hilaire Belloc. (Belloc was at the time considered something of a pundit on war matters. His reputation did not long survive his persistent errors of judgement.) The conversation at Ciro's Club was mainly devoted to Churchill and the Dardanelles. Hankey was subject to much 'fishing' about the doings of the War Council but kept his mouth firmly shut. 'Some of these women', he noted sourly, 'talk too much *and* know too much!' In mid-June Hankey was present at E. S. Montagu's residence to meet the political secretaries to Asquith, Balfour, and Kitchener ('the "real Cabinet" as the Asquiths call it"): 'Late in the evening a bevy of Montagu's society friends came in for supper, fearfully made up and rather over-dressed . . . there was a general exodus of "the real cabinet".' Soon after, Montagu was telling the nation that it would have to stint on consumption and must limit its extravagant spending on luxuries. Asquith too discoursed in public on the necessity for personal economy – a homily that some felt accorded ill with reports of his own daughter's lavish wedding.

Such instances of high living continued to the end of 1915 and beyond. In the first week of January 1916 Lady Scott found herself in the company of two visiting Serbs, a Government Minister and his military attaché. Hunger was much on the visitors' minds, for they related how the Italians were commandeering food intended for starving Serbs. Yet it was thought appropriate to dine these visitors at the Carlton and then to repair to the Pavilion, where the show, apart from an outstanding dancer, was 'appalling'. Lady Scott commented: 'It was I know rather terrible to those Servians to see hundreds of people eating oysters & drinking champagne & then going on to these asinine performances.'[26]

The people who behaved thus were not, as a rule, repudiating the war, only seeking to preserve as much of 'normal' life as possible. Nevertheless, in all classes there were some who went a good deal further. In so far as circumstances permitted, they turned their backs on the conflict. Those best known for doing so were the articulate: in particular, the members of literary circles that did not just shy away from the war but consciously refused to acknowledge it. Prominent among these was the Bloomsbury

[25] Sir George Young to Hilton Young, 28 November 1914, Kennet papers.

[26] Lady Scott's diary, 6 January 1916, Kennet papers. Lady Scott, the sculptor and widow of the Antarctic explorer, married Hilton Young (later Lord Kennet) in 1922. She was an acquaintance of Asquith, who in the latter part of 1915 and during 1916 used to discuss at length his political problems with her.

group. The war did violence to 'all they had stood for, the new age of tolerance and enlightenment inaugurated in G. E. Moore's Cambridge'.[27] Their response is indicated by a letter of Vanessa Bell, written in April 1915. It was addressed to Hilton Young, a Liberal MP now serving with the Grand Fleet, who had been on the fringes of Bloomsbury since coming down from Cambridge. The epistle was intended, Vanessa wrote, for someone who did not want to hear anything about the war (which is presumably the sort of letter Young had requested). Certainly, it reflects the ostentatious refusal of Bloomsbury to render the international struggle even nominal obeisance:

> We spent a very gay winter in London – far gayer than usual. Ottoline [Morrell] – do you know her? – took it upon herself to keep us all merry & gave a party every week, at which you might see Bertie Russell dancing a horn-pipe with Titi (Hawtrey's young woman)[,] Lytton & Oliver & Marjorie Strachey cutting capers to each other, Duncan [Grant] dancing in much the same way that he paints, John & Arnold Bennett & all the celebrities of the day looking as beautiful as they could in clothes seized from Ottoline's drawers – & Ottoline herself at the head of a troup of short haired young ladies from the Slade prancing about . . . . you can imagine us doing that every Thursday evening. Then we spent another evening reading plays which is a very good way of spending an evening – & another listening to Belgian music at the Omega which wasnt always such a good way. When we had had about enough of all this we came here to a funny little house by the sea, where Duncan is at this moment our only visitor. Here we live without newspapers – at least they come at moments when I at any rate can ignore them – & no horrors of any kinds.[28]

Living without regard to newspapers was the essential condition of those who refused to recognize the war.

V

As 1915 proceeded the gulf between the two sections of the nation – the fighting part, and the part that backed up the fighters or chose not to – was diminishing. It remained wide. But it was narrowing perceptibly.

Among many people who, by virtue of age or sex, would never don uniform, a great dread was forming. They now had to confront the possibility that loved ones, who until quite recently had seemed unlikely ever to participate in battle, might soon be dead. For many generations, fighting had been no part of the life experience of ordinary Britons. And in the first phase of this war its toll had fallen principally on the regular army, the rank and file of which belonged to a particular, decidedly lowly, socio-economic group. From now on, to a noteworthy degree, the battlefield would be exacting its casualties from a different social stratum.

Something of the difference is suggested by a letter of September 1915 written by Robert Saunders, a schoolmaster in Sussex, to his eldest son in Canada:[29] 'You would find a great change everywhere in England as regards the attitude towards soldiers since the war broke out. Everyone tries to do all they can for them.' Saunders indicates the reason for the change: 'the majority of them are from decent homes' (which no one would have said of most regulars) and were finding camp life 'very hard'; 'and those who had boys of their own naturally set the example in welcoming other peoples boys.'

By the time Saunders wrote this the first of Kitchener's recruits were beginning to

---

[27] P. N. Furbank, *E. M. Forster: A Life*, one-volume edition but retaining page numbering as in two volumes (Oxford: Oxford University Press, 1979), vol. 2, p.1.

[28] Vanessa Bell to Young, 15 April [1915], Kennet papers.

[29] The Saunders letters are in the Imperial War Museum.

move to Flanders, and 'decent homes' increasingly had a personal concern in the course of the war. Saunders had three sons serving, one in India, one in the navy, and one (Ron, aged 18) on the Western Front. In mid-October he wrote of the anxiety they were feeling: 'Every day there are the terrible lists of casualties that you feel you must look through, and then you are always hearing of someone you know who is missing, wounded, or killed, and you can't help feeling, sometimes that Ron's turn may come as well. . . .' He related the names of several lads, known to them or from their district, who were among the killed or missing. They included a young man named Paine, who when last seen was cut off and being bombed by Germans. 'Poor Carrie Paine's letter to Ma about it was heartbreaking.' This letter so heightened Mrs Saunders's anxiety over her own son in France that, Saunders recounted, 'this morning [she] had to come out of Church during the Service.'

Even for those who adopted the stance of wishing to have nothing to do with the war, the pressure to make some contribution might prove irresistible. One who succumbed, at least in a measure, was the novelist E. M. Forster. In a personal sense he was a conscientious objector. That is, he simply could not participate in the taking of life. But he did not generalize from this. He regarded someone who enlisted as his superior (or anyway said he did). To Hilton Young, in March 1915, he too wrote a letter of non-involvement.[30] 'Since I failed to come with you to the Scapa Flow I have done nothing for Britain, and now that my cup of shame is full have an increasing tendency to throw it in her face.' He was working four days a week at the National Gallery and spending the other three on literary projects and journalism, or listening to César Franck's Violin Sonata, or pursuing a stormy friendship with D. H. Lawrence ('mit frau').

Yet Forster was not managing wholly to stand aside. He and his mother felt called on to offer hospitality to refugees. The first was a Belgian, who proved unsatisfactory. Mrs Forster complained that he ate up all the marmalade and never stopped playing the piano. Undeterred, they tried again. This time they secured 'a *v.* nice Armenian . . . recovering from a complexity of diseases'. Simultaneously Forster was being harassed to put on uniform. Among his tormentors was the mother of his old school friend William Beveridge. Forster severed relations with her after receiving a hectoring letter. In May he became ill, 'able to think of nothing but young men killing one another while old men praised them.'[31]

Soon Forster was seeking about for some non-combatant work at the front. In November he left England for Egypt, to take up a position as a Red Cross 'searcher'. This meant interviewing wounded soldiers about comrades who had gone missing in action and of whom no more was known. (There Forster would spend the rest of the war. By a fine piece of irony, one of his reports was printed by the jingoistic press lord Northcliffe in *At the War*, with the encomium that it exemplified the 'labour of love' by which the Red Cross were 'easing the sorest wounds of warfare'.)[32] So, though he had failed to go with Hilton Young to Scapa Flow, Forster soon found himself 'doing something for Britain'.

The timing of his doing so was, from his own viewpoint, felicitous. For by November 1915 the right of deciding whether or not to join the armed services was slipping away from men of military age. This meant that, in a very direct way, the war was impinging on an increasing number of families. The achievement of voluntary recruiting in the first year of the war had been prodigious. As Asquith told the House of Commons in mid-September 1915, 'not far short of three millions of men, first and last . . . had

[30] Kennet papers.
[31] Furbank, *E. M. Forster: A Life*, vol. 2, p. 18.
[32] Ibid., pp. 23–4.

Plates 14a and 14b   *Two stages on the road to conscription.*

14a   *Filling up the National Register form in a common lodging house.*

offered themselves to the country.' What Asquith did not go on to say was that the voluntary system had now shot its bolt. Either the army must cease getting men on any but a trivial scale or it must get them by other means.

Well before this situation developed some official recruiting activities were exceeding authorized forms of appeal. From Fletching in Sussex, Robert Saunders wrote in June: 'On Saturday a big motor with an important official and a Recruiting Sergeant came round to the houses where men of military age had not joined [,] so they are beginning to look up the slackers.' The deed (which can hardly have been legal) was ominous enough. Even more so was the term used to describe those who exercised their right not to volunteer. Even to a fairly tolerant man like Saunders, who supported the voluntary system, those tardy about enlisting were 'shirkers' or 'slackers'.

In August came the National Register. This compelled every citizen aged 16 to 65, male and female, to supply details of age, sex, and occupation. And it gave respondents the opportunity to state whether they could and would perform work of national importance. Supposedly it was a census of the nation's human resources, not a prelude to conscription. But as Walter Long, the Conservative Minister who introduced the Bill to Parliament, said on 5 July, it would afford the necessary information if the need for conscription did arise. And although it compelled nobody to serve on the battlefield or in the factory, added Long, 'it will compel them to declare that they are doing nothing to help their country in her hour of crisis.'

The National Register was no sooner gathered (an undertaking that required the services of thousands of unpaid distributors and collectors) than it was being employed to test the voluntary system of recruiting. In October the Derby recruiting scheme was launched. It drew from the Register the identity of every eligible male not engaged in essential work. Each was then approached, by letter and in person, to 'attest' under the scheme: that is, to affirm his willingness to accept military service when called upon to

14b   *Woman clerks taking particulars of men 'attesting' their willingness to join up under the Derby scheme.*

do so. This form of canvass was no small undertaking. For example, in Leeds some 42,000 men were revealed by the Register to fall into the eligible category: they were of military age, had not enlisted, and were not employed in essential occupations. No fewer than 99 per cent of these reluctants were canvassed, many more than once. Altogether in Leeds volunteer recruiters paid 200,000 visits, chiefly in the evening and often in inclement weather. The whole endeavour, as had been made clear at the outset, was 'the last effort on behalf of voluntary service'.

VI

In one interesting respect, the opening weeks of December 1915 were akin to the opening weeks of August 1914. The recruiting offices were doing a roaring trade. Men queued for long hours to enlist. The medical services were overwhelmed. Some recruiting stations stayed open all night.

But the similarity was largely illusory. The nature of the transaction was not the same in the seventeenth month of the war as in the first. Married men attesting under the Derby scheme had an assurance that they would not be called up until the turn of their particular class came around. And the class to which they were assigned, although based partly on age, was primarily a matter of marital status. An undertaking had been given that no attested married man would be called up until all eligible bachelors had entered the services, voluntarily or against their will. No such stay of execution would apply once the Derby scheme closed on 12 December. Thereafter both single and married men, either volunteering or being compelled to enlist, would be liable for immediate call-up. So it is a nice point whether the married men who crowded the recruiting stations in early December were indicating their eagerness to serve or their desire to delay serving until the last possible moment.

Even the single men who joined at this time were hardly making a free decision. It had been stated quite explicitly, by both the Prime Minister and Lord Derby (the Director-General of Recruiting), that the choice before these bachelors was only voluntary enlistment or compulsory enlistment. G. H. Hardy, a Cambridge academic, recalls that under the Derby scheme 'hundreds of thousands "volunteered" because they regarded conscription as certain and supposed (quite wrongly) that voluntary attestation would entitle them to preferential treatment. I can say this the more easily as a "Derby man" myself.'[33]

In the large majority of cases the men who came forward at this late stage, like those who even now held back, were not opponents of the war. They wanted it to be won. What they did not want was themselves to run a severe risk of being killed or maimed – which, it had become quite evident, was a likely fate of those delegated to win it. Young men taxed with their failure to enlist were reported not as expressing a refusal to serve but as offering temporizing replies: 'I will wait until I am fetched' or 'I am quite ready to go when we are all called, but I don't see why I should give up my job when Tom is allowed to stick to his.'[34]

The Derby plan was designed so to press these reluctants that the authorities would be saved the unpleasantness, and the possible divisiveness, of actually doing the fetching. It failed in its object. In the last days of 1915, when the figures of attested men were set against the statistics provided by the National Register, it became apparent that a significant number of bachelors preferred still to delay enlistment until the authorities came to take them.

This was only one matter that rendered gloomy the closing weeks of the year. In no respect was the war proceeding in a way that could be deemed thoroughly satisfactory. In several the course of the year had been marked by calamity. The reputations of revered leaders had been seriously tarnished. The manner in which the military situation might be redeemed without terrible cost was difficult to envisage.

Yet in all these causes for unease there was nothing decisive. At sea Britain's command was unchallenged. On land, in terms of the marshalling of its manpower and its industrial resources, the nation had scarcely begun to fight. Holcombe Ingleby, in a letter of Christmas Day 1915 to his son, summed up the pros and cons of the war and found them not particularly good. But, he went on: 'every one is quietly content to persevere – even unto the end. One never hears a murmur in England – which is really wonderful.'

---

[33] G. H. Hardy, 'Bertrand Russell & Trinity', printed for the author at the University Press, Cambridge, 1942.
[34] Armitage, *Leicester 1914–1918*, p. 86; *Nation* (New York), 30 September 1915.

16

ECHOES OF THE WAR IN AN ENGLISH VILLAGE: GREAT LEIGHS, ESSEX, IN THE FIRST YEAR OF THE CONFLICT

I

On 22 January 1915, in the account he was keeping of his impressions of the war, the Rev. Andrew Clark of Great Leighs, Essex, wrote that everything around them was a constant reminder of war. This seems an exaggeration.

In addition to being the representative of the Established Church in a small Essex village, Clark had wider contacts. He was an examiner for Oxford University and visited there regularly. He also had acquaintances who brought him details of happenings in various Essex towns and elsewhere, and a relative who wrote often from Scotland. Anything bearing on the war that he gleaned from informants – as distinct from newspapers and official bulletins – he set down in a series of large volumes.[1] Much of his narrative, it must be said, amounts to pretty small beer. But it does suggest the war experience, direct and indirect, of both a particular member and a tiny sector of the home front.

II

One thing emerging plainly from Clark's record is that, from early in the war, England was beset by rumours. A populace eager for drama fed readily on improbable tales, whether chilling or reassuring in nature. (The fact that Clark set them down is not necessarily evidence that he himself gave them much credence.) There were several tales of aliens planted long since in key parts of the country to poison the water supply of large urban centres. One Great Leighs mother heard from her daughter, in domestic service in London, that five foreigners had been seized attempting to poison the great reservoir at Chingford, Essex, from which London drew much of its water. The following day a further missive from the daughter placed the number of villains at six. All had been convicted and shot. In another story a leading chemist in Braintree, Essex, was asked for poison by a foreigner. The chemist kept his customer waiting long enough for the police to be summoned and to remove the suspect.

Clark also heard the tale, already noted, that Prince Louis of Battenberg was being

---

[1] These are to be found in the Bodleian Library, Oxford, where they were unearthed for me by Dr Philip Bull.

held prisoner on suspicion of espionage. In his version, Battenberg had as companions in the Tower such luminaries as Princess Henry of Pless, the financial magnate Sir Ernest Cassel, and Mrs G. Cornwallis-West, 'a Society person'.[2] Clark also picked up a number of those widely circulated stories about Russian troops having landed on the coast of Yorkshire. According to his informants, all East Coast trains had been commandeered to speed the Russians on their journey to France. A surgeon in Braintree was able to affirm that the visitors had been fed in Colchester on 30 August. This medico also put forward the view that the naval action in the Heligoland Bight had resulted from an attempt by the Germans to intercept them. Again, Clark was assured that the whereabouts in Britain had been established of Belgian girls and Belgian babies whose hands had been hacked off by German soldiers.

A rumour that caused much perturbation in Essex concerned a 'tragic happening' at the Marconi works in Chelmsford, an institution that was seen as a key target for saboteurs. On 5 November it was said that one of the sentries guarding the works had been shot dead. He was supposedly the victim of German agents in a motor car, and hasty telephoning had prompted troops to close all outlets from Chelmsford. The next day a less colourful account supervened. Apparently the alarm had arisen from the accidental discharge of a revolver. No one had been hurt, and no sentry had been shot at; nevertheless, the alarm had spread like wildfire. Clark noted: 'People are nervous, owing to the alarmist instructions issued by the police, and the absence of any satisfactory precautions.' (According to this view, the police seem to have been in error both in trying to take precautions and in not taking them.)

Great Leighs managed to generate some ill-founded tales of its own. On 18 August there occurred, quite unexpectedly, a march through the village of a brigade of Territorials in full equipment. The children from both the church and the council schools were speedily sent to vantage points to witness the spectacle. ('There's never been a sight like that in Great Leighs,' stated Old Collins, whom Clark described as an ex-under-gamekeeper and the village patriarch.) But the long trek from Chelmsford in great heat severely affected two of the regiments, which the next day were able to make very little progress; and popular imagination fed on their infirmity. Two days after the march Clark noted a report that two of the Territorials were dead, one of pneumonia and one of blood poisoning after having a foot crushed by a horse. Both fatalities proved to be fictitious. Clark subsequently learned that the soldier supposedly dead of pneumonia was back with his regiment, and the man with the damaged foot was able to get about.

Given the excitable mood of the country, this was clearly not a good time to have either an occupation or a name out of the ordinary. Clark records that members of the Royal Commission on Ancient Sites and Buildings, visiting outlying farms and houses in the vicinity of Great Leighs in September 1914, found themselves viewed with suspicion amounting to violence. 'By the life of Pharaoh, Ye are spies!' was a text that summed up the popular attitude. The following month, in the neighbouring parish of Great Waltham, the reviser of the Ordnance Survey was, in the space of a few days, arrested six times as a spy by special constables, and finally had to implore protection from a local Justice of the Peace, Colonel Tufnell. Meanwhile at Little Waltham the schoolmaster was unwise enough to complain that soldiers had damaged the school's piano. The piano proved to be of German origin, whereupon the soldiers took to

---

[2] All but the last-named presumably qualified for inclusion in popular demonology by virtue of their German or Austrian origins. Mrs Cornwallis-West, a prominent figure in Welsh landed society, was of Irish birth. (She was subsequently to figure in a considerable wartime scandal. It concerned not espionage but her passion for a young wounded officer of upright character who resisted her advances.)

deriding him as 'the pro-German' and to jeering at 'the great care he takes of the Kaiser's goods'.

Clark's correspondence also includes several missives from firms with un-British names seeking to establish their patriotic credentials and purposes. One of particular note came from the wine merchants Ehrmann Brothers. They were disadvantaged by both occupation and name. As has been noted, the war produced many exhortations that people should demonstrate their patriotism by abstaining from luxuries, not least alcohol. Ehrmann Brothers argued that, at the reasonable prices they were charging, their goods were not 'luxuries'. They also held that the 'panic economies advocated in certain quarters' were as undesirable as the 'panic hoarding of cash or foodstuffs', because 'unessential economies by the well-to-do' caused 'unemployment, suffering and penury' among the labouring classes. Anyway, a little drink was good for the health:

> Moderate use of sound wholesome wine is at all times beneficial, specially during a time of stress and anxiety. It and the following of customary healthy habits, enable us to pass through such a period with little of the nerve-racked wear and tear to which the total abstainer is subject.

The case for imbibing as usual could hardly have been put more seductively.

Ehrmann Brothers' second problem concerned their name. To offset it they described themselves as 'Supplier to His Majesty's Flagships and Royal Navy'. They also issued the following disclaimer:

> *Notice* – To prevent misconception, we beg to say that ours is an English firm, and all members thereof are British Subjects, and none Subjects of any Foreign State. The whole of our large staff is British.
> While we own vineyard property *in France*, and are financially interested in businesses *in France*, we own no property and have no interests in Germany or Austria.

A similar repudiation of alien origins reached Clark from the furniture and china shop of Oetzmann & Co., of Tottenham Court Road:

> The Directors of *Oetzmann & Co. Ltd.* beg to announce that the business was *founded in 1848* by the late John R. Oetzmann a British-Born Subject and that the Directors, Shareholders and Staff are all British Subjects.

And even Boot's the Chemist thought it desirable to state 'The Truth about Eau de Cologne'. This commodity, it was affirmed, did not come from Köln or anywhere else in Germany. It was of purely British make.

III

From correspondents, verbal informants, and his own observations Clark received indications of the war's early impact on a number of communities other than Great Leighs. Many districts experienced the billeting of soldiers during this period when the forces were being assembled for France and camps were not yet available. Not all communities relished the experience. From Bedford came an account of the billeting of Scottish troops, many of whom were fisher folk and 'smelt as if they had never washed. It was just awful for the poor people in whose cottages they were billeted.'

Chelmsford also was not happy with the conduct of a Territorial division of the Warwickshires. These were reported as having behaved in a disgraceful manner; not only men but officers had been seen drunk in the streets night after night. It was suggested that the offenders consisted of that section of the Territorials who had declined overseas service, and who were therefore 'the scum of the county'. However, another account reached Clark that suggested that there were faults on both sides: that Chelmsford, being 'a thoroughly illiterate place', with the conceit of a county town when it was not one, had proved very unfriendly to its visitors. The citizens, in this view, were 'possessed with the idea that all men who enlist are the waifs and strays who enlisted in the old evil days of the army. They have not yet awoke to the fact that the men of the new army are gentlemanly fellows, and expect gentlemanly treatment.'

The experience of neighbouring Braintree was much happier. Even here the strain of constant billeting began to tell; yet when a body of Notts and Derby soldiers departed, tears were shed among the townfolk. ('The men have been extremely popular.')

The war, Clark learned from his brother-in-law, John Paterson, brought an early transformation to the small village of Cupar Fife, near St Andrews on the east coast of Scotland. Ten days after the start of the conflict Paterson wrote that these were stirring times for Cupar. The 'wee village' was being used as the army depot for that part of Scotland, and it had become a big military camp, with troops arriving and departing daily. Nearly every home had officers billeted on it, while rank-and-file soldiers were occupying the schools, halls, barracks, and riding school. 'None are in camp as the tents are too good a mark for Bombs from aeroplanes.' The streets were scarcely passable on account of motors, wagons, and soldiers; the fields were full of horses; and guns occupied the local park. Sentries were stationed everywhere, and anyone out after 9 p.m. had to give an account of himself. Furthermore, no woman was allowed out after 10 p.m.

The female section of Cupar Fife had been singled out in another respect, this time by the leaders of their own community. All had been set to work knitting socks. 'No woman dares to appear in the evening without a sock in her hand. . . . I tell them it is martial law now. They are all very good & very willing.'

However, much of this transformation of Cupar proved short-lived. The troops departed to France, and the fear of air raids on army camps receded. By the end of the year Paterson was reporting: 'Things are much as usual here. We were threatened with having 100 men & horses billeted on the village. But . . . this is to be done only in case of emergency.' The knitting activities continued, however – 'Every one knits on Sundays now, even the parson's wife.'

Clark himself gained direct experience of the effects of the war on Oxford. Here the changes wrought on the composition of the community were dramatic. As he found when he stayed there in October 1914, even 'the Commerical Travelling circle' was being depleted by the war. But the really noteworthy falling-off was among the undergraduates. The Bursar of University College told Clark: 'the clientele of that College belong chiefly to the idle rich, and are therefore very largely gone on service. . . . There are this term 55 sets [of rooms] empty in Univ. Coll.' At Queen's College, according to a porter, some 100 students – nearly half of the total – were in the services, leaving 22 sets empty. The same drop of nearly 50 per cent of students was reported at Jesus and Merton Colleges, while Balliol was without one-third of its students as well as two of the Fellows and some lecturers.

Clark preserved some press cuttings from the early part of 1915 concerning the war effort of his old University. In February the *Daily Express* had an article headed 'Varsity Men at the Front. Fine Patriotism of the Universities'. And a report in the *Oxford Times* on 24 April stated that the number of students expected for the summer term was 891, as against the pre-war number of over 3,000.

IV

Great Leighs itself avoided the experience of billeting. Clark explains that, although only 37 miles by road from London, and in close proximity to such centres as Chelmsford and Braintree, the village was isolated. It was quite away from any railway station; no through traffic came to it by road; and none of its residents went regularly to London. The work of the village was self-centred: on the farm, in the smithy, among the wheelwrights and carpenters. It was not a prosperous community. Official appeals to practise economy, he noted in January 1916, were not appropriate to 'a village like this where no one has ever done anything else'. In common with other members of the clergy, Clark received appeals from the War Office to search out members of his congregation who might join the Officer Training Corps (OTC). He could only reply that his was a parish of farm labourers and farm bailiffs and had 'no one of position or means to enter an O.T.C. corps.'

How then did the war affect Great Leighs? Motor cars and horses were commandeered; a consignment of light reading was assembled for wounded soldiers; a Red Cross instruction class was instituted that attracted a small number; and a considerably larger group was established, under an 'admirable committee of management', to create endless garments for members of the armed forces and their families (and also, in due course, for Belgian refugees). A force of special constables was enrolled to aid the regular police in enforcing restraints on aliens and mounting a watch against saboteurs. And for particular families the war soon loomed very large indeed. These were the families with menfolk already in the armed forces or Merchant Navy and those that included males of military age.

From a handful of the residents of Great Leighs the war speedily began to exact its ultimate cost. In mid-October 1914 Clark noted that Mrs Fitch, whose husband was an agricultural labourer, had lost a son killed in action with the 2nd Essex Regiment. A lad of 19, he had enlisted in the regular army some 16 months earlier. Mrs Fitch was the mother of 12 children, all of them living at the outbreak of war. She soon suffered a second bereavement. In January 1915 a son who had been in the navy for nine years – and who, according to his mother, was the kindest of all her family to her – went down in HMS *Formidable*.

At the same time the war claimed a victim from much higher in the social scale of Great Leighs. J. M. Tritton, the squire of Lyons Hall, had three sons serving as officers. On 26 December 1914 one of them, a captain in the Coldstream Guards, was killed. According to one of his brothers, there was no fighting at the time: 'He was passing along a trench, and being a very tall man, incautiously exposed his head, so that a "sniper" shot him through the head.' (It may be noted that the Trittons, so Clark wrote some months later, were 'most unpopular among the country-lads' and the death of their son does not seem to have softened this feeling. When his loss was offered at a recruiting meeting as a reason why others should enlist, it produced the response from the farm hands that, as he had been in the army, it had been his job to go and fight.) On 10 January 1915 Clark held a memorial service for the three village men whom the war had already claimed.

If a handful of Great Leighs men were in the armed forces from the start, many more were required. It was the job of those in authority or of social standing to persuade eligible males to 'do their duty'. Sometimes this took the form of pretty direct coercion. Employers terminated the services of their hands and directed them to recruiting sergeants – Clark even referred, in February 1915, to certain farmers 'who have kept on all their hands & not forced any to enlist'. Such coercion was not always appreciated. On 1 September 1914 it was reported that the village lads were not pleased at the pressure exercised by the squire on his two footmen to enlist: 'To use the phrase of one of the lads, the "idle son" of the house ought to have set the example of going, though married, with children, and something over the age.' And when, six weeks later, Stoddart the land agent (or bailiff) at Lyons Hall 'approached some of the farm-lads with an admonition that they ought to enlist', he was met with 'a counter-thrust that they were waiting for the farmers' sons of the district to show them the example'. (Stoddart's own son was deemed to be among the backsliders.)

Men who could not be coerced into enlisting had to be appealed to: and so, for almost the first year and a half of the war, the recruiting meeting became a feature of British life. What form did this ritual take? Great Leighs had its first such gathering on the afternoon of 6 September 1914. A panel of notables of varying political hues, along with a representative of the Territorials, addressed the gathering, with J. H. Tritton in the chair. One speaker, a Boer War veteran, stressed the difference between Britain, where people were peace-loving and the Government was responsible to them, and Germany, where men were seen only as potential soldiers and became almost indistinguishable from machines. A former member of the Liberal Government then laid stress on the Belgian issue, without which Britain would not now be at war. And a gentleman of more conservative persuasion spoke of Britain's long-standing obligation to Belgium and more recent engagement to France, and observed that the path of honour was also the path of Britain's interest – namely, preserving its very existence.

The military representative then explained the conditions of enlistment; the need for six months of training before 'that trip to France'; the various occupations in the army awaiting blacksmiths, carpenters, and those fond of horses; and the more than sufficient provision being made for the dependants of recruits. 'To working men, who may think of serving their country at this crisis, I would say: don't worry about your family in your absence; they will be well looked after.'

Oddly enough, no volunteers were called for at this gathering, whose purpose presumably was to instruct and encourage. Five days later the actual recruiting meeting was held, with a full colonel present. Who attended the gathering? Clark noted: 'The School was moderately well filled. Women were present in considerable numbers. A good few lads crowded together on the back seats.' The colonel seems not to have been happy with this composition, for he observed: 'It was their experience on this tour that at a meeting, at which ladies were present, young men held back from shyness, and that for one who came forward at their meeting, four or five offered themselves next day.' Plainly something in the situation imposed reticence on the males in the 'back seats', for apart from two men who had already sent in their names only two came forward while Clark was present, although he gathered that others did so later.

Certainly, the response of eligible men in Great Leighs was not what everyone thought it should be. Four days after this meeting Clark noted: 'There is a great village outcry against lads who are of age & physique to enlist, and who have not done so', giving the names of three defaulters. In November Mrs Tritton, after extolling the patriotism of the village in such respects as knitting garments for the troops, wrote: 'I do wish we could see it also amongst the young men as regards enlisting.' And the following May, after two further recruiting meetings had drawn poor audiences from among eligible males and had aroused resentment among those who did attend, Tritton told Clark that Great and Little Leighs did not look well in the recruiting lists. Although about three dozen had volunteered, there were still some 36 men of military age in the two villages who had not come forward.

What stands out about these observations is their obtuseness regarding the inequality of sacrifice that the war was demanding. The squire's wife might wax lyrical over the patriotism of village folk who knitted socks, and deplore, by contrast, the unwillingness of local lads to place themselves in the firing line. A dispassionate observer would hardly consider the two forms of service on the same plane. And it would seem that a measure of sympathy would not have been out of order for such cases as the young man who did not want to enlist because 'His mother is old, & has practically lost her sight, and would grudge his going abroad.' (He went anyway, after several false starts.)

But perhaps this is to over-state the favoured position of those ineligible for military service. Many of them, even this early in the war, were linked by personal ties to events on the battlefield. On 19 May 1915 news began coming in of the battering taken by the Essex Yeomanry in what was soon being referred to as 'the late disastrous action' – 'the men were thrown away by incompetence of the superior officers.' Clark wrote: 'The village is much agitated about the heavy loss reported in the Essex Yeomanry, and anxiously waits for details. Practically everyone has relatives or intimate acquaintances in that regiment.'

V

How did the war affect the Rev. Mr Clark himself? As a man above military age, and anyway a member of a reserved occupation, he could not have participated in battle even had he wished to. Yet as a person of standing in the community he needed to identify himself with some war-related activities.

One that immediately presented itself was participation in the force of special constables. The purpose of such a body was explained to a gathering of potential members on 31 August 1914 by Sir Richard Pennefather, a former member of the Metropolitan Police. He told them: 'A specially onerous, but most important duty . . . is that of watching "spies".' There were at least 50,000 enemy aliens in the country, and the police would have to keep a close watch on them. Chelmsford was now a prohibited area, and Great Leighs fell within its district, so no enemy alien might live there without special permission, and every alien, of whatever origin, must be registered. Further, special constables must aid in protecting all roads, the abutments of bridges, telegraph posts, and the like. 'The hired agents of the enemy may try to do damage; and if our fleet or army suffer any reverse they are sure to be very much bolder and more active.' No person, native or foreigner, was to be allowed to loiter on or near any bridge or main roadway. Notice should be taken of all persons passing along the main road; the credentials of all foreigners were to be checked; and those foreigners who failed to produce identification were to be handed over to the police. 'Special Constables also are to arrest, and hand over to the police all persons speaking to the dishonour of this country.'

At the same time Pennefather stressed that special constables were not to employ unnecessary violence, prove officious, or employ firearms. They should make arrests only for breaches of the peace actually performed in their presence; offences reported to them should be referred to the regular force. They would in due course be issued with a warrant card and, when available, a baton. But again a note of restraint was sounded. 'This baton is not to be carried in any provocative way: but in a pocket inside right leg of trousers, like a carpenter's pocket rule.'

Some 40 individuals, including many farmers, attended this meeting. (Men of military age were initially deemed ineligible. But it was soon concluded that those with 'very special reasons' for not joining the army ought to enrol with the constabulary – 'very special reasons' including at this stage young dependent children and also teeth in such bad repair that they could not cope with 'the hard biscuit and hard beef of camp fare'.) By the time the swearing-in took place in early September the number offering had fallen to 25, and it diminished further in the following weeks. This falling-off was matched by a lowering in morale.

The problem, at least in part, was the gulf that existed between the ostensible duties confronting the special constables and anything that those in Great Leighs might actually perform. For example, their first duty was to draw up a list of foreigners resident in the district. But, Clark wryly observed: 'As there is not a single foreigner in Great or Little Leighs, this return will not take long to compile.' They were also set to work learning elementary drill, 'so as to know what to do if ever ordered to do duty in a body'; this activity was not conspicuously successful or appreciated. Then they were directed to patrol the streets of Great Leighs throughout the night, keeping watch for spies and saboteurs and paying particular attention to hayricks that the enemy might seek to set on fire. Each special constable, acting as one of a team of two, must once a week undertake a four-hour stint (either from 9 p.m. to 1 a.m. or from 1 a.m. to 5 a.m.). Although this does not seem onerous, the task was resented on account of its futility.

To begin with, Clark and his fellows ignored the directive about night patrols. But they were called to order at a meeting on 30 October 1914. First, Pennefather caused a state of near-collapse when he justified the protection of hayricks against incendiarism by relating how a tramp had been discovered sleeping under one on a wet night. Then Captain Finch, the county officer, addressed them. Clark recounts; 'Captain Finch, in giving this order, attempted to justify it by the most inconsequential remarks about soldiers in the front serving in the trenches, and by foolish drivel about an army of German mechanics who were shortly to be launched against Essex & Suffolk to destroy waterworks.'

Notwithstanding his scepticism, Clark agreed to go on patrol. His first night left him convinced that this activity was 'absolutely unnecessary', there being nothing that an enemy would want to destroy. And from the local police constable he learned that the patrols caused great alarm to some villagers. They heard the sound of measured footsteps pacing past their houses and lay trembling, wondering whether these were tramps or invaders.

By early in the new year the special constables had become so indignant that the patrols were confined to two hours from 11.30 p.m. Yet now they were beginning to serve some purpose. Following the raids by units of the German fleet on three coastal towns, there was a brief revival of invasion talk, and in January the special constables were summoned to learn of the intended movements of civilians in the event of an invasion. But it was the other form of threatened intrusion, from the air, that was mainly to exercise them. As early as mid-October 1914 lighting restrictions were introduced for Chelmsford on account of the importance of the Marconi works. (Under the restrictions, shops were to show only 'minimum' lights, and car headlights were to be turned off in the town.) These regulations applied also to Great Leighs, as lying on the route that hostile airships might take. Then, following the first air raid on Britain of any note on 19 January 1915, lighting restrictions in Great Leighs were extended to private dwellings. At first Clark and his companions found a number of villagers most unreasonable. One lady, refusing to darken her windows, informed them that she was 'not afraid of Zeppelins'. But as air raids became a fact, if still a minor one, of life during 1915, the community grew more co-operative. Enforcement of the lighting regulations gave the special constables a sense of purpose that, at least in Great Leighs, they had hitherto lacked.

Activity as a part-time policeman was one of the few ways in which citizens of standing in this Essex village could contribute directly to the war effort. But Clark himself had a further way, as a minister of religion. In his pastoral capacity he was called on to give advice and comfort, not only to the bereaved but also to young men exercised over the question of enlisting. Further, from the pulpit and in other ways he presented the views on the war taken by himself and by the leaders of the Church.

Early in the war Clark received from the Bishop of Chelmsford a form of intercession for those in the armed forces and a pastoral letter. These made it clear that the bishop, while endorsing the nation's involvement in the struggle, was not in the grip of jingoistic passions and had not forgotten the Church's role as an agent of reconciliation. 'All our hearts are full of grief at the call to arms,' he wrote. And his form of intercession included the petition 'that we may be brought through strife to a lasting peace; and that the nations of the world may be united in a firmer fellowship'. The bishop exhorted the populace to be 'calm and quiet', neither falling into undue depression in the event of defeat nor indulging in 'undue and unworthy exaltation if God gives us the victory'. And he stressed that the Christian God was the Father not only of the peoples of Britain but also of 'the men with whom we are at war'; 'it was for them, equally with ourselves, that Christ bled and died upon the Cross.' 'These facts once realized will help our people to refrain from bitterness in spirit and will also, I trust, lead them to pray, as they have never done before, for their enemies.'

But as time went on a more strident note entered the bishop's communications – a stridency directed not against the nation's enemies but against backsliders within. On 1 June 1915 he wrote to his clergy that there had been a splendid response to the call from king and country, but that even now there were numbers of people who did not realize the terrible issues at stake or acknowledge their duty to help to bring the war to a speedy and successful conclusion. (Helping to bring the war to a speedy conclusion was a much employed euphemism for joining the armed forces.) 'In some cases even our own people do not attend the Services of Intercession as they did in the earlier stages of the war.' This pointed, said the bishop, to the necessity for arousing people in our parishes to a sense of their responsibility: 'I have no hesitation in asking you to urge, all men of a military age, as a religious duty, to take their stand with their brothers at the Front; but above all to keep before men the great moral and spiritual aspects of the struggle now being waged.' He urged that an open-air meeting should be held, in association with the Nonconformists, so as to attract as large a number as possible. And he included, to be read in church, a pastoral letter from the Archbishops of Canterbury and York solemnly calling on all churchmen, and their fellow citizens, to meet whatever demands of service and sacrifice the Government might make of them (which they hoped would be considerable).

Clark's records make it clear that not only the episcopate but also a number of the clergy in neighbouring parishes felt entitled to identify their office with patriotic directives. At the end of August his daughter attended evening service at Fairstead, where the rector 'preached a harrowing sermon, on the horrible scenes on the battlefield, and exhorted all the young men to join the army. He had a big union-jack hung in front of the pulpit, instead of the pulpit-hanging.' Again, in the first six weeks of the war the rector of the parishes of South and West Hanningfield (according to statements he made to the Chelmsford Recruiting Committee) 'preached twelve "recruiting sermons" but had not been able to raise one recruit from either of his two parishes'. In Little Leighs the rector early in the war soundly berated an individual who was refusing to resume his position as a sergeant in the Territorials, and at special services in July 1915 he 'drew a harrowing picture of the imminence of invasion, and horrors in Essex worse than in Belgium, and urged all unmarried men to enlist at once'.

Whether Clark himself appealed directly for recruits he does not make clear. But if he did not, that was because of the unfriendly view he took of voluntary recruiting. So on 22 December 1914 he wrote:

> P.C. Coles, on his round, obligingly left me specimens of recruiting hand-bills; officially issued in November. They show the obstinacy with which, to save itself the confession of past error, the Government shirks its plain duty of compulsory service. The Country lads say, and to my mind say justly, 'if so many men are needed by the country, let the country say all *must* go.'

Certainly, Clark saw it as his role to endorse the utmost patriotic endeavour. This is apparent from the first reference he made to the war from the pulpit. He was in Oxford on 2 August 1914 and had arranged to preach in a neighbouring village. Learning that Germany had declared war on Russia, and taking it for granted that Britain would soon be involved, he set aside his intended sermon. Instead he 'mentioned the grave news and spoke for a little on the impending war, & the sacrifices it would call for'.

Clark from the outset had invoked the key word that would enable a Church whose founder was deemed the Prince of Peace, whose saving message was to all peoples, and whose tenets included love for one's enemies to endorse the waging of war against the nation's adversaries. That word was 'sacrifice'. The basis of Christianity was that its founder had made the supreme sacrifice. He had allowed his life to be taken from him even though, by invoking the heavenly hosts, he could have put his enemies to rout. Now Britain's fighting forces were placing themselves in a situation in which they might have to make the supreme sacrifice on behalf on their country and its ideals.

Of course, the supposed identity between the one use of the word 'sacrifice' and the other hardly bore investigation. There was no equivalence between the action of Christ, who was in a position to preserve his life but did not do so, and that of soldiers killed in the Great War. They did not 'lay down their lives' but were rudely deprived of them. British soldiers were not, in fact, when they underwent military training, being prepared for sacrifice. They were being prepared to preserve their lives in all ways commensurate with fighting effectively, and to impose death and injury on those fellow human beings (including, where applicable, fellow Christians) who belonged to the side of the enemy.

Yet this use of the word 'sacrifice' to identify what happened at Calvary with what was happening on the battlefield was necessary for a churchman like Clark. It enabled him whole-heartedly to endorse the nation's war effort and to demand that every eligible male be compelled to involve himself in the business of taking life. And it provided him with the means of offering a special consolation to those whose loved ones had been killed: that the fallen, by the manner of their dying, were directly emulating the founder of Christianity, who was the first to rise from the dead.

VI

By the time the war had run its first year it was making a distinct, if not necessarily lasting, impact on this corner of Essex. The womenfolk had now extended their range of knitting and sewing activities to include sandbags for use in the front line. Some inhabitants, among them a farmer who had failed to make his holding pay, had removed to munitions works in the towns and were prospering. The billeting of soldiers had not affected Great Leighs directly, but it was a source of sufficient discomfort to neighbouring communities to impinge on the consciousness of this village also.

Air raids affected Great Leighs directly. Certainly, no enemy aircraft would wittingly select it as a target. But the village lay on the path that bombers were likely to follow, and so it must keep its streets darkened and house lights sealed from view. After special constable patrol early in August 1915 Clark recorded: 'No lights in any windows, so far as I went.'

A week later the village had its first experience of a Zeppelin passing directly overhead. The intruder was on its way to bomb Chelmsford, where it did little damage, and London, where it did more. A few days later Clark viewed a house in Chelmsford that had been struck by a bomb, though fortunately for the occupants the missile had failed to explode. And his regular companion on special constable duty, F. R. Lewin, actually witnessed the unexploded bomb – reportedly of a novel type and so of great interest to the authorities – being extracted from the ground by an expert from the Woolwich Arsenal. ('Mr Lewin's badge as Special Constable obtained him a foremost place of observation.')

The same air raid revealed that, although after a year of unsubstantiated rumours its penchant for spy stories had diminished, the village could still embrace far-fetched tales. It was soon generally believed that the Zeppelin that had bombed Chelmsford had been directed to its destination by a motor car speeding along the main road with headlights blazing. Even Clark found this story difficult to doubt, supported as it was by dovetailing accounts coming independently from different sources. He felt that the authorities were much to blame for not setting up barriers, with sentries, at successive points along the main roads.

The war was starting to have an impact, if a mild one, on the economic and social structure of Great Leighs. Rising prices meant a good deal to a community most of whose members lived pretty near subsistence. But the lower classes were in a position to meet this problem by exacting higher wages. They could also afford to be less amenable than heretofore. A farmer told Clark in July 1915: 'Even the old hands will do only what they like.' If a labourer were given a task that needed doing immediately but that did not suit him, then he would simply neglect it; and if rebuked 'he will tell you that he is master now, and you cant do without him.'

This truculent attitude was, of course, facilitated by the scarcity of labour. In part the shortage resulted from the emergence of war-induced employment in the towns. But, far more, it reflected the movement of able-bodied men into the forces. So far military service had not impinged too greatly on the inhabitants of Great Leighs. Some 40 or so had enlisted, and a tiny number of those already in the services had died. But there was mounting evidence that the conflict would hereafter demand much more in human terms. Plainly, the war was nowhere near completion – J. H. Tritton spoke of the labour shortage as being likely to intensify unless the war ended suddenly, 'of which there seems no hope'. Equally plainly, it would prove for most participants a grim experience. Clark in mid-1915 could still note a report from Colchester that those men of Kitchener's army who had completed training were champing to get overseas: 'Everybody is very disgusted at the want of action.' But at about the same time he referred to an account from Braintree hospital of soldier patients 'making themselves as ill as they can' because they did not want to leave; and the same day he reported 'a general feeling that the soldiers met casually on the roads are much more depressed than were the troops formerly in these parts'.

The failure of the war to proceed towards victory, and the fact that 'every day' (in the words of one of Clark's associates) the struggle was producing 'big lists of casualties, and nothing to account for them', meant that the voluntary system was coming under strain. Not only was it apparently ceasing to produce the number of men required, as that number kept increasing; it was also being undermined by mounting resentment of what was considered its inherent inequality of 'sacrifice' – that is, the inequality between those adult males who came forward and those who did not. This constituted an ominous situation for men loath to enlist, and also for women dreading the removal of menfolk on whom (it seemed to them) the family structure depended.

One event, as the war had just ended its first year, pointed plainly to an approaching change. All adult villagers were confronted with a significant extension of state authority: the National Registration form. Theoretically, although completion was compulsory and wilful misinformation carried penalties, this National Register was in the nature of a census designed to estimate the nation's human resources. As such, it carried no compulsionist implications. But it was not so regarded. Clark was told by one prominent citizen assigned to distribute and collect the forms: 'the women were terribly afraid that the Register was the beginning of a plan to take away their menfolk.' Their fears would soon prove well founded.

17

COMMITTEE OF INQUIRY:
LORD BRYCE'S INVESTIGATION INTO
ALLEGED GERMAN ATROCITIES IN BELGIUM

It was a great idea of the PM's to ask you to do this piece of work, which will stand as an historic indictment – hideous enough, God knows. And I wish – as I have no doubt you wish – that you *could* have disproved the evidence or brought in a verdict of 'Not Guilty'. But as it was *true* – the world must learn it; that it may *never* occur again.

C. F. G. Masterman to Bryce, 7 June 1915

I

The first half of 1915 was a special time of hate in Britain. For in this phase of the war atrocity-mongering reached its peak. Tales of outrages committed by Germans, whether well founded or ill, replenished the queues at the recruiting offices and triggered off indiscriminate violence against residents of German origin or (supposed) pro-German sympathies. But, most important, they reinforced the conviction that, although the end of the struggle might be much farther off than had initially been expected, no resolution of the conflict was acceptable short of total victory.

The principal atrocity, of course, was war itself. The grievous casualties (if small by later standards) suffered by British forces at Second Ypres and Neuve Chapelle and Cape Helles imposed on a growing number of British families severe deprivation, and one only tolerable because it could be seen as a stepping-stone to their nation's triumph. But outside the established round of death by gunfire, a series of events rendered Germany peculiarly repugnant at this time. These were the use of poison gas against British combatants; the first Zeppelin raids upon British cities; the sinking of the passenger liner *Lusitania*; and the publication of the Bryce Report, which proclaimed German forces guilty of sadistic outrages during the invasion of Belgium. It was a particular stimulant to hate that, in all but one of these exceptional categories, a significant proportion of the victims were women and children.

Concerning the use of poison gas against combatants, of torpedoes against passenger ships, and of aircraft against cities, all that need be said is that the Germans did employ these measures and that Britons did deem them atrocious. But the Bryce Report of May 1915 has a different sort of interest – as an example of the manner in which the pressures of war could affect the standards of conduct of honourable, enlightened, fastidious Britons.

II

In December 1914 the British Government appointed a committee to investigate charges that German soldiers, either directed or condoned by their officers, had been guilty of widespread atrocities in Belgium. It was headed by Lord Bryce, formerly a highly respected British ambassador to Washington and author of a standard work on the American Commonwealth. The selection of Bryce seemed a guarantee both that the report would be a carefully weighed judgement and that it would carry conviction. The latter expectation was entirely fulfilled by the reception of the report, not least in the USA. A résumé of the American press, compiled by Britain's propaganda headquarters at Wellington House on 27 May 1915, stated: 'Even in papers hostile to the Allies, there is not the slightest attempt to impugn the correctness of the facts alleged. Lord Bryce's prestige in America put scepticism out of the question, and many leading articles begin on this note.' And C. F. G. Masterman, who was in charge of British propaganda, wrote to Bryce on 7 June: 'Your report has *swept* America. As you probably know even the most sceptical declare themselves converted, just because it is signed by you!'[1]

Was such confidence in Bryce warranted? On the basis of a wide range of his actions and attitudes, not only before but also during and after the war, it would seem that it was. A former student at Heidelberg, a sympathizer with German rather than French culture, and a recipient of the highest honour that the Kaiser could award (the Pour le Mérite), Bryce before the war was no uncritical admirer of the Triple Entente. At the end of June 1914 he expressed to C. P. Scott (editor of the radical newspaper the *Manchester Guardian*) his antipathy to the ruling forces in Russia. That country, he said, was 'rapidly becoming a menace to Europe'; Germany was 'right to arm and she would need every man'.[2] A month later, with Europe on the brink of war, he was acting with Lord Loreburn, a strong Liberal dissenter from Grey's foreign policy, in preparing opposition to any move to involve Britain in the conflict. And in the following days he came out as a supporter of the British Neutrality Committee, which was rallying opinion in the same direction.

Only the violation of Belgium converted Bryce from the neutralist position. By this action (so H. A. L. Fisher writes in his biography of Bryce), 'German militarism disclosed itself to him as the enemy of all that he valued most in European civilisation'; Bryce was convinced that there was 'no alternative but to fight and to fight to the end'.[3] Yet, despite his endorsement of the Allied cause, he did not lose a sense of proportion in his view of Germany. This is made clear in a letter that he wrote to Fisher himself on 15 October 1914, when the war had been in progress for over two months.[4] (The letter may throw some doubt on Fisher's own qualifications to serve on the Bryce Committee.) Bryce warmly congratulated Fisher on his lectures on the war. But he asked what evidence there was that Germany's learned and commercial classes, or the German people in any sense, had adopted the doctrines of Treitschke and Bernhardi – such doctrines as that state necessity could justify any action, including breaches of faith and the destruction of the innocent. He would, he wrote, believe this of German soldiers and politicians, but he doubted that ethics and religion could have vanished from the universities and the Church in Germany, even though he was aware of 'her decline from the Germany I remember as a student'. And he pointed out that neither

---

[1] All letters to Bryce quoted in this chapter are to be found in the Bryce papers, Bodleian Library, Oxford.
[2] Trevor Wilson (ed.), *The Political Diaries of C. P. Scott 1911–1928* (London: Collins, 1970), p. 88.
[3] H. A. L. Fisher, *James Bryce* (London: Macmillan, 1927), vol. 2, p.127.
[4] H. A. L. Fisher papers, in the Bodleian Library, Oxford.

Fisher nor himself would want to be judged by the jingo press in Britain and the ravings of the (arch-reactionary) *National Review*.

So it was not inconsistent with his support for Britain's involvement in the war that Bryce resisted proposals for retaliatory measures against German non-combatants;[5] that he devoted much effort during the war to working for the establishment of an international organization that would banish future conflicts; and that after the war he deplored the peace settlement as unduly vindictive towards Germany, describing the peace conference as an event 'where negotiators might have done so much good, and have done so much evil'.[6]

Bryce's qualifications, then, for conducting – if not an impartial – at least a careful and scrupulous inquiry into alleged German atrocities in Belgium would seem to be secure. And yet it is difficult to avoid the conclusion that, once committed to the task, he took pains to avoid any course of action that might oblige him to disbelieve in the main body of these tales. And the same appears to have been true of all but one of the members of his committee, notwithstanding the fact that it consisted of H. A. L. Fisher, the liberal historian; Sir Frederick Pollock, the distinguished jurist and historian of the law; three eminent lawyers, Sir Edward Clarke, Sir Alfred Hopkinson, and Sir Kenelm Digby; and Harold Cox, the editor of the *Edinburgh Review*. Only Cox, a Cobdenite Liberal who had abandoned a seat in Parliament in 1909 in protest against the 'socialist' tendencies of the Lloyd George Budget, seemed ready to probe the evidence thoroughly, even at the risk of finding it inconclusive.[7]

III

The principal material for investigation by the Bryce Committee consisted of 1,200 depositions recounting acts of atrocity by German troops in Belgium. Most of the depositions had been made by Belgian civilians living as refugees in Britain (there were 180,000 such refugees in April 1915), the rest by British and Belgian soldiers stationed in Britain or France. The large majority of the depositions had been taken by a team of barristers appointed for the purpose, but not under oath.

The only other material before the Bryce Committee consisted of diaries found on German soldiers who had been killed or taken prisoner. These diaries freely recounted the execution of civilians, allegedly for shooting at German soldiers or for aiding the forces of the Allies. ('The second burgomaster is shot, as he has telephonic communication with the French Army and thus betrayed our movements'). They also related many instances of looting, especially for liquor. ('There was a shop in the house where we plundered thoroughly'; 'They [a body of Dragoons] struck the teacher on the head with a violin because he would not give them wine.')[8] But although the Bryce Report states that the diaries are in one respect 'the most weighty part of the evidence', being exempt from the charge of bias, and that they 'recorded incidents just such as those to which the Belgian witnesses depose',[9] in fact they do not contain accounts of the

---

[5] Bryce withdrew a preface he had written for a book on the conduct of the German army in France when the author of the book, in an article in *The Times*, advocated retaliation against German non-combatants.
[6] Wilson (ed.), *The Political Diaries of C. P. Scott*, p. 380.
[7] According to his entry in *Who's Who*, Cox once 'spent nearly a year working as an agricultural labourer in Kent and Surrey in order to gain an insight into the life of English labourers'.
[8] *Appendix to the Report of the Committee on Alleged German Outrages* (London: HMSO, 1915), Appendix B, pp. 164, 166.
[9] *Report of the Committee on Alleged German Outrages* (London: HMSO, 1915), pp. 4–5.

sexual-sadistic outrages against women, children, and the aged that feature so largely in the Belgian accounts.[10]

If this collection of depositions and diaries were to substantiate the heavy charges being laid against German authorities, it would require thorough investigation. Yet from the outset Bryce was under pressure to forego any such investigation. This is plain from the terms in which, in a letter of 4 December 1914, he was asked to head the committee by the Liberal Attorney-General, Sir John Simon (who in the first days of August 1914 had come close to resigning in protest against Britain's entry into the war). Simon stressed that the 'value of this investigation entirely depends upon the known impartiality and authority of those who compose the Committee'. But he was also at pains to indicate that much of the groundwork of the inquiry had already been done. Some 'trained staff investigators at Scotland Yard', in co-operation with the Public Prosecutor's department, had begun collecting evidence. 'Certain members of the Bar, who volunteered their assistance', had then 'used their special training to sift the stories thus selected, rejecting mere rumour, and exposing what remained to the severe scrutiny which is traditional in British legal procedure'. Thus 'a limited number of stories of outrage' had been subjected to 'a very precise test'. Whether or not Simon was conscious of the fact, he seemed to be leaving the proposed Committee with very little to do. And certainly his statement on this aspect was notably imprecise: the members of the Committee were to study these selected cases and 'report what are the conclusions at which they arrive on the evidence available'.

Asked by Bryce whether the Committee was itself to hear evidence, Simon's reply was discouraging. This, he wrote on 8 December, was for the members of the Committee to decide, 'but the matter has been so prepared that they can pass a judgment on it without themselves undertaking the work of interrogation'. The Committee might wish 'in some isolated case' to interrogate witnesses. 'But primarily the idea was that a suitably constituted Committee would express in moderate language the impression which a study of the documents put before them leaves upon their mind.' Thus was the scene set for a Committee of Inquiry into alleged atrocities which did not itself select the cases it would investigate and did not come face to face with any of the persons making the allegations.

Bryce had plenty of warning that not all tales concerning German atrocities were well founded. This might have given him pause, even though he had Simon's assurance that the cases to come before him would not be of this type. H. D. Chalmers, one of the English barristers who prepared an interim report for the Committee based on evidence received from Belgian refugees in England, wrote to Bryce on 29 December: 'I find my Belgian friends discount a great deal of the evidence of sensational outrages which please the public. We have left those over . . . & have only dealt with official and ordered violations of the laws of civilised warfare.' In a postcript he added: 'As a curiosity of war, we have had 6 addresses given us where Belgian children have been seen with their hands cut off. No such children have been seen or heard of at any of those addresses.' And Grimwood Mears, one of the secretaries of the Bryce Committee (he too had played a part in the initial investigations), wrote on 9 March 1915 that all information given him of addresses where he would find Belgian girls rendered pregnant by rape had proved unfounded. This seemed to be the case – unless, that is, 'there is a determination to keep the matter secret' – even when the address was that of a Member of Parliament supposedly 'sheltering two young pregnant girls' and the informant was 'a man of high position'. Given such warnings,

---

[10] In the extracts from the diaries of German soldiers quoted in Appendix B to the Report there is only one rather opaque observation that may be describing an incident of this type.

Bryce had ample cause to wonder to what extent these spurious cases differed (except in being capable of disproof) from others supposedly well founded.

Probably each member of the Committee did in truth recognize that even among the sifted cases passed on to them some were of dubious validity. Their letters to Bryce bear witness to this. Sir Frederick Pollock, after studying the preliminary evidence, found it 'of every degree of value from O upwards', and he wrote of 'wilful blackening the enemy's conduct' and 'mere hysterical fiction or delusion'.[11] Again, Sir Kenelm Digby questioned whether 'the most horrible cases of mutilation . . . are so firmly established as to be safe to mention'. Writing to Bryce in March he took it to be a 'fallacy [that] the method of examination may afford a guarantee of the truth of the evidence'. It seemed to him that 'we must admit, what is certainly the fact, that in so large a body of evidence taken ex parte there is probably a good deal of exaggeration and inaccuracy in detail which cannot be discovered by the examiner.'

But, apart from Harold Cox, the response of members of the Committee to this problem was not to look carefully at dubious cases to see what light they might throw on the reliability of the mass. It was, rather, to reject the doubtful items without further inquiry, and to argue that reliance should be placed not on particular cases at all but on the totality of cases. Fisher (partly as a way of meeting Cox's objections) advocated stating in the report that 'although the Committee is not prepared to aver the accuracy of every detail attested to, it sees no reason to doubt the general truth of the picture presented by the whole mass of the depositions.' Digby also invoked the doctrine of the 'general truth': 'we ought as much as possible to avoid the appearance of relying on individual cases . . . and rest on the broader facts where you have concurrent testimony and also the entries in the diaries which are substantially not in dispute.'

Only Cox insisted that 'broader facts' are grounded on 'individual cases', and argued that the Committee must actually examine some of the witnesses whose depositions were before it. Otherwise, he wrote on 1 March 1915, the report could state only that the Committee had been through large numbers of printed statements professing to be depositions by Belgian refugees and British soldiers, some of which appeared incredible while others were probably true. To this statement, he added, a German critic might reply that the British Government was known to be capable of issuing fraudulent documents, as instanced by copies of the Navy List that included the battleship *Audacious* when that vessel was at the bottom of the sea. Soon after, Cox was able to offer clear instances of the hazard of a 'general truth' approach that ignored 'individual cases'. At least some of the depositions were submitted without comment by the barristers who had taken them, and yet when inquiry was made about two of these cases the barristers replied that they ought not to be treated as evidence. The Committee, he pointed out, did not know of how many depositions this was true.

Cox soon became alarmed at the gulf between his attitude and that of the chairman of the Committee. Regarding the draft report that Bryce circulated at the beginning of March 1915, Cox wrote to Bryce on 5 March that it impressed him 'immensely' on account of its clarity but that it raised some of the points about which he had been writing:

> *page 2.* You say: 'These instructions[12] have, as we believe, been scrupulously observed.'
> The Committee has had absolutely no evidence on this point.

---

[11] Pollock even wrote, in this letter of 31 December 1914, of 'direct evidence that German officers sometimes summarily shot men who were misbehaving. But I fear this was exceptional'. More often, the soldiers were encouraged to get out of hand, 'as in Louis XIV's dragonnades'.

[12] Probably the instructions given to the barristers who took depositions from Belgian witnesses.

page 3. You say: 'The lawyers who took the depositions . . . assure us, etc.' We have seen none of the lawyers, and have received no such assurances from them.

At the bottom of the same page you say: 'nothing admitted except such as a judge sitting in an English court would allow to be laid before a jury.' This is clearly inaccurate.[13]

page 4. You say 'that the diaries [taken from German soldiers] have been deciphered and translated into English with great care'. We have no evidence at all on this point. All we know is that Brodrick and Mears [the committee's secretaries] have given us various printed statements, but so far as we are officially aware they may have invented the whole.

Cox speedily found himself at odds not only with Bryce but also with the rest of the Committee. Sir Frederick Pollock, for one, wrote on 6 March that he was amazed at Cox's state of mind over dealing with testimony. In Pollock's view, Cox seemed to require a far higher degree of probability than a court of justice ever got, and to think that every statement of fact must be absolutely true or false. (It is interesting that an eminent jurist should consider that, on such a matter as the alleged amputation of children's hands, any finding could be other than true or false.) 'If history had to be revised on his principles most of it would become blank, including every document not expressly cited by some contemporary.'[14] Fisher was less openly hostile to Cox but no more encouraging. Regarding even Cox's proposal that they examine the barristers – not the witnesses – he wrote on 7 March: 'I do not myself feel that I should be assisted by such a proceeding but I would not stand in the way of any member of the Committee who might be of another opinion.'

For a brief spell it seemed that Cox would stand his ground and refuse to endorse the report, a course that, as Fisher realized, would be 'a calamity'. Cox wrote to Bryce on 9 March 1915 that the difference between himself and the rest of the Committee concerning the need to examine witnesses was fundamental and that it would be quite impossible for him to sign the report. But the next day he saw Bryce and, after reflection, agreed on a sort of compromise that in fact abandoned the essence of his position. He gathered, he wrote on 11 March, that Bryce was willing to call the barristers who had received the depositions and to 'ask them generally about their method of procedure and their impressions of the witnesses, but not to ask them to go through all the cases individually'. Cox was prepared to accept this as long as, when a barrister or some other receiver of depositions was before them, it would be permissible to ask for 'information on any special case of importance'. For each barrister, he added, this would not take more than ten to twenty minutes at the outside and, in many cases, five minutes. 'If the Committee will agree to this I will not press for the calling of the actual witnesses, provided it is made clear that our report is based upon depositions and not upon oral evidence given to us as a Committee.'

It is plain that Cox's protests had made little or no impact on the thinking of the rest of the Committee. Fisher is a case in point. As mentioned earlier, he was alarmed at the possibility that Cox would refuse to sign the report. But his response, as he related to Bryce on 11 March, was to write Cox 'some sedative words and hope that we shall bring him along with us'. Fisher went on: 'His scruples seem to me to be excessive for our evidence is far better both in quality and quantity than that upon which most of our histories have been built.' Two days later, in respect of those cases that Cox considered

---

[13] In a letter of 3 March 1915 Kenelm Digby also pointed out to Bryce, if in less trenchant tones, that the Committee was receiving evidence that would not be acceptable on an English court.

[14] For his part, Cox was critical of Pollock's view of acceptable evidence. He pointed out to Bryce in his letter of 1 March that Pollock was prepared to regard as satisfactory the evidence of witnesses about whom the examining barristers commented: 'This man would, I think, prove a credible witness' and 'I think what he says is true' – showing, in Cox's view, in the first instance that the barrister did not regard the examination as final, and in the second (typical of many) that the barrister himself was uncertain of the witness.

doubtful, Fisher expressed the view that 'our friend H. C.' should be allowed to make inquiry if he so wished of the barristers and even of the deponents; but he also said that he himself was satisfied that 'we have more than enough sifted information to justify the general conclusions of our Report'. And when Fisher submitted his particular section of the report, on the highly emotive issue of alleged ill-treatment of women and children, it transpired that he had failed to amend it to take into account the cases that Cox had challenged. W. J. Brodrick, in his capacity as a secretary to the Committee, pointed out to Bryce on 4 April that Fisher had stated that he did not want to use any cases that had been called in doubt. Yet very many of the 116 cases that he cited as evidence of German brutality had been rejected by Cox, and others had been queried. To overcome this inconsistency, Brodrick wrote, Fisher's essay would require serious modification.

In the upshot all that Cox achieved was some minor toning-down in the conclusions of the report and the replacement of some questionable cases by others not yet questioned. His plea for a serious inquiry into at least some of the allegations on which the Committee was supposed to be basing its report accomplished nothing. And his quest for truth earned him considerable disfavour with other members of the Committee. This is plain in their references to him. So Bryce wrote to Fisher on 8 April, regarding one of the revisions in the final draft of the report made in Fisher's absence: 'Pollock's conclusion is certainly more effective, in a literary sense, than the one which was adopted to humour Cox, but for the sake of peace we adopted the latter, modifying it however; it is now passable if not powerful.'

IV

The Bryce Committee did not produce a dishonest or fraudulent report in the sense that it reached conclusions shown by the evidence to be unsound. What it did do was carefully to avoid verifying the evidence. So it escaped placing itself in a situation in which, while seeking to establish Germany's guilt, it might be obliged to deem the more notorious charges, if not false, then at least unproven. Having carefully disqualified itself from reaching final conclusions either way, the Committee proclaimed Germany guilty in the most sweeping terms.

This failure by the Bryce Committee to undertake the sort of inquiry that alone would justify such a verdict was not an oversight. When the Committee was appointed, *The Times* had urged that it make a thorough investigation, including the examination of witnesses, of a limited number of test cases. 'Findings based upon direct testimony of this kind are usually more satisfactory than those arrived at upon testimony taken by third parties.'[15] If the members of the Bryce Committee did not read this journal, they had in Harold Cox a member urging the same considerations upon them. Yet Simon appears to have been seeking to dissuade Bryce from following this course when he asked him to head the Committee. And Bryce, although to begin with he spoke of examining some of the deponents,[16] soon became steadfast in opposing a painstaking investigation. Among dissenters from the Committee's procedure, Cox capitulated under pressure; and *The Times*, when Bryce's report was published, did not recall its earlier admonitions.

---

[15] *The Times*, 18 December 1914, quoted in James Morgan Read, *Atrocity Propaganda 1914–1919* (New Haven: Yale University Press, 1941), p. 205.
[16] This at least was how Cox understood Bryce's position at the beginning of their correspondence: Cox to Bryce, 1 March 1915.

Why did men of known integrity behave like this? In particular, why did Bryce hazard his enviable reputation by such a proceeding? Fisher, in his biography of Bryce, gives it as his impression that when Bryce began his investigations he hoped, if not to acquit Germany, at least to contain the charges against it within a small compass; but the weight of evidence forced him to a contrary conclusion.[17] This is consistent with the glimpse we get of Bryce, two months before he was asked to undertake his inquiry, taxing Fisher himself as to whether he was justified in saying that the German people had embraced the doctrine that state necessity overrules all other considerations. Yet it is difficult to reconcile with the clear view we get of Bryce failing to confront, let alone cross-examine, the persons upon whose unsworn statements he was prepared to convict Germany of 'murder, lust and pillage . . . on a scale unparalleled in any war between civilized nations during the last three centuries' – deeds committed not because of indiscipline but 'on a system and in pursuance of a set purpose'.

Was it that Bryce, in the course of chairing the committee, himself came to embrace the doctrine of state necessity? Did he cease to see any need for probing evidence that at best could only confirm, and at worst might serve to discredit, the conclusions that he was determined – for the good of his country – to reach? This conjecture seems to gain support from the mysterious fate of the depositions themselves. Although the Bryce Report contained no details of the identities of the deponents – supposedly so as to protect their relatives in occupied Belgium – it did state that the original documents would be retained in the Home Office for inspection in peacetime; but after the war the documents could not be traced.[18] Yet the obvious implication of this, that Bryce never intended to let his sources be investigated and even took trouble to cover his tracks, is hard to reconcile with a question that Bryce put to Simon when the report was being published. He asked whether the original depositions could forthwith be made available for inspection by individuals who had no improper purpose to serve. It was Simon, after consultation with the Home Office, who concluded that this was incompatible with the promise made to deponents that, for the safety of their families, their names would not be revealed. And it was Simon who suggested that the Committee's report might state that the evidence would be retained by the Home Office for inspection after the war. Whatever else he was doing, Bryce does not seem to have been acting with a conscious intention to deceive.

V

Perhaps to comprehend Bryce's conduct it is necessary to spell out just what was at stake. As far as Britain's place in the war was concerned, anything touching on the issue of Belgium was of great moment. Germany's violation of that country had been the ostensible – and for important sections (among them Bryce himself) the actual – determinant of Britain's intervention in the war. Further, this was the issue that most commended British participation in the conflict to important neutrals, especially the USA. Anything that would heighten awareness, in Britain and overseas, of the enormity of German behaviour deserved to be exploited. But there was an important corollary. Anything that might devalue the Belgian issue was to be avoided.

Given the many tales in circulation about German outrages against Belgian civilians, it seemed the path of wisdom to have their validity confirmed by a group of respected

---

[17] Fisher, *James Bryce*, vol. 2, pp. 132–5. It is no aid to discovering the inwardness of Bryce's conduct that his biographer should have been a member of the Committee.

[18] Read, *Atrocity Propaganda*, p. 206.

individuals. The potential value of such tales in hardening the resolve of Englishmen, and in arousing the sympathies of neutrals, was enormous. But this gave rise to a problem that, although not mentioned, appears to have been recognized by Simon at the time he gave Bryce his commission. How much would be lost, in British resolve and neutral sympathy, if the atrocity stories proved unfounded?

Now, in a world of rational values this would not have been a problem. German atrociousness towards Belgium was flagrant, and it was far more subversive of civilized standards than brutal acts perpetrated upon women and children by bands of soldiers. The German state's unprovoked aggression towards its neighbour had been on a scale and in a manner that, unless repelled, would terminate for good Belgium's existence as an independent country. Under whatever legal fiction, the population of Belgium would hereafter be a subject people. Further, in pursuit of this policy the German authorities had prepared and, when it suited them, had put into effect a deliberate policy of terrorism against Belgian civilians. It included the cold-blooded execution of civilian hostages and the destruction of towns and buildings of great historic and emotional significance. In the words of the American historian James Morgan Read (who clearly viewed atrocity stories with a heavy scepticism): 'Some thousands of Belgian civilians were massacred by the invading German armies. The Germans never made any pretenses about the matter, admitting the "execution" of hundreds at a time.'[19] And all of this, it should be stressed, was high policy, not soldierly excess.

Yet, by a strange perversion of values, these things paled into insignificance once tales became current of raped women and mutilated children. In some quarters of the USA even the American dead of the *Lusitania* could not match the supposed Belgian victims of sexual outrage. It so happened that the Bryce Report appeared only days after the sinking of the great passenger liner. And the Wellington House survey (quoted earlier) which related the American response to the report remarked how newspaper editorials 'invariably bring the treatment of Belgium into connexion [sic] with the sinking of the "Lusitania".' It quoted the *New York Tribune* as saying: 'While our own women were only slain those of Belgium were outraged.' And the survey continued: 'the thought is repeated in a cartoon, representing America sitting in mourning for her dead, while Belgium, laying her hand on her shoulder, says: "They only drowned your women."' If it should emerge that the Germans had not 'outraged' Belgian women – only, with great deliberation, executed numbers of its menfolk, destroyed precious buildings, terminated a whole people's independence – then the conviction that the Kaiser had behaved shamefully towards Belgium would be seriously impaired; and so, consequently, would be Britain's moral warrant for intervening in the war.[20]

This strange quirk of human psychology was referred to obliquely in two pieces of Bryce's correspondence. The first was the remark (already quoted) by the lawyer H. D. Chalmers that there might be no truth in accounts of 'sensational outrages *which please the public*' (emphasis added). The second was an observation by Simon when he was discounting Bryce's suggestion that the depositions be immediately opened for inspection. He said that he hated to think what might happen if some enterprising reporter got hold of them and endeavoured to make people's flesh creep. By the time that Bryce began compiling his report, much of the British case against Germany had

---

[19] Read, *Atrocity Propaganda*, pp. 82–3.
[20] After the war, when the tales of sexual-sadistic actions committed by the Germans in Belgium were discredited, there ensued widespread scepticism about the whole concept of German frightfulness towards that country; so that in 1941 James Read felt it necessary to write: 'Some people, having become so thoroughly convinced of the nonexistence of Belgian babies without hands, have forgotten that the treatment of Belgians was, in the words of General Moltke himself, "certainly brutal".' Ibid.

come to depend on his ability to function as any journalist on a popular Sunday paper: to tell a tale that would make his readers' flesh creep and so 'please' (at the same time as it repelled) 'the public'.

That is, a situation had developed that threatened to approximate the experiences of Sir Charles Dilke and Oscar Wilde (a later generation might add Alger Hiss and Dr Wladyslaw Dering). The British Government, when it put Germany on trial for committing a particular brand of atrocity in Belgium, had put itself on trial as well. In the event that the charge against Germany of instituting 'people-pleasing' outrages should prove insubstantial, the central moral case against the German Government concerning Belgium would be severely (and unjustifiably) shaken. Bryce did not have the choice of telling the truth or telling a falsehood. If he proved so scrupulous in his investigations that he might deem the tales of sadistic crimes unproven, then, inadvertently but inescapably, he would be helping to propagate a larger untruth: that the whole notion of deliberate and calculated atrocity perpetrated by Germany upon Belgium was unfounded. It is perhaps permissible to infer that Bryce – preceded by Simon, and accompanied by the rest of his Committee (including ultimately the reluctant Cox) – perceived that these alone were the options. So he went to great lengths to avoid endorsing the second, greater, untruth by unreservedly embracing the first.

18

FROM LIBERAL GOVERNMENT TO FIRST COALITION

I

When war broke out, Britain was governed by the Liberal ministry of H. H. Asquith. A Yorkshireman of modest origins and commanding intellect, he had risen by means of manifest ability up the ranks of politics and society. By August 1914 the Liberals had been in office for almost a decade. They had come to power in 1905 and had won a staggering electoral victory in 1906. They had gone on to win two further general elections – though by no similar margin – in January 1910 and December 1910. Their years in office had been marked by fierce political passions and by the mismanagement of some important episodes. Nevertheless, in 1914 the Asquith Government had to its credit an astonishing series of constitutional and social reforms.

Opposing the Liberals, as the only other party capable of aspiring to office, was the Conservative or Unionist party. Its leader was a rather dour Scottish-Canadian businessman, Andrew Bonar Law. The expression 'Unionist' had nothing to do with trade unions. It reflected the more nationalistic, imperialist slant of the Conservatives. In particular, it expressed their determination to preserve the 'union' with Ireland, as against the Liberal policy of Home Rule – that is, the concession to Ireland of a limited measure of self-government.

As a result of the elections in 1910, the Liberals lacked an absolute majority in the House of Commons. (The second 1910 election secured them 272 seats, the same number as the Conservatives.) This, however, did not imperil Asquith's position. For he could count on the support of the two minor parties, the Irish Nationalists with 84 seats and the Labour Party with 42. Each of these parties saw the Liberals as the guardians of the causes nearest to their hearts: Home Rule in the case of the Irish, the preservation of the bargaining power of trade unions in the case of Labour.

Initially – and contrary to what promised to be the case in the opening days of August – the onset of war worked to the advantage of the Liberal Government. In the dramatic events surrounding the declaration of war and the rush to the colours, Asquith and his colleagues were at the centre of things. The political controversies that had been working to their disadvantage were pushed to the sidelines. The destiny of the nation hung on their decisions. In March 1915 'Toby, MP' (i.e. Sir Henry Lucy, formerly private secretary to two Conservative Ministers and himself an unsuccessful Conservative candidate) wrote in *Punch*: 'A special Providence ordains that at such a crisis we have at head of affairs a strong man endowed with gift of lucid speech, which . . . rises to height of eloquence.' Rarely, if ever, wrote Lucy, had the House of Commons found its convictions and aspirations 'so faithfully, so fully, so forcefully' expressed as on several occasions when Asquith talked to it about the war. 'His personality is worth to the Empire an army in the field, a squadron of *Queen Elizabeths* at sea.'

Yet almost from its outbreak some of the circumstances engendered by the war were working powerfully against the Government. Many dearly cherished Liberal principles became inapplicable in war and seemed unlikely to revive in peace. In March 1915 Sir Maurice Hankey found himself dining with Sir George Paish, editor of the *Statist*. Paish explained to him the difficulties of the financial outlook and (Hankey recorded) 'astounded me by advocating a tariff, though he has been a lifelong free trader. How war changes people's ideas!'[1]

Ian Hay, the author of *The First Hundred Thousand*, was also noticing how political attitudes were changing. He was eager to assist the process with his pen. Among its lesser attributes, his vastly popular book is a powerful exposition of right-wing attitudes.[2] One of its minor heroes is a former model Boy Scout who rapidly proves himself to be a model private soldier. 'In short,' Hay tells us, 'he was the embodiment of a system which in times of peace had served as a text for innumerable well-meaning but muddleheaded politicians of a certain type, who made a speciality of keeping the nation upon the alert against the insidious encroachments of – Heaven help us! – Militarism!' These 'muddleheaded politicians of a certain type', with their ill-conceived warnings against militarism, would be instantly recognized as Liberals.

Hay also recounts a conversation between a group of officers and NCOs that points a number of political morals. The much praised Captain Wagstaffe remarks: 'War is hell, and all that, but it has a good deal to recommend it. It wipes out all the small nuisances of peace-time' – among which he instances suffragettes, futurism, the tango, party politics, and golf maniacs. What is meant by the wiping out of party politics becomes clear when members of the company relate the advantages they have derived from the war. One of the company, Borrodaile, says that he has no complaints about the war. In private life he is a 'prospective candidate'. (He does not say for which party, but no one could fail to recognize him as a Conservative.) For several years he has been nursing a constituency:

> That is, I go down to the country once a week, and there reduce myself to speechlessness soliciting the votes of the people who put my opponent in twenty years ago, and will keep him in by a two thousand majority as long as he cares to stand. I have been at it five years, but so far the old gentleman has never so much as betrayed any knowledge of my existence.

(It is probably no accident that in Hay's account the Conservative hopeful is a young man in uniform, while his opponent is an 'old gentleman'. One term of abuse soon to be freely employed against Asquith and his colleagues was 'the old gang'.) Wagstaffe remarks that this situation must be galling, but Borrodaile indicates that, thanks to the war, it is not so any longer:

> 'Ah! but listen! Of course party politics have now been merged in the common cause – see local organs, *passim* – and both sides are working shoulder to shoulder for the maintenance of our national existence.'
>
> 'Applause!' murmured Kemp.
>
> 'That is to say,' continued Borrodaile with calm relish, 'my opponent, whose strong suit for the last twenty years has been to cry down the horrors of militarism, and the madness of national service, and the unwieldy size of the British Empire, is now compelled to spend his evenings taking the chair at mass meetings for the encouragement of recruiting. I believe the way in which he eats up his own previous utterances on the subject is quite superb. On these occasions I always send him a telegram, containing a kindly pat on the back for him and a sort of semi-official message for the audience. He has to read this out on the platform!'

---

[1] Hankey's diary, 29 March 1915.
[2] *The First Hundred Thousand* began serialization in *Blackwood's Magazine* in 1914 and was published in book form in December 1915. Quotations are from the Penguin edition of March 1941.

In response to a 'delighted' inquiry, Borrodaile gives some examples of his telegrams. One of them is: 'All success to the meeting, and best thanks to you personally for carrying on in my absence.' Borrodaile observes: 'I have a lot of quiet fun composing those telegrams.'

It is plain from this account that party politics had not been submerged by the war. Rather, the war had altered the climate of political debate in a way that enhanced the prospects of this formerly hopeless Conservative candidate. For it had made it an offence on the part of his Liberal opponent ever to have inveighed in peacetime against militarism, national service, and an over-large Empire.

There is another private soldier in *The First Hundred Thousand* considered deserving of approbation. He is 'a dour, silent, earnest specimen, whose name, incredible as it may appear, is McOstrich'. Hay describes him thus:

> He keeps himself to himself. He never smiles. He is not an old soldier, yet he performed like a veteran the very first day he appeared on parade. He carries out all orders with solemn thoroughness. He does not drink; he does not swear. His nearest approach to animation comes at church, where he sings the hymns – especially *O God, our help in ages past!* – as if he were author and composer combined. His harsh, rasping accent is certainly not that of a Highlander, nor does it smack altogether of the Clydeside. As a matter of fact he is not a Scotsman at all, though five out of six of us would put him down as such. Altogether he is a man of mystery; but the regiment could do with many more such.

The mystery is not very profound. Most of Hay's readers would realize that McOstrich is an Ulsterman, and that he 'performed like a veteran the very first day he appeared on parade' because he had been training with the Protestant Ulster Volunteers to resist Home Rule by force.

Should any of Hay's audience fail to take this point, it is spelled out for them. 'Once, and only once, did [McOstrich] give us a peep behind the scenes.' This was when a 'contemptuous and ribald reference' was made concerning Sir Edward Carson and the Ulster Volunteers. It emanated from Private Burke, 'a cheery soul, who possesses the entirely Hibernian faculty of being able to combine a most fanatical and seditious brand of Nationalism with a genuine and ardent enthusiasm for the British Empire'. (Irish nationalism, it will be observed, is 'seditious', however cheery its advocate. Ulster nationalism is not.) McOstrich's response to the ribald comment about Carson was swift. He 'promptly rose to his feet, crossed the floor in three strides, and silently felled the humorist to the earth. Plainly, if McOstrich comes safe through the war, he is prepared for another and grimmer campaign.'

II

What Ian Hay's account shows is that, in the heat of this conflict, many cherished Liberal principles were becoming discredited, while those of their opponents were appearing to be vindicated. Not only had Liberal ideals of international conciliation and a low level of armaments been rendered inappropriate. It was coming to be seen as an offence ever to have striven for them. Certainly, Liberals might feel warranted in reconciling a belief in internationalism with participation in the war by regarding the conflict as a struggle between democracy and autocracy. Nevertheless, belief in internationalism was bound to be eroded by the burgeoning mood of national hate, and its advocates were necessarily seen as feeble exponents of the nation's resolution. 'I meet many good Liberals in Midlothian and elsewhere', wrote a prominent Scottish

Liberal in December 1914, 'who are prone to take the view that we pacifists made a mistake and the Jingos were right all along.'[3]

For the moment the classic Liberal notions of freedom were, in part or in whole, being placed in cold storage or subjected to growing challenge. Free trade was certainly in suspense as far as enemy countries were concerned, and many even of its former devotees could not imagine themselves wanting it restored. Free speech was seriously curtailed, so that it became an offence to express opinions on politics or international relations that might prove prejudicial to recruitment for the army. Freedom of the press was subject to restraint – if not in the expression of opinions hostile to the Government, then certainly in the reporting of a wide range of war news. *Punch* in February 1915 related: 'Apropos of newspapers, we are beginning to harbour a certain envy of the Americans. Even their provincial organs often contain important and cheering news of the doings of the British Army many days before the Censor releases the information in England.' (At least one item of news regarding the British navy that was important, but not cheering, was denied publication for the duration of the war. This was the sinking of the battleship *Audacious* by a mine in October 1914.) As for free service in the armed forces, it was from the outset of the war (as Ian Hay's Conservative candidate makes plain) subject to severe challenge. For a while the army might have more recruits than it could handle. But the view was gaining currency that absence of compulsory peacetime training was symptomatic of the nation's unpreparedness for war. So *Punch*, in a dreadful piece of verse, referred to the campaign for national service that Lord Roberts, the Boer War hero, had conducted since 1905:

> He knew, none better, how 'twould be,
>   And spoke his warning far and wide. . . .
> His every word proves true today
>   But no man hears, 'I told you so!'

If Lord Roberts did not proclaim his prescience, many publicists on the right of politics were making good his omission.

'Unpreparedness for war', carrying the implication that this was a necessary offence of a 'Little England' Government, was a major charge levelled against the Asquith regime from early in the conflict. As it happened, it was justified only to a limited extent. Indeed, in the most vital area of all, that of naval preparations, it lacked substance. The army was, at least superficially, a different matter. The Liberal Government had not made Britain a conscript state, immediately capable of fielding a mass army with all the logistic support it would need. But no political party before the war had been envisaging such an outpouring of money as this would have required. Some politicians may have talked about training more men. They did not propose stockpiling appropriate quantities of guns and shells and rifles. In terms of the sort of force that the nation had been prepared to pay for, the BEF was superbly trained and well equipped. Further, to provide the base for a great expansion of the British army in the event of war, the Liberal Government had established the part-time, 'weekend' Territorial force, numbering 14 divisions. Certainly, it transpired after 4 August 1914 that this body of semi-trained citizens was not to be used as the foundation for the mass army that, it was swiftly decided, Britain must have: Kitchener chose to put it on one side and raise the New Armies from scratch. But this action does not invalidate what the Liberal Government, and in particular R. B. Haldane, had accomplished. Rather, it

---

[3] Alex Shaw to A. G. Gardiner, 9 December [1914], Gardiner papers, Library of Political and Economic Science, London School of Economics.

is a reminder that those who plan for war can control only up to a point the inspirations and actions of those called upon to conduct it.

But if the charge of unpreparedness, as a crime peculiar to this sort of Government, was not very substantial, it was nevertheless made – with telling effect. And Haldane, the last Minister against whom it should have been directed, was its chief victim. Certainly, he had in the past commended Germany for the high quality of its philosophers. And in 1912 he had sought to negotiate with the rulers of Germany a mutual scaling down of naval armaments. But it was an indication of the feverish, unwholesome spirit of wartime politics that such things could be regarded as evidence of crypto-treachery on the part of this Minister. And it was evidence of how the condition of political conflict was turning against the Liberals, and in favour of their opponents, that remarks made by the Conservative leader that could equally have been employed as evidence of pro-Germanism did not damage him in the least.

It was taken to be in the nature of things that a Liberal Government would be soft on enemy aliens and other 'traitors' in the nation's midst, that it would be reluctant to force 'slackers' to do their duty, and that it would be wedded to economic practices inappropriate in wartime. Nothing that the Government might actually be doing could quite offset this handicap.

At the same time there were soon powerful reasons, quite apart from its liberalism, for discontent with the Asquith Government. The war, with its grim stalemate and terrible casualties, was a profoundly shocking event. Nothing that the country's leaders could do would alter this. All the participants were trapped by the equal balance between the contending forces and by the killing power of modern weapons. But, as Governments claim credit when wars go well, however small their contribution, so they must suffer discredit when wars go ill, whether or not they are blameless. In mid-March 1915 Lord Crewe observed that they were experiencing peaceful days in Parliament and added: 'The general military and naval outlook is now tolerably cheering.'[4] As the outlook thereafter ceased to cheer, so the Government's stocks fell.

Anyway, in important respects the Asquith ministry was plainly open to criticism. For some weeks before May 1915 MPs were becoming aware that military operations were being conducted with insufficient ammunition. It was no reassurance to be told by the Prime Minister (in an address, moreover, to munitions workers) that this was not so. Certainly, when Asquith made this claim in Newcastle on 20 April he was speaking on the basis of information supplied by Kitchener, who in turn had been misled by Sir John French. And anyway the purpose of Asquith's address was to convince munitions workers of the need for increased endeavours. But a contented statement on the munitions issue ran counter to what too many people knew to be the case. It was hard to reconcile with statements made earlier by Lloyd George, that excessive drinking and bad timekeeping among munitions workers were hindering the war effort. And it seemed evidence of complacency on the part of the country's leader at a time when what was needed was awareness of past inadequacies and a stern resolve towards greater energy, more dedication, and a larger vision.

Moreover, that the nation's decision-making apparatus was faulty at the highest level seemed evident from the series of botched moves that had produced the impasse at the Dardanelles. It was widely believed, if not quite justly, that Churchill, in convincing his colleagues of the wisdom of the undertaking, had acted in defiance of his professional advisers. It seemed plain that the naval attack had been a mistake and had jeopardized the military operation that followed. It appeared questionable whether the country

---

[4] Crewe to Hardinge, 19 March 1915, Crewe papers.

should be employing its resources against Turkey at all. These considerations, when taken together with misgivings about the operations in France, concern about the navy, fears (however ill-founded) about enemy agents at home, and a sense that drive was wanting in the direction of affairs, raised ominous questions. Were the right men in charge of the country? And were they in a position both to receive the best advice and to employ it so as to reach a considered decision? For the moment the answers to such questions seemed to lie in the personnel of the government rather than in the machinery of decision-making. This was bound to imperil the Liberal Ministry.

III

Any course of events that was undermining the position of the Liberal Party and the Asquith Government was fraught with consequences for the other political groups: the pre-war allies of the Liberal Government, Labour and the Irish Nationalists; and its opponents, the Conservatives.

The Irish Nationalists found themselves in a situation full of menace. At the outbreak of war they had embraced the British cause. Yet recruiting in Ireland never revealed the grass-roots endorsement of the war effort apparent in the rest of Britain (including Ulster). And once more the Nationalists were confronting a situation in which the long journey to Home Rule had been halted short of its destination. Certainly, the Home Rule Bill was at last on the statute book. But it had been made plain that it would not, anyway for an initial period of several years, apply to Ulster: that is, it envisaged a divided Ireland. And its operation was suspended for the duration of the war – which, it was becoming apparent, might constitute a long delay indeed. A sense was developing among the Irish that they could be cheated even yet.

Nor was this an idle fear. As Ian Hay's eulogy of McOstrich indicated, the war was enhancing the standing of those who had for so long thwarted Home Rule. Hence a strong possibility was developing that, before Irish self-government could ever be established, the 'Unionists' might triumph at a general election and halt the whole process. This danger had serious implications for the standing of the Irish Nationalists within Roman Catholic Ireland. For anticipation of the betrayal of Home Rule undermined the position of the Nationalists vis-à-vis Sinn Feiners and republicans, who rejected the policy of Irish self-government within the British connection and demanded the complete severance of Ireland from Britain. These sections repudiated Redmond's call for their nation to rally behind Britain in its hour of need. Rather, they embraced the historic policy that England's difficulty was Ireland's opportunity. Those who let this opportunity slip, they proclaimed, were no fit guardians of the Irish cause.

The war also placed a severe strain upon the Labour Party. The large majority of its MPs accepted the necessity for British intervention in the struggle. Yet for the Labour Party, as for the Liberals, this course conflicted with a tradition of internationalism and a suspicion of militarism. And the war was soon raising alarming possibilities of the erosion of working-class liberties. Moreover, the party did not escape division as a result of its endorsement of the war – and division in more than one direction. The resignation of Ramsay MacDonald from the chairmanship of the parliamentary party and the critical stance taken by Keir Hardie indicated that a small but weighty section of Labour denied the propriety of Britain's involvement in the war. Other elements moved in the opposite direction. They demanded of Labour a decidedly jingoistic stance. These tensions became evident when Keir Hardie died in September 1915. For, as has been related, in the ensuing by-election for his working-class seat the victor was not the official Labour candidate who, like MacDonald and Hardie, was identified with the ILP. The seat went to a former Labour candidate and miners' leader now representing a ferociously nationalistic breakaway group called the British Workers League.

Yet there was a restriction on how far the war could damage the Labour Party. For the political Labour movement had a limited by definite link with trade union organizations. And it was becoming evident that organized labour was going to be a vital element in prosecuting this war to victory. Some commentators might extol labour for responding to the call of patriotism. Others might condemn it for failing to amend workshop practices to meet the nation's needs. Either way, they had to recognize that it possessed the power to make or mar the war effort. By the same token, no blow that might be struck in the world of politics could be permitted to damage the Labour Party so grievously that it might arouse trade union resistance.

If the war carried with it a certain menace for Liberals, Labour, and Irish Nationalists, it was full of promise for the Conservatives. This may not have been immediately obvious. For one thing the Conservatives were restricted in waging party warfare or even in testing the tide of political opinion. At the outset of the war they agreed to the institution of a party truce. Hence when a constituency fell vacant only the party holding it would put up a candidate at the ensuing by-election; the other parties would voluntarily refrain. (The truce, of course, could not prevent independent candidates or those of splinter parties from standing.) In addition, Conservative MPs agreed to appear on platforms with those of other persuasions in support of the recruiting drive.

Yet a truce mentality never fully obtained, and this was to the Conservatives' benefit. The public was not allowed to forget that, for long before 1914, the Conservative Party had treated the probability of war with Germany as the cornerstone of its foreign policy and had demanded sterner measures of preparedness. Newspapers favourable to the Conservatives made much of this foresight. (So did John Buchan in his novel *The Thirty-Nine Steps*, published in 1915.) The right-wing press also grew frantic at the Government's supposed indulgence towards British residents of alien origin who, implicitly, constituted a nest of spies, and they connected this with the number of former aliens within the Liberal Party's own ranks. And notwithstanding the party truce, these journals subjected certain members of the Government to unrelenting persecution. On only the second day of the conflict the *Daily Express* set the scene for one of the war's most noteworthy hate campaigns by referring to 'elderly doctrinaire lawyers with German sympathies'. The reference was to Haldane, formerly War Minister and now Lord Chancellor, whom Leo Maxse of the *National Review* managed to convince himself was 'a very clever German . . . a German superman', and so a fair recipient for all the pent-up fury generated by the war.[5]

This type of journalism, in so far as it carried conviction, would have enhanced the Conservatives' cause even if members of the party had played no part in stimulating it. But it is plain that such partisan activities were welcome in at least some of the highest Conservative circles. The Unionist Central Office spurred on Leo Maxse in his campaign against prominent Liberals of alien origin, and the director of the Central Office, Arthur Steel-Maitland, expressed serious displeasure when J. L. Garvin in the *Observer* defended the actions of the Home Office in its handling of the aliens issue.[6]

---

[5] Quoted in Stephen Inwood, 'The Role of the Press in the First World War, with Special Reference to the Period 1914–1916', D.Phil. thesis, Oxford University, 1971, pp. 109–10.

[6] Ibid., pp. 129–30.

Yet despite the apparent trends in their favour, these were not easy times for the Conservative leaders. They felt the patriotic urge to maintain a united nation, and so ·were inhibited in prosecuting party warfare. Yet they recognized that they were in danger of being pushed to the political sidelines if they carried the practice of the party truce too far. And they did not doubt that they were better fitted than their opponents to be in charge of affairs, most of all at a time of great national endeavour. One historian refers to their 'deeply-running, but ill-defined, feeling that, in an infinite variety of ways, the Liberals were much less suited than the Unionists to deal with questions relating to war'.[7] This feeling reflected itself in the claim, which the Conservative leaders started making with little justification, that they had exercised a decisive influence upon the Government in its decisions both to go to war and to appoint Kitchener War Secretary.

The role of patriotic opposition was, in truth, difficult to define and fraught with pitfalls. If the Conservative leaders went too far in operating the party truce by acting jointly with the Government, they might be identified with deeds unpopular generally or unpalatable to their own followers. This danger became apparent in November 1914, when Austen Chamberlain agreed to engage in private discussions with Lloyd George over details of the Budget. Only six days later he gave up, on finding that the Chancellor of the Exchequer was proposing a tax on beer. Given the Conservative Party's associations with 'the trade', Chamberlain was not prepared to accept responsibility for such a measure. Patriotic enthusiasm, in short, had not wiped out sectional allegiances.

Nor had it diminished party animosities. One Conservative wrote in his diary of the anomaly both of acting jointly with a Government 'incapable of honesty or truth' and of 'going on tour with little-navyites, traducers of the Army and peace-at-any-price men to raise recruits and explain the war to the people': nevertheless 'we have certainly done it whole-heartedly'.[8] The only Conservative (A. J. Balfour) who did go far in acting with the Liberal Government, by participating regularly in ministerial discussions of war policy, soon came to be regarded by his own side as a doubtful member of the Conservative camp.

From early in 1915 a strong current was running in the Conservative Party towards adopting a more combative political posture. One manifestation was the formation of the Unionist Business Committee, a largely back-bench body that met for the first time in January. It contained only one of the party's major figures: Walter Long, a Tory squire who possessed strong links with the party rank and file. (He saw it as his role to prevent the leaders and the Business Committee from getting too far out of phase with one another.) Twice in early 1915 the party leaders and these back-benchers seemed likely to clash. The first time concerned Lloyd George's abortive proposal for state control of the drink traffic. Initially Bonar Law, rather surprisingly, was not hostile to the idea, and so came dangerously close to losing his hold on his followers. The second occasion concerned munitions supplies. In the House of Commons on 21 April Bonar Law seemed readier to accept the Government's explanations than his followers deemed was warranted.

Such a trend, should it continue, might seriously imperil Law's position. Hence he could not afford to remain inactive when, early in May, disturbing developments occurred in respect to both the Admiralty and the War Office.

---

[7] John Stubbs, 'The Conservative Party and the Politics of War 1914–1916', D. Phil. thesis, Oxford University, 1973, p. 101.

[8] W. Bridgeman's diary for 29 November 1914, quoted in Stubbs, ibid., p. 98.

IV

In the first fortnight of May 1915 the grim succession of failures in the conduct of the war occasioned upheavals in the upper ranks of the ministry.

One disturbance was the long-developing rupture at the Admiralty between Churchill and Fisher. The latter justly possessed an enormous reputation on account of his role, from 1904 to 1910, in equipping Britain to confront the German naval challenge. Hence it was not readily apparent that, by early 1915, he had ceased to be an asset to his country. Yet his part in the inception and implementation of the Gallipoli operation was not to his credit. If it is possible to divine any consistent attitude on Fisher's part, it was the same as Jellicoe's. That is, the navy must be concentrated in the North Sea to await a sortie by the German fleet. Diversionary operations, however modest in conception, that might make growing demands on naval resources should be rejected.

But although Fisher expressed such views to Jellicoe, he failed to do so to Churchill or the War Council. And there was a short-lived but crucial moment when he came round to supporting the operation, to the extent of agreeing to include the *Queen Elizabeth* in the squadron bombarding the Dardanelles forts. It is difficult to find a rationale for Fisher's behaviour. Probably, despite his fundamental agreement with Jellicoe, he was reluctant to appear an advocate of what, given the inaction of the German fleet, seemed a negative policy. He was regarded, and like to see himself, as a man of action, loudly proclaiming the merits of boldness in war. His attempts to reconcile this stance as a go-getter with his antipathy to the Dardanelles operation led him to adopt one position after another. Sometimes he would claim that the ships being employed at the Dardanelles were needed for a (quite hare-brained) plan of his own for invading northern Germany from the Baltic. Sometimes he claimed to approve of action at the Dardanelles but not on the terms being offered. He soon fell to complaining that he was always being out-argued by Churchill, ignoring the speciousness of the arguments that he was putting forward and that the First Lord made the mistake of taking seriously.

In mid-May 1915 Fisher at last fled from a position he had helped to render intolerable. He resigned over a fairly trivial matter of naval reinforcements for the Dardanelles, after his principal demand, for the withdrawal of the *Queen Elizabeth*, had been granted (to Kitchener's chagrin). No doubt he imagined that his purpose was to drive out Churchill, with some amenable person (or even himself) as his successor. But his subsequent conduct ensured that he would not be reinstated. First he refused – despite a directive from the Prime Minister – to return to his post until a replacement for himself had been found. Then he issued a set of intolerable demands as the price for his resumption of office.

Churchill felt himself to be on firm ground in dealing with this upset. He failed to recognize that on larger matters his position was much enfeebled. Lacking any solid body of support in the Government ranks, detested by large sections of the Opposition, he was also being widely suspected of engaging in conspiracies against the leaders of the Government. But, most of all, he was irredeemably associated with the operation at the Dardanelles. At crucial stages he had put forward the view first that it would be a straightforward proceeding to force the Dardanelles by ships alone, then that there would be no problem about effecting a military landing on the Gallipoli peninsula. These were serious misjudgements for the occupant of so important a post.

Another ministerial reputation, and one but lately high in stature, now stood at something of a discount. Kitchener was proving a good deal of a disappointment, if not to the general public, then to those in high places – to his colleagues, to prominent members of the Opposition, and to much of the press. He was not an amenable member of the Government. He resisted giving the Cabinet the information to which, under the British constitution, it was plainly entitled. Sometimes, when under pressure, he deliberately misinformed it. On other occasions, such as over the matter of French and the shells, he misled his colleagues because he had been misled himself, but on a subject about which it appeared he should have known the facts.

In important respects it was not Kitchener's fault that he was failing to give satisfaction. He was expected to perform a variety of tasks that, in such a war as this, were wildly beyond the capacity of one individual. He was not to blame that the members of the General Staff, a body of military experts who were supposed to advise the War Secretary, had gone off to France in August 1914 to participate in the expected speedy victory. Nor was he culpable because no preparations had been made for munitioning a large and ever-growing army engaged in a static conflict conducted by the methods of siege warfare.

Where he was open to criticism was in the tardiness of his response to these difficulties. He was not anxious to make good his lack of well informed and independently minded advisers. He seemed to prefer self-effacing and overly respectful assistants. And although, with commendable speed, he recognized the importance of weapons and munitions in this kind of warfare, it took him time to make the appropriate response: that of seeing this as a matter concerning heavy industry, to be dealt with by civilian experts and not by soldiers.

Kitchener may, as has been claimed (probably with exaggeration), have possessed a commanding stature that placed his cabinet colleagues in awe of him. Nevertheless, he was from the outset occupying a terribly exposed position, comparable only with that of Churchill. Territory that was lost, attacks that failed to regain it, and the swelling lists of casualties, all came home directly to him. His position was exposed in another sense as well. He seemed to be occupying several key posts in the Government: those that dealt with strategy, recruiting, weaponry. Any thrusting and ambitious political figure, interested in political advancement or the progress of the war, would be eager to take over one or more of these roles.

Lloyd George was a man much concerned with both the progress of the war and his own part in it. This development had not been predictable: he had paused long before committing himself to the conflict. But, once engaged, his commitment was whole hearted. And from the moment the country went to war he began scoring some noteworthy successes. His financial arrangements for tiding the country over the initial emergency aroused much admiration. His speeches on the war appealed particularly to those who, like himself, had begun by entertaining doubts about the righteousness of Britain's cause and were eager to have their doubts laid to rest. His first war Budget, in November 1914, achieved a most satisfactory double: it required only a modest level of sacrifice and yet was hailed as proof of the nation's determination to stint nothing in prosecuting the struggle. By February 1915, whereas a number of his colleagues were undergoing savage attacks in the press, it was being said of Lloyd George that 'all men speak well of him.'[9]

From early in the conflict Lloyd George revealed that he was not so overawed by Kitchener that he would keep silence on army matters. He protested furiously at what he deemed slights by the War Office upon Welshmen and Nonconformists. He gave voice to highly independent views on military strategy. And he began involving himself

---

[9] *Liberal Magazine*, February 1915.

in a number of aspects of munitions production, not least in the area where he possessed qualifications enjoyed by no member of the military establishment and few civilians: labour relations. By March 1915 he was making it clear that he would endure Kitchener's control over munitions matters no longer. Moreover the personal relations between the two were sometimes lamentable. 'Terrible row at Cabinet between Ll. George & K.', Hankey noted in his diary for 16 April 1915. That is, if Lloyd George had not set his heart on becoming director of munitions production, he was revealing a marked capacity for the job. He was also insisting that the present incumbent be unseated.

Kitchener, meanwhile, had acquired dangerous enemies outside the ranks of the Government. Some powerful Conservatives were becoming disillusioned with him: among them Curzon, who had had no cause to love Kitchener since their spectacular feud in India a decade earlier, which had forced Curzon to resign as Viceroy; and Walter Long, who listened sympathetically to French's complaints about the way in which the War Secretary was starving him of troops and shells. Kitchener had also done much to alienate newspaper proprietors and journalists by the way in which he was denying the press access to the battlefield. In particular he had alienated Northcliffe, the proprietor of one very popular and one highly respected newspaper (the *Daily Mail* and *The Times*).

Northcliffe was a quite unstable personality. As a merchandizer of newspapers he knew that it was his job to tell the public what it was already thinking. But as a wildly successful self-made man he sometimes became convinced that he could determine what the public would think. By the early months of 1915 he held two firm views concerning Kitchener. The first was that he himself had been responsible for elevating Kitchener to his present position. The second was that Kitchener had betrayed him, both by his ban upon press reporters at the front and by his ill-usage of Sir John French (with whom Northcliffe, according to the Liberal *Daily News* on 22 May, had a 'special friendship' which had been 'notorious for some time'). On the matter of reporters at the front, Northcliffe went to see Kitchener direct but without success; after a heated exchange he was shown the door. Regarding the second matter, Northcliffe wrote to French on 1 May urging him to put his grievances before the public.[10] This led to the opening less of a door than of a Pandora's box.

Eight days later French, already fearful that Kitchener was planning his removal, launched the attack on Aubers Ridge. It failed completely. Lest this further setback be used to unseat him, he chose to act first. He attributed his failure to want of munitions and held Kitchener to blame. This view he imparted to Kitchener's most devoted adversary in the Government, Lloyd George, and also to the Conservative leader Bonar Law and ex-leader Balfour. In addition he communicated it to Northcliffe, using the military correspondent of *The Times* (a former ally of Kitchener, now disgruntled) who chanced to be staying with French. On the strength of this prompting, *The Times* on 14 May ran a strong report and a leading article on the munitions question. It did not directly name the individuals concerned. But it warmly praised the role of command in the recent operation ('The attacks were well planned and valiantly conducted'). And it laid the responsibility for failure at the door of the War Office ('The want of an unlimited supply of high explosive was a fatal bar to our success'). The appearance of so patently inspired a piece could not pass without consequence.

The very next day, the breakdown of relations between Churchill and Fisher (of which for weeks rumours had been rife) came to a head. Fisher resigned. Two days

---

[10] For these events, see George H. Cassar, *Kitchener: Architect of Victory* (London: Kimber, 1977), pp. 350–2.

later Bonar Law received oblique intimation of this fact from Fisher himself. Law was already confronting a situation in which his more vociferous followers were demanding a parliamentary inquiry into aspects of the conduct of the war that were 'giving rise to much anxiety'.[11] On receiving the news about Fisher, he repaired to Lloyd George to seek confirmation. This being provided, he warned Lloyd George that unless the Government were 'reconstructed' he could not prevent a resumption of full-scale party warfare.

Bonar Law's choice of Lloyd George as the recipient of this view was probably not accidental. Some three months earlier Lloyd George had spoken to both Law and Austen Chamberlain about 'the memorandum which he had drawn up in 1910' concerning 'the possibility of a Coalition of the two great Parties'. He had pressed copies of it upon them.[12] At that stage Law had not responded favourably to the idea of a coalition, although he was of the view that it would come 'in time'.[13] Now, unless he was to wage party warfare on the Government or lose hold on his followers, he saw no alternative.

Lloyd George went to Asquith to express the need for a change of Government. The Prime Minister quickly agreed. It was only a week since he had told the House of Commons, in response to an inquiry from a Liberal MP well known both for his affinity to Lloyd George and for his hankering after a coalition, that no such move was under consideration. But apparently the emergence of the munitions issue (with all its manifestations) and the Fisher resignation were serving to convince him both that some large action was imperative and that he would have to consult the Conservative leaders on 'the steps to be taken'.[14] Now he was confronted with the threat of all-out party warfare, and the possibility of an association between Lloyd George and Bonar Law. And over all hung the menace that, with the life of Parliament due to expire in the next nine months, these matters might – at great cost to the unity of the country and the fortunes of the Liberal Party – be shortly transferred to the constituencies.

So in mid-May 1915 Asquith decided to dissolve the Liberal Government and form a coalition ministry in which Liberals, Conservatives, and Labour would all hold places. (The Irish Nationalists were invited to come in, but could not run the risk of joining.)[15] Yet at the time he did so Asquith's position as head of the Liberal Government had not deteriorated beyond redemption. He was, among purely political figures, the largest in the land, whose steadiness of character and intellectual capacity were widely acknowledged. His opponents made much of his evident personal shortcomings; but it may be speculated that a good deal of the hatred they felt towards him was excited less by his failings than by his manifest abilities – particularly when contrasted with the qualities of their own rather ordinary leader.

Unless Asquith voluntarily relinquished the headship of the Government, it would be rash at that moment for anyone else on his side of the House to seek to replace him. Lloyd George certainly did not yet possess the stature to do so. He was showing great

---

[11] This particular demand came from Lord Robert Cecil. See Stephen Koss, *Asquith* (London: Allen Lane, 1976), p. 184, quoting from the diary of Austen Chamberlain for 14 May 1915.

[12] Lloyd George had not forgotten about his coalition scheme in the years between 1910 and 1915. In a letter to Garvin on 31 December 1913 he referred to the Conservative leaders' failure to respond to the idea in 1910 as 'their great refusal' (Lloyd George Papers). The response of the Liberal E. S. Montagu to the proposal, when Lloyd George showed it to him in November 1914, was one of amazement. 'Well!' he said. 'I always thought you weren't really a Liberal!' A. J. P. Taylor (ed.), *Lloyd George: A Diary by Frances Stevenson* (London: Hutchinson, 1971), p. 15.

[13] Quoted in Stubbs, 'The Conservative Party and the Politics of War 1914–1916', p. 118.

[14] Winston S. Churchill, *The World Crisis 1911–1918* (London: Odhams Press, n.d.), vol. 2, p. 767.

[15] Their credibility in southern Ireland was further weakened by the fact that two 'legal' posts in the new government went to Conservatives (Edward Carson and F. E. Smith) identified with the most extreme forms of Ulster's intransigence.

capacity for innovation and improvisation. But his judgement was far from sure. There was much that was courageous about the way that he had sounded the cry against excessive drinking among munitions workers. But so carried away did he become by the matter that he managed to give much offence to organized labour, cause Cabinet colleagues to doubt his grasp on financial realities, and alarm Conservative defenders of the drink traffic.

As for the Conservative leader, it might be courting disaster for him to grasp at power at this time, notwithstanding the urgings of firebrands in his own party. Too reckless an attempt to pursue party warfare could easily backfire. And even if Bonar Law did manage to seize office, what sort of Government could he form that would be adequate to deal with this many-faceted crisis? A purely Conservative ministry would be ill-equipped to impose measures of national organization – decidedly in keeping with its own principles and at odds with those of the other parties – in face of the hostility of Home Rulers, militant trade unionists, and devout Liberals. Admittedly, Bonar Law rarely expressed concern for the sensibilities of such bodies as Irish Nationalists, organized labour, and Nonconformists. Yet it may be speculated that he recognized the unwisdom of embarking on a course that would severely antagonize such groups. This left him ill-placed actually to seek the overthrow of a Prime Minister who, even if diminished in stature, could still invoke the allegiance of these sections.

As it happened, events in the days that followed Asquith's decision to form a coalition – and while posts were still being haggled over – marginally strengthened Asquith's hand. It became apparent, even before the fierce public backlash against Northcliffe's attacks on Kitchener, that the War Secretary could not be removed from office. That made the 'shells scandal' a difficult weapon for the Conservatives to wield, should they not get what they wanted in a coalition and contemplate embarking on party warfare instead. And it rendered Asquith yet more difficult to replace. For Kitchener in office (despite his 'conservative' views on politics and the fact that Asquith had contemplated removing him) was Asquith's man, not Bonar Law's.

Nor did Lloyd George prove anxious to conciliate Bonar Law. He was soon working closely with Asquith in deciding how offices in the reconstructed Government should be apportioned. And when the Conservatives proved reluctant to accept what was being offered them, Lloyd George was prepared – or anyway claimed to be prepared – to give up the whole idea of a coalition Government. He suggested keeping the bulk of the Liberal Government in office, strengthened (if that is the word) by some 'independent' members of the House of Lords – a proposal that, once again, suggests how variable was his political judgement. The part that Lloyd George played in pressing Bonar Law to take a post in the coalition Government well below what was appropriate for the Conservative leader constituted an astonishing sequel to their entente of 17 March. For long it secured him Bonar Law's enmity.

Hence the outcome of the Government upheaval was strangely paradoxical – and so proved less than satisfactory as a resolution of the nation's political difficulties. The coalition Government was formed by a Prime Minister acting under the duress of untoward circumstances and political challenge but not of dire and inescapable necessity. It left Asquith unrivalled at the head of affairs and Kitchener at the head of the War Office, yet with their reputations damaged and their assurance of command shaken. The same sort of anomaly applied to the Liberal Party. It remained the strongest party in Government. Yet it had been humiliated, as was driven home by the fact that Haldane, plainly the subject of a scurrilous campaign, was denied a place in the new ministry. And its most cherished principles, already eroded by the war, now seemed in considerable peril.

The position of the Conservatives was similarly equivocal. They had scored a political success and were back in office after a decade. Yet their share of offices was not grand, and it seemed smaller to themselves than it did to their opponents. For example, Liberals might note with unease that not only the War Office but also the Admiralty now rested with a person usually classified as a 'Conservative'. Followers of Bonar Law, by contrast, doubted if either Kitchener or Balfour should be counted on their side of the ledger. They were more aware that the Liberals still held a majority (if by no means an overwhelming one) of posts in the Cabinet, and that many of these were positions of importance – certainly by comparison with that of their leader, who was relegated to the Colonial Office.

Given its equivocal nature, the new Government was scarcely equipped to confront head-on the great issue that the war was now presenting to the country. This issue was stated explicitly by Garvin, who was both an influential Conservative editor and an associate of Lloyd George. He claimed that the 'chief cause of the political revolution' – by which he meant the change to a coalition Government – was 'the question of munitions, involving the vaster question of organising the entire nation for the industrial as well as the military purposes of the war'. What had happened in the May 1915 crisis, wrote Garvin, was this:

> A purely party Cabinet had shown itself to be incapable of dealing with the questions of Drink and Munitions. It would be the less capable afterwards of dealing with other questions bound to arise in connection with what Mr. Asquith has called 'the full mobilisation and organisation' of the country for war. . . .[1]

If the 'purely party Cabinet' had failed to master the issue of mobilizing the country for war, it did not seem certain that its successor, the Asquith coalition, was well fitted for the task. Certainly, the reconstruction had placed Lloyd George, now emerging as a dedicated mobilizer, in charge of the most crucial of all internal posts, munitions. But the ejection of Haldane and the downgrading of Churchill had effectually disposed of two other Liberal advocates of mobilization. Again, the introduction of a contingent of Conservatives had brought in an important, but not undiluted, body of supporters for the cause of 'mobilisation and organisation'. But they found themselves alongside a goodly number of Liberals who dreaded the economic disruption and threat to basic liberties that this cause implied.

Nor did the entry of Labour members into the Government make clearer its course in this matter. Their accession might betoken much at a time when circumstances were requiring increased state direction of the workforce. Yet the Labour Party was as devoted as most Liberals to those individual liberties that such direction was bound to undermine. As for the unwillingness (indeed, inability) of the Irish Nationalists to join the Government, this was striking evidence of the fact that, in one part of the British Isles, no central Government any longer possessed the authority to mobilize resources. Finally, there was the question of where the Prime Minister himself stood on this issue of 'mobilisation and organisation'. Although it was he whom Garvin was quoting, it might be thought that his inclinations lay with those who longed to fight the war by methods of free choice and individual initiative, and who viewed the imposition of contrary methods with dread.

Did Asquith, when he allocated posts in the Government, deliberately maintain a balance between the advocates of compulsion and the devotees of freedom? This may have been so. Yet it is difficult to see how, given the many pressures which had to be

---

[16] *Observer*, 23 May 1915. For this matter see Alfred Gollin, 'Freedom or Control in the First World War', *Historical Reflections*, vol. 2, no. 2, 1975.

taken into account, he could have come up with a very different Government. Certainly, he might have handled some individuals differently. For example, he could have downgraded McKenna and upgraded Samuel instead of doing the reverse, but that would have signified little. In larger respects the state of parties and politics demanded most of what he did: a few places for Labour; several places for the Conservatives; a slender majority of places for the Liberals; a major role for Lloyd George and no great role for Churchill; the retention of Kitchener at the War Office but with diminished powers; and the retention of Grey at the Foreign Office but with the post ever-diminishing in importance. For the rest there remained great uncertainties defying prime ministerial calculation: because thanks to the pressures of war it was ceasing to be predictable where, at any point on crucial subjects, particular individuals would stand – with Lloyd George the most particular individual of all.

In sum, the composition of the new Government was appropriate to the political circumstances of this moment. But that did not produce a ministry geared to directing the country through the stressful times ahead. Probably, given the issues then developing or soon to develop, May 1915 was not a moment well chosen for a Government reconstruction. But matters were pressing. And no better time was in prospect.

19

THE COURSE OF THE ASQUITH COALITION

A new phase has been reached in the Conscription controversy, and the burning question appears to be whether the necessary men are to be compelled to volunteer or persuaded to be compulsorily enrolled.

Punch, *October 1915*

I

The course of politics following the institution of the coalition in May did not run smoothly. Ultimate authority still rested in a Cabinet of 25. From early in the War so large a number had been recognized as unwieldy. So in November 1914 a sub-committee, known as the War Council, had been instituted. With the change of Government it was replaced by a body of different name (the Dardanelles Committee) but identical function. Under whatever title, this instrument proved inadequate. It was itself too large for rapid decision-making. (The Dardanelles Committee numbered nine at its inception but soon rose to 12 and then 14.) And it lacked final authority. Its conclusions went as recommendations to the full Cabinet, where the arguments pro and con might again be rehearsed before a decision was reached.

These defects in the instruments of government were aggravated by matters of personality. Asquith's continuance as Premier, and so as chairman of both Cabinet and Dardanelles Committee, ensured that there would be no driving man at the helm. This had been a deficiency in the last years of peace. But it had in a measure been offset by his skill in co-ordinating an able, though wilful, body of colleagues. It was proving much more of a shortcoming in war, when events would not always tarry on Asquith's methods of striking a balance or working towards a compromise; and when the nation, sometimes without reason, felt the need for a thrusting figure in command.

Again, there was little cohesion in the coalition Government between new Ministers and old or between their groups of supporters. Asquith, at the outset, took a dim view of the former opponents he was admitting to office. Hankey records: 'He said that Balfour, Curzon, and possibly Bonar Law were the only ones with brains.' (Hankey himself, after a first meeting with the new Ministers, did not dissent: 'Not a very bright lot, except Balfour I thought.')[1] On the Treasury benches the various sections of Ministers seemed less than eager to cohere. And their attitude was mirrored among their parliamentary followers. The Liberal rank and file felt resentful at the abrupt and ill-explained demise of the late Government and, not least, at the apparent sacrifice of Haldane to a right-wing witchhunt. The Conservative back-benchers had little cause to be satisfied with a political arrangement that gave them neither a commanding place in government nor a clear role in opposition.

---

[1] Hankey's diary, 21 May and 12 June 1915.

There was another large factor now operating in politics that might imperil the Asquith coalition. The creation of a Ministry of Munitions had done more than give Lloyd George new responsibilities; it had placed him in a new position politically. As yet he possessed neither the following nor probably the desire to bid for the premiership. But he could at any time place the Government's continuance in jeopardy. And, wittingly or not, he did by public statements and well canvassed attitudes profoundly aggravate its problems. For example, he made no secret of his distinctive views on strategy, of his disrespect for Kitchener and the administration at the War Office, and of his differences with most of his Liberal and Labour colleagues over conscription. His displays of independence culminated in December, when he delivered a well pondered speech in Parliament condemning the general prosecution of the war as always 'too late': 'the footsteps of the Allied forces have been dogged by the mocking spectre of "Too late".' The utterance caused a vast sensation and was widely taken to be an expression of no confidence in the Government of which he was a member.

Did Lloyd George will the political turbulence that flowed from such actions? At the time his private secretary, Frances Stevenson, described him as deeply distressed at the way in which events were dividing him from Asquith and the Liberals. As for the 'Too late' speech, she called it 'the charges which he was unable to help bringing' against the War Office.[2] (The charges, in fact, struck at more people than that.) Lloyd George spoke similarly to Seebohm Rowntree, when in November this noted Quaker and social reformer called on him. Rowntree was bearing an appeal from his father, the cocoa magnate, that Lloyd George should not forsake democracy or allow the disfavour of his own party and the adulaton of the Tories to turn him from his Liberal convictions. Lloyd George offered ample reassurance. He had not only taken up the cause of the people, he said, but he was '*one of them*'. And although he was working in conjunction with Curzon and others, 'he loathed the Curzon set, and all that they stood for – loathed their mannerisms, their ideals, their customs, their mode of life.'[3]

Rowntree appears to have departed satisfied. Yet the remarks that had been made to him were not free from ambiguity. First, the association between Curzon and Lloyd George, which had flourished three months earlier, was by November at a discount. A sharp difference over the Gallipoli operation, which Lloyd George wanted abandoned and Curzon was determined to maintain, had caused a falling out. Hence this denunciation of Curzon may not have been saying very much about Lloyd George's political position. Secondly, immediately after vowing that he had not merely taken up the cause of the people but was '*one of them*', Lloyd George described Bonar Law as 'also more or less of humble origin'. Was he, then, only countering the suggestion that he was slipping away from his former principles by replying that he stood by 'democracy' in the sense that Bonar Law did? If so, it was questionable reassurance.

This personal matter must not be over-stressed. Lloyd George's conduct would hardly have loomed so large but for the divisive issues confronting the Government. The removal of Churchill and Fisher from the Admiralty had not eliminated the problem that occasioned their falling out: the deadlock at the Dardanelles. Nor was the infusion of new blood into the Government of assistance here. The Conservative leader, Bonar Law, soon became vehement in demanding withdrawal from Gallipoli. Curzon, as already mentioned, was equally determined in resisting this course. Again, although munitions had been largely taken out of Kitchener's hands, he continued in charge of the War Office despite the growing conviction in high circles that he was not

[2] A. J. P. Taylor (ed.), *Lloyd George: A Diary by Frances Stevenson* (London: Hutchinson, 1971), pp. 57, 87.
[3] Ibid., p. 76

competent to administer so important a department or to exercise a large role in strategy.

At the same time weighty issues that had scarcely begun to disturb the old Government were rising to the point where they might disrupt the new. There was the strategic question: not just the prosecution or abandonment of the Gallipoli operation but whether or not to renew the assault in France and what (if anything) to do about the Balkans. Another and much greater issue, which all along had been in the background, was now demanding consideration: compulsory service. For the first nine months of the war this matter had been in a sense academic. More men had been offering themselves to the army than it could equip or train. From mid-1915 this was ceasing to be the case. The number coming forward was proving insufficient. Anyway, there was an increasing body of citizens who felt that, irrespective of the sum of volunteers, adult males should not be allowed the choice of deciding whether or not to serve their country. Early in May the rector of Great Leighs reported, regarding his Essex village: 'indignation is felt at the supineness of the authorities in not *taking* the loafers of military age. Mr. Barker, who brings the morning mail from Chelmsford, says he hears everywhere the saying "England expects that every man should be made to do his duty."' At a more exalted ecclesiastical level, in June the Archbishops of Canterbury and York issued a pastoral letter espousing a similar view. It stated that they looked ('with confidence') to the Government to take, 'and with courage', whatever steps it considered necessary 'to summon and control every possible resource which we have of body and brain, of wealth and industry'.[4] From an opposing viewpoint the radical newspaper the *Manchester Guardian* warned on 1 June: 'The attempt to stampede the country into conscription is now in full swing.'

II

The nation's leaders endeavoured to grapple with these problems. In November, under pressure from some of his colleagues, Asquith again reorganized the small body advising the Cabinet on war matters. Its name was changed a third time: from the Dardanelles Committee to the War Committee. And its number was pruned to five. Yet in no time the same complaints would be heard: that too many additional members or temporary advisers were attending its meetings; that the need to refer its conclusions to the Cabinet hindered decision-making; and that the Prime Minister lacked drive.

One person was accorded no seat on the new War Committee in November: Churchill. He thereupon resigned from the Government (although remaining an MP). For a spell he even took up military duties on the Western Front. He gave as his grounds for going that he declined to remain in well paid inactivity. But there was an even more potent reason. Nothing he now could do, in office or out, would save the Gallipoli expedition. Its abandonment was only a matter of time. That resolved one issue of strategy. But the question of the Balkan alternative, which so exercised Lloyd George, continued to plague the Government.

In another area matters were working out more to Lloyd George's satisfaction. The demotion of Kitchener, begun in May, was carried several stages further in the ensuing months. This was a painful, and a delicate, proceeding. Certainly, it caused no division in the Cabinet. Opinion there was well-nigh unanimous that Kitchener was unfit for his post: that he was incapable of heading a team, a poor guide on matters of strategy, and frequently downright untruthful in what he told his Cabinet colleagues. The

---

[4] Copy among the papers of the Rev. Andrew Clark, in the Bodleian Library, Oxford.

Conservatives in the Government, who might have been expected to respond to his cast of mind, had a further grievance against him: his refusal to come out clearly for conscription.

Yet Kitchener remained difficult to jettison. For one thing, his stature among the public continued high. The Northcliffe newspapers (*The Times*, the *Daily Mail*, and the *Evening News*), which, at their proprietor's bidding, had attempted to topple him, paid for their temerity in waning circulation. Once more the diary of our Essex clergyman offers a grass-roots opinion. Late in May Andrew Clark recorded the impressions of a parishioner in business who commuted regularly to London. This individual reported mounting indignation among his travelling companions at the 'abominable pretensions' of the Northcliffe papers to direct the War Office and the Admiralty. Formerly many had carried the *Daily Mail*. Now he never saw anyone with it. And on the return journey Northcliffe's once-popular *Evening News* had been quite superseded by other journals.

Hence Asquith faced the problem of preserving Kitchener in a position of eminence while depriving him of real authority. This, by the much derided method of choosing his moments, the Prime Minister accomplished with great skill. In September he requested Kitchener to reconstitute the General Staff. This body was supposed to be giving considered advice on military matters to the War Minister and, through him, to the Cabinet. But at the outbreak of the war its expert advisers had mostly gone to France, and their replacements had proved utterly subservient to the War Minister.

Hankey witnessed the General Staff in action on 23 September and was not impressed. Kitchener, he wrote in his diary, 'sits at the head of the table and talks a lot, and bludgeons everyone into agreeing with him'. The Chief of the Imperial General Staff, Wolfe Murray ('or "Sheep" Murray as Winston calls him'), merely mumbled assent, while the Director of Military Operations just agreed. 'Then K. proceeds to dictate, and it is dished up next day as a Memo. by the General Staff.'

As the beginning of change Wolfe Murray was replaced. Then, in November, the War Minister's position was further eroded. Kitchener was out of the country, viewing the impasse at the Dardanelles and trying to redeem something from the dismal situation in the Balkans. (His colleagues hoped – in vain – that he might prolong this roving commission indefinitely.) Asquith seized the opportunity to make two alterations. Final control over the supply of war material was transferred to the Minister of Munitions, so confirming contemptuous references to the War Office's administration that Lloyd George had made in Parliament in July. Yet more important, Kitchener ceased to be the Government's adviser on strategy. That role was taken over by the Chief of the Imperial General Staff, a post now assigned to Major-General Sir William Robertson. A blunt, forceful character, 'Wully' Robertson shared Lloyd George's humble origins and had risen in a profession even more resistant than politics to the advancement of members of the lower orders. Starting out on the bottom rung of the army ladder, he had ascended by sheer devotion to the business of being a soldier. He was every bit the professional.

On two issues Robertson was not in doubt; and his appointment as CIGS, with powers never before accorded to that post, settled them at least for the moment. One was the matter of strategy. In his view the war could only be won on the Western Front, and to it Britain must direct its endeavours. The other concerned Kitchener. If Robertson had ever regarded him as competent, he did so no longer. The terms in which he indicated to the War Secretary that the duties of military adviser to the Government now rested with himself were brutally frank. It was a tribute to Kitchener's patriotism that, with all authority gone, he agreed to remain in office.

III

If the resolution of the problem of Kitchener proved painful in a personal sense, the largest issue hanging over the Government during these months, conscription, was agonizing in many ways.

The idea of conscription, for army or industry, might appear to have much to recommend it in wartime, but it ran contrary to Britain's liberal traditions. Military conscription seemed a violation of the right of free-born Englishmen to choose whether or not to take up arms. And it constituted a formidable extension of the powers of the state in the interests of those conservative forces with which military authority was traditionally aligned. As for the enforced direction of labour, this threatened to reverse any advance towards independence that wage-earners had accomplished since the legalization of trade unions.

Certainly, it could be argued that these strong measures were being proposed only temporarily and to meet a national emergency. But would liberties, once surrendered, ever be restored? The attitudes of some of the earliest and loudest advocates of conscription, in Parliament and press and the community, were hardly reassuring. These people might oppose Prussia, but they were plainly enamoured of some aspects of Prussianism. To them a militarily trained populace and a regimented labour force were not unwelcome wartime necessities. They were elements in an ideal world.

Yet, plainly, this was not true of many Conservatives. At most, they did not balk at enforced military service should danger from without seem to require it – a situation that they deemed to be the case by the second half of 1915. Most Liberals, by contrast, along with their Labour colleagues, found conscription in any circumstances deeply repugnant. Their opposition, certainly, was not unqualified. However reluctantly, they would agree to compulsion for military purposes if the nation could be saved in no other way. But it seemed to many of them that the pressure now mounting for conscription sprang from quite different sources: the malevolent influence of the jingo press and the marked swing to the right in the balance of political forces.

One development might have assuaged the discomfort of Liberal and Labour members on this matter: the fact that a Liberal luminary, but recently regarded as well on the left of the party, was now endorsing compulsion. In his first public address as Minister of Munitions, Lloyd George in June stated that industrial conscription might become necessary, and that he accepted military conscription in principle although it was not required as yet. But this development, far from offering the Liberal Party guidance through its dilemma, only increased its agony. Some Liberals, it is true, were responsive to Lloyd George's lead. But many, including former close associates, were not.

For the truth was that Lloyd George, on good grounds or ill, was not always regarded as having a firm grasp on Liberal principles. For not a few years, doubts had been expressed as to whether he might not go the way of Joseph Chamberlain, the one-time radical leader who had found his final home among the party's enemies. Lloyd George's endorsement of military compulsion, along with his eagerness for a coalition with the Conservatives and his hankering (as he put it in a private letter to a Conservative editor) for a 'properly disciplined nation',[5] could be interpreted as evidence of infirmity of allegiance to the Liberal cause.

So, in a letter of 12 June 1915, a prominent Nonconformist much in accord with the Minister of Munitions was compelled to admit: 'There has been much jealousy of

---

[5] See below, p. 215.

Lloyd George, and there are not a few of his own party who would like to see him destroyed.'[6] At the same time the Liberal editor J. A. Spender was reporting members of his own party as being 'very disgruntled with L. G.': 'They believe he is going the way of [Joseph] Chamberlain and are much perturbed at a sentence in one of his recent speeches, in which he foreshadowed the extinction of party politics and indicated the possibility of men standing side by side who had hitherto been bitterly opposed to each other.' According to Spender: 'Our people do not feel like that. They intend that after the war Liberal principles shall be maintained and advocated as strongly as ever.'[7] The fears that Lloyd George's turn towards conscription, industrial as well as military, had aroused within his own party became apparent in the House of Commons on 7 June, during a debate on his Munitions of War Bill. There was 'a tremendous explosion against any notion of labour compulsion.'[8]

Asquith responded to the mounting pressure for conscription by temporizing. Personally, it is clear, he loathed the notion of enforced military service. But in public what he said was that it should not be implemented until its necessity had been proved and until the nation was agreed on its adoption. Strangely, he found an ally in Kitchener, who for much of 1915 insisted that military conscription was not required. Perhaps for him it was not a case of principle. Rather, he did not wish to surrender the one task in which he had proved truly successful: that of persuading men to volunteer. Yet, if all unwittingly, Asquith and Kitchener had already conceded the game to the devotees of conscription. The War Secretary had declared that Britain must raise an army of 70 divisions. The Prime Minister had not dissented. So large a quantity of soldiers could be obtained only if all eligible men joined up. Yet as long as a significant number of eligibles remained unwilling to volunteer, be it on grounds of conviction or domestic need or simple unwillingness to place themselves at risk, then the 70–division goal could be obtained only by conscription.

The great question was when. In September Lloyd George published a volume of his war speeches, to which he contributed a preface. This caused something of a sensation, for it made it plain that he, for one, was not prepared to wait for conscription much longer. Then, in company with such prominent Conservatives as Curzon and Austen Chamberlain, he set about driving Asquith to capitulate. For his purpose he was even prepared to employ the powers of the House of Lords. The authority of that body had been seriously depleted since 1911, when it lost its perpetual veto. But the Lords could still delay any non-financial measure for two years. As it happened, the term of the existing House of Commons was due to expire in January 1916. If the Government were to avoid an election at that date, it would have to pilot through both Houses a Bill extending the life of the existing Parliament. Lloyd George and his associates took steps to ensure that no measure prolonging the term of the Lower House would pass through the Upper unless accompanied by a first instalment of military conscription.

Asquith can have been in no doubt that, in the political climate then prevailing, an election fought on the issue of conscription would disrupt his party and terminate his hold on office. That a colleague of the standing of Lloyd George, with whom he had waged the successful campaign against the House of Lords, should now use that institution of privilege as a weapon against him, and for such a purpose, can hardly have been other than repugnant. Arguably, it was during these months that the

[6] William Robertson Nicoll to St Loe Strachey, 12 June 1915, Strachey papers, House of Lord Records Office.
[7] *Lord Riddell's War Diary 1914–1918* (London: Ivor Nicholson & Watson, 1933), p. 104.
[8] Christopher Addison, *Four and a Half Years* (London: Hutchinson, 1934), vol. 1, p. 91.

separation of Asquith from Lloyd George, which was to be a potent factor in politics for many years to come, really took hold. Certainly, by mid-October each man in private was speaking of the other with marked hostility.

The Prime Minister was not without resources in dealing with this menacing situation; but these resources had to be deployed in terms of Lloyd George's timetable. Early in October Asquith persuaded Lord Derby to become Director-General of Recruiting in a last great voluntary campaign. But it was an appeal that clearly envisaged a resort to force. On 2 November Asquith publicly assured Derby that unmarried men who failed to come forward would be compelled to serve.

Neither the first action, which seemed intended to rejuvenate the voluntary system, nor the second, which decreed its partial abandonment, appears to have come before the Cabinet. Indeed, the three most active Conservative conscriptionists pointedly drew Asquith's attention to the fact that the Derby scheme had been launched 'without any reference to or consent of the Cabinet'.[9] Asquith's decisiveness at this stage is deserving of note. He may have been a waning force. But, at least on one level, the resolute manner in which he fought his way out of these difficulties compels admiration.

Before 1915 ended it was apparent that the Derby scheme had failed and that a Bill conscripting the single men must be prepared. Given the reluctance of a significant body of bachelors to volunteer and the threat from Lloyd George to force a dissolution, the Prime Minister was in the comfortable position of having no choice. Yet he still had to contend with profound misgivings about conscription among Cabinet Ministers from the Liberal and Labour parties. Labour, as the ensuing weeks would reveal, could be won over by assurances that this measure would not be used to implement industrial conscription. (And as long as industrial conscription was what the Labour Party feared most, then Asquith, of all potential Prime Ministers, seemed the surest bulwark against it.) The opposition from within the Liberal Party was more complex, and by late December it had brought four of his leading colleagues to the point of resignation.

On 29 December the Prime Minister related the situation to his friend Lady Scott, who recorded the matter in her diary. Only one of the four, Sir John Simon, was actually taking his stand on the issue of individual liberty. He was 'convinced that forcing anyone [to bear arms] is wrong'. Grey, whose eyesight was failing and who had been pondering resignation anyway, felt he ought to go because so many of his close friends were leaving. (Lady Scott judged Grey's letter on the matter 'stupid & selfish'.) Runciman and McKenna, according to this record, 'had come blustering to see the P.M. They were excited & not very nice[,] McK. saying we couldnt afford this enlargening army & Runciman saying we couldnt spare the men from industry.'

These objections were sufficiently various as not to constitute a united front. Runciman and McKenna were querying Britain's capacity, in terms of financial resources and the demands of production, to contribute 70 divisions to the battlefield. But this weighty question had never been explored when Kitchener promulgated the need for so many men. Asquith could argue with cause that the matter should be gone into thoroughly (which did not necessarily mean that it ever would be), and that Runciman and McKenna should be present when it was. Yet such an inquiry could hardly be carried out before Asquith's pledge regarding the call-up of single men fell due. So McKenna and Runciman were persuaded to stay on. (Some said that the eagerness of Lloyd George and others to be quit of them had helped to influence their

---

[9] Joint letter of Curzon, Chamberlain, and Selborne to Asquith, 3 November 1915, Selborne papers, in the Bodleian Library, Oxford.

decision.) And as Grey had decided to go primarily because these close associates were departing, his resignation also lapsed. Hence only Simon, full of reluctance and misgiving, departed from office, to offer unavailing defence for an ideal that the war was fast undermining: that victory could be won without compelling the less than eager to contribute.

So by the beginning of 1916 Asquith was able to bring his coalition ministry to agree, for the loss of only one member, to the conscription of unmarried men. This was no small achievement. But it was an achievement that was flawed in important respects. The Bill proposed that single males should be conscripted because only thus could married men be persuaded to volunteer. But the Government contained devotees of conscription who had no wish to preserve the voluntary status of wedded males. (The numbers of those entering wedlock, it was noted, were fast increasing.) As Chamberlain, Curzon, and Selborne pointed out in joint letters to Asquith, the demand for an army of 70 divisions still stood, and to it they attached supreme importance. If this required the conscription of married as well as single men, then they held themselves free to urge it on the Cabinet.[10] Asquith's own position on this matter was hardly well based. On 7 November he had informed this trio of Conservatives that he was quite prepared to work towards 70 divisions but doubted if such a recruitable reservoir existed. Yet when, in January 1916, he introduced the conscription Bill to Parliament, he stated that he would be no party to compulsory service for married men – which suggested that he was prepared to leave part of the reservoir untapped.

As well as this ambiguity and this unresolved issue, there was a further reason why the Cabinet's near-unanimous endorsement of conscription seemed less than a triumph for the Prime Minister. In the last days of December, as the decision was being taken, the press carried seemingly inspired tales that Lloyd George had delivered an ultimatum to Asquith: if conscription were not immediately endorsed, the Minister of Munitions would resign. And the enactment of the measure itself occurred in the very month when, had the House of Lords tarried over the extension Bill, the life of the Lower House would have expired. So it seemed questionable whether Asquith, in persuading his colleagues to conscript the unmarried, was really demonstrating his political mastery. From one viewpoint he appeared to be capitulating before the threat of a general election and intimidation from his most conspicuous colleague.

---

[10] Joint letters by Chamberlain, Curzon, and Selborne to Asquith, 3 November and 29 December 1915, Selborne papers. Asquith replied to the first letter on 7 November 1915.

20

MEN AND MUNITIONS

The whole of this very serious and menacing trouble [unrest in the labour world] is but part of the price we are paying for running a great war on what is known as the 'voluntary' system. An undisciplined nation is fighting the best-disciplined country in the world, and some of our politicians think this terrible handicap is a real advantage. I wish they could have a few weeks experience of the Munitions Department. Were this a properly disciplined nation I could almost have doubled the output in a very short time.

Lloyd George to R. D. Blumenfeld, 25 October 1915

One thing is clear: the dispute [i.e. the 'disastrous and regrettable' strike on the Clyde] must be ended and the men got back to work at once. We who are pacifists dare not interfere with the essential supplies needed by the Army and Navy until the nation gives the word to 'stop the war'.

Herald, 30 March 1916

I

Britain had made no economic or industrial plans for war. Nor, when war broke out, did it begin to plan industrially and economically. Certainly, arrangements had been made as far back as 1871 whereby, on the commencement of hostilities, the Government would take command of the railways, so important were they to the mobilization and dispatch of any army. And, in order to keep Britain's merchant fleet at sea, the Government underwrote a war risks insurance scheme. It also acted to preserve the food supply – for example, by taking control of the purchase and import of sugar, a commodity hitherto largely supplied by the Central Powers. But these were isolated actions, not parts of a master plan.

That the Government failed to do more can only partly be attributed to the British predilection for just muddling through. Two other considerations were more important. One was the general conviction that the war would be a short affair. A military type in a *Punch* cartoon of 1909 trusted that any war would run its course 'between the polo and the huntin' ', so as not to interfere with the normal sporting round. Even the railways were taken over for one week only, so that for the next four and a half years the ritual of requisition had to be repeated every seven days.

The second consideration that had precluded economic planning for war was the part envisaged for Britain in any conflict. The British contribution, it had been assumed, would be twofold. The navy would both command the seas and, by means of the blockade, would gravely impair Germany's war-waging capacity. And Britain's great financial resources would be employed to support its allies in the land war. What is noteworthy about this scenario is the role that Britain was not expected to play. It would not, to any notable extent, contribute to the land battle on the Continent.

215

Plate 15   *David Lloyd George addressing a 'Women's Right to Serve' demonstration in London.*

In so far as Britain would be participating in the clash of armies in Europe, it would be doing so economically, out of its great surplus wealth. But to accomplish that, it must maintain its profitable trading position. That is, it must maintain 'business as usual'.[1]

If the war was going to be brief and Britain's contribution predominantly non-military, then established British industry and finance could provide the nation's needs for armaments and money, as well as being able to subsidize Britain's allies. In so far as the war was likely to be costly, it was agreed that it should be financed by borrowing, with repayment spread thin over future generations. At the commencement of hostilities a major concern was that a financial crisis would develop, as people withdrew their cash from banks and hoarded it and as international financial movements – with which Britain's economy was vitally involved – became disrupted through 'the one economic world [being] split into two opposed groups.'[2]

The run on banks did not develop. Nevertheless, the paper money (the £1 and 10/- notes) issued to meet it soon proved that it had come to stay. It carried a reassuring inscription promising to pay on demand its equivalent in gold, a promise that, fortunately, the Bank of England was not called on to honour. A show of firmness by the Chancellor of the Exchequer and the Bank authorities, and sensible measures (like those designed to support financial institutions whose debts in enemy countries were at present irrecoverable), served to forestall any serious crisis. For the rest, Government and industry strove to preserve an equable pattern of supply and demand by promoting confidence.

But economic expectations soon started to go awry. Although a financial crisis had been averted, Britain now lacked its valuable markets in countries that had become its enemies. It was also suffering a diminution in the lucrative financial transactions handled by British banks and insurance firms. But most of all, by raising a mass army of

---

[1] For this line of argument, see two writings of David French: *British Economic and Strategic Planning 1905–1915* (London: Allen & Unwin, 1982), and 'The Rise and Fall of "Business as Usual"', in Kathleen Burk (ed.), *War and the State* (London: Allen & Unwin, 1982).

[2] William Ashworth, *An Economic History of England 1870–1939* (London: Methuen & Co., 1965), p. 266.

young and fit males the country had jettisoned the fundamental principle on which pre-war planning (including 'business as usual') was based. For a Continental-scale army meant withdrawing a highly productive element from the labour force. It also required the country to divert some of its productive capacity to feeding, clothing, sheltering, transporting, and munitioning these unplanned hundreds of thousands of soldiers. Yet it was in no position to supply such needs by reducing its volume of exports, for from them came foreign exchange of which Britain had growing need as the exigencies of war forced it to increase its imports of raw materials and manufactured goods.

All this might be managed, and business might proceed somewhat as usual, as long as the war did not go on for too long. But it has already been observed that the Government was showing itself wiser than conventional military orthodoxy by pressing ahead with the raising and training of an army whose only role could be in a long war. Where it was delinquent was in refusing to acknowledge the corollary of its wisdom: that a mass army meant a prolonged conflict, and a prolonged conflict urgently demanded a powerful Government initiative in unanticipated parts of the economy.

The obvious place where its initiative was needed was in provisioning the army. Two problems presented themselves. What types of supply were needed? And how were they to be procured? Only as the conflict froze into the immobility of trench warfare did an answer to the first question (and a very uncomfortable one) start to emerge. A war of movement, however prolonged, made little use of heavy guns or high-explosive shells – heavy guns being difficult to move about in a hurry and hence of use only when the front stabilized for a time. But very soon this war had removed the limitations on the usefulness of heavy artillery by presenting a stable front that failed to yield even to vast pitched battles. If it was to be prised open and mobility restored, large numbers of heavy guns must be employed.

The same was true of the type of shell needed. The army used high explosive only against fortifications and equipment. Its weapon against personnel was shrapnel, and seemingly with good reason: for the killing and maiming of troops in the open it was most effective. A shrapnel shell has been described as a 'flying gun' containing some 250 to 350 lead balls and a charge of gunpowder. The gunpowder was set off not by impact but by a fuse timed to explode while the shell was still above its intended victims. The 'explosion of the powder would blow out the balls in an expanding cone at high velocity, delivering hundreds of lethal missiles onto the unprotected heads below'.[3] Technical developments in the nineteenth century, particularly the substitution of the elongated shell for the cannonball, had made shrapnel much more deadly by ensuring that its content of lead balls would always be driven in the direction towards which it was travelling.

Trench warfare, however, changed this. Trenches were a form of fortification, offering their occupants fair shelter from bullets whether fired by rifle, machine-gun, or shrapnel shell. Against troops in the open shrapnel would hit a man if the range was accurate within 150 yards. Against trench-dwellers the required degree of accuracy became 5 yards. That level of precision was rare indeed. This did not mean that shrapnel no longer had any uses, as evidenced by the fact that to the end of the war it constituted, by choice, at least 50 per cent (and usually nearer 70 per cent) of the army's artillery requirements. It was deemed more effective than high explosive against barbed wire, if fired with sufficient accuracy and decently fused. And it continued deadly against troops in the open, particularly those delivering an attack.

---

[3] Ian V. Hogg, *The Guns 1914–18* (London: Pan-Ballantine, 1973), pp. 16–17.

But during 1915 the Germans on the Western Front (except in the minor operation of Second Ypres) were standing on the defensive. If the artillery was to dislodge them, it would need high explosive to dig them out.

Yet the change from shrapnel to high explosive could not be accomplished just by altering a requisition order. Shrapnel could be manufactured fairly easily by an industrially advanced nation, and if the products were faulty, they would not (because of the limited quantities of explosive involved) cause much damage. The production of high-explosive shells that could be trusted not to detonate during manufacture and firing, and yet were certain to do so on contact with the enemy, was a skilled and perilous undertaking. Failure to acquire the necessary expertise beforehand could produce a variety of mishaps: explosions in munitions factories (each of which had its danger zone where high explosive was poured and packed into shells); premature detonations of shells in the gun barrels, destoying or damaging weapons and sometimes the men who tended them; failure of shells to explode on reaching their destination. The French suffered from many of these misfortunes in 1915 as a result of a crash programme of production – 1,000 guns were destroyed by faulty ammunition and 600 more put out of action pending repairs. Clearly, it would require more than businessmen of push and go, free from the trammels of military obtuseness, before Britain's needs in guns and shells could be satisfied.

While these supplies were pending, and the problem of whether or not they could blast a way through the enemy lines remained unresolved, other sorts of *matériel* were needed in prodigious quantities. British trenches must be rendered habitable and defensible. This required revetting posts, sandbags, barbed wire, and machine-guns; and in due course gas masks, and after that tin helmets (the head being the most attackable part of a trench-dweller). One statistic will serve for the rest. By the end of 1914 the army's requirements of sandbags, used chiefly in the construction of trenches and dug-outs (not least in Flanders, where the high water level prohibited digging to any great depth, so that trenches had to be built upwards), had reached the formidable figure of 250,000 a month. By May 1915 the monthly figure had reached 6 million.

Along with their need for these commodities wherewith to defend themselves, British soldiers required the means by which they could aid the artillery in rendering the enemy's trenches indefensible and uninhabitable. Among them were trench mortars, hand grenades, and periscopes; and later tunnelling equipment and poison gas.

Where were these things to come from? The military authorities expected the process of supply and demand to provide them. After all, whenever the War Office decided it needed men – half a million on 6 August 1914, another half million a month later, a further 1 million two months after that – Parliament promptly voted the necessary sums and the men came forth. It was presumed that appeals to industry would function similarly. The War Office would assess its needs; Parliament would provide the finance; and private enterprise would seize the proffered contracts.

In applying these principles the War Office had certain fixed procedures. There existed government ordnance factories to tide the army over the initial period. Simultaneously contracts were being placed with those manufacturers who were experienced in supplying the army's needs. It was considered that the best way of marshalling the untapped munitions-making resources of the country was by delegating to firms with knowledge the responsibility of bringing them forth through sub-contracting.

This proceeding was inadequate in two respects. In the short term private industry failed to deliver on schedule. In particular, sub-contractors who had eagerly taken on work either fell behind with deliveries or produced items that did not pass inspection tests. They were lacking in skilled labour, which may have been sufficient at the time when they accepted contracts but ceased to be so as skilled employees volunteered for the army or accepted better-paid positions elsewhere. They lacked the necessary machinery, principally because the delivery of machine tools that had been ordered in North America also fell behind schedule. And they lacked experience, a commodity that only time would provide. In these respects it is idle to apportion blame for munitions shortages in the early months of the war.

But in the longer term, War Office attempts to munition the army were bound to break down as long as reliance was placed on market forces – that is, on private industry's willingness, as long as the price was right, to produce whatever the army needed. 'Within a few months of the war's beginning it was clear that no money offer on the market however high could call out supplies large or fast enough to meet the State's urgent need to train, equip and maintain by July 1915 an army of two million men.'[4] If munitions in the required quantities were to be forthcoming, the peacetime form of large sectors of industry would need to be distorted. They must cease production for established customers, even though they might be under contract to them. They must expand workshop space and machinery and the labour force. They must introduce untrained workers into processes of production formerly reserved for the experienced and qualified. They must aid in the establishment and management of factories set up and owned by the government. And all this must be done in order to provision a market that, it was devoutly hoped, would disappear in short order. Whatever the terms or prices offered, no version of market economics would justify such a proceeding.

The tale has often been told – it is a particularly good tale – of how, in the case of the army's sudden need for enormous quantities of sacks for making sandbags, the War Office discovered in March 1915 that private industry was not going to meet its requirements. So it set about commandeering not only the country's stocks of sacks but also its productive capacity, even though this meant that the manufacturers must dishonour existing contracts. Then the War Office found that it must determine the price structure not only of the finished articles but also of the goods at every stage of production from the raw material upwards. After that it discovered that there were domestic industries of great national importance (like meat-packing) that it would be perilous to deprive completely of sacks, so that it must begin apportioning the supply between military and civilian needs.

Private initiative and the profit motive had proved inadequate to the army's needs in this instance. And what was true in the matter of sandbags must in time be true of munitions in general. Industry would have to be told what to produce. It must be assured of a profit but also be prevented from profiteering. It must be equipped with the necessary productive capacity. And, certainly not least, it must be guaranteed a sufficient supply of labour – and labour allocated in ways that served the cause of maximum productivity rather than the established codes of the labour force.

II

At least in the matter of providing sandbags the War Office had shown more adaptability than, in general, it has been given credit for. And the strictures delivered against its attempts overall to munition the army in the first ten months of the war

---

[4] W. H. B. Court, *Scarcity and Choice in History* (London: Edward Arnold, 1970), p. 94.

rather ignore the great technical-industrial obstacles that only time could overcome. But this is not to deny that the production of munitions needed to come under new direction. There must be a state authority empowered to control production and determine priorities. By delegating to certain manufacturers the task of releasing (through subcontracting) the nation's untapped capacity for making munitions, the War Office admitted that it did not possess the necessary expertise. Either it must be reconstituted so as to include a core of civilians who were expert in all phases of munitions production, or the matter must be transferred to a new ministry.

Powerful forces were pressing for the adoption of the second alternative. First, there was the conviction that the War Office, in what it regarded as a military affair, would never accord to a civilian group within its midst the authority and trust that they were going to need. (This conviction was not held without cause.) Secondly, the heavy casualties suffered by British forces in the first half of 1915 were giving rise to a demand for an explanation and a scapegoat. The War Office (not in the person of Kitchener but in the form of the bungling military bureaucrat) provided these – with or without good cause. And there was a third reason why the country should establish a Ministry of Munitions separate from the War Office. This was the way in which Lloyd George had become identified with the demand that munitions production be given a new incentive under a new direction. If Lloyd George were to take charge of such a body, then clearly it must be constituted as a full ministry – and one, given their strained relations, outside the orbit of Kitchener.

From the early weeks of the war Lloyd George had been active in munitions matters. In September 1914, in his capacity of Chancellor of the Exchequer, he had started removing financial restrictions that might hamper industry in undertaking the manufacture of munitions. So he provided advances for contracts to purchase plant, and he guaranteed firms against loss in the event of an early return to peace. Behind the scenes – but not so far behind that his activities could not be divined – he began pressing on his colleagues the need for greater application to the problem of increasing military supplies. In Parliament he spoke out in support of an amendment to the Defence of the Realm Act that gave the Government powers to appropriate factories and convert them to producing munitions. Outside the House he expounded the desirability of setting up National Munitions Factories, and joined in negotiations with trade union leaders to facilitate increased production. His translation from the Exchequer to the Ministry of Munitions in May 1915 – whatever misgivings, false starts, and backtracking accompanied it – looked, from the outside, like the necessary end to an irresistible course of events.

Lloyd George's contributions to munitions production during the first two years of the war were many. But one was pre-eminent. He rang down the curtain on the charade of 'business as usual'. At Bangor in February 1915 he dubbed the conflict 'an engineer's war', to be fought in the workshops as well as on the battlefield. On the same occasion he sounded the call for direct civilian sacrifice: the potato-bread spirit in Germany, he warned, was a thing to dread, not to mock at. After two months as Minister of Munitions he renewed these admonitions. In England, he said, there was too much disposition 'to cling to the amenities of peace – business as usual, enjoyment as usual, fashions, lock-outs, strikes, ca'canny, sprees – all as usual.' The place that he was now occupying as a public figure was proof enough that matters already were changing.

The person with whom Lloyd George most deserves comparison at this stage – and it is a flattering comparison to them both, although neither would have thought so – is Kitchener. From the outset the latter had embodied the truth that this was to be a war not just of the professional army plus a leavening of recruits but of the able-bodied manpower of Britain. Lloyd George summed up the other great military truth of the conflict: that the war could not be confined to established war-producing industries and their employees plus some appropriate additions. All of industry must be bent and shaped by war's demands. Not least must this be true of its labour force.

III

The first six months of the war, according to a well informed publication of 1922, were a time of peace in the labour world such as the country had not known before or since.[5] There is no need grossly to exaggerate the transition from peace to war by believing that, just prior to August 1914, a large section of British workers were hell-bent on social revolution through the medium of the general strike.[6] Nevertheless, the industrial quiescence of the opening phase of the war deserves mention. After all, in many respects the war created ideal conditions for strike action. Deeply felt grievances, such as the miners' demands for a living wage and for national (instead of regional) wage levels, remained unsettled. The war, after a few months, converted labour into a scarce commodity, so that potential strikers need not be inhibited by a ready availability of blackleg labour. Moreover, the commodities and services provided by labour in such key industries as coal-mining, engineering, shipbuilding, and the railways were so essential to the war effort that the authorities could not afford to let a dispute run its course until starvation forced strikers to capitulate.

But if, in these respects, conditions seemed ripe for industrial disturbances, one powerful force was thrusting in the opposite direction: patriotism. British workers, there is no reason to doubt, were convinced as fully as the rest of the country that their nation was fighting in a righteous cause against a malicious and devoted adversary. They had much desire to aid, and none to hinder, the prosecution of the struggle. Any consideration of labour in wartime must begin at this point.

This may seem painfully obvious. Yet discussions of labour in the war tend not to highlight the influence of patriotism. It is perilous to try to explain why strikes did not happen and so to adduce forces such as love of country or of liberty as having caused them not to happen. But unless this is said it is possible, by encapsulating into a few paragraphs such wartime events as the unrest in South Wales, the shop stewards' movement, the 'revolt' on the Clyde, and the Leeds conference of June 1917, to convey an impression of constant unrest. Yet any such impression is misleading. Working days lost by stoppages, which had reached an unprecedented 41 million in 1912, and there-after had stood at 10 million in 1913 and again at 10 million (virtually all before August) in 1914, fell to 3 million in 1915, 2.5 million in 1916, 5.5 million in 1917, and under 6 million in 1918.

The transition was marked late in August 1914 by the declaration of an industrial truce. A meeting representing the industrial and parliamentary sectors of the labour movement passed a resolution calling for the termination of all existing industrial disputes and for an effort thereafter to seek an 'amicable settlement' of any 'new points of difficulty' that arose 'during the war period'.

Yet if the urge to close the nation's ranks against a common enemy was strong in the world of labour, it could not – especially once it became evident that the war must be

---

[5] *History of the Ministry of Munitions* (London: HMSO, 1922), vol. 1, pt 2, pp. 31–2.
[6] See Henry Pelling, *Popular Politics and Society in Late Victorian Britain* (London: Macmillan, 1968), ch. 9; and G. A. Phillips, 'The Triple Industrial Alliance in 1914', *Economic History Review*, 2nd series, vol. 24, no. 1, February 1971.

long – wholly suppress forces making for unrest. The causes of disturbance were four-fold. First, war-induced inflation was producing an absolute decline in living standards for some and a relative decline, *vis-à-vis* other sections of labour, for others. Secondly, the spectacle of war profiteering reminded wage earners that, for at least some capitalists, the espousal of patriotism did not suppress the quest for personal gain. Thirdly, some communities in Britain were sufficiently detached from the nation as a whole that patriotism did not take them as far along the road of industrial truce as it did most others. Finally, there were key groups whose socio-economic position, already under stress, was further threatened by changes brought about by the pressures of war.

One thing that early soured labour's patriotic enthusiasm was the spectacle of capitalists doing very nicely out of the conflict. Speculation in goods that the War Office was anxiously seeking became notorious in the early months of the war. E. M. H. Lloyd recounts: 'Any one who could offer supplies could name his own price; and in order to get a contract, it was not always necessary even to possess the goods. An option was sufficient. The banks were quite willing to advance money on a War Office contract and thus enable the contractor to buy what he had already sold.' The same writer cites a case early in the war of 'a complete stranger to the wool trade, with next to no capital, [who] made £150,000 in six months by speculation in yarn.'[7] Yet Lloyd George, in the first two war Budgets, did nothing to discourage such conduct by imposing punitive taxation.

In addition to the deliberate profiteers, there were investors and producers who found themselves profiteering whether they wanted to or not. For example, the diversion of most imported meat to military needs created a shortage on the civilian market. Prices rose, and the producers of home-killed meat gained automatically. Shipping also was making huge war-induced profits. An embarrassed Bonar Law had to tell Parliament on a number of occasions that he thought them excessive. (In two years, from 1915 to 1917, he earned nearly £7,500 on an investment of rather more than £8,000.) Labour was less conscious of the distress that this might cause capitalists than of the fact that such windfalls from the national endeavour, whether unsought or schemed after, did not come the way of the working classes.

While profits were rising at random but often spectacularly, prices were rising also. War-induced shortages, as in the case of meat just mentioned, were one cause. Government actions in response to the war were another. The state had to provide wages for soldiers, separation allowances for their families, sometimes pensions for their widows. It had to employ vast numbers of others in servicing its armed forces. It had to subsidize Britain's allies. These could not be done without some resort to inflationary measures.

Yet if these trends caused general working-class resentment, occurrences of labour unrest during the first year and a half of the war were pretty much confined to two geographically distinct regions: South Wales and the Clydeside. Neither region thrilled upon hearing the name of Britain to the extent that most other parts of the country did. (As for the name of England, it did not thrill them at all.) Yet there were few districts more essential to the continuance of the war effort. South Wales was a quite special coal-mining district, for it serviced the Royal Navy and merchant marine. And the Clydeside was unique in its concentration of railway workshops, engineering, and shipbuilding. Yet although their regional separateness and their capacity for provisioning the war-machine gave these two areas a deal in common, it is important to consider them apart in order to understand the course of events.

---

[7] E. M. H. Lloyd, *Experiments in State Control* (Oxford: Clarendon Press, 1924), pp. 26, 32.

It had been evident since 1912 that, come 1915, a dispute might well occur throughout the mining industry. The wages contracts negotiated after prolonged dispute in the former year were due to expire in the latter. The Miners' Federation expressed itself determined to stand firm on demands to which the mine owners were utterly opposed. This does not mean that there would certainly have been a miners' strike in 1915 had the war not intervened. It does indicate that miners and owners existed in a state of avowed hostility, and that any agreement between them would constitute a treaty between antagonists rather than a *modus vivendi* between two elements in a single enterprise. Miners in general constituted a race apart, separated physically from other sections by the setting of their work, by the location (not to say the quality) of their dwellings, even by the effects of their labour upon their physical appearance. Their levels of pay were generally higher than in other industries, but this in no way bridged the gulf between employers and employed. Their toil was different in kind from most other types of work: in the dangers attendant upon it, the combination of skill and physical strength that it required, and its effects upon health. Miners did not doubt that it required special renumeration.

The imperious attitude of the employers' organizations, coming on top of the miners' physical isolation from the rest of the community, produced among this section of workers an unusual obstinacy and determination to see a conflict through to the bitter end. Among long-standing demands that had been denied them were those for a living wage and a national wage scale. The owners were adamantly opposed. They held rigidly to district wage levels tied to the profitability of particular areas. Their attitude was determined not just by local particularism. Given the wide variations in richness of seams and in ease of extraction, a national wage was unattainable unless the country's hundreds of mine owners formed a cartel. This would so generally be regarded as a violation of free enterprise principles, and hence as a ground for nationalization, that the owners would not entertain it. The miners were equally aware of the implications. They felt no such reservations.

Despite this unpromising background, in April and May 1915 the negotiation of new wage agreements was accomplished in seven of the eight districts into which the British coal industry was divided. Agreement on higher wages was facilitated by the great profitability of the industry in wartime. But there still could have been no settlement if the Miners' Federation had not made a huge concession. It set aside during the war its demand for national wage levels.

The new wage rates were rejected in one district: South Wales. What was true of the mining industry generally, its apartness, applied with particular force here. With its large admixture of 'immigrant' elements of English, Irish, and Scots, the Welsh mining community was seen – admittedly by an unfriendly observer – to be 'rapidly developing a civilization and a political morality of its own', much influenced by 'foreign and socialistic' forces. Its actions were informed by the 'savage ferocity' of those 'obsessed with the idea that they are being wronged and deprived of their just reward by those whose wealth they have helped to create'.[8] The separateness of the Welsh miners was multi-faceted. It embodied the separation of Wales from England, of industrial Wales from rural Wales, of the mine workers from the rest.

On 15 July 1915, in defiance of the recommendation of the Miners' Federation of Great Britain, the South Wales miners rejected the proposals of a government commissioner who had been sent to arbitrate. Instead, they struck. Their action, involving a serious threat to Britain's command of the sea and so its national survival,

---

[8] Rev. J. Vyrnwy Morgan, *The War and Wales* (London: Chapman & Hall, 1916), pp. 281–7.

aroused widespread indignation. Major Bonham-Carter, occupying a staff post in France, wrote home:

> What is filling our minds most is the strike of the South Wales Coalminers, which fills us with rage. I must acknowledge that I dont think it right that we should receive higher dividends from Nixon's than we should if the war were not taking place, but to strike is inexcusable all the same. I trust the Government will sit on it with a very firm hand.

The manner in which Bonham-Carter could mildly deprecate the sins of capital, while finding those of labour 'inexcusable' and to be sat on (in a choice mixed metaphor) with a firm hand, serves as a reminder that in war, even more than at other times, the dice were loaded against labour.

The Government, in the person of its recently appointed Minister of Munitions, seemed ready to take the firm action against strikers that the Major required. Under the Munitions of War Act, which had become law only a few weeks before, the South Wales coalfield was proclaimed a 'controlled' industry. Automatically, the strike became illegal.

Plate 16   *The beginning of the South Wales coal strike. Miners leave the pithead at the expiration of their strike notices.*

IV

The Munitions of War Act, as it applied to labour, was the culmination of more than six months' wrestling with a problem imposed on the country by the nature of this particular war. Armaments in the quantities required could be achieved only by the conversion of major industries from producing for peace to producing for war and by a huge expansion in their output of certain commodities. The problems involved in such an undertaking were not only technological. High among the human problems was the pattern of labour relations in the engineering industry. So before completing the tale of the South Wales coal struggle, it is necessary to say something about the engineering labour force.

Engineering in 1914 was still one of Britain's most dynamic industries. Levels of change in the processes of production continued high. Yet the workforce was rigidly stratified, both vertically and horizontally. Vertically, workers at the same level of expertise, and enjoying the same status, were separated by an intricate set of distinctions concerning which aspects of the work process belonged to which crafts. Herein lay the source of limitless demarcation disputes: that is, disputes not between labour and management but within the same grade of labour. Horizontally, the workforce was divided between those who, through serving the required six- or seven-year apprenticeship, had qualified as skilled labourers and those who had not. In industries like mining and the railways a labourer might hope in time to work his way right through the workforce. In engineering there was no such mobility. The separation between the skilled and the rest was, as a rule, insurmountable. And clear benefits attached to membership of the skilled sector: command of the more important elements in the work process; status; and high levels of pay. (Wages for skilled work ran at between 75 and 100 per cent above those for unskilled labour.)

Consequently, the most powerful sector of workmen in the engineering industry had a strong vested interest in maintaining the *status quo*. Yet before 1914 technology and the demands of the market were constituting powerful forces for change. As the USA – which had no entrenched body of skilled labourers – was showing, machinery requiring only semi-skilled workers to attend it could supply many of the necessary skills. This development of a category of semi-skilled employees complicated the hitherto simple horizontal segregation between skilled and unskilled. And it further soured relations, both within the workforce and between the skilled labourer and the section of employers attracted to mass-production methods.

If by 1914 the skilled workers were still holding at bay the more unwelcome innovations, they were in the process developing a siege mentality. This was evident in the chaotic internal arrangements and defensive actions of their principal organization, the Amalgamated Society of Engineers (ASE). The most powerful among a multitude of engineering unions, the ASE nevertheless included only about one-third of the skilled engineers and almost none of the semi-skilled and unskilled. An attempt had been made in 1907 to widen its membership by admitting the semi-skilled. But this had been stultified from the outset by resistance from within the skilled ranks.

It was to this somewhat embattled sector of skilled workers, among all industrial groupings, that the war presented its most serious challenge. The struggle on the Western Front made it imperative that they abstain from demarcation disputes, substitute arbitration for strike action, and suspend union-imposed restrictions on output. It also required them to assist in the process that became known as dilution – that is, the introduction of unskilled and semi-skilled workers into some of the skilled workers' preserves, so that the limited supplies of skilled labour could be made to go further. To the already hypersuspicious skilled men, such a course seemed full of menace. Once the work process had been reshaped to accommodate a smaller element of the skill that they provided, what prospect was there that former practices would be restored after the war? J. T. Murphy, a leader of the dissidents, asked whether they were so credulous as to believe that 'all the new machinery, all the new processes of production, and all the new labour which we have trained to work at cheaper rates than ourselves, would be discarded, and the shops reorganised on the 1914 pattern?'[9] But

---

[9] J. T. Murphy, *New Horizons* (London: John Lane, 1941), p. 46.

opposing Murphy's particularist brand of industrial militancy were the force of public opinion, the pressures of government, and the skilled labourers' own consciousness of the national need.

In March 1915 representatives of employers and employees in a wide range of war-related industries were brought together at the Treasury by a group of Ministers, of whom Lloyd George (still Chancellor of the Exchequer) was the most notable. It so happened that they gathered in a large room where a throne of Queen Anne was situated. Lloyd George, for one, was struck by the contrast between this item of furniture and the 'stalwart artisans' who leaned against it or sat on its steps, 'on equal terms negotiating conditions with the government of the day upon a question vitally affecting the conduct of a great war'.[10]

Whether all of the 'stalwart artisans' were as convinced as Lloyd George that this proved 'Queen Anne was indeed dead' is an open question. For nearly all the concessions had to come from their side. The Government did agree – under pressure from the ASE, which otherwise refused to co-operate – to confine dilution to war work, to limit the profits of firms engaged in engineering and shipbuilding to a fixed percentage above the pre-war level, and to put in statutory form the promise that dilution arrangements would terminate the moment the war ended. Nevertheless, the positive achievement of the gatherings was that the unions signified their conviction that the nation's need was imperative and that they must temporarily abandon their constraints on productivity. The terms whereby they promised to do this were quaintly called (in the *History of the Ministry of Munitions*) a 'treaty' – the Treasury Agreement.

But in the engineering industry the agreement was, from the outset, inoperative. Its terms required close oversight at the workshop level. Yet no authority had been established to implement it. Any attempt by the employers to do so would be anathema to the skilled engineers. Any attempt by the unions would smack of treachery. Already it was becoming apparent that in some districts the shop stewards – that is, the representatives of the skilled engineers at the shop-floor level – were developing as a force independent of the union leaders. They were serving as the mouthpiece of rank-and-file suspicion that, in the negotiations at the Treasury, the ASE representatives had been gulled by employers using the rhetoric of the nation-in-peril. So if an authority were required to direct the implementation of dilution, only the Government could supply it. And, clearly, it would be advantageous if this authority were under the charge of an individual who possessed the common touch, had played the part of conciliator in industrial disputes, and yet could tell labour its duty in unmistakable terms. Once more, although from a different direction – that of labour relations in the engineering industry – a strong pressure was manifesting itself for the creation of a Ministry of Munitions under the direction of Lloyd George.

Thus in July 1915 the ailing Treasury Agreement was rejuvenated as the Munitions of War Act. It gave the Minister power to proclaim any industry that he deemed essential to the production of munitions a 'controlled' establishment.[11] The rights of labour in these establishments were seriously curtailed. Strikes were outlawed, the settlement of disputes by arbitration becoming mandatory. Workers who struck unofficially were liable to be fined. So were employees who absented themselves from work without good cause – among which the after-effect of consuming alcohol was not one. The Act further laid down that the dilution of the skilled labour force by semi-skilled and unskilled workers must be implemented when required. And the movement

---

[10] Quoted in Henry Pelling, *A History of British Trade Unionism* (London: Macmillan, 1972), p. 152.

[11] Initially 134 firms were so designated. By the end of the war the number exceeded 6,000, and among them were some involved only at one remove in war production (e.g. firms erecting houses for munitions workers).

of skilled labourers to other establishments, usually in response to offers of higher wages, was hampered by the introduction of leaving certificates. Unless an employer provided one of these to a departing employee, the latter could not take up a position in another controlled establishment until six weeks had elaspsed.

V

As the dilution clauses bore witness, the Munitions of War Act was designed principally for the engineering industry. And there was one industry to which its terms presumably did not apply: coal-mining. For although the miners had been represented at the Treasury meetings, their union leaders had refused to sign the Treasury Agreement. They would try, they said, to discourage stoppages and to keep up output. But they would not consent to strikes being outlawed. Yet it was in confrontation with the most troubled part of this troubled industry that the Munitions Act's attempt to prohibit stoppages encountered its first great test.

The strike of the South Wales miners in July 1915 was not initially a matter that fell within the writ of the Ministry of Munitions. Nor need it have become one, had the Ministry not so chosen. Admittedly, South Wales coal was a matter of great import to the navy, and so to the war effort as a whole. But the Admiralty had not gone out of its way to co-operate with the new Ministry even on matters of naval munitions. And the Ministry of Munitions was not intended to take the whole nation as its parish. Why, then, did Lloyd George directly involve himself in this dispute by 'proclaiming' the South Wales coalfield a controlled establishment in which strikes were forbidden? Doubtless he was stung by the fact that this blot on the nation's sacred unity was occurring in Wales. Doubtless he was convinced that a dispute in any major industry challenged the principle that the Munitions Act was seeking to establish. But Lloyd George had shown from early in the war that his devotion to the struggle could not be confined within the limits of his particular portfolio. And the ill-considered zest with which, early in 1915, he had sought to vanquish the demon drink suggested an enthusiasm for propounding drastic solutions first and only contemplating their application afterwards.

South Wales was to teach the Ministry of Munitions a lesson that was to govern its approach to strikes thereafter: that the severity of its action against strikers must vary in inverse proportion to the size of the dispute. The more general the strike, the more restrained must be the Ministry's attempt to prosecute the strikers. For South Wales posed a problem already quite apparent to the experienced industrial commissioner, Lord Askwith, but yet to be appreciated by the fledgling Minister of Munitions: that not even in war, and not even when armed with extraordinary powers, could a British Government mete out punishment to a whole community. It may have seemed that the mere threat of enforcement of the law, coming on top of public indignation, would prove action enough. This overlooked the fact that the only public with whom the South Wales miners came into contact was their own kind, and it conveyed no condemnation. As for the threat of legal penalties, the miners already regarded the law as an instrument of the bosses, which they would probably have to combat if they challenged the mine owners.

The practical difficulty of punishing the strikers mounted. The Munitions Act was deficient (the deficiency was soon made good) in that it could be employed only against strikers, not against union officials – be they local or national – who urged strike action. As the legal officer whom Lloyd George sent to South Wales to institute proceedings pointed out: 'To prosecute only the dupes while the real offenders escape will I am afraid cause great heart burning.' But there was a much more serious difficulty, as the same correspondent admitted: that the 'dupes' were so many in number. 'It is of course impossible to summon and try 200,000 men'; the process of dealing with them in manageable batches was bound to be lengthy, and the interval "before there can be any real enforcement of the sentence will, I fear, only lead the men generally to regard the Act as ineffective'.[12] This was not the end of the difficulties. The Miners' Federation of Great Britain had been as good as its word when it had said that it would seek to discourage stoppages: the South Wales miners had struck without its authority. But the Federation had also refused to come under the Act with its provision to outlaw strikes. It would not now stand by while one group of miners was forced within the jurisdiction of the Act. Robert Smillie, the miners' president, warned that if attempts to prosecute the South Wales miners continued, there would be a nation-wide stoppage.

For the Ministry of Munitions, as far as this dispute was concerned, the game was up. Happily, Lloyd George possessed the virtue of knowing when he was beaten and the ability abruptly to change course. He made a lightning visit to South Wales, entered into negotiations with the miners, and by conceding nearly all of their original demands achieved a settlement. By so doing he maintained his reputation both as a man of action and as a conciliator. But the Munitions Act, and its author, could not afford many such rebuffs.

VI

Another great test of strength was looming for the Ministry of Munitions. This time there could be no doubt that it was faced with precisely the sort of challenge that it had been created to overcome.

The Clyde had already been the scene of the first breach of the industrial truce. Back in February 1915 skilled engineers had struck. Some of them had been reacting to an attempt by one particularly aggressive employer to introduce American engineers – symbols of mechanization and mass production – at bonus rates. The large majority had been rebelling against a new pay award that did not keep pace with the rising cost of living. Under what one of their leaders called 'the most terrific barrage ever directed against a strike',[13] including a sharp salvo from Lloyd George, they had gone back to work for rather less than their full demands. But they had established the Clyde's reputation as a major centre of disaffection.

There were good reasons why the Clyde should be a scene of unrest. With its large numbers of immigrants from Ireland and the Highlands, and its reliance on tenements as the main form of housing, it was arguably the worst-housed and most violent area in the land (certainly if Ireland was excluded). As a centre of war industries, it soon became subject to a fresh influx of the dispossessed seeking lucrative employment. This aggravated the pressure on dwelling space and encouraged landlords to raise rents. From mid-1915 they were countered by a spreading refusal of tenants to pay up. By November there was an estimated 20,000 tenants on rent strike, including five Labour councillors. The most affected districts were those housing shipyard workers. So when eighteen tenants were summonsed, five of the largest shipyards downed tools. Asquith's coalition Government had little choice but to act – either against the landlords or against the tenants. Urged on by Lloyd George, if discouraged by some of its Tory members, it rushed a Rent Restrictions Bill through Parliament to curb the activities of 'profiteering' landlords.

---

[12] Quoted in Iain McLean, *The Legend of Red Clydeside* (Edinburgh: John Donald, 1983), p. 30.

[13] William Gallacher, *Revolt on the Clyde* (London: Lawrence & Wishart, 1936), p. 47.

These events seemed to show the Clyde as an ideal setting for industrial unrest on a community-wide basis. But this was what the 'Revolt on the Clyde' never became. Even the rent strike was not a general movement, and the industrial action that grew out of it did not spread to engineers. By the same token, the purely industrial disputes did not embrace the railway workshops or most of the shipping workers. These disputes were confined to the engineering industry, and to only a segment within it – the skilled labourers. Behind the rhetoric of revolution and class war there existed a body of skilled craftsmen at odds as much with other sections of labour (the semi-skilled and unskilled) as with the employers and the Ministry of Munitions.

Three things gave the resistance to dilution on the Clyde between December 1915 and March 1916 the appearance of a communal uprising. It appeared – although the appearance was deceptive – to be occurring in the same locality and among the same people as the rent strike. It was led by a group of militant shop stewards, the Clyde Workers Committee (CWC), who justified opposition to dilution in socialist and class war, not in craft, terms. And the most memorable episode in the struggle, the reception given to Lloyd George on Christmas Day 1915, had much of the appearance of a popular outburst.

The Ministry of Munitions had made haste slowly in implementing dilution. It had been hoped that enough skilled workers would join the ranks of what were called War Munitions Volunteers – craftsmen prepared to take work wherever they were directed – to obviate the need for enforcing dilution. When this did not happen the Ministry began applying dilution to the more amenable districts. It was noticed that during the rent strike no offence was being given by the Ministry to the engineers on the Clyde. Only in the last month of 1915 did it direct its attention there. Lloyd George (in company with Arthur Henderson, who was the principal spokesman of Labour in the coalition Government) decided personally to visit both the Tyne – where resistance was also anticipated – and the Clyde. It was hoped that a direct appeal would convince the engineering shop stewards of the urgency of dilution.

The visit to the Tyne passed off without incident. That to the Clyde did not. The central event of Lloyd George's appearance on the Clyde was a meeting with some 3,000 shop stewards on Christmas Day. (This was not a public holiday in Scotland. Lloyd George had offered to compensate those attending for wages lost.) From the outset the audience proved unsympathetic. Henderson, who spoke before Lloyd George, made much of the Belgian issue, which he called the violation of a brave and independent people. This had little effect. A voice called out: 'Oh heavens, how long have we to suffer this?' Lloyd George, for his part, did not help his cause by being at his most specious. He attempted to win over his listeners by referring to Ramsay MacDonald as 'one of my greatest personal friends' and by calling the national munitions factories 'great Socialist factories'. All he elicited was a storm of denuncia-tion. He made a bid for sympathy by saying that 'the responsibility of a Minister of the Crown in a great war is not an enviable one.' This provoked the inevitable response: 'The money's good' and howls of laughter. Amidst mounting uproar Lloyd George adopted a franker, not to say more combative, approach: opposition to dilution was 'haggling with an earthquake'. Soon after, the meeting broke up in disorder.[14]

These events did not retard plans to impose dilution on the Clyde. Rather, the Ministry of Munitions set about the task with renewed vigour. When the Independent Labour Party journal, *Forward*, published a factual account of the Christmas Day meeting, it was suppressed. Lloyd George (who emerged from his Christmas Day

---

[14] This account is drawn from McLean, *The Legend of Red Clydeside*, ch. 5.

experience in remarkably good spirits)[15] was full of fight. In conversation he asserted that his adversaries were 'ripe for revolution' and 'completely out of hand'; also 'there is German money up there.'[16] In Parliament he justified the suppression of *Forward* with a provocative utterance unhampered by concern for accuracy. A new weapon was to hand in the struggle to enforce dilution. January 1916 saw the enactment of the first instalment of conscription. Certainly, it had been fundamental to the campaign to increase the output of munitions that skilled engineers were needed in the factories, not in the army. But this might not be true of engineers who hampered the munitions drive.

On the Clyde the Ministry advanced on two fronts: close co-operation with skilled labourers during the institution of dilution, so allaying much of their fear for their position as craftsmen; and a vigorous offensive against the CWC. The Committee's journals were suppressed. Its leaders were imprisoned (for seditious writings) or deported from the area. Any workers who struck in protest were prosecuted and fined. It had been axiomatic since the South Wales fiasco that the Ministry would act only against strikes that enjoyed limited support. Its firm handling in March and April 1916 of those engineers who did strike in support of the deported shop stewards shows that it was not anticipating a widespread stoppage. This calculation proved correct. The Clyde did not rise in defence of the CWC leaders. The latter had never tried to merge the grievances of the skilled engineers in a broader movement such as the rent strike. Perhaps, given the particularist nature of those grievances, there was no point in trying. But this meant that their only power base was a body of skilled workers whose sectional anxieties were in the process of being set at rest. Notwithstanding Lloyd George's assertions, these workers were not eager – thanks to the stimulus either of revolutionary conviction or of German gold – to cripple the war effort. And anyway they lacked the communal endorsement for resistance that had been the strength of the South Wales miners.

With the rout of the CWC, dilution on the Clyde was able to proceed uninterrupted. The Committee's hopes of bringing forth from the war a new order proved insubstantial once its adherents had come to the conclusion that the pre-war order could after all be restored.

VII

The events of 1915 and early 1916 established a pattern of relations between Lloyd George and the labour movement that persisted until the end of his life. He had qualities unique in the wartime Governments for relating with labour. As the issue of rent restrictions showed, he was prepared to thrust aside doctrines and prejudices if thereby he could ally the grievances of the 'common man'. He was willing to speak to labour face to face – in however daunting circumstances – about its duties and shortcomings, confident that, whatever the strains produced thereby, he would still be on speaking terms with them afterwards. As Lord St Davids put it in a letter to Lloyd George in October 1915, urging him to speak out against unwarranted rent increases in munitions districts: 'You have had lately to pitch into the Trade Unionists a good deal and to point out the ways in which they and their rulers have been damaging the

---

[15] A. J. P. Taylor (ed.), *Lloyd George: A Diary by Frances Stevenson* (London: Hutchinson, 1971), p. 87. On the train coming back from Glasgow, Lloyd George held a Christmas dinner and a madcap concert – evidence of his extraordinary resilience.

[16] Ibid., p. 87.

National Cause. They have put up with it from you in a way they would not have done from anybody else because of your championing them on so many previous occasions.'[17]

But there was another side to this coin. Lloyd George might champion labour or chastise it, but either way he was not of it. He himself seemed to take this for granted, as in the terms he used in appealing for the co-operation of the Trades Union Congress in 1915: 'without you our cause is lost . . . with you victory is assured.' Admittedly, he could use the language of labour's dearest aspirations. But as his Christmas Day utterance showed, he was too palpable in the way he debased such language by employing it as a counter in a game he meant to win by one means or another. However strongly he might acknowledge labour's contribution to the production of munitions and other war-winning commodities, his deeper expressions of gratitude went elsewhere: to business magnates like William Weir and Andrew Weir and Eric Geddes. Labour knew these men, and did not warm to them. The Ministry of Munitions was designed by Lloyd George as a 'businessman's organization'. The relations between such an institution and its labour force, however harmonious, must ever be those of separate and potentially opposed bodies.

The forces of labour would have been ungracious not to admire Lloyd George's achievement in guiding them along the way in which, with respect to production for war, they needed to go. But he made it clear to them that, although happy to guide, he was – in so far as it was possible – prepared when necessary to command and even to intimidate. Not for nothing, in his first public utterance as Minister of Munitions, did he announce that he fully endorsed industrial conscription in principle and would advocate its introduction if present measures failed to meet the country's needs. As he told Parliament, he had fallen back on the Munitions of War Bill only because the country had not accepted the wider view that 'a perfectly democratic State has . . . the right to commandeer every resource, every power, life, limb, wealth, and everything else for the interest of the State'. Faced with this threat of so ultimate a weapon, labour had good cause to set aside misgivings about the milder methods he was proposing. It had no cause to regard as one of its own the individual who employed the threat.

---

[17] Quoted in McLean, *The Legend of Red Clydeside*, p. 24.

21

THE LARGEST BUYING AND SELLING CONCERN IN THE WORLD

Thus by the time the Ministry [of Munitions] was founded the principle of Government control of munitions materials was admitted, and the War Office had already introduced many of the methods which were later established as part of the ordinary machinery. . . . But the remaining three years of the war saw great developments.

History of the Ministry of Munitions

The war was declaring itself a struggle between peoples, and, more to the point, between industrial and manufacturing peoples. The need for unlimited munitions was perceived by a statesman who to Chatham's will for victory added something of Chatham's disdain for its cost, and vast new industrial armies were created to supply them.

The 'Manchester Guardian' History of the War

I

It is not surprising that the Ministry of Munitions has attracted much attention. There was the outstanding stature – not to mention the ability to seize the headlines – of the first Minister. There was the crucial nature of the Ministry's undertakings. And there was the mounting scale of its operations.

R. J. Q. Adams has summed up Lloyd George's way of going about things:

> as the Minister of Munitions decided further powers were required for the production by his Department of munitions, those powers were acquired by the Ministry. That Department grew until, by mid-1916 and the close of Lloyd George's tenure as Minister, it controlled virtually the entire process of armaments production: from research and development, procurement of raw materials and machinery, supervision of both private and State factories, to the provision to the War Office of finished guns, shells and other warlike stores.[1]

The War Office was a conspicuous victim of this process of expansion. It is necessary to stress that Kitchener, prior to the upheaval of May 1915, had been establishing under War Office aegis new instrumentalities for dealing with munitions. These were directed by expert civilians like Lord Moulton and George Macauley Booth. That is, control of production was already moving out of military hands and into those of qualified managers and scientists.

The formation of the Ministry of Munitions greatly accelerated this process – among other things by annexing these civilian-run bodies. But it did not end all War Office authority in munitions matters. So a most unsatisfactory situation resulted, in which

---

[1] R. J. Q. Adams, *Arms and the Wizard: Lloyd George and the Ministry of Munitions 1915–1916* (London, Cassell: 1978), p. 43.

War Office obstructiveness to some hopeful developments, such as the Stokes mortar, became marked.

This state of half-and-halfness was not to Lloyd George's liking. Consequently it did not last. First his Ministry annexed direction of the Royal Arsenals. Then it secured control of design, offering as justification the failure of the War Office to develop an effective high-explosive fuse. Soon after, the technical department that the War Office had attempted to maintain in rivalry to that of the Ministry of Munitions was taken over. Lloyd George's next target was 'inventions' – that is, research and development. So in July 1915 he established his own Munitions Inventions Department (MID), and in November he insisted that the Inventions Department of the War Office be merged with it.

Kitchener and his aides were helpless to resist these proceedings. Lloyd George was everywhere regarded as the man who could 'solve' the munitions problem. And although Asquith might blanch at the directness of some of his methods in dealing with the War Office, the Prime Minister was prepared, by one means or another, to see that he got his way.

II

Terminating the last vestiges of War Office control over munitions production was only clearing the ground for the Ministry's really large expansion: into one facet after another of the British economy. Soon its empire embraced considerable regions of production, domestic and overseas purchase of key commodities, and even major aspects of imports and exports.

We have seen how Lloyd George secured himself a large, and fairly controlled, workforce. This was only one of his necessities. Another was a sufficient supply of materials. For this purpose the Ministry set about commandeering existing stocks, placing a lien on future output, establishing a centralized system of purchase in foreign markets, and developing new sources of supply. Following upon precedents already established by Kitchener, Lloyd George began to requisition the stocks and forthcoming output of home suppliers in a wide range of commodities. According to the *History of the Ministry of Munitions:*

> The method of purchasing in advance the whole output of an industry, at first for a definite term and later for the duration of the war, was widely adopted by [the Ministry's] Explosives Supply Department; practically the whole output of certain materials obtained as by-products in important industries like the gas industry, the coke industry, the soap trade and the dye industry, were taken over by the Ministry for the duration of the war.

Also secured were 'the whole British output of non-ferrous metals, of optical stores and glass, of linen and flax, and a very large proportion of the output of the iron and steel trades'.[2]

Again building upon a War Office initiative, the Ministry of Munitions for its overseas transactions employed a system of centralized buying. This reduced competition with other British and Allied agencies, brought down prices, and opened up new sources of supply. The most important overseas source, needless to say, was the USA, where (until the last months of the war) the banking firm of J. P. Morgan acted as the Ministry's agents. But there were also commercial firms appointed to secure commodities such as mica from India, magnesite from Greece, ferro-silicon from

---

[2] *History of the Ministry of Munitions* (London: HMSO, 1922), vol. 7, pt. 1, p. 14.

Norway, and special iron and steel from Sweden: the last-named country being a major supplier of ball bearings, in which Britain – having been largely dependent on Germany up to the outbreak of the war – was seriously deficient. (Dependence on Swedish ball bearings actually increased during the conflict owing to the development of the war in the air. In 1916 and 1917 one-third of the ball bearings required for aircraft production came from this source.)

Plate 17   *Women war workers taking part in a patriotic demonstration.*

The scale of these purchasing activities, at home and abroad, became gargantuan. Overall, the Ministry of Munitions – despite occasional residual competition with the Admiralty and the War Office – established its authority as the purchasing and distributing agent for explosive materials, non-ferrous metals, materials for chemical warfare and glass manufacture, and the materials of iron and steel. 'Thus the Ministry became the largest buying and the largest selling concern in the world, with a turnover amounting to hundreds of millions yearly.'[3]

The range of the Ministry's activities did not end here. It played an important role in initiating or, where this was not necessary, in encouraging the application of science and technology to war. It soon equipped itself with a Trench Warfare Department, involved in developing such items as mortars, bombs, grenades, and metal helmets. And it took over the already established Explosives Department run by the septuagenarian jurist and scientist Lord Moulton. Moulton was in large measure responsible for ensuring that Britain's capacity to produce high explosives would not suffer too severely from the meagreness of its supply of toluene (a basic element of TNT). This he did through his 'fight for amatol', a combination of TNT and ammonium nitrate in the proportions of 20 to 80 per cent. This compound produced 'a new explosive as

---

[3] *History of the Ministry of Munitions* , p. 16.

powerful bulk for bulk as pure TNT'. And in that ammonium nitrate was freely available (as long as Britain commanded the seas) in the form of Chilean saltpetre, amatol provided the solution to Britain's toluene deficiency.[4]

Associated for a time, if not always amicably, with Moulton (and, even earlier, with the Admiralty) was the Russian Jewish refugee Chaim Weizmann. By 1914 a British citizen and Reader in Biochemistry at Manchester University, Weizmann met Lloyd George through C. P. Scott of the *Manchester Guardian*. His purpose was to further the cause of Zionism. But as a by-product he offered his expertise in the production of acetone, an essential component in the manufacture of the cordite that propelled shells and other weapons of destruction at the enemy.

While men like Moulton and Weizmann were contributing in that area for which the Munitions Department had especially been called into existence – shells – the Ministry was also looking about for radically new devices with which to wage war. Its Munitions Inventions Department (paralleled by the Admiralty's Board of Inventions and Research of the same year, 1915, and the Air Inventions Committee of 1917) incorporated university and industrial laboratories, existing military experimental grounds and private workshops, and the experimental facilities of other government laboratories. In so doing (in the judgement of Michael Pattison) it achieved unprecedented integration of the scientific and military communities.[5] (Among the many distinguished scientists who contributed their expertise to the war effort were J. S. and J. B. S. Haldane who, in response to an appeal from Kitchener following the appearance of poison gas, produced a viable respirator within a fortnight; the experimental physicist J. J. Thomson; the physicist and chemical engineer Sir Richard Threlfall; the physiologist A. V. Hill; and the students of aeronautics Henry Tizard and F. Lindemann, both of whom learned to fly so as to put their investigations to the test.)

One task confronting the MID and similar bodies was to sift through the imposing number of 'war-winning' devices put forward by members of the general public. The vast majority had to be rejected as hare-brained or at best impractical.[6] By contrast, a few devices were deserving of encouragement. The most noteworthy, which had been cold-shouldered by the War Office, was the Stokes mortar, devised by the managing director of an engineering firm. In time it would become the most widely used of British trench howitzers. Again, the MID distinguished itself by aiding the development of a weapon that had emanated independently from a number of sources but would need all possible assistance to reach the battlefield in effective form: the tank.

Nevertheless, the achievements of the 'inventions' bodies thrown up by the war must not be exaggerated. Science and technology might refine the means of prosecuting the conflict, but they proved incapable of changing the face of the battlefield. Indeed, Michael Pattison tells us, 'in their efforts to produce war-winning inventions, they were largely ineffective.'[7] Thus in two of the areas in which the MID became most heavily

---

[4] H. Fletcher Moulton, *The Life of Lord Moulton* (London: Nisbet & Co., 1922), ch. 7.
[5] Michael Pattison, 'The Munitions Inventions Department: a Case Study in the State Management of Military Science, 1915–1919', unpublished thesis, Teesside Polytechnic and University of London, 1981, Introduction.
[6] All told, the MID received 48,000 suggestions, of which only 226 possessed any potential for implementation. Among the more bizarre were proposals to fill shells with bubonic plague germs, or (so as to place the enemy at a disadvantage when being attacked) with red pepper and snuff; the freezing of clouds on which would be mounted machine-guns for use against Zeppelins; the equipping of balloons with magnets that would snatch away the guns from German soldiers; the employment of electricity to project a deadly heat ray; and the training of cormorants, carrying timed explosives suspended from their necks to land on enemy airships. To facilitate gas attacks one 'inventor' professed himself able, at two hours' notice, to summon a wind from any direction.
[7] Pattison, 'The Munitions Inventions Department', p. 123.

engaged it played little or no part in affecting the outcome of this war. One was its anti-aircraft activities. These secured it much insight into the use of land-based guns against aeroplanes. But its discoveries had not influenced practice when the war ended. The other was an effort to emulate the Germans in the fixation of nitrogen from the air (lest supplies from Chile should be severed by the U-boat). The principle was in time mastered. But the factory intended to render Britain self-sufficient had not entered production at the cessation of hostilities.

Science and technology, then, contributed to war-making but without changing its basic forms. And this was true of the proceedings of the Ministry of Munitions as a whole. The truly significant aspect of that organization's history was the ever-mounting production, in marginally more sophisticated versions, of weapons with which the world was already distressingly familiar. According to the Ministry's *History*: 'In spite of the development of newer weapons of war, the production of guns and gun ammunition absorbed quite half of the Ministry's productive energy down to the end of hostilities.'[8] In short, the great achievement of Britain in the matter of munitions production in this war lay in sheer bulk of output: of artillery pieces and shells and machine-guns and bullets and grenades and mortars.

To achieve so much required three things of the home front. One was the conversion of peacetime industries to the business of manufacturing for war. The second was the widescale expansion of many of the enterprises so employed. The third was the construction, from the ground up, of state-initiated enterprises for the sole purpose of producing instruments of death. In the words of a contemporary account:

> The demand for munitions caused new towns to spring up, while it gave new leases of life to old ones; and when the demand for munitions became more especially a demand for high explosives, the manufacture of which requires seclusion and a wide elbow space, there broke out in many of the pastoral and idyllic landscapes of England – in that of Hereford for one, and of Gretna for another – an extensive industrial blistering, showing itself in acres of corrugated iron, and the gathering together of great populations engaged, as was obvious from their hands and complexions, in chemical processes quite foreign to the *genius loci*.[9]

The nature of this industrial transformation can best be indicated by some examples. One is an account (written early in 1918) of the changes that the war had wrought in a major British manufacturing centre. Its authors were a party of journalists representing newspapers in Britain, the Dominions, and the United States.

> No turn of the kaleidoscope ever produced a more startling change than the total conversion accomplished in Birmingham. Jewellers abandoned their craftsmanship and the fashioning of gold and silver ornaments for the production of anti-gas apparatus and other war material; old-established firms noted for their art productions, which had found a permanent home in most of the museums of the world, turned to the manufacture of an intricate type of hand grenade. Cycle-makers devoted their activities to fuses and shells; world-famous pen-makers adapted their machines to the manufacture of cartridge clips; and railway carriage companies launched out with artillery wagons, limbers, tanks and aeroplanes, and the chemical works devoted their energies to the production of the deadly T.N.T....
>
> We have walked through miles of workshops and watched the manufacture of shells and fuses at all stages, from the steel billet and rough brass forging to the finished and tested product. We have visited factories where rifles are made by the million and Lewis guns by the thousand. We have inspected works which produce artillery limbers by hundreds. Monster aeroplanes have been built up under our eyes. Aeroplane engines and big guns

---

[8] *History of the Ministry of Munitions*, vol. 2, pt. 1, p. 97.
[9] *The 'Manchester Guardian' History of the War* (Manchester: John Heywood, 1920), vol. 9, p. 159.

we have watched in the making. We have examined chemical processes by which from the colourless liquid called 'gas tar toluene' clever men produce the reddish, flaky, terribly explosive substance called tri-nitro-toluol, or T.N.T.[10]

The historians of wartime Birmingham make reference to the experience of a 'well-known motor company, engaged in pre-war days upon touring cars, commercial vehicles, electric lighting installations', and the like. During the war it increased its number of employees from 2,300 to 25,000: and it transferred its output to such commodities as 4.5-inch howitzers, armoured cars, aeroplane engines, and shells for 8-and 9.2-inch howitzers and 18-pounder guns.[11]

More was required than the conversion and extension of existing industries. Entirely new undertakings, usually under government sponsorship but managed by business-men, were called for. One of the largest was the National Shell Filling factory at Barnbow, near Leeds. It blossomed forth on what, in mid-1915, were 400 acres of farmland lacking electricity, gas, water, sanitation, roads, and connections with the railway. Its first shell-filling plant was complete by April 1916, and output soon reached 6,000 shells a day. Other buildings were swiftly erected. Ultimately the Barnbow factory possessed a roof area of 127,000 square feet, and it had absorbed in its construction 6 million bricks, 5,400 tons of cement, and service mains running a distance of 33 miles.

In its two and a half years of production the output of this National Factory was impressive. According to its historian, by the end of the war 'over 36,000,000 breech loading cartridges had been charged and nearly 25,000,000 shells filled, apart from 19,250,000 shells completed with fuses and packed in boxes, making a grand total of 566,000 tons of finished ammunition despatched overseas'. At the height of these activities over 16,000 workers were employed, 93 per cent of them women. On three occasions explosions in the factory claimed lives. The most serious occurred on the night of 5 December 1916. A shell in the process of being fused exploded, causing others to detonate. Thirty-five young women were killed outright. Sir Douglas Haig, the Commander-in-Chief, in a special Order of the Day, mentioned the incident as exemplifying the loyalty and determination of the munitions workers.[12]

III

There would be no more shell scandals in Britain after May 1915. By the time, in mid-1916, that Lloyd George left the Ministry, the increase in output was already impressive. (Some of this, no doubt, sprang from initiatives taken earlier by the War Office. As for the question of how much of the total improvement would have occurred had the War Office retained control, this is a rather pointless speculation. By May 1915 – if less whole-heartedly – the War Office system was itself in the process of changing.) R. J. Q. Adams offers the following estimates of increases in shell production. June 1916 saw an advance in output over June 1915 of 9½ times for lighter shell, 7 times for medium, and 12½ times for heavy. On the basis of the first twelve months of the war, by mid-1916 a year's output of shells was being produced in 2 to 3 weeks for light guns, 11 days for medium, and 4 days for heavy.[13]

[10] Reginald H. Brazier and Ernest Sandford, *Birmingham and the Great War 1914–1919* (Birmingham: Cornish Bros., 1921), pp. 123–4.

[11] Ibid., p. 140.

[12] W. H. Scott, *Leeds in the Great War* (Leeds: Libraries and Arts Committee, 1923), pp. 182–8. Scott had earlier written 'The Story of Barnbow', the official record of the enterprise.

[13] Adams, *Arms and the Wizard*, pp. 172–3.

Nevertheless, in terms of the task ahead, a sufficiency of guns and shells would not prove easy to come by: so that if 1916 would see no shell scandal, it would witness episodes of decided shell shortage. For one thing, much of the ammunition produced in the first year of the Ministry was of such poor quality that it might have been saved the trip to the battlefield. But, more important, if the number of guns and shells was increasing, so was the need; as a result of the mounting number of Britons in uniform, the escalation in the scale of the operations they would be called on to perform, and the elaborate preparations being made by their adversaries to thwart their best endeavours.

So although the number of guns possessed by the BEF on the Western Front increased between April 1915 and June 1916 from 1153 to 3721 (with a disproportionate increase in the number of badly needed heavy guns), the task required of them had also leapt ahead.[14] For the British were holding only 36 miles of the front at the earlier date, as against 85 miles at the later. Again, the smaller number of guns of April 1915 had to service but 14 British divisions; the thrice times larger number in June 1916 were being employed by 43 divisions. And the heavier calibre of gun available in 1916 had a much more onerous task to perform than any attempted the year before. For the quality of German defences on the Western Front was at least keeping pace with the quality of the weapons that Britain was developing against them.

In sum, if the labours of Britain's burgeoning munitions industry would in time equip the nation to participate successfully in a Continental war, that time would not be soon in coming.

---

[14] I am indebted to Dr Robin Prior for assembling statistics employed in this paragraph.

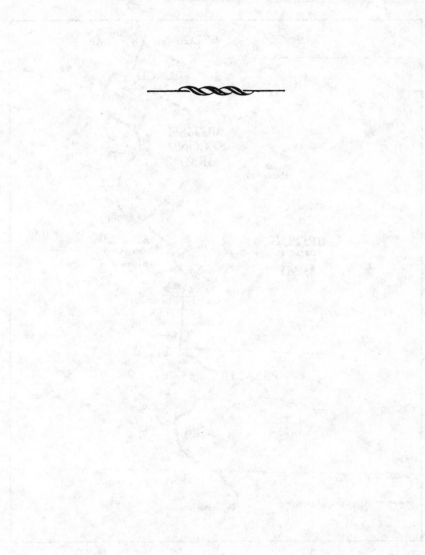

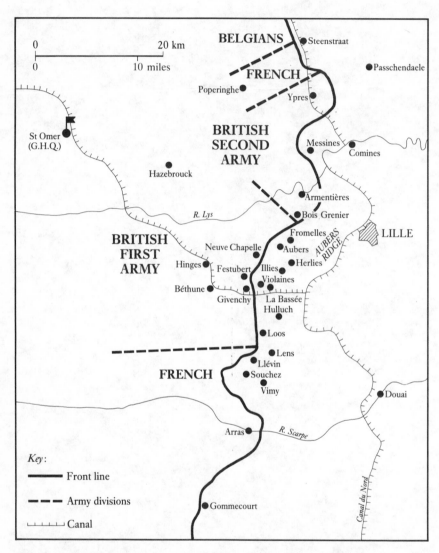

Map 4 *British offensives on the Western Front in 1915, showing the sector of front occupied by the BEF at the time of the battle of Loos.* Source: *John Terraine,* Douglais Haig: The Educated Soldier, *p. 138.*

PART FIVE

Battlefronts
July–December 1915

22

KITCHENER'S MEN

On Saturday, August 1st [1914], the officer in charge of the principal recruiting office in London, Great Scotland Yard, attested only eight recruits; the two days succeeding were a Sunday and a Bank Holiday; the 4th of August saw a seething mass of men waiting to enlist and it took twenty minutes and twenty policemen to enable the astounded recruiting officer to force his way into his own office, after which he was kept at work without intermission. . . . Many men tramped for miles and slept under hedges for the chance to join up, others stood for hours waiting in queues. There was little cheering, little excitement, but an undercurrent of deep earnestness.

The story of the first three new Armies is a story of muddle which evolved into method; of a confused crowd of men who settled down into an army; of enthusiasm which, starting with a cruelly cold douche of lack of arms, lack of uniforms, lack of quarters, lack of officers, dirt, overcrowding, vermin, and terrible weather conditions. . . continued to be enthusiasm. . . .

V. W. Germains, The Kitchener Armies
(London: Peter Davies, 1930), pp. 57–8, 107

I

While Britain's regular army had been holding the line at Ypres and assailing the beaches at Cape Helles, the men who would in time take their places were making the transition from civilian to soldier.

Nothing revealed the British people's commitment to this war better than the way in which so many of the country's young men volunteered for military service. There was no inevitability about this. It is quite possible for people to proclaim the justice of their country's involvement in a war and yet not intend themselves to participate, either by risking their lives or by paying higher taxes. From the first day Britain's endorsement of the struggle was not of this order. Doubtless scarcely any of those who rushed to the recruiting stations divined what sort of a conflict they were in for. This is no reason for presuming that, had they known, they would have held back.

What moved men to enlist? Reference to the famous Kitchener poster explains little. Upon what responsive chord did it strike? Some recruits spoke of the call of 'duty' and 'national honour'. These were expressions that, in the Britain of the time, could possess great emotional power; but they also functioned as stock phrases doing service for an explanation where none lay easily to hand. Some named a yearning for adventure, but did not explain why only this particular adventure had summoned them. There were those who said that their pals had gone off to enlist and they had not wanted to be left out, and others who claimed to have signed up after taking a drop too much to drink. Probably members of neither group appreciated that they had been strongly predisposed to enlist before they succumbed to the impetus of comradely

Plates 18a and 18b   *Training the men of Kitchener's armies.*

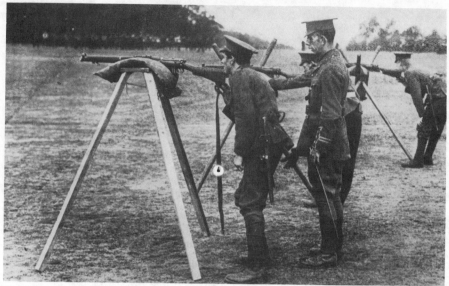

18a· *Sighting a rifle.*

feeling or Dutch courage. In truth the outbreak of this war stirred feelings deeper than many men were able to articulate. So outraged by Germany's actions was one excellent liberal and opponent of war, C. E. Montague of the *Manchester Guardian*, that he determined to join the army even though it meant concealing his age (he was 47) and dyeing his white hair. The only explanation his wife could offer was that 'he wants to kill a German!'[1]

The fact was that by the time Britain went to war the case for intervention was so compelling, and the reasons for intervening so various, that men of quite unlike opinions might feel the urge to enlist. For the jingo and the internationalist, the authoritarian personality and the democratic personality, the man ever eager to throw a punch and the person unwilling to strike a blow except under extreme provocation, the course of action required at this moment seemed the same. Prussian militarism must be stopped, and only violent deeds would stop it. Certainly, two things probably held true of most of those who enlisted. First, they would not have chosen personally to participate in an overseas conflict had not the reasons for going to war seemed overpowering. Secondly, they were convinced of the special worthwhileness of their own country. Yet even this latter sentiment could be the expression of widely varying attitudes. To Britons of insecure or domineering disposition, foreigners in general and 'Hunnish' foreigners in particular were likely to arouse emotions of fear and even terror. Hence taking up arms against them – vindicating one's national superiority – constituted less a leap into danger than a grasping after security. To those of more equable temperament and more democratic bent, the object of distaste was, rather, authoritarianism in any of its guises. It just so happened that, in August 1914, that guise was a national one. In consequence the British way of life, whatever its illiberal aspects, seemed deserving of armed support against that other way of life which was seeking to impose itself upon Western Europe.

---

[1] David Ayerst, *Guardian: Biography of a Newspaper* (London: Collins, 1971), p. 376.

II

For many who volunteered in the opening weeks of the war, the initial experience of army life proved disappointing. They could not all be equipped with a uniform, the talisman that set them apart from and – at least in wartime – above their fellow citizens. They received no rifles, the symbols of their new-found authority eventually to perform deeds of violence. There was a severe shortage of officers to train them, most having hastened to France. And their camps lacked basic amenities.

George Coppard, a working-class lad who joined up late in August 1914 aged only 16½ years (he misstated his age at the prompting of the recruiting sergeant), soon became aware of some of these deficiencies. He drank his initial serving of cookhouse tea out of a soup plate ('not an easy task at the first attempt') because of a shortage of mugs, and spent miserable nights under canvas because of overcrowding in the tents. (His fellow enlistees, he observes, were a motley crowd, including several near-tramps.) He relates:

> As tents were in short supply, the maximum number of recruits were allotted to each one. If I remember correctly the number was twenty-two, and not having been in a tent before, I had no idea that it had twenty-two separate pieces of canvas sewn together to form the roof. The flap was the point of entry and, with twenty-two men stampeding to get in, somebody had to get the flap division as his portion of territory. I got it. This meant that I couldn't lie down at night until everyone was in the tent. There were forty-four feet built up in tangled layers converging in the general direction of the centre pole. Nights were a nightmare to me and I dreaded them. Outside the tent flap within a yard of my head stood a urinal tub, and throughout the night boozy types would stagger and lunge towards the tent flap in order to urinate. I got showered every time and, worst of all, it became a joke. At last revulsion overcame me, and one night I suddenly went berserk and lashed out violently at someone. There followed a riotous eruption and the tent collapsed. Luckily more tents became available, and from then on I managed to avoid the entry flap.[2]

In the ensuing months many shortcomings were gradually made good. By early 1915 uniforms and weapons were beginning to reach the troops, although there was still insufficient .303 rifle ammunition and a paucity of hand grenades. And wooden hutments were being constructed to house them, though these were not immune to winter flooding.

By various means the shortage of officers was in a measure overcome. In addition to those wounded in action, who were retained in Britain, some unscathed officers were withdrawn from the BEF – much to the indignation of French and his aides. (Sir John's argument that every experienced man was needed at the front was entirely valid; so, unfortunately, was the counter-argument that a large number of experienced men were needed in Britain to train raw recruits.) For the rest, resort had to be made to the over-aged and the youthful. Senior posts were offered to retired officers, so that each new battalion could have at least a commanding officer of experience. And a call was made to young men of 'good education' to take junior posts; it being anticipated that their social and educational backgrounds would confer on them a bearing of authority that would compensate for their lack of experience. Word of mouth helped further to swell the ranks of young officers. V. M. Lunnon was nearly 20 at the outbreak of war and had been educated at Alleyn's School in Dulwich. Having joined up in September 1914 with no previous military experience, by December he found himself being invited by the commanding officer of an Essex regiment to apply for a commission and

---

[2] George Coppard, *With a Machine Gun to Cambrai* (London: HMSO, 1969), pp. 2–3.

serve with him. Apparently a relative of Lunnon had recommended him to someone who knew this CO.[3]

It need hardly be added that a strenuous time lay ahead for such fledgling officers. During the day they offered basic training to the rank and file; late into the night they sought to master their new calling, studying such matters as discipline, regulations, and more advanced aspects of military training. The old regular army tradition that officers never talked shop over meals vanished instantly. These men could afford to talk little else.

18b   *Trench digging.*

As for meeting the army's need for fresh supplies of NCOs (sergeants, corporals, and lance-corporals), any private soldier who seemed to possess aptitude and initiative might be in line for quick promotion. Ian Hay describes one of these – it may be thought an idealized portrait – in his novel *The First Hundred Thousand*, which recounts the training of a raw Scottish division.[4] His subject is a former Boy Scout 'of no mean repute': 'clean in person and courteous in manner', 'truthful, and amenable to discipline', he 'could be trusted to deliver a message promptly', 'could light a fire in a high wind with two matches, and provide himself with a meal of sorts where another would have starved'. For Hay this is 'the true scout breed', and he scoffs at those who at one time detected in the Boy Scout movement incipient militarism – not noticing how many of the qualities that he applauds have military overtones.

Not all the disappointing aspects of military life were the result of haste and improvisation. New recruits chafed at performing routine tasks apparently unrelated to their passion for ejecting the Germans from Belgium: peeling potatoes, scrubbing floors, carrying coal. A private soldier in Ian Hay's novel is brought before the company

[3] Philip Warner, *The Battle of Loos* (London: Wm Kimber, 1976), p. 208.
[4] See note 2, p. 193.

officer for refusing to obey an order – the order being to scrub a floor. The soldier defends himself on the ground that he joined the army to fight Germans, not to clean floors, something that he did not do in civilian life and that would have affronted his wife. In this area of disgruntlement no redress could be forthcoming. Such tasks were seen as an inherent part of army life, and private soldiers who viewed the matter differently just had to knuckle down. In the case of the dissenter from floor scrubbing in *The First Hundred Thousand*, the attitude of his commanding officer is stern but kind. The officer remarks in an aside: 'That chap's all right. Soon find out it's no good fussing about your rights as a true-born British elector in the Army.' He tells the private that, laudable as is his desire to fight the Germans, he must do many dull jobs first, even as must a company commander. As for refusing to obey an order, it is the most serious crime a soldier can commit, and the offence must not be repeated. The recalcitrant private, being 'all right', duly forgets about his 'rights as a true-born British elector' and conforms to army routine.

III

What were the army authorities seeking to do with the human material with which they were so suddenly deluged? First, the recruits had to be brought to a state of physical fitness in which they would be able to transport themselves by their own two feet over long distances, to remain steadfast in face of the enemy, and to be capable of pursuit of orderly retreat. Even if potentially fit, as medical inspection prior to enlistment had presumably established, this standard of endurance would not ordinarily have been present among a city-bred population. Even the Territorial forces, who had at least done a certain amount of weekend drilling, could fail the test of long marching. In mid-August 1914 an Essex village eagerly turned out to witness a route march by a brigade of 6,000 Territorials in full equipment. But not all the soldiers proved equal to the undertaking. The Rev. Andrew Clark recounts:

> Two of the regiments were exceedingly footsore. One of the young soldiers explained that the march was an amusement for him, accustomed daily to tramp over miles of ground in ordinary farm-work – but it was desperate hard for shoplads and clerks, who for years had never been off pavements, and were in the habit of nothing more than jumping on & off a tram.[5]

The next day these two regiments were so footsore that they could not proceed far. Opinion in the village was that the military authorities had erred in attempting a route march so long as 19 miles, on bad roads and in blazing weather, this early in the piece.

As well as marching, much army activity took the form of hard physical labour. Provisions and ammunition must be loaded on and off carts and manhandled to forward positions, and trenches must be dug – for it did not take the authorities long to recognize that mastering the art of siting and constructing trenches capable of withstanding artillery bombardment had become the *sine qua non*, if not of victory, then certainly of survival. If new recruits were to perform these tasks, then they must be fit. As it happened, the initial shortages of arms and equipment allowed a good deal of time for the physical training needed to bring them up to standard.

Then, as rifles became available, recruits were directed in mastering what it was assumed would be their prime weapon: for in 1914 (if for not much longer) it was still possible to believe, with Ian Hay, that at a range of 200 yards 'British rapid fire is the most dreadful medium of destruction yet devised in warfare.' So while only dummy

---

5 'Echoes of the 1914 War in an Essex Village', vol. 1, entry for 18 August 1914, in the Bodleian Library.

ammunition was to be had, long hours were spent on becoming familiar with the care and handling of the rifle: how to hold it when standing, kneeling, and lying; how to aim, to press the trigger without jerking, to re-load. Time was also spent on target identification, so that the fire of a section could be concentrated against an enemy promptly upon detection. Then, as live ammunition at last came to hand, long sessions were spent at rifle ranges. For no one doubted that the Kitchener recruits must approach as nearly as possible the hallowed standards of fire of the old regular forces: 15 aimed rounds a minute.

There was another form of activity that the army authorities deemed of prime importance. The recruits of 1914 must be trained to move as units: that is, to carry out manoeuvres of rising degrees of complexity, involving increasing numbers of men, without the components becoming irrevocably separated or hopelessly entangled. In order to master such manoeuvres the recruits first practised drilling as squads (of about 20 men), then as platoons (of some 50 men), then as companies (consisting of four platoons), and then – but only after about four months – as battalions (of 1,000 men).

Drill served many purposes. One of them, indeed, was to familiarize the soldier with his rifle; to 'make it a part' of him, as one recruit of 1914 put it. For the rifle, a heavy and rather unwieldy implement (it weighed 14 pounds), took a deal of getting used to as a constant companion. But the prime purpose of drill was even more fundamental than this. It was to weld the human components of the army rank and file into units that moved according to a single rhythm and a single spirit, so that its members felt themselves to be not individuals but elements in a larger whole. This objective is set out explicitly in an army handbook of the Great War, using as its example a party of men learning to drill with arms.[6] Initially each man, giving the command to slope arms, 'obeys the command individually as best he can'. Then, with some experience, the action of sloping arms becomes smarter and more uniform; but each soldier is competing against his comrades, and this produces 'an air of hurry in the movement'. It is only a fully trained group of men who obey the command 'without anxiety or haste', knowing that their comrades will respond in precisely the same way, and so produce 'a rapid and precise but unhurried movement', with deliberate pauses between each stage, conveying 'the strongest possible impression of trained and controlled collective power'. The handbook says of this process:

> Drill at this stage is a perfect embodiment of all the qualities of soldierly discipline – prompt and methodical obedience, skill at arms, confidence in comrades, and pride in the unit to which the soldier belongs. It is the basis of all sound training for battle, and the surest method of drawing men together and giving them confidence in each other and themselves. Its steadying power in action has been proved in military history again and again.

The key phrase in the foregoing paragraph is 'soldierly discipline'. Drill was seen as a vital element in achieving this quality, deemed so essential in preparing men for battle. Military discipline, of course, was designed to serve many functions. Negatively, it helped to safeguard the positions of bungling or vicious officers and to reconcile rank-and-file troops to low pay, poor conditions, and unwarranted ill-treatment. Positively, it helped to raise up the more unwashed and uncaring elements of the army to standards of conduct that made them tolerable companions, and it served to ensure that they possessed weapons fit to function when required. But, primarily, discipline was designed to condition the individual soldier, upon encountering the shock of battle

---

[6] *Notes for Commanding Officers* ('a collection of some of the circulars which were issued from time to time at the Senior Officers' School, Aldershot'), Aldershot, 1918, pp. 5–7.

with all the powerful emotions it engendered, not to make the particular, instinctual responses – either that of taking flight or that of striking out in a disordered, random fashion. In circumstances in which the compulsion to act instinctually and as an individual was well-nigh overpowering, the army required human material that had been rendered proof against these urgings. As the afore-quoted handbook puts it: 'Discipline confers on troops the power of rapid, corporate action and of movement in formed bodies of great strength without loss of cohesion, even in difficult country and under heavy fire.' Much military training consisted of gearing men, still far from the battlefield, to behave in just this way when at last they found themselves under fire.

Discipline required of rank-and-file soldiers many other things than ordered conduct on the parade ground. They must pay due attention to their appearance (for example, they had to shave daily) and conduct (they might not take beer to bed with them). They must lavish great care on their weapons and accoutrements, which would be closely inspected for shortcomings. And they must adopt the correct bearing towards their superiors. In regard to officers, this meant saluting them, calling them 'sir', standing stiffly to attention when addressed by them. In respect to NCOs, it meant accepting their orders and their rebukes without indicating dissent. Young George Coppard early in his army career grew indignant at repeated reprimands for petty failings over matters not always within his control. Aware that he had better not answer back, he tried scowling instead. He found himself marched off to the guardroom and charged with dumb insolence. The next morning he received a dressing-down from the company commander and a sentence of four days CB (confined to barracks), which involved him in a succession of 'fatigues' such as emptying urinal tubs, peeling potatoes, and washing countless dishes. 'In a sense it was an important part of my army training learning how to be fly and cunning.'[7]

In establishing a disciplined force, pains and penalties could not accomplish more than a certain amount. By and large, the army functioned only by the consent of those involved. Its rank and file must come to identify with the units in which their whole lives were now immersed (apart, that is, from letters to and from home and occasional spells of leave): the platoon and the company for those of limited horizons, the regiment for those of wider view. They must come to regard officers not only as wielders of irresponsible authority but as persons meriting admiration. Coppard, notwithstanding the four days CB, viewed his company commander as 'undoubtedly the handsomest and smartest soldier in the battalion' and regarded his platoon commander, who 'looked a distinguished and powerful man', as 'sincere and kindly, with a cultured voice which I can hear in my memory to this day' ('this day' being half a century later).[8] And they must continue to accept that what they were doing was somehow related to what Ian Hay calls 'the Cause which has brought us together'. Hay describes this happening in his own small section of Kitchener's army: to him it is the process by which 'the soul of a soldier is born'.

> Presently fresh air, hard training, and clean living begin to weave their spell. Incredulous at first, we find ourselves slowly recognising the fact that it is possible to treat an officer deferentially, or carry out an order smartly, without losing one's self-respect as a man and a Trades Unionist. The insidious habit of cleanliness, once acquired, takes despotic possession of its victims: we find ourselves looking askance at room-mates who have not yielded to such predilections. . . . We begin, too, to take our profession seriously. Formerly we regarded outpost exercises, advanced guards, and the like, as a rather fatuous form of play-acting, designed to amuse those officers who carry maps and notebooks. Now we begin to consider these diversions on their merits. . . .

---

[7] Coppard, *With a Machine Gun to Cambrai*, pp. 6–7.
[8] Ibid, pp. 5–6.

Furthermore, Hay records, the troops are becoming less individualistic – 'beginning to think more of our regiment and less of ourselves'. At first this new-found loyalty takes the form of criticizing other regiments for slovenly marching, dirty accoutrements, and (significantly) bad discipline, which is taken to be a sign of poor officers. Suddenly it comes home to them that this means their own officers must be a good lot, and they find themselves taking a queer pride in the company commander's 'homely strictures and severe sentences the morning after pay-night'.

> Here is another step in the quickening life of the regiment. *Esprit de corps* is raising its head, class prejudice and dour 'independence' notwithstanding.

For those of Ian Hay's bent of mind, it is very nearly the promised land.

IV

The business of training Kitchener's first New Army, as Hay recounts it, occupied some seven months. During that time much sorting out of individuals took place. A handful of undesirables – drunkards and habitual troublemakers – were ejected from the army altogether. The less obnoxious ne'er-do-wells found themselves on semi-permanent CB. By contrast, private soldiers who showed that they could command respect and obedience rose to become NCOs; the 'quick-witted and well-educated' joined the Orderly Room staff or became scouts or signallers; the handy joined the transport section or became machine-gunners; the sedentary became cooks and tailors and officers' servants. (Coppard found himself 'picked out of the blue' for a machine-gun reserve team. 'This was a welcome surprise and I became a keen and willing learner.' He found the Vickers .303 water-cooled gun a wonderful weapon. 'Devotion to the gun became the most important thing in my life for the rest of my army career.')[9]

To many soldiers the business of training seemed unduly protracted. At the mid-way point spirits were sagging. Winter had set in; the novelty had worn off; the business of fighting mock battles with blank cartridges and non-existent shells had become tedious. But with the coming of spring (not yet recognized as harbinger of the campaigning season's rendezvous with death) spirits rose. The soldiers had learned all they could without actually doing battle, and were confident that they knew enough. They could march, dig, manoeuvre, act on orders without being coached, unleash 'fifteen rounds rapid', take food and seize the opportunity to sleep as and when these were offering. They had participated without disaster in mock operations involving the elements of a whole division, which meant not only thousands of infantrymen but an headquarters staff, cavalry, artillery, ammunition columns, signallers, a transport train, and field ambulances. It was all make-believe, but there was no reason to think that the real thing, despite live bullets and actual casualties, would be so very different. It would certainly be more exciting and more purposeful.

The New Army divisions that left Britain between May and July 1915 were, whatever the doubts and hesitations of particular individuals, raring to go.

---

[9] Coppard, *With a Machine Gun to Cambrai*, p. 14.

23

LOOS AND AFTER

We are coming to anxious time.
Henry Wilson's diary, 21 September 1915

I have never seen the men more cheeful [than on the evening before the Loos operation]. . . . There was an atmosphere of confidence and victory in the air. We all sang!
G. W. Grosmith, captain in 2nd Leicestershire Regiment, to his fiancée, 27 September 1915

I lost my sweetheart at Loos. . . .
Miss Palmer (aged 89) to Philip Warner, May 1975

I

The force whose training is recounted in *The First Hundred Thousand* was in fact the 10th Argyll and Sutherland Highlanders, constituting a part of the 9th division of the BEF; in it Ian Hay, otherwise John Hay Beith, held the rank of captain. As described in the climax of the book, these Kitchener recruits saw action for the first time on 25 September 1915. The occasion was the battle of Loos.

II

By mid-1915 Sir John French's situation was not enviable. Even in March he had become so anxious to acquire fresh laurels that he had sought to filch from Haig some credit for the success – such as it was – of Neuve Chapelle. This aroused the lofty scorn of Haig, who no doubt managed to convey to his chief the sense of moral superiority he so regularly entrusted to his diary. French had good grounds for fearing Haig. Whether the operations of Haig's First Army went well or ill, they seemed always to bring advantage to its commander, increasingly less to the Commander-in-Chief. Charteris noted that important people like Asquith, and people who coveted the company of the important like Esher, were now calling on Haig. He concluded that Sir Douglas was a coming man.

French's attempts at self-rescue availed him nothing. The total failure of his forces at Festubert on 9 May caused him great alarm. A week later he was described (by Henry Wilson) as having lost confidence in Haig and himself and as dreading further losses. So he resorted to using friends in the press to let it be known that Kitchener, not he, was to blame. This served greatly to embarrass his political masters, but did not remove Asquith or Kitchener from their posts. Hence French was left serving a Prime Minister and a War Secretary – and, as it happened, a monarch – deeply hostile to him and looking to Haig as a likely successor.

251

Plate 19   *The main street of Loos, immediately after it had been captured by the British.*

Nor had French's trafficking with the newspapers commended him to his senior officers. Wilson wrote of one press attack on Kitchener: 'This is Sir Js work & very bad work it is too.' And Haig said of his chief's use of newspapers to criticize Kitchener: 'A most disgraceful state of affairs.' Haig was in the happy position of being able to draw attention to the fact that the military correspondent of *The Times*, who had spent much time with French and was his main contact with the press, had printed information of value to the enemy. He urged that this person be kept away from the front.[1]

So by the middle of the year talk of French's approaching fall was common. Rawlinson, according to Wilson, was discussing the matter openly. Nor was it confined to French's enemies. In June F. E. Guest, a soldier-MP whom Sir John had employed to inform politicians of Kitchener's failings, said that French's reputation at home and in the army would not stand another check. He urged that the fairly minor operation about to take place at Givenchy be called off.[2] In July both Kitchener and the King began to move against French. The former urged Haig to assert himself more and 'to insist on French proceeding on sound principles'. And both of them wanted Haig to send them confidential letters 'regarding the situation and doings of the Army in Flanders'.[3] (Kitchener might have been surprised to learn that this was not the first time Haig had been asked to report clandestinely on his chief in the field. He had done so 17 years before, during operations in the Sudan. His commander then had been Kitchener himself.)

Confronted with this growing threat, what was French to do? He badly needed a success, yet he dared not risk another calamity. On balance, and no doubt wisely, he decided against further large efforts that year. Yet his cogitation was wasted effort. He

---

[1] Henry Wilson's diary, 15 and 21 May 1915; Robert Blake (ed.), *The Private Papers of Douglas Haig 1914–1919* (London: Eyre & Spottiswoode, 1952), p. 93.
[2] Henry Wilson's diary, 10 and 20 June 1915.
[3] Blake (ed.), *The Private Papers of Douglas Haig*, pp. 97–8.

found that he must mount another offensive even though no success was likely to flow from it. Yet there was no suggestion that, in such circumstances, he would escape culpability for the expected disappointing result.

III

There were good reasons against a further major offensive by the Western Allies in France and Flanders in the second half of 1915. Already in mid-May Kitchener had told the War Council: 'The optimistic view that Germany was becoming seriously weakened by the prolongation of the war has been entirely disproved by facts' – in particular, Germany's heavy blows against Russia. As for the situation on the Western Front: 'Our attempts to break through the German lines in Flanders, for which long preparations had been made, have entirely failed.' The French, Kitchener added, had done somewhat better, but their advance had been slow and without any serious strategic effect. His conclusion was that 'experience has shown that the German lines cannot at present be seriously forced along our or the French front.'[4] Therefore it was necessary to remain on the defensive.

For the British in particular, the want of trained troops (as distinct from troops in training) and, even more, of munitions seemed decisive in this matter. A conference in June at Boulogne attended by the British and French Ministers of Munitions, Lloyd George and Albert Thomas, decided that they were gravely short of the war's most important implements, heavy artillery and shells. They concluded that there should be no major operation against the German lines before 1916. The same view was taken by the British Cabinet, at a meeting of 3 July attended by Sir John French. While affirming that 'the western theatre was the principal one for our efforts', it decided that the most the BEF could do for the moment was to take over further lengths of the line from their ally. This would release French troops 'for offensive or defensive purposes'; nevertheless, 'it should be strongly represented to the French that they should defer any offensive operations.'[5] Two days later Kitchener told the Dardanelles Committee that their ally was most anxious to take the offensive in the West but that 'For his part, he intended to do his utmost to prevent the French from doing anything of the kind.'[6]

The French high command, however, was in no mood to agree. Joffre was not simply being obtuse. Certainly, by disposition he yearned for the offensive. Otherwise he would not have attained the post of Commander-in-Chief before the war or the eminence he now enjoyed on account of his counter-attack on the Marne. Again, he was more of an optimist than circumstances warranted. He recognized that there had been shortcomings in his operations in the spring. And he assumed too easily that but for them the operations would have succeeded. But there were strong objective reasons for his attempting another major Western offensive in the second half of 1915. With the war not a year old and so much of France overrun, the French home front was not inclined to accept a long period of quiescence. And Joffre had good reasons for believing, whatever the Munitions Ministers might say, that in important respects France's prospects looked worse for 1916 than for the latter part of 1915. He now had manpower as great as when the war began and much more ammunition. And he was facing an enemy distracted by commitments in the East to an extent it had not been in 1914 and was unlikely to be, given Russia's misfortunes, in 1916.

---

[4] War Council Minutes, 14 May 1915.
[5] Quoted in Paul Guinn, *British Strategy and Politics 1914 to 1918* (Oxford: Clarendon Press, 1965), p. 89.
[6] Minutes of the Dardanelles Committee, 5 July 1915.

These were weighty considerations. If hindsight confirms that Joffre's judgement in resuming the offensive in the autumn of 1915 was wrong, it does not show that a decision for the opposite course would certainly have been correct.

Joffre's strategy for the autumn was virtually a repetition of that in the spring: to strike in Artois and the Champagne, seize the rail communications behind the German lines, and jeopardize the enemy's retention of the Noyon salient. He proposed to apply the 'lessons' of his earlier failures, including the near-success at Vimy Ridge. A major feature of the attacks launched by the French in September 1915 proved to be meticulous preparation: at the rear, in the front line, and also between them. This was revealed in the sapping forward of trenches, the building of roads and railways in the rear to ensure ample supplies for the front, the laying of telephone lines, a long preparatory bombardment employing all available heavy guns, and the placing of reserves well up so as to avoid further 'lost opportunities'.

Events were to reveal, however, that all of Joffre's refinements in the methods of assault were being countered on the German side by refinements in the methods of defence. Only in numbers of men at the point of impact would Joffre be allowed a superiority. And this would not be decisive, given the 'natural' advantages of defence over attack in the existing technology of war and the maximizing of those advantages by the Germans. The latter enjoyed superiority in heavy guns, and were developing new artillery fire patterns calculated to make the progress of an attack yet more difficult. And they were constructing second lines of trenches that were certain to minimize the effect should their forward trenches be overrun. As September and October 1915 in Artois and the Champagne were to demonstrate, nothing the French could accomplish with existing resources was going to wring a victory out of this unequal contest.

IV

The part in this operation assigned by Joffre to the British – assuming they were willing to participate – lay alongside the French offensive in the Artois. This was in the district of Lens and Loos (just to the south of Aubers Ridge and Festubert of unhappy memory). Apart from its contiguity to the French attack, the area had little to recommend it. As Haig, whose First Army was again to make the assault, early pointed out, the British would be operating across open space, offering the enemy good observation and clear fields of fire. The German side of the front, by contrast, consisted of ruined villages, slag heaps, mines, and coal pits all ideal for defence. French, who had begun by seeing merit in an attack here, grew ever more disenchanted. By early August he was proposing to limit the British contribution to a predominantly artillery exercise, unaccompanied by large infantry attacks 'liable to result only in the sacrifice of many lives'.[7] For this conception of his task he had at the time the authorization of the British Cabinet. But in mid-August, thanks to the intervention of the French commander and a change of mind by the British War Minister, he lost it.

This was a grim time for Kitchener. Early in August Warsaw had fallen, apparently heralding fresh disasters for the Russians. Simultaneously, the climactic British thrust at Gallipoli had failed decisively. Kitchener may earlier have made private promises to Joffre that he would support a French offensive in these circumstances. Certainly, he now described the state of Russia as providing imperative reason why the Western Allies must forego the desired policy of 'active defence' and instead 'act vigorously'.[8]

---

[7] Blake (ed.), *The Private Papers of Douglas Haig*, p. 100.
[8] Ibid., pp. 101–2.

The French too, he informed the Dardanelles Committee on 20 August (after visiting Joffre), needed to take offensive action to preserve the morale of their army, amongst which there was a good deal of peace talk. He feared – or claimed to fear – that if Britain remained on the defensive, there was some chance of both Russians and French making a separate peace in October. 'The French were beginning to have grave doubts about us.'

Yet Kitchener took the decision in no spirit of optimism. He told the Committee: 'We must make war as we must; not as we should like.' Asked by Curzon if there was a reasonable chance of success for a great offensive in the West, he replied that there was 'a *reasonable* chance', but 'the odds were against a great success.'[9] And he told Haig that British forces must do their utmost to help the French, '*even though, by so doing, we suffered very heavy losses indeed*'. This conclusion, however irresistible, sealed the doom of many thousands of Kitchener's recruits, of Sir John French's command, and of Kitchener's remaining authority as war leader.

Haig, as has been seen, had not approved of the area of the forthcoming assault in his report to the British C.-in-C. And in informing the commanders of his I and IV Corps (Gough and Rawlinson) on 6 September that they were to undertake this operation, he made no bones about the fact that the Western Allies had been 'forced . . . to abandon their defensive attitude' by the 'losses incurred by the Russians'. Yet he was by then warming to the task. In mid-August he had given Kitchener no hint of the misgivings he had expressed to French, telling him, 'my Army was all ready to attack. All we wanted was ammunition.'[10] And although it became apparent that he would not get sufficient heavy artillery to blow a hole in the German lines, he believed he saw a way of overcoming this deficiency: by relegating shells to a supporting role and using poison gas as his main preparatory weapon.

Although the first use of gas had been passionately condemned in Britain, the decision to reply in kind was speedily taken. Five days after its initial employment at Ypres on 22 April, Kitchener had asked the Cabinet (so one Minister recorded) 'whether he should give orders for the preparation of poisonous gases, as he wished Cabinet assent "before he fell to the level of the degraded Germans"'. The Cabinet proved ready to accept such degradation. 'We agreed he should use anything he could get invented.'[11] There remained people of note hostile to this course. The Archbishop of Canterbury expressed (to Esher) 'an almost violent hope that we should not retaliate'. But his position was shared by few. The King, when Esher reported the Archbishop's comments, took 'a diametrically opposite view, and rightly holds that the question is purely military, and that ethical considerations will not enter into it.'[12] Yet the condemnation of Germany for first employing this weapon had apparently been based precisely on ethical grounds.

Haig's plan to use gas as the main bludgeon of attack at Loos was a hazardous undertaking, and quite unlike the action of the Germans on 22 April. Their operation had not been part of a major offensive, had not involved the use of reserve troops whose presence might have attracted shelling, and had been capable of postponement until the wind was favourable. Haig was bound to attack on the day selected by the French, without regard to the wind. And he had to assemble troops in such large

---

[9] Minutes of the Dardanelles Committee, 20 August 1915.
[10] Anthony Farrar-Hockley, *Goughie* (London: Hart-Davis, MacGibbon, 1975), p. 166; Blake (ed.), *The Private Papers of Sir Douglas Haig*, p. 102.
[11] Edward David (ed.), *Inside Asquith's Cabinet: From the Diaries of Charles Hobhouse* (London: John Murray, 1977), p. 239.
[12] Esher's diary for 9 May 1915.

numbers that their presence might well bring down on his front lines – and his gas cylinders – a devastating bombardment.

Up to a point the gamble succeeded. The Germans, although they knew that an attack was coming in the Loos district, failed to divine what was in store for them. Doubtless they were concerned more with the threat from the French sectors than with that from the British. But Haig's First Army staff went about their business with considerable skill. The word 'gas' was excluded from all communications, lest these fall into the wrong hands; its place was taken by 'accessory'. And although 150 tons of gas, in more than 5,000 cylinders, were transported to the British front lines, they escaped enemy vigilance. All movement of the gas took place at night during the week preceding the attack. Wagons with muffled wheels conveyed the cylinders to advanced dumps. Each cylinder was then slung on to a pole and carried by men on whose shirts had been sewn a number that corresponded with the number of the bay in the front line where the cylinder was to be placed. The carriers were formed into parties, which were led by guides from the advanced dumps to the communication trenches and so to the front line. 'The only sound was the creaking of the slings and the grunts and muttered oaths of the men, for the cylinders weighed about 200 lbs. each and constant halts were necessary.'[13]

In order that the gas should be released in No-Man's-Land rather than in the British trenches, long pipes were attached to the cylinders. These pipes also had to be taken to the front line, with two men carrying six pipes between them. One participant wrote soon after:

> I shall never forget that journey down the communication trench. In order to localise the effect of shell explosions, the communication trench is zig-zag from beginning to end. The result was that we had to carry the pipes right above our heads in order to get them along the trench, otherwise at every corner they would get stuck. The communication trench is 3½ miles long and the journey took us between 7 and 8 hours. Rain was falling during the whole of the journey. In many places the trench was over a foot deep in water.[14]

The success of these preparations for the Loos offensive was a creditable achievement. Given that the battle is often seen (and by no means without reason) as an example of bungling by the British command, it is worth noting that this military curate's egg contained some very good parts.

Yet infiltration of the gas cylinders into the front line left important problems unsolved. Gas would not remove the enemy wire, and it was questionable whether the available artillery bombardment would be adequate for this task. And Haig had no control over the elements without whose aid the gas would not reach the enemy's positions. Yet there was no question of waiting for a day when the wind was favourable: the attack must go ahead on 25 September to coincide with the operations of the French. In these circumstances Haig was bound to have at hand an alternative plan. Under it the attack would be made on a much smaller front and be supported just by the available artillery. But Haig had few hopes for this scheme, as it would enable the defenders to concentrate their superior fire power against a lesser target. And the nearer it got to 25 September, the more difficult it became to arrange a last-minute adjustment.

Consequently, by the morning of the attack Haig could hardly avoid authorizing the release of the gas if circumstances proved even barely propitious. These were precisely the circumstances he encountered. Nothing more substantial than the drift of a

---

[13] Quoted in Philip Warner, *The Battle of Loos* (London: Wm Kimber, 1976), p. 86.
[14] Quoted in ibid., p. 54.

cigarette's smoke and a rustling in some poplar trees suggested the presence of a favouring wind. Yet on this basis (though with aweful misgiving) the go-ahead was ordered. As a result, the gas achieved far less than it might have done had the elements been kinder. At some points it did reach the enemy front line and, taking the Germans by surprise and providing concealment for the attackers, it helped to suppress resistance. At others it came to a stop in No-Man's-Land or moved across so slowly that the attacking troops (under heavy fire and so not inclined to dally) outran it. At yet others it blew back into the British trenches.[15] This indifferent performance by the 'accessory', coupled with the spasmodic impression made by the artillery on the enemy wire, doomed all chance of a swift penetration on a broad front.

Plate 20 *A former German trench just after it had been captured by the British and before the wounded and prisoners had been removed.*

The three divisions of Gough's I Corps, on the left of the main attack, gained little or no help from their gas. In the case of one division, the 2nd, the wind was in the wrong direction; but when one of the officers in charge of the gas refused to accept responsibility for releasing it, the divisional commander (Horne) delivered the remarkable directive that 'the programme must be carried out *whatever* the conditions.' His attack failed utterly. The other two divisions (one of them the aforementioned 9th division) did, despite heavy losses, claw their way into several German strongpoints, including the menacing Hohenzollern Redoubt. But they lacked efficient hand grenades, which were the most effective of all weapons in close-quarter trench fighting. And with no large-scale reserves coming to their aid, they were able to do no more than cling on by their finger tips.

On the right of the attack, in the sector assigned to the three divisions of Rawlinson's IV Corps, the performance of the gas was better but again spasmodic. The most

---

[15] There is good evidence that, overall, the British suffered heavier casualties from their gas than it inflicted on the Germans.

spectacular success was achieved by the two right-hand divisions. One of them (the 47th) was a Territorial force that had seen enough action earlier in the year to know what it was about. The other (the 15th) was a force of Scots receiving their first taste of battle but fighting with exemplary courage and enthusiasm. Again at great cost, they overran the front German lines and the town of Loos (in effect a forward post of the German defence system). In diminished numbers they then ascended the crucial Hill 70 to the east of Loos. But on the reverse slope of this hill was an undamaged second line of defence, and here the attackers were first pinned down and then driven back.

In fact, the most promising advance that day took place not at the township of Loos but on the left of Rawlinson's front, before Hulluch. Here sections of his 1st division, notwithstanding casualties from both their own gas and enemy machine-guns firing in enfilade, broke through the Germans' first and into their second trench system. By soon after 9 a.m. there seemed to be developing in this sector, if only on a front of three-quarters of a mile, the sort of breach that would allow of exploitation.

But the thrust of the first wave of attackers was now exhausted. The most that they could do was hold on while reserves were fed through them. But the supporting forces did not come. The tactical reserves under the hand of the divisional commander were wasted in renewed attacks against strong points where the initial assaults had failed. As for the general reserve, consisting of the three divisions of Haking's XI Corps, it did not appear on the field of battle at all this day. In its absence such fleeting promise of success as the battle of Loos had ever offered melted away.

V

If the general reserve was not on hand when needed, the responsibility lay with Sir John French. His difficulties were great. He had been thrust into an offensive that he did not want, that was likely to incur grievous casualties (something, to his credit, at which he balked), and that could lose him his job. And should his worst expectations not be fulfilled, he personally had little hope of benefit. The credit for what went right was likely once more to accrue to Haig.

Yet there was always the possibility that the battle of Loos would prosper. And there was one way in which he might expect to secure some of the credit if it did: by controlling the reserve force that was bound to be involved in any favourable development. So, despite repeated requests from Haig direct, as well as representations that Haig sought to make through Kitchener and others, he insisted on retaining control of the reserve divisions under his own hand. (According to Wully Robertson, French was jealous of Haig and wanted to fight an action on his own.)[16] What French did not then do was to think through the implications of this decision. On 25 September he positioned himself at a point where he could not possibly keep in close touch with developments on the battlefield. And he placed the reserves where they could not be thrown into the fray as opportunity beckoned.

So it was only during the night of 25–6 September that the two reserve divisions, the 21st and 24th, reached the scene of the struggle. And by the opening of the second day all chance of using them to advantage had gone. But this did not mean that they went unused. Late in the morning of the 26th, without aid of gas or significant artillery preparation, they were directed to advance across 1,500 yards of No-Man's-Land towards solid banks of barbed wire and well sited machine-guns. So hopeless was their task, and so atrocious the resulting slaughter, that when at last the battered remnants

---

[16] This anyway is Wilson's report of what Robertson told him; Henry Wilson's diary, 24 September 1915.

abandoned the attempt and began to stumble back, numbers of German machine-gunners and riflemen stopped shooting because they had not the heart to continue the massacre.

Even in a war so rich in episodes of purposeless sacrifice, the travails of these two divisions on 26 September seem cause for indignation. They consisted not of professional soldiers but of former civilians who had volunteered in August and September 1914, in the first flush of enthusiasm for the conflict. They had trained amidst all the improvisation and disarray that had perforce accompanied the military authorities' attempts to create a mass army. Having landed in France only a fortnight before the battle, they were seeing action for the first time on 26 September. The circumstances in which they did so ensured that, without their having a chance to strike a blow at the enemy, their lives would be squandered by the thousand – along with the patriotism, enthusiasm, and spadework that had gone into making them soldiers.

The responsibility for this débâcle was not French's alone. Certainly, but for his ineptitude the reserves would probably have been committed the previous day, when their task might not have been so hopeless. But for the quite independent decision to initiate an attack at 11 a.m. on the 26th, as if all the hopeful aspects of 24 hours earlier still existed, responsibility lay also with the corps commander and especially with Haig, the chief of the First Army. It is right that Haig should no longer be employed by historians as a whipping-boy for all the intrinsic horrors of the Western Front, or be denied credit for his substantial achievements. It is not commendable that, aided by a resort to circumlocution ('the raw New Army Divisions received a terrible baptism of fire'),[17] his blunders should be passed over without comment.

It is worth noting that there are discrepancies in the accounts of how the two reserve divisions behaved during this 'baptism of fire'. According to one view, they soon became a disorganized rabble. According to another, they advanced steadily and with exemplary courage towards near-annihilation. This discrepancy is not to be explained by assuming that the sources are tainted – that the former account emanates from defenders of the military command, the latter from its critics. As we shall see, bitter remarks were made about the performance of some English divisions by members of the New Armies who had themselves first gone into battle on the previous day. And some of the strongest praise for the unfortunate reserves came from combatants who happened to be well placed to observe – and wonder at – their tenacity under fire: the German troops who inflicted death upon them.[18]

Obviously, this discrepancy in part tells us only that, over a wide field of battle, the performance of the reserve divisions was not uniform. But two things more may usefully be said. The first is that these troops were unlikely to respond as well to their first ordeal by battle as had those of the day before, because they were less well handled by circumstances and their commanders. They went into battle worn down by nights of gruelling route marches and days of inadequate rest and the persistent neglect of their need for sustenance. They moved into a front line already occupied by many British and German dead, an experience that 'shocked' them. ('We were new to the sight of still stiff bodies, staring eyes and mutilation.')[19] They had undergone none of the careful rehearsal that preceded the first day of the battle, and had only a vague idea of what they were to do. And they were sent into action without the reassurance of seeing enemy positions softened up by gas and shells: 'An occasional shell from our gunners whistled towards the German line,' one survivor of 26 September recorded, 'and I

[17] John Terraine, *Douglas Haig: The Educated Soldier* (London: Hutchinson, 1963), p. 159.
[18] For the German view see G. C. Wynne in *The Fighting Forces*, 1934.
[19] Warner, *The Battle of Loos*, p. 216.

wondered if the RFA ammunition and our rations and rum were still somewhere back near Montreuil.'[20]

The second point is this. In a situation where the fog of battle mingled with inept command, it was not wonderful that raw troops behaved inappropriately. What is noteworthy is that this applied not only to those who broke too easily. It is true also of those who stuck to their task when circumstances demanded its abandonment. Troops who have learned their business do not panic readily. But neither do they adhere too devotedly to orders emanating from Cloud-Cuckoo-Land. The heroism of those who pushed on under terrible fire to uncut wire that they then struggled to surmount was magnificent; but it was not war of a sort that Britain could afford to fight.

VI

Something of the heroism, ferocity, and blighted hopes of the opening days of the battle of Loos are conveyed in a long letter home, written four days after the start of the operation, by a Scottish infantryman.[21] His surname is unknown. He signed the letter Howard and, from internal evidence, was a member of the 7th Cameron Highlanders, a battalion of the 44th Infantry Brigade, 15th division. He fought throughout the first day of the battle and most of the second, by which time his battalion had been virtually annihilated. At the head of the letter, as an afterthought but in order that nothing might be in doubt, he wrote:

> It was our Brigade that took Loos and Hill 70 and our Division which held it. All Scotch and proud of it.

His narrative begins about 3 a.m. on the morning of 25 September, when the 7th Camerons left their reserve trenches and moved into the front line.

> The Black Watch and Seaforths were over the parapet and we followed. The Germans had bombarded our trenches which were covered with blood and a few dead lying. Once over the parapet our platoon officer was shot dead in front of me and the place [became] a pure shambles of dead and dying. We had given them gas and it came back on us. I got a dose but it didn't lay me out. On we went over the German trenches[,] and what sights. German shells and even our own were falling amongst us and time and again I was bowled over but not struck.
>
> We came to Loos village where machine guns played on us and we had to lie down. Our bombers went first and did great work in cellars and round about the houses. There were scores of Germans and a few hundred surrendered. Isolate[d] parties of them we bombed, shot or bayoneted.

It is not crystal-clear from the last sentence whether these 'isolated parties' were Germans still attempting to resist or prisoners receiving summary execution. In a later stage of his narrative there is no ambiguity; and Loos was to gain a certain notoriety for the number of occasions on which British forces dispatched their prisoners.

The narrative continues:

> we made a left incline out of the village and got into line near the foot of Hill 70. For miles there was open country and we advanced in a long line and up the hill. It was an irresistible line and two chaps alongside me took out mouth organs and played the 'March of the Cameron Men' and nearly all of us lit cigarettes and pushed on.

---

[20] Warner, *The Battle of Loos*, p. 217. RFA was the Royal Field Artillery.

[21] A typed copy of the letter is in the Imperial War Museum. There are no paragraphs in its account of the battle; these have been inserted. In addition, a few spelling errors have been corrected and some abbreviations expanded.

It is not surprising that observers described them as 'a magnificent Border rabble' and 'looking like a bank holiday crowd'. Seemingly they thought the battle was almost won. They were misled.

> We were supposed to dig in on our side of the hill but we kept on right over the ridge for a few hundred yards down the other side on to another village and there we were met with an intense machine gun fire. The Germans had a trench dug in front of the village and had it lined with guns. Our line was fairly thick and although we fired until our rifles were too hot to hold it was no use and we were getting it stiff as we lay quite exposed. Their guns were firing very low and although we kept our noses in the ground they were catching us every time. For what seemed like two hours we held on[,] and as no reinforcements came our left flank had to retire and then our turn came. Instead of seeing a whole crowd get up[,] there were only about 6 or 7 near me who got up, the others had been hit.
> A chum of mine, a Paisley lad, was lying alongside me when he gave a groan, bullet in the arm. I cut off his sleeve and shirt and got out my dressing. It [had] got him on the muscle which came right out and blood gulped out. Before I had finished I was drenched in his blood and the smell of it was sickening. By the time I had finished my tunic sleeves were holed with bullets but I never felt any hitting. My chum started to crawl back and glad to say he managed alright.

As Howard himself made off to leave, a bullet passed through his kilt and struck him a glancing blow above the knee, knocking him over. He looked back to see advancing Germans not 50 yards behind him. He started to run, losing his rifle as he did so, but after 10 yards 'I was completely done out.' With the ridge still 300 yards away, he gave himself up as hopeless but nevertheless put his head down and staggered on.

> Bullets whistled past my ears and half deafened me, others went through my equipment and smoke helmet which I was wearing as a cap[,] but devil a one actually got me. I never looked back to see where the Huns were and it seemed I was never going to get to the ridge. However I came to it and was so pleased I started to run. Our reserve Brigade . . . had dug a little trench along and I fell into it and could not speak for about half an hour.

A handful of British machine-guns on the ridge 'mowed the Huns down and held them up'.

By this time it was about 3 p.m.; 'we had kicked off about 6 a.m. so you can imagine how we felt being under fire the whole time.' Rain was falling heavily, adding to their discomfort. As it got dark he went seeking other Cameronians and found two. 'Of our Battalion there were not more than 20 left in the line.' About midnight 'the Germans came on again and we mowed them down again.' The British wounded came streaming back, among them 'some ghastly sights': men holding on arms, legs broken, heads smashed. 'Until I got another rifle I dressed some.'

It was now the morning of Sunday, 26 September. An officer of the Argylls informed the three Cameronians that 'our lot had been relieved the night before'; the message had not reached them.

> We did not move back until an English Brigade came up and just at that time the Germans made another attack[,] and Holy God what did those damned English do but turn back and as they were in the open they got it stiff. There were about 200 Kilties and about 1,000 English and yet they turned.
> We held on with machine guns and to see the Germans piling up was sickening. They came in mass formation and must have left hundreds piled up dead and wounded and had to retire[,] and for a while we had only shell fire to contend with, some of it once more our own.

It was about 7 a.m. on the second day of the battle, and the three Cameronians were 'half dead with exhaustion'. The officer in charge told them to go, and 'we went willingly.'

> We made for the village [Loos] and the open part before it was strewn with our dead. Once in the village we were safe from rifle fire but the shells were coming over one after another. The Germans were lying thick and in some of the cellars where our bombers had passed they were like mince meat, heads, legs, arms, etc. lying about.
>
> At one part we dodged into a house as we heard a shell coming. It burst on top and smothered us but still our luck held good. I can safely say this was where we got the biggest fright. It stunned us and as we lay a door leading up [from] a cellar opened and what came out but three French women and when they saw us they threw themselves at us thanking and merci(ing) us and crying awful. We simply gaped and could not move for about 5 minutes.
>
> One of them pointed to a cellar out in their garden and we went forward to see what was in [it] when out trooped a German officer with hands up and 'Mercy Kamerad' etc. We searched him and one of the women brought us a jug of milk and in case there was anything wrong with it I made the German drink it first and as he showed no signs of being any the worse of it we drank ourselves. We sent the women back saying they were safe and showing them the way. The German we did not know what to do with so we sent him on in front and as he got a few yards away I shot him.
>
> At another part of the village we came across three of our lads who had discovered some Huns in a cellar hiding. One lad was fair mad and wanted to bayonet each one as they came up the stair. We held him back for a little but the fourth Hun was a huge chap and as he came up his brains were scattered along the wall by a shot from this chap. The others we eventually disposed of. I could tell you hundreds of other such incidents but they are all too gruesome.

In marked contrast to this ruthless treatment of prisoners, the three Cameronians, as they made their way back to the starting point of the day before, were moved to compassion by the sight of their own dead and wounded.

> We came right back over the battlefield and our wounded were still shouting for stretcher bearers. We attended some until we had not the strength to do any more. Some dead were lying in weird positions and oh it was awful recognizing some of our own pals.
>
> We got back to headquarters and reported ourselves present and at that time only 75 of our Battalion had turned up. We got tea and rum and two hours sleep and then [were] sent back to reserve trenches[,] and were almost right back again as our left flank composed of those cursed English regiments had retired almost right back to where we had started from. It was galling for us to see them lose the ground we had so hardly won[,] but the 6th boys[22] regained it again. The whole of Sunday night we dug ourselves in and were relieved early in the morning and marched back to a little town where we lay that day and night in the rain, dead beat, nervous and miserable. The gas was having its effects. Altogether it was rotten but how thankful to be back out of the fire zone. Any gun that went off fair made us jump[,] in fact any unusual noise had its effect.

On the day he wrote the letter, Wednesday, 29 September, Howard and his companions were 'a few miles back in billets and going further back'. During that day some two dozen of the brigade were 'knocking about' at a crossroad when Sir John French came by. The Commander-in-Chief's solicitude for his troops was much in evidence at this time. Three days earlier he had spent two hours talking to the wounded in a British dressing station, which cannot have been an enjoyable experience. It can only be conjectured how he felt about these Scottish soldiers who, in the town of Loos and on the slopes of Hill 70, had seemed on the verge of giving him the triumph he so badly needed. Certainly, his demeanour towards the Cameronians was above reproach. Howard relates:

---

[22] I.e. the 6th Camerons, part of the reserve brigade that, on 25 September, had held off German counter-attacks on the near side of Hill 70.

He stopped and said he wished to speak a few words. He said he was proud to thank us for what we had done and we were quite fresh as soldiers and by magnificent courage had gained a glorious victory and finished off by thanking us again (each individual one) and saying our country would be proud of us indeed. It was like a tonic and we did cheer.

The same day messages also came from the Army Corps commander (Rawlinson) and other commanders 'with another dose of praise', their colonel being specially mentioned. But, as Howard reflected, many acts of valour would go unreported because the slaughter of their officers had been so great.

There were hundreds of brave deeds done but nothing will come of them as all our officers were killed. We have not an officer in our Company left and only four lieutenants out of the Battalion came back. Strange all our Sergeant Majors, Platoon Sergeants and N.C.O,s wiped out. About 5 Sergeants left. Battalion including those who were not in the charge about 200 strong.

Howard concluded his letter with personal messages to friends, an apology for not writing more, a request for comforts – cigarettes, a shirt, socks, and 'a pair of short blue pants' –, and an account of a galling incident.

A draft arrived today and one of the officers actually gave one of our men gip for having a dirty rifle[,] and all our rifles are thick with rust and the barrel almost blown to bits. It does get on one's nerve to see a joker coming the tin man after what we have come through. However such is life.

Then, in a postscript, the letter writer's mind turned again to that critical stage on the far side of Hill 70, when the battle from seeming almost won turned against them:

At our furthest point of advance about 3 miles on[,] when we had to lie for an hour or two[,] we managed to get a smoke. Some of our boys never got it finished.

VII

The battle of Loos did not end on the second day, although all prospect of a success had by then vanished. During an attack north of Loos on 28 September, the Coldstream Guards were almost wiped out. And in close-quarter trench fighting on 3 October the Germans managed, thanks to their superior hand grenades, to regain the Hohenzollern Redoubt. But a general offensive by the Germans on 8 October was beaten back. Thereafter British efforts were confined to trying to improve the line. Haig was contemplating a larger move for early November, but the rain began in earnest. So the British army and its commanders were left facing a second winter of war in which to plan something better.

This battle had not been all loss. British forces had wrested a little territory from the enemy. And, on their first appearance upon the battlefield, some of Kitchener's new armies had revealed great fighting qualities. There was no doubt that the British civilian was capable of being transformed into an efficient warrior.

Yet this was poor reward for casualties of 60,000, especially as the French had not managed any advance as a result of British exertions. Furthermore, the German troops in this sector had provided no evidence of a decline in fighting quality, despite Germany's commitments elsewhere. Henry Wilson, early in the afternoon of the first day, learned that the French on the British right had made very little progress and had lost some of their modest gains to German counter-attacks. He noted: 'This is something new as we thought the German Inf: was becoming inferior.' And on 3 October, upon hearing that the Germans had recaptured the Hohenzollern Redoubt, Wilson was moved to comment: 'Stout fellows these Boshes.'

At the level of the British command the Loos operation sealed the doom of Sir John French. There was no gainsaying that on the first and second days the reserves had been grievously mishandled, both by not being available when opportunity offered and by being sent in when no opportunity remained. Although French's particular responsiblity applied only to the first, he was bound to carry discredit for both. Haig's staff was soon assiduously collecting information from German prisoners and diaries about the proximity of a breakthrough on the first day that the absence of reserves had supposedly rendered abortive. And, to French's further discomfiture, in London wounded survivors of the reserve divisions were letting it be known that many lives had been squandered on a hopeless task. (One of the best-known stories concerning the second day of Loos tells how the commander of the reserves moved among the survivors asking, 'What went wrong?' He is said to have got the invariable reply: 'We did not know what it was like. *We will do all right next time.*' If this tale is accurate, then it is worth noting that, very soon, some of the survivors were offering a different explanation – and one that placed responsibility at a more elevated level.)

French, now the subject of awkward inquiries, was almost bereft of defenders in high places. A month after the battle the Prime Minister, replying confidentially to a Cabinet colleague, wrote that both he and Kitchener had gone as carefully as possible into the vexed question of who, if anyone, was to blame for 'the undoubted fact that our recent operations in France were not brought to a more definite and decisive success'. It was, he concluded, a question that turned entirely on the use of the reserve forces, concerning which French and Haig took opposed views. Asquith wrote:

> The stories which are current are highly over-coloured, but there is no doubt that the Reserve was late in being ordered up, that through bad staff work some of the units took the wrong road, that the new troops were tired & hungry when they reached the scene of action, and that a number of them ran away.
>
> My own view is (I regret to say) that the main responsibility rests with Sir J. French, and a very serious one it is. K's judgment (wh. of course is much more important) inclines in the same direction, but not to the extent of thinking that a case has been made out for removing him from the Command. He [French] seems still (unlike I.H.) to possess the general confidence of his Army. I have no doubt myself that before long Haig will have to take his place: but this is for your own ear only.[23]

It seems odd (though entirely in character) that Kitchener, having been prepared to dismiss French in May, balked at doing so now. But, plainly, if the Commander-in-Chief depended for survival on Kitchener's goodwill, then he was doomed.

What of the 'general confidence' that French (unlike Ian Hamilton) was supposed still to enjoy among his forces? In some measure, confidence may have remained among the rank and file – as witness the letter quoted in the preceding section. It was certainly lacking among his senior officers. With the partial exception of Henry Wilson, whose fate at that moment was tied up with French's, the Commander-in-Chief had lost the support of his principal subordinates.

Nor did he recover it when he engaged in a piece of public self-justification almost as ill-conceived as his earlier action over shells. In his account of the Loos operation he misstated the time at which Haig secured command of the reserves. Haig demanded a retraction. And he did not stop there. When the King set about asking high-ranking officers whether the time had not come to replace French, Haig's reply was brutally frank: he 'thought strongly that, for the sake of the Empire, French ought to be removed.'[24] (He also told the King that 'I, personally, was ready to do my duty in any

---

[23] Asquith to Lord Selborne, 26 October 1915, Selborne papers.
[24] Blake (ed.) *The Private Papers of Douglas Haig*, pp. 108–9 (diary entries for 17 and 24 October 1915).

capacity, and of course would serve under anyone who was chosen for his military skill to be C. in C' – a piece of self-abnegation in which it was safe to indulge, seeing that no one could challenge his claim to succeed French.)

Early in December the deed was done. The Government informed Sir John that it desired his resignation. With the utmost reluctance, this was eventually submitted.

24

SIDESHOWS MORE AND LESS: GALLIPOLI, SALONIKA, AND MESOPOTAMIA

Things have not been going well in the East.

> Punch, *December 1915*

. . . this Brobdignagian Bumstunt. . . .
Major-General Julian Byng, recently arrived at the Dardanelles, on the Gallipoli operation,

> *3 October 1915*

I

One of the events that had precipitated the political crisis in May was the deadlock at the Dardanelles. And one of the first acts of the new Government was to establish a sub-committee of the Cabinet that, although soon concerning itself with the war as a whole, was called the Dardanelles Committee. In short, the new Government recognized that it must do something about the Gallipoli campaign.

There was one decision it did not take: to run down Britain's commitment on the Western Front so as to provide massive quantities of men and ammunition for operations elsewhere. Although in mid-1915 there was no eagerness for a further offensive in Flanders that year, nothing about the state of the Western Alliance or the prospects of an Eastern campaign seemed to warrant a major change in priorities. So the Cabinet agreed early in July that 'the western theatre was the principal one for our efforts'.[1] But it was still possible to decide that the time had come to send additional manpower and naval support to the Dardanelles. This might even be in accord not with what was left over from elsewhere but with what could be thought the expedition's real needs. It was indicative of the new spirit that, where Hamilton asked for an additional three divisions, he found himself presented with five. The Government wanted the matter of Gallipoli to make progress.

And if Hamilton was still not being offered vast forces, this may have been no great deprivation. For there was a limit to the number of troops he could employ if he was going to work from the positions already established. The territory held by the Allies on the peninsula was severely confined. And Hamilton's choice of options was narrowing. A series of abortive offensives at Helles in June and July had all but eliminated that area as a credible choice for further endeavours. That left only Anzac, where the beach-head was so small that it placed its own limitations on the number of fresh troops that could be employed.

---

[1] Sir Maurice Hankey, *The Supreme Command 1914–1918*, 2 vols. (London: Allen & Unwin, 1961), vol. 1, p. 343.

Hitherto Hamilton had seen Anzac as subsidiary. Now it became central to his hopes. What he planned was a break-out from the Anzac beach-head to seize the Sari Bair ridge. This might not only imperil the Turkish forces in the south of the peninsula but, much more important, might also gain some sort of oversight of the Narrows Forts. Then, if sufficient artillery fire could be brought to bear against the forts (which was far from certain), the Dardanelles might be opened to the passage of the fleet. This transit, an age before, had been the entire purpose of the endeavour: although whether (given de Robeck's reservations) it remained so any longer was a question someone needed to be asking.

Plate 21   *Troops in the cover of a small beach in the Suvla bay region awaiting the order to attack.*

An attack on the Sari Bair ridge faced formidable problems. Surprise was of the essence in the undertaking. It was only because the Turks saw the peaks as well-nigh impregnable that they were leaving them lightly defended, so giving Hamilton his chance. If they divined his intention, they could bring up reinforcements that would render any attack there abortive. Two things would give Hamilton's game away: the detection of large numbers of fresh troops and stores arriving at Anzac, and the inception of movement from the Anzac beaches along the tortuous valleys leading to the Sari Bair ridge. To avoid the first of these, Hamilton directed that the 20,000 reinforcements to be employed at Anzac should be landed over three nights during the hours of darkness. In the daytime they were to be kept concealed. (This phase of the operation was carried out with commendable skill.) The second problem he also planned to overcome by using stealth. During a single night the assaulting troops must find their way along the valleys leading to the peaks and seize them before the Turks were alerted. If this timetable went awry, there would be no chance for amendment.

There was, however, a limit to what secrecy could achieve. The Turks were bound to know that a major offensive was in the offing. In order to deceive them further, diversionary operations were planned that might pin down their forces and attract their reserves. The first of these would take place at Cape Helles; the second at Lone Pine on Anzac, to the right of the main operation.

Nor did Hamilton's improvisations stop there. On the left of the Anzac operation he instigated an attack at a point where no Allied soldier had hitherto set foot. This was at Suvla Bay, to the north of the Anzac position. The purpose of this landing, except to employ troops that he could not accommodate elsewhere, is unclear. Hamilton assigned to it a variety of purposes. One aim was to establish a base. (This suggests that he was not expecting his thrust from Anzac to wind up the Gallipoli campaign; it would be only the first in a series of pushes across the centre of the peninsula.) A second aim was to advance rapidly from Suvla Bay and seize a couple of hills to the east that were believed (erroneously) to be heavily armed and so to constitute a threat both to the proposed base at Suvla and to the left wing of the Anzac attack. A third aim was to proceed south from these hills against the flank of the Turks confronting the Anzacs, so assisting the main operation.

The man whom Kitchener sent to command at Suvla was General Stopford, who was elderly and inexperienced. Ever since, it has been usual to blame the ineptitude of Stopford, and the want of initiative on the part of his troops, for the failure of the Suvla undertaking. This appears unwarranted. The landing at Suvla, as has been made clear, had no single purpose. The most modest of Hamilton's intentions, to establish a base, would in due course be accomplished. As for the most ambitious – that Stopford's force (of less than two divisions) should in short order make a night landing on an unfamiliar beach, advance against and capture two hills possibly well defended, and then cover a lot of ground to assault the Turkish right flank at Sari Bair – a commander well short of his dotage could reasonably have regarded this as impractical.

As a result of representations from Stopford, Hamilton somewhat amended his proposals for Suvla. Emphasis was now firmly placed on the first and second objectives: the securing of the base and (if possible) of the two hills so as to render it safe. At this point the landing at Suvla ceased to have more than a tangential bearing on the assault out of Anzac. What happened at the former could scarcely affect the fate of the latter.

Much heart-searching has been lavished upon the Suvla episode, as if a great opportunity was lost there. Probably this is because, elsewhere in the August attacks, there proved to be so few opportunities for the losing. The diversionary attacks at Cape Helles and Lone Pine (the latter a decidedly ferocious action), designed to keep Turkish attention away from the main assault, failed to divert large numbers of enemy troops. As for the attempt to seize the Sari Bair range by a night march and early morning assault, it proved, despite near-successes at two isolated points, to be too ambitious for accomplishment. The hours of darkness were insufficient – or, put another way, the distances to be covered in them were too great. The Turkish forces remained intrepid, their leaders resilient. Only on the second day of fighting did a party of New Zealanders manage to claw their way to the top of Chunuk Bair, one of the key peaks of the Sari Bair range; and then only to be driven off by weight of numbers and their own exposed position.

An account of the fighting the following morning, in an effort to retake this peak, must serve as illustration of the ferocity of this culminating struggle for Anzac. Digger Craven, a New Zealand private, was among those crossing The Farm, on the near side of Chunuk Bair, when the fury of the Turk counter-attack descended upon them. (His figures of the totals of men involved are clearly exaggerated.)

In all, we were some five thousand men on Chunuk Bair and within a quarter of a mile of its summit at the Farm. And against us were the Turks' reinforcements – some fifteen thousand men.

They descended upon us in a dense, black, screaming mass, so thickly ranked that they could advance shoulder to shoulder, and six to eight deep. They came and we sprayed them with machine-gun bullets, threw bombs in the packed mass, tore gaps into them with volley after volley of rifle-fire. From our miserable holes and bits of breast-works we annihilated their advance line. Then we rose to meet the second with bayonets, knives, entrenching tools, cut and battered them to bits despite their overwhelming superiority of numbers. The din of battle was deafening. . . .

They came on us in storming waves. The third line broke us, forced us back on our pitiful apology for trenches, leapt into our holes and hacked right and left in a confused jumble of destruction and death. The remnants fell back to the second line of trenches, rallied, stiffened, fired into the charging wall of men, killing and wounding hundreds in a deathly hail of musketry. But we could not hold them. Nothing could stop that dense multitude. . . .

Nothing in the world is as loathsome as the sight of human beings who have forgotten they *are* human beings. It is no mere expression to say we caught one another by the throat. We rolled about the dirt locked in death grips. We used stones, knives, bayonets, clubs, even fists, hurled ourselves upon one another in a fiendish bestiality such as the battlefield rarely sees. And the hullabaloo we set up was the concerted snarling of wild beasts in the jungle around The Farm.

The Turk counter-attack was brought to a standstill. Both sides forsook The Farm, leaving it to 'the dead and the dying and the carnivorous birds of the air'. But there was no doubt that the Turks had triumphed.

Chunuk and its road to victory was not for us. We had fought from Friday night to Tuesday evening in a wilderness of tangled scrub and precipitous rock and innumerable gullies, in blazing sun and in pitch darkness, without rest, with very little food, and an appalling lack of water, on hills afire and crags that rotted to our tread – and in all that effort of pain and blood and sweat and wasted gallantry we gained not a single position of any tactical or strategical importance.[2]

Ultimately, what had been true of Gallipoli in April remained every bit as true in August. The peninsula was heaven's gift to a defending force. Unless aided by great good fortune and indifferent opposition, neither the courage and discipline of the Anzac troops (admittedly a good deal blunted by August) nor Hamilton's strategic imagination could overcome this.

II

The main action in this renewed Gallipoli offensive took place between 6 and 10 August – although the failure to take Sari Bair on the night of 6–7th all but settled the matter. The attacks continued until the end of the month. But already by 17 August Hamilton was telling Kitchener that, in face of Turkish reinforcements, he would need a large increase in forces. And a week later he wrote: 'it is only possible for me to remain on the defensive. . . . it must be stated plainly that no decisive success is to be looked for until such time as reinforcements can be sent.'[3] (He failed to indicate what use he thought he could make of them.) This request only went further to call in question an operation that appeared to have lost all justification.

---

[2] Digger Craven, as told to W. J. Blackledge, *The Peninsula of Death* (London: Sampson Low, n.d. [*c.* 1937]), pp. 157–60.

[3] Hamilton to Kitchener, 17 and 23 August 1915 (copy in the Crewe papers). Kitchener spoke in the Dardanelles Committee of Hamilton's 'rather despondent' telegram of 23 August.

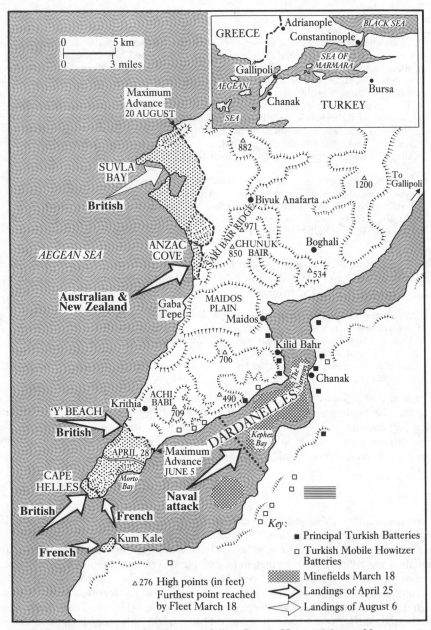

Map 5   *The Dardanelles, 1915*. Source: *Gilbert*, Recent History Atlas, *p. 33*.

Yet for a moment the Dardanelles operation received a promise of new life. An offer of large support came from an unexpected quarter – the French. France had participated in the campaign from the outset, but on a very limited basis and against the unrelenting hostility of Joffre, the Commander-in-Chief. The ambiguous position of the French is not to be wondered at. They had stronger cause than the British for keeping their gaze fixed on the German forces encamped in France. Yet, as in Britain, some important figures concluded that the Western Front was a situation of deadlock and that somewhere in 'the East' must lie a 'back door' into Germany. And as 1915 wore on there was alarm at the failure of Allied offensives in France to render aid to the flagging Russians. Furthermore, France, like Britain, had 'interests' in the Middle East that might be advanced by the destruction of the Turkish Empire, as well as disaffected Muslim subjects whose allegiance might be shaken by the collapse of the Dardanelles enterprise.

The tendencies in France to act somewhere in the Eastern Mediterranean, possibly at the Dardanelles, were reinforced by an internal difficulty. In July Joffre dismissed for incompetence the commander of his Third Army on the Western Front, General Sarrail. Sarrail happened to be Joffre's main rival for the post of Commander-in-Chief. He was also one of the few eminent military figures who were republican and anti-clerical in their sympathies, and so enjoyed much support on the left of French politics. His dismissal threatened French political unity and the security of the French Government. It was therefore deemed desirable to find another command for Sarrail, as far from Joffre as possible. The Dardanelles seemed a distinct possibility, except that Sarrail (tempted though he might be to lead a victorious march on Constantinople) refused to take charge of a meagre French force in an operation whose overall commander was British.

Here were good grounds for the French Government's decision to increase their role at the Dardanelles. But the decision was not unequivocal. The failure of the British August offensive raised doubts about whether any action could redeem the situation at Gallipoli. And Joffre refused to relinquish forces for Sarrail's new command until after his own offensive in September, which meant that they were unlikely to affect the situation at the Dardanelles before the onset of winter.

As quickly as the rulers of France began evincing an interest in Gallipoli, circumstances turned their attention elsewhere (with results that would leave Hamilton no choice but to remain on the defensive). These circumstances were events in the Balkans in late September and October 1915. The long-feared strike of Germany and Austria-Hungary against Serbia, which had been in abeyance while Germany's attention was directed against Russia, was about to take place, and in circumstances in which it could scarcely fail. For Bulgaria, aching for revenge against Serbia since the Second Balkan War in 1913, was prepared to throw in its lot with the Central Powers now that Germany was ready to move south. This meant that the Serbs were about to be attacked simultaneously from the north and east.

If any glimmer of hope existed for Serbia, it must come from Greece. Officially, the Greeks were treaty-bound to take Serbia's part against Bulgaria as long as the Serbs contributed 150,000 men to the Bulgarian front. This the Serbs could not do. But the Greek Prime Minister, Venizelos, who was anxious for his country to enter the war on the Allied side, suggested that Britain and France should provide the 150,000 men and so activate the treaty. This seemed a small price for the Entente to pay to secure a new ally and bring succour to a present one. But it terminated all prospect of a large French action at the Dardanelles, and even entailed a diversion of British troops away from the peninsula.

In the outcome it was all to no avail. Venizelos did not speak for the Greek King, Constantine, or for other important elements in the Greek community. At the very moment when Allied forces began disembarking on Greek soil, Venizelos was driven from office. The new Government announced that, notwithstanding its treaty obligations to Serbia, it would remain neutral – an attitude attributed by the Allies to King Constantine's pro-German inclinations, although, given the armed might of the Central Powers, it may have been the result of prudence. (Constantine told Kitchener that he was anti-German but not prepared to go to war with the Central Powers. He would go to war with Bulgaria when it did not mean embroiling himself with Germany.)[4]

This turn of events left the position of Serbia beyond redemption, whatever Britain and France might do. Given this military reality, along with their questionable position in international law, it appeared that the Allied forces disembarking in Greece would be advised promptly to re-embark, galling though it might be simply to leave Serbia to its fate. The British Government – if not quite all of its members – took this view; Asquith considered the Balkans campaign 'a wild goose affair'.[5] But the French Government, having found in the Balkans a suitable command for General Sarrail, did not.

This divergence speedily manifested itself in the actions of the forces landed at Salonika. The French troops swiftly moved north into Serbia. Considering their ignorance of the terrain and lack of equipment for mountain warfare, not to mention the quality of communications, their performance from a military point of view was commendable. The British force, by contrast, was instructed to remain at Salonika until Greek intentions became clear. Only late in October was it dragged north by the momentum of the French advance and the awareness among British authorities that otherwise they would appear to be leaving not just one but two allies in the lurch. By the time British troops reached Serbian soil, in mid-November, fierce winter storms reduced them to immobility.

Anyway the Allied rescue mission was in vain. The Bulgarians had cut the Serb line of retreat to the south. The only way of escape for the Serbian army lay to the west, across the snow-bound and gale-swept mountains of Albania. The most the Entente forces could do to help was to relieve some of the pressure by engaging the Bulgarians. By late in November, however, the French and British were themselves being driven out of Serbia by weight of numbers and their own dangerously exposed position. By mid-December they were all back on Greek soil. This rendered all the more anomalous their occupation of Greek territory.

A month before, the commander of the British force, Lieutenant-General Mahon, had reported to Kitchener: 'Although the Greeks are perfectly friendly, they are not helpful, and are obstructing in many ways.' Soon after, he appealed to London for clarification of his position: 'I should be very glad to know the general scheme and plan of campaign. The uncertain attitude of Greece makes the position of our weak force somewhat difficult and dangerous.'[6] He was going to have to wait for enlightenment.

Yet the British authorities knew quite well what they wanted. They had authorized the advance from Salonika only in the remote hope of aiding the Serbs and only under pressure from the French. (Kitchener wrote of 'the mistaken policy we have followed,

[4] So Kitchener wrote to Asquith on 20 November 1915 (copy in the Crewe papers).
[5] Quoted in J. K. Tanenbaum, *General Maurice Sarrail 1856–1929* (Chapel Hill: University of North Carolina Press, 1974), p. 70.
[6] Sir Bryan Mahon to Kitchener, 4 and 13 November 1915 (Crewe papers).

at the dictation of Frence'.)[7] It had clearly been understood that, should Serbia prove past redemption, the expedition to Greece would be abandoned. This conclusion was swiftly reached first by the British General Staff, then by the Cabinet. It seemed that for once a decision on strategy was about to be taken, and acted upon, without delay. But the process was rendered nugatory by the strongly contrary views of the French, egged on by that member of the British Government most prone to criticize his colleagues for evading ruthless decision-making.

Lloyd George at the end of 1915 was remembering vividly that he had urged British intervention in the Balkans – which meant Greece – early in the year so as to rally the Balkan states to the Allied side. He was less mindful of the obstacles he had encountered: the fierce animosities between those states that had rendered joint action by them highly unlikely; the refusal of Romania to act unless Russian military power were being asserted in the region (as it was not being in 1915); and the unwillingness of Greece to move until Romania did, culminating in the decision of the Greek rulers in March not to become involved.

Aided by the partiality of his recollection, Lloyd George was convinced in the later part of the year that a decisive chance had been lost in the Balkans. And lost though it might now be, he was determined to maintain a presence there. When, with the fall of Serbia, McKenna and others in the War Council argued that the Balkan episode should end, Lloyd George protested that the decision must wait on the General Staff. When the British General Staff came down firmly for abandonment, Lloyd George fell back on the French. 'The French', he told the Cabinet, 'are a proud race, and it hurts their pride to have to withdraw under the protection of the miserable little traitor, Greece.'[8] And he rather offensively told Kitchener: 'it seems that you and the Germans want the same thing' – whereupon (according to Lloyd George's account) 'Kitchener turned red and Asquith white.'[9] (Actually at least one important German, their Commander-in-Chief Falkenhayn, was delighted for the Allies to retain a large force immobilized at Salonika.) Lloyd George, in conversation with the French Minister of Munitions, let the French Government know that there was at least one prominent dissenter from the British Cabinet's firm resolve to be quit of Salonika.

Perhaps the French did not need this encouragement. A change of Government in France had brought into office a Prime Minister (Briand) and a Minister of War (Gallieni) both of whom favoured action at Salonika. And Joffre recognized the peril to his own position if he further antagonized the political supporters of Sarrail. The British dared not run the risk of provoking a further ministerial crisis in France, least of all one that might discourage the French socialists from participation in the wartime Government. So although Asquith and Kitchener took a firm stand at a conference at Calais on 4 December and got the French to agree to abandon Salonika, they were forced to climb down within a matter of days in face of dire warnings about possible internal consequences for France. (The French authorities also rallied expressions of support for the Salonika operation from the Russians, Italians, and Serbs.) Once more the British were finding that they must forgo the course of military wisdom for the sake of mollifying their badly bruised allies.

The outcome, militarily, was an absurdity. Just as at Gallipoli in April, the Entente powers were involved in an operation in a distant clime for which no calculation of need had been made. Ludicrously, the size of the Anglo-French force at Salonkia was

---

[7] Kitchener to Asquith, 22 November 1915 (Crewe papers).

[8] A. J. P. Taylor (ed.), *Lloyd George: A Diary by Frances Stevenson* (London: Hutchinson, 1971), pp. 62, 79, 84–5.

[9] Trevor Wilson (ed.), *The Political Diaries of C. P. Scott 1911–1928* (London: Collins, 1970), p. 161.

based on nothing but a figure struck in a pre-war bargain between Greece and Serbia. And the operation, if proving less costly than Gallipoli, made less sense. The Allies had gone to Salonika in the first instance at the invitation of the Greek Prime Minister for the purpose of aiding Serbia. They were now proposing to remain there even though the Greek authorities were antagonistic and Serbia had been overrun. Their only role was to stand on the defensive – 'Salonika is clearly defined as a defensive operation,' stated the War Office on 21 December – against an enemy that was not proposing to attack.

III

The Salonika operation, nevertheless, further invalidated the campaign at the Dardanelles. The British troops sent to Greece in October had been withdrawn from the peninsula. It was a small diversion, but it pointed the way to winding up the Gallipoli expedition.

There was another pointer that same month. Hamilton was dismissed. He had conducted a succession of failed offensives. And the way in which he exercised command had come under increasing criticism from men on the spot, among them a son of the Prime Minister. But it was noteworthy that those in London most eager to get rid of him were also those (like Lloyd George) anxious to close down the expedition – which the man in charge would never recommend as long as he continued to be Hamilton. Simultaneously, in London the Dardanelles Committee was reconstituted as a smaller War Committee, from which the devotees of the Dardanelles operation (especially Churchill) were excluded. And General Monro, sent out to command in Hamilton's place and to report on what should be done, was most assuredly a Westerner.

The matter hung fire throughout November. After all, if Gallipoli seemed hopeless, Salonika looked no better; attacks on the Western Front had failed; and the only hopeful sideshow, in Mesopotamia, had suddenly taken a turn for the worse. Further, it was believed that heavy losses would be sustained during the evacuation of Gallipoli. And it was said that the humiliation of having to wind up the operation would damage British prestige, particularly in imperial trouble spots. None of this could affect the ultimate conclusion. But it ensured that the agony of decision-making would be prolonged a little further. First Monro advised evacuation. Then Kitchener, who resisted this advice (fearing, or claiming to fear, the effect on Egypt), went out to see for himself and came round to endorsing evacuation. The last serious note of dissent came from the navy – which, given its long spell of relative quiescence, might well have kept silence. It argued that Cape Helles should be retained so as to facilitate the actions of British submarines against the Turks. This advice was taken seriously, if only because it enabled the Cabinet to make the necessary decision without altogether making it. On 7 December the Cabinet agreed that Anzac and Suvla should be evacuated but not Helles.

What this entailed was that 80,000 men, together with large quantities of stores and animals, should be removed from under the noses of the enemy. The staff planned a withdrawal in three phases, each independent of the others so that the intervention of bad weather would not cause utter disruption. First the forces surplus to a purely defensive holding of Anzac and Suvla would be removed; then the defensive forces would be pared to the bone; finally the remnants of the defence would be spirited away. It was accepted that at some stage the Turks must divine what was happening and that eventually the skeleton force remaining would be too small to hold them. But every endeavour would be made to delay discovery.

As with the landing of reinforcements at Anzac in preparation for the August attack, so with its evacuation: all unusual activity had to take place at night. During the day the diminution of numbers must be concealed. The soldiers remaining busied themselves conspicuously, as if preparing for a winter sojourn; and breakfast fires were lit for troops no longer present. In the course of a fortnight it was done. On the last night, as the remnant of the defenders left their positions with feet muffled and made their way to the shore along paths covered with flour, the tension was hard to endure. But at least, unlike so many First World War operations, it was an undertaking with a clear-cut ending.

In the outcome the Turks did not divine even at the last that Anzac and Suvla were being evacuated. The entire British force was taken off; there were no casualties. This settled the question of what was to be done about Cape Helles. Far from evacuation of Gallipoli proving a fearful blow to British prestige, when carried out with such success it constituted a mild form of face-saving. As for the navy's objections, there was little left for British submarines to do in the Sea of Marmora now that the expedition had been run down this far. It was assumed that the evacuation of Helles could not go so well, because the Turks must now recognize that such action was on the cards. But as it happened, if the Turks guessed that evacuation was occurring, they failed to divine the critical point at which the defenders would be too few to resist them. Helles, also, was evacuated without loss.

It is often said that only in abandoning Gallipoli did the British bring to this theatre of war the skill in preparation that earlier might have brought success. Yet it is a questionable judgement. For it is not plain that greater flair and expertise were revealed in planning the evacuation than in some phases of the assault on Gallipoli: for example, the undetected landing of reinforcements at Anzac in August. The difference in outcome lay in the fact that invasion and evacuation were operations of a different order. The invasion of Gallipoli constituted an attempt by a force possessing command of the sea to seize control of a formidable piece of land; the troops, as they came ashore, were leaving their power base behind them. And if they succeeded in the first phase of the operation, by getting ashore, that did not mean that they had achieved a victory, only that they must go on to the second phase and then the third. It required many 'victories' before they would be immune from danger. And even then it would not be certain that they could accomplish the purpose for which they had come. None of this was true of evacuation. Here British troops were falling back on their power base. Once aboard ship, nothing more was required of them, and the Turks could not touch them.

There was another vital difference between assault and evacuation. The Turkish soldiers who had fought with such tenacity in defence of their homeland proved much less enthusiastic about getting themselves killed so as to dispose of an intruder whose invasion was clearly melting away. One may surmise that it was not only British skill that allowed the Turks not to divine that an evacuation was occurring. For on 7 January 1916, while the evacuation of Cape Helles was proceeding (British forces there were fewer than 20,000), the Turk command sought to launch a major offensive. The great majority of Turkish troops refused to leave their trenches. Their prudence was justified. On that and the following nights the last British soldiers slipped away from Gallipoli.

IV

While the sideshow in Gallipoli was being wound up and that in Salonika was settling into immobility, a third, which had been looking quite hopeful, was turning sour. This was the operation in Mesopotamia.

It will be recalled that British action in Mesopotamia had occurred prompt upon the severance of relations with Turkey in November 1914. Its main object was to protect supplies of oil from Persia vital to the British navy. But it was also intended to impress Arab opinion in Mesopotamia and to give reassurance to those sheikhs sympathetic to the British cause. British forces first occupied Turkish territory opposite Abadan and then advanced to the port of Basra, at the confluence of the Tigris and Euphrates.

These forces came from India. The point is important because, although the first impetus for action in Mesopotamia emanated from Britain and ultimate authority for what happened thereafter rested with the British Cabinet, the conduct of the operations fell upon the Indian army. Further, the strong initiative to extend the operation beyond its original limits came not from Britain but from the civil, and in particular the military, authorities in India. Yet for many reasons stemming from British policy towards India before 1914, the Indian Army lacked the expertise and resources needed to mount a sustained operation well outside its usual sphere of activities.

For anything greater than the limited object of securing the head of the Persian Gulf, Mesopotamia was unwelcoming to an invader. Its climate ranged from atrocious heat to extreme cold and spawned many diseases. If Basra was a potentially good port, it was severely lacking in the dock facilities necessary to service a military expedition. And the interior of the country lacked communications for a major campaign. Owing to the number of months during which the country was subject to flooding, river craft were the only feasible means of transporting an army. Yet outside the seasons of the flood the principal waterways were so shallow that only special forms of craft could operate there. It followed that, before any decision was taken to convert the operation from its original purpose (safeguarding oil supplies and staging a demonstration) to that of overthrowing Turkish power in Mesopotamia, much preparation was needed; in particular the creation of an efficient port and the acquisition of a fleet of vessels for use inland.

This was not done. The authorities in Britain, civil and military, were too preoccupied. The Government of India also had concerns enough. That left the matter to the military authorities in India and the men on the spot. Two things lured them into folly. The first was that, as long as British forces in Mesopotamia remained where they were, the Turks were in a position to send forces down the great rivers to threaten them. The second was that, whenever British forces set themselves to meet these threats by advancing from their existing bases, they accomplished their objects comfortably enough. And if the British Government, nevertheless, felt inclined to restrain them, it could not be wholehearted in its attitude. For a countervailing factor existed. Arab opinion was not proving as favourable to Britain as had been anticipated. In February Crewe, the Secretary of State for India, writing to the Viceroy, expressed his disappointment in the attitude of the Arabs. He had been 'led to suppose that there was a general impatience of Turkish domination, and its methods of exercise . . . which would cause many Arabs both in Arabia and Mesopotamia to adopt a friendly neutrality even if they did not actually join us'; but of this there had been little sign.[10] In these

---

[10] Crewe to Lord Hardinge, 11 February 1915, Crewe papers.

circumstances it was not simple for the British Government vigorously to discourage its soldiers in Mesopotamia when they moved forward a step at a time, and the steps proved easy to take.

Already in December 1914 British forces had advanced some 46 miles north of Basra and occupied Qrna (where a branch of the Euphrates flowed into the Tigris) to deprive the Turks of one strong point for attack. Then in March 1915 a move northeast up the Karun river was called for, after the Turks had incited local tribesmen inside Persian Arabistan to cut the pipeline. The oil was soon flowing again, and by mid-1915 the Turks were ceasing to show much aggression. But the British forces did not settle down. For a change of emphasis was affecting the British operation in Mesopotamia, not inspired by London but evident in the attitudes of the military authorities in India and the commander in Mesopotamia, Sir John Nixon.

Nixon, who took control in March 1915, was a cavalry officer who had seen service in India. He was not wanting in enterprise. What he lacked was the organizing ability to put his inspirations into effect. For one thing, he never equipped himself with sufficient staff to look beyond day-to-day requirements. Hence he did not set about providing the facilities that an expedition going ever further inland would need. And even when Nixon perceived the necessity for additional river craft and transmitted his wishes to India, he did not delay further advances until the fulfilment of his requests. Nevertheless, for the forward policy that he soon came to adopt he had the endorsement of the military authorities in Delhi, who were proving equally unmindful of basic matters of logistics. Their instructions to him played down the matter of safeguarding the oil supply. His first task was defined as being 'to retain complete control of the lower portion of Mesopotamia', which was specified as the province (*vilayet*) of Basra.

At the time, Nixon did not happen to have 'complete control' of this province. To get it he would need to push his forces almost 90 miles up river and to take two major towns. As an added incitement to action, Nixon was told to submit plans for 'a subsequent advance to Baghdad' – over 400 miles upstream from Basra. This he took, justifiably or not, to constitute a firm instruction.

None of this conformed with the thinking of the British Government. In April Crewe deemed the British position 'strategically a sound one and we cannot afford to take risks by extending it unduly. *In Mesopotamia a safe game must be played.*'[11] Nixon, to his credit, perceived a difference of emphasis in the attitudes of London and Delhi. But an inquiry to India in May produced an assurance that this was not so; it was just that the British Government wished to stress that it could not provide reinforcements. His conquest of the whole of the Basra province was to proceed.

The events of June and July 1915 removed any lingering caution on Nixon's part. The remaining Turkish strongholds within the province, Al Amarah on the Tigris and Al Nasiriyah on the Euphrates, fell with comparative ease. Indeed, the advance to Al Amarah of Major-General Townshend, commander of the 6th Indian division, reads like a tale from a boys' storybook written by a propagandist of empire. A suitably romantic setting was provided by the fact that most of the fighting had to be done on water. The infantry, after some weeks of training in the art of punting, made their attack in large native canoes (*bellums*), while artillery support came from a flotilla of sloops, armed launches, naval horseboats, and gun barges. Just above Qrna the back of the Turkish resistance was broken by weight of fire power, and the Turks' positions were stormed by amphibious troops. Then the naval flotilla – with Townshend and his

---

[11] Quoted in A. J. Barker, *The Neglected War: Mesopotamia 1914–1918* (London: Faber & Faber, 1967), p. 80.

staff aboard but his army falling well to the rear – set off on a 100-mile dash in pursuit of the fleeing enemy.

As the regatta steamed north its larger vessels were forced to drop out because of the shallowness of the river. Townshend and his companions transferred to launches and thus proceed to Al Amarah, which promptly surrendered. It was a decidedly exotic event. The town, its 20,000 inhabitants, and its garrison (which included a crack Turkish infantry regiment) capitulated to just a general, a naval captain, a political officer, and about 100 soldiers and sailors – who spent a rather anxious 24 hours awaiting the arrival of the rest of their force. Perhaps it is not surprising that the British in Mesopotamia began seriously to underestimate the calibre of their adversaries.

Nixon was by now obsessed by the prospect of advancing on Baghdad. He was not, of course, alone in considering it a desirable acquisition. The British Cabinet, the War Office, and the authorities in India were agreed that, although of negligible military value, its capture would greatly raise British prestige at the expense of the Turk, so helping to offset the misfortunes of Gallipoli. Nixon's particular contribution was the belief that, with the men and craft he had available, he could take Baghdad – which was not the view of Townshend, the man who would actually be conducting the advance. Eventually Nixon managed to bring the Indian authorities round to his view, despite misgivings on their part concerning the adequacy of his river transports. (From mid-1915, as the number of troops in Mesopotamia was increasing and the supply of river transport was not keeping pace, the mobility of the force there was actually on the decrease.)

This doubt was not conveyed to the British Cabinet: indeed, a special committee set up by the latter noted that it understood the existing supply of vessels on the Tigris was sufficient for the operations. Thus misinformed, the committee decided in favour of the advance to Baghdad; but only if, once taken, it could be retained. The Cabinet (with Kitchener a noteworthy dissenter) concluded that the benefits to be gained from taking Baghdad justified running the risk of a possible eventual withdrawal. The terms in which this decision was conveyed to India are revealing: 'We are therefore in need of a striking success in the East. Unless you consider that the possibility of eventual withdrawal is decisive against the advance . . . we are prepared to order it.'[12]

Nixon received the go-ahead on 24 October. A month earlier, Townshend had already advanced beyond Basra province and taken the fortified town of Kut, 120 miles upstream of Al Amarah. It was to prove his last triumph. On 22 November, still 20 miles short of Baghdad, he attacked a well entrenched Turkish position near Ctesiphon (soon to be dubbed 'Pistupon' by his soldiers). The attack stuck dead, at a cost of one-third of his troops: 4,500 casualties out of a force of 12,000. With his capacity for further advance clearly exhausted, three days later he ordered the withdrawal. There followed seven-and-a-half days of arduous marching, during which the Turks snapped at his heels and much of his naval flotilla came to grief. At last his force reached Kut. There Townshend, although bound to be surrounded, decided to remain and await relief from Nixon.

It is unlikely that anyone in Britain at the end of 1915 anticipated the dire calamity that awaited both Townshend's force and many of the soldiers sent to its relief. But once more a sideshow that had seemed to promise large results for a small commitment was becoming a cause for deep anxiety.

---

[12] Quoted in Major-General H. H. Rich, 'Ctesiphon: Townshend's Pyrrhic Victory', in *Purnell's History of the First World War* (London: Purnell & Sons, 1969–71), issue no. 42, p. 1169.

PART SIX

Brief Encounter at Sea:
the Battle of Jutland, 1916

Map 6   *The battle of Jutland, 31 May 1916.* Source: *Arthur Banks,* A Military Atlas of the First World War *(London: Heinemann, 1975), p. 256, map 1.*

25

BEATTY VERSUS HIPPER

I

The battle of Jutland, which occurred during the afternoon and evening of 31 May 1916, fits uneasily into any account of the Great War. Unlike the land campaign on the Somme, which opened a month later, it was not the end-product of a mounting crescendo of decisions, preparations, and actions. Jutland could have occurred at any time in the war. It could, by the same token, never have occurred at all.

A conflict between the opposed naval might of Britain and Germany was something for which the British navy had been yearning ever since the outbreak of war. It is true that Jellicoe, as commander of the Grand Fleet, had made it clear early on that he would not accept battle in circumstances in which the Germans might be seeking to lure him into a snare of mines and submarines; and from this view he did not budge. Nevertheless, it is anything but the case that fear of the submarine had reduced the Grand Fleet to paralysis.

As evidence of this, it is necessary only to observe the circumstances in which the battle of Jutland came about. The German Commander-in-Chief sought to arrange a trap for units of the British fleet, and the first element in his plan was a screen of submarines awaiting the British forces as they left their bases. British naval intelligence was not ignorant of this. On the contrary, it was its awareness of a concentration of U-boats in the northern part of the North Sea, accompanied by no attacks on merchant shipping, that first alerted the Admiralty to the fact that something big was in the offing. This did not prevent the Grand Fleet from putting to sea on 31 May, determined – notwithstanding the danger from submarines – to turn that something to their own advantage. (In the event, the U-boats made no successful attacks and were not able even to give warning that the Grand Fleet was coming out. So this aspect of the German plan failed utterly. However a mine laid – in the wrong place – by one of the U-boats did, a few days later, accomplish the demise of Lord Kitchener.)

That no major sea battle had hitherto occurred was the consequence of German, not British, attitudes. The rulers of Germany had the strongest aversion to losing any of their great vessels. And the commanders of the High Seas Fleet did not doubt that they would have the worse of any meeting with their British counterparts. This attitude was not remarkable, given the British superiority in numbers of warships, weight of fire, and range of gunnery (for which possible British inferiority in other respects, such as ship armament, range-finding, and quality of shell, was unlikely to compensate). The question that Jutland posed was whether, even when the side eager for battle managed to bring off an encounter with the side determined to avoid it, any sustained conflict would eventuate.

Plate 22   *The guns of a battleship in action.*

In January 1916 the German fleet had acquired a new commander, Reinhard Scheer. He was determined to discover a more active role for his warships, most of which had spent the last year in near idleness. Yet he recognized that any such role must not involve an encounter with the main British fleet. His policy was, if on a subtler level, a revival of that with which the German navy had started the war. Piecemeal, elements of the British fleet must be lured to their doom until the point was reached at which Britain's forces no longer outnumbered their enemies. It remained to be seen whether Scheer could prove so cunning or Jellicoe so foolish as to commence, let alone carry through, this programme. The events of 31 May 1916 would hardly suggest that this was the case.

Scheer devised various schemes for entrapping elements of the British fleet. The one which he sought to apply on 31 May was as follows. The German battle cruisers under Hipper would ostentatiously proceed to Scandinavian waters, as if to interfere with the British blockade, while the main force of German battleships followed more secretively. This would bring the Grand Fleet out of its bases in Scotland and into the waiting arms of the U-boats, which would both inflict losses and report British movements. And, with any luck, Beatty's battle cruisers would dash across the North Sea, expecting only to resume the clash with Hipper that had ended abortively at the Dogger Bank in January 1915. Instead Beatty would find himself embroiled with Scheer's battleships, and would suffer accordingly. Should anything go wrong, Scheer would be in a position to make a swift journey home and so avoid any encounter with Jellicoe.

Fatal to the success of this plan, the British decoders were managing to piece together at least an outline of their enemy's intentions. By late in the afternoon of the 30th they were aware that Scheer would be leaving harbour next day. At 5.40 p.m. Jellicoe received the order to take his fleet to sea with the object of forcing an engagement. (For the men on Jellicoe's battleships, who had yet to see any significant action, the news was received with unrestrained glee.) By late evening on 30 May Jellicoe, with his 16 Dreadnoughts, had left Scapa Flow. Also putting to sea were the 8 Dreadnoughts of the 2nd Battle Squadron, stationed to the south at Cromarty. Further south still, Beatty with his Battle Cruiser Fleet set out from Rosyth. His force, apart from light vessels, consisted of 6 battle cruisers, plus the 5th Battle Squadron (consisting of 4 super-Dreadnoughts) commanded by Rear-Admiral H. Evan-Thomas.

Thus by the time the various elements of the German fleet, in the early morning of the 31st, began putting to sea, not only their intended victims but also the battleship force they had no wish to encounter were well on the way to meeting them. If the two groups should clash *in toto*, as Jellicoe (but not Scheer) intended, it would prove a decidedly unequal contest. The British had at sea 28 Dreadnought battleships, as against the 16 Dreadnoughts and 6 pre-Dreadnoughts (these last more a liability than an asset) of the Germans. There were also 9 British battle cruisers to the Germans' 5; 34 armoured and light cruisers to the Germans' 11; and 78 destroyers against the 61 of the enemy. Beatty even had a seaplane carrier attached to his battle cruisers (although Jellicoe's main seaplane carrier had been left behind in ridiculous circumstances), whereas no German airships were on hand owing to unfavourable weather.[1]

On leaving harbour Jellicoe did not immediately concentrate his force. Each of his three units set out in a generally easterly direction, on gradually converging courses. Rendezvous was to be a point 100 miles west of the entrance to the Skagerrak, which Jellicoe planned to reach at 2.30 p.m. on 31 May. By that time the 8 Dreadnoughts of the Second Battle Squadron would have joined up with his 16 Dreadnoughts. But Beatty's force (the Battle Cruiser Fleet) of 6 battle cruisers and 4 super-Dreadnoughts would still be some 70 miles to the south. Beatty's prime task, with his speedier vessels, was to establish the whereabouts of the enemy. If by 2.30 p.m. he had failed to locate them, he was to turn north and meet up with Jellicoe.

The most Jellicoe and Beatty expected to encounter at this stage were Hipper's battle cruisers. They were confident that Scheer with the main German battlefleet was not yet at sea or was still well to the south. For this misapprehension the naval authorities in London were to blame. The Admiralty's Operations Division, grotesquely misinterpreting the information they were receiving from their decoders, informed Jellicoe and Beatty that by near midday, although Hipper was out, Scheer had not yet left harbour. (By that time he was already nine hours at sea.)

At 2.15 p.m., having proceeded almost as far east as he was supposed to go, Beatty had still found no trace of the enemy – which, equally unaware of his presence, was sailing north straight towards him, its leading battle cruisers only 50 miles distant. In accordance with his instructions, Beatty prepared to turn north and make rendezvous with Jellicoe. What dissuaded him was a succession of messages from one of his light cruisers still probing eastward. At 2.20 p.m. he learned: 'Enemy in sight. Two cruisers probably hostile bearing ESE. Course unknown.' Yet more dramatic was the signal received 15 minutes later: 'Urgent: have sighted large amount of smoke as though from a fleet bearing ENE.' Beatty now knew that Hipper's battle cruisers were at hand. He turned to engage them.

The first phase of the battle of Jutland took the form of the 'run to the south'. Hipper, on sighting Beatty, veered away to the south-east. To all appearances he was

---

[1] In the event the only British seaplane that got airborne saw little – before it broke down – owing to the low cloud. The most notable aspect of its endeavour, apart from the fact that it was the first aircraft ever employed in a sea battle, was the name of its pilot, F. J. Rutland. Inevitably, if without royal *fiat*, he became 'Rutland of Jutland'.

taking flight, just as he had done at their last meeting at the Dogger Bank. Beatty promptly gave chase. That he failed to suspect that he was being led towards the German battlefleet is not to his discredit, since he had the Admiralty's assurance that Scheer, if he was at sea at all, could not possibly be this far north.

More questionable was the unrestrained nature of Beatty's pursuit. Thanks to inept signalling when he changed course to follow the enemy, he had parted company with his most powerful vessels, the 5th Battle Squadron, and he did not pause to let them catch up. Certainly, he had a small numerical superiority over his opponents anyway (six battle cruisers to five). But he did not know this, for the Admiralty had informed him that Hipper also had six battle cruisers at sea. If Jackie Fisher's unkind epithet after the event, 'Balaclava Beatty', exaggerates Beatty's willingness to disregard the odds, it justly reflects a degree of recklessness in his conduct.

Criticism of Beatty's performance at this moment, however, sometimes goes much further. It is suggested that his failure to convene his forces before engaging Hipper was a major reason why the British fleet missed a 'victory' at Jutland. There appears little warrant for this. If Beatty had waited for the 5th Battle Squadron, he would have had less time in which to engage Hipper before running into Scheer. So it is unlikely that Hipper would have sustained many losses. What is more, any openings Beatty missed now he secured not long after. For later in the battle Hipper proved incapable of performing his key function – that of warning Scheer that he was heading straight towards Jellicoe. And responsibility for this achievement rested largely with Beatty's combined forces. So, in the long view, Beatty's early conduct in the battle had little adverse effect on its overall outcome.

In the short term, however, the gunnery exchange that developed between the battle cruisers from 3.48 p.m. revealed that Beatty needed all the help he could get. Very soon the German fire began to tell on his ships, while the British gunners were finding it difficult to get the enemy's range. This might not have mattered too much but for one thing: British battle cruisers were vulnerable in a way that their German counterparts (though they had once been) were not. At the time of the Dogger Bank encounter in early 1915 the battle cruisers of both sides had been subject to a serious structural defect. A shell bursting on a gun turret could start a fire that, by means of exploding cordite, might be transmitted down the ammunition hoists. If the doors of the magazines (situated in the bowels of the vessel) were open – as they were likely to be during a battle – there might follow an explosion producing total destruction. At the Dogger Bank this fate had nearly overtaken Hipper. The event had alerted the Germans to their danger, and by the time of Jutland their battle cruisers were no longer subject to this hazard. Beatty's battle cruisers most certainly were.

During the run to the south Beatty himself came within an ace of annihilation. At 4 p.m., after less than a quarter of an hour of shooting, a heavy shell struck the Q-turret of the *Lion*, igniting the cordite in the loading cages and producing an explosion. The fire spread down the supply hoist, causing further explosions of cordite. Fortunately for the *Lion*, an officer in the gun turret, with both legs blown away and near to death, saved the ship by ordering the closing of the magazine doors and the flooding of the magazines. Beatty's survival was almost a rerun of Hipper's experience at the Dogger Bank.

Others of the British battle cruisers proved less fortunate. A few minutes after 4 p.m. the last ship in Beatty's line, the *Indefatigable*, suffered a succession of hits on its turrets, was rent by a terrible explosion, and vanished from sight. The number of British battle cruisers engaging the enemy was now only the same as Hipper's. Beatty turned away to widen the range.

Help, however, was already at hand. The 5th Battle Squadron, consisting of four of the most powerful battleships in the British fleet, had now caught up and began immediately to register a telling fire on the rearmost German ships. Beatty thereupon turned towards Hipper again and resumed the gunnery duel. Once more he suffered a severe loss. At 4.26 p.m. the third ship in his line, the *Queen Mary*, which had been shooting with considerable accuracy but had come under the fire of two of its opponents, was rent by two great explosions. It disappeared in a cloud of smoke rising to 1,000 feet. This evoked from Beatty what, for so patent a statement of the obvious, remains a curiously gripping remark: 'There seems to be something wrong with our bloody ships today.'

Yet, to all appearances, it was Hipper who was in really serious trouble. His five ships were still engaged with eight of the British, including four super-Dreadnoughts that he could scarcely touch. Appearances, however, were on the point of changing dramatically. Indeed, the whole nature of the encounter was about to be transformed. Scouting ahead for Beatty was a light cruiser squadron commanded by W. E. Goodenough. At 4.38 p.m. it sent Beatty (and also Jellicoe) the following message: 'Urgent. Priority. Have sighted Enemy battle fleet bearing approximately SE, course of Enemy N.' The Admiralty's misleading signal now stood corrected. Beatty at last knew that he was on a collision course with the naval might of Germany.

Beatty's task thereupon was entirely altered. It was no longer his business to seek the destruction of Hipper. His prime responsibility was to bring Scheer's battleships into contact with the battlefleet of Jellicoe. That object, as well as the elementary matter of survival, required him to bring his force round towards the north. The first phase of the battle of Jutland, the run to the south, was at an end.

It ended somewhat later for the 5th Battle Squadron of Evan-Thomas than it did for Beatty. Once again this force was unable to read Beatty's flag signals (which ought to have been duplicated by searchlight). So Evan-Thomas was in the process of passing the battle cruisers before he realized that he too was to alter direction. As he did so he became engaged in a heated exchange with Scheer's leading vessels – the first exchange of fire ever to occur between Dreadnought battleships, with each side inflicting much punishment but without appreciable effect. For a spell the 5th Battle Squadron proved at a serious disadvantage. As it turned to follow Beatty, it was ill-placed to return the heavy fire that it was receiving. Then, as Evan-Thomas proceeded north in Beatty's wake, his gunnery duel with Scheer's leading ships was resumed. All told, the British super-Dreadnoughts took much battering. And it is worth noting that they did so without calamity. Had Evan-Thomas been so minded, he could well have observed that there was a great deal right with his bloody ships that day.

II

In the run to the north the situation moved steadily to Beatty's advantage. In one respect all the British ships engaged in it fell short of their task. None was sending Jellicoe information of the enemy's whereabouts, so that the C.-in-C., now hastening south-east from the rendezvous position to fall on his prey, was having the greatest difficulty in deciding on his deployment.

Nevertheless, a highly favourable situation was being created for him. Beatty's battle cruisers and, in particular, the 5th Battle Squadron were having the better of the gunnery duel. And they were aided by the sudden intervention of Admiral Hood's 3rd Battle Cruiser Squadron, which had been stationed temporarily at Scapa Flow when the fleet set out and so was part of Jellicoe's force. The C.-in-C. now sent it ahead to assist Beatty. Hood's appearance, combined with a skilful change of direction by Beatty towards the north-east and the severe pummelling Hipper was continuing to take from the British guns, forced the German battle cruisers back towards Scheer. Consequently, Hipper (as already mentioned) was unable to perform his crucial function: that of providing Scheer with advance warning of the great danger forming up just over the horizon.

Jellicoe, meanwhile, despite inadequate information, was managing to deploy ideally to meet the Germans. In forming his fleet into line of battle he veered slightly more towards the east. This gave his gunners the advantage of the light (which was not, however, ideal for either side), while still keeping him on a course to cut off the enemy from their bases. But, most important of all, his manoeuvre enabled him (to employ naval parlance) to cross the enemy's T. That is, his warships were placed at rightangles to Scheer's oncoming force, which found itself constituting the stem of the T. This meant that the whole weight of Jellicoe's broadside could be brought to bear on Scheer's foremost ships, which could reply with nothing but their relatively small complement of forward-firing guns.

It is difficult not to speculate on Scheer's emotions when, shortly before 6.30 p.m., he became aware that he had accomplished what each German C.-in.C. since the outbreak of war had vowed to avoid. He had placed the German navy in the same stretch of water as the British battlefleet. The battle of Jutland proper was about to begin.

III

It has been necessary to relate the battle-cruiser phase of Jutland in relative detail, not because of its intrinsic importance (which was hardly marked) but because of the vast weight that has since been attached to it. Mainly on the strength of what happened between these subsidiary elements of the two fleets, particularly in the period 3.45 to 4.30 p.m., large conclusions have been reached. It is argued that British warships were fatally inferior in construction to German warships; that the quality of British shells, range-finders, and fire-control systems fell significantly below those of their adversaries; and that these shortcomings sprang from severe deficiencies in British industrial and technological know-how, which were placing the nation at a grave disadvantage vis-à-vis its adversary.

Now, it is possibly the case that all these assumptions are warranted. British armour may have been inadequate, either because of poor craftsmanship or because of Jackie Fisher's obsession with speed and fire power at the expense of protection. British range-finders and gunfire directors may not have been comparable with those of the enemy. And British shells may have lacked the penetrative power of German shells. The British educational system – expressing the values of British society – may have set at a discount those scientific and technical skills without which Britain could not remain a great power in the twentieth century. But what seems absolutely certain is this. The battle-cruiser phase of the battle of Jutland – or, more strictly, the run to the south, for the run to the north tells a different story and so is disregarded – provides no sufficient evidence to establish any of these assertions. And as no subsequent sea engagement, either during the remainder of 31 May 1916 or later in the war, put these matters to the test, these claims must be deemed unproven.

Too often, commentators on Jutland have been mesmerized by the failure of Beatty's battle cruisers to get the range of the Germans from the outset; by the inability of British ships to sink any of Hipper's battle cruisers; and by the calamities that befell the *Indefatigable* and the *Queen Mary* (and would later befall Hood's battle cruiser, the *Invincible*). 'There seems to be something wrong with our bloody ships today' has appeared more than an indication of Beatty's sang-froid. It has been deemed to epitomize the experience of the entire British fleet at Jutland and even of the British nation in the Great War.

Such extrapolation is without warrant. The inaccurate shooting that characterized Beatty's battle cruisers early on was not evident in the 5th Battle Squadron when it entered the fray, or among Hood's battle cruisers when they joined in during the run to the north. Indeed, at no stage in the Jutland conflict following the run to the south did the British have the worse of the gunnery exchanges. Beatty, when he first engaged the Germans, had a severe disadvantage of visibility, owing to mist obscuring the enemy and the fact that the wind was blowing his smoke in their direction. His opponents, by contrast, had the British ships in silhouette and suffered no interference from smoke. Further, the British vessels were proceeding at a faster rate and having to make more changes of course than their adversaries, thus increasing their problems of accurate shooting.

At the same time it is quite likely that Beatty's gunners were not unduly proficient. And by being stationed at Rosyth they had been denied the opportunity to improve. It is worth noting the reason why Hood's battle cruisers were at Scapa Flow, not Rosyth, when the fleet put to sea. They had been sent there to get the gunnery practice that the Rosyth anchorage had been denying them. Their performance on the day suggests that they had benefited from the experience.

As for the failure of Beatty's force to sink German vessels while some of his own were being dramatically destroyed, an obvious explanation lies to hand. There was in truth 'something wrong with our bloody ships', as long as it is understood that the remark applies only to the battle cruisers. But as exactly the same 'something' had been wrong with German battle cruisers at the beginning of the war, there is little ground for making weighty generalizations about the technical incompetence of the one country as against the other. As has already been indicated, with inadequate protection of its magazines a battle cruiser was vulnerable to a shell striking one of its gun turrets. On this account, Hipper's flagship had almost come to grief at Dogger Bank, and Beatty had a very close call at Jutland. In consequence each commander after the event ensured that protective devices were installed. The difference in the experience of the two fleets was that at Jutland not only did the *Lion* come near to destruction but three British battle cruisers were actually destroyed.

Yet if we set aside this significant weakness, a noteworthy point emerges. In all other respects there is no convincing evidence provided by Jutland of inferiority between British and German vessels, even in the battle-cruiser class. Excluding the three battle cruisers destroyed by internal explosion, the damage wreaked by German shells on British ships was not greater than that inflicted by British shells on German ships. On the contrary, it was a good deal less.

To establish this it is necessary only to compare the state of the two battle-cruiser forces about 6.30 p.m. – that is, early in the battleship stage of the conflict. Hipper's five vessels were, in Marder's words, 'in a very bad state'. Hipper's flagship, the *Lutzow*, was listing heavily, 'her bows deep in the water,' and could not remain in the line. The *Derfflinger* too was 'in a sorry condition, with water streaming in through a large hole in her bows'. The *Seydlitz* was 'awash up to the middle deck forward'. The

Von der Tann had no turrets in action. 'Only the *Moltke* remained serviceable', and to this ship Hipper eventually managed to transfer his flag.[2]

None of the British battle cruisers that avoided internal explosion was reduced to these sorry conditions. It is instructive to look at Beatty's flagship, the *Lion*. It had come close to destruction. And it had sustained repeated heavy shelling. Yet it remained to the end of the battle a powerful fighting ship, its speed unaffected and with all its guns except Q Turret (eliminated by a direct hit) in action. Given the relative condition of Beatty's and Hipper's flagships by the time the battle-cruiser phase was over, what grounds are there for claiming that, compared with the Germans', British shells could do little damage and British vessels were unable to withstand heavy punishment?

The lesson that the battle of Jutland wrote large was not the vulnerability of British warships in general nor even, except in the one particular that has been detailed, the vulnerability of British battle cruisers. The lesson was altogether different. Jutland established the relative invulnerability of both British and German warships. The only weapons that stood much chance of disposing of Dreadnoughts were those that could strike heavy blows below the waterline: that is, torpedoes and mines. And the vessels that principally delivered these weapons – the submarine, the destroyer (or torpedo boat), and the mine layer – were unable, on any but the most random and infrequent occasions, to come to grips with Dreadnoughts. This much the failure of Scheer's submarine trap in the preliminaries to Jutland, like the failure of his destroyer attacks in its later phases (to which we shall turn shortly), indicated clearly.

As for shell fire, the Dreadnoughts – as long as their magazines were adequately protected – could absorb an enormous amount without suffering fatal injury. If one of these vessels was to be put out of action by shelling, it would have to be brought to battle not only by superior numbers but also over a lengthy encounter. Anything less was unlikely to encompass its destruction. One aspect of the events so far studied establishes this forcefully. As we have seen, by about 6.30 p.m. all four of Beatty's surviving battle cruisers had been much knocked about, and four out of Hipper's five were in a quite grievous condition. Nor was their participation in the battle by any means over. Nevertheless, eight out of these nine battle cruisers, British and German, returned to their respective harbours on the following day. (The sole casualty was the *Lutzow*.)

These considerations deserve to be borne in mind as we move to the Jutland contest proper: the encounter between the battleships of Jellicoe and Scheer. If Jellicoe was to achieve a 'decisive victory' (to employ an expression ill-used by some naval historians) or, in other words, if he was virtually to eliminate his enemy's fleet, he would need a long passage of arms with it. As for Scheer, if he was to deny Jellicoe such a victory, his prime concern must be to ensure that no such passage ever took place.

---

[2] Arthur J. Marder, *From the Dreadnought to Scapa Flow*, 2nd edn (Oxford: Oxford University Press, 1978), vol.3, pp. 116–17.

26

JELLICOE VERSUS NOBODY

We keep the sea, which denotes a victory.

Samuel Pepys

Everything right through the ship went well, JRJ was as he always is! my God, what a man.

Tom Calvert, officer in a gun turret of the Iron Duke *during the battle of Jutland, in a letter of*
9 June 1916

I

By 6.30 p.m. of 31 May Jellicoe had all but completed his deployment across the bows of the oncoming Germans, and firing had commenced. Scheer, for his part, had at last gathered that he was in action with the Grand Fleet. The tasks confronting the two commanders were, in outline, straightforward. Jellicoe must both wreak damage upon such enemy vessels as came within range and prevent the remainder from escaping to the east. Scheer, on the contrary, had to break off contact with the British and find a way home.

In the very short run Jellicoe's purpose was already accomplished. He had crossed the enemy's T on a course running south-east and was pouring into the Germans' forward units a hail of fire. Scheer's response was to execute a speedy withdrawal. He ordered a 'battle about-turn': that is, each vessel in his line turned 180°, so that what had been his last ship now became his first, while his previously foremost vessel found itself in the rear. The German fleet sped off to the south-west. Scheer thus accomplished the first of his objectives, that of breaking contact with the British, but not the second. His flight was carrying him away from the German coast.

Scheer's skilful use of the 'battle about-turn' reveals much about the situation of the German fleet relative to the British. Jellicoe's ships had no experience in this manoeuvre. If they wished to reverse course, each vessel followed its leader in going about. That could be an uncomfortable business if a British force ran into a superior body of Germans and needed to remove itself quickly, as Evan-Thomas had discovered at the end of the run to the south. Had Scheer's ships followed each other in line ahead when trying to disengage from Jellicoe, they would have remained much longer under British fire and must have suffered heavily as they passed through the point of turn. By mastering the 180° manoeuvre to the last detail, the High Seas Fleet escaped serious injury.

Yet what this signifies above all is not that the Germans were more inventive in seamanship than their adversaries. Rather, it exemplifies how the two navies envisaged their parts in a sea engagement. The British anticipated bringing the enemy to battle, pressing home the conflict, sinking many German ships, and driving the rest from the high seas. The Germans had no such vision. They were eager vigorously to engage minor British forces. But they recognized that the North Sea was not a No-Man's-Land. If sometimes they trespassed upon it, nevertheless it was the territory of the British fleet. The German commander was aware that should one of his poaching expeditions bring him into contact with the gamekeeper, his only course must be flight. Hence the 180° turnabout was bound to have a priority in German calculations –and so in training activities – that it would not have in British. Jellicoe's course might be a bold or a cautious advance, depending on the commander's temperament and the actual dangers ahead. But precipitate retreat was not a prospect for which he felt the need to plan.

That the German fleet had managed to break contact was not readily apparent to Jellicoe. With his observation hampered by mist, funnel smoke, and enemy smoke screens, he did not observe the Germans' departure; and those British vessels that saw it failed to inform him. When he did grasp the situation, he set his force towards the south at a moderate speed. This established him firmly between the High Seas Fleet and its bases.

It was not long before Jellicoe encountered the enemy again – or, more accurately, before the enemy ran into him. Shortly before 7 p.m. Scheer ordered another 180° about-turn, so pointing towards home. Once more, his much injured battle cruisers were now leading the way. This brought him, after about ten minutes, into another collision with the British fleet. Jellicoe a second time, if somewhat unwittingly on this occasion, was across the German T.

Again the British battleships brought down a savage fire on their opponents, and once more Scheer made haste to disengage. In order to distract the British guns from his battleships, he first sent his battle cruisers on a death ride straight at Jellicoe, but as quickly diverted them. More effectively, he then sent his destroyer flotillas (or torpedo boats as they were called in the German navy, which indicated their prime function) into the attack, accompanied by a smoke screen. Most effectually of all, he ordered his battleships into another 180° about-turn and set off to the west. (Soon after he changed course to the south-west.) So by 7.30 p.m. contact between the two fleets was once more at an end.

One of the things that hastened the loss of contact, though it certainly did not cause it, was Jellicoe's response to the German destroyer attack. Threatened by the possibility of confronting a swarm of torpedoes, Jellicoe ordered a change of course – in effect, from south-south-east to south-east – away from the enemy. This manoeuvre succeeded utterly. The German flotillas were unable to deliver their attacks, or did so from too great a distance. Several British battleships were endangered by torpedoes, but, owing to the distance, they were able to outrun or evade them.

Few actions in modern naval history have excited so much controversy, or aroused such fierce condemnation, as Jellicoe's turn away from the torpedo threat. At this point the High Seas Fleet disappeared for good from British sight. In the view of Jellicoe's critics, had he turned towards the enemy, whose closest ships were in some disarray, and entered into a hot pursuit, he stood a chance of claiming several victims.

This is highly speculative. It takes no account of the much greater possibility that Jellicoe, not his enemies, would have been the loser from such a manoeuvre. There are no grounds for assuming that, because in one set of circumstances the German torpedoes gained no victims, therefore they would have failed equally in other circumstances. A turn towards the German destroyers would have increased the threat from the torpedoes that were delivered and enabled the enemy flotillas to deliver a great many more, and at a number of different angles, so making the problems of evasion possibly prohibitive. It seems unwarranted to speculate that Jellicoe would have got off scot-free. (In fact, one scholar argues that six British ships would have suffered torpedo hits.)

Jellicoe had never made any bones about the fact that, threatened in this way, he would open the range. At Jutland, he was in good company. During the run to the south, both battle-cruiser commanders had sent destroyers against each other, and Hipper ('the outstanding sea officer of the war', according to A. J. Marder)[1] as well as Evan-Thomas had responded by turning away. Nor can we be confident that Beatty, had he been in command, would have acted any differently. Five days before Jutland the Torpedo Sub-Committee of his Battle Cruiser Fleet had recommended a turn-away in the event of a torpedo attack.[2] And it should be recalled that at the Dogger Bank Beatty had ordered turns-away from mines and submarines that were not even there.

To say this is not intended as a hit against Beatty. But it does raise the question of whether the whole Jellicoe versus Beatty controversy, which has been something of a pastime ever since Jutland, is anything short of preposterous. Their temperaments as naval warriors (and in some private aspects) may have been very different. But the circumstances of this war, at sea as on the battlefield, were time and again so overpowering as to compel unlike individuals to behave in near-identical fashion.

Had Jellicoe not turned away from the enemy, and had he managed to escape a severe check from torpedoes, it is unlikely that much would have been accomplished. Once again he did not see the enemy depart, and in the failing light, mist, and smoke it took him some time to discover that Scheer had gone. Anyway, there was scarcely any prospect that, by plunging regardless towards the enemy, he could – in the one remaining hour of daylight – have overhauled Scheer, engaged him, and inflicted great losses.[3]

Jellicoe did, however, alter course to the south-west, and then to the west, so as to force the enemy yet further from their bases. Scheer, meanwhile, had altered course from south-west to south. So the two fleets were on a converging course. At 8.15 p.m. the forward units met, and fire was exchanged for about 20 minutes. Then the Germans veered away into the mist. This last brush before darkness settled had a fortuitous significance. British and German capital ships would not again exchange fire during the Great War.

II

By 9 p.m. night had fallen upon the North Sea. Jellicoe therefore turned to a southerly course, hoping to present his fleet as a barrier between the Germans and their bases. He had no intention of trying to seek out the High Seas Fleet in the dark. Night fighting was not something in which his ships were practised – and this for what were deemed good reasons.

---

[1] Arthur J. Marder, *From the Dreadnought to Scapa Flow*, 2nd edn (Oxford: Oxford University Press, 1978), vol.3, p. 44.

[2] I am indebted to Dr Robin Prior for this information, drawn from the papers of the sub-committee held by the Admiralty.

[3] Some writers who take a contrary view are unnervingly imprecise about what they think might have been the outcome. So one book, after stating that 'Jellicoe did not seize this opportunity to finish off the High Seas Fleet', elaborates thus: 'A ruthless British attack would at the very least have finished off the German battlecruisers.' The collapse in aspiration from 'finish[ing] off the High Seas Fleet' to 'finish[ing] off the German battlecruisers' (even if 'at the very least') is breathtaking. See John Costello and Terry Hughes, *Jutland 1916* (London: Futura Publications, 1976), pp. 190–2. This book, it should be added, provides a very useful account of the battle of Jutland and is not unduly hostile to Jellicoe.

A night action was precisely the sort of battle that Jellicoe did not wish to fight. In conditions of limited visibility there could not be a conflict between one battlefleet and the other, only a mêlée between isolated units. In these circumstances a group of enemy ships might join action with a smaller number of British vessels and overwhelm them. Moreover, the German torpedo boats might in the dark get within striking range of the British battleships. Jellicoe had no cause to run such risks. He possessed the essentials of naval dominance already. Should it be his forces, not the Germans', who had the better of a succession of scraps in the dark, nothing about his overall situation would be improved. If the reverse occurred, he could be in danger of losing his margin of superiority – and Scheer might be on the way to achieving his objective.

Yet however good the reasons for shunning a general action at night, the British fleet proved to be at a disadvantage, in the last Jutland encounters, for having neglected this facet of naval warfare. Those vessels that encountered the Germans lacked the techniques of night fighting. They also lacked the equipment. Their searchlights were poor; their binoculars were inadequate; and they were altogether wanting in star shells. Hence the German ships usually managed to strike the earliest and heaviest blows. Moreover, some commanders of British ships were so convinced of the undesirability of a night action that they made no response upon sighting isolated enemy vessels. And painfully few felt any obligation to inform their C.-in-C. of the whereabouts of units of the German fleet.

All this mattered a good deal in a situation where some form of night encounter was bound to occur. For Scheer simply could not afford to be still at sea, and on the wrong side of Jellicoe, when day dawned. If this made it necessary for him to barge through the British lines, possibly at cost to himself, then such a prospect was infinitely preferable to a fleet-to-fleet action on the following day. The fact that the Grand Fleet was having to stretch its forces over a considerable distance to cover all likely escape routes gave him a good chance of success. And his chances were improved by the fact that German wireless intelligence could give him some indication of Jellicoe's movements.

In the event, luck and good management and the relative simplicity of his task all told in Scheer's favour. Jellicoe had to guess the route that the Germans would take on their homeward journey and place his most powerful vessels accordingly. In the event he guessed wrongly. Scheer drove south-east towards the Horn's Reef instead of following a more southerly course, as the British commander had expected. Hence the High Seas Fleet had only to breach the most thinly held part of the British line, namely its rear, to which Jellicoe had sent his destroyers. But this was not wholly a matter of chance. German intelligence had decoded Jellicoe's message to his destroyers sending them to the rear and had passed it on to Scheer. The German C.-in-C. accordingly altered direction somewhat more to the east to make sure of encountering only this part of the British line. So perhaps if he had not already adopted the Horn's Reef route, this information would have sent him there anyway.

The British destroyer flotillas, unsupported by battleships and under the considerable handicaps involved in night fighting, encountered the German warships piecemeal. They managed some noble acts of resistance. At no small cost to themselves, they sank several German light cruisers and one pre-Dreadnought battleship. But they had no prospect of halting Scheer's progress eastward, which by early morning had been securely accomplished.

Jellicoe's performance during this phase was not impressive. He was ill-served by those of his craft that encountered enemy ships and did not inform him. And he was yet more badly served by the Admiralty. A number of messages from Scheer came to it that, rightly interpreted, laid bare the German fleet's homeward route. But their significance was not appreciated. The reason was that the sort of trained academic mind that from such particular trees could divine the shape of the wood was not present – and was not welcome – in the Operations Division of the Admiralty. It could be found among the decoders. But they were expected only to translate, not to interpret. Hence the information that might have alerted Jellicoe to Scheer's course was not passed on to him.

Nevertheless, Jellicoe's own response to the information he did receive was hardly inspired. (He must, of course, have been near exhaustion.) He had no cause to be absolutely confident in his interpretation of Scheer's intentions, which meant that he had strong reason to seek out indications confirming or contradicting it. This he did not do. He made no response to the sporadic instances of gunfire, indicating a series of unexplained actions, that were occurring to his rear. Certainly, they could have been clashes between the rival destroyer flotillas. And Jellicoe had a right to expect that if larger German units were involved, he would be informed. But he had already had warning that his subordinates did not necessarily tell him what he needed to know. Yet during the night action he neither interpreted correctly the encounters taking place between his destroyers and German warships nor sent demands to his rearward units for information. It is arguable that Jellicoe was so averse to the prospect of a night action that he did not wholly confront the likelihood that this was the only sort of action he would now be allowed.

But once again it must be said that, had Jellicoe responded differently, not a great deal would probably have been changed. If he had altered direction towards Horn's Reef, it is likely that Scheer would soon have been apprised of the fact. So the German fleet might also have opted for another course. And even had Scheer pushed on to the Horn's Reef, the circumstances for a 'decisive' battle were unlikely to have been present. Thanks to fog, visibility at daybreak was down to 2 miles, which offered no prospect of a fleet-to-fleet encounter. Scheer could hardly have failed to increase the speed of his battleships, which were hanging back so as not to lose touch with his slower pre-Dreadnoughts in the rear. Several of the latter, at least, might have succumbed to encounters with British units. But it is difficult to believe that practically the whole German fleet would have been annihilated in a battle in the fog; and not even certain that all the losses would have been on the German side.

This remains speculation. For Jellicoe did not receive the necessary stimulus – from the Admiralty, his own ships, or himself – to change course. As dawn broke on 1 June the members of the Grand Fleet remained convinced that they stood between Scheer and safety, with a full day in which to force him to action or drive him ever further towards Britain. It could not be less than a heavy disappointment when Jellicoe learned from the Admiralty, on the basis of intercepted messages, that the High Seas Fleet was back in harbour.

III

From the British viewpoint, many aspects of the fighting at Jutland had proved unsatisfactory. Beatty's battle cruisers had revealed a structural weakness. The Grand Fleet's shells had failed to wreak great destruction, and their range-finders and fire-control systems were open to criticism. At every level, moreover, performance had not lived up to what the situation required. Beatty's gunnery had seemed inadequate, and his principal signalling officer – not for the first time – had proved inept. The Operations Division at the Admiralty had sent information that was wrong and had omitted to send some intelligence that might have been highly valuable. Repeatedly, units of the fleet in contact with enemy ships or sighting their movements had failed to enlighten Jellicoe. British vessels and seamen were neither equipped nor trained for night fighting. One consequence was that during the night action some commanders did not avail themselves of opportunities to engage enemy ships. Indeed, lack of initiative on the part of those in command of subordinate units was apparent at Jutland on many occasions.

The historian and one-time naval captain Stephen Roskill, drawing on his own youthful experience, bears witness to the deeply authoritarian spirit of the British navy. It manifested itself in a passion for suppressing originality and imposing conformity. This spirit, in his judgement, found an expression in the incredible detail of Jellicoe's Grand Fleet Battle Orders – the instrument by which the C.-in-C. sought to ensure that, when battle was joined, his great force would perform to his will.

Two things, however, must be said about this. In the first place, the passion for conformity in the navy, and the dismal absence of initiative that sometimes resulted at Jutland, should not be seen as the mainspring of Jellicoe's conduct. Underlying all else was his determination not to lose – or allow his subordinates to lose for him – Britain's naval dominance by playing into German hands. To permit some of his units to go their separate ways in a fleet action was to run the risk of creating the very situation that Scheer was seeking. A section of the British fleet might become embroiled with a substantially larger body of Germans and not survive the encounter. Certainly, by keeping his forces under his own direction Jellicoe might miss the chance of accomplishing the reverse: the chance of a British unit's wiping out a section of the German fleet. But the latter would not constitute a strategic gain for Britain. It would simply confirm British command of the seas. The former might so diminish Britain's numerical lead as to advance Scheer towards a strategic victory.

The second point that needs to be made is this. There may have been a number of shortcomings in the material equipment of the British fleet and in some aspects of its performance at Jutland. It is not evident that these made much difference to the outcome. Had all things been done well by the Grand Fleet, the number of enemy ships sunk would probably not have been much greater. Certainly, some of Hipper's battle cruisers needed much luck, and a good deal of British ineptitude, to survive. But although their demise might have caused the tally of losses to work out more to British satisfaction, that would have had no strategic significance. It would matter only if the Battle of Jutland were viewed as a sporting fixture characterized by low scoring on both sides. Perhaps it is in the nature of sea battles that they are subject to such trivialization. But the realities of sea warfare are concerned with different questions altogether.

The score card of casualties seems to point to a German success. The British lost 14 ships totalling 111,000 tons, while the Germans lost 11 ships of 62,000 tons. The tale of damage tells a somewhat different story. The Grand Fleet, notwithstanding its losses, was ready to put to sea again almost immediately. The High Seas Fleet would require several weeks before it was in a fit state to leave harbour. But none of this is really to the point. The losses and damage to both sides were, in terms of the mighty forces involved, of no account. The balance of naval power was not remotely affected. What alone signified was that on 1 June 1916 the Grand Fleet was scouring the North Sea seeking its enemy. The German fleet was not. It was once more at rest in harbour.

Much breast-beating has since occurred in British naval circles, as well as among historians, because even this degree of success was enjoyed by the Germans. The British navy, it has been argued, let slip the chance not just to win a numbers-game victory over the High Seas Fleet but to annihilate it. And the failure to do so was supposedly fraught with the gravest consequences. For, according to this view, had Scheer and his entire force gone to the bottom, the history of the world would have been changed.

What then, to follow this line of argument, might have been the consequences of a total naval victory? First of all, the British fleet from mid-1916 would have been free to go where it pleased; and so it could have taken command of the Baltic, cutting off iron-ore supplies from Sweden to Germany and facilitating an invasion of Germany from the north. Secondly, the German U-boat campaign that was to assume such menacing proportions in the year that followed Jutland could never have accomplished what it did. For had the High Seas Fleet been absent, the British navy could have blocked the U-boats in their harbours, and many destroyers employed for protecting battleships could have been diverted to protecting merchant ships. Thirdly, the large numbers of soldiers kept in Britain to guard against invasion would immediately have been available for service overseas.

This does not end the suggested consequences of a thoroughgoing British victory at Jutland. With the Baltic open to British shipping, supplies of weapons and ammunition could have been hastened to Russia; hence 'it is possible that the Russian revolution would have been delayed, or even avoided altogether.'[4] More than this, the shattering blow to German morale occasioned by the loss of their fleet 'might easily have shortened the war by a year' (in one estimate), or by 'six months, eighteen months, perhaps two years' (in another).[5] Taking these together – or even separately – it seems that more opportunities were available to Jellicoe on 31 May 1916 than merely to lose the war in an afternoon.

What is to be said of all this? Even, for the moment, admitting the possibility that Scheer's force could have been wiped out, some of these speculations are difficult to take seriously. Most of all this applies to the notion that a British armada bearing munitions (presumably filched from Kitchener's under-supplied armies on the Somme) could have changed the course of events in Russia. This type of speculation has a familiar ring. It is the extension into absurdity of the idea that a naval force fighting its way up the Dardanelles to Constantinople would have occasioned the disintegration of the Turkish Empire. The ills besetting the Tsar's regime would not swiftly have been put to rights by such military hardware as the British could spare. Indeed, it has been suggested that by 1917 the Russian Government was no longer lacking in war material. What it lacked was the command structure to place such material where it was needed. The notion that Britain in general, and the British fleet in particular, ever had it in its power to transform the situation in Russia is jingo history (of the send-a-gunboat variety) in its most unreflecting form.

Equally insubstantial is the claim that the loss of Scheer's fleet would have dealt so heavy a blow to German morale that the war thereby would have been appreciably shortened. German morale had held up well enough during two years in which its fleet had accomplished practically nothing. The demise of that fleet must have proved a profound shock; but not insupportable to a country that placed its trust in military, not naval, might.

As for the notions that a 'decisive' victory at Jutland might have caused Britain to attempt an invasion of northern Germany, and might have prevented the German U-boats from provoking American intervention in the war, these are indeed sobering

---

[4] Richard Hough, *The Battle of Jutland* (London: Hamish Hamilton, 1964), p. 56.
[5] Russell Grenfell (quoted in Marder, *From the Dreadnought to Scapa Flow*, vol. 3, p. 256) offers the first estimate; Hough, *The Battle of Jutland*, p. 56, offers the second.

speculations. They raise the question of whether Britain could have afforded a triumph at sea that first would have led it into military folly in Pomerania and then would have forestalled the Germans from engaging in naval folly against the USA. If these speculations have any substance, then apparently Germany also would have reaped decided benefits had Scheer gone to the bottom.

None of this is meant to deny that a complete success at Jutland would have brought tangible benefits to Britain. German trade with Sweden might in good measure have been curtailed; plainly, the morale of the contending sides would have been affected; and the U-boat threat would have been much diminished. Yet the strategic consequences would have been limited because strategically Britain held command of the seas already, and the results actually achieved at Jutland were great enough to confirm this. A wipe-out of the German fleet would only have made assurance triply sure.

There is, of course, a further point to be made. All speculation about what would have happened had Jellicoe annihilated the German fleet is idle. Certainly, Jutland had its share of lost opportunities – opportunities, that is, to sink some more German ships. No opportunity was missed to sink the German fleet, for none ever presented itself. Dreadnought battleships, as already indicated, proved inordinately difficult to destroy with the weapons that could actually be brought against them in a fleet action. Jellicoe's guns could have finished off Scheer only had the German commander been agreeable to remaining under fire for a long time. Instead Scheer declined to remain for any time whatever. On the two occasions in daylight when he made contact with the Grand Fleet, he severed it immediately. Only at night, when lack of visibility rendered a fleet-to-fleet engagement impossible, was he prepared (if he must) to meet up with some of Jellicoe's units, and then only so as to ensure that there would be no third encounter with Jellicoe's combined force.

The British C.-in-C. did not have it in his power to alter this. Even a reckless pursuit into enemy smoke screens – had he been so rash as to engage in one – would not have enabled him to compel Scheer to stand and fight, broadside against broadside, battlefleet against battlefleet. Jutland, in short, was not a great naval battle at all. It was a non-battle, the clearest possible indication that the Germans did not intend to engage in such a transaction and that they could not be forced to do so.

It was, nevertheless, a great naval victory. This becomes evident as soon as the notion of Jutland as sporting fixture is dismissed. At the end of the day, as at the beginning, the British navy, in Samuel Pepys's words, held the sea. The German attempt to loosen that hold had failed decisively. This might not have amounted to much if Scheer's action had been a naval *jeu d'esprit*, or anyway marginal to Germany's vital concerns. But this was not so. The battle of Jutland was the consequence of two great needs pressing upon Germany. First, the High Seas Fleet hoped to end the deleterious effects that the British blockade was having on German economic life. Secondly, the High Seas Fleet was endeavouring to advance Germany to the stage where it could starve Britain and strangle it economically; for this was Germany's only alternative to defeating Britain by means of another great blood-letting on land.

In its attempt to further these objectives on 31 May 1916 the German fleet, far from succeeding, had found itself courting disaster. That is, it failed in such circumstances as held out no prospect that a better result might be anticipated on some later occasion. Given that Germany's need to drive Britain from the war remained as compelling as ever, other means for its accomplishment must be looked for. Either so large a proportion of Britain's young manhood must be slaughtered on the battlefield that the nation could no longer function as a military power; or Britain must be defeated at sea by some means other than the High Seas Fleet.

For Germany these were terrible prospects. Eliminating the armies that Britain was now in the process of training and equipping would not be less painful for the Germans than their current attempt to bleed France white at Verdun. As for mounting a blockade of Britain, that could now be accomplished only by a U-boat offensive against all merchant shipping, Allied and neutral, approaching its shores; and this would mean adding the USA to the ranks of Germany's enemies. In short, the clear failure of Scheer's attempt even to start the process of undermining Britain's dominance at sea was among the most portentous events of the war.

Few people in Britain, when they first learned of the naval encounter, perceived this. Such headlines as that in the *Daily Express*, 'Heavy and Unaccountable British Losses', hardly suggested a British success. In the fleet also few could rejoice at the outcome. Only further reflection, aided by some fantasizing about the extent of German losses, provided Britons with a measure of satisfaction. But it would require a longer perspective still for the real import of what had taken place to become apparent.

27

AFTERMATH

I

The experience of Jutland produced no startling changes in British naval affairs. Jellicoe remained determined that, in any subsequent fleet action, he would again employ his forces as a single unit, and convinced that, in face of a torpedo-boat attack, his battleships should turn away. Certainly, Jutland had driven home the point that the enemy fleet would never participate in a gunnery duel if it could possibly disengage, so making the likelihood of a 'decisive' encounter all the more remote. But this did not prove to Jellicoe that any other way existed of doing battle in circumstances that would not threaten Britain's already established dominance at sea. So although some encouragement was given to units within his force to exercise more initiative during an engagement, it was only with the proviso that they should not exercise much initiative.

On the level of material, changes were instituted – immediately or gradually – as a consequence of Jutland. First and foremost, the matter of protecting the magazines of the battle cruisers during action was undertaken thoroughly. The second change concerned extension of the system of director firing, whereby all guns on a vessel were operated by a single control. This system already existed on the major units of the Grand Fleet at the time of Jutland and was thereafter introduced into the remainder. Thirdly, the fleet was issued with star shells, an essential element in night fighting. And strong pressure was exerted on the Admiralty to set about producing a type of shell that would achieve greater penetration before exploding. (These last were not actually issued to the fleet until April 1918.)

In the matter of intelligence appreciation an important reorganization took place. It was at last recognized that the decoders in Room 40 were experts at more than deciphering enemy messages. They were equipped to interpret the meaning of such messages and to estimate their importance. So Room 40, whose expertise had been sadly misused during some episodes of the Jutland conflict, became an integral part of the Operations Division.

It would be interesting to know whether these amendments greatly affected the Grand Fleet's competence. But this is not possible. For the changes were never put to the test. The opposed navies did not meet in battle again.

Scheer had not yet reached the stage where he was loath to take his Dreadnoughts to sea at all. But he was absolutely determined not to repeat the sort of miscalculation that would cause him to meet up with Jellicoe. Hence he would venture far from harbour only if he could be covered by sufficient airships and submarines to warn him of the Grand Fleet's approach. For various reasons such occasions proved rare.

The weather, and Scheer's resources, appeared to provide him with the opportunity he was seeking on 19 August 1916. Atmospheric conditions allowed a force of 10 Zeppelins to accompany the High Seas Fleet for observation. And Scheer had 24 submarines available to lay across the path of any oncoming British units. So he set out with 18 Dreadnoughts, sundry light forces, and his only two battle cruisers fit for sea following their Jutland pounding. His intention was to apply a plan that he would have employed on 31 May but for the intervention of bad weather. He would sail west towards the coast of northern England, with his cruisers leading the way and serving as bait. They would advertise their presence by bombarding Sunderland, while the German battleships remained over the horizon. On each of Scheer's flanks a line of U-boats would both attack approaching British vessels and warn him of their advent. The airships also would alert him to likely victims and sound the alarm should the Grand Fleet come into view.

On the British side, Room 40 soon realized that Scheer was planning to move, although it did not manage to divine his objectives. So, early on the morning of 19 August, Jellicoe yet again put to sea ahead of his enemy. His course was due south, with Beatty's battle cruisers leading the way. The British C.-in-C. was very conscious that Scheer might be setting a U-boat trap. And he took it as possible confirmation when, at 6.50 a.m., he learned that one of Beatty's light cruisers had fallen victim to a mine or a torpedo. (It was actually the latter, from one of Scheer's U-boats.) So Jellicoe turned away north until convinced the way was clear. Nevertheless, when he resumed his southerly progress at 9 a.m. he was still, according to Admiralty information, in good time to encounter Scheer. At 2.15 p.m., on the strength of an Admiralty reading of Scheer's course, Jellicoe was confident that the two fleets were about to clash. To his forces he sent a suitably Nelsonian message: 'High Seas Fleet may be sighted at any moment. I look with entire confidence on the result.'

But the High Seas Fleet was not sighted, at that moment or any other. The Admiralty prediction of Scheer's course was based on an extension of his progress as it had been established about 12.30 p.m. But not long thereafter the German fleet had changed direction, away from Jellicoe. It had done so because one of Scheer's airships had sighted, to the south-east, a body of British ships coming northwards. This was Admiral Tyrwhitt's force of light cruisers and destroyers, whose base was Harwich on the Essex coast, moving up to assist Jellicoe. But the Zeppelin observer imagined that he espied more than light craft. He reported large cruisers and battleships as well. This appeared to be precisely the sort of quarry that Scheer had all along hoped to ensnare: a segment of the Grand Fleet separated from its main body. So he set off south-east to make the kill.

In the event the German C.-in-C. was not able to locate Tyrwhitt, let alone any larger game. And at 2.13 p.m., just as Jellicoe was informing his ships that a fleet encounter was imminent, Scheer – now well to the south – received a disturbing intimation from one of his submarines: that the Grand Fleet was 65 miles to his north and heading in his direction. So, well in advance of Jellicoe's arrival, Scheer headed for home.

It was not until 4 p.m. that Jellicoe abandoned the hunt and turned back towards his base. The journey north took him into the path of the U-boat screen, and in running this gauntlet the Grand Fleet had a number of anxious experiences. A second of Beatty's light cruisers succumbed to torpedo attack.

Scheer, once again, had failed in his purpose. He had not eliminated any major unit of the Grand Fleet, and had not altered, even marginally, the naval balance of power. So, in the only respects that mattered, the non-encounter of 19 August reaffirmed the message of Jutland. Yet for Jellicoe and also for Beatty (who responded identically), the experience of 19 August had been deeply unsatisfying. They had proceeded south under repeated observation of enemy airships, which seemed to eliminate all chance of their catching Scheer unawares. And they had been forced at Scheer's bidding to enter an area infested by enemy submarines; and this in circumstances in which the British fleet did not possess sufficient destroyers to guard its lighter vessels from U-boat attack. In a situation where they had enjoyed little hope of getting at Scheer, and his submarines some chance of getting at them, it was becoming a nice point which side was playing cat-and-mouse with the other.

Jellicoe and Beatty therefore proposed that they should not, henceforth, invariably respond to Scheer's forays, if these were made into the more southerly or easterly parts of the North Sea. As long as there was little or no chance of catching Scheer, and a real danger of being drawn towards submarines or mines without sufficient destroyer cover, a move by the Grand Fleet was deemed unwarranted. It would remain a different matter, in Jellicoe's words, 'when there is a really good chance of engaging [the High Seas Fleet] in daylight'.

The Admiralty, unable to meet the demand for more destroyers, indicated its agreement to this proposal. It was a decision that might have signified the first stage in a major shift in policy. Parts of the North Sea could indeed have become a No-Man's-Land – anyway unless the German fleet was attempting a lengthy incursion. But in fact the ensuing weeks would reveal no real qualification to British dominance at sea. Certainly, when the German fleet left harbour on the morning of 19 October Jellicoe was only placed on alert and did not, as heretofore, set out in an attempt to intercept. Consequently Scheer, after a modest sweep towards the Dogger Bank, returned home uneventfully. But the situation remained that, if the Admiralty believed that the Germans were coming out with serious intent, the Grand Fleet would still try to catch them.

On 23 October the Operations Division detected what was thought the harbinger of a major movement by Scheer. No fewer than 24 German destroyers moved out of base. (In fact, they were transferring to a Belgian port for a raid into the Channel unaccompanied by big ships.) The Admiralty took this as portending an assault by Scheer on the Thames Estuary or the Straits of Dover. So Jellicoe was ordered to place the Grand Fleet in a state of readiness, in the hope that he might get a chance to cut off Scheer on his way back.

But Scheer did not set sail on this occasion. Nor would his fleet put to sea for a great many months after that. Hence the question of whether the Grand Fleet was prepared to limit its command of the North Sea was never put to the test.

Two considerations were obliging Scheer to abandon the last vestige of that more assertive role which he had been seeking for the High Seas Fleet. First, he was learning that submarine traps could be set by both sides. On 19 August, and again on 19 October, one of his ships was torpedoed by a British submarine; and although neither blow proved fatal, they did constitute a salutary warning. Early in November he received another. He sent some of his battleships to rescue two U-boats stranded on the Danish coast. During their return journey a British submarine managed to torpedo two of his battleships. Again, both vessels succeeded in returning to harbour. But this near-escape earned Scheer an expression of royal displeasure.

Of considerably more importance, the key weapon in German attempts to whittle away the Grand Fleet's capital ships was now being turned to other purposes. The only element in the German navy equipped to strike at Jellicoe's force, if the High Seas Fleet was not to be placed at risk, was the U-boat. And on neither 31 May nor 19 August had this weapon actually achieved its purpose of sinking – as distinct from frightening – British Dreadnoughts. The moral was plain. If Germany was to impose an economic blockade on Britain, this could not be done by aiming blows at the Royal Navy. The U-boats must be turned loose against merchant shipping.

Without submarines at hand to threaten Jellicoe, there was no point in Scheer's taking the High Seas Fleet to sea at all. So, on a decided note of anticlimax, the period of passing encounters and near-meetings between the two great navies came to an end. It left the British blockade on Germany not only unimpaired but without serious challenge. What remained unsettled was a different, and potentially far more decisive, question. Could Britain, while still dominant at sea, nevertheless itself be blockaded into starvation and economic collapse?

II

In the course of 1916, Britain's naval authorities continued to grapple with the threat to merchant shipping posed by the U-boat. Success continued to elude them.

New anti-submarine instruments began making their appearance. The paravane – a load of explosive attached (at a distance) to the side of a moving ship and maintained by a rudder at a constant depth – was brought into use. Listening devices, known as hydrophones, were introduced. In favourable circumstances, these might detect the presence of a submerged U-boat. And depth charges, designed to detonate at pre-set levels under water, started to become available, although only in small quantities. The potential value of some of these devices was demonstrated when, on 6 July 1916, a German submarine was detected by several hydrophones and destroyed by depth charges.

Yet, at least for the moment, neither separately nor together did these measures constitute a breakthrough. The paravane was too dependent on a chance encounter or on a U-boat rashly remaining in the area where it had already made an attack. The depth charge required to make a near-direct hit to destroy a submarine and could be brought into play only once a U-boat was detected. The hydrophones were as yet too rudimentary to discern their quarry with any frequency. This meant that the crucial problem in destroying U-boats – that of location – remained largely unsolved.

In a sense the Q-ship – that is, the armed trawler disguised to look like a helpless merchantman – was nearer the mark tactically than most other offensive measures. Certainly, on an absolute judgement the Q-ships did not achieve much. Up to the end of 1916 they eliminated only five U-boats. (However they damaged others, and probably inhibited submarine attacks on merchant ships which were actually un-armed.) Yet at least the Q-ships bore witness to an important truth. At this stage anyway, the conquest of the submarine could not be accomplished by a policy of seek and destroy. Both vertically and horizontally, the ocean offered the U-boat too much hiding space. So either enemy submarines must be obliged to make contact with British vessels (such as Q-ships) equipped for their destruction, or else their quarries needed to be rendered less vulnerable to attack.

One step in the latter direction was the arming of merchant ships. During 1916 cargo vessels equipped with guns proved much more capable of surviving encounters with submarines than those which were not. (This was an indication, of course, that most attacks by U-boats were still being made on the surface.) Admittedly, the armed merchant ship hardly ever managed to dispose of its assailant. But as long as no effective means existed for the large-scale destruction of U-boats, then the next best thing was to render hazardous the submarine's approach to its potential victim. The problem in 1916 was that the supply of guns for arming merchant ships fell far short of the quantity needed.

The Grand Fleet had recognized all along that the best way of countering the submarine at this stage was by denying it safe access to its targets. At sea Jellicoe's great ships were guarded by a gauntlet of small, fast craft that U-boats were unable to penetrate. The same sort of protection was provided for troopships and other vessels whose cargoes were too vital to place at risk. But, as the events of 19 August 1916 bore witness, there were not enough destroyers available to guard even some of the lesser units of the Grand Fleet. So no one in 1916 was considering providing this sort of protection to merchant shipping.

What followed from this, however little recognized at the Admiralty, was ominous. Huge numbers of merchant ships engaged in servicing Britain were vulnerable to submarine attack. What alone stood between them and potential destruction was a factor beyond Britain's control: namely, the misgivings among Germany's rulers, owing to the attitude of the USA, about employing U-boats indiscriminately against civilian targets. But that safeguard was proving precarious. Early in 1916 the leaders of Germany, believing that American attitudes were softening, authorized a stepping up of the U-boat campaign. The effect was dramatic. In April Britain lost 37 merchant ships to submarines and six more to mines – mine laying being an increasingly important aspect of U-boat activity. This was almost as great as the scale of loss sustained in the worst month of 1915. But it straightway became evident that the attitude of the US Government had not changed. The endangering of American lives consequent upon the sinking of the cross-Channel steamer *Sussex* caused such an outburst from Woodrow Wilson that in May the German authorities once more called off the campaign.

Then came Jutland, with its clear message that Germany must either employ U-boats against merchant shipping or abandon all hope of blockading Britain into submission. In the last quarter of 1916 the U-boat campaign, if still under constraints, was resumed. From the viewpoint of the British Admiralty, two things became starkly clear. First, no effective means of destroying submarines had been discovered. Germany's U-boat losses for the whole year numbered only 15, a small deprivation for a force that had increased from 58 vessels at the beginning of 1916 to 140 at its end. Secondly, measures designed to deny victims to the U-boats were failing. The rate of British tonnage sunk by submarines and mines, which had jumped to 140,000 in April 1916 and then dropped to 37,000 in June, soared in October to 175,000. This was accompanied by a sharp increase in the sinking of neutral (particularly Norwegian) ships trading with Britain, which, if continued, might cause neutral vessels to withdraw their services. None of this meant that Britain was nearing starvation. But the nation's war effort was being threatened with serious impairment.

These events were received with dismay in Britain. Coming on top of what, however questionably, was deemed the missed opportunity of Jutland, and then of some raids by German destroyers in the Channel, the U-boat successes cast doubt on the whole conduct of naval affairs. The immediate victims of criticism were Balfour, the First Lord of the Admiralty, and Sir Henry Jackson, the First Sea Lord. Their regime, it was claimed, was too lethargic and too removed from actual experience of the war at sea. In November Jackson surrendered his post. The Government prevailed on Jellicoe to leave the Grand Fleet and to take over at Whitehall the task of defeating the submarine. Soon after, Balfour too was removed – from the Admiralty, if not from high office. But this change was part of a larger upheaval. Uneasiness concerning events at sea merged with far more grievous disappointments regarding those on land to sweep the Asquith Government from power.

PART SEVEN

Blooding the New Armies: the Battle of the Somme, 1916

Map 7   *The Somme campaign, 1 July – 18 November 1916.* Source: *Gilbert,* First World War Atlas, *p. 56.*

28

INCEPTION

The attack is to go for the big thing. I still think we would do better to proceed by shorter steps; but I have told D. H. I will carry out his plan with as much enthusiasm as if it were my own.

Sir Henry Rawlinson, 30 April 1916, quoted in Frederick Maurice,
Life of General Lord Rawlinson of Trent

It is a gamble to go for an unlimited offensive but D. H. apparently wants it and I am prepared to undertake anything within reason.

Rawlinson diary, entry for 23 May 1916

I

The events of 1915 had determined, within severe limits, the course that Britain's involvement in the war in 1916 would take.

The past year had not brought the war any nearer to a conclusion. And Britain had suffered some noteworthy setbacks. Yet nothing had occurred seriously to impair the nation's capacity to wage a sustained campaign. And much had happened on the home front – at recruiting stations, in training camps, throughout industry, within the ranks of government – to bring the country for the first time to the point where it could make a major contribution to the war on land. By the end of 1915 it was plain that that contribution could not be foregone: that the men who had offered their services would be required to fight, and the munitions now in production would need to be expended.

If Britain's fighting capacity at the start of 1916, far from being impaired, was considerably enhanced, this was not true of its allies. Serbia had been crushed, even though the remnants of the Serb army remained a force in the Salonika campaign. The Italians, having entered the war on the Allied side in May 1915, had launched costly and fruitless offensives against the Austrians. These established beyond doubt that the struggle would be quite unlike anything they had contemplated. The Russians had suffered a succession of defeats that had robbed them of territory and cost them heavily in manpower, especially among their irreplaceable junior officers. And the French, in their great offensives of the spring and autumn of 1915, had incurred terrible casualties that they would be hard put to it to make good. Certainly, it was still possible to look for major efforts from Britain's principal allies, and even to speak with enthusiasm concerning their powers of recuperation – as Lloyd George, in November 1915, was doing about the Russians.[1] But there was no prospect of the war's being won unless Britain in 1916 assumed a much greater share of the burden.

Where was Britain to make this military effort? Late in 1914 and early in 1915 great doubts had been expressed about the feasibility of launching successful attacks on the

---

[1] Trevor Wilson (ed.), *The Political Diaries of C. P. Scott 1911–1928* (London: Collins, 1970), p. 159.

Western Front. Since then all the offensives that had been delivered there, by the British and even more by the French, had seemed to justify these misgivings. Yet, paradoxically, by the start of 1916 Britain's military operations were more, rather than less, tied to that area.

For this there were several reasons. In the first place, despite the strategic flexibility that sea power supposedly bestowed, Britain did not possess so large a margin of naval superiority that it could employ many vessels aiding operations outside the North Sea.

Plate 23   *British troops on the Western Front early in 1916 wearing their new splinter-proof helmets. (Compare the soft caps still being worn late in 1915 by the soldiers in plate 20.)*

Secondly, the experience of 1915 had confirmed that there were few, if any, places where sea power could be used to bring effective military pressure to bear on an enemy bestriding the centre of Europe. Thus the operations at Gallipoli and Salonika, while requiring much British endeavour, had produced virtually no direct response from the Germans – something that could not be said of the otherwise disheartening actions at Neuve Chapelle, Aubers Ridge, and Loos. Finally, what in early 1915 had looked like the two most promising areas for an 'Eastern' strategy had produced only disappointments: an operation that had been abandoned, and an operation that all but a fragment of the Cabinet were eager to abandon.

Changes in personnel reinforced, but were not the source of, the impetus that was directing Britain's military endeavours towards the Western Front. As regards this matter, it was not of major importance that Haig had replaced French as commander of the British forces in France and Flanders. Whoever commanded there would press for the concentration of Britain's strength in that theatre. Nevertheless, it doubtless helped the politicians, in making their decisions on strategy, to have a commander in France who aroused a measure of confidence – something his predecessor had long since ceased to enjoy. Even Lloyd George, after a visit to France at the turn of the year, reported that 'things are much more business-like than in French's time. There is a new spirit. Haig seems very keen on his job and has a fine staff.'[2]

Admittedly, from December 1915 the official adviser to the Government on military matters was Wullie Robertson, a devoted Westerner and supporter of Haig. And it is clear that the War Committee and the Cabinet were prepared to pay Robertson and the re-formed General Staff much attention; Asquith in December called the new CIGS 'a man of first rate capacity'.[3] But it did not follow that the civilian rulers had abdicated direction of strategy to military men who happened to be Westerners. Indeed, at times Robertson felt keenly the suspicion with which at least some members of the Government viewed him. He wrote to Haig on 26 April 1916: 'They regard me as an optimistic ass when not as a stupid soldier. They think – and many say – that all soldiers are stupid.'[4] And members of the War Committee were not tardy both in expressing misgivings about the proposed offensive in France and in suggesting other courses.

In December 1915 the military representatives of the Allies, meeting at Chantilly, had concluded that the strategy for the following year must be a series of offensives on the principal fronts (the Western, the Russian, and the Italian), delivered as near as possible simultaneously. Thus the enemy would not be able to move his reserves from one front to another. In line with this resolution the War Committee, prompted by Robertson, agreed on 28 December that Britain should make its major effort for 1916 on the Western Front. But Balfour, a reluctant assenter, soon began agitating against the decision, something Robertson found 'all very unsettling'; 'much of my time is taken up in *talking*, and in explaining what these people cannot understand and sometimes do not wish to understand.'[5] Nor, in the short run, did Balfour talk in vain. On 13 January the War Committee amended its resolution. Preparations were to go ahead for an offensive in France and in the greatest possible strength. But 'it must not be assumed' that offensive operations 'are finally decided on'.

Yet as long as British forces must engage the enemy somewhere, and in 'the greatest possible strength', this temporizing amendment would accomplish nothing unless the dissenters could offer a convincing alternative course. There was no shortage of alternatives: what each of them lacked was the power to convince. Robertson wrote to Haig on 13 January concerning the Cabinet opponents of 'offensive operations on your front': 'One wants to go to the Balkans, another to Baghdad, and another to allow the Germans to "attack us." I have used all the arguments which you or any other soldier could use, but not with complete success.'[6]

Yet in the long run he was bound to succeed against proposals like these. Britain had already suffered humiliations enough in the Balkans and Mesopotamia, and these at the hands of non-German forces. And no one could provide a formula that would induce the Germans 'to attack us' in the West. Balfour's own notion of an alternative strategy, offered late in December 1915, was even more bizarre. Given the strength of the enemy's defences in the West, he proposed to the War Committee that they transfer all possible troops to the Russian Front. Coming from the First Lord of the Admiralty, who should have known better than most the fearful problems of transportation involved in such an undertaking, it is not surprising that Robertson (so he recounted to Haig) lost his temper.[7] Nothing more was heard of that scheme.

---

[2] *Lord Riddell's War Diary 1914–1918* (London: Ivor Nicholson & Watson, 1933), p. 146.

[3] Wilson (ed.), *The Political Diaries of C. P. Scott*, p. 164.

[4] Victor Bonham-Carter, *Soldier True* (London: Muller, 1963), p. 168.

[5] W. Robertson, *Soldiers and Statesmen* (London: Cassell, 1926), vol. 1, p. 256.

[6] Ibid., p. 257.

[7] Bonham-Carter, *Soldier True*, p. 168.

One individual was no longer present in the Government to offer his strategic insights: Churchill. Would it have made a difference if he had been? His post-war memoirs hardly suggest so. They contain a powerful argument against making Britain's major effort on the Western Front in 1916. But the alternative that he supports could have been received with nothing but derision had he been in a position to advance it: a renewed attack on the Gallipoli peninsula. The task of those urging a British offensive in the West might be strewn with obstacles. But they were bound to succeed eventually as long as the obstacles were not more substantial than these.

The last trace of strategic flexibility vanished in February 1916. For then the Germans commenced their operation against the fortress of Verdun, designed to wear down the French army to breaking-point. The change that occurred in Lloyd George's attitude is illuminating. A month earlier, so Robertson reported indignantly to Haig, the Minister of Munitions had been one of a number in the Cabinet who were arguing that the offensive should be delayed 'until we are at full strength, which they say will not be until well on in the summer'. Lloyd George was to confer with the French munitions authorities about how much ammunition would be needed and how long it would take to get it. 'This is the thin end of the wedge for deferring matters.'[8] Late in March, however, by which time the attack on Verdun had been proceeding for a month, Lloyd George attended a hurriedly convened conference in Paris. On his return he discussed his impressions with Lord Riddell, who noted:

> L.G. says . . . that the feeling in France concerning England is not happy. The French think they are making all the sacrifices and we are endeavouring to preserve our trade and carry on as usual. This he thinks may prejudice the alliance. He feels we should make strong efforts which will dispel this feeling.[9]

Whether or not Lloyd George recognized the logic of this statement, it pointed directly to a British offensive on the Western Front. For only there was planning under way for making 'strong efforts'.

Regarding that proposed operation, Robertson told the War Committee on 31 March 1916: 'It is now necessary . . . to decide, at once and definitely, whether they do or do not approve.' On 7 April the British Government finally authorized Haig to concert an offensive with the French.

II

If the logic of the Allies' situation required that the British army should launch a major offensive in France in 1916, why did it occur in the sector of the Somme?

There were many factors that rendered this an acceptable area for an Anglo–French offensive. Most of them, certainly, were only relative. That is, there were compelling reasons against any other sector of the Western Front. The northernmost region, Flanders, if not ruled out, was placed at a discount by its high water level, which rendered it liable to be turned into a quagmire if much subjected to bombardment. The southernmost sector, from below Verdun to the Swiss border, was heavily wooded and broken up by hills and valleys, so that a sustained advance over a wide front was practically impossible. (It remained a quiet sector for the last three and a half years of the war.) Many areas in between were also ruled out. For example, two that might have looked promising, Artois and the Champagne, had been the scenes of large-scale and

---

[8] Robertson to Haig, 13 January 1916, in Robert Blake (ed.), *The Private Papers of Douglas Haig 1914–1919* (London: Eyre & Spottiswoode, 1952), p. 124.
[9] *Lord Riddell's War Diary*, p. 168.

utterly fruitless French offensives in 1915. They could not within a year be regarded with any hope.

The Somme sector had none of these disadvantages. It had seen no large action since 1914 and so was not associated with failure. Its chalky sub-soil, topped by loam, made it good campaigning territory as long as the weather remained fine. It was free of heavily built-up areas such as had hampered the British at Loos, and it possessed no dominating features as imposing, in enemy hands, as Vimy Ridge or the Chemin des Dames. The region contained much open countryside free of trees and hedges, and it was fairly flat. As Sir Henry Rawlinson noted when his forces started moving into the area: 'The country resembles Salisbury plain, with large open rolling features, and any number of partridges which we are not allowed to shoot. It is a great improvement on the flat muddy plains of Flanders.'[10] The principal study of First World War battlefields concurs: 'The most striking characteristic of the Somme battlefield is its monotonous succession of low, rolling plain.'[11] It had the additional advantage of being the point where the British and French sectors joined, for during late 1915 and early 1916 the British, with their growing forces, had taken over further lengths of the front from the French. This clearly would facilitate the planning of a joint operation by the armies of the two nations.

Certainly, a great many things could be said against choosing the Somme as the area for an offensive. If not hilly, it was by no means devoid of rising ground near the front lines. This lay in German hands, so placing the attackers in an uncomfortably exposed position. Further, the fact that there had been no fighting here since 1914 meant that the front had not moved and the Germans had enjoyed ample opportunity to organize their defences. Again, the chalk sub-soil that made it good territory over which to campaign made it even better for constructing underground defences: the Germans had been methodically excavating dug-outs well below the penetrative powers of artillery bombardment. Finally, if much of the region was open, there were neverthe-less several woods that could hold up an advance, as well as numerous small villages – 'dense clusters of houses', as they have been described, 'whose walls and cellars formed veritable forts'.[12]

Hence if an absolute judgement was to be made, it might be concluded that the demerits of the Somme as a region for an offensive outweighed its advantages. But the men who had to plan the offensive were not in a position to make absolute judgements. An attack must take place somewhere. The Somme appeared better than anywhere else.

It was Joffre who first proposed this region, at a time when Haig was contemplating a British operation in Flanders. But it is not the case that Haig was averse to Joffre's proposal. Rather, the decision seemed to rest on what sort of action the French and British decided upon. If they chose to launch simultaneous but quite distinct operations, then Haig was drawn to a British attack in the north. If they participated in a single operation, then the Somme had clear advantages. So Haig wrote to Joffre on 1 February 1916 suggesting that the British contribution might be as many as 25 divisions and form part of the main attack, in which case he would agree with Joffre's proposal that the battle should take place astride the Somme.

The events of the next few weeks, which had finally driven the Cabinet to decide that an offensive would take place, also decided its locale. As we have seen, on 21 February 1916 the Germans, for the first time since the opening months of the war, launched a

---

[10] Rawlinson to Wigram, 27 February 1916.

[11] Douglas Wilson Johnson, *Battlefields of the World War* (New York: Oxford University Press, 1921), p. 96.

[12] Ibid., p. 112.

major offensive in the West. It was directed against the French fortress of Verdun, which had held out in 1914 and so had materially helped to thwart the German advance in the southern part of the front. The German objective in 1916 was, by means of massive artillery bombardments, either to take the fortress and so deliver a shattering blow to French morale or to inflict such heavy casualties on the French that their army would cease to exist as a fighting force. The terrible blood-letting that resulted rendered the French incapable of launching an offensive on their own. But they were still able to participate in a joint offensive with the British. That left the Somme as the only viable area of operation.

Haig explained the matter to Kitchener four days after the assault on Verdun began. If the French proved 'unable or unwilling' to contribute to an offensive, then the British operation would occur in Flanders. 'If, however, the French have sufficient troops left for the general attack, then we should make our attack alongside of theirs, say, astride the Somme (as already proposed by Joffre).'[13] As the struggle at Verdun proceeded and French losses rose, Joffre's promised participation in the coming offensive diminished. But it never vanished altogether. As late as 24 May an aide of Joffre told Haig that, although on account of Verdun the French commander 'had not the number of Divisions available for a combined attack which he had hoped', nevertheless he estimated that the minimum number of French divisions participating would be '22, or possibly 26' – just about the same number as the British. He also indicated that 'the French would prefer to lose their casualties in an offensive attack rather than to melt away while sitting still.'[14]

In the following weeks the situation at Verdun became so grave that the size of the French participation on the Somme fell from '22, or possibly 26' to only 13 divisions. But this was still a significant contribution. And anyway, with the survival of Verdun – and, by implication, of France as a fighting force – in such jeopardy, it had become a matter of the utmost urgency that the British launch the only operation that had reached an advanced stage of planning.

Did Verdun have another effect – that of fundamentally impairing the Somme offensive as originally conceived? On a cursory view, it did. The French were obliged to scale down their contribution to the point where, from being the major partner, they became decidedly the minor. As a result, the whole scale of the offensive was reduced; and so, by implication, was its capacity for achieving a major advance.

But this argument is not conclusive. The French were not alone in having to devote to Verdun many divisions that otherwise might have fought on the Somme. The same was true of the Germans. This may seem obvious. But the corollary is often overlooked. The French and British commanders were agreed in early 1916 that what lay in the way of a successful breakthrough was the existence of large numbers of enemy reserves, held back well beyond the range of the bombardment and capable of plugging any gap or establishing a new defensive line. As Robertson put it, with adequate artillery preparation 'there is no insuperable difficulty in overwhelming the enemy's troops in the front line and in support', but the enemy's reserves could prevent this success from being exploited. Consequently sufficient force must be employed to make the enemy use up his reserves: 'then, and then only, the decisive attack which is to win victory should be driven home.'[15] Haig took this view, and so did Joffre. Indeed, a considerable tussle developed between them early in the planning of operations for 1916 because the French commander intended that the British should spend some

---

[13] Blake (ed.), *The Private Papers of Douglas Haig*, p. 133.
[14] Ibid., pp. 143–4.
[15] Robertson, *Soldiers and Statesmen*, vol. 1, p. 244.

months wearing down the German reserves, after which the French would launch the decisive attack. The British commander resisted this notion of his army's contribution.

Verdun, in a sense, ensured that Haig, not Joffre, had his way: that the French and not the British wore down the German reserves. Robertson, indeed, welcomed the German attack for this very reason. He wrote to Joffre:

> It seems to me that we can desire nothing better than that the enemy should continue his attacks, as they will use up his troops to a much greater extent than the operations of 'usure' which you had proposed that we should employ against him. I am strongly of opinion that, by attacking, the enemy is playing our game.[16]

Before long the German operation at Verdun ceased to look like an exercise in playing the Allied game. And in time it would be invoked as a major reason why that game did not prosper as it should. But Robertson's point remained. If the French forces falling at Verdun would not be available for the Somme, neither would the Germans being ground down in almost equal numbers. The German strike against the French fortress, in short, did not rob the Somme of its larger prospects for the Allies. It simply decided that the Allied (and German) tragedy in France in 1916 would be divided between two regions instead of being concentrated in one.

III

So the range of choices facing British strategists in 1916 was narrow. And the imperatives demanding a great offensive in an area like the Somme were powerful. What, then, is to be said of the actual operation that they planned?

The first thing that seems plain is that the operation sprang from an uneasy amalgam of ideas. There were the notions held before 1914 about the right conduct of battles. And there were the lessons that had been learned from the first 18 months of the Great War.

Some of Haig's pre-war ideas are illuminating in this context.[17] In 1907 he had written: 'The real objective in war is a decisive battle'; and in 1909: 'Decisive success in battle can be gained only by a vigorous offensive.' The prerequisite of the successful offensive was deemed to be a matter less of fire power than of morale – the determined thrusting home of the advance, the imposition of the will of the attacking force upon the defending. The culmination of offensive action, and the stroke that would convert a successful into a decisive battle, was the cavalry charge. For here was the means whereby retreat would become rout and the defending force, its lines of communication severed, would become incapable of functioning as a fighting unit.

Some of these views looked decidedly out of place even in the light of British experience in South Africa. For the Boers had demonstrated the toll that defensive fire power could levy on troops attacking frontally in the open. But Britain's military authorities had seized on the subsequent Russo-Japanese war as grounds for discounting the lessons of South Africa. The Japanese were deemed to have shown that the frontal assault delivered with sufficient vigour remained the means of victory. We may note the views in 1910 of Brigadier-General Launcelot Kiggell, later Haig's Chief of Staff. He wrote that the notion had developed as a result of the Boer War that fire power was decisive in battle and that the sword and the bayonet no longer counted. But, happily, 'this idea is erroneous and was proved to be so in the late war in

---

[16] Paul Guinn, *British Strategy and Politics 1914 to 1918* (Oxford: Clarendon Press, 1965), p. 138.
[17] See T. H. Travers, 'The Offensive and the Problem of Innovation in British Military Thought 1870–1915', *Journal of Contemporary History*, vol. 13, no. 3, July 1978.

Manchuria. Everyone admits that. Victory is now won actually by the bayonet, or by the fear of it.'[18]

These preconceptions were much battered by the events of 1914 and 1915. Encounters on the Western Front showed that defensive fire power could wreak such havoc on an attacking force that superior morale would avail it nothing. As for cold steel (or 'the fear of it'), the attackers might never manage to get close enough to the enemy to bring it into play. Further, it transpired that an offensive battle might not produce a decision even when the attackers managed to eliminate a crucial proportion of the original defending force. For the defender could feed more and yet more forces into the battle zone, restocking old positions or creating new, and so denying the attackers either a breakthrough or – in traditional terms – a 'victory'.

In planning their offensive on the Somme Britain's military leaders sought to take account of these developments. They recognized that it was pointless to send infantry or cavalry into the contested zone while enemy fire power remained unsuppressed. And, as we have seen, they recognized that the power of the enemy to feed in reserves made the conduct of an offensive altogether more complex and more protracted than in the past. What they did not do was to conclude that there could be no such thing as a decisive battle, or that they should cease employing cavalry as the instrument of an attempted breakthrough. Haig still wrote and talked about launching an offensive that would be decisive, and still hankered after an infantry advance on so wide a front that he would be able to pour his cavalry through the gap. Three weeks before the Somme offensive began, he was urged by the King to reduce the size of his cavalry because it was proving, in monetary terms, so costly. Haig 'protested that it would be unwise, because in order to shorten the war and reap the fruits of any success, we must make use of the mobility of the Cavalry.'[19] And a week later he was urging the commander of his Fourth Army, which was playing the major role in the operation, to keep the cavalry close up in case the enemy's resistance broke and it proved possible to get through into open country.

How was it imagined that this could be accomplished? It was assumed that the Germans, because of their four-month offensive at Verdun in addition to their commitments on other fronts, were in the process of exhausting their reserves. And the answer to the problem of sending infantrymen across a contested zone without suffering annihilation lay in the very force that so far had been thwarting them: fire power. Hitherto British attacks had been halted by the weapons of the German defenders. Now those weapons and the men wielding them were to be rendered inoperative by the weight of British gunfire. So the way would be open for British foot soldiers, and ultimately horse soldiers, to cross No-Man's-Land and break through the enemy's lines.

IV

The man whom Haig chose to convert these principles into actual operations was Sir Henry Rawlinson, commander of the British Fourth Army. This army was to occupy all but the most northerly part of the 18-mile sector that the British were to attack (in conjunction with the French on their right). Although Rawlinson's troops contained a fair stiffening of experienced forces, both regulars and Territorials, they were predominantly a force of Kitchener's New Armies making their debut on the field of

---

[18] Quoted in Travers, 'The Offensive and the Problem of Innovation in British Military Thought 1870–1915'.
[19] Blake (ed.), *The Private Papers of Douglas Haig*, p. 147.

battle. Rawlinson seemed the right man to lead them. Unlike Haig and most of the other prominent figures in the British army, he was by origin not a cavalryman but a commander of infantry. He was also an efficient administrator with an effective staff.

This was important. With a great campaign to wage and half a million men under his command, Rawlinson must first set in motion a prodigious work of organization and preparation. This was done commendably. Sites were chosen, as far as possible from the counter-fire of the enemy (but there could not be total immunity), for the hundreds of guns that were to carry out the work of destroying the defenders. Observation posts to direct the fire of these guns were established well forward. To facilitate communication between observers and gunners, telephone lines were laid at a depth of 6 feet, to withstand all but the worst of the German shelling. Further, enough fighter squadrons were moved into the region to secure command of the air, so denying oversight of the preparations to enemy aircraft as well as observing the fall of British artillery fire on the German rear positions.

In addition, a new town had to be constructed behind the British lines for the huge population that was being moved into the district. Not only accommodation must be provided, but also washing and toilet facilities – no small matter in a region not over-endowed with water – as well as food and drink. There was also the need for medical services, to deal with the wear and tear of daily life accompanied by spasmodic bombardment, and to provide against the maiming on a vast scale that battle would shortly bring.

The insatiable requirements of men and guns demanded the employment of great quantities of transportation, which meant providing large numbers of horses and vehicles and seeing that they in their turn received adequate shelter and nourishment (be the last of these fodder or petrol). Ensuring sufficient transportation also involved the construction of a great number of roads and railways – a heavy undertaking in an area where roads crumbled easily under continual use and where the stone with which to construct additional railbeds and to render roads durable was at a premium. (Some of it had to be obtained from as far away as Cornwall.)

The attack on the first day alone would be made by some 120,000 men; to hold and launch this number a trench system of enormous complexity had to be constructed and rendered secure. Further back, to ensure that the guns would never want for ammunition, a series of supply dumps, each replenishing the one ahead, was established.

British preparations for the battle of the Somme constituted a mighty feat of organization and administration, carried out with a considerable degree of efficiency. But a large question remained. Were the operational orders that these preparations were designed to facilitate equally well devised?

In one respect the choice of Rawlinson to direct the Somme campaign seemed anomalous. As long ago as March 1915 he had concluded that breakthrough operations were doomed to failure and that the best policy of attack was one of 'bite and hold': that is, deliver a series of sharp blows against limited objectives that the enemy would wear himself out seeking to recapture. Yet here was Rawlinson directing an operation that was to 'go for the big thing'. By his own account he went about it with a will, as if the plan were 'my own'. But he diverged from Haig's notions in important respects. He did not plan to break through both German defensive systems at the first go, or expect to be able to employ the cavalry immediately (although at Haig's bidding he kept them on hand should the opportunity arise). Instead, he proposed, on most of the front attacked, in the opening phase of the offensive to capture only the first German system. When that had been accomplished his resources would be advanced and the attack launched on the German second line. Ultimately, the entire enemy defensive system would be overrun, and at that stage break-in could become breakthrough and the cavalry make its advance.

It may be thought that this conception was a good deal sounder overall than Haig's more grandiose notions. Whether Rawlinson had either the tactical insights or the resources to carry it out was another matter. Haig for one had misgivings about what seemed the unimaginative use to be made of the infantry. Rawlinson was apparently convinced that untested and undertrained troops, who until recently had been committed civilians, could not be trusted to act on received infantry tactics. French infantrymen on the right of the attack, advancing under fire, would form into small groups and proceed by rushes from one piece of dead ground to another, each rush being covered by the fire of other groups. Kitchener's novices, it seems to have been assumed, could not be trusted to act like this. They would either take cover and stay there or else disintegrate into unrelated units, losing the momentum of the advance. So both the men of the New Armies, who made up some 60 per cent of the attacking force, and the more experienced regulars and Territorials, were directed to advance in a succession of waves 100 yards apart. Each wave was to consist of a line of men, at intervals of two or three paces, moving across No-Man's-Land at a steady walk.

Such tactics seemed to be setting up the infantry for massacre, in particular by the scythe-like sweep of enemy machine-guns and the curtain of death rained down by enemy artillery. But Rawlinson was convinced that in this instance the enemy's weapons would not be operating. For he proposed to bring down upon the German positions such a weight of fire power as would obliterate them. As he assured his corps commanders: 'nothing could exist at the conclusion of the bombardment in the area covered by it.'[20] This was a pretty tall order. It assumed that along a 15-mile front his 1,437 guns (one for every 17 yards of front) could deliver a bombardment that would accomplish three things: at the furthest point, suppress the German artillery; at the nearest, destroy the German barbed wire; and in between, render the occupants of the German trenches incapable of wielding their machine-guns, rifles, and grenades.

What grounds were there for such an assumption? It may seem axiomatic that for any given area of defended territory there must be a weight of bombardment that will render the defences inoperative. And it may have appeared, from the early successes of the British at Neuve Chapelle and of the Germans at Verdun, that this war had already shown that such a ratio of bombardment to space lay within Rawlinson's reach. Yet each of these successes had been facilitated by special circumstances – surprise in the first instance, ill-prepared defences in the second. These could not be hoped for on the Somme. Anyway, the required weight of bombardment must alter from place to place according to important variables. These would range from the type of soil in which the enemy had constructed his defences to the degree of skill of the officers conducting the British bombardment. (In no respect did the inexperience of Kitchener's army count more heavily against it than in its lack of trained artillery officers.)

It is unlikely that any precise calculations, embodying not only the quantities of shell proportionate to the area attacked but also the role of local variables, were ever made by the Fourth Army authorities. Probably it was not even possible to make them. All that was done was that a great many shells were accumulated, and it was then concluded that these would be sufficient. And that conclusion was maintained in face of mounting evidence that it was quite unwarranted.

The enemy defences in the area were indeed formidable. The Germans had

---

[20] Sir John Edmonds, *Military Operations France and Belgium 1916* (London: Macmillan, 1932), vol. 1, p. 288.

occupied this region since late in 1914, giving them ample time to secure their position. There was also plenty of incentive for them to do so. Their leaders were not planning to attempt an advance here. And they had good reason to assume that the Allies would shortly seek to drive them out. During the first half of 1916 evidence of the movement of British forces into the area – a good indication of the location of the expected Allied offensive – had accumulated. And the fact that Falkenhayn, the German supreme commander, was sceptical on this score only caused his local commanders to look more keenly to their defences. They set up barbed-wire entanglements, thoroughly staked and employing the type of wire that did not spring apart should the stakes be uprooted by bombardment. They dug trenches in the accommodating soil to a depth of 10 feet. And, perhaps of greatest importance, beneath their trenches they constructed dug-outs to a depth of 30 feet or more. These dug-outs were not just hidey-holes. Many had electricity, piped water, forced ventilation, and living quarters.

At intervals in this trench system were a series of strong points of a most formidable nature. These were generally located in the cellars of the 13 villages that had been integrated into the German lines. Where disused villages were not available, they consisted of intricately constructed redoubts giving almost the same degree of strength. Implanted in them were machine-gun posts of great killing power, which were acutely difficult for attacking artillery to pinpoint.

Finally, behind the first system of defences was an array of artillery pieces. Most of them would not be brought into play (and so reveal their positions) until Allied troops were crammed into their forward trenches preparatory to going over the top.

How aware was the British command of the nature of these obstacles? Direct observation would reveal the existence of the barbed wire and system of trenches, and aerial observation would discover some at least of the big guns. And there were a number of indications that, beneath the trenches, lay a thorough sytem of dug-outs. A portion of German trench containing these underground shelters had been captured by the French while they still occupied this sector. It was handed over to the British, who were using it as a company headquarters. Again, a group of British miners, tunnelling well below the German lines to lay an explosive charge, had actually broken into a German dug-out. And German prisoners, taken in raids or deserting in anticipation of the British offensive, had acknowledged the security of their underground positions. Some of this information reached the highest levels. A trench raid on 5 June that produced telling evidence of the depth of the German defences was written up in the Fourth Army Intelligence Summary.

What grounds had the commander of Fourth Army for assuming that these defences could be eliminated? Rawlinson planned for a protracted bombardment, lasting five days and directed by ground observers and airmen. Haig was reluctant to agree, arguing for a shorter, whirlwind bombardment followed by a rush of infantry. Rawlinson opposed this on several good grounds. There was, he argued, little if any chance of securing surprise; 'effective wire-cutting [could] not be carried out in five or six hours' and could not be accurately observed if undertaken at the same time as the bombardment of trenches and strong points; and a long bombardment, preventing German front-line troops from being relieved and denying them food and sleep, would have an effect on their morale that a short bombardment could not, 'bearing in mind the existence of numerous dug-outs and cellars in the enemy's lines'.[21] His case against a shorter bombardment seemed irrefutable. What he did not demonstrate was that a protracted bombardment would achieve his object.

---

[21] Frederick Maurice, *Life of General Lord Rawlinson of Trent* (London: Cassell, 1928), pp. 157–8.

There were good reasons for thinking that it might not. Of the 1,500,000 shells being fired, about 1 million were shrapnel. It is hard to believe that this proportion had been chosen as appropriate to the task in hand. Rather, it reflected the limited quantities of high explosive that British industry was as yet capable of manufacturing. Shrapnel shells were of slight value against troops under cover and could not significantly damage earthworks. Their only function in an operation against entrenched troops was to cut up barbed wire. But that could be achieved only if they had been manufactured, and were fired, with a high degree of precision, and this was something of which neither British manufacturers nor British gunners were yet capable. A significant proportion of these shells (possibly a quarter or even a third) did not explode at all. A larger proportion, owing to the lack of skill among the artillerymen, detonated too soon or too late, leaving the barbed wire unharmed.

Plate 24   *A heavy howitzer in its gun pit on the Somme.*

To eliminate the German trench dwellers and collapse their dug-outs and knock out their machine-guns was the task of the high-explosive shells. Yet when one deducts the shrapnel from the total, the quantity of high explosive being employed does not seem over-large, and it was again effactually reduced by the high proportion of 'duds'. Yet this matter of quantity was of especial importance. For most British gunners had not reached the standard of expertise to pinpoint targets like machine-gun posts. They could hope to hit them only by blanketing fire. But the deficiency went further. The explosive charge in the shells was simply insufficient to penetrate to the German dug-outs. Consequently, the very most that the bombardment was likely to accomplish was to cave in the German trenches and close up, temporarily, the exits from the dug-outs. But for this to serve the purpose of the attackers, they would have to make a speedy crossing of No-Man's-Land. Yet Rawlinson had not planned for an advance at speed. And none was possible if the barbed wire remained in place.

During June evidence mounted that artillery preparations for the offensive were proving inadequate.[22] Certainly, reports were not uniformly pessimistic. From some sections to the south they were very hopeful. Yet observers in the more northern parts of the front line were aware that the barbed wire was but little damaged or, notwithstanding the supposedly annihilating bombardment, was being repaired during the night. Along the chain of command strong resistance existed to the reception of these more pessimistic reports: it was sometimes suggested that those delivering them were becoming 'windy'. Nevertheless, even at the higher level there was a recognition that all was not well. German prisoners examined in the first week of June revealed, according to the Fourth Army's Intelligence Summary, that they had never known a shell to penetrate into a dug-out. And as late as 29 June, the day on which – but for bad weather and misgivings about the success of the bombardment – the attack should have gone ahead, the Intelligence Summary recorded: 'The dug-outs are still good. The men appear to remain in these dug-outs all the time and are completely sheltered.' As for the enemy wire, there was uncomfortable evidence from at least three of the five corps under Rawlinson's command that the wire-cutting was not complete.

The British commanders remained, by and large, impervious to these warning signs. Haig, at the top of the command structure, wrote in his diary for 30 June 1916: 'The wire has never been so well cut, nor the Artillery preparation so thorough.' Yet he did enter one caveat. He entertained a doubt about VIII Corps, the northernmost of the five corps in Fourth Army, which 'has not carried out one successful raid'. Whether he appreciated that its raids had failed on account of uncut wire is not clear. As for Rawlinson, who had planned and was directing the operation, he too was full of confidence, although indicating rather more doubts. Reviewing the situation on the eve of the attack, he enumerated the number of men and guns that had been accumulated and the number of rounds fired; the high quality of his corps and divisional commanders; the condition of German prisoners, some of whom admitted that 'they have not had any food for 48 hours as no parties could get through our barrage to bring it up to [the] front trenches'; and the progress of the bombardment: 'The Arty work during the bombard[t] and the wire-cutting has been well done except in the VIII Corps which is somewhat behindhand.' Yet he recognized that there were shortages of heavy ammunition and heavy trench mortars (both vital for destroying enemy trenches). And he added this noteworthy qualification: 'I am not quite satisfied that all the wire has been thoroughly well cut and in places the front trench is not as much knocked about as I should like to see it in the photos. The bit in front of the 34 Div.[n] has been rather let off.'[23] Yet the offensive would go ahead as if all that was needful had been accomplished.

V

It is plain why, as the bombardment moved to its climax, the higher ranks failed to act on such unfavourable information as they received. Plans had been drawn up for launching an offensive on the presupposition that the bombardment would succeed. No provision had been made for its failure. Those plans must now be put into effect.

Certainly, Haig had laid it down that the artillery preparation should continue until the officers commanding the attacking units were satisfied that the obstacles had been destroyed. But there was no appreciation of the logic of this directive. It appeared to be

---

[22] See Robin Prior, *Churchill's 'World Crisis' as History* (London: Croom Helm, 1983), pp. 217–18.

[23] Rawlinson diary, in Churchill College, Cambridge, entry for 30 June 1916. All quotations hereafter are from this diary, not from the notebook diary of which a typewritten version is in the National Army Museum.

saying one of two things. If the attack were to take place on a predetermined date, it should do so only in those areas where the conditions for an advance had been satisfied. Or, alternatively, if the attack were to take place along the whole front, then the date would depend on the arrival of reports from all sectors that the conditions had been satisfied. Nothing about the conception of the Somme offensive allowed for such flexibility. When the day came to launch the offensive, it was simply assumed that the bombardment had succeeded and that such shortcomings as plainly existed would not prove significant.

The reason for this was that the British were committed to embark on a general advance at a particular time, give or take a couple of days. (The last-minute delay in the attack from 29 June to 1 July resulted in a slackening in the rate of artillery fire, which was unlikely to make good the deficiencies of the bombardment.) They were so committed in part because of the imperilled condition of their principal ally; but in much greater part because the British commander had decided on a particular sort of offensive. It would be a 'decisive' operation, and that could only mean a broad-front attack directed at a major objective. In the region of the Somme there was only one major objective offering: a breakthrough followed by exploitation.

So, although Haig might tell Robertson, for the benefit of Cabinet Ministers, that the sole object of the operation was 'relieving the pressure on Verdun',[24] a few days later he was urging Rawlinson to keep the cavalry close up in case enemy resistance broke and it proved possible to get through into open country. And on 28 June, almost on the eve of the attack, he was disputing hotly with Joffre and Foch about the direction in which his forces should go once they had reached Bapaume (9 miles behind the German lines and well beyond the third German defence system). Should they swing northwards to enhance the British position or turn south-east to enhance the French? Haig wrote in his diary: 'Foch seemed anxious that the British should do all the fighting required to get the French on to the open ground between Bapaume and Peronne, and he ignores the danger to our left flank which is very real if we do not enlarge the gap northwards as soon as possible.'

Within a matter of days, at unprecedented cost in British lives, it was plain that such argumentation had been without purpose. Objectives like Bapaume and Peronne, and concepts like 'enlarg[ing] the gap northwards as soon as possible', belonged in the realm of strategic Cloud-Cuckoo-Land.

---

[24] Prior, *Churchill's 'World Crisis' as History*, p. 216.

29

FIRST DAY

God, God, where's the rest of the boys?
Lieutenant in the 4th Tyneside Scottish on 1 July 1916, having reached the German front line with only
two other men

But the German dug-outs! My word, they were things of beauty, art, and safety.
Letter from a serving soldier in The Times, *8 August 1916*

I

For the British the first day of the Somme offensive was a calamity. On the greater part of the front attacked no advance was registered. Such territory as was gained did not lie in the area where progress was most needed. And the level of casualties suffered would scarcely have been warranted by an advance of real significance.

It is possible to describe the events of the day in a few brief sentences because in terms of ground changing hands there is so little to describe. What cannot be conveyed is the swift death or long agony sustained on a vast scale by men who had joined the army in the early enthusiasm of recruiting, had trained with inadequate resources under barely adequate instructors, and had approached – with mingled hope, enthusiasm, misgiving, dedication – this moment of high endeavour. For many it was a short moment indeed. Of the 60,000 men who went over the top in the first waves, half had become casualties within 30 minutes. Of the 120,000 who attacked altogether during the day, casualties were again almost 50 per cent.

The cause of this calamity is not far to seek. The German dug-outs had not collapsed under the weight of the British bombardment. At one point where the British did overrun the German front line that day, they found the electric light in a dug-out still burning. And a soldier whose job it was, following the capture of Contalmaison nine days later, to clear out the dug-outs recalled: 'In the whole course of clearing I did not come across a single dug-out which had been broken into from the roof by our artillery fire. Several of them had had the doorways smashed in by our fire, but never a shell had gone through a roof.'[1] Consequently on 1 July the German occupants of their front lines were not dead or entombed or wanting in serviceable weapons. As the British infantry went over the top near Gommecourt, a German bugle could be heard summoning the defenders from their dug-outs.

So, as the attackers advanced deliberately across No-Man's-Land, they were met by a pitiless stream of rifle and machine-gun fire. Nor had the German artillery been

---

[1] Private G. M. Sturgess in *I Was There!*, issue no. 18. (*I Was There!* is an anthology of participants' accounts of the Great War, edited by Sir John Hammerton and published in 51 weekly parts during 1938–9.)

Plate 25   *The entrance to one of the elaborate German dug-outs.*

suppressed. This had already become apparent during the forming-up period for the attack, as high explosive and shrapnel began bursting upon the crowded British trenches. Now, with the attack under way, an artillery barrage descended like a curtain upon No-Man's-Land, thinning out each wave of attackers. Those British infantrymen who managed to pass through it found, not on all but on too many parts of the front, that the German wire was intact or had been severed in only a few places, which immediately became death traps. In face of such obstacles the slow-moving, heavily burdened, regularly spaced-out British infantry was bound to sustain prohibitive losses.

On the left wing – that is, the northern one-third of the front under attack – no progress was made, and the German lines were scarcely ever entered. The attack was wiped out in No-Man's-Land. (It was at one part of this sector, as we shall see, that Private Surfleet waited most of the day to go over the top in support of the early waves, until at last the attack was cancelled.) In the centre of the offensive, where most of the cavalry awaited their opportunity, small groups of British forces did manage to penetrate the German front line. Sometimes they pressed beyond. But behind them enemy fire continued to dominate No-Man's-Land. The telephone lines they had brought across, like the runners they sent back, too often did not survive. Hence knowledge of success and failure was denied those seeking to direct operations. And when fresh infantry and fresh supplies, especially of the hand grenades that dominated trench fighting, were sent forward, most never got through. Denied these supports, the men who had entered German positions gradually succumbed to the enemy or expended all their munitions. The story of the Ulster division, which managed to occupy the powerfully defended Schwaben Redoubt, is a saga of unrelieved heroism. Yet by the end of the day, with casualties mounting, bombs gone, and counter-attacks growing in effectiveness, they had been driven from the redoubt and left holding only a small section of the German front line.

Only on the British right, and on the French sector of attack still further to the right, was there anything to show in terms of captured territory; and, because of the correspondingly shorter time spent in No-Man's-Land, a much reduced level of casualties. The British here were, in fact, much aided by the success of the French: a success attributable first to surprise, in that the Germans did not think the French capable of making an effort on the Somme given their sufferings at Verdun; secondly to the much greater weight of the French bombardment, which in proportion to the area covered was four times as heavy as the British (along with the greater skill with which it was fired); and thirdly to the superiority of French infantry tactics, which included the use of lightly loaded bombing parties that rushed into the German trenches in the immediate aftermath of the bombardment. (It was noticeable that the British infantry on the right made some approach to the rushing tactics employed by the French instead of the regular, unconcealed advance enjoined by the British command.)

The sum total of territory gained by the British was a stretch of 3 miles on their right to a depth of 1 mile. This left them in possession of only three of those 13 villages integrated into the German line that it had been intended to take. It nowhere brought them on to the German second line of defence or gave them any of the raised ground overlooking their centre. And it certainly did not hold out to Rawlinson any prospect of a breakthrough. At 12.15 that afternoon he concluded: 'There is, of course, no hope of getting the cavalry through today.' Rawlinson, indeed, with his plans gone so desperately awry, seemed unable to grasp such limited opportunities as the fighting did offer. He refused permission during the day for the forces on the right to go beyond their first day's objectives despite the tempting open spaces that lay beyond them. And the next day, when Haig questioned him about advancing on his right instead of his left, Rawlinson 'did not seem to favour the scheme'.[2]

The cost to the British for so small a gain had been atrocious: 57,000 casualties, of whom more than one-third were dead. German losses were a relatively trivial 8,000. Haig, presented next day with an approximation of these figures – estimated casualties of 'over 40,000 to date' – consoled himself with the reflection: 'This cannot be considered severe in view of the numbers engaged, and the length of front attacked.'[3] At first sight the obtuseness of this remark is astonishing. If the loss, for so little apparent gain, of over one-third (actually it was more like a half) of his attacking force was not to be considered 'severe', what level of casualties would Haig deem excessive? But that may be unjust. Presumably the commander of so badly failed an operation had to grasp at such straws of comfort as he could find. More important than his facile reflections on what had already happened were the decisions he would now take on what to do next.

II

In the story of the misfortunes of the British army that attacked on the Somme on 1 July 1916, a particular place belongs to the wounded. Certainly, the nature of wounds was not more grievous than during other episodes of action. But because the attack failed so heavily, leaving No-Man's-Land still outside British control, many of the wounded there could not speedily be rescued. And the scale of wounding was so great that, at the casualty clearing stations behind the lines, the process of evacuating seriously injured men to the base hospitals went awry. Many of them, suffering deeply, were left lying for hours in the blazing sun because the casualty stations were overflowing and the ambulance trains which were supposed to collect them did not appear.

The severely wounded man in this, as in any, action constituted an anomaly. Unlike the dead, he could not be disregarded or used for cover if in No-Man's-Land, or roughly ejected if in his own or a captured trench. Unlike the walking wounded, he could not take himself to the rear, content that he had done his duty and free from fear of reprisals by the authorities. He had some sort of claim on the attention of his compatriots; yet, unless they were stretcher-bearers or medical officers, it was not their business to render aid, and the operation would have come to an even earlier halt had many tried to do so. This meant that most of the helpless injured in No-Man's-Land would have to wait long for succour. In addition to pain, they would often be subject to intense heat, thirst, fear, and constant sniping. Many stretcher-bearers themselves became casualties, while those who did not must eventually give way to exhaustion after aiding a relatively small number – for it could take two stretcher-bearers over an hour to carry one wounded man to a dressing station.

Even those wounded in their own trenches or able to return so far were often in sorry state, owing to their sheer numbers, the constant German shelling, and the coming and going of masses of troops who often had no alternative but to trample on them. On the front of VIII Corps, where the attack had been totally repulsed, it was later recorded: 'Our original front and support lines were full of wounded men from all

---

[2] Duff Cooper, *Haig* (London: Faber & Faber, 1935), vol. 1, p. 334 (quoting Haig's diary for 2 July 1916).
[3] Robert Blake (ed.), *The Private Papers of Douglas Haig 1914–1919* (London: Eyre & Spottiswoode, 1952), p. 154.

the various units and it took three days to clear them. Heavy rain came on 2 July and made the trenches impossible, and many wounded were actually drowned.'[4]

R. H. Tawney, who went over the top with the first waves on 1 July 1916, experienced the plight of the wounded in No-Man's-Land as both object and subject.[5] A Workers' Educational Association lecturer at the outbreak of war and a man of left-wing and Christian convictions, he had enlisted in November 1914. This was not because he felt identity with the British social structure but because he saw in Prussianism a state of mind and attitude to human affairs against which all his endeavours were directed. Enlisting as a private, he had soon been offered a commission but had refused, feeling that the proposal was based not on his merits but on his educational background (namely Rugby and Oxford). Nevertheless, his qualities as a leader of men had quickly asserted themselves, and by mid-1915 he had been promoted to full sergeant.

The Somme battle found Tawney serving with the 22nd Manchester Rifles. This was one of the 'Pals' battalions, whose rank and file consisted largely of men drawn from the same geographical area and possessing the same social status, customs, and manners of speech. (Such an arrangement served to soften the transition from civilian to army life and helped to cohere the elements in Kitchener's army. But it was to give terrible geographical concentration to the lists of dead and wounded.) The 22nd Manchester Rifles were part of the 7th division, which attacked between Fricourt and Mametz. Here good progress was made.

At 7.30 a.m. on 1 July Tawney and his men went over the top, formed up in front of their wire, and began to advance:

> not doubling, but at a walk. For we had 900 yards of rough ground to the trench which was our first objective, and about 1,500 yards to a further trench where we were to wait for orders.

He found to his surprise that he had no fear of becoming a casualty:

> I hadn't gone ten yards before I felt a load fall from me . . . . I had been worried by the thought: 'Suppose one should lose one's head and get other men cut up! Suppose one's legs should take fright and refuse to move!' Now I knew it was all right. I shouldn't be frightened and I shouldn't lose my head. . . . I knew that I was in no danger. I knew I shouldn't be hurt; knew it positively, much more positively than most things I'm paid for knowing. I understood in a small way what St. Just meant when he told the soldiers who protested at his rashness that no bullet could touch the emissary of the Republic.

For the moment, his conviction proved justified. The Manchester men crossed three lines that had once been German trenches and reached a fourth. 'If it's all like this, it's a cake walk,' said a little man beside Tawney.

Nevertheless, it was here that Tawney had his first encounter with the problem of the casualty – as object:

> On the parados lay a wounded man of another battalion, shot, to judge by the blood on his clothes, through the loins or stomach. I went to him and he grunted, as if to say, 'I am in horrible pain, you must do something for me; you must do something for me.' I hate touching wounded men – moral cowardice, I suppose. One hurts them so much and there's so little to be done. I tried, without much success, to ease his equipment, and then thought of getting him into the trench. But it was crowded with men and there was no place to put him. So I left him. He grunted again angrily and looked at me with hatred as

---

[4] Martin Middlebrook, *The First Day on the Somme* (London: Allen Lane, 1971), p. 248.

[5] His famous account of his experiences on 1 July 1916 was first published, anonymously, in the *Westminster Gazette*, 24–5 October 1916. It is reprinted in Guy Chapman (ed.), *Vain Glory* (London: Cassell, 1968), pp. 319–25.

well as pain in his eyes. It was horrible. It was as though he cursed me for being alive and strong when he was in torture. I tried to forget him by taking a spade from one of the men and working fiercely on the parapet.

The advance was resumed, but they had fallen behind the British barrage, and this time it was no cakewalk. Topping a little rise, they walked straight into a zone of machine-gun fire.

The whole line dropped like one man, some dead and wounded, the rest taking instinctively to such cover as the ground offered.

One hundred and fifty yards away the Germans could be seen plainly, for instead of firing from the shelter of their trench they were kneeling, or even standing, on the top of their parapet. The 'palaeolithic savage' rose in Tawney. He confesses that from the age of catapaults to that of shotguns he had always enjoyed aiming at anything that moved, 'though since manhood the pleasure has been sneaking and shamefaced'.

Now it was a duty to shoot, and there was a splendid target . . . . One couldn't miss them. Every man I fired at dropped except one. Him, the boldest of the lot, I missed repeatedly. I was puzzled and angry . . . . Not that I wanted to hurt him or anyone else. It was missing I hated. That's the beastliest thing in war, the damnable frivolity. One's like a merry mischievous ape tearing up the image of God.

When the remaining Germans dropped back in their trenches, Tawney looked around. On every side were the dead and dying. 'D'you think there's any chance for us, sergeant?' a man whispered to him, and Tawney assured him that it would be all right, that reinforcements would be coming in an hour. 'All the same it looked as if they wouldn't find much except corpses.' He set about crawling along the line to rally the living and establish contact with the company that should have been on their left, imagining that between them they could organize a rush on the German trench. His sense of personal immunity remained.

One couldn't believe that the air a few feet above one's head was deadly. The weather was so fine and bright that the idea of death, if it had occurred to me, which it didn't, would have seemed absurd.

This delusion was to bring Tawney once more into intimate contact with the problem of the casualty – this time as subject:

Then I saw a lot of men lying down away to the right and waved to them 'Reinforce.' When they didn't move, I knelt up and waved again.
    I don't know what most men feel like when they're wounded. What I felt was that I had been hit by a tremendous iron hammer and then twisted with a sickening sort of wrench so that my back banged on the ground, and my feet struggled as though they didn't belong to me. For a second or two my breath wouldn't come. I thought, 'This is death,' and hoped it wouldn't take long.

Gradually it dawned on him that death was not yet his lot. He tried to turn on his side, 'but the pain stopped me dead'. He was now craving the sort of comfort that he had been unable to give the wounded soldier earlier.

After a few minutes two men in my platoon crawled past at a few yards distance. They saw me and seemed to be laughing, but they didn't stop. Probably they were wounded. I could have cried at their being so cruel. It's being cut off from human beings that's as bad as anything when one's wounded, and when a lad wriggled up to me and asked what was up, I loved him. I said, 'Not dying, I think, but pretty bad,' and he wriggled on. What else could he do?

Tawney tried raising his knees to ease the pain in his stomach, whereupon bullets came over, so he put them down.

> Not that I much minded dying now. By a merciful arrangement when one's half dead, the extra plunge doesn't seem very terrible.

So, though reason told him to keep his legs straight, the pain in his stomach made him raise them again. He did not even mind when German heavy guns started shelling the trench 80 to 100 yards behind him.

> Then there was a thump, and I was covered with earth. After about the thirteenth thump, something hit me in the stomach and took my wind. I thought, 'Thank Heaven, it's over this time,' but it was only an extra heavy sod of earth. So the waiting began again.

It was very hot, and reluctantly he drank the last of his water bottle. Longing for the evening, he kept looking at the sun from under his tin helmet, but it seemed stationary above him 'as though performing a miracle for my special discomfort'. He began shouting feebly for stretcher-bearers, ignoring the fact that any man who tried to aid him would be committing suicide. And he yearned to lose consciousness but could not.

Eventually he must have fainted or fallen asleep, for he awoke to a 'lovely evening' to find a man standing beside him: 'I caught him by the ankle in terror lest he should vanish.' The man, a Royal Army Medical Corps (RAMC) corporal, summoned a doctor. After looking at him they went off to attend to someone else, promising to return shortly.

> That was the worst moment I had. I thought they were deceiving me – that they were leaving me for good. I did so want to be spoken kindly to, and I began to whimper, partly to myself, partly aloud.

But the doctor returned, and the moment he spoke to his orderly

> I knew he was one of the best men I had ever met. He can't have been more than twenty-six or twenty-seven, but his face seemed to shine with love and comprehension.

The doctor listened 'like an angel' while Tawney told him a 'nonsensical yarn' about being hit in the back by the nose cap of a shell, and then explained that in fact he had been shot by a rifle bullet through the chest and abdomen. A stiff bandage was applied, and morphia administered.

> There were no stretchers available, so it was out of the question to get me in that night. But after I had felt that divine compassion flow over me, I didn't care.

Tawney was lucky in the sector of the front on which he was serving. While he lay wounded the attack was proceeding, driving the Germans out of Mametz, obliging them to retire during the night from Fricourt. Hence it was possible for RAMC personnel to seek out the wounded on the battlefield. On the northern two-thirds of the front, where the Germans had hardly been forced back at all, much of the old No-Man's-Land was No-Man's-Land still and remained under German fire – for informal truces to aid the wounded were rare. So only in the few hours of darkness was it even relatively safe to seek out the wounded, and the chances of discovering them were correspondingly less.

The record for survival in such circumstances, 14 days, lies (so far as is known) with Private A. Matthews.[6] He was a member of the 56th (London) division, which attacked at Gommecourt, a diversionary operation at the very north of the offensive. Initially the

---

[6] Matthews's account of his experiences is reprinted (from the *London Scottish Regimental Gazette*) in *I Was There!*, issue no. 17.

Londoners broke into the German lines, but no supports could reach them, and by the end of the day they had been driven back to their starting point.

In the course of the early advance Matthews was sent back with a party of captured Germans. In No-Man's-Land he was hit in the thigh by a bullet and suffered a compound fracture, which rendered him immobile. He was dragged into a disused trench by an officer and given a drink of water, and later in the day he received another drink from a runner. For the rest he was left quite alone, while shells burst around him. During the night he shouted for help but to no avail. During daylight on 2 July, still under bombardment, he smoked up his supply of cigarettes. The following day he finished up his iron ration of bully beef and hard biscuits. It was on the fourth night, as far as he could later recollect, that a party of men approached and, in response to his shouts, stumbled into his ditch. All of them, like himself, had been wounded on 1 July. They had been living off the iron rations of the dead, of which there was no shortage, and they provided Matthews with a supply. Then they set off in search of their lines, promising to send him aid. Some hours later they were back, having failed in their quest, so they set off in another direction. The next night footsteps again approached, but it was the same group of men, bringing him more supplies but still lost and in a deteriorating condition; one of them was 'actually crawling on his hands and knees'. They set off once more and vanished for good.

Matthews woke the next morning to find that a shell had blown part of the trench on top of him, burying his biscuits and puncturing his water can. For two days he was without any sustenance, then rain brought some relief. Days passed.

> At times I must have lapsed into unconsciousness, for I had very clear visions of some of my own pals finding me and carrying me off on a stretcher to safety. Several times this happened, and when I recovered my senses and found I was still lying in the trench I nearly went mad with frenzy . . . .
> Then I began to feel that I was dying, and would read again and again letters I had received from dear friends at home, whom it seemed destined I was never to see again. I had lost all count of time, when in the darkness I was awakened by the shuffle of feet, and I managed to call out. Somebody came towards me, nearly treading on me, and it proved to be an officer on patrol with a party of NCO's of the London Scottish.

The officer, on learning the situation, secured a group of men with a stretcher and a shovel who dug Matthews out ('it proved very painful') and took him on the 'perilous journey' across No-Man's-Land. His wound proved in a bad state but, 'wonderful to relate, not septic'. It took a year to heal.

The victims of wounding whose experiences are known at first hand always, in the nature of things, survived. Those who bled to death, or died of pain and shock, or lingered like Matthews but for whom help never came, or possibly ended their agony by means of a self-inflicted wound that permanently removed them from the battlefield, did not leave records. Perhaps the helpless man whom Tawney encountered, shot through the loins or the stomach and looking 'with hatred as well as pain' when he was abandoned, will serve to suggest the grim fate which so many encountered.

30

CONTINUATION

I had tea at the headquarters of the Fourth Army with Sir Henry Rawlinson, a very agreeable man, in a charming park and chateau. There is a general hopefulness – he and the Commander-in-Chief both seeming to believe that the Germans are now getting to their last legs, with few reserves, and doubting – even their officer prisoners – whether they can escape defeat.

Lord Bryce in a letter from General Headquarters, France, 29 July 1916

I

Gradually the truth dawned on the British command that their hammer blows of 1 July had failed. That meant that they must start afresh. For there could be no stopping here. The needs of their allies, the need to preserve Britain's credibility as a military power, the need of British commanders to justify retention of their jobs, the need to employ the vast army that had been assembled, not to mention the need to end the war by the only means that was generally acceptable – victory: all determined that the struggle would go on. The first of July was, ultimately, just another day (if not one of the good days) in this long conflict.

The only question facing the command was where to resume the Somme offensive. There could be no question of another thrust along the whole front. And Haig had no intention of trying again on its more northern part. So the choice lay between the centre, where the most important objectives lay, and the right, where progress had been made. Rawlinson opted for the centre. So did Joffre, who during an astonishing display before Haig on 3 July (so the British commander recorded in his diary) positively '*ordered* me to attack Thiepval and Pozières'. Haig, rendered determined by failure, overrode Rawlinson and told Joffre that he, not the Frenchman, was in command of the British army and would decide on modifications to the Allied plan 'to suit the changing situation'. The attack would be directed towards the village of Longueval. This lay well along the eastern part of that ridge of raised ground that was now becoming – irrespective of the design of commanders – less the first objective of the battle of the Somme than its *raison d'être*.

On both sides of the front a process of replacement and reconstitution was occurring – as would be the case continually during the campaign. The Germans had suffered heavily under the preliminary bombardment, and on 1 July had lost parts of their front defensive system, particularly to the French. They hastened to bring in from other regions (including Verdun) fresh infantry divisions, replacements for smashed-up artillery, and new machine-gun companies. They also brought in enough squadrons of aeroplanes, if not to secure air superiority, then to give them some power of overseeing British rear positions.

Plate 26   *British officers taking observations from what was once a German front-line trench.*

The British also were taking out worn divisions and bringing in fresh, as they had always intended to do – although the new forces would not be employed where originally planned. In one arm, however, there was not much replacement: among the heavy artillery. The gunners, though exhausted, had sustained relatively few casualties in the preliminary bombardment. They had gained much experience. This was now turned to advantage. With the aid of aerial observation they bombarded areas where German counter-attacks were forming up. And in support of British attacks they were developing the enormously valuable – but, in less than skilful hands, highly dangerous – techniques of the creeping bombardment.

On 14 July the British launched their second substantial blow of the Somme campaign, preceded by some days of protracted pushing forward into areas that had lain invitingly empty on the afternoon of 1 July. The second stroke was a decidedly more modest undertaking than the first. The attacking force consisted of 22,000 men, and their objective was Longueval Ridge. But if more modest in scope, it was also more imaginative in conception. Perhaps because it came nearer the idea of 'bite and hold', it showed the Fourth Army commander at his best. For if Haig had determined the area of attack, it was Rawlinson who decided on its nature. This time he intended to go for surprise. After a deceptively short bombardment the attack would take place in the early dawn. Neither the French nor the British Commander-in-Chief was disposed to agree. The French staff considered it an attack organized 'for amateurs by amateurs' and refused to participate (except by providing some useful artillery fire from the flank). Haig informed Rawlinson that the plan was unsound and 'declined to discuss the matter further'.[1] Rawlinson managed to bring his chief to further discussions and, after some face-saving but unimportant concessions, won him round.

The attack was preceded by thorough use of aerial photography to secure intimate knowledge of the layout of the German trenches. The final bombardment was of only five minutes' duration (artillery ammunition was anyway running low at this stage) and employed no shrapnel, allowing the infantry to get perilously close to their own gunfire.

---

[1] John Terraine, *Douglas Haig: The Educated Soldier* (London: Hutchinson, 1963), p. 211.

The idea of a night attack was sufficiently unusual that, at least on the first occasion, it stood a good chance of catching the enemy napping. Nevertheless, it was a hazardous undertaking. Forming up even experienced troops in No-Man's-Land in the dark would be risky, and most of these forces were far from experienced. In the main they were New Army soldiers served by New Army staffs.

On the day fortune favoured the attackers. Assembling along prearranged tapes at 3 a.m., they remained undiscovered. For half an hour they waited anxiously. ('All the time I was saying to myself "You're there. You're there, boy. Right in the middle of No Man's Land and no one else can see you, no one's firing."')[2] By the time their waiting was over they were standing in bright moonlight with only patches of mist. This meant that the danger of losing their way while advancing was minimized, yet on account of the earliness of the hour the enemy remained unsuspecting. The brief, whirlwind bombardment drove the defenders underground, and most of them were still there when the first British rush entered their trenches. By 10 a.m. Rawlinson's forces had taken 6,000 yards of what, on 1 July, had been the second German lines.

This success opened up distinct possibilities just beyond Longueval. High Wood – which, as its name suggests, was of particular importance in this raised sector (and which would soon occupy a special place in the Somme campaign's demonology) – was deserted. Repeated messages from Royal Flying Corps (RFC) pilots announced this. Yet for several reasons, among them a predisposition to wait for the cavalry – which had to come forward 12 miles over difficult territory and so had no chance of an early arrival – the corps commanders allowed the opportunity to go begging. By late afternoon, when a forward move was at last organized, German resistance was hardening.

Nevertheless, the early-morning success contributed significantly to French celebrations of Bastille Day.

II

In the following days there was less to celebrate. The problem awaiting any limited-sector attack was that it soon attracted all the enemy's reserves. What this meant became terribly apparent next day when, belatedly, the British sought to overrun High Wood.

Graham Seton Hutchison commanded a company of machine-gunners who participated in this attack on the morning of 15 July.[3] He relates:

> The objective was firstly High Wood and Martinpuich [village], and thence an unlimited field of advance through the city of Bapaume.

Late in the afternoon of the 14th he had talked with a major of Indian Horse and learned that

> the Cavalry were concentrating in Caterpillar Valley and would break through, so soon as High Wood was captured, and this, the last line of German defence, had been pierced.

On the morning of the 15th, under cover of a thick mist, the assaulting brigade formed up in a valley 800 yards west of High Wood. All was silent.

> Men spoke in whispers. Their faces were pallid, dirty, and unshaven, many with eyes ringed with fatigue after the night, hot and foetid, gaseous and disturbed by shell-fire, in Bazentin. Few there were whose demeanour expressed eagerness for the assault. They

---

[2] Quoted in A. H. Farrar-Hockley, *The Somme* (London: Pan Books, 1966), p. 187.
[3] Lt.-Col. Graham Seton Hutchison, *Warrior* (London: Hutchinson, 1932), pp. 126–32.

were moving into position with good discipline, yet listless, as if facing an inevitable. Their identity as individuals seemed to be swallowed up in the immensity of war: devitalized electrons.

As 9.30, zero hour, approached the sun burst through the last remnants of the disappearing mist:

> all the landscape, hitherto opaque and flat, assumed its stereoscopic vivid form. The wood seemed quite near, just above us up the hill-side . . . . The village of Martinpuich, jagged ruins and rafters all askew, broken walls and shattered fruit trees, looked down. Both trees and village appeared Gargantuan, and the men waiting to attack like midgets from Lilliput.

Directly in front of Seton Hutchison the attack was led off by a company of Glasgow Highlanders.

> I raised my head as the Highlanders rose to their feet, bayonets gleaming in the morning sun. My eyes swept the valley – long lines of men, officers at their head in the half-crouching attitude which modern tactics dictate, resembling suppliants rather than the vanguard of a great offensive, were moving forward over three miles of front. As the attackers rose, white bursts of shrapnel appeared among the trees and thinly across the ridge towards Martinpuich.
>
> For a moment the scene remained as if an Aldershot manoeuvre. Two, three, possibly four seconds later an inferno of rifle and machine-gun fire broke from the edge of High Wood, from high up in its trees, and from all along the ridge to the village. The line staggered. Men fell forward limply and quietly. The hiss and crack of bullets filled the air and skimmed the long grasses. The Highlanders and Riflemen [troops of the 16th King's Royal Rifles] increased their pace to a jog-trot. Those in reserve clove to the ground more closely.

Across the valley to his left Hutchison could see attacking infantry passing up the slope to Martinpuich, then being halted by a low wire entanglement.

> Some two hundred men, their Commander at their head, had been brought to a standstill at this point. A scythe seemed to cut their feet from under them, and the line crumpled and fell, stricken by machine-gun fire. Those in support wavered, then turned to fly. There was no shred of cover and they fell in their tracks as rabbits fall at a shooting battue.

The attack had been brutally stopped in the 800 yards between the start line and High Wood, and throughout the morning it remained there. The chance of the cavalry had not come. Some of the cavalrymen came, nevertheless. Hutchison, at the time pinned down in No-Man's-Land, recounts:

> Towards noon, as my eyes searched the valley for reinforcements or for some other sign of action by those directing the battle, I descried a squadron of Indian Cavalry, dark faces under glistening helmets, galloping across the valley towards the slope. No troops could have presented a more inspiring sight than these natives of India with lance and sword, tearing in mad cavalcade on to the skyline. A few disappeared over it: they never came back. The remainder became the target of every gun and rifle. Turning their horses' heads, with shrill cries, these masters of horsemanship galloped through a hell of fire, lifting their mounts lightly over yawning shell-holes; turning and twisting through the barrage of great shells: the ranks thinned, not a man escaped.

A similar fearful experience was being undergone in nearby Delville Wood, on the north-east corner of Longueval, by the South Africans – one of those 'colonial' forces whose contribution to the ensuing phases of the Somme campaign would become legendary. Hard on the heels of the success of 14 July, the South Africans were sent in to take Delville Wood. By the time they were withdrawn six days later, having occupied most of the wood and then been driven out by ferocious counter-attacks, their numbers had been reduced from 3,000 to 800.

Soon after that came the turn of the Australians. First they were engaged in fighting far to the north of the Somme campaign; then at its very centre.

In the last fortnight of July the British commanders, conscious that limited advances like that of 14 July attracted a disproportionate weight of resistance and counter-attack, sought to activate a large sector of the British front. Doubtless this was also intended to test their conviction that the Germans 'are now getting to their last legs'. The first consequence was an attack in Flanders near Aubers Ridge. The operation was conducted with 'chilling ineptitude' (Farrar-Hockley) and was so barren of results that it had to be written off in official communiqués as 'some important raids'. (It has been claimed that the Australians, having participated, never again trusted British head-quarters communiqués.) The second consequence was the renewal, in the Somme region itself, of attacks in parts of the centre as well as the right of the original offensive. (These were by way of piecemeal operations rather than a grand advance.) The attacks on the right, towards High Wood and Guillemont, failed. The attack in the centre, by Australians and English Territorials, did not. On 23 July Pozières fell.

An Australian private wrote of that day:

> the shellfire was now hellish & the noise deafening, but just to show you how cool the boys were, why, some of them were walking up with rifle's at the slope & singing 'I want to go home'.[4]

Then for two days they endured counter-attacks; and, for six weeks after that, so murderous a bombardment that Birdwood, the Australian commander, was moved to write on 9 August:

> it seems almost impossible that a mouse should be able to live through it.

A sergeant wrote in his diary for 25 July:

> Heavy firing all morning – simply murder. Men falling everywhere . . . . 23 men smother-ed in one trench. Dead and dying everywhere. Some simply blown to pieces. Shells falling like hail during a storm. Five left in trench.

Another, five days later, yearned for the arrival of the relief, which was overdue. When the barrage lifted and it arrived,

> half dazed, we climb from the trenches and make a wild rush to get away while we have the chance.

A veteran of Gallipoli wrote in his diary for 24 July:

> All day long the ground rocked & swayed backwards & forwards from the concussion. . . . men were driven stark staring mad & more than one of them rushed out of the trench over towards the Germans. [A]ny amount of them could be seen crying & sobbing like children their nerves completely gone. . . . we were nearly all in a state of silliness & half dazed but still the Australians refused to give ground. [M]en were buried by the dozen, but were frantically dug out again some dead and some alive.

But, at whatever cost, Pozières – recognized as one of the vital points on the crest – remained in British hands.

III

As long as a suitably modest view was taken of what the Somme offensive was supposed to be about, the situation on the last day of July looked decidedly better than on the

---

[4] Quotations in this paragraph are from Bill Gammage, *The Broken Years* (Ringwood, Victoria: Penguin Books Australia, 1975), pp. 163–6. Gammage has retained the spelling and punctuation employed in the original documents, without the use of 'sic'.

first. Bit by bit British forces were clawing their way up and along the ridge that had overlooked their earlier preparations. And every advance attracted furious counter-attacks that, for limited or no success, cost the Germans dear. Gradually the toll of casualties for the two sides, so unfavourable to the British at the outset, was becoming more equal. Whether any of this indicated that enemy morale was not only declining but doing so at a faster rate than that of the British, and was proving less able to recover, was another matter. But it is unlikely that those on the British staff who perceived a serious decline in German morale were making similar assessments regarding their own side.

There were those, however, who were asking awkward questions – and about the campaign as a whole. In London some members of the Government remembered that large things had been promised of the Somme campaign, without they themselves having necessarily believed the promises. At the end of July Robertson wrote Haig a warning letter.[5] 'The Powers that be are beginning to get a little uneasy.... The casualties are mounting up and they were wondering whether we are likely to get a proper return for them.' Robertson was trying to meet this by referring to the effects of the campaign on Britain's allies. But he was obviously in a difficulty when pressed to say 'whether *I* think a loss of say 300,000 men will lead to really great results, because if not we ought to be content with something less than what we are now doing'. The critics of the campaign were arguing that 'the primary object – relief of pressure on Verdun – has to some extent been achieved'; that the British had as yet insufficient big guns; and that it was not clear which side was sustaining the heavier casualties. He urged Haig to let him know his views, about which Robertson was in the dark. He also warned that if matters continued as in the last fortnight, Haig might be asked to appear before the War Committee.

Haig, doubtless convinced that he had concerns enough, and not appreciating the mounting pressures upon the Government (and so upon Robertson as intermediary between Government and army), wrote unfeelingly on this missive: 'Not exactly the letter of a C.I.G.S. He ought to take responsibility also. I have no intention of going before the War Committee while this battle is going on.' But he did pen a long appreciation of the situation for Robertson and the Government. What had been accomplished, in his view, was as follows: the relief of Verdun; the retention on the Western Front of German divisions that otherwise could have prevented the recent successes of the Russians over Austria-Hungary; a demonstration to the world that the Allies could make and maintain a vigorous offensive and drive the enemy's 'best troops from the strongest positions'; and the infliction of 'very heavy losses' on the enemy, so that in 'another 6 weeks, the enemy should be hard put to it to find men'. (Haig rather detracted from this last point by saying, a few sentences later, that they could not bank on German resistance being completely broken 'without another campaign next year'.) He also argued that British losses so far – 'about 120,000 more than they would have been had we not attacked' – did not impair 'our ability to continue the offensive'. The conclusion of all this was entirely predictable. 'Principle on which we should act. *Maintain our offensive.*'

It is hard to see how this could have satisfied Haig's critics. They had already made the point that Verdun had been relieved. They were concerned about how limited was the advance against the enemy's 'strongest positions'. They wanted to know how the balance of 'very heavy losses' was working out between the two sides. And before long they would know that the Germans were transferring divisions to the Eastern Front. Haig nevertheless carried the day. His appreciation of the situation, Robertson

---

[5] See Farrar-Hockley, *The Somme*, pp. 204–7.

reported, pleased the War Committee 'very much indeed'. On 5 August they sent him a message 'assuring him that he might count on full support from home'.[6]

Haig's strength lay less in the power of his own arguments than in the weakness of his critics' position. If they thought that the British 'ought to be content with something less than what we are now doing', how much less were they proposing? Whether Britain's allies were doing well or ill – and Verdun could be threatened by a renewed attack at any time, just because the defenders had been forced so far back – it was unlikely that the French and Russians would continue fighting devotedly if the British opted for quiescence. And it was difficult to envisage an operation by the British of any significance that would be much smaller than what Haig now seemed to be proposing – in effect, a series of hammer blows against selected targets. The key to all this lay in the fact that no voice was as yet being heard in governing circles challenging the view that, in some form or other, the British must (in Haig's words) *'Maintain our offensive.'*

---

[6] Robert Blake (ed.), *The Private Papers of Douglas Haig 1914–1919* (London: Eyre & Spottiswoode, 1952), pp. 158–9.

31

MOTOR-MONSTER

Never mind the heat.
Never mind the noise.
Never mind the dust.
Think of your pals in the infantry.
Thank God you are bullet-proof and can help the infantry, who are not.

Tips to tank crews, mid-1916

I managed to get astride one of the German trenches . . . and opened fire with the Hotchkiss machine-guns. There were some Germans in the dug-outs and I shall never forget the look on their faces when they emerged . . . .

Captain H. W. Mortimore, commander of the first tank to go into battle on 15 September 1916

I

Throughout August and early September the grim process continued on the Somme of piecemeal advances along that blood-drenched crest of ground that had once enabled the Germans to overlook the British positions and might one day enable the British to overlook theirs. The following quotation provides what for both sides was the rationale of these endeavours. It comes from a German directive, late in the Somme campaign, ordering one of a series of 11 counter-attacks in 20 days against a single point on the upland.

> Men are to be informed by their immediate superiors that this attack is not merely a matter of retaking a trench because it was formerly in German possession, but that the recapture of an extremely important point is involved. If the enemy remains on the ridge he can blow our artillery in the Ancre valley to pieces, and the protection of the infantry will then be destroyed.[1]

Bit by bit, objectives fell to the British. Guillemont succumbed between 18 August and 4 September, and on 9 September, when Ginchy was occupied, the Germans at last relinquished their hold on Delville Wood, where the South Africans had striven a month and a half earlier. But the British task was far from accomplished. Thiepval on the left of the crest, High Wood in the centre, and other points on the right, all remained in German hands. And summer was giving way to autumn, and rain was beginning to fall. As Haig, exhorting Rawlinson to 'bold action', observed ominously on 10 September: 'the season for fighting is nearly over.'[2] (Whether he recalled this point in the following months is another matter.) So if the British commander was still dreaming of piercing the enemy lines and making an advance that would be visible on a map, he would need to act soon.

---

[1] Quoted in Douglas Wilson Johnson, *Battlefields of the World War* (New York: Oxford University Press, 1921), p. 153.
[2] John Terraine, *Douglas Haig: The Educated Soldier* (London: Hutchinson, 1963), p. 224.

Such was Haig's intention. He planned a third great blow for mid-September, with five divisions of cavalry well up to exploit the breakthrough. Yet it should not be thought that he was contenting himself with the mixture as before. He was constantly seeking after the extra element, the new ingredient that might convert forward push into decisive breach. He believed that he had found it this time: in the tank.

Plate 27 *A tank in action.*

II

The tank was the most striking innovation of the war. As a concept, of course, it had many precursors, the knight in armour being one. The penetrative power of the bullet had long since become greater than any sheet of metal capable of being carried by a man, walking or mounted, could withstand. So the employment of metal protection by infantry and cavalry had been abandoned. But by 1914 the prohibitive losses that could be inflicted on attacking infantry – not to say horse soldiers – by machine-guns and rifles, employed by defenders sheltering in trenches and screened by barbed wire, had created an utterly new situation. This led a number of Englishmen independently to inquire whether it might be possible to interpose a shield of metal between soldiers attacking in the open and the weapons of the defenders.

Obviously, no soldier or group of soldiers could carry metal of the required weight and thickness. But the development of the engine-powered motor vehicle suggested a different answer. The sheet of metal could take the form of a steel box, capable of crushing barbed wire and immune from machine-gun bullets. There remained a further problem. The motor vehicle had been designed to run on tolerably smooth surfaces, not over land cratered by shell holes and severed by trenches. But, again, some men of insight perceived that a solution might already lie to hand: in the caterpillar tractor.

There remained the problem of what precise function the steel box was intended to perform. If it was meant to negate the killing power of automatic weapons, then it was possible to see the armoured vehicle as providing infantry with a means of reaching the enemy without having to emerge into the open. But this was to prove a serious misconception of what, technically, was feasible at the time. In the existing state of technology, any vehicle capable of making the transit of No-Man's-Land would have a capacity for carrying only a handful of men. Its task, therefore, must be to clear the way for the mass of infantry, first by crushing the wire, then by destroying the enemy's machine-gun posts with its own fire power. The armoured tractored vehicle must be, primarily, a weapons platform.

It was no easy matter to put the pieces of the jigsaw together in this way. Several men – some in high places, like Churchill and Hankey – divined at least a good part of the picture. The person who envisaged it whole was Lt.-Col. Ernest Swinton. He had the right qualifications and experience and the ability to employ them. He was a trained engineer in the regular army. From experience in South Africa, and from an extensive study of the trench stalemate that developed in Manchuria in the later stages of the Russo-Japanese war, he had developed a 'machine gun complex'.[3] During the opening months of the Great War he was official correspondent for the British forces in France, and so had had plenty of opportunity to observe the nature of the stalemate there. In addition, he could express himself effectively on paper.

Late in October 1914, while the high commands of the contending powers in the West still believed in the possibility of a war of movement, Swinton wrote to Hankey about devising armed caterpillar tractors to breach the trench barrier. Hankey took up the matter in his 'Boxing Day memorandum'. Indeed, compared with the vagueness of some of his suggestions on strategy, Hankey was admirably precise in his references to 'numbers of large heavy rollers . . . propelled from behind by motor engines', the wheels fitted with caterpillar gear 'to grip the ground', 'the driver's seat armoured, and with a Maxim gun fitted', whose task would be 'to roll down the barbed wire by sheer weight' and to support the infantry advance with machine-gun fire.[4] Asquith responded affirmatively, and Kitchener, though querulous, appointed a War Office committee to inquire. Churchill also acted on the proposal, undeterred by the fact that it hardly seemed an Admiralty matter (or that calling the proposed vehicles 'landships' did not make it one). In an important respect Churchill was barking up the wrong tree. For it was the Trojan horse idea – an infantry carrier – that attracted him. Nevertheless, he too set up a committee, with a trained engineer in the chair and other forceful individuals, such as Albert Stern, among its members. He even authorized a sum of money to finance experiments.

As Churchill's committee began meeting in February 1915, the War Office committee was temporarily losing interest. A trial was held of a caterpillar tractor, towing a truck with a weight of 5,000 lbs (to represent the vehicle's armour) over a simulated battlefield. It proved a failure. In extremely muddy conditions the tractor, having overrun barbed wire successfully, proceeded into a trench and was unable to get out. However, in mid-1915 Swinton returned to the task. He enrolled the support of Sir John French, who informed the authorities in Britain that the proposed machine

---

[3] E. D. Swinton, *Eyewitness* (London: Hodder & Stoughton, 1932), p. 24.
[4] Sir Maurice Hankey, *The Supreme Command 1914–1918*, 2 vols. (London: Allen & Unwin, 1961), vol. 1, p. 246.

would be of 'considerable tactical value'.[5] This revived the interest of the War Office, which contacted the Admiralty committee. The two bodies merged, pressing ahead with a vehicle on War Office (and Swinton) lines – that is, not an infantry carrier but a lightly manned vehicle employing fire power.

Many technical problems lay ahead. Developing caterpillar tractors of sufficient strength to carry so much weight over cratered territory was a major difficulty. Ultimately, tracks of American design had to be employed. Devising a vehicle that would climb out of a trench was another problem. Guns mounted above the vehicle made it top-heavy, so these had to be attached to the sides. And to increase the length of the tracks, so as to get sufficient grip on the sides of a trench, it was decided to run the caterpillars not just around the wheels but around the entire hull. The shape of the vehicle, moreover, was altered from square to rhomboid, so as to provide extra tracking. There was one problem, clearly foreseen by Swinton, that the designers could not overcome: the likely vulnerability to shell fire of the slow-moving vehicle – it had a projected speed of only 4 m.p.h. *on roads*. Unless supporting artillery could silence the enemy's guns, there was no way that the tank could escape this menace.

So secret was the whole undertaking that the firm of Foster's, the manufacturers of caterpillar tractors being employed for the purpose, was not officially designated an armaments firm. Also in the interests of secrecy, the vehicle was given the name of a water-carrier: the tank. According to Swinton: 'We rejected in turn – "container" – "receptacle" – "reservoir" – "cistern". The monosyllable "tank" appealed to us as being likely to catch on and be remembered.'[6] In view of the need for increased water supplies in areas where troops were gathering, this was not a bad subterfuge. As a further device for secrecy, during manufacture the machines carried the legend 'With Care to Petrograd' in Russian letters 12 inches high.

Swinton was given the task of commanding the new tank detachment – which, again for reasons of deception, was called the Heavy Section, Machine-Gun Corps. This meant raising the necessary personnel; making decisions about the most suitable armament to be carried by the vehicles; and, as the finished product gradually rolled out of the factories, training the crews under simulated battle conditions. In a very secluded part of Suffolk, on 15 square miles of the shooting estates of some titled persons, a model battlefield was constructed. Its depth equalled the distance that a tank must travel from the British support lines to the German third defensive position. And its features included breastworks, wire entanglements, shell craters, communication trenches, dug-outs, and machine-gun emplacements – 'in fact every sort of work, which, according to the latest information, might be met with in the defensive zone'. To give the tanks experience of climbing under conditions as near to the real thing as possible, the shell craters were made not by digging but by exploding mines, 'since soil is shattered by explosive in a way which cannot be imitated by the shovel'.[7] (Supplying water for the large additional population being brought into this out-of-the-way place was itself a problem – and, of course, the 'tanks' were not of help. An artesian well was sunk.) The War Office, the Ministry of Munitions, and even, when called on, the Home Defence Command stinted nothing in preparing the new weapon for the battlefield.

The inception and development of the tank was a prime indication of Britain's considerable war-making capacity in a long-drawn-out struggle. The country possessed the industrial resources and the skills that could convert the ideas of visionaries

---

[5] Quoted in Robin Prior, *Churchill's 'World Crisis' as History* (London: Croom Helm, 1983), p. 234.

[6] Swinton, *Eyewitness*, p. 187.

[7] Ibid., p. 244.

and designers into functioning machines. It also possessed the political structure appropriate to producing a positive response to the insights of men like Swinton. Those occupying the key positions for furthering or thwarting the inception of the tank either actively supported the undertaking or at least refrained from hampering it – in particular Asquith, Kitchener, Churchill, and Hankey. Certainly, there were instances of obstructionism along the way: for example, the speed with which the War Office committee on tanks went cool on the idea in February 1915 after one unsuccessful trial. More noteworthy is the momentum, developing from several quarters, which ensured that such halts would be brief.

Equally deserving of comment is the ready acceptance of the concept of the tank in another key quarter: that of the high command. Haig, a week after supplanting French, read of the new machine for the first time in a paper written by Churchill. He was immediately interested. Soon the inquiries he instituted were favoured with a hopeful report. On 29 January 1916 and again on 2 February, on Lord Salisbury's estate near Hatfield, the Mark I tank underwent a successful trial over a formidable obstacle course. On the first occasion, only the men who had been closely connected with its development were present. On the second, an array of notables who included key Cabinet Ministers and representatives of GHQ were on hand. Only Kitchener among them seemed less than enthusiastic. And even this may have been a subterfuge on his part to still the loquacity of his civilian associates (whose babbling tongues on military matters caused him much pain). The following day he told the War Committee that he had been 'impressed by the trials', and he appointed Stern, of the old landships committee, as head of a War Office department whose remit was to produce tanks. (Stern, along with the task of production, was speedily annexed by Lloyd George and the Ministry of Munitions.)

Haig immediately began incorporating the tank into his preparations for the opening of the Somme battle. Forty were ordered, and this number was soon increased to 100. On 7 April he told the commander in the sector where he proposed using them: 'we must be fully prepared to take advantage of the surprise and demoralizing effect which [they] seem likely to produce the first time they are used.'[8] Haig's enthusiasm was running away with him. Neither the tanks nor the crews to operate them would be available by the middle of the year.

That difficulties were encountered in the production of tanks is not to be wondered at. Equally formidable was the problem of recruiting and training crews. The British nation was not well endowed with drivers of motor vehicles, which had remained largely playthings of the well-to-do. It was better off, to its fortune, in motorcyclists and people engaged in the manufacture and repair of these vehicles, and from their ranks quite a number of tank crews were drawn. But they usually knew nothing of war and had a vast amount to learn about the handling of a vehicle that placed intense strains on its crews.

Four men operated the tank (another four worked its guns), one commanding, one driving, and two manipulating the separate gears that served to steer it. The noise of the engine and tracks was so deafening that the commander had to issue directions by means of hand signals. Discomfort was intense. There was insufficient room for the crew to stand up; the progress of the vehicle caused unpleasant jarring; and conditions became suffocating as the air grew foul and the heat level rose to 100°F. Nor was it easy learning to employ the vehicle under simulated conditions of war: keeping to a timetable, conforming to an artillery barrage, co-ordinating with the movements of

---

[8] Terraine, *Douglas Haig*, p. 220.

infantry. (Other, yet grimmer, forms of experience could be acquired only in battle: manoeuvring under shell fire, sustaining a hail of bullets from machine-guns, deciding on appropriate action when all sense of direction was gone, and accepting the necessity of sometimes running over wounded soldiers – one's own as well as the enemy's – because it was impossible to avoid them.)

Haig, denied the use of tanks for the opening of the campaign, continued to plan for their eventual appearance. In mid-April he understood from a conversation with Swinton that he might have 150 by the beginning of August; a month later it became apparent that only half this number were likely to be ready by that date. When the time came to launch his third big push in September the number had fallen to two-thirds of the lower figure. But Haig was not to be deterred. His frame of mind is apparent from a comment he made when he learned on 11 August that tanks would not be available until early in September: 'This is disappointing as I have been looking forward to obtaining decisive results from the use of these "Tanks" at an early date.'[9] A man who, after so many setbacks, was still bent on achieving 'decisive results' must clearly invoke – in whatever quantities – any device that might convert failure into success and meagre advance into breakthrough.

Yet strong pressure was being exercised against the use of the tank at this stage of the Somme campaign. It came not from obscurantists but from men like Hankey, Churchill, and Lloyd George. Their arguments were powerful. The tanks available were too few to strike a heavy blow. Yet their use now would mean that the advantage of surprise hereafter would be lost. Again, the shell-torn, cratered battlefield of the Somme presented an obstacle course too great even for a tank to contend with. And given the tanks' admitted vulnerability to shell fire – a point to which Swinton made frequent reference – it appeared folly to employ them in an area that had drawn to itself a vast quantity of enemy artillery. There was a further reason for delay. Haig's subordinate commanders showed little appreciation of how the tanks should be used. Rawlinson, who anyway appeared unenthusiastic about the new weapons (and whom Hankey at the time deemed 'a dull man with rather a dull staff'), was choosing to spread them out in driblets along the front of attack.[10] That meant they would be an appendage to, rather than the spearhead for, the infantry. Haig, whether or not he approved, was not intending to overrule Rawlinson.

These voices of wisdom went unheeded. When Lloyd George, at Asquith's suggestion, took his protests to Robertson, the CIGS 'answered in his most laconic style, "Haig wants them."'[11] When Hankey sought to reason with Kiggell, Haig's Chief of Staff, and Butler, his deputy, they were 'not very receptive'.[12] Nor did Asquith get any further with Haig himself. The Commander-in-Chief proved unwilling to act on the wisdom of the men who had conceived the armoured vehicle.

It is not difficult to see why. He needed a striking success at this moment, after all that he had staked on the Somme campaign. He needed it on the Somme because he was not in a position to act elsewhere. And he needed it on a reasonably wide front, not a narrowly concentrated one, otherwise his cavalry would not be able to penetrate. Necessity, not the wisdom of the tank pioneers, would be Haig's master.

For this action Haig has received the castigation that awaits a gambler who throws

[9] Robert Blake (ed.), *The Private Papers of Douglas Haig 1914–1919* (London: Eyre & Spottiswoode, 1952), p. 159.
[10] Hankey's comment is in his diary for 6 September 1916, after lunching at Rawlinson's headquarters. (As he dined with Haig in the evening and found him 'a terribly bad conversationalist', Hankey's meals that day must have been rather an effort.)
[11] *War Memoirs of David Lloyd George*, 2-volume edn. (London: Odhams Press, 1938), vol. 1, p. 385.
[12] Hankey's diary, 7 September 1916.

important stakes on the table and loses the round – a round that anyway, given the advanced stage of the year, he had virtually no hope of winning. The charge levelled against him is that, for no substantial purpose, he revealed a secret that had been well kept despite the myriads of people involved in the tank's manufacture and development. As a result, the chance of later springing the weapon unannounced on the enemy, in large numbers and over appropriate terrain, was lost. This gave the Germans time to develop weapons and tactics against the tank before having to encounter it in significant numbers. Further, the performance of the tank on the Somme confirmed the prejudices of those members of the British military establishment who were sceptical of any newfangled device.

Yet the case against Haig is not as heavy as this indictment suggests. For one thing, the tank did gain some benefits from its early experiences under fire. Shortcomings in the vehicles were made apparent, and a nucleus of crews with battle experience was developed. Anyway events were to prove that, over a year hence, it would still be possible to take the enemy by surprise with a full-scale tank attack. Nor was this the only way in which the German commanders failed to benefit from the premature employment of the tank. For they deduced from its disappointing early performance what it suited them to deduce: that the weapon would always prove ineffective and need not be emulated.

Of course, it does not excuse Haig's misjudgement that the enemy failed to capitalize on his mistakes. Yet the contrast between his response to the tank and that of the German high command deserves to be stressed. When confronted with a startling new weapon he immediately recognized its potential. His opponents did not. Their obtuseness was not peculiar to their own side. There were not a few members of the British military hierarchy, and some of them not much junior to Haig, whose response to the tank was decidedly unfriendly. Britain was fortunate in having a commander who was not among them.

III

The fifteenth of September 1916 witnessed the début of the tank on the battlefield and so marked a large day in the history of warfare. It did not mark a large day in the history of the campaign on the Somme.

Despite Haig's efforts, this attack was basically the mixture as before. Only 49 tanks were available for the action, and 17 of these broke down or were ditched before they reached the start line. Of the 32 able to participate, 14 were soon out of action with mechanical or other troubles, so that only 18 tanks effectively participated in the assault. On one part of the front, Flers, where several of them operated together, they contributed signally to the advance. On another, where the Canadians were attacking, the slow-moving vehicles (capable of a speed of only 0.5 miles per hour over the battlefield) could not even keep pace with the advancing infantry. By and large the contribution from the tanks was marginal. The infantry on 15 September had to struggle forward as they had done on all previous occasions: with the support of artillery fire and their own resources.

All along the front of attack, except on the far right, the British forces pushed forward, and shortly before midday High Wood fell at last. This progress mattered. Bit by bit the imposing defensive system that the Germans had constructed prior to the Allied campaign was being wrested from them. But none of this signified a break-through. When it seemed that the last German defences must have been taken, always a line remained, or strong points held out catching the attackers in enfilade, or German reserves moved into new positions – however sketchy – to halt the advance. So it was on 15 September. The British chalked up fresh successes. And soon the newspapers were ringing with accounts of their new weapon: variously described as 'Land Dreadnought', 'Motor-Monster', 'Touring Fort', 'Travelling Turret', and – more imaginatively – 'Giant Toad' and 'Jabberwock with Eyes of Flame'. But on the morning of the 16th the cavalry divisions (or anyway three out of the five of them) that had been awaiting the breakthrough went back into reserve.

32

CONCLUSION

I sometimes dread coming back to normal life with so many gaps – especially of course
George Butterworth [killed at Pozières on 5 August 1916]. . . out of those 7 who
joined up together in August 1914 only 3 are left – I sometimes think now that it is
wrong to have made friends with people much younger than oneself – because soon
there will only be the middle aged left. . . .

Ralph Vaughan Williams to Gustav Holst, n.d. (autumn 1916)

I

By the second half of September the rain was setting in, and it was 10 days before
serious fighting could be resumed. This time a push forward was managed on the
right, where resistance had proved too strong on 15 September. There was also an
advance on the centre left, where the Canadians had taken over the storming role of
the Australians, and farther left still, where Thiepval was taken. So by the end of
September, except for a small section north of Thiepval, the whole of that crest of
ground which had lain in the centre of the Allies' objectives on 1 July was in British
hands. Whatever case there may have been for continuing the campaign up to this
point, none existed hereafter.

The weather provided a compelling reason against continuation. It broke emphati-
cally on 2 October, and rain continued for most of the month. The surface of loam that
overlaid the chalk of the Somme district turned the battlefield into a sea of mud, which,
with a devotion that even the Germans could scarcely match, halted movement and
took a steady toll in casualties. Writing home in December an Australian artillery
captain recalled:

> Last time we were here one of our officers rode into a Shell hole. His horse disappeared in
> the mud & he was only rescued with great difficulty. He had to be pulled out with ropes &
> in doing so they strained his internal organs. He is now in Blighty & it will be 3 months
> before he is fit to rejoin his unit. It is a common sight to see men pulling one another out of
> the mud – it clings like glue.

And in November a lieutenant recorded how, under shelling, the side of the hole in
which he was sheltering started to cave in:

> It struck me in the act of rising and completely buried me. The weight of my tin hat
> pressed me down irresistably and forced my chin into my chest. After struggling a little I
> found that it only settled the earth closer around me. . . . Then the realization came of
> what was gradually but surely ending things. The soft earth at first yielded slightly to my
> struggles, but was slowly settling down and compressing under the weight above, so that
> the movement of my ribs was becoming more and more constricted. It was as though an
> iron band were tightening round my chest and preventing any movement. Then I heard
> the Sergeant Major speaking, and calling me, as though he were a long way off. . . . I

346

heard him say, 'Good God, I believe the man's buried! Come here two men with shovels. – Now gently – don't maim him.' At last the terrible weight was relieved, and they lifted me out and laid me on the floor of the trench.[1]

Delivering attacks under such conditions was a heartbreaking undertaking. The rain made observation for the artillery, and therefore accurate shelling, well-nigh impossible. The infantry, often wet to the skin, with mud the size of footballs clinging to their feet, could scarcely discern, let alone reach, their objectives. Supply problems were daunting. Behind the front line lay 'a strip of sheer desolation':[2] 4 miles of sodden landscape, served only by battered country roads, up which the British had clawed their way since 1 July.

With nature so devoted an adversary, and with the only realistic objectives already achieved, the case for terminating the campaign seemed irresistible. The British command, nevertheless, managed to resist it. At the end of September Haig defined a further series of objectives on the central part of the front. For each of them there was, on narrow tactical grounds, a sort of justification. But they offered no reward commensurate with the sufferings involved in assaulting them. The objectives were not taken.

However, Haig also decided to return to the attack on the more northerly part of the front, where failure had been total on 1 July and where there had been little activity since. And it was here in mid-November that the British achieved their last success for the year. Attacking from the same positions as on 1 July, and so not burdened with the difficulties of getting supplies forward over a front of advance (because there had been none), British troops took Beaumont Hamel. They failed, farther left, to take Serre – where, as we shall see, Private Surfleet had his second experience of the Somme offensive. On 19 November the Somme campaign was brought to an end.

Haig's determination to maintain the offensive during October and most of November, when it had plainly become an exercise in futility, appears so obtuse that it raises doubts as to whether his sounder decisions were the result of chance or good judgement. Of course, there were arguments of a sort for what he was doing. The Somme campaign was placing a fearful strain on German forces, and Haig was acutely aware of this. He wrote to Joffre on 11 September concerning the enemy, 'evidence of a growing deterioration in his morale accumulates daily'; and to Robertson on 7 October, 'It is not possible to say how near to breaking point the enemy may be but he has undoubtedly gone a long way towards it.'[3]

But the evidence concerning German morale was not one-sided. Hankey, during his visit to the Somme region, wrote in his diary for 9 September:

> On the whole I think our people have an exaggerated opinion of our superiority over the enemy. The Germans are undoubtedly still very strong. They dig better than our men . . . and consequently their losses are probably far less. The prisoners, of whom I saw hundreds on the roads, are fine, well set-up, intelligent looking men, with no sign whatsoever of indifferent morale or physique. They work as well as or perhaps better than British or French labourers, I am told – and certainly they seemed to work well.

Anyway, Haig's judgements on German morale existed in a vacuum. He was making no corresponding calculations about what was happening to the morale of his own forces. Nor was he inquiring whether, in the conditions of the Somme battlefield, it was even possible to capitalize on any falling off in German fighting capacity.

---

[1] Bill Gammage, *The Broken Years* (Ringwood, Victoria: Penguin Books Australia, 1975), pp. 173–4.
[2] John Buchan, *The Battle of the Somme: Second Phase* (London: Thomas Nelson, n.d.), p. 34.
[3] Robin Prior, *Churchill's 'World Crisis' as History* (London: Croom Helm, 1983), p. 220.

There is good evidence that Haig, whatever rationalizations he cared to offer, had reached the stage where he was persisting in fighting simply because he was fighting. On 19 September Rawlinson reported Haig's Chief of Staff as saying that the C.-in-C. 'means to go on until we cannot possibly continue further either from the weather or want of troops'. (Rawlinson, to his credit, added: 'I'm not so sure that he is right.') And on 6 October the Fourth Army commander wrote: '[Haig] is bent on continuing the battle until we are forced to stop by the weather indeed he would like to go on all through the winter.'[4] It must be wondered whether the British commander, ensconced in his *château*, understood what – in military, let alone human, terms – concepts like 'want of troops' and 'go[ing] on all through the winter' really meant.

II

The Somme campaign had failed. It had attempted to inflict a strategic defeat on the enemy and had not done so. In order to break through the German front and render a large segment of enemy forces incapable of further action, it had first been necessary to overwhelm an intricate defensive system. That system now lay in Allied hands. But it had not been taken at a blow or following a swift succession of blows. The process of advance had been so halting and gradual that the Germans had always secured time to put together some new, if inferior, forms of defensive. And meanwhile the campaigning season had run out, leaving the Allies stuck in the mud. Certainly, they were now much better placed to attack the Germans in this region in the coming spring than they had been in the high summer of 1916 because they now occupied the central crest. But that expectation depended on the Germans playing their game by continuing to regard every yard of French soil as precious.

Yet in this respect the Western Allies had the dice loaded against them. Britain and France must attack the enemy in regions where the Germans had chosen to make their stand because the Germans were occupying Allied territory. The enemy, by contrast, was under no compulsion to hold on to one part of occupied France as against another. In fact, following their repulse on the Marne in 1914 the Germans had often fallen back until they had established themselves in good defensive positions. Certainly, since then some of those positions had become hallowed ground to them because their commanders had directed that every yard of it must be held or recaptured at whatever cost. But these directives had concerned territory of tactical importance. On the Somme the tactically important ground was now in Allied hands. And anyway this consideration of hallowed ground signified much less to the German command after August 1916. For Falkenhayn, who had issued the directive of no retreat, was no longer in his post. The men who replaced him, Hindenburg and Ludendorff, were concerned not to endorse his fighting methods but to show that they had been erroneous. For them abandoning territory on the Somme where the British and French were now in a favourable position, and withdrawing to new areas of France where they would not be, was a relatively easy matter. When the time came for the British to strike again at the German lines outside Bapaume, the Germans would not be there.

Yet a campaign that does not accomplish its prime objective may still accomplish a great deal. Was this true of the British endeavour on the Somme? One thing was certain. The pressure on Verdun had been relieved. Indeed, the French in the last part of the year had gone over to the attack there, recapturing all the territory they had lost.

---

[4] Ibid.

But the relief of Verdun had been accomplished early on. In order to dissuade the Germans from resuming the offensive there, it was not necessary to engage in the sort of operation persisted in on the Somme. In fact, that operation itself contributed to the growing enfeeblement of the French by costing them some 200,000 casualties, over half the number they sustained during their blood-letting at Verdun. Nevertheless, the fact that Verdun had survived was a major Allied success and one to which the Somme campaign had contributed significantly.

There was a larger achievement at the Somme, as far as the British were concerned, than the question of taking pressure off Verdun. It was necessary, by this stage of the war, for the British to demonstrate, to friend and foe alike, that they were now prepared and able to make a major contribution to the war on land. The French needed to be reassured that they would not have to win in the West on their own strength. The Germans, in making their plans and calculating their chances, must be obliged to take into account the resources and the determination of Britain. The Somme had accomplished this. Certainly, the way in which it had been accomplished was in many respects unsatisfactory. Yet there was no one who could argue convincingly that a campaign on some other front, directed by some other commander, would have resulted in a much happier outcome.

Moreover, the Somme offensive, in driving the Germans step by step from positions they had tried to render impregnable and had sought devotedly to hold, had imposed a terrible toll on the defenders. This was of no small importance. During 1916 the experience of Germany (disregarding its allies) on all fronts apart from the Western Front was that of gaining victories at moderate cost. Only on the soil of France was a radically different tale being told: huge casualties were suffered by the Germans, for no tangible gain, both while attacking the French at Verdun and while being attacked by the British and French on the Somme. German casualties on the Western Front in 1916 cannot have fallen much below the 1 million mark. Such losses were little short of calamitous.

Yet much the same can be said of the Western Allies. They too had suffered terrible losses. They too had little tangible to show for it. Did these blood-lettings work more to the advantage of one side than the other? Did they, to be specific, advance Britain and its allies towards victory by plainly tilting the balance of military resources against the enemy? Haig argued (after the failure to break through had robbed his operations of their prime justification) that it had. He claimed that the Germans had suffered much heavier casualties than the British. His critics – among them Churchill and Hankey while the campaign was actually proceeding – denied this.

The debate, transferred to historians, has continued ever since. And on it has hung the judgement of whether the Somme campaign was, for Britain, a victory or a defeat. It is a debate about facts, but the facts are in dispute. There seems to be general agreement that British casualties on the Somme were about 420,000 and French casualties about 200,000. The disagreement concerns the German figures. These were put by the Germans at about 500,000, significantly fewer than those of the Western Allies. But the British official historian, arguing that the Germans had excluded a whole category of wounded that the British had included in their figures, claimed that in terms of equivalents the German figure was 680,000. Thus the Somme could be judged a British success. The grounds for making this calculation have been subjected to severe scrutiny and deemed to be without foundation.[5] Although the raw material on which to assess German casualties no longer exists, and so a final total may

---

[5] See M. J. Williams, 'Thirty per cent: a Study in Casualty Statistics', *Journal of the Royal United Services Institution*, February 1964.

continue to elude us, there seems no firm ground for doubting that the Allies lost more heavily than the Germans.

Yet to conclude from this that the Somme must be regarded as a British defeat is unwarranted. This is for the good reason that the whole basis on which the argument has been conducted is specious. A simple example will show this. The Australians made a significant contribution to the Somme campaign by their part in the battle for Pozières. Possibly, in so doing, they inflicted heavier casualties on the Germans than they themselves suffered. If this were so, then it would follow in terms of the 'Blood Test' (Churchill's expression) that the Australians had secured a victory, and that if the victory were repeated often enough Australia would ultimately triumph over Germany. It is, of course, quite apparent that nothing of the sort would have been true. Enough such victories and Australia would have been denuded of active males and rendered unable to continue fighting. Germany, meanwhile, would have had many armies still in the field. Certainly this is a *reductio ad absurdum*. The point that needs to be made is that the absurdity is present all along.

Another example – a real one this time – will indicate the complexity of the issue. Who won the battle of Verdun? Based on crude figures of total casualties (i.e. the 'Blood Test'), it was a drawn match or a very modest German success, as by a narrow margin the French lost more men than the Germans. Yet another factor seems to need taking into account: total resources of manpower. On this basis it was more definitely a German victory. For France, with its smaller population, could not afford to trade casualties even on a man-for-man basis.

Yet if this consideration takes us a stage nearer reality than the crude counting of heads, it is still unreal in an important respect. Like the hypothetical succession of conflicts between Australia and Germany, it treats the war as if it were being fought by only two powers: in the case of Verdun, France and Germany. Certainly, only Frenchmen and Germans died at Verdun. But the fate of two great alliances was involved in that struggle. Seen in this larger context, Verdun may well appear an Allied, not an enemy, triumph. For the alliance of which Germany was a part was arguably less able to afford the losses suffered at Verdun than was the alliance of which France was a part.

How do we apply these considerations to the struggle on the Somme during July to November 1916? That campaign, it must be stressed, was one large episode in a protracted war that was grinding down the fighting capacity of both sides. Whether it advanced or retarded the victory of the Allies would depend not just on absolute figures of casualties but on the relative capacity of the two sides to afford their losses. And that relative capacity did not consist in fighting men alone. It involved also human resources that would not appear on the battlefield and a wide range of non-human resources, including industrial capacity and access to raw materials.

It follows that the Allies could have inflicted heavier casualties on the Germans during the Somme campaign than they themselves suffered and yet have ended the campaign further from victory than at the start: because they were less able to sustain even a lower rate of losses. But the contrary may have been true. The British and French may have suffered heavier casualties than the Germans – almost certainly, they did. Yet in so doing they may have advanced the Allied cause towards victory, because the Allies could better afford their larger number of casualties than the Germans could afford their lesser number.

How does one choose between these alternatives (assuming agreement on the actual totals of casualties)? How does one assess the entire war-making resources not of two countries but of two power blocs, even in terms of adult males of military age – to say nothing of industrial capacity, supplies of raw materials, the efficiency of the administrative structure, the viability of the state system, and various other quantifiables and non-quantifiables? Is it even realistic to say that a male of military age from one combatant country equals a male of military age from any other combatant country? To put that question specifically: given the successes that Russian troops usually achieved over Austro-Hungarian troops, and the defeats that Russian troops usually suffered at the hands of German troops, is it warranted to assume that one German soldier equalled one Russian soldier equalled one Austro-Hungarian soldier? (On the other hand, for one side to assume in advance that its fighting men were inherently superior to those of another side could prove a discouraging business. The British discovered this when they set about ejecting the Turks from Gallipoli.)

The problems do not end here. If we are to deal in the resources not of particular countries but of the two alliances, what weight should we attach to the resources of Russia, seeing that that country left the side of the Allies rather early, and to the resources of the USA, given that it joined the Allied side rather late?

It is clear why, in assessing the outcome of the Somme campaign, neither participants at the time nor historians since have cared to ask these questions. The issues are so difficult, the calculations so complex, that it appears impossible to arrive at any answer. It is much easier to regard the battle as being in the nature of a sporting fixture, in which each side scores a point for every casualty it inflicts on its adversary, and victory goes to whichever side accumulates the more points. Admittedly, those making the judgement, being usually somewhat partisan, have had difficulty in agreeing on the final totals, and have even accused each other of cheating. And as some of the score sheets have gone missing, it has anyway been necessary to indulge in a bit of guess-work. But at least the judges, whatever their dissensions, have been of one mind about the rules of the game. And within the terms of those rules they have been able, individually, to enter firm verdicts.

This may seem better than requiring a set of calculations that cannot ever be made and so will leave us without any firm verdict. But it is not better. Historians must ask the real questions. And if the questions cannot be answered, then they must say so and, to the best of their ability, make a calculated guess. If that seems an untidy and unsatisfying proceeding, then nothing could be more appropriate for so ambiguous an event as the battle of the Somme.

So, for what the guess is worth, the estimate offered here is that the Somme harmed the Germans more than it harmed the British and the French, and advanced the Central Powers nearer to defeat than it advanced the Entente Powers. For the Central Powers depended utterly on Germany for survival, and Germany did not have the wherewithal to outlast its adversaries while sustaining losses on the scale of the Somme, even granting that its losses were somewhat fewer than those of its enemies.

But this is no more than a guess. No one at the time could know, given the incomplete information available about casualties, not to mention all the other information (some of it intangible) that needed to be brought into the calculation, which side could stand this degree of strain the longer. The commanders on both sides of the Western Front claimed success for themselves. As far as the Somme is concerned, on the basis of the 'Blood Test' Haig was probably wrong. On a wider calculation of resources he was probably right. But if at this second and more decisive level his claim was correct, that is not evidence of greater insight or a better intelligence service on his part. Rather, he happened to have made the correct call on the toss of a coin.

Haig's intelligence service could inform him, with justice, that he had inflicted a large number of casualties on the Germans. And it might conclude that the Germans could not go on sustaining such losses indefinitely. But the actual extent of enemy casualties, and whether at the current rate of loss Germany would fail in the battle of resources earlier than the Allies, Haig neither knew nor had any way of discovering. Time, and the course of the war, would vindicate his claim to have achieved a victory or expose it to be fraudulent. What the Somme had plainly shown was that the time would be long and that the number of young lives required of Britain while it discovered which side could outlast the other would be very great indeed.

33

ONE PRIVATE'S SOMME

We see human heroism broken into units and say, this unit did little – might as well not have been. But in this way we might break up a great army into units; in this way we might break the sunlight into fragments, and think that this and the other might be cheaply parted with. Let us rather raise a monument to the soldiers whose brave hearts only kept the ranks unbroken, and met death – a monument to the faithful who were not famous, and who are precious as the continuity of the sunbeams is precious, though some of them fall unseen and on barrenness.

George Eliot, Felix Holt

I

Arthur Surfleet – he was Archie to his friends – was 17½ years old when the war broke out. His home was in Hull, in the north-east of England, where his father was a laboratory manager. He attended Hull Grammar School until he was 15, served for a year as a junior reporter on a local newspaper, and then embarked on an apprenticeship with the same firm of manufacturing chemists as employed his father. In January 1916, on turning 19, Surfleet volunteered for service in the East Yorkshire Regiment. He was a young man of upright character and firm principles. And despite his youth he possessed enough independence of mind to disregard the army regulation that forbade privates to keep diaries.[1]

When he joined the army he had never visited London or imbibed alcohol. He had his first sight of London in transit to France. His company's training was completed at the beginning of May 1916 – or, if not completed, was brought to a halt by the demands of the Western Front. Most of Surfleet's company were as ignorant of the south of England as he was, so on the march through London to Victoria Station they were taken past a number of historic places. 'I quite enjoyed it' was Surfleet's only comment.

His introduction to alcohol came two months later. At the end of an exhausting route march he found that the only refreshments available were beer and wine. To the accompaniment of much leg-pulling from his comrades on the subject of going to the devil, he drank his first glass of beer. 'I suppose,' he wrote in his diary, 'if I admit the truth, I did have some sort of conscience-stricken feeling at this deliberate step from the path of strict temperance, but I must say I did not find it unpleasant and, so far, I have not felt any of the "after-effects" usually attributed to this stuff!' This fall from grace occurred early in the battle of the Somme. By its end he was unashamedly grateful for a tot of rum to put himself to sleep.

Yet the devil cannot be said to have claimed him. In essentials the war impaired neither his sobriety nor his strength of character. In July 1916 he wrote an appreciative description of his pal Marshall, a man who could always manage to produce a dixie of tea or a snack when it was most needed. Marshall was 'a religious chap' who 'says his prayers on his knees every night, sometimes with a bit of jeering from a few, though I

---

[1] A. Surfleet, 'Blue Chevrons: An Infantry Private's Great War Diary' is in the Imperial War Museum. Biographical information was provided by his widow, Mrs Anne Surfleet.

think, like me, most of the lads admired his pluck'. Marshall was far from being a robust or athletic man, and it was his great faith, according to Surfleet, that explained his indifference to danger and death. Similarly, Surfleet wrote admiringly of the Church of England padre, 'one of the finest types I have ever known', 'always with us – at play, in the trenches, at celebrations and even "over the top"'. The qualities that Surfleet found admirable in such men he continued, in no small measure, to reveal in himself.

In later years he recalled that the company with whom he travelled to France were tough lads: dustmen, fish-dock workers, trawler hands, merchant seamen, casual dockside labourers, plus a sprinkling of white-collar types. 'As civilians, most were as poor as crows – and we were all poor together as privates in the Infantry.' But as comrades under the most miserable conditions 'you would have to go a long way to find better lads than those with whom I served in France.' His was not, he admitted, one of the elite scrapping divisions, but in trench digging and working parties they did their share and more.

Surfleet spent May and June 1916 in France during the preparations for the Somme offensive. For several weeks he was part of a pioneer battalion, engaged in carrying munitions to the front and constructing trenches. Sometimes the work proved so exhausting that the company was driven to the limits of its endurance. 'I have seen fully grown men with the tears of hopelessness in their eyes,' he wrote; yet they always saw the job through to the end.

'Then,' as he noted graphically, 'dawn came on July 1st.' Surfleet's division (the 31st) was in the northernmost part of the Somme offensive, where its failure was most complete. Twice, on the first day of the Big Push and again in its waning stages, his division was engaged in full-scale attacks against Serre. Both failed at fearful cost. As it happened, he did not himself go over the top on either occasion, except to bring in the wounded. But his experiences were grim enough.

A little after daybreak on 1 July he watched the men of other brigades disappearing into the smoke of No-Man's-Land. Then for an age he and his companions waited, wondering how long before they would follow. 'We waited hours; news kept filtering through – good news, bad news, news of captured trenches, of casualties, of our part to come in the attack – dozens of rumours of all kinds.' At noon he and some others were dispatched to fetch water: a thankless job, he wrote, but '[a]nything in the line of *action* seemed preferable to that terrible, interminable waiting for the unknown.' The location of the water supply had been detected by the Germans, who bombarded it steadily. There was a long queue for water, and the tap, when reached, ran at a trickle. But the worst part of this journey for Surfleet was not the personal danger, or the thick mud hampering his progress that was already becoming a feature of the Somme trenches. It was the sight of men who had been over the top and were now coming back, 'with blood-stained faces – hands – bandages; some limping, some being helped along by a pal; all with a look of indescribable fear in their eyes. I know, now, I *hate* this warring business.'

Back with his platoon, he endured several more hours of 'horrible uncertainty' expecting to join the attack. Eventually, to his surprise and 'intense relief', they were ordered back to base. The reason soon became apparent:

> That those poor lads of the attacking parties had a real hell of a time is obvious from the lists of those who returned. From what I hear, the enemy were waiting for them with hundreds of machine-guns, bombs and rifles and it seems that the Germans met our attack with real courage. I can only record what I have been told by those who took part: that the Germans stood on the top of his [sic] trenches so that he could mow down our

boys more readily, and, Heaven knows, he did that only too well. Our men went down like grass beneath a scythe.[2]

One ruse employed by the Germans, he was told, was to remain underground while the attacking troops passed over and then slaughter them from behind.

> It is not for me to question the whys and wherefores of this affair; Jerry is a cunning devil, but it would seem to me that the authorities should have known the possibility of this ruse. Perhaps they did, and expected our barrages to clear the way; I don't know.

A few days later the Corps Commander visited the 'remnants of the Division' in person.[3] Addressing them on horseback, he told them that the main object of the attack had been accomplished ('they speak very impartially, these Brass Hats,' Surfleet noted) and that the good work of this division had enabled others, particularly the French, to push forward. 'He said a lot of nice things to us and everyone seemed to take a fancy to him.' There was something sincere, Surfleet felt, in the way he talked. It would perhaps be unfair to question Surfleet's judgement, even though most of the general's remarks were misleading. After what the troops had experienced, they needed this measure of deception.

For Surfleet's company the next four and a half months consisted of desultory scrapping, trench raiding, and working parties, interspersed with rest periods behind the lines. Then on 13 November the assault on Serre was resumed in earnest. The troops viewed the coming of this event with dismay, and for Surfleet the day before the attack was 'the most thoroughly miserable day I ever remember. The morning broke dull, foggy and wet; everything was in a hopeless hubbub and bustle; even the mud seemed stickier and thicker.' Once more he was to miss the first wave of the attack. A sergeant tossed a coin between him and his friend Bell to see which of them would remain behind as a 'detail', that is, as part of a skeleton force that stayed to provide a nucleus for new drafts coming in. Surfleet won the toss and Bell, with a shrug, went off to die.

With sad hearts the 'details' watched the rest of the battalion move up to the line. 'There was an artificial air of jollity about . . . but it was the thinnest of veneers, a very feeble covering over the sense of grim reality which I felt the whole battalion was feeling.' Throughout the next day, 13 November, news kept coming in of the progress of the attack. The troops had advanced but with heavy losses and the certainty of counter-attack. Late in the afternoon Surfleet set out for the front line with a party of 30 new arrivals from England ('Poor devils! What a start for them!'). They were heavily shelled along the way as the Germans sought to impede reinforcements. By the time they reached the front line the only task left for them was to care for the wounded: getting the dead and injured out of the forward trench (which was 'no longer a trench; it was a bloody ditch') and carrying those not beyond hope back to the first aid post.

Surfleet and another man set off for the rear with a severely wounded soldier on a stretcher. As they proceeded the mud got worse, until approaching a position under constant fire it became almost impassable.

> Each pace meant that your boot sank slowly into the churned up mud until, the knee almost submerged, an effort had to be made to drag that leg out. This, of course, necessitated putting all your weight on the other leg, which promptly sank in the quagmire. Each pace took us nearer those rending crashes as the shell burst and before we had gone

---

[2] According to the official history, losses in the two battalions attacking Serre were close on 50 per cent: 3,600 casualties (killed, wounded, missing, and prisoners) out of a force of roughly 8,000.

[3] The Corps Commander was Sir A. Hunter-Weston, who had commanded the 29th division (with no marked distinction) at Gallipoli.

far, the continuous dragging of our legs and the suction on our boots tore the skin off our heels. The stretcher, naturally, lurched and swayed precariously all the time; our 'burden' [the wounded man] got windier with every step. The drumfire – a shell every half-minute – continued; each shell landed with terrifying regularity almost in the same spot, right in the trench. . . . We drew nearer, waited for the shriek, the crash, ducked so low that the stinking mud touched our faces; took another pace or two, ducked again, and again, sweating and tearing our legs frantically out of that dreadful mud. The horror of that passage remains indelibly stamped on my mind. . . .

The scene at the first aid post, when at last it was reached, provided little relief. The medical officer, sleeves rolled up, 'looked about finished'. The place was jammed with bleeding men. On all sides were blood-stained bandages and the sickly, penetrating smell of iodoform (a compound like chloroform) and iodine.

That, and the look on the faces of some of those lads down there made me hurry out into the fresh air; it was something not unlike the scene and smell of a slaughter-house. . . .

Then came the long trudge back to the front. Just as Surfleet arrived there a shell burst among the waiting men.

Four of the new draft who had only just arrived were killed and some of the other new lads wounded. . . . It seemed like Fate that these poor lads should be put out of it all so soon; someone said they were lucky.

When a call went out for men to go over the top Surfleet and his friends, imagining it to be a raiding party, were reluctant to offer. On finding that it was an expedition to rescue the helpless wounded, 'each one of us went about that job with real enthusiasm.' He and three others, carrying a stretcher, set off in the blackness, 'the watery moon, seemingly, being too sad to shine any more on such a scene of desolation'. The cries of the wounded and dying were frightful to hear: 'it was awful to pass some of these men who shouted for us to take them back, but we had orders to leave anyone who could possibly get in on his own'. They reached very close to the German front line; 'they were collecting their wounded, too, and a sort of mutual tolerance was being observed.' After falling into a number of shell holes and over much debris, they came upon a soldier with both legs broken and a shattered elbow. 'We gradually got the stretcher beneath him by dint of carefully raising first one part of him and then the other. This took quite a time; then we raised the stretcher, one of us at each corner and set off back to our lines.'

But the care taken getting the wounded man on to the stretcher had caused them to lose their sense of direction. 'God only knows how we got back. It took two and a half hours of the most awful, desperate struggle against dreadful odds in such circumstances as I have never known before.' For the first three-quarters of an hour they stumbled down what proved to be the centre of No-Man's-Land. Then on his right Surfleet spotted a landmark he recognized, and they headed in that direction. 'After falling into shell-hole after shell-hole . . . tripping over barbed wire, telephone lines, dead bodies, discarded equipment, rifles and the like', they encountered a forward British outpost and secured directions. For the sake of their greatly suffering burden, who mercifully 'lapsed into unconsciousness for part of the way', they kept on over the top trying to follow the line of the trenches. But 'the lines were so badly blown up and battered, we were soon lost again. Trenches we once had known did not now exist and those which remained were so altered in character as to be unrecognisable.' The rest of the stretcher party halted while Surfleet, following 'some old light-railway lines', went on ahead to try and locate their trench. 'After struggling along through the mire for about a mile', he found himself in a communication trench he recognized ('it seemed like home to me at that time') and hurried to the nearest RAMC post for help. To his amazement, 'those damned "stretcher-bearers" . . . told me they could not leave their post!' His feeling was that their post was 'a bloody sight too safe and comfortable to be left'. So he had to make his way back alone to his comrades:

> they listened with open mouths to my report and after a few moments of profound and prolonged profanity, we picked up the stretcher and, spurred by the very anger in our hearts, hurried along to that R.A.M.C. Post. We handed our burden over to them; I can still see those swine sitting there, smoking and drinking tea while that lad lay there on the stretcher; I can still feel my blood boil (and I am not easily roused to anger) and still hear, without the slightest blush, the flow of abuse we poured out to them until, eventually, they did put the lad on a trolley and set off with him to the Dressing Station . . . .

Surfleet and his companions then made their way back to their front line, 'expecting another job'. But their sector was being relieved by another battalion, and so they withdrew to their support position, 'dog-tired, foot-sore with the skin off both heels, blood-stained, utterly muddy, ready to fall in our tracks'. When they got there they found their lieutenant (who was also a 'very able' quarter-master) waiting for them with hot tea, soup, bread, 'and last but not least, a *heavy* tot of *rum*'. Then Surfleet fell asleep, and he and the rest of the battalion slept as if in a trance. When eventually they were roused for roll call, it became plain that this force could participate in no more offensives that year. Not only the actual attackers but even the 'details' ('we lucky devils who were, originally, left behind') had suffered dreadfully. Of the 30 men, fresh from England, whom Surfleet had led forward on the 13th, nearly half had disappeared: six were dead, and another six or seven missing.

II

Private Surfleet was not among the outstanding combatants in the battle of the Somme. Among divisions employed in this campaign, his was quite untypical in that it attacked on only two occasions. Yet he encountered the realities of this phase of the war in a number of ways: as a member of gruelling work parties sometimes reduced to a delirium of exhaustion; as a victim of the mud that came increasingly to oppress trench life on the Somme; and as a much-shelled inhabitant of the trenches or the regions behind the lines. His response to the Somme may be thought fairly typical of the civilians-recently-turned-soldiers who constituted the main body of the army involved in this operation.

Surfleet's main response was proclaimed, passionately, on 1 July: 'I know, now, I *hate* this warring business.'[4] In the weeks preceding this outburst he had endured his first experience of working under a heavy bombardment ('the hell through which we had just passed'; 'The feeling was so utterly indescribable that I cannot hope to portray it; God alone knows how awfully afraid I was') and the 'agonising' sight of wounded pals, 'some badly in need of medical aid: others, alas, beyond all earthly assistance'. For long stretches, too, he had endured the utter dreariness that characterized so much of military life: the lice that tormented them whenever their bodies grew warm in bed, the stinking lavatories (which, if near the front, could be prime targets for German snipers), the unnourishing stew that served as staple diet, and the ceaseless route marches and work parties. 'I don't mind saying we all are fed [up] as hell with this lot,' he wrote while the British guns were still booming their prelude to the Somme offensive.

---

[4] It is noteworthy that he expresses no similar sentiments about hating Germans.

Had the attacks that began on 1 July yielded tangible results, no doubt Surfleet's attitude would have changed. Their failure to do so added a new dimension of horror and despondency. Within a few days of the opening of the offensive he was writing: 'For my own part, every hour has been spent fearing to be sent back to that hell up by Serre.' The very name of the Somme, he wrote three months later, 'conjures up a picture of miserable wastes, mud and devastation; surely no place (except, maybe, the Ypres Salient, which God forbid we ever see) could be more trying to patience, temper and comradeship.'

In mid-October he described how his company were marching back from a rest period singing heartily. (It was perhaps no accident that 'It's a Long Way to Tipperary' had been ousted in popular favour by the infinitely more poignant 'There's a Long, Long Trail a' Winding'.) Then they found themselves in familiar territory. The singing faded, and 'the whole lot of us had that characteristic depression which these parts induce. I could not make out exactly where we were, but past, miserable experience in that sector told us we were too near the enemy to be pleasant and just about opposite that ominous blackness near Serre.' Soon the troops were engaged in mock battles, 'capturing many miles of white-taped trenches under distinctly "red-tape" conditions'. These exercises caused great disquiet, for they could only be the prelude to another Big Push. 'I know all the lads here will go wherever they are told in spite of the fear we cannot help, but I don't know anyone who would not welcome with open arms news of our departure to some less devastated and dangerous part.'

One manifestation of the despair induced by the Somme battles appears in the preceding passage: growing hostility to the wielders of red tape. Sometimes this took specific form. It showed itself in resentment against the irritations of petty discipline, as on finding that one of their company, who had been accidentally stabbed in the bottom by a comrade while returning from a raid in No-Man's-Land, had been classified as receiving a self-inflicted wound because the wound had not been inflicted by the enemy. There was even deeper indignation at the effrontery of major discipline. Early in the Somme operation Surfleet's company were out on a march when they came, almost to their unbelief, on a soldier lashed cruciform-fashion to a wheel, his arms and legs wide apart, his head lolling forward 'as he shook it to drive away the flies'. This was the notorious Field Punishment Number One. Surfleet recorded: 'I don't think I have ever seen anything which so disgusted me in my life and I know the feelings amongst our boys was very near to mutiny at such inhuman punishment . . . . I'd like to see the devils who devised it having an hour or two lashed up like that.'

Specific indignation at such actions was accompanied by a general distrust of the brass hats. He described in October the preparations for a tank attack that was supposed to sweep away wire entanglements and machine-guns, 'so making it a perfect doddle for the Infantry following.' The remarks of their corporal on this plan, he wrote, did not bear repeating but they described well enough the feelings of the rank and file. 'Those stunts may look lovely on paper, worked out from a safe seat way back in some chateau accommodating Corps H.Q., but its not all beer and skittles for the P.B.I.' The initials, it is perhaps unnecessary to add, stood for Poor Bloody Infantry.

III

Here, then, was one part of a conscientious soldier's response to the Somme campaign: frustration, resentment, anguish, and a deep resistance to further involvement. But if this had been his total response, it would be hard to explain how the British army lasted out the offensive – and went on to endure others no less testing. Offsetting these feelings were sentiments that served to maintain such soldiers as effective fighting units.

For one thing, hostility to the higher command never reached the level where it might impair a soldier's willingness to fulfil orders. It constituted a good grouse but carried no suggestion that foolish directives might be defied. We have seen that, in writing of the anguish with which his companions viewed a renewal of the offensive, he nevertheless added: 'I know all the lads here will go wherever they are told in spite of the fear we cannot help'. Further, hostility to the brass hats lacked sting because it never became personalized. It constituted disquiet about a body of people higher up, but these people never took on identities. It was a long step from this measure of dissent to the questioning, independent spirit of a man like Siegfried Sassoon who, in his poem 'The General', could point the finger directly at Sir Douglas Haig. Dissent of the latter calibre was rare.

Yet north-of-England conformism is not a sufficient explanation of why the East Yorkshire soldiers went on fighting. It is plain that although the months of the Somme were hell, they were not unrelieved hell. For one thing, soldiers made adjustments that lessened the impact of their miseries. Aiding their attempts to cope with the constant presence of death was a dulling of their anxiety to live and a growing fatalism about their prospects of survival. Surfleet remarked on this at the beginning of October, when the probability of a renewal of the offensive was beginning to confront them.

> I think, too, we are becoming more or less fatalistic; you get like that. I, for one, cannot imagine this blasted war ever ending without most of us being killed or so wounded that we go home to Blighty for good . . . . It boils down to this: we've got to the stage when we don't dare to think of the future. If we are alright today – if we are alright this hour, almost – it is enough.

Accompanying this fatalism was the merciful development of a certain insensitivity to the horrors that, initially both shocking and novel, were now part of everyday life. This applied equally to personal danger and the misfortunes of others. Recounting the frightful injuries suffered by a companion in No-Man's-Land who, while relieving himself in a shell hole, had apparently detonated a grenade, Surfleet wrote:

> The poor lad was hysterical most of the time; Hurste and I had to hold him down forcibly and he shrieked for us to 'put him out of his misery'. It was awful . . . . Hurste and I were somewhat upset; it really was a bloody business (as witness my tunic which was in a dreadful mess) but what surprised me was that I did not feel nearly so 'shocked' as might have been expected. In civilian life, a much milder scene would have turned me up ; it must be the excitement.

Early in 1917 the sight of hideously decomposing corpses caused him to thank God for the remarkable ability to put such sights out of his mind 'just as soon as a little peacefulness comes into life again'. He had come far since his first sight of the dead and wounded.

Equally, he became in a measure inured against distress at danger to himself. In mid-June 1916 his first experience of heavy shell fire had produced appalled terror. A month later, while on sentry-go in the trenches, he was constantly menaced by snipers and the periodic scythe of an enemy machine-gun. 'Yet we became used to the sweep of that gun and almost careless of the sniper. I cannot understand it: I actually found myself waiting for the commencement of that gun's round of fire and timing the moment I should duck to avoid being hit!' A different sort of indication of his changing attitude to death was provided in the weeks before the renewed attacks in November. Surfleet and his friend Bell were inspecting a graveyard next to their waterlogged camp. (Buried there was Basil Hallam, a music-hall star whose song 'Gilbert the Filbert' had been one of the hits of 1914.) They noticed many fresh graves being dug and discovered from the grave diggers the identities of their intended occupants.

> They were actually digging graves in preparation for our coming stunt and if that is not callous, I don't know what is. The very fact that we turned away and sludged and squelched our way into the filthy huts, *merely disgusted*, makes me think a curious change must have come over us all since we got out here.

The dangers and suffering of war produced not only this gradual dulling of sensitivity but a positive response as well: a heightening in the enjoyment of the pleasures of normal life whenever these became available. Four days after the fearful commencement of the Somme attacks Surfleet's battalion marched to Beauval, 'one of the most beautiful little places I have ever seen', with its fine, well preserved church; 'to come to such a place after that dreadful period in the line has cheered us all up quite a lot, despite the very hard-going, long march; we always march well, going away from the line! Lovely billet, too: a barn with clean straw, a door and a roof which is intact!' Subsequently he remarked that men going away from the line were often 'windier', more concerned for their safety, than the 'more stolid, indifferent, come-what-may sort of crowd going in'. The latter were responding to the prospect that faced them: death, wounds, certainly danger. Ahead of the former, on the other hand, if they could but survive the journey back, lay 'the vision of *pay*, of eggs and chips, of beer, of wine and of a good sleep in some wholesome straw in a nice clean barn'.

During these spells away from the line Surfleet also gained pleasure from simple encounters with French civilians: 'the villagers are kindness itself,' he wrote on one occasion, 'and do everything they can to help us to be comfortable.' This was especially the case during his happiest period in billets. In October he was stationed in a little village called Merville, with plenty of shops, lots of food, and again a fine old church (though he was a bit surprised to find urinals built into its side, 'even allowing for the broadmindedness of the average Frenchman – and woman'). Merville was untouched by war: 'What is really grand about this place is its *intactness*.' On one occasion he and his mates sat for ages on a bridge gazing down a tree-lined road, 'which seemed to lead to a land of peacefulness we have not known for such a long time'; on another he messed about mending bikes – 'Just like being at home'. When he and some friends called at a house in an outlying village to see if they could buy a meal, they were welcomed with open arms, shown into the best room, and served a beautiful meal for which 'these kindly folk absolutely refused to accept anything at all . . . one does not meet many like that in any country.' The happy interlude at Merville lasted four days, and they left this place, 'where we were treated with such consideration and kindness', in a fitting manner, with the regimental band playing and the soldiers marching proudly behind and the crowd out to see them off. 'It was a glorious feeling whilst it lasted; that was until we were packed into those damnable trucks and jolted through the night to Candas.'

There was one form of relief from the miseries of war in which Surfleet did not indulge: sex. He may have been untypical in this respect, but in later life he claimed that literary accounts placing much emphasis on the amorous adventures of the troops were misleading. In general French women were not available – they were 'too old or too tired doing a man's job to be interested'. And although in the larger towns brothels were available, the menace of venereal disease helped to keep the troops away. Probably Surfleet was an innocent in these matters. But his point was not without some substance. Not only was VD likely to have dismal medical consequences, about which soldiers were soldiers were warned at length, but by contracting it a soldier was committing a military offence in rendering himself unfit for service. It was Surfleet's view that those who 'caught a dose' suffered in so many ways that the urge in others was quenched.

Certainly, Surfleet would not have behaved in any way that might have unfitted him to serve with his companions. For here perhaps was the greatest solace that army life had to offer him and that made it bearable and sometimes even worthwhile – comradeship. This, it may be conjectured, is why the question of disobeying orders never entered his mind. It was not the fear of punishment that caused him to participate in offensives he thought ill-advised. Failure to do so would have seemed a blow struck not against the military establishment but against his own mates. He would have been leaving them in the lurch and causing them to shoulder his share of a common burden that he ought to be bearing with them.

His attitude is made plain by an incident on the dread 13 November 1916. Late on that day of the renewed offensive he led a party into the battle zone and was waiting for a lieutenant to give them instructions. At that point some of the party ('thank God there were not many') slipped down a side trench and stayed there until all the work had been done and the rest of the group was returning. 'Then the miserable devils slipped back into the file, no one of any importance being any the wiser.' For Surfleet these men had not beaten the system or got the better of the authorities he sometimes criticized. They had betrayed their companions. He wrote:

> There are some things one can understand: I must never sneer at a man who is afraid, for I have been more frightened out here than it is necessary for me to record. That is one thing; scrounging to the detriment of your pals is another and we who saw those rotters have not forgotten; I don't suppose we ever shall.

As we have seen, Surfleet himself during this phase of the battle was to spend long spells, in awful exertion and considerable danger, giving aid to the wounded. Then he slept as if in a coma, and it was midday on the 15th before he learned of the terrible losses – including those of close friends and admired officers – suffered by his battalion. Yet he was glad, he wrote, to have participated in the way he did and not to have been absent while the rest of his company was suffering. As he had fallen asleep after that long spell in No-Man's-Land, a quite indescribable feeling had come over him, 'esprit de corps or comradeship – I don't know what it was'. What he did know was that he felt glad he could 'look the rest of the lads in the face and claim to be one of them'. This seemed foolish to him, 'for I have said many times how nervous I am and I should have no wish to fraternise with the *real* warriors'. Still, that was his feeling.

In Private Surfleet's strange elation at having stood with his comrades in this culminating disaster of the Somme operation may lie the explanation of how the British army kept fighting during those desperate months and how it could face another year prepared to do the same.

34

THE WAR OF THE SKIES

You've no idea what you're missing. Come and see men like ants crawling.
Captain Eustace Lorraine to Major H. M. Trenchard, c. June 1912 (these sentences persuaded
Trenchard, then well into his fortieth year, to take up flying)

I

The Somme campaign was the first climacteric of Britain's involvement in the Great War. It also marked an important phase of one noteworthy, if minor, aspect of that conflict: the struggle for mastery of the air.

Aircraft had revealed themselves as a useful adjunct to the land forces from the outset of the war. The BEF took with it to France in August 1914 what has been called 'the first organised national force to fly to a war overseas'[1]. Admittedly, the numbers were puny by later standards: 63 flying machines (of bewildering variety), along with 105 pilots and observers, 755 mechanics and administrators, and sundry motorized vehicles. But even though not large, the Royal Flying Corps (RFC) probably provided the BEF, relative to its size, with as much air support as was available to the armies of France and Germany. What Britain lacked *vis-à-vis* its principal ally and principal adversary was the basis for rapid expansion: an aeroplane engine industry. Germany, it is true, had before 1914 devoted unwarranted resources to the development of the airship as against the aeroplane. But the effort put into devising the large engines required by the Zeppelin would in part explain why, for so much of the war, German pilots flew more highly powered aircraft than did British.

To speak of air power in this conflict is somewhat misleading. The fragile machines that flew to France in 1914 were not equipped to strike directly at the enemy. They lacked the carrying capacity to convey bombs and guns in any quantities. And although this would change as the war proceeded, it would not do so to any large extent in terms of the forces engaged in the land war. Where aircraft could make a distinctive contribution, as had become clear in pre-war manoeuvres, was in the gathering of 'intelligence'. That is, to an extent far beyond what had ever lain within the capacity of the traditional arm of observation – the cavalry – aircraft were capable of detecting what was taking place on the other side of the hill.

Yet performing this task, anyway with consistency and to a high standard of efficiency, was not easy. In the early stages of the war it was largely a matter of chance what airman saw, how much of it they recalled by the time they reported to base, and how accurately they interpreted it. Yet a handful of events in the opening weeks demonstrated the potential worth of aerial observation. The fledgling RFC brought Sir John French at Mons the ominous news of von Kluck's approach from the north and

---

[1] Sir Walter Raleigh, *The War in the Air* (London: Hamish Hamilton, 1969), vol. 1, p. 287.

the French withdrawal on Sir John's own right. And Allied airmen helped to alert Joffre to the developing gap between the German First and Second Armies that made possible the counter-stroke on the Marne.

Early in September 1914 the RFC performed another service for the forces on the ground. With the enemy dug in on the Aisne, aircraft helped to direct British artillery fire on to German positions. First they took artillery officers aloft to establish the whereabouts of the German guns. Then they began observing the fall of British shells and reporting back on its accuracy. Few aircraft at this time were capable of taking aloft the bulky wireless sets (weighing some 75 lbs) of the day, anyway with an observer also on board. But occasionally a pilot, flying solo, was able to observe the fall of shell and report it by wireless. A sequence of messages telegraphed from the air on 24 September 1914, during the battle of the Aisne, by one Lieutenant Lewis (who would lose his life while observing in 1916) has entered aerial folklore. The series began at 4.2 p.m.: 'A very little short. Fire. Fire.' It continued at 4.12: 'A little short; line OK,' and at 4.15: 'Short. Over, over and a little left.' Then at 4.22 it proclaimed: 'You have them,' and at 4.26: 'Hit. Hit. Hit.'

Thereafter, in the interests of efficiency, artillery observation messages lost this dramatic quality. Plain English gave way to hieroglyphics referring to positions on what was termed a clock code. By means of just a letter and a number, the observer in the sky could indicate in what direction and by what distance the artillery were diverging from their target. So the Morse message 'E5' signified that a shell had fallen 400 yards south-south-east of its intended destination.

In the opening weeks of combat, then, the RFC established what would remain its major contribution to the First World War. The air force would not, in any large respect, be capable of waging an independent campaign. Air strategists might dream of

Plate 28 *A British air fleet drawn up for inspection. This assemblage of early RFC aircraft suggests their varied nature, flimsiness, and limited carrying capacity.*

bombing missions against Berlin and other principal centres. And, on the basis of quaint notions concerning the German as against the British 'national character', they might envisage the devastating effects wrought upon enemy morale by a few tons of bombs directed at civilians. The war would end with such notions unfulfilled. As aircraft grew larger, structurally stronger, and more highly powered, they would become capable of bombing missions and machine-gun attacks against ground targets. In so far as these could be directed at communications facilities and enemy troops beyond the range of land-based guns, they extended the strike capacity of the British war machine. But their effectiveness lay very largely in tactical support of operations on the ground. And the total weight of bombs and bullets that aircraft could dispatch remained trivial by comparison with what the contenders down below were flinging at each other. Where the air force could make its unique contribution was as the eye in the sky, warning of the activities of the enemy and making ever more effective the activities of its own side.

II

As 1915 and 1916 witnessed a huge expansion in British ground forces, a corresponding need emerged for the growth of the air arm. Given the nation's lack of an aircraft industry and tardiness in development of the motor vehicle, this was a tall order. By August 1915 it was noted that, while the number of divisions in the BEF had expanded from 4 to 30, the number of squadrons in the RFC had advanced only from 4 to 11. Early on, to secure engines and even designs for aircraft, Britain was obliged to look across the Channel, for the only arsenal of aircraft construction available to the Allies lay in France. So of the additional 50 aeroplanes acquired by the RFC in the last four months of 1914, 26 were supplied by the French and the remainder, though British-made, were powered by French engines.

Not until 1916 did Britain's dependence on its ally in this area pretty well cease. By then firms once quite outside aircraft production, like Daimler and Weir, were producing aeroplane engines on a large scale, while makers of furniture and pianos were constructing complete air frames. Statistics for August 1916 reveal that 114 firms, employing 20,000 personnel, were engaged in the manufacture of aeroplane engines; and that, all told, some 491 firms with a labour force of 60,000 were contributing to some aspect of aircraft production.

The other crying need was for trained personnel: not only pilots and observers but also mechanics. For the last of these the engineering industry had to be scoured. As for flyers, Britain possessed – particularly in its public schools – a considerable reservoir of young men eager to take to the air in the nation's interest. Its deficiency lay in the area of training. There was a lack of suitable aircraft, of appropriate training methods, and of men with the flying ability and instructional skills to convert novices into competent pilots. For three years, until R. Smith-Barry was appointed in 1917 to carry out a wideranging reorganization of training methods, Britain paid heavily for its attempts to create airmen in a hurry. According to one account, 'official figures at the end of the war listed 14,166 dead pilots, of whom 8,000 had died while training in the U.K. In other words more pilots died training at home than were killed by the enemy.'[2]

As the numbers of machines and personnel grew, an appropriate command structure and a suitable manner of grouping the aircraft had to be devised. So there came into existence the flight (consisting of four machines), and then the squadron (initially

---

[2] Denis Winter, *The First of the Few: Fighter Pilots of the First World War* (London: Allen Lane, 1982), p. 36.

consisting of three flights), and then the wing (of two to four squadrons). Different squadrons were assigned to different authorities: those under corps command carried out principally the task of close observation, while those under army command roamed further afield.

In the actual practice of aerial warfare 1915 saw the initiation of many developments that, for Britain, would come to fulfilment only in the great struggles of the ensuing years. Early in 1915 it became evident that much aerial observation for the artillery was going unregarded by those on the ground. Following one attack the commander of First Wing had the galling experience of being asked by an artillery officer: 'Don't you see, Colonel Trenchard, that I'm far too busy fighting to have time for playing with your toys in the air?'[3] Plainly, signalling by lamp and such devices would not serve. The first necessity was a wireless set light enough to be carried in an aircraft along with an observer; and by the autumn of 1915 this had been accomplished with the introduction of the Sterling set weighing under 20 lbs. Secondly, these sets had to be married to ground receiving stations that were themselves in direct contact with the artillery.

That year witnessed another major advance in air reconnaissance. The early battles had shown that, if pilots and observers witnessed some things of importance, they missed others or reported them misleadingly. Clearly, what was happening on the ground needed to be captured in permanent form, thereafter to be studied and deciphered by trained interpreters. This need grew with the unrelenting development of anti-aircraft guns, driving pilots and observers from the low levels at which they had originally operated to heights of several thousand feet. Consequently (again with much assistance from the French), British observation aircraft came to be equipped with cameras of increasing sophistication and reliability. From this small beginning a huge war industry blossomed. Enemy areas were photographed not only comprehensively but repeatedly, in order that what might not be evident from an isolated viewing revealed itself through the changes occurring between one visit and the next.

As early as February 1915 aerial photography played a notable part in an infantry attack. Pictures taken in advance of a limited assault by British and French forces revealed a feature of the German defences that had hitherto gone unobserved. The plan of attack was amended accordingly. By the end of the same month the RFC was providing a photographic portrait of the whole German defence system at Neuve Chapelle.

The battle of Aubers Ridge in May 1915 saw a further development – a novelty at least for the British – in aerial observation. To assist the British attack the French made available a kite balloon: that is, a tethered balloon manned by highly skilled observers. (The occupants of balloons could, in an emergency, make their departure by parachute, a facility not available to any RFC pilots throughout the war.) The balloon, within the limits of its vision, proved extremely useful. Unless molested by enemy aircraft, against which it was protected by a great deal of weaponry, it could remain aloft practically all day, while aircraft needed refuelling every couple of hours. And the balloon observer could communicate with the battery by telephone, whereas the wireless transmitter in an aeroplane was strictly one-way. Hence the RFC set about acquiring its own balloon sections, thereby substantially increasing its capacity to serve the artillery. (It was while acting as a balloon observer that Captain B. H. Radford – otherwise the entertainer Basil Hallam who was much admired by Private Surfleet – met his death. In a high wind on 20 August 1916 the balloon that he was occupying broke free and set off towards the trenches. Hallam and his aid jettisoned their maps and instruments and jumped for it, but Hallam's parachute failed to open.)

---

[3] Andrew Boyle, *Trenchard* (London: Collins, 1962), p. 136.

In one respect aerial observation continued to fall short of requirements throughout 1915. During an infantry attack an overriding problem for the command and the artillery was to establish the whereabouts of the advancing troops. On the face of it, the air force was equipped to supply this information. Yet as late as the battle of Loos in September airmen still proved, despite considerable preparation, ineffective in this matter. Attacking infantry, even when able, were usually unwilling to try to attract the attention of their own aircraft for fear of attracting hostile attention as well. And from the heights at which, in the interests of self-preservation, aeroplanes were now required to fly the distinction between khaki and field-grey uniforms simply was not apparent.

One aspect of the war increased dramatically in the closing stages of 1915: combat in the skies. Quite evidently, aerial observation was a boon not to one contestant but to both. Each side, therefore, wished not only to possess this advantage but also to deny it to the adversary. To accomplish the latter it was necessary to devise means of driving opposing aircraft from the skies. Anti-aircraft fire was one method, and was increasingly employed. But plainly aeroplanes, if suitably armed and in sufficient numbers, were the most effective way of denying airspace to the opposition. What was needed was a flying machine that, if not necessarily of great service for the primary function of observation, could accomplish two subsidiary purposes: to drive away or destroy the observation planes of the enemy and to hold at bay enemy aircraft themselves bent on attack.

From this situation there emerged the fighter plane (or scout, as it was initially called). In short order these aircraft and the men who flew them established a grasp on the public imagination that since that time has scarcely been relaxed. The fighters, it needs to be insisted, were not performing the central function of the air war. That remained with the reconnaissance machines, taking their photographs, guiding the artillery, flying an undeviating course, enduring much tedium, and finding the skies increasingly perilous. But for those who wished to perceive warfare as combat between warriors, aerial reconnaissance was not inspiring. If performed unmolested, it seemed as unglamorous as the Grand Fleet beating the waters of the North Sea (another, and even more crucial, task that failed to rivet the imagination). And if the observation craft came under attack from a fighter, the contest was too unequal to satisfy the public craving for combat. By contrast, in the activities of the fighter pilots the heroic notion of warfare might find ample satisfaction.

Only in the second half of 1915 did technology manage to convert the flying machine into a true fighting machine. Admittedly from an early stage some pilots and observers had carried with them pistols and rifles. But so slim was the chance, when firing a single-shot weapon from one moving vehicle towards another, of striking a vital spot that this hardly constituted aerial fighting. Something more was required: first, an aircraft sufficiently powered that it could manoeuvre effectively when burdened with the weight of a machine-gun; and, secondly, an efficient means of bringing the bullets of the machine-gun to bear on the intended victim.

By the middle of 1915 all the combatants on the Western Front had developed aircraft capable of taking a machine-gun aloft. But no one on the Allied side had really mastered the problem of employing the weapon to deadly effect. The most propitious manner, plainly, of shooting down an opposing aircraft was when the enemy lay directly ahead: here the problems of aiming at a moving target from a moving gun platform were minimized. For the pusher aircraft, in which the engine and propeller were situated in the rear, forward firing was a simple matter. But the pusher planes of 1915 were slower and less manoeuvrable than the tractors (with their engines in the front) and hence not well equipped to get the latter in their sights. As for the tractor (or puller) machine, its foremost object was its propeller, so that firing a machine-gun directly forward was likely to be more hazardous for the attacker than the attacked. One solution was to place the machine-gun alongside the fuselage, or (in the case of a biplane) on the top-wing mounting, thus allowing the bullets to clear the propeller. And it was in a machine so equipped that, on 25 July 1915, L. G. Hawker scored the run of successes that won him the Victoria Cross for valour. Nevertheless, it was not a very satisfactory solution. For one thing, the gun was too remote for the pilot easily to change ammunition drums or to clear the jams that developed in the frequently malfunctioning weapons.

It was the Germans, as all the world soon knew, who first effectively married the machine-gun to the tractor aircraft. So dramatic was their success that on 20 January 1916 the son of Earl Beauchamp, on the eve of returning to France, wrote privately to the editor of the *Daily Express*: 'It is not too much to say at present that the Germans have got absolute mastery of the air. Why not say it? – but don't quote me!'[4] The enemy success was twofold. In the Fokker monoplane they developed a fighter that, if not outstanding, was capable of an almost vertical dive and so could make a swift pounce on reconnaissance craft. And the weapon with which the Fokker was armed was a forward-firing machine-gun synchronized with the propeller, so that the firing mechanism halted whenever the propeller reached the vertical. Hence when the Fokker pilot aimed his aircraft at his quarry he was also aiming his gun. The outcome was frequently decisive.

In one important respect the Germans were unlucky in the timing of this development. It was late October 1915 before the Fokkers began appearing on the British sector of the Western Front in large numbers. Their supremacy continued through the first half of 1916 but by mid-year was decisively ended. That is, their dominance coincided with a period in which no major operation was launched by the British. Hence the Fokker's influence on the land war (to which, it cannot be said too often, the air war was only an adjunct) was negligible.

Nevertheless, the 'Fokker scourge' marked an important stage in the development of aerial warfare. It indicated that, at any moment, a combination of technological developments could transform the situation in the skies. The air force that slipped behind in these respects would not only cease to be able to do its job efficiently; it might find itself unable to do its job at all.

The RFC, certainly, was not reduced to this extremity during the Fokker period. But it lost aircraft at the distressing rate of one a day between November 1915 and June 1916. And it suffered a shrinkage in effectiveness that far exceeded the total of planes damaged or destroyed. For the only way that observation craft could now operate was if they were accompanied by a strong force of fighters – which meant that the fighters were not free to operate elsewhere. So on 14 January 1916 a directive went out that, in the absence of an aircraft capable of dealing with the Fokker, 'it must be laid down as a hard and fast rule that a machine proceeding on reconnaissance must be escorted by at least three other fighting machines.' In order to make this protection effective, 'Flying in close formation must be practised by all pilots.' Early the following month a proposal was put forward for a reconnaissance of German railway activity. It envisaged employing 12 fighter escorts for a single observation machine. Although the scheme was not implemented, it provided a clear indication of the way in which the Fokker was constricting the activities of which the RFC was now capable.

---

[4] R. D. Blumenfeld papers, in the House of Lords Record Office.

The Fokker period marked an important transition in another respect. It brought a large new element of death, injury, and capture into the RFC's experience of the war – an element that, if fluctuating, would be present unrelentingly hereafter. From the start, admittedly, flying in this war had been a dangerous occupation. Simple errors would place any pilot, and particularly the novice, at serious risk. And every flyer faced the threat of betrayal by ill-designed or ill-made machines. Moreover, once over the battle lines there was the further hazard of fire from machine-guns and artillery on the ground.

But the creation of an aircraft that constituted not just a chance menace but a potent weapon against other aeroplanes added a new dimension of danger to aerial activity. The sky ceased to be friendly or even neutral. Within it might lurk, concealed by clouds or the sun, a single adversary or – increasingly as the war progressed – a whole flock of adversaries. Their onset could encompass sudden death as a spray of bullets extinguished life. But death might be protracted if the bullets shattered part of the machine, causing it to disintegrate or spiral downwards to the ground.

The worst prospect confronting the airman was that an enemy attack might fire his engine. The light-weight aircraft of the day made a relatively leisurely descent, and the pilot had little prospect of bringing his machine to ground before the flames engulfed him. (Some might choose to jump to their deaths or, if they carried a pistol, to make their quietus that way – as Mannock, the greatest of British aces, made it plain he would do.) Death by burning, it is said, is among the forms of dying to which humans are least able to reconcile themselves. For airmen in this war it proved sufficiently common to become an obsession with many of them. Mannock and, across the lines, Richthofen dwelt on it increasingly. Just before his death, Mannock wrote:

> To watch a machine burst into flames is a ghastly sight. At first a tiny flame peeps out of the tank as if almost ashamed at what it is about to do. Then it gets bigger as it licks its way along the length and breadth of the machine. Finally, all that can be seen is a large ball of fire enveloping in a terrifying embrace.

For not a few airmen the dread of death by fire followed them into sleep. One British pilot wrote in his diary:

> Had a terrible nightmare last night. Jumped out of my bed eleven times even though I tried to stop myself by tying my pyjama strings to the bed. . . . It was the usual old business of being shot down in flames and jumping out of my aeroplane.[5]

Plainly, combat in the air exacted a heavy price from those who became engaged in it.

III

Notwithstanding the dominance that the German air force seemed to have established in the first half of 1916, by the time British infantry went over the top on 1 July the situation in the air had been quite transformed. The skies above the battle lines were under Allied control.

Fundamental to this change was the defeat of the Fokker. By May 1916 the RFC could call on a range of aircraft that were more than its match. The French were supplying their ally with the Nieuport single-seater, a purely fighting machine in which Albert Ball cut a swathe through his opponents and became his countrymen's first air hero. The Royal Aircraft Factory provided the FE2b and private enterprise the DH2.

---

[5] Quotations in Winter, *The First of the Few*, pp. 163, 145.

Both were pusher aircraft, a species that had no great future but served well enough in mid-1916. Fairly fast and manoeuvrable, with an excellent field of fire, they fulfilled a crucial purpose in the hands of men like Hawker. Rawlinson reported late in May that since the DH2s had started taking on the Fokker, his corps aircraft had photographed all of the German trenches on a front of 20 miles 'without being once attacked by the Fokkers'. (Also making its appearance at this time was a Sopwith two-seater, the first of a notable breed. A tractor aircraft, with a forward-firing machine-gun equipped with interruptor gear, it clearly heralded the type that the RFC would need in mounting numbers. But in mid-1916 it was not available in sufficient quantities to account for the demise of the Fokker.)

The role assigned to the RFC in the Somme campaign required not only better machines but many more of them. At last British industry was going some distance towards meeting the requirements of its air force. So by the start of the Somme battle the four squadrons on the Western Front of August 1914 had risen to 27, consisting of 410 aeroplanes of which a majority were still reconnaissance craft but with a mounting proportion of fighters. Their tasks, for which preliminary training was intense, were primarily what they had been in previous offensives but on a greatly magnified scale: above all, aerial photography of enemy positions in advance of and during the battle, and observation for the artillery. In addition, tactics of formation flying were developed. Their purpose was to render bombing more effective by concentrating upon a limited number of targets. And close liaison was at last successfully established between groups of observation planes ('contact patrols') and the advancing infantry, so that for the first time the RFC managed to provide headquarters with accurate information regarding the progress of the attack. Finally, squadrons of fighters drove the reconnaissance and fighting aircraft of the enemy well away from the British lines.

The burgeoning number of fighter planes was accompanied by the adoption of a doctrine that would be a feature of the air war hereafter. It laid down that the RFC must, as a matter of course, fly patrols deep into enemy territory. No longer would British fighters provide close protection for the observation machines. Their parish lay in the air space of their adversaries, acting as cover for long-distance bombing missions, seeking battle with enemy aircraft wherever they could be found, and engaging, day in and day out, in 'offensive sweeps so meticulously timed that Fokker intruders were said to "set their watches by them"'.[6]

The author of this doctrine was H. M. Trenchard, who had taken over command of the RFC in France in August 1915 and would prove the dominating figure in British air policy to the end of the war. In earlier life, as a soldier and administrator in foreign parts, Trenchard had often driven himself to and beyond the limits of physical endurance. Now he set about driving the flying men of Britain to the limits of their country's capacity for producing aircraft and flyers. In the outcome, it could fairly be said, no military operation was launched on the Western Front to which the air arm was not able to make its necessary contribution. Whether, in doing so, it was really needful for the airmen to pay so high a price, in young lives and unfulfilled talent, is an altogether different matter.

The doctrine underlying Trenchard's forward policy received its classic statement in a memorandum written by him on 22 September 1916 – a document that, notwithstanding its unrelenting incoherence, evokes expressions of admiration even to this day. Fundamental to it are two assertions: that 'the aeroplane is not a defence against the aeroplane'; and that 'as a weapon of attack' the aeroplane 'cannot be too highly

---

[6] Boyle, *Trenchard*, p. 184.

estimated'. From these points it draws the conclusion that, regardless of developments in German air policy and performance, the RFC must go on 'attacking' and 'continuing to attack'.

Neither of Trenchard's premises is argued by him. Neither, it must be said, is capable of argument. The havoc wreaked on the RFC by the relatively small number of Fokkers had already made it apparent that the aeroplane was a highly effective weapon against other aircraft. The same thing would be demonstrated many times thereafter, as in Bloody April of 1917 and in the Battle of Britain of 1940: so making Trenchard's reputation as a prophet of aerial developments hard to comprehend.

As for the doctrine that as a weapon of attack the aeroplane 'cannot be too highly estimated', as it stands it is meaningless. If the reference is to attack on distant ground targets such as industrial centres, then in the context of 1916 the assertion was the reverse of true. Indeed, to the end of the Great War the aeroplane's powers of attack were ridiculously easy to overestimate. If the reference is to attacks on other aircraft, then nothing is left of Trenchard's assertion that the aeroplane is no defence against the aeroplane. But then if the statement really does refer to attacks upon enemy aircraft, it is hardly discussing an offensive policy at all. Rather, it is saying that, for protecting British reconnaissance aircraft and ground positions, the forward defensive is a more effective proceeding than the close defensive. And that, it might be thought, was a question not dependent on large strategic generalities (let alone a misconception of what constitutes an offensive). Instead it required a close inquiry into a variety of tactical matters: for example, the relative numbers and fighting qualities of the opposing air forces at any particular time; the direction and strength of the wind on any day; and the state of activity or inactivity on the battlefield.

Yet on the basis of these ill-supported dogmas British fighter pilots henceforth would be sent relentlessly into enemy territory and into the waiting arms of the German squadrons. There they sustained a level of casualties that, if impossible accurately to compute, seems well to have outrun those they were able to inflict. (According to the official historian, 'it would appear that the offensive which was relentlessly pursued in the air by the British air service was about four times more costly than the defensive policy adopted by the Germans.')[7] No doubt many flying men were as convinced as Trenchard of the merits of proceeding into enemy air space regardless of cost. But this was not invariably the case. 'I have lost, as you know, eight machines at low bombing,' Trenchard wrote early in July 1916 to the director of air organization at the War Office. 'I am afraid some of the pilots are getting a bit rattled, and it's not popular.'[8] One who did not appreciate the casualty rate was Hugh Dowding, then a wing commander (and in time one of the heroes of the Battle of Britain). Early in August 1916 he insisted that one of his squadrons, half of whose original rota of pilots were by then dead or wounded, be withdrawn from the line – causing Trenchard to write him off as a 'dismal Jimmy' and to make plans for his replacement.

To single out Trenchard's doctrine of the 'offensive', of course, is to consider only one part of his contribution to the air war. He gave the RFC determined leadership and a clear sense of direction. He won for it the admiration and devoted support of the army command, and played an important part in drawing from the authorities at home reinforcements both in aircraft and in personnel. No other individual in the RFC

---

[7] H. A. Jones, *The War in the Air* (Oxford: Clarendon Press, 1935), vol. 5, p. 471. This statement, unfortunately, is not elaborated in the text or the statistical tables.
[8] Boyle, *Trenchard*, p. 183.

offered the driving power that he brought to it. Much would have been lost had his dynamism been absent – even though a good deal was lost because of its presence.

IV

July and August 1916 proved an ambiguous period in the history of the RFC. Superior numerically and in the quality of their aircraft, British flyers kept the skies over the battle lines free of the enemy. And they furnished prodigious support for the artillery and infantry and high command, to which the enemy air force could provide no counter. But they lost 141 men killed or missing (and about another 90 wounded) in the process. And British forces down below, after first sustaining a terrible setback, were at no stage proving able to accomplish their larger objectives. Ultimately, the opening of the Somme campaign served to show that the most the RFC could contribute must remain a small part of the whole. Command of the air in this war would never make the difference between success and failure on the ground.

By September command of the air was receding. As the Germans abandoned the Verdun operation, there occurred a large increase in the number of enemy aeroplanes stationed in the Somme region: by October one-third of the German air force was to be found there. Again, the Germans were now bringing to the front new classes of aeroplane, particularly the Albatros D and the Halberstadt, which could outfly anything the RFC had in the sky. Finally, these new aircraft coalesced into special pursuit squadrons, made up of hand-picked flyers and commanded by leaders of the calibre of Oswald Boelcke.

On 17 September Boelcke with five of his pilots, among them Manfred von Richthofen, fell in with a force of eight British bombers and six fighters, all of the pusher variety. Without loss, Boelcke's squadron dispatched four of the fighters and two bombers. All told, that month 105 RFC flyers went killed or missing, nearly three-quarters of them in the second half of the month. Haig on 30 September sent home an urgent request for 'a very early increase in the numbers and efficiency of the fighting aeroplanes at my disposal'. For three months, he wrote, the RFC had maintained 'such a measure of superiority over the enemy in the air that it has been enabled to render services of incalculable value'. But the Germans had been making great efforts to increase the number, speed, and power of their machines, and had 'unfortunately succeeded in doing so'. They were now in possession of 'a considerable number of fighting aeroplanes which are faster, handier, and capable of attaining a greater height than [with a handful of exceptions] any at my disposal'. Haig did not anticipate losing air predominance in the next few months, but 'the situation after that threatens to be very serious unless adequate steps to deal with it are taken at once.'

So 1916 drew to a close with the RFC facing an ominous situation. It had achieved notable successes during the Somme campaign. Rawlinson, on 29 October, reported that airmen had observed 1,721 shoots on enemy batteries and 281 bombardments of enemy trench systems, and on each day of attack had furnished reports on the whereabouts of British and hostile troops that were 'remarkably accurate'. Moreover, despite Flying Corps casualties between July and December of some 419 killed or missing and more than another 250 injured, the number of pilots and the size of the force was larger by a quarter when the battle ended than when it began. But the wastage rate was higher than these figures suggest, as another 250 men had left the strength without becoming casualties. (It may be wondered how many of these had fallen victim to physical and nervous breakdown.) And the German air force, if always numerically inferior, was closing the gap in numbers – on 15 October the figure was 434 German planes on the British sector to the RFC's 563 – and more than bridging it in organization and quality of aircraft. The newest German fighters as yet constituted a small proportion of the whole. But it was a proportion that was sure to grow. And the British had nowhere in sight, anyway in appreciable numbers, an aeroplane with which to redress the technological balance.

Two events symbolized the grave situation confronting the RFC at the end of 1916. On 16 November Haig and Trenchard made another appeal to the War Office, this time for 20 squadrons of fighters in addition to what had already been calculated as required for the approaching spring. This meant that two squadrons of fighters were now envisaged as necessary to enable each reconnaissance squadron to perform its work.

A week later Lanoe Hawker met his death. The first Briton to be awarded the Victoria Cross for air fighting (the two earlier recipients in the RFC had been engaged in bombing activities, one against a railway station and the other against a Zeppelin), he had also been the first commander of a purely fighting squadron. The best-qualified British ace, on 23 November he fought an isolated duel with the emerging German master Richthofen. In skill there was nothing to choose between them. In quality of aircraft there was much. Richthofen was flying one of the new Albatroses, Hawker a now sadly obsolescent DH2 pusher. (The Englishman, flying over enemy territory with the wind, as usual, against him, also had constantly to manoeuvre for home before he ran out of petrol.) It was evidence of Hawker's superb flying skill that for 30 minutes he held his opponent at bay, time and again tugging his aircraft just clear of the path of Richthofen's synchronized machine-guns. But always the Albatros's greater speed and rate of climb placed the German slightly above and behind his adversary, driving Hawker lower and lower until there was almost no air space left. At last the duel between equal opponents in unequal aircraft reached its climax. Hawker, unable to vanquish his adversary, perforce made a dash for his own lines. Richthofen momentarily got him in his sights and shot him through the head.

PART EIGHT

On The Peripheries
1916

35

SHADOWS OVER THE SIDESHOWS

I

The sideshows brought Britain no comfort in 1916.

The Allied involvement in Salonika continued during this year. But it did so against the wishes of Britain's political and military leaders. Only Lloyd George among them thought the operation made sense once Serbia had been overrun. And even he was not ardent in pressing for much activity there. But the French were determined to remain. And as Ward Price, the official war correspondent in Salonika, observed: 'in every coalition something has to be sacrificed now and then to solidarity.'[1]

Hence Britain agreed not to pull out of Macedonia. But it also refused to send there large numbers of reinforcements. For these the French must look to their other allies: the Russians, the Italians, and especially the Serbs. It was to Macedonia that the remains of the Serbian army were eventually transferred, to become once more a powerful fighting instrument.

The situation of the Salonika force *vis-à-vis* the Greek authorities was awkward. King Constantine and his Ministers expressed their determination to remain neutral, but their sympathies appeared to lie with the Central Powers. For example, in May they handed over to Bulgarian invaders a key position to the north of the Allied camp. This provoked a strong response from Sarrail, the Allied commander, who had little regard for the niceties of Greek neutrality. He brought Salonika and its environs under his own control, so making it 'an occupied city as effectively under alien military administration as Brussels or Warsaw or Belgrade'.[2] (But Salonika, it should be noted, had come under Greek control only two years earlier, making its situation less than comparable with these capital cities.) Sarrail did not halt here. He exerted pressure, in the form of a naval blockade, on the Greek King to give his Government a less pro-German complexion.

As yet the French stopped short of trying to unseat Constantine or instal in office their favoured Greek politician, Venizelos. But they had gone far enough to create uneasiness in Britain's ruling circles. George V objected to the anti-monarchist slant of Sarrail's behaviour. And Robertson and the military hierarchy deplored all forms of involvement in the Balkans. Nevertheless, the British Government did not repudiate its ally's actions. Its members deemed it wiser to go along with the French so as to preserve a right of restraint over Sarrail. In the process they became consenting parties to some pretty squalid deeds.

In military terms, the Salonika front remained quiescent for much of 1916. Sarrail, prudently enough, spent the early part of the year securing his position against a

---

[1] G. Ward Price, *The Story of the Salonica Army* (London: Hodder and Stoughton, 1918), p. 193.
[2] Alan Palmer, *The Gardeners of Salonika* (London: André Deutsch, 1965), p. 67.

possible Bulgarian invasion. However, these precautions proved unnecessary. Apart from some border incursions, the Bulgarians did not invade. So from May the Allied commander sought a more combative role for the 300,000 Allied troops (90,000 of them British) under his direction. His view was endorsed in Paris. Joffre hoped that a Salonika offensive would divert German forces from the Western Front, as well as rendering the principal Balkan neutrals, Greece and Romania, more accommodating.

For a while the authorities in London continued to resist this course. But events on the Eastern Front forced them to reconsider. Thanks to the successes in mid-1916 of the Russian forces against Austria-Hungary, Romania developed a strong inclination to intervene on the Allied side. But its Government specified, among other conditions, that Sarrail must launch an offensive from the south so as to pin down the Bulgarians. So eager were the Allies to secure Romania's aid that this demand could not be gainsaid.

Nevertheless, the British authorities insisted that their own forces at Salonika would make only a limited contribution to any Balkan operation. So when Sarrail planned his attack he placed his main effort not on his right wing, where the British contingents were situated, but on his centre and left. As it happened, he was beaten to the punch by the Bulgarians. In mid-August 1916 they struck against both the British and French forces on his right flank and the Serbs on his left. This double assault enjoyed early success but by the end of the month had been held. Thereafter, from mid-September to mid-December, Sarrail's offensive went ahead. On his right he conducted only holding operations. On his left the Serb contingents, aided by the French, Russians, and Italians, pushed back the Bulgarians as far as Monastir on Serbian territory. (One hotel in Monastir, dubbed the 'Hôtel de la Nouvelle Serbie' in 1912 on the termination of Turkish rule, and retitled 'Hôtel de la Nouvelle Bulgarie' in 1915 when Serbia was overrun, now judiciously opted for 'Hôtel Européen'.)

With the capture of Monastir the Allied offensive against Bulgaria petered out. It was something that, with the onset of another Balkan winter – 'always a time of rain overhead and mud underfoot'[3] –, a corner of Serbia had been liberated. But in its primary purpose, that of assisting the newest ally, this operation had failed. As it proceeded, the forces of Romania were suffering catastrophe at the hands of the Central Powers. By the end of 1916 most of Romania lay under enemy occupation.

In other respects little had been achieved on the Salonika front in 1916. Far from being driven out of the war, Bulgaria had warded off Sarrail's assaults with little loss of territory and only modest assistance from Germany. As for Greece itself, by and large it remained obstinately neutral. At the end of 1916 the notion of a Balkan confederation marching shoulder to shoulder against Austria-Hungary – or was it against Turkey? – remained as much a pipe dream as ever.

II

If the campaign in Macedonia in 1916 brought no success to British arms, at least it did not inflict any great humiliation. Matters were otherwise with the campaign in Mesopotamia.

As related earlier, in November 1915 the British advance up the Tigris had been roughly halted at Ctesiphon. Townshend's force had been driven into retreat, coming to rest at Kut. Townshend judged that his troops were too exhausted to retreat any

---

[3] Ward Price, *The Story of the Salonica Army*, p. 187.

further, so he decided to render Kut secure and await relief. The prospect of being besieged may not have dismayed him too much. Early in his career, as an officer in the Indian army, he had been holed up in similar circumstances. After 46 days he had emerged, unvanquished, to find himself a hero.

Events would turn out differently in Mesopotamia in 1916. The problems of relieving Kut were considerable. The harbour at Basra was not as yet properly equipped to speed ashore such reinforcements of men and weapons as were becoming available. The movements of the relief force were tied to the river, given the absence of roads and motorized transport, yet river craft were in painfully short supply. And the Turks had established a strong series of defensive positions, downriver from Kut, that it would be necessary to breach.

Townshend severely underestimated the difficulties that awaited his rescuers. Hence he made at the outset no close investigation of the food supplies that might be available to him. After a quick check he informed Basra that he could last out for only 60 days, which meant not much beyond the end of January 1916. He also made it clear that he placed little reliance on the staying power of the Indian contingents under his command.

This information forced the organizers of the rescue operation to act with greater dispatch than was warranted. So instead of waiting to maximize their resources before moving against the Turks, they decided to press upriver with such men and equipment as lay to hand. In consequence, the under-strength and under-supplied rescuers were pushed into a succession of frontal assaults against well entrenched positions. The resulting cost was prohibitive: in the attacks of January one-third of the British front-line forces became casualties and in April one-quarter. All told, 23,000 casualties were sustained in the attempt to rescue a besieged force of 13,000. The losses were much aggravated by the inadequacy of the medical services and of transportation for the wounded. This not only inflicted wanton suffering but also lowered morale throughout the entire force.

Only once did the relief operations approach success. During the night of 7–8 March a British force of 20,000, undetected by the enemy, marched a distance approaching 7 miles to a position where they might turn the Turkish flank. By dawn the companies were poised to attack a completely unprepared foe. But detailed orders had stipulated that the assault must be preceded by an artillery bombardment. More than three hours passed before this could be mounted, and then its principal effect was to alert the Turks and send them hastening to reinforce their positions. There followed the customary failure of a frontal assault against entrenched positions.

Townshend meanwhile had scoured Kut for food, had cut down rations, and had even prevailed on his Indian troops to set aside their scruples about consuming horseflesh. Thus he had considerably extended his forces' staying power. And the morale of his troops proved a good deal sturdier than he had anticipated. But it was all in vain. By mid-April his food supplies had reached exhaustion; his troops had become desperately weak and were succumbing to various illnesses; and all hope of early rescue had vanished. A medical officer within Kut writes of these last days:

> Though we jested and joked and made light of each other's vanishing figures, yet it was a time of misery – a long-drawn-out agony of suspense and disappointment, and of not a little suffering. . . .
> General Hoghton lay dying. He could not eat the horse-meat and became a shadow of his former robust self. He was one of the first victims of an acute intestinal trouble, a sort of cholera, that was fatal to so many in those last three weeks. He died on the 13th and was

buried the same day.... A military funeral is always impressive, but under those conditions it was doubly so.[4]

As a last resort Townshend, armed with an authorization from the British Government to offer £1 million in cash, sought to negotiate with the Turks. The effort was fruitless and the proposal of money rejected with derision. On 29 April Kut surrendered unconditionally. Many of those who passed into captivity would not survive the long trek across the desert that awaited them or the neglect and frequent ill-usage that lay beyond that.

The fall of Kut, if hardly a major setback to British arms, sent shock waves all the way to Whitehall. Coming so soon after the abandonment of Gallipoli, this further humiliation at Turkish hands appeared inexcusable. Plainly, the conduct of operations in Mesopotamia must be transformed.

The principal change to be instituted was that London took over responsibility for a campaign hitherto directed, with quite inadequate resources, from India. Secondly Major-General F. S. Maude, who had commanded a division with distinction, found himself elevated to the command of the entire Mesopotamian campaign. Some notable acts of reorganization had already been instituted before Maude's appointment. But he possessed the necessary personal qualities to bring them to completion, as well as the unstinted confidence of Robertson, the CIGS, in London.

In the aftermath of Kut large changes took place in the command structure of the Mesopotamian force, from which flowed many practical consequences. Efficient port facilities were at last established at Basra. Sufficient river craft, and craft appropriate to the vagaries of the Tigris, were made available. The narrow parts of the river were illuminated and placed under telephone control so as to render them usable at night. Railways were constructed to supplement river transport, and a metal road was laid from Basra to the front.

An enhanced transport service was, among other things, crucial to another vital improvement: a reorganized medical system. An increase in the number of river craft meant that the wounded could more speedily be transferred from the front to hospital. At the same time, the quality of medical services and of nursing staff was considerably upgraded.

Up-to-date fighting equipment, in ample quantities, also began making its appearance. To quote A. J. Barker:

> Stocks of the latest type of grenades, Verey lights, machine-guns, mortars and guns were all welcome additions to the Expeditionary Force's armoury – especially the medium guns and howitzers so essential to deal with the Turks' earthworks. Reserves of ammunition started to accumulate and bridging material to eradicate one of the most severe handicaps that the Tigris Corps had been suffering from – [lack of] freedom to manoeuvre – was also either collected or manufactured.[5]

Command of the air also changed hands during these months. In May 1916 the Turks, with German machines, could easily outfly the five antiquated aeroplanes available to the British forces. By the end of the year Maude had at his disposal 24 modern aeroplanes capable of bombing and, far more important, photographing enemy positions.

This transformation signified one thing above all else. The military authorities in London continued to have no love for the Mesopotamian operation. But they were prepared to devote to it command personnel, manpower, and materials in sufficient

---

[4] Lt.-Col. C. H. Barber in *I Was There!*, issue no. 23.
[5] A. J. Barker, *The Neglected War: Mesopotamia 1914–1918* (London: Faber & Faber, 1967), p. 317.

numbers and of sufficient quality to ensure that whatever was undertaken stood a reasonable chance of success.

Maude's next task was to convince London that something, indeed, ought to be undertaken – that the shame of Kut must be countered by some aggressive action. Robertson wanted no more progress up the Tigris and talked of withdrawing one division from Mesopotamia. But Maude managed to convince Sir Charles Monro, the new C.-in-C. India (and the man who had recommended the evacuation of Gallipoli), that a forward move was warranted. As India still supplied a majority of the fighting men in this region, Monro's word carried weight in London. So the War Committee authorized Maude to organize an advance, if with no grand objectives. By mid-December 1916, almost coincident with the change of Government in London, the British forces in Mesopotamia began moving on to the offensive once more.

III

There was one other region where, in 1916, British forces were sporadically engaged against the Turks: Egypt and Arabia. But here there were no big actions, and Britain sustained no calamities.

It was firm British policy that the Suez Canal must never be in danger. So whatever was required there to hold the Turks at bay would be supplied. British commanders in Egypt usually overestimated wildly the forces available to the Turks. Hence the Canal was at most times more than amply stocked with Allied troops. The Turks, for their part, were fighting on many fronts, had limited communications, and must cross the Sinai Desert to attack Egypt, so they never managed to pose a serious threat to the Canal.

During 1914 and 1915 the British in this region were inhibited from carrying the war to the enemy by their concern over the attitude of the Egyptian populace. Only by early 1916 was it plain that, little love though the people of Egypt might have for their British rulers, they would not rise against them just so as to bring back the Turks. In 1916, therefore, General Sir Archibald Murray, who from March was sole commander in Egypt, moved towards a more offensive stance. Instead of resting his defence on the Canal itself, he decided to push across the Sinai Desert and establish himself in good watering places just south of the frontier of Palestine.

Crucial to such an undertaking were communications and the supply of water. So Murray instituted the construction across Sinai of a railway, a pipeline, and even a sort of road. He encountered some Turkish resistance and also a quite heavy attack aimed at the Canal in August, but these were defeated with comparative ease. By the end of 1916 the Sinai peninsula was firmly under British control.

This success raised a question. Should the advance be halted here? Or should what had begun as an operation for securing the Canal be transmuted into an invasion of Palestine? There seemed one good reason for pursuing the latter course: restiveness against Turkish rule in parts of the Arab world. Should this escalate, it might prove a serious drain on Turkish resources.

Early in June 1916 Sherif Hussein, the Arab prince who was keeper of the Holy Places of Mecca and Medina, launched a rebellion against the Turkish rulers of Arabia. Hussein had fallen foul of the authorities even before the outbreak of war, and gave further offence after it by failing to endorse the Sultan's call for a Holy War of Islam against the Allies. During 1915 he entered into active negotiations with British representatives that were designed to bring about the end of Turkey's overlordship.

These negotiations were not easy. Hussein was envisaging the establishment of an independent Arab state, presumably under his own rule. This seemed a somewhat grandiose scheme, given his own limited territorial authority and the deep divisions within the Arab world. And it ran counter to ambitions nursed by the Western Allies. For as Turkish rule dwindled, important elements in Britain and France hankered to inherit the role of imperial overlord in parts of Arabia. France had its sights set on most of Syria and Britain on Mesopotamia, with some sort of special status envisaged for Palestine. These imperialist designs acquired tangible form in May 1916, when a secret agreement was concluded between Sir Mark Sykes and M. Georges-Picot on behalf of the Governments of Britain and France.

Nevertheless, if only with a measure of embarrassment and ambiguity, a sort of arrangement was struck between Hussein and the British. The Turks were not unaware of all this. Early in 1916 they began mounting a punitive expedition to bring Hussein's region, the Hejaz, firmly under control. Hussein was already receiving arms and ammunition from the British, but in insufficient quantities to warrant a rising. However, against the advice of British authorities in Cairo (who included some pretty formidable experts on Middle Eastern affairs), Hussein decided to strike.

In Mecca the rising enjoyed immediate success. And, with the aid of British naval craft, Hussein's forces overran some of the main Red Sea ports. But the Turks hit back savagely in Medina. And, thanks to the railway constructed by the Germans before the war (which ran as far as Medina but not to Mecca), they were soon drawing in reinforcements from Damascus. The rebels sought to impede this by action against the railway, but without success. By late 1916 the amalgam of Arab tribes that made up Hussein's supporters was starting to disintegrate.

With the British now established across the Sinai Desert, there were good reasons why they should mount further advances themselves and also devote greater resources to Hussein's movement. As yet only a part of the Arab world had responded to the rebellion. Yet here was the potentiality for a large uprising that might seriously strain the Turks without placing a corresponding (or larger) drain on the British. Certainly, this sideshow, like the others, would cause only limited heartache to the principal enemy, Germany. But at least it might, for a moderate investment of British manpower and weaponry, persuade a local population to tie down large numbers of the troops of one of Britain's lesser adversaries. That was something the other sideshows, despite lofty promises, had manifestly failed to do.

36

SMUTS VERSUS LETTOW-VORBECK

At the outbreak of war Germany possessed an imposing number of colonies. But, lacking command of the sea, it was in no position to retain them unless its colonial troops could live off the land and the Allies were not prepared to bring overwhelming forces against them. By 1916 there was but one German colony whose resistance continued unsubdued.

This was German East Africa (present-day Tanzania), a territory that adjoined British and Belgian and Portuguese possessions. (Portugal entered the war on the Allied side in March 1916.) For both British and Germans, campaigning here was full of obstacles presented by nature. There were tsetse flies and wild bees, a great range of tropical diseases, torrential seasonal rains (of which General Smuts would write, 'I have never in all my life dreamt that rain could fall as it does here'), and bush often so thick that two considerable forces could pass unbeknown to each other at a distance of a mile. Added to these were the problems of transportation in a region where motor roads scarcely existed.

Up to 1916 the war in this region went much in favour of the Germans. They possessed a highly gifted commander in Colonel von Lettow-Vorbeck. And they were employing the right type of troops for these conditions. The German forces were overwhelmingly black. Hence they were inured against the local diseases and were *au fait* with the country. Further, their use of large numbers of porters was the most effective solution to the problem of supply. The War Office, by contrast, had no faith in the fighting quality of the native inhabitants. To begin with the British employed ill-trained and inexperienced troops from India. Then they brought in white South African and better-trained Indian troops – admirable fighting material but terribly prone to malaria and similar scourges.

A further consideration aiding the Germans was the type of war Lettow-Vorbeck chose to fight. He had drawn first blood in 1914 when a British landing at the port of Tanga was repulsed in circumstances humiliating to the invader. And he had followed this up with a minor incursion into Kenya. Then in January 1915 Lettow scored a further success at Jasin on the Kenyan coast, but at a cost in officers and ammunition that he concluded he could not afford. He therefore chose to eschew set-piece battles and to employ guerrilla tactics instead. By striking across the border at the railway line running from Uganda to the coast of Kenya he reckoned that he could oblige the British to use up reinforcements required in other theatres.

On a limited scale, this strategy prospered. At the beginning of 1915 Kitchener had made it plain that reinforcements were not available for this region and that British troops in Kenya and Uganda should stand on the defensive. Given the length of the border and inexperience of the British forces, this gave Lettow ample opportunity to raid the railway. In two months some 30 trains were derailed and 10 bridges destroyed. Coupled with a high incidence of sickness among the British forces, these events forced the War Office to reconsider. It agreed to supply experienced Indian troops from France, and yet more experienced white South Africans who had just completed the conquest of German South-West Africa.

So 1915 had gone very much as Lettow intended. The next year proved more equivocal. With the British reinforcements there came, early in the new year, a new commander. General Smuts was a South African statesman who, having fought against Britain in the Boer War, would spend 1917 and 1918 as a member of Lloyd George's War Cabinet. His year commanding the British forces in East Africa left the enemy in a much depleted condition.

Certainly, Smuts's accomplishments in 1916 were not as great as he claimed when, on departing from East Africa in early 1917, he stated: 'the campaign is over . . . all that now remains to be done is to sweep up the remnants of the enemy force!' In fact, he had not fulfilled his strategic design. Smuts's initial intention was to hem the enemy in by co-ordinated movements from the north (Kenya and Uganda), the west (the Belgian Congo), and the south (Nyasaland). This, according to Cyril Falls, proved 'one of those elaborate enveloping movements which so often promise more on paper than they provide on the ground'.[1] The Germans, eluding each of the advancing prongs, were never brought to confrontation. And if this kept battle casualties low for the British, their losses from tropical diseases proved prohibitive. Smuts, from a force of 20,000, lost through sickness some 12,000 to 15,000 men between October and December 1916. (He also lost, from the same cause, prodigious numbers of transport animals.)

Even so, Smuts's achievement by the end of 1916 was considerable. He drove Lettow far inside German territory, so ending the threat to the Kenya–Uganda railway. The German commander lost control of his colony's north-eastern region, where the economic resources and European population were concentrated, and of all the ports, which included the capital Dar-es-Salaam. (Earlier, with the aid of two British gunboats transported overland from South Africa, the Allies had gained command of Lake Tanganyika, bordering the Belgian Congo.) Smuts's forces then pressed on to overrun the central railway system, and by the end of 1916 they had crossed the Rufiji river, which was as far as the British Government had asked Smuts to go. Lettow was now the leader of a hunted force within a steadily contracting homeland.

Smuts's period of command witnessed another large achievement, which came to fruition only following his departure. Emulating the Germans, he set about converting this war in the Black Man's Continent into a struggle primarily between black forces. That is, 1916 saw a steady increase in the recruitment and training of indigenous soldiers in the King's African Rifles (as well as the introduction of substantial forces from West Africa and of a contingent from the West Indies). This facilitated the withdrawal of the South Africans and Indians, on whom the brunt of the fighting had hitherto fallen.

So by the start of 1917 neither of the German commander's twin objectives was any longer proving capable of attainment. He was not able to carry out guerrilla raids into British territory. And he was not holding down British forces that otherwise would have been employed elsewhere: for – to labour an obvious point that is often disregarded – even had Lettow been forced to capitulate, the bulk of the troops engaging him in 1917 and 1918 would never have been transferred to other theatres.

To look ahead, Lettow managed to remain in the field to the end of the war. In the course of 1917 he was driven out of German East Africa altogether. But he promptly

---

[1] Cyril Falls, *The First World War* (London: Longman, 1960), p. 233.

invaded Portuguese African territory. There he replenished his supplies of ammunition, food, and medical stores at the expense of well provisioned but ineffective Portuguese forces. Only the capitulation of Germany in November 1918 caused him to lay down his arms. From beginning to end of the war, his was a courageous and skilful performance, absolutely attuned to the circumstances in which he found himself. And it was bound to place him, in German estimation, on the heroic plane to which Britons soon elevated Lawrence of Arabia.

But, even more than is the case with Lawrence, this display of gallantry and resourcefulness has somewhat concealed the limited nature of his achievement. His exploits were possible only because the essential war was occurring continents away. And from the end of 1916 his continued resistance contributed virtually nothing to the outcome of that larger struggle.

PART NINE

Home Front
1916

37

HOME AFFAIRS

English people, taken as a whole, are only just beginning to realize the magnitude of the struggle we are engaged in, and of course want to blame somebody else that greater things are not being done to the end the War.

... since the big offensive started we hear the guns all day sometimes, and can't forget that Ron is there. And we are dreading the Telegram that so many have received lately.

Robert Saunders to his son in Canada, 3 February and 16 July 1916

I

1916 was the year in which the great endeavours that Britain had been making in the mobilization of resources – human, industrial, and financial – began to come to fruition. By chance, at the end of May the great fleets of Britain and Germany met in battle for the first time. By design, in July the British army engaged a major part of the military might of Germany. Indeed, as in no previous phase of the war, the main blows falling on the Germans were being delivered from mid-1916 by the armed forces of Britain.

These events affected the home front very nearly. 'There was little need in June 1916 for the old fretted cry that most people were living as if there was no war on.'[1] The burden of taxation, the air raid, conscription for men, the movement of women from being occasional participants to forming a major component of the workforce, and (not least) the sorrow imposed on countless families by the ubiquitous War Office telegram – 'the terror by day'[2] –, all brought the war home to civilians. Admittedly, most of these elements had been present to a degree in 1915. But the difference in scale in 1916 was moving the impact of war on to an altogether higher plane.

The reward for all this effort seemed disappointingly small. In some respects, certainly, British citizens found causes for satisfaction in 1916. Chief among them, in September, was the unveiling on the battlefield of the tank. For the first time Britain had shown itself able to devise and employ an entirely new weapon of war, for which the enemy, notwithstanding Germany's supposed technical superiority, had no equivalent. And it had managed to do this with complete secrecy, covering the identity of the new weapon by a trick of terminology that tickled the public fancy. The whole episode was taken to characterize what Britons liked to think was their undemonstrative efficiency.

But in only one other respect was the same satisfaction to be derived from the year, and this in an area that, up to September, was a cause of great disgruntlement. The air raid in 1916 brought both dismay and elation to the home front. The raids for this year

---

[1] R. H. Gretton, *A Modern History of the English People 1880–1922* (London: Martin Secker, 1930), p. 993.
[2] E. S. Turner, *Dear Old Blighty* (London: Michael Joseph, 1980), p. 129.

began on the night of 31 January. An attempt was made to bomb as far west as Liverpool, with the object of disrupting merchant shipping. No Zeppelin, in fact, discovered that city (although one did reach Shrewsbury, 40 miles to the south). But the inadequately blacked-out Burton-on-Trent received a good deal of attention, and bombs also fell on some crowded Birmingham suburbs.

This was the first time air-raid alarms had sounded in the West Country. And although the casualties were not great (70 killed, 113 injured), public feeling in the Midlands was outraged by the paucity of resistance that had been offered. Strong opinions were expressed in Parliament, with demands for the appointment of a Minister for Air – someone akin to Lloyd George being specified. The authorities responded by instituting a number of improvements. Responsibility for air defence was at last shifted from the navy to the army; an early warning system was established; and yet more gunnery expertise was diverted from the fighting zone to the home front. (Kitchener went so far as to indicate that in this last respect civilians were being given priority over the army, a statement that had hastily to be amended.) In addition, from mid-February a sequence of air bases was set up equipped with night-fighting aircraft. Their armament, however, remained inadequate. The machine-gun was judged ineffective against the Zeppelin. So most interceptor aircraft were equipped with incendiary bombs intended to be dropped on the raiders.

In the following weeks public indignation on account of air raids did not abate. On the night of 5 March a force of Zeppelins, intended for the Firth of Forth but much buffeted by the weather, dropped bombs on Hull. 'No guns or planes defended the town. The helpless population, in ugly mood, relieved its feelings by stoning a Royal Flying Corps vehicle in Hull, and a flying officer was mobbed in nearby Beverley.'[3] On 10 March a sensational by-election occurred in East Herts, a district that lay on the track of airships approaching London. In a strongly Conservative area the official Unionist candidate was defeated by a flamboyant Independent, Pemberton Billing. Having served in the air force, Billing was campaigning for 'better air defence' and 'a strong air policy'. His success, it was remarked, 'effectually drew the attention of the Government to the popular demand for a more elaborate defence against Zeppelin raids'.[4]

With the airships extending their area of attack, the lighting restrictions that hitherto had applied most rigorously to London and the East Coast were enforced far more widely. To the amusement, it was said, of rural inhabitants, the town dweller was discovering that 'a moonless night can be so dark that no one can see his way about.'[5] As it happened, town dwellers were inclining anyway to staying at home on moonless evenings, because dark fine nights constituted 'Zeppelin weather' – only in such conditions did the raiders deem it safe to come. In London theatre attendances fell as the moon waned, to the point where some proprietors began drawing attention to 'moony nights' as carrying no risk of attack. In what must have been the war's most excruciating attempt to make light of a serious matter, the Alhambra, where the enormously successful *Bing Boys Are Here* was running, proclaimed: 'Come and see the Bing Boys: it is full moon to-night so you need not fear the "Bang Boys".'[6]

In the first week of April, raids were made over a wide area. Scotland received its first experience of attack from the air, the most damage occurring when a whisky

[3] Douglas H. Robinson, *The Zeppelin in Combat* (London: G. T. Foulis, 1962), pp. 131–2.
[4] *Annual Register for 1916*, p. 83.
[5] Gretton, *A Modern History of the English People*, p. 981.
[6] Michael MacDonagh, *In London during the Great War: The Diary of a Journalist* (London: Eyre & Spottiswoode, 1935), p. 143.

warehouse in Leith was set on fire. Altogether, civilian deaths in this week of raids numbered 84, with 227 injured. This constituted a pretty small toll. And for the first time a Zeppelin fell victim to the London defences: a combination of anti-aircraft fire and aeroplane attack brought it down in the sea a mile off the Kentish Knock lightship. Only one more raid occurred in the spring, and that proved farcical. Some fires started on the Yorkshire moors and a few windows broken in a Highlands castle were all that resulted from an attempt to devastate the naval base at Rosyth on 2 May. And again the Germans lost one of their airships, which came to rest in a Norwegian fjord when it ran out of fuel.

During the summer the short nights kept the raiders away. Their reappearance in the autumn brought the Zeppelin attacks to a blazing climax. Improved British defences were now in a position to demonstrate the airship's terrible vulnerability. For, despite its technical accomplishments, the Zeppelin remained basically an enclosed series of gasbags filled with highly inflammable hydrogen. It could not maintain a height beyond anti-aircraft fire or the climbing ability of improved British aeroplanes. And it was becoming increasingly dependent on radio directions to find its targets, so giving the defenders ample warning of its approach. Moreover, the Ministry of Munitions was now equipping British aircraft with machine-guns loaded with a new type of explosive ammunition.

On the night of 2 September the largest airship raid of all was launched against London. Sixteen Zeppelins, both army and navy, set out. On account of the weather many of the raiders did not reach the capital, and those that did enjoyed no success. Only four people were killed and 12 injured (none of them in London) by this formidable array of bombers. And, even more noteworthy, an aeroplane piloted by

Plates 29a and 29b   *Death of a Zeppelin.*

29a   *Part of the remains of the German airship set ablaze by Lieutenant Robinson. It came to earth near the village of Cuffley in Hertfordshire, about 7 miles north of the London boundary.*

29b   *Some of the great crowd which had gone out from London to view the wreckage seen scrambling for a train to get them back home.*

Lieutenant Leefe Robinson managed to engage an army Zeppelin of the older design. Employing the new explosive ammunition, Robinson set it ablaze. The gradual death fall of the flaming airship, according to *Punch*, 'gave North London the most thrilling aerial spectacle ever witnessed'. Robinson became the hero of the hour and received the Victoria Cross, and the small hamlet of Cuffley, where the burning raider came to rest, was soon overrun with sightseers arriving on foot and in every description of vehicle. The authorities went to considerable lengths to conceal their new means of countering the Zeppelin. Readers of the *Annual Register for 1916*, published the following year, were told that Robinson had dropped a bomb on his victim.

Further such spectacles were soon provided. Peter Strasser, the chief of the German navy's Zeppelins, refused to believe that what had happened to an older-style army airship could threaten his more experienced crews and new super-Zeppelins. His force attacked again on 23 September. This time London was bombed successfully, and most of the casualties (40 dead, 130 injured) occurred there. But two of the newest Zeppelins fell victim to the combined attentions of guns and aircraft. One, holed by shells and losing gas as it limped back to the coast, came to earth in Essex and was set on fire by its crew, who were duly taken in charge by a special constable. (An Essex couple, blessed with the birth of a daughter that night, christened her Zeppelina.) The other came down in flames, its awesome descent providing good viewing for what must have been literally millions of people. (Its fate was also witnessed, with less appreciation, by the crews of other raiders, one of them all of 150 miles distant.)

In the following weeks the toll of Zeppelins was unremitting, and the amount of damage they managed to inflict absurdly small. A raid on the Midlands on 25 September achieved for the attackers a modest success without loss. But then on 1 October Heinrich Mathy, the most experienced of Zeppelin commanders, and one greatly admired not only by his comrades but by British defenders, was shot down in flames over London. Subsequent raids further afield demonstrated that no safety was to be found by avoiding the capital. On 17 November 1916, on a night not nearly dark enough to provide the airships with the necessary concealment, British pilots brought down one Zeppelin at West Hartlepool and another at Great Yarmouth.

If once the Zeppelin had proved a threat to British morale, it was now having the contrary effect. In material terms the airship scarcely mattered either way. It could accomplish little destruction, and Germany could easily bear the cost of its decimation. Yet the very evident spectacle of these great creatures in defeat provided British civilians with a keen sense of satisfaction – such as the really substantial naval victory of Jutland failed to give, owing to the paucity of German ships that actually went to the bottom. As 1916 drew to a close the threat from the air remained for Britons a source of discomfort. It was also, however, proving a cause for self-congratulation.

II

For the rest, little about the course of the war in 1916 gave civilians much reason to rejoice. It was not a good year for the nation's allies. In the first half of 1916 the French, instead of taking the battle to the enemy, were fighting for existence at Verdun. It was some cause for reassurance that they survived. But the spectacle of France barely holding its own seemed less than the steady accomplishment of victory.

The case of Russia was different. The campaign waged by General Brusilov in June against the Austro-Hungarians enjoyed astonishing success. (There was no comparable progress by the Russians in the northern sector, against the Germans.) But in the first fortnight of August the Russian advance ground to a halt as the new leaders of Germany – exercising a strategic flexibility of which, owing to their hammering on the Somme, the Germans were now supposed to be incapable – came to the aid of their ally. Worse followed. In the last days of Brusilov's success Romania had entered the war on the Allied side. In September and October the 'sleepy Rumanian generals' and their unenthusiastic soldiery were routed.[7] By December Bucharest had fallen. This peremptory elimination of a new ally produced widespread dismay in Britain.

The exercise of Britain's own military and naval power was not wholly reassuring. The disaster at Kut, according to one diary-keeping civilian, was 'a bitter blow to British prestige'.[8] In April German cruiser squadrons slipped across the Channel to bombard two East Coast towns, if to little effect, and got off 'Scot free again'.[9] Yet more alarming, at Easter rebellion broke out in Dublin and took a week to suppress.

If fomented by Germans, the Dublin uprising sprang from the situation within Ireland. It signalled the end of that 'great reconciliation' between Britain and Roman Catholic Ireland that the outbreak of war had supposedly inaugurated. Already in January 1916 the exclusion of Ireland from the Conscription Act had demonstrated that this was not Ireland's war in the sense that it was Britain's. For the one people it was far from being the life-and-death struggle that it was for the other. The Easter Rising took this process of separation a further stage. It revealed that for the republican section of Irishmen the struggle against Germany offered Ireland an opportunity to sever the ties with Westminster for good. And if the republicans were only a minority, there proved to be a much larger section of the Irish who did not view their rebellion

[7] *Annual Register for 1916*, pp. 43–5.

[8] First World War diaries of F. A. Robinson, 30 April 1916, in the Imperial War Museum. Robinson was a businessman living in Cobham, Surrey, who from 1914 to 1918 devotedly recorded events concerning the war.

[9] Ibid., 25 April 1916.

with abhorrence. For whereas most Britons deemed it appropriate that manifest treachery in wartime should be stamped out with severity, Southern Ireland dissented. In short, Roman Catholic Ireland was placing such limitations on its allegiance to the British crown as effectually to take it outside the British connection.

In the history of Ireland the Easter Rising was a major event. In the history of wartime Britain it was a minor occurrence – and one quite devoid of terrible beauty. The historian of Leicester in the war writes: 'in these tremendous days [by which he means the Great War, not the Easter rebellion] such incidents, though disturbing, made but a superficial impression on the public mind. The Irish, at any rate many of them, always were difficult to understand.'[10] Such a judgement demonstrates, if unwittingly, both the extent to which Britain and Ireland were distinct countries and how inappropriate was the rule of the latter by the former. But that was not the conclusion being generally drawn on the British side of the Irish Sea – or in the Protestant counties of Ireland.

Other aspects of the war caused uneasiness in the first half of 1916. There was dissatisfaction at the conduct of the naval blockade of Germany, with allegations widespread that substantial quantities of supplies were getting through to the enemy. Then, early in June, came the first, chilling reports of the clash of the fleets at Jutland. The Admiralty, with almost excessive regard for telling the truth, baldly stated British losses. For the moment it could provide no details of German losses. One home-front diarist recorded:

> We have experienced to-day what is probably the greatest shock we have had since the declaration of war. On opening our papers we hear that a big Naval Engagement has taken place, that some of our finest ships have been sent to the bottom, and that thousands of our brave seamen have been lost. . . . All the facts are not known yet, but from such as are available it is bad enough. . . . it is almost impossible to believe it can be true.[11]

The following day a reassuring account of the outcome of the battle was issued. It came, by request of the Admiralty, from the pen of Winston Churchill (a jettisoned First Lord). This gave some comfort – 'but *why* Mr. Churchill?'. In the ensuing days, with the release of further information, 'a better feeling' set in.[12] Jutland became (in the view of *Punch*) a 'glorious if indecisive battle' that might yet prove to have ended the German fleet's pretensions to put to sea.

Nevertheless, the effect of the blow dealt by the first Jutland communiqué was never quite expunged. And certainly the battle did not provide the occasion for rejoicing so generally expected from a fleet action. Probably, given the facile but widely held view that exercise of command of the sea consisted in sending enemy ships to the bottom, Jutland never could have proved such an occasion, even had the events been more alluringly presented in the first instance.

Within days of the first Jutland dispatch the sea brought a yet more evident cause for dismay. On 5 June Kitchener, on his way to Russia, was drowned. Soon after leaving Scapa Flow, in raging seas, the cruiser on which he was travelling struck a mine and sank. For the British public, which had no reason to know that Kitchener was out of London, this was a considerable blow: 'In its abrupt suddenness the news was as shocking as anything in the war.'[13] A witness from the war years, who was then a schoolgirl in an Essex village, identifies this as the only major public event of the conflict which she

---

[10] F. P. Armitage, *Leicester 1914–1918: The War-Story of a Midland Town* (Leicester: Edgar Backus, 1933), p. 132.

[11] Diary of F. A. Robinson, 3 June 1916.

[12] Ibid., 4 and 5 June 1916.

[13] Gretton, *A Modern History of the English People*, p. 991.

vividly recalls; she fled home to tell her parents that Britain had lost the war, for Lord Kitchener was dead. Michael MacDonagh, in London, saw the first newspapers bearing the tidings arrive soon after lunch on 6 June and recorded in his diary:

> The newsman was immediately surrounded by an excited group of passers by, struggling to get a paper. Vehicles pulled up on the roadway. Traffic was stopped. The drivers helped to block the pavement also. . . . The scene I witnessed must have been repeated a thousand times throughout London as the news spread. Over the man in the street Kitchener maintains a supreme ascendancy. Public opinion is a fallible and erratic thing, especially so in war-time. It remained steadfast in support of Kitchener from the beginning. Very few knew of what was going on behind the walls of the War Office, and of what the politicians thought of Kitchener.[14]

For those to whom Kitchener symbolized the national resolve to make war his death was not the accidental departure of a supernumerary. At best it was a shocking piece of mismanagement. At worst it suggested treachery in high places.

In the following months the conduct of the war at sea took on a further disturbing aspect. U-boat activities grew ominously. Most dramatic was the appearance of Germany's ocean-going submarines. The first, acting as a commercial vessel, crossed to the USA and back without being apprehended by British patrols: 'an extraordinary achievement of pluck and seamanship', as one British diarist described it.[15] Early in October another U-boat crossed to the USA, then put to sea and sank about a dozen merchant ships.

Far more menacing in reality, however, was the sharp rise in sinkings nearer home. The upturn began in September and jumped yet higher in October. Only 'the other day', noted F. A. Robinson in his diary for 9 October, it had been accepted that the U-boat menace was at an end. For 'people who know' had given assurance that most of these vessels were resting in Davy Jones's locker. 'Now there has been a sudden revival of activity.' It coincided with two German destroyer raids in the Channel, which, if they achieved little, showed the limitations of Britain's command even of this most important sea lane. For civilians in Britain such demonstrations were the cause of widespread dissatisfaction.

Yet these events at sea, like the rise and fall of Allied hopes on the Eastern Front, were overshadowed in the second half of 1916 by awareness of the mighty British offensive in France. Even before newspapers began carrying reports of the Somme operation, civilians were becoming aware of its approach. Vera Brittain's brother was home from France for a brief leave in June. She relates:

> in a quiet interval, when we were alone together, he spoke in veiled but significant language of a great battle impending. It would start, he told me, somewhere near Albert, and he knew that he would be in it.

As a dweller in London, and a Voluntary Aid Detachment (VAD) nurse, she soon had further evidence of the approaching struggle:

> At the end of June, the hospital received orders to clear out all convalescents and prepare for a great rush of wounded. We knew that already a tremendous bombardment had begun, for we could feel the vibration of the guns at Camberwell. . . . Hour after hour, as the convalescents departed, we added to the long rows of waiting beds, so sinister in their white, expectant emptiness.[16]

Thereafter the newspaper accounts of the fighting, the sight of the wounded, the lists of the casualties – 'No one who lived through that time will ever forget the casualty lists

[14] MacDonagh, *In London during the Great War*, p. 109.
[15] Diary of F. A. Robinson, 25 August 1916.
[16] Vera Brittain, *Testament of Youth* (London: Virago, 1978), pp. 272–4.

of the Somme'[17] –, and for those who lived near the South-East Coast the pulsation of the guns impinged constantly on British civilians. According to *Punch* in the first month of the offensive:

> July has brought us a new experience – the sound fifty or sixty miles inland in peaceful rural England, amid glorious midsummer weather, of the continual throbbing night and day of the great guns on the Somme, where our first great offensive opened on the 1st, and has continued with solid and substantial gains, some set-backs, heavy losses for the Allies, still heavier for the enemy.

Whatever the optimistic interpretations placed on the various phases of the Somme campaign, two things were evident to British civilians. One was the fearful cost: F. A. Robinson noted that *The Times* on 31 July carried casualty lists occupying two whole pages, with each page consisting of six columns and each line containing three to four names. The second was that this great endeavour was yielding but modest rewards. On 17 July the *Leicester Post* had hailed news of the British advance with a leader entitled 'Smashing Through'. But before long, according to the historian of wartime Leicester, it was being recognized that the process of 'smashing through' would prove long and arduous. As September passed, so did general confidence that the end was near.[18]

This was bound to have important implications in the area of government. Nothing that happened during the Somme campaign provided clear proof, should other evidence suggest the contrary, that the direction of the country's affairs was in the best possible hands. In this regard events on the Western Front were bringing the day of reckoning appreciably nearer for the nation's rulers.

III

Other far-reaching changes were occurring on the home front that year. In 1916 Britain became a conscriptionist country. The process began in January with a measure confined to unmarried men that Asquith claimed was designed to save the voluntary system. This pretence was to prove short-lived.

The Military Service Act of January imposed conscription on single men and childless widowers between the ages of 18 and 41. It excluded certain categories: the population of Ireland, ministers of religion, the medically unfit, those employed in essential work, and men with a conscientious objection to combatant service. Resistance to this first measure of conscription, in the House of Commons and the country, proved negligible. The impassioned opponents of all war, or this particular war, or this degree of intrusion into personal liberty, remained firm in condemning it. But they had become a tiny company. Asquith had said that conscription must wait until the nation was united in its support. Effectually, such unity now existed. (Perhaps, as his critics alleged, it had been in existence for some time. But this is far from certain.)

At one stage significant opposition to conscription had been anticipated from the labour movement. But labour, in joining hands with Asquith in his endeavours to save voluntary recruiting, had endorsed his warning that the Derby scheme was that system's last chance. At a large meeting of labour organizations in Birmingham in support of the Derby appeal, a resolution was carried unanimously that contained the warning: 'Failing a satisfactory response from all classes it will not be possible for

---

[17] Gretton, *A Modern History of the English People*, p. 998.

[18] Armitage, *Leicester 1914–1918*, pp. 137–43.

trades unionism further to oppose compulsory methods.'[19] Here was clear notice that labour opposition to military conscription was not absolute. It was conditional upon the voluntary appeal bringing forth at least all the unmarried men.

When, at the start of 1916, the Government concluded that the Derby scheme had failed to do this, the Labour Party went through the motions of dissent. The parliamentary party on 6 January decided it must withdraw its support from the Government, and the three Labour Ministers sent in their resignations. Six days later Asquith met Labour MPs and offered them assurances that enabled them to reconsider. He said that there would be no conscription of married men, that the measure was for the war only, that the Bill would be amended to obviate the possibility of industrial conscription, that the tribunals dealing with exemptions would be civilian and not military bodies, and that Parliament would have the opportunity to strengthen the exemption of conscientious objectors. The party then decided to resume its support for the Government. And the resignations of the Labour Ministers were withdrawn pending a party conference at the end of January.[20]

When this conference met it followed the fairly predictable course of registering its dissent while acquiescing in what was occurring. A resolution hostile to any form of conscription was carried overwhelmingly. But it was decided not to agitate for the measure's repeal. Nor were Labour members asked to leave the Government. The 'moderate attitude' of this conference was cited by Lloyd George, one of the strongest advocates of compulsion, in discussion with the anti-conscriptionist C. P. Scott. Lloyd

Plate 30   *The Labour Party conference on the conscription issue: a view of the delegates.*

---

[19] Reginald H. Brazier and Ernest Sandford, *Birmingham and the Great War 1914–1919* (Birmingham: Cornish Bros., 1921), p. 21.

[20] Minutes of the National Executive Committee of the Labour Party, 12 January 1916; microfilm copy in the University Library, Cambridge.

George derided Labour opposition 'as proceeding only from [a] small and noisy group and as virtually negligible'.[21]

Yet the persistence of misgiving over conscription in Liberal and Labour ranks did produce one of the Bill's most noteworthy, if most controversial, provisions: that conceding exemption from combatant service to conscientious objectors.[22] Its application gave rise to innumerable difficulties. The Act contained no definition of conscientious objection and perhaps would have erred in doing so. For any definition was likely to prove either too narrow, so applying only to a few well defined religious groups, or too sweeping, so discrediting the whole concept. What proved more unfortunate was the fact that no bodies were called into being especially to administer this provision. Responsibility was assigned to tribunals set up some months earlier under the Derby scheme for a quite different purpose: that of considering the appeals of men who had attested their willingness to join up but who believed they had special grounds for delay. In performing that function the members of these tribunals (many of whom had earlier been engaged in recruiting campaigns) had been under official urging to secure as many men for the army as possible. It is not wonderful that, when given the task of passing judgement on those claiming conscientious objection, they might be uncomprehending in response and arbitrary in decision – not to say sometimes downright cruel.

Certainly, the applicants for exemption were not drawn exclusively from the ranks of the high-minded. Some had taken jobs in munitions factories, believing that this would keep them out of the army; only when this manoeuvre failed did they discover a conscientious objection to taking life. Others may have been sincere enough, but their position was hopelessly confused. Michael MacDonagh tells of an applicant who, of his own volition, was at the time employed in the War Office. He argued that he had gone there at God's behest and was concerned with the resettlement of servicemen, not with the business of killing. But it is perhaps not surprising that the tribunal rejected his claim.[23]

In the case of some conscientious objectors whose claims were rejected, it is plain that they fell victim to tribunals that were simply mean-spirited and conformist. The very nobility of some of the applicants for exemption was bound to antagonize the less than noble individuals who were administering this aspect of the law. One may instance the case of the Quaker Stephen Hobhouse. He took the absolutist position of refusing any form of involvement in the war – including submission to a medical examination, which would probably have discharged him as unfit. He was imprisoned for failing to obey military orders or accept alternative service. Such an action spells out the crudity of the ethos of patriotism. By any humane definition, Hobhouse was already engaged in work of national service. Some years before the outbreak of the war he had renounced both his considerable inheritance and his secure position in the Civil Service and had embarked on 'a life of poverty and social work in London's East End'.[24] It is unlikely that any of those who passed judgement on him could approach his contribution to the nation's well-being.

Yet the deplorable ill-treatment of some worthy individuals should not rank as the

---

[21] Trevor Wilson (ed.), *The Political Diaries of C. P. Scott 1911–1928* (London: Collins, 1970), p. 176.

[22] For a thoroughgoing study of this subject see John Rae, *Conscience and Politics* (London: Oxford University Press, 1970). Dr Rae estimates that, all told, the war produced 16,500 conscientious objectors in Britain. He also points out that, contrary to a popular view, they did not consist almost exclusively of Quaker pacifists and socialist internationalists. A great many belonged to non-mainstream religious groups, such as the Plymouth Brethren, Christadelphians, and Jehovah's Witnesses. Some of these were not at all pacifist in their beliefs.

[23] MacDonagh, *In London during the Great War*, pp. 100–1.

[24] Rae, *Conscience and Politics*, p. 208.

principal aspect of this question. Two much larger issues deserve primacy. First, it was a noteworthy event that the concept of conscientious objection was admitted into legislation in 1916. Given the widespread communal contempt for any male resisting participation in the war and the powerful pressures to impose conformity, it was evidence of the strength of Britain's liberal ideals that provision nevertheless was made for this deeply unpopular minority. Secondly, it is the fact that, for all their shameful lapses, the tribunals did not generally act to deprive conscientious objectors of their rights under the law. John Rae, after careful study of the statistics, concludes:

> The tribunals granted some form of exemption to over 80 per cent of those conscientious objectors who were the subjects of their decisions. The figure may be consistent with the view that the tribunals' investigation of claims was perfunctory; it is not consistent with the view that the majority of tribunals allowed prejudice or intolerance to dictate their decisions.[25]

In a number of respects the application of this first Conscription Act soon came under attack. Opponents of conscription were quick to allege that the measure was being applied too widely: men who were the sole support of widowed mothers were being denied exemption by the tribunals, and the medical certificates of men who had previously offered themselves for attestation and been declared unfit were being torn up or confiscated by the military authorities. But a different sort of complaint was soon emanating from Lord Derby. He argued that so many bachelors were gaining exemption that the pledge to attested married men was in danger of violation – for example, many single men were remaining in essential jobs that could be performed by the married or by women. And too many forms of employment were being deemed

Plates 31a and 31b *The hunt for soldiers.*

31a *A 'round-up' at the Newmarket races.*

---

[25] Ibid., p. 131.

essential – he instanced the rural sector (to the wrath of the Conservative Minister of Agriculture). Derby even claimed that men were evading military service fraudulently. Certificates of medical exemption were said to be changing hands for money.

These complaints were loudly taken up by the married men who had attested under the Derby scheme. For by April call-up notices had begun going out to those who fell into this category, first to the younger age group and then to the rest. They responded with indignation: against Derby, whom they argued had misled them; against those single men who were securing exemption; and even against married men who had not attested and whom they almost seemed to think should be taken first as a penalty for their unwillingness to serve.

These events pushed the country a sizeable step towards military conscription for all males. By March the right-wing press was loud in its demand. And it soon became an open secret both that the nation's military planners were calling for such a number of men as could be met by no other means and that powerful elements in the Government would rest content with nothing less. In the second half of April, in circumstances of the utmost humiliation, Asquith bowed to this pressure. The second Conscription Act applied to married men on the same terms as had the first to the unmarried. It also provided for a review of the medical certificates of those already exempted. And it kept in the army, or recalled to it, those regular soldiers under the age of 41 whose period of service had expired. However, the measure was amended during its passage to provide that enlisted men short of their nineteenth birthdays would not be sent out of the country except in an emergency.

The hunt for men did not stop there. In September the military authorities began taking strong action against the supposedly large numbers of unexempted men who were evading the net. Parties of soldiers swooped on the exits from railway stations, parks, football fields, cinemas, theatres, and prize fights. All males who looked of military age and were not in uniform were apprehended. Those among them who could not produce exemption papers were taken off for examination. This 'revival of the Press Gang', as the *Annual Register* called it (with no great accuracy), aroused much indignation among ordinary citizens, for whom the delays in crowd movement caused some inconvenience. That is, the female and the more senior male, although often eager to impose military service on youthful men, resented suffering any measure of military interference themselves. The round-ups were soon abandoned, at least on a large scale. The hostility they inspired proved too great, the number of defaulters they netted too few.

These actions by the authorities had not been generated solely by officiousness. The nation was setting itself a target of men required for the front that would not be reached without yet severer measures. At the end of May Churchill pointed a finger at the army itself. He claimed that too many soldiers who were fit for combat never came within the sound of gunfire. Soon after, the authorities established the Women's Army Auxiliary Corps. This was one step in the process by which uniformed men were displaced from desk jobs or duties as chauffeurs and made available for service at the front.

As losses mounted on the Somme, so did the pressure for further recruits. One obvious source, Ireland, hardly bore contemplation in the aftermath of the Easter Rising – except among devoted haters of the Southern Irish. Another, men who had passed their forty-first birthday, seemed too plainly a course of desperation. So attention fell on those men of military age hitherto exempted on grounds of occupation. A manpower committee appointed by the Government reported in October in favour of what would prove the first of many 'comb-outs'. Except in munitions and

31b *A batch of recruits on their way to the railway station following a 'comb-out' in a large industrial centre.*

coalmining, it declared, fit men in the younger age group must cease to be eligible for exemption from the army, however important their work. The Civil Service and agriculture were indicated as two areas for particular attention. But within a month the Asquith War Committee was prepared to look even further. The decision was taken to establish compulsory service of one kind or another for all adults, male and female: that is, conscription would now apply to all forms of employment, not just to the army. Hence two large sectors of the community formerly exempt from state direction would now lose their freedom of choice: women, and men hitherto not liable for military service.

As far as human resources were concerned, Britain appeared poised in November 1916 to take one of the decisive steps towards total war. But the Asquith Government, having proved reluctant to embark on some of the earlier steps, did not survive to complete its process of conversion. And Lloyd George's Government, having appeared converted already, would soon reveal that it was prepared to settle for something less.

IV

Nationalistic fervour did not abate in 1916. A further crop of enemy 'outrages' served to aggravate it. These included reported ill-treatment of British prisoners of war, the deportation of civilians from occupied Belgium to perform forced labour in German industry, and the execution of a captured merchant seaman, Captain Fryatt, for once nearly ramming a U-boat that had threatened his ship.

Such misdeeds by the Germans were grist to the mill of the Northcliffe press and other jingo newspapers, which fed the mood of hate with unremitting zeal. Their attacks, needless to say, were not confined to the enemy. Campaigns, supposedly patriotic in inspiration, were waged against selected members of the Government, conscientious objectors, aliens resident in Britain (including Jews and even Belgians), and bearers of foreign-sounding names. In August the press harried an individual who had been appointed vice-consul in Rotterdam. Although a British subject, he had the misfortune to be named A. G. Holzapfel. So venomous was the abuse rained on him that he was obliged to relinquish the post. Newspapers were also active in stimulating popular adulation for the jingo Prime Minister of Australia, Billy Hughes, during his five-month visit to Britain. And they acted to circulate the sentiments of 'A Little Mother.' This lady, responding to a letter from 'a common soldier' who had had enough of bloodshed, wrote to the ultra-Conservative *Morning Post* affirming that 'we women, who demand to be heard, will tolerate no such cry as "Peace! Peace!" where there is no peace.' 'There is only one temperature for the women of the British race,' she proclaimed, 'and that is white heat. . . . We women pass on the human ammunition of "only sons" to fill up the gaps, so that when the "common soldier" looks back before going "over the top" he may see the women of the British race at his heels, reliable, dependent, uncomplaining.' Her letter, reprinted in pamphlet form, sold 75,000 copies in less than a week.[26]

Yet, as these circulation figures suggest, the role of the press was to stimulate (as well as to feed on) the more malevolent aspects of the wartime mind: it scarcely created them. As the *Annual Register for 1916* observed, the significance of the Holzapfel affair lay in revealing 'the sensitiveness of public opinion in this country'. This sensitivity was evident among commercial and financial sections: the Baltic Exchange led the outcry against Holzapfel. And it was by no means absent among prominent academics and high-ranking police officers. In mid-1916 the world of historical scholarship suffered a notable blow when the editors of the *Cambridge Medieval History* decided to exclude all German contributors, including those under contract, from its volumes. One of the co-editors, in a pseudonymous letter to the *Nation*, accused the German people of 'wanton massacres' and 'devilish deeds' placing them 'below the level of savages', and concluded that a country could not be trusted 'which will not be bound by treaties'. He did not say whether the same principle applied to academic editors who declined to be bound by contracts.[27]

If prominent scholars were not immune from indulgence in wartime spite, neither were high authorities in the police force. The Commissioner of the Metropolitan Police, Sir Edward Henry, instituted an investigation into 28 cafés set up by Belgian exiles in central London near the Tottenham Court Road.[28] These rather seedy institutions, it was suggested, might be a meeting place for spies masquerading as refugees. Henry's inquiries revealed a fair degree of squalor, including basements that reeked of urine and bedrooms where prostitutes were entertaining British and Canadian soldiers. But for the rest the cafés consisted of cramped rooms serving Belgians with coffee, ale, and mineral water. A few had automatic pianos; there was little disorder or drunkenness; and the clientele tended to depart about 10.30 p.m. The cafés closed by 11.30 p.m. Of evidence of spying, or even of serious crime, there was none.

It might be imagined that an overworked Commissioner of Police in wartime London would have more with which to concern himself than these trivialities. But Henry appeared to see his duties differently. From this information he drew large and

---

[26] See Robert Graves, *Goodbye to All That* (Harmondsworth: Penguin Books, 1965), pp. 188–91.

[27] P. A. Linehan, 'The Making of the *Cambridge Medieval History*', *Speculum*, vol. 57, no. 3, 1982.

[28] For information on this matter (including the quotations in the following paragraphs), see Peter Cahalan, *Belgian Refugee Relief in England During the Great War* (New York: Garland Publishing, 1982), pp. 394–8.

reckless conclusions. The automatic pianos playing 'late into the night' (!) seemed to him to symbolize these 'squalid' places. The cafés clearly harboured 'prostitutes and other undesirables'. The appearance of both the premises and their customers gave rise to the belief, 'probably with justice', that 'immorality and other irregularities take place and that these restaurants are the meeting places for alien enemies and spies'. In consequence action was taken (through a tightening up of the Aliens Restriction Order) to place alien-owned premises under stricter control.

One interesting aspect of this preposterous spy hunt is the way in which the discovery of 'immorality and other irregularities' was used to support references (otherwise quite without substance) to 'alien enemies and spies'. Patriotism thus became the justification for seeking to enforce conventional morality. Henry belonged to a stream of opinion that, before the war, had manifested itself in groups like the Duty and Discipline Movement. Enjoying the support of such personages as the founder of the Church Army, the headmaster of Eton, and the originator of the Boy Scouts, this movement had inveighed against the prevalence of the 'new softness' and the 'new sentimentality' in the rearing of juveniles. Its advocates had trembled to think what sort of young manhood would (in the words of one of its publications) emerge from 'the children who have looked upon themselves as entitled to go to the kinematograph every evening and to visit the sweet shop seven times a week'. And they had expounded their views in publications some of whose titles bear an uncanny resemblance to a certain type of pornography: *British Discipline* by Lieutenant-General Sir R. S. S. Baden-Powell; *The Value of a Certain 'Hardness' in Education* by Mrs Arthur Philip; and *Endure Hardness* by the Rev. and Hon. E. Lyttelton, headmaster of Eton. (The imagination boggles at the ribaldries that the last of these titles must have aroused among the headmaster's youthful charges.)

At the start of the war the devotees of Duty and Discipline had taken comfort from the fact that at least Britain's cause would not rest in the hands of a generation reared in the kinematograph and the sweet shop. And they had believed that the demands of war would recall a backsliding nation to the very qualities it had been neglecting. But by 1916, if not earlier, the conflict in important respects seemed to be letting them down. The 'new sentimentality', if in retreat, was (they complained) manifesting itself in talk that Britain should not crush and humiliate Germany. And instead of a resurgence of 'morality', these disciplinarians felt that they were observing a mounting tide of laxity and vice. Its causes were taken to be the war's enforced severance of family ties and the greater personal and economic freedom of young persons, as well as a sense of impermanence consequent upon the proximity of death in battle. Manifestations of this unhappy trend were to be seen in those districts where uprooted people of both sexes congregated. Not least was this true of London, with its burgeoning nightclubs and the 'vulgar and suggestive' tone of its stage performances, as General Smith-Dorrien publicly protested in the autumn.

The conclusion was easily reached that such lapses, by subverting Duty and Discipline, were undermining the war effort. It followed irresistibly that enemy agents would in some way be involved. Sir Edward Henry was simply acting out the assumptions of crusaders after moral improvement when he managed to envisage a connection between 'enemy aliens and spies' on the one hand and cafés for Belgian refugees, containing a sprinkling of prostitutes and serenaded by automatic pianos, on the other.

V

In various ways the war bit deeper into the Home Front in 1916. Guy Fawkes night passed uncelebrated, by direction of DORA. The Whitsun and August Bank Holidays were cancelled so as to expedite production of munitions for the great offensive. (*Punch* even managed to print a cartoon showing the munitions worker in a favourable light. This was noteworthy in a journal that, when not treating members of the working classes as figures of fun, usually made them seem somewhat disreputable.) The Budget made further large inroads into the citizen's spending power. The income tax and excess profits tax were both raised, and a levy was introduced on matches and admission tickets to entertainments. In addition, the cost of licences for cars and motorcycles was increased, as were the imposts on sugar, cocoa, and coffee. The House of Commons, according to a Conservative MP, became positively jocular during the unveiling of these proposals, each section laughing heartily as another was hit. He related: 'I am bound to say the Chancellor bestowed his favours in the form of knocks with the most undeviating impartiality. We none of us had a sound skin when he had finished.'[29] In addition, citizens accepted a voluntary reduction – albeit only for the duration and at a handsome rate of interest – in their available supply of money by making large purchases of the new War Savings Certificates.

Various forms of shortage were making themselves felt. Middle-class families had great difficulty in securing servants, as working-class women found better openings elsewhere. Import restrictions on commodities such as paper and building materials helped to produce thinner newspapers, a scarcity of matches, and an ever-growing shortage of houses. (Tales were told of people having to pay 'key money' in order to secure a dwelling.) The Government also set about curtailing the consumption of fuel for lighting. Shops were required to close earlier. And an hour of daylight saving was introduced during the summer. This last measure was not welcomed by farmers, but it proved a great boon to the growing number of town dwellers tilling allotments.

Travel also was suffering restrictions. Shortage of petrol caused buses in some cities to be fitted with gasbags, which propelled them well enough but caused a lot of back-firing. The owners of private cars were obliged to secure petrol licences. Late in July F. A. Robinson applied for 25 gallons per month, which he estimated was about half his pre-war consumption. He received an allocation of only 24 gallons per three months. With this, he concluded, he must try to be content, given the information then being published about petrol consumption at the front.

Train travel also, having been somewhat restricted in 1915, was further diminished. Services were trimmed, some inner surburban stations closed, tourist tickets withdrawn, and restaurant cars reduced. Yet the railway companies persisted in seeking after civilian customers – even though, with profits fixed for the war, they gained nothing financially. They devoted labour to the design of new types of engine, including passenger types. And they solicited vacation customers with enticing brochures such as 'Holiday Haunts' and 'Through the Garden of England'. What was more, the holidaymakers continued to appear: in August, despite the cancellation of the Bank Holiday, the seasonal peak was unaffected. And, as of yore, they brought with them ample luggage despite appeals from the Railway Executive Committee. Railway clerks at Paddington Station were sometimes obliged to double as porters.[30]

Prices of essential commodities continued to rise. The 4lb loaf of bread, which had cost less than 6d. in 1914, reached 10d. towards the end of 1916. The cost of potatoes was much affected by a bad harvest: having remained stable from the opening of the war until April 1916, potato prices doubled in the course of the next eight months.

---

[29] Holcombe Ingleby to his daughter-in-law, Muriel, 5 April 1916.

[30] For this subject, see J. A. B. Hamilton, *Britain's Railways in World War I* (London: Allen & Unwin, 1967).

Milk and butter also increased in price by 100 per cent during 1916, as did sugar. The last of these was also becoming difficult to procure. Complaints began to be heard that shopkeepers would sell sugar only to customers making substantial other purchases.

None of this meant that luxury was vanishing from the face of the land. Holcombe Ingleby dined at Boodles Club with some other parliamentarians in April and reported: 'I came away a more full-blooded animal than I went in – they do you well there!'[31] And Lady Scott once more found herself dismayed by an encounter with London high living. She wrote in her diary for 6 May:

> Dined with Major Smith at the Piccadilly of all awful places. I was shocked to death to see the extravagance of the womens dress – & we eat foie gras, I eat it too with a feeling of disgust at the gaudy brilliantly lighted place.

Golfing at Formby (near Liverpool) on Christmas Day, the convalescent Siegfried Sassoon noted:

> They say the U-boat blockade will get worse and there will be a bad food-shortage in England in 1917. The sideboard in this Formby golf-club doesn't look like it yet; enormous cold joints and geese and turkeys and a sucking pig and God knows what, and old men with their noses in their plates guzzling for all they're worth.[32]

Among the needier sections most reports suggest that, notwithstanding rising prices, living standards continued to improve. Tramps, according to a police report, had vanished from the country. In one Midlands city, following a fall of snow a foot deep in mid-February, only a dozen casual labourers could be found to deal with it, and the army had to be called in. In the same area the Distress Committee found so little to do that it indefinitely postponed its meetings, and the Charity Organization Society reported that it received 1,432 applications in 1916 as compared with 2,223 in 1913.[33] In July, in a review of the work of the Local Government Board in wartime, its President Walter Long stated that unemployment was non-existent and pauperism very low. The health of the country, he claimed, was being wonderfully maintained: enteric fever was steadily decreasing, and little anxiety was now caused by cerebro-spinal fever. During the same period great satisfaction was being expressed at the steady decline in convictions for drunkenness, although this was in a measure offset by a notable increase in the use of cocaine, leading to a prohibition on its import except under licence.

Yet these accounts of lessened distress and better consumption can hardly have brought pleasure to those members of the middle and working classes living on fixed incomes and pensions. For them this was a time of falling living standards. Sylvia Pankhurst, toiling among the children of the poor in the East End of London, observed not general trends towards improvement but the way in which rising prices weighed down those families with several young children.

She was also receiving many appeals for aid from another section: the families of soldiers recently invalided out of the army. When a man was discharged as unfit for further service his army pay ceased and so did the separation allowance to his family. Very often, especially if he had previously been engaged in heavy work, he was not capable of returning to his former occupation, and maybe could not work at all. But the authorities, perhaps because they wanted to see whether a discharged man was able to earn, took their time about awarding pensions to the disabled. By so doing they

---

[31] Ingleby to Muriel Ingleby, 5 April 1916.
[32] Rupert Hart-Davis (ed.), *Siegfried Sassoon Diaries 1915–1918* (London: Faber & Faber, 1983), p. 106.
[33] Armitage, *Leicester 1914–1918*, pp. 146–7.

imposed at least temporary destitution upon many families – and these the families of wounded 'heroes'.[34]

Not only Miss Pankhurst felt indignant. By August MPs of all parties were loud in condemning this scandal. They showed their feelings again in November when the Government, to meet the complaints, brought in legislation to establish a Pensions Board. So little did parliamentarians like the proposals that they forced the Government to accept a radically different scheme put forward by a back-bench Liberal MP.

VI

If 1916 proved a year of half-successes, lessened expectations, and severe disappointments, this did not dispel the nation's resolution to prosecute the war to victory.

Certainly, even in governing circles some were beginning to entertain doubts. Among them was the Conservative elder statesman Lord Lansdowne. It seemed to him dubious that Britain could stay the course to victory; or, if it could, that it would be recognizable as the Britain he cherished. But such sentiments were being expressed only discreetly. McKenna, the Chancellor of the Exchequer, might tell his colleagues of his alarm at the erosion of Britain's financial resources. But in Parliament he insisted that British finance could stand any demand that might be made of it. A similar contrast may be found even in the case of Lloyd George. At the beginning of the year, in conversation with C. P. Scott, he foresaw without distaste the possibility of the USA's imposing itself as mediator 'when both sides were getting exhausted'.[35] But he never gave a hint of this in public. And in September, in a public interview with an American journalist, he repudiated Woodrow Wilson's promised intervention. The British were not disposed to stop the war 'because of the squealing done by Germans or done for Germans'. 'The whole world – including neutrals of the highest purposes and humanitarians with the best of motives – must know that there can be no interference at this stage.' He recognized that the end of the war was not in sight. But peace was 'unthinkable' without 'the final and complete elimination' of the menace to civilization posed by 'Prussian military despotism'. 'The fight must be to a finish – to a knock-out.'

When Lloyd George defended this outburst in Parliament he was strongly supported. On the same day (11 October) a speech by Asquith repudiating any peace not founded on complete Allied victory was welcomed by G. H. Wardle on behalf of the Labour Party. As for those who spoke out in favour of a negotiated settlement, they followed a lonely and sometimes perilous course. Their infrequent public meetings were usually broken up by gangs of rowdies, often men in uniform. Nor could the opponents of war *à outrance* find comfort even in a gathering like the Trades Union Congress (TUC) at Birmingham in September. 'Labour,' proclaimed Harry Gosling, the chairman, 'has been the personification of real patriotism.' And by a two-to-one majority this gathering rejected a proposal from the American Federation of Labour that, whenever the time came for the warring nations to assemble at a peace conference, a congress of labour should be held simultaneously. The delegates to the TUC did not doubt that Labour's voice should be heard on such an occasion. But they were simply not prepared to parley, even at the end of hostilities, with working-class delegates from Germany.

---

[34] E. Sylvia Pankhurst, *The Home Front* (London: Hutchinson, 1932), pp. 351–9.

[35] Wilson (ed.), *The Political Diaries of C. P. Scott*, p. 177.

Summing up the year, the *Annual Register* observed that most classes in the community had been 'called upon to bear sacrifices little anticipated at the commencement of the war', and that yet greater deprivations lay ahead.

The prospect of these sacrifices, however, appeared to be quite powerless in effecting any modification of the national resolution to prosecute the war to a successful conclusion.[36]

A similar judgement was passed by the schoolmaster Robert Saunders, in a letter to his son in Canada on 23 December. The war, he said, had been brought home to them very clearly during the past year. 'Every day almost brings sad news and we can't help feeling depressed.' Yet he reported general resentment towards the peace overture of President Wilson, which was regarded as a pro-German action:

public opinion is dead against Peace at present, we are only just getting our 5,000,000 Army ready for business, and mobilizing our resources of men and munitions for real business. People naturally think the Germans are aware of this and want the War to end while they hold the spoils, but to quote our Tommies, Fritz has got to take his medicine before we have finished with him.

---

[36] *Annual Register for 1916*, p. 215.

38

THE COURSE OF POLITICS

I wonder what the news is this m[ornin]g. I've come to think that the Asquith regime means certain & moderate disaster, the L1. G. [regime] either absolute disaster or success.

Barbara Hammond to J. L. Hammond, 7 December 1916

I

During the first 18 months of the war Asquith's achievements had been considerable. It is appropriate, as we enter the period when his grasp decisively failed, to take note of this.

As long as he was alive and engaged in politics, Asquith in the opening stages of the conflict was the essential Prime Minister. In a way that was true of nobody else, he could guarantee the political unity of the nation. This quality he demonstrated in the last days of peace. By insisting, right up until the violation of Belgium, that Britain remained free to decide its own course of action, he was able to carry his Cabinet and parliamentary followers into the war without serious dissent. By contrast, the premature action for which the Conservatives had been pressing might have proved deeply divisive.

What was true in August 1914 continued to be true up to the beginning of 1916. The parties that had kept Asquith in office before the war – Liberals, Labour, and Irish Nationalists – felt secure in accepting drastic wartime measures only while he was in command. Lord Selborne, a Tory member of the coalition Government who came to regard Asquith as 'quite hopeless as a War P.M.' ('the worst chairman I ever sat under at any committee'), nevertheless admitted that the Liberal and Labour parties 'believed in him thoroughly'.[1] And their sentiments could not be ignored if the unity of the nation was to be preserved. The remodelling of the Government in May 1915 may have meant a large concession to the Conservatives, the party that least admired the Prime Minister. But it had also confirmed his ability to appeal to Labour, which the Conservatives plainly lacked.

Moreover, Asquith's early achievements as war leader were not inconsiderable. Even Selborne, while deploring Asquith's 'desire on all occasions to avoid a decision', observed: 'Asquith was intensely patriotic & cared with his whole soul for England's victory.' And during his premiership the fundamental strategies by which the war was to be conducted were established. These were: command of the North Sea as the first priority of the Grand Fleet; the steady escalation of the naval blockade of Germany; the preservation and extension of the entente with France and, in lesser measure, with

---

[1] Selborne's views are contained in a sketch of the Asquith Cabinet written shortly after he resigned from it (on the Irish issue) in June 1916. The document resides in the Selborne papers, Bodleian Library, Oxford.

Russia; the rallying of Britain's financial resources to the Allied cause and their employment to marshal a sector of America's productive capacity for Allied purposes; and the concentration of the rising military capability of Britain upon the Western Front as the pre-eminent area of combat. Nothing that happened after Asquith's fall would invalidate these strategies.

In order to pursue them, Asquith led Cabinet, Parliament, and nation to endorse a series of strong measures. Pre-eminent among these was the mobilization for war purposes of a considerable part of Britain's adult manpower and much of its adult womanpower. Under Asquith the voluntary recruiting campaign was initiated that was one of the most memorable aspects of the first phase of the war. And when the voluntary system began to run down he accomplished, if not without a battle against his personal inclinations, the transition from voluntary to imposed enlistment. Moreover, he managed to do this in a way that kept his Cabinet intact and avoided the threatened resistance of labour.

Plate 32   *H. H. Asquith inspecting the Royal Flying Corps.*

This was but the most evident of a series of actions by which Asquith made it plain that he would not let Liberal beliefs stand in the way of wartime necessities. From the start there was the Defence of the Realm Act, with its grave intrusions into personal liberty, and such early violations of laissez-faire economics as state control of the sugar supply and state insurance of shipping. Then free trade was breached with the McKenna duties of 1915. And the state actually launched productive enterprises: the dyestuffs corporation, and the many instrumentalities connected with the Ministry of Munitions. Concerning the last of these, it should be remembered that Asquith's was the guiding hand that steadily withdrew control of munitions from Kitchener and the War Office and established a new Ministry with large powers under Lloyd George. And at the same time that he was removing effective power from the War Minister

Asquith was managing to preserve Kitchener as a symbol of the Government's determination to prosecute the war to victory. This list of accomplishments could be added to. All told, and notwithstanding failures and inadequacies, it is decidedly impressive.

In sum, for about a year and a half Asquith had clear merits as a wartime Prime Minister. He was able to carry through, or to provide others with the opportunity to carry through, essential measures of national mobilization. And among potential leaders he was the one who, when he did not unite the country, divided it least. As the Conservative F. E. Smith put it in a letter to Churchill of 25 February 1916: 'The Government is not popular but indispensable & I think that the PM is firmer in the saddle than ever. LG is still very much alone.'[2] Nevertheless, in the ensuing months Asquith's usefulness to the nation steadily became exhausted. Too many setbacks were being sustained. Too many hopes were failing of fulfilment. A growing section of the nation was coming to see his style of government as a cause for these misfortunes, and to yearn for a more decisive, ruthless, committed type of leadership.

To a degree, Asquith was becoming discredited on account of events that were beyond his control and that no successor would prove able to amend. But this was not wholly the case. In political terms Asquith, as Selborne recognized, may have been devoted to Britain's cause in the war; but his way of expressing it was too dispassionate, too considered, too remote from the market place. The situation required a leader better able to embody nationalistic fervour and more given to public rage, not only against the enemy but also against compromisers within and conciliators abroad. Perhaps this style of leadership could be provided only by a Conservative or by someone not separated from the Conservatives by any firmly fixed political allegiance.

Moreover, in both his approach to his job and his personal life Asquith rarely seemed to appreciate that the tasks of a leader in wartime might be more exacting than those of an Edwardian Prime Minister. This criticism was not confined to those outside his circle of intimates. It was sometimes expressed, if only in his diary, by the loyal Hankey. Back in January, after a weekend at the Prime Minister's country residence, he had warmly summed up Asquith's merits:

> P.M. is an awfully good host, and his simple, honest, and fearless character, devoid of any trace of 'swank' and 'side' never shows up more clearly than in his own home. It is a great privilege and satisfaction to me that he always confides in me, and asks my advice in difficult times. . . .

But Hankey was soon having to notice another side to the Prime Minister's character. On 19 May 1916, following Asquith's return from Ireland, Hankey endeavoured to persuade the Prime Minister to meet a visiting Russian dignitary anxious to see him about Kitchener's impending visit to Russia. These efforts were in vain:

> Nothing would induce him to see Gourko, and first on one excuse & then on another he wriggled out.

Hankey dined at 10 Downing Street that evening, but so large was the company that he was unable to talk with Asquith. His account continues:

> Afterwards the inevitable 'bridge' in which I did not join. I could not resist the thought that if the P.M. would give one quarter of the time and thought to the War Ctee. that he gives to 'bridge' we should be in a better position in the war. The solemn rite of Bridge occupies about 2 hours of his time every day of the week and nothing is allowed to interfere with it. We are lucky if we get 4 hours in a week for the War Ctee!! 'Bridge' is the vice of the P.M. and of most Cabinet Ministers.

---

[2] Martin Gilbert, *Winston S. Churchill*, Companion Volume 3 pt. 2 (London: Heinemann, 1972), p. 1436.

The next day, a Saturday, Hankey found further cause for complaint:

> Saw P.M. to ask for an early War Ctee. to consider some urgent questions. He would not give me one until Wednesday, which will be 6 days since the last. The only reason was that the Cabinet must meet Tuesday – on some political point, I suppose. What is one to do with a P.M. who doesn't like meetings on Saturday, Sunday, or Monday or on any afternoon or evening, and whose morning does not start until 11.30 a.m.! I am not happy about it.

Not only was Asquith loath to spend his weekends on the nation's business but he sometimes passed them in company little appreciated by much of the community. For example, he continued a frequent visitor to the country residence of Philip and Lady Ottoline Morrell. In the same month that Hankey wrote so critically of the Prime Minister's inattention to business Lytton Strachey observed Asquith among the company at Garsington. Writing to his brother, Strachey described the Prime Minister as 'a fleshy, sanguine, wine-bibbing, medieval abbot of a personage – a glutinous lecherous cynical old fellow'. He went on:

> you should have seen him making towards [Dora] Carrington – cutting her off at an angle as she crossed the lawn. I've rarely seen anyone so obviously enjoying life: so obviously, I thought, *out* to enjoy it; almost, really, as if he'd deliberately decided that he *would*, and let the rest go hang. . . . One looks at him, and thinks of the war. . . .[3]

During the very weekend that Hankey was failing to have the War Committee summoned, Asquith participated in a small drama at Garsington. According to Clive Bell's account, while Lady Ottoline and her guests were away picnicking in the woods, one of the maids got into difficulties in the lake and was in danger of drowning. No one left in the house could swim. However, in the nick of time Asquith drove up in the company (among others) of Mrs Keppel, one-time lover of Edward VII, and Robbie Ross, one-time lover of Oscar Wilde. Ross jumped in and saved the maiden, and Asquith – indulging his fondness for the company of young ladies – summoned the prettiest of the 'maillotties mermaids' and questioned her about the incident.[4]

In the present context what is striking about this domestic drama is the company Asquith was choosing to keep. Philip Morrell was a Liberal MP utterly opposed to intervention in the war and a leading campaigner against conscription. And his wife's circle was a centre of anti-war opinions. Among the regular *habitués* of Garsington were conscientious objectors like Clive Bell and Aldous Huxley, 'honorary gardeners' employed by the Morrells to do 'work of national importance'. (According to Robert Skidelsky, the supply of eggs fell off suddenly after one of them had been put in charge of the poultry.)[5] Other frequent visitors were agitators against the war like Bertrand Russell, who had recently been fined £100 for publishing a pamphlet judged injurious to recruiting.

It was also the case that many in this circle repudiated conventional sexual morality. Marriage for them was anything but a fixed state. And a number were well known for their homosexuality. This inclination, it may be thought, had no bearing on the war. But, as has been suggested earlier, a good many people felt otherwise. They held that sexual 'laxity' went hand in hand with setbacks to the British cause. The sadly unbalanced Lord Alfred Douglas was proclaiming to anyone who would listen – and it seems a good many would – that Britain's failures in the war were attributable to the

---

[3] Quoted in *The Times Saturday Review*, 15 January 1972.
[4] Clive Bell to Hilton Young, 5 June 1916, Kennet papers. Cf. Lady Scott's diary, 24 May 1916, relating a conversation with Asquith: 'Robby Ross jumped in to save a drowning maid of the Morrells.'
[5] Robert Skidelsky, *John Maynard Keynes* (London: Macmillan, 1983). vol. 1, p. 329.

'vice' practised by Oscar Wilde. Robbie Ross was a particular victim of Douglas's enmity, to the extent that Ross brought action for libel against him. The action did not succeed. What it did accomplish was to make it public knowledge that Ross was a frequent visitor to 10 Downing Street.

Asquith no doubt believed that the company he kept on his days off work was his own business. His presence at Garsington did not mean that he approved of anti-war agitation or the more flagrant forms of homosexuality. He deemed Bertrand Russell 'a crank, gnarled mentally & morally'. And when Ottoline Morrell appealed to him to intervene on behalf of Roger Casement, who was to be hanged for his part in the Easter Rebellion, Asquith replied that Casement (whose homosexual diaries had been uncovered during the investigation) was 'a depraved and perverted man'.[6] It may be surmised that what attracted the Prime Minister to Garsington, apart from the fact that he had once conducted a lengthy flirtation with Lady Ottoline, was the enjoyment he derived from associating with cultured, creative people. If such people were sometimes wayward in their private conduct and their attitudes to public affairs, this was not unusual among outstanding writers, artists, and thinkers. The fact that Britain was at war did not seem to Asquith any reason for foregoing such company. To a later generation this attitude may seem warranted. But it happened to be at odds with the feelings of many people at the time, for whom these associations were evidence of half-heartedness towards the war, if not of downright traitorous intent.

II

The decline of belief in Asquith's special fitness for his post was accompanied by other powerful political tendencies. These too served to undermine the Government. The increasing attractiveness of Conservative attitudes, evident since August 1914, continued perceptibly in 1916. And the will to resist among the non-Conservative parties became steadily enfeebled.

The overt nationalism with which Conservatism was identified, and the particular sorts of state control over the individual and the economy of which Conservatives approved, rose steadily in favour. These tendencies were evident even among men who, in strictly party terms, remained firmly outside the Conservative ranks. Asquith and Runciman, for example, did more than agree to breaches of free trade for the duration of the war. They began talking about an Empire self-sufficient in certain vital commodities after the war. And they came back from an Allied Economic Conference in Paris in June with proposals to place Germany outside regular trading relations when peace was restored.

While the hold of even some devoted Liberals on their principles seemed to be waning, a section of the Liberal Party in the House of Commons was going much further. From early in 1916 a body of about 40 Liberal MPs were forming themselves into what they called the Liberal War Committee, although the popular name was 'ginger group.' They made no secret of their dissatisfaction with the Government as a whole and Asquith in particular. They demanded more ruthless measures of national mobilization – particularly the hunting out of shirkers and disloyal elements. And in so

---

[6] Lady Scott's diary, 24 May 1916; Sandra Jobson Darroch, *Ottoline: The Life of Lady Ottoline Morrell* (New York: Coward, McCann & Geoghegan, 1975), p. 165. Asquith, it should be noted, expressed to Lady Scott a desire to see Casement hanged as early as 26 April (only five days after the arrest). That is, it was Casement's treasonable activities within Germany and attempt to extend them to Ireland that aroused Asquith's enmity, quite apart from the subsequent discovery of Casement's diaries.

far as they revealed allegiance to any prominent Liberal, it was to the man whose own relations with his leader and party seemed most in question: Lloyd George.

The ginger Liberals were acting in a way distinct from the rest of their party in Parliament. Yet many Liberals who deplored their divisiveness plainly shared at least some of their attitudes. They too felt the need for a less ambiguous direction of affairs and a more forceful figure at the top. In consequence, outside the ginger group there was no tightening of the Liberal ranks.

At the same time Conservative back-benchers also were establishing a War Committee, whose principal figure was Carson. If to a lesser extent than its Liberal counterpart, this body likewise was out of sympathy with its party leader. The principal cause was forcefully stated (in the document quoted earlier) by Lord Selborne: Bonar Law clung to the theory 'that Asquith was indispensable as War P.M. and that therefore under no circumstances must the Coalition Cabinet be allowed to break up'. In one respect the Unionist War Committee was potentially more menacing to the Government than its Liberal equivalent. Its base, actual and potential, was much wider. By March 1916 it numbered 150 Conservative MPs. And in some measure it appealed to nearly the whole party. Referring to a special Conservative conference in August, the *Annual Register* observed that the coalition Government, 'although it appeared to represent nearly all shades of opinion in the country', was never really popular with the Unionist Party. Conservatives 'thought they were still keeping up a Liberal Government by being members of it'.[7]

Time and again during 1916 it seemed evident that Asquith's control of his colleagues and of the House of Commons was failing. The clearest display occurred in April, with conscription once more the issue. The question of its extension to married men brought the Cabinet to deadlock. 'Of course Lloyd George is the villain of the piece,' Asquith told Lady Scott, '& you know what I think of him.'[8] The dispute among Ministers became a matter of public knowledge. *Punch* wondered if the reference in one newspaper to the 'leekage' of Cabinet secrets was not an appropriate misspelling; but journals hostile to Lloyd George were also proving well informed. Indeed, the indiscretions from within the Government became so blatant that DORA had to be invoked to prevent further such publications – a sad admission that the Prime Minister was unable to stem the flow at source.

So complete did the impasse in the Government become that on successive days Asquith had to inform the Commons that he could not keep his promise to present the Cabinet's proposals on recruiting. On the second occasion he admitted that the Cabinet was on the verge of break-up. Then, at the last minute, compromise proposals were devised. These preserved free enlistment for married men (although not for some other groups, such as lads turning 18). But, as in the case of bachelors under the Derby scheme, the right of married men to volunteer would now depend on their doing so in sufficient numbers by specified dates. If they failed, then they too would be fetched. At this point it was the turn of the House of Commons to rebel. Rank and file MPs, both conscriptionist and anti-conscriptionist, rounded on the Government's proposals and rent them. With almost indecent haste the Cabinet accepted general conscription for men of military age.

Simultaneously other events were shaking Asquith's command of Parliament. The Easter Rising in Ireland, and the ensuing revelations of long-standing administrative indulgence towards subversive activities there, gave a field day to the enemies of Home Rule. And Asquith before long suffered further harm from his attempts to redeem the

---

[7] *Annual Register for 1916*, pp. 160–1.

[8] Lady Scott's diary, 18 April 1916.

situation in Ireland. Initially, he responded boldly. He appointed Lloyd George to try to secure a settlement between the contending groups in Ireland. With great energy and ingenuity Lloyd George managed to bring Redmond and Carson – both of whom had been dismayed by the rebellion – to an agreement. But the terms of the proposed settlement outraged those diehard Conservatives who were determined not just to safeguard Ulster but to deny self-government to southern Ireland. Their representatives in Asquith's ministry threatened resignation unless the scheme was amended in a way unacceptable to Redmond. (Selborne, prematurely, resigned anyway.) Asquith capitulated to this demand, so dooming any hope of a settlement.

By his action Asquith once more escaped the possible break-up of his Government. But he damaged his standing among those parliamentarians who particularly owed him allegiance. Many Liberals were conscience-stricken by Ireland's long denial of any degree of self-government and oppressed by the recent bloody events there. To them Asquith's surrender was shameful. And the Prime Minister's action fatally alienated the Irish Nationalists (whose own position within Ireland was becoming terribly endangered). In the House of Commons on 24 July Redmond denounced the Government for a disgraceful breach of faith. He said that his attitude to the war was unchanged. But his party would henceforth adopt an independent position in criticizing the procrastination of Ministers, not only concerning Ireland but regarding the whole conduct of the war. With these words a fundamental breach was signified in the old association of parties upon which Asquith had depended up to May 1915.

In mid-1916 rebuffs to the Government came thick and fast. In July a fierce attack on the conduct of the Mesopotamian campaign, including a demand for a commission of inquiry, was launched by Carson and strongly supported by Redmond. Asquith resisted the proposal for an investigation, stating that the military authorities considered the time inopportune. The House was not convinced, and on 20 July the Prime Minister was obliged to capitulate. He announced the appointment of committees of inquiry into both the Dardanelles and Mesopotamian operations. Still Parliament was not appeased. It insisted on widening the terms of reference of the proposed committees and adding members of its own choice.

At the same time MPs were pressing the Government for proposals regarding a new electoral register. This would facilitate an early election – something that appealed only to Asquith's enemies. Meanwhile the Government's request for a further extension of the life of Parliament was granted grudgingly and for a lesser period than asked. At the beginning of August Waldorf Astor, a Conservative MP and proprietor of the *Observer* (he was also an American millionaire), wrote privately: 'It looks as if the A regime might crumble at no distant date. The old man has had 2 black eyes & his wind knocked out over the Registration, Mespot, & Irish incidents. He is obviously rattled & has certainly for the time lost his hold on the House.'[9]

In the autumn the fractiousness of Parliament continued. The direction of affairs at the Admiralty, and in particular Balfour's performance as First Lord, came under constant attack. The Government's measure for an electoral register, which evaded the issue of votes for serving soldiers and sailors, failed to give satisfaction, and the Bill had to be withdrawn. The proposals for establishing a Pensions Board, as mentioned earlier, so little pleased the Commons that the Government was obliged to adopt the scheme of one of its critics. And Carson mounted strong attacks on the role still supposedly occupied in Britain's business affairs by enemy representatives. His

---

[9] Astor to J. L. Garvin, 2 August 1916, Garvin papers. I am indebted to Dr Stephen Inwood for transcripts of letters from the Garvin papers.

campaign on this matter – and, by implication, his challenge to Bonar Law's control over the allegiance of Conservative MPs – reached a climax on 8 November.

The issue was the sale of captured enemy property in Nigeria. The Government proposed to accept bids from British and Allied citizens and also from genuine neutrals. Carson moved that only British subjects should be allowed to participate. Bonar Law met the challenge head-on, announcing that this was a motion of censure on the Government. Nevertheless, only 72 Conservative Members (including holders of office) voted with the Government, as against 65 who divided against it and about 35 who, although present, abstained. This was a solemn warning to the Conservative leader. As he himself remarked, many of those who sided with Carson had previously been his own staunchest supporters and had aided him in securing the party leadership five years before. Bonar Law emerged from the debate (so Asquith told Lady Scott) 'with his teeth chattering'. It was a sound that boded the Prime Minister no good.

Up to this stage, notwithstanding the serious threats to Asquith's position, two things had ensured his continuance in office. One was the Conservative leader's conviction that the unity of the nation required Asquith at the helm. The other was the seeming absence of any individual apart from the Liberal leader who could command a broad following. By November 1916 all this was changing. Bonar Law could hardly go on assessing Asquith's usefulness so highly when the unity of his own party was in danger. This raised in acute form the question: was there no person, agreeable to most Conservatives and also to a wider political spectrum, available to supplant Asquith?

III

One politician only since August 1914 had addressed himself to war matters with conspicuous success: Lloyd George. This had aroused much appreciation in the country. He had enhanced it by trenchant utterances delivered apparently without regard to the sensibilities of his colleagues: the 'too late' speech and the snub to the American President ('a fight to a finish – to a knock-out').

Yet Lloyd George seemingly lacked some of the qualifications necessary for the post of national leader. His eagerness for conscription and apparent willingness to regiment working people, his associations with pressmen engaged in attacking Liberal colleagues, and the apparent slightness of his attachment to party and principle had antagonized many devoted Liberals. And in the ranks of labour, both political and industrial, he was regarded with much suspicion. One of the most experienced of civil servants, Robert Morant, referred to this in no uncertain terms in a private letter of 7 January 1916. Lloyd George, in his view, had done 'very grave mischief.'

> His rash promises, his failure to carry them out, his prevarication, his mishandling of the Munitions Act and its Amendment and lastly his suppression of 'Forward' . . . – all this has made the workers *very* bitter and they are convinced that Ll-G is filled with vindictiveness against them and is trying to arrive at compulsory powers (via conscription) for smashing their industrial possibilities.

Morant regarded the hostile decision of the recent Labour congress towards conscription as being as much a vote against Lloyd George and 'the suspicions that he arouses' as it was a vote against the Bill itself. As for the threatened general election, Morant feared it for the passions it would arouse and also because anything putting Lloyd George 'into a *more* dominant position just now would certainly make Labour revolt badly': 'Even the good labour leaders are utterly disgusted with Lloyd George.'[10]

---

[10] R. Morant to J. L. Garvin, 7 January 1916, Garvin papers. Transcript provided by Dr Stephen Inwood.

Among Conservatives also sentiments were divided. Some were loath to believe that the nation had come to such a pass that an individual of Lloyd George's lowly birth and pre-war record should be accorded the first position. For those in the upper ranks of the party these misgivings had sometimes been reinforced by association with Lloyd George since the formation of the coalition. Austen Chamberlain had collaborated with him in the first conscription crisis and had been dismayed by his unpredictability. In December 1916 he would write of Lloyd George as 'a man who does not seem crooked because he wants to [be], but because he does not know how to run straight'. Lloyd George, in his view, had 'tired out the patience of every man who has worked with him and most of those who have worked for him'; he 'let his Unionist colleagues down about conscription at the critical moment and then took up the question again when he thought the audience more favourable and the limelight more concentrated on himself'.[11]

But the most serious enmity that Lloyd George aroused among Conservatives was that of Bonar Law. The two men had acted together to bring about the change of Government in May 1915. Yet in the allocation of offices Law found himself, seemingly with Lloyd George's connivance, fobbed off with one of the lowlier positions in the Cabinet. This had deeply offended the Conservative leader. Thereafter Lloyd George did not go out of his way to recover Law's favour. In September 1915 Law suggested that, given his status in the Conservative Party, he ought to be deputy leader of the Commons. The Prime Minister agreed. Lloyd George, who had held the title of deputy leader for some years, was not pleased and intimated as much to Law.

By such conduct Lloyd George aroused a resentment that, on Law's part, was to continue unabated right up to the end of October 1916. In that month Sir Edward Goulding, an influential Conservative back-bencher strong in Law's friendship, tried for a *rapprochement* between them. He failed utterly. As he recounted privately:

> I am of opinion there is a wide and widening gulf between the two men. He [i.e. Law] had no word of praise for him and much prefers Squiffy [Asquith], Grey, or even Runciman. He says that if Lloyd George was head of a Cabinet it would not last three months and he would not serve in it.[12]

Many aspects of Lloyd George's behaviour in 1916 reinforced Conservative doubts about him. Time and again in the first half of the year he talked as if determined to resign from the Government but then always found an excuse for staying. His motives must remain a matter for speculation. He may genuinely have disliked breaking off relations with Asquith and the official Liberal Party and falling back on the Conservatives for his main support. But he may have been oppressed by the possibility that, once out of office, he would find it no easy matter to get back. For the moment he had no certain power base and many devoted opponents. As a man who had not been born into governing circles, he could never assume that office was his by right, simply on the grounds of talent. So resignation was bound to constitute a daunting prospect. Yet by so often talking as though he could not remain in Asquith's company a moment longer and then choosing to do so, he helped to confirm a reputation for instability and waywardness.

In the aftermath of Kitchener's death in June 1916 Lloyd George further antagonized powerful Conservatives. He wanted the post that Kitchener's demise had

---

[11] Quoted in John Stubbs, 'The Conservative Party and the Politics of War 1914–1916', D.Phil. thesis, Oxford University, 1973, p. 391, and Sir Charles Petrie, *The Life and Letters of the Right Hon. Sir Austen Chamberlain* (London: Cassell, 1939–40), vol. 2, p. 63.

[12] Goulding to Garvin, 24 and 29 October 1916, Garvin papers. Transcript provided by Dr Stephen Inwood.

rendered vacant. And, given his accomplishments, he could not be denied it. But he wanted it with its former powers restored. This was a different matter. The arrangement by which the Cabinet took its military advice from Robertson, the CIGS, seemed at this stage eminently satisfactory. Few members preferred to receive Robertson's guidance through the medium of a civilian War Minister harbouring peculiar views on strategy, of which the only fruit so far had been the barren operation at Salonika.

So Lloyd George received the War Office only with the limited authority that Kitchener had latterly possessed. This arrangement was hardly appropriate. Kitchener had come to this point by his manifest failures; Lloyd George by his many successes. There was no reason why the new head of the War Office should behave with the self-abnegation latterly displayed by his predecessor. Yet if he did not, he was bound to run into trouble.

Robertson's position was a powerful one. Belief in the CIGS's strategy, now to reach fulfilment on the Somme, was at a peak. Belief in the sideshows was very low. Should Lloyd George try to adopt a line at odds with that of Haig and Robertson, the military leaders had allies at Buckingham Palace, in political circles, and on the newspapers. Robertson had no scruples about leaking to appropriate journalists any developments in the Government that alarmed him. And Haig, in person and through Philip Sassoon, his ingratiating private secretary, was cultivating pressmen for all he was worth. (Haig invariably dubbed those press figures ready to do his bidding as 'anxious to be useful to the Country' and 'anxious to play the game'.)[13] From these activities Haig reaped a full reward. Northcliffe, after visiting British headquarters at the beginning of August, wrote to the editor of *The Times*: 'He and his entourage inspire me with absolute confidence.'[14] Therefore, Northcliffe intimated, *The Times*'s military correspondent should be restrained from criticizing Haig.

Lloyd George soon received warning of what might befall him if he stepped out of line. From outside the Government, Churchill sought at the end of July to convince the Cabinet that the Somme campaign was a failure. Northcliffe was immediately apprised of this by Haig. The press baron thereupon directed to Lloyd George, both privately and by means of a *Times* editorial, strong warnings that he should counter Churchill's move. For the moment Lloyd George proved accommodating. In Parliament on 22 August, while warning that there could be no 'early victory', he offered a positive account of what the British offensive was accomplishing: 'We have captured the ridge; we can see, at any rate, the course of the campaign. I think in the dim distance we can see the end.'

But the new War Minister could not maintain this stance for long. The huge casualties and small advances on the Somme, well founded doubts about the toll being exacted upon the Germans, and the revival of the Balkan issue with Romania's entry into the war, all renewed his hostility to the Western strategy. He soon began acting as something other than a mouthpiece for Haig and Robertson. In September, when visiting the front, he intimated to French generals that he much preferred the way in which they were conducting the offensive. Alarmed, they conveyed news of this to Haig, who passed it on to his allies in the press. On 28 September the high-Tory newspaper the *Morning Post* delivered a furious attack on Lloyd George. It told him to stick to his desk in Whitehall. And it warned him that if he repeated the sort of 'gaffe'

---

[13] Haig's diary for 1 June and 25 July 1916, quoted in Stephen Inwood, 'The Role of the Press in the First World War, with Special Reference to the Period 1914–1916', D. Phil. thesis, Oxford University, 1971, pp. 344–6.
[14] Quoted in ibid., p. 348.

he had made recently in France, 'we shall feel it our duty to publish the facts of the occurrence.'

At the same time Lloyd George was pressing for the dispatch of troops to the Balkans. On 9 October he urged the Cabinet to send eight divisions to Salonika for an invasion of Bulgaria. Robertson apprised Northcliffe of the fact. This time the press baron decided on actions as well as words. He stormed into the War Minister's office and, finding him absent, left a message that if Lloyd George did not stop interfering with strategy, then 'I will break him.'

Northcliffe did more. He sent word to Asquith promising him support as long as he allowed the generals a free hand. At the same time H. A. Gwynne, the editor of the *Morning Post*, wrote to the Prime Minister appealing to him personally to intervene to protect Haig's position. Thus Asquith was in the agreeable situation, early in October, of having two prominent adversaries in the right-wing press rallying to him against Lloyd George.

The Prime Minister was perhaps to be excused if he failed to recognize that his downfall was at hand.

Plate 33   *'Wullie' Robertson and Lloyd George arriving at the War Office during the political crisis.*

IV

But if Asquith was a better Westerner than Lloyd George, this was just about his sole remaining asset. And in the circumstances it was barely sufficient. Neither the high command nor its press allies had it in their power to make of the Somme campaign a mighty victory. By October, as has been suggested earlier, a cold awareness was developing of the limited achievement and grievous cost. As Haig's private secretary admitted in a letter to Northcliffe on 30 October: 'Now that almost everyone has lost someone in the war, it is very easy to arouse criticism.'[15]

Recognition that the Somme campaign, whatever its achievements, had left the country facing further such terrible operations coincided with a succession of events bound to create despondency. The calamity suffered by Romania, the setback on the Russian front, rising food prices and the beginning of shortages at home, and deep concern about the course of the naval war (particularly the latest U-boat successes), all came together in a general conviction that the nation's affairs were not being directed with grip and determination. In such circumstances it required more than Lloyd George's apparent instability of party allegiance and political intent, along with his unwelcome interventions in military matters, to preserve Asquith's position.

Something of the fragility of this late rally to Asquith is evident in the conduct of Gwynne, the editor of the *Morning Post*. On 11 October, the day on which he appealed to Asquith to safeguard Haig, he wrote to Lloyd George. His purpose was to urge the War Minister not to place people like himself in 'an awkward dilemma':

> you are the only man in the Cabinet who sees clearly that we have to beat the Germans thoroughly or go under. The rest of your colleagues are already whispering the words 'Armistice', 'peace'. But why on earth can't you let the Army alone? With it enthusiastically on your side victory over Germany becomes easier while if you quarrel with it, you will jeopardize the issue and lose influence in the country. And all the time we want a man who is all out for beating the Germans.[16]

In the course of the next six weeks Gwynne, at least for the moment, resolved his 'awkward dilemma'. On 23 November the *Morning Post* called on its readers to rally behind Lloyd George. And early in December it denounced Bonar Law for standing by Asquith. Northcliffe too, in the opening days of December, made his peace (if that is the right expression) with Lloyd George. Clearly, this was no case of the 'Napoleon of Fleet Street' master-minding events. He was having swiftly to change direction so as to keep up with them.

At the same time, Bonar Law was reappraising his position. The mounting threat both to Conservative unity and to his own standing as party leader, signalized by the Nigeria debate of 8 November, left him little choice. 'He had once said that unless he was entirely backed by his supporters he would resign,' he reminded Asquith; now he was faced with being in opposition to 'his own people.'[17] The next day Law told Hankey that the political situation was very precarious: 'Lloyd George is at the same time the right hand man to the Prime Minister, and the leader of the Opposition.' (Asquith too noted, in a rather disgruntled way, that Lloyd George had dined with Carson on the night of the Nigeria debate.)[18] The conclusion, reluctantly reached by the Conservative leader, was irresistible. As Law put it later in the month to one of Lloyd George's keenest Liberal supporters: 'One cannot go on like this, Addison, do you think?'[19]

So Law allowed himself to be reconciled with Carson, the leading Conservative dissident, and with Lloyd George, simultaneously the 'righthand man to the Prime Minister' and the 'leader of the Opposition'. This *rapprochement* could occur only at Asquith's expense. For Carson was bent on having Asquith out of office. And Lloyd

---

[15] Quoted in Inwood, 'The Role of the Press', p. 364.

[16] Lloyd George papers, in the House of Lords Record Office.

[17] Asquith's account to Lady Scott; Lady Scott's diary, 8 November 1916.

[18] Hankey's diary, 9 and 10 November 1916.

[19] Christopher Addison, *Four and a Half Years* (London: Hutchinson, 1934), vol. 1, p. 269.

George, if not necessarily wishing to go this far, was determined to end Asquith's exercise of power.

Law's turn to Lloyd George late in November found the latter more than usually dismayed. The doom of Romania was sealed. And the War Minister was painfully aware of how little control he possessed over the CIGS and the Commander-in-Chief. But it was against Asquith, not against Robertson and Haig, that he chose to move. On 22 November Lloyd George outlined the first version of his plan to Hankey, who recorded in his diary:

> He wants to present a pistol at the P.M.'s head in order to secure a new inner War Ctee. – himself, Carson (!), Bonar Law, & Henderson – the latter in order to conciliate labour. . . . I told Ll.G. that I liked his proposal in principle, but not his personnel. I said frankly that I had not a high opinion of Carson or Bonar Law in council. After thinking it over I added that the net result would be to put absolute power in his (Ll.G's) hands. . . .

Certainly, the arrangement was intended to leave little or no power in the hands of the Prime Minister. As Lloyd George's private secretary summed up the scheme that day, Lloyd George and Carson and Bonar Law (there is no mention of Henderson) would 'arrange to run the War Committee & leave the P.M. to run "his show", i.e. the Cabinet which would not then count for much.'[20]

Law, egged on by his ally Sir Max Aitken, became a party to these discussions. To begin with he jibbed at the proposed exclusion of the Prime Minister from what plainly must become the most important instrument of government. So in the scheme as initially put to Asquith, the Prime Minister would be president of the new body and Lloyd George its chairman – which meant that the latter would preside whenever Asquith was absent. All the members of the committee would be Ministers without departments. Asquith resisted the proposal. He alleged the unworkability of a war committee without the heads of the Admiralty and the War Office. And he raised problems of personnel. The inclusion of Carson, 'our most formidable parliamentary critic', would be seen as 'a manifest sign of weakness and cowardice'. As for the elevation of Lloyd George, it could be construed only as a stage in his own displacement, 'not perhaps at the moment, but as soon as a fitting pretext could be found'.[21] This response shook Bonar Law's resolve. He also became aware of hostility to the course on which he was embarked among other Conservative Ministers.

But Lloyd George this time was not inclined to retreat. He revised the proposals to the Prime Minister, but not all in one direction. The war committee would now be a three-man body including the Ministers responsible for the War Office and the Admiralty (the latter of whom would not be Balfour). But it would not include Asquith, who at most was to retain a shadowy power to refer the committee's decisions to the cabinet. On 1 December Asquith replied, agreeing to the formation of a body of the size Lloyd George was proposing, but holding off on the matter of personnel and insisting on himself as chairman. Lloyd George spent much of the next morning drafting his letter of resignation.

The news that Lloyd George really meant to go, conveyed to Asquith by E. S. Montagu (who was seeking to prevent a breach), brought Asquith hurrying back from the country the following day. As 3 December was a Sunday, this was clear evidence that he appreciated the seriousness of the situation. On his arrival he found it to be even graver than he had supposed. Bonar Law informed him that a meeting of Conservative Ministers had decided that Asquith should hand in the Government's resignation. If he disagreed, then they would resign their posts.

[20] A. J. P. Taylor (ed.), *Lloyd George: A Diary by Frances Stevenson* (London: Hutchinson, 1971), p. 127.

[21] Roy Jenkins, *Asquith* (London: Collins, 1964), p. 426.

This did not necessarily mean that the Conservative Ministers had swung round behind Lloyd George. Some were utterly averse to the scheme he was proposing. Robert Cecil said of it, in rage: 'This means that George is practically dictator!' ('So it does!' was Lloyd George's comment when he related the story to Frances Stevenson – who agreed.)[22] And the Conservative Ministers were indignant at a detailed account of the crisis contained in a Sunday newspaper owned by a close ally of Lloyd George – only the latest in a series of plainly inspired press articles. But their conclusion was that an intolerable situation must be resolved one way or another. They probably did not greatly fancy any of the likely outcomes, although some seem to have believed that the Government's resignation would aid Asquith by forcing Lloyd George to face the consequences of his conduct. It is not certain that Law made all this clear to the Prime Minister. It is unlikely, anyway, that Asquith would have considered his own resignation any sort of a scheme for out-manoeuvring his subordinate. In haste he arranged a meeting with Lloyd George.

At this gathering, late in the afternoon of 3 December, the Prime Minister largely capitulated. He agreed that a small committee to direct the war should be formed under Lloyd George's chairmanship. His own relations with this body would be indeterminate. He might attend on occasion, and could withhold approval of its decisions. The question of how far Asquith was prepared to back down on the matter of personnel remained uncertain.

Clearly, the Prime Minister had gone a long way, while retaining the shadow of office, towards endorsing his own supersession. The extent of his surrender was spelled out to him next morning in some well informed articles in *The Times*. (Asquith presumably suspected Lloyd George of being their inspiration and of acting through Northcliffe, whom Lloyd George had seen on the three preceding days. In fact, the immediate source of information was Carson, who was in communication with the editor of *The Times*, Geoffrey Robinson.) *The Times* made much of the fact that the crisis had been brought to a head by Lloyd George. He had become 'gravely dissatisfied with the dilatory and irresolute manner' in which the Cabinet and War Committee were directing the war, and he would 'play a large and perhaps controlling part in the drama of reconstruction'. The newspaper also stressed that Carson was being imposed on Asquith at the insistence of Lloyd George, who had in these matters the support of Bonar Law. And a leading article emphasized the degree of expediency in Asquith's conversion to the new arrangement, as well as the small role he would occupy under it.

Stung by this attack, or perhaps shocked by it into realizing the humiliating conditions to which he had agreed, Asquith early on 4 December informed Lloyd George that he was reconsidering. During that morning, as he came to appreciate how small was the support for Lloyd George's actual scheme among Liberal and most Conservative Ministers, he reconsidered even further. That evening he wrote to Lloyd George insisting that the Prime Minister must be chairman of the proposed committee. He also refused to jettison Balfour or accept Carson. Lloyd George replied with a long and pungent letter of resignation. He laid stress on the shortcomings of the Government in the conduct of the war. And he insisted that Asquith was abandoning an arrangement to which he had agreed.

Asquith received this missive on the morning of 5 December. In a moment his position had crumbled. He could not about-turn once more, accepting for a second time a scheme that the press proclaimed was degrading to himself and that most of his Cabinet colleagues condemned. Yet Lloyd George's departure on this issue involved

---

[22] Taylor (ed.), *Lloyd George: A Diary by Frances Stevenson*, p. 131.

that of Bonar Law. And the two-day-old decision of the Conservative Ministers in favour of resignation, whatever its meaning or intention, still stood.

That evening Asquith went to Buckingham Palace and resigned as Prime Minister. Whatever may have been the views of those in the upper echelons of politics, he no longer had the base on which to maintain a Government. The departure of Bonar Law and his new-found association with Carson must have large implications for Conservative MPs generally. Already, on the Nigeria issue, about 100 of them had failed (by vote or abstention) to support the Government despite Bonar Law's stand on its behalf. And the Unionist War Committee had been estimated to number some 150 MPs, a total that was bound to grow now that its chief figure was allied with the party leader.

Among Liberal MPs no such large defection from Asquith was to be anticipated. But it was likely – as Addison was relaying to Lloyd George – that a good many more than the 40 MPs associated with the Liberal ginger group would support a change of Premier. And the handful of anti-war Liberals would never rally to Asquith. Something of the same applied to the Labour Party. A majority of Labour MPs would continue to give Asquith lukewarm approval. But the most devoted supporters and opponents of the war would be glad, if for different reasons, to act against him. As for the Irish Nationalists, they were already voting in opposition to a man. This they had demonstrated in the Nigeria debate, when their support for Carson's motion had clearly not been based on the merits of the issue.

These points deserve to be noted. It is possible to become hypnotized by the manoeuvres at the top, and so not to connect Asquith's fall with the attitudes of rank-and-file parliamentarians. Yet the political crisis of early December was the culmination of a succession of rebuffs to the government in the House of Commons. Certainly, the counting of heads could not be conducted down to the last MP. But it was quite evident by the evening of 5 December 1916 that Asquith no longer had the numbers in Parliament to remain Prime Minister. As a *Manchester Guardian* correspondent had put it three days earlier, 'The House of Commons is ready to create another Ministry.'

The principal question remaining was whether anyone else was in a happier position. As leader of the next largest party, Bonar Law was invited to attempt to form a Government. He had little to recommend him except that, like Asquith before him, he might serve as a unifying force. But this he proved unable to do. Asquith and most of the leading Liberals would no more serve in a Bonar Law Government than in a Lloyd George Government. So Law gave up the attempt and advised the King to send for Lloyd George.

By this time all the leading figures in the Conservative Party could be persuaded to serve under Lloyd George. Some, certainly, would join only on terms: that there would be no posts for the ill-trusted Northcliffe and Churchill, and no attempt to supplant Haig. Here was evidence of Conservative uneasiness about the change. But even the most reluctant had come to prefer Lloyd George under restraints to any alternative. As for the Liberals, none of his former colleagues in the upper ranks of the Government would serve with him. But a number among the lower order of Liberal MPs – reinforced by a distinguished import in H. A. L. Fisher – were prepared to accept office. This gave the Government a Liberal element.

That left the Labour Party. Henderson, only days before, had spoken out publicly in support of Asquith. But this meant less that he was enamoured of the Asquith Government than that he feared some of its critics and took it to be in the national interest to bolster up the existing regime. Now Lloyd George was appealing to Labour from the vantage point of being the only individual with any prospect of creating a viable Government. At least some of the considerations that had prompted Henderson to uphold Asquith now pointed to his agreeing to serve with Lloyd George.

The process by which the new Prime Minister persuaded a gathering of Labour MPs and the party's Executive Committee to join him in office has sometimes been adjudged a 'doping session'. Lloyd George, almost by his own admission, was 'at his craftiest': 'They asked him awkward questions, & he put them off with chaff.'[23] In his address he held out imprecise but attractive-sounding promises about state enterprises and post-war reconstruction. More concretely, he proposed immediately to establish a Food Controller and a Ministry of Labour, and offered the party several posts in his Government (including one in the five-man War Cabinet). According to Beatrice Webb, whose husband had been there, the 'main motive' (or anyway the most conscious) of Labour members for accepting was 'the illusion that the mere presence of Labour men in the Government, apart from anything they may do or prevent being done, is in itself a sign of democratic progress'. She instanced J. R. Clynes, who came round to supporting entry into the Government so that Labour might have some say in the terms of peace. 'Poor Labour men,' observed Beatrice Webb, 'they will not get much say in the terms of industrial peace at home, leave alone those of the peace of the world!'[24]

Yet there is no need to believe that the Labour representatives who responded to Lloyd George's coaxing were just being simpletons. Organized labour supported the war and wanted it to be won. Only the day before this meeting the parliamentary committee of the TUC had passed a resolution making this clear. It regretted that certain statesmen, under the influence of the press campaign, had entirely failed to observe the 'loyalty and self-sacrifice they have repeatedly urged upon the workers during the War'. And it called on them to cease 'the present unseemly quarrel' and so to 'set a better example to the workers, who, we trust, in spite of the wrecking tactics adopted, will continue to give of their best in the national interest'.[25] For 'the national interest' to be upheld a resourceful Government was required. By 7 December 1916 only Lloyd George could provide it.

It is unlikely that the Labour representatives expected of the new Prime Minister much sympathy for organized labour. His tastes, pretty plainly, ran more to thrusting, self-made businessmen. And it would have been difficult to overlook the powerful anti-Labour forces that constituted the backbone of his present support. But as long as he must be Prime Minister these were not sufficient grounds for refusing to enter his Government. There was an important difference here between the Labour Party and the followers of Asquith. The latter could decline to serve in the new ministry without making impossible a continuance of strong government. Labour could not. Its abstention from office would threaten Britain's war endeavours at the centre, for it would tend to dissociate a vital segment of the workforce from the direction of affairs. That such a solemn responsibility rested on Labour's decision indicated how powerfully, in the forcing-house of war, the party's status was rising.

The affirmative decision of Labour, coming on top of the endorsement – if not always wholehearted – of the entire Conservative Party and the unstinting support of a section of Liberals, confirmed Lloyd George as Prime Minister. In its issue of 9 December the left-wing *Nation*, while deeply repelled by him, came close to explaining his success. The journal called him 'a true personality of the hour': 'It has made him; his audacities of manipulation excite and please, and even inspire men with hope.' In the prevailing circumstances hope was the vital commodity.

[23] Taylor (ed.), *Lloyd George: A Diary by Frances Stevenson*, p. 134.

[24] Margaret Cole (ed.), *Beatrice Webb's Diaries 1912–1924* (London: Longman's, Green, 1952), p. 73.

[25] Minutes of the Parliamentary Committee of the TUC, 6 December 1916.

PART TEN

The Killing Time
1917

39

THE SHADOW OF THE PERISCOPE

Then called on Carson at Admiralty . . . . still deeply depressed about submarine war.
C. P. Scott, 2 May 1917

I

Lloyd George had become Prime Minister at what for Britain was one of the supreme testing times of the war.

Up to January 1917 the naval and military forces of Britain had generally been taking the war to the enemy. On the water the Royal Navy had instituted a blockade of Germany and had forced the High Seas Fleet to keep off the high seas. On land Britain had launched offensives against the Germans in Flanders and France and against the Turks at Gallipoli and in Mesopotamia.

Germany, by contrast, had so far made no direct attempt to knock Britain out of the war. Twice around Ypres during the first year of the struggle German forces had dealt savagely with the relatively small British army. And at sea in 1915 the limited number of U-boats had sunk a considerable body of British merchant ships. But these blows were not of the same order as those Germany had launched against France in the opening weeks of the war and again at Verdun in 1916 – blows intended to eliminate the French from the ranks of the combatants.

In January 1917 this situation changed. The rulers of Germany determined that Britain should now become the adversary destined for swift elimination. This would not be done on land, given Britain's continued strength in manpower and in industrial resources. Instead advantage would be taken of Britain's acute vulnerability to naval blockade. Germany's enlarged submarine force would be employed to sink a large proportion of the merchant shipping approaching and leaving Britain's shores. This would have a double effect. Neutral vessels would soon refuse to run the U-boat gauntlet and so would cease trading with Britain altogether. And British shipping would become so depleted that it could no longer adequately supply the nation's civilian population, war machine, and expeditions abroad. The calculation was that the destruction of 600,000 tons of British shipping a month, combined with the total withdrawal of neutral shipping, would force Britain to sue for peace within six months.

The German plan depended on the adoption of unlimited submarine warfare. That is, every merchant ship of Allied or neutral origin, within a large area of sea, would be considered fair game. And no regard was to be had for the safety of their passengers and crews. Attacks would be carried out without warning and, where appropriate, from beneath the sea.

Developments in the submarine war had, in any case, been pointing the Germans in

427

this direction. The new U-boats that Germany was building had a considerably increased torpedo capacity, thus facilitating many more submerged attacks. And Britain's growing practice of arming its merchant ships, along with its use of Q-ships, was rendering submarine attacks on the surface both more perilous and less rewarding. As long as the U-boat could strike from beneath the sea, the weapons of merchantmen and Q-ships held no dangers.

Technical evolution, then, was directing German thinking towards the unrestricted use of the U-boat. What the country's rulers contributed was the calculation that the consequent sinking of neutral vessels would not be an unfortunate corollary. Rather, it would be the most lucrative part of the whole campaign. For whereas attacks on British shipping would deprive Britain only of that proportion of its merchant fleet that actually went to the bottom, the campaign against neutrals would accomplish far more. It would drive all neutral shipping from Britain's shores.

Germany's leaders, of course, were not under the illusion that in adopting this course they had nothing to lose. The United States would certainly become a belligerent. President Wilson might be prepared to retreat from his stand on the *Lusitania* and kindred incidents, whereby he had refused to tolerate the sinking even of Allied passenger ships if American lives were thereby endangered. But he would never back down so far as to tolerate the course that was now being contemplated: the indiscriminate sinking of American-owned and -manned merchant ships. Nevertheless, the Kaiser's advisers calculated that this would not matter greatly. In their view, American industry and raw materials were already at the disposal of the Allies. So the only further contribution the United States could make was in manpower. But the USA had for the moment no army deserving consideration. Hence its intervention would signify only if the war went on long enough for the Americans to raise and train an army that they could then transport to Europe. If all went according to German plans, this would never happen. The U-boat campaign would ensure that the war ended much earlier. And anyway, by the time the USA possessed a considerable army, the shipping required to carry it to the battlefield would have ceased to exist.

II

Events from 1 February 1917 to the end of July would test the validity of the calculation that the U-boat could force Britain to sue for peace within six months. Two things rapidly became evident. The first was that Germany could now put to sea considerably more submarines than at any previous time. The second was that the U-boats, employing unrestricted methods, were capable of exacting a greater toll than at any earlier stage of the war.

As a monthly average, between February and April 1917 there were 41 U-boats at sea out of 121 operational. (Those not at sea were refitting, undergoing repairs, or resting their crews.) This may not appear a large number, but proportionately it was a considerable advance. For example, in February, the first month of the unrestricted campaign, the 36 German submarines at sea constituted 11 more than in January and 19 more than the monthly average for 1916. Given that they could now strike without warning or restriction of targets and (because attacking increasingly from beneath the surface) with relative immunity, this constituted a substantially increased force.

Its effectiveness rapidly became apparent. In January 1917, the last month of the restricted campaign, Britain had lost 49 merchant ships to enemy action, and its allies and neutrals 122. This made a total of 171 ships sunk, constituting a tonnage of about one-third of 1 million. (These, it should be noted, are total losses to submarines, mines, and surface raiders. But the U-boat claimed 85 per cent of the victims, and that proportion increased in the following months.) In February and March, with the opening of the unrestricted campaign, the total of ships destroyed rose dramatically – by not much short of 100 per cent. Britain lost 105 merchant ships in February and 127 in March, its allies and neutrals 129 in the former month and 154 in the latter. Total tonnage sunk was in excess of 500,000 in February and 600,000 in March.

Even these losses paled by comparison with the events of April, when the destruction of merchant shipping became a holocaust: 169 British vessels and 204 of other nationalities went to the bottom, constituting a total of 870,000 tons. This meant that in the third month of the campaign one-quarter of merchant ships leaving Britain's shores would never complete the round trip. The cargoes lost in consequence were heavy enough. But far worse was the depletion of vessels capable of carrying future cargoes.

Nor did the cost of the U-boat campaign to Britain end there. In April a further one-third of 1 million tons of world shipping was damaged by German action, choking the repair yards and ensuring a considerable delay before these vessels could be got back to sea. Again, the known proximity of U-boats was reducing the effectiveness of undamaged ships by causing them to shelter in harbour or to adopt evasive routing. Already from January the toll exacted by submarines in the Mediterranean was forcing merchantmen from the Far East to take the longer journey around South Africa. And some neutral shippers were refusing to run the U-boat gauntlet, so that in April the volume of neutral vessels calling at Allied ports fell to one-quarter.

In the next three months the number of U-boats at sea declined somewhat, as did their toll of victims, although hardly significantly. Total losses (British, Allied, and neutral) in this period were as follows: in May 287 ships of 600,000 tons; in June 290 ships of over 680,000 tons; and in July 227 ships of 547,000 tons. Hence in the half-year that the rulers of Germany had allowed themselves, they had destroyed 3.75 million tons of world shipping, had reduced the efficiency and so the carrying capacity of much that survived, and had persuaded a significant (although not constant) body of neutrals to shun Britain's shores. No one could doubt that it was an imposing – and, for Britain, deeply threatening – accomplishment.

III

If the raw statistics of the U-boat campaign are chilling enough, they convey little of the terrible human drama that this form of warfare involved. The battle between U-boats and merchant ships, to which mines, patrol craft, and all the normal perils of the sea also contributed, was not an agreeable experience for the participants on either side. The occupants of the submarines would sometimes have the satisfaction of witnessing the death throes of their victims; and in this war few conquests can have been more evident than the sight of a merchant ship vanishing beneath the waves. Yet the strain of life in a U-boat was plainly intense, and was one reason why only about one-third of Germany's submarines could be at sea at any time. According to a German account:

> submarine men were likely to break down with nerve strain of some kind or other and were constantly being sent away to recuperate. . . . Some men went mad. Others, after periods of rest and medication, came around and were, or perhaps were not, fit for undersea service again. All felt the grinding pressure.[1]

---

[1] Quoted in Edwyn A. Gray, *The Killing Time* (London: Pan Books, 1975), p. 148.

For the U-boats' intended victims, the tension of living for days on end in peril of sudden attack was also powerful. The greatest terror was the prospect of being caught below decks when a torpedo struck. Some who found themselves at sea for only a brief period preferred not to run this risk. An officer on a merchant ship making the disagreeable journey to Russia and bearing 'important officials on secret missions' recalls:

> On our first run across we carried more than 400 passengers, among them high military officers with the most imposing records for gallantry. Yet I remember how several of them refused to turn in, but spent the whole trip standing by the lifeboats in case a submarine got us. No amount of persuasion would get them to go below until we were safely inside the Marsden Fiord.[2]

For the crews and for less notable passengers (such as troops and nurses aboard transports) the choice of remaining above deck was not available. It would be mere chance whether or not they were in a position to abandon ship when a torpedo struck. And this might happen even to a vessel under escort. Early in April 1917 Trooper Reginald Huggins (18 years old at the time, having given a false age on enlistment) was a cavalryman on his way to Egypt aboard the troop transport *Arcadian*. A Japanese destroyer accompanied it. Nevertheless, for three days a U-boat kept it bottled up in a north African river. Although it was then able to reach Salonika and disembark troops there, luck soon ran out for the men going on to Egypt. One day out of Salonika:

> Without one moment's warning, a terrific explosion occurred, made hideous by the splintering into matchwood of great timbers, the crash of falling glass and the groaning of steel girders wrenched asunder, followed by the hissing rush of escaping steam from the ship's boilers.

Huggins discarded his boots, donned a life-belt, and descended by rope into the water, badly burning his hands in the process. There, a non-swimmer, he remained helpless, waiting to be sucked below in the wake of the ship.

> The suspense, fortunately, was brief. For a moment or two the *Arcadian* partly righted on her keel and then with much hissing of escaping steam and explosions from the boiler rooms, she slid for ever out of sight of human eyes, carrying with her hundreds of troops and her own crew caught like rats on the lower decks.

Huggins, although dragged below, was moments later shot back to the surface. He remained clinging to wreckage for several hours before being picked up by a Q-ship.[3]

Of necessity, those who have left accounts of being torpedoed at sea, however gruelling their experiences, in the end came through safely. Many others did not, even when they managed to survive the disappearance of their ships. Some, it is fair to speculate, lingered for hours or days in the water or in lifeboats before exposure or hostile seas ended their struggles. Others fell victim to the very U-boats that had already destroyed their ships. For the attitude of U-boat commanders to the survivors of vessels they had sunk varied widely. Some behaved with courtesy and even practical concern. The crew of the sunken Q-ship *Tulip*, once in their lifeboats, were offered extra provisions by the submarine captain who had vanquished them. But the crew of the SS *Addah*, which, though not a Q-ship, did carry a gun (and tried unavailingly to use it), were less fortunate.[4]

---

[2] Captain J. R. Murphy in *I Was There!*, issue no. 33, p. 1326.

[3] Reginald Huggins, 'Torpedoed in the Aegean Sea', in C. B. Purdom (ed.), *Everyman at War* (London: J. M. Dent, 1930), pp. 406–10.

[4] Accounts of the contrasting experiences of the crews of the *Tulip* and *Addah* are to be found in *I Was There!*, issues no. 26 and 30.

The fate of the *Addah*, torpedoed off Brittany on 15 June 1917, is related by its second mate, Edgar Stauffer. (This was his third such experience.) He found himself in command of one of the two lifeboats that left the stricken ship. And he was ordered by the captain of the surfaced U-boat to take a German officer (who spoke good English) back to the sinking *Addah* to secure the breech-block from its gun. The young officer informed Stauffer that his commander regarded sailors on an armed merchant ship as the equivalent of *francs tireurs*, who merited execution for engaging in acts of war (even though only in self-defence) when out of uniform. Events bore this out. After the German officer had been returned to the U-boat, its commander ordered the lifeboats to draw away. He then set about shelling them with great deliberation. Stauffer's boat was subjected only to protracted harassment, because (he speculated) the young officer had interceded on their behalf. But the other lifeboat, including the ship's captain, was completely destroyed, and its survivors were then shelled to death in the water.

Compared with the casualties of the war on land, the loss of life among the crews and passengers of merchant ships was never large. Yet in absolute terms it was substantial enough. And the rise in the figures is a further indicator of the growing effectiveness of the U-boat campaign. In January 1917, the month before unrestricted warfare began, 227 British merchant seamen lost their lives. In April, when it reached its highpoint, the figure was 1,150. Again, deaths from sinkings of British merchant ships for the whole of 1916 were only 1,225. The first six months of the unrestricted campaign claimed 3,833 lives.

IV

By mid-1917, therefore, there was no doubt that Germany's submarine offensive had achieved considerable success. But something else was not in doubt. This success had proved less than decisive.

Britain at the end of July 1917 was not suing for peace. Though its food and oil supplies were not secure, neither its civilian population nor its war industries were facing serious deprivation. As for British military operations, they were far from running down for want of supplies. On the contrary, the BEF was on the point of launching a massive new offensive in Flanders, supported by unprecedented artillery bombardments. Perhaps Britain's range of strategic choices was becoming limited by a shortage of shipping. Yet even this is not certain. The shipping problem may have been a convenient excuse for curtailing operations that, but for political embarrassment, would have been scaled down on grounds of merit.

In every respect German calculations regarding the U-boat war were proving over-optimistic. Only in one of the designated six months (April) did the sinking of British merchant shipping approach the required total of 600,000 tons. As for neutral shippers, far from abandoning Britain's shores altogether, most of them were soon being prevailed upon – by '[d]iplomatic skill, hard bargaining and pressure exerted in various other ways' – to resume their service.[5] So by July the volume of foreign ships supplying Britain was only 20 per cent below normal. And it was transpiring that Britain was better equipped to survive shipping losses than had been predicted. It was able to prune extravagances in military shipping, further restrict imports to absolute necessities, employ internal transport in place of coastal shipping, enhance the efficiency of its ports, and economize on sea miles. Thus the day of Britain's collapse was certain to be delayed well beyond its enemies' anticipation.

---

[5] Vice Admiral Sir Arthur Hezlet, *The Submarine and Sea Power* (London: Peter Davies, 1967), p. 91.

In this last matter of economizing on sea miles, the British authorities were greatly aided by what, for the Germans, was the supreme negative effect of the submarine campaign: the USA's entry into the war.

This development was ironical. During the second half of 1916 a decided deterioration had occurred in Anglo-American relations. Britain had stepped up its economic warfare against Germany in ways that deeply offended President Wilson. For example, the British authorities had issued a 'blacklist' of US and Latin American firms with which, on account of pro-enemy affiliations, British subjects were forbidden to deal. Moreover, Wilson was not pleased to discover, as he approached the presidential election late in 1916, that the British did not intend to call upon him to mediate between the warring powers. The ill-feeling engendered by these events was brought home powerfully to Walter Hines Page, the deeply Anglophile American Ambassador in London. In August and September 1916 Page was in Washington to confer on the situation. Five weeks passed before he was accorded a private interview with the President, and what transpired there gave him no joy. Page wrote in his diary: 'The P[resident] said to me that when the war began he and all the men he met were in hearty sympathy with the Allies; but that now the sentiment toward England had greatly changed. He saw no one who was not vexed and irritated at the arbitrary English course.'[6]

There was little likelihood that this cooling in Anglo-American relations would ever have led to actual conflict. But there was at least a possibility that the US Government would refuse clearance to British ships discriminating against the goods of the blacklisted firms. And, what was far more serious, by the beginning of 1917 Britain was ceasing to be capable of purchasing goods from American suppliers. The excellent credit position with which Britain had entered the war *vis-à-vis* the USA was now at an end, thanks to the vast purchases Britain had been making not only on its own behalf but also on that of its allies. On 5 March 1917 Walter Hines Page, now returned to London, sent his Government an urgent telegram. It warned that Britain had absolutely reached the end of its resources for securing credit in the USA, and that unless the US Government was prepared to guarantee a large loan, or itself supply the credit, the Allied war trade with the USA would cease.

By the time Page sent this message Wilson had already responded to the Kaiser's declaration of unrestricted submarine warfare by severing diplomatic relations with Germany. But the President hoped that this would be sufficient: that the Germans would realize he meant business and would back down. In short order British diligence in securing and deciphering German diplomatic messages helped to disillusion him. On 25 February the Foreign Office passed on to him the contents of the Zimmerman telegram. In it the German Foreign Minister proposed to Mexico that, in the event of war breaking out between Germany and the United States, the Mexicans should take Germany's side and receive a handsome reward in US territory. But not until 18 March did the President's last hope of preserving neutrality depart. On that day U-boats sank, without warning and with heavy loss of life, three American merchant ships. Six days later Wilson authorized his Secretary for the Navy to open conversations with the British Admiralty regarding the co-ordination of their naval operations. On 7 April the United States declared war upon Germany. At this moment the U-boat campaign was accomplishing, in a sense quite contrary to the intentions of its originators, its most considerable contribution to the outcome of the war.

Nor was it the case, as Germany's rulers had calculated, that America's intervention

---

[6] Quoted in Arthur S. Link, *Woodrow Wilson and the Progressive Era 1910–1917* (New York: Harper Torchbooks, 1963), p. 222.

could be of no immediate benefit to the Allies. The struggle against the U-boat was straightway affected. In the first place, the American navy included a significant number of destroyers, and these were promptly diverted to anti-submarine warfare. Secondly, America's merchant shipping ceased to fall into the neutral category, so that there could be no question now that it might be scared away from trading with Britain. Thirdly, there was locked up in American harbours some half-million tons of German cargo ships. These were promptly seized by the authorities and employed in the Allied cause. Finally, the British Admiralty, in deciding on cargoes and routes so as to make the best use of available shipping, no longer needed to be inhibited by economic considerations.

Plate 34   *The most substantial consequence of the U-boat campaign: William McAdoo, Secretary of the US Treasury, signs a warrant for a loan of $200 million to the Allies – the first American government (as distinct from private) loan to Britain during the war. On the left of the picture are Lord Cunliffe, the governor of the Bank of England, and Sir Cecil Spring-Rice, the British Ambassador to Washington. (The latter is best remembered for his wartime hymn 'I vow to thee my country'.)*

Some examples will indicate the weight of this last factor. Hitherto, for purposes of the balance of payments, Britain had devoted much shipping space to the importation of raw cotton and the export of manufactured cotton goods. Now, with American credit at its disposal, it felt obliged to do neither, so reducing its shipping needs. Again, Britain could now secure from the USA commodities that it had hitherto been importing from more distant sources. So, having purchased the whole of Australia's export wheat crop, the British authorities decided to leave it there. The length of voyage was plainly excessive once it had become possible to secure wheat from America without economic restraint.

V

What all this meant was clear, but also what it did not mean. Germany's attempt to accomplish the defeat of Britain within a specified time had failed. The U-boat could not attain the required killing rate. Britain possessed greater resilience than its enemies had allowed for. And America's intervention was enhancing British resources.

But it did not follow that, on an adjusted timescale, Germany's expectations might not yet be fulfilled. If the toll inflicted by the U-boat between February and July 1917 could be repeated in the ensuing six months, and perhaps for a bit longer, the outcome would not be in doubt. A point must be reached when the number of merchant ships available to supply Britain would be inadequate to sustain the country's livelihood and war effort. The question confronting Britain was whether, before that stage was reached, the Royal Navy could master the U-boat.

In the opening months of the unlimited submarine campaign the response in the Admiralty and in governing circles was less than adequate. Jellicoe, having been transferred from Scapa Flow to Whitehall to confront precisely this menace, failed immediately to rise to the occasion. His political chief, the supposedly fire-eating Carson, proved ill-equipped to make good Jellicoe's deficiencies. And the new Prime Minister, for all his mistrust of the service chiefs, did not rush in to fill this gap.

The elevation of Jellicoe to the Admiralty in December 1916 ultimately proved a misfortune. Possibly he was pleased to leave the Grand Fleet after two exhausting years involving dire responsibility and no spectacular success. But his positive qualities had proved more than sufficient to the tasks he had encountered there. And in that post such shortcomings as he possessed were no great disadvantage. At Whitehall this situation was reversed. Qualities that had been an asset in the one post proved no help in the other. And what had simply been demerits in a commander of the Grand Fleet became serious deficiencies in a First Sea Lord.

As an individual Jellicoe was resolute but averse to daredevilry, inclined to pessimism, and much given to centralization. With these qualities he had, from August 1914 to December 1916, preserved Britain from the gravest danger facing it: that of hazarding its naval supremacy in some reckless enterprise. And the absence of decentralization can hardly be judged a serious shortcoming. For only too often, when subordinate members of the Grand Fleet were presented with opportunities calling for the exercise of initiative, they proved unable to seize them.

At Whitehall the requirements of the time were dissimilar. In the crisis of the submarine war the First Sea Lord needed to be a man of boldness rather than caution, and to be innovative rather than dogged by pessimism and misgiving. But, even more, he must be ready to employ the services of an expert staff. Only thus could he free himself from the trivia of paperwork to take stock of large issues. And only so would he receive the types of information that pointed the way to sound decisions. Jellicoe's tardiness, in his early months as First Sea Lord, in perceiving the solution to his problems derived most of all from a lack of competent advisers feeding him with hard facts and considered assessments regarding a wide range of shipping matters.

Carson, as First Lord of the Admiralty, was no help here. Had Jellicoe been engaged in taking harsh and unpopular decisions that were nevertheless appropriate, then Carson would have been ideal as his political chief. He possessed the same cast of mind as Jellicoe. And he was prepared to stand loyally by his professional advisers, especially against interfering politicians and disgruntled subordinates. But this meant that he reinforced Jellicoe's shortcomings, not least his proneness to pessimism. He did not complement Jellicoe's merits with virtues that the First Sea Lord lacked.

Jellicoe's predominant response to the U-boat menace was that of his predecessors: seek and destroy. If British anti-submarine ships were failing to locate their quarry, then his answer was to double and redouble their number. Theoretically this was a positive, 'offensive' response. Practically, it was a waste of resources. As long as British patrols lacked equipment whereby to establish the whereabouts of U-boats, it was immaterial how many such patrols were roaming the seas.

Plainly, a different solution must be sought. If the submarine could not be found, then it must be denied victims. After all, it was not essential to destroy U-boats in order to thwart an underwater blockade of Britain, any more than it was necessary to sink Germany's battleships to prevent them from blockading Britain on the surface. A U-boat fleet unable to gain access to merchant ships would be of no more use to Germany than a High Seas Fleet permanently confined to harbour.

No one doubted that, in most circumstances, there was a way of preventing submarines from attacking surface vessels. If a particular unit of the fleet were deemed important enough, it could be safeguarded from U-boats by the provision of a screen of destroyers – that is, by convoy. This practice had assured a large measure of immunity to the battleships of the Grand Fleet and also to troopships. And since January 1917 it had been extended to the cargo ships serving the vital coal trade to France.

That the merchant fleet was essential to Britain's war effort, and indeed to its very survival, was evident enough. Hence the unrestricted U-boat campaign seemed to create an irresistible case for extending convoy to Britain's overseas trade. The chiefs of the Admiralty, however, judged that there was an overriding argument against this course: namely, that it was impractical. Three aspects in particular weighed with them. First, many owners and captains of cargo ships agreed that an aggregation of merchantmen simply could not keep station – that is, a convoy would soon disperse itself. Secondly, it appeared that convoying on a large scale must reduce the ports of Britain to chaos by producing gluts and dearths of vessels requiring servicing. Thirdly, the navy chiefs argued that they simply did not possess the numbers of destroyers and similar craft needed to safeguard the huge volume of shipping travelling to and from Britain.

These seemed weighty objections. Yet each was speculative. Only wide-ranging investigation could establish whether they were soundly based. This meant the accumulation of statistics concerning the amount of shipping coming to Britain from overseas, expert consideration of the management of the nation's ports, experiments regarding the sea-keeping qualities of merchant seamen, and a careful calculation of the advantages of using patrol craft in hunting operations or in defence of cargo ships.

Britain's naval chiefs were ill-equipped for this varied exercise. They were imbued with a proud tradition, according to which going hunting for the enemy seemed a proper course and chugging along in support of merchantmen did not. They were already overwhelmed with a multitude of tasks. And they lacked ready access to hard facts about the practicality or otherwise of instituting a convoy system.

Some big event, or some big person, was needed to overcome these obstacles to the adoption of what, in truth, was the decisive counter to the U-boat. According to popular legend, it was a person rather than an event that accomplished the break-through. In regard to the sea war, as to the land war, Lloyd George (in this view) possessed the insights and the freedom from professional constraints needed to unravel the crucial problems. In what some have judged his greatest single contribution to Britain's survival, he marched across Whitehall on 30 April 1917 and imposed convoys on the resisting Lords of the Admiralty.

This tale, it has to be concluded, is without substance. To say this is no necessary criticism of the Prime Minister, who had other matters on his mind. But whatever one's judgement about that, it is clear from the evidence that Lloyd George was not ahead of the Admiralty on the issue of convoys. This was not because he lacked appropriate guidance. There were junior figures in naval circles who recognized, in advance of their more hidebound chiefs, that convoys were the way to salvation. And some of them, at whatever cost to naval protocol, were courageous enough to convey this view to the head of the Government.

Further, close to Lloyd George's hand there was Sir Maurice Hankey. From the beginning of February Hankey was urging the case for convoys. But Lloyd George was slow to respond, as Hankey's diary makes clear. Regarding a meeting of the War Cabinet on 28 March Hankey recorded:

> Appalling waste of time, the whole morning slipping away over some trivial and quite unimportant question connected with anti-submarine inventions of slight immediate importance. . . . I am quite in despair about the unbusinesslike methods of the War Cabinet. They will not buckle too [sic] on their Agenda papers, but day after day they wander off on any by-path. . . . Meanwhile vitally important war questions affecting the food supply of the country, shipping, the army at Salonika, the supply of men for the army etc etc remain on the Agenda paper for weeks together. . . .

Two days later found Hankey

> much worried about the shipping outlook owing to submarines and the inability of the Adty. to deal with it, and their general ineptitude as indicated by their stickiness towards every new proposal. I have many ideas on the matter, but cannot get at Ll. George in regard to it, as he is so full of politics.

Not until almost a month later (22 April), during a visit to France, did Hankey find Lloyd George responsive to his urgings on shipping matters – and, clearly, this was a recent development. Hankey records that Lloyd George, after reading one of his papers on the subject,

> at last seemed to have grasped the danger of the submarine question – though earlier in the trip he had said 'Oh well, I have never regarded that matter as seriously as you have.'

So it was not a person that shocked the chiefs of the British navy into reconsidering their resistance to convoys. It was an event; or, more accurately, a succession of events: the massacre at sea in April 1917. This made it starkly evident not only that existing methods of combating the U-boat were failing but also that this deficiency would shortly encompass Britain's defeat. Hence it became imperative to look with greater sympathy, and on a sounder basis of knowledge, at the only course of action still untried. Imminent catastrophe at last dispelled the prejudice against using ships of the Royal Navy as guardians for merchantmen. The statistics suggesting that there were far too many merchant ships coming from overseas to make convoys practicable had to be subjected to searching inquiry – whereupon they were found to yield a quite different message. As for the claim that merchant ships could not hold their place in convoys, it was at last recognized that this matter had better be put to the test – a proceeding that would soon ensure that no one in authority would make that claim again.

So at the end of April 1917, following a decision arrived at independently by the Admiralty but powerfully underwritten by Lloyd George's visitation, the decision was taken to institute convoys as an experiment. On 10 May, a crucial day in the history of Britain's involvement in the First World War, a collection of 17 merchant ships with various escorts set out from Gibraltar. Their experience was instructive. Twelve days later every one of them reached port in Britain. The time of their journey proved to be two days less than it would have been had they sailed independently. And in the course of the journey not only did the enemy fail to make a kill but not a single U-boat was sighted. If there are such things as 'decisive events' in this war, the first Gibraltar convoy must rank high among them.

Time would pass before convoys could become fully operative. Their institution required a large feat of administration: the planning of routes, the diversion of naval craft from futile searchings after U-boats to this new protective role, the gathering together of merchant ships of like seagoing capacity to form a coherent entity, the reorganization of ports. While this was happening, the U-boats continued to find victims. In the second six-month period of the unrestricted campaign, from August 1917 to January 1918, 2.25 million tons of merchant shipping was sunk. But that was well short of Germany's minimum requirements. And it was a sum total that masked a steady decline: 211 ships went to the bottom in August, only 150 in January. Moreover, a large majority of the ships sunk were travelling individually, so that with every extension of the convoy system the potency of the U-boat declined.

Already by mid-1917 the merchant traffic of inward-bound ships across the north Atlantic was fully under convoy. In August and September the system was extended to traffic from Gibraltar and the south Atlantic, and also to outward-bound ships (whose losses had begun rising sharply). By the end of the year the Mediterranean trade had also come under convoy, to such noteworthy effect that shipping from the Far East, which had been driven to taking the longer route around South Africa, once more began using the Mediterranean. The accomplishment was remarkable, if not by any means complete. By the end of 1917 rather more than half of Britain's overseas trade had been brought under convoy.

What made the system so effective? It did not contribute significantly to the destruction of U-boats. Certainly, sinkings of enemy submarines were on the increase. But mainly these were due to such factors as the development (at last) of an efficient British mine and the more effective sowing of minefields as submarine traps; the action of patrol craft against U-boats operating ever closer to the British coast in the search for targets; and the use of British submarines against their German counterparts. By these means the destruction of U-boats reached a point where it more than equalled Germany's acquisition of new submarines.

The especial contribution of the convoy lay not in destroying U-boats but in rendering them ineffective. This it did by denying them victims. Increasingly from May 1917 U-boat commanders who earlier had looked out on seas swarming with merchant ships now found themselves gazing at empty oceans. Given the limited stretch of sea visible from a submarine, a convoy of 20 ships was not much easier to spot than a single vessel. And, of course, the convoy reduced drastically – to one-twentieth – the number of possible sightings. In addition, the Admiralty's wireless intelligence soon became effective in establishing the whereabouts of the enemy, either from messages sent by U-boats to their headquarters and to one another or from the distress signals of their victims. Convoys were diverted from these areas.

The effectiveness of the convoy went further. On the occasions when a U-boat did run in with this accumulation of ships it could make nothing like as many kills as when encountering the same number of merchantmen individually. In the daytime it could only risk an attack submerged; at night it might also attack on the surface using a torpedo. In either circumstance employment of the gun as the main instrument of destruction was out of the question. Admittedly, this form of attack had been declining anyway because of the increasing arming of British merchantmen. But that did not apply to neutral ships, which were never armed and so had hitherto been defenceless against U-boats. The convoy constituted the first, and a highly effective, form of protection available to neutral merchant shipping.

Again, the convoy did more than limit the types of attack that the submarine might employ against such ships as it managed to encounter. It seriously limited the number of attacks. By the time the U-boat had claimed one victim, or at the outside two, the remaining merchantmen in the convoy had departed the scene. The patrol ships with their depth charges were now occupying it. The U-boat might survive this hazard. But it had to remain well below periscope depth for so long that all contact with the convoy was lost.

What all this signified for Britain was not early appreciated. And confidence in the Admiralty, having been badly shaken by the gravity of the situation in April, continued low for the rest of 1917. The depredations of the U-boat seemed to be continuing on a large, even if diminished, scale. Moreover, on two occasions in late 1917 German surface raiders struck at Scandinavian convoys with devastating effect. And the yearning for a great battleship engagement that would put paid, 'finally' and 'gloriously', to the German fleet persisted unassuaged. One small engagement did occur, but it brought no comfort: 17 November witnessed the last big-ship encounter of the war. A force of British battle cruisers and cruisers sought to surprise some German heavy ships protecting a minesweeping operation in the Heligoland Bight. The enemy were certainly taken by surprise. But, by the use of smoke screens and zig-zagging, they managed to extricate themselves without loss. The outcome, if not disgraceful, did no great credit to Britain's naval staff or its commander on the spot.

Yet notwithstanding these negative aspects of the war at sea, only one thing really signified, and that was most certainly positive. The threat confronting Britain of being strangled by a submarine blockade, having been held at bay in the first half of the year, was decisively surmounted in the second half. The U-boat, on whatever timetable being employed by the enemy high command, would not bring Germany the victory.

40

STRATEGIC EXPEDIENTS I:
THE AFFAIRE NIVELLE

I

Lloyd George had become Prime Minister at a key moment for the conduct of military operations. One campaigning season had just ended. Plans were being made for the next. The planning, so far as it had proceeded, gave him no joy. Haig and Joffre seemed bent on repeating the operations of 1916. The Anglo-French offensive on the Somme was to be resumed but on a wider front. Lloyd George concluded that he had not obtained direction of the nation's affairs just to preside over these barren expedients.

Yet the new Prime Minister's range of choices was acutely circumscribed. One alternative, seemingly attractive in retrospect, did not lie open to him at the beginning of 1917. He could not afford to decide that British forces should simply go on to the defensive. It might seem a good idea to let the enemy batter themselves unavailingly against British positions. But with Hindenburg and Ludendorff, the victors of the Eastern Front, now in command in Germany, this was unlikely to happen. They intended to defeat Britain by means of the U-boat. If they chose to attack anywhere on land, their obvious victim would be Russia. By the start of 1917 the condition of Britain's Eastern ally was plainly precarious. Indeed, in January Milner, one of the War Cabinet, was delegated to lead a mission there to discover what could be done. Plainly, it was even more true by this stage of the war than in 1915 that the Western Allies could not stand back and witness Germany's exercise of the initiative.

If this was true generally, it was particularly true of Lloyd George. He may, when he came to power, have been disgruntled with Britain's high command and its views on strategy. But that was not why he had come to power. His accession reflected the nation's wish for a more forceful, ruthless conduct of the war – for an end to 'wait and see'. Any resort to a defensive strategy, accompanied by the piecemeal elimination of Britain's allies, would not have fulfilled these expectations. It would have looked like 'waiting and seeing' with a vengeance.

This point needs to be borne in mind when reviewing the events of the coming months. The high standing that Lloyd George had acquired during the war sprang from his devotion to providing first money, then munitions, then conscripts for a mass army. And it had been reinforced by his trenchant dismissal of any proposal for a peace short of victory. This, he had proclaimed in July 1916, must be 'a fight to a finish – to a knock-out'. When President Wilson again sought to act as mediator, within days of Lloyd George's becoming Prime Minister, the response was the same. The British Government specified war aims that would never be agreeable to the Central Powers until they had been brought to defeat. Among them were the evacuation of invaded territory in Belgium, France, and Russia, and the liberation of subject peoples, including those of Alsace-Lorraine. (The statement is often made that a good opportunity existed for a negotiated settlement of the war at the end of 1916. This is not borne out by the evidence. The feelers about negotiations put out at this stage, first by the Germans and then by the Americans, were concerned with the imminent breakdown in relations between those two countries. Like the British, the Germans would not consider calling off the war except on terms that their adversaries would never accept short of defeat. The German Government was not even prepared to meet Britain's minimal demand: the unconditional restoration of Belgian independence.)

Lloyd George, having become Prime Minister, did not balk the implications, in military terms, of this situation. His purpose was to seek victory with all dispatch, and that meant taking the war to the enemy. Yet in terms of grand strategy, this left him with very few options. The operation from Salonika against the Bulgarians was hopelessly stalled. No one – except perhaps Churchill, who had been omitted from the new Government – proposed trying again at the Dardanelles. And other possible operations against the Turks, if more promising, appeared so peripheral as to have only a slight bearing on the central struggle. Moreover, the accelerating shipping crisis threw doubts on any operations that required to be supplied by sea. These considerations underlined the dilemma of a Prime Minister averse to incurring heavy British casualties but bent on victory. He might be repelled by a further offensive in France. Yet in terms of supply, and in terms of striking against the main adversary, there seemed to be no other course.

During the first six months of 1917 Lloyd George, in an attempt to square this strategic circle, gave his support to some of the war's most unpromising operations. (Where an attempt was made to implement them, they would also prove to be among its most tragic.) In spite of the many setbacks suffered by the Italians in their attempts to scale mountains against Austrian resistance, he proposed yet another such undertaking. It should, in his judgement, be this year's main operation in the West. Again, despite the fragile condition of the Provisional Government in Russia, which came to power in March following the disintegration of tsarist rule, Lloyd George exhorted it to new offensives against the Germans. And notwithstanding the terrible batterings that French forces had suffered over the past two and a half years, he came wholeheartedly to endorse a further French offensive on the Western Front. It was to be delivered in a sector where Joffre had tried twice, with no success, in 1915.

There is sometimes a misunderstanding about the differences over strategy between Lloyd George on the one hand and the 'brass hats' on the other. It is not the case that they differed in early 1917 on the fundamental aspect: namely, that the Allies must continue to launch offensives. The difference, in so far as it was more than a matter of temperament, concerned a subordinate matter. Lloyd George preferred that the forces of Britain should be employed against the lesser adversaries, Turkey or Austria-Hungary. Britain's allies should be left to engage the Germans. This would not reduce total Allied casualties, and so was not a scheme for saving lives. At most it was a scheme for saving British lives at the expense of other members of the alliance. Lloyd George admitted as much in June, when he was once more arguing for an offensive on the Italian front. If the Germans came to the assistance of the Austrians, he argued, this would mean fighting and wearing out the Germans: 'But this would be taking place at the expense of the Italians and not of our men. . . . It would be the first time that the Italian resources of manpower had been properly utilized to pull their weight in the War.'[1]

---

[1] Meeting of Cabinet Committee on War Policy, 21 June 1917, quoted in John Terraine, *The Road to Passchendaele* (London: Leo Cooper, 1977), p. 166.

Such a view may be judged deplorably cynical or blessed with great (if rather parochial) wisdom. That question need not concern us. Either way, Lloyd George's view was not appropriate to the circumstances of 1917. The combatant forces of France, Russia, and Italy would soon be revealing that, having fought so devotedly hitherto, they were not now capable of waging a fight to a finish. If the process of knocking out Germany were to be significantly advanced in 1917, that burden must fall upon Britain. Lloyd George might rage against the plans served up by Britain's military command. But the plans were intended to fulfil his own policy and his own public promises. And he had no schemes of any substance to put in their place.

It is a truism that the Great War was a vast impersonal force, which dominated and compelled those who thought that they could make it do their bidding. Nowhere is this more clearly exemplified than in Lloyd George's attempts to exercise the strategic initiative in 1917. He had come to the pinnacle of office determined that military affairs would henceforth be conducted differently: the atrocious human toll of operations on the Western Front would be levied no longer. As he told his secretary in mid-January: 'Haig does not care how many men he loses. He just squanders the lives of these boys. I mean to save some of them in the future. . . . I am their trustee.'[2] Yet the events of the next 12 months were to reveal that the emergence of this new man, with his new methods, would signify little change in that area. For the 'boys' on the fields of battle, the squandering of lives would proceed as before.

II

Lloyd George made his first bid to alter the direction of strategy at an Allied conference in Rome early in January 1917. As the main operation in the West for the year, he advocated a large Italian offensive against the Austrians assisted by a generous supply of British artillery. The proposal fell on stony ground. Lloyd George received no encouragement from his own military advisers or from the civil and military representatives of France. And the Italian commander, Cadorna, showed no enthusiasm for the proposal. His response cannot be deemed surprising. Although no one raised the point directly, it was plain what would happen if the Italians launched an offensive when no major operation was occurring in France or Belgium. They would attract to their front, in imposing quantities, contingents of Germans. (Cadorna's rejection of the Lloyd George proposal is sometimes ascribed – especially by Anglocentric historians – to the fact that Robertson, who opposed the scheme, got to the Italian commander ahead of Hankey, who was prepared to advocate it. Yet it is difficult to believe that the chief of Italy's forces was this susceptible to British guidance – or that he could not exercise his own judgement on a matter so nearly affecting his countrymen.)

The French did not support Lloyd George on this occasion because they had plans of their own. At the end of 1916 Joffre, whose failures by this time were many, had been superseded. The direction of the French forces went to General Nivelle, who had commanded in the Verdun sector during the later phases of that campaign. In October and December 1916, on what for the enemy was now a quiet sector, Nivelle had launched two set-piece attacks that robbed the Germans of their principal gains at Verdun. These limited-objective operations riveted the attention of his countrymen. On the strength of them the French Government was prepared to believe that Nivelle

---

[2] A. J. P. Taylor (ed.), *Lloyd George: A Diary by Frances Stevenson* (London: Hutchinson, 1971), p. 139.

could conduct an offensive of an altogether different sort – that he could accomplish a large-scale rupture of the enemy line leading to a decisive victory over the Germans.

The main area of Nivelle's offensive was to be the Chemin des Dames, well to the south (and east) of the area where Joffre and Haig had been proposing to act. Hence it would be a predominantly French undertaking. Nevertheless, the British were expected to make a twofold contribution. First, they would take over a further stretch (of about 20 miles) of the Western Front so as to release French forces for Nivelle's operation. Then, in advance of the great French offensive, they were to launch a considerable attack out from Arras in the direction of Cambrai. The latter undertaking was intended, in its early stages, to hold German forces away from the main area of advance. Ultimately, it would aid in exploiting the huge success that Nivelle was anticipating.

In the weeks following the Rome conference Britain's military and political leaders indicated their assent to this proceeding. Haig insisted on entering certain caveats. With the departure of both Joffre and his notion of a coterminous Anglo-French offensive, Haig was no longer held to the Somme area. So his mind began reverting to a scheme that he had contemplated much earlier: a mainly British offensive in Flanders. Consequently, he stipulated that, while co-operating fully with the Nivelle plan, he expected that a new course would be followed if that plan failed in its larger objectives. The British would then switch over to the Flanders scheme. And they would receive from the French the same co-operation as they were now offering Nivelle.

Haig's attitude may suggest disbelief that Nivelle would really enjoy a success so much greater than had awaited the Somme operation in 1916. But his doubts went hand in hand with the intention to fulfil the role assigned to him for as long as the offensive proceeded according to plan.

Lloyd George went very much further. Indeed, at this point he revealed an apparent confusion between means and ends. Initially his hostility to Haig and Robertson had sprung from his aversion to the Western Front as a suitable area for large-scale offensives. But during the battle of the Somme he had begun to qualify this position. Such operations remained deplorable when conducted by British generals, but not certainly otherwise. This transition he now carried much further. He gave his unqualified endorsement to a particularly grandiose Western Front offensive under a scarcely qualified French commander.

His support became quite apparent when Nivelle visited London in mid-January. Lloyd George began making blunt observations to Haig about the superiority of French generals over British. And he insisted on treating discussions about aspects of the forthcoming operations as though they were a contest between Haig and Nivelle – a contest in which Nivelle would receive his unstinted support. So, when a difference arose between the two commanders about the timing of the offensive, Lloyd George allowed himself to be easily convinced by Nivelle's view that it should commence within a month. 'But in any case,' as he told Frances Stevenson, 'I should have backed Nivelle against Haig. Nivelle has proved himself to be a Man at Verdun; & when you get a Man against one who has not proved himself, why, you back the Man!'[3]

Quite apart from the *Boy's Own Paper* language employed here – how much torment was inflicted on the young male of that generation under the guise of ensuring that he became 'a Man!' – this zeal for Nivelle was plainly ill-considered. Certainly, the aura of his recent (small-scale) successes clung to him. And Lloyd George doubtless found him personally agreeable. As the offspring of an English mother and a French father,

[3] Taylor, *Lloyd George: A Diary by Frances Stevenson.*

Nivelle spoke fluently in two languages – in happy contrast to Haig, who was not articulate even in one. Yet the evidence simply did not exist to suggest either that Nivelle was Haig's superior in conducting a large-scale offensive or that his schemes converted the Western Front from a deplorable into an ideal place for such an operation. Lloyd George, in concluding otherwise, was grasping at straws.

It should be stressed that the Prime Minister's misjudgement did not lie in consenting to British participation in this campaign. Haig, after all, was doing the same. The Rome conference had refused to support any other course. And the French were plainly determined to embark on what would be predominantly their show. So however slim its chance of anything like full success, the British had little choice but to agree. What was inappropriate was Lloyd George's quite immoderate enthusiasm for an operation of the sort he claimed most to hate, and his efforts to use it as the occasion for pursuing a vendetta against the British commander. By so doing he staked on Nivelle's success both his own credibility as a judge of military matters and his resources for exercising judicious control over Haig and Robertson. Nothing in the situation warranted such a gamble.

III

So great became Lloyd George's enthusiasm for Nivelle that the Prime Minister did more than agree to Britain's involvement in yet another Western Front offensive. He determined that Nivelle should command not only the French forces but also the British.

Lloyd George soon secured an opportunity to act in this direction. The French complained that Haig was proving tardy in taking over the new stretch of front assigned to him. The British commander argued that the delay sprang from severe shortcomings in the French rail system, and in this he was supported by Eric Geddes, an expert on transportation earlier assigned to him by Lloyd George. The Prime Minister arranged, for late in February, a conference at Calais between the military and political leaders of the two countries. Ostensibly it would discuss the railway situation and general questions of strategy. Its actual business would be to elevate Nivelle to command of the British forces in France.

In preparation, Lloyd George encouraged Nivelle to formulate the demand for a single direction of the French and British armies. And at a meeting of the War Cabinet on 24 February the Prime Minister secured a measure of endorsement for this arrangement. But he could not thus prepare the ground without acting in devious ways. Neither Derby, the War Minister, nor Robertson, the CIGS, was asked to attend this meeting of the War Cabinet. And neither they nor the King – who, as titular commander of the British army, had a right to know what was happening – were promptly informed of the decision.

When the Anglo-French conference met, the question of railways was soon relegated to a sub-committee. Lloyd George then called on the French commander to formulate his larger requirements. For one so verbally adept, Nivelle proved inadequate to the occasion. He talked at length without coming to the point – 'walking round and round the porridge and not sticking the spoon in', as one of the French Ministers present later recounted.[4] Only during a break for food did Nivelle and his political associates present their proposals – in writing. This time the spoon was indeed stuck into the porridge. Under Nivelle's requirements, Haig's functions virtually disappeared. In the words of E. L. Spears:

---

[4] Ibid., p. 147.

Not only was all military initiative taken from the British, but even food, munitions and weapons were to be distributed under the authority of the French Commander-in-Chief, his heirs and successors. The one power to be left to the British Commander-in-Chief was that of administering discipline. He would only differ from the Provost Marshal in that, presumably, his would be the duty, over and above that of court martialling delinquents, of seeing that everyone in the British Army obeyed the orders of his French master.[5]

Predictably, this proposal did not recommend itself to Robertson and Haig. Their dismay at receiving it soon increased. They were bluntly informed by the Prime Minister that the War Cabinet had already agreed to some such arrangement. (If this was a trump card, Lloyd George could only play it at cost. He was revealing that he had known all along what was coming, and had been holding out on his military associates.) A menacing state of deadlock developed within the British camp.

It was left to Hankey – who knew, and told Haig, that Lloyd George was claiming more for the War Cabinet resolution than it merited – to work out a sort of compromise. (He was aided by General Maurice, who had accompanied Robertson.) Nivelle's proposals were modified in important respects, employing the analogy of relations between the British and French commanders at Gallipoli. As the French there had possessed the lesser force, so their commander had exercised a lesser authority. During the Nivelle offensive this principle would be applied in reverse. But it was stipulated that Nivelle's direction of British forces would obtain only for this one campaign. And Haig would both direct the operations within his own sector and have a right to appeal to his own Government against any instruction that he believed might endanger his army. This arrangement did not satisfy Haig and Robertson. But they submitted to it as the best they could secure.

It was not long, however, before they began securing more. Back in London Lloyd George encountered much criticism, both for subordinating the British army to a French commander and for the manner of his doing it. Derby, along with other important Conservatives, was decidedly resentful. And sharp words passed between the Prime Minister and the King, who did not expect his army to be placed under foreign control without his being informed. Further, Lloyd George seems to have received less than total support from his own War Cabinet.

In these circumstances the conduct of the French did not prove helpful. Nivelle began writing to Haig in a somewhat officious manner. And, when Haig failed to respond in the tones of a subordinate, the French War Cabinet (on 7 March) requested of its counterpart in London that Haig 'be ordered to conform, without delay, to the decisions of the Calais Conference and to the instructions given him by General Nivelle'.[6] Presumably, the French Government assumed that such sentiments would prove acceptable to Lloyd George. The response from London made it plain that the Prime Minister, whether of his own volition or under pressure from his colleagues, was now revising his position.

The War Cabinet concluded that a further conference on this issue must be held. To make its own attitude clear, it called attention to the tendency of the French to treat Haig 'as a subordinate of General Nivelle rather than as an equal who has temporarily and for a specific operation been placed under the orders of the French Commander-in-Chief'. It also referred to Haig's 'considerable sacrifices', and wanted the French Government to know that Haig had its 'full confidence.' Such language could point in only one direction. At the renewed conference held in London in mid-March Nivelle's

---

[5] E. L. Spears, *Prelude to Victory* (London: Jonathan Cape, 1939), p. 143.
[6] Ibid., p. 179.

authority over Haig was further defined and further restricted. As part of the proceedings, it fell to Lloyd George to reiterate that Haig possessed the full confidence of his Government and was 'regarded with admiration in England'.[7]

The Prime Minister's misfortunes in this matter were not yet complete. Within days of this second conference a change of Government occurred in France. The men who departed office had fully believed in Nivelle's plan. Those who supplanted them did not. In common with important figures in the French military hierarchy, they seriously doubted his promise of a decisive victory. The operation, nevertheless, would go ahead: if only because it had the enthusiastic support of the British Prime Minister, and because for this one occasion the BEF came under French direction. But the offensive would proceed under a cloud of misgiving.

So, with Nivelle's attack not yet launched, Lloyd George was receiving clear indications that the man whom he had intended to direct the forces of Britain might soon lose control even over the forces of France. There is a concerned entry in Frances Stevenson's diary for 10 April ('D' in the following passage stands for David i.e. Lloyd George):

> Painlevé, the new French Minister for war, came over to consult D. about the military operations. It appears that the new Fr. Gov. have their doubts about Nivelle, as to whether his plans are sound. I do hope he will not fail, for D. has backed him up against Haig, & it will rather let D. down if he proves to be a failure.[8]

It would soon become apparent that even more was at stake in this operation, especially for the long-suffering French infantrymen, than letting down Lloyd George.

IV

There is no reason to believe that, had circumstances been entirely propitious, Nivelle would have achieved his promised breakthrough. His methods did not point to success of that order. But, as it happened, circumstances proved less than propitious. One of the factors that told against him was the German withdrawal to the Hindenburg Line.

This so-called line was in fact a powerful defensive system that the Germans had begun constructing late in 1916. It lay behind their positions in part of that north–south section of the Western Front shared by the British and French. It ran from just below Arras to a point somewhat east of Soissons, a distance of 70 miles: that is, it was situated to the rear of both the Somme battlefields and the large salient that pointed so menacingly towards Paris.

The Allies were not unaware that the Germans had constructed this defensive system. Their problem lay in divining its purpose. Was it there as a highly prudent safeguard lest the Somme offensive be resumed and the Germans be forced back once more? Or did the enemy mean actually to abandon the considerable stretch of territory lying between his front and this new system? There would be advantages for the Germans in executing a withdrawal. This would deny the Allies on the Somme the opportunity to attack defensive positions weaker than those that had confronted them in July 1916. And by flattening out much of their great salient the Germans would be shortening their line and economizing on the forces needed to hold it. Yet such a retirement would mean abandoning territory that many German soldiers had died to

---

[7] David R. Woodward, *Lloyd George and the Generals* (East Brunswick, New Jersey: Associated University Presses, 1983), p. 152.

[8] Taylor (ed.), *Lloyd George: A Diary by Frances Stevenson*, p. 150.

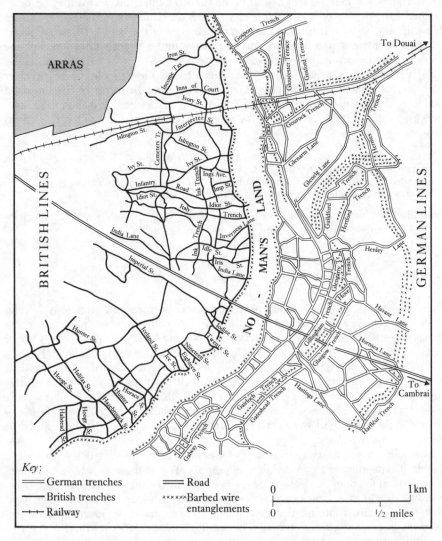

Map 8   *Trench warfare: a section of front south east of Arras, February 1917.* Source: *Arthur Banks, Military Atlas, p. 175.*

hold. And a withdrawal would take the Germans yet further away from an objective that ultimately they must reach if they were to win the war: Paris.

By late in February 1917 it was becoming apparent that the German command had indeed opted, at whatever risk to morale, for the immediate advantages of retirement. Places burned into the consciousness of those who had fought on the Somme were surrendered without a struggle. Among them were Serre and Bapaume, which had been included in the British objectives of 1 July 1916 but were still in German hands when the campaign ended; and Mont St. Quentin, described by Spears as 'the wicked hill to the north of [Péronne] from which the Germans had watched and plagued us during the whole of the Battle of the Somme'. (His 'us' refers more properly to the French than the British.)

Spears, a liaison officer with the French in the area of the withdrawal, has left a vivid account of this episode. He relates that by the start of March 1917

> There were many signs [of withdrawal]: persistent sounds of convoys at unusual places at night; special activity where dumps were known to exist, only explicable if they were being removed; extraordinary noises of hammering as if machinery was being dismantled, and outbreaks of gunfire where obviously no attacks were intended. These were assumed to be meant to cover the rumblings of transport which could nevertheless be heard. The Intelligence reported that several German Army Headquarters were falling back; twenty-five localities were said to have been evacuated by the civil population, and several bridges over the Oise in the neighbourhood of Noyon had been blown up.

As the Allies advanced into the evacuated areas, Spears almost persuaded himself that he was 'taking part in the victorious advance the *communiqués* were describing'. Yet the move forward carried its own miseries – not least in the many hazards the Germans had left behind. Land mines, timed to go off anything from hours to weeks after the Germans had departed, kept the engineers busy. On occasion these devices escaped detection:

> some of them inflicted considerable casualties, as for example when the Town Hall at Bapaume blew up a week after the British had occupied the place, killing two French Deputies and some Australians who were sleeping there.

In addition there was the experience of towns and villages laid waste: not destroyed by gunfire – a sight that was familiar enough – but torn down, as it were stone by stone, 'evidently at the cost of immense labour'. 'It was as if Satan had poured desolation out of a gigantic watering-can.'[9]

Soldiers in less responsible positions also reacted to the German retirement with mixed feelings. On the last day of February the youthful Graham Greenwell reported home that things were happening on the Western Front. At last the Hun was weakening; all the talk was of his evacuation, and they were preparing to rush through. But what followed proved less than a rush. Soon they were in deserted German trenches 10 or 15 miles in advance of their old positions, and open warfare was in full swing. Yet Greenwell recognized that the enemy was retreating in good order, as evidenced by the difficulty in making contact with the German rearguard. And he was aware that the enemy forces were falling back on a strong defensive system.

The experience of open warfare soon ended. On 30 March Greenwell reported that his company was billeted in leaky cellars and ruined barns quite close to the enemy and was preparing to '*dig trenches*'. 'Isn't it too ghastly. But the Staff is nothing if not cautious and the Bosche is developing a certain power of resistance.'[10]

---

[9] Spears, *Prelude to Victory*, pp. 204–28.
[10] Graham H. Greenwell, *An Infant in Arms, War Letters of a Company Officer 1914–1918* (London: Allen Lane, 1972), pp. 157–70.

Greenwell's reference to the cautiousness of the staff suggests that the Allies might have caused the Germans some discomfort had the retreat been followed up more vigorously. Yet too much should not be made of this. The perils were too great to warrant a headlong pursuit. And any blows that the enemy might have been dealt could only have been of modest dimension.

Upon the forces of France the German withdrawal imposed the worst of both worlds. The retreat seriously impaired the plans of the new French commander, but not to the extent of requiring his operation to be abandoned.

Had Joffre still been in command, a different situation would have obtained. The scheme devised by Haig and himself would have placed the main attack in the region of the German withdrawal (although their attack might have pre-empted it). Only a subsidiary operation was intended for the east–west sector of the French front clear of the Hindenburg Line. Nivelle's plan placed the emphasis the other way round. His main operation fell in the east–west sector. There his principal objective was the plateau of the Chemin des Dames, an obstacle that Joffre, from bitter experience, had proposed to circumvent.

Nevertheless, with the object of holding German forces away from the main area of assault, Nivelle had also prepared a strong thrust by British and French forces between Arras and the river Oise in the north–south sector. Except in the region of Arras itself, this part of the scheme was thrown into disarray by the German withdrawal. Plainly, it would not be possible, in the time available, to mount more than a feint attack across the German-devastated area. So Nivelle moved large quantities of men and munitions away from the region of the Oise to the district around Reims. There, on the right of his main attack, they would engage in a somewhat impromptu operation. Thus the German retreat had undermined the careful planning and orderly procedure that was intended to characterize Nivelle's scheme.

It had done more. The establishment of the Hindenburg Line had both shortened the German front and created a defensive system requiring fewer men per mile. In consequence, about a dozen German divisions had been set free to meet the coming offensive. And during March it was becoming quite evident that these reinforcements were being placed in precisely those areas where Nivelle would be making his main attack. The French, therefore, would be launching an offensive without the advantage of either numbers or surprise.

For this last aspect, loss of surprise, the French commander was himself in good measure responsible. In discussing his scheme with Haig early on, he had stressed the importance of secrecy. But since then, no doubt in reaction to the practices of Joffre, he had emphasized another element: the importance of informing his forces fully of the nature and purpose of their operations. By this means he secured their confidence. But he did more. He raised large expectations among his troops. And he left the enemy in no doubt about where he would be making his main endeavours.

41

STRATEGIC EXPEDIENTS II:
THE BATTLE OF ARRAS

I

Before recounting Haig's part in the Nivelle operation, some general remarks are called for about the British army on the Western Front at this time.

The British forces in France and Flanders in early 1917 consisted of five armies comprising 62 divisions. This constituted a total strength of 1.5 million men. If one thing had changed markedly since the opening of the Somme battle, it was in respect to artillery. The increase in both quantity and quality was noteworthy. The 761 heavy guns and howitzers possessed by the BEF in mid–1916 had advanced by April 1917 to over 1,500. And the ammunition available to them had increased more than proportionately. In the three months April to June 1916 the BEF had received something over 700,000 rounds of heavy ammunition; for the same quarter of 1917 the figure exceeded 5 million. In field artillery the number of guns available had made no such advance, but the supply of ammunition increased almost as much.

The import of this should not be exaggerated. At 20 heavy guns and howitzers per division, Britain's forces enjoyed only half the number available to each French division. And at no stage in 1917 could operations be planned without paying careful attention to ammunition supplies, as well as to the rate at which guns were wearing out. (It would not be until 1918 that shells might be fired practically without regard to the question of availability. And it is the case that Haig's ultimate objective regarding artillery pieces was never fulfilled. He looked forward to a time when he might possess such an abundance of guns that, as a prelude to launching an offensive, he would not need to move artillery to the sector he proposed to attack – for such movement entailed the risk of advertising his intentions. This ideal state would prove unattainable.)

Nevertheless, it is still the case that in 1917 the artillery situation of Haig's forces had improved markedly over the position in 1916. This might have a distinct bearing on the success of military operations – but only if these were so devised that the artillery's contribution could decisively affect them.

It was not only in quantity that the improvement was evident. The effectiveness of artillery fire was also improving, not least in suppressing the artillery of the enemy. This was consequent on the development by scientists, mathematicians, and gunners of such devices as flash-spotting and sound-ranging, the latter 'one of the most potent factors in the development of counter-battery work towards the excellence it eventually attained.'[1] Thanks to these devices, it was possible to locate enemy guns in the act of firing both by their muzzle flashes and their reports. The sound-rangers, in addition,

[1] Brigadier Edgar Anstey, 'The History of the Royal Artillery (from 4th August 1914)', n.d., unpublished volume in the Official History series, galley proof 138, copy in the Royal Artillery Library, Woolwich.

Plate 35   *Canadians dig themselves in under fire on Vimy Ridge.*

could follow the path of single British shells to their destination and correct the range accordingly. As a supplement to (or, in unfavourable weather, a substitute for) aerial observation, these innovations would prove of mounting importance.

Further, the actual quality of British weapons improved during 1917. The old ⊤./-inch gun of Boer War days finally gave way to the 60-pounder. The clumsy 30-hundredweight 6-inch howitzer was replaced by the 26-hundredweight. At various stages in 1917 several notable weapons made their debut: the 6-inch Mark XIX gun, the 9.2-inch Mark II howitzer, the 8-inch Mark VIII howitzer, and the 12-inch Marks III, IV, and V howitzers. As for ammunition, British bombardments were no longer plagued by the high proportion of dud shells that had littered the Somme battlefield in 1916. Moreover, finer-quality fuses were being introduced that caused shells to explode on impact rather than after burying themselves in the ground. And the development of the gas shell gave poison gas a usefulness it could never possess as long as it was discharged from cylinders dependent on the vagaries of the wind.

What all of this signified is clear. British fighting men were now drawing substantial benefits from the endeavours apparent on the home front since 1915: the conversion of peacetime industries to war purposes; the creation of new national factories for the production of implements of destruction; the diversion of scientists, managers, and labourers into war-related activities; and the marshalling of a segment of the industrial capacity of countries like the USA and Canada, as well as the raw materials of some less developed nations, to the service of the Allies.

II

The British contribution to the Nivelle offensive was to be conducted out of Arras by the Third Army under General Allenby, a cavalryman of fierce disposition and a meticulous planner. On the left he was to be aided by the Canadian Corps of General Horne's First Army, which was to assail the Vimy Ridge. On the right he would be

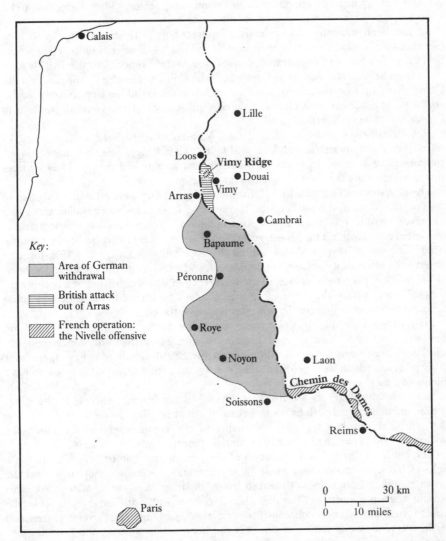

Map 9 *The German withdrawal and the battle of Arras.* Source: *Gilbert*, First World
War Atlas, *p. 89.*

assisted by elements of General Gough's Fifth Army. Vimy Ridge, it might be noted, lay outside Nivelle's original plan. The French commander feared that its inclusion would pull the British advance towards the north-east, whereas he was proposing a thrust south-east. But Haig insisted that in order to secure his left flank, and on account of the intrinsic importance of this dominating feature, Vimy Ridge had to be included.

As has been indicated, the primary purpose of the British assault was to hold German forces away from the main area of Nivelle's offensive. Hence Haig would commence his part of the operation a week before the French. But the British were also expected to advance as far as Cambrai. If the French offensive on the Chemin des Dames lived up to expectations, a quite new situation would develop. Nivelle's drive north would intersect with Haig's advance south-east, and the German position in France would be entirely dislocated.

The British operation opened on Easter Monday, 9 April 1917, on a front of 15 miles. Ten divisions attacked at Arras and four at Vimy Ridge. The first phase enjoyed commendable success. In terms of dislodging an entrenched enemy, Haig's forces surpassed anything they had achieved so far in the war.

The British were fortunate in that, for the most part, they were attacking a section of the German front to the north of the Hindenburg Line. This latter system was sited, wherever possible, on reverse slopes. And it employed what was called 'elastic defence' or 'defence in depth'. The advantages of these arrangements may be briefly summarized. The use of reverse slopes limited the opportunities for an attacking force to observe the effect of its artillery bombardment; and when its infantry reached the brow of the hill they presented a perfect target. Defence in depth consisted of a lightly held forward zone, where the force of an attack might be blunted, succeeded by more formidable barriers supported by powerful counter-attacks.

Haig's forces, for the most part, were not facing this system. On Vimy Ridge and opposite Arras the main defence lines were situated on forward slopes, and the German forces were massed within range of the British bombardment – apart from their reserves, which were held far to the rear on the expectation that they would have plenty of time to come forward.

Yet such advantages as the British enjoyed had not brought success to the Allies during the many earlier offensives launched in this area. What made the difference on this occasion was in part the high quality of the commanders who planned the operations and in part the human and material resources available to them.

The battle of Arras was a revelation of the paramountcy of artillery fire upon the field of battle. The decisions made by the commanders before the battle, and the courage and resourcefulness displayed by the fighting men during its course, must remain of great importance. But these had to operate within the parameters set by the effectiveness of artillery bombardments in clearing a path into and through entrenched positions. One manifestation of this was the burgeoning of staffs and organizations attending to artillery matters throughout the British army. These extended from Haig's chief artillery adviser, Major-General Noel Birch, down through each stage of the military organization to the men actually operating the guns. These artillery officers, it has been said, were of necessity 'educated men of the highest calibre', 'the rising generation of technologists who had come to dominate the war'. If the traditional commanders and staffs still laid the central plans for attack, it was the artillery commanders and their staffs who were the virtual dictators of policy: 'In their immensity they were now omnipotent.'[2] The Canadian Corps, for example, had the

---

[2] Kenneth Macksey, *Vimy Ridge* (London: Pan/Ballantine, 1973), pp. 68–9.

support of six British and two Canadian Heavy Artillery Groups. Without them an infantry assault on Vimy Ridge could never have begun.

In the artillery preparations for Arras the conundrum that had posed itself at the opening of the Somme was again present. What weight of shell was required for each yard of enemy trench in order to smother the defences? As before, military science had no precise answer. It could only go on pursuing a process of trial and error. But some things were evident enough. The weight of shell employed must be a good deal heavier than that used in preparation for the Somme. And it had to be both of a higher quality and of a kind more appropriate to the job in hand.

Simply in terms of the quantity of shells fired, Arras signified a further stage in Britain's capacity for waging war. Upon the Vimy sector some 50,000 tons of artillery ammunition were released, employing one heavy gun for every 20 yards of front – almost treble the density on the Somme prior to 1 July 1916. For the heavy and medium guns the improved type of fuse, destroying wire with an efficiency hitherto unattainable, was now available. And the delivery upon the enemy, in shells and flying canisters, of a considerable quantity of poison gas reduced the effectiveness of the defence. For gas, even though it could be guarded against, impaired the efficiency of men forced to wear masks for long stretches of time and often killed animals bringing up supplies from the rear.

Again, the pattern of the preliminary bombardment revealed growing sophistication in planning and greater skill in execution. The heavy guns were concentrated upon the rear positions, battering German artillery and supply routes. The medium guns and mortars took on the wire and the enemy trenches. During the actual attack a barrage of machine-gun bullets, fired indirectly over the heads of the advancing troops, swept the ground in front, while a creeping bombardment of artillery fire engaged first one defensive system and then the next. This was not the first appearance of the creeping bombardment on the British sector. It had emerged during the Somme attacks. But that campaign had been fought by a new army, and it took artillery men a long time to learn their craft. At Arras it was evident that the men operating the guns were acquiring the necessary skills.

Consequently, a noteworthy phase of this action was the confidence with which the infantry were prepared to follow close behind the barrage. 'All you have got to do,' a sergeant instructor was reported as telling an inexperienced young Londoner, 'is to hang on to the back wheel of the barrage, just as if you were biking down the Strand behind a motor 'bus; carefully like, and not in too much of a hurry; and then when you come to Fritz, and he holds up his hands, you send him back to the rear.'[3] Whether sergeants were really this solicitous about the welfare of defeated Germans may be doubted. But the rest rings true enough.

The infantry side of the operation was also prepared with skill. Tens of thousands of maps of the areas to be overrun were distributed. These were obtained at heavy cost in airmen, for although at this stage the RFC had a considerable superiority in numbers, their aircraft were decidedly inferior. In consequence, they were out-fought by the Germans. (Not for nothing were the first weeks of the battle of Arras known to the RFC as 'Bloody April'.) But, from the viewpoint of the men on the ground, the price in airmen was warranted. The infantry's objectives could be clearly delineated and its attacks thoroughly rehearsed.

The town of Arras itself provided Allenby with a singular advantage, which he exploited thoroughly. Underneath the town, whose suburbs ran almost to the front

---

[3] Frank Fox, *The Battle of the Ridges* (London: C. Arthur Pearson, 1918), p. 33.

line, lay a great many tunnels, from which stone had once been quarried, and also a system of sewers. These were extended and linked up to provide a labyrinth capable of housing an army of 30,000. Electric lighting, water, and a light railway were laid on. By this means the attacking infantry could be brought right up to the jumping-off point, unobserved by the enemy.

Something similar occurred on Vimy Ridge, although there the caves owed nothing to history or civilian requirements. They were the work first of British and then of Canadian forces preparing for the attack. The chalk soil of the ridge enabled tunnels to be dug so deep that no shell could reach them. Hence here also the assault forces could be assembled free from enemy observation.

As a result, although five days of steady bombardment gave clear warning that a British offensive was at hand, the enemy remained unaware of the imminence of zero hour until the British infantry were well into No-Man's-Land. Even the wretchedness of the weather did not thwart the attackers. On the left success was virtually total. In the space of just two days (9 and 10 April) the Canadians, in one of the war's most memorable actions, seized Vimy Ridge. In the centre also 9 April was a decidedly good day. Aided by a handful of tanks, many deeds of valour, and some collapse of morale among the defenders, Alienby's Third Army tore a large gap in the German front and advanced to a depth of 3½ miles – the greatest distance accomplished since the onset of trench warfare.

At this point, with the German reserves being held so far back, all sorts of opportunities seemed to beckon. If they existed, they were not taken. This is not surprising. All preparations for the offensive had laid emphasis on the taking of definite objectives in accordance with a definite timetable. As long as the creeping barrage was deemed the key to success, it was essential that infantrymen stick to the plan, neither falling behind the barrage and so denying themselves its aid nor getting on too fast and so becoming its victims. This procedure amply justified itself on 9 April. But it left men, at all levels, ill-prepared to take advantage of fleeting opportunities.

A further problem intervened at this stage. An arm of exploitation was believed to be on hand when it was not. Once more, this role was assigned to the cavalry. Yet with winter persisting right into these April days ('the severity of the season,' according to a contemporary, 'established a record for nearly a hundred years'),[4] the cavalry were more than usually ill-equipped to function on the Western Front. The horses had already suffered greatly from the climate, as well as from a shortage of feed. And they were being held well back under cover, in expectation that their moment would arrive on the second day. Instead it came, if in fact it came at all, within the first 24 hours. By the time the cavalry could be got forward over shattered terrain on 10 April the German lines were mending, and all that awaited the horse soldiers was the familiar slaughter. Only a blinding snowstorm – hardly ideal circumstances for a mounted attack – enabled the remnants of the cavalry to withdraw.

Given the ineffectiveness of the mobile arm, it was bound to be only a short time before the advance came to a halt. The artillery, plainly, could make only laborious progress over ground that its own shells, aided by the infamous weather, had thoroughly disrupted. The enemy, meanwhile, was strengthening his rearward defences and rushing forward strong forces of reserves unblunted by the opening phases of the battle. Rather than constituting a tale of lost opportunities, the successes at Vimy Ridge and opposite Arras revealed that the transformation of break-in to breakthrough continued as elusive as ever.

---

[4] Fox, *The Battle of the Ridges*, p. 21.

The story just related, of early advance followed by waning momentum, applied only to the left and centre of the British offensive. On the right there was no early success. Gough, the Fifth Army commander, was facing exceptional difficulties. He was up against the Hindenburg Line proper with its bristling defences. And at his back, as a supply route, lay a stretch of German-induced desolation. Further, because his contribution was deemed subsidiary, he had been relieved of much infantry and artillery. As a consequence, his preliminary bombardment was not effective against the German wire.

Gough's objective was the strong point of Bullecourt, initially intended for attack on the second day of the offensive. The failure of the bombardment caused him to contemplate delay. But then the successes on the left and centre on 9 April rather turned his head. He allowed himself to be convinced that with a sufficient force of tanks (which had played a small but not insignificant part on Vimy Ridge and before Arras) he might still attack on the 10th. The tanks would destroy the wire where artillery had failed, and the guns would open up only as the infantry went forward. This attempt to introduce strikingly new tactics of assault says something for Gough's imagination. But it reflects also a serious failure to appreciate that inspired methods must be accompanied by careful staff preparation.

In the outcome the tanks never reached the start line on 10 April, and once more the attack had to be called off. It went ahead the following morning with calamitous results. The few tanks that managed to reach the battlefield largely failed to get as far as the wire. Hence the Australian infantry, which was supposed to follow them, had to breach the wire unaided. This it somehow accomplished, in spite of terrible enfilade fire. But, having entered the first two German lines, it was marooned there. With failing ammunition and under attack from front and flanks, it was at last driven out with heavy loss.

After two days therefore, along the entire front of attack, the British operation in support of Nivelle's offensive had lost all potentiality for a considerable advance. Yet large-scale attacks continued at regular intervals for another six weeks. In most instances they achieved little, and on some occasions were calamitous failures. One costly success deserves to be noted. Undeterred by the fiasco of 11 April, the Australians of Fifth Army returned to the attack on Bullecourt, gaining first a foothold and eventually a secure position on the Hindenburg Line.

What had been accomplished? Plainly, the Arras operation, running from early April until mid-June 1917, was not without its achievements. The capture of Vimy Ridge was an enormous moral victory over the enemy, as well as securing a position of outstanding tactical importance. The ridge denied observation to the Germans and gave the British oversight of the Douai plain. It also provided a strong point against the day when the Germans must, if they were ever to win the war, come this way again. Simultaneously, the advance beyond Arras had driven the enemy out of strong positions and removed the threat to an endangered rail centre. And the capture of Bullecourt demonstrated, if at heavy cost, that even the Hindenburg Line was not impregnable. More than this, the British in the course of these six weeks had imposed yet another heavy drain upon German manpower. The enemy's casualties were well in excess of 100,000.

But against this reward must be set a considerable expenditure of resources. The British, whose own supply of men was not inexhaustible, had suffered casualties in the order of 150,000. They had fired off prodigious amounts of ammunition. In the last stages of the offensive they had used up some weeks of fine weather, in a year that would be blessed with precious few of these, to the detriment of subsequent operations. And the rank and file could not fail to notice that the offensive had been maintained long after it had lost all potential for further advance – a process certain to sap faith in their high command.

Haig was plainly disappointed that, after such a hopeful start, few strategic advantages had been gained. For this he regarded Allenby, with whom he did not enjoy good relations, as being in a measure blameworthy. (Haig can hardly have been disappointed when, soon after, Allenby was transferred to the Palestine front.) Yet there were powerful reasons for concluding that a well conducted operation was not going to accomplish more than this: that the cavalry was doomed as a weapon of exploitation, that artillery could not hasten forward over territory it had just devastated, and that consequently the whole notion of strategic advance was a pipe dream. It was not to Haig's credit – nor would it prove to his army's good fortune – that he seemed loath to ponder this possibility.

But a summing-up of this operation requires more than an account of what the forces of Britain did and did not achieve, and of the cost to the enemy and to themselves. As explained earlier, the primary British objective was to make easier the way of Nivelle by pinning down German forces away from the area of the main French attack. However unrewarding such a proceeding may have appeared to the British forces engaged, this objective was worthwhile and it was accomplished. The Germans were not free to divert troops from the Arras area. Admittedly, Allenby's forces did not carry success to the projected second stage. They did not advance as far as had been hoped, and so were not in a position to help exploit a French breakthrough. But in the event this hardly mattered. No French breakthrough occurred.

Indeed, by late April and early May the initial *raison d'être* for the Arras operation had vanished. Now the British offensive was continuing for a quite different purpose. This was to shore up the waning offensive spirit of their ally, about which Haig was commenting with alarm as Nivelle's star waned and that of Pétain rose. And by the last weeks of the British action it was a nice question whether they were not attacking for quite another reason again: to prevent the Germans from finding out why so little offensiveness was apparent on the French front. That is, the justification for the Arras operation in its last phase was one that would have been unimaginable when it started. The British were having to deny the Germans the opportunity to search out and exploit the growing demoralization among the fighting forces of France.

III

The Nivelle offensive had achieved the reverse of what it promised. Instead of rupturing the German line, it had reduced the French infantry to mutiny.

Nivelle's failure had not proved total. He had taken many prisoners and had secured a large chunk of the Chemin des Dames. But, essentially, this was the unpalatable mixture as before – what Joffre had described as 'nibbling'. It was not a breakthrough; it was not decisive; and it was not accomplished within 48 hours. Furthermore, in terms of French lives it was not cheap.

The effect of this grievous disappointment was conclusive. Any army, when its numbers, fighting spirit, and hopes have been worn beyond a certain point, will lose the will to fling itself against terrible barriers. That now happened to the forces of France. Instances of 'collective indiscipline' began growing to menacing proportions. One form was predominant. Troops that had been in the front line and had then gone into reserve refused to obey the order to return. French generals at the time found it convenient – as have some military historians since – to interpret this as meaning that soldiers away from the front were falling victim to subversive propaganda. Such an explanation trivializes a profound malaise. The French rank and file, having escaped momentarily the toils of offensive battle, found themselves observing the gulf between what the military command was promising and what flesh and blood had any chance of accomplishing. They refused to participate in this fraudulent undertaking any further.

Fortunately, before the troops went on strike the 'mutiny' had already begun among France's political rulers. They recognized that performance was falling far short of promise, and set about constricting Nivelle's opportunities to persist. Only after that did the withdrawal of confidence clearly manifest itself among the French soldiery. The consequence was irresistible. After having his powers restricted by late April, Nivelle suffered their termination in mid-May. His authority was transferred to Pétain. The latter, although an authoritarian, was both a paternalist and a pessimist. Consequently, he would care for his troops and show no fondness for rash adventures.

This course of events was observed with dismay on the British side. The extent of the disaffection in the French ranks was a well kept secret. But both Haig and Lloyd George became aware that the French had lost the heart for a continuation of large offensives. They resisted this trend to the utmost. It is probably not wonderful that a man of Haig's limited vision should have hastened to Paris to urge that the campaign must go on. It may appear more surprising that Lloyd George should have accompanied him, not so as to contradict him but in order to echo his every word: 'We must go on hitting and hitting with all our strength.'

On an unkind view, the Prime Minister was again revealing that, if determined to economize on British lives (although Arras had scarcely proved bloodless), he was not equally solicitous for the sons of France. But a more charitable interpretation is probably nearer the truth. Lloyd George at this moment was simply without resource. His master-stroke against Haig had proved such a calamity that it appeared to leave him at the British commander's mercy. So he told the conference in Paris on 4 May (according to Haig's account) 'that he had no pretensions to be a strategist, that he left that to his military advisers, that I [i.e. Haig], as C.inC. of the British Forces in France had full power to attack where and when I thought best'.[5] This volte-face continued as Lloyd George, in the ensuing days, visited Haig's headquarters. According to Charteris, the Prime Minister's 'line' was 'outspoken praise of everything in the British Army in France, and especially of D. H. He compares us now with the French, very much to the disadvantage of the latter.'[6] The meaning of all this was summed up by Frances Stevenson, who wrote in her diary for 12 May:

> In the meantime, Nivelle has fallen into disgrace, and let D. [i.e. Lloyd George] down badly after the way D. had backed him up at the beginning of the year. Sir Douglas Haig has come out on top in this fight between the two Chiefs, & I fear D. will have to be very careful in future as to his backings of the French against the English.[7]

The comment was more than a fitting epitaph to the military improvisations now concluding. Unwittingly, it set the scene for the process of decision-making that must soon be undertaken regarding Britain's military operations in the second half of 1917.

---

[5] Robert Blake (ed.), *The Private Papers of Douglas Haig 1914–1919* (London: Eyre & Spottiswoode, 1952), p.228.

[6] John Charteris, *At G.H.Q.* (London: Cassell, 1931), p. 223.

[7] A. J. P. Taylor (ed.), *Lloyd George: A Diary by Frances Stevenson* (London: Hutchinson, 1971), p. 157.

42

STRATEGIC NADIR: THIRD YPRES, PART I

In this week of our reprieve [i.e. out of the line], there has been a chance to adjust oneself to the facts of life – and, for that matter, of death. For out there, it is not just the Valley of the Shadow, but the very home of Death itself, where neither trees, nor plants, nor birds, nor even soldiers can hope to keep alive for very long. . . .

In this strange world, the Psalms can be a very present help in time of trouble; particularly as they were written by a fighter who knew what it was to be scared stiff. It's really amusing to find how literally some of them apply to life in the Ypres salient in 1917. 'I stick fast in the deep mire where no ground is' (Psalm 69). 'The earth trembled and quaked: the very foundations also of the hills shook' (Psalm 18). 'The clouds poured out water, the air thundered: and thine arrows went abroad.' (Ps. 77). 'Thou shalt not be afraid for any terror by night: nor for the arrow that flieth by day. A thousand shall fall beside thee, and ten thousand at thy right hand, but it shall not come nigh thee' (Ps. 91). Very comforting that one, so long as you are sure you won't be among the unlucky 10,000! But David was obviously whistling to keep his courage up.

[4 a.m.] Weather awful. Cold. Sheets of rain. Clothes wet already. Just off to work. Are we downhearted? Very!

Huntly Gordon, artillery officer in the Ypres salient, to his mother,
19 August and 28 August 1917

I

The question facing British strategists following the Nivelle débâcle could be simply expressed. What was to be done next? If Lloyd George was serious when he told the French on 4 May 1917 that he left strategy to his military advisers, and that Haig had full powers to attack when and where he thought best, then the answer would also be simple. The British, with such support as the French could muster, would forthwith mount a major campaign in Flanders. Its intention would be to drive north-east from Ypres to the Belgian coast. Haig had been contemplating such an operation since he first became Commander-in-Chief. And it had received a measure of Cabinet approval in the last weeks of Asquith's ministry.

The reasons in favour of this particular operation were not few. Greatest of all, it would initiate, by the most direct means, the liberation of Belgium, the objective that at the last had induced Britain to go to war. Further, it would take from the Germans the ports of Ostend and Zeebrugge, which posed a threat to cross-Channel communications and were something of a haven for U-boats. (This last aspect was much played up by the Admiralty. It is unlikely that it counted greatly among the civil and military leaders.) Again, no large British offensive had hitherto been launched in this region. The first and second battles of Ypres had been defensive actions. Hence no aura of past failure hung over an attack here – except in so far as any operation on the Western

Front tended to assume the character of any other operation there. And even among those who doubted whether Haig could achieve his full objectives a further argument obtained. As long as the British were determined to hold on to the vulnerable Ypres salient, with its steady toll in casualties, there was much to be said for driving the Germans from the commanding heights around the town.

Since March a fresh reason for making Belgium the location of the next British offensive had presented itself. It was stated succinctly by Sir Maurice Hankey – who is not remembered as an advocate of the third battle of Ypres. The Somme offensive of 1916, if it had achieved nothing else, had driven the enemy from a strong, carefully

Plate 36   *Glencourse Wood and Inverness Wood in mid-August 1917 (at the time of a German counter-attack).*

prepared defensive position. But the Germans had negated this achievement by their retreat to the Hindenburg Line. That is, by abandoning a slab of occupied France now of no use to them, they had recovered the tactical advantage in the Somme area. Hankey, in conversation with General Maurice, urged the importance of 'striking the enemy somewhere where he could not withdraw without surrendering to us some object of value such as the Belgian coast'.[1] Maurice, who happened to be Robertson's chief offsider, had no hesitation in agreeing.

Yet if a Flanders offensive had all these things to be said in its favour, there was one big thing to be said against it. It promised to be nothing more than another hideous assault on entrenched positions, incurring a crushing toll of British casualties.

Certainly, the proposed operation was meant to be accompanied by some tactical novelties. In particular, Haig was planning that, as his forces advanced on the Belgian ports, he would launch a supporting attack both along the coast and from the sea. But

---

[1] Hankey's diary, 26 March 1917.

all such inspirations presupposed a great initial success for what would be nothing more than a conventional Western Front offensive. And since the end of 1914 offensives on this front had never accomplished a strategic advance. The most that had been achieved were attritional successes. And to claim even this much it was necessary to employ the term attrition in its bleakest sense: not the wearing down of the enemy at little cost to the Allies, but the wearing down of the enemy at equal or greater Allied cost.

Haig insisted that his Flanders operation would not be like this. He based this claim on two assertions. First, an offensive out from Ypres would not be a blow in the void or an attack with limitless objectives. It offered clearly defined geographical goals relatively close to hand. Secondly, the process of attrition had now reached a decisive stage. The Germans had come to a condition of fragility; one more good push would start them sliding into collapse. Yet both were questionable assertions. The Belgian coast might present clear objectives, but they lay well beyond the range of any advance so far accomplished on the Western Front. And Haig's assumption that the Germans were nearing exhaustion was based on little more than his own wishful thinking and the information supplied by his Intelligence Department. In that this department, by virtue of the men he had selected to staff it, was largely a device for reflecting his own thoughts, this constituted one inadequate source rather than two.

Some men in key positions were unconvinced by Haig's promises. They did not believe that Germany was on the point of collapse. And they resisted putting the matter to the test by a further Western Front offensive – or, anyway, a Western Front offensive under Haig's direction. Most prominent among them was Lloyd George.

In the process of decision-making now taking place, the Prime Minister held the key position. Ultimate responsibility for matters of grand strategy rested with him. In exercising that responsibility he must secure the agreement of his Cabinet colleagues, and he must weigh carefully the judgements of his military advisers – particularly Robertson. But the members of the War Cabinet held their posts by his choice. And his military advisers received and retained their positions by will of their civilian masters. When a decision was made about British strategy for the second half of 1917, the person finally making it (as had been abundantly clear concerning the first half of 1917) would be Lloyd George. If he was determined that there would be no further offensive on the Western Front or that it would take a far more constricted form than Haig desired, then that would settle the matter. No offensive, or only a limited one, would take place.

Of course, when arriving at his decision Lloyd George – to reaffirm a point made several times already – would be acting under severe constraints. He was set upon securing victory in the war, and with the greatest possible dispatch. Sometimes during 1917 he talked as if this was not so; as if he were prepared to wait for the Americans or to negotiate a settlement with the Germans at the expense of the Russians. But these were signs of his desperation, and his agony, as he viewed the strategic choices before him. Ultimately he would not tarry for the Americans, for to do so – given their unpreparedness – would involve much 'waiting and seeing'. Nor would he chase the pipe dream of a negotiated settlement.

In appreciating Lloyd George's flirtation with such ideas, it is instructive to note a conversation he had had with C. P. Scott and Christopher Addison back in November 1916. Asked by Addison who was to be the new 'Food Dictator', Lloyd George remarked ('quite seriously', Scott records): 'I think the job would rather suit me – to provide for the food of the people, instead of this bloody business.'[2] Lloyd George did

---

[2] Trevor Wilson (ed.), *The Political Diaries of C. P. Scott 1911–1928* (London: Collins, 1970), p. 239.

not act upon this inspiration. Within a fortnight he had moved from the War Office to the premiership in order to involve himself yet more thoroughly in the 'bloody business'. Nevertheless, the outburst to Scott and Addison should be viewed with sympathy: not as a statement of any intention to change course but as an expression of his revulsion against the cost of the war to those waging it – and to himself as an humanitarian and social reformer. Yet, however much the war repelled him, he would press on with it.

That the war must be prosecuted, and that this should not be through a process of 'waiting and seeing', were major constraints on Lloyd George in mid–1917. They were not alone. The strategic options had narrowed since January. The French army was for the moment a spent force; except, gradually, as an instrument for conducting limited attacks with strictly defined objectives. The new Russian Government was on the offensive against the Germans, yet this was plainly a precarious (as it would soon prove a catastrophic) undertaking. The Italians – with the Germans occupied elsewhere – had also gone on to the attack against the Austrians, but once again it was proving an arduous business. And if the British were having successes against the Turks, it was palpable that the expedient of 'knocking away the props' held out small promise. Germany was surviving in spite of, not on account of, its allies.

Lloyd George, to all appearances, did not appreciate this. The failure of Nivelle was causing him to turn his eyes not from the French to the British sector of the Western Front but once more to the Italian front. He believed that a heavy blow there would drive Austria-Hungary out of the war, so cutting what he called the 'umbilical cord of the Central Alliance'.[3] In saying this Lloyd George appeared to disregard the ferocious geographical obstacles awaiting any offensive from Italy, as well as the reluctance of the Italian commander to embark on a course likely to attract against himself great numbers of Germans.

By taking up this position Lloyd George determined the outcome of the argument over strategy. For he was creating a situation in which only two choices lay open: Haig's Flanders offensive and his own (probably chimerical) Italian campaign. To pose the alternatives thus was to guarantee a decision for Haig.

Hankey – if all unwittingly – makes this plain. In his diary for the later part of June 1917, he recounts a 'regular battle royal (conducted in the best possible spirit) between Lloyd George on the one hand and Robertson and Haig on the other':

> The two latter want to make a great attack on the Belgian front, which Ll. G. objects to as having no decent chance of success. Russian & French cooperation are too insufficient; our superiority in men & guns too slight; the extent of the advance required in order to secure tangible results (Ostend & Zeebrugge) too great in his opinion to justify the great losses which must be involved, losses which he thinks will jeopardise our chance next year, & cause great depression. All this they dispute. Ll. G. wants to mass heavy guns on the Italian frontier, making use of Italian manpower, and dealing a blow which will compel Austria in her exhausted state to make peace. Robertson, however thinks this very risky, owing to the danger of a German counterstroke in the Trentino which will stop our attack and possibly cut off the whole Italian main army including our guns. He dreads to transfer the war to the Italian front, where he considers the Italian army unreliable and our communications inferior to those of the enemy.

What seems so evident in this verbal passage-of-arms is the success of each side in

---

[3] See John Terraine, *The Road to Passchendaele* (London: Leo Cooper, 1977), p. 164. The notion of the 'umbilical cord', with Germany as the mother sustaining the foetuses Turkey and Bulgaria, has one noteworthy feature. It implies the plain opposite to Lloyd George's other figure of speech, 'knocking away the props', which portrayed Germany as being in a state of dependence on its allies. This confusion aptly illustrates the dangers of basing strategy on flights of imagery.

invalidating the scheme put forward by the other. Lloyd George's arguments against the Flanders plan were utterly compelling. So were Robertson's against the Italian scheme. The difference lay in the fact that the Flanders plan at least existed as an operation that could be tried, because the resources required for it were under British control. Lloyd George's scheme, which depended on 'making use of Italian man-power', was little more than a speculation, which would have to be sold to the principal executants. Such an exercise in salesmanship was unlikely to succeed. According to Robertson: 'It is notorious that the Italians are miserably afraid of the Germans. They themselves have confessed as much.'[4] So the decision was bound to go to the former plan.

But all this assumed that there were, in truth, no other forms of operation that merited consideration. Yet plainly there was another way of proceeding. It offered less than Haig was promising but as much, and at smaller cost, than he had so far shown any capacity to deliver. It would not set either Germany or Austria sliding to early destruction, but it held good chance of producing tangible successes, to the comfort of the Allies and the injury of their opponents. The course being referred to was that by which Nivelle had made his reputation at Verdun late in 1916, and by which Pétain would soon be heralding the recuperation of the French army. On the British side, Horne at Vimy Ridge and Allenby at Arras on 9 April 1917 had made this way of proceeding clear enough. And their message was reinforced in literally devastating fashion on 7 June 1917, just a fortnight before the 'battle royal' between the Prime Minister and his military advisers. Plumer's Second Army, which occupied the Ypres area, carried off one of the great limited-objective operations of the whole war when it stormed the Messines Ridge 5 miles south of Ypres.

In one respect Plumer was blessed for this operation with an ally that would not be available for similar such attacks. He had had time, and to spare, in which to make his preparations. For two years he and his army had sat in the same place. Among the ways it had occupied itself was in tunnelling deep under the German positions at Messines and in planting there a score of great mines. The explosion of these mines on 7 June – audible as far away as 10 Downing Street – provided the ideal starting pistol for the infantry's advance.[5] But that was not the infantry's only ally. Careful artillery preparation, crashing down in their support, contributed greatly to the triumph at Messines; as earlier it had done for Nivelle and Horne and Allenby and, before long, would do also for Pétain.

Here, then, was a true alternative to Haig's Flanders plan. Rawlinson, after Neuve Chapelle in long ago 1915, had called it 'bite and hold'. It consisted of a series of set-piece operations whose extent and frequency would depend on the range and mobility of the artillery. The objective of any infantry attack must lie within the hitting limit of the guns. Once the objective had been taken, that phase of the operation would be over. As soon as the artillery could assume new positions and register upon fresh targets, another blow would be struck.

Lloyd George did not embrace this proceeding. He less rejected it than acted as if it barely existed. Yet having been so impressed by Nivelle's Verdun successes and having, as Prime Minister, presided over the exemplary victories at Vimy Ridge and Messines, he can hardly have been unaware of it. Nor, had he opted for it, would he have lacked powerful endorsement, not only from outside military circles but also from

---

[4] Terraine, *The Road to Passchendaele*, p. 172

[5] This finest achievement of the tunnelling war on the Western Front was also the last. The development of listening devices to detect mining activities beneath the lines now reached the point where tunnelling operations hereafter ceased to be cost-effective.

within: from Rawlinson, commander of Fourth Army, from Horne, commander of First, from Plumer, commander of Second, and from Byng, who had been in charge of the Canadian Corps at Vimy Ridge and was now commander of Third Army. And, closer to home, Robertson was plainly uneasy about Haig's grand designs, and was urging him to contemplate more modest objectives and to make more responsible promises. (Haig would reveal that he had not forgiven this display of common sense on Robertson's part when, early in 1918, the sands were running out for the CIGS.)

The manner in which Lloyd George chose to see the strategic alternatives at this stage placed Robertson in a dreadful dilemma. (Robertson's way of trying to deal with the situation, it should be added, was sometimes highly devious.) The CIGS was receiving from his own Intelligence Department none of the fanciful calculations concerning Germany's near-collapse that Haig was offering. Yet if Robertson wavered in his support of Haig, he was confronted with a Prime Minister apparently eager to rush forces away from the Western Front – the only area, Robertson did not doubt, where they could be usefully employed. Given the necessity to choose between Haig's grand design for fighting the Germans and Lloyd George's seeming enthusiasm for taking the war to the Austrians or the Turks, Robertson was bound to opt for the former. It was his misfortune that Lloyd George effectively allowed him only these choices.

On the face of it, the rationale of Lloyd George's conduct is difficult to divine. If he was so devotedly opposed to Haig's Flanders plan, why did he not seize upon any viable alternative? If a big operation outside the Western Front was not available, then the next best thing would appear to have been a handful of limited operations within it. Yet at the meetings of the War Policy Committee (a sub-committee of the War Cabinet set up in June to hammer out the strategic question), Lloyd George gave this latter course the most cursory attention. In effect, what could have appeared to the opponents of the Flanders plan to be an attractive option was allowed to go by default. For this there can be only one explanation. The Prime Minister wanted it so.

In another respect also Lloyd George's conduct at these crucial discussions appears perverse. At the meeting of 21 June, when he made his principal statement, he began by taking up the position he had adopted with the French on 4 May 1917: that the ultimate decision on grand strategy rested not with the Government but with the military. The record of these proceedings finds Lloyd George saying early on:

> His view was that the responsibility for advising in regard to military operations must remain with the military advisers. Speaking for himself, and he had little doubt that his colleagues agreed with him in this, he considered it would be too great a responsibility for the War Policy Committee to take the strategy of the War out of the hands of the military.

He went on that if, after hearing his view, the military leaders 'still adhered to their previous opinion', then the civilian rulers of the nation 'would not interfere and prevent the attempt'. And, as he began, so he ended. After a long exposition against Haig's plan and in favour of an Italian operation, he concluded by saying that he would not be willing to impose his strategical views on his military advisers. He felt that he would not have been doing his duty had he concealed his misgivings. But if they advised against his suggestions, he would concur.

As long as Lloyd George was prepared to begin and end like this, he might as well have saved himself the trouble of further utterance. Plainly, Haig would not budge from his plan, and Robertson would not allow his reservations to place him in Lloyd George's camp. With whatever qualifications and after however many delays in authorization, the campaign in Flanders would go ahead.

If Lloyd George was in truth allowing Haig and Robertson to make this vital decision, in despite of his own judgement, then he was engaged in abdicating his constitutional responsibility. The ultimate decision rested with him, and he had neither the right nor the power to transfer it. Yet it may be guessed that, notwithstanding his own statements, this was not what Lloyd George was doing. As long as he was almost ignoring the existence of a plain alternative to Haig's scheme, it is legitimate to doubt whether he was singleminded in his opposition to the Flanders offensive. After all, that offensive was not so very different from the French operation on the Chemin des Dames and the British attack at Arras, which earlier that year he had enthusiastically sponsored.

No doubt there was a part of Lloyd George that utterly resisted another great blood-letting on the Western Front. This same part of him had pondered, on 1 August 1914, opposing Britain's intervention in the war. And it had caused him in November 1916 to consider escaping the 'bloody business' of the War Office by becoming food controller. But, consistently, when the time for contemplation ran out the war-rejecting side of Lloyd George was not uppermost. Always, in the end, he concluded that the war must be fought, and to a finish. He had already provided the wherewithal, in men and weaponry, for great offensive battles. He would also, however reluctantly and even resentfully, provide the go-ahead.

Haig, and Haig's plans, may not have been what Lloyd George wanted. But Haig saw the war big, as did Lloyd George (and, early in 1917, as had Nivelle). The aspirations of Rawlinson and Plumer, as of Pétain, to 'bite and hold' were small-scale by comparison. A war pursued by their means might continue for not much short of forever. It is not marvellous if, at the War Policy Committee, Lloyd George gave their views cursory attention. Nor does it defy comprehension that he failed to employ his undoubted powers to veto Haig's endeavours.

In his war memoirs Lloyd George provides a (much quoted) description of how on 19 June Haig advocated his plans to the War Policy Committee:

> he spread on a table or desk a large map and made a dramatic use of both his hands to demonstrate how he proposed to sweep up the enemy – first the right hand brushing along the surface irresistibly, and then came the left, his outer finger ultimately touching the German frontier with the nail across.[6]

This demonstration clearly made a profound impression on Lloyd George – as evidenced by his vivid recollection of it. By the time he came to write about it his response was one of rage. Nearer the event, Haig's exposition may have aroused in him – however unwillingly – some responsive chord. Indeed, it is quite probable that it got home to him much more nearly than to the more stolid Robertson. After all, when on other occasions Lloyd George had expounded his own strategic views, his hands must have moved with similar fluency over maps of the Balkans and southern Austria, sweeping across mountain peaks and rivers as if they presented little obstacle.

The ability to conceive strategy in large terms, to crave for big results, to welcome a campaign only if it promised to eliminate one adversary or another, bound Lloyd George to Haig in June 1917. It ensured that, with whatever expressions of dismay, the Prime Minister would employ his authority for Haig's purposes.

II

It has been noted that four out of Haig's five army commanders possessed expertise in

---

[6] *War Memoirs of David Lloyd George*, 2-volume edn (London: Odhams Press, 1938), vol. 2, p. 1277.

the 'bite and hold' type of operation. None of them was chosen to initiate the Flanders battle.

Rawlinson, following what was adjudged his success in the Somme campaign, believed late in 1916 that Haig had promised him the job. In his diary for 30 December he referred to 'my big push at Ypres' intended for the following July (and wondered if the Germans would hold out that long). By January 1917 Haig was reconsidering. Rawlinson was being relegated to direction of the coastal operation. The primary attack, it seemed, would be initiated by the man who had spent so long in the Ypres salient: Plumer. But despite Plumer's subsequent success at Messines, he in turn was passed over. This was not because Haig's favour had meanwhile fallen on Horne or Byng, on account of their coup at Vimy Ridge. The choice fell on the comparatively youthful cavalryman, Hubert Gough.

Not until 6 September 1917 did Rawlinson discover (as he recorded in his diary) 'why D. H. put Goughy in to do the attack instead of me': 'It was because he thought Goughy the best man he could choose for the *pursuit.*' The Australians who had fought at Bullecourt could have spoken pungently about the likelihood that Gough would create such a breach in the enemy line as would facilitate a pursuit. And the forces engaged at Arras on 9 and 10 April could have drawn on experience to say whether, even if a breach was accomplished, any pursuit was likely to follow. In short, by choosing Gough, Haig was embarking on the Ypres campaign determined to disregard the lessons offered by the fighting so far that year.

With the change of man there occurred a shift in objective. Had Plumer been in overall control, the success at Messines would presumably have been followed fairly shortly by an attack on the next obvious target: the Gheluvelt plateau, to the east of Ypres. This would have advanced the process of freeing Ypres from constant oversight by the enemy. Haig, in transferring direction of the campaign to Gough, was making it plain that his prime concern was not the security of Ypres. It was those large goals about which his hands had spoken so eloquently to the War Policy Committee.

Gough responded by seeking to accomplish not a limited push east but a considerable thrust north-east. In a sense he had little choice. Starting late in July, he had not much more than a month in which to get forward towards the Belgian coast; for September, according to the calculations of the Admiralty, was the latest date when conditions would be suitable for a landing from the sea. Yet, as Haig was coming to realize, an advance in the direction Gough was proposing would not be secure as long as the German artillery could harry it from its position on and behind the Gheluvelt plateau.

While this change in the director and in the direction of the campaign was taking place, time was being lost. Six weeks passed between Plumer's blow at Messines and the opening of Gough's offensive. This was to prove a heavy deprivation. Precious fine weather passed unused. And the Germans further strengthened their defences.

The enemy defences, in any case, were considerable. Gough's preparatory bombardment, of a fortnight's duration, drew a severe rejoinder from its adversaries. And although the British artillery – blessed with the information provided by a real, if sometimes precarious, superiority in the air – delivered a great many shells upon the German guns, it did not vanquish them. When the time came for the attack the infantry encountered punishing enemy barrages. And, further on, other grim obstacles awaited them. The machine-guns in the German forward zone were housed in concrete pill-boxes, immune to all but a direct hit from a heavy shell and exceedingly difficult for the attacking forces to suppress. And the enemy had to hand highly trained counter-attack troops, to be brought into battle as the depleted British infantry were still endeavouring to consolidate new positions.

While the offensive was only a matter of hours old, a further barrier to British success presented itself. Seating himself at a conference with his corps commanders on the evening of 31 July, Gough burst out: 'What a perfect bloody curse this rain is!' It should be said that the rain, falling with little interruption for the ensuing fortnight, was a two-edged sword. It brought no joy to the German fighting men: water rose in their trenches; signals for artillery support sometimes went unseen; and the movement forward of supplies, reserves, and counter-attack troops was severely hampered. But the encumbrances created by the downpour weighed much less heavily on the forces seeking to sit tight than on those endeavouring to struggle forward. In the rains of early August the Flanders terrain, with its clay soil and high water level, and with its drainage system wrecked by the preparatory bombardment, became in itself a cruel obstacle to any British advance.

In the outcome the first month of the attack accomplished little towards Haig's larger objects. In the early stages Gough, anxious to progress north-east in accord with the overall plan but harried by Haig to make sure of the plateau to his east, spread his guns and troops evenly along the whole front of attack. This reduced his chances of succeeding anywhere. Only the opening day, 31 July, yielded anything tangible. Gough attacked with nine divisions on a 10-mile front, with flank support on his left by the French and on his right by Plumer. A push of 2 miles on his left, with similar progress by the French, was the furthest advance that could be retained against German counter-attacks; although a somewhat smaller advance on his centre-right was probably more useful, as it captured German observation positions.

But even this modest progress only drove home the conundrum that Haig had set Gough. No secure advance could be made towards the north-east while the Germans held the Gheluvelt plateau. But if too much effort were devoted to taking out the plateau, there would be insufficient campaigning time left that year for an advance north-east.

Willy-nilly, Gough (along with Haig) found himself being forced to settle for smaller goals. But thereafter even limited progress proved elusive. Large efforts on 10 and 16 August were pretty dismal failures (again, except on the left). Heavy German shelling, the wretched condition of the terrain, and determined counter-attacks by the enemy were more than the assault forces could overcome. Gough thereupon drew the obvious conclusion. According to his own account,[7] he informed Haig that 'tactical success was not possible, or would be too costly under such conditions, and advised that the attack should now be abandoned'.

Haig resisted this conclusion. He did not allude to the great prospects that had but recently beckoned him. He simply claimed that 'we have no alternative. We must continue.' He evidenced the precarious state of the Russians, Italians, and French; along with the submarine menace, air raids on southern England, and his own difficulties with Lloyd George. The only army that could be relied on to go on fighting and wearing down the enemy, he asserted, was the British. So the campaign must continue.

These considerations would hardly have convinced the Commander-in-Chief had he not already been determined to maintain the offensive. It is sometimes claimed that what particularly influenced Haig was the enfeebled condition of the French army. He needed therefore (this argument runs) to go on attacking the Germans, however vainly, so as to keep them from assaulting the French. No evidence has been adduced for this view. What is plain, on the contrary, is that he often justified these operations by

---

[7] Anthony Farrar-Hockley, *Goughie* (London: Hart-Davis, MacGibbon, 1975), pp. 224–5.

claiming that the French were prepared fully to participate in them. As for his assertion that the British now had the only army left capable of fighting the Germans, this might appear to require precisely the opposite course from that he was advocating. For if Haig was in truth commanding the Allies' only reliable sword, that seemed cause enough for not further wearing it away in costly offensives.

Ultimately, in any consideration of the grounds for attacking or calling off the attack, reason very easily merged into rationalization. Arguments pro and con were so compounded of hopes and fears, of inspired guesses and misgivings, that any decision-making was in considerable measure a game of chance. Haig, having gambled on an offensive, would continue to place his stakes on that course for a considerable time yet.

More curiously, his civilian masters did not intervene to stop him. When the War Cabinet had belatedly approved the offensive, it had done so with the proviso that it would not accept 'protracted, costly and indecisive operations as occurred in the offensive on the Somme in 1916'. Should the results not seem to be commensurate with 'the effort made and the losses incurred', then the War Cabinet would re-examine the whole question 'with a view to the cessation of this offensive and the adoption of an alternative plan'. The fighting in August had produced minimal advances at a cost of nearly 70,000 casualties. So the War Cabinet apparently had ample grounds for calling an immediate halt. It failed to do this. In time Lloyd George would argue that his military advisers had fed him with misleading information. Given the state of civil-military relations, he can have expected nothing else. Anyway, no cheerful colouration could make it seem that the British had secured key objectives when these clearly remained in German hands.

Yet the same apparent infirmity of purpose that had caused the Prime Minister to authorize the offensive now seemed to prevent him from giving it the *coup de grâce*. The reason is plain. Lloyd George's endorsement of the campaign was a good deal more

Plate 37   *An artillery observation post in a shell crater.*

positive than he cared to recognize. The limitations placed by the Cabinet on its authorization were in large measure play-acting. They provided an appearance of responsible decision-making. They looked well on the record. But no actions were intended to flow from them.

The War Cabinet, like Haig, had made its gamble. And like him, it would persist in the course it had chosen, hoping – if with increasing disbelief – for some return.

III

The first month of Third Ypres, though it imposed most of its suffering on the infantry, was primarily an artillery battle. The bombardment that preceded the first assault on 31 July was fired by over 3,000 guns, of which nearly 1,000 were heavy – that is, one gun for every 6 yards of front.

One artillery officer who served under Gough's command penned, not long after the war, a tribute to the weapons he tended:

> What a dignified old autocrat a gun was! What a suite of servants and attendants he required to wait on him. He could go nowhere and do nothing without a whole retinue of attendants. We were all his servants – we were there for no other purpose than to wait on him. That is all we had been trained for, that is all we had come to France for. A battery of four 6 inch Howitzers demanded the services of a Major, a Captain and at least four Subalterns and about 120 other ranks to wait on them, also four F.W.D.s [four-wheel drives] to draw them and a column of about 15 three ton lorries with the necessary A.S.C. [Army Service Corps] drivers and officers. All of these just to wait on four guns. You would see a battery on the road, – the four guns in front, looking very solemn and dignified, with all this following in attendance.

The author of these words, Lieutenant E. C. Allfree, was not a professional soldier.[8] Fourteen months before the opening of Third Ypres, he had been a practising solicitor in south-western England. (So he would be again in 1920 when, aided by a diary kept at the time, he recorded his war experiences.) A married man with four children, he was 36 years of age when, following his attestation under the Derby scheme, he was called up in June 1916. In the ensuing year he trained as an artillery officer, took part in the later stages of the Vimy Ridge operation, and was present throughout the battle of Messines. Then, late in June 1917, his battery was transferred to XIV Corps of Gough's Fifth Army and moved to a position 5 miles north of Ypres.

By the time Allfree arrived there it was apparent on every side that a big push was on hand. The Germans responded to their appearance with heavy shelling, which knocked out some neighbouring guns as soon as they were installed. The position where the guns were to be sited had already been assigned. The major in charge of the battery, with considerable prescience, objected to the directive that the guns be placed in pits, arguing that, should it rain, the pits would fill with water and the trails of the guns become buried. The colonel who had given the order proved oblivious to this wisdom.

Throughout the night of 13–14 July Allfree was engaged in getting guns, men, and stores into their forward positions. The road up was under constant shelling and several breakdowns occurred, but by the early morning all was in place. On 15 July they got down to business. There followed 'a most intense artillery bombardment of the Enemy's trenches, wire and strong points for about a fortnight before the Infantry

---

[8] Allfree's account of his war experiences is in the Imperial War Museum.

attack. He [the enemy] is very strongly entrenched here with masses of wire entanglements.'

Allfree's battery was sited on the extreme British left, adjacent to the French, in flat country leading up to the Yser canal (which here ran parallel to the front line). On the far side of the canal the ground rose to Pilckem, a low ridge providing the Germans with good observation. His battery was placed in a small copse, where some huts and shanties provided accommodation for the officers. The rank and file were supposed to sleep in slightly excavated pits, it being impossible to make dug-outs in this wet, low-lying country; but they were soon shelled out and had to be provided with a reinforced basement in an old house.

Allfree spent 17 July in the observation post (OP) 3 miles ahead of the battery. This was a key position for the gunners, and the officers, in rotation, spent a whole day there. It was also an object that the enemy searched for devotedly. Allfree went forward equipped with glasses, telescope, maps, compass, and protractor. He was accompanied by two telephonists, whose job it was to seek after and to repair breaks in the line so that the OP could maintain contact with the battery. The officer's task was to select targets that he could observe and whose position was known on the map, and to direct fire upon them. Once the battery was firing accurately at these, it could shoot at more distant objectives just by reference to the map. The varying atmospheric conditions made it necessary to go through this procedure every day and sometimes more than once a day.

During these weeks of preliminary bombardment the OP was situated in a ruined house in the deserted town of Boesinghe. The periscope used for surveying the enemy lines was disguised with a sandbag. 17 July proved relatively safe in this forward position.

> There was one continuous and unceasing whistle of our shells passing over the whole day. I counted 150 large shells pass almost immediately over the O.P. in five minutes, that is 1800 in an hour. The same thing was going on all along this front, all day and every day for a fortnight before the attack! . . . A certain number of Boche shells were bursting behind me. But the number coming our way was not to be compared with the number we were sending over.[9]

Nevertheless, enemy shelling cut the telephone line, and it was some time before repairs could be effected. And on his return that evening Allfree found that the battery had been under heavy fire. Indeed, enemy shelling recommenced as he returned at 7.30 p.m. (he had started out at 6 a.m.) and kept him from his dinner for two hours. Thereafter they remained in the mess until 1 a.m. as their huts were under constant fire, and then a gas attack kept them in their masks for another hour. After that Allfree was able to retire and 'slept soundly till 8.30 A.M.'.

On the next two days the harassment by shells and gas recurred. But thereafter until the opening of the offensive they received less attention. However, the enemy located the observation post and made its occupancy so precarious that a new position had to be found.

Zero hour for the infantry assault was dawn on 31 July. Exactly on time all the batteries opened up, 'and the stillness of early dawn was rent by the sudden roar'. Allfree's job was to ensure that the guns were lifted from line to line in accordance with the timetable of the attack. Yet even in these last hours of relatively fine weather, the moist, clayey soil rendered the alterations difficult. 'The trails [of the guns], after firing a number of rounds, would become very deeply buried, necessitating much digging

---

[9] In the bombardment leading up to 31 July the BEF fired 4.25 million shells – 4.75 tons for every yard of front.

with pick and shovel and strenuous heaving to get them out – thus some time was unavoidably lost, and the full allotment of rounds on each target could not always be got off in the time.' Nevertheless, in this northernmost part the British attack made progress. Pilckem Ridge was taken. The Germans counter-attacked, and the artillery received many SOS calls. Locating these, pulling out the guns, aligning them on the new targets, and commencing firing, all with the least delay, kept the battery 'pretty busy'. The counter-attacks failed.

Allfree's account of 31 July concludes: 'Towards the end of the day it came on to rain hard and continued throughout the night.' Of 1 August he says: 'A soaking wet day following a beastly wet night. A real brute of a day!' The battery was supposed to move forward that night, so he was sent to Boesinghe – no longer deserted as it had been when it had housed their OP – to find cellars for their accommodation. On his way he observed that the mud was already hampering movement. A horse harnessed to a wagon was up to its stomach in mud, with its front legs stretched out before it along the ground: 'It had to be dug out.' And in Boesinghe Allfree encountered stretcher-bearers bringing in the wounded from mud swamps on the other side of the canal. A stretcher party of six men took four hours to bring in a single wounded soldier.

Allfree, after appropriating cellars from infantry in the process of moving out, returned to his battery. There, to his relief, he learned that the move forward had been delayed. On 2 August rain was constant, and the battery's advance was again postponed. On 3 August: 'Still raining. Great difficulty experienced with the guns owing to the trails and wheels sinking so deeply into the soft, wet ground.' Only on the afternoon of 5 August did the weather clear temporarily.

At 6.30 the next morning Allfree set off for the battery's new observation post, in company with telephonists and a recent arrival who was replacing one of their number sent home with a nervous breakdown. This OP was across the canal, about 4 miles forward. In early morning mist and through dreadful mud they could find their way forward only by following the telephone wire – which anyway had been cut in five places and needed joining and binding. It was 9 a.m. before they reached their destination (Captain's Farm). Within minutes they were under heavy shelling. They tried some alternative locations but all came under fire. The visibility was now much improved, and to get good observation Allfree moved into a shallow trench 100 yards in front of the farm. They were in full view of the enemy and continued under bombardment through the day. Somehow they survived.

The new position, despite its hazards, provided good observation. Thanks to his now considerable experience, Allfree was able to expose himself only momentarily when spotting the fall of shells. By counting from the word 'Fired!' at the other end of the telephone and employing his knowledge of the time of flight, he needed to witness the journey of the shell only in its last two seconds. Jackson, the new man, remained calm and cool.

At 5.15 p.m., with their telephone line out of action, they decided to call it a day. This meant returning over some 500 yards of exposed ground; in the course of their journey a shrapnel bullet struck Jackson in the back. He remained able to walk and, with Allfree's aid, was conducted to a dressing station, the first staging-post on the way back to Blighty. Allfree repaired to dinner and bed: 'It had not been a pleasant day.'

At last the battery was able to move forward, although a caterpillar tractor had to be summoned to extract the well settled guns. A period of relative freedom from German bombardment followed. The greatest cause of misery was the regular visits to the OP. Allfree was there again on 14 August. This time he contented himself with remaining in Captain's Farm and did not try to reoccupy his forward trench. The shelling, if not as bad as on the previous occasion, was considerable. His comment regarding his safe return is illuminating:

> There is no doubt that one's pleasures in life depend to a great extent on contrasts. It was a real pleasure to get back to the comparative safety of the mess in the evening, with cheery company, a few whiskeys and a game of cards and some dinner after a bad day at the O.P. all on your own.

On 16 August another big infantry attack was launched. Allfree had devoted the previous day to working out lines and elevations, and spent the early morning of the 16th firing in support of the infantry, lifting the barrage at the appropriate times. Once more on this left wing of the British attack – but only there – a measure of success was enjoyed.

For the artillery, of course, progress had its disadvantages. The guns had to be moved forward yet again, and a new observation post had to be established. In some ways it proved the most disagreeable so far. They were to occupy it for the next two months, and Allfree calls it 'the chief bugbear of my life. I measured time from one O.P. day to another.' The post consisted of a former German machine-gun pill-box, situated in a desolate battlefield swept by shell fire. It could be reached only by means of an interminable walk over duckboards winding between shell craters. The post itself, once attained, provided fairly extensive observation, and it was strongly constructed. But its isolation was oppressive. And it was not a savoury spot. Two dead Germans and a dead Briton lay close at hand, and in the improving weather blue-bottle flies swarmed over them. (These creatures also attacked the sandwiches of the living.) Yet the position was too dangerous to justify an attempt to bury the corpses.

So Allfree and his companion gunners passed the remainder of August 1917. On the 25th they were badly strafed by heavy shells and their position was much knocked about, but their guns were not damaged. On the 26th a replacement arrived for the wounded Jackson: he was an artist in civil life, 'and I don't think he appreciated soldiering in the Great War very much'. On the 31st Allfree had a day off in St Omer. A band was playing in the park, and the elite of the town were out in their Sunday best. It was a lovely summer's day.

IV

The meagre gains of the August fighting, coming on top of months of struggle at heavy cost, did not escape criticism. This was to be heard even in military circles. Rawlinson, in his diary for 5 September, records a conversation with Archibald Montgomery, his devoted Chief of Staff: 'Archie tells me he hears the Army is beginning to lose faith in D.H. I hope this is not so.' It was to be heard yet more loudly in political and journalistic circles. In London on 19 August Rawlinson noted: 'People criticise D.H. for being too optimistic.'

There is no way of gauging the extent of such feelings. But on occasions they were expressed with great (if intemperate) pungency. A single letter must serve as illustration.

Ellis Ashmead-Bartlett was a newspaper correspondent who had seen war, often from a headquarters position, in many parts of the world. He had been a witness of the Graeco-Turkish war of 1898 (when, accompanying the Turkish army, he had been taken prisoner by the Greeks), the Russo-Japanese war, French and Spanish operations in Morocco, the Italian invasion of Tripoli, and the first and second Balkan wars. He had himself fought (with the rank of lieutenant) against the Boers. He had also engaged in political conflict, having contested both general elections of 1910 in the Conservative interest. In 1915 he had been chosen by the National Press Association to represent London newspapers throughout the Gallipoli campaign, but his blunt comments on the British command had brought him into conflict with Sir Ian Hamilton, who had sought to suppress his views. In 1916 he had represented the London press with Joffre's headquarters.

On 1 September 1917 Ashmead-Bartlett wrote a letter to R. D. Blumenfeld, editor of the *Daily Express*.[10] If hardly the product of a dispassionate or judicious mind, it serves to indicate that the blood toll of these battles was being keenly felt, and that responsibility for British losses, whether justly or not, was being laid at the door of the military command.

> Dear Blumenfeld,
>   These d— optimistic generals, who live in French Chateaux, who can save their pay, who are having the time of their lives, who are covered with variegated ribbons, who do not have 'to go over the top', who are, with some few exceptions, men of the most indifferent intellect, who long to keep the war going as long as the Government will send them human fuel – so as to prolong their own feeble hour of imaginary glory – have succeeded in the last five months in killing[,] permanently maiming or wounding
>   21,727 Officers
>   344,614 N.C.Os & Men.
>   They have hardly moved the Hun an inch.
>   Each of these 376,341 human beings has, or had, a soul, a family & his own particular interest in life. The entire population is in fact being handed over to Executioners in Red & Gold who in normal times might earn after many years service from £400 to £500 a year as Clerks to those whose destinies they now control.
>   The World is full, and is fed up with, swaggering Nonentities.
>   Yours
>   E. Ashmead-Bartlett

It is unlikely that 'the World' was as convinced of the validity of his views as Ashmead-Bartlett believed. But the expression of such judgements in influential circles did not bode well for the British command as the Ypres campaign entered its second phase.

---

[10] The letter is among the Blumenfeld papers, House of Lords Record Office.

43

'THE AWFULNESS OF IT ALL':
THIRD YPRES, PART II

As a runner, finding your way around in that sea of mud was the worst part. . . .
  The moment you set off you felt that dreadful suction. It was forever pulling you down, and you could hear the sound of your feet coming out in a kind of sucking 'plop' that seemed much louder at night when you were on your own. In a way, it was worse when the mud didn't suck you down; when it yielded under your feet you knew that it was a body you were treading on. It was terrifying. You'd tread on one on the stomach, perhaps, and it would grunt all the air out of its body. . . . The smell could make you vomit. And you could always tell whether it was a dead Jerry or a dead Tommy. The Germans smelt different in death.
  Reminiscence of Charlie Miles, a private in the 10th Battalion, Royal Fusiliers, during
  Third Ypres

A party of 'A' Company men passing up to the front line found . . . a man bogged to above the knees. The united efforts of four of them with rifles beneath his armpits, made not the slightest impression, and to dig, even if shovels had been available, would be impossible, for there was no foothold. Duty compelled them to move on up to the line, and when two days later they passed down that way the wretched fellow was still there; but only his head was now visible and he was raving mad.
  Major C. A. Bill of the 15th Battalion, Royal Warwickshire Regiment

I

In one respect Haig responded positively to the failure of August. Late in that month he took overall direction of the Ypres campaign out of Gough's hands. Criticism of Gough's sharp temper and overbearing, inefficient staff was widespread. It went hand in hand – as we have seen Rawlinson noting with concern – with a deal of criticism of Haig himself both at home and in the army. Not for the last time, Haig would see the demotion of Gough as a way of repairing his own position.
  It was hardly the case that Gough had failed. Rather, he had been given a task that lay beyond the realms of possibility. And, increasingly, he had then been harried by his chief to perform a quite different task: a set-piece assault upon the Gheluvelt plateau. For this he had no obvious qualifications. Now Haig handed the direction of the operation to Plumer. This meant a return to the step-by-step methods that alone had yielded some success that year.
  At the same time Rawlinson received a first hint that his coastal operation, which was an integral part of Haig's grand design, might never take place. Kiggell, Haig's Chief of Staff, told him on 23 August that the risk of a landing on the Belgian coast was not worth the candle: for, should it fail, the War Cabinet would seize the opportunity both to remove Haig and to send British divisions to Italy. Another month would pass before

this decision became official. But this first intimation, coincident with the change from Gough to Plumer, had a clear meaning. Only in one set of circumstances might the Flanders campaign still retain some potentiality for achieving 'decisive' results (to employ a much used, and desperately imprecise, expression): if the German army really were on the verge of collapse.

Plate 38   *The environs of Passchendaele after their capture by the British.*

Hitherto, Gough's Fifth Army had embraced the British forces on the left and in the centre of the attack. Plumer's Second Army on the right had conformed to Gough's plan. Hereafter the forces in the centre became part of Second Army, and Gough on the left conformed to Plumer's plan. Only with reluctance did Plumer agree to take over direction of the operation. And he laid down firm conditions. Although time in which there was reason to expect good weather was running short, he insisted on his customary careful preparations. This demand, given the ill-repute of Gough's allegedly slapdash methods, Haig could not reject. Plumer also required a much greater concentration of guns and men, for a lesser area of attack, than Gough had been allowed. By the device of drawing resources from Rawlinson, Horne, and Byng, he was able to bring against the enemy, on but half the length of front, a weight of fire twice that earlier available to Gough.

Plumer also paid attention to the employment of his infantry. He placed an Anzac corps in his centre, so bringing against his key objective some of the most offensively minded troops now at the disposal of the British army. And he employed new infantry tactics. These thinned out the troops attacking his first objectives, which – having been battered by his artillery – were not expected to offer a stiff resistance; employed rather more troops against his second objectives; and brought the largest complement of infantry against his third, where maximum resistance might be anticipated. Further, the infantry were to attack not shoulder to shoulder but in small groups. Each group had a specific purpose, such as the capture of a particular strong point or pillbox. And they were to be followed closely by moppers-up so as to consolidate what had been gained.

Plumer planned to launch four distinct operations, each with a limited objective lying inside artillery range. He believed that, when completed, these would deliver into British control the whole of that ridge which almost semi-circled Ypres: from Messines in the south (already in his hands), through the Gheluvelt plateau in the centre, to Passchendaele and Westroosebeke in the north.

Plumer's first blow did not fall until 20 September. The weeks of fine weather that preceded it raised morale and made the battlefield more manageable. And the strong forces of infantry were supported by a weight of artillery fire that, once again, set a precedent in war. Thus the barrage that went ahead of the attacking forces consisted of five belts of fire to a depth of 1,000 yards: three belts of high explosive, one of shrapnel, and one of machine-gun bullets. As long as the infantry could keep in step with the careful timing of this barrage, they were unlikely to encounter prohibitive resistance.

The result was a commendable success. The attack began at 5.40 a.m. In the centre, by midday, all but one of the planned objectives had been taken, and the advance could halt. More than three hours passed before the German counter-attack forces appeared, and these – with the RFC providing a flood of information to the British artillery – were stopped dead in their tracks. On the left of the operation Fifth Army, with a larger frontage of attack and a smaller concentration of artillery, also achieved most of its objectives.

Plumer struck next on 26 September, after a pre-emptive attack by the Germans on the previous day had been warded off. Once more the combination of massed artillery, a strong leavening of enthusiastic infantry, and limited objectives ensured success in good time. Once more the German counter-attack troops appeared late, had to advance into a hostile fire zone, and failed completely.

Here were undoubted successes. For the forces engaged they provided the plain satisfaction of having participated in operations that were skilfully conducted and whose objectives had been certainly accomplished. Even so, these attacks should not be accorded credit for more than they had achieved. The gains in territory were decidedly restricted. And the losses sustained were considerable: some 35,000 British casualties between 20 and 26 September. The German artillery, if sometimes silenced, was never vanquished. And the narrow area of Plumer's advances provided the enemy gunners with a concentration of targets.

Plumer struck again on 4 October. This time he fired no preparatory bombardment, bringing down his barrage only as the assault troops went over the top. His guns did not want for targets. The German command had been disturbed by its failure on the two previous occasions to get its counter-attack troops forward soon enough. So it had brought into the fire zone large numbers of men to make an attack themselves. A bombardment laid down by the Germans in anticipation of their own assault caused many casualties among the Anzacs assembled for the advance. But Plumer's attack proceeded nevertheless. And the German troops, awaiting their own zero hour, were hit first by the intensive shelling and then by the assaulting infantry. They were overwhelmed. 'It was the barrage that made them break,' according to the contemporary account of the journalist Philip Gibbs. (Gibbs found it 'agony' to be in proximity to one of the 'big-bellied howitzers' when it was firing. 'It rose like a beast stretching out its neck, and there came from it a roar which clouted one's ear-drums and shook one's body with a long tremor of concussion.')[1]

---

[1] Philip Gibbs, *From Bapaume to Passchendaele 1917* (London: Heinemann, 1918), pp. 313–16. This book consists of Gibbs's dispatches as a war correspondent with the British army.

The attack was a decided success. According to General Monash, commander of one of the Australian divisions: 'We got absolutely astride of the main ridge.' And one Australian captain related how some of his forward troops had looked on 'green fields and pastures, things of course we had never seen before in the Ypres sector'.[2] The centre of the ridge, due east of Ypres, was now with minor exceptions in British hands.

Yet 4 October was in every sense a limited success. On average the British advanced only 700 yards, to a maximum of 1 mile in the centre. That left the northern part of the ridge firmly in enemy hands. And the cost was mounting unrelentingly: 26,000 casualties for the one day. The heaviest losses, as ever, were among the infantry. But they were increasing disproportionately among the artillerymen. Their guns also, which anyway were wearing out in large numbers, were falling victim to enemy shelling. Philip Gibbs described the peril under which the gunners were operating:

> .... I saw the enemy's shells searching for them, flinging up the earth about their batteries, ploughing deep holes on either side of them. They worked in the close neighbourhood of death, and at any moment, between one round and another, a battery and its gun teams might be blown up by one of those howling beasts[3]. . . .

Infantrymen on their way to the front line sought to get clear of the artillery positions as speedily as possible, such was the weight of fire that these were attracting.

In these circumstances it is not certain that, even had conditions remained propitious, further attacks by Plumer would have proved quite so successful. The thrust of his artillery weapon was becoming blunted. And the Germans were adjusting their tactics in response to his methods. In view of the limited advances that he was seeking to accomplish and the reduction in his artillery preparation, they were once more strengthening their forward positions in preparation for his next effort.

Haig, it need hardly be said, saw the three blows of 20 and 26 September and 4 October as the prelude to greater things. He had more or less decided to call off the coastal operation. But he was bringing into the Ypres sector six fresh infantry divisions. And he was placing two divisions of cavalry in their rear, with another three close at hand. These reflected his belief that German resistance was about to collapse. In that event, he calculated, the railway bottleneck in Flanders would restrict the enemy's powers to rush in reinforcements. 'I am of opinion,' he told Plumer and Gough on 28 September, 'that the enemy is tottering, and that a good vigorous blow might lead to decisive results.'[4]

Rawlinson had a long talk with Haig the following day, and found him 'v. pleased with the recent successes East of Ypres'. He would attack again on 4 October, but his next big effort – 'for which he means to bring up the Cavalry' – would be on the 10th. The French would participate on the left, and Haig was also hoping (as it proved, in vain) for a large diversionary effort by them on the Chemin des Dames. Rawlinson's diary entry goes on: 'If only the weather will last till then we shall do a big thing. . . . Any way D.H. is v. optimistic.'

Haig's optimism, it is pretty clear, was outrunning that of his army commanders. Rawlinson saw Plumer on 6 October and 'congratulated him and his army on their great success'. 'He was in capital form and very pleased but had some difficulty in resisting the Chiefs endeavour to push on further beyond the agreed objective.' Yet it seems that Plumer himself was becoming a deal less cautious as a result of his three

---

[2] Quoted in John Terraine, *Douglas Haig: The Educated Soldier* (London: Hutchinson, 1963), p. 366.
[3] Gibbs, *From Bapaume to Passchendaele*, pp. 321–2.
[4] Haig's diary for 28 September 1917, in John Terraine, *The Road to Passchendaele* (London: Leo Cooper, 1977), p. 274.

successes. It fell to Gough, chastened by his experiences in August, to sound a real note of caution.

From early October he had good reason to do so. For a terrible adversary had re-entered the lists. Rawlinson, in his diary for 29 September, had described as 'phenomenal' the 'spell of dry weather during so long a time in Sept.' October would provide no repetition of this phenomenon. A drizzle accompanied the attack on the 4th. Within days it had become a downpour, rendering the battlefield a 'porridge of mud'. No let-up in the weather thereafter was likely much to improve the condition of the ground.

Argument still rages as to whether the command was blameworthy for pressing ahead as if nothing had changed. One view exculpates Haig. It claims that the unrelenting rain was a cruel trick of fate. An opposite view holds that such downpours were entirely predictable for this time of year. Yet this argument about weather forecasting is pointless. It is the business of command to estimate the viability of operations in terms of whatever obstacles actually obtain. The commanders had been warranted in attacking while luck was on their side – while the 'phenomenal' dry spell in September lasted. So they had an obligation to cease attacking once luck had plainly turned against them. Moreover, the substitution of Plumer's methods for Gough's meant that the British could delay action until circumstances were propitious. The attacks of October 1917, when circumstances were anything but propitious, are hardly to be justified on the ground that fate had played a cruel trick.

Haig ignored these considerations. Making the most lamentable decision of his lengthy – and sometimes distinguished – command, he chose to press on. He had given his political masters such lavish promises that it was doubtless embarrassing to consider calling a halt with so little accomplished. (Even the notion of a coastal operation was refloated briefly in mid-October, before its final abandonment.) So he grasped at reports that German reserves were coming to an end as justification for one further blow; and, if that did not do the trick, then for a further one after that.

The hopeful information he so plainly craved was certainly being supplied him. Charteris, his head of intelligence, was seeing to that. Rawlinson records a conversation in mid-October with Kiggell, Haig's Chief of Staff, who reported that the Germans had 'used up' 48 divisions in the Ypres area since 31 July, while 'we have only had 23 in the line so far.' (Only German divisions, it will be noted, got 'used up' when they took part in this fighting.) Rawlinson commented: 'This is very satisfactory but it comes from Charteris I fear!!' Nor was this the sole occasion on which he expressed disbelief in, and alarm at, Charteris's optimism – 'doing D.H. a lot of harm' and 'really a serious danger' had been his remarks in mid-August. Yet it says nothing for Haig's judgement that, while others perceived the falsity of Charteris's estimates, the Commander-in-Chief allowed himself to be deluded.

Anyway, Charteris was not without an element of caution. He could see good reason in early October for stopping the offensive at that stage. And he was aware that, before many months were out, it would not be a case of the British pushing on. They would have their work cut out to withstand the threat posed by German reinforcements from the Eastern Front. Haig was open only to the optimistic side of Charteris's perceptions. That was because he wanted to hear nothing but the information that would support the course he was determined to take.

Admittedly, the claim has been made that, quite apart from the enemy's possible collapse, the offensive had to be continued. This view has been stated – it was certainly not argued – by Charles Harington, Plumer's (highly efficient) Chief of Staff.[5] It rests

---

[5] See ibid., pp. 298–9.

on the assertion that the British 'advanced troops' could not have spent the coming winter in the positions they had secured by 4 October. Consequently, great and costly exertions had to be made to conquer Passchendaele ridge to the north. That the British, having gained the south and centre of the ridge, would be at an advantage if they also secured the northern section is not to be doubted. But it does not follow that they could not have remained where they were during the winter. For they did precisely that during the whole of October, despite calamitous attempts on their part to push on. The German occupancy of the northern part of the ridge no doubt was a source of inconvenience, and some cost, to the British. So was the British occupancy of the centre and south of the ridge to the Germans. It is difficult to see why that situation must prove unendurable for the one side and advantageous for the other, and so had to be rectified by a terrible blood-letting.

II

Thanks to the weather, the next stages of the offensive involved a quality of misery that almost beggars description.

On 9 October, after almost five days of steady rain that had turned into a downpour, a further attack was delivered. Once more Plumer's Second Army played the main role, with the crucial area of attack – two spurs leading up to Passchendaele Ridge – assigned to the Anzacs. On the left the Fifth Army, with assistance from the French, was to move north and take Poelcapelle. It says much for the failure of the main endeavour that it was by the name of this subsidiary objective, Poelcapelle, that the day's fighting came to be known.

Conditions for the advance simply did not exist. The long journey up to the forward zone must proceed over sheets of duckboard secured as best could be upon the mud. Heavy use and enemy shelling caused many of the boards to sink, or become slimy, or break up. Hence the movement of pack animals and pioneer groups bringing up supplies, and of infantry moving up for the attack, proved more than ever gruelling and precarious. Animals became frantic or stubborn. The shells being brought forward acquired a coating of mud which the batteries had to clean off one by one. As for the infantry who were to make the attack, their wretched journey to the start line took hours longer than the timetable allowed. A lieutenant in a Lancashire regiment recalls:

> It was an absolute nightmare. Often we would have to stop and wait for up to half an hour, because all the time the duckboards were being blown up and men being blown off the track or simply slipping off. . . . We were loaded like Christmas trees, so of course an explosion near by or just the slightest thing would knock a man off balance and he would go off the track and right down into the muck.[6]

In consequence, large numbers of the infantry had no sooner completed the long haul to the front than they had forthwith to go into the attack – whereupon they lost even the unreliable support of the duckboards and entered the mud proper. A private in the same Lancashire regiment states:

> As dawn approached I could see the faint outline of a ridge about four or five hundred yards in front, and we then left the duckboards and moved to the white tape fastened to iron stakes. It was knee-deep in slush, and then I heard the sound of a heavy gun firing and immediately our barrage started; but we had not then arrived at the jumping-off point. Heavy German shells were already falling amongst us and shrapnel was flying all over the place. There were shouts and screams and men falling all around. The attack that should have started never got off the ground.[7]

---

[6] Lyn Macdonald, *They Called it Passchendaele* (London: Michael Joseph, 1978), p. 197.
[7] Ibid., p. 198.

Another burden weighed down the infantry. Their artillery support was now proving woefully inadequate. Even when the gunnery was accurate, the waterlogged earth absorbed the high-explosive shells before they detonated, thereby much reducing their effectiveness. (Equally, of course, the condition of the terrain lessened the impact of German shelling, to the benefit of the attacking infantry; but hardly to an extent that offset the additional difficulties being imposed on them by the state of the ground.) But what hampered the attack far more was the fact that the prevailing conditions told heavily against accuracy of artillery fire. The *sine qua non* of Plumer's method happened to be precise and overwhelming shelling of enemy positions, destroying wire, suppressing machine-guns and artillery pieces, and forcing the survivors in the German front lines to keep their heads down while the British infantry got forward. On 9 October this quality of bombardment was quite lacking. Weather conditions rendered aerial observation for the guns impossible. And particularly among the field artillery, which had to be further forward and so got the worst of the ground, the weight of the weapons and the impact of their recoil caused the guns to sink. Some, indeed, vanished out of sight: a flag marked the point of their submergence.

For the infantry the results were calamitous. It might have been thought that the tales of troops advancing without effective artillery cover, to be stopped dead by uncut wire and massacred by undamaged machine-guns, belonged to the inexperience of 1915 and the vainglory of 1916. Yet they were repeated in, of all deplorable places, the Ypres quagmire on 9 October 1917.

On the following day Charteris, to his credit, found himself oppressed by the human misery inherent in these operations. When attacks were going well, he wrote, it was possible to pass 'without much thought all the horrible part of it – the wounded coming back, the noise, the news of losses, the sight of men toiling forward through mud into great danger'. When they did not succeed, 'somehow one sees and thinks of nothing but the awfulness of it all.' He 'got back very late and could not work, and could not rest'.[8]

It may have been true at other times that Charteris went out of his way to buoy up Haig's confidence. The reverse was certainly the case at this stage. Charteris describes Haig that evening as 'still trying to find some grounds for hope that we might still win through here this year, but there is none'.

The process of 'winning through' was nevertheless resumed three days later, despite Gough's urging for a postponement. The sorry decline that was occurring in the quality of preparations and in the confidence of those engaged is epitomized by the diary entry of a 'senior and experienced officer' of the New Zealanders: 'We all hope for the best tomorrow, but I do not feel as confident as usual. Things are being rushed too much. The weather is rotten, the roads very bad, and the objectives have not been properly bombarded. However, we will hope for the best.'[9] Guns could not be got forward, so that the infantry, in C. E. W. Bean's telling expression, 'attacked virtually without protection.'[10] Uncut wire, unsuppressed defenders, and mud once more reduced the endeavour to futility. The same New Zealand officer wrote, after the event: 'My opinion is that the senior generals who direct these operations are not conversant with the conditions, mud, cold, rain and no shelter for the men'; 'the Germans are not so played out as they [the senior generals] make out'; and all recent

---

[8] John Charteris, *At G.H.Q.* (London: Cassell, 1931), p. 259.
[9] Quoted in H. Stewart, *The New Zealand Division 1916–1919* (Auckland: Whitcombe and Tombs, 1921), p.292. The officer is not identified.
[10] C. E. W. Bean, *Official History of Australia in the War of 1914–1918* (Sydney: Angus and Robertson, 1938), vol. 4, p. 912.

attacks 'lack preparation, and the whole history of the war is that when thorough preparation is not made, we fail.' This diarist concluded: 'You cannot afford to take liberties with the Germans. Exhausted men struggling through mud cannot compete against dry men with machine guns in ferro-concrete boxes waiting for them.' As an indictment of the command, this was complete.

In the aftermath of these impoverished gambles, the directors of the campaign decided to halt attacks until an improvement in the weather at least permitted artillery participation. And the Anzacs having been driven as far as they could go, the Canadians were now called in to provide the shock troops for further advances. Relatively fine weather supervened in the middle of the month and continued to the eve of the next big effort on 26 October. But with midnight came a change. 'Great clouds gathered across the moon. It began to rain gustily, and then settled down to a steady, slogging downpour.'[11] Once more Gough appealed in vain for delay. But at least on this occasion the assault forces were in position well before the time of attack. And the artillery situation was as much improved as the dismal terrain would allow. The guns had been got forward, 'out of one bog into another bog – those monsters of enormous weight, which settle deeply into the slime.' It was a considerable achievement:

> Not only the gunners, but all the transport men, all the pioneers and working parties have done their utmost. Battalions of fighting men, busy not with their rifles but with shovels and duck-boards, worked in the mud – mud balking all labour, swallowing up logs, boards, gun-wheels, shells, spades, and the legs of men, the slime and filthy water slopping over all the material of war urgently wanted for this morning's 'show'.[12].

On the Fifth Army front the advance was again defeated by the terrain. But the Canadians in Second Army managed by great exertion and against strong opposition to struggle forward about one-third of a mile. So a footing was secured on one of the spurs leading towards Passchendaele.

The effort was resumed on 30 October. The rain, having desisted for three days, did not begin in earnest until noon. Yet even without it the condition of the ground remained a severe obstacle, and on the left proved quite prohibitive. The Canadians, again at abysmal cost, got ahead once more. They were now on drier ground and within 500 yards of Passchendaele.

The two Canadian divisions that had spearheaded these attacks of late October were replaced by two others. On 6 November, following some overcast but not too wet days, the culminating bid for Passchendaele was launched. Aided by powerful artillery support, the Canadians stormed the ruined village. On 10 November an attempt was made to extend the British hold on this part of the ridge. It progressed between one-third and half of a mile on a very narrow front. These two Canadian divisions were then also withdrawn, having suffered nearly 16,000 casualties.

The conquest of the ridge was not complete. To the north lay its final stretches – 'the eastern wall of the Ypres bastion'[13] – with Westroosebeke and Staden as significant objectives. But on 12 November Haig, having recently stated his intention to 'continue the offensive on the Flanders front for several weeks yet',[14] at last decided to halt the operation.

---

[11] Gibbs, *From Bapaume to Passchendaele*, p. 359.

[12] Ibid., p. 358.

[13] Douglas Wilson Johnson, *Battlefields of the World War* (New York: Oxford University Press, 1921), p. 74.

[14] Haig to Robertson, 31 October 1917, in Terraine, *The Road to Passchendaele*, p. 314.

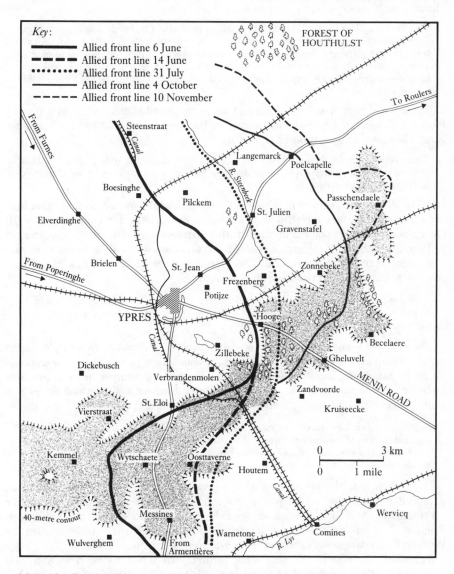

Map 10 *British offensives in Flanders, June–November 1917: Messines (commencing 7 June) and Third Ypres (31 July – 10 November)*. Source: *Banks*, Military Atlas, *p. 173*.

III

In terms of territory captured, it was no telling achievement. On 15 November Haig bluntly admitted as much in a letter to Robertson:

The positions already gained on that front fall short of what I had wished to secure before the winter cessation of active operations. Our present position about PASSCHENDAELE, and between that place and the YPRES–STADEN Railway may be difficult and costly to hold if seriously attacked. Although the German losses have been severe this year I think this latter contingency must be expected as soon as the enemy realises that he has regained the initiative.[15]

At the same time Rawlinson, who had taken command of Second Army following Plumer's transference to Italy, was surveying the new British line and finding it not good. He wrote in his diary on 12 November:

There is no cover for the men in the forward areas and in the low lying parts the mud & shell holes are appalling – it is worse than the Somme was last year and we shall have heavy losses from sickness.

Least of all was the position in Flanders satisfactory in the overall situation that now obtained – a situation foreshadowed for many months. In a memorandum of 10 December Rawlinson pointed out that British divisions were now well below strength and would remain so in the spring, whereas the Germans in the West would soon gain large reinforcements from Russia. The Germans were likely to attack as early as possible to forestall the Americans. Rawlinson wrote:

That this policy is the right one from the German point of view there can be little doubt. It is, so far as can be seen, his last chance of achieving a victory with superior numbers at the decisive point.

The most likely target, Rawlinson considered, was the Second Army front, 'owing to the very sharp salient at Passchendaele, and the consequent possibilities of concentrating an overwhelming fire of artillery against it'. The present position, he reiterated, was 'defective, not to say dangerous'. For it constituted a salient against which the enemy could concentrate his larger artillery pieces on two-thirds of the arc.

Nothing we can hope to do can make the line now held a really satisfactory defensive position. We must therefore be prepared to withdraw from it, if the Germans show signs of a serious and sustained offensive on this front, or if an attack elsewhere necessitates the withdrawal of more troops from the front of the Second Army.

Here, then, was the outcome of Haig's great effort in Flanders. His forces had advanced to a position whose partial evacuation was, in a matter of weeks, under consideration. And so meagre an accomplishment had been secured at terrible cost. The toll of casualties, at least for the immediate future, left the British army on the Western Front dangerously short of men *vis-à-vis* their enemy.

Moreover, the cost to the army went further than actual losses. A gunner who participated in the fighting of 11 October recalls how a 'month of incessant attacks', with little progress, appalling casualties, and severe fighting, was having 'a bad effect on the morale of everybody concerned'. 'Reinforcements of the new armies shambled up past the guns with dragging steps and the expressions of men who knew they were going to certain death. No words of greeting passed as they slouched along; in sullen silence they filed past one by one to the sacrifice'.[16] In December the Minister for

---

[15] Transcript provided by Professor David R. Woodward.
[16] Aubrey Wade, *The War of the Guns* (London: Batsford, 1936), pp. 57–8.

National Service, in a Cabinet document written with the concurrence of General Macready (Adjutant-General to the Forces), wrote of increases among soldiers of drunkenness, desertion, and psychological disorders. Men home from the front, he said, frequently spoke with great bitterness about 'the waste of life during the continued hammerings against the Ypres Ridge'.[17] And Philip Gibbs, in retrospect, noted: 'For the first time the British Army lost its spirit of optimism, and there was a sense of deadly depression among many officers and men with whom I came in touch.'[18]

One aspect of this 'deadly depression' was a waning of confidence in the military command. It was by no means universal. But it was manifesting itself, to a degree not previously apparent, in political circles, in the press, and among the fighting forces. It is astonishing that, with the fearful consequences of Nivelle's great promises and scanty achievements before him, Haig acted as he did: first proposing objectives that had little chance of accomplishment, and then hammering away when all belief in their attainment had vanished.

Certainly, it can be argued that responsibility should not be sheeted home to Haig alone. He acted in the context of an ill-considered craving for victories among the populace. And, as has been said more than once, he could never have proceeded without the endorsement, however grudging, of a Prime Minister whose strategic visions were probably more grandiose, and certainly more insubstantial, than his own. Yet the responsibility of Haig, as conceiver and chief executor of the campaign, cannot be put aside. If he is entitled – as is plainly the case – to a measure of credit for the victories of 1918, he can hardly be excused a good share of the discredit that attaches to the calamities of Third Ypres.

Offsetting these calamities, it is important to notice, lies one element of profit. Not only British (and some French) troops endured martyrdom in the Ypres campaign. German gunners perished under British counter-battery fire. German front-line troops crouched in pill-boxes and shell holes and what remained of trenches, there to be set upon by savage bombardments followed by determined infantry assaults. And German counter-attack forces, also needing to move forward through quagmires, were flung repeatedly into withering artillery barrages and against devoted infantry resistance. Many died or were maimed or became prisoners. The morale of the remainder can hardly have been unaffected. If it is tempting to deplore battles of attrition, it is at least important to recognize that they are games in which both sides, if not necessarily to the same extent, are the losers.

Which side lost the more heavily in this instance is a disputed question, and one to which a definitive answer may never be forthcoming. It is likely that German losses fell markedly below those of the Allies: 200,000 German casualties as against 250,000 British (plus a considerably smaller number of French) is probably as close a figure as we are likely to get. As with the Somme, some authorities wish to raise the German total so as to take account of the 'lightly wounded', a category that they argue was present in Allied but not in enemy computations. It is easy to dispose of this view. If we set aside the wounded altogether and look only at figures of the dead, these show a clear discrepancy between the two sides, in line with the overall totals given above. And not even the British official historian has suggested that German figures omit a category of 'lightly dead'.

Yet it remains a fact that, viewed absolutely, the blood cost of Third Ypres to the

---

[17] David R. Woodward, *Lloyd George and the Generals* (East Brunswick, NJ: Associated University Presses, 1983), p. 230.

[18] Philip Gibbs, *Realities of War* (London, Heinemann, 1920), p. 396.

Germans was heavy. Plainly, it contributed substantially to the long-term debilitation of German fighting strength. Assuming the Allies did not run dry first, Germany could not go on indefinitely sustaining this erosion of its human resources.

Nevertheless, from the British angle two further points need to be made, and they detract considerably from the force of this one positive achievement of Third Ypres. The first is this. In the short term, following the collapse of Russia, Britain had more important objectives to serve than shedding German blood at heavy cost to itself in casualties and morale. It needed all the fighting men it could rally for the defensive. And it needed them in good heart and in strongly prepared positions, so as to ward off a temporarily more numerous adversary.

The second point concerns the longer term. If the enemy, to employ the words of Rawlinson, should miss out on 'his last chance of achieving victory', his 'superior numbers' would steadily become inferior. For, as America mobilized, the forces opposing Germany would mount. If the burden of inflicting casualties on the enemy, at similar cost to the Allies, had not already been borne by Britain and France, it must in time fall on the Americans. And the USA, given its much greater resources and its so far negligible human involvement in the war, was far better equipped to bear these losses than were its 'associated powers'. It was part of the culpable folly of Third Ypres that it caused the British army to pay a greater share of the blood cost of ultimate victory than either the military circumstances of the moment or the long-term resources of the British people could in any way justify.

44

RINGING OF BELLS, WRINGING OF HANDS: CAMBRAI, NOVEMBER–DECEMBER 1917

Byng's victory yesterday near Cambrai very comforting. . . . A good comment upon L. G.'s sarcastic references to the Western front.

Colonel Repington's diary, 21 November 1917

The Germans claim to have taken 6000 prisoners and 100 guns from Byng. . . . The War Cabinet naturally asked questions about the loss of German moral[e], upon which Haig and Kiggell were always harping. . . .

Colonel Repington's diary, 4 December 1917

. . . . one of the most ghastly stories in English history. . . .

Northcliffe on Cambrai, 12 December 1917

I

As Third Ypres ended the British command was looking elsewhere for a success on the Western Front. It had good reasons for so doing.

Certainly, it was now very late in the campaigning year. But Haig was badly in need of a victory, however modest. His political chiefs, with reason, were raging against the dismal outcome of his Flanders offensive. Less reasonably, they were also employing another stick with which to beat him. In October Italy's defences had collapsed temporarily at Caporetto, and this was somehow seen as a judgement on Haig, who earlier had opposed an Italian offensive. The British commander's position appeared precarious.

Nevertheless, Haig would probably not have agreed on a last fling for 1917 if the prospects had not looked hopeful. The overriding considerations were military. To the south of the bog-ridden Flanders battlefield lay a stretch of ground that still constituted good campaigning territory. And both artillery and tank officers had been devising plans for an attack there – plans that might employ artillery to better use than ever before and tanks to good use for the very first time.

Out of these considerations emerged the battle of Cambrai. Conducted by elements of General Byng's Third Army, it had been in preparation since September. The attack went in on 20 November, and the ensuing struggle continued for a fortnight. Its results fluctuated wildly. The initial assault was highly successful. Indeed, church bells were rung throughout Britain to celebrate the victory. Then, ten days later, events turned sharply against the British forces, and before long the War Cabinet was instituting an inquiry into the setback.

II

Cambrai has gone down in history as the first great tank battle. Apart from the fact that only one side was employing tanks, this description requires qualification. The part played by armoured vehicles was substantial and without precedent. Yet, as has been justly said, 'In no case were tanks able to accomplish anything lasting by themselves.'[1]

All arms, and not least the artillery, made a vital contribution. Prior to 1917 the gunners had rarely been able to deliver an effective blow against enemy defences – and especially against enemy artillery – without much preparatory ranging and blanketing fire. So, in preparing a way for the infantry, the artillery had advertised the imminence of an attack. In the course of 1917 such preliminary firing had become less and less necessary, thanks to developments already referred to: flash-spotting and sound-ranging. This mattered greatly at Cambrai, where surprise was of the essence of the operation. Byng's artillery, having got the new methods down to a fine art, would open up only as the infantry and tanks started forward, confident that its shells would fall with savage effect upon their designated targets. As even an historian of the armoured vehicle admits, this employment of an unregistered artillery bombardment was 'an innovation as important as the tank'.[2]

But if the tank contributed less to the early success of Cambrai than is sometimes supposed, this operation is rightly regarded as a milestone in the development of the armoured fighting vehicle. For one thing, this was the first occasion when tanks were available in substantial numbers. For another, at long last they were being employed in a manner appropriate to their particular attributes.

Perhaps it is not surprising that a year had elapsed before the tank was used creatively. Much military prejudice (from which Haig, to his credit, was exempt) persisted against it. In the case of one divisional commander, such prejudice would again be evident on the opening day of Cambrai. But there were also the tank's undeniable limitations: its proneness to breakdown, the inexperience of its crews, and the amount of gunfire that it attracted from the enemy. On this last account, it is worth noting, the infantry had usually been giving tanks assigned to help them a wide berth.

What remained to be seen was how much the tank could achieve if employed in terms of its own capabilities. Hitherto tanks had been used only in driblets, not *en masse*. And they had never been employed on level ground, only on terrain cratered by shell fire and often soaked by rain. That the tanks had not distinguished themselves during the Third Ypres campaign is hardly surprising. Of the opening day one participant has written:

> Although they gave valuable assistance to the infantry, they could not swim. Most of the day's history for tank commanders could be summed up in the fateful words, 'Bellied in boggy ground.' Many, by use of their unditching beams, managed to struggle out of the oozy slime, but the majority sank lower and lower, until the water came in through the sponson doors and stopped the engines.[3]

And as the Third Ypres campaign began, so it continued. The tanks were committed to a sequence of actions 'without adequate preparation in unsuitable conditions and with a complete disregard of the characteristics of the machine'.[4]

Yet the year since the tank's début had not been wasted. For one thing, the Mark IV

---

[1] Major-General H. De Pree, 'The Battle of Cambrai', *Journal of the Royal Artillery*, vol. 55, July 1928, p. 253.

[2] Kenneth Macksey, *Tank Warfare* (London: Rupert Hart-Davis, 1971), p. 46.

[3] Lieutenant F. Mitchell in *I Was There!*, issue no. 31, p. 1253.

[4] Major-General H. L. Birks in the *Royal Armoured Corps Journal*, vol. 3, October 1945, p. 207.

model, which began making its appearance in April 1917, was a considerable improvement on its predecessors. Its infirmities, certainly, were many. Like previous models, it was prone to breakdown. With a maximum speed of 4 m.p.h., its progress across the battlefield was cumbersome; according to one account: 'It moved so slowly across country that if you were watching a tank attack you would often find it difficult to tell if the tanks, a few hundred yards away, were moving or not.'[5] A change in direction required the endeavours of four out of its crew of eight and brought the vehicle to a halt for something like 15 seconds – 'a long time when under fire'.[6] It remained as vulnerable as ever to shelling, and small-arms fire could send a shower of metal sparks flying around its interior. (The crew were issued with chain-mail masks, but these could so impair vision as to become unusable.)

Even so, compared with its predecessors the Mark IV possessed an improved motor, extended range of travel, and – in the 'male' version – more effective fire power. (The installation of Lewis machine-guns in the 'female' version proved a misjudgement.) And its stronger frontal armour gave a measure of immunity from what had become increasingly dangerous armour-piercing bullets.

But of greatest significance was the fact that only now had tank production in Britain reached a level at which this weapon had the weight of numbers largely to affect a military operation. This matter of numbers, depending on the painful development of productive capacity, needs to be stressed. For it bears on a judgement by Winston Churchill. He writes in *The World Crisis*:

> Accusing as I do without exception all the great ally offensives of 1915, 1916, and 1917, as needless and wrongly conceived operations of infinite cost, I am bound to reply to the question, What else could be done? And I answer it, pointing to the Battle of Cambrai, '*This* could have been done.' This in many variants, this in larger and better forms. . . .

Such a judgement, though often quoted with approval, is downright absurd. In the necessary absence of great number of tanks, *this* could not remotely have been done in 1915, 1916, or most of 1917. (Even in 1918, as events would show, the British army could repeat only on a few occasions the massive tank strike of Cambrai.)

It was not only in respect of enhanced quality and quantity that, by late 1917, the tank was at last equipped to make a considerable impact on the battlefield. In October 1916 Haig had established a Tank Corps (although not initially giving it that name). Its job was to devise proper organization and employment for the new weapon. Its chief was Hugh Elles, an early enthusiast for the tank and a man who, if not of outstanding ability, aroused great confidence in his force. Seconding him was J. F. C. Fuller, a staff officer who combined administrative efficiency with a capacity for creative thought on military matters. Both of these qualities he began applying, with all the fervour of a convert, to his new task. Under the aegis of Elles and Fuller, the Tank Corps acquired a body of trained personnel blessed with considerable *esprit de corps*. And they were soon equipped with a set of tactics for the right employment of their vehicles in battle.

III

With the cessation of fighting in Flanders, the moment was at hand to put machines, men, and tactics to the test.

The area chosen for this operation lay in the Somme sector, to the south of Arras. In

---

[5] 'Cambrai', Part 3, in the *Royal Tank Corps Journal*, June 1936, p. 37.
[6] Ibid.

certain respects it was well suited for an offensive. The country consisted of rolling uplands, its valleys and ridges not too abrupt. The ground was chalky and hard and had not been cratered by constant shelling. Its surface of strong grass was ideal for the progress of tractored vehicles. Further, this area was lightly held by the Germans, who treated it as a rest zone for worn-down troops ('the sanatorium of the Western Front'), on the assumption that the Hindenburg defences would render it immune. Finally, just to the rear of the British front line lay a number of features, particularly Havrincourt Wood, providing excellent concealment for the instruments of a massed assault.

Yet an offensive here would be no walk-over. On its right and left the area was constricted by two canals, 6 miles apart, that, when reached, would impede further progress. Within the region of initial attack lay a number of villages and two considerable ridges, Flesquières and Bourlon, which must pose serious obstacles to an advance. And still closer to hand lay the Hindenburg system, 5½ miles deep. These defences, exploiting the configurations of the ground, presented a series of hazards: 'vast barbed-wire aprons, still unrusted and in sunlight giving off a blue sheen intimidating to behold';[7] then concrete dug-outs housing batteries of machine-guns; then trenches of a width and depth seemingly beyond the capacity of any tank to surmount; and, finally, a variety of artillery. One British officer called it 'the most perfect system of trenches I saw during the whole time I was in France'.[8]

If the British were to attack here, it must be with a clear intent. Fuller's initial scheme was for no more than a raid of a few hours' duration. Spearheaded by tanks, it would take prisoners, disrupt the enemy's defences, and shake German morale. It would not retain ground or exploit any initial success. Such a conception had little to recommend it. The raid, for little gain, would reveal the tank's mounting potential and so invite enemy counter-measures. And, given that many tanks (on past performance) would break down during the advance, Fuller's scheme would present to the Germans good specimens of the latest British model.

The plan adopted by the Third Army staff was altogether grander. Without doubt, the attack would be intended to capture territory. More, this was meant to lead to full-scale penetration and exploitation, principally by the cavalry. The communications centre of Cambrai was to be a prime objective, followed by a great drive north-westwards. This plan also invited criticism, although for different reasons. It assumed that a considerable early success, for which planning was meticulous, would lead to a major break-out, for which planning was vague. And it disregarded the fact that, by this waning stage of a terrible year, the British army was desperately drained of numbers and fighting resolve (as well as being engaged in reinforcing the Italians). Of the six divisions available to Byng for this undertaking, five had already seen much fighting that year. In short, for the moment there simply did not exist the manpower for a further large campaign.

Haig was a good deal nearer the mark when he urged an advance with limited objectives. Not Cambrai and points beyond but the proximate Bourlon Ridge (offering excellent oversight of enemy positions) seemed to him sufficiently ambitious. But although he amended, he did not veto, Byng's scheme. He was reluctant to restrict the army commander's freedom of action. And, as ever, he was tempted to believe optimistic reports about the enemy's failing morale and inability quickly to reinforce this sector. So the most he did was to lay down that he would curb the offensive after 48 hours unless it revealed clear progress.

---

[7] Cyril Falls, *The First World War* (London: Longman, 1960), p. 296.
[8] Quoted in Bryan Cooper, *The Ironclads of Cambrai* (London: Pan Books, 1967), p. 62.

Crucial to all these proposals – small, large, and medium – was the element of surprise. Several factors, some of which have already been noted, contributed to it. The proximity of Havrincourt Wood enabled huge numbers of guns and tanks and shells to enter the sector unobserved. The employment of tanks in force spared the artillery the job of cutting the wire in preparation for the advance, which would certainly have alerted the enemy. And the gunners were making their own significant contribution by firing an unregistered bombardment.

But there may have been another factor, less often remarked upon, that contributed to surprise. It is usually argued that the initial success of the Cambrai operation was wasted because Byng had no reserves on hand to exploit it. But that same lack of reserves may have contributed largely to his early success by helping to conceal from the enemy the imminence of an attack. The Germans seem to have known quite a bit about the forces opposite them. When a medical officer captured on the fourth day refused, under interrogation, to reveal the name of his brigadier, the reply came back: 'He is Pelham Burn, and he goes on leave next week!' This officer remarks: 'They knew more than I did!'[9] If the enemy were that well informed, there is every reason to suppose that he would have detected the movement of British reserves into this sector and drawn the obvious conclusion. So what helped to thwart Byng after his initial success may have aided him in making that success possible.

IV

The Cambrai assault opened at 6.20 a.m. on 20 November. A thousand hitherto mainly silent guns poured down smoke, high explosive, and shrapnel upon the German positions, shrouding the battlefield and obliging the defenders to keep their heads down.

Simultaneously the tanks went forward. All told, there were 476 of them. Ninety-eight were reserved for special duties: bringing forward supplies, reporting by wireless from the battlefield, removing barbed wire with grappling irons so as to facilitate the passage of the cavalry. The remaining 378 were fighting tanks, of which none, when it came to the day, was held in reserve. (This made the action of Elles, in riding conspicuously into battle at the head of his forces, less foolish than it would otherwise have been.) Their task was not only to crush the barbed wire and shoot up enemy forces but also to cross the German trenches. To accomplish this last, each tank was equipped with a fascine of 3 to 4 feet in diameter. It consisted of 60 bundles of brushwood, weighing 1½ tons, bound together by a chain. (The park railings of Britain, among other sources, had been plundered for this last commodity.) A trigger mechanism inside the tank released the fascine into the enemy trench. Fuller had devised a ritual whereby the tanks advanced in groups of three, using only one fascine per group for each trench. That enabled the trio to cross a succession of three trenches.

Behind the tanks, and also just about as the bombardment opened, came the six divisions of infantry. For ten days before the assault these divisions had trained with the tanks; thereby their scepticism towards the motorized arm had given way to marked confidence in it. 'For the actual attack the utmost care was taken to ensure that the assault of the two arms should be simultaneous, that the tanks and infantry which were grouped together should not miss one another, and that they should as far as possible work together throughout the advance.'[10] Again by Fuller's devising, the infantry

[9] Captain R. Tennant Bruce in *I Was There!*, issue no. 37, p. 1466.
[10] Major-General H. De Pree in *The Army Quarterly*, vol. 29, October 1934, p. 21.

(except at Flesquières, thanks to the obstinacy of the divisional general) went forward not in line abreast but in single file, so as to avoid the worst fire that would befall the tanks.

Also engaged in the attack were 14 squadrons of the RFC, not only for observation and bombing but also to harry German ground forces. Further back, and not to proceed until two and a half hours after zero, were five divisions of cavalry. Byng still believed that here lay the potential to convert a savage punch by the other arms into something more far-reaching: the unhinging of the German defences over a considerable area.

In the opening stages the progress of the attack proved irresistible. Followed by their columns of infantry, the tanks rolled ponderously onward through what the enemy had assumed was impregnable barbed wire. Then they reached trenches supposedly too deep and broad to allow their transit, unloaded their fascines, 'dipped their noses in, and came up and over'.[11] While their enfilading fire harried the trench dwellers, the British infantry moved in to complete the conquest.

John F. Lucy, now a commissioned officer, was that morning in charge of a platoon detailed to fill in British and German trenches so that the artillery could get forward. He relates: 'we witnessed the astounding sight of whole sections, and even platoons, of our infantry strolling up the opposite enemy slopes behind [the tanks].' German soldiers were fleeing or streaming forward in surrender: 'We watched the scene fascinated.' As the day progressed Lucy's platoon wandered about, smoked, and chatted in what only hours before had been 'a formidable enemy defence system': 'I collected the silly fellows and marched back gaily to bivouac.'[12]

The British assault on 20 November established a significant point. The Hindenburg system was not impregnable, at least against a skilful attack delivered in propitious circumstances. By 8 a.m. British tanks and infantry had overrun the Hindenburg Main Line over the 6 mile stretch between the two canals. By 11.30 a.m., except in the centre at Flesquières, they had taken the Hindenburg Support Line as well. By early afternoon an advance to a maximum depth of 4½ miles had been accomplished, and at least two German divisions had been put out of action – many of them taken prisoner. British casualties, by contrast, amounted to about 4,000.

But although an astonishing achievement, it remained circumscribed. For one thing, tank losses for the day – 179 altogether – were heavy, though more from mechanical breakdown and ditching than from enemy action. A good many other tanks were in need of repair, their crews in a state of exhaustion. Further, the advance had not brought into British hands any strategically important territory, and had certainly not accomplished a breakthrough. The cavalry did not start out until after midday and reached the new front line only as darkness was approaching. There enemy machine-guns awaited them. Byng's vision of a great cavalry penetration expired forthwith.

In the ensuing week little more was accomplished despite fierce exertions. The Germans abandoned Flesquières during the night of 20–21 November, but progress towards Bourlon Ridge proved arduous and costly. In truth, the conditions that had produced early success no longer obtained. The artillery lacked the mobility, the ammunition supplies, and the registered targets to repeat the compelling effect of the first morning. And the early co-ordination between guns, tanks, and infantry waned

---

[11] 'Cambrai', Part 4, in the *Royal Tank Corps Journal*, July 1936, p. 69.

[12] John F. Lucy, *There's a Devil in the Drum* (London: Faber & Faber, 1938), pp. 379–81. Lucy's Cambrai experiences did not continue in this happy vein. On 3 December, having been withdrawn from the line and then thrown in again to meet the German counter-offensive, he received severe injuries from a bomb blast that kept him in hospital until well after the end of the war.

steadily. The armoured vehicles, with their limited range of vision, passed by many enemy machine-guns (of which there were great and increasing numbers), which then wreaked havoc upon the foot soldiers. This rendered advances nugatory, for tanks on their own had no capacity to hold the territory they overran.

Haig, by the time his 48-hour deadline was over, recognized that no prospect of a breakthrough existed. Hence he terminated the attack on the right wing. But the lure of Bourlon Ridge on his left drew him on. It was to prove an unfortunate decision. The enemy were bringing in large bodies of infantry, artillery, and aircraft. Despite the aid of two divisions intended for Italy and dismounted cavalry employed as infantry, Byng could not match these numbers. Even now his troops, aided by a diminishing supply of tanks and hastily assembled artillery, might accomplish piecemeal advances. But they could make no decisive progress.

On 27 November Haig decided to call a halt. Most of Bourlon Wood had been taken, but the high ground to the west and Fontaine Ridge to the east had not. This was less than satisfactory, for it gave the British no clearly defensible line. Rather, they had secured a salient, 'a death trap in which it would have been impossible to keep troops, especially artillery, without great loss, and without the continual danger of their being cut off'.[13]

Haig, if he did not want another Ypres salient on his hands, must in time decide on a withdrawal. It was the enemy who ensured that the time would be soon.

V

On 30 November 1917 the Germans went on to the offensive at Cambrai. Their object was to entrap the British troops in their newly won salient. Although they did not achieve this purpose, the enemy inflicted heavy losses and wiped out British elation.

The main German blow was aimed at the southern part of the British advance. Byng had some inkling that an attack was coming. But he concentrated his fresh troops and most of his guns in the disputed Bourlon area to the north. So the principal enemy thrust fell upon weary troops stretched thin.

Soon after 7 a.m. on 30 November, and preceded by an intense bombardment of only an hour, the German assault descended upon this sketchily held sector. The enemy employed some strikingly novel infantry tactics – novel, anyway, for the Western Front. (They had already been applied with effect against Russians and Italians.) Their primary forces attacked in groups, infiltrating through parts of the front knocked out or weakened by the bombardment, by-passing areas of resistance, and falling with great speed on the artillery supports. By 10.30 a.m. an 8 mile stretch of the British front in the southern sector had been driven in. That placed the enemy well beyond what had been the original British line prior to the commencement of the Cambrai offensive.

Much worse threatened. For a while it looked as though the Germans would manage to swing north and achieve their purpose, that of severing the base of the salient. But soon exhaustion took its toll. And British resistance stiffened as reinforcements arrived in the form of dismounted cavalry. (Even a section of tanks – having begun entrainment on the assumption that the year's fighting was over – came hurrying in.)

---

[13] De Pree, 'The Battle of Cambrai', p. 249. Military historians are sometimes slapdash in their use of statistics, and the Cambrai salient is a case in point. According to Cyril Falls, it was 6 miles deep by 7 miles wide. According to the official history, it was 4 miles deep by 9 miles wide. As a depth of 6 miles would place the British right through the Hindenburg system and a depth of 4 miles would not, the difference seems of some importance.

The Germans attacked also in the northern sector, against the head of the salient, but with no comparable success. The crest of Bourlon Wood went to them that day, and a few places of minor note thereafter. But by 3 December both sides were prepared to call a halt. However, the German counter-offensive had rendered yet more awkward the salient produced by the initial British advance and made mandatory a partial withdrawal. This was completed by 7 December. In terms of fighting, if not of post-mortems, the Cambrai episode was at an end.

For the British it was hardly a satisfactory conclusion. They had retained marginally more ground, and of more tactical importance, in the northern part of the sector than they had relinquished in the southern. But it was a trivial advantage from a battle that had engaged more than a quarter of their forces on the Western Front (20 divisions, five of them cavalry, and three brigades of tanks). They had suffered 45,000 casualties, at least as many as those sustained by the enemy. And they had lost one-third of the tank personnel and two-thirds of the actual tanks. Nothing was left of the heady assumption of the first day that a great success, and the special favour of the Deity, were at last being bestowed on British arms.

Not least was the outcome disillusioning for the men on the ground. One infantryman who, having been engaged in the early advance, was called back to stem the Germans relates of the last phase:

> When we . . . looked across towards the positions now held by the Germans, there was none that could not help thinking of the great and successful work of our troops during those four splendid days from the 20th November onwards, of the ground that had been captured from the enemy, of the comrades who gave their lives for that ground. And now that territory no longer belonged to us, but was once again in the hands of the foe.[14]

All told, Cambrai had proved an ambiguous episode. And its ambiguity lay in more than the fact that, for the British, success had been followed by setback. The achievement of the opening day had sprung from a mixture of the particular and the general. For this occasion, as perhaps for no other, the British had been blessed with means of concealment and good campaigning territory. Yet in other respects the opening strike appeared the harbinger of a new sort of offensive: in the employment of an unpredicted bombardment, the co-ordination of artillery, infantry, and tanks, and the use of armoured vehicles *en masse*. What remained unclear was which elements had tipped the balance: the particular or the general.

One thing, however, was not in doubt. Neither the British on 20 November nor the Germans 10 days later had revealed any capacity to convert early success into wide-scale exploitation. After everything, stalemate dominated the Western Front as 1917 drew to its unlovely close.

---

[14] 'Cambrai, 1917 – the Impressions of an Infantryman' pt. 3, in the *Royal Tank Corps Journal*, 1927–8, p. 327.

45

MIXED FORTUNES ON THE PERIPHERIES

I

In addition to these struggles against the naval and military power of Germany, British forces in 1917 were engaged in battles with Bulgars and Turks.

The war with Bulgaria absorbed little of Britain's attention. This remained primarily a French concern, with aid from Serbs, Italians, and Russians as well as Britons. It was the French who took the initiative in planning military operations. And it was the French who decided to resolve the political situation confronting the Allied forces in this region.

Ever since their arrival in Salonika the troops under Sarrail's command had been standing on neutral – and increasingly unfriendly – Greek soil. In mid-1917 Sarrail decided to settle this matter by carrying to the ultimate stage his intervention in Greek internal affairs. The King of Greece was forced to abdicate in favour of his second son, whose views on politics – in so far as he had any – were considered acceptable. The dissident Greek politician Venizelos was swiftly installed as Prime Minister, and one of his first acts was to declare war on the Central Powers. From the Allied point of view, these less than noble events constituted the only positive achievements in the Balkans for 1917.

The military situation improved not at all. The prospects at the beginning of the year were summed up some months later by the newspaper correspondent Ward Price. With the coming of spring and the drying of the mud, he wrote, the Allied force in the Balkans stood at the highest point of efficiency it had yet reached. During the winter of 1916–17 reinforcements had arrived, reserves of ammunition been accumulated, and new roads been placed under construction. So everything was prepared for a spring offensive, 'which should test whether, with the means then at the disposal of the Allies in the Balkans, it was possible to dislocate the Bulgar front at any point in such a way as to compel their whole line to fall back, and so win not a local tactical advantage, but a larger strategic one.'[1]

Yet from the start, according to this account, there were grounds for doubting whether such a result could be achieved. The weight of enemy effectives was as great as or greater than those of the Allies. And the enemy had incomparably the advantage of positions. Moreover, the Bulgarians could await a spring offensive confident that, if they did sustain much of a reverse, Germany would be swift to react:

> for the Germans would not spare any effort to maintain the present position in the Balkans. Hitherto they have had considerable reason to be satisfied with the existing state of affairs. The Salonica Expedition is not doing them any vital harm; it is Bulgars, not Germans, who are being killed by our attacks.

---

[1] G. Ward Price, *The Story of the Salonica Army* (London: Hodder & Stoughton, 1918), p. 191.

Map 11 *The Balkan states and the Salonika campaign.* Source: *Charles and Barbara Jelavich,* The Establishment of the Balkan National States, 1804–1920, *Volume VIII of* A History of East Central Europe *(Seattle and London: University of Washington Press, 1977), p. 262.*

In Ward Price's view, the presence of Allied troops near the borders of Bulgaria actually served Germany's turn. For it kept the Bulgarians firmly in the German camp and so ensured communications between Berlin and Constantinople. 'Moreover, the German General Staff knows that Salonica is a heavy drain upon the resources of the Allies.' They were therefore well content to preserve the existing deadlock.[2]

It is plain that the situation of early 1917 placed Sarrail, as Allied commander, in an unenviable position. He was in charge of an enterprise that (Ward Price admitted) had not yet 'achieved anything of striking utility from the standpoint of the major aims of the war'.[3] Consequently, it enjoyed little endorsement from the Allied Governments. Admittedly, Britain's new Prime Minister had once been much excited by operations in this area. But in 1917 other regions were arousing his enthusiasm – Italy, Palestine, even (for a spell) the Western Front. Hence he had neither much attention nor great resources to devote to Macedonia. So if Sarrail were to rescue this region from continued neglect, he needed to pull off some striking success. Yet, given the limited resources available to him and the ability of his opponents to match any increase he might be granted, it was not evident how he could bring this about.

In the spring of 1917 Sarrail, undeterred by this uncomfortable logic, made his greatest effort on the Salonika front. He planned to employ his multi-national forces along a 140-mile line in five distinct attacks. Thereby he hoped to open the way to an advance on Sofia.

Unlike in previous offensives in this region, the British were intended to make a major contribution: an attack on the Allied right against the hill positions adjoining Lake Doiran. Sarrail had been prevailed on to give them this task by Sir George Milne, commander of the British Salonika Army. It was a formidable undertaking. The Bulgars opposing the British had a slight advantage of numbers and a huge advantage of position; for Doiran, it has been said, was 'one of the most formidable natural fortresses in Europe'. It consisted of a succession of rocky ridges climbing to more than 2,000 feet above the lake, heavily fortified and ideal for observation.[4]

In an attempt to overcome these disadvantages, both the first British assault on 24 April and that which followed a fortnight later were launched in the dark. But the enemy countered this by skilful use of searchlights. And the Bulgarians again proved themselves formidable warriors. As the British forces struggled up the rocky slopes during the first attack, their adversaries could be heard calling through the din, 'Come on, Johnny.'

In the event, although British troops on both occasions managed to get a footing in the enemy's trenches, their limited gains proved untenable and had to be abandoned. The cost of these gallant but abortive assaults – some 5,000 British soldiers killed or incapacitated – was small by Western Front standards. But it was considerable in terms of Britain's commitment to this region. Indeed, these two attacks were responsible for one-quarter of the casualties suffered by British forces in the three years of the Balkans campaign.

What was true of the British sector proved to be the case along the whole line of attack: 'nowhere was it found possible to drive the desired wedge into the Bulgar front.'[5] In short, Sarrail's spring offensive had failed utterly. Its single accomplishment

---

[2] Ward Price, *The Story of the Salonica Army*, p. 192.
[3] Ibid., p. 193.
[4] Alan Palmer, 'Salonika: Sarrail's Spring Offensive', in *Purnell's History of the First World War* (London: Purnell & Sons, 1969–71), issue no. 81, p. 2256.
[5] Ward Price, *The Story of the Salonica Army*, p. 205.

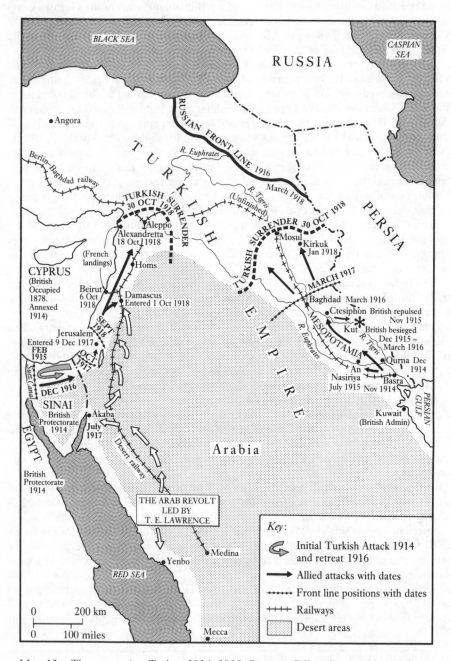

Map 12   *The war against Turkey, 1914–1918.* Source: *Gilbert*, Recent History Atlas, p. 35.

was to reduce yet further his waning reputation and to confirm British disbelief in the whole undertaking.

Sarrail would have no opportunity, between this setback in the spring and the end of 1917, to redeem his position. In the interval two of the six British divisions that had participated in the offensive were removed, along with much heavy artillery. That was evidence enough of Lloyd George's lack of enthusiasm for both the campaign in Macedonia and its French commander. Only Sarrail's political following in Paris enabled him to survive a while longer. Then in November 1917 Georges Clemenceau, a devoted opponent both of the Salonika expedition and of its commander, became Premier of France. That sealed Sarrail's fate. On 10 December he was abruptly recalled.

II

If Macedonia had even less to offer the Allies in 1917 than it had done in 1916, the same was not true of Mesopotamia. There what had earlier been a saga of mismanagement and humiliation was transmuted into a succession of victories. In the process General Maude became a national hero.

This happier course sprang largely from the availability of resources. The British in Mesopotamia now possessed a three-to-one superiority in men, a clear preponderance in river craft and flying machines, sufficient land transport to enable them to manoeuvre away from the river, and – perhaps most important of all – a weight of artillery that could in time crush any Turkish position. Nevertheless, success in this region still had to be earned. The land of Mesopotamia provided a fiercely hostile setting for offensive operations. And the Turks, especially early in the year, continued to be devoted adversaries holding well prepared positions.

Maude's first task was to recapture Kut on the left (northern) bank of the Tigris. During February he outflanked the powerful defences below Kut by advancing up the southern bank of the river until he was above the fortress. Then, by means of pontoon ferries and in face of considerable resistance, he established a bridgehead across the river. This forced the enemy to abandon Kut in haste. The event was more than symbolic. It was a telling demonstration of British superiority in numbers and supplies. The morale of the Turkish soldiery and the credibility of the Turkish Commander-in-Chief (who had limited his forces opposing the British because he was planning a grand sweep through Persia) had sustained a severe check.

Maude was no longer under restraint from London. Whatever Robertson's objections, the Government would not be denied further successes in a region recently associated with calamity. Hence the pursuit up the Tigris proceeded, delayed less by the enemy than by the long haul of supplies up the tortuous river. At the start of March British forces, virtually unopposed, entered Ctesiphon, scene of Townsend's first setback. In the ensuing days, just downstream from Baghdad, they encountered some determined resistance. But soon they were thrusting into, and also threatening to outflank, their opponents. At this point the Turkish commander recognized that he must abandon Baghdad before his escape route to the north was closed.

On 11 March Maude's forces entered Baghdad. According to an Arab commentator, this was the thirtieth time the city had fallen to a conqueror during its history, and never before had the event passed off so quietly. Back in Britain, needless to say, jubilation was considerable.

At this point the authorities in London were ready once again to call a halt. An advance beyond Baghdad promised to be limitless, making escalating demands at a time when the country's ability to supply overseas campaigns was being gravely threatened. Still, just to consolidate his hold on the city Maude must go a bit further. Otherwise the enemy might break down the retaining banks on the main rivers, so reducing Baghdad to an island surrounded by floodwaters.

By the end of April the flood-control points had been secured and the enemy driven yet further away. (As it happened, these were particularly uncomfortable actions for the British troops. They were still clad in rough serge winter uniforms, and the hot season had arrived prematurely.) The intense summer that followed prevented nearly all campaigning between May and August – and should have prevented what little did take place. In September action was resumed to push the Turks still further away. But this was of minor import. The one noteworthy event in Mesopotamia in the second half of 1917 was the death of Maude, from cholera. Not everything about his conduct of military operations had been praiseworthy. But overall, with an adequately supplied force facing a numerically inferior enemy, he had shown what a rigorous and efficient staff officer could accomplish in an inhospitable environment.

On a larger view, the merit of what took place in Mesopotamia in 1917 was open to question. We have seen that the Balkan campaign was allowed to languish because no one in authority in Britain believed that what could be accomplished there justified the expenditure of the men, weapons, shipping, land transport, and medical supplies necessary for success. By the same token, it was not evident that avenging the shame of Kut or acquiring even so glamorous a prize as Baghdad was the wisest use of British resources. As A. J. Barker points out, had the Turks been employing against Maude a force at least as big as his own, the undertaking might have been worth while. But this was not the case. In the eighteen months following Townshend's surrender at Kut, the Turks with about 50,000 men held down a British force with a ration strength nearly ten times as great, constituting a heavy drain on Britain's shipping; 'from the Turkish point of view this must have been very well worth while.'[6]

Of course, had Britain been engaged only in a war with Turkey, it could doubtless have afforded such expensive successes. But Turkey, far from being its sole, was not even its primary adversary. The action taken in Mesopotamia back in 1914, designed to safeguard Britain's oil supplies, had made sense in the context of an Anglo-German war. That was hardly the case with the operations that followed. These weighed on Turkey less than they did on Britain, and they weighed on Germany scarcely at all. Ward Price's judgement on the Salonika campaign, that it played the German game by imposing casualties on the British at a cost not to Germany but to one of its allies, applied equally to Mesopotamia.

In short, unless one subscribes to the notion that Turks, like Bulgarians, were props without whose support Germany would collapse, it is difficult to perceive the wisdom of purchasing costly if sometimes glamorous victories in Mesopotamia. Britain could ill afford to devote huge quantities of resources to defeating non-German adversaries in an Anglo-German war.

III

It is a moot point whether a similar judgement is to be passed on the other campaign which the British were waging against the Turks in 1917: that in Palestine and the Hejaz.

At the year's opening the War Cabinet, despite the change of Prime Minister, did

---

[6] A. J. Barker, *The Neglected War: Mesopotamia 1914–1918* (London: Faber & Faber, 1967), p. 362.

not opt for any large movement in this region. Murray, the Commander-in-Chief in the Middle East, was enjoined to some activity in southern Palestine. But he was also informed that, far from securing reinforcements, he would be relieved of one division. This left him with five divisions: three infantry and two cavalry. (The latter, one Anzac and one British Yeomanry, were by now very experienced.)

Given that a modest advance was expected of him, Murray's obvious course lay in the direction of Gaza. This fortress of long standing, situated on a low hill 2 miles from the sea, commanded the coast road into Palestine. But capturing it would not be easy. Its natural defences against an attack from the south were strong. And British movements were constricted by the problem of supplying water (not least for the 9,000 horses) beyond the railhead. To surmount the latter problem, an attack must capture Gaza, where wells could be found in abundance, within 24 hours. Otherwise the assault forces would have to withdraw to their starting point.

The operation against Gaza on 26 March was skilfully planned and well executed. The infantry pressed up from the south with determination. Meanwhile the cavalry first outflanked the town on the landward (eastern) side and then swung west to encircle it. Within the allotted time Gaza was cut off, and its capture was imminent. But the inadequacy of available communications, and poor work by the staff in trying to keep touch with events on the battlefield, converted near-success into failure. With the coming of sunset the point had been reached where it seemed that the forces must be withdrawn for lack of water. Further, the British command had learned that Turkish reinforcements were approaching from the north. As it happened, neither threat was substantial. The cavalry had already reached water. And the oncoming Turks had halted for the night. Ignorant of this, the command ordered the withdrawal. The cavalry officers responded with disbelief; some even demanded the order in writing. But it was not to be gainsaid, and so the chance to take Gaza by *coup de main* vanished. It had not been without cost: 4,000 British casualties as against only half that number of Turks.

Murray rashly sent London an optimistic account of what had transpired. This caused the War Cabinet to request a further advance, this time to Jerusalem. Consequently, Murray was obliged to make a second attack on Gaza, which he did on 19 April. By then the situation had changed to his disadvantage. The Turks had been reinforced and their defences improved and extended. The British lacked the artillery required for a direct frontal assault, which was the only course now offering. The outcome was a total failure, and at heavier cost than on the previous occasion.

London now realized that Murray had misled them and ordered his recall. Yet his achievement over the preceding year had not been negligible. He had rendered the Canal impregnable. And by his systematic crossing of the Sinai he had, in the words of his successor, 'brought the waters of the Nile to the borders of Palestine'.

The setbacks at Gaza did not cut short the attempted thrust into Palestine. For Lloyd George, denied his Italian campaign and disillusioned with the prospects in France, was now coming to adopt this distant shore as his preferred sphere for a British offensive. As he told Murray's successor, he wanted Jerusalem 'as a Christmas present for the British nation' – an aim that was possibly an inspired exercise in morale boosting but hardly central to the life-and-death struggle in which Britain was engaged.

In pressing this region upon his colleagues as appropriate for a major British effort, Lloyd George used some strange arguments – strange, certainly, for the man who had established himself as the nation's prime exponent of a victorious war. (If anything, they foreshadowed his advocacy of a compromise peace in 1940.) Thus he told the War

Cabinet, according to its minutes, on 1 May: 'we could not disregard the possibility that in a few months' time we might be confronted with an insistent demand for peace. If Russia collapsed it would be beyond our power to beat Germany. . . .' Before entering a Peace Conference at which the enemy would be in possession of a large slice of Allied territory, he concluded, it was necessary to have conquered Mesopotamia and Syria.

On 9 May, again urging on the War Cabinet the case for a campaign in Palestine, Lloyd George spoke gloomily of Russia's impending collapse, which would neutralize the British blockade and allow the Germans to concentrate against France and Italy. Unless Austria-Hungary dropped out, he said, 'he could see no hope of the sort of victory in the War that we desired.' So it might be necessary to bargain with Germany for the evacuation of Belgium. He urged that, instead of sacrificing men on the Western Front, it would be better to concentrate against Turkey, adding vaguely: 'To continue the process of releasing subject peoples from Turkish oppression would be to gain considerable advantage.'

Did these counsels of near-despair represent a real assessment of the war's prospects? Or was Lloyd George grasping at any argument that might move British operations to the peripheries? Either way, his attempt to concentrate attention on Palestine faced great difficulties. The War Cabinet was not prepared to regard the war as unwinnable. Moreover, a diversion of effort to the Middle East would exacerbate the shipping crisis. And Lloyd George was confronted with the devoted opposition of Robertson, the Government's chief military adviser, to this as to every sideshow. In October Robertson went so far as to encourage Murray's successor, Allenby, to pitch his requirements for a Palestinian campaign at the highest level. Allenby obliged with what has been termed 'one of the most absurd appreciations ever presented to a British government'.[7] He requested an additional 13 divisions to meet a supposed enemy force of 20 divisions, two of them German. (There were in fact no German divisions in this region, only three German battalions.)

In the outcome Lloyd George's attempt – or was it only a *cri de coeur*? – to shift the main weight of Britain's military endeavours away from the forces of Germany came to nothing. Allenby was accorded only such reinforcements as could be secured from Salonika or from within the Middle East.

Nevertheless, a successful campaign in Palestine resulted. Allenby's force, after all, now stood at seven infantry and three cavalry divisions – 'a big army for a side-show'.[8] This constituted a superiority over the Turks of two to one in infantry and eight to one in cavalry. Moreover, however much Allenby might wish to co-operate with Robertson against the politicians, he had good cause for engaging in offensive action. He had come to Palestine from France with his reputation somewhat tarnished. As commander of the Third Army in the battle of Arras, he had presided over the stunning success at Vimy Ridge on 9 April 1917. But thereafter he had kept the attacks grinding away, at grievous cost to his troops, for long after they had lost all prospect of success. This had done more than earn him the displeasure of Haig (with whom he had not been on good terms anyway). It had caused three of his subordinate generals to enter a formal written protest.

Allenby now had the chance to redeem himself in a theatre where the formidable conditions – and formidable adversaries – of France did not obtain and where

---

[7] David R. Woodward, *Lloyd George and the Generals* (East Brunswick, NJ: Associated University Presses, 1983), p. 206.
[8] Cyril Falls, *The First World War* (London: Longman, 1960), p. 305.

opportunities existed for the use of horse soldiers. He was well equipped for the job. The possessor of a ferocious temper (he was nick-named 'The Bull'), he was recognized as an expert cavalryman and a skilled director of men and operations. In short order his strong personality, along with his decision to move headquarters from Cairo to the front, began improving his forces' shaken morale – which anyway was bound to rise as the reinforcements started appearing.

Late in October Allenby launched the third British attempt upon Gaza. His force was thoroughly prepared: among other things he had gained air superiority, enabling him to mislead the enemy in a crucial respect. His initial purpose, while maintaining pressure on Gaza so that it would seem as if he meant to attack there, was to capture Beersheba, 25 miles to the south-east and an important source of water. (The British attack force, both men and animals, was consuming 400,000 gallons a day.) On 31 October this town fell to combined infantry pressure and a thrilling cavalry charge. Then, on the night of 1–2 November, Allenby increased his feint attack against Gaza and broke through between the coast and the town. Threatened by a double envelopment, the Turks abandoned the fortress. In the following days the whole of the Gaza–Beersheba line, which had brought Murray to grief, fell into British hands.

Allenby's forces pressed on up the coast of Palestine and then swung east towards the Judean hills. The Turkish resistance – directed, of all people, by Eric von Falkenhayn, whose status had subsided somewhat since he launched the Verdun operation in 1916 – proved stubborn for a while. But the Turks were seriously under-manned, and their position was ultimately hopeless. On 8 December the British began their direct thrust for Jerusalem. Next day, after 400 years of occupancy, the Turks slipped away from the Holy City, and the municipal authorities solemnly handed over the keys to Allenby.

This phase of operations had been costly: some 18,000 casualties. But for once Turkish losses had been higher. And the capture of so prestigious, if strategically insignificant, a centre provided a glowing finale to the year's endeavours.

It was not the only romantic aspect of the war in this region. Throughout 1917 the Turks were being forced to divert increasing numbers of troops to the Hejaz. Overwhelmingly, their opponents here were Arabs; this aspect of the war is far more an episode in Arab than in British history. But the British did supply money, arms, ammunition, and naval bombardments, as well as military experts and political advisers. Among the last of these was T. E. Lawrence. Not yet 30 and hitherto a student of Middle Eastern archaeology and Arab affairs, Lawrence would soon rank among the few legendary figures of the war.

His subsequent fame is no cause for wonder. For Britain, it is true, the essential war lay far from the Arabian desert: in the mass engagements on the Western Front and the impersonal vigil of the Grand Fleet. But the public mind craved tales of solitary individuals transforming events by personal skill and courage. Only on the peripheries – in the air or in the desert – could such individuals function. For only here was it impossible to concentrate monster weapons and soldiery in the mass. Consequently, along with the air aces, Lawrence has ever since attracted – whether he wished it or not – attention out of all proportion to anything he accomplished or had the opportunity to accomplish.

The Arab revolt was a 'sideshow within a sideshow'. Its contribution to the defeat of Germany was nil and to the defeat of Turkey not great. But in terms of cost-effectiveness – of resources (especially British resources) employed to enemy forces eliminated or neutralized – it was highly successful. That is, the number of Turkish soldiers pinned down by the revolt far exceeded the forces brought against them. In part this was because of the strategy that Lawrence recognized as appropriate to the situation.

By early 1917 Lawrence had established good relations with Feisal, the most able of the Sherif of Mecca's sons; at Feisal's urging he took to wearing Arab garb in place of his British officer's uniform. He had also developed a keen appreciation of the merits and shortcomings of the Arabs as a fighting force against the Turks. As a mass, he wrote, they were not formidable, for they possessed no corporate spirit or discipline. But:

> Man by man they are good: I would suggest that the smaller the unit that is acting, the better will be its performance. A thousand of them in a mob will be ineffective against one-fourth their number of trained troops: but three or four of them in their own valleys or hills would account for a dozen Turkish soldiers.[9]

From this appreciation Lawrence deduced an effective course of action against the Turks. A harassing warfare would be waged upon their railway lines, which were hated by the Arabs anyway as rendering Turkish overlordship more effective. Such sporadic action would not completely sever the Turks' communications or force them to abandon the Hejaz. Rather, it would occupy large numbers of Turkish troops in protecting the line to Medina. 'Our ideal,' Lawrence was to write later (he may have been making a virtue of necessity), 'was to keep his railway just working, but only just, with the maximum loss and discomfort to him.'

As the raids on the railway north of Medina (much aided by British demolition experts) grew in success, it became possible for Lawrence to push his base farther up the coast. This drew in additional Arab tribes and so escalated the enemy's problems. In mid-1917 Lawrence planned his most ambitious coup: a strike against Aqaba, near the head of the Red Sea and its only port in Turkish hands. Aqaba was well defended against attack from the sea. Lawrence therefore chose an assault from the desert: a great wheeling movement involving him and a party of Arabs in a journey of 600 miles across utterly desolate territory during the hot season. He set out on 9 May. Two months later his force appeared before Aqaba from the landward side, and the port surrendered.

The success at Aqaba did more than carry the Arab uprising, and consequent pressure on the Turks, a large step northwards. It enlisted Allenby's wholehearted support for the war in the desert. He proved generously forthcoming in arms, ammunition, and money for the tribesmen. He also provided officers to train the slowly developing regular army that was being formed out of captured Arab soldiers earlier conscripted by the Turks.

The British commander next presented Lawrence with another task against the railway. He was to strike still further north to coincide with Allenby's own thrust against Gaza. This undertaking failed. And Lawrence's experiences during it, coming on top of his previous gruelling activities, left him for the moment seriously impaired. Yet the setback was not all that important for the Arab campaign. Within its decided confines, this most remote and limited of the sideshows had enjoyed a markedly successful year.

---

[9] Quoted in Major-General James Lunt, 'Lawrence and the Arabs', in *Purnell's History of the First World War*, issue no. 86, p. 2398.

PART ELEVEN

Home Front
1917

46

A Land No Longer Merry

I

For the civilian population of Britain 1917 was a grim year: even if grimness, when set against the experiences of the fighting forces, must be deemed relative. In the 'once merry month of May', *Punch* described England as 'no longer merry though not downhearted'.

For many reasons 1917 was bleak for civilians. It was necessary that the great endeavours in productivity of the past two years be continued, yet confidence in the victory they were supposed shortly to bring was hard to maintain. Comforting news from the battlefronts was rare. No great sea encounter came to complete the work of Jutland, and the naval command was increasingly criticized for lack of offensive spirit. The slaughter of merchant ships, particularly in the first half of the year, seemed to the navy's discredit and directly threatened the home front. As late as 6 December Barbara Hammond, in a letter to her husband, remarked: 'Rather bad abt 16 big boats sunk.'[1]

The opening months of 1917 were also notable for the heavy toll among Britain's airmen. 'Bloody April' was exceptional only for its severity. A 'grave statement' in March of the RFC's losses and increased German air activity, admitted *Punch*, had 'created some natural depression'.

As for the war on land, only in a few peripheral campaigns did British arms clearly prosper. Nearer home the exhilarating brief successes of Vimy Ridge and Messines were soon overshadowed by the protracted bloodbaths of Arras and Third Ypres. Nor did the Prime Minister's Paris speech at the end of the year, in effect denying confidence in Britain's commanders while failing to end their command, uplift the spirit of the public.

The military misfortunes of 1917 were crowned by the deep disappointment of Cambrai. The church bells set ringing at the behest of the bellicose Bishop of London had scarcely fallen silent before the triumph was snatched away. A. G. Burn, a 60-year-old lieutenant-general (currently unemployed), wrote in his diary for 16 December 1917:

> The German papers are laughing over the premature joy bells of St. Paul's over our supposed victory. It is said that only 4 tanks remain of those engaged.[2]

And Barbara Hammond wrote to her husband on 8 December:

> How one dreads the papers. Bourlon Wood [which the British had just abandoned] was a great blow. I suppose the whole enterprise is one more instance of our incapacity to think

---

[1] The papers of Barbara and J. L. Hammond (who jointly wrote distinguished works of social history) are in the Bodleian Library, Oxford.
[2] The Burn diary is in the Imperial War Museum.

& plan a thing out. After what [an informant] was saying abt Paschendaele it strikes one chill. What is the good of having the best troops in the world if there is no one who can lead them?

When oh when will the Bp of L/n be interned?

Among Britain's allies little went well in 1917. The fall of the Tsar in March initially excited some enthusiasm. But the feeling was not universal. P. M. Yearsley, in London, records that on 'Russian Flag Day' (15 May) 'people refused to buy.'[3] Thereafter, as military collapse was followed by a second revolution (which to some had alarming social implications), Russia brought only dismay. As for France, the army mutinies that began in April may have been a well kept secret. But the impairment of French fighting capacity and growing civilian discontent were common knowledge. Yearsley reported in May 'a rumour that France was unable to do much more. She had lost 20,000 in her last big battle and must soon come to a standstill for lack of men.' Then in October Italy suffered the crushing setback of Caporetto. The German and Habsburg forces advanced in one day as far as the Italians had managed to do in two and a half years, and a prodigious number of Italian troops abandoned the struggle. To offset these events, certainly, there was the accession to the Allied ranks in April of the USA, which would prove of momentous long-term significance. But except in the important sphere of credit facilities, it would be a considerable time before any tangible results, comforting to British civilians, ensued.

All of these sources of discouragement were compounded at home by the deep misery of particular families: those whose menfolk were in the firing line or were numbered among the casualties. Some of the ways in which events on the battlefield could strike at civilians are apparent from the letters sent by Robert Saunders, the headmaster of a Sussex school, to his son in Canada. On 14 July he refers to the presence in the village of wounded men back from the front and clearly dying; of a man of 80 who had just received a telegram from the War Office informing him that his son was wounded and, it seemed plain, beyond hope; of witnessing an aeroplane out of control and apparently crashing (Saunders learned later that it had managed to land); and of the oppression caused by the sound of the incessant bombardment from Flanders. On 23 July he wrote:

> One of the mothers [of a former pupil] brought me her boy's Photo & apologized because he didn't call on me when he was home from the front where he had been 2 years before getting Leave. He is in the 16th Lancers & she said she nearly cried to see the change in him, all the Boy being gone. He couldn't bear to come down through the Street to see anyone & was very downhearted to go back. She said the sound of the Guns all day long when she was alone nearly drove her mad thinking of her boy out there.

In August Saunders witnessed a cricket match at Piltdown between a local team and an 'Arms & Legs' side – the latter consisting of soldiers who had lost limbs. He watched for a while, but found it too worrying observing a man with only one leg trying to bat, even though the opposing side had been instructed to bowl easy. And he wrote: 'All the time the big guns were roaring in Flanders so we could hear the War & see the sad results of it.'

For those living in London and on the East Coast, experience of war's injuries could be yet more direct. The Zeppelin had practically been defeated. On account of its range it was still employed sparingly on some (fairly ineffective) raids against the Midlands, but that was all. However, against closer targets, and particularly London,

---

[3] P. M. Yearsley, 'The Home Front 1914–1918' (unpublished account based on his wartime diary), in the Imperial War Museum.

its place was taken by the Gotha aeroplanes; accompanied, from late September, by a handful of Riesen (Giant) aircraft, the largest aeroplanes employed against England in either world war. Unlike the Zeppelins, which needed to hug the darkness and so had difficulty in finding their targets, the Gothas were used first by daylight and then, as the defences stiffened, by moonlight.

Plates 39a and 39b   *The lovely and the unlovely faces of the home front.*

39a   *Allotment holders helping to counter the food shortage.*

The early daylight raids were especially dangerous, in that they found civilians in exposed positions. The first against London was the costliest air raid of the war: 162 civilians died and 432 were injured. Liverpool Street Station was the main target. But the victims also included 16 children killed and 30 badly wounded in an East End school, where a bomb penetrated through three floors before exploding in the cellar in which they were sheltering.

As the Gotha raids switched to moonlight and continued into September and October, the lives of many Londoners became seriously disrupted. Especially in the poorer districts, whose homes offered less shelter, whole families (sometimes accompanied by pets) took to crowding into the tube stations for the night. Increasingly they did so in anticipation of raids, until the authorities forbade this. (They also banned the pets.) Other Londoners departed the capital altogether. A report to the Cabinet on 17 October referred to 'the movements of large numbers of workers who have been upset by air raids. This has particularly affected the clothing firms in the East End of London who have lost many of their workers.' The report also spoke of 'the large numbers of machinists temporarily at Brighton'. And a visitor to that resort in September observed: 'Thousands of people have left London till the end of the Harvest Moon so as to be out of the danger Zone. Brighton is simply packed with Jews from the East End.'[4]

---

[4] Saunders to his son in Canada, 30 September 1917, in the Imperial War Museum.

Something of the effect of these raids may again be gleaned from the letters of Robert Saunders. Three days before the 13 June raid he wrote with concern of his married daughter Em: 'She will worry herself to a shadow over Air Raids & never sleep, if she stays in London.' A week afterwards he reported: 'Em & Elsie came down after the Big Raid, completely washed out.' A month later small Elsie, his grand-daughter, came running home in terror of an approaching raid. It was actually a heavy bombardment in Flanders.

Yet outside London and the south-east – which meant for the large majority of Britons – the principal anguish caused by air raids remained not the bombs but the lighting restrictions. These occasioned not a few discomforts: the early closing of shops and places of entertainment, the grim and sometimes dangerous aspect of darkened streets, and the inconvenience of preventing light escaping from houses – not to mention the indignity of prosecution for many who failed, or were negligent, in the attempt. In some parts of the country the approach of winter stimulated protests against the compulsory darkness. The chief constable of Bristol, a city well beyond the likely range of bombers, even prevailed upon the Home Secretary to allow a relaxation of the rules.

This points to the predominant fact about air raids. For all the attention they aroused, the large majority of Britons were not in danger from them. *Punch* felt called upon to remark in October: 'the space which our Press allots to Air Raids moves Mr. Punch to wonder and scorn. Our casualties from that source are never one-tenth so heavy as those in France on days when G.H.Q. reports "everything quiet on the Western front."'

The Press Bureau at the time was seeking to curtail excessive attention to the raids. On 6 September it sent to newspapers a message from the C.-in-C., Home Forces: 'elaborate reports of casualties and damage are a direct encouragement to the enemy to repeat and extend the raids'; 'it is the British Press which acts as the enemy's observer.' These strictures proved unsuccessful, and on 28 September the Press Bureau returned to the attack: 'In consequence of representations from the Commissioner of Police the Press are very urgently requested to refrain from publishing further articles which may add to the feeling of apprehension which is already prevalent specially amongst the poorest and most ignorant classes of the people of London.'

What occasioned this journalistic obsession with air raids? In part, presumably, the newspapers were letting themselves go upon violent incidents of war that, for once, did not have to pass the War Office censors. In part they were simply recognizing that disasters, however trivial, always make good copy: in war as in peace, the dramatic destruction of property, and the killing or maiming of the female and the young, ensure large sales.

But the matter may be thought to go further. The stress on air raids in the press reflected a deeply held conviction among the public: that a clear divide ought to exist between the warrior and the civilian – especially the civilian as woman and child. The fighting man was equipped for battle and so was eligible for death therein. The civilian had no place in combat and therefore should be exempt from its slaughter. Clearly, the random bombing of cities violated this conviction. It did more. It opened up a vision of a new and dreadful type of warfare, a type that, if not yet accomplished, might be practicable before long. Such a style of war had little to do with the clash of armies, and much to do with the devastation of whole nations.

To such a prospect, even in embryonic form, Britons had yet to adjust themselves. In the meantime they responded with feelings of distress and indignation. Nor was it only civilians who experienced these. An officer on leave was at the Gaiety theatre in

London when the explosion of a bomb nearby caused dust and plaster to fall on the audience. The officer clutched the arm of the girl accompanying him, stared at her as if hypnotized, and said over and over: 'It's no business to happen here you know, it's no business to happen here.' He told her afterwards that being bombed in England seemed to 'destroy something in him'.[5]

39b *A crowd breaking up an alleged pacifist meeting in Stockport, Cheshire.*

II

In 1917 the war began seriously to inconvenience train travellers. Given the large demands on internal rail services of both the military and essential industries, it may seem surprising that this had not happened earlier. But Britain began the war with a considerable excess of railway capacity. It had not, like the Continental powers, built railways for military purposes. But competitive building by private companies in the nineteenth century had produced a plethora of lines. And these were lavishly stocked and staffed. In every type of rolling stock, Britain was vastly superior per route-mile to other countries, including heavily industrialized Belgium. As for manpower, this was so abundant that when one inner-suburban London station (which anyway had been losing traffic to buses and trams) was closed during the war it released a staff of 25. This excess capacity would require severe rationalization after the war, especially in face of the growing competition of road transport. But it proved a boon in wartime.

Nevertheless, in 1917 it became necessary to end the relative normalcy that had so far obtained for train travellers. On the Continent the French Government had hitherto been meeting the British army's needs in locomotives. They now required the return of more than 600 trains. Replacements could come only from Britain's civilian

---

[5] Mrs C. S. Peel, *How We Lived Then, 1914–1918* (London: John Lane, 1929), p. 152.

services, and as a first instalment 370 mainline locomotives were removed. At the same time, the army needed extra track for its offensive operations. This required the closure of branch lines in Britain. Simultaneously, there was a mounting need to divert coal supplies to military purposes, not least to meet the deficiencies of Britain's allies; the Italian railways were wholly dependent on British coal.

This could mean no good for civilian rail services. Up to 1916 these, although reduced, had borne a recognizable affinity to the services of 1914. In 1917 they were changed out of sight. Some whole services vanished. On many others – although there were exceptions – trains were cancelled or decelerated. Restaurant services all but vanished, and 400 stations were closed – often (unlike earlier closures) in areas where alternative forms of transport were not available. At Easter the Railway Executive took the drastic step of announcing that no extra trains would run and that tickets would be sold only to the capacity of the carriages. Two years earlier this body, defending the decision to maintain race specials, had stated: 'we are bound to carry passengers who present themselves at the stations.'[6] Now the days of travel-as-usual were ended.

<h1 style="text-align:center">III</h1>

In numerous ways simple pleasures disappeared in this year. Race meetings, the University boat race, and the football league final all went into limbo. And dismal shortages started to develop. In April coal supplies ran short in the capital. The wife of a Conservative MP, moving to London from her Yorkshire residence, wrote:

> When we arrived here there was no coal & the weather was bitter – in fact there was hardly any coal in London & now they are only allowed to give one ton at a time & it takes about 3 weeks to get the one ton.[7]

The *Observer* on 8 April recorded:

> In South London trolleymen with coals were besieged by people who had requisitioned all types of receptacles, including perambulators, wheelbarrows, go-carts and trucks, while others brought sacks, baskets and boxes. At a railway coal-siding the would-be purchasers assembled soon after seven o'clock in the morning and the queue of waiting women and children extended to a great length within an hour or so. Several policemen regulated the crowd. . . .[8]

By October continuing shortage and the approach of another winter prompted the application of coal rationing to London. (For the rest of the country 'moral suasion' was 'the only agent applied'.)[9] Under this system consumers had to register with particular dealers and were allocated quantities according to the number of rooms in their houses. A house of one to four rooms was entitled to 2 hundredweight of coal a week, a house of five or six rooms to 3 hundredweight, and so on.

As a means of overcoming the scramble for supplies, this proved satisfactory. But it did not reduce consumption to the extent expected. Two hundredweight of coal constituted an increase in consumption for many working-class families. 'There is no doubt,' writes the historian of the wartime coal industry, 'that, before the War, the working classes could not in many instances afford a reasonable allowance of coal, and

---

[6] J. A. B. Hamilton, *Britain's Railways in World War I* (London: Allen & Unwin, 1967), ch. 6.

[7] Jane Ingleby to Clement Ingleby, 23 April 1917, Ingleby papers.

[8] Quoted in Arthur Marwick, *The Deluge* (London: Bodley Head, 1965), p. 192.

[9] Sir R. A. S. Redmayne, *The British Coal-Mining Industry During the War* (Oxford: Clarendon Press, 1923), p. 112.

could not obtain it even if they could afford it.'[10] Now increased earnings meant that they had the resources to buy a tolerable amount. And rationing provided them with an entitlement that dealers were obliged to fulfil.

Paper at this time started to run short. One consequence was more expensive and less ample newspapers: for example, the *Leicester Post*, from late in 1916, was reduced from eight pages to four, and in March 1917 the price of several leading newspapers doubled. Waste paper became a marketable commodity. From Leeds it was reported that customers of whatever social standing were expected to bring their own bags or sheets of paper when shopping, 'waste paper being by this time nearly as valuable as the perfect product itself'.[11]

The matter that caused most anguish, however, was food supply. In May it was said to be the one subject the House of Commons cared about. In part the problem was rising prices. These caused hardship to people on fixed incomes, and aroused a sense of betrayal among those whose higher earnings brought little or no advantage. At a public meeting called in Leicester late in January 1917 to protest at excessive prices, the mayor quoted the Book of Wisdom: 'He that withholdeth corn, the people shall curse him, but blessing shall be on the head of him that selleth it.' A resolution was passed condemning the exploitation of food and demanding action by the Government.[12] (The mayor's diligence in this matter, not to say his familiarity with Scripture, did not save him from becoming the subject of unfounded rumours. It was soon being said that he had half a ton of sugar stored at his house, and that his cellar was so well stocked workmen could not open the door.) A visitor to London in April noted butchers' shops as apparently well supplied, but with prices so high that 10/– would buy only the equivalent of 3/6d. before the war. In December *Punch*, waxing heavily facetious, observed that bloaters had now reached 6d. each, so dispelling the hope that they would remain within the income of the upper classes. Soon afterwards P. M. Yearsley, finding himself with guests, could obtain no red meat and had to pay the 'preposterous sum' of 13/4d. for 'a rather forlorn duck'.

The other aspect of the food problem was shortage, whose visible manifestation was the queue. Sometimes the deficiency did not run the whole year. Potatoes were in short supply in the first half of 1917. But thereafter a good harvest over a much increased area rendered them available (at a price) in larger quantities than the market could absorb.

Other commodities, particularly sugar and butter, continued hard to obtain throughout the year. Saunders reported in May that they had been unable to get either butter or margarine for a week: 'Bert tried 3 shops & the girls 3 more in Uckfield to no purpose.' As for sugar, its distribution gave rise to so much discontent that, before the year's end, several municipalities had led the way in introducing rationing. And the central government had decreed a national system of rationing from the New Year.

By that time the authorities had more problems than this. In the last weeks of 1917 shortages in a whole range of important foodstuffs, including meat and tea, came together with a rush. Queues reached ominous proportions. In Leicester:

> On one day towards Christmas there were some two or three thousand people outside the Home and Colonial Stores. The notice 'sold out' was exhibited after some of the crowd had waited two hours. The police had to send for reinforcements.[13]

---

[10] Ibid., p. 115.

[11] W. H. Scott, *Leeds in the Great War 1914–1918* (Leeds: Libraries and Arts Committee, 1923), p. 51.

[12] F. P. Armitage, *Leicester 1914–1918: The War-Story of a Midland Town* (Leicester: Edgar Backus, 1933), p. 206.

[13] Ibid., p. 213.

Under the heading 'Workers' Demand for Rations' (by which it meant 'Rationing'), *The Times* reported on 17 December 1917:

> The food queues continue to grow. Reports from some parts of London state that outside the dairy shops of certain multiple firms women began to line up for margarine as early as 5 o'clock on Saturday morning, some with infants in their arms and others with children at their skirts. Over a thousand people waited for margarine at a shop in New Broad-street, in the heart of the City, and in Walworth-road, on the south-eastern side of London, the queue was estimated to number about 3,000. Two hours later 1,000 of these were sent away unsupplied.

Nor was it only customers who were having to line up. At the beginning of January 1918, butchers at Smithfield market were standing in queues to the number of 500 people.

By this time the food situation was beginning to undermine public order. On 12 January 1918, according to Yearsley, munition workers at Leytonstone whose wives were unable to secure food looted the closed shops and were brought to heel only by the military. On the same day a big provision shop was smashed at Wembley. Sometimes the authorities even took the side of the disturbers of the peace. Barbara Hammond reported from Hemel Hempstead on 13 January: 'There was a quasi-riot at Chennell's the Sat before last & the police made him produce margarine from his cellar & sell it.'

It is important not to exaggerate the significance of all this. The British people were going short of some important commodities. They were in no sense facing famine. More exotic items like tinned fish were in plentiful supply, though the price may have discouraged some purchasers, and others were put off by unfamiliarity with fish in this form. (Reluctance to amend eating habits to what foods were available was considered a major cause of the discontent over shortages.) As for the staple item of mass consumption, bread, it was freely available. Moreover, in September 1917 its price was actually lowered to the level of a year earlier.

Certainly, bread was becoming less palatable. Regulations forbade its sale until 12 hours after baking. And to make the supply go further, a quantity of unusual substances was introduced. These included the husk of wheat, flour from other cereals, and even an admixture of potatoes. For a while bakers endeavoured to preserve the whiteness of bread, but eventually they had to give up the struggle.

But what mattered was not that bread seemed less enjoyable or that people were saying of it, 'I can't eat the stuff', 'It is only fit for pigs', and 'Its very colour annoys me.'[14] The crucial fact was that bread was available; that, however unlovely, 'war bread' was as nutritious as the peacetime variety; and that people, whatever they said to the contrary, were eating it. Bread consumption was higher, not lower, in 1917 than in the pre-war years – even if, as *Punch* remarked in December, 'the stuff is now eaten by itself instead of being spread thinly on butter, as in pre-war days.' (Perhaps this had only ever been the case with *Punch*'s rather select clientele.)

What the disturbances of late 1917 and early 1918 revealed was far less hunger than anger. Its cause was resentment at the unnecessary hardship being occasioned, especially for women and the young, by an inefficient system of distribution that the authorities were tardy to amend. It was aggravated by the way in which some shopkeepers were taking advantage of a situation where (for once) they had the whip hand. Their manner was sometimes proving uppity. One shopkeeper was quoted as telling a dissatisfied customer: 'Go and get your groceries where you can.'[15] When

---

[14] Ibid., p. 210.

[15] Sir William H. Beveridge, *British Food Control* (London: Oxford University Press, 1928), p. 242.

workmen downed tools to assist their wives in queueing or stormed shops to force the release of commodities in store, they were delivering a message to those in authority. They knew the commodities they wanted were available in at least some quantities, and they expected these to be distributed justly and in a way that avoided hardship. So a Leicester Labour leader told a workers' gathering in the local Trades Hall: 'If our Government will not listen to the wishes of the workers, they will have no alternative but to use the only weapon they have in their hands and stop work.... The Government must take over complete control of the production and distribution of food to secure an equitable distribution among all classes.'[16]

Some government control of food consumption did exist in 1917, and it impinged on the lives of ordinary citizens in ways that caused them discomfort or even prosecution. It became an offence to use food in a wasteful manner. J. R. Clynes recalls: 'A man who fed his pigs with bread-crusts, discarded by navvies building a new aerodrome, was fined £50. A woman convicted of feeding her Peke regularly with rump-steak was fined £20.'[17] (Perhaps the seeming discrepancy between the offence and the scale of punishment in these instances is evidence that, to British magistrates, ladies who kept Pekes were a more desirable class of person than men who kept pigs.) Again, William Beveridge relates:

> it became a crime for a workman to leave a loaf behind on the kitchen shelf of the cottage from which he was moving (£2 fine), for a maiden lady at Dover to keep fourteen dogs and give them bread and milk to eat (£5), for another lady in Wales to give meat to a St. Bernard (£20), for a furnaceman dissatisfied with his dinner to throw chip potatoes on the fire (£10), and for a lady displeased with her husband to burn stale bread upon her lawn (£5).... A Lincolnshire farmer finding himself able to buy seven stone of rock cakes cheaply from an Army canteen used them to feed pigs; as the food executive officer and a police sergeant were able to pick some of the cakes out of a swill-tub and taste them without bad consequences, the farmer was fined £10 for wasting human food. Another farmer in Yorkshire made up for shortage of cattle-cake by feeding his stock on bread: his exclamation, 'Well, I'll tell you straight, my cattle is going to have something', put a point of view deserving of sympathy, but he suffered three months' imprisonment.[18]

Regulations against food hoarding also struck nearly at the freedom of the individual. Under them the authorities might enter any premises believed to contain food exceeding the amount required for ordinary consumption. This restriction must have inhibited would-be hoarders from the time of its promulgation in April 1917, although the wave of prosecutions under it did not begin until the following year.

Again, government regulations prevented producers and retailers from selling at the prices and upon the conditions that they wished. In September 1917, for selling large quantities of potatoes above the maximum price, one farmer was fined £5,500 plus costs, and another was fined £3,700 and given two months' imprisonment. Shop-keepers likewise were fined for purchasing potatoes at more than the proclaimed price (they argued that otherwise farmers would not supply them), for selling bread while it was fresh, and for refusing to supply scarce commodities to customers who were not 'regulars'. Those who offended on too considerable a scale or showed no inclination to mend their ways might go to prison without option of a fine. A grocer in Stepney charged with selling margarine above the permitted price replied: 'It is my shop, my margarine and I shall do what I like with it.' His old-fashioned libertarian notions earned him a fine of £50 and six weeks in prison.[19]

---

[16] Armitage, *Leicester 1914–1918*, p. 212.

[17] Quoted in Frank P. Chambers, *The War Behind the War 1914–1918* (London: Faber & Faber, 1939), p. 559.

[18] Beveridge, *British Food Control*, pp. 238–9.

[19] Ibid., pp. 237–8.

Yet if government regulations were in some circumstances a source of misery to producers, wholesalers, retailers, and consumers, this did not mean that the public desired their removal. On the contrary, the queues and disorders at food shops and the mounting public outcry for compulsory rationing showed, as 1917 drew to a close, that the nation recognized (in advance of its leaders) that it required a thoroughgoing system of control. In a situation where commodities were available but not in sufficient quantities to meet normal demand, the discomforts of a free market were far worse than any inconveniences resulting from state regulations.

IV

The shopkeeper in Stepney who thought he should be free to do what he liked with his own margarine was ignoring one of the grimmest facts of life in 1917. Men in the age group 18 to 40 were not free, in most instances, to do what they liked with their own bodies. Barbara Hammond wrote to her husband on 26 September: 'Do you know that you can't now get a passport to go to Italy if you are an able bodied? Only those w. doctors certificates may go.'

In no respect did the encroaching misery of war extend its grip more harshly than in this matter of manpower. The willing men – be they moved by idealism, a grim sense of duty, an unreflecting readiness to conform, an eagerness for adventure, or a yen to engage in legalized slaughter – had all gone. Now the reluctant and the positively averse must be brought forth – 'combed out' in the current, scarcely flattering, phrase. Men of military age hitherto exempt because they were engaged in essential services discovered that substitute workers, not eligible for the firing line, had been found to take their places. Their exemption, consequently, vanished. Men once deemed unfit were re-examined. Some were informed that their physical inadequacies were no longer judged important. Others learned that, if still unfit for combat, they were considered eligible for base duties, so enabling enlisted men in posts behind the line to be moved closer to the enemy.

Little sympathy was felt in the community for those who sought to escape military service. Robert Saunders, not an intolerant man, wrote in April 1917 of a man, previously exempted, who was now placed medically in the first class yet still managed to remain among the 'Rabbits'. In Saunders's view, he would not do so much longer: 'the Military will see to that, if public opinion doesn't.'

The reference to 'public opinion' was not necessarily rhetorical. The local community might seal the fate of a man bent on evading military service while any hiding place remained. An incident reported in the newspapers concerned a young man who had been handed over to the military authorities and, on the eve of his departure for France, had decamped from his unit and fled home. The police, as a matter of course, called at his mother's house; for young men who had not lived away from home and who had no expertise in changing identities or forging papers usually had nowhere else to hide. The mother had gone to great efforts to conceal her son, hiding him in a locked box in the attic. But it was all to no avail. The authorities had cause to know that he was there, because it had been noticed that the mother was purchasing an extra two loaves of bread a day. A prolonged search of the house at last flushed out the occupant of the box, who was taken off to serve his country. The mother was prosecuted for harbouring a deserter, and only on account of her health escaped a prison sentence.

If the civilian community was prepared to impose such misery on these reluctants, the army held no welcome for them. Haig, in October 1917, reflected sourly on his conscript forces:

The influence of these men and their antecedents generally are not such as to foster any spirit but that of unrest and discontent; they came forward under compulsion and they will depart the Army with relief. Men of this stamp are not satisfied with remaining quiet, they come from a class which like to air real or fancied grievances, and their teaching in this respect is a regrettable antidote to the spirit of devotion and duty of earlier troops.[20]

No doubt, from the perspective of wartime, the civilians who helped to flush out the young man hidden in the attic acted properly. He seemed to them contemptible. On a longer view it is appropriate to reflect on the sufferings of men who wanted to escape military service this badly and were undone by neighbourhood resentment. It is also in order to wonder whether they were invariably so inferior to those ready to 'do their duty'. Certainly, there was much nobility among the men who had volunteered for their country's service. Yet some among the volunteers were not, on any wide view, particularly noble. They included small-minded jingoes, eager to play out the fantasy that theirs was top nation and so was entitled, whenever it chose, to deal out a thrashing to inferior peoples, be they Russians, Maoris, Zulus, Egyptians, Boers, Chinese, or Germans. The world has not become a finer place because, in one country and among one race after another, such attitudes have been widely adopted.

Similar variations must also be noted among those who sought to escape military service. Some were spongers on the community, ready and eager that other men should perform a necessary task but disinclined to risk their own necks. But others were simply people burdened with a heightened awareness of the terrors and miseries that combat would hold for them, and conscious of their inability to confront battle in the appropriate, and required, manner. They were appalled by the prospect of military life, with its demands to conform to standards of conduct that repelled them or lay beyond their capabilities. They were desperately aware that they possessed only one life, and that they could contribute nothing to the prosecution of the war that would be commensurate with the cost of losing it.

No doubt during this conflict the British community simply could not take account of such sensibilities or deem these people deserving of consideration. It was not only the enemy who must be reduced to stereotypes. The same had to be true of adult British males. They must be divided into men of noble character who were ready to serve their country and men of ignoble character – though with varying degrees of ignobility – who must be driven into following the way of duty. Recognition of the needs of those ill-equipped to participate in the clash of arms, and unable to identify with its ethos, was a luxury Britain could not afford.

Yet although the historian must recognize the pressures directing the community towards these harsh judgements, it is no part of the historian's business to don the blinkers or endorse the pretences of the time. The imposition of these stereotypes was doing violence to the sensibilities of particular men. The war was supposed to be making equal demands, if not upon all citizens, then upon all fit males within the military age group. Yet in truth the demands of war were grossly unequal; because human beings, even those of the same sex, age group, and general state of health, were and are so differently constituted. These differences become acute in a situation requiring of men first the regimentation of military life, which to some will prove

---

[20] Quoted in Stephen R. Ward (ed.), *The War Generation: Veterans of the First World War*, National University Publications (Kennikat Press: Port Washington, N.Y., 1975), p. 28. It is permissible to wonder whether Sir Douglas saw himself as belonging among those 'satisfied with remaining quiet' and not given to airing 'real or fancied grievances'.

attractive and to others repugnant; then the prospect of danger, which will evoke varying responses from excitation through mild apprehension to profound dismay; and ultimately the proximity of widespread maiming and death, which will wear most men down eventually but will reduce some to immediate prostration.

It may be true that the 'comb-out' of 1917 was necessary. The supply of men eager or prepared to fight was exhausted, while the war's demands upon the manpower of the country was nowhere near an end. But that is not all that should be said on the matter. There was a decided, if unquantifiable, increase in the degree of cruelty that the war was imposing when it became necessary to take this sort of action against the unwilling.

47

THE MOOD OF LABOUR

The unequal distribution of food has brought more discontent and dissatisfaction to the people of East London than anything we have known since the war started. Although less terrifying than the air-raids, the food scarcity has produced an amount of exasperation which German terrorism never did. At the back of it all is the feeling that there is plenty of food in the country but that the apportioning of it has been unequal and unjust.

East London Advertiser, 11 January 1918

I

In the early phases of the war the response of the masses had, by and large, been all that their social superiors could have wished. The rush of working men to the colours had been noteworthy. And this was not, as with so much pre-war recruitment, simply a case of the army being the last resort of men bereft of a job. The volunteers came more from industries where employment was buoyant than from those where it was slack. Certainly, the rush to the recruiting stations was even greater among white-collar workers than among labourers. The former, with generally middle-class aspirations that caused them to marry later and breed less and to identify passionately with mother country and Empire, had both stronger incentives to enlist and fewer domestic responsibilities to restrain them. It was also the case that the working class contained most of the poorest and least well nourished in the land, and so included the large majority of those who, eager or otherwise to enlist, would never qualify medically. Yet the voluntary acceptance of military service by large sections of the working class was still a noteworthy event, and one that some social observers found remarkable, given how few were the material possessions most workers had to defend.[1]

Even a devoted opponent of the war like the socialist George Lansbury admitted to experiencing a strong pull towards donning uniform. In a *Herald* pamphlet, whose main purpose was to argue that it was a crime for the workers of Europe to be killing each other at the bidding of militarists, he described an occasion during a visit to the front when he had found himself surrounded by fighting men:

> every troop or regiment of troops on the march created a longing in me to get out and march with them. I had no sort of feeling about killing or being killed. There was a sense of danger and service – impersonal service – which, as men swung past, made me wish to be with them.[2]

---

[1] See B. L. Hutchins in the *Sociological Review* for 1915. I owe this reference, and very much else in this chapter, to the writings of Bernard Waites, particularly his (at present unpublished) manuscript on 'The First World War and Working-Class Consciousness in England'. The studies of Bernard Waites are a signal contribution to understanding of a little researched subject.

[2] Quoted in Caroline Playne, *Society at War 1914–1916* (London: Allen & Unwin, 1931), p. 58.

519

   This sense of identity early on between the working class and the nation at war soon
became apparent also in the factories. There developed a decided preference among
workers, and not just those who were males of military age, for taking employment in
government establishments where they would be 'badged' as participants in essential
industry. This caused a difficulty in the manufacture of the first tanks. So secret was
the undertaking that the firm employed for the task, being the principal manufacturers
of caterpillar tractors, was not designated a government establishment. Hence its
workers were not provided with badges. In consequence, skilled labour started moving
to other factories whose association with the war effort was publicly recognized.

Plate 40   *A demonstration of munitions workers at the Town Hall, Manchester, in January 1918,*
urges the adoption of a national scheme of food rationing.

   Again, late in 1915 a prominent official in the Ministry of Munitions recorded that
some manufacturers, upon encountering labour unrest, asked to have their industries
declared controlled establishments.[3] It was not just that the Munitions Act provided
ways of circumventing strikes. Workers in essential industries were not so willing to
down tools lest they appeared to be betraying relatives and fellow workers at the front.
For, in circumstances of large-scale worker participation in the army, those in the
factories were linked personally with the struggle in the trenches: quite apart from the
psychological urge that caused them to identify with King and country and to feel grief
and rage (manifested by incidents of working-class violence towards German-owned
shops) when civilians drowned in the *Lusitania* and Kitchener perished with the
Hampshire.
   But during 1917, with the war completing its third year and victory still nowhere in
sight, and with Britain's ally, Russia, in social turmoil, a question began to assert itself.
How secure was the adhesion of the British workforce to the conflict?

---

[3] Report of the Labour Department of the Ministry of Munitions by Llewellyn Smith, 3 December 1915,
cited in Waites, 'The First World War and Working-Class Consciousness in England'.

Among those who felt that they needed to know were the members of the Cabinet. So, from mid-April 1917, detailed reports were prepared for them on the labour situation. These recounted all strikes and potential strikes and their settlement, summarized 'labour propaganda' (by which was meant comments in working-class and left-wing publications), and offered 'a general appreciation of the labour situation'. Notwithstanding the partiality of those who compiled them, the reports prove illuminating documents.[4]

Of particular interest is the report for the week ending 6 June 1917. This was a time of great anxiety in governing circles regarding the labour situation. In the previous month there had been a rash of unofficial stoppages (the 'May strikes'). Then at the beginning of June, under the auspices of two anti-war groups, the Independent Labour Party and the British Socialist Party (BSP), a convention was held at Leeds to welcome events in Russia. Many trade unionists attended. One of the resolutions passed at the convention seemed especially ominous: it called for the establishment in Britain of Workers' and Soldiers' Councils on the Russian model.

The report on the labour situation for 6 June dealt in some detail with this Leeds conference. The gathering was deemed a 'distinct success' for the promoters. It had been 'large and orderly', and 'its composition as reported even in *The Times* could not but impress uncritical opinion as representative'. Of the 1,150 attending, according to *The Times*, there had been large delegations from trades councils and local Labour parties, from trade union executives and branches, and from the ILP, as well as smaller groups from the BSP, women's organizations, the Council for Civil Liberties, and the Union of Democratic Control. The cost of the conference, £7,000, had already been largely met.

The report on the labour situation sought to soften this account. It argued that, despite appearances (and the judgement of 'uncritical opinion'), the conference had little claim to be 'in any sense representative of Labour'. Trade union leaders like Smillie and Robert Williams were there 'in their pacifist and revolutionary capacity respectively, rather than as representatives of the unions to which they belong'; and the same applied to 'the very large majority of the 580 quasi-labour delegates'. The fact that trade unionists got permission from their branches to attend the conference did not mean that they spoke for 'the men in the shops'. As for the trades councils, they 'carry very little weight in the Labour world'.

Nevertheless, the report felt it would be a mistake to dismiss the conference as negligible. It was intended as 'the starting point of a widespread agitation'. Unless the views it proposed to spread were 'ignored by the responsible leaders of the Labour movement', they could become dangerous.

So, in one possibly large respect, this report of early June 1917 conveyed what, for the rulers of the country, was an ominous message. Some sections of labour were looking to the upsurge of a unified working class – including soldiers as well as civilians – to wrest power from the hands of constituted authority. Yet other parts of this same report seemed to be telling a different tale. Unlike the report of the previous month, it contained no section on strikes. What it did contain was a section on 'settlements', a 'large number of disputes' having been settled by the Munitions Department, none of them of special importance. Other items suggested a tendency away from working-

---

[4] These documents are in the Public Record Office. The reports are partial in the sense that their authors invariably disapprove of strikes and applaud industrial quiescence. But they reveal no signs of distorting the facts as a result of these attitudes, either by inventing or exaggerating industrial unrest so as to prove the working class malevolent or by playing down industrial militancy so as to show it placid and deferential. As a repository of information and of fairly balanced comments, the reports are of decided value.

class militancy and cohesiveness. Disunity within the workforce between the various grades of labour was continuing. In Coventry 'skilled men on time-rates' remained discontented because 'learners and women are able to earn higher wages at piece work.' A study of the press revealed that the general secretary of the Amalgamated Society of Engineers (ASE), the organ of the skilled engineers, was extolling the formation of 'workshop committees, truly representative of the men', whereas J. Clynes, Labour MP and a spokesman for unskilled workers, deplored the setting up in workshops of 'quite new, unofficial and unauthorised forms of representation'. Meanwhile working-class activists were still not immune from the appeals of patriotism. In South Wales 'general satisfaction' was evident owing to the fact that three prominent labour figures ('noted agitators' who 'exercise much influence') had received invitations from the Government to 'visit the front in France'.

The impression provided by these aspects of the report, that the labour force was not moving irresistibly in a pacifist and class-conscious direction, is reinforced by two further items. In Leeds events other than the socialist conference had been occurring. There had been 'a good deal of anti-Jewish rioting on [the] 3rd and 4th, due mainly to the number of Jews who have evaded military service. A great deal of damage was done to property.' And among the small disputes resolved by the Munitions Department was one which the report considered an 'interesting case'. At a factory manufacturing bullets, 50 toolsetters and labourers had threatened to strike owing to the promotion to the rank of foreman of a man who was a conscientious objector. 'The man was dismissed and the matter thus settled.'

So it appears that in mid-1917, notwithstanding war-weariness at home and social upheaval in Russia, the British working class was far from shedding its powerful internal divisions on the basis of skill, status, and sex. And it remained subject to the strong pull of patriotic zeal – not to say racial bias – that had been so much in evidence since the outbreak of the war.

II

Events in the weeks following the Leeds conference of June 1917 revealed that this gathering would not prove a turning point in the history of wartime Britain or the British working class. The resolution to establish Workers' and Soldiers' Councils throughout the country was never implemented. Labour organizations such as the London Trades Council, which had agreed – on a divided vote – to send delegates to Leeds, declined to act on the decision taken there. Other working-class bodies were positively hostile. The executive of the Dockers' Union called the proposed councils 'bogus organizations' to be created 'at the instigation of moneyed and middle class people whose mischievous exploitation of the labour movement is disruptive in character'. (The dockers' leader, Ben Tillett, had earlier told his members that the Leeds conference 'did not represent working class opinion and was rigged by a middle class element more mischievous than important'.)[5] And where attempts were made to establish these councils, they failed. The opposition was too devoted, the rank and file of labour too indifferent, for the movement to take root.

In a good many instances meetings for setting up Workers' and Soldiers' Councils

---

[5] *Dockers Record*, June and August 1917, quoted in Julia Bush, *Behind the Lines: East London Labour 1914–1919* (London: Merlin Press, 1984), pp. 150–1.

were broken up by mobs incited by the jingo press. (According to these journals, the supporters of the movement were 'German agents' and 'traitors to their country'.) The owners of halls, both public and private, seized on this unruliness as reason for refusing to make premises available for further meetings. The left-wing press fulminated and threatened retaliation. The *Merthyr Pioneer*, after three out of six attempted meetings were broken up at the end of July, stated: 'London, Newcastle, Swansea – three new smears and three of the ugliest, soiled the pages of English constitutional history last Sunday.' Perhaps, it said, 'when we drop our quiet acceptance of incitement against us', public opinion would follow its usual course of siding with 'the best armed force' and would concede the right of free speech. Another Labour journal, the *Herald*, also warned the authorities that 'miners and railwaymen, engineers and boilermakers' would not be denied 'the full right of organization and free speech. It is certain these great organizations of labour will not tolerate mob law.'[6]

Nothing followed from these denunciations. For on the issue of establishing Workers' and Soldiers' Councils these journals did not speak for 'miners and railwaymen, engineers and boilermakers'. Prepared though such bodies were to exercise industrial muscle and vindicate their rights on some issues, they did not choose to do so on this. The 'quiet acceptance of incitement' continued, presumably because the rank and file of labour did not identify with the council movement and so did not see the incitement as directed against themselves. Indeed, the report to the Cabinet on the labour situation for 8 August claimed: 'On the whole it appears probable that the general opinion among the workers is turning against these Councils.' And a week later, despite some activity, the report concluded: 'the Councils are attracting little attention and show little sign of becoming important.' For a short while longer sporadic attempts were made to organize the councils. Usually they fell under banning orders from local authorities grown intransigent as a result of the evident weakness of the movement. Soon the attempts ceased altogether.

The generality of workers, in short, were little inclined to embrace movements whose origins lay in revolutionary Russia. This was borne out by the fate of the proposal for holding an international socialist conference at Stockholm (that is, a conference that would be attended not only by Allied and neutral socialists but by Germans and Austrians as well). This proposal gained a measure of official Labour endorsement such as the movement for Workers' and Soldiers' Councils never secured. The Labour representative in Lloyd George's War Cabinet, Arthur Henderson, was one of the leading figures in favour of the scheme. And a special Labour Party conference on 10 August approved sending British delegates by a large majority. Henderson, it has been shown,[7] was initially opposed to the Stockholm conference, but he changed his mind as a result of a visit that he paid to Russia at the request of his Cabinet colleagues. What he discovered there caused him great concern. He recognized that the democratic forces would need all the outside support they could get if they were to survive and keep Russia in the war. And the democratic forces in Russia were committed to the Stockholm conference. So he urged the Labour Party conference on 10 August: 'remember poor struggling Russia whose great miracle we welcomed with such delight a few weeks ago. . . . Let us remember poor Russia, and if we cannot give the newest Democracy, the infant of Democracies, all she asks, I beseech you not to give her an entire point blank refusal.'[8]

---

[6] Quotations included in the report on the labour situation for 8 August 1917.

[7] See J. M. Winter, 'Arthur Henderson, the Russian Revolution, and the Reconstruction of the Labour Party', *The Historical Journal*, vol. XV. no. 4, 1972.

[8] Quoted in ibid., p. 769.

But in basing his actions on the needs of the democratic forces in Russia, Henderson was embarking on a hazardous course. It was open to question whether what happened in that far-off country concerned Britons nearly, except in so far as it assisted in the prosecution of the war – and that, by this time, the upheaval in Russia was clearly failing to do. Certainly, on the right of British politics any sympathy for the Russian revolution as heralding a Russian military renaissance had evaporated. Conservative newspapers like *The Times* and the *Morning Post* welcomed General Korniloff's attempted overthrow of the constitutional Government. Could Henderson expect that, among British workers, there would be such concern for the situation in Russia that they would welcome a proposal for British representatives to confer with German Social Democrats?

Plate 41   *At the Labour Party conference on the issue of British representation at Stockholm: George Lansbury and Ben Tillett appear in good humour, whatever their differences regarding the war.*

It rapidly became apparent that, even with official Labour endorsement, the Stockholm proposal lacked the approval of many among the organized working class.[9] The division of opinion became most manifest at a conference of shop stewards in Manchester, where 'at one time the proceedings became so stormy that a free fight seemed imminent.' (It appears to have been a seriously divided gathering, with one section of shop stewards adhering to the 'Craft Union spirit and supporting Trade Union methods', while the other 'aimed at complete industrial unionism and revolution'.) The strongest support for the Stockholm proposal came from the Clyde and South Wales, where – probably not coincidentally – the ILP had much of its following. In many areas of England opinion among the workforce was divided or definitely

[9] The matter is considered extensively in the reports on the labour situation for August 1917.

hostile. The Durham Miners Association – and Henderson represented a Durham constituency – reversed the decision of its executive in favour of Stockholm, and at various mining branches resolutions were passed demanding the resignation of representatives who had voted for the proposal. Other bodies of miners took the same line. Those in Warwickshire 'sent delegates to London . . . to proclaim their strong protest against the Stockholm conference directly to the Prime Minister'.

But all these manifestations of hostility were outshone by the indignation of British merchant seamen, who happened to be in a position to take practical steps to ensure that British delegates did not reach Stockholm. At a meeting of seamen in South Wales a resolution was passed unanimously rejecting the decision of the Labour conference to send delegates. Ominously, it demanded 'a referendum of the rank and file of Trade Unionists'.

Even among supporters of the Stockholm conference there were deep divisions about what a British delegation was supposed to accomplish. Those of the ILP persuasion plainly saw Stockholm as an episode in a stop-the-war movement; while for those who shared Henderson's viewpoint the conference was intended to strengthen the commitment to the struggle of the Allied working class. The latter was the view taken by the miners of Aberdare in South Wales, who supported sending delegates and for whom the conference would serve two purposes: to 'place our position clearly before the Russian delegates' and to tell the delegates of the Central Powers that 'Germany is responsible for the war and . . . Germany alone is the stumbling block in the way of its settlement.' It was presumably the latter position that British representatives would be taking up at Stockholm; for at a second Labour conference on 22 August to reconsider the earlier decision it was decided to exclude the ILP from a place on the British delegation.

As it happened, no British delegates ever reached Stockholm. The Government refused them passports. This rebuff the Labour movement took tamely. It was in no position to do otherwise. The strong protests against the conference among sections of labour, the hostility of the Seamen's Union and their threat to appeal from the Labour conference to the trade union rank and file, the evident divisions among supporters of the conference about the objects of a British delegation, and the anger of the ILP at its proposed exclusion (something, wrote Philip Snowden, 'the ILP will not accept for a moment'), had already rendered the conference a source of deep embarrassment to the Labour movement. The fact that, at the second conference on 22 August, the majority in favour of sending a delegation fell, on a card vote, from the 1.3 million of 10 August to a beggarly 3,000 was evidence enough of this. The Government's diktat saved Labour from further humiliation and possible disruption.

The Labour débâcle over Stockholm showed that, however well Henderson had assessed the situation in Russia, he had misjudged the temper of British workmen. That his standing in the labour world did not suffer too heavily over the incident was in part the result of a further aspect of the matter that was wholly British: the manner of his treatment by his Cabinet colleagues. While still a Cabinet member, Henderson was kept waiting outside the door of the Cabinet Office so that his colleagues might discuss his conduct. He was then summoned in to be rebuked by the Prime Minister. This course did not recommend itself to the ranks of labour. It seemed too plain that no upper-class member of the Cabinet, whatever his misdemeanors, would ever be treated like that. As the report on the labour situation for 22 August noted: particularly in Lancashire but in 'the whole country in varying degrees', 'there is considerable resentment about the Government's treatment of Mr. Henderson, both among his supporters and opponents. It is by many regarded as a slight to the Labour movement.'

III

Events in Russia, then, were not exercising a powerful impact upon labour. British workers showed no great inclination to wrest power from the central government by establishing Workers' and Soldiers' Councils. And they seemed less than eager to discuss their war aims with German delegates. Yet it is still the case that this year witnessed growing discontent in the ranks of labour. In a bad week, like that ending 26 September, 75 strikes were reported. In a good one, like that ending 29 August which produced no major stoppages, it was still possible to conclude that 'the labour position and outlook cannot be deemed satisfactory.'

Much of this unrest had no national implications. There were complaints from workers in parts of the Midlands about the employment there of Chinese labour. There were demarcation disputes between rival unions within the same industry: so in August a strike almost developed on account of the 'considerable bitterness' between the Locomotive Engineers and Firemen's Union on the one side and the National Union of Railwaymen on the other – exacerbated, it was said, by personal hostility between the secretaries of the two unions, John Bromley and J. H. Thomas. And there were protests from members of long-established unions who saw their special status being undermined. Miners in the Black Country demanded a heavy wage increase because, among other things, of 'the high wages paid to munition workers'. Skilled workers in engineering complained that wage adjustments were eroding the differentials that distinguished them from the semi-skilled and unskilled. Indeed, in many instances the semi-skilled, employed on piece rates, were earning more than skilled workers occupying more onerous positions but paid only on time rates. And there was a further issue that caused serious discontent among the 'aristocrats of labour': the 'comb-outs' by the Ministry of National Service that were designed to reduce the number of skilled men exempt from military service.

The most important of the strikes in May had occurred among the skilled engineers. Of the two principal causes, one was the Government's decision to abolish the Trade Card scheme, whereby members of the craft unions (but not of other unions) engaged in munitions work were guaranteed exemption from military service. The other was a new Dilution Bill, extending the practice of dilution to private factories. Here again the issue of military service loomed large. According to one of the reports on the labour situation a few months later (15 August 1917), a chief ground of objection to this extension of dilution had been 'a lively fear that that measure was intended as a means of further recruitment from the ranks of the skilled engineers', a sentiment 'expressed at the time of the strike with an openness which suggests that it is held by no inconsiderable body among the engineers'.

Even more serious, according to the same source, was the attitude towards military service among the coal miners. The executive of the Miners' Federation, acting on the precept that it was better to serve as a recruiting officer itself than to leave its members to the mercies of the state authorities, had agreed to produce from its ranks 21,000 further recruits. But such was the 'difficulty experienced in carrying it out' that the exercise had, at least temporarily, to be suspended. In 'the most important of all the coalfields', South Wales, 'opinion is undoubtedly hostile to any further combing out.' Similar, if less widespread, feelings were reported from Lanarkshire, Yorkshire, and Leicestershire. The most that gatherings of rank-and-file miners were prepared to concede was the calling up of men who had entered the pits since the outbreak of war. These were not regarded as 'bona fide miners'.

This last point makes it clear that resistance to the call-up among the miners did not constitute an attempt to prevent any more men from passing into the army, only a particular group of men. The same was true of the skilled engineers. As one of the militants in Sheffield put it in May: 'we say that we are the people to say who shall do the skilled mechanics' work and who can be spared for the Army.' More succinctly, some of the strikers shouted, 'Don't take me, I'm in the ASE' (that is, the chief of the craft unions). Again, in the following January the militant engineers in Sheffield, echoing the miners, passed a resolution threatening drastic action unless, among other things, 'all men who have started in munitions factories since the commencement of the war are taken first'.[10] Plainly, such exercises in self-preservation among miners and skilled engineers were not actions of the whole working class or likely to foster working-class cohesion. Rather, they tended to be most divisive. In Sheffield, during the May strike, a song called 'A Prayer to Lloyd George' was chanted that mocked the particularist slogan of the Amalgamated Society of Engineers:

> Don't send me in the Army, George,
> I'm in the ASE.
> Take all the bloody labourers,
> But for God's sake don't take me.
> You want me for a soldier?
> Well, that can never be –
> A man of my ability,
> And in the ASE!

The only way in which the privileged sector could avoid this appearance of looking after itself at the expense of other workers was by making its opposition to conscription universal. That is, it must argue that no further men at all should be forced into the army. This could only mean the closing down of the war. All along, on the Clyde and in Sheffield, there had been some militant shop stewards who were hostile to the war (incongruously, perhaps, given that they were employed in munitions works). Briefly, towards the end of 1917, it seemed that their view might be gaining currency: that a stop-the-war movement was developing among the skilled engineers. But this never had real substance. It was a grasping at straws by men who, in circumstances of deteriorating manpower, wished to preserve their own immunity from military service without incurring the stigma of doing so at the expense of their fellow workers. But the price of trying to universalize their particularist demands was plainly too high. If war-weariness might turn some of the engineers' minds to an early peace, the sort of peace settlement that Germany was imposing on Russia was bound to turn those same minds sharply away. By January 1918 the stop-the-war tendency among the labour aristocrats had vanished. Consequently, the rift dividing the skilled from the less skilled, and those claiming military exemption from those with no grounds for claiming it, remained.[11]

But if hostility to combing out was always sectional, the authors of the labour situation report for 15 August 1917 feared that it had large implications for the war effort. 'There can be little doubt,' the report stated, 'that much of the early enthusiasm for military service has evaporated. . . . It is also no doubt the case that the voluntary system having exhausted most of those who were keen to fight, the later drafts under conscription consist mainly of men averse to doing so.' The report suggested two

---

[10] Quotations in this paragraph are from James Hinton, *The First Shop Stewards' Movement* (London: Allen & Unwin, 1973), pp. 209–10.

[11] James Hinton, in the introduction to his excellent *The First Shop Stewards' Movement*, says that in January 1918 the shop stewards came within a hair's breadth of initiating a strike movement against the continuance of the war. His thorough account of the events hardly suggests that they came within 100 miles of doing so.

causes of this aversion. One was doubts about whether 'the ideals which were in men's hearts in the first months of the war have been forgotten by the governing classes'. The other was the feeling 'that a man forfeits too much of his citizenship on becoming a soldier, that he is not treated with human sympathy and consideration by the military authorities'. (There may have been a further reason for resisting the call-up that the authors of the report preferred not even to consider: the speed with which especially fit men, entering the army at this advanced stage of the war, were likely to become casualties.)

There were other causes of discontent among groups of wage earners: trends that struck at their living standards. During the war the income tax, which hitherto had fallen only on the upper class and part of the middle classes, began reaching down into the working class. It did so because the level at which income tax became payable was lowered and because wage levels – in monetary if not in real terms – were raised. Social historians have noted this diffusion of direct taxation as tending to dissolve class rigidities. Perhaps it did. Nevertheless, many of the entrants to the select world of income tax payers did not welcome their achievement. The income tax robbed them of a part of wage increases that often were doing no more than restoring wage levels to their former value. And it struck in particular at that part of their earnings secured by working overtime – and overtime usually meant work in excess of 54 hours a week, which was truly money gained by the sweat of their brows. Furthermore, as so often in wartime, the income tax brought the workers into contact with an aspect of state authority that they found disagreeable and even intimidating: its form-filling, bureaucratic aspect. So it was said of north-eastern England in early August: 'A strong feeling against payment of income tax is reported to exist among the workers and a large number of prosecutions for non-payment have been observed in the local press.' And a week later: 'The agitation against the present basis of the income tax, which is now equal to a pre-war assessment of about £75, has spread to the Clyde. . . .'

Yet income tax struck at only a section of wage earners. The force that hit at them all was rising prices, and especially rising food prices. Here was the factor that rendered the wartime experience of so many workers deeply frustrating. In many ways the war seemed to shower them with opportunities absent in peace: full employment, ample overtime, more remunerative forms of work, and a market for war-oriented goods that appeared limitless and demanded satisfaction regardless of cost. But every improvement in wages was rapidly undermined, and generally negated, by advances in the cost of living. Certainly, the war had given to many workers unaccustomed industrial muscle. The nation could not afford to allow bodies like the engineers, miners, and railwaymen to down tools for any length of time. Seeking an explanation for what it called 'the ever-growing and apparently illimitable demand for large increase in wages', one report sourly concluded that the 'rise in the cost of living affords its excuse, the practical impossibility of resisting the demand its explanation'. What the authors of this judgement failed to notice was that every step up the wage scale was promptly eroded by rises in the cost of living, so that the successes won in wage negotiations crumbled away almost as soon as they had been achieved.

The labour reports themselves sometimes suggest that mounting prices were the cause of, and not just an excuse for, industrial militancy. On the Clyde in August the Shipbuilding and Engineering Trades Federation were putting in a claim for 'an increase equivalent to the increase in the cost of living, i.e. 100% on pre-war rates, less 27½% advance already granted'. In the Yorkshire textile industry at the end of September, 50,000 workers, most of them women, voted to hand in their notices early in the next month following an unsatisfactory wage award. 'The workpeople say that their earnings have only increased by from 30% to 50% during the war while the cost of living has risen nearly 100%.' It is difficult to believe, anyway in these instances, that the rise in the cost of living was merely a cloak for industrial blackmail.

As 1917 wore on (and this choice of expression seems apt for the greyest year of the war) it was not only the cost of food but also its availability that was giving rise to deep discontent. As we have seen, sugar had begun to be in short supply even in 1916, and in the course of 1917 margarine, butter, tea, and bacon joined it. According to the historians of Birmingham in wartime, 'the queues outside the grocers' shops became a pathetic and alarming spectacle as the winter approached.'[12] This phenomenon aroused profound working-class resentment, which spread even to soldiers serving at the front. And working-class organizations began drawing conclusions that, however much in tune with wartime notions of equality of sacrifice, severely challenged the existing structure of society. At Nottingham late in September, a report on the labour situation recorded, 'an important joint meeting' of miners and railwaymen passed with enthusiasm a resolution calling on the Food Controller to 'take all the foodstuffs in the country and share them out equally to every household in proportion to the number of the family'.

Such a demand for an equal sharing out of resources contrasted sharply with the visible inequalities between social groupings. Queues outside food shops were not nearly so apparent in middle-class districts. And as for the wealthy, they remained conspicuous consumers. Lady Scott in her diary for 25 May 1917 recorded attending an immense dinner party at the Berkeley followed by the theatre. 'Rather shocking, champagne, strawberries etc.' These indulgences did not pass unnoticed among a working class afflicted by rising prices and shortages. The report on the labour situation for the end of November referred to 'wide advertisement of the facility with which the rich obtain luxuries, the cost of which precludes the working class from their enjoyment'.

Resentment among wage earners at these developments focused on a number of targets, but on one in particular: the war profiteers. These were people alleged to corner markets in scarce commodities, so forcing consumers – be they labourers, industrialists, or government departments – to pay through the nose. How many there were of them, or how wealthy they became, was scarcely known. But the word 'profiteering' entered working-class language as one of the war's most potent terms of abuse. 'By dint of harping on "profiteering", "the inequality of sacrifice", and "the capitalists' war",' lamented the labour situation report for 2 January 1918, 'a great deal has been done to destroy the spirit of unity which permeated the country in the early stages of the war.' What particularly excited indignation among the masses was the conviction that profiteers, in addition to the offence of growing rich through the circumstances of war, were acquiring wealth in ways that struck at the workers directly. One of the commissions of inquiry into industrial unrest appointed in the aftermath of the May strikes referred to the 'deep-seated conviction in the minds of the working classes that the prices of food have risen not only through scarcity, but as a result of the manipulation of prices by unscrupulous producers and traders'.[13]

Rising prices, food queues, profiteering, and the evident contrasts between affluence and deprivation on the home front constituted a potent combination of forces that served to canalize a sense of working-class apartness. Events like the refusal of passports to British delegates to Stockholm or the disruption of meetings intended to

---

[12] Reginald H. Brazier and Ernest Sandford, *Birmingham and the Great War 1914–1919* (Birmingham: Cornish Bros., 1921), p. 210.

[13] Quoted in Waites, 'The First World War and Working-Class Consciousness in England'.

set up Workers' and Soldiers' Councils might arouse little working-class indignation (and some working-class approval). The efforts of skilled workers to preserve differentials or to safeguard their immunity from military service might cause division rather than cohesion within the labour force. But the concourse of a rising cost of living, queues at the food shops, and a suspected group of manipulators getting rich quickly produced a mood of indignation that permeated the working class.

Soon this indignation began to express itself in industrial action. In Lanarkshire in August a one-day strike involving 50,000 miners took place 'as a protest against the rise in food prices.' In Coventry in November indignation against food queues produced a one-day strike there. Within two months this sort of protest was reaching alarming proportions. According to the report on the labour situation for early February 1918: 'The number of workers involved in the short strikes which are occurring all over the country as protests against the food situation is becoming a matter of serious national importance.' And sometimes the strikes were accompanied by yet more ominous events. In Birmingham (where, except for meat, foodstuffs in short supply were already being rationed on a municipal basis), butchers' shops were raided by indignant mobs.

These events, and the strong feelings from which they sprang, had important class implications. They tended to unify the disparate elements of the working class. They tended to sharpen hostility between the workers on the one side and the possessing classes on the other. And they tended to call in question some basic tenets of industrial capitalism. For outrage against profiteering impugned the profit motive. And demands for equal shares of food challenged the inequalities that lay at the heart of the private enterprise system.

How powerful these radicalizing tendencies were, and how lasting, only time and the further strains of war would decide.

48

THE ROLE OF GOVERNMENT

I

Lloyd George's accession to the premiership witnessed more than a change in the personnel of the Government. It saw the institution of a new sort of Cabinet.

Under the pressures of war Asquith had set up, in parallel to the established Cabinet, a sequence of committees drawn from it to deal exclusively with war matters. These had been called, successively, the War Council, the Dardanelles Committee, and the War Committee. Lloyd George now dispensed with the larger body and elevated the smaller into the Cabinet proper. It was dubbed the War Cabinet to indicate its overriding purpose. And its handful of members, apart from Bonar Law (Chancellor of the Exchequer), had no departmental responsibilities. Their job was to exercise oversight of all areas of the conflict.

The extent of the change need not be overstated. Like the Cabinet proper of the Asquith coalition, Lloyd George's five-man War Cabinet faithfully reflected the Government's diverse following in the House of Commons. As at first constituted, it consisted of three Conservatives, one of whom was that party's leader; one Labour man, who was plainly there as his party's representative; and a Liberal who, though the country's outstanding war leader, was doubted in some quarters to be firm in his party allegiance.

Again, if this Cabinet proved more decisive and less prone to division than its predecessor, that was not primarily on account of its reduced size. Other factors, like the personality of the Prime Minister, counted for more. This is not to say that Lloyd George proved – as he has sometimes been portrayed – a sort of populist dictator, disregarding his parliamentary followers and riding roughshod over his ministerial colleagues. But he possessed none of the aversion to reaching decisions that (according to Selborne and others) had characterized Asquith's direction of affairs. On the contrary, Lloyd George was determined to lead; and this counteracted any tendency to fractiousness in his Cabinet. Yet a strong director at the top was no peculiarly wartime development. It was in line with the burgeoning authority of the Prime Minister's office over many decades of peace, even if exaggerated by a war-induced craving among the populace for determined, and above all demonstrative, leadership.

Moreover the large issues that had threatened to tear apart the first wartime coalition posed no threat to the second. When even Asquith's War Committee, in its last days, could propose compulsory service (military or industrial) for every adult male, then plainly the conscription issue had lost all power to paralyse the nation's rulers. As for the question of what size of army Britain could afford, financially, to keep in the field, that was settled within five months of Lloyd George's accession to the premiership. The entry of America into the lists ended the mounting peril that Britain's credit would shortly run out. Again, no question of strategy such as had racked the Asquith coalition over what to do about the Gallipoli operation confronted Lloyd George's administration, anyway in disruptive form. On the contrary, however little Lloyd George liked (or was even prepared to admit) the fact, he was engaged in a war that presented no viable strategic alternatives.

There was another respect in which the Lloyd George Cabinet, irrespective of numbers, was unlikely to suffer the disruption of Asquith's. No member serving within it possessed either the will or the stature to function simultaneously as a leader of malcontents, and so to appear an alternative Prime Minister.

To say this is not to deny that the new style of Cabinet (like the new man at the top) was a great improvement on the old. The small War Cabinet could and did meet frequently – over 500 times between its formation and the end of the war. It was free to call in other Government Ministers and departmental experts when matters of their special concern were under discussion, while dispensing with their presence when they had nothing pertinent to offer. (A rather different proceeding occurred in the run-up to the Calais conference in February 1917. Then the War Minister and the CIGS were excluded because what they were likely to say would be pertinent but not welcome.)

On some issues, not even the entire War Cabinet was the guiding body. 'Committees' composed of only some of its members were assigned to tackle particularly serious matters. Principal among these were the War Policy Committee of mid-1917, convened (according to John Turner) 'to intimidate Robertson and Haig into changing their plans'; and the 'X' committee of 1918, apparently designed to give the Prime Minister 'control of the fighting in France'.[1] Neither committee, it has to be said, proved markedly successful. The former, as we have seen, neither prevented nor even brought to a halt the Third Ypres campaign. And (contrary to Dr Turner) the 'X' committee did not 'supervise strategy until the armistice'. Rather, as will be shown, Lloyd George's Government in 1918 became the only British administration in this war, if not in modern history, to allow control of strategy in the principal theatre largely to pass out of civilian hands.

To underpin, and to reduce to manageable proportions, the activities of the War Cabinet, a great many (generally useful) bodies were established. It is their existence that explains John Turner's description of the Cabinet's evolution during the war as being one of transformation 'from a political committee into a complex administrative system'.[2] Periodically *ad hoc* sub-committees, usually presided over by members of the War Cabinet, were established for long or short periods. Their job was to advise on new problems or on problems over which departments were at odds with one another. So General Smuts (who entered the War Cabinet in June 1917) was appointed chairman of a sub-committee on air policy. It produced a highly influential report, whose principal – if questionable – achievement was the foundation of the Royal Air Force.

Other sub-committees, dealing with matters like domestic legislation and post-war economic policy towards Germany, existed on a more permanent basis. The most noteworthy were those that dealt with the allocation of scarce resources, such as shipping space and raw materials. One of them, the War Priorities Committee, has been called 'a model of devolved administrative responsibility'.[3] At its head a committee of eight Government Ministers (chaired by the ubiquitous Smuts) presided

---

[1] John Turner, 'Cabinets, Committees and Secretariats: the Higher Direction of War', in Kathleen Burk (ed.), *War and the State: The Transformation of British Government, 1914–1919* (London: Allen & Unwin, 1982), pp. 66–7.

[2] Ibid., p. 57.

[3] Ibid., p. 68.

over several sub-committees dealing with the main groups of resources in short supply. Under these were 16 allocation sub-committees responsible for specific commodities. Difficulties at any one level were referred to the level above, with the War Cabinet as the ultimate court of appeal. This structure proved one of the war's decided successes.

Two other bodies were called into existence to support the War Cabinet with specialist services. A private secretariat to the Prime Minister (dubbed the Garden Suburb) was set up to employ some able men whom Lloyd George wished to occupy and whose advice he appreciated. It provided expert – and in some instances useful – opinions on a rather random group of matters, such as Ireland and shipbuilding. It never functioned as the Cabinet-outside-the-Cabinet that it was sometimes reputed to be.

More noteworthy was the Cabinet Secretariat, under Hankey. Its task was to keep minutes of Cabinet meetings and records of Cabinet decisions. Thereby Ministers (in and out of the War Cabinet) were apprised of which matters had been discussed and what had been resolved. And departments received a clear indication of the consequent actions that were expected of them. Much of the confusion of Asquith's day regarding what, if anything, had been agreed on was thus eliminated. And the diligence of this secretariat ensured that the War Cabinet would never want for matters requiring its attention.

II

The formation of Lloyd George's Government was speedily followed by the institution of a number of new Ministries: among them Ministries for Labour, National Service, Food, and Shipping. The first of these may have been 'largely a gesture'.[4] Such ill-defined functions as the Ministry of Labour possessed, like control of the employment exchanges, tended to complicate the activities of other Ministries dealing with the same areas. But by and large the new instrumentalities reflected a will to grapple with major problems. In company with the reconstituted War Cabinet and other already established Ministries, they considerably enlarged the role of the state in directing the economy, controlling manpower, and guarding communal welfare.

These developments may be variously interpreted. One of the major issues confronting Governments in wartime was the tension between freedom and control. So it is possible to view the changes of Government in May 1915 and December 1916 as phases in the advance of the latter at the expense of the former. That Lloyd George, upon becoming Prime Minister, established new Ministries and extended the powers of old appears evidence that his Government possessed a much stronger commitment to the philosophy of state control at the expense of individual freedom.

Yet it is necessary to enter caveats to this interpretation, which may not invalidate it but do qualify its simplicities. Several of the changes instituted by Lloyd George can equally be interpreted – as, in a sense, can the change of Government itself – as pragmatic responses to the mounting crises of the war. That is, it was less the change of Government than the changing nature of the conflict that determined these new forms of action. For example, the manpower situation was once more acutely difficult because of the heavy casualties suffered during the Somme offensive in France – not to mention that offensive's failure to bring the war anywhere near to termination. Consequently, the army would need another 450,000 men by the end of March 1917. But the country must also increase the size of the labour force in munitions so as to keep the army better supplied than in 1916.

---

[4] R. H. Gretton, *A Modern History of the English People 1880–1922* (London: Martin Secker, 1930), p. 1015.

How well the Asquith Government would have dealt with the manpower problem created by the heavy losses and stalled offensives of 1916 must be a matter for speculation. But it is worth noticing that in its last weeks of office it was not inactive in the matter. Fit men of military age working as unskilled and semi-skilled operatives in essential industries began to be released for the army whenever substitutes could be found for them. And exemption from service, under the Conscription Act, on exceptional financial or business grounds was largely withdrawn from men under 26. (The age limit was raised to include men under 31 early in 1917.) Even more notably, on 30 November 1916 the Asquith War Committee decided to accept the principle of compulsory national service for all men up to the age of 55 years. This was, on the face of it, a momentous decision. Asquith and his closest colleagues were thereby committed to conscription not only for the army but also for industry.

Whether Asquith's War Committee possessed the resolve to carry this proposal through both Cabinet and Parliament, and whether they would have pressed on with it in the face of labour resistance, are open questions. But it is noteworthy that the Lloyd George Government, though claiming to hold compulsory national service in reserve, did not persist with this bold course. The Ministry of National Service that it set up was equipped with only vague powers, and was to proceed initially by means of voluntary appeals – what a biographer of the first director of National Service caustically describes as 'a scheme for industry . . . corresponding to the Derby Scheme for the army, which had so signally failed'.[5]

In the matter of foodstuffs, also, it is important to recognize that no crisis requiring drastic action appeared to exist before the second half of 1916. Up to that stage it had been a case of 'feeding as usual'. Only the comparative failure of the American harvest (as against abundance in 1915), the inadequacy of Britain's potato crop, a possible shortfall in its cereal crop, and the mounting submarine campaign radically altered by August 1916 what had seemed a secure situation. Again, the Asquith Government showed preparedness to act. Even the arch-devotee of *laissez-faire*, Runciman, announced his conversion to a large degree of state intervention in the matter. Lord Crawford, Minister for Agriculture in the closing months of Asquith's premiership, took powers to enforce the cultivation of unoccupied urban land, so increasing the area available for allotments. And the Government not only announced its intention to appoint a Food Controller but offered the post to a Conservative proponent of state action, Lord Milner (who declined it).

Once more it is a matter for debate whether the will on Asquith's part would have been followed by any remarkable deeds. But Lloyd George's own first appointee as Food Controller, Lord Devonport, fell well short of Milnerism in his approach to the food question. In fact, his period in office also was seen as equivalent to the Derby scheme: a last attempt to work the voluntary system. Devonport's activities did include some developments in the organization of food control, as well as the institution of one meatless day per week for hotels and restaurants. But mainly they consisted of appeals to the public to keep food consumption within prescribed limits.

Indeed, one of the most striking things about the new Government's handling of the food problem, during months of lengthening queues and mounting discontent, was its tardiness in resorting to general rationing. No doubt practicalities had a lot to do with this. A rationing scheme required the services of a considerable body of administrators at a time when personnel was short. Yet it is still noteworthy that the central authority tarried, while local bodies were being driven by popular indignation to inaugurate their own rationing schemes. This remains a signal qualification to any description of the

---

[5] Keith Feiling, *The Life of Neville Chamberlain* (London: Macmillan, 1946), p. 64.

second coalition as implementer of a statist philosophy. It is even possible to envisage Lloyd George applying the expression 'too late' to government action in this field, had anyone but himself been First Minister.

III

Having suggested that the change from the first coalition to the second was not, in policy matters, so abrupt a transition as may seem the case, it is necessary to make a further point. In the increasingly desperate fields of manpower, shipping, and food supply the achievements of the Lloyd George Government were considerable.

As the decision by the Asquith War Committee, late in November 1916, to impose national service on all adult males bore witness, the new Government was heir to a grave manpower crisis. The army's losses must be made good. This meant that the stage had been reached when even essential industries must be obliged to disgorge fit males. As far as was possible, substitutes would be found for them. In part this would be done by regulation. Early in 1917 a directive was issued under DORA forbidding non-essential industries (except those with special permission) to hire males aged between 18 and 60. This was an important step towards the indirect control of manpower outside the armed forces. But it was not all-embracing. These non-essential industries were not obliged actually to surrender male employees in this age group; nor were they prevented from taking on females, boys, and old men, some of whom might have been of use in essential industries. For the rest, substitutes for men taken into the army would, to begin with (and it proved a long beginning), be secured by voluntary appeals.

But what is noteworthy is the determination to summon into the army fit men hitherto exempted, whether or not substitutes for industry could always be found. For this purpose existing schemes by which 'badged' men could be combed out of essential industries were put aside as inadequate . A thoroughgoing administrative system was set up throughout the country to allocate certificates of exemption and to hear appeals from those in the process of being denied them. Such immunity as was granted to fit males of military age ceased to be unqualified. It could be terminated whenever substitutes became available or military needs became imperative.

From August 1917 this proceeding was greatly assisted by the reorganized Ministry of National Service. In the form that this body was first established in December 1916 it proved a considerable fiasco. Its role was exhortatory rather than executive. It found itself confined to matters of civilian manpower only, and even there it was in competition with well established bodies like the Ministry of Munitions and the newly established Ministry of Labour. It had no control over the employment exchanges, 'the machine upon which the whole Government system of labour supply rested'.[6] The man appointed as Director of National Service, Neville Chamberlain, did not prove agreeable to Lloyd George, who disregarded his proposals.

In August Chamberlain resigned, and the department was reconstituted under Auckland Geddes.[7] It now had the confidence of the War Cabinet, and it had the whole field of manpower, military as well as civilian, as its province. It was in a better position to work through the employment exchanges. And it was able to tell established bodies, such as the Ministry of Munitions, if not which men they would relinquish then what number of men. So exhaustive and convincing were its inquiries that in time the

---

[6] Humbert Wolfe, *Labour Supply and Regulation* (Oxford: Clarendon Press, 1923), p. 22.

[7] A brother of Sir Eric, Auckland Geddes in peacetime had been a professor of anatomy with a long-standing interest in military matters. From early 1916 he had been Director of Recruiting.

Ministry of National Service was able to go further. It established the principle of the 'clean cut', whereby specified industries would, without guarantee of substitutes, be obliged to release all fit males within a particular age limit. This was the basis of a new Military Service Act introduced in February 1918. That labour agreed to it was evidence of the growing recognition that, by the fourth year of the war, the country was confronting a situation of the utmost gravity.

The adoption of this principle of the 'clean cut', by which even essential industries could be deprived of specified sectors of their fittest personnel, was noteworthy. In time it might lead to a running down of industrial output. But during the approaching military crises of 1918, when the country would be calling up both younger and older men than it had hitherto deemed warranted, it was able to throw into the fray at least some men of the highest level of fitness and belonging to the most militarily desirable age group.

Yet although during 1917 the Government extended its grasp over men of military age, it continued to fall well short of imposing national service upon all adult males. In response to working-class resistance – the May strikes, involving 200,000 men and the loss of 1.5 million working days – it gave up its plans to extend dilution in the engineering industry to private work. And in the aftermath of these strikes it actually surrendered a power that the state had been exercising since the passing of the Munitions Act back in mid-1915. It agreed to abolish the hated leaving certificate, which prevented skilled men from selling their services to the highest bidder.[8]

So while in some ways the spectre of industrial conscription seemed to be moving closer, in others it had been stopped in its tracks or even forced to retreat. The adherence of Lloyd George's Government to the philosophy of state direction over labour was not single-minded – or perhaps it would be more accurate to say that the country's rulers recognized that they were practising a branch of the art of the possible.

IV

If shortage of manpower was one of the major problems confronting Lloyd George's Government, shortage of shipping was another.

From early in the war the supply of merchant shipping had come under strain because of Britain's mounting commitments. The severance of relations with customers and suppliers in Central Europe made it necessary to go further afield for markets and raw materials. A growing proportion of Britain's shipping had to be diverted to supplying its allies – to the tune of 3 million tons of cargo space by late 1917. During the first two years of the war a great many merchant ships were requisitioned for the nation's military campaigns across the Channel and much further afield. Meanwhile the ports were suffering growing congestion: on account of the threat from the submarine, heavy enlistment of dock labour, and the redirection of shipping away from the vulnerable East Coast ports. Then there were the mounting losses to the U-boat.

One of Lloyd George's first actions was to create a Ministry of Shipping, which also embraced ship building. The man appointed as Minister was Sir Joseph Maclay. A prominent shipowner and a driving businessman, he was one of a type whom Lloyd George regarded as high among the potential saviours of the nation. And for the task set him, he proved ideal. He formed an advisory committee, also peopled by

---

[8] The leaving certificate regulation had decreed that a workman in an essential industry could not, without a certificate of release from his last employer or the munitions tribunal, be taken on by another employer until after the passage of an interval of six weeks.

shipowners. He incorporated into his Ministry the organization and personnel of a number of committees formed under Asquith to deal with aspects of the shipping problem. And for his departmental aids he had available an experienced body of civil servants. On this basis he carried state direction of the mercantile marine to a high level.

Under Maclay all merchant shipping was requisitioned at fixed rates, and all shipping space allocated. Non-essential imports were prohibited, and essential imports and exports rationed. Shipping was directed to secure commodities from the nearest sources of supply, especially North America, at whatever cost to established trade patterns. And in order to economize on space, wheat was imported from the USA not in its unmilled condition but in the form of flour.

The activities of the Ministry invaded many other areas. Pressure was put on the service chiefs to curtail the amount of tonnage employed for the more remote campaigns; although about a quarter of merchant shipping was still diverted to these activities, this was a reduction. The problem of the ports was also assailed, not least by employing a large body of servicemen as dock labourers in especially congested areas. Efforts were also made to relieve the bottleneck in and out of the ports on the land side caused by the overcrowding of the railways.

At the same time endeavours to secure fresh tonnage were increased. In one important respect these were successful. An ambitious policy of construction, aiming at 1 million tons per annum as against the 630,000 tons of 1915, was undertaken. Despite shortages of steel and of labour, strikes, and heavy calls for repairs of ships that had broken down under the hands of inexperienced crews or had suffered from enemy action, the programme was fulfilled. Another aspect of the attempt to secure new ships was less fortunate. Large orders were placed with shipyards in the USA. However, as soon as America joined the combatants its Government proceeded to requisition all shipping under construction.

No actions by government could alter the fact that throughout 1917 a grave situation was obtaining. The demands on Britain's shipping were constantly increasing. For example, the USA could not offer vessels sufficient to carry what ultimately it would be able to provide in equipment and manpower. At the same time, thanks to the depredations of the U-boats, the number of ships reaching Britain was falling alarmingly. And the building schedule, at least until the middle of 1918, was not making good the vessels lost.

This alarming reduction in the quantity of shipping reaching Britain was befalling a country with no great room for manoeuvre. Non-essential trade had already been practically eliminated. Whatever was being brought in and sent abroad was badly needed: for the waging of war, economic survival, and the feeding of the populace. In 1917, 46,000 tons of meat were lost at sea. In less than five months, between February and June of that year, 85,000 tons of sugar went down, reducing the country at one point to four days' supply. In this same period stocks of wheat and flour were so low that they would suffice for little more than two months. Clearly, government initiatives in other areas were also required.

V

State control of shipping and action against the U-boat were two ways in which the Government strove to preserve the nation's food supply. But other courses were open to it. It could act to increase the output of home-produced food. And it could take charge of distribution so as to avoid intolerable hardship and uncontrollable discontent.

The onset of war had steadily reduced rural output in Britain: on account of such factors as the disappearance of farm labour into the army and into industry, the requisitioning of horses by the military (at a time when mechanization was conspicuous by its absence), and the diversion of phosphates into the manufacture of munitions. With poor harvests in many parts of the world in 1916 and the mounting threat from the U-boat, there was already by the beginning of 1917 a vocal demand that Britain should reduce its dependence on imported food. This meant restoring to grain production much of the land that had gone over to grass since the 1870s. But if farmers were to undertake this without risking heavy losses, they must be assured of a market not only during but for several years after the war, which entailed a state-guaranteed price for their produce. In return farmers would have to accept a measure of supervision to ensure that they farmed efficiently, and would have to pay a more appropriate wage to their labourers than they had so far been inclined to do.

To achieve this package of guaranteed prices, supervision of farming, and living wages, the Government added regulations to DORA, secured the passage of a Corn Production Act, and established a wideranging administrative machinery that stretched all the way from Whitehall to the localities. Thereby it became possible to combat inefficiency, to direct farming towards producing the required commodities, to bring derelict areas back into production, and to allocate such scarce resources as labour, fertilizers, implements, and feedstuffs.

By the end of 1917 the food-production policy had already achieved some success, in terms of increased output of cereals and potatoes – but only at the expense of decreased meat, milk, butter, and cheese. More rewarding in the short run was the Government's food-control policy, whose purpose was to enhance the amount of food derived from a given quantity of farm produce – in particular, by securing more bread from the same amount of wheat. This was achieved in two ways: by employing a higher extraction rate, so that more of the grain became flour and less went into animal feed; and by diluting wheat flour with flour derived from such substances as barley and maize.

This combination of high rates of extraction and admixture secured impressive results. 'In April 1918,' Peter Dewey tells us, 'out of every 100 lbs. of flour milled, 54 lbs. represented that part of wheat which had always gone to human consumption, 17 lbs. that part of the grain which had formerly gone to animal feed, and 29 lbs. came from admixture with other cereals or with potatoes.' In his judgement, this food-control policy increased supply by 3.7 billion calories in 1917 and by 7.5 billion in 1918 (1 billion being 1 million × 1 million) – 'much larger than the net gains due to the food production policy'.[9]

VI

The Government's actions in the other areas of food supply – that is, control of the price and allocation of food – were (as has been suggested already) less than happy. Its first appointee as Food Controller, Lord Devonport, was not a success, and by the time of his resignation in April 1917 he had become something of a laughing-stock. Yet the cause of failure did not really lie with him. The government was still not accepting that

[9] See P. E. Dewey, 'Food Production and Policy in the United Kingdom, 1914–1918', *Transactions of the Royal Historical Society*, Fifth Series, vol. 30, London, 1980, pp. 71–89. This article contains much valuable information, although parts of its central argument require closer investigation.

the day of voluntary appeals had passed. No doubt the complexities of devising a rationing system, and the considerable number of persons who would be needed to administer it, presented daunting problems. But these were reasons for taking the matter in hand without delay, and this the Government failed to do. Lloyd George justifies his reluctance on grounds of public, and in particular working-class, hostility to rationing. The Government, he says, therefore 'decided to approach it – as had previously been done with compulsory service – along the line of first exhausting the possibilities of voluntary control.'[10] Given the resentment that he had himself expressed towards just this proceeding on the matter of military service, his conviction that it was appropriate to the food crisis of 1917 seems a strange lapse in judgement. His view was not shared by one of the people actively engaged in the administration of this area. William Beveridge writes:

> The new Government, though they had threatened drastic control of food and had made weakness in relation to food one ground for overthrowing their predecessors, were not themselves prepared for strong measures . . . .
> In retrospect, it seems clear that the public would have been ready for compulsory rationing of sugar and of other articles, as need arose, at any time after the end of 1916.[11]

Devonport's successor (who took the post against his doctor's orders) was Lord Rhondda, a Welsh colliery owner on a huge scale and a former Liberal MP. His acquaintanceship with food distribution was negligible. But he had large experience of business and administration, possessed a flair for publicity, and assembled an effective staff.

Fundamental to Rhondda's policy was the precept that, if at all possible, there must never be a shortage of bread. This was the prime article of mass consumption, and so must be available both in sufficient quantities and at a reasonable price. For the latter purpose, the Government took the extreme step of introducing a bread subsidy. Thus the tax-paying classes found themselves required to aid the less wealthy in the procurement of this item. On 1 September 1917 the Government decreed that the price of the 4-lb. loaf, which had risen from 5½d. in 1914 to 1 shilling three years later and was about to rise again, would be reduced to 9d.

To ensure a sufficiency of supply the Food Ministry needed not only increased home production but also an adequate allocation of shipping space. This it managed to secure, and to signal effect. Indeed, weekly bread consumption in 1917 proved to be ½ lb. per head above the pre-war level.

But if shipping space was being reserved for wheat, other commodities must go short. A prime case was sugar. After bread it was the article most generally consumed by all classes. But it was wholly imported, and on account of the U-boat campaign the supply began to fall short of demand. So whereas bread consumption in 1917 was higher than before the war, sugar was down by about one-third. This led to abuses. Shopkeepers took to supplying customers according not to the size of their families but to the depth of their pockets. So, in Leicester, 'A woman with eight children could obtain no more than 2 lbs., whereas a small well-to-do family could increase the amount by the purchase of tinned fruits and other luxuries.'[12]

When the authorities made this practice illegal they facilitated a different sort of abuse. Those who were fit and able could travel from shop to shop buying nothing but sugar, and shops that tried to deter them became liable to prosecution. Semi-control by

---

[10] *War Memoirs of David Lloyd George*, 2-volume edn (London: Odhams Press, 1938), vol. 1, p. 788.

[11] Sir William H. Beveridge, *British Food Control* (London: Oxford University Press, 1928), pp. 45–6.

[12] F. P. Armitage, *Leicester 1914–1918: The War-Story of a Midland Town* (Leicester: Edgar Backus, 1933), pp. 207–8.

the state, in short, could solve nothing. Only a thoroughgoing system of rationing could meet the situation.

By the end of 1917 Rhondda's administrative structure for food control was just about complete. Fundamental to it was a large measure of decentralization. A network of food-control committees was established all over the country, appointed by the local authorities but responsible only to the Ministry. Between the committees and the Ministry Rhondda established Divisional Food Commissions, originally 12 in number but growing in time to 15. These commissions were the agencies through which the central authority transmitted to the localities its ideas and instructions on such key matters as the registration of all retailers of controlled foods, the administration of controlled prices, thorough inspection of the dealings of manufacturers and distributors, and the development of a rationing system by the registration of households. So efficient and devoted did some food committees become that late in 1917, as commodities became scarce and national rationing tarried, they instituted their own rationing schemes. Most noteworthy in this regard was Birmingham, where by the end of the year ration cards for tea, sugar, butter, and margarine had been distributed to 300,000 families, so abolishing queues for these commodities.

At the centre a large machine of control was being developed. It combined the expertise of businessmen with the skills of civil servants. It employed scientifically qualified advisers to guide it on matters such as nutrition. It inquired into the anxieties and peculiarities of consumers. And it possessed as its chief spokesman in the House of Commons a Labour MP, Clynes, with direct experience of the least skilled and (in normal times) least well paid among the organized workers. The objectives of the Ministry were four-fold: to stamp out profiteering in food, to keep the prices of basic foods at levels that the public could afford and would tolerate, to maintain adequate supplies, and to see that what was available was distributed justly to retailers and eventually to individual consumers. This would involve the Ministry and its agencies in taking over the business of purchasing, transporting, and distributing both the imported and the locally produced food of the entire nation. In time 85 per cent of all food eaten by civilians would be bought and sold by government instrumentalities, and 94 per cent of all food and drink would be subject to price control.

Once brought fully into operation, the effects of this machine of state control would be dramatic – with the disappearance of queues their most visible sign. The reason was not that the Food Ministry had it in its powers to provide much larger supplies of food. But this was not the key aspect of the problem. A sufficiency of food still existed overall, whatever the shortfall in particular commodities. What was lacking was control over supply and distribution to ensure that all citizens got what seemed a reasonable share of the amount available.

As 1917 ended the necessary machinery of control had just about been developed. But to ordinary people queueing in miserable weather, this was far from evident. What appeared to be occurring was a dramatic deterioration in the food situation. As a consequence, the standing of both Government and Food Ministry was falling markedly.

PART TWELVE

Battlefronts
1918

49

THE EVE OF THE STORM

I

1918 opened in the shadow of the previous year's failures. Certainly, the worst calamity threatening Britain – defeat by the U-boat – had been averted. And the entry of the USA into the lists held out the promise of eventual massive military assistance.

Nevertheless, 1917 had not, in respect to the war on the Continent, been a good year for the Allies. The great French offensive of the spring had fared disastrously. The major British operations from April onwards had fulfilled none of their larger promises and had cost the nation dear. Italy had suffered a savage rebuff late in the year, causing five British divisions under the nation's outstanding army commander (Plumer) to be rushed to the Italians' aid. Most calamitous of all, Russia had gone out of the war altogether. This placed Germany in a position not only to extract plunder from its conquests but also to transfer huge numbers of troops from the Eastern Front.

In these circumstances confidence in an early victory was difficult to maintain. Tubby Clayton, the clergyman who established Toc H as a rest centre for troops out of the line, recounts how at the start of each year a debate was held on the progress of the war. The voting, he says, was generally more instructive than the speeches. The motion was 'That this House is decidedly [or 'firmly' or 'profoundly'] convinced that the war will be over this year'. In January 1916 it had passed by 150 votes to 8. In January 1917 it had succeeded by 200 votes to 15. In January 1918 it was carried only on the casting vote of the chairman after the two sides had tied at 80 votes each.

One event of January 1918 deserves mention. Lloyd George embarked on a definition of war aims. Hitherto there had been no strong call for such an exposition. The prime British war aim was unequivocal: to clear the invader off the soil of Belgium and France. This might be reiterated, with suitable embellishments, in season and out. But anything more wide-ranging had, up to now, seemed injudicious. There was the danger of revealing that Britain's allies had territorial ambitions that were in conflict with one another, or contrary to Britain's ostensible ideals, or calculated to prolong enemy resistance. It might even transpire that Britain itself had ambitions inconsistent with its high professions; or, on the contrary, that it was not coverting enemy territory to the extent that British jingoes thought appropriate.

However, by January 1918 three powerful impulses were compelling clarification of this matter: President Wilson's pronounced views on the subject; the Bolshevik action in publishing the Allies' secret treaties so as to depict the two sides equally as predators; and the feared development within Britain, consequent upon weariness or the Russian 'infection', of disenchantment with the war.

The setting of Lloyd George's utterance was noteworthy. He spoke not to the House of Commons or his political supporters or a public gathering. His venue was a conference of trade unionists. This ensured that he would be at his most 'idealistic'. But the trade unionists were gathered to consider matters concerning manpower – that is, the continuing mobilization for war. Hence the Prime Minister could address himself to war aims, not to the issue of a negotiated peace.

Lloyd George began by saying what Britain was not fighting for: the destruction of Germany or its demotion from the great position it had occupied in the world. (Even the establishment of democracy in Germany, though desirable, was deemed a matter that must be decided by the German people.) He then moved to positive war aims. The restoration of Belgium and other conquered countries was pre-eminent, and the 'reconsideration' of Alsace-Lorraine was something for which Britain would 'stand by the French democracy to the death'. Concerning Russia, he said that Britain would be proud to fight alongside its new democracy but could not save it if its present rulers were bent on destruction.

Plate 42   *Lloyd George in Paris in November 1917, indicating his disenchantment with Britain's military command and calling for the creation of an Allied War Council.*

Lloyd George touched also on issues less central to Britain. Austria-Hungary should be required to grant self-government and democratic forms to those of its nationalities seeking them, and its Italian and Romanian subjects should be united with their co-nationalists. Turkey might retain Constantinople and its genuinely Turkish parts but not the remainder of its empire. And Poland should recover its independence.

There were three final points. Germany's former colonies must be placed under Governments acceptable to their inhabitants. The victims of violations of international law – Britain's merchant seamen principal among them – must receive reparation. And an international organization must be established so as to diminish the burden of armaments, the growing evil of military conscription, and the probability of wars in the future.

The immediate impact of this utterance proved limited. It may have helped to reassure the doubters at home and allies abroad. But it was bound to have little influence upon the enemy. For to Germany's rulers even the *sine qua non* of Lloyd George's utterance – full restoration of Belgium – was out of the question. And now more than ever the purpose of all their endeavours was not to trade peace packages but to achieve swift and total military victory.

Even in Britain the need to enunciate war aims as a means of stiffening war resolve soon vanished. Before March was out, any rallying of the nation that was required had been accomplished by the drama of the battlefield – by what the left-wing periodical the *Nation* called 'the gigantic events of such a week of war as the world has never known and, pray Heaven! may never know again'.

II

While Britain awaited the war's culminating onslaught, some noteworthy changes were occurring in its upper military echelons. First to go were Haig's intelligence adviser Charteris and Chief of Staff Kiggell. It was none too soon. Their optimistic accounts of the enemy's decline had lost them the trust of almost everyone (except Haig) inside military circles and without. Then in February 1918 Robertson, who at the last played his hand very unskilfully, was manoeuvred out. He had advised persistently in favour of the Western Front, and after the experiences of 1917 the Western Front was decidedly out of favour among the nation's political leaders.

But far more striking was the change in the military hierarchy that did not take place. The occupant of the post of Commander-in-Chief on the Western Front remained undisturbed.

This is remarkable. In one respect at least the battle of Cambrai, which had closed 1917 so discouragingly, had seemed a decisive operation. Here, surely, was the end of the line for Sir Douglas Haig. Lloyd George could seek no better grounds for dispensing with him. Certainly, Cambrai was a less profound calamity than Third Ypres – concerning which Lloyd George had told an audience in Paris (and the world) on 12 November: 'We have won great victories. When I look at the appalling casualty lists I sometimes wish it had not been necessary to win so many.' But Cambrai was more galling because of its great early promise, followed by retreat and humiliation.

The decline in Haig's prestige by the start of 1918 was manifest. Those devoted weathercocks of public opinion, the press barons Northcliffe and Rothermere, concluded that the time had come to abandon him. When, on 13 December 1917, Philip Sassoon wrote once more to Northcliffe seeking his support for Haig, he received a different reply from that which had been customary. Northcliffe answered: 'There is the memory of a dead man, or the knowledge of a missing or wounded man, in every house. Outside the War Office, I doubt whether the Higher Command has any supporters whatever.'[1] These views Northcliffe did not keep to himself. On 12 December *The Times*, his most prestigious newspaper, called for the removal of every blunderer. And on 21 January the *Daily Mail*, his biggest-selling journal, fiercely attacked the general staff for squandering British manpower.

Even in military circles, though he retained the loyalty of his army commanders, Haig's standing was not unimpaired. Henry Wilson (Robertson's successor as CIGS) remained, of course, unsparingly critical. Characteristic entries in his diary during January 1918 read: 'Haig really is incurably stupid' and 'The man is a FOOL.' But

---

[1] Reginald Pound and Geoffrey Harmsworth, *Northcliffe* (London: Cassell, 1959), p. 598.

military figures of sounder repute were coming to a like judgement. Tim Harington, Plumer's highly regarded Chief of Staff, expressed himself to Wilson on 28 January as favouring the removal of Haig, in whom he had no confidence –and in whom, he said, the troops had no confidence either. By late March Wilson was receiving an even stronger opinion from Major-General Tom Bridges, commander of a division until he had lost a leg at Passchendaele. Wilson reported him as saying, 'the Army would give a "sigh of relief" if Haig was removed.'

Nevertheless, Haig survived. It has already been noticed that Lloyd George in November 1917 discountenanced the 'great victories' won by the 'appalling casualty lists' with which Haig was identified. This public disparagement of the Commander-in-Chief was endorsed by Auckland Geddes, Director-General of National Service, in January 1918. The Government, he declared, was 'determined that carelessness with regard to human life, and thoughtlessness with regard to casualties, shall be stamped out wherever it appears'. But stamping out the consequences of Haig's operations did not, it transpired, mean stamping on Haig. Admittedly, he had suffered some loss of supporters, but this did not imperil him. With fine political judgement, if seeming lack of gratitude, he witnessed Robertson's demotion without a murmur of regret. And although the new CIGS was plainly a Lloyd George man, Haig neither appeared alarmed nor had cause to be. Henry Wilson might regard Haig with disdain. But he would never, when the crunch came, nerve himself to insist that Haig should go.

As for Lloyd George, he was active in the name of Allied unity in designing new bodies intended to lessen Haig's authority. In November 1917 he helped to establish a Supreme War Council of the Allies, which he hoped would provide an alternative source of strategic advice. As it could do no more than make suggestions, this signified little. Then, late in January 1918, an effort was made to give it some teeth. It was proposed that an inter-Allied force, called a general reserve, be created. This would be controlled by an executive committee under Foch, who so might emerge as an Allied generalissimo. But Haig and Pétain (backed up by Clemenceau) put paid to that proceeding. The British and French commanders believed they were already short of troops to meet the threatened German onslaught. So they refused to relinquish a single division to the proposed reserve. Haig made it clear that he would resign rather than bow to such a requirement. Lloyd George, with astonishing consistency, once more passed up the chance to get rid of him.

Haig's survival, after the awesome failures of 1917 and this latest display of fractiousness (not to mention the near-disaster that lay just round the corner), may seem puzzling. In the central respect there is no puzzle. Haig survived because the Prime Minister willed that he should survive. The real point at issue is why Lloyd George, possessing the political power and constitutional authority to be quit of him, chose to let him stay. Two explanations have been offered. It is said that Lloyd George, had he sought Haig's dismissal, would himself have been hurled from office. And it is said that no high-ranking soldier competent enough could be found to replace Haig.

It is difficult to keep patience in face of these absurdities. Haig, it is true, had important friends: at court, in the army, in political circles, and (though diminishingly) in the press. These did not render him invulnerable – least of all when (in Northcliffe's not greatly exaggerated phrase) 'every house' in Britain had suffered loss on account of his operations. Of only one man in the country could it be said that, as long as he was alive and active, he was irreplaceable: Lloyd George. For only he could hold together a Government embracing Conservatives, Labour, and a fair section of Liberals, thereby preserving the national unity. If Lloyd George cared to make it clear that either he or Haig must go, the Commander-in-Chief would vanish as if he had never existed.

No more is to be said for the view that a suitable replacement for Haig could not be found in early 1918. General Plumer had produced one of the few gripping victories of 1917 on the Western Front when he blew the top off Messines Ridge. He had then rescued a good deal from the wretched opening phase of Third Ypres. These accomplishments did not escape the attention of the War Cabinet. When in November 1917 disaster befell the Italian Front – about which Lloyd George cared inordinately – the Government rushed Plumer to Italy to help redeem the situation.

It was not only the War Cabinet and serving soldiers who knew of Plumer's qualities. By March 1918 he was back in command in Flanders, where it was thought the German blow might fall. It descended instead on the Fifth Army, and Gough lost his post. The radical weekly the *Nation*, after a critical review of Gough, wrote on 6 April:

> Plumer is again reported on the Western Front, and we should have welcomed him as Gough's successor. His Staff is ever as orderly as Gough's was reputed to be the reverse. He discovered one of the best staff officers we have [Harington], and the difference between his and Gough's calibre was conspicuous at Ypres.

So there certainly was available a replacement for Haig. Plumer enjoyed the confidence of any force he led, had noteworthy successes to his credit, favoured conducting operations on the Western Front only with limited objectives, and possessd a clear mark of approval from the Government.

It may even be said that, as long as Lloyd George was prepared to strike down one tallish poppy in the military hierarchy, he would have done well to retain Robertson and remove Haig. Certainly, the supersession of Robertson by Henry Wilson had little to recommend it (as Lloyd George, who was soon referring to Wilson as 'Wully Redivivus', was not long in discovering). Wilson may have possessed an engaging personality. But he had nothing like Robertson's talent for the job of CIGS, least of all when it came to controlling Haig – who was soon telling all and sundry how much he preferred working with Wilson to working with Robertson. Had Lloyd George decided to keep Robertson and substitute Plumer for Haig, they might well have formed an admirable team. Haig and Wilson were no team at all; only a combination in which Haig called the tune and Wilson danced to it. This, presumably, had not been Lloyd George's intention.

So the question remains: Why did Lloyd George, while expressing strong disapproval of Haig, nevertheless choose to retain him? It may be conjectured that the Prime Minister divined that further military setbacks lay ahead, and quailed at the responsibility that would befall him if the Commander-in-Chief were his own nominee. Haig, according to this view, was needed as a convenient whipping boy. Again, it may be speculated that the Prime Minister was more at ease in striking down a man of Robertson's humble origin than one of Haig's lordly demeanour. But another possibility, more to the credit of the Prime Minister, strongly suggests itself. Notwithstanding his distaste for Haig, it may be that intuition told Lloyd George that all the experience Haig had gained during his command on the Western Front should not be lightly cast aside and that, when the opportunity presented itself to win the war, Haig would possess the qualifications for the task.

III

If Lloyd George failed to remove Haig, did he express his antipathy in a way that placed British forces at peril? It has been argued that the Prime Minister starved the Western Front of reinforcements, which were freely available, and so brought his country near to calamity.

A part of this charge may be easily dismissed. There were not large numbers of first-class troops at the Prime Minister's beck and call. Given the vast and competing demands for British manpower, any reinforcement of the Western Front must be made at the expense of some other region or activity. Certainly, there were active British divisions that could have been placed at Haig's disposal and were not. One may instance those in Palestine and Italy. But, plainly, Lloyd George had not sent them there just to keep them out of Haig's clutches. These regions engaged his sympathy in a way that the Western Front did not. He believed that the forces there would advance Britain's cause as they would not do in France and Flanders. This may be deemed a serious misjudgement, and to that extent the Prime Minister can be held responsible for Haig's impending setback. But that is to say much less than that Lloyd George was deliberately starving Haig of troops.

Equally, it would have been possible to send more men to France had the Government not accorded a higher priority to activities like coal-mining and ship-building and munitions-making. The nation's rulers, it is plain, did not recognize the imminence of Ludendorff's onslaught, and suspected Haig of a ruse to secure men for another ill-starred offensive. So on 22 January Smuts and Hankey visited Rawlinson, who had taken over command in Flanders while Plumer was in Italy. Rawlinson recorded in his diary: 'I gather they do not think the Boch will make a really big attack in the West.' And as late as 14 March Haig spent an hour at Downing Street with Lloyd George and Bonar Law, during which (according to Haig's diary entry) 'They did their best to get me to say that the Germans would not attack.'

Clearly, if no German offensive was pending, then Lloyd George was entitled to deny Haig additional first-class troops. For he had no intention of letting Haig use them. Haig might be aching to resume his Flanders campaign as soon as the weather permitted. (He even said as much to the War Cabinet on 7 January, alleging a desire to take the pressure of the coming German offensive off the French.) But Haig would ache in vain. The Prime Minister would see that the Flanders operation was not resumed. The veto that he had shirked in mid-1917 he would certainly employ now.

Hence, from the War Cabinet's viewpoint, it was logical to leave Haig's forces at their existing strength (apart from offering him – as was done – such troops of lower quality as were available in Britain). For the nation's leaders had no hope of an Allied victory before 1919, by which time the Americans would be contributing large numbers of fighting men. In the interval British males would be employed in the production of war materials and on campaigns against the lesser adversaries.

Unfortunately, the basis of this calculation was absurd – the basis being that the Germans would not attack in the West and that this left the War Cabinet free to allocate Britain's manpower as it chose. The unrelenting movement of German divisions from the defunct Eastern Front to what, from Britain's point of view, was the only crucial region of the land war accorded the Government no options whatever. This it was sadly tardy in recognizing.

By and large, the Government's military advisers saw the peril much earlier and pressed for an appropriate response. But their reputation was tarnished by more than two years of lavishing resources on the Western Front (even though for offensive, not defensive, undertakings). And they did not have in Haig an ideal spokesman. Fundamentally, this was because the Government distrusted him and so did not respond when he talked good sense – as when, on 14 March, he parried Lloyd George's suggestion that the Germans 'would not attack' with the solemn warning: 'we must be prepared to meet *a very strong attack indeed on a 50 mile front, and for this drafts are urgently required.*' But it was also the case that Haig's position was not unequivocal.

Sometimes he talked as though the Germans might not attack. Sometimes he seemed concerned to take the offensive himself. And sometimes he appeared confident that he could thrash the enemy with the forces already at his disposal. For example, on Saturday, 16 March, he conversed with George V, who passed on the discussion to the CIGS. Wilson noted in his diary: 'The King told me that Haig had told him on Sat. that he could smash any attack. I hope Haig is right!'

To comprehend Haig's gusts of optimism and the Government's disregard for the rising peril in France, it is necessary to recall the context. The men who made these misjudgements had lived through a succession of Western Front offensives – by the French, the British, and (at Verdun) the Germans. It seemed axiomatic that any onslaught Ludendorff might mount would not make anything but halting progress, such as Haig had accomplished on the Somme and in Flanders. That would leave the defenders ample time in which to take counter-measures.

This expectation swiftly proved unwarranted. The events of 21 March revealed that the war of stalemate and unyielding positions was coming to an end. For this, in the initial battle of 1918 as in each of those that followed, there were particular reasons. But a general reason also applied thoughout this year. At least in part, operations on the Western Front in 1918 differed from their predecessors because this was the fourth – not the first, second, or third – year of a war that had been swallowing up lives at a prodigious rate. Vast numbers of the fittest males of Britain, as of France and Germany, had been killed, broken, or worn down. The tenacity evident on the Somme in 1916 on both sides required combatants with great fitness and motivation. No country could produce these in unlimited numbers. By 1918, on every side, the supply was approaching exhaustion.

Britain, certainly, was now having to dip deep into its barrel of manpower (and its circumstances must have been happier than those of Germany and France). Consequently, British males entering the conflict were often less than ideal military material: because they had already passed through the furnace of war too often, or suffered from physical or emotional shortcomings, or were of a type that failed to see why they should lose their lives for their country, or were simply too old or too young for the job. One accepts that Rawlinson might refer to his forces as 'boys', because that was part of the language of the time. But late in April 1918 he was using a chilling refinement of this expression to describe his reinforcements – who had just been under heavy German attack involving artillery fire and gas shelling. He called them 'young boys', 'young troops', and even 'children'. No one would have used these terms of the Kitchener armies of 1916.

An indication of how physically drained Britain's manpower had become by early 1918 is provided, if only by contrast, in the recollections of Vera Brittain. At a desperate stage in the German spring offensive she observed a company of marching men. They did not appear to have come from the bottom of the barrel, nor to be once-fit men ground down by combat. The impact was profound.

> They looked larger than ordinary men; their tall, straight figures were in vivid contrast to the under-sized armies of pale recruits to which we had grown accustomed. At first I thought their spruce, clean uniforms were those of officers, yet obviously they could not be officers, for there were too many of them; they seemed, as it were, Tommies in heaven. . . .
> Then I heard an excited exclamation from a group of Sisters behind me.
> 'Look! Look! Here are the Americans!'
> I pressed forward with the others to watch the United States physically entering the

War, so god-like, so magnificent, so splendidly unimpaired in comparison with the tired, nerve-racked men of the British Army.[2]

IV

The effect that this erosion of Britain's manpower exercised on the course of battle is difficult to estimate. It has been argued that among the fighting men who encountered the German onslaught in March 1918 the determination to endure all and hazard all was less evident than in the past. And some participants do refer to failures of morale on 21 March and the following days. A captain in the field artillery, writing in the 1920s, related how by 11 a.m. on 21 March a 12-inch howitzer not under fire had been 'abandoned by its detachment on orders from the officer' – 'the most disgraceful instance of panic I ever came across'. He saw it as an example of a 'tendency to come back rather than to fight to the last that contributed largely to the *débâcle* of the Fifth Army. No one felt confident that the people on his right and left would stand firm.' A private soldier in an infantry battalion, recalling 21 March nearly 60 years afterwards, admitted: 'When the Jerries came towards our line in large numbers, they were firing from the hip and I thought, 'Tosh. Do what some of the others are doing. Hop it back.' So I did. I was not alone, I can assure you, otherwise I don't think I should be able to write this.'[3]

The ensuing days brought further such incidents. Captain E. D. Ridley of the Grenadier Guards, in his diary of the time, refers to instances of 'wind' among the forces with whom he was involved. So on 26 March: 'Pretty windy. I thought wind pretty bad at Arras but this Corps seems ready [?] to bolt. . . . Road packed with retiring troops. . . . by 4.30 [we] were ordered to withdraw. . . . It is nothing but wind. No attack no nothing.' Some weeks later Ridley wrote home: 'Did I tell you one of the Corps here has a sign, a Bull-dog. . . . After their exhibition in March, they were asked to change it to a grey-hound, but they did not like the suggestion.'[4]

The problem is to estimate the importance of such incidents. Probably every battle reveals instances of 'wind'; it is just that if no disaster occurs, they are not singled out for attention. And the heavy casualties imposed upon the Germans in their March offensive is proof enough that British troops offered devoted resistance. Some, in fact, expressed satisfaction that at last they could actually see the enemy they were shooting at.

If, nevertheless, the British line broke in March, explanations other than demoralization lie to hand: new German artillery and infantry tactics; the consequent breakdown of the defenders' trench barrier with resulting confusion; and, above all, the facts that, on the crucial sector, the British had recently taken over ill-made trenches, found their lines stretched thin, and possessed both inadequate reserves and insufficient artillery. (Brigadier Anstey calls attention, in his unpublished history of the artillery, to the marked contrast in artillery resources between the sector where the line held and that where it gave way.)

Falling morale, therefore, may not have been of great moment among Britain's forces as they awaited the German offensive. Certainly, Haig's army was unlikely to fail

---

[2] Vera Brittain, *Testament of Youth* (London: Virago, 1978), pp. 420–1.

[3] Quotations in this paragraph are from Martin Middlebrook, *The Kaiser's Battle* (London: Allen Lane, 1978), pp. 257–9.

[4] Documents in Cambridge University Library.

in operations, defensive or offensive, that carried a reasonable prospect of success. At most it might give way when the odds were too evidently hopeless, or the demands of the high command beyond reason, or the needed systems of support clearly wanting. Plainly, it was in just such circumstances that parts of the British army confronted the ordeal of 21 March.

50

LUDENDORFF'S DAY

We must beat the British.

Ludendorff, 11 November 1917

However long I may be destined to survive my friends who went down in the Flood, I shall never forget the crushing tension of those extreme days [following 21 March 1918]. Nothing had ever quite equalled them before – not the Somme, not Arras, not Passchendaele – for into our minds had crept for the first time the secret, incredible fear that we might lose the War.

Vera Brittain, Testament of Youth

I

At least two courses appeared to lie open to Germany at the start of 1918. For one, the Germans could seek to negotiate their way out of the war. While retaining their huge acquisitions in the East, they might offer to call off the U-boat campaign and withdraw from their conquests in the West. This would have several advantages. It would challenge the Western democracies to go on fighting when their prime objectives were attainable by negotiation. And it would give Germany a breathing space in which to strengthen its defensive positions in France and Flanders, exploit its unrealized acquisitions in Russia and Romania, and get its fast-crumbling railway system back in order.

A further benefit might flow to Germany from this course. While standing on the defensive and seeing how its adversaries responded, it could set about improving its food situation. A proportion of its military manpower and of the nitrates going into producing explosives could be converted (respectively) into farm labour and fertilizers. For if it was true that the Allied war on land and the British blockade at sea were depriving the German countryside of workers and nitrates, it was also true that Germany had the means to make good these needs. But the potential farm labourers were in the army, and the home-produced nitrates were going into munitions.

Yet if this was a course available to the German people, it must have seemed no choice at all to that nation's rulers. Neither the Kaiser nor the military caste was disposed to leave the military initiative to their adversaries. And they would never agree to relinquish their conquests in the West. Had they contemplated doing so, the probable consequences at home would have stopped them short. Germany as a national entity might have benefited from such a dénouement to the war. The political and social regime of William II and Ludendorff could hardly have done so.

Anyway, the men with the power to decide these things had made up their minds before 1918 dawned. Having won in the East, Ludendorff would now conquer in the

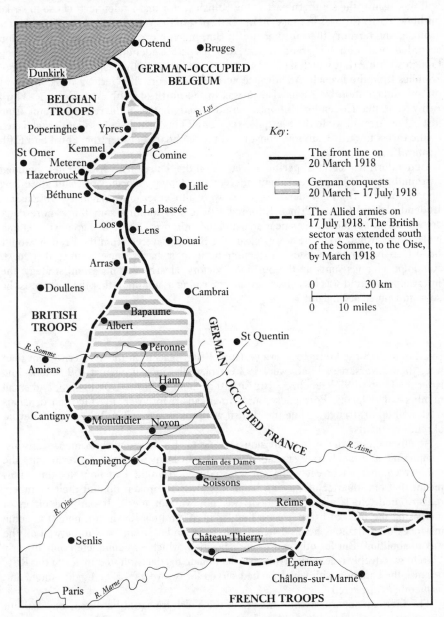

Map 13   *The German offensive against the BEF and the French, March – July 1918.*
Source: *Gilbert*, First World War Atlas, *p. 110.*

West. He would deliver such blows against the British forces early in 1918 as to shatter them. As a consequence, French resistance would collapse. And American intervention would never eventuate.

It was against the southern part of the British sector that Ludendorff chose to strike his blow. Partly this was because, in the early part of the year, this region offered better campaigning territory than further north. But, much more, it was because this region accorded best with his grand design. On his left Ludendorff would be attacking Gough's Fifth Army, which had but recently – and reluctantly – taken over a stretch of 28 miles from the French. An advance here would secure the German flank and ward off any intervention by Pétain. But it was to the north of Fifth Army, on the Third Army front, that Ludendorff's hopes were directed: that is, in the region running from just below Arras down to the Flesquières salient. (This British-held salient, established by the thrust towards Cambrai, constituted the boundary between the Third and Fifth Armies.)

Ludendorff had certain specific objectives on the Third Army front. They included surrounding the Flesquières salient, thereby entrapping its occupants, and advancing upon Bapaume. But his general objectives were altogether more visionary. 'In Russia', Ludendorff told Crown Prince Rupprecht (who was wanting something more concrete), 'we always merely set a near goal and then discovered where to go next.' Yet in a general way 'where to go next' was clear: the British, severed from the French, would be driven in a north-westerly direction until their backs were against the coast. Randolph Hennes sums up the position: 'Victory, clearly, was his grand strategy; the intervening ground was less clear beyond the ruling assumption that the blow must be soon and aimed at England.'[1]

II

By March 1918 the Germans were certainly better placed on the Western Front than were their adversaries. There were 192 German divisions as against 169 Allied – the latter made up of 98 French, 57 British (10 of them from the Dominions), and small numbers of Belgians, Portuguese, and Americans. Moreover, the German divisions were well up to strength, while the British were undermanned and the French devoid of reinforcements.

At this moment the British divisions, owing to the deficiencies in men, were just completing a difficult reorganization. On the insistence of the Government, the infantry component in each division was reduced from 12 battalions to nine. This meant that one-quarter of existing battalions must be broken up and their members redistributed. Such a rearrangement was not without merit. It had the effect of increasing the ratio of fire power to foot soldiers. And (as Rawlinson noted) in some instances the battalions being disbanded were so under strength as to be well on the way to abolition. But for others the reorganization, which was completed only in early March, was deeply resented. Private Surfleet made his decision to transfer to the RFC because the battalion with which he had served for two years was being disbanded and its members dispersed.

The German superiority in numbers in the West, it should be noted, was real but not overwhelming. However, other factors served to enhance it. The German forces that had spent 1917 on the Eastern Front or on the French sector of the Western Front had generally not been engaged in protracted slogging operations. They might even

---

[1] Randolph York Hennes, 'The March Retreat of 1918: an Anatomy of a Battle', Ph.D. Thesis, University of Washington, 1966, pp. 157, 172 (for Ludendorff's remark to Rupprecht).

have passed a year relatively free from combat. Nothing of the sort applied to the British. The engagements of Arras, Third Ypres, and Cambrai had drawn in virtually every British division. Indeed, it has been said that only nine of them had escaped just the Third Ypres campaign.

The Germans had a further advantage. Now that they were going on to the attack, they could concentrate on the sector of their choosing, so maximizing their numerical advantage. Theoretically, it is true, the Allies could retaliate by moving additional forces to the threatened sector. But this proved impractical. Apart from the Belgians, Portuguese, and Americans, who were all under independent commands, the 98 French and 57 British divisions were separate national forces operating in clearly defined sectors. Neither command was eager, however great the threat to its ally, to move troops from its own sector before the enemy's hand was thoroughly revealed. Otherwise the French might weaken their defences before Paris or the British theirs covering the Channel ports, only to find that they were responding to the first, but not the principal, German attack. Neither Haig nor Pétain would run this risk. And it is the fact that, through guile on the part of the enemy and misjudgements among the Allies, uncertainty about the intended direction of the major German blow continued to a late stage. On the evening of 21 March, with the storm well and truly raging, Henry Wilson still had doubts whether this was the Germans' main effort.

The events of that day made it plain that, if Ludendorff was after a large initial success, he had chosen well the region to attack. This applied particularly to the Fifth Army's sector. Neither Allied commander accorded it high priority, for it did not guard the road to Paris or the approaches to the Channel. So if a shortage existed of troops and artillery to hold the trenches, of labour to construct defensive positions, and of material to lay roads and railways, Gough's front would be most poorly served. The one thing not lacking, in the event, was the attention of the enemy.

Gough's problems were exacerbated by both a particular and a general consideration. The particular consideration concerned supply on his sector. This was especially arduous because it lay across the area ravaged by the Germans in their withdrawal a year before. As to the general consideration, the British on the Western Front had done little before the beginning of 1918 to establish a complex defensive system. For this there was a reason. They had launched many offensives, but they had rarely been attacked (apart, that is, from enemy counter-strokes to recapture positions the British had just taken). Not since the small-scale operation of Second Ypres in April 1915 had the Germans attempted to break the British line. So when, late in 1917, the British command became aware that it might soon sustain a massive assault, a great work of preparation lay ahead.

The response was marred by inexperience and lack of time. A scheme of defensive arrangements, supposedly based on the latest German model, was set in train – the Germans on the Western Front having had plenty of cause to work out defensive systems. In fact, the model had failed the enemy a year before and been abandoned. Worse, the British amended it in ways that rendered it still less efficacious: they packed additional troops into what was supposedly an expendable forward zone. Moreover, owing to shortage of time and manpower, the system was incomplete when the attack came.

Theoretically, the British would confront the enemy with a three-tier defence: a Forward, a Battle, and a Reserve Zone. But the Forward Zone had little power to slow down the enemy, though much to supply him with a fine bag of prisoners. And the Reserve Zone was so little developed that it scarcely existed. That placed on the central Battle Zone a disproportionate burden, which it was unlikely to sustain unless adequately manned, gunned, supplied, and provided with a sufficiency of counter-attack and reserve forces.

In particular, on the Fifth Army sector preparations and resources were woefully deficient. Out of the 126 miles of front held by the BEF, Gough was responsible for 42 miles. Yet to hold it he possessed only 12 infantry and three cavalry divisions. (The latter, if dismounted – the only way in which they were likely to be useful – would add up to one division more.) That is, the Fifth Army was holding one-third of the British front with between one-quarter and one-fifth of the BEF's troops. Its situation may be compared with that of Third Army on its left, holding 28 miles with 14 divisions.

The superiority in numbers of the attacking Germans was overwhelming. The two British armies under assault numbered roughly 300,000 men, their adversaries 750,000 – with the disproportion weighing much more heavily against the Fifth Army sector. Nor could Gough hope for much assistance from the eight divisions held by Haig in GHQ reserve, most of which were intended for Third Army. His only prospect of assistance was from the French.

The disproportionate thinness of the Fifth Army's line resulted from a definite calculation by Haig. He felt that he could not afford to give ground above Arras and, least of all, in Flanders. Therefore if some part of his front must be left at risk on account of the shortage of men, it would have to be Gough's. For, as has just been mentioned, at Fifth Army's back lay a considerable stretch of territory of no strategic value: the stretch adjoining the old Somme battlefields that the Germans had abandoned in 1917. Haig's estimation of priorities made sense. But he did not appreciate the extent of Fifth Army's plight. Consequently, he failed to recognize that an enemy advance might make such substantial progress as indeed to threaten him with serious damage – such as splitting the British from the French, or imperilling the rail centre of Amiens.

Within days of 21 March, Haig was confronting just these prospects. The German attack had employed novel, and extremely effective, tactical methods. They were not exactly untried, having been used against the Russians at Riga and the Italians at Caporetto, as well as in the counter-attack at Cambrai. (Gough had felt certain that he was being selected for attack when von Hutier, who had commanded at Riga, appeared on the front opposite him.) But this was the first time that the new German tactics had been employed on a large scale on the Western Front.

Central to the German assault were three elements: surprise, attained by the most stealthy assemblage of artillery and infantry; a short-lived but quite overwhelming artillery bombardment, aimed at incapacitating both front-line troops and the artillery; and infiltration. For the last of these the German infantry were spearheaded by storm-troopers. Their task was not to advance in a steady line, maintaining contact with each other and eliminating all pockets of resistance. Rather, they were to penetrate where the British defences had crumbled and to bypass those strong points that were still holding out. (These could be attended to by the follow-up forces.) The main object of the storm troopers was to get forward in a hurry so as to strike at the vitals of the British defence by overrunning its artillery positions.

For the day, the German artillery on the frontage of attack numbered 6,600 guns plus 3,500 mortars (as against only 2,800 guns and 1,400 mortars available to the defenders). For five hours a devastating onslaught rained down on the British Forward Zone. According to one artillery officer, rudely awakened in his bed: 'At half-past four in the morning I thought the world was coming to an end.'[2] What did come to an end

---

[2] Aubrey Wade, *The War of the Guns* (London: Batsford, 1936), p. 89.

was the hut which he was occupying, only moments after he had vacated it. The effect of the bombardment on the front line troops was intense. As one recollected:

Artillery was the great leveller. Nobody could stand more than three hours of sustained shelling before they start[ed] falling sleepy and numb. You're hammered after three hours and you're there for the picking when he comes over. It's a bit like being under an anaesthetic; you can't put a lot of resistance up. The first to be affected were the young ones who'd just come out. They would go to one of the older ones – older in service that is – and maybe even cuddle up to him and start crying.[3]

Fortune, in the form of the weather, favoured the Germans on 21 March (and the following day). Fog blanketed the battlefield. While the German bombardment was falling on predicted targets, the storm-troopers were able to form up in No-Man's-Land unobserved. Then, as the artillery lifted at 9.40, the still undetected assault forces moved forward to their objectives. Their experience was in stark contrast to that of the British attackers on 1 July 1916, who in clement weather withered before the observed fire of German machine-guns and artillery. The first waves of German infantry on 21 March 1918, whose main weapon was the hand grenade, crossed No-Man's-Land and brought their grenades into play almost before they were visible to the British front line.

Within an hour and a half the Forward Zone on all of Fifth Army's front, and much of Third Army's, had been overrun. This meant a loss of almost one-fifth of the fighting strength opposing the attack (and nearly one-third on Gough's sector). The large majority had been taken prisoner. This was clearly preferable to injury for those involved – although the experience of near-starvation in the prisoner-of-war camps of a semi-starving nation would prove an experience that not all would survive. But from the point of view of the army command, men taken prisoner were a more serious loss than those going wounded: for a proportion of the wounded would in time return to the firing line, but the prisoners, like the dead, would not.

In the course of 21 March the situation, though seeming to stabilize on the Third Army front with its superior artillery resources, deteriorated further on that of Fifth Army. It was gravest on Gough's right, in the poorly defended and thinly manned region so recently taken over from the French. The Fifth Army was now fighting in its Battle Zone, with little more than paper defences behind it and almost all its reserves committed. In time aid might come from Pétain, as Haig had arranged it would. But it would be delayed; for the French had been convinced to the last that the real assault would come much further south and that they would be its victims. So at the end of this day Gough concluded he must draw his right wing well back, which meant some further withdrawal of his centre also. After only 12 hours of fighting, the March retreat was under way.

The British army, in one day, had suffered a stunning setback. The enemy had overrun 98½ square miles of territory and had penetrated, at the furthest point, to a depth of 4½ miles. That was virtually equal to the advance that the British and French had made, in much the same region, during the entire Somme campaign of 1916. Moreover, the loss of territory was plainly not over, for at the end of the day another 40 square miles were being evacuated.

In terms of casualties, admittedly, nothing that happened on 21 March was comparable with the Somme campaign of 1916. But for a single day's fighting, and for a force enjoying the advantage of standing on the defensive, the losses were bleak enough. According to the figures calculated by Martin Middlebrook (which necessarily

---

[3] Martin Middlebrook, *The Kaiser's Battle* (London: Allen Lane, 1978), p. 161.

involve a modicum of guesswork), on 21 March the British suffered casualties of 38,500. At first sight that was marginally fewer than the losses of the Germans, which were about 40,000. But the advantage lay with the enemy. Two-thirds of the German casualties were wounded, and a fair proportion of these would again appear in the firing line. Fully 28,000 of Britain's 38,500 never would: 7,000 of them were dead, and a staggering 21,000 had been taken prisoner.

Nevertheless, all this was much less than Ludendorff had aimed for. His intention for the day was to overwhelm the complete British defensive system on the front under attack. This he had not done: on Third Army's front he was held up in the battle zone, and the Flesquières salient had yet to be cut off. He had sustained heavy casualties and, while taking many British prisoners, had captured surprisingly few guns. And he had made least progress on his right, which was just where he needed to do best if he was to sweep the British towards the north-west and the sea. His most noteworthy advance had been on his left, where all he had been planning to do was to secure his flank against the French.

So at the end of 21 March the situation remained ambiguous. The Germans had accomplished much. But had they accomplished enough to be of any use to them?

Plate 43   *A roadside scene during the German advance.*

III

The next two days underscored the parlous circumstances of the Fifth Army. By the morning of 22 March, thanks to the retreat, it was holding an extended line with diminished forces. Worse, its front was no longer continuous. There was, for example, a 4-mile gap between the 20th and 24th divisions. Such breaks in the line facilitated enemy infiltration, so imposing further retreats, rising losses, and increasing disorganization. By the end of the second day the Fifth Army was out of touch with the Third

Army on its left and the French on its right, had committed all its reserves, and had no fewer than eight of its divisions down to brigade strength. The situation of Third Army was never quite this desperate, but it was far from good. In mid-afternoon on 22 March, after it had seemed that the line was holding, the centre began to give way under fierce enemy pressure, pulling back the sector to its right and exposing the left flank of the Flesquières salient. Arthur Behrend, an artillery officer stationed on the Bapaume–Cambrai road, describes a scene 'fixed indelibly in my mind's eye':

> I was standing on a high bank which commanded a fine view up the Cambrai road as far as Frémicourt. The light was just beginning to fail. . . . Along the road a slow stream of traffic was moving towards Bapaume and beyond, first waves of the tide which rolled westwards for days and days. Here and there a battery in column of route, walking wounded in twos and threes, an odd lorry or two, a staff car carrying with undignified speed the dignified sign of Corps Headquarters, a column of horse transport, and a biggish batch of German prisoners captured by 51st Division. The procession reminded me of a film; it was with something approaching a shock that I realized everything was in retreat.[4]

The greatest peril in this region concerned the Flesquières salient. Byng was reluctant to part with the only remaining gain from his short-lived success at Cambrai. Yet with Fifth Army out of touch on its right and now with its left flank in peril, the salient must soon become a trap for its occupants. So on the night of 22–23 March, the withdrawal there at last began.

Haig, meanwhile, was having difficulty appreciating the full import of events. On 23 March he simply could not understand 'why Fifth Army has gone so far back without making some kind of a stand'. Yet he was certainly responding to the emergency. Quite apart from throwing in GHQ reserves, he was bringing down divisions from the Flanders front to aid Third Army and seeking additional support from the French for Fifth Army. More than this, he was calling into existence a whole new defensive system to the rear of his threatened sectors. Where previously Gough had had to beg for labour, writes Randolph Hennes:

> suddenly under the lash of impending disaster the British rear area began to teem with activity and to sprout waves of fortifications. Before the spring crisis would pass 5,000 miles of new trenches would emerge inside a steel thicket of some 23,500 tons of barbed wire.[5]

This matter is worth dwelling on. For it highlights the factor that, in this war, must ultimately render absurd the concept of victory by breakthrough. A devoted assault might get into a defensive system. And very occasionally, as happened in March 1918 on the front of the Fifth Army, it might drive right through it. But the consequence proved to be much less than a breakthrough.

For this the explanation lies in two crucial elements. One was the slow-moving world of attacking forces in this war. The launching pad of any great offensive was the railway, which made possible a fairly swift accumulation of men and weapons and ammunition. But once the offensive was launched, trains and railheads receded into the distance. The speed of the attack was then tied to the rate at which foot soldiers could advance and horses could drag forward guns and shells.

The second crucial element invalidating the notion of breakthrough was the nature of trench defences. A trench system is quite unlike a system of fortresses. A fortress, once overrun or surrounded, is virtually irreplaceable owing to the time involved in

---

[4] Arthur Behrend, *As from Kemmel Hill* (London: Eyre & Spottiswoode, 1963), p. 77.
[5] Hennes, 'The March Retreat of 1918', p. 304.

constructing another. This was anything but true of a trench system in a war that had rendered the cavalry obsolete. As long as the defending side possessed the labour to dig new lines and the infantry to occupy them and the weaponry and barbed wire with which to equip them, a whole new protective system could forthwith be called into being.

So, for all their impressive achievements, Ludendorff's soldiers found themselves engaged in a struggle with the interminable quality of a nightmare – or a game of 'Space Invaders'. However often they overwhelmed their adversaries, there was always a new set of adversaries, in a new set of strongholds, requiring to be dealt with. (The analogy, admittedly, must not be pressed too far. The electronic game can presumably produce forces for the battlefield to infinity. In the Great War one side or the other must in time discover that its resources were finite: that it was running out of the human and material commodities required to construct, man, and equip further defensive positions.)

Something of Ludendorff's response at the end of the third day suggested a man who, though enjoying his finest hour, was indeed experiencing a nightmare. But perhaps that is to exaggerate. He had set his forces clear, if distant, objectives. But he had also said that he would follow wherever opportunity beckoned. There was an inherent contradiction here, and it was now closing in on him. He might seek to achieve his great aim of driving the British forces north-west towards the sea; but that would mean hammering away on his right, where he had been making least progress. Or he could take advantage of the success befalling his left, and follow it to no clear purpose.

The dilemma proved too great for the German leader. He decided that the assault on his left would continue; and he seemed to reinforce this decision by pointing his centre more towards the south-west, as if that would now be the direction of his thrust. But he also determined that preparations would go ahead for a great hammer blow on his right, with Arras as its first objective and the sweep towards the coast to follow. Such wide ranging decisions might have been appropriate for a commander possessing unlimited forces and dealing with a failing adversary. Ludendorff was not in that position.

IV

On 24 March and the ensuing days retreat and disorder remained the lot of the Fifth Army. It had become a series of independent columns, each making its individual stand until overwhelmed or outflanked, then retreating once more. Its communications system had been shattered at the outset, so that there was no possibility of the central command trying to draw back its elements on to a contiguous front.

Help, certainly, was on the way. It came from the French – to such an extent that by the end of March the Fifth Army sector would be under French command. Pétain sent the initial six divisions he had promised Haig, and soon began funnelling in a further six as well. (This makes short work of the still widely held view that Pétain subjected Haig to a display of cold charity. It also disposes of the notion that the existence of a general reserve, which at most would have contained only 13 French divisions, would have made all the difference.) But the situation required greater speed than the French could manage, in part because they had been anticipating an attack in Champagne and in part because the rapidity of the Fifth Army's retirement had exceeded all expectations. Hence the French reinforcements, instead of being able to take up ordered positions in rear of the British, found themselves being introduced straight into the conflict and caught up in the retreat.

The Third Army's position, if never so grave, continued serious for some days more. It is true that reinforcements, not only from GHQ reserve but also from Plumer's Second and Horne's First Armies, were making their appearance. And Byng's left flank was holding firm in its original Battle Zone. But on the right the whole of the Flesquières salient was being relinquished so as to retain some semblance of contact with the Fifth Army, and this pulled back Byng's centre also. One consequence was the abandonment of Bapaume, for which the British had fought unavailingly in 1916 and which they had then acquired gratis following the enemy withdrawal in 1917. Worse followed. Just as the front was beginning to stabilize, Byng's forces managed to relinquish Albert, which had been in British hands before 1 July 1916.

These withdrawals across the old Somme battlegrounds were a bleak experience, especially for those men who had once fought their way in the opposite direction:

> It was by no means a happy coincidence that brought the Civil Service Rifles back to this battlefield, where, eighteen months previously, they had paid such a high price for the capture of High Wood. On their previous visit to this area they had been filled with confidence and the offensive spirit. They had felt they were really doing something towards winning the war. To retreat across the same country now made it seem as though all the labours of the past eighteen months had been wasted – the lives lost in vain.[6]

But the experiences of the enemy were far from cheering, despite their progress. They were now deep into the wasteland they had created a year earlier, described by one German participant as 'these accursed regions without tree or shrub, without meadows and fields, without cities and villages, without bird song and flowers' bloom'. With the streams wrecked and wells poisoned during the earlier German withdrawal, water was soon a scarce commodity. And the meagre roads constructed by the British since they had occupied the area had fallen victim to the renewed shelling. Hence while the British were falling back on reinforcements and gun parks and supply points, their enemies were encountering mounting problems of supply. If the German foot soldiers could advance only at a walking pace, that was still faster than the overburdened horses could drag forward the big guns and shells. As a consequence, the German infantry, which had been so well served by the gunners at the outset, were now having to attack with inadequate artillery support. In an event that must have intrigued the shade of Lord Kitchener, on 25 March one German army corps was obliged to restrict the daily consumption of ammunition to a half. It is little wonder that, on 26 March, the German advance slowed down against the Fifth Army and came to a halt against the Third.

Ludendorff's dilemma was now acute. The advance on his left had so prospered as to bring within grasping distance a considerable prize: the city of Amiens. Into it there seemed to flow almost every rail system that serviced the Allied forces. Its capture would disorganize all movements north and south by the French and British forces. But, even so, it was small beer when compared with the original German objectives.

Once more, Ludendorff could not accept the failure of his grand design or even settle for a single goal. He directed a frontal offensive against Amiens, along with a strike south-west against the French. But at the same time, on 28 March, he launched a great blow on his right. His immediate objectives were Arras and the southern terminus of Vimy Ridge, along with the river Scarpe running between them. His larger

---

[6] *The History of the Prince of Wales Own Civil Service Rifles*, quoted in Hennes, 'The March Retreat of 1918', p. 323.

purpose was what it had been since he had decided to strike in the West: to 'beat the British'.

Ludendorff's drive towards Arras settled matters. By comparison with 21 March, his bombardment was more hurried and less accurate, and his counter-battery work particularly inadequate. This was crucial. For he was attacking not the Fifth Army, which through all these battles was lamentably weak in field artillery, but the Third Army. Its artillery, according to Brigadier Anstey, was strong, well placed, amply supplied with ammunition, and not blinded by fog. Its ammunition expenditure at this stage equalled anything in the war: in the 24 hours from the morning of 28 March the 18-pounders fired 750 rounds per gun and the 4.5-inch guns fired 650 rounds. Equally important was the role of the heavy batteries, whose targets came to include even German infantry at short range – for with the enemy as close as 600 yards the gunners stuck to their posts.

Yet the chief honours, Anstey suggests, rested with Third Army's machine-gunners. Protected by deep dug-outs and occupying short frontages, they were present in strength and took savage toll of the attackers.

The twenty-eighth of March was one of the decisive days of the Great War. In the German endeavour to drive the BEF from the battlefields of Europe, the sector around Arras occupied a central place. On this day Ludendorff made his culminating effort to subdue it; and on this day he failed conclusively.

On the other side of the front the import of the event was not appreciated. For Haig, the conflict had already become – as it now must become for Ludendorff – simply a struggle for possession of Amiens. And that battle raged for another week, during which the Germans advanced perilously close to the great rail centre. But by 4 April Ludendorff's endeavour had failed in its lesser purpose as in its larger, and the next day it was 'temporarily discontinued'.

So came to a close an operation that had shaken Britain to its foundations. What the enemy had accomplished was, from the viewpoint of the BEF's own offensives in 1916 and 1917, unimaginable. At the furthest point the Germans had advanced 40 miles. They had taken 1,200 square miles of territory. They had inflicted on the British 160,000 casualties, no fewer than 90,000 of whom had been taken prisoner, and on the French possibly 80,000 casualties.

Yet, on a wider perspective, the Germans had purchased a tactical success at the price of a strategic calamity. They had sustained irreplaceable casualties to the tune of 250,000 men. And they had overrun territory that, a year before, they had gone to great trouble to abandon. Of course, if they were to eliminate the BEF from the ranks of their adversaries, then they must come this way again. But an advance that did not accomplish that object only saddled them with an extended front for whose retention they now possessed a diminished force. In the course of acquiring it they had learned that the process of defeating the British simply could not be accomplished – least of all before the arrival of the Americans. This meant for Germany that the war could not be won.

51

RECOVERY

By the end of the March–April battle of 1918, the British Army had met 109 German divisions and fought them to a standstill, without any strategic gain by the Germans whatsoever.

John Terraine (R.U.S.I. Journal, 1982)

I

In London, and at Haig's headquarters, the crisis of late March and early April produced stirring responses.

Lloyd George, by common consent, rose heroically to the occasion. His conversation was spiced with backbiting against Haig and Woodrow Wilson for what he deemed their failures to act, with praise for Henry Wilson's alleged prescience regarding the course of events, and with laments over the absence of a general reserve that, supposedly, would have made all the difference. But his demeanour was that of a man determined to hold on now and to triumph in the long run. Early in April Hugh Trenchard, then Chief of the Air Staff, was summoned to Downing Street. A number of Ministers were present, none of whom impressed him. Milner looked ashen and drawn. Bonar Law gazed into space and reminded him of a 'psalm-singing saint'. Only Lloyd George, according to Trenchard's later reminiscence, looked and talked 'like a man who had not lost heart': 'He met me in the passage, though I knew he disliked me, and said, "Well, general, though we shan't win this year, we shall win next year instead." He showed courage at that moment far outweighing that of all the rest of them.'[1]

Broadly, the Government decided on two courses of action. More Britons must be supplied to Haig. And America must be urged to enter the fighting.

There were 170,000 troops in Britain in late March who were deemed immediately available for the fighting zone, and during April another 52,000 were accumulated. About one-third of these were under 19 years and so, except in an emergency, not to be sent out of the country. And possibly a good many of the others were not in prime physical condition. (Regarding this last point, we may note a remark made about a group of novices who broke before the German onslaught in April: 'One of them has thick glasses and looks like a musician.')[2] Yet, irrespective of their youthfulness or want of fitness, they were sped to the Continent. In addition, two divisions in Palestine and one in Italy were transferred to the Western Front.

Even more Draconian measures followed. Essential services such as munitions, mines, and the docks were scoured; wounded men in the course of recuperation were

---

[1] Andrew Boyle, *Trenchard* (London: Collins, 1962), p. 274.
[2] R. H. Kiernan, *Little Brother Goes Soldiering* (London: Constable, 1930), p. 70.

bundled off to France; and the standard of eyesight required to place soldiers in the first category was lowered. The age limit for conscription was both reduced (to 17½) and raised (to 50 or, if need be, 55). And powers were taken to extend conscription to Ireland by order in council. This last action doubtless seemed warranted as a sop to opinion in England, Scotland, and Wales: the compulsion of Irish 'slackers' being a *quid pro quo* for the calling up of youngsters and the middle-aged in the United Kingdom. But seen from the Irish side of the border it was beyond justification – and would prove incapable of application.

Plate 44   *A scene in the battle area during the German offensive. A Canadian Corps tramway runs through a shelled village.*

The remaining major act by Lloyd George in response to the March crisis was an appeal to America. He urged President Wilson to dispatch 300,000 men in the next three months, to fight as American battalions in British brigades. The reply was reassuring. Wilson offered, in the course of four months, almost 500,000 men. But he stipulated that Britain would have to provide a considerable proportion of the shipping. Lloyd George responded with alacrity. Raw materials and foodstuffs must for the moment take second place to the need for soldiers on the Western Front. Here was evidence of how thoroughly the Government was adjusting its priorities; and of how gamely Lloyd George was responding to brutal realities.

Haig too was doing some adapting. One of the shocks he received during the March crisis was the reaction of the French commander. With respect to Haig's appeal for reinforcements Pétain behaved well – and certainly better than Foch ever would. But when they met on 23 March Pétain indicated that the two armies might have to separate, the French south-west to cover Paris, the British north-west to guard the coast. This appalled Haig. (The British commander chose not to notice that he himself had been regarding the protection of the Channel ports as his first priority and that for this reason he had left the junction between the two armies palpably weak.)

But there was another aspect of Pétain's response that distressed Haig, and with more justification. Pétain's resolution seemed to be crumbling before Ludendorff's blows. The British commander, to his credit, was unshaken by misfortune. As has been said: 'The same characteristics which kept Haig battering away at Third Ypres and the Somme, courage, faith and a desperate want of imagination', now buoyed him up 'in a sea of troubles'.[3] Pétain, by contrast, was unnerved by the turn of events. For that we have the testimony of not only Haig but also Clemenceau and Poincaré. Pétain even told an outraged Clemenceau that the British were about to be beaten in the open field and that the French would be lucky to avoid the same fate.

Pétain's failure of nerve, along with his contemplation of a possible breach in the Anglo-French line, brought Haig to a severe decision. If France were to be kept fighting, and French forces to be interposed in growing numbers between the enemy and Amiens, then Pétain must be overruled. Haig could hardly suggest that he be sacked. But the same effect might be achieved by giving some individual the authority – nominal in the one case, actual in the other – to direct the operations of both the British commander and the French. The obvious man for the job was Foch, combative and unquenchable as ever.

Others were coming to the same conclusion, if not always for the same reason. Clemenceau's position approximated Haig's. He was dismayed by Pétain's defeatism. Up to now he had favoured Pétain against Foch. But he was so relieved by the latter's determination that (he recounts in his memoirs) he was almost moved to embrace him. And as a good French patriot Clemenceau doubtless welcomed the prospect of appointing a French general as overall commander on the Western Front.

As for the British Government, it came to the same decision by a different route. From its viewpoint, the problem was not Pétain but Haig. Yet even this latest setback would not cause Haig's head to roll. The chopping block was reserved for Gough. He may not have been responsible for his army's defeat. But after his ill-conduct of operations in 1917 he had no credit balance to fall back on. So he made a convenient scapegoat.

Yet if Haig were to remain, some change in the command structure was considered called for. And the obvious course was a repetition of Lloyd George's manoeuvre of a year before, only with two variations: Foch would occupy the role then assigned to Nivelle; and the Allied commander would subordinate a French as well as a British Commander-in-Chief. Foch would have overall direction of the Allied armies in the West, would control the general reserve, and would be responsible for proposed operations. This meant that he would have the authority to veto or approve Haig's military initiatives. Such an arrangement, of course, came close to a renunciation by Lloyd George's War Cabinet of its own control over the British commander. It was based on two assumptions: that virtually any French general was superior to any British; and that no French general would share Haig's eagerness for launching offensives on the Western Front. In the case of Foch neither assumption was warranted.

At conferences held at Doullens on 26 March and Beauvais on 3 April, the deed was done. Present there were high-level political and military representatives of France and Britain, as well as, on the latter occasion, General Pershing on behalf of the Americans. It was concluded that Foch would 'co-ordinate the action of the Allied Armies on the Western Front', and that for this purpose he would be entrusted by the three Governments with 'the strategic direction of military operations'.

---

[3] Randolph York Hennes, 'The March Retreat of 1918: an Anatomy of a Battle', Ph.D. thesis, University of Washington, 1966, p. 347.

It was an arrangement shot through with ambiguities – and so would work out very differently from what some of the parties had intended. Foch had two elements of strength: control of the general reserve, and the authority to lay down general strategy. But he had no comprehensive staff with which actually to devise operations; only a handful of men to plan the actions of four national armies. And echoing the Nivelle arrangement, the national commanders were free to appeal to their own Governments against Foch's directives.

But the ambiguities went deeper. For much of 1918, notwithstanding the dogged contribution of the French and the rising participation of the Americans, the British were the major fighting force on the Allied side of the Western Front. Hence it was rather anomalous for so devotedly French a general as Foch to be exercising ultimate direction. This was particularly the case when neither Haig nor Lloyd George necessarily shared Foch's view of the part the British army should play.

For Haig, Foch was there to overrule Pétain in his hour of defeatism and to direct French forces to the British front in its hour of danger. Haig was not anticipating that his own direction of British operations should be seriously curtailed, except as had been necessary all along in this war run by a coalition. And he certainly did not believe that British forces should be thrown improvidently into operations of French devising – operations that, if contributing to Allied victory, would drain away the last reserves of British manpower.

As for Lloyd George, he envisaged that once the crisis in the West was over he would be able to divert British forces away from France to remoter and less bloody fields. The American troops flowing to Europe would replace the British, while the French remained where they were. Of course, Haig would not approve and would strive to retain his divisions and employ them in new offensives. But Haig was no longer an independent commander.

This, however, took no account of Foch. If hardly at one with all of Haig's views, Foch was far removed from Lloyd George's. He was more devoted to offensives on the Western Front than Haig – to say nothing of Pétain. The German onslaught that had brought him to his present office he regarded as a temporary interruption to a succession of Allied assaults. These he envisaged as employing the British in full measure. The American reinforcements – irrespective of whose ships had brought them from over there to over here – would be employed largely on the French sector, not the British. So the French would be safeguarded from a repetition of the Nivelle experience.

Given this divergence on fundamentals between the Allied commander and the British Premier, it is little wonder that Foch, as 1918 proceeded, became in Lloyd George's eyes a greater villain than Haig. The consequence was one of the war's crowning ironies. Far from the appointment of a supreme commander constricting Haig or terminating his influence upon strategy, it gave him a leeway he had never enjoyed before. For whereas Haig had previously had one master, he now had two – at odds with each other – and therefore none.

It is not the case that during 1917 and the opening months of 1918 Haig had been exempt from political control. As has been argued earlier, he had been able to act only with Lloyd George's active or tacit approval. But from April 1918 he became in good measure free from that control except where he chose to invoke it. Yet the overlordship by Foch which largely took its place was in good measure nominal. For if Foch sought to compel him to undertake operations of which he disapproved, Haig held a trump card that Foch dared not let him play. The British commander simply threatened to appeal to London.

Foch had no counter to this. Haig might disapprove of particular operations that Foch planned for the Western Front. But Haig was at one with him in wanting to fight there. Lloyd George was not. From Foch's viewpoint, therefore, it was altogether wiser to bow to Haig's wishes than to let Lloyd George have the last say. Hence one major consequence of the Doullens and Beauvais arrangements was something that no one could have foreseen. Under 'unity of command', Haig was about to embark not only on his finest military accomplishments but also on his period of least trammelled authority.

II

All this would only become evident when the time came once again for the Allies to take the war to the enemy. That was not the situation when Foch acquired his new responsibilities, nor would it be for some months yet. The immediate position was better expressed by an exchange between Foch and Clemenceau (whose new-won amity remained fragile) in the aftermath of the Doullens conference. Clemenceau remarked chidingly, 'Well, you have had you own way.' 'Yes!' retorted Foch. 'A nice mess! You give me a lost battle, and tell me to win it.'[4]

That was an exaggeration. On this same day, 26 March, the German offensive on the Third Army front ground to a halt. And in the ensuing week, in a dénouement that owed nothing to unity of command, the whole Somme battle ended with the enemy having accomplished not one of Ludendorff's large objectives.

But if the battle was not lost, it was far from won. Ludendorff, having committed himself to victory by means of the offensive, could not turn back now. He must hold his extended front on the Somme and seek to defeat his adversaries elsewhere. And, for a while longer, the adversaries he chose would be the British.

So developed the second phase of the Ludendorff offensive. It is known as the battle of the Lys, after a sluggish stream on the Flemish plain. Beyond the stream lay an important objective: the rail centre of Hazebrouck, 'through which ran the lines on which the British front in Flanders depended for, probably, half its daily food and munitions.'[5] According to one view, Ludendorff had always wanted to make his first and main effort here; he had been dissuaded by the muddy terrain (and Haig's experiences in attacking there) in the wintry months. This is open to question. An attack in Flanders might give Ludendorff a substantial success, but not the over-whelming victory over Britain's forces that drew him to the Somme. The attack further north bore witness to the fact that his brightest visions had already departed.

In this second phase the enemy was aided both by good fortune and by failures of the Allied command and some of the rank and file. The early cessation of winter rains had turned the northern sector into tolerable campaigning territory for the Germans ahead of British expectations. As for Haig, although anticipating a second attack, he was awaiting it further south. So the British sector chosen by Ludendorff was under-manned and held by divisions worn down by the March battles. And the Germans' initial blow was aimed at a stretch of front occupied by demoralized Portuguese troops – conscripts who (with good cause) had little comprehension of what they were doing there. The inadequacy of these soldiers to withstand an attack was recognized by the British command, which was in the process of replacing them when the blow fell.

The manner of the German attack followed, though on a much reduced scale, the

---

[4] John Toland, *No Man's Land: The Story of 1918* (London: Eyre Methuen, 1980), p. 94.
[5] C. E. W. Bean, *Official History of Australia in the War of 1914–1918* (Sydney: Angus & Robertson, 1939), p. 434.

pattern of 21 March. Twenty-four hours before it went in, the 11 miles of front between Armentières and Béthune were drenched with mustard gas. This had the effect of incapacitating large numbers of the defenders, yet the gas would have somewhat dispersed before the storm-troopers went forward. Then, on the early morning of 9 April, 900 German guns (against 200 British) bombarded the sector of attack for four and a half hours. After that eight German divisions, aided once more by an obliging mist, went into the attack. Against them were one British division on their left, another (which had been through the March retreat) on the right, and the Portuguese in the centre.

On the German left the British division covering Béthune held firm – and even captured a German regimental band assigned to accompany the intended victors into that town. But the Portuguese in the centre, except in small pockets, gave way completely. Many, indeed, had departed during the bombardment. This presented the attackers with an uninterrupted advance for 3 miles, so enabling them to get around the British division on their right. It also had to fall back. Only the rushing in of two battered British divisions, which had been sent here for a rest, halted the advance. Nevertheless, despite this impressive start the Germans at the day's end were across the Lys at only one point, whereas they had been intended to overrun it completely.

On the following day, while continuing pressure on this sector, the Germans also attacked further north, against Plumer's Second Army, on a front of 6 miles. Again, they had a heavy numerical advantage. General Maurice, Director of Military Operations, wrote on 10 April of Plumer's front: 'we have skinned it for the Somme and have nothing left of much use.'[6] This meant that six relatively fresh German divisions were up against three British divisions that had just been through the Somme battles – where they had lost 'more than half of their fighting strength'.[7] The losses already sustained by these British divisions had been made good by mere youngsters, whose condition shocked the Australians they had just replaced in the firing line: 'the thin ranks had been expanded by a flood of very young recruits who, to the harder Australians, appeared as mere children, pink cheeked, soft chinned, giving the impression of being dazed by the grim conditions into which they were suddenly plunging.'[8]

In short order these Second Army divisions were driven back over Plugstreet Wood, of unlovely memory, and across Messines Ridge, scene of Plumer's triumph less than a year before. The retreat on both sides of Armentières rendered the town untenable, and in the course of the day it was abandoned.

By the third day of this northern attack Haig was finding the situation decidedly uncomfortable. The enemy were now across the Lys in force and within 10 miles of Hazebrouck. And there were limits to how far the British commander could redeem the situation by bringing up reinforcements to the north. For the Germans were still within shelling distance of Amiens and might attack there again at any moment. And a further assault upon Arras was a distinct possibility. As for appeals to Foch, they availed nothing: his eyes also were fixed on Amiens, as well as on the possibility of a German attack further south.

So Haig issued an appeal to his forces to keep fighting: 'Every position must be held to the last man: there must be no retirement. With our backs to the wall, and believing in the justice of our cause, each one of us must fight on to the end.' It is impossible to assess the effect of this unusually frank document. Some troops responded cynically:

[6] Nancy Maurice (ed.), *The Maurice Case* (London: Leo Cooper, 1972), p. 81.
[7] Sir James Edmonds, *Military Operations France and Belgium 1918* (London: Macmillan, 1937), vol. 2, p. 204.
[8] Bean, *Official History of Australia in the War of 1914–1918*, vol. 5, p. 419.

'What ruddy wall?' H. Essame, then a captain in the Amiens sector, wrote seventeen years later: 'to many who had fought in the March retreat its tone was insulting. It infuriated my own commanding officer who refused to publish it to the troops and said that if the morale of the higher command was low, his at least was not.'[9]

But according to C. E. W. Bean: 'Among the Australians . . . it had precisely the result intended – that of stringing them to the highest pitch of determination.'[10] And we have the testimony of Vera Brittain that, among nurses driven to the limits of exhaustion by the flood of wounded, Haig's missive revived their resolution to keep at their task. After three weeks of days and nights 'lived without respite or off-duty time under the permanent fear of defeat and flight', the staff of the Etaples hospital had been reduced to the negative conviction that 'nothing mattered except to end the strain.' But, Vera Brittain continues:

> On April 11th, after a dizzying rush of wounded from the new German offensive at Armentières, I stumbled up to the Sisters' quarters for lunch with the certainty that I could not go on – and saw, pinned up on the notice-board in the Mess, Sir Douglas Haig's 'Special Order of the Day'. . . .
>
> [A]fter I had read it I knew that I should go on, whether I could or not. There was a braver spirit in the hospital that afternoon, and though we only referred briefly and brusquely to Haig's message, each one of us had made up her mind that, though enemy airmen blew up our huts and the Germans advanced upon us from Abbeville, so long as wounded men remained in Etaples, there would be 'no retirement'.[11]

The crisis of the battle came in the next few days. By 12 April the advance by the Germans had secured them a salient, subject to heavy flanking fire, bulging out from the pivots of Ypres in the north and Béthune in the south. This was still not a breakthrough. So the German command brought in one of its best corps to transform the situation. Yet on 13 April it managed an advance of only half a mile. On the 14th it did better, capturing Wytschaete and Bailleul. But the attackers were still buying hundreds of yards of ground at a cost of thousands of casualties. And the forces confronting them were growing: they included two French divisions, an Australian division withdrawn (under intermittent shelling) from Amiens, and several British divisions arriving from Italy, Palestine, and Egypt.

Only towards Ypres was the enemy making progress that showed up well on the map. That was on account of a decision by Plumer, who was now in charge of the whole battlefield. In order to shorten his line and so reinforce the part of his front that was in danger, he decided to abandon Passchendaele ridge and other 'prizes' of the Third Ypres campaign. (These had all along been recognized as untenable should the Germans attack there, as clearly they were planning to do.) So, in the account of William Moore:

> On the 15th the elements of five divisions holding the line outside Ypres trailed back over the greasy duckboard tracks, past the loathsome stagnant pools, the rusting wrecks of tanks, the still unburied bodies. Four out of the five divisions of the withdrawing troops had participated in the gruesome attacks to seize this unspeakable wilderness, and now the survivors of the earlier disasters covered in two nights the ground that had taken them three months to win.[12]

Contemporary writers were dismayed by the abandonment of such 'sacred ground'. The troops, according to the war correspondent Philip Gibbs, were overjoyed.

---

[9] Quoted in William Moore, *See How They Ran* (London: Sphere Books, 1975), p. 218.

[10] Bean, *Official History of Australia in the War of 1914–1918*, vol. 5, p. 437.

[11] Vera Brittain, *Testament of Youth* (London: Virago, 1978), pp. 418–20.

[12] Moore, *See How They Ran*, p. 228.

Haig too was revealing a heightened quality of flexibility – something that would be evident in his conduct of operations, offensive as well as defensive, for the remainder of the war. He took it as essential to maintain the junction with the French, which meant he could not reduce further his forces between Arras and Amiens. In the north he must hold the ports of Calais and Boulogne and the rail centre of Hazebrouck; but he concluded that this gave him room to manoeuvre in the area now in danger. If need be, the whole Ypres salient could go and his forces could fall back at least to a line running south from Dunkirk, an area for whose inundation preparations were in train. So when, right at the end of April, he received alarming (but, as it proved, unfounded) news of German progress against Plumer, he responded – according to his diary – with the injunction that Plumer 'must carry out the plans laid down for him and fall back from the salient . . . as he judges necessary'.

As long as the British front was being commanded with this degree of flexibility, the enemy had little prospect of a mighty success in the north. They might inflict heavy casualties and capture positions of importance. But their prospects of persuading Plumer to let his army be cut off and driven into the sea were slim.

In the event, the second half of April offered scant success to the Germans. Their efforts were now directed less against Hazebrouck than Mount Kemmel, the eastern high point of 'Flemish Switzerland' – a chain of peaks running west to east and *in toto* dominating the Flanders plain. Furious attacks on 17 and 18 April accomplished nothing, and a lull followed for almost a week. During it, with 'unity of command' now functioning belatedly in the way the British had intended, French divisions replaced British – some of the latter reduced from an original complement in excess of 10,000 to a bare 3,000. Plumer meanwhile was further shortening his line, so securing additional troops by relinquishing ground from the original Ypres salient.

On 25 April Ludendorff scored what would prove his last success in the north. A strong attack on a French division took Mount Kemmel, to the fury of the British. But the rest of this succession of high points was denied the enemy, and after a further effort on 29 April Ludendorff concluded that the cause was lost.

The German accomplishment had again been impressive. Hazebrouck had been threatened, Plumer obliged to relinquish hard-won territory, heavy casualties imposed on the British, and Haig driven to utter an uncharacteristic *cri de coeur*. Yet in terms of his principal objectives, Ludendorff had achieved nothing. The Allies' rail communications remained intact; their ports continued inviolate; and no great bodies of British or Belgian troops had been isolated and overwhelmed. Two German armies had exhausted their offensive powers in securing a lengthening of their line and another salient – one that, apart from Mount Kemmel, left the Germans 'in ill plight . . . entrenched in low wet land and badly overlooked'.[13]

III

While making their main effort in the north, the Germans in the latter half of April had not quite done with Amiens.

East of that city lay three plateaus: Gentelles, Villers-Bretonneux, and Moreuil. The last of these was already in German hands. If the enemy could secure the other two, Amiens would be under direct artillery fire and could be battered to pieces.

On 24 April the Germans launched a heavy attack against these positions. Opposing them was a British division that had lost heavily a month earlier. Its casualties (in the

---

[13] Bean, *Official History of Australia in the War of 1914–1918*, vol. 5, p. 655.

words of Rawlinson quoted earlier) had been made good with 'young boys' and 'children'. Now there fell upon them the usual preliminaries to a German offensive: mustard gas and high explosive – not to say fog. Then came something quite novel: an assault not only by German infantry but also by German tanks. This was the first time the latter had been used for spearheading an enemy attack. There were 13 of them: larger and yet more cumbersome than the British variety, but heavily armed, advancing over good terrain, and (thanks to their novelty) opposed by no special defences. However, they were roughly handled by several Mark IV and Whippet tanks in what proved history's first tank-to-tank combat.

By the end of the day the Germans had captured the Villers-Bretonneux plateau and were approaching the Gentelles upland. It was to prove the farthest point of their Somme advance. And the success was short-lived. A moonlight counter-attack led by two brigades of Australians drove them back, and by the end of 25 April the British had recovered nearly all that had been lost on the previous day.

The action of Villers-Bretonneux, along with the dying stages of the Flanders offensive, marked an important terminus. During March and April 1918 the BEF had been subject to unrelenting German attack. Except for a few divisions, this would not again be their experience for the remainder of the war. That was not – if we are to accept Ludendorff's later account – because the German command did not intend to complete the business then begun. And it is the case that many good German divisions remained in the Flanders sector, as if to renew the offensive there. But for the moment, with his attempts to rout the BEF at a standstill, Ludendorff was prepared to turn his attentions to the French. His intention, or anyway his rationalization, was that thereby he would draw Foch's reserves to the southern sector, so improving his prospects for a renewal of the attack in the north.

This new phase of German offensive operations would continue from May to July. And by the time it was done, Ludendorff's initiatives would have ended for ever. Thereafter the story of 1918 would become for the BEF what in essence it had been in 1916 and 1917: unrelenting assaults upon the German lines. But these attacks would not be confined to one sector of the British front. And in their outcome they would be quite unlike the endeavours of previous years.

IV

Meanwhile the setbacks of March and April were producing a minor political crisis in Britain. Questions were being asked as to why Britain had sustained these misfortunes. And one explanation being offered was that Haig had been subject to interference. His political masters had obliged him to occupy a longer front than he considered safe, with fewer troops than he considered necessary.

Lloyd George and his colleagues stoutly denied these charges. They alleged that the BEF confronting Ludendorff's attack had been stronger than a year before. They claimed that the number of white (as distinct from coloured) troops being employed in distant theatres, and so not available to Haig, was negligible. And they argued that Haig had been free from political pressure when he agreed to take over additional miles of front from the French.

Each of these assertions, broadly interpreted, was false. In some instances Lloyd George and his colleagues may have been under a misapprehension. In others they were plainly twisting the facts.

None of this, given that the Germans had failed in their efforts, mattered by the end of April, except in one particular. Probably Lloyd George, in seeking to slough off responsibility for his actions, was just trying to safeguard himself. But to some it appeared that he had a deeper purpose: that of casting blame for the recent setbacks on the high command, with a view to dismissing Haig.

One who came to the latter conclusion was Major-General Sir Frederick Maurice. (He had been recently set aside as Director of Military Operations and was about to take up a command in France.) Maurice determined that Lloyd George must be thwarted. So on 7 May a letter by him appeared in the press. It claimed that the Government, contrary to its public statements, had kept Haig's forces undermanned, had lavished white troops on distant theatres, and had obliged Haig to extend his front. This seemed an extraordinary action for a serving officer, who in the British way of doing things should not intervene publicly in political matters. And it did not excite the approval even of some in the military hierarchy – including Haig. On the other hand Maurice recognized that he was destroying his military career, and acted on the conviction that this was an occasion 'when duty as a citizen comes before duty as a soldier'.[14]

Maurice's charges, although soundly based, had not been put together with such care that they could not be circumvented. This would have mattered little as long as they were subject to a thorough investigation. But that never happened. Momentarily the Government announced that there would be an inquiry by judges, but it quickly changed its mind. Lloyd George decided to settle the matter by a debate in the House of Commons. This took place on 9 May 1918.

The debate was opened by Asquith. Unaware that all prospects of an inquiry had already vanished, he moved that the promised investigation should be undertaken not by judges but by a select committee of the House. His speech was devoted to these technicalities and offered no comment on the rights and wrongs of Maurice's charges – or the propriety of Maurice's action. Lloyd George then demolished both Maurice and Asquith. His speech was skilful, if hardly creditable. He evaded the point that the extension of the front had been imposed on Haig; used figures that he knew to be incorrect to show that the BEF had been stronger in early 1918 than a year before; and made it appear that Maurice had up to now endorsed Government statements about the paucity of white troops in the sideshows. Yet for all its sophistries, the speech had a strong underpinning: resentment against public intervention in political matters by a serving soldier with access to privileged information.

Lloyd George's trump card, however, was not his bravura display of questionable statistics and *ad hominem* irrelevancies. It was his announcement that Asquith's motion constituted a vote of censure, which, if carried, would bring down the Government. That settled the matter. The House would never embark on a course that might imperil Lloyd George and restore Asquith.

The sensible course for Asquith at this juncture, having delivered no attack on the Government, was to abandon his motion. Since his fall he had studiously refrained from leading an opposition to the Government. Only recently he had refused to do so, despite pressure from some of his supporters, on an issue that touched Liberal consciences nearly: conscription for Ireland. But in the House on 9 May Asquith would neither go forward nor back down. Doubtless he thought it unfair that Maurice, whatever his breach of military discipline, should be condemned unheard. And probably he felt that the Government should not be allowed to discredit Haig on spurious grounds. But it can hardly be doubted that Asquith's futile stubbornness

---

[14] Maurice, *The Maurice Case*, p. 60.

betrayed his deep – if publicly unexpressed – resentment against the man and the methods that had driven him from office.

In consequence the Liberal leader brought on himself the worst of both worlds. None of his close associates tried to counter Lloyd George's utterance. Yet Asquith pressed his motion to a division. Only 106 MPs voted for it, the great majority of them being Liberals; and it is permissible to speculate that some of these would have abstained had there been any prospect that the motion might be carried. 293 MPs voted against him: the overwhelming body of Conservatives, a good complement of Liberals, and several from the Labour Party.

The Maurice debate is sometimes regarded as a large event in wartime Britain. It is variously said to have sundered the Liberal Party, determined Lloyd George's future political course, exacerbated the rift between soldiers and civilians, and yet (paradoxically) to have saved Sir Douglas Haig. All of these are questionable assertions. There was already an incipient split in the Liberal Party between followers of Asquith and followers of Lloyd George (as well as potential divisions on quite other grounds, ranging from economics and social questions to foreign policies). But whether the antipathy between the two leaders would result in a rupture in the party, embracing the rank and file as well as the upper echelons, would not depend on the short-lived passage of arms on 9 May. Most of all, it would rest upon Lloyd George's judgement about his political future – a judgement that would be based on matters larger than Maurice's *démarche* and Asquith's muted endorsement.

As for relations between the Government and the high command, nothing changed in the aftermath of Maurice's action. Admittedly, the War Cabinet had been talking about sacking Haig and never got round to doing so. But this was running terribly true to form. At most it is speculation that, but for Maurice, the Government would have gone beyond considering Haig's dismissal and would actually have dismissed him. Apart from its impact on the career of the author of the letter, the Maurice incident appears to have been largely a non-event.

V

For most British divisions on the Western Front, the months of May, June, and July 1918 formed a respite from battle. The approach of summer also brought rest, recuperation, retraining, and re-equipment. For a battered army, all this proved a considerable restorative.

Other factors aided the process of recovery. Despite continuing manpower problems, the divisions were gradually built up to something approaching their nominal strength. And Haig appointed Major-General Sir Ivor Maxse, an incisive thinker on matters of tactics, as inspector-general of training. Under him methods of training for the more open style of warfare now obtaining were standardized.

Meanwhile a new sort of junior officer was emerging, replacing the public-school and university-trained men who, ever since the development of Britain's mass army, had fulfilled this role. The ranks of the nation's 'born leaders' were wearing thin. Some, having been adjudged officer material on the basis of social class or education, had broken down or been relegated to other spheres. And many, proving adequate to their tasks, had lost their lives while fulfilling, or striving to live up to, the public-school stereotype. Now the army was perforce drawing its junior officers from the products of social groups that had been deemed inappropriate at the war's outset: men of middling and humble origin, who under stress had displayed initiative and a readiness to take charge.

While death and injury and strain were bringing changes in the lower rungs of leadership, other forces had acted to reconstitute the upper echelons. The mediocrities and conformists whom Haig had found so agreeable were at last out of harm's way. Now his chief administrators – some of whom he had appointed but several of whom he had had thrust upon him – were at least competent and often much more than that. Two among the better sort may be instanced. Travers Clarke was Quartermaster-General and so directed an organization whose complexity 'vied with the great industrial organizations of a later age such as ICI, Shell and General Motors'.[15] Among its great range of administrative duties were transportation, veterinary services, pay, war graves, canteens, labour, and postal services. Clarke's rank was that of major; but, H. Essame tells us, 'no general ever made sterner demands on his officers and men or overrode more obstacles'. 'He had one rule to which he never permitted an exception – that it was "the fighting man who must be considered first and last". He was quite willing that his staff should labour to the extreme point of endurance to take any load off the man in the trenches.'

The artillery side of GHQ was directed, as it had been since May 1916, by Major-General Noel Birch. With the aid of his by now considerable experience, he had become possessed of great expertise – an important matter, given the magnitude of his coming task and the large resources at his disposal. By the second half of 1918, so Birch told Colonel Repington (military correspondent of the *Morning Post*), 'our artillery are now from 30 to 40 per cent. of our fighting strength': a signal indication of the role the guns were expected to play in clearing a way for the depleted infantry.[16]

Meanwhile the BEF's gunners had attained a high standard of professionalism. In the previous two years, it is true, they had suffered many casualties. But they had never endured the martyrdom imposed on the infantry. Their consequent expertise is suggested by the following accomplishment of late summer 1918: 'In a single month more than 13 per cent. of the German artillery in the West was completely destroyed by counter-battery fire.'[17]

Behind the gunners, moreover, lay the productive resources of the home front, now more than equal to meeting the insatiable demands of the battlefield. Churchill, at this time Minister of Munitions, relates how, immediate upon the setback sustained in the Ludendorff offensive, he gave an assurance that 'all losses in material would be immediately replaced.' To this end 'the Munitions Council, its eighty departments and its two and a half million workers, men and women, toiled with a cold passion that knew no rest.' Factories everywhere forewent their Easter holidays, and those not asked to make this sacrifice had to be provided with a ministerial explanation. 'One thought dominated the whole gigantic organization – to make everything good within a month. Guns, shells, rifles, ammunition, Maxim guns, Lewis guns, tanks, aeroplanes and a thousand ancillaries were all gathered from our jealously hoarded reserves.' By the end of March Churchill was able to inform the War Cabinet and GHQ that 'nearly two thousand new guns of every nature, with their complete equipments, could be supplied by April 6 as fast as they could be handled by the receiving department of the Army. In fact, however, twelve hundred met the need.'[18]

Perhaps, in the circumstances, it is not surprising that Churchill himself was becoming the subject of unwonted praise among the high command. Repington,

[15] H. Essame, *The Battle for Europe 1918* (London: Batsford, 1972), p. 25.
[16] C. à C. Repington, *The First World War 1914–1918* (London: Constable, 1920), vol. 2, p. 365.
[17] *History of the Ministry of Munitions* (London: HMSO, 1922), vol. 2, pt 1, p. 98.
[18] Winston S. Churchill, *The World Crisis 1911–1918* (London: Odhams Press, n.d.), vol. 4, pp. 1263–6.

visiting GHQ late in August, noted: 'They all say that Winston has been very good and very helpful in the late hard times.'[19]

VI

This period of renewal for the British army (barring certain divisions to whom reference will be made shortly) was enormously to its benefit. But others had to pay the cost. While the BEF recuperated, the French nation was passing through its culminating struggle for survival. For it was against the armies of France, between late May and the middle of July, that Ludendorff directed his next three offensives.

The British were not wholly absent from the fighting during this phase. Nine British divisions participated in it, four by design in the later stages, five by sheer ill-fortune at the outset. The involvement of the latter stemmed from the fact that Foch, from April 1918, was busy establishing his general reserve. The British were so exhausted that they could not be asked to contribute directly, especially as the reserve would go to wherever the fighting developed. So Foch proposed that some of Haig's most drained divisions be moved to a quiet part of the French front, thereby releasing French divisions for his reserve. The British commander consented.

Consequently, five British divisions that had been through some of the worst fighting of March and April and had been reinforced by the very young and the doubtfully fit, were transferred in May. Four of them went to what was known as the 'sanatorium of the West': the Chemin des Dames on the river Aisne, a region where British forces had last fought in September 1914. (The fifth division was placed a bit further east; but not for long.) The new arrivals were agreeably impressed, one of them writing to a wounded mate in hospital:

> Well, we have not heard a shell for five days, nor a bomb for four days. We are now on virgin soil and in a beautiful part of the country. I think it is the best we have been in yet. When we go forward, I believe it is a comparative health resort – so look sharp old boy and return to enjoy the beautiful scenery and the wine of the country.[20]

Soon these divisions would experience more than attractive scenery and good wine. By the time they left the French sector (in mid-June), two would enjoy the unhappy distinction of having sustained the heaviest casualties of any British divisions since 21 March: between 16,000 and 17,000 each, well in excess of 100 per cent of their original establishment. Half of these casualties were the consequence of their transfer to the 'healthy' Chemin des Dames.

The Aisne was the region chosen by Ludendorff for his third offensive. He believed that by attacking the French he could persuade Foch to draw away divisions from the British sector, so making it worth his while again to strike in the north. Still, now as ever Ludendorff would seize whatever openings presented themselves, even though they did not accord with this principal purpose.

The French preparations on the Chemin des Dames were lamentable. The three British divisions in the front line, along with their artillery, were packed well forward within easy range of the German bombardment. They were situated with their backs to a river – 'one of the classic prescriptions for defeat'[21] – and there was virtually no organized rear zone. Had Pétain had his way, this would not have been the case: his

---

[19] Repington, *The First World War*, vol. 2, p. 365.
[20] Quoted in Essame, *The Battle for Europe 1918*, p. 56.
[21] Ibid., p. 58.

formula was elastic defence in depth. But Duchêne, who commanded in this area, was a disciple of Foch. And the generalissimo still resisted surrendering a yard of territory, in which respect he supported Duchêne against the French C.-in-C.

Once more the Allied command was caught napping as to the whereabouts of the coming blow. Somehow 30 German divisions, 4,000 guns, and a like number of mortars were assembled unobserved. When, at 1 a.m. on 27 May, the guns opened up for a bombardment of three hours, the effect was annihilating:

> Never, even on 21 March, had there been a bombardment as accurate and terrible as this. Not a single forward position, dug-out, communication trench, command post, head-quarters, dump or battery position was missed.

Then, at 4 a.m., 14 assault divisions fell upon the hapless defenders. The German progress proved irresistible. H. Essame writes:

> By nightfall the Germans had reached the river Vesle on a nine-mile front. In one day, the German Seventh Army had crossed two, and in places three, rivers; they had driven a salient 25 miles wide at the base and extending nearly 12 miles into the Allied line. They had destroyed four of the divisions originally in the line and nearly wiped out four more sent up from the reserve.[22]

By the day's end only one of the four British divisions fighting in this area existed as an integral force. (Nevertheless, the remnants of the others would still be in action 11 days later.) As for the fifth of the divisions which had come to the French front for a rest, it entered the fray on the third day – accompanied by abuse from French civilians who held the British responsible for the collapse. Along with the survivors of the initial onslaught, this division became engaged in a fighting retreat along paths whence the original BEF had advanced following the battle of the Marne in 1914.

A young private engaged in this phase recounts how, with his heels 'cracked and caked with blood' and his nose and mouth bleeding, he reached the point where he could walk no further. When he told this to a ranker officer he received the reply: 'If you don't march, you stay bloody here, and we go on.' His account continues:

> Four of us who cannot march follow behind the short column. The M[edical] O[fficer] rides behind us on a horse. After a time he tells the others to march on. Me he puts on a lorry. The lorry soon puts me down, and when the column comes up I fall in and struggle along. I could scream or tear my head with pain. We march many kilos. We come to a great broad river. They say it is the Marne. We cross and halt on the other side. So I have crossed the Marne. We march on – they are singing a song:
>
> > Forever on the march, our song so let it be,
> > We've crossed the Aisne, we've crossed the Marne,
> > We'll soon reach gay Paree,
> > And in this cruel strife, we live from hand to mouth,
> > And nightly pitch our box-latrine –
> > A day's march further South.'[23]

Ludendorff's achievement was formidable. He had placed German forces once more within sight of Paris. This had shaken France profoundly, causing even the ferocious Premier, Clemenceau, to contemplate evacuating the capital, – although 'as to making peace, never!' If but temporarily, the nerve of Britain's leaders also was shaken. On 31 May Henry Wilson noted: 'The news is bad, there is no question of that.' Some rumoured losses of territory suggested that the French were not fighting.

---

[22] Essame, *The Battle for Europe 1918*, pp. 60–1.

[23] Kiernan, *Little Brother Goes Soldiering*, p. 92. The day following this march, Kiernan was found to have a temperature of 104° – the result of gas poisoning.

'If this is so we are done, and Lloyd George and Milner at once went on that assumption and talked of – nonsense.' By next morning Wilson was not beyond talking nonsense himself: 'Writing now, before breakfast, I find it difficult to realize that there is a possibility, perhaps a probability, of the French Army being beaten. What would this mean? The destruction of our army in France? In Italy? In Salonika? What of Palestine & Mesopotamia, India, Siberia & the sea? What of Archangel & America?' Fortunately for Wilson the news during the day, if not good, suggested that his anticipation of a global catastrophe was premature.

For the truth was that this latest endeavour of Ludendorff's was following the pattern of his previous offensives: an impressive early start earning him, at heavy cost, a large salient but no strategic success. This was not to his purpose: it gave him an extended front to be held with diminished forces. For the start of this third offensive he had been able to draw on additional divisions from the Eastern Front. But that well of manpower was now dry of good quality troops; and anyway it was necessary to maintain a huge force in Russia if the Germans were to secure the wheat and oil and other good things they so eagerly anticipated.

By the early days of June Ludendorff was once more confronting a dilemma. At least for the moment his drive on Paris had come to a halt, with his advance guard just across the Marne. Should he make a further effort here, with the French capital – and the collapse of France – his goal? Or should he revert to his original view that the operation here was a diversion and turn once more against the British in Flanders? While leaving his options open, he inclined for the moment towards the first alternative. He even brought reserves from the north to assist his next blow.

On 9 June the Germans attacked on the river Matz, a sector of the front lying to the west of their new salient. As well as enhancing the threat to Paris, they hoped to engulf a railway system needed to supply their forces on the Marne. This time Ludendorff could not conceal his intentions. The hurried movement of his artillery uncovered his hand. Nevertheless, the French commanders again served his purpose by keeping their forces well forward to fall under the lash of his high explosive and gas. So on the opening day the Germans pushed south a distance of 6 miles, and on the following day, 10 June, made further progress.

Thereafter, however, little went according to Ludendorff's plan. On 11 June his forces were held on the eastern sector of the Matz offensive, while on the western side General Mangin, with five divisions, launched a briefly successful counter-attack. By the following day the whole episode had ground to a halt. There was no doubt who had come out of it the better. The French, if only on a small scale, had revealed that they could once more mount a counter-attack in unpromising circumstances. Ludendorff, needing a big success, had gained almost nothing.

A month later these conclusions were driven home with a vengeance. Now turning his attention to extending the eastern side of the salient jutting towards Paris, Ludendorff on 15 July launched what he termed his 'peace offensive' – peace, in this context, being envisaged as the consequence of victory. (Given that he was still holding back forces for a great thrust in Flanders, this title, on the most optimistic view, appeared premature.) As on 9 June, the Germans could not maintain secrecy; although that was a price that could hardly be avoided if Ludendorff's offensives were to be cumulative rather than (as with the first three) widely dispersed and so non-supportive. For once the French did not play into his hands. On a good part of their front they applied defence in depth. Hence the terrible German bombardment fell on almost empty positions, and the storm-troopers, after making what appeared good progress, came upon unbroken defences against which they withered. Only on the French left, where elastic defence had not been instituted, did the attackers enjoy some success, so extending their bridgehead across the Marne.

On 16 July, the second day of the offensive, little went well for the Germans. They made scant progress where on the previous day the going had been reasonable, and none where it had been bad. Ludendorff concluded that his peace offensive had nothing more to offer. This left him with but one hope to cling to: that he might now succeed against the British in Flanders.

Ludendorff's three efforts against the French had attracted many Allied divisions away from the British sector. In fact, as soon as the Germans opened their offensive against the French late in May, Foch – if not meeting all of Pétain's demands – had brought in reserves with an alacrity denied to Haig during the Flanders crisis of April. Not only were French divisions withdrawn from the north, but they were followed by five American divisions then training behind the British lines.

This was a pointer to an important development. It would be on the French sector of the Western Front, not the British, that American military involvement in this war would develop. To begin with it took the form of American divisions being employed within the French command structure. Pershing, the American C.-in-C., did not find this a comfortable experience. It confirmed him in his determination that thereafter his army would fight as an independent force. Yet whatever the strains of such close co-operation between allies, in June and July the appearance of American and French troops fighting shoulder to shoulder profoundly affected morale on both sides of the front. It convinced the French that unlimited help was at hand. And it left the Germans in no doubt that the balance of forces had moved irrevocably against them.

Foch's initial withdrawal of French reserves and unblooded Americans from the British sector had not been endorsed by Haig; for the British commander had not been consulted, only informed after the event. This displeased both Haig and the War Cabinet, although for different reasons. Haig felt he should have been consulted. Lloyd George was alarmed to discover that unity of command might signify greater effort, not less, for the British on the Western Front. Nevertheless, Haig did, despite his own continued peril, fall in generally with Foch's wishes on this matter. He even, at the generalissimo's request, dispatched four of his own divisions to the French sector in mid-July.

Contrary to expectation, these four divisions were employed not in defence but in attack. Ludendorff on 17 July, following the meagre progress of his 'peace offensive' against the French, had himself set off to the north. He directed to be sent in the same direction the heavy artillery and mortars that, having done their worst from the Aisne to the Marne, would now blast a way from Ypres to the sea. But his deliberations regarding a new campaign in Flanders were cut short. What halted them was an event on the Marne so compelling as to shake profoundly the morale of himself and his forces. On 18 July, on the west side of the German salient, General Mangin launched a counter-offensive. Far from running down, as Ludendorff had intended, the struggle on the French sector was proceeding in a quite new direction.

For the area of attack, the French had assembled 24 divisions (including 4 American divisions containing double the prevailing infantry strength) and 750 tanks. Opposing them were 11 German divisions and few if any tanks. Moreover, the French and American divisions were of high quality, whereas the Germans were not first-class troops and their numbers were well below establishment. By the end of the day, the attack had progressed 4 miles along the whole western side of the salient.

Next morning, 19 July, the Allied forces on the eastern side also went on to the attack. But after the first day progress was not spectacular. The tanks were almost eliminated in the early stages; the Allied artillery found difficulty in adjusting to open warfare; and the enemy devotedly established new defensive positions. So the four British divisions employed piecemeal around the salient participated in ill-prepared and costly assaults of little consequence.

One of the things these endeavours made apparent was the acute difficulties involved in mingling units of separate nationalities. Differences in organization, equipment, and – above all – language hampered the employment of British troops within a French structure. Few British officers, even though possessing a smattering of French, could make themselves understood over the telephone. And as the French commander would not accept even Morse messages in English, the problems of communication were severe. Further, French ways of doing things seemed slapdash or chaotic by British standards.

> Almost without exception troops were committed to battle in a hurry without being given time for reconnaissance or for ensuring that all concerned knew what they had to do. This would have been excusable if the element of surprise had been present; now that it had gone the wasteful expenditure of British life on the orders of foreign generals was a bitter pill to swallow.[24]

Yet for the Germans, this counter-offensive was a parting of the ways. And it was fitting that the French, who between 1914 and 1916 had borne so onerous a share of the war's burdens, should at this moment occupy the principal role. To the Germans it had become swiftly evident not only that the road to Paris was barred but also that the territory overrun in the preceding seven weeks was untenable. First the bridgehead over the Marne had to be abandoned. Then, step by step, all of the salient wrested from the French was relinquished. By 7 August the Allies were back on the start line of 27 May.

Something else vanished in the aftermath of the second battle of the Marne. On the afternoon of 18 July Ludendorff had cancelled the movement northwards of the guns and mortars for his projected Flanders offensive. He then hurried back to the French front. From there, on 20 July, he telegraphed to his army group commander in the north. The planned attack in Flanders, he stated, would 'probably never come into execution'.

However, it was not just Mangin's counter-thrust that had brought the German command to this conclusion. It is permissible to speculate that the prospect of attacking again at Ypres, where he had failed in April, gave Ludendorff pause. But of that we have no evidence. What he offered as grounds for his decision were two other factors. One we have noted: the French counter-attack on the Marne. The other was 'the possibility of a British offensive action'. That is, the shadow of an approaching blow by Haig had fallen upon the German commander. And a dark shadow indeed it would prove.

---

[24] Essame, *The Battle for Europe 1918*, p. 98.

52

A HUNDRED DAYS I: AMIENS

> Night came on cloudless and windless and braced with autumn's first astringent tang of coolness. Above, as I lay on my back in the meadow, the whole dome had a stir of life in its shimmering fresco, stars flashing and winking with that eager air of having great things to impart. . . . We were all worked up, you see. Could it be coming at last, I thought as I went to sleep – the battle unlike other battles?
>
> *C. E. Montague, concerning the eve of the battle of Amiens, 8 August 1918*
>
> I think we have given the Bosche a pretty good bump this time.
>
> *Rawlinson to Henry Wilson, 9 August 1918*

I

The reversals of fortune on the Western Front between March and November 1918 seem to impel historians to resort to metaphor. Conventionally, the proceedings of the German army are equated with the motions of the sea. The onrush of March to June becomes a great tidal movement, reaching high-watermark outside Amiens and Hazebrouck and Paris. Then, inevitably, the tide turns.

This resort to imagery no doubt seizes the imagination. But it has little else to recommend it. If anything is certain, it is that the movements of the ocean do not cease; the tide, having ebbed, will flow again. That was not the circumstance of the German army in the second half of 1918. Nor do the exertions and ultimate triumphs of the Allied soldiers deserve to be equated with something as inert as the seashore, experiencing but hardly repelling the pounding of the waves.

What is required at this point is not colourful prose but an attempt to unravel a crucial issue. Why in 1918 did the struggle on the Western Front, having been static for so long, become a war of movement and decision? In earlier chapters it has been shown how, owing to the state of military technology and the fairly even balance between the contending forces, the war in France and Flanders persisted in stalemate from late 1914 to the end of 1917. The problem is that this explanation seems to hold good for 1918 – except that in 1918 the static war vanished. What, then, made the difference?

Often it is said that a new instrument had entered upon the battlefield that revolutionized the technology of warfare. With its aid the dominance that weapons of defence had exercised up to this point was broken. Consequently, the offensive, instead of being an essay in self-destruction, became a means of vanquishing the foe. The tank is the obvious candidate for this role of war-winning innovation. Prior to 8 August 1918 (except for the mismanaged operation at Cambrai) it had been given no opportunity to show its potential as an instrument of attack. But at Amiens on that day it took charge of the battlefield and accomplished 'the strategical end of the war; "the rest was minor tactics".[1]

On close inquiry this explanation will not suffice. For one thing it ignores the achievements of the Germans in the first half of 1918, virtually without tanks. (Whatever the British accomplished in August, they never made a breakthrough equal to Ludendorff's in March.) Yet it is hardly likely that the Germans secured their successes by totally different means from those of the Allies, even though particular weapons, as well as particular circumstances, may have brought variety to basically similar events.

Plate 45   *German prisoners marching past advancing British artillery.*

Anyway it is plain that the tank, though contributing powerfully to the British victory of 8 August, was less of a force thereafter. The reason was its high casualty rate. Even at its most successful, the tank not only was prone to mechanical failure but also suffered severely at the hands of the enemy. In the words of Shelford Bidwell:

> the mathematics of combat operate with peculiar force for tanks, which are easily identified, easily engaged, discrete, much-feared targets which attract all the fire on the battlefield. When all is said and done, a tank is a small steel box crammed with inflammable or explosive substances which is easily converted into a mobile crematorium for its highly skilled crew.[2]

The consequence of the tank's vulnerability is revealed by its waning part in the British successes of 1918. Some 430 were employed in the initial assault on 8 August (with almost 200 more acting as supply tanks or gun-carriers or providing a mechanical

---

[1] Douglas Orgill, *The Tank* (London: Heinemann, 1970), p. 84, quoting (with approval) J. F. C. Fuller.
[2] Shelford Bidwell, *Modern Warfare* (London: Allen Lane, 1973). p. 227.

reserve). But thereafter their numbers fell dramatically. Only 155 went into the assault on 9 August, and in the ensuing days the total was well below 100. From then on, during 13 weeks of unrelenting British victories, tanks were never again available on the scale of 8 August. In the renewed British assaults on 21 and 23 August, they numbered 183 and 103. And from then to the end of the war there was only one occasion, 29 September, when more than 100 were available, and only four others when the number exceeded 50.[3]

These relatively small complements of tanks would make a valuable contribution to the British successes after 8 August. But they are plainly too few to explain why the saga of victories proceeded unabated. The devotees of the tank simply evade this point when they call Amiens 'the strategical end of the war' and relegate later events like the seizure of Mont St Quentin to 'minor tactics'.

It is necessary to go further. The termination of the Great War was too complex an event to be accounted for by any single-cause explanation. For, it should be noted, we are trying to account for two things: not only the development of mobility on a hitherto static battlefield; but also why successful offensives by first one side and then the other brought the Germans no lasting benefits but for the Allies opened the way to victory.

Part of the answer must be found on the German side of the lines. Ludendorff's triumphs from March to June were achieved by numerical superiority at the point of attack, together with tactical innovations facilitating surprise. But these successes were not of a type to win the war for Germany. They secured no strategic objectives. And the losses in manpower inflicted on the Allies were not, especially with growing American intervention, decisive.

Yet anything less than complete victory left the Germans in a desperate condition. The temporary advantage in fighting men bestowed by the collapse of Russia soon departed; for the German army, having suffered prodigious casualties in previous years, sustained a terrible battering during Ludendorff's offensives. The picked troops used in the forefront of these assaults were irreplaceable. The losses could be made up, if at all, only by inferior substitutes. The upshot was that, by mid-1918, the balance of resources had turned irreversibly against the Central Powers. Defeat seemed only a matter of time.

This was bound to affect German resolve to continue fighting; including the resolve of the German ruling classes. The latter, of course, feared an Allied victory. But there was something else they had to fear: that an unwinnable war, if unduly prolonged, might engulf Germany in a communist revolution. From mid-1918 this appeared a growing possibility. There was no longer comforting news from the battlefront. And the internal situation was deteriorating alarmingly – thanks to the steady breakdown of an overburdened railway system, mismanagement of the war economy, and the deprivations imposed on the civilian population both by the Allied blockade and, even more, by the diversion of productivity from the German home front to war needs.

In these respects the ending of the war lies somewhat outside the scope of this book. It is a large episode in Germany's internal history, requiring an acute assessment of that nation's economic resources, social cohesion, political stability, and war direction.

But the end of battles was not just a German capitulation. It was also a compelling triumph for the Allies, in which they imposed their will on a still powerful military adversary. In this culminating process Britain played a large and even predominant part. Confronting a major segment of Germany's fighting men and weapons, Haig's

---

[3] These figures apply to tanks actually engaged in battle. They do not include supply tanks, or reserves not called into action. They are drawn from a document 'Tank Corps – Summary of Actions' in the Imperial War Museum. I owe this reference, and very much else in these 1918 chapters, to Dr Robin Prior.

armies drove their enemies from one stronghold to another. Within three months it was evident that this proceeding would not end short of an Allied victory. The German army might choose to abandon the contest while still on conquered territory. Or it might capitulate only when forced back into its homeland. But those were the sole choices that would be allowed it.

II

That British arms managed this succession of victories must appear a cause for wonder. For the manpower crisis confronting the nation at the beginning of 1918 did not abate as the year proceeded. The British army continued undermanned and with some half of its troops below 19 years of age

Yet in all sorts of ways this battered or inexperienced force was conducting the war with greater skill and sophistication than ever before. For one thing, its commanders were employing a variant on the Germans' use of storm-troopers. The most combative soldiers available – in particular, the Australians and the Canadians – were given the central role in any attack and received the lion's share of equipment. But perhaps even more than this, the effectiveness of British operations was enhanced both by an improved range of weapons and by their more effective deployment. Developments that had been taking place over the past two years, in the nature of arms and in their use, now came to a powerful fulfilment.

It is sufficient to outline the main improvements in weaponry. Two new types of tank appeared in 1918. There was the Mark V. It was still slow-moving, with a maximum speed of 4½ m.p.h. and an average speed of 2½ m.p.h., and it was anything but shell-proof. But it was more heavily armoured than its predecessors, and it could be driven by one man (out of a crew of eight) instead of four. And there was the Whippet, a lightweight tank, short on fire power but requiring a crew of only three and twice as fast as other tanks.

Among more conventional arms, the machine-gun was now established in two basic forms. One was the lightweight Lewis gun, capable of being carried by advancing infantry and so greatly increasing their fire power. The other was the heavy Vickers weapon, which served as a form of artillery firing pre-arranged barrages over the heads of advancing troops. Such barrages could have a telling effect on enemy infantry who, in the din of battle, were barely able to detect the existence of this menace.

Arguably, the most impressive developments were taking place among the artillery. To gauge their extent we may contrast the role of artillery on 1 July 1916 and on 8 August 1918. On the Somme in 1916 the artillery had given up all hope of locating and knocking out the enemy's guns, which were probably the greatest of all threats to the attacking infantry. Instead it had concentrated – with scant success – on the German wire and trenches. On 8 August 1918 two-thirds of British shells were directed at the German artillery – what is termed counter-battery fire. With devastating effect, the British gunners unleashed an unregistered bombardment on enemy batteries. (These had but recently been relocated in the hope of concealment.)

The capacity to hit a target without preliminary ranging fire, and so without revealing the intention to attack, sprang from the endeavours of the survey battalions. They developed the means of fixing, on what were termed artillery boards, the positions of enemy targets relative to the batteries that were to bombard them. And they devised a proceeding by which guns could be laid on these targets without registration.

But it was also necessary to know the location of the targets at the moment of attack. In the case of fairly static objects like trenches and strong points and barbed wire, this was not too much of a problem. But the enemy's guns were likely to be moved about in anticipation of hostile action, and no offensive could succeed if its supporting bombardment fell on empty gunpits. As mentioned earlier, various means had been developed to deal with this. Aerial observation was one, now reaching a high art. Flash-spotting was another: an enemy gun in the act of firing was observed from a number of positions under a central control, and its whereabouts thereby established. A third means was sound-ranging. A series of microphones picked up the sound wave made by an enemy gun, which was then translated on to film. This could be read to establish the position of the gun. Furthermore, the flash-spotters and sound-rangers could also track the passage of shells fired by British guns, and so aid in directing them on to their targets.

Any one of these methods for suppressing enemy artillery was liable to fail under unfriendly conditions. Rain might baffle the airmen and mist the flash-spotters. A strong west wind would defeat the sound-rangers by carrying the report of the enemy gun into the upper air and out of the range of their microphones. But it was rare for all these devices to fail simultaneously. The days before Amiens, when as it happened the Germans had changed the positions of their guns extensively, were very misty. This hampered observation by airmen and flash-spotters. But these were ideal conditions for the sound-rangers. For, according to an expert: 'Mist or fog is no obstacle to sound. In fact, conditions are ideal in misty weather both because the wind is generally light and the temperature of the air is very uniform.'[4] Hence the Amiens battle opened, despite poor visibility, with British shells falling with deadly precision upon the enemy's carefully concealed artillery pieces.

But it was more than developments in the separate arms that now gave British forces such enhanced striking power. What was particularly noteworthy in the operations of these last 100 days was the co-ordination between the various elements. Infantry, artillery, machine-guns, tanks, aircraft, and wireless telegraphy all functioned as parts of a single unit. As a result of meticulous planning, each component in the offensive was integrated with, and provided maximum support for, every other component. Here, more than anywhere else, was the great technical achievement of these climactic battles. It was not that the British had developed a war-winning weapon. What they had produced was a 'weapons system': the melding of the various elements in the military arm into a mutually supporting whole.

The importance of this development may be illustrated as follows. To force the Germans into retreat, it was essential that their defended positions be overrun and retained by attacking infantry. That is, the role of the foot soldier was crucial. But, among other adversaries, the infantry could make little progress against uncut barbed wire and unsuppressed machine-guns. A number of devices, from heavy shells to wire-cutters and hand grenades, might assist in overcoming these. But the tank had a particular facility: it could run down barbed wire and engage machine-guns at close range. Hence the integration of tanks with infantry was a key element in many advances. But the tanks, as we have seen, suffered terribly from the attentions of the enemy's artillery. (So did the infantry.) Hence it was vital that the British guns suppress the fire of their opposite numbers while men and armoured vehicles got forward. As a writer on the role of the artillery on 8 August observes:

It should be realised that many of the enemy batteries had been withdrawn far to the rear a

---

[4] John Innes (compiler), *Flash Spotters and Sound Rangers* (London: Allen & Unwin, 1935), p. 129.

week before the attack took place, and it was not the Tanks who found out where these guns were hidden and silenced them. It was the Sound Rangers who discovered where they had gone; the artillery who silenced them; and the Topo. Sections of the Survey Battalions who made it possible for the artillery to hit these targets without previous registration.

. . . If these guns had remained unlocated, and if our guns had not been able to engage them effectively throughout the day, would the gallant fellows who manned the Tanks have been able to achieve as much as they did?[5]

At its most powerful, this method of proceeding would not prove capable of rupturing the enemy's defensive system. For one thing, parts of that system lay beyond shell range. So once the front had been penetrated, painful delays must occur while the artillery was being hauled forward and its fresh targets delineated – delays during which the enemy, with characteristic resilience, would be taking measures to reinforce his battlefront. Consequently, no breakthrough was possible, nor would the opportunity ever arise for Haig's cavalry to pour into open country. But what the British army could now accomplish was to render the most strongly defended position ultimately untenable. That is, the great advantages that, formerly, defence had possessed over offence had been whittled away to a crucial extent. As a result the Allied armies could impose upon a now inferior adversary a series of reverses, none decisive in itself but mounting irresistibly to a conclusive control of the battlefield.

III

The events of 8 August had been foreshadowed on two occasions: at Cambrai in November 1917 and, more recently, by the minor action at Hamel on 4 July. For a number of reasons the latter engagement deserves comment. It constituted the first occasion on which Rawlinson, the chief of the Fourth Army, used as his spearhead the Australian Corps under its newly appointed commander John Monash. In peacetime a highly qualified engineer as well as a part-time soldier, Monash brought to the conduct of battle important qualifications: intellect, organizing ability, fixity of purpose, and a determination not to squander his forces. Infantry, he wrote, should be 'relieved as far as possible of the obligation to *fight* their way forward'. They should 'advance under the maximum possible protection of the maximum possible array of mechanical resources' – 'guns, machine-guns, tanks, mortars, and aeroplanes'.[6] This made especially good sense at a time when manpower was at a premium, in stark contrast to the 'array of mechanical resources' that was pouring forth from Britain's factories.

Hamel, lying between Villers-Bretonneux and the Somme, constituted an enemy salient overlooking British positions. The operation on a 3½-mile front that resulted in its elimination was noteworthy for the integration of the various arms. Infantry and tanks trained together, each tank being assigned to a particular infantry commander. And when the foot soldiers and the armoured vehicles went forward on 4 July, they did so in the closest possible proximity to a creeping barrage – which, in addition to firing high explosive and shrapnel, was employing a lot of smoke shells to facilitate concealment. At the same time particular squadrons of aircraft were assigned to the separate arms. Some searched out and attacked the enemy's anti-tank weapons; others air-dropped ammunition to the advancing infantry.

Not everything at Hamel went according to plan. In the dust and smoke, infantry

[5] Ibid., p. 15.
[6] Quoted in John Terraine, *The Western Front 1914–1918* (London: Arrow Books, 1970), p. 185.

confronting uncut barbed wire found themselves separated from their tanks. But such misadventures were the exception. Overall, what was remarkable was how closely the plan approximated its execution. Within an hour and a half all objectives had been secured. Tank casualties were few, and the number of enemy soldiers taken prisoner was significant. Despite the small scale of the operation, this success attracted a lot of attention. Clemenceau paid the Australian division a congratulatory visit. And Monash wrote home concerning the battle, 'All England is talking about it and me.'[7]

Amiens a month later transferred this proceeding to a larger canvas. (In effect, Rawlinson was seeking to repeat the happy opening phase of the Cambrai operation nine months before, without its regrettable sequel.) Where Hamel had involved 64 tanks and 10 battalions of infantry, the first day of the Amiens attack would be made by over 400 front-line tanks, 11 divisions of foot soldiers, and 3 cavalry divisions – quite apart from the large contribution (7 divisions of infantry) of the French First Army on Rawlinson's right.

Even so, this was not to be an operation on the scale of Third Ypres. The 2,000 guns available to the Fourth Army at Amiens constituted only one artillery piece for every 29 yards of front, as against the one gun for 5 yards sometimes employed at Passchendaele. But Rawlinson's objectives were fairly modest, and the Germans' defences – in territory they had but recently overrun – were not comparable with those of Flanders a year before. Anyway Rawlinson was not under the illusion, which had seized him on the eve of the Somme campaign in 1916, that artillery could annihilate the opposition. The task assigned to the gunners now was to pin down the defenders while men and tanks got forward.

To accomplish even that much, surprise was vital. And the movement of two substantial forces into this sector, if detected by the Germans, would assuredly give the game away. One was the cavalry (for the dream of 'exploitation' continued to exercise a spell over the British high command). The other was the Canadian Corps. This powerful body of soldiers had so far avoided the fighting of 1918, and its appearance on any sector would betoken an approaching offensive.

Even though the Germans were anticipating – and were apprehensive about – an imminent blow, the time and place of the coming attack eluded them to the end. Only at night did Rawlinson's staff allow reinforcements of troops, tanks, and horses (not to mention ammunition and fodder) to enter the Fourth Army sector. During the day RAF pilots scoured their own side of the front, searching out evidence of abnormal activity that might alert the enemy. Deception was much practised, especially to convince the Germans that an attack was pending in the north to recapture Mount Kemmel. So there was unusual air activity in the north, but none around Amiens. (Yet on 8 August 800 aircraft would participate in the British attack.) And, with a modest amount of display, some of the Canadians were moved from Arras north to the Ypres sector, where thereafter a stream of wireless messages conveyed the impression that the whole corps was in residence. Meanwhile the Canadians were moving south; but they would not enter the Amiens zone until the day preceding the attack, nor the front line until two hours before zero.

For all the skill of these deceptive practices, it suggests a failing of German expertise on this sector that the enemy divined so little of what was going on. In other respects also the Fourth Army was fortunate in the circumstances of its opponents. The Germans here were outnumbered and were not of storm-trooper quality: in many instances they consisted of worn-down divisions occupying recently overrun and ill-prepared positions.

---

[7] Geoffrey Serle, *John Monash: A Biography* (Melbourne: Melbourne University Press, 1982), p. 336.

The region selected for the attack lay astride the Somme river in an area where it ran roughly east to west. It was here, back in March, that the Germans had threatened to split apart the forces of Britain and France. Now the Allies' primary concern was to end the enemy threat to the Amiens rail centre. So Rawlinson planned an advance of 6 or 7 miles, to what had once been the outer defence line covering Amiens. But Haig became seized of larger objectives, and Foch of larger still. Hence they doubled the extent of the proposed penetration for the first stage, and looked even beyond that: to the line where the Somme, between Ham and Péronne, ran in the direction of south to north.

For the British forces engaged, the Amiens offensive opened along a 13-mile front at 4.20 a.m. on 8 August. (The French attack on the right of the British, on a 7-mile front, did not commence until 45 minutes later.) On the British left, north of the Somme, III Corps made only limited progress. Consisting of battered divisions that had been reinforced with fledglings, it had in the past couple of days been heavily engaged by good-quality German forces. Further, this Corps was operating in poor country for tanks and anyway had only a small supply of them – 36 tanks as against the 144 each for the Australian and Canadian Corps.

South of the Somme matters went quite differently. The Australian Corps in the centre and the Canadians on their right made remarkable progress. They attacked with enormous spirit. They were operating in ideal tank country. And the offensive opened in dense mist, which served to blind their adversaries. Certainly, the mist also presented the attackers with problems in keeping direction, but they were helped here by the racket of their own creeping barrage (to which was devoted one-third of the artillery fire).

At some places the enemy, overwhelmed by the weight of the barrage and the onrush of tanks and infantry, gave way with barely a struggle. H. R. Williams, an Australian infantryman going forward in the second wave, noted the number of German prisoners coming in and the paucity of Australian wounded accompanying them. But there were also instances of enemy machine-gunners offering spirited resistance. (Sometimes Australian and Canadian infantrymen, having lost their tanks in the mist, had to quell machine-guns by deeds of exceptional valour.) And the German field-gunners, sticking to their posts, inflicted severe losses on the tanks. In short, for the attackers nowhere was the contest a walkover. Nevertheless, as bright sunlight replaced the mist around 10.30 a.m., it found the Australians already occupying their designated objective: the old Amiens defence line. Half an hour later the Canadians came up alongside them.

H. R. Williams recounts the transformation that now overtook the road running from Villers-Bretonneux to Warfusée-Abancourt. For many months no vehicle had run along this road, for the former place was in British hands, the latter in German. But in the morning sun of 8 August all was changed.

> Coming along with all haste were motor lorries, loaded with ammunition, stores, and tools, horse-drawn limbers, cookers, water-carts, dispatch-riders on motor bicycles, heavy guns, here and there an armoured car; mounted men regulated the traffic; and only a mile or so forward could still be heard the spasmodic rattle of machine-guns. The traffic along the road so close to the moving battle was possible only because all the German batteries which yesterday supported their front-line infantry had been captured in the advance.
>
> Monash's clear vision had foreseen all this when he planned the attack. To overrun and destroy the German infantry in the front-line trenches had been done during previous advances. But to overrun and destroy in addition the German artillery swung open wide the gateway to a great victory.[8]

---

[8] H. R. Williams, *The Gallant Company* (Sydney: Angus & Robertson, 1933), p. 219.

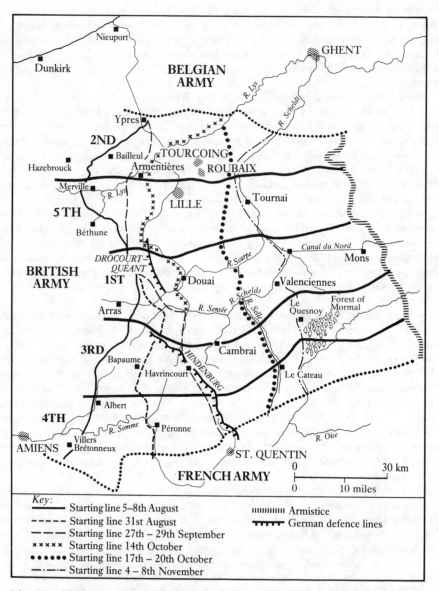

Map 14   *The British advance to victory, 8 August – 11 November 1918.* Source: *James E. Edmonds and R. Maxwell Hyslop*, Military Operations France and Belgium 1918. History of the Great War, volume V (London: HMSO, 1947), frontispiece.

Apparently the moment of exploitation, by the cavalry acting in concert with the Whippet tanks, was at hand. This proved a pipedream. Despite the overall collapse of the enemy's resistance, pockets of their machine-gunners continued active. Once more, the willing spirit of the cavalrymen could not compensate for the weakness of horseflesh against modern weapons. Some of the Whippets and armoured cars, by contrast, achieved minor wonders. Penetrating into the German rear, they wreaked havoc upon retreating infantry, troop trains, horse transport in columns, and even staff officers at lunch.

For the enemy 8 August was a heavy setback. As on 18 July against the French, they had failed to divine the moment or whereabouts of an impending attack. In a matter of hours they had been driven back to a depth of 7 miles on an 11-mile front, losing territory overrun in a victorious hour and full of strategic promise. And they had sustained heavy losses in guns and material but above all in manpower. As far as can be ascertained, German casualties on 8 August amounted to 27,000, including over 15,000 taken prisoner and so a total loss. Two things were of particular note about these figures. The British, though attacking, suffered comparatively lightly: fewer than 9,000 casualties. And the number of Germans taken prisoner indicated a plain crumbling of morale, anyway when their forces were powerfully attacked in disadvantageous circumstances. Churchill summed up the matter when, on 10 August, he wrote to a less than receptive Lloyd George: 'It seems to me this is the greatest British victory that has been won in the whole war, and the worst defeat that the German Army has yet sustained.'[9]

IV

Among those who made a small contribution to this outcome was A. W. Bacon, a tank driver. Only at 7 p.m. on the evening of the 7th did he learn that the attack would be taking place the following morning. Bacon recounts that the news was welcome. The tank men had not had a free evening for nearly a week, and 'this preparation business was getting on our nerves.'[10]

Despite the arduous day confronting them, Bacon and his colleagues were then set to work loading up their tanks with petrol and supplies. In pitch darkness they had to hump 8-gallon cases of petrol across 100 yards of unfamiliar territory. They also had to remove the ordinary lorry petrol already in the tanks so as to make way for the Number One aviation spirit specially allocated for battle. 'The only way to get the old stuff out of the tanks was by siphoning, and the only way to start the siphon going was by lying down on the ground below the level of the petrol and sucking for all you were worth – it always meant getting a mouthful of dirty petrol. . . .' This operation was followed by a hot meal of soup and bread and an issue of cigarettes.

Soon after midnight the tanks began moving forward along crowded roads. For several hours Bacon 'swerved and swung the monster' in the dark as he avoided wagons, limbers, and groups of infantry. Overhead the drone of low-flying aircraft drowned out the noise of the vehicles' approach. Near the front the tanks stopped to receive final orders. They were operating with the Canadians on the British right wing. Starting time would be 4.20 a.m., and their objective was Cayeux, 5 miles inside the German lines. On reaching it, they were to await further orders.

---

[9] Quoted in David R. Woodward, *Lloyd George and the Generals* (East Brunswick, New Jersey: Associated University Presses, 1983), p. 328.

[10] Bacon's account is in *I was There!*, issue no. 44.

The tanks then proceeded to the jumping-off point, just in rear of their front-line trenches. Once in position, the men got out to stretch their legs and await zero hour.

Officers kept peering at their wrist-watches, gazing intently at the radium-coated hands as though they feared they had stopped. Men were standing behind the buses, having a last whiff of fresh air and looking into infinity with unseeing eyes; no one spoke at all, the momentousness of the occasion had laid hold of everybody.

Very quietly the order was given to take up positions for action. The engines were set purring. The last minutes dragged terribly. Then at 4.20 a.m. the bombardment opened and 'the heavens seemed to fall.'

The noise was like that of a colony of giants slamming iron doors as fast as they could go. All the pent-up longing to avenge the March retreat went into that moment.

The tanks crept forward, Bacon's the second in a sequence of three. Just as they were deploying, a blinding flash knocked him backwards. He fell on steel bolts which cut his head, and he was temporarily blinded. An instant later he was thrown forward as his tank collided with its leader and began to mount it. 'I threw out the clutch and rubbed the dirt and muck out of my eyes.' There was another crash. Smoke rose from the tank ahead, 'its left trackband rearing into the air like a cobra preparing to strike'. 'The officer of that bus dashed round to me and said: "Swing out and pass us. My driver's killed. Got a direct hit." Poor Sergeant Sutton.' Himself somewhat shaken, Bacon manoeuvred his craft around the stricken vehicle and set off for the battlefield.

Mist enveloped everything, but his compass and the sound of gunfire pointed the way to the front. The tank crossed the British forward trenches and made for the sound of the nearest enemy machine-gun. The going was slightly downhill, and Canadian infantry were on all sides.

The tank crushed the German wire defences like so much paper, and left a clear pathway through which the infantry followed. As we cruised over No Man's Land several erratic strings of bullets flashed across my driving window plate as some enemy machine-gunner blindly traversed our front.

The German artillery was at sixes and sevens, they were shelling behind our lines, but their own trenches which we were now storming were being left untouched.

In the mist Bacon collided head-on with one of his own tanks but without serious consequence. Soon he was through the enemy's front line, dealing with some of their machine-gunners in the process, and advancing over ground that was firm and (unlike the northern battlefields) unspoiled by shell craters. They reached the German support position:

as I straddled the bus across the main trench my machine-gunners got busy from both sides and caught several of the enemy scuttling for cover.

We climbed right over and went blindly on, several times running into batches of Canadian infantrymen, who were getting ahead in places.

Another German machine-gun was now firing very close to us, so I swung the bus and made straight for it.

Suddenly I noticed a brick wall right up against the nose of the tank, but as we had been through so many of them before I did not hesitate, but just trod on the gas and charged straight through.

A terrific rumble of masonry followed, and when the old bus regained level keel I opened my window and peered out. Gosh, we were inside a church, and had routed a machine-gun nest!

On the other side of the church the tank encountered a serious menace in the form of a German field gun but managed to put its crew to flight. However, from then on enemy artillery became a mounting danger. The mist lifted, and German observation balloons directed a high-explosive barrage against them.

> Suddenly we observed a German field-gun firing from a spinney almost in front of us. Driving the bus on a zigzag course I made for the gun, and we were within twenty yards of it when CRASH! – a flash – and merciful oblivion.

Bacon recovered consciousness 'to find myriads of pale stars gleaming in the night sky above me'. Around him lay hundreds of men in differing stages of sensibility. 'Some were groaning, some sobbing, and others crying out for water – water. A strange voice arose from a figure lying next to me intoning: "Mutter, O Mutter!"' Bacon's 'throat and guts were burning'. He called for water, but in vain. An aeroplane flew overhead and dropped bombs. Again he sank into oblivion.

But in time rescue came, and he survived. He had certainly played a part in avenging the March retreat.

V

The second day of the Amiens battle did not, for the British forces, repeat the success of the first. The gap that had opened on the enemy front seemed, at first glance, full of promise. But the weapon of exploitation had already failed, which meant that only infantry and tanks could be used. A great deal of organization was needed to prepare the infantry for a further advance, and Fourth Army staff did not rise to the occasion. Reserve divisions were not got forward with dispatch. And co-ordination was not achieved between the corps, or even the divisions, required for the next actions. Consequently, by the time the infantry were ready to attack German reinforcements had taken up position.

Furthermore, the tank corps was seriously depleted. Crews were exhausted, sometimes to the point of delirium, after a high summer's day in their oven-like boxes. And tank losses had been heavy, even though a good many of those damaged or broken down could in time be repaired. Hence where 430 tanks had gone into the attack on 8 August, only 155 were available on the following day.

In the circumstances the accomplishments of 9 August were substantial. On the left, aided by a regiment of Americans, III Corps took the main objective that had eluded it the day before, so securing the left flank of the Australians. And on the centre and right the Australians and Canadians advanced a further 3 miles.

By the end of that day, however, it was evident that little more could be immediately accomplished. A meagre 85 tanks remained. Ten weary British divisions were confronting 12 German divisions that had been fed into the battle since its inception. And the struggle must now proceed not in open country but in territory giving every advantage to the defender: the torn ground, old trenches, and rusted wire of the first Somme battlefield.

Up to this point Haig and Foch had been in agreement. Where Rawlinson had proposed a modest advance securing immunity for Amiens, they had envisaged driving the Germans all the way to the Somme river where it flowed at the enemy's backs. But now an important divergence developed. Foch was prepared to disregard the mounting British casualties, the problems of providing effective artillery support from new positions and against fresh targets, and the stiffening German resistance. He concluded that the enemy was demoralized and would crumble before a little more pressure.

Haig no longer felt like this. He had at last come to recognize that persistence in attacking on the same sector, after all the prerequisites of initial success had departed, was fruitless. What was required was a sequence of operations on the lines of 8 August but on different parts of the front. Such actions might not result in the seizure of great objectives, any more than the Amiens battle had done. But they would accomplish the piecemeal yet inexorable elimination of the German army's dwindling resources.

This was a crucial moment in the war on the Western Front. As an army commander in 1915, and as Commander-in-Chief in 1916 and 1917, Haig had planned offensives with large strategic aims. Not only had these aims proved impractical. More, they had been inimical to sound tactics: namely, the employment of surprise and the limitation of objectives to the effective range of artillery. Such tactics secured maximum support for the attacking infantry and heavy losses for the enemy, even though they could not secure great objectives.

It suggests the limitations of Haig's military capacity that he had taken so long to accept this fundamental aspect of warfare on the Western Front. (Rawlinson had divined it, early in 1915, in the aftermath of Neuve Chapelle.) And to the end he jibbed against what he had discovered. During an action at the end of October, infantry reinforcements urgently needed in the front line found their way obstructed by cavalrymen waiting to exploit a non-existent breakthrough. Yet it is still the case that what Haig learned at Amiens decided the pattern of his operations thereafter, and that it was to his credit that he was still capable of learning. Certainly, he was well ahead of Foch, for whom the lure of the 'decisive victory' beckoned even now. (Of course, Foch's obtuseness may have functioned more powerfully when it was the troops of his ally, not those of his own nation, with whom he was proposing to gamble.)

The divergence between the two men raised a key question. It concerned unity of command. As Rawlinson bluntly put it to Haig on 10 August, when Haig informed him that Foch required the offensive to continue: 'Are you commanding the British Army or is Maréchal Foch?' (At least we have the authority of the official history, 'which tapped liberally on private sources',[11] that this exchange took place. It is not recorded in Haig's diary or Rawlinson's. But each was writing with an eye to posterity, and perhaps they felt that this instance of near-insubordination should not go beyond themselves.)

The British commander's answer to Rawlinson was delivered by stages – to Foch. After further action at Amiens on 11 August had accomplished almost nothing, he postponed operations there for some days. A telegram from Foch on 14 August, seeing 'no necessity for delay', failed to move him. He 'much regret[ted]' that he could not alter his orders. His preference, he made it clear, was for a new attack further north, on his First and Third Army fronts. Foch wanted this operation as a supplement, but intended that Rawlinson's attack should continue. When they met Foch barraged Haig with questions regarding his intentions. This brought to a head the issue of who commanded the British army. According to Haig's diary:

> I spoke to Foch quite straightly and let him understand that *I was responsible to my Government and fellow citizens for the handling of the British forces.* F.'s attitude at once changed and he said all he wanted was early information of my intentions so that he might co-ordinate the operations of the other Armies, and that he now thought I was quite correct in my decision not to attack the enemy in his prepared position.

Haig was only partly mollified. As he confided to his diary, Foch – whatever he said now

---

[11] Gregory Blaxland, *Amiens: 1918* (London: Frederick Muller, 1968), p. 196.

– had for five days been most insistent that Haig capture the Somme bridges above Péronne, 'regardless of German opposition, and British losses'.[12]

The situation was now plain. The British army would follow Foch's directives when these agreed with Haig's inclinations. Should Haig take a contrary view, then Foch, far from commanding Britain's forces in the West, would 'co-ordinate the operations of the other Armies' on the basis of 'early information of [Haig's] intentions'.

What had enabled Haig to make this stand was his implied threat to appeal to the British Government – whose leader was viewing Foch with mounting disfavour. There is much irony here. For in the lead-up to the Amiens operation Haig had shown how he interpreted his responsibility to his own Government. Information of the coming attack was never conveyed to Britain's civilian leaders by the Commander-in-Chief. They learned of it only by accident. On 1 August, at a gathering of Dominion Prime Ministers, Lloyd George was dismayed by an inquiry from R. A. Borden of Canada regarding the participation of Canadian forces in an imminent offensive, as well as by Henry Wilson's admission that 'he knew nothing of any forthcoming operation.' The Prime Minister spoke bitterly of Foch, who 'had always been somewhat reckless of human life'. And the Empire's leaders then agonized over 'their constitutional position' vis-à-vis the supreme commander. What they discovered, and found difficult to accept, was that they could not intervene in Foch's operations unless they received an appeal to do so from Haig.[13] The latter's success, two weeks later, in taming Foch ensured that no appeal from him would ever be forthcoming.

It is not wonderful that Haig was now attaining his apogee as military commander. He was confronting a failing, if not yet vanquished, enemy. He was able to devise operations without supplicating for the endorsement of Foch or Lloyd George. And he had at last divined the manner of proceeding on the Western Front: that he should not seek a strategic triumph but should deliver a sequence of limited, tactical, but ultimately mortal hammer blows.

---

[12] Robert Blake (ed.), *The Private Papers of Douglas Haig 1914–1919*, (London: Eyre & Spottiswoode, 1952), pp. 323–4, dates this diary entry 14 August, although 15 August seems correct.

[13] See Woodward, *Lloyd George and the Generals*, pp. 325–6.

53

A HUNDRED DAYS II:
TO THE HINDENBURG LINE AND BEYOND

The front line changed every day. Spying eyes saw the flat-brimmed English or
American helmets rising out of trenches which had contained the round German ones
the day before.

German airman's account of late October 1918

Then, one grey, sombre autumn day, the news began to flash through the soldier
grapevine. 'They're cracking. They're ready to cry off. It's true. *Can* it be true?'
Richard Lloyd George, serving soldier 1914–18, and son of the Prime Minister, reminiscing in old age

I

The month of August 1918 had begun well for British arms. It concluded in the same
manner; and this turn of events persisted into September. The methods employed at
Amiens proved applicable again and again, notwithstanding the diminishing availability
of tanks. It became evident that, anyway as long as the enemy remained in their
recently conquered territory, they were serving themselves up for destruction.

Yet in the view of the official history, there is an anomaly about these operations. As
far as any strategic purpose was concerned, the attacks were taking place in the wrong
part of the Western Front. Between Arras and the Somme no important objectives
beckoned. The Germans were simply being forced back upon their lines of communication, towards the formidable Hindenburg system of defences. Moreover, this was
territory quite inhospitable for an offensive, and it contained a large majority of the
German divisions in the West.

What strategic sense demanded, in the view of the official history, was a great
offensive in the east–west sector of the Western Front, beyond Reims. A thrust from
there might get behind the Hindenburg system where it ran north to south, outflank
the main concentration of German divisions confronting the British, and sever the
supply railway running close behind the enemy front.

It is difficult to assess the validity of these arguments. Certainly, an attack north from
Reims would imperil German communications in this region. But to get at them it was
still going to be necessary to break through powerful defences reinforced by natural
features like the Argonne forest. That is, at one point or another a breach would be
needed in the Hindenburg system. As for the notion that the Germans would keep the
bulk of their troops opposite the British sector while they were being attacked
elsewhere, it is unlikely that they now lacked the adaptability to transfer their forces
towards any serious menace.

Nevertheless, it is clear that, in terms of strategy, there was little to be said for the region chosen for the principal offensives of August and September. The main Allied effort occurred there for only one reason: because this was where the British armies were located. The sector east of Reims was manned by French and American forces, the former too worn down to take the major part in assaulting the enemy, the latter still far from ready to do so.

What we are seeing is the closing stage in a drama that had opened in March. Then Ludendorff had attacked on the Somme – not because it offered real strategic opportunities but because to win the war he must 'beat the British.' In August and September the same calculation applied in reverse. If Foch and Haig were to end the war forthwith, as they recognized was now a possibility, then the British – not solely, but primarily – must take on the job of beating Ludendorff.

Plate 46   *A British advanced dressing station in what was once the German front line.*

II

Britain's forces on the Western Front were now divided into five armies. The two northernmost were Plumer's Second Army, adjoining the Belgians on the coast, and the recently reconstituted Fifth Army under Birdwood. In the operations designed by Haig for August and September, neither of these armies was assigned a considerable role. Certainly, early in September they made a substantial advance in territory. But that was because Ludendorff, under the stimulus of events further south, felt obliged to abandon all the ground he had overrun during his drive for the coast in April.

On the right of Fifth Army was Horne's First Army, standing east of Vimy Ridge and Arras. Then came Byng's Third Army, confronting an area (including Bapaume) that had not been much fought over in the British offensives of 1916 and 1917. Finally there was Rawlinson's Fourth Army, now hard up against the old Somme battlefields. Separately or together, these forces undertook the major engagements on the British sector between 21 August and 25 September. (There was also a good deal of offensive activity on parts of the French front. And on 12 September the American army fought its first independent operation, when it eliminated the St Mihiel salient adjoining Verdun.)

The accomplishments of these three more southerly British armies, attacking over usually blighted battlefields ideal for defence, were formidable. During the five weeks up to 25 September, 34 British divisions mastered 66 divisions of the enemy, advanced on average some 14 miles, and overwhelmed positions on which Ludendorff had decided his forces would stand for the winter. The casualty figures for the period, in what remained an attritional struggle, were of paricular moment. For heavy though British losses remained, it was the enemy who was sustaining an insupportable drain. The three British armies in these operations suffered 89,000 casualties, their adversaries 116,000. But the disproportion is much greater when we take into account the figures for prisoners: 46,000 Germans but hardly any British. In this respect it is worth reiterating the distinction between prisoners and wounded. A good proportion of the wounded would in time resume active service. For the war as a whole, in the British army 82 per cent of the wounded returned to duty, 64 per cent of them to duty in the front line. The prisoner, by contrast, was a total loss to his side. Rawlinson no doubt was conscious of this when he proudly informed Henry Wilson in mid-October that, since 1 August, his army had taken one prisoner for every one and a half casualties it had sustained.

This new series of operations began on 21 August. Third Army attacked in an area lying between the Somme battlefields of 1916 (on the right) and the Arras battlefield of 1917 (on the left). Aided by fog and employing the methods of 8 August – including the practice of leapfrogging divisions – the infantry this day achieved all of its reasonably modest objectives. On the following day the left wing of the Fourth Army also moved, retaking the ruined town of Albert and so restoring British forces to about the starting point of 1 July 1916. Then, between 23 and 25 August, against a usually much reinforced enemy, both Third and Fourth Armies maintained such progress as to convince Rawlinson that enemy morale was in truth seriously declining. In response to this advance Ludendorff, having earlier set his face against any withdrawal, agreed to a retirement of 10 miles on Fourth Army front, so placing his forces behind the Somme in the region where that river ran south to north.

On 26 August First Army entered the fray. The Canadian Corps, having distinguished itself on Rawlinson's front on 8 August, had now returned to its old stamping ground near Arras. It straightway captured Monchy-le-Preux, a hill whose crest 'dominates a wide stretch of country to the east and west, as well as the valleys north and south'.[1] Three days later, as the Germans withdrew, the New Zealand division of Byng's Third Army entered Bapaume. (This prime objective of the 1916 Somme campaign had eluded the British to the end of that year and had only been occupied – for a while – following the Germans' first retirement in 1917.)

By 29 August the enemy had gone back as far as Ludendorff intended. They were now placed on a sequence of strong positions including, from south to north, the Somme river, the Canal du Nord, and the Drocourt-Quéant line – the last of these 'one of the strong positions on the western front and, because of the skill with which its defenses were adapted to the topography, entitled to rank with the Hindenburg Line,

---

[1] Douglas Wilson Johnson, *Battlefields of the World War* (New York: Oxford University Press, 1921), p. 165.

of which it was a northern continuation'.[2] Yet, during the first week of September, Haig's forces successfully assailed both the first and third of these obstacles.

It was Monash's Australians, on the Fourth Army front, who began the process. Confronting them, from Péronne southwards, lay the Somme, consisting of 1,000 yards of marsh and stream – an all but impassable barrier. But as they approached Péronne the Australians stood astride the Somme where it ran east to west. Their problem lay in the fact that, at the point where the river turned at a rightangle, it was commanded by Mont St Quentin, 140 feet high, utterly bare, occupied by elements of five German divisions, and guarded by a sequence of trenches and barbed wire.

Monash concluded that, rather than try and cross the Somme opposite or below Péronne and so get around the bastion of Mont St Quentin, he would take the bastion and so outflank the line of the river. In the half light of early morning on 31 August a mere 1,320 Australians, with no tanks but substantial artillery support, fell upon an unsuspecting enemy and secured themselves on the mountain. Reinforcements were fed in during the ensuing night, and after two days of ferocious fighting not only Mont St Quentin but also Péronne were in British hands – 'the greatest infantry exploit of the war'.[3] The line of the Somme had been convincingly turned.

As Péronne fell, to the north other elements of Fourth Army and the whole of Third Army were making progress. And on the left of the offensive the Canadians of First Army were poised for another compelling blow: against the Drocourt–Quéant line. Aided by only 50 tanks and in face of fierce opposition, the Canadians on 2 September stormed their way through this succession of barriers and into open country beyond.

These events drove Ludendorff to a conclusion he had rejected in the aftermath of Amiens: that, by stages, he must abandon all the territory taken in his March offensive and fall back upon the Hindenburg Line as his bastion for the winter. Hence the spell of fierce encounters that had opened on 21 August ran down after 3 September, as the British probed forward after a departing enemy. But harsh fighting flared up again on 12 September, when only with effort did elements of Third Army seize Havrincourt by getting across the Canal du Nord. (It was said often during these months: 'The Boches are trying to get behind water.') And there was another stern engagement on 18 September, as the Fourth Army broke into what had been the British front line of late 1917, since much fortified by the enemy. This, Rawlinson wrote to Henry Wilson, secured him important ground from which to attack the main Hindenburg positions. He added that in most of their divisions Boche morale was still very low.

III

In the closing days of September the British First, Third, and Fourth Armies embarked on the decisive battle of the Hundred Days: the assault upon the most formidable section of the Hindenburg Line. Its rupture might not leave the Germans naked to their enemies: other defensible positions, and in particular a succession of waterways, lay to their rear. But a British victory here would be crucial in two respects. It would establish that the Germans' recent reverses were not to be accounted for by the fact that they had been occupying extended lines in recently overrun territory. And it would rob them of the most powerful defensive system that they would ever possess. If the Hindenburg Line could not keep out their adversaries, nothing would.

On more than this central sector were the Germans having to withstand attack. Foch

---

[2] Ibid., p. 198.

[3] H. Essame, *The Battle for Europe 1918* (London: Batsford, 1972), p. 149.

had proclaimed 'tout le monde à la bataille', and virtually from the Channel coast to Verdun the forces of Belgium, Britain, France, and the USA – 12 armies comprising 6 million men – moved all but simultaneously against the German defences. The far right of this great push lay between Reims and Verdun, on the east–west part of the Western Front, in a region rendered ideal for defence by nature and long German preparation. Here the French and Americans set in motion what would prove an arduous process on 26 September. The far left of the offensive was undertaken by the Belgian Army, some French divisions, and Plumer's Second Army, which opened a powerful thrust on 28 September. In what has been termed 'the last Battle of Ypres' these Allied forces overran in a couple of days all that, back in 1917, British troops had managed to capture in the long months of Third Ypres. By the end of 29 September Plumer once more held Messines, and the Belgians had taken Passchendaele Ridge.

But both the assault in the south by Americans and French and that in the north by the Belgian–French–British forces constituted the lesser aspects of this climactic thrust. For one thing, at least to begin with, the greater number of German divisions were not to be found in these sectors. Ludendorff was relying on the Argonne forest to hold off the nine American divisions and had placed only five of his own there to meet their initial attack. And he had been thinning his front in the north, allowing the Allies a numerical superiority there of almost two to one. The German command's purpose was to ensure the impregnability of the Hindenburg Line on its most important – and most highly developed – sector: opposite the British First, Third, and Fourth Armies.

As has often been observed, the word 'line' is a misnomer to describe the Hindenburg system. Between Cambrai and St Quentin, where it was most powerful and where the main British attack was being made, it consisted of defensive positions 10 miles deep. These were designed to withstand – where they did not lie beyond the range of – the most powerful artillery bombardment, and to annihilate in stages any attempted infantry penetration.

Basically the 'line' consisted of three successive positions: an outpost line, lightly held and intended to blunt an assault without great cost to the defenders; a central line, held in force by troops kept immune from bombardment in great underground barracks; and a reserve line. Each position was covered by a forest of barbed wire – as many as eight or nine belts each – geometrically sited so that attacking troops would be taken in enfilade by machine-guns in concrete emplacements. The artillery had been placed, wherever possible, on reverse slopes. Thus it escaped observation from the ground and could wreak havoc upon forces coming over the crest of any hill. Deep ditches had been constructed against tanks. And the whole system had been carefully incorporated into such pre-existing obstacles to an attack as the Canal du Nord and the St Quentin Canal.

The British command was not ignorant of what confronted it. During the Amiens attack Fourth Army had captured a complete plan of one sector of the Hindenburg defences. But whether the wit of the military planners and the fighting qualities of British troops could actually surmount so formidable a barrier only the test of battle would reveal.

On 27 September, 24 hours after the Americans attacked in the Argonne and a day before Plumer moved in the north, the first phase of the assault on the central Hindenburg system opened. The thrust was towards Cambrai, by the First and Third Armies on a front of 13 miles. Lying opposite a good part of this sector was a still unvanquished stretch of the Canal du Nord. The attackers had little tank support. But they could call on much artillery, with the field guns now employing the efficient fuse that rendered shells far more effective against barbed wire.

The German forces, on this and the ensuing days, revealed that their fighting capacity was by no means at an end. Not only their machine-gunners, who for most of the following weeks stuck to their task with terrible devotion, but also their infantry firmly resisted the British assaults. Nevertheless, the Canadians on 27 September, attacking the canal on a narrow front where it proved least of an obstacle, forced their way across and fanned out, pulling along a neighbouring division in the process. They then proceeded to advance beyond the furthest point attained in the first Cambrai operation of the previous November.

Plate 47 *The Canal du Nord.*

Elsewhere on the front matters did not go quite so well. But all along the line the attacking infantry made some progress, and its yield, as we learn from the account of the South African Deneys Reitz, was maximised by earlier careful preparations. Reitz was second-in-command to a Scottish battalion fighting to the right of the Canadians. They enjoyed the advantage of starting with the Canal du Nord already just behind them; to get across it they had needed to employ scaling ladders. The infantry went over the top and, if only with heavy loss, managed to advance. Then, Reitz recounts:

> . . . British batteries from the rear began to come by, to take up fresh positions nearer the enemy. That they were able to cross the Canal du Nord so soon was due to the careful manner in which the battle had been thought out beforehand. A bridge had been built in sections, and the moment the German barrage lifted that morning, the R.E.'s [Royal Engineers] were seen coming down from Hermes with the bridge-lengths on wagons, and in a short time they had erected a trestle-way from bank to bank, over which guns and ammunition limbers and ambulances were now pouring on to ground which scarcely an hour before was held by the enemy.
>
> By 8 o'clock practically every British battery had moved up, and along the lip of the Hindenburg Trench the guns stood in unbroken line, firing as fast as they could load.

Being so near to us, the roar of all these pieces was magnificent. General Fisher [commander of 8th Brigade, 3rd Division] stood eagerly watching the guns belching forth, and he turned to us and cried: 'Men, do you remember Lloyd George's speech: "We will put the guns wheel to wheel and pound home the lessons of democracy"?'

For Reitz, they were witnesses to a great event: 'the mighty Hindenburg Line was going at last.'[4] By the end of the next day (the 28th), although Cambrai was holding out, a penetration to a depth of 6 miles had been made on a 12-mile front.

The following day, 29 September, would test the significance of everything that had happened since the Allies went over to the offensive. Now Rawlinson's Fourth Army was ready to strike at the toughest of all obstacles the enemy could offer: the 12 miles of Hindenburg Line to the north of the town of St Quentin (not to be confused with the recently conquered hill of the same name). The core of the defence lay on the St Quentin Canal, bristling with wire and guns, impervious (except where it ran underground) to tanks, and a most formidable barrier to infantry.

Haig was employing all the mechanical and scientific innovations that lay at his disposal. He had saved 181 tanks – a large proportion of those remaining to him – especially for the occasion. And in the opening stage of the bombardment he was for the first time using mustard gas (which it had taken British industry a year to develop). Yet in many ways this was an attack in the old style: that is, the style of the Somme and Arras and Third Ypres. For one thing, the number of tanks available was substantially lower than at First Cambrai or Amiens; and anyway at the outset there was not much of the front where tanks could operate. As for the element of surprise that had proved so potent at Cambrai and on 8 August 1918, it was – apart from the day and the hour – quite lacking. The objective was just too obvious. Anyway the attack was heralded by several days of bombardment – which began on the evening of the 26th – because nothing less could make a dent in such obstacles.

In the culminating 24 hours before zero almost 1 million shells, to a total weight of 25,000 tons, rained downed upon the German positions. Major-General Maurice relates:

So the guns again came into their own. It was long since the Germans had been subjected to such a dose of shelling, and many of their troops having come from the Eastern front, or being fresh drafts from Germany, had never experienced a really intense and prolonged bombardment. The moral effect of this cannonade was therefore very great. It drove the enemy into his deep dug-outs and tunnels, and prevented his carrying parties from bringing up food and ammunition.[5]

Even this scale of shelling did not achieve the purpose for which Rawlinson had striven in the run-up to the Somme in 1916: to render uninhabitable the area under bombardment. But such grandiose ambitions had now vanished. It was enough that the enemy defences, along with their occupants, should at the moment of attack be seriously impaired.

The most promising stretch to attack seemed to be where, for over 3 miles, the canal ran into a tunnel: for here tanks could be employed. Hence Rawlinson entrusted this sector to Monash. But for once the Australian commander did not have a good day. The enemy had recognized the danger here and had provided this sector with particularly dense defences. And the tunnel had served as a haven for the German forces during the preliminary bombardment. Hence the attackers here encountered stout resistance. Tank losses soon exceeded 50 per cent. Moreover, because two of the

---

[4] Deneys Reitz, *Trekking On* (London: Faber & Faber, 1934), p. 260.
[5] Sir F. Maurice, *The Last Four Months* (London: Cassell, 1919), pp. 160–1.

five Australian divisions were utterly exhausted and a third could be used only in support, Monash's attack was spearheaded by two inexperienced American divisions – the only Americans serving on the British sector. Woefully short of officers, these troops were soon baffled by fog, barbed wire, and their own unfamiliarity with combat. Consequently, the Australians who were intended to leapfrog through them became embroiled in the early fighting.

But further right along the front of attack, in what had seemed less propitious circumstances, it proved a different story. Here the British forces were up against the canal proper, seemingly unfordable under fire. And the task of crossing it had gone not to one of the elite Dominion forces but to a Midland division with no record of spectacular achievements. Nevertheless, they combined valour with daring on this occasion. They were aided by the facts that the enemy was less expectant of serious endeavour here and that Rawlinson's artillery preparation – which continued until the very last minute – wreaked havoc among the defences. Moreover, the early-morning fog, which was serving to baffle the Americans, here proved a boon in providing concealment. And the preparations for the crossing had been both thorough and imaginative. The infantry were supplied with novelties like life belts (3,000 had been commandeered from cross-Channel vessels), floating piers, collapsible boats, mud mats, life lines, and scaling ladders.

So, contrary to expectations, it was the Midlanders who provided Fourth Army with its most striking success on 29 September. First they overran German trenches on their own side of the waterway. Then (writes Maurice), 'the majority dropped down the sheer sides of the canal, swam across, clambered out and stormed the German trenches on the top of the eastern bank.' After that they turned south, surprising the enemy 'before he had realised the new direction of the attack'.[6] By 3 p.m. this division had achieved its objective for the day. A penetration of 3½ miles for minimal cost (the Midlanders sustained under 800 casualties), against the best defences of which the Germans were capable, could have only one meaning. That day had not fulfilled all of Rawlinson's hopes. But it had placed beyond doubt the vulnerability of the Hindenburg system on its strongest sector.

Despite much German resistance, which included sometimes successful counterattacks, Fourth Army maintained its momentum on the following days. On 30 September, on the centre left, the Australians set about completing the unfinished business of the day before. On the right the canal was forced just north of St Quentin. In between, the advance made feasible by the Midlanders was pressed further. By the end of the first week of October, on First and Third as well as Fourth Army fronts, the task was all but done. Some fragments of the Hindenburg system continued to hold out. (Cambrai did not fall until 9 October.) But in the main not only the outpost zone but also the enormously strong central segment had been conquered, and the sketchy reserve position was in the process of succumbing. Between 29 September and 5 October Fourth Army alone had taken 15,000 prisoners. Before it now lay 'open country bearing few traces of war: there were no prepared lines of defence ahead.'[7]

IV

Even now, the game was not quite up for the Germans. They had lost their finest defensive system and were in retreat along the entire Western Front. But at least they

---

[6] Ibid., pp. 161–2.
[7] Essame, *The Battle for Europe 1918*, p.191.

were still falling back across occupied territory, and could with impunity booby-trap buildings and devastate communications. And to their rear lay a succession of rivers and canals on which they might establish strong lines of resistance.

Certainly, if the Allies could press them close enough then the retreating forces would be denied the chance to convert these water barriers into truly powerful positions. But, from the sea to Verdun, the victorious Allies were hardly in a position to make swift pursuit. The problem confronting them was not just one of enemy rearguards. Even more acute were difficulties of supply. For example, behind Haig's armies lay a wilderness. Backing his northernmost forces, in this rain-drenched season of the year, was the dreaded Flanders quagmire. As for his more southerly armies, to their rear lay a region desolated by numerous great battles and two German withdrawals. Over these abysmal areas must be conveyed all the food, weapons, munitions, and stores required by the front-line forces.

Admittedly, the enemy also had communication problems. Any enforced retreat, not least by the converging forces pouring out of Belgium, was likely to produce clogged roads and bottlenecks at bridges. But at least the Germans were retiring over areas long untouched by battle, as witness the momentary return to prominence in mid-October of the almost forgotten name Le Cateau, where four years earlier British forces retreating from Mons had made a brief stand.

In the event, however, the Germans were unable to turn this seemingly favourable aspect to substantial advantage. It is true that Haig's forces never broke through the German front and that their 'pursuit' proved a slow, slogging business. But they maintained sufficient pressure to deny the Germans the opportunity to convert the rivers and canals at their disposal into really formidable obstacles. In fact, nothing revealed better the standards of professionalism that the British army had now attained than its present accomplishments in the areas of transportation and supply – from engineers who oversaw the construction or restoration of roads and railways and river crossings to lorry drivers spending exhausting hours negotiating crumbling, rain-soaked roads so as to provision front-line forces.

The course of events of this last month and a half of fighting may be briefly related. It found German forces still capable of stern, if sometimes fragile, resistance. And it took large numbers of British lives – among them that of the poet Wilfred Owen, who had come to perceive so clearly, and to express so tellingly, the war's fundamental outrage upon human dignity. Just one week before the gun's monstrous anger was at last stilled (and one month after he had been awarded the Military Cross for 'conspicuous gallantry and devotion to duty'), he was killed while encouraging his men during the crossing of the Sambre. Altogether the month of October inflicted 120,000 casualties upon the British army, so maintaining the rate of loss for August and September. But at least this month, coming on top of the two preceding, ensured that the German forces would find no refuge where they might stand for the winter. Hence there would be no 1919 campaign, with its potentially appalling blood-letting.

Ludendorff's ultimate backstop was the river Meuse, running all the way from Verdun on his left, through Namur (opposite Haig's main thrust) on his centre, to Liège in eastern Belgium on his right. If his forces could fall back so far, in good order and at their own pace, then he would shorten his line, secure strong natural defences, and still find himself on conquered territory. But he would need to be able to show that he was capable of establishing more than another halting place in a succession of retreats.

For the British Ludendorff's withdrawal had two dissimilar consequences. In the north he was falling back a considerable distance, pausing in the first instance on the river Scheldt. So he abandoned the entire Belgian coast and much of French Flanders. As a result, the two northernmost British armies, Plumer's and Birdwood's, were able to execute an opposed but not too heavily resisted advance. On 17 October Fifth Army entered the great manufacturing centre of Lille. Three days later the whole of Second Army was across the river Lys.

By contrast, no easy progress was accorded the three British armies further south. Here Ludendorff could not afford to give ground too readily, lest a swift British advance cut off his forces retreating south-west out of Belgium. Hence he sought in the first instance to fall back only to the river Selle, reinforcing this line with the troops being released by the shortening of his front elsewhere.

Yet it was on this centre sector, most of all, that his retreat failed to go according to plan. As his forces clogged the roads and bridges, their withdrawal became increasingly disorderly, and an element of despair started to manifest itself. On the British side of the line it was a different story. Despite imposing difficulties the engineers relaid railways, got bridges across canals, and rendered the roads passable. Hence Haig's forces received supplies and so were able to press the enemy nearly. The advance to the Selle yielded 12,000 prisoners.

Then, from 17 to 24 October, these three British armies – comprising 24 British and two American divisions – forced the line of the river, in the process defeating 31 enemy divisions. It was not an easy undertaking. Generally, conditions favoured the defenders. Heavy rain hampered the advance, and the lie of the land provided both good cover for the enemy's machine-guns and elevated positions for his artillery. And, for a declining adversary, the German forces sometimes offered stern resistance. But the outcome, if costly for the attackers, was unequivocal: an advance of 6 miles on a wide front, the capture of Le Cateau, a bag of 20,000 prisoners, and the elimination of Ludendorff's first river position.

The blows that the British had dealt the enemy in this week coincided with an advance by the Americans in the Argonne at a vital point for German communications. In the view of the Official History, the result of so many setbacks upon the German armies was cumulative, 'both moral and material'.

> Their difficulty in replacing the enormous losses in guns, machine guns and ammunition had increased with every fresh attack, and their reserves of men were practically exhausted. . . . Although enemy troops could still be found to offer stout resistance from good cover, the infantry and machine-gunners were no longer reliable, and cases had been reported of their retirement without fighting ahead of the artillery barrage.[8]

On 26 October, in the aftermath of these defeats, Ludendorff resigned.

So by the end of October German prospects of retiring to the Meuse according to plan had markedly waned. The opening days of November extinguished them. In the northern sector the Second and Fifth Armies were advancing at a pace that gave the enemy little opportunity to withdraw in good order or to wreak great destruction. Almost without a struggle, the Germans abandoned their obvious halting place here, the river Scheldt.

On the front of Haig's other three armies the Germans had taken a stand that, on the British right, lay on the river Sambre – almost the last major natural obstacle before the Meuse itself. And, where the Sambre swung away from the front, the enemy had the services of the forest of Mormal and other obstacles like the long-established fortress of Le Quesnoy. In early November the Fourth and Third Armies, aided by the

---

[8] James E. Edmonds and R. Maxwell-Hyslop (compilers), *Military Operations France and Belgium 1918* (London: HMSO, 1947), vol. 5, pp. 383–4.

French on their right and First Army on the left, pressed against this line. As ever, it was a daunting prospect. On Rawlinson's sector the canalized Sambre was 70 feet wide for much of its length and 6 feet deep, and it was protected by strong defences. Erecting bridges and passing over infantry, all under intense fire, could not be accomplished without cost.

But by the end of 4 November the Fourth Army had crossed the canal on a front of 15 miles to a depth of 2 miles and were driving the enemy from the forest of Mormal. For Third Army the New Zealanders took Le Quesnoy by scaling its outer walls with ladders and then doing the same with the inner walls. Apart from the type of assistance received from the artillery, this might have been an episode from a different war altogether.

The stage was now set for the Western Front's climactic engagement: that of the river Meuse. But the climax was never accomplished. Despite some episodes of conflict, by the end of the first week of November British forces were having difficulty in bringing their adversaries to battle. And on 11 November, with the Meuse still distant, the fighting simply terminated. If the Germans even now possessed a consecutive front line, behind it their armed forces were disintegrating. And this collapse, resulting directly from military failure, was yet more evident in their navy and on their home front. So, virtually on any terms they could get, the military leaders of Germany opted to lay down their arms.

Only chance provided a fortuitous symmetry to the war's untidy ending. In the early morning of 11 November British forces entered Mons, where back in 1914 the BEF had first done battle with troops of the enemy.

V

In appearance, the ending of battles was the outcome of negotiations between the adversaries. The German authorities did not simply surrender. Rather, they appealed to President Wilson for an armistice, which carried the implication of a possible resumption of hostilities. And they stipulated a peace settlement on the basis of Wilson's 14 Points.

Yet, despite these formalities, what occurred on 11 November 1918 was the capitulation to the Allies of a defeated adversary. There were good reasons why the German authorities, in seeking to abandon the war, should first approach the American President and should make obeisance to his peace formula. Given America's limited participation in the conflict, Wilson was unlikely to view the enemy with the depth of antipathy felt by Clemenceau and Lloyd George. Consequently, his terms were likely to be less severe than theirs. But it is a myth that the 14 Points offered Germany a 'soft' (or, as it is sometimes termed, an 'impartial' or 'idealistic') peace. As Walter Rathenau, one of the architects of Germany's wartime mobilization, bluntly observed, the 14 Points were far from friendly to the Central Powers. And they became even less so following further stipulations by the Allies to which the German Government consented.

In consequence, the fighting ended with Germany confronting a peace settlement involving the dismemberment of its major allies and serious reverses for itself. The latter included the attribution of responsibility for the war to the 'aggression of Germany'; the restoration to France of Alsace-Lorraine; the reconstitution of Poland with a corridor to the sea; and the levying from Germany of large reparations for damages inflicted upon civilians. No German Government would have endorsed these proposals if its military situation had been anything but calamitous.

As for the terms of the Armistice, they precluded any renewal of hostilities. The Germans were required to evacuate all occupied territories – not only those in the West where they had been defeated but also those in the East where they remained victors. They had to surrender such prodigious numbers of weapons, aircraft, locomotives, and motor lorries as stripped them of their fighting power. They were obliged to hand over all of their submarines, and to submit for internment most of their battlefleet. And they had to withdraw their forces even from an important slice of German territory that would come under Allied occupation: the whole left bank of the Rhine, the principal crossings over that river, and the bridgeheads on the other side.

Plate 48   *British troops crossing the Rhine at Bonn.*

These terms, plainly, left Germany with no capacity to resume the struggle. In all but a nominal sense, what transpired on 11 November 1918 was not an armistice. It was Germany's unconditional surrender.

For a section of Britain's forces, this mighty accomplishment reached its fulfilment a month later. Brigadier General Bonham-Carter wrote home on 12 December that he had just taken part in an historic event: 'the march of a British Cavalry Division across the Hohenzollern Bridge over the Rhine at Cologne'.

> Imagine old Plumer with his Corps Commanders by him & a crowd of staff officers behind them, standing for two hours in front of the statue of the Kaiser, & with the statue of the Emperor Frederick in front of them while a continuous column of British Cavalry, Artillery & transport passed by, saluted & passed underneath the great stone archway that stands at the end of the Hohenzollern Bridge, & then onto the great bridge which spans the 300 yards of the swiftly flowing Rhine, to debouch from a second archway into Germany East of the Rhine. It seemed to me to be the culminating point of the soldiers life of everyone of us. Never shall I forget the sight of the leading squadron acting as an escort to the Divisional Commander, as it breasted the slight rise towards the bridge, advancing towards us with lances at the carry and red & white pennons fluttering in the wind.[9]

---

[9] Papers of Charles Bonham-Carter, Churchill College, Cambridge.

54

CONTROLLING THE SKIES

The numerical superiority of the enemy increased from day to day. Eight to one were the usual odds now. The English and Americans fought ruthlessly, for they had inexhaustible reserves of men and materials.

German airman's account of the closing stages of the war

I

When the British forces launched their attack outside Amiens on 8 August 1918, the Royal Air Force (as it had become earlier in the year) on the Western Front numbered 93 squadrons consisting of 1,782 aeroplanes. And three months later, when the war ended, the figures were 99 squadrons and about 1,800 machines. These numbers are fairly impressive. Yet it should be noted that they are not much more than what Haig and Trenchard had been clamouring for two years earlier, in the closing days of the Somme campaign. And they fall well short of the revised figures that, in July 1917, the War Cabinet had agreed were required.

In truth, there are a number of sorry aspects to the story of British aircraft production and air policy in 1917 and 1918. This is not all that surprising. The possible uses of the aeroplane – as a support for ground troops in France and also much further afield, as an adjunct to the navy, as a defence of the homeland against air raids, and as an instrument of independent bombing missions – greatly exceeded the supply. The attempt to reconcile these conflicting calls was likely to have some unhappy consequences.

Again, the aircraft was developing so rapidly in respects of technology that some risks in production had to be taken. The demand for machines capable of attaining higher altitudes, greater speed, swifter rates of climb, and deadlier fire power was unrelenting. Nothing comparable was to be found (except perhaps among subsidiary weapons like the tank) on land or sea. The army was, as one historian of industry points out, still using in 1917 guns that had been designed before 1914. So standardization of parts and quantity production were straightforward matters. 'But by 1917 there were no 1914 aircraft still flying.'[1] Hence one crying need by 1917 was for rationalization of the aircraft industry: the manufacture of fewer types of airframes and engines, leading to increased scales of production. And in some measure this was attained. But another urgent demand was for the development of new types of aircraft capable of superior performance.

Moreover, whatever the shortfall in output in terms of military requirements, the mobilization of industry and workers and the corresponding levels of production were

---

[1] W. J. Reader, *Architect of Air Power: The Life of the First Viscount Weir of Eastwood* (London: Collins, 1968), p. 58.

Plate 49　*An aeroplane of the Royal Air Force returning at sunset.*

impressive. It has been shown earlier that, by August 1916, 114 firms employing a labour force of 20,000 were engaged in making aircraft engines. By October 1918 the figures had jumped to 323 firms and nearly 100,000 employees. If attention is directed to firms engaged in every aspect of aircraft production, the figures again reveal a striking increase. In August 1916, as shown earlier, there were 491 firms and a labour force of 60,000. By October 1918 these stood at 1,529 firms and 347,000 employees. So by the end of the war the British aircraft industry was employing more than three times the number similarly employed in Germany.

The consequent output of aircraft was considerable. Back in 1915 Britain had produced 2,500 aeroplanes and in 1916 6,600. For 1917 output was 14,800 aircraft and for 1918 30,800. These production figures, admittedly, fell well below those of France. But they exceeded, if not by a great margin, the overall output of Germany. This ensured that the Germans, confronting the joint endeavours of Britain and France, were always overall – if not on sectors of their own choosing – heavily outnumbered.

Furthermore, some of the British-made aircraft acquitted themselves with distinction. Private enterprise produced the Sopwith Camel, which entered service in June 1917 and continued in action to the Armistice. (In a sense it is airborne still, if only in the imagination of a cartoon dog.) And the Royal Aircraft Factory produced the SE5 and SE5A, which appeared a month or two earlier than the Camel and also saw out the war. Contemporaneous with them, in date of appearance and longevity, was the Bristol F2, a two-seater reconnaissance machine that, amazingly, possessed the manoeuvrability, performance, and fire power to take on German fighters; 'it went down in history as the most versatile aircraft in the First World War.'[2]

---

[2] Alan Clark, *Aces High* (London: Weidenfeld & Nicolson, 1973), pp. 91–4.

These technical achievements would not prevent British airmen from dying in large numbers: because of the nature of air fighting, their own inexperience, the policy of the German command to concentrate its air force against the British sector of the Western Front rather than the French, and Trenchard's requirement that RFC fighters relentlessly intrude into enemy air space. But never in the last 18 months of the war would they be at the mercy of the enemy as in the heyday of the Fokker or the Albatros.

Nevertheless, as has been indicated, aircraft production and administration went through some unhappy phases in 1917 and 1918. A number of dreadful errors were made regarding the types of aircraft engine chosen for mass production. Models were selected that, though looking most attractive on the drawing board, were not sufficiently developed to warrant the decision to manufacture in bulk. A sequence of modifications became necessary that caused delays in production and shortfalls in delivery – to the point, in one instance, where the engines had become obsolete by the time they made their appearance.

Other matters bedevilled the air force in these two years: questions of organization and policy. This was no doubt inevitable. The army and navy were rivals for air support, and they were now competing also against civilians demanding aeroplanes both for home defence and for retaliatory bombing expeditions against Germany. Somehow a structure of control had to be devised in order to maximize output and adjudicate between these competing requirements.

Following the raids on London in June and July 1917, the War Cabinet appointed Smuts to investigate not only defence against air raids but also the much larger questions of organization and direction of aerial resources and operations. His conclusion was that the day was not far distant when aircraft would be not just adjuncts to military and naval forces but the instruments of an independent campaign against the enemy. Indeed, he said, a stage might soon be reached when devastation of an enemy from the air might become 'the principal operations of war', with military and naval activities 'secondary and subordinate'. This judgement, it must be said, was quite inapplicable to the war of 1914–18. The aircraft of the time had no capacity to devastate the enemy. And it was based on a double misconception: that the stalemate on land would continue, and that Britain would soon produce aircraft far in excess of its military and naval needs.

Yet, however wide of the mark, Smuts's report proposed lines of action that were in some measure implemented. Between November 1917 and January 1918 the existing Air Board was transformed into a Ministry with an air staff. Lloyd George, unwisely, offered the post of Minister to the press baron Northcliffe, who declined in a manner embarrassing to the Prime Minister, then to Northcliffe's brother Rothermere, also a press baron. Rothermere accepted, but by April 1918 he had abandoned, or been levered out of, the office. The appointment then went to Sir William Weir, an industrialist who during the war had become much engaged in aircraft manufacture. He proved sufficient to the task.

The second consequence of the Smuts report was that the military and naval arms, the Royal Flying Corps and the Royal Naval Air Service, were amalgamated. On 1 April 1918 the Royal Air Force (RAF) officially entered into existence.

Among those who viewed this proceeding with misgiving was the Commander-in-Chief in France. Haig feared that the new RAF would be dominated by the circumstances of its immediate origin: the demand for a large-scale bombing campaign against Germany. He need not have worried. In June 1918 an Independent Force (that is, a force independent of military or naval operations) was indeed set up, under Trenchard. Its purpose was to raid targets inside Germany. But its numbers were never large: 140 aircraft at the end of the war. It managed to drop just 543 tons of bombs during its five months of existence, and more than one-third of these were on aerodromes rather than industrial centres. Losses, to hostile weather as much as enemy action, were considerable: 109 bombers went missing and another 243 were wrecked, a rate of wastage of one aircraft for every 1½ tons of bombs dropped. This was an absurdly heavy cost for the small results achieved by the independent bombing campaign.

II

For the rest, the air war continued as before. The transition from RFC to RAF provided no discontinuity in the conflict being waged for the skies.

At the last, on all fronts, Britain's flying forces attained dominance in the air. In the more remote regions it became virtually complete. Most of all was this so in Palestine, where Allenby's closing campaign has been called 'as perfect an example of the proper application of air power as the German blitzkreigs in 1940 or the Israeli campaign of 1967'.[3] On the Western Front, to which attention must perforce be directed, command of the skies was never so conclusive. Nor was it so easily come by. Rather, during 1917 and 1918 Britain's flying men clawed their way by painful stages to an overall dominance.

1917, in truth, opened for the RFC with the worst phase of the entire war. Only an advantage in numbers of almost two to one explains how, in face of the superior German machines, British airmen managed to continue serving the forces on the ground. A disproportionate share of losses was borne by the observation craft, which the enemy, eluding British fighters, shot down in large numbers. So, of Richthofen's 30 victims in March and April, no fewer than 12 were of a single type – the BE reconnaissance machine: 'These slow, stable and obsolete aeroplanes attained their final martyrdom at Arras.'[4]

In addition to the British aircraft that fell to the enemy, a considerable number were wrecked by their pilots – evidence both of the intense strain being imposed on the more experienced flyers and of the desperate inexperience of the novices being rushed to the front. One squadron, No. 60, sustained losses of 105 per cent in April, and this proportion rose to nearly 200 per cent for the eight weeks from late March to early May. Their replacements were men who had never flown in the type of machine being employed by the squadron, none of which (being of French manufacture) was available in Britain.

One feature of the deteriorating situation was the RFC's inability to confine the Germans to their own air space. Of the 120 RFC planes shot down in March (according to the Official History), 59 fell in the British lines.[5] RFC fighters were still making regular patrols into German-occupied territory, but the manoeuvre was not effective. Aided by cloud, the German fighters were evading these patrols and wreaking havoc among the observation planes. So despite its much vaunted 'offensive' policy, the RFC was gradually driven to provide more direct support for its observation aircraft. But this was done with reluctance. Official policy, according to an head-quarters memorandum of 15 April, remained 'very strongly opposed to anything in the

[3] Robin Higham, *Air Power* (London: Macdonald, 1972), p. 41.

[4] R. H. Kiernan, *The First War in the Air* (London: Peter Davies, 1934), p. 99.

[5] H.A. Jones, *The War in the Air* (Oxford: Clarendon Press, 1931), vol. 3, p. 322.

nature of a local escort'. However, it did recognize that, for the moment, fighters must act in closer proximity to the observers.

The deadly days of April 1917 had scarcely passed when the RFC sustained a severe personal loss. On 7 May, after participating in a prolonged engagement, Albert Ball was seen to fly into a cloud in pursuit of an enemy machine. Shortly after, for reasons never established, his aeroplane fell out of the sky on the enemy side of the lines. Ball was the epitome of the lone flyer. Well-educated, courteous, if somewhat temper-amental and impatient of discipline, he had a natural aptitude for anything mechanical and seemed assured of a civilian career in electrical engineering. Only his passion for marksmanship had suggested that he was anything but a man of peace. But as a pilot over the Western Front he proved the reverse of peaceful. Early in 1916, while flying observation planes, he revealed a dangerous predilection for doing battle with the enemy. So for his own good (or that of his observer) he was transferred to fighters.

By his death in May 1917, still only 21 years of age, Ball had 44 conquests to his credit. By preference he flew alone, ever eager to tear into the enemy regardless of the odds, shattering his victims by the violence of his onslaught and departing before the survivors had adjusted to his presence. One of his favourite forms of encounter was to go for his adversary head-on, convinced that his opponent would be the first to pull away ('play chicken' is the modern expression) and so offer a brief but sufficient target for his deadly fire.

By the time of Ball's death the air war held a steadily receding place for his style of fighting. The instrument of aerial operation was now the unit rather than the single machine; the method of proceeding, at least until the mêlée of a dogfight, was by formation. The RFC's outstanding figures of the latter part of the war, James McCudden and Edward Mannock, were formation leaders. The manner in which, on 23 September 1917, McCudden orchestrated his seven planes to deal with the solitary German master Werner Voss, who was seeking to take them on in precisely the Albert Ball manner, clearly indicated the passing of the lone flyer's day.

This was not because McCudden and Mannock were anything less than superb fighters. Mannock, with 73 kills to his credit, was the highest-scoring British ace; and his tally would have been higher had he not so often allowed an unblooded British flyer to deliver the death blow to an enemy plane that he had already crippled. But, even more, these men welded their squadrons into complete units, guarded their novice pilots until they were ready for battle, and stimulated in their companies an extraordinary *esprit de corps*. Again, neither McCudden nor Mannock possessed a passion for taking on overwhelming odds – perhaps surprisingly for Mannock, whose resentment against the injustices of the British social system was outweighed only by his near-pathological detestation of the Germans. Like Richthofen, they preferred to give battle at moments of their own choosing, with the weight of numbers favouring them or with their adversaries at a disadvantage. Hence, although neither survived the war, they did not fall to opposing airmen. McCudden was killed in a flying accident; Mannock fell to a chance shot from the ground.

One feature of this period was the way in which the RFC was having to widen its net to secure additional personnel, mechanics as much as flying men. An extensive recruiting campaign was conducted within the ranks of the army (with Haig's blessing, if not with that of some of his subordinates), in industry, and – not least – in the Dominions. The last source had already begun to prove particularly rich, and it continued to do so. Canada, indeed, brought forth some of the outstanding pilots of the second half of the war, as aces like William Bishop and Raymond Collishaw (respectively second and third highest scorers in the RFC) bear witness. Of the 25

British pilots who brought down thirty or more enemy aircraft, no fewer than 10 were Canadians. One way and another, the day was past when aerial combat was, for Britain, largely a preserve of its great fee-paying schools.

III

By mid-1917 the dreadful time for the RFC was receding. Losses of flyers remained high: according to one compilation, in the period June to November between 153 and 214 airmen went killed or missing every month. Hence 'the training facilities did not catch up with Western Front requirements until the year was well spent.'[6] But the steady appearance of new breeds of fighters changed the whole aspect of air fighting.

During the brief, set-piece battle at Messines in June, with newly acquired aircraft and a numerical superiority of two to one, the RFC dominated the skies. Trenchard's ADC rejoiced in the outcome of the first day: 'The air reports read like a fairy-tale. It all went like clockwork. It is the finest day in the air we have ever had.'[7] The operation was, after its initial mine explosions, predominantly an artillery affair. The airmen served the limited but valued role of observing for the guns and chasing off enemy aircraft. Notably, for this occasion they were not asked to roam far afield but concentrated their efforts within 10,000 yards of the front line.

There followed the prolonged agony of Third Ypres and the brief episode of Cambrai. In both, the contribution of the flying arm was curtailed by the weather. The rain that bedevilled the first and third months of the Flanders campaign and the mist that was a feature of much of the fighting at Cambrai imposed decided limits on the role that the RFC might play. Its part, even so, was far from negligible. For example, in the clement middle month of Third Ypres the RFC ranged the artillery on nearly 10,000 targets, conducted 226 bombing attacks, and exposed 14,500 photographic plates (from which one-third of a million prints were distributed).

A development much in evidence at Cambrai, and employed by both sides, was the execution of low flying attacks on ground forces. Carried out in co-operation with an infantry attack, and especially when employed against troops on the move (be it in retreat or advance), these proved decidedly effective. But they could not be engaged in without cost. During Cambrai the RFC's ground-strafers suffered losses of 30 per cent per day, which meant that a squadron of highly skilled and difficult-to-replace pilots was eliminated in the space of four days. For the moment this form of activity was undertaken only on a small scale. But in the crisis-ridden, no-cost-too-high days of four months later it proved a major feature of the RFC's contribution to Allied survival.

The prelude to the German offensive of March 1918 was an ominous time for the RFC. During 1917 the enemy had made great exertions to increase his output of aircraft, and was now doubling the allocation of petrol to the air service. By judicious concentration the German air force was outnumbering the RFC in the sector of attack: 730 German aircraft (326 of them fighters) against 579 British (of which 261 were fighters).

On 21 March and again on the 22nd fog hampered flying in the morning for both sides, but in the later part of each day aerial activity was intense – if with little effect on the course of events. By 25 March, with disaster seemingly confronting the Allied cause, the resort to desperate measures appeared warranted. RFC squadrons were directed, wherever possible, to launch low-level attacks on enemy troops and

---

[6] H.A. Jones, *The War in the Air* (Oxford: Clarendon Press, 1935), vol. 5, p. 469.
[7] Andrew Boyle, *Trenchard* (London: Collins, 1962), p. 220.

transports. Major-General Salmond, commander of the airforce in France since January, ordered the leader of 9th Wing: 'bomb and shoot up everything. . . . Very low flying is essential. All risks to be taken. Urgent!'

The low-flying aircraft did not want for targets. In the account of the Australian official historian:

> On the Monday [25 March] every road leading to Bapaume, and all the other main roads south of that place behind the German front, were crowded afresh with transport. The German drive had so far proceeded mainly on the strength of such food and ammunition as the infantry could carry with them. Now supplies were wanted forward, and guns had to be brought up. The enemy's wheeled-transport was obliged in most places to keep to the roads, for the fields alongside were wet and holed and boggy. The Bapaume–Cambrai road was one of the main arteries for the supply of the advancing German front in this region. Over that road the machines of No. 4 [Australian] Squadron made a sort of ant-trail in the sky. Pilot after pilot recorded that his bombs burst in the middle of troops or transport, and so thick was the traffic that any block in it must prove serious. The airmen blew craters in the road-surface with their bombs, and then concentrated their attack on the traffic, which became bunched at such craters in the effort to make the narrow passage round them. With machine-gun fire the airmen ditched motor-lorries, blocked the road with broken waggons and maimed horses, set field-gun teams into panic-gallops away from their route, and played all possible havoc with the German rear-services.[8]

The low-level attacks continued unabated for six days. At their peak, on 27 March, they delivered 300,000 bullets and 50 tons of bombs upon the enemy. How large a part this played in halting the German advance is impossible to assess. Salmond on the night of the 26th reported:

> When I was at G.H.Q. to-night I heard a telephone message. . . saying that without doubt the concentration of aircraft in the south had frozen up the attack there temporarily. Similarly Cox (Intelligence). . . considered that the concentration of aircraft west of Bapaume had had the same effect.[9]

Against this it must be remembered that the strike capacity of aircraft, particularly in bombs, remained small and that the German advance on its fifth day had other reasons to be running out of steam.

The months of March and April 1918 severely tested the British air arm. Among unusual (and unwelcome) experiences, aerodromes were overrun, requiring the destruction not only of petrol and stores but also of aeroplanes awaiting repair or grounded by the weather. So on 9 April, owing to fog, the commander of 208 Squadron was obliged to burn his 18 Sopwith Camels and evacuate the personnel by motor transport. Consequently, new airfields had to be located and established and supplies rerouted. Losses in these months were heavy: 439 airmen killed and missing, and over 1,000 aircraft written off (the large majority of them 'wrecked beyond repair') out of a force that on 21 March had stood at 1,232.

Yet such was the extent of the nation's mobilization that none of this crippled its air arm. The intense search for potential airmen that had been launched early in 1917 was just now bearing fruit in trained flyers. And British industry was accomplishing new feats of output. According to Denis Winter, 'during the great German offensive of March 1918, the RFC requested 1,993 machines to replace those lost and got 2,259.' This reflected less an heroic response to a particular crisis than the general gearing up of industry to meet war-created requirements. Back in 1914 annual production of

---

[8] F. M. Cutlack, *The Official History of Australia in the War of 1914–1918* (Sydney: Angus & Robertson, 1938), vol. 8, pp. 235–6.

[9] Boyle, *Trenchard*, p. 273.

Plate 50   *Aeroplane engines ready for dispatch at the Wolseley works.*

magnetos had been 1,140 and of sparking plugs 5,000; 'when the war ended the figures were 128,637 and 2,148,726 respectively.'[10]

On the enemy side, no similar resilience was possible. The German air force might establish superiority in numbers in a particular sector at the outset of an offensive. It lacked the Allies' ability to rush in reinforcements to maintain that balance. Again, the Germans might still be able to produce a new aircraft marginally superior to the best of the Allies, as they did with the splendid Fokker DVII. But commodity shortages, not least of petrol, were forcing them to ration flying hours; for example, those devoted to the training of new airmen, with all the unhappy consequences that had befallen inexperienced RFC pilots early in 1917. In the actual offensives the heavy losses sustained by the Germans could only slowly be made good; their supply organization failed to meet requirements; and the problem of establishing new aerodromes and wireless installations in devastated regions proved even more severe than those confronting the retreating British. There was a failure also in the area of command. According to one account:

> the rapid pace of the ground battle apparently bewildered staffs grown slow-thinking in almost four years of siege warfare, and hitherto unaccustomed to thinking in terms of close co-ordination between ground and air. The German squadrons found themselves miles behind the front, seemingly forgotten. . . . orders, when they came, bore little relation to current needs of the battlefield.[11]

In a symbolic sense, if in no other, this phase of the air war culminated in an engagement over the Somme on 21 April. It witnessed the death of Manfred von

---

[10] Denis Winter, *The First of the Few: Fighter Pilots of the First World War* (London: Allen Lane, 1982), pp. 202–3.

[11] Thomas G. Miller, 'The Air Battle over Lys', *Purnell's History of the First World War* (London: Purnell & Sons, 1969–71), issue no. 97, p. 2702.

Richthofen. The argument continues as to who delivered the single bullet that, traversing his chest, brought him down. What is plain is that, under the unrelenting pressure of aerial combat, the Red Baron on this occasion exercised less than the rigorous caution that had enabled him to survive so far. In close pursuit of his intended eighty-first victim (an inexperienced pilot whose guns had jammed) he committed two errors. He allowed a Sopwith Camel piloted by a Canadian to get, unnoticed, on his tail. And he came close enough to the ground to place himself in range of the Lewis guns of an Australian artillery battery. Both the Canadian pilot and the Australian gunners were able to fire bursts at the red Fokker triplane. It went out of control and struck the ground. If there was doubt about who had accomplished its demise, there was none that its occupant was dead.

IV

If the great German offensive of March and April 1918 saw the fall of the Red Baron, the British counter-stroke of August occasioned the destruction of the elite force that still bore his name.

On 8 August aircraft were employed on an unprecedented scale. In the attack out of Amiens some 800 British and 1,100 French machines were active on a 25-mile front. Soon the commanders perceived a prospect so alluring that all endeavours were diverted to it. The retreating Germans were crowding along the roads leading to the Somme. If the river crossings could be destroyed, the enemy forces would be trapped. So all aircraft capable of bombing were thrown against the Somme bridges. For two days the attacks continued round the clock. The consequences were negligible. The bridges, if damaged, remained intact. And the cost was severe: 97 RAF planes were lost or wrecked on 8 August and a further 45 on the 9th.

But the endeavour had its positive consequences, which helped further to tilt the balance of air power against the enemy. The onslaught of 8 August so menaced German ground forces that their air arm was bound to respond. Reinforcements, including the Richthofen squadron under Herman Goering, were hastened into the region. In circumstances not of their choosing, they fought unrelentingly. Like the RAF, they lost heavily. Unlike it, they could not hope to make good these losses. In short order the Richthofen squadron was reduced from 50 aeroplanes to 11, and before long another 4 went down. Although a force bearing the Red Baron's name would in due course reappear, its day as an elite unit ended here.

Thereafter, in order to achieve an effective concentration in the regions considered crucial, the German air force was obliged to leave uncovered important sectors of the front. So, late in August, 'for days in succession every Australian patrol reported no German machines seen anywhere north of the Scarpe. The rare appearance of a few two-seaters only emphasised the fact that the enemy had left the air in this region.'[12]

Moreover, enemy flyers were rarely in a position to wreak havoc among ground forces as the RAF was regularly doing. R. H. Kiernan instances the case of a company of British infantry that occupied forward positions throughout the six months April to September 1918. In April they were at Ypres, in May at Reims (on the French front), from July to September first on the Somme and then advancing from Thiepval to St Quentin. During all that time they only twice witnessed German aircraft at close quarters, both of them observation planes, one of which was shot down. And on only one occasion did this same company observe, a good distance away, anti-aircraft fire

---

[12] Cutlack, *The Official History of Australia in the War of 1914–1918*, vol. 8, p. 351.

being directed against a German machine behind the British lines. The majority of men in the company, according to Kiernan, never considered the possibility of being attacked from the air because they never experienced it. And meanwhile the pilots of the RAF – sometimes as many as 70 machines at a time – were flying continuously over their heads towards the enemy.[13]

Yet it was never the case that the Germans were wholly driven from the skies. The RAF in September and October 1918 could perform all the tasks asked of it: bombing railway stations, dropping smoke bombs upon enemy machine-gun positions as British infantry were about to go forward, air-dropping food supplies to advanced forces, mercilessly harrying German soldiers crowding the roads in retreat. But British flyers could do none of these unopposed. Many of their activities brought them up against strong fire from the ground. And they also encountered spasms of intense opposition in the air, often delivered by the powerful Fokker DVIIs. So in September 235 RAF aircraft went missing, the heaviest losses for any month of the war. And although in October the toll (164) was less, it was still above that of March and April 1918 and (possibly) Bloody April 1917.[14]

Anyway, the reduction in October may be accounted for by the limitations on flying imposed by the weather. There were still episodes of intense aerial activity. For example, on 14 October in the northern sector where Plumer was attacking:

> The air work was almost entirely offensive. . . . The bomber and fighter squadrons flew from aerodrome to target, and then back again to replenish their fuel and to reload with ammunition. All day the destruction went on.

But on the two ensuing days rain and mist hampered flying in Flanders, and from 18 October they did so for a stretch of 10 days. H. A. Jones writes:

> The air superiority of the Allies was overwhelming, the targets which streamed towards the bottle neck into Germany were innumerable, the retreating troops were depressed in body and mind, the setting indeed was such as to ensure the most awesome effects for the rigorous employment of air power, but the quality of mercy rained from the clouds.[15]

One air contest of these last days deserves mention. On 27 October, over the southern part of the British front, the Canadian ace William Barker in a Sopwith Snipe (intended to become the successor to the Camel) fought an epic battle single-handed against a horde of Fokker DVIIs. In what was intended anyway to be his last appearance on the Western Front (he was now commander of a combat school in England), Barker shot down four enemy aircraft, was wounded in both thighs and an elbow, and twice fainted in the air. Yet he managed to crash-land on his own side of the lines: unconscious, his cockpit awash with blood, but still alive.

For the rest, owing to inclement weather flying was severely curtailed in the last days of the conflict. The air war, rather than coming to a grand finale, somewhat petered out. Perhaps this was appropriate. It served to indicate that the war of the skies remained to the end an ancillary to the struggle on the ground. A climactic air battle was no prerequisite of an Allied victory.

---

[13] Kiernan, *The First War in the Air*, pp. 181–3.
[14] The statistics offered by authorities on the air war for losses in April 1917 are so various as to leave the general historian bewildered.
[15] Jones, *The War in the Air*, vol. 6, pp. 539–41.

55

LATE SUCCESSES IN THE SIDESHOWS

I

In the view of the 'Easterners' (otherwise the advocates of the 'indirect approach'), the sideshows would do more than drive Germany's allies out of the war. In the process they would encompass the fall of Germany. It was never plain why the one event should lead to the other. Anyway, this was not what happened. Not until Germany had first lost all prospect of winning the war, and then was confronting – gradually but inexorably – certain defeat, did its allies abandon the struggle. The conflicts on the peripheries did end for the Western powers in a spate of victories. But these did not occur until it had been clearly demonstrated that victory – that is, triumph over the major adversary – was only a matter of time.

During 1918 little happened in the sideshows before September, by which time Germany's 'black day' at Amiens was already a month old. This was not because Lloyd George had lost enthusiasm for employing British forces in relatively bloodless struggles against the Turks rather than in bloody conflicts with the Germans. But in the spring and summer of 1918 the essential reality of this war had asserted itself with a vengeance in France and Flanders: the reality first of threatened defeat and then of imminent victory. Whatever Lloyd George's predilections, he was too responsible a war leader to disregard the menace and then the hope here confronting him.

II

Hence it was only in the autumn of 1918 that the sideshows saw any dramatic action. In the case of Macedonia the action, when it came, was dramatic indeed. For three years, from early October 1915 to mid-September 1918, the Allied campaign there had hung fire. Then in a fortnight the situation was transformed.

Britain's contribution in this area, it should be stressed, continued limited and grudging. The British military command, including Henry Wilson, had no wish to activate the Balkan front. And the only theatre that aroused Lloyd George's enthusiasm was Palestine. So it was from the French that any initiative must come for an offensive from Salonika. And, given Clemenceau's want of sympathy, such initiative could not be great.

Sarrail's successor as commander of the Army of the Orient, from December 1917 to June 1918, was General Guillaumat, who had commanded the French Second Army at Verdun. His half-year in Macedonia did not witness any large operations. But he brought greater coherence to the various national elements he commanded than had been possible under the fractious Sarrail. And he greatly improved communications leading up to the front.

In June Guillaumat was succeeded by Franchet d'Esperey ('Desperate Frankie' to the British), a cavalry commander of fierce temper, considerable dash, and much personal magnetism. 'I expect from you savage vigour,' he announced on taking up his new command. He also brought to his task a familiarity with the region gained from travels before the war and belief in the viability of an Eastern strategy. Hence he straightway put preparations in train for a major offensive. His problem lay in convincing London and Paris and Rome that such an undertaking was warranted. Paris (with Guillaumat now in a key position to influence it) soon came round. But it was 4 September before Lloyd George succumbed and 10 September before the Italians gave their endorsement. All of them insisted that neither additional troops nor additional shipping would be placed at d'Esperey's disposal.

The Allied commander was prepared to go ahead without these. And as soon as he received authorization, he was ready to move. Instead of making his main thrust, as the enemy anticipated, on the right of his front, down the Vardar Valley, he struck first on his left-centre. This was mountainous territory that provided the Bulgarians with powerful natural defences. But d'Esperey was banking on surprise to carry him over the peaks that constituted his opponents' front lines. Beyond, there lay valleys running in precisely the direction he needed to advance to breach the enemy's main defensive system.

Despite the handicaps of geography, the French commander managed to get his artillery forward to the chosen point of attack, and to do so unobserved. He also accumulated there a superiority of manpower (consisting mainly of Serbian and French forces) of three to one. The bombardment, extremely heavy by the standards of this front, opened on 14 September. Early next morning the Serbs and French went forward. Only after two days of severe fighting did they manage significant progress. But with the mountain obstacles taken, the situation was becoming hopeful.

D'Esperey's problem now was to prevent the enemy's withdrawing troops from other parts of the front to shore up the threatened sector. So on 18 September he ordered an advance by the British and Greeks on his right wing. As they had done twice in 1917, the British forces in Macedonia assailed the terrible high points above Lake Doiran. Once more these positions proved impregnable, at a cost to the attackers sometimes as high as 30 per cent. Only in a negative sense was this endeavour rewarded. It pinned down Bulgarian forces badly needed further west.

The enemy command now made a serious decision. It opted to withdraw along the whole front. The calculation was that the Allied supply lines would become overstretched and could then be attacked from the flanks. Consequently, three days after the British had struggled in vain to take the positions north of Doiran, they found them to be abandoned. Soon the RAF was harrying Bulgarian soldiers retreating along the narrow mountain roads, reducing the devoted adversaries of a few days before to a disorganized rabble.

This was not the only respect in which the enemy withdrawal was proving a serious miscalculation. The bleak prospect of the war now confronting the Central Powers had eroded Bulgarian morale to a crucial degree. Their front-line troops had remained steadfast in defence, but behind them lay a situation of the utmost fragility. Hence the notion of luring d'Esperey's forces to their doom proved a pipedream. Once in retreat, the Bulgarian forces lost all coherence. Unprecedented opportunities for the Allied cavalry suddenly presented themselves. A dramatic 60-mile ride by French colonial forces carried them around the enemy resistance and on to Skopje, second largest city in Serbia and the crucial railway centre between the Central Powers and the front. On the morning of 29 September Skopje surrendered, after some resistance from the small German forces but virtually none from the Bulgarians.

By then, anyway, Bulgarian officials bearing white flags had appeared on the British sector, and armistice negotiations were under way. The fall of Skopje settled the matter. On 30 September Bulgaria withdrew from the war. A grand Allied advance followed. Serbian and French forces swept north across liberated Serbia and crossed the Danube. British forces moved into unresisting Bulgaria and swung east towards Turkey. Visions of conquering Budapest, Vienna, and Constantinople seized d'Esperey and Milne.

Their aspirations were not to be fulfilled. The same factors that had brought Bulgaria so swiftly to collapse were now carrying away the Hapsburg and Ottoman empires. Their capitals surrendered without a struggle. Both at the time and subsequently (in their uncritically received memoirs) Germany's war leaders – with Ludendorff principal among them – stressed Bulgaria's demise in explaining their own decision to abandon the war. This self-indulgence is excusable. But it is hardly deserving of the endorsement of historians. The German forces in France had been experiencing defeat for nearly two months before the Bulgarians acted on the awareness that the cause of the Central Powers was truly lost.

III

Unlike that in Macedonia, the sideshow in Mesopotamia simply petered out. To say this is not to detract from the courage and endurance revealed by the British, and in particular the Indian, forces who fought in this region, frequently under the most gruelling climatic conditions. But it now transpired, especially with the collapse of Russia, that strategically the advance to Baghdad in early 1917 had led nowhere. Discovering this had occupied half a million men, half a million tons of ocean shipping, and large quantities of railway track and river craft – 'an extraordinary exertion for a single campaign removed by nearly the entire breadth of the Middle East from the enemy's major political and economic centers'.[1] During 1918 it was evident that, given the crisis in France and the promise of Palestine, such a volume of resources could no longer be spared for Mesopotamia. So by mid-summer the British army there had become 'a much diluted force'.[2]

Not until the second half of October was a fresh advance ordered, on Mosul. Before this objective could be reached Turkey capitulated, but the British commander insisted on occupying the city anyway.

IV

The ending of affairs in Palestine was altogether more stirring. Again, however, 1918 was well advanced before these events developed. For eight months following the capture of Jerusalem in December 1917 Allenby's front was fairly quiescent. To begin with, winter rains prevented any advance. Then the demands of the Western Front in the spring caused the removal of nearly 60,000 men. In time these deprivations were made good, overwhelmingly by Indian troops, and in respect to cavalry Allenby's force was increased to four divisions. But the summer was over before he was ready to strike another blow.

---

[1] Howard M. Sachar, *The Emergence of the Middle East: 1914–1924* (London: Allen Lane, 1970), p. 226.
[2] A. J. Barker, *The Neglected War: Mesopotamia 1914–1918* (London: Faber & Faber, 1967), p. 454.

On Allenby's flank the Arab forces of Feisal and Lawrence also made only limited progress up to September 1918. Early in the year an advance took place (at Allenby's request) into southern Trans-Jordan, a corn-producing region important to the Turks for supplying their forces. Tafila within this area was taken by Arab troops, who then managed to hold it against a fierce Turkish counter-attack. (This episode gave Lawrence his only opportunity to fight a set-piece battle, a form of activity he himself disparaged. He acquitted himself with distinction.) But thereafter, for several months, the desert war enjoyed only limited successes. Stretches of railway were demolished, but direct assaults on railway junctions by regular Arab forces came to nothing.

Allenby meanwhile was planning his next large push, to come in the autumn. Commanding the Turks opposing him was the German Liman von Sanders, of Gallipoli fame. Sanders had taken the place of Falkenhayn, who had fallen out of favour with the Turks. The exchange did not prove to their advantage. Falkenhayn had practised defence in depth, whereas Sanders kept the bulk of his forces – along with himself – well forward. This played into Allenby's hands.

The British commander intended to place the main weight of his thrust on his left wing, that is, on the coastal side. He went to great lengths to conceal this, establishing in his centre not only fake camps but also an array of dummy horses. And on his right he directed Lawrence and the Arabs to step up their attacks on rail centres.

The offensive opened on 19 September. By then the advantages enjoyed by the British were considerable. They possessed a splendid communications network in their rear. They enjoyed overwhelming superiority in cavalry – a key consideration for the type of attack Allenby was planning. They were facing an increasingly demoralized enemy, short of food, afflicted with disease, and subject to a high incidence of desertion. Moreover, the British had secured command of the air and so could prevent observation of their areas of concentration. Thanks to this, and to various deceptive activities, the enemy was thoroughly misled regarding Allenby's intentions. A Turkish intelligence map captured two days before the start of the offensive showed the Turks to be expecting the main thrust not on the coast but in the centre of the front. This enabled the British greatly to outnumber them in men and guns in the chosen sector.

The assault began in the early morning. By late afternoon the Turks' right wing on the coast had been overwhelmed. The British infantry advanced up to 14 miles, so that, from facing north at the outset, they ended the day facing east. Between them and the sea lay an open corridor, to be employed by the cavalry in accordance with Allenby's ambitious plan. Leaving the infantry far behind, and living off the country and such rations as they could carry, the cavalry struck at the main communications routes in the rear of the enemy. Such was their speed that Liman von Sanders, in his headquarters at Nazareth, barely escaped capture. By the end of the second day the Turks' lines of retreat – which meanwhile were being pounded and machine-gunned by the RAF – had been severed. Three days later the Turkish Seventh and Eighth Armies, occupying the front from the sea to the river Jordan, had ceased to exist as fighting units.

Meanwhile on the east side of the Jordan the Arabs were taking heavy toll on the railways around the crucial junction of Dera. Hence the Turks could neither withdraw their forces from the Hejaz nor bring down reinforcements from Damascus. Then on 28 September units of Allenby's forces crossed the Jordan to take Dera. This obliged the one Turkish army still operating in the region to retreat towards Damascus. But it could not match the speed of the Australian cavalry and of the Arab irregulars. Damascus fell to elements of both these forces on 1 October, and the Turks' last force was cut off and doomed.

Thereafter Allenby's advance was an almost unimpeded procession. Before the month was out Turkey had capitulated.

This campaign was a victory above all for Allenby and for the cavalry with whom he was identified. Nevertheless, especially in the opening phases, artillery and infantry made a key contribution. And all the time the free-roaming air force was harassing Turkish command centres and helping to convert enemy withdrawals into routs. Allenby had proved an exemplary commander: visionary in his awareness of how much the cavalry could accomplish in suitable conditions, imaginative and yet thorough in making preparations, both an inspiration and a goad to his men by his constant presence near the front.

How important was the contribution of the Arab contingents to this victory? Plainly, it was not decisive, and it was of less moment during this year than in 1917. Yet it had not been inconsiderable: in protecting Allenby's right flank, helping to mislead the enemy concerning the whereabouts of his initial thrust, and disrupting the Turks' communications. According to General Wavell, when Allenby launched his attack in September 1918 half the Turkish troops in the operational zone were on the far side of the Jordan, occupied by Lawrence and the Arabs. And a yet larger body of Turks were strung out down the Hejaz railway, trying to preserve the route to the Holy Places. In the opinion of General Glubb, the Arab revolt was an extraordinary example of what could be achieved by guerrilla tactics. Tens of thousands of regular Turkish troops had been pinned down by an adversary barely capable of engaging a brigade of infantry in pitched battle. Such economy of force was rare on either side in this war.

V

The events of 1917–18 had not enhanced Britain's position in the Balkans. But they had left it the dominant power in the Middle East. This was not a role Britain had coveted. During the nineteenth century it had preferred that the Ottoman Empire should survive and, by governing well (instead of ill, as was its custom), maintain stability in the region. Thereby the British route to India – a region that in 1913 had accounted for nearly 10 per cent of Britain's total trade – was assured at minimum cost.

Hence when the Arab revolt prefigured itself shortly before the war, it had received no encouragement from Britain. In April 1914 one of the Sherif of Mecca's sons had approached Kitchener, then effective ruler of Egypt, seeking aid for a rising against the Turks. He had been told that such a plan 'presupposed a break-up of Turkish authority', which was no part of British policy.

At the end of that year the Turkish Empire doomed itself by entering the war on the losing side. By 1918 its role in Arabia was at an end. The resulting great-power vacuum demanded a response, be it to intervene or to abstain, from Britain. The nation's rulers had no doubt what this response should be: they must take over much of Turkey's role. After all, they had no wish to see France – let alone communist Russia – greatly extend its authority here. And the safety of the route to the East could hardly be allowed to depend on the whims of the inhabitants of Arabia, any more than on those of the inhabitants of Egypt.

Two areas in particular seemed to require a measure of British direction. Palestine, including the Trans-Jordan, was precariously close to the Suez Canal. For Lloyd George, Palestine was 'really the strategic buffer of Egypt'. He held that its control by a group of powers (as foreshadowed by the Sykes–Picot agreement of 1916) 'would be quite intolerable to ourselves'.[3] The other area of particular concern was Mesopotamia (soon to become Iraq), which both lay at the head of the Persian Gulf and promised to alleviate Britain's need for a secure source of oil.

It was recognized that Britain could not gain control of these ex-Turkish territories without offering a *quid pro quo* to its allies. Anyway, from early in the war France and Russia had made it plain that they looked to gains in this region as reward for their military exertions. The most grandiose request of all had been made by, and conceded to, the Tsar: the demand for Constantinople. Happily, the Tsar's demise had obviated this factor from post-war complications. The established regime in France, by contrast, had survived the war in good order. It was determined to secure the fulfilment of at least a major part of the Sykes–Picot agreement: that by which France had been accorded control of Syria.

But these matters were not straightforward. The withdrawal of Turkish authority had not left a simple vacuum into which one or other of the European allies could move. Among the Arab inhabitants, the war had generated aspirations to self-government – be it on the grand scale of a united Arabia or on an altogether more fragmented basis. Not least, of course, was this the case in the Hejaz, where revolt against Turkey had come earliest and proved most effective (and where none of the Allies had great designs). But it was evident also in those areas – which had not necessarily contributed much to their own liberation – that Britain and France were determined to rule.

Moreover, the view that Turkey's former subjects merited self-government found much support even within the victor powers themselves. Nor was it confined to the America of Woodrow Wilson and a handful of 'idealists' in Britain and France. The very politicians in Paris and London who were bent on dominating parts of the Middle East were also applying to these regions the language of self-determination. It might be thought that this was simply a fraudulent device for stirring up the Arabs against the Turks. But this is an over-simplification. Early in November 1918, following the capitulation of Turkey, the rulers of Britain and France issued a proclamation to the Arabs promising them emancipation and Governments of their own choice.

Significantly, one of the authors of this proclamation was Sir Mark Sykes, a Tory MP and Middle Eastern 'expert' who had co-authored the Sykes–Picot agreement of two years before. In the interval Sykes's views had undergone much amendment. (A recent biography traces his course from 'pre-war Turcophilia and anti-Semitism to become a leading champion of the Arabs, Armenians and Zionists'.)[4] By mid-1918 Sykes was striving to convince Picot that their agreement of 1916 was, as it stood, of 'positive harm' to the Allies. Democratic forces, he said, regarded it as 'an instrument of capitalistic exploitation and Imperialistic aggression' and as 'contrary to President Wilson's policy'. And Arabs gained from it the impression 'that we were intent upon annexation'.[5] What Sykes failed to notice was that, although diminishing, there were still forces in Britain and France intent upon 'Imperialistic aggression' and 'annexation'.

The complexities of arranging a settlement in the Middle East did not cease here. In the case of Palestine there was the matter of the Balfour Declaration. In November 1917 Balfour, as Foreign Secretary, had publicly announced that the British Government sympathized with Zionist aspirations to establish in Palestine a national home for the Jews. He had added, certainly, that nothing would be done that might 'prejudice

---

[3] See Sacher, *The Emergence of the Middle East: 1914–1924*, p. 188.
[4] Roger Adelson, *Mark Sykes: Portrait of an Amateur* (London: Jonathan Cape, 1975), p. 11.
[5] Ibid., pp. 267–8.

the civil and religious rights of existing non-Jewish communities in Palestine'; but he did not appear to consider that the second statement might be in conflict with the first. This declaration meant that the British Government was committed, if to an ill-defined extent, to the ideal that Judaism should regain a geographical identity in its homeland of long ago. (There were, at the outbreak of the war, already 85,000 Jews settled in Palestine. They had no legal status or representation in the Ottoman Parliament, but they were beginning to prosper in self-contained, Hebrew-speaking communities.)

As far as Britain's leaders were concerned, Balfour's action had many causes. Not only Balfour himself but also Lloyd George and Smuts had an Old Testament-derived admiration for the Jews. They also thought, in the context of November 1917, that the Declaration might rally support for the war both from Russian Jewry (in the process of falling out) and American Jewry (deemed tardy in becoming involved). And, in the longer term, it seemed that a Jewish home being established under British aegis would create widespread support for Britain's control over this region.

What these complexities make plain is that, within British political circles, the war had both perpetuated old views and stimulated new ones. It had underpinned the traditional notion that a country engaged in a long and costly struggle might expect some territorial reward at the end. Especially was this so when the reward was being secured from a palpably spent empire, incapable thereafter of launching a campaign of *revanche*. But at the same time, the war was powerfully inspiring the notion of national self-determination for populations previously subject to alien rule. And it markedly stimulated the idea of bringing together from many lands – to a territory with which they were associated by religion and ancient history but that happened to be occupied by others – a scattered people of common identity.

It is not remarkable that Britain's rulers were responsive to these varied aspirations. But that they solemnly endorsed schemes arising from each of them, as if these in no way conflicted, is more surprising. Had these matters concerned the struggle against Germany and the crucial territories of Western Europe, it could hardly have happened. Only regarding the peripheries, which engaged their attention spasmodically and without long reflection, were responsible individuals likely to enter into such varied undertakings.

Theoretically, it is true, there might be no inconsistency between the three elements in the situation: British and French aspirations to rule over some Arab territories; the promise of self-government to the inhabitants of those same territories; and the fostering of Zionist ambitions with respect to one of them. Possibly the Arabs of Syria would welcome French overlordship and the Arabs of Palestine and Iraq British overlordship, as providing sound administration forthwith and a promise of eventual self-government. And it might be that the Arab inhabitants of Palestine would manage to live in accord with the Jews already settled or shortly to migrate there.

This last presupposed that the Palestinian Arabs would recognize themselves as a backward people in an undeveloped land, and so would welcome new inhabitants blessed with drive, advanced economic techniques, and capital. (At the outset this presupposition was endorsed by some prominent Arabs, including Feisal, but it was swiftly abandoned.) It took for granted two other points. The first was that Jewish immigration would occur at so modest a rate that it could be absorbed on reclaimed coastal areas and former Turkish property. The second was that the Jewish settlers would not – as many Zionists plainly did – envisage the Jewish national home as soon becoming a Jewish national state, in whose governance neither Arab nor Briton would play much part.

In important respects these expectations were not fulfilled. Outside the Christian section of Lebanon, French rule in Syria was hardly ever more than an imperialist regime imposed – in clear violation of wartime promises – on an unwilling people. And British rule in Iraq, established very much on the authoritarian pattern of India, rapidly encountered armed resistance. As for the British attempt to establish an 'impartial' regime in Palestine, this proved unwelcome to both major elements. It soon became evident that the Jews might not only come to dominate the economy but also, in due course, constitute a numerical majority, with aspirations towards self-government. They did not see it as Britain's role to interfere with these trends. By contrast, the Palestinian Arabs, whose cause was swiftly adopted by much of Arabia, looked to the mandatory power to apply forthwith at least one important aspect of self-government. They pressed that the will of the existing (i.e. Arab) majority should be decisive on the matter of immigration; and, thereby, that the Jews should remain a permanent minority.

It lies beyond the scope of this book to relate how these matters worked themselves out. What needs to be stressed is that, in terms of a short view (which nevertheless spanned more than the quarter of a century following the Great War), Britain did enjoy a satisfactory position in the Middle East. Its chain of imperial communications was preserved. Its access to a share of Middle Eastern oil was assured. The unwished-for demise of the Ottoman Empire had been made good in a way that upheld these important interests.

Even the impasse developing in Palestine did not invalidate Britain's presence there. Indeed, it seemed to necessitate rule by a power that was neither Arab nor Jew. As for Iraq, the early difficulties encountered there soon led to a more indirect (and much cheaper) style of government. This provided a façade of Arab rule while preserving the reality of British control. Many Iraqis found this fairly acceptable, anyway for a while. The conservative elements ('kings and pashas and rich merchants'), being wary of the more turbulent sections in their own people, welcomed a firm British presence.[6] And after decades of ill-rule by the Turks, the population found that the British administered their mandates devotedly and efficiently. This helped – at least while memories were strong of what had gone before – to reconcile subject peoples to Britain's oversight of affairs.

In time Britain's dominance in these parts would be eroded: by the emergence (or re-emergence) of other great powers; and by developments in Arab nationalism that were exacerbated by the ever-worsening situation within Palestine. But in large measure these events lay beyond what, at the end of the Great War, any British Government could have envisaged or taken action to prevent.

---

[6] Elizabeth Monroe, *Britain's Moment in the Middle East 1914–1956* (London: Chatto & Windus, 1963), p. 82.

56

VICTORY AT SEA

I always told you they would have to come out.

Admiral Beatty on receiving the surrender of the German fleet in Rosyth harbour,
21 November1918

I

Between January and November 1918 Britain's triumph over the naval forces of Germany was brought to completion. It was a double victory – over the High Seas Fleet and over the U-boats. Yet for many, not only among the general public but also in the naval service, it provided little cause for rejoicing. One episode only in the sea war aroused great enthusiasm in this year: the attempted *coup de main* against Zeebrugge, an event that affected the outcome of the naval conflict scarcely at all.

By the opening of 1918 important changes had occurred in the higher direction of Britain's naval affairs. Basically, Lloyd George during 1917 came to regard Jellicoe as a liability – indeed, as being no improvement on the members of the military hierarchy whom the Prime Minister loathed. The First Sea Lord, in Lloyd George's view, had first dragged his feet over the inception of convoys and thereafter did not show sufficient zest in their application. There was also Jellicoe's persistent pessimism, aggravated by his ceaseless combat against a mountain of paperwork. And Jellicoe in mid-1917 had blotted his copybook irreparably by proclaiming – if probably to little effect – the absolute necessity for the Third Ypres campaign.

Lloyd George also became convinced, before 1917 was far advanced, that Carson was misplaced. As First Lord of the Admiralty he would neither correct Jellicoe's failings nor assist in his removal. So, by stages, the Prime Minister set about unseating first Carson and then Jellicoe. As a preliminary stage, in May 1917 he appointed Sir Eric Geddes Controller of the Navy. Geddes was a thrusting, self-made businessman and expert in railway management, who had achieved wonders in meeting the communication needs of the British army in France. (As part of his reward, Lloyd George had made Geddes an honorary major-general. Now he made him also an honorary vice-admiral. Doubtless this was an instance of the Prime Minister cocking a snook at service pretensions. But Geddes, a dedicated *arriviste*, actually took to wearing an admiral's uniform.) As Controller of the Navy, Geddes brought with him a bevy of railway officials and other civilian experts. Thereby he sought to counteract the centralization that bedevilled Jellicoe's regime, provide clear estimates of the navy's losses and requirements, and take the business of supplying its needs into civilian hands.

In July 1917 Lloyd George took the plunge of substituting Geddes for Carson. The device was employed of elevating Carson (or kicking him upstairs) to the War Cabinet.

Plate 51 *The British White Ensign flies above the German flag on a surrendered U-boat following the cessation of hostilities.*

This was doubtless intended to save his face and escape his enmity. It had limited success in both respects.

The new First Lord of the Admiralty pressed ahead with reorganizing naval administration. In the process Geddes became convinced that Jellicoe would never provide wholehearted support. So at Christmas 1917 he seized the opportunity to make a change. The First Sea Lord was a staunch ally of Admiral Bacon, who commanded the Dover Patrol and was supposed to have rendered the Straits of Dover impassable to U-boats. Early in December it was established that many German submarines were still using this shorter route into the Atlantic. The revelation provided grounds for demanding Bacon's removal. Jellicoe stood firm, whereupon he also was sacked.

So in January 1918 a fresh triumvirate presided over Britain's naval destiny: Beatty as C.-in-C. of the Grand Fleet (as he had been since December 1916), Geddes as First Lord, and Admiral Sir Rosslyn Wemyss as Jellicoe's replacement in the post of First Sea Lord. Wemyss was hardly a stellar figure. In time he would be chosen as Britain's delegate at the signing of the Armistice on 11 November 1918, with the result that it is often forgotten that Britain even had a delegate there. But Wemyss proved effective enough in running the navy on the lines required of him: never submerging himself in technical detail, allocating responsibility to his deputies, and so keeping in view the larger questions. And he was adept at preserving good relations with a wide range of colleagues; including even Beatty – at least till almost the war's end – who, as his frustrations mounted, became increasingly self-assertive and fractious. (Beatty's inspiring leadership of the Grand Fleet, it should be added, played a notable part in preserving naval morale during these long months of inaction.)

One development did not follow upon Jellicoe's sudden exclusion from all part in Britain's naval affairs. There was no adoption of a more adventurous strategy. The fundamentals of the policy that Jellicoe had established continued to the end. Indeed, in the first half of 1918 the Grand Fleet, at Beatty's insistence, took up a rather more cautious stance than at any other stage in the war. In a memorandum of early January Beatty stated that it would be 'to our general interest to adopt measures which would tend to postpone a Fleet action' – unless one could be arranged in clearly favourable circumstances. He offered several reasons for this. The Grand Fleet was having to devote a portion of its resources, particularly from among its destroyers, to the protection of commerce from submarines. Again, the improved type of shell that was required for a fleet action had yet to appear. Further, the Grand Fleet had no clear superiority over the enemy in battle cruisers. And the Germans, thanks to the collapse of Russia, were now free to transfer naval forces from the Baltic to the North Sea.

Beatty's proposal was endorsed without resistance by the Admiralty and by Downing Street. Perhaps this is not too surprising. Beatty was proposing at most a slight shift in the balance of policy. And there continued to be little sign that the High Seas Fleet would ever become active enough to make a live issue of what should be the appropriate response.

In the event Scheer did take his armada to sea on one more occasion while hostilities lasted. Late in April he set out for Scandinavia in an attempt to intercept and destroy a convoy guarded by a British battle squadron. The response of Beatty was not defensive. As soon as Scheer's movement was divined the Grand Fleet left harbour, in full battle array, for what would prove the last time in the war. Indeed Beatty, who had but recently transferred his base from Scapa Flow to Rosyth, managed despite thick fog to get out 193 ships in record time.

The outcome of this flurry of activity was disappointing for both sides. Scheer's

Map 15 *The North Sea.* Source *Gilbert,* First World War Atlas, *p. 75.*

attempt to catch and destroy a British convoy, with its attendant warships, proved unavailing. No convoy was at sea that day. So he returned empty-handed (and with one of his battle cruisers damaged by a torpedo from a British submarine). Nor was Beatty better rewarded. For the first time in the war, the Admiralty's decoders had been unable to give the C.-in-C. advance warning of a German sortie. The enemy were using a new cypher, which had yet to be broken. And anyway Scheer, chastened by previous mishaps, was employing wireless with the utmost caution. On this occasion he also refrained from undertaking airship reconnaissance or mine-sweeping in preparation for the expedition, so as to avoid arousing suspicion. And although the early progress of his force was witnessed by one British submarine, its captain came to the preposterous conclusion that these must be Beatty's vessels and hence sent no signal. As a result, by the time the Grand Fleet got to sea the enemy were well on their way home.

The one point that this non-encounter apparently demonstrated was that the restrictions Beatty had proposed for his fleet's movements at the start of the year did not amount to very much. And in mid-1918, with the appearance of the new armour-piercing shell and the waning of the U-boat menace, his memorandum of January was withdrawn. Nothing of consequence followed. As far as capital ships were concerned, the Great War would end as it had begun: with the Grand Fleet in effective control of both the North Sea and the ocean approaches to Britain. The German battleships, for all their advanced technology and fine seamanship, proved to the last an ineffective and increasingly demoralized spectator of the war.

II

There was, of course, another sea war that had emerged during the course of the conflict: the attempted U-boat blockade of Britain. During 1918 it too went steadily in the Allies' favour. Mainly this was the achievement of the convoy, which denied victims to the U-boats and placed in jeopardy any submarine that attacked. Other forms of action against U-boats contributed, but to a much smaller degree.

One episode of the campaign against Germany's submarines excited great enthusiasm in 1918. This was the raid upon Zeebrugge and Ostend in the early morning of 23 April. Its purpose was to neutralize the port of Bruges in German-occupied Belgium, lying 8 miles inland and harbouring a considerable force of U-boats and destroyers. The port was connected to the sea by a large canal with exits at Zeebrugge and Ostend. It appeared that if the exits could be blocked, the port would become unusable.

The driving force behind the raid was Roger Keyes, who had supplanted Bacon in command of the Dover Patrol. His purpose was to sink a number of his own light cruisers, loaded with cement and rubble, in the mouths of the canal. No one doubted that this would be a formidable task. The harbours were protected by quantities of heavy artillery, as well as by nets and such natural hazards as shifting sandbanks. Zeebrugge, the more capacious of the two exits, presented a further hazard. Some decades before the war the Belgians had created an artificial harbour by building a mole that came straight out from the shore and then curved east to cover the canal opening. This had been extended and heavily fortified by the Germans. So the blockships would have to run a severe gauntlet of fire from the sea before ever approaching their destination. To have any chance of success, they would need to approach under cover of darkness or smoke, even though that would increase the problems of finding the passage through shallows and sandbanks. For this purpose, smoke screens of a sophisticated type were developed.

Keyes's plan for Zeebrugge was as follows. The batteries on shore would be engaged by two large monitors armed with 15-inch guns. To neutralize the fire from the mole, other means would be employed. A force of marines and bluejackets would be landed on the tip of the mole from the seaward side and would set about putting the guns there out of action. And two submarines loaded with explosive would blow a gap in the landward end of the mole, so preventing German reinforcements from reaching their gunners. Thereupon three blockships would circumvent the mole, sail into the canal entrance, and sink themselves. (Small craft would be on hand to pick up the crews from the submarines and blockships. But as Keyes insisted that the crews of the blockships consist entirely of unmarried men, he plainly recognized that their lives would be much at risk.)

For Ostend, where no mole existed, the plan was less complicated. Monitors would engage the land defences. Small craft would lay down smoke screens in advance of the two blockships being employed there. After the latter had made their run and settled in the canal entrance, the small vessels would pick up their crews.

In all sorts of ways the day and hour of the assault had to be carefully chosen. The attack must be made at night, at high tide, and preferably without a moon. Twice in mid-April Keyes set out, but each time he was forced back as the weather changed against him. On 22 April he decided to try again. The weather report was favourable and the tides right, but he was now in the full-moon period and so dependent on favourable winds to carry his smokescreen inland. His wife assured him all would be well: with the coming of midnight it would be St George's day and 'St George can be trusted to bring good fortune to England.'

St George did nothing of the sort. As the vessels approached Zeebrugge, low visibility and a favouring wind promised well. But just before midnight the wind swung round, blowing back the smokescreens and revealing the incoming force to the Germans. The *Vindictive*, which was the vessel supposed to land the assault parties on the mole, came under punishing fire, which inflicted heavy casualties and put it off direction. It managed to get alongside the mole and was held firm against it by a support ship. But it was sadly out of position, so that the marines and bluejackets had the utmost difficulty in effecting a landing and no chance of getting at the guns at the end of the mole.

By contrast, one of the two submarines assigned the task of blowing a hole in the landward end of the mole was completely successful. It completed its run under heavy fire, crashed into the girders supporting the bridge, and disembarked its crew before exploding. This was only a limited accomplishment, as the German gunners at the outer end of the mole were not in need of reinforcements. But it did cut communications between the mole and the shore, leaving the gunners on the latter uncertain whether the approaching blockships were friendly or hostile.

Nevertheless, the leading blockship, as it rounded the mole, had to proceed in the full glare of searchlights and star shells and under heavy fire. In consequence, it fouled one of the safety nets and ran aground well clear of the canal entrance. But its journey did secure an uninterrupted passage for the second blockship, which managed to gain entry to the canal. The third blockship had an altogether more hazardous journey but also reached its destination. Hence two out of these three craft did achieve the astonishing feat of sinking themselves just about as directed. But that did not prove sufficient. In the positions where they had come to rest they did not effectively seal up the canal.

The attempt on Ostend was even less successful. Again the wind turned against the attackers at the crucial stage of approach, causing the smoke laid by the small craft in the van to blind not the enemy but the approaching blockships. Further, although light craft had laid markers to the harbour entrance, these were demolished by the German guns. So only a permanent marker was visible to the blockships, and this (by German design) had been recently moved from its correct place. In consequence, the blockships ended up on sandbanks well clear of their objects. (On 10 May another attempt was made on Ostend. One blockship did manage to sink itself in the entrance to the canal, but not in a position to prohibit its use.)

The raid on Zeebrugge on St George's day cost the attackers some 700 casualties. Among the wounded was Lieutenant Commander Hilton Young, whose handwriting at this time underwent an abrupt transition from the adult to the novice: having lost his right arm during the *Vindictive's* dash towards the mole, he had to master writing with his left hand. In material terms the rewards were slight. At no time was the movement of smaller U-boats in and out of Bruges affected. And in a few weeks, following the widening of the channel around the blockships, the Germans could employ Zeebrugge for their larger craft as well.

The only gain, from the British viewpoint, was a considerable boost to morale at a sorely needed time. It was believed that a great deal had been accomplished. And it appeared to seamen as well as to civilians that this was the way the navy ought to be going about its business. In other circumstances such a view could have proved dangerous, and Zeebrugge counter-productive. For it fed the delusion that the ultimate counter to the U-boat lay in 'offensive' action. It was to Britain's advantage that no further operations on these lines lay to hand.

Fresh measures against the U-boat were constantly being tried, with decidedly mixed results. In the Mediterranean the naval command actually deprived convoys of all but the barest sufficiency of protective craft so as to pursue 'aggressive' action. This consisted of blocking the Straits of Otranto with minefields and patrolling them in force. The object was to oblige U-boats on their way to the Mediterranean to make the passage on the surface, where they could be attacked. Geddes told the Allied Naval Council in February 1918: 'we think it desirable to devote more of our limited resources [in the Mediterranean] to attack submarines in the Straits even if that means to a certain extent reducing the number of craft on escort duty. . . .'[1] This was specious to an extraordinary degree. Britain's prime purpose was to keep its merchant shipping afloat, not to attack U-boats. And there was no real distinction between obliging enemy submarines to give battle when passing the Otranto Straits and when assaulting a convoy. The difference lay in the area of effectiveness. The Otranto policy proved a failure. It neither brought U-boats to destruction nor prevented their egress into the Mediterranean.

The wonder is that the Mediterranean convoys, despite severely diminished support, continued getting through almost unscathed. Yet this they accomplished. In the twelve months from November 1917, 11,509 ships were convoyed in the Mediterranean, of which only 136 were sunk. In addition, convoy escorts accounted for 8 of the 12 U-boats destroyed in the Mediterranean from mid-1917 to the end of the war.

(These aberrant views about offence and defence, it may be added, were not confined to Geddes and the Mediterranean command. In January 1918 Beatty was wanting to abandon the Scandinavian convoys, at least for the winter, so as to have vessels available 'to carry out more offensive form of sweeps and so deny the initiative

---

[1] Quoted in A. J. Marder, *From the Dreadnought to Scapa Flow* (London: Oxford University Press, 1970), vol. 5, p. 32.

to the Enemy which he most certainly holds at the present time'.[2] This piece of misappreciation does no credit to Beatty's judgement. During 1918 some 4,230 ships sailed in the Scandinavian convoys, of which a mere 15 were sunk – an adequate comment on the notion that 'the Enemy' held the initiative there.)

If the blocking operation at the Otranto Straits failed in its purpose, a similar undertaking nearer home enjoyed much success. On Keyes fell the task of completing Bacon's attempted closure of the Straits of Dover. By the establishment of a deep barrage of mines, constant sea and air patrols, and the provision of bright illumination at night, the Straits became unusable for enemy submarines. This meant that U-boats operating against shipping in the Atlantic had to spend an extra 10 days travelling to and from their destination by the longer northern passage. Given that a submarine's total cruising time amounted only to three or four weeks, these 10 lost days constituted a telling reduction in the submarine's striking power.

A devoted attempt was made in the course of 1918 to deny the Germans the use of the northern passage also. A mine barrier, part of it patrolled, was laid across the 240 miles between northernmost Scotland and the territorial waters of Norway. More an American than a British undertaking – 56,000 American mines were laid as against 15,000 British – it enjoyed no great success. American mines were ill-constructed. Whereas British mines, until a year before, had seemed reluctant to explode in any circumstances, those of the USA were quite likely to go off on contact with water. Further, the patrols were insufficient to prevent U-boats from passing on the surface. And the enemy took to evading the minefields by travelling illegally through Norwegian territorial waters. All told, this northern mine barrage probably disposed of six U-boats, as well as lengthening and rendering more precarious the passage of others. Such a contribution was welcome enough. But it hardly constituted an effective use of resources.

Overall, the destruction of U-boats – by mines, 'offensive' patrols, and 'defensive' convoys – was considerable but in no sense decisive. In the last nine months of the unrestricted campaign (February to October 1918) some 60 U-boats were sunk. This was below the rate of destruction for the previous six months, and less than the delivery to the German fleet of new submarines (which numbered 83). However, the cost to the enemy was higher than these figures suggest. Germany was losing its experienced crews and replacing them with others less well trained. What this signified is suggested by the fact that, of the 400 U-boat commanders employed in the war, a mere 20 of them achieved 60 per cent of all Allied sinkings.

But what had been true of the second half of 1917 applied equally to 1918. The declining effectiveness of Germany's attempted blockade by submarine was not primarily the result of the falling quality of U-boats crews or of Britain's mine barriers and hunting patrols. It remained, first and foremost, the achievement of convoy. A handful of statistics bears witness to one of the Great War's most compelling, and least bloody, weapons of victory. Excluding the Mediterranean, nearly 49,000 merchant ships sailed in convoy during the nine-month period February to October 1918. Only 120 of them fell victim to U-boats. In the same period and regions 357 vessels not in convoy were sunk by submarines.

During 1918 convoy was extended in all sorts of ways, and the failure of the U-boat correspondingly enhanced. To prevent the picking off of merchant ships before they joined a convoy or after it dispersed, the proportion of each journey spent under escort was extended. Increasingly, therefore, the U-boats transferred their attentions to local

---

[2] Ibid., p. 97.

shipping sailing independently on Britain's east coast. The Admiralty responded by implementing convoy for this category of vessel also. From mid-January 1918 over 16,000 merchant ships sailed in the east coast convoys. A mere 35 were sunk.

Coastal convoys, and also ocean convoys as they approached the British Isles, began receiving the additional assistance of air cover – at least during daylight and in fine weather. This had a considerable effect. Indeed, once a convoy was enjoying both sea and air support it became virtually immune from attack. (According to Professor Marder, 'Only 5 ships were sunk which had AIR as well as SURFACE escort.')[3] Aircraft did not manage to sink any U-boats. But they provided early warning of their presence. And they forced submarines travelling on the surface (so as to get into attack position) to submerge and so lose their quarries.

In May 1918 the German naval authorities made their only substantial effort to reverse the U-boat's mounting defeat by attempting a systematic assault on convoys. In that month they got as many submarines to sea as in their great killing time of April 1917. And they assigned a group of them to concentrate on the south-western approaches to Britain. By 10 May eight U-boats were on station. Yet on that day nine convoys passed through the danger zone without a single encounter taking place. This set the pattern for the following fortnight. On 11 May the U-boats scored their first success, but that was against a merchant ship that had left its convoy. On 12 May the tables were turned with a vengeance. Two of the U-boats were destroyed, one being rammed by a surface ship and the other torpedoed by a British submarine. The number of U-boats on the scene was soon restored to eight, and on 17 May they managed to sink three ships well protected by escorts. But those were their only successes against convoyed ships before the U-boat concentration dispersed, as it had done by 25 April.

For Britain this was one of the most telling episodes in the naval war. A force of 10 U-boats had concentrated, in what a year earlier had been one of their most lucrative killing grounds, expressly to engage convoys. The statistics of the outcome proclaim their failure. (These details, it should be said, are drawn from more than one authority, and there is no complete concordance between them.) Thirty-six convoys passed through the chosen area, yet U-boats made contact with only five of them. Put another way, nearly 300 convoyed ships made the transit for the loss of only three vessels. Even had the U-boats got off scot-free, this would have constituted a telling defeat. The destruction of two submarines out of 10 raised the whole transaction to the level of a calamity for the Germans.

It was not one that the Allies could proclaim aloud – if only because they dared not reveal to the enemy how well they were monitoring the U-boats' movements. But those in authority recognized only too well what had been achieved. Late in May French naval intelligence (which, along with the British, had been following the struggle through wireless intercepts) summed it up:

> To our knowledge this is the first time that the enemy attempted such an operation in compact formation. . . . Not only did these successive waves of submarines in close order fail to hinder the arrival of the convoys in any way whatever, but also the units in question were immobilized, so to speak, and completely wasted for two weeks, since in these waters, where traffic was very heavy, they succeeded in torpedoing only three steamers.[4]

The events of the war at sea in May 1918 are summed up with appropriate enthusiasm by the official historian. At last the construction of merchant shipping was

---

[3] Marder, *From the Dreadnought to Scapa Flow*, vol. 5, p. 114.
[4] Quoted in Robert M. Grant, *U-Boat Intelligence 1914–1918* (London: Putnam, 1969), p. 48.

exceeding the losses inflicted by the U-boat. And the amount of tonnage available was sufficient to the nation's 'tremendous military exertions'. Henry Newbolt writes:

During the last four weeks [i.e. May 1918], 192,330 British officers and men had been moved to and from the various theatres of war; 750,267 tons of military supplies had been carried to the British armies in France, 38,000 tons of stores and supplies had been delivered to the Allies. More than that, the transportation of the American armies was proceeding without a hitch and at great speed; during the same period 116,404 American officers and men, 1,914 animals and 20,221 tons of stores had been carried across the Atlantic. . . . British sea power was making its greatest exertion at its moment of greatest trial.[5]

III

In severely limiting the effectiveness of the U-boat and keeping the German battleships bottled up in harbour, the British navy was accomplishing all that lay within its competence. Whether the saga of the war at sea would contain one further chapter – a clash of the battlefleets – must depend solely on the enemy.

In the outcome the Germans elected to close this aspect of the conflict with a whimper rather than a bang. Only when all else had failed were their naval chiefs prepared to send their fleet on a death-or-glory operation. And by the time they had come to this resolution, they had passed the stage where they could carry it out. Rank-and-file German sailors, having been denied opportunities to risk their lives when it might have seemed to some purpose, refused to do so with the war clearly lost. So, while the men of Britain's fleet looked on with mounting disgust and despondency, the battleship war ran its course without any conclusion of arms.

In mid-October the Germans were forced to evacuate the ports of Zeebrugge and Ostend on the Belgian coast, scuttling a number of U-boats in the process. Then on 20 October, bowing to President Wilson's demand for the abandonment of attacks on passenger ships as a precondition for armistice negotiations, they called off the whole U-boat war against merchant shipping. This meant that the High Seas Fleet could once again make a sortie with submarine reconnaissance. The German command proposed to strike on 30 October. Light forces would carry out raids in the southern part of the North Sea, bringing out Beatty and the Grand Fleet. First the British would blunder into a trap of U-boats and mines. Then the High Seas Fleet would fall upon it.

Several days in advance the Admiralty became aware that something big was afoot. Destroyer reinforcements were hastened to Rosyth. And Beatty was alerted that 'it seems now absolutely clear that the enemy wishes you to come out to the Southward over a submarine trap.' However, it was not yet appreciated that the German command intended a fleet action.

In the end the High Seas Fleet never put to sea. During the 24 hours prior to its dispatch, insubordination among the crews mounted to a stage where it became impossible to go ahead with the operation. It was another week before the British authorities learned enough to draw an inescapable conclusion: that all prospect of a climactic sea battle had now departed.

For Britain's naval chiefs the prospect of so tame an ending was galling. And they were determined that if the German fleet were simply to call off the war, it should do so under the most humiliating conditions – so humiliating, Beatty and Keyes hoped, that the enemy would elect to fight rather than swallow them. Their demand was the surrender of Germany's principal surface ships and all the U-boats that could put to

---

[5] Henry Newbolt, *Naval Operations* (London: Longmans, Green & Co., 1931), vol. 5, pp. 277–8.

sea. Neither Lloyd George nor Haig was prepared to go this far. Unlike the naval chiefs, the Prime Minister and the principal army commander had seen battles enough. They felt no unfulfilled yearning for a good scrap. Nor would Britain's allies endorse naval terms of great stringency. Foch wanted to push the Germans as far as they would go on military terms and so proposed moderation in naval demands. As for the Americans, they were less conscious of Britain's maritime anxieties than of Britain's maritime pretensions – and so had no wish to present an intact German fleet to the principal 'associated power'.

Yet in the end matters worked out closer than expected to Beatty's demands. The Armistice, as drafted, required the Germans to hand over only their submarines to Britain. Their major surface vessels would be interned in neutral ports. However, at a late stage it occurred to the Supreme War Council that neutral Governments might decline to offer hospitality to Germany's naval might. So it was further stipulated that if this course failed, internment would be in Allied ports. In due course it became apparent that no neutral was prepared to welcome the High Seas Fleet. Britain therefore became the country of internment and Scapa Flow the chosen harbour.

This was still less than Beatty had demanded. Internment was not surrender. But it made possible a fairly spectacular coda to the sea war. Ten days after the signing of the Armistice, Beatty put to sea to receive the High Seas Fleet into his custody. An assemblage of 370 British vessels, plus units of the French and American navies, steamed out in full battle array. Just to be on the safe side, their guns were loaded and crews at action stations. Then the German warships approached, led by a diminutive British light cruiser. No final act of defiance emanated from the enemy command, and the ritual passed off without incident. It proved a sombre occasion even for the victors, who regarded as almost unnatural this passive capitulation by an unscathed opponent. At sunset, by Beatty's orders, the Germans hauled down the flags on their ships: they were 'not to be hoisted again without permission'.

Three days later, with winter fast approaching, the German fleet set off to experience what Beatty ironically referred to as 'the pleasures of Scapa'. There it would find, in due course, a last resting place.

PART THIRTEEN

Home Front
1918

57

HOME AFFAIRS

They are sending very young, untrained soldiers at once into the fighting line – the
need for men being so great.

Diary of the Rev. Andrew Clark, 12 October 1918

I

In many respects the story of the home front up to 11 November 1918 continues that of
preceding years. Themes that had been present throughout, or had emerged to
prominence in 1917, worked themselves out during what – in the expectation of few –
proved to be the last year of the war.

But the period from January to the Armistice also has a quality of its own, if only in
the intensity of events. There was at this time an alternation between nobility and
squalor that, if apparent throughout the war, was now evident to a special degree. In
the category of the noble or the creative one may instance the enthusiasm, early in the
year, for the educational proposals of H. A. L. Fisher. And, late in the year, there was
the decision to accord women the right to stand for Parliament on exactly the same
terms as men. This provision, which exceeded the greatest hopes of pre-war
reformers, theoretically entitled some women to become elected who were still not
eligible to vote.

A further instance of the creative side of British life in this year was the Exhibition of
British Scientific Products held at King's College, London, from 12 August to 7
September. Organized by the British Science Guild, it was intended to demonstrate
that Britain was now capable of producing a wide range of commodities for which it
had previously relied on Germany. Some 250 firms participated; over 30,000 people
paid for admission during the four weeks that the exhibition ran; and the conclusion
seemed plain that scientific industry in wartime Britain had made remarkable
developments.

On the side of squalor a high place must be accorded to the libel case in May and
June involving the right-wing MP Pemberton Billing. Billing published a journal in
which he purported to reveal the existence of a 'mysterious influence' that lay behind
'all the "regrettable incidents" of this war'. His actual intention was to gain notoriety
for himself by playing on the fervour of a puritanical society – especially at this grim
stage of the war – for tales of sexual irregularity in high society. For the prudish,
interest in such tales could be deemed permissible on patriotic grounds: these
salacious stories supposedly revealed the cause of Germany's successes.

According to Billing, there existed in Germany a Black Book containing the names
of 47,000 Britons, among them 'Privy Councillors, youths of the chorus, wives of
Cabinet Ministers, dancing girls, even Cabinet Ministers themselves', as well as

'diplomats, poets, bankers, editors, newspaper proprietors, and members of His Majesty's household'. Their names were in the book because they had engaged in sexual activities of a sort that 'all decent men thought had perished in Sodom and Lesbia'. Brought to trial on the grounds of libelling a prominent dancer whom he had impugned with encouraging such practices, Billing reduced the proceedings to farce. In the course of his antics he put into the mouth of his star witness, as appearing in the Black Book, the names of prominent individuals whose careers happened to be at a discount: Asquith, Mrs Asquith, Haldane, and the presiding judge. His frequent offences against the dignity of the court brought him no penalties. (It is not difficult to imagine, by contrast, what would have happened to a conscientious objector or a purveyor of anti-war pamphlets who had behaved thus.) When he was acquitted pandemonium broke loose in the court, and on his emergence he was mobbed by at least 1,000 admirers.[1]

Plate 52   *American troops crossing Westminster Bridge during a march through London.*

Among this year's most unlovely aspects was a frenzied campaign against enemy aliens resident in Britain. It is safe to say that those persons of German and Austrian origin who might have constituted any sort of danger, along with many who did not, had long since been interned or deported. Those who had escaped the round-up were mainly people whose lives were identified entirely with Britain. They included, according to a contemporary, 'many pitiful cases of Germans long years in this country, married to English wives and having sons fighting in the British Army. Some came to this country in infancy and have not since been back to Germany. A large number did

---

[1] For the quotations from Billing's writings and a lively account of the trial, see Joseph Dean, *Hatred, Ridicule, or Contempt* (Harmondsworth: Penguin Books, 1964), ch.1. It may be noted that Billing's star witness, Mrs Villiers Stuart, was not so fortunate on her next appearance in court. Three months after this trial she was sentenced to nine months' imprisonment for bigamy.

not know they were of German nationality until the issue of the alien regulations when the War began.'[2] These people were now to be subjected, as the only victims available, to a sustained campaign of Hun-hating.

Nor was it only enemy aliens who suffered. So indiscriminate did this outburst become that a Frenchman wrote to *The Times* complaining that the expression 'alien' should not be applied to people of his nationality. And the Press Bureau actually issued a 'D notice' urging newspapers not to apply the term 'aliens' to Belgian refugees, who had a 'great objection' to it. (A 'D notice' is an official request to the press to refrain from publishing material deemed not in the public interest.)

This outburst of xenophobia took many forms. Street names with German connotations, having been tolerable for nearly four years of war, now ceased to be so. Hence in May the Leicester Council, responding to a petition of residents, solemnly converted Hanover Street to Andover, Saxe-Coburg Street to Saxby, and Gotha Street (certainly a name inappropriate to the times) to Gotham. The Royal Society passed a resolution expelling enemy aliens from its membership. And as late as 25 September 1918, with the end of the war barely six weeks away, a crowd numbering 1,000 people demonstrated outside the residence of Sir Eyre Crowe, an official of the Foreign Office. They were prevented from forcing an entry only by the police. Crowe's alleged offence was that, although a British subject with an English father, he had been born in Germany of a German mother and had received much of his education in Europe. The demonstrators demanded his replacement by 'someone of purely British blood'. (Ironically, as a member of the Foreign Office from 1885, Crowe had followed a line decidedly unfriendly to Germany. After the war he would become a *bête noire* of some historians for his supposedly large part in the deterioration in Anglo-German relations after 1900.)[3]

Twice in London vast crowds assembled to demand strong action against the enemy within. On 13 July what *The Times* called 'the biggest crowd seen in [Trafalgar] square since the outbreak of the war' – in 'spirit and temper' it was also 'the most determined' – demonstrated against the supposed presence of huge numbers of enemy aliens on the loose in Britain. A mass meeting soon after at the Manchester Free Trade Hall took up the demand, and local councils at Liverpool, Newcastle, and other centres weighed in.

By late August a monster petition 2 miles in length and bearing 1¼ million signatures was ready for dispatch to 10 Downing Street. It received its send-off from a huge gathering in Hyde Park, and was escorted to the Prime Minister's residence by a procession of bands and banners accompanied by thousands of marchers. Lloyd George was not at home to receive this reading matter, but he had left with his secretaries an assurance that it would receive his serious attention. It is probable, in fact, that the Prime Minister felt little sympathy for this gross exercise in self-delusion. Yet he made a signal contribution to it by a statement in the House of Commons on 11 July. He claimed that there was never an occasion, when Britain suffered a set-back, on which 'I do not get anonymous letters written by Germans in this country crowing over it. The letters have British postmarks upon them. . . . the writers say they are Germans. Where are they? I feel that that sort of thing has got to be stopped.'[4] A more obvious incitement to spy-hunting fanatics to press ahead with the persecution of available victims could hardly have been offered.

---

[2] Michael MacDonagh, *In London During the Great War*, quoted in John Terraine, *Impacts of War 1914 & 1918* (London: Hutchinson, 1970), p. 184. Terraine's book, pp. 177–84, gives an excellent account of these events.
[3] For Crowe's career see Richard Cosgrove, 'The Career of Sir Eyre Crowe: a Reassessment', in *Albion*, vol. IV, no. 4, 1972.
[4] Quoted in Terraine, *Impacts of War 1914 & 1918*, p. 182.

But there was also a more profound sense in which, it may be thought, the Government contributed to this phase of unreason. The nation had passed through a terrible sequence of events – the reverses on the battlefield in March and April. It was entitled to expect from its leaders a clear explanation. None was forthcoming. From critics of the Government came dark suggestions that the military leaders had been let down by their civilian chiefs: the Maurice letter was only the most startling of these. From members of the Government there were pretty clear indications that they lacked confidence in the country's military commanders – and these intimations came not only from Lloyd George but also from Ministers such as Auckland Geddes and the lamentable Rothermere. But none of this bore fruit in frank explanations or strong, plainly appropriate actions. Even the question of whether the enemy onslaught had been fully expected or had taken the authorities by surprise called forth contradictory ministerial statements.

This meant that the responsible leaders were failing to take the nation into their confidence regarding events about which the community had a need to be informed. It may be speculated that the public, realizing that it could not afford to dispense with either its political or its military leaders, responded by indulging in wild action against token villains – action that was as deplorable as it was irrelevant to the nation's needs.

II

The home front during the first half of 1918 existed under the shadow of the great German offensive. Although the storm did not break until 21 March, it was common knowledge from the start of the year that big events were in the offing. *Punch* observed in January: 'already there is a talk of a German counter-offensive on a colossal scale on the Western front. So that Mr. Punch's message for the New Year is couched in no spirit of premature jubilation, but rather appeals for fortitude and endurance.'

But although the nation was prepared for grim events, it was no more geared than its military and political leaders for the setback that occurred. For three years the British people had been exhorted to hail as major successes what plainly were very limited advances. The scale of the German progress from 21 March did not lie within this frame of reference. Yet anxiety, and the sense of having been thrust into uncharted territory, never passed over into despair. The nation could, if only with an effort, jerk itself out of the pattern of thought established by the fighting of 1915–17 and cast its mind back to August 1914. And, indeed, it was the circumstances of that first 'great retreat' that came to the mind of many observers as they saw crowds of anxious people awaiting the arrival of newspapers and the posting of bulletins. In that earlier crisis the German tide, seemingly irresistible, had been stemmed. As the initial reactions of dismay and bewilderment passed, it became possible in these weeks of 1918 to believe that the same fate would befall this latest – and, surely, last – German bid for victory. So at Easter the Labour Party's most prominent figure, Arthur Henderson, stated publicly that, by their offensive, the Kaiser and the war lords had drawn the British people together in a consecrated and determined effort to secure the destruction of militarism.

Yet the crisis of March and April completed the war's erosion of glib notions about the inherent superiority of Britain's fighting men and the cowardly nature of their adversaries. Much crude nationalism was still in evidence on the home front. But it concentrated on the savagery, not the inferior fighting quality, of the enemy. So it was noted at this time:

The old Music Hall hits about anyone daring to tread on the tail of the British lion, or about a British Tommy being quite able to face a score or so of the soldiers of any other nationality no longer appealed. Audiences responded freely enough to jokes about the Kaiser or 'Little Willie' and they were prepared to laugh heartily at the discomforts of the fighting men; but patriotic fervour was not to be stimulated by singing or flag wagging.[5]

What was more, these setbacks in the field imposed additional and very tangible burdens upon a severely tested people. A further call must be made on the nation's males, and for this purpose a new Manpower Bill was rushed through Parliament early in April. At whatever cost to production, a 'clean cut' was introduced to munitions works and coal mines, removing all exempted males within certain age groups; above this age limit the more selective 'comb-out' operated. On the land those soldiers promised for temporary release to aid the harvest were withheld; instead, hitherto exempted men were called up. The manpower authorities secured the right to take men forthwith from certain occupations where hitherto they had been obliged to negotiate. For example, they could now remove school teachers without the endorsement of the Board of Education. Nor did the hunt end here. Youngsters, as they turned 18, became immediately liable for combat overseas. And the age of conscription was raised. It now applied to men in the category 41 to 50 years, and for those in particular occupations, especially the medical profession, it went higher still.

The new Act turned its attention to two other groups hitherto exempt: the clergy and the Irish. It proposed to conscript both, though the former only for non-combatant service. The decision about the clergy was reversed while the measure was still before Parliament. That about the Irish was not. In a sense this aspect of the Manpower Act scarcely belongs here, for it has less to do with the call-up of males for the British army than with relations between England and Ireland. The attempt to conscript Ireland completed the alienation of a supposed British possession that, even in March, *Punch* had admitted was becoming ungovernable. Possibly the provision did serve one positive function concerning recruitment. It may have made enforced service tolerable for middle-aged Englishmen who did not see why fit young Irishmen should continue to escape. But as a device for securing recruits from Ireland it was the most purposeless of gestures. (In the outcome, the measure was never applied. After all, as long as Britain was suffering from a shortage of troops, it could hardly afford – for whatever ostensible purpose – to open a fresh battlefront in Ireland.)

As for the suggestion that the Government might, as a corollary to conscription in Ireland, forthwith institute Home Rule there, this was a sorry mockery. For Home Rule could mean nothing if it did not grant Irishmen the power to decide something as basic as whether or not theirs would be a conscriptionist society. (This proposal also, in the event, fell by the wayside.)

The extension of conscription to men in the age group 41–50, by removing the 'breadwinner', struck hard at families that so far had managed to maintain a settled existence. In the nature of things, many exemptions had to be granted, for much of the key personnel in science and industry and business and government fell within this category. Yet the measure still had the effect of disrupting small businesses and established careers. This was pointed out in a letter to *The Times* by Wilfred Ashley and Josiah Wedgwood, respectively a Conservative and a Liberal MP. (The latter had served with distinction in the war.) They warned that vital export trades were being undermined and that a sense of injustice was being created. The well-to-do were gaining exemption because their work was plainly indispensable. The small man, the

[5] F. P. Armitage, *Leicester 1914–1918: The War-Story of a Midland Town* (Leicester: Edgar Backus, 1933), pp. 264–5.

traveller, the journeyman, and the shopkeeper were being taken from their homes to serve at 1/3d. a day. Yet their new job was not fighting. It was to serve in home garrisons against an invasion that was manifestly impossible, and 'to fill semi-civilian jobs as servants, batmen, clerks – jobs that discharged men or even women could often do'.[6]

Yet the men in the over-40 group were at least escaping direct contact with the enemy. That was anything but true of the fit men from essential industries whose exemptions had been withdrawn; and, not least, of the youngsters who were being not only sucked into the army but flung into combat the moment – if not in advance of the moment – the law allowed. A witness from these years, who early in 1918 was an art teacher, recalls that at one art school she was particularly impressed with the work of two young men (whom she judged to be nearer their middle than their late teens). When she returned to the school later in the year these particular students were not in evidence, and she inquired after them. 'They're both dead' was the chilling reply.

The war, it may be thought, had few greater cruelties to bestow on British civilians than this: that youngsters who were barely of secondary-school age when the conflict began would be lying dead in France in its last months.

III

If the war was making yet further demands on Britain's manpower, so it was on the country's financial resources. Bonar Law spoke of his Budget in April as 'a great taxing budget'. It sought to impose additional taxes of £114 million – though one of its provisions, a luxury tax, never came into effect. The standard rate of income tax rose by 1/- (from 5/- to 6/-), although with increased allowances for dependents. Farmers, who had been getting off rather lightly, had their taxes doubled. Super-tax was made more onerous, and a stamp duty was placed on cheques.

Other provisions of the Budget fell on a wider section of the populace. Both matches and tobacco were taxed more heavily, and this measure, combined with the fact that both commodities were in short supply, diminished the joy of the smoker. The duties on beer and spirits were doubled, at a time when the alcoholic content of both was being steadily reduced. The Budget also terminated the penny post: letter rate was raised to 1½d. (and postcard rate to 1d.). From one point of view, this rise merely brought the rate of postage in line with the level of earnings. But such an assertion is questionable. For the war was requiring the frequent writing of letters by families, especially among the working classes, who previously would have written but rarely, so that this was an impost placed upon an impost. To appreciate the change, it may be noted that during 1918 the post to soldiers in France every week consisted of 10 million letters and 350,000 parcels.

Another means by which the authorities drew money from the populace was through the war loan and the war bond. These were less onerous than taxation for the donors, who could expect their money back in time at a satisfactory rate of interest. Nevertheless, the sums that these appeals brought forth were prodigious and must, in some instances, have represented a forgoing of present comforts. Altogether between October 1917 and September 1918 war bonds raised £1,000 million. Various special appeals were made to attract this money. In March a Businessman's Week was launched with the endorsement of the King. Its aim was to raise £100 million, and within its allotted seven days that target was over-fulfilled. Some of the larger cities

---

[6] Quoted in Caroline E. Playne, *Britain Holds On 1917, 1918* (London: Allen & Unwin, 1933), p. 343.

staged a Tank Week, in the course of which a tank proceeded through the main streets. This also proved highly successful. The Tank Week in Leicester in January appealed for £1 million; it brought in twice that amount. It was duly followed by a War Weapons Week. Then, in October, to reinforce the Feed the Guns campaign, Trafalgar Square was converted into a replica of a shell-shattered French village. The statue of General Gordon disappeared inside a ruined church tower, and the ornamental fountain was absorbed into a shattered farmhouse.

> About 20,000 sandbags were used to make emplacements and trenches, along which the visitors walked to feed the guns with Bonds and Certificates. The breech-loaders and howitzers were ranged along the north side of the square, facing the National Gallery, and each War Bond purchased was specially stamped by a device fitted within the guns for this purpose.[7]

During the eight days that the village stood, £29 million was invested in London in war loan.

Plate 53   *Trafalgar Square transformed into a battlefield.*

IV

If on the principal battlefront much occurred for the worst in the first half of 1918, the British public even then could find some hopeful features. In April, which for *Punch* provided 'the darkest hours of the War', two events of at least symbolic importance gave a distinct lift to civilian morale. On the 21st Richthofen died. Two days later – on St George's day, as every commentator remarked – came the navy's daring raid on Zeebrugge, arousing wild enthusiasm quite out of proportion to anything achieved. These events seemed almost to make it true, as in so many schoolboy tales, that 'pluck',

---

[7] *Annual Register for 1918*, pp. 148–9.

'daring', and 'the Nelson touch' really could shape the course of events. *Punch* said of Zeebrugge: 'here at least is a magnificence of achievement and self-sacrifice on the epic scale which beggars description and transcends praise.' (Was there, even so, a note of doubt in this journal's remark that the 'hornet's nest. . . if not rooted out, has been badly damaged'?)

Also a source of comfort, the air raid was ceasing to pose the threat to Londoners that it had done but recently. The capital was raided on the night of 28–9 January, resulting in 58 dead and 173 injured. In one incident a bomb exploded in the cellar of an Odhams printing works, where 500 people were sheltering: the explosion and subsequent fire killed 38 and injured 85. Yet of the 13 Gothas and one Giant that had set out, only the Giant and six of the Gothas reached England. One of the latter was shot down, and four more were destroyed in crash landings on their return. It took the Gothas some time to reorganize, and thereafter they were fully engaged in the military offensive in France. That left only the Giants, never more than six in number, for use against London. They came once more in January, twice in February, and once in March, with negligible results. Then in May, sandwiched between offensives, the Gothas returned in force, causing nearly 200 casualties. But they encountered strong resistance, and anyway the German authorities in France could no longer spare them for such diversions.

This was the last appearance of the bomber over London. Against other parts of Britain air raids ceased at the same time. On three occasions in March and April Zeppelins attempted raids on the Midlands and the north of England. All told, they managed to kill a meagre 16 people and to injure 49 more.

One other attempted raid by Zeppelins, in August, deserves notice even though the raiders never got as far as the coast. Leading the attacking force was Peter Strasser, the driving figure behind the Zeppelin campaign against Britain. His airship, L70, was engaged by a British aeroplane whose pilot, Egbert Cadbury, had already been instrumental in the destruction of one Zeppelin. Strasser's death in the ensuing holocaust seems a fittingly symbolic end to the airship campaign against Britain. (It is less evident what symbolism lies in the fact that the one British pilot to bring down two Zeppelins belonged to a distinguished Quaker family.)

Another clear change for the better at home during this year occurred in the matter of food distribution – notwithstanding much continuing hardship. By the middle of the year the food situation had been transformed from that of January, when in Manchester 100,000 workers marched in protest to the Town Hall, and *Punch* (taking feeble inspiration from the reported activities of Q-ships) observed that for housewives this was becoming a 'queue-war'. Although in February Parliament remained agitated on this topic, by then the great improvement was commencing. Not only did local food committees exist throughout the country that could administer a rationing system, but also the basis of a system had been developed. Two steps were essential. First, the consumer must be provided with a document of entitlement – to begin with a separate card for each rationed commodity, then a comprehensive book of coupons. The second step was to tie consumers to particular retailers for rationed goods. Each retailer would then be supplied, by a specified wholesaler, with only so much of a commodity as was appropriate to the number of registered customers. In this way the holders of ration cards would be certain to receive their entitlement, and shopkeepers would be unable to supply favoured customers with more than the permitted amount.

On 25 February the Ministry of Food established a rationing system for meat, butter, and margarine in London and the Home Counties. Once shopkeepers had mastered the novelty of dealing with ration cards, the queues vanished. On 7 April all of Britain was required to have meat rationing of some sort, and in mid-July a uniform system was established throughout the country. By this time national rationing applied also to sugar, butter, margarine, and lard, while other commodities like tea, jam, and cheese might be rationed on the decision of local food committees. In some respects the system went out of its way to ensure equality. So all districts, however rich or poor, got equal shares of better-quality and poorer-quality meat, to be sold at one and the same price. And people who took meat meals at restaurants had to surrender coupons. In other respects it recognized inequalities. Children under 6 got only half the meat ration of adults, while adolescent boys and 'heavy workers' received extra allowances of meat.

So during the first half of 1918 Britain established a system of control over 'nearly everything eaten and drunk by 40,000,000 persons'. 'The civilian population [was] catered for like an army; nothing [was] left to chance or private enterprise.'[8] It was not only the enthusiastic Beveridge (who, in addition to being the historian of this course of events, was one of its architects) who believed that this accomplishment was extremely popular. *Punch* remarked in June that, now the Food Controller had got into his stride: 'the nation has begun to realise the huge debt it owes to his firmness and organising ability, and is proportionately concerned to hear of his breakdown from overwork. The queues have disappeared, supplies are adequate, and there are no complaints of class-favouritism.' When Rhondda died the following month this journal observed: 'It is to be hoped that he realised what was the truth – that he had won not only the confidence but the gratitude of the public.'

No doubt, as Beveridge does not try to conceal, this gratitude might have been less had rationing not seemed such an improvement on the miseries of queueing that preceded it. And what is yet more to the point, rationing in Britain was not, as with the Central Powers, a means of spreading evenly a great and deepening hardship. Soon after its introduction the value of the meat ration was raised. And bacon, thanks to over-production in the USA, became freely available. As evidence that the populace did not feel themselves seriously underfed – although examples of children plainly suffering from insufficient sugar and fats were remarked on – the fate of the supplementary meat ration is noteworthy. Under half of the men and adolescent boys eligible ever applied for it. And in Birmingham, of the 100,000 who applied for and were granted the extra rations, more than a quarter never took them up.

In another way local authorities assisted citizens in receiving adequate food – by the provision of national kitchens. Started in one of the poorer parts of London, these spread rapidly. By June, according to Clynes (who was in the process of replacing Rhondda), there were 535 of them, and by August 623. (Not all of them were in the less affluent districts.) These institutions were kitchens rather than restaurants in that, although they might have dining facilities, most meals purchased there were eaten at home. A typical kitchen is recorded as offering, at modest prices, a range of oxtail soup, Irish stew, potatoes, beans, bread, jam roll, and rice pudding: 'Using food-stuffs on the large scale they could prepare meals, in exchange for coupons, far more appetising and nourishing than a wage-earner's household could manage for itself'.[9]

V

Yet 1918 continued paradoxical. In other respects life on the home front grew more straitened and more anxious. With the call-up of miners and the demands of allies, the

---

[8] Sir William H. Beveridge, *British Food Control* (London: Oxford University Press, 1928), p. 2.

[9] R. H. Gretton, *A Modern History of the English People 1880–1922* (London: Martin Secker, 1930), p. 1069.

quantity of coal available for civilians decreased. Restrictions on its use, directly or as gas and electricity, mounted. From March, under what was dubbed the Curfew Order, restaurants and other eating places had to cease cooking meals at 9.30 p.m. and turn off lighting half an hour later. Places of entertainment must end performances by 10.30 p.m. In April tram and train services were curtailed further, and the cost of travel was again raised. By June the misery of train travel had reached a point where a mass meeting was held of those who commuted regularly to and from London. And, in other parts, Railway Travellers' Protection Societies were formed.

It was all to no avail. Further restrictions on the civilian supply of coal, gas, and electricity, and so further curtailment of public transport, lay ahead. From the middle of the year all of England and Wales came under a coal-rationing scheme similar to, but less generous than, that introduced for London in 1917. The Minister responsible frankly told the House of Commons that consumers of coal would have nothing like the degree of comfort they had enjoyed before the war. Again, it was the middling and more affluent householders who suffered particularly. The historian of the coal industry in the war writes: 'probably at no time has the very small consumer of household coal been better served with coal than he was during the period of control.'[10] But other writers tell of consumers having difficulty in finding coal dealers to register them and of delays in deliveries when they did get registered. By September even industry was becoming affected: on Teeside, shortage of fuel was reported as affecting the furnaces. Train services were reduced yet again, and travel on public transport, especially at rush hours, became yet more of a nightmare.

These discomforts, directly attributable to the war, did not complete the nation's misfortunes during the second half of 1918. At the same time it was being assailed by a fearsome epidemic. (In one city, during the last week of October, the wholesale price of hothouse grapes jumped from 2/6 to 5/- a pound, a sure sign of widespread malady.) The nature of the ailment was a subject of universal comment. On 26 October Holcombe Ingleby MP wrote to his son from Norfolk: 'If any of yr. household get the "flue", isolate the culprit & pass the food through the door! It is rather too deadly an edition of the scourge to treat it anything but seriously.' The next day, from Sussex, Robert Saunders wrote: 'Influenza is rampant in Sussex, nearly all schools round are closed & there is hardly a house that isn't affected.' When he had opened school at the beginning of that week, he related, he had found 92 pupils absent; so, after wiring the Medical Officer, he had closed the school for a fortnight. 'There have been several distressing deaths in the district, of mothers, who while nursing other members of the family, suddenly died of heart failure caused by Influenza.'

The epidemic struck first in June and was a major cause for alarm by July, when 700 Londoners died in a week, and miners in Northumberland and Durham had to be laid off. Then it abated somewhat, only to return ferociously in the autumn, when 18,000 Londoners died. Its depredations continued until the end of the year, and it did not disappear finally until the spring of 1919. Estimates of the total number who died in Britain of the scourge, from its first appearance until its final extinction, vary from 150,000 to 230,000.

Much unsettlement, as well as a good deal of downright heartbreak, was caused by this phenomenon during the last weeks of the war. In many areas apart from Sussex schools had to be closed. A medical officer in Manchester recalls children during a school inspection falling 'like poisoned flowers' across their desks. Attendances at church services and places of entertainment fell off markedly, and many districts

---

[10] Sir R. A. S. Redmayne, *The British Coal-Mining Industry During the War* (Oxford: Clarendon Press, 1923), p. 120.

seriously contemplated prohibiting such gatherings. The strain on the diminished body of medicos was acute. In Leicester a doctor called to 25 patients in one street wrote a single prescription and told the recipient to pass it on. In Stepney one doctor on his rounds 'jingled like a locksmith; always his pockets were stuffed with the latch-keys of houses where everyone was laid up.'[11] Undertakers were also burdened beyond their resources – although it was a French newspaper that commented, 'Having queued to live, now we must queue to be buried.' In Woolwich harassed undertakers had to call in soldiers to help them make coffins.

The origins and treatment of the disease baffled medical science. Sir Bertrand Dawson, physician to the King and to the British armies in France, announced after a lengthy diagnosis of a victim: 'I fail to see any explanation.'[12] Many aspects of its incidence remain, even today, decidedly curious. Where German soldiers on the Western Front were seriously afflicted, British soldiers there were not – although British soldiers in Italy decidedly were. Again, while it was claimed in the USA that fatalities were greater among the lower-income groups, this was denied for Britain. In London the residents of prosperous Chelsea and Westminster suffered as severely as the slum dwellers of Bermondsey and Bethnal Green. In the spa town of Bath the incidence was slightly higher than in industrial Birmingham. It was also noteworthy that, although most of the distinguished victims of the plague were elderly – among them were the composer Sir Hubert Parry and the actor Sir Charles Wyndham – the epidemic was not directed primarily against the aged. A considerable majority of its victims were under 35. The dead included Canada's youngest VC, aged 19, and Captain W. L. Robinson, the first man to bring down a Zeppelin on British soil, aged 23. (Robinson had suffered much as a – decidedly recalcitrant – prisoner in the hands of the Germans. He died soon after his repatriation.)

The scourge of the 'Spanish lady', as it has been called (although there is no reason for placing its origin in Spain), did not necessarily owe anything to the war. At the time the assumption was general that the disease had fertilized among the unburied corpses of the European battlefields, and was striking down people weakened by war's privations. But, in fact, it was a world epidemic, in a sense that the conflict of 1914–18 was never a world war. Even on the very rough statistics available, its principal victims were not in Europe at all. They were in Asia and especially India – the last-named country, according to one computation, suffering 12.5 million fatalities out of a world total of 21.5 million. In terms of percentages of population, India also led the way.

It is purposeless to speculate whether the British total of those stricken would have been different had the nation not been in the fifth year of a terrible war. The greater availability of doctors to civilians might have made a difference, although in the state of medical knowledge it is difficult to be confident. In peacetime there might have been more leeway for allowing people to rest and for preventing them from congregating. (The Armistice celebrations themselves are said to have led to a sharp increase in the death rate. A single church service of thanksgiving in a Cumberland town possibly caused widespread infection in an area hitherto free of it.) Yet there is no reason to doubt that, even apart from the war, the country would have been afflicted and many people would have died. What alone can be said with confidence is that the epidemic served as a further cause for anxiety and grief among a people who already had cause enough. It is one of history's ironies that the 'plague' struck just at the time when, in other respects, Britons might have been indulging in cautious hopefulness.

---

[11] Richard Collier, *The Plague of the Spanish Lady* (London: Macmillan, 1974), p. 240.
[12] Ibid., p. 20.

VI

It was late in the day before awareness dawned on British civilians that the war was fast approaching conclusion. No bells rang to celebrate France's second great victory on the Marne or the 'bad day' inflicted by British forces on the Germans on 8 August. (The expression is from *Punch*. If less graphic than Ludendorff's 'black day', it has the merit of being contemporary with events.) But perhaps, after the fiasco of the bell-ringing following Cambrai, it seemed inadvisable to presume again on the Almighty's favour.

Certainly, it was apparent by the middle of the year that the crisis of the spring was past and that victory had, for good and all, eluded Germany's grasp. Moreover, Britons had mounting and tangible evidence that an Allied triumph was only a matter of time. It was provided by the steady arrival of American troops. The fourth of July became in Britain the occasion for many Anglo-American ceremonies, as well as for demonstrations of hospitality to American servicemen. And deep regret was felt in August at the retirement, through failing health, of W. H. Page who, as American Ambassador, had striven throughout the war to promote the unity of the two nations.

Yet the promise of limitless reinforcements and the steady pressing back of the enemy did not point to a speedy termination of the war. As long as the Germans were just retreating across territory they had recently captured and still had the Hindenburg Line to fall back on, there was little cause for expecting their early collapse. Meanwhile at home the unceasing toll of casualties from the battlefield, the influenza menace, the darkened streets, and what was taken to be (with considerable exaggeration) an epidemic of strikes kept any tendency to exult in check. But at the end of August the capture of the Drocourt–Quéant switch revealed that the Hindenburg Line was not impenetrable. And in September, with the whole Allied line from the coast to Verdun on the move, a new timescale for the termination of hostilities began to suggest itself.

At home, it has been said, in grey weather and encroaching darkness, appearances did not differ. Yet the expectation that the war might be over by Christmas began to be voiced for the first time in years. And even people not inclined to excesses of optimism were prepared to admit that the situation was changing. In October, in an observation that must rank high in the annals of understatement, G. H. Roberts, the Minister of Labour, announced: 'the happenings of the last six weeks justify us in the belief that peace is much nearer than it was during the earlier part of the year.'

58

THE MOOD OF LABOUR

I

It would be satisfying if the historian could discern in Britain an ascending pattern of social unrest, labour discontent, and agitation against the war that commenced during the bleak year of 1917 and reached a climax in March 1918. The pattern, it could then be argued, suffered disruption as a result of events on the battlefield: the heavy military setbacks of late March and April 1918 restored Britons to full patriotic fervour.

The evidence, however, does not support this hypothesis. That there was mounting discontent during 1917 has already been established. One cause, almost certainly, was simply the strain being placed on the workforce by the length of the conflict. So the report to the Cabinet on the labour situation, at the end of October 1917, referred to the large number of strikes and disputes in munitions factories involving small numbers of workers acting for seemingly trivial reasons: 'probably in the majority of these cases the real reason for the stoppage is overstrain and the desire for a short rest, even if it lasts but a few days.'

There were other, more specific reasons for developing unrest during 1917, and these deserve recapitulation. One was the fact that the grim human toll of the war posed a threat to the well-being of every ablebodied male who had so far escaped active service. (At one remove, it also posed a threat to his family.) In addition there were food shortages and the resulting hardships of queueing; the rising cost of living and consequent lack of finality in any wage settlement; a growing housing shortage; restraints on the mobility of labour; and the further attack on real wages – and a particularly hard-earned section of wages – by the imposition of the income tax. These causes of discontent often gave rise to class-conscious utterances. One was the charge of profiteering. Another was the claim that there was no enforced billeting of migrant workers and soldiers on well-to-do homes, only on the homes of labourers. A third was the allegation that food shortages were unknown among the better-off: the *Herald*, for example, ran articles under the slogan 'How they starve at the Ritz'.

But these manifestations of class-consciousness did not, to any great extent, take a general form. Even at the severest periods of discontent there was no widespread tendency to describe the war as something created by, and in the interest of, the ruling classes. Nor was it being generally suggested that the proletarians of the warring nations should make common cause against their masters. At the end of October 1917, with regard to one of the most unsettled sections of the country (South Wales), it had still been possible to write: 'There can be no question that, as a whole, the mining population is sound and solid in its determination that Germany shall be defeated.' As evidence it was recorded that even in the South Wales village of Tonypandy ('a hotbed

653

of pacifism') a meeting addressed by General Smuts on war aims had proved a decided success. The attempt to organize opposition by the 'pacifist party' had failed. So large had been the audience that an overflow meeting had become necessary, and 'the streets were full of crowds equally enthusiastic, gathered to greet General Smuts.'[1]

So perhaps it is not remarkable that industrial unrest was on the decline even before the opening of the German offensive on 21 March 1918. For one thing, some of the specific grievances, if they could not be wholly remedied, were being mitigated. A concession to married men on the income tax took the sting out of the agitation, even if it did not quieten some prominent agitators – who, it was suggested, were unmarried. Even more effective was the Government's tardy resort to food rationing, which left-wing journals like the *Herald* had been demanding for weeks before its piecemeal introduction. This not only removed the physical discomfort of queueing but also met the charge that the wealthy classes never had to go without. The fact that meat rationing was by value, and not by weight, was recognized as depriving the better-off classes of a possible advantage.

There was also benefit gained from the Government's seemingly bungled measures of wage increases for engineers. Admittedly, discontent was caused by the manner in which a 12½ per cent rise was given to skilled men so as to restore differentials and then a smaller but still substantial rise had to be conceded to the less skilled. Yet in the upshot these arrangements helped to allay much of the unrest caused by the falling purchasing power of wages.

But underlying all this was the continued commitment of all sections to the view that the war must be carried on to victory, and that even disagreeable measures introduced by the Government must be accepted if they were necessary for its attainment. Only in this context did it make sense to say that a main factor in the abatement of industrial unrest was 'the firmness of the Government in the matter of its manpower proposals'.[2]

The report on the labour situation for the end of January reveals a waning in manifestations of working-class discontent. Opposition to the new manpower proposals was intense 'only among the younger members of the A.S.E.', whose attitude was 'much resented by the other unions' – and the latter's 'feeling of hostility [was] growing'. 'It is improbable that the man-power proposals are popular everywhere, but a feeling of loyalty to the nation exists generally, and it is being fortified by the opposition of what is termed "the autocratic union".' The Labour Party conference, it was also noted, had once looked like being a success for the pacifist, revolutionary, and ILP elements; but it proved 'a victory for the orthodox and loyal' sector. A week later the report recorded 'a considerable increase in the expression of support of the Government in the matter of the manpower proposals', even from quarters 'where opposition has hitherto been most pronounced'. The 'overwhelming bulk' of organized labour, it averred, was 'loyal and temperamentally conservative'.

The same sort of comment runs right through the labour reports for February. On the Clyde the general situation was deemed 'materially improved', partly as a result of press and government propaganda, but primarily on account of 'the national loyalty of the majority of the workers'. The penultimate report for February positively rejoiced that 'the unrest in the industrial world has perceptibly continued to abate. There have been no strikes or labour troubles of any importance.' And the final report for the month continued to find cause for joy:

Again abnormal quiet is reported from all parts of the country. Opposition to the manpower provisions has weakened everywhere, and on the Clyde, where the opposition

---

[1] Report on the labour situation, 31 October 1917.
[2] Ibid., 20 February 1918.

was in the first instance extreme, it is now reported that the Clyde Workers Committee have resolved not to call a strike in protest against the arrangements. As practically all the Workers' Committees look to the Clyde for a lead in the matter, it is clear that no concerted action to 'down tools' need now be expected.

Yet if a setback on the battlefield was not needed to bring about a transformation on the home front, it may still be true that events on the Continent, of which the great German offensive was only the culmination, helped to abate labour unrest. In the later part of 1917 the war really was beginning to look like a life-devouring stalemate, which held out no prospect of victory for either side. As such, it was being repudiated by the emergent forces within Russia. And it also appeared to have lost its attraction for significant sections within Germany. In a famous resolution the Reichstag espoused the formula of a peace without annexations and without indemnities.

Plainly, by the early months of 1918 all this was false. On the Eastern Front nothing was left of stalemate. The Germans had conquered utterly. Further, the forces that had come out on top in Russia's internal struggles were ceasing to look like appropriate models for reformist sections within Britain. The Bolsheviks were in the process of capitulating ignominiously to a predatory foe. And within the territories left to them they were establishing a regime that set liberty at nought and crushed movements for self-determination. These events did not pass unnoticed among British workers. It was observed that not even the leaders of the ILP were prepared 'to come out boldly in support of the Bolsheviks'. And late in March a survey of the labour situation in Scotland (which employed the term 'improvement' as a synonym for industrial quiescence) reported: 'The remarkable improvement which has undoubtedly occurred on the Clyde during the past two months has been attributed locally to the Bolshevik failure to stay the German advance.'[3]

As for the notion that any section of Germans would strive to hold their rulers to a peace without annexations and without indemnities, this was placed out of court by the response of the German parties to the treaty of Brest-Litovsk. As a Labour Party document, drafted by Arthur Henderson and imbued with a sense of disillusionment, put it: 'in spite of four years of warfare the German Socialists [are] not animated by any new spirit.'[4] So the report on the labour situation for 20 February 1918 could suggest that a main cause for Britain's industrial quiescence was the Brest-Litovsk negotiations and the 'chaotic position of the Russian Republic'. Regarding the first of these it said: 'It has been impressed upon the minds of all thinking men . . . that the German Government is just as much imbued with militarist imperialism as it was before the passing of the famous Reichstag resolution.' The action of the Russians in disarming and then negotiating had 'simply enabled [the Germans] to carry out their annexationist programme to the letter'.

II

These trends towards industrial quiescence culminated with the German onslaught in March. This halted virtually all industrial disturbance at home. Indeed, before long April 1918 was being looked back on as a sort of ideal time of industrial harmony. Resistance to the comb-out among engineers and miners evaporated. In the last eight

---

[3] Ibid., 23 January and 26 March 1918.

[4] Private and confidential memorandum by Henderson relative to the decisions of the Inter-Allied Socialist Conference of 20–4 February 1918, contained in the Minutes of the National Executive Committee of the Labour Party.

Only a month before, Ramsay MacDonald had told an extremely well attended meeting on the Clyde that the German Social Democrats would see to it that the Russian Revolution would not be allowed to go down.

months of 1917, 68,000 munitions workers had been recruited into the army, and in the first three months of 1918, 32,000. By contrast, just five weeks following 1 April produced 40,000, and by mid-July this figure had risen to 100,000. As for the miners, there occurred a positive rush to enlist on the part of young men who up to that moment had been seeking to escape military service – a movement particularly noted in the supposed pacifist strongholds of South Wales. At a national conference of shop stewards in mid-April, according to a labour situation report, representatives from Sheffield were reported as saying that the workers were 'war mad', and that 'men who had left jobs at £12 a week and accepted others at 30sh. a week in order to escape military service, were now anxious to join up.' The same source (which remained keenly on the look-out for manifestations of discontent) also noted: 'The proceedings of this Conference, past meetings of which have almost invariably led to serious trouble, may be regarded as significant, not only of the temper in this district [the north-west], but of that of the workers throughout the country.'

In the munitions industry, according to notes circulated by the Minister of Munitions: 'The response to the appeal to munition workers to work over the Easter holidays was excellent, and indeed almost embarrassing.'[5] Strikes in the munitions industry in April dwindled to vanishing point. And the report on the labour situation at the beginning of May observed that 'a threat to national security, such as has been experienced during the past month, suffices to reduce the extremist section to almost total eclipse. It may be that such an experience of national danger is required to enable an accurate judgement of the forces in the labour world to be formed.'

None of this meant that a condition of industrial benevolence would reign to the end of the war. Forces tending to produce unrest soon began to operate. By the end of June the sheer endeavours of the preceding three months were considered to be causing a reaction among some who had driven themselves hardest. Again, the emergency measures introduced by the Government to secure more men for the army meant that the call-up was now reaching older men, who had hitherto served as a steadying force; some were suspected of slowing down output so as to avoid becoming available for the army. And government measures in engineering appeared to be favouring dilutees over skilled workers, so reinforcing doubts among the latter as to whether their privileges would ever be restored.

Late in July (by which time it was becoming apparent that the German thrust on the battlefield had spent itself) there was a brief but serious upsurge of discontent among skilled engineers in parts of the Midlands and the north of England. The Government introduced a regulation – soon dubbed the 'embargo' – which in effect reimposed the hated leaving certificate abolished the previous August. The embargo differed in that it did not prevent skilled men from offering their services to fresh employers but forbade the employers from hiring them. Those affected were not impressed by the subterfuge. (Even some managers were suspected of trying to sabotage it.) Skilled engineers in Coventry and Birmingham downed tools – although, it was felt, with some reluctance – while other centres threatened to follow suit. This action was widely unpopular – even, it was reported from Coventry, among the wives of the strikers. The Prime Minister, spurred on by his Minister of Munitions (Churchill), issued a stern warning that men absenting themselves from work would be liable for induction into the army – an unprecedented direct use of military conscription as a strike-breaking weapon. But the Government also offered a committee of inquiry into the embargo scheme.

This combination of threat and cajolery was successful. A return to work followed

---

[5] Labour position in munition industries, 8 May 1918.

promptly, and the press lauded the Government for its firmness. Yet on the substantive issue victory lay with the strikers. Under cover of the promised inquiry, the embargo scheme was in effect abandoned. Skilled engineers retained their private-enterprise right to sell their services to the highest bidder, whether or not this was deemed in accord with national necessity. To the end the Government, even in the crucial area of munitions-making, was obliged to stop short of industrial conscription. As Humbert Wolfe laments: 'the last attempt to check the liberty of movement died when certain workmen ceased work at Coventry on the 23rd July 1918.'[6]

This has been deemed (by the same writer) 'the last serious strike of the war'. Yet two disputes subsequent to it deserve brief mention, if only because they occurred where stoppages were not expected. One was in the cotton industry, where (an official tribunal discovered) 'relatively to the cost of living the operatives are substantially worse off than before the war' – and so would remain, in that their week-long strike availed them nothing. The other strike, in the last days of August, was among the London police force. During the preceding four years the economic situation of its members had steadily fallen, both absolutely and relative to that of many unskilled workers. When asked by his superintendent why he was striking, one constable replied: 'We want more pay, Sir. I don't get sufficient money to keep my children in food and boots. My second son has just been called up by the Army and I have to go caretaking to keep out of debt.'[7] Another member of the force, recollecting the event in after years, said that when he fell sick in 1918 the divisional police surgeon stated that his condition was at least partly attributable to malnutrition. By the time the policemen's situation had deteriorated to this point, another issue had become involved: whether or not they had the right to belong to a union.

The police strike was widely condemned ('deserters' was the judgement of the *Morning Post*) but, at least in respect to wages, marvellously effective. The right to form a police union was not conceded. But at a hastily assembled gathering at 10 Downing Street on 31 August, the Prime Minister did agree to a substantial advance in pay, and also to allowances for the policemen's children and pensions for their widows.

Of greater long-term significance in these last months of the conflict, there was clear evidence in two major industries of an assertiveness that, though it might be held in check until the Armistice, was unlikely to remain so thereafter. On the railways sporadic disturbances gave warning of an approaching crisis over wage rates. And in the mining industry an increasingly radical stance was evident. In July the conference of the Miners Federation of Great Britain was considered 'remarkable for the extreme character of some of the resolutions which were passed':[8] among them were demands for a national system of wages (to replace the hated district system) and a thorough-going restructuring of the working week to the advantage of the miners. These, quite apart from the traditional call for nationalization, were frankly recognized by the delegates as involving the expulsion of the coal owners from the industry. According to an unfriendly observer: 'Ever since they were excluded from the Munitions of War Act, the miners have felt that they have the whip-hand of the Government, and have used their position to force concession after concession without encountering any effective opposition.'[9]

But apart from the miners, and to a lesser extent the railwaymen, these manifesta-

---

[6] Humbert Wolfe, *Labour Supply and Regulation* (Oxford: Clarendon Press, 1923), p. 234.
[7] Quoted in G. W. Reynolds and A. Judge, *The Night the Police Went on Strike* (London: Weidenfeld & Nicolson, c. 1968), p. 46.
[8] Report on the labour situation, 17 July 1918.
[9] Ibid., 7 August 1918.

tions of working-class discontent in the months following the German spring offensive had no on-going quality, and did not challenge the fundamentals of the industrial system. Generally they revealed a concern for established working-class rights, or constituted attempts by unmilitant groups – whose passivity was being taken for granted – to get a better deal. The latter applied to the cotton operatives and the police force; it was also true of women workers on buses and trams, who became resentful when males were accorded a wage increase that they were denied.

As such actions did not threaten industrial capitalism, so they revealed no falling-off in the determination that the war should be prosecuted to victory. In this respect 1918 saw no extension of the flickerings of hostility to the war that had appeared in 1917.

Various commentators at the time remarked on the warlike temper of the workers, even in areas where it was not always expected. The gathering of the Trades Union Congress in Derby, according to the report on the labour situation for 11 September, 'derived its importance in the opinion of the general public mainly from anticipation of its pronouncements on War and Peace, and from the indication of the views of Labour on these subjects which it was expected to provide'. The indications, in the opinion of this source, were not in doubt: 'it may be concluded with some confidence, from what actually occurred, that organised Labour as a whole is unshaken in its determination that the destruction of the German military machine is an essential antecedent to a satisfactory and lasting peace.' Even the official resolution, which was designedly non-committal so as to embrace 'men of extreme pro-war views equally with extreme pacifists', urged that peace negotiations should be opened 'only when the enemy, voluntarily or by compulsion, evacuates Belgium and France. Organised labour is therefore pledged to support the war, at any rate until this consummation.'

But it was 'incidental circumstances' at the TUC, rather than official resolutions, that seemed most to demonstrate the feeling of the members. There was the 'extraordinary enthusiasm' shown when the President announced news of the fall of Lens and Quéant. There was the especially warm welcome offered to the American Samuel Gompers, whose passion for war à outrance and hostility to any meeting with labour delegates from enemy countries were well known. And there were the telegrams of congratulations to the armed forces dispatched to Haig and other service leaders, and 'the loud and general cheers which greeted the replies thereto'. The writer of this report also picked up a pointer to political events of a few months later: evidence of discontent with the existing arrangements in the Labour Party. These arrangements were 'felt to allow excessive influence to a comparatively small, but compact and well-organised, "intelligentsia" clique'. The conclusion drawn from this was prophetic: 'The dissatisfaction which has been expressed at the Conference is perhaps an indication that the next General Election will disclose an absence of cohesion in the Labour vote.'

In October and November further evidence of the war-like mood prevailing among the workers was provided by another source. Basil Thomson, the Bolshevik-hating Assistant Commissioner of the Metropolitan Police, was at this time sending the Cabinet a fortnightly report on 'Pacifism and Revolutionary Organisations in the United Kingdom'. His report for 21 October detected little that was either pacifist or revolutionary:

My correspondents all over the country report the *morale* of working men to be now probably at its highest point. In Liverpool, conversation in the workshops is all on winning the War. 'We must give the German b[uggers] socks now we have got them on the run.' Even Shop Stewards have been heard to talk like this, but what is most interesting is that many who were formerly advocates of a round table conference, are now not only determined to beat the Germans, but also to make them pay the cost of the War, 'even if it takes a thousand years to do it'. They say, 'If the Government does not make Germany pay for the War, we (the workers) will have to find the money, and we don't see why we should. The Germans made the French pay in 1870, and they must pay now.'

It was observed that even those formerly prepared 'to find excuses' for the Germans were now justifying a demand for indemnities, on the grounds that 'this War has been fought more for the democracy of Germany than for anyone else. It will result in their emancipation: instead of being ruled by the Military class, they will rule themselves.' As the Germans were to receive these benefits, they ought to pay 'the market value'.

The prevalence of this mood, according to Thomson, was making things grim for the opponents of the war: 'A woman who is in close touch with the directors of the Women's Peace Crusade says that they have come to the conclusion that house to house visiting in the cause of Peace is useless, for the visitors are often subjected to abuse, and the doors are shut in their faces. They are, in fact, very despondent.' A dissenting report, he noted, was received from the Clyde. His correspondent there recorded opposition to the League of Nations, on the grounds that it would 'really be a "world capitalist combine" to shackle the working classes'. The same correspondent found industrial conditions on the Clyde 'fairly quiet at present', but he was anticipating a 'big upheaval' on the least provocation. 'He says that allowance is not made for the bad conditions under which the workers live. Many of the men go to work in the morning on dry bread. "This", he says "does not tend to make men run about the streets with Union Jacks in their hands, shouting for carrying on the War."' Yet Thomson's report of two weeks later (4 November 1918) suggests that even the Clyde had now ceased to be exceptional. He wrote: 'My Glasgow correspondent says that the pacifists, who were so very noisy a few weeks ago, are practically dead. . . .'

At the same time as this network of informants was sending what, from the Government's point of view, were such encouraging reports, the position on the industrial front appeared equally reassuring. In mid-October the report on the labour situation described it as 'abnormally tranquil'.

It may be concluded that, whatever slackening of feeling had occurred in mid-war, the last weeks of the struggle found Britain in the same mood as the first: a mood of committed, sometimes frenzied, devotion to the national cause.

59

POLITICAL DÉNOUEMENT

I

For some six months before the end of the war Lloyd George had been contemplating an early general election. Its purpose would be threefold: to confirm in power his coalition Government with its predominantly Conservative power base; to perpetuate the exclusion from office of the Asquithian Liberals (if not necessarily of Asquith himself); and to wage political war upon those elements in the Liberal and Labour ranks whom he deemed less than fully patriotic – or, anyway, less than enthusiastic about his Government. It was not intended to be a 'victory' election, because in mid-1918 victory still seemed a long way off. But its justification would be the promise that Germany's defeat, whether soon or late, would under this administration certainly occur.

Events outpaced Lloyd George. By the time the electoral register had been brought up to date and he himself had come to the sticking point, the end of the war was upon him. So, on the day after the Armistice, the Prime Minister held a meeting of those Liberal MPs whom he chose to regard as his followers. There he informed them – and, at one remove, the nation – that an election would be held forthwith.

II

The face of politics had changed markedly since, back in far-distant 1910, the nation had last gone to the polls.

In part the changes had been accomplished by parliamentary enactments. Under a wideranging redistribution measure, electorates – to an extent unknown in the past – approached equality in numbers of voters. (However, rural areas were still, by design, over-represented.) Again, many people hitherto denied the vote were now enfranchised. The Representation of the People Act of 1918 had raised the size of the electorate from 8 million to 21 million. This was achieved by several noteworthy changes in the qualifications of those entitled to vote.

In a couple of respects, it should be noted, the change was in the direction of lessening qualifications. Conscientious objectors, unless certified as having performed work of national service, were disfranchised for five years. (However, wives of conscientious objectors who might now be entitled to vote on account of their husband's local government qualifications were spared this obloquy.) The second class to suffer diminution – and who, unlike the first, were generally deemed to be Conservative in allegiance – were the plural voters. Instead of being allowed to vote in

660

every constituency for which they possessed a residential or business or university qualification, this well endowed section could now vote in at most two constituencies.

If opposition to war service temporarily cost some males the franchise, performance of combatant duties secured it for an exotic group. Under the new Act, the age of eligibility for the vote remained for males 21 years. But men on active service in the age group 19–20 were considered an altogether exceptional body, who had already established their qualifications as electors. (Servicemen in Western Europe could vote by post, those further afield by proxy.)

As against these relatively minor reductions and additions to the ranks of voters, electoral rights were now accorded to two large sections previously ineligible. Before the war four out of 10 males of voting age (although not always the same four) had been effectively disfranchised. Electors hitherto had been required not only to place themselves on the electoral register but also to remain in the same constituency – or, in the case of lodgers, in the same actual residence – for between one and two years. This arrangement excluded a great many younger, and in particular working-class, males. (A working-class male, it should be noted, was not necessarily a potential Labour voter.) Now the required period of residence was shortened to between six months and a year. And, of yet greater import, the notion of residence ceased to be a single dwelling place. It embraced the same, or even a contiguous, parliamentary county or borough. 'This provision meant in general that a man would have to move a long way to break his qualification'. It 'had almost as much to do with enlarging the register as any other clause of the Act.'[1]

The second major innovation in voting rights was the extension of the suffrage to females. In what was both a large step towards democratization and a clear refusal to carry the step too far, the vote was accorded to women aged 30 and above, as long as they or their husbands were qualified to vote in local government elections. (A local government elector owned, or paid rent on, a dwelling.) Again, war service produced an exceptional category. Women lacking, in their own right or by virtue of marriage, this local government qualification received the vote if they had joined the auxiliary services and had attained the age of 30. But servicewomen under the legal age, unlike their male equivalents, were not thought to merit this privilege. And the great numbers of female 'war workers' – in factories, the Land Army, government offices, and the nursing services – were (whatever their ages) denied any special expression of Parliament's gratitude.

The new Representation Act was the product of recommendations (usually unanimous but in the case of female suffrage only by a majority) of a Speaker's Conference set up late in 1916. Yet one of that conference's unanimous recommendations failed to secure enactment, possibly with large consequences. This proposed the institution of a system of proportional representation (PR) for the larger boroughs. Under it parties would secure members from urban districts proportionate to the number of votes they received. The House of Lords went further, resolving that this arrangement should apply to practically the whole country. But the House of Commons would have none of it.

On the other hand, the Lower House did propose – if by very narrow majorities – to introduce the alternative vote (AV) for single-member constituencies; which meant for all but a handful of borough electorates. Under this arrangement electors would vote preferentially, the votes accorded to the least successful candidates being distributed among the front-runners. That proposal failed in the Upper House.

---

[1] *The 'Manchester Guardian' History of the War* (Manchester: John Heywood, 1919), vol 8, p. 272.

So, in the words of The 'Manchester Guardian' History of the War: 'the irrational system of election was maintained by which a candidate could be returned representing only a minority of the constituency.' It did so in circumstances where the 'irrationality' of minority representation was likely to occur on an unprecedented scale, thanks to the changing face of party relations.

III

In certain crucial respects the position of parties vis-à-vis one another in 1918 was quite unlike what had obtained before the war. Most of all, the 'progressive alliance' that had ensured Asquith's retention of office between 1910 and 1915 had disintegrated beyond recall.

One of the three parties to the alliance, the Irish Nationalists, was now at death's door. On its home ground it was being entirely supplanted by Sinn Fein, the party of Irish separation. The Sinn Feiners refused to associate with any British party or, indeed, to occupy such seats as they might win in the Parliament at Westminster.

A second of the three parties to the progressive alliance was in the process of being riven in two. (This was quite apart from its dissensions over matters like pre-war diplomacy, wartime intrusions upon individual liberty, and post-war economic policy.) Primarily, this impending rupture was the consequence of Lloyd George's determination to perpetuate into peace, and ultimately to render permanent, the fissure within the Liberal ranks resulting from the events of December 1916: the supersession of Asquith as Prime Minister and Asquith's refusal to serve in a Lloyd George ministry. Much animosity had been generated in the party, and especially in its top echelons, by these events. And Asquith's indignant rebuffs to subsequent attempts to draw him into Lloyd George's Government, along with the brief fracas of the Maurice debate, had done nothing to assuage ill-feeling.

Yet there was no hard-and-fast line of ideology and policy, certainly regarding the peace settlement and the post-war world, to render this division permanent. The wartime split in the Liberal Party would carry over from war into peace only should one or more of the men at the top find advantage in making it do so. What became increasingly evident as victory approached was that one key man – Lloyd George – saw the utmost advantage in accomplishing this.

The Prime Minister's decision was to have a powerful effect on the condition in which the Liberal Party faced the end-of-war world. In 1914 the Liberals had been one of the two securely established parties that vied for office. When not His Majesty's Government, they had assuredly been His Majesty's Opposition. The fact of being either the party in government or the only prospective alternative Government had proved a huge asset – especially at general (as distinct from by-) elections. The events of November 1918 robbed the Liberal Party of this asset. One section of Liberals, including its most eminent figure, had become an adjunct to the now dominant, and still impressively united, Conservative Party. The other section, including the party's official leader, had become so demoralized, so uncertain of its position in the political spectrum, and so conscious of impending disaster that it was not even pretending to challenge Lloyd George's occupancy of office.

This signalized an astonishing fall. Three and a half years before, Asquith and his associates had been rulers of the country. Yet by November 1918 Asquith was telling the electors that he was not even attempting to unseat the existing Government. So, just as Lloyd George was confirming his own movement from the left wing to the right wing of the political spectrum, the official Liberals were failing even to bid for recognition as the nation's alternative rulers.

IV

Yet the position of opposition to the dominant Conservative Party had not fallen vacant. For, at this very time, the third party to the now defunct progressive alliance was making a determined bid to occupy the place of alternative Government.

Between late 1917 and mid-November 1918 the Labour Party took a series of decisions that gave public notice of this determination. Its actions cut it off from all other parties and established its ambition to function as a national party in its own right. It set itself the goal of at least 500 candidates at any forthcoming general election. It adopted distinctive policies on the peace settlement and on internal reconstruction, including a (highly generalized) endorsement of a socialist objective. While the war was still proceeding it repudiated the party truce in by-elections. And, close upon the Armistice and Lloyd George's announcement of a general election, it took the culminating step of breaking with the coalition Government and standing forth as an independent party in its own right.

This meant that instead of contesting, as in 1910, only a few score of seats, most of them by arrangement with the Liberals, Labour intended to fight every constituency where it could mount a campaign and produce a candidate. The possibility that, in so doing, it might on many occasions be handing probable Liberal seats – and, by provoking retaliation, probable Labour seats – to the Conservatives on a split 'progressive' vote was not regarded as any sort of constraint.

It may be the case that, already before the war, the political Labour movement was approaching this condition of independence; and that, even without the war's upheavals, the Labour Party would eventually have got the better of the Liberals. That issue cannot be reviewed here. But it would hardly seem to be in doubt that, on the most modest appraisal, the events of 1914–18 markedly influenced the timescale (whether or not it influenced the ultimate course) of events.

The war, for example, called in question widely held assumptions about the special fitness to govern of the established ruling groups. Their presumed qualifications seemed difficult to reconcile with such cataclysmic events as the unheralded plunge into conflict, the humiliations sustained by British arms in far-off places, the ill-rewarded bloodbaths across the Channel, and some of the squalid aspects of wartime diplomacy. The Labour journal the *Herald*, for one, saw this as evidence that the days of the nation's established rulers should end. In November 1917 it proclaimed: 'Liberal, Coalition and Lloyd George Governments have failed – then let Labour try its hand.'

Again, wartime stress on equality of sacrifice, and even on the equal rights of citizens to a basic minimum of food, seemed to invalidate the once accepted deprivations and inequalities of the pre-war world. Awareness of these anomalies was reinforced by the war's demonstration of the essential role that labour must play if the nation was to survive. As the left-wing academic G. D. H. Cole observed in June 1919: 'never before has the extent to which the whole community depends upon the working class been so fully realised, either by the other classes *or by the workers themselves.*'[2]

As Cole's use of emphasis suggests, these changing perceptions of the wage earner's place would influence politics only when entertained by the labouring classes

---

[2] *Daily Herald*, 30 June 1919, quoted in Julia Bush, *Behind the Lines: East London Labour 1914–1919* (London: Merlin Press, 1984), p. 195.

themselves. And there is much evidence for his view that this was becoming more the case. One manifestation was the mounting enrolment of wage earners (and their membership would not prove transitory) in trade unions. Between 1914 and 1918 union membership rose from 4 million to 6.5 million. Of particular significance was the fact that the largest proportionate increases occurred among those hitherto least responsive: the most poorly paid (including females).

This burgeoning of trade union membership was accompanied by mounting political awareness within the trade union movement. The politicization of the unions was a complex process, with no inevitable follow-through from growing numbers of unionists to rising adherence to the Labour Party. But these years required of organized labour much participation in social problems arising from the conflict. This was a form of activity that bridged the gap between social action and political involvement.

War-induced issues claiming the attention of working-class organizations included: rent increases; relief of those affected by dislocations of trade; the administration of separation allowances to the families of servicemen and of pensions to the families of the dead and maimed; the claims of those seeking exemption from military service; and (above all) matters relating to rising prices and scarcity of commodities. The fact that, when queueing was at its peak, the requisitioning and rationing of food was widely instituted by municipalities in advance of any action by the central government owed much to the pressure of labour representatives. This was exercised in part through their membership of committees instituted at the levels of local and central government. But it was also made effective through such bodies as the War Emergency Workers National Committee and the network of offshoots of trade unionism known as the trades councils – described by their historian as 'spokesmen and representatives of working people on a wide range of political and social issues', including 'all matters relating to the welfare of the poor'.[3]

This involvement of working-class organizations in questions of social administration – not to mention their frequent dissatisfaction at the way things were turning out – constituted an important element in Labour's emergence as a party aspiring to rule. From 4 August 1914 there were potential rifts in the Labour movement over foreign policy matters, ranging from Britain's involvement in the war to the desirability or otherwise of trying to negotiate a peace. But, simultaneously, social questions were emerging that closely affected working-class welfare, and upon these Labour's 'patriots' and 'pacifists' could co-operate effectively and conspicuously. The outcome was an evident growth of political involvement among sections of organized working people. As one of the key figures in London Labour politics, Herbert Morrison, put it in March 1918: 'We do not remember a time when there was so much enthusiasm of the right sort in the London Labour Movement. If we can only steel ourselves against red herrings and hot-heads, and we can only determine that we will get down to detailed organisation as well as rejoice in the contemplation of great ideals – heaven help the capitalist foe!'[4]

This process is well summed up (from an intensive study of one segment of working-class Britain) by Julia Bush. The war, she writes, had certainly produced no fundamental transformation of British society. But the 'only too obvious absence' of such a transformation was 'a prime reason for Labour voting'. For it existed alongside a major change in the level of popular expectations.

---

[3] Alan Clinton, *The Trade Union Rank and File: Trades Councils in Britain, 1900–40* (Manchester: Manchester University Press, 1977), p. 4.
[4] Quoted in Bush, *Behind the Lines*, p. 85.

Social inequality had been spot-lighted. So too had the power of government to take ruthless and effective action in chosen directions. Most important of all, a new political leadership for working people had acquired the conviction, experience, funds and organisation which it needed to challenge the existing parties.

With particular regard to the dismal East London area – once so impervious to the activities of trade union recruiters and social reformers – Dr Bush writes:

> Labour Party re-organisation during the final year of the war was not primarily the outcome of the national leadership's decisions on policy and party structure. It is important to recognise that such decisions reflected, rather than caused, important changes in the labour movement and in working class attitudes at local level. It is no coincidence that the raw material for building strong new constituency Labour Parties lay ready to hand in East London. This was the result of patient local political activity throughout the war, as well as of increasingly receptive public opinion in 1917–18.[5]

V

The disintegration of the Liberal Party and the collapse of the Irish Nationalists proclaimed themselves in the election results.[6] The emergence of Labour as a major force did not – except to those who noticed how often a Labour candidate, when failing to win a seat, came second on the poll, so relegating the Liberal to third place.[7] It would require the local government elections of 1919 and the general election of 1922 to establish Labour's success in bidding for the position of alternative Government. (Its bid to become the actual Government, with a majority of seats in the House of Commons, would prove a good deal longer in coming. In the short term, given the absence of the alternative vote, the chief beneficiary of Labour's refusal to make electoral pacts with the Liberals would be – as the *Manchester Guardian* had foreseen – the Conservatives. They reaped a rich harvest in constituencies won on minority votes.)

Certainly, in the context of November–December 1918 Labour's moment was not at hand. For this was Lloyd George's day – or, rather, the Conservatives' day, with Lloyd George their willing ally, instrument, and spokesman. His arrangement with the Conservatives for the continuance of the coalition into and beyond this election constituted a frank endorsement of their political dominance at the parliamentary level. This was evident in the timing of the election (which made sense only if a Conservative victory was intended); in the candidates (a large majority of whom were Conservatives) receiving the Prime Minister's imprimatur; and in his bargain with Bonar Law over sensitive policy matters (such as imperial preference, the postponement of Irish Home Rule, and financial compensation to the Church of England in Wales).

This calculation by the Prime Minister regarding his political future appears prudent – anyway if his pre-war stance on the radical side of politics be overlooked, and if the success of his manoeuvre be judged only in the short run. (Judged in terms of his repudiation at the hands of his allies four years later, a different conclusion may

---

[5] Ibid., pp. xxii, 85.

[6] The results for the principal groups were as follows:
(i) on the Government side, Conservatives 384, Lloyd George Liberals 138, Coalition Labour 14;
(ii) on the Opposition side, Labour 58, Asquithian Liberals 27, Irish Nationalists 7;
(iii) on neither side, Sinn Fein 73.

[7] There were altogether 144 single-member constituencies contested by Liberals (couponed or uncouponed), Conservatives, and Labour candidates. (In a few of these there were also Independents who did so badly that they do not muddy the picture.) The Liberals won only 12 and came second in but 40. They came third on 92 occasions. For the Liberals this was probably the most calamitous, and for Labour the most hopeful, feature of the election results.

suggest itself.) In an election at this moment fought in association with the Conservatives, he could not lose. Had he chosen, instead, to terminate his wartime Government as having served its purpose and to resume a purely Liberal stance, it is hard to believe that his manna could have secured a majority for a discredited, even if reunited, Liberal Party. It is hardly necessary to recall the fate of Winston Churchill in 1945 at the head of a discredited Conservative Party to appreciate this. There are no grounds for believing that, single-handed, Lloyd George in 1918 could have carried to victory any Government, irrespective of its party composition.

This was not how it seemed at the time; nor how it would be portrayed for many years thereafter. To all appearances, whatever happened politically in these weeks occurred because the Prime Minister willed it: political parties prospered or disintegrated at his touch; the electorate danced to his bidding; matters of great moment appeared at one instant in elevated form and the next were relegated to the gutter.

Two aspects of Lloyd George's behaviour gained a particular notoriety. One was what Asquith dubbed his use of a political coupon. The coupon was a letter signed jointly by Lloyd George and Bonar Law and addressed to selected candidates throughout the country. It told the recipient that he or she had the coalition's blessing. Hence any other candidate fighting in the same constituency fell – by implication and soon very explicitly – under the Prime Minister's ban. This letter seemed to dictate the outcome of the election. A great majority of these *billets doux* went to Conservatives; Liberal recipients were in a decided minority. When the results were announced it transpired that the Conservatives had won a massive victory. As for the Liberals, only the recipients of the coupon enjoyed any measure of success. Liberal candidates lacking this endorsement, including many probably well disposed to the Prime Minister, suffered almost total rejection.

The other aspect of the election that rendered it notorious was the Prime Minister's handling of issues of policy. When addressing his Liberal followers on 12 November he had spoken like the Lloyd George of old. He had placed himself firmly on the left of politics: 'Revolution I am not afraid of. Bolshevism I am not afraid of. It is reaction I am afraid of.' He had taken his stand unswervingly with the cause of Liberalism: 'I was reared in Liberalism. . . . I am too old now to change. I cannot leave Liberalism.' He had proclaimed a policy of wideranging social reform, adherence to free trade, and Home Rule for Ireland (excluding Ulster). And regarding the peace terms he had come down firmly against a settlement patterned on that of 1871, which had been dictated by a sense of revenge and greed. Rather, the peace must embody the doctrines of righteousness: 'a settlement which would be fundamentally just' and would point towards 'the reign on earth of the Prince of Peace'. (Asquith called this 12 November utterance a perfectly clear and satisfactory exposition of Liberal policy, in no way impairing Liberal unity. It would be the last time he praised his former lieutenant for quite a while.)

The manner in which Lloyd George closed the election was altogether different. Indeed, in the course of the campaign he all but ran the gamut of political positions. Social reform, after rising to dazzling insubstantialities ('a fit land for heroes to live in'), all but vanished from sight. The peace settlement became a vehicle for an orgy of Hun-hating, with Germany's conduct towards France in 1871 now translated into a model to be followed. ('When Germany defeated France she made France pay . . . . that is the principle we should proceed upon.') There were no more protestations of his fidelity to Liberalism. Electors were told to investigate 'ruthlessly' the claims of Liberals (outside his chosen group) to be supporters of his Government. And Asquith and his associates were likened to German soldiers who first sniped at, gassed, poisoned, and machine-gunned British troops and then cried, 'Comrade.' Nor did Lloyd George remember for long that it was 'reaction', not 'revolution', that he feared. The communist bogey was trotted out in his final election speech, during which the leaders of the Labour Party were denounced as a 'Bolshevik group' who had taken Labour out of his Government because 'what they really believed in was Bolshevism.'

Not surprisingly, this unbridled style of electioneering, coming together with his novel electoral arrangement regarding candidates, riveted attention. That, in short order, Asquith and all his leading colleagues had been swept from the Commons; that the parliamentary Labour Party should lose many of its leading members and make painfully little of the anticipated headway at the polls; that the only Liberals to retain their seats in any numbers were his couponed followers; and that the Conservatives should take unchallengeable control of the Lower House – all this seemed the product of the Lloyd George coupon and Lloyd George's demagoguery.

Yet that appearance was quite misleading. The outcome of the election had been foreshadowed well in advance of these events. From early 1915, by which time it had become evident that the war was going to be long and arduous, the whole trend of politics had been towards a convincing Conservative victory whenever the nation polled. The parties to the former progressive alliance were bound to suffer electorally from their pre-war hostility to large-scale rearmament, their wartime resistance to the introduction of conscription, and their insufficient enthusiasm, regarding the post-war world, for harrying aliens at home and milking the defeated enemy abroad. The discredit of Liberals and Labour was simply underscored by the fact that the war-winning Government proved predominantly Conservative, and that their own leaders had (in December 1916 and August 1917 respectively) been expelled from office. Whatever the issues presented to the electorate and whatever the utterances of the men at the top, the outcome of an election in the immediate aftermath of this war could hardly be other than a Conservative victory. Everyone remembered the Khaki election of 1900, and accepted that another contest similarly timed would have an identical result.

Lloyd George's conduct made sense in this context. He wanted to stay in power by making common cause with the Conservatives. But he did not care to become their puppet. And he was concerned to safeguard the future of his association with them. The best way, apparently, of doing so was to provide himself with a strong bargaining counter: a solid body of his own Liberal adherents in the new House of Commons. The Conservatives had good reasons for consenting. As director of a victorious war, Lloyd George was a national leader of commanding stature. And his adherence to the present arrangement of parties would complete the discomfiture of the Liberals and would help to stem the pretensions of Labour. So the deal was struck. To the extent that Conservative headquarters could arrange it, about 150 Liberals designated by Lloyd George would contest the election free of Conservative opponents. That is, any swing to the right on the part of the electors would in these constituencies come to rest upon the Lloyd George Liberals – which is the explanation, far more than the receipt of the 'coupon', for their great measure of success.

But Lloyd George yielded, as the price of securing these safeguards, all the points that really mattered: his concessions on policy issues like imperial preference and the postponement of Irish Home Rule; and, above all, his explicit commitment to a House of Commons with a Conservative majority. That he should then go on to denounce the Liberal and Labour parties was simply to accept the logic of what he had surrendered. The thing that made his platform performances during the campaign appear aberrant was their contrast with the 'idealistic' address he had delivered to the gathering of selected Liberals on 12 November. But that had been intended to serve a particular, and non-recurring, purpose. Among those present were 'good' Liberals like H. A. L. Fisher, who wanted to go along with him but doubted the propriety – in Liberal terms – of such a course. It was necessary to assuage their consciences. Lloyd George accomplished this by his heartfelt assurances that he would never leave Liberalism, and by his promises of major social reforms and 'the reign of peace'. More significant, in fact, than anything he said on that occasion was what he did not say: his silence concerning the bargain already struck over candidates, which entailed the proscription of a majority of Liberals and a proposed Conservative dominance in the new Parliament.

Once his 12 November address had served its purpose by securing endorsement for his proposed course, it was for Lloyd George a matter of taste and circumstance whether he returned to or abandoned the themes then foreshadowed. There was an element of consistency here. On almost every occasion, his utterances concerning the peace settlement were adjusted to the composition of his listeners. When he had spoken to trade unionists on this matter back in January 1918, he had taken the line of President Wilson. When he addressed a predominantly 'patriotic' and affluent audience at the Lord Mayor's Banquet on 9 November, he stressed the punishment that Germany so deeply merited.[8] Speaking (as we have seen) to his Liberal supporters three days later, he appealed for their aid in resisting those forces at home that would seek to bully him into pursuing a course of revenge and greed, so betraying the strict principles of right. Thereafter, during the election campaign, he found himself increasingly among 'bullying' audiences eager to hear him speak about revenge and greed: and he had no difficulty in satisfying them. So he promised to expel every enemy alien from Britain, to punish the Kaiser, and to demand from Germany 'the whole cost of the war' – 'we shall search their pockets for it.'

In a measure, what these oscillations were doing was exposing the terrible ambiguity that would confront any attempt to make a viable peace settlement. The placing of severe restraints upon manifest wrongdoers and the levying of recompense for their victims constituted one, totally warranted, side of the coin. Reconciliation with the vanquished, and a bid to establish a stable German democracy, constituted the other side. Even a master-expositor like Lloyd George could hardly, in the heat of an election campaign, have achieved a perfect balance between these rival aspects – assuming, which is highly doubtful, that any point of balance actually existed. What was culpable about his conduct was his evident lack of concern even to seek for some type of balance; and his almost perverse demonstration that – within the parameters set by his chosen political arrangements – what he would say about the peace settlement would be whatever his audience of the moment wanted to hear.

VI

In his conduct of November and December 1918 Lloyd George dealt his reputation irreparable damage. This was not immediately evident. He had achieved his short-term objectives. His adversaries, actual or designated, in the Liberal and Labour parties were routed. Their leaders, Asquith and Henderson, along with eminent colleagues like Simon and McKenna and MacDonald and Snowden, would have no seats when the new Parliament assembled. The old Liberal Party had gone, to all appearances beyond recall. And the new Labour Party, anyway in the House of Commons, was far from having acquired an elevated stature. Rather, it would be so

---

[8] See below, pp. 831–2.

weak in debating talent as to appear a shadow of its predecessor. Lloyd George's supporters had fared differently. His group of nominated Liberals had been elected almost to a man. And a great company of Conservative MPs securely occupied the Government benches.

But all this meant that, henceforth, Lloyd George and his Liberal followers would be dependent on the suffrance of their one-time enemies. A withdrawal of Conservative support in Parliament and the intrusion of Conservative candidates into their constituencies would leave them helpless. Once Lloyd George's accomplishments as war director ceased to count for much and the nation confronted difficulties at home and abroad, his usefulness to his allies might wane. For it would become evident that he was no longer needed to keep the Liberal Party in its diminished circumstances, and that the Conservatives could check Labour's advance without the dubious aid of the Coalition Liberals. Lloyd George then would have nothing to fall back on except an appeal to Conservative gratitude for past services. And a Prime Minister whose own loyalty to persons and parties and principles had seemed so insubstantial in 1918 might find that such an appeal aroused little response.

In a wider context, Lloyd George's conduct in the coupon election grievously undermined his standing as a statesman. He had promised to establish 'a fit land for heroes' and to make Germany 'pay to the uttermost farthing'. Neither promise was fulfilled; if only because, in the state of the post-war British economy and in the absence of an on-going will to impose a severe peace, neither promise was fulfillable. But the promises would be remembered: in the one case as describing the sort of better world that should have emerged from the war and did not; in the other as evidence of the lengths to which a vote-seeking demagogue would go in deluding a gullible public. With these millstones of recollection around his neck, Lloyd George's capacity to do good – or, increasingly, to do anything at all – would be seriously impaired in the post-war world.

Yet plainly it would be inappropriate to end here our narrative of the war and of Lloyd George's part in it. An attempt must be made to sum up his place in the events of 1914–18. During the election he was proclaimed 'The Man Who Won the War'. The expression, clearly, is absurd (if not much more so than others that remain current: for example, calling the Great War a 'total war', when all that is meant is something like 'bloody big war'). It was not given to any individual to 'win' so cataclysmic a conflict as this.

For one thing, the war was not won by Britain. Victory was the achievement of a coalition of powers in which Britain was a single, if vital, component. For another, the struggle was so all-encompassing that the role of individuals, however highly placed, rarely determined the way things turned out. Finally, it is plain that other individuals played distinguished parts in Britain's contribution to the Allied victory: men like Kitchener and Asquith and Henderson, and Haig and Robertson and Jellicoe. The contribution of at least two among that half-dozen deserves to be stressed (loath though Lloyd George might have been to find their names coupled with his). Kitchener perceived earliest that Britain would need to raise a mass army and helped to call it forth in a great voluntary movement. And Haig – pre-eminently, if not solely – recognized that for all sorts of compelling logistical reasons the German army could not be vanquished by any sort of 'indirect approach' and that Britain must fight the enemy to a standstill on the Western Front.

Yet, after every appropriate qualification to the characterization of Lloyd George as war-winner has been entered, his contribution as national leader cries out for acknowledgement. He alone occupied, and without flagging, a central position in

Britain's Government from start to finish of the war. He dealt, first as Chancellor of the Exchequer, then as Minister of Munitions, then as War Secretary, and ultimately as Prime Minister, with a great range of problems to which he brought rare qualities of insight and perseverance – most of all in the mobilization of Britain's resources of industry, finance, manpower, and woman-power to the purpose of waging war. His contributions to the debate on strategy, admittedly, rarely rose above the specious, and his conduct towards Britain's military leaders was often not to his credit. But, at the least, when it lay within his power to make potentially calamitous alterations in his country's strategic direction, he chose to believe that he did not possess such powers and so did not act on his inspirations. In consequence, when the moment of ultimate opportunity presented itself in mid-1918, the nation's forces were situated in the decisive region, amply supplied and under an efficient command structure.

One other contribution on Lloyd George's part remains to be noted. Sometimes, and especially in the horror months of 1917, he spoke privately as if the war were unwinnable. Yet always in his public persona he epitomized the nation's determination to endure all and overcome all. Time and again – and not least in December 1916 and March–April 1918 – when there might have seemed good cause for the national resolve to fail, his display of resolution gave grounds for hope and persistence. One fleeting incident encapsulates this aspect of his contribution. It is his remark to Trenchard in those darkest of all days, the Ludendorff offensive: 'Well, general, though we shan't win this year, we shall win next year instead.'

Lloyd George may not have been the man who won for Britain its triumph. But more than any other individual – more than Kitchener, more than Haig – he made the outstanding contribution to its accomplishment.

PART FOURTEEN

Some Participant Views

60

WARRIORS AND VICTIMS

What did they expect of our toil and extreme
Hunger – the perfect drawing of a heart's dream?
Did they look for a book of wrought art's perfection
Who promised no reading, nor praise, nor publication?
Out of heart's sickness the spirit wrote. . . .

Ivor Gurney, 'War Books', in Poems by Ivor Gurney *(London: Hutchinson, 1954)*

The enduring is not a substitute for the transient,
Neither one for the other. But the abstract conception
Of private experience at its greatest intensity
Becoming universal, which we call 'poetry',
May be affirmed in verse.

T. S. Eliot, 'A Note on War Poetry', in Collected Poems 1909–1962
(London: Faber & Faber, 1963)

I

What use do literary works concerning the war have for the historian? Some would argue very little; others, without arguing, write as if this were so. It is clear why. The poets, novelists, playwrights – and, very often, writers of memoirs – deal with the individual and the particular. They do not enable us easily to generalize. A poet may convey how hideous was death by poison gas:

> If you could hear, at every jolt, the blood
> Come gargling from the froth-corrupted lungs,
> Obscene as cancer, bitter as the cud
> Of vile, incurable sores on innocent tongues. . . .[1]

But this does not help us to estimate the effectiveness of poison gas as a weapon of war. Again, creative writers may relate aspects of life in the trenches that were of moment to those who existed there: the depredations of lice, which came to life as the body of an exhausted soldier began to grow warm in sleep; the strain of sentry duty, which required a man, without exposing himself to snipers, to establish visual mastery over a stretch of territory in which nothing could move without his knowledge; or an encounter at daybreak with a 'queer sardonic rat' of 'cosmopolitan sympathies', which having touched an English hand 'will do the same to a German'.[2] But all of this is at a level too minuscule to enable the historian to make generalizations. And it does not help us to answer the key question: why did one side win in the outcome and the other lose? Or even: What happened next?

---

[1] Wilfred Owen, 'Dulce et Decorum Est'.
[2] Isaac Rosenberg, 'Break of Day in the Trenches'.

But the historian is not entitled to exploit the past: to mine it for what appear its few precious metals and otherwise disregard it; to employ it only as an aid for finding out how we reached the present and what supposed lessons may be learned about the future. The past exists in its own right. The historian's task is to know it as completely as is possible. The experiences of poison gas, and lice, and sentry-duty, and a chance encounter with a rodent, are part of the fabric of the life lived by a particular body of people during this segment of the past. Where we cannot easily generalize about that segment, the historian has cause to welcome the opportunity to provide particular instances that, although they cannot be incorporated into generalizations, seem to illuminate an area much wider than themselves. Creative writing is a prime source for this general-embodied-in-the-particular concerning one of the war's most intense areas of experience.

II

Yet the creative writers are often partial witnesses. And it is important that this be recognized, if only because they are such compelling witnesses, difficult to approach with reserve. They tend to be partial because they are witnessing to the war so largely from the viewpoint of the serving soldier. (No member of Haig's staff, or the Civil Service, or the shipyard labour force wrote anything comparable.) And they tend to be partial because the personal qualities that enable them to feel so deeply, and to express their feelings so tellingly, are bound to heighten their outrage at what they are experiencing.

In consequence, much creative writing portrays the common soldier as someone upon whom war, and its horrors, are imposed. In other words, he is presented as victim. This is evident in some of Wilfred Owen's best-known poems:

> What passing-bells for these who die as cattle?[3]

and:

> Move him into the sun –
> Gently its touch awoke him once,
> At home, whispering of fields unsown.
> Always it woke him, even in France,
> Until this morning and this snow.[4]

The common soldier is the victim first of a technology which has reduced him to the condition of a helpless recipient of cruelty inflicted from remote distances by monstrous weapons. Owen clearly feels this even when the weapon is one of his own:

> Be slowly lifted up, thou long black arm,
> Great gun towering towards Heaven, about to curse; . . .[5]

But the soldier is victim also of his own countrymen. He is the victim of a community – not least in the form of parents, womenfolk, schoolmasters, clergy – who have moulded him to see participation in this struggle as the finest expression of his nature, or are prepared to intimidate him into acting as if this were so. He is the victim of press barons who find in the trumpeting of jingoism and the pedalling of atrocity stories an easy path to money and power. He is the victim of politicians who embark on wars they

---

[3] Wilfred Owen, 'Anthem for Doomed Youth'.
[4] Wilfred Owen, 'Futility'.
[5] Wilfred Owen, 'Sonnet'.

do not have to fight. He is the victim of generals who plan on paper battles that will bring glory to themselves if they succeed and 'acceptable' levels of casualties if they do not. And this state of victimhood embraces friend and foe, so that the common soldier sees across No-Man's-Land not an alien but a sufferer like him. E. A. Mackintosh, who was killed in action in 1917 after earlier being wounded, expresses these attitudes in a poem called 'Recruiting':

'Lads, you're wanted, go and help',
On the railway carriage wall
Stuck the poster, and I thought
Of the hands that penned the call.

Fat civilians wishing they
'Could go and fight the Hun.'
Can't you see them thanking God
That they're over forty-one?

Girls with feathers, vulgar songs –
Washy verse on England's need –
God – and don't we damned well know
How the message ought to read.

'Lads, you're wanted! over there,'
Shiver in the morning dew,
More poor devils like yourselves
Waiting to be killed by you.

Go and help to swell the names
In the casualty lists.
Help to make the column's stuff
For the blasted journalists.

Help to keep them nice and safe
From the wicked German foe.
Don't let him come over here!
'Lads, you're wanted – out you go.'. . .

Leave the harlots still to sing
Comic songs about the Hun,
Leave the fat old men to say
Now *we've* got them on the run.

Better twenty honest years
Than their dull three score and ten.
Lads, you're wanted. Come and learn
To live and die with honest men.

These poets were telling the truth. The anger of the guns was monstrous, and their victims did die like cattle. Equally, 'fat civilians' like Horatio Bottomley, and 'blasted journalists' like Northcliffe, and a great regiment of tarted-up females conveniently saw it as their duty to enjoin sacrifice upon others at no small profit to themselves. But nevertheless these poems tell a partial truth. For one thing, the soldiers were not alone in their victimhood. Among civilians who were not male or were not of military age were a great many parents and wives and offspring and lovers for whom the bells that tolled for the fallen diminished them also. And none of the seemingly irresponsible decision-makers and propagandists was free from terrible constraints. Politicians and generals often had only dreadful evils to choose between – and were not always free to choose the lesser evil. They must satisfy a public that expected them not to conserve lives but to 'get on with the war', wage 'a fight to a finish', and press on 'no matter what the cost' – which would not spare the decision-makers from ruin if they failed to satisfy fanciful expectations, or if their forces sustained casualties beyond a circumscribed level (for 'whatever the cost' did not mean 'whatever the cost'). Even press magnates were inhibited in what they could write by what their customers were prepared to read. Northcliffe's disastrous attempt to 'tell the truth' about Kitchener was a salutary reminder that newspapermen are the reflectors, rather than the creators, of their readers' opinions.

By the same token, the serving soldiers were not only the victims of war. They also ranked high among its makers. In a responsibly run community, such as Britain was, politicians do not declare wars when they have no menfolk eager to wage them, and generals (if they value their jobs) will not launch offensives that their soldiers are unlikely vigorously to prosecute. Even pressmen are aware that a mass army constitutes a large body of customers, and are concerned to keep them satisfied. Certainly, most of the killing in this war took place at long distance and was grimly impersonal. But a good deal was not: it took place at close quarters, was brutal and bloody, and often gave considerable satisfaction to the soldiers who dispensed it. That, nevertheless, the serving soldier is so often portrayed as the bearer, not the inflictor, of pain and death –

> In a far field, away from England, lies
> A Boy I friended with a care like love;
> All day the wide earth aches, the cold wind cries,
> The melancholy clouds drive on above. . . .[6]

– is really a reminder that this war betrayed expectations in a way that men, and in particular sensitive men, found outrageous.

III

The finest of the creative writers, particularly if they lived long enough to make a balanced statement, usually recognized this duality. It is especially manifest in the war novel of Frederick Manning. (This was for long known as *Her Privates We*, the title of the expurgated edition. It is bound to become better known by the name of the unexpurgated version, *The Middle Parts of Fortune*).[7]

Quite apart from its interest in the present context, Manning's book merits attention as a remarkable achievement. It has flaws. There are too many characters who are insufficiently delineated, and a few tedious episodes that appear to serve no purpose. But these are far outweighed by its power to illuminate the human dimension of war. The novelist Ernest Hemingway has called it 'the finest and noblest book of men in war', and a leading military historian, Michael Howard, considers it 'without doubt one of the greatest books about soldiers in the whole of western literature'. Its author, interestingly enough, although born in Australia and raised in England, was as far as one could get from either the dinkum Aussie or the typical Tommy. A friend, Peter Davies, has described him as an 'intellectual of intellectuals – poet, classical scholar, and author of the exquisite *Scenes and Portraits* – delicate in health and fastidious almost to the point of foppishness'.[8] Yet he enlisted as a private soldier and served in

---

[6] Robert Nichols, 'Boy'.

[7] All the quotations are from Frederick Manning, *The Middle Parts of Fortune* (London: Peter Davies, 1977).

[8] Introduction to the 1943 edition of *Her Privates We* (see note 7).

that capacity on the Somme in 1916. Then he went on to write what Davies calls 'a profound and truthful picture of the ordinary Englishman standing up to the perennial ordeal of war' – an achievement that should lay at rest the notion that creative writers are, by virtue of their sensitive natures, unreliable guides to the experiences of the common soldier.

Manning certainly portrays the soldier as victim. There are many bitter remarks about civilians, particularly politicians and sections of the workforce.

'They don't care a fuck 'ow us'ns live,' said little Martlow bitterly. 'We're just 'umped an' bumped an' buggered about all over fuckin' France, while them as made the war sit at 'ome waggin' their bloody chins, an' sayin' what they'd 'ave done if they was twenty years younger.'

Bourne, the book's central character, reflects:

Men were cheap in these days, that is to say men who were not coalminers or ship's riveters, to whom war only meant higher wages.

And one of the minor characters, Glazier (who opines that it might be a good thing if the Huns did land a few troops in Britain: 'Show 'em what war's like'), tells a lively tale of sitting in a pub with his mate Madeley when they are offered a drink by a loud-mouthed coalminer. This individual is waving about a week's wages for which he boasts he has only worked eight hours – 'I don't care if the bloody war lasts for ever.' Glazier recounts:

I looks up an' sees Madeley lookin' white an' dangerous. 'Was you talkin' to me?' says Madeley. 'Aye', 'e says. 'Well, take that, you fuckin' bastard!' says Madeley, an' sloshes 'im one in the clock.

A fine old brawl develops between the allies of the two protagonists, during which Madeley drags the chief offender into the urinal

'an' gets 'im down an' rubs 'is face in it . . . . 'There, you bugger,' 'e says; 'now go 'ome an' talk to yourself.'

When asked to confirm this tale Madeley, although demurring somewhat out of a sense of modesty, endorses his friend's hostile opinion of civilians.

But it's all true what 'e says about folks at 'ome, most on 'em. They don't care a fuck what 'appens to 'us'ns, so long as they can keep a 'ole skin. Say they be ready to make any sacrifice; but we're the bloody sacrifice. You never seed such a windy lot; an' bloodthirsty ain't the word for it. . . . The only person as 'ad any sense was me mother. She on'y fussed about what I wanted to eat.

Equally, Manning's novel portrays the ordinary soldier as a victim of the military staff. Certainly, there is one passage in which Bourne tries to put the 'brass hat's' point of view:

He's not thinking of you or of me or of any individual man, or of any particular battalion or division. Men, to him, are only part of the material he has got to work with; and if he felt as you or I feel, he couldn't carry on with his job.

But even Bourne cannot defend all of the staff's grotesqueries. As for his companions, they see the staff as men who devise operations knowing nothing of the mentality of the ordinary soldier or the realities of battle. On the eve of an offensive, an operational letter is read out to the troops telling them what they are to do and what course the battle (supposedly) will take. Two passages in it jar badly with the rank and file. One states that 'men are strictly forbidden to stop for the purpose of assisting wounded'; the other that, owing to the weight of the preliminary bombardment, 'It is not expected that the enemy will offer any very serious resistance at this point.' One melancholy soldier comments on this:

> The bloody brass-'at what wrote that letter 'as never been in any big show 'isself, that a dare swear. 'e's one o' them buggers as is never nearer to the real thing than G.H.Q.

Manning's account of the rehearsal for this offensive portrays an unbridgeable gulf between staff and combatants, with the 'brass hats' cutting a sorry figure.

> Presently arrived magnificent people on horseback, glancing superciliously at the less fortunate members of their species whom necessity compelled to walk.

Bourne, who loved horses, warmed to the animals but not to some of their riders:

> 'That bugger will give his horse a sore back before the day is out,' he said, as one of the great men cantered by importantly.

As the rehearsal itself proceeded, the men became increasingly aware of its unreality.

> The files of men moved forward slowly, and, when they reached the tapes, followed the paths assigned to them with an admirable precision. Their formations were not broken up or depleted by any hostile barrage, the ground was not pitted by craters, their advance was not impeded by any uncut wire. Everything went according to plan. It was a triumph of Staff-work, and these patient, rather unimaginative men tried to fathom the meaning of it all, with an anxiety which only made them more perplexed.

Then the plan went slightly awry. The 'attack' was proceeding past a cottage – 'little more than a hovel' – and over a patch of sown clover that constituted winter feed for three cows. Of a sudden the door of the hovel was flung open and a furious woman appeared.

> 'Ces champs sont à moi!' she screamed, and this was the prelude to a withering fire of invective, which promised to be inexhaustible. It gave a slight tinge of reality to operations which were degenerating into a series of co-ordinated drill movements. The men of destiny looked at her, and then at one another. It was a contigency which had not been foreseen by the Staff, whose intention had been to represent, under ideal conditions, an attack on the village of Serre, several miles away, where this particular lady did not live. They felt, therefore, that they had been justified in ignoring her existence.

Now however the 'men of destiny' recognized that something must be done.

> 'Send someone to speak to that woman,' said the Divisional General to a Brigadier; and the Brigadier passed on the order to the Colonel, and the Colonel to the Adjutant, and the Adjutant to Mr Sothern, who, remembering that Bourne had once interpreted his wishes to an old woman in Méaulte when he wanted a broom, now thrust him into the forefront of the battle. That is what is called, in the British Army, the chain of responsibility, which means that all responsibility for the errors of their superior officers, is borne eventually by private soldiers in the ranks.

IV

Yet Manning is not saying that his long-suffering soldiers are in essence men of peace, and that war is being imposed upon them by bloodthirsty profiteers and armchair strategists. The urge to wage war – or anyway to wage this war – comes from within themselves. And so does the urge to go on prosecuting it, however shaken their illusions about its nature and however strong their resentment against non-combatants.

No sympathy is indicated for Lance-Corporal Miller, who fled on the eve of an offensive.

When Miller disappeared just before the attack, many of the men said he must have gone over to the Hun lines and given himself up to the enemy. They were bitter and summary in their judgment on him. The fact that he had deserted his commanding-officer, which would be the phrase used to describe his offence on the charge-sheet, was as nothing compared to the fact that he had deserted them. They were to go through it while he saved his skin. It was about as bad as it could be, and if one were to ask any man who had been through that spell of fighting what ought to be done in the case of Miller, there could only have been one answer. Shoot the bugger.

Nor is Miller portrayed as having redeeming features personally. 'He had a weak, mean, and cunning face' and the 'physical characteristics' of a Hun; 'after one glance at that weak mouth and the furtive cunning of those eyes, Bourne distrusted him.'

More fundamentally, Manning is not saying that the common soldier is acting contrary to his nature, or that he is waging war only because he has been brainwashed or intimidated. Manning observes that there was a question that each soldier put to another on first acquaintance: 'What did you do in civil life?' It was a question full of significance; in part because it implied that, for the time being, civil life for them had been obliterated:

Men had reverted to a more primitive stage in their development, and had become nocturnal beasts of prey, hunting each other in packs: this was the uniformity, quite distinct from the effect of military discipline, which their own nature had imposed on them.

War in this book is not an affront to human nature. It is a natural activity. But the activity has taken on a life of its own.

There is nothing in war which is not in human nature; but the violence and passions of men become, in the aggregate, an impersonal and incalculable force, a blind and irrational movement of the collective will, which one cannot control, which one cannot understand, which one can only endure. . . .

Here Manning perceives what for him is the central tragedy of the war: that war emanates from the wills of individual men but assumes a nature that, as individuals, they cannot control; and yet it still remains a part of themselves.

Whether it were justified or not. . .the sense of being at the disposal of some inscrutable power, using them for its own ends, and utterly indifferent to them as individuals, was perhaps the most tragic element in the men's present situation. . . .There was no man of them unaware of the mystery which encompassed him, for he was a part of it; he could neither separate himself entirely from it, nor identify himself with it completely. A man might rave against war; but war, from among its myriad faces, could always turn towards him one, which was his own.

The book begins in the aftermath of one offensive; it ends in the aftermath of another. Little of it is devoted to relating battles. Yet all hinges on its episodes of conflict. During the first offensive, which is described only in retrospect, the men are said to have been subject to a

moral impetus which thrust them into action, which carried them forward on a wave of emotional excitement, transfiguring all the circumstances of their life so that these could only be expressed in the terms of heroic tragedy, of some superhuman or even divine conflict with the powers of evil. . . .

In the days following the offensive their whole psychological condition changed:

all that tempest of excitement was spent, and they were now mere derelicts in a wrecked and dilapidated world, with sore and angry nerves sharpening their tempers, or shutting them up in a morose and sullen humour from which it was difficult to move them.

For most of the novel the troops are in billets behind the line, recuperating. But when they find that they are once more to participate in an offensive, the 'moral impetus' begins once more to take hold of them.

> It was very curious to see how the news affected them; friends grouped themselves together, and talked of it from their individual points of view, but the extraordinary thing was the common impulse moving them, which gathered in strength until any individual reluctances and anxieties were swept away by it. A kind of enthusiasm, quiet and restrained because aware of all it hazarded, swept over them like fire or flood. Even those who feared made the pretence of bravery, the mere act of mimicry opened the way for the contagion, and another will was substituted for their own, so that ultimately they too gave themselves to it.

It is in this second offensive that the book makes its most intensive statement about the effects of war upon individuals: about men reverting to 'a more primitive stage in their development'. The principal character Bourne (clearly in some measure modelled on Manning himself) does not belong, by class or breeding, among the rank and file. But he has stubbornly remained there, relating to ordinary soldiers even though, in such matters as the use of expletives, he does not emulate them. The first offensive had thrown him together with Shem, an 'archetypal Jew' (according to Julian Symons), and Martlow, a chirpy young Cockney. Their friendship becomes more profound during the weeks of recuperation. They determine, in so far as the circumstances of battle allow, to stick together this next time.

Waiting to go over the top, they endure a relentless bombardment.

> Bourne's fit of shakiness increased, until he set his teeth to prevent them chattering in his head; and after a deep, gasping breath, almost like a sob, he seemed to recover to some extent. . . . His eyes met Shem's, and they both turned away at once from the dread and question which confronted them. More furtively he glanced in Martlow's direction; and saw him standing with bent head. Some instinctive wave of pity and affection swelled in him, until it broke into another shuddering sigh, and the boy looked up, showing the whites of his eyes under the brim of his helmet. They were perplexed, and his underlip shook a little. . . .
>
> 'Are you all right, kid?' Bourne managed to ask in a fairly steady voice; and Martlow only gave a brief affirmative nod.

A spoken order breaks the awful tension, and the three friends look at each other more quietly. 'We've stuck it before,' says Shem. As they prepare to go up the assault ladder, they shake hands. 'Good luck, chum. Good luck. Good luck.'

Once over the top, Shem is early wounded in the foot and has to crawl back. Through mist and heavy shelling the others press on.

> Bourne, floundering in the viscous mud, was at once the most abject and the most exalted of God's creatures. The effort and rage in him, the sense that others had left them to it, made him pant and sob, but there was some strange intoxication of joy in it, and again all his mind seemed focused into one hard bright point of action. The extremities of pain and pleasure had met and coincided too.

They penetrate the German wire and enter the first German trench, which they secure after some sharp bombing. Bourne – in an incident that will contrast acutely with the events of a few moments later – encounters two German prisoners, 'their hands up, and almost unable to stand from fear', being threatened by British soldiers 'with a deliberate, slow cruelty'.

'Give 'em a chance! Send 'em through their own bloody barrage!' Bourne shouted, and they were practically driven out of the trench and sent across no-man's land.

Bourne's company, now much depleted, moves out of the German front trench and presses forward.

> They had only moved a couple of yards from the trench, when there was a crackle of musketry. Martlow was perhaps a couple of yards in front of Bourne, when he swayed a little, his knees collapsed under him, and he pitched forward on to his face, his feet kicking and his whole body convulsive for a moment. Bourne flung himself down beside him, and, putting his arms round his body, lifted him, calling him.
> 'Kid! You're all right, kid?' he cried eagerly.
> He was all right. As Bourne lifted the limp body, the boy's hat came off, showing half the back of his skull shattered where the bullet had come through it; and a little blood welled out on to Bourne's sleeve and the knee of his trousers. He was all right; and Bourne let him settle to earth again, lifting himself up almost indifferently, unable to realize what had happened, filled with a kind of tenderness that ached in him, and yet extraordinarily still, extraordinarily cold.

Bourne moves on and again encounters Germans attempting to surrender, 'holding their hands up and screaming'. But the death of Martlow has changed him:

> he lifted his rifle to his shoulder and fired; and the ache in him became a consuming hate that filled him with exultant cruelty, and he fired again, and again. The last man was closest to him, but as drunk and staggering with terror. He had scarcely fallen, when Bourne came up to him and saw that his head was shattered, as he turned it over with his boot.

Bourne's teeth are 'clenched and bared, the lips snarling back from them in exultation'; the restraints on language that class and upbringing have hitherto imposed on him vanish:

> 'Kill the buggers! Kill the bloody fucking swine! Kill them!'
> All the filth and ordure he had ever heard came from between his clenched teeth; but his speech was thick and difficult.

In a scuffle immediately afterwards a Hun goes for one of his officers, and Bourne bayonets him, 'under the ribs near the liver, and then, unable to wrench the bayonet out again, pulled the trigger, and it came away easily enough. "Kill the buggers!" he muttered thickly.'

> He ran against Sergeant Tozer in the trench.
> 'Steady, ol' son! Steady. 'ave you been 'it? You're all over blood.'
> 'They killed the kid,' said Bourne, speaking with sudden clearness, though his chest heaved enormously. 'They killed him. I'll kill every bugger I see.'

But by this stage the attack is as good as over. The offensive has failed, and the troops who have advanced into German-held territory are obliged to fall back to their own lines. For Bourne this is almost the end of fighting. A few night's later, returning from a raid on a German trench, he is killed. In the last sight of him he is propped against the side of a trench, dead.

> Bourne was sitting: his head back, his face plastered with mud, and blood drying thickly about his mouth and chin, while the glazed eyes stared up at the moon.

Sergeant-Major Tozer regrets his passing:

> He was a queer chap. . . . There was a bit of a mystery about him; but then, when you come to think of it, there's a bit of a mystery about all of us.

It is rare, in even the finest imaginative works about this war, to have the hero presented with this sort of insight: floundering in viscous mud while shells hiss and shriek about him, and yet not only abject but exalted, not just panting and sobbing but experiencing 'some strange intoxication of joy', a meeting place of the 'extremities of pain and pleasure'. It is even rarer to have him portrayed as a man seized with bloodlust, uttering 'filth and ordure', exulting in slaughter as mindless and gratuitous as the massacre of helpless, terrified prisoners: the hero not just as victim – although he is that as well – but also as luster after revenge, war lover, killer.

61

'THE SUPPOSED INACTIVITY OF THE GRAND FLEET'

Geoffrey Coleridge Harper was born into a middle-class, church-going family in November 1894.[1] Educated in New Zealand, he became convinced when he was 15 that the navy was 'the only life worth living'. He joined it in 1913. Reflecting, a year later, on the question he was often asked as to how he liked life in the navy, he said the inquiry was pointless. He might as well be asked how he liked living. 'The Navy is life – it is beyond the region of argument altogether – how can it be "disliked". I may not be clear to outsiders but naval people will understand what I mean. I did not find it out till I was 15 – that the Navy is everything to me.'

Almost as strong as his passion for the navy was his distaste for civilians – as a body, if not as individuals. This sentiment grew as the war proceeded. He did not often comment on politics, but when he did his remarks were pretty caustic. He rejoiced at the death of Keir Hardie in September 1915, and his solution to the political crisis of December 1916 was to make a clean sweep of civilian politicians: 'Civilians are such hopeless fools in general.' The one exception he allowed to this rule was Lloyd George, 'the only energetic politician who wants to get on with the war'. In his view the war should be run by a triumvirate of Lloyd George, General 'Wully' Robertson, and Admiral Jellicoe.

Even stronger than his views about politicians were his opinions of civilian labourers. At the end of 1916 he penned a swingeing account of the conduct of workers in the shipyards.

> We have heard a lot of twaddle in the papers & elsewhere of the patriotism of the dockyard workers & how hard they are working – so I thought you would like to hear a few facts. I have been in contact with shipbuilders a lot this year. . . . On the Clyde an enormous lot of work is done but it takes an army of men to do it and they are frequently threatening to strike. There have been one or two strikes of a minor kind. How can men be called 'patriotic' when they will strike over shipbuilding work in war time which is our vital industry? At Liverpool there were glaring instances of the awful way these men are wasting the country's time – and money. . . . The men as usual spent most of their time on board sleeping & eating – & it always took twice as many of them to do a job as were necessary. At Newcastle they were even worse – they even *made* work so as to delay the ship & get more pay & work overtime. . . . Their method of walking is so slow that when an ordinary Englishman [sic!] wants to get past one he has to push him out of the way – I have often done so – it is no use telling them to hurry up – they dont listen. After my experiences this year I simply can't stand the sight of a shipyard labourer without getting angry. They have simply brought timewasting to the summit of perfection as a fine art. And yet people want to be Socialists (like Aunt Agnes).

---

[1] Harper's Papers are in Churchill College, Cambridge.

'A civilian,' he concluded, 'is a nasty thing to contemplate at any time but a shipbuilding civilian is the nastiest.'

How, then, did the war at sea look to this young man for whom the navy was the centre of all things? He began the war as a cadet, became a midshipman after a month, and by 1918 had reached the rank of lieutenant. In those four years he served in a variety of vessels, among them a superannuated cruiser, a respected if somewhat elderly battleship, a mine-sweeper, and a brand-new, experimental, high-speed cruiser. He was involved in blockading, mine-sweeping, and convoying. He participated in the destruction of an enemy submarine and in an attempted strike at a large German naval force. And for most of these years he was situated at the heart of British sea power in the Scottish waters inhabited by the Grand Fleet. Yet for G. C. Harper the naval war was never to fulfil the soaring expectations with which he greeted it in August 1914.

Harper was a naval cadet at Devonport on the south coast of England when war broke out. During the evening of 3 August 1914:

> we had a temporary depressing feeling that perhaps after all England would remain neutral. A week ago the very last thing I wanted was a war because it would have interrupted our training & stopped our much deserved summer leave - but having got this far I saw it was the chance of a lifetime - besides being an excellent thing for the country. . . .

Harper's 'chance of a lifetime' was soon upon him. Next day he was sailing for an unknown destination as part of the crew of the 'two funnelled, two masted old armoured cruiser' *Endymion*, 'a comfortable old ship – but frightfully old'. By 6 August they were in Scapa Flow, 'a very large bay with about 3 narrow entrances – a fine anchorage', although apart from a small town nearby 'there is not much habitation.' It was as well for Harper, and many like him, that the war began in summer.

Although he could not be expected to know it, Harper was doubly lucky in his introduction to Scapa Flow. For, as well as arriving in summer, he made the journey by sea. The alternative means of getting there was by one of the troop trains (the 'Jellicoes', as they became known), 'crammed, cluttered, cold, and interminable', which carried their human cargo from one end of the British Isles to the other and then deposited them at the northern tip of Scotland to complete the last few miles of the journey by ferry. It so happened that those remaining miles constituted one of the most turbulent areas of water anywhere, for the Pentland Firth is the channel where the North Sea and the Atlantic meet and clash.[2]

Right from the start, the naval war failed to develop along the lines Harper had expected. No noteworthy battles occurred. The fault, of course, lay entirely with the Germans: 'how anyone could be such skulking cowards we cant understand.' But it still denied him the experience he craved. Instead of engaging in a shooting war, the *Endymion* formed part of the Northern Patrol searching the sea lanes for cargo vessels. Its only perils were the weather, mines, and torpedoes. Only once during its four months of service did it actually destroy enemy ships, and then the circumstances were not dramatic. On 8 August 1914 the *Endymion* apprehended two German trawlers (which may not even have known that a war was on) and, after taking off the crews, sank them. 'It was the first time I had seen ships sunk by gunfire,' remarked Harper, '& it was jolly interesting.' Thereafter the German mercantile marine disappeared from the seas, and the *Endymion* spent its time seeking out neutral merchantmen and inspecting them for contraband. In the course of its 110 days of service – 80 at sea and

---

[2] See Malcolm Brown and Patricia Meehan, *Scapa Flow* (London: Allen Lane, 1968), chs. 2 and 3.

30 in harbour – the ship patrolled 20,000 miles, sailed as far east as 45 miles off the coast of Norway, and intercepted a great many merchant vessels. Three of these proved to be on the Admiralty's wanted list and were forced to repair to British harbours.

The work of the cruiser squadron of which the *Endymion* was part in maintaining the Northern Patrol during these early months of the war has won high praise from naval historians. Harper, from a less detached position, was not so enthusiastic. He had not gone to war to exhaust his energies and eyesight searching grey northern seas for cargo ships and enemy underwater devices. After one week he concluded that the work of a patrol cruiser was rather a rotten job. After a month, he was sickened by the thought that the war might have nothing more to offer: 'That is what is depressing us a good deal now – there seems an awful chance that we may go through the war without an action.' And meanwhile life aboard this 'rottenest and oldest cruiser in the Navy' was proving uncomfortable. There was a shortage of water to bathe in or even to drink; the food was fancy but not filling; and sleep was never sufficient to ward off the prevailing tiredness. Once during a middle watch he fell asleep while walking up and down and woke only as he began to fall. Life aboard was 'incessant noise – incessant work – incessant watch, watch, watch – incessant motion – sleeplessness – hunger – dirt etc etc'.

Action was what Harper pined for. In harbour he watched with envy Seaforth and Cameron Highlanders marching off 'with much cheering and bagpipes' to serve in France. And to begin with he was not even dismayed by the menace of mines and torpedoes. Certainly, the indiscriminate sowing of mines was further evidence of German cowardice and barbarity. 'The fact simply is,' he wrote, 'that every German is – under his civilized clothes & human skin – an awful loathsome beast.'[3] But the possibility that his ship might strike a mine 'merely makes life less boring'. And when he learned in September 1914 of the torpedoing of the three Cressy cruisers his feeling was one of envy rather than dismay: 'they are lucky beggars – the survivors – except that they lost their belongings. We are longing – now – even to get blown up by a mine – *anything* rather than spend the whole war doing nothing. The only trouble about being sunk is that you lose your personal gear.' Given that 1,400 of the 2,200 men aboard these ships had lost their lives, Harper's response might be thought quixotic.

Two weeks later this attitude sustained a heavy blow. The loss of the three cruisers caused far stricter precautions against submarines to be introduced. When out on patrol the ships in Harper's squadron were ordered to take on mail from the supply vessel one at a time, not all bunched together as hitherto. And when the *Endymion* sent a boarding party to inspect an apprehended vessel, the cruiser no longer remained stationary but circled round at a good speed and zig-zagged.

Despite these precautions, one ship in Harper's squadron, the *Hawke*, was torpedoed on 15 October. It sank in eight minutes with the loss of 500 men. The first Harper knew of the matter was that radio contact with the *Hawke* had been lost; then next day wreckage was washed ashore. When he learned of the losses in lives he wrote angrily:

> The news which concerned us most was bad – very bad. Dickson and *all* the midshipmen of the Hawke went down. Perhaps I shouldn't have minded so much if it had been in fair fight – but it is the beastly underhand way of doing it that is so awful. . . . It is rotten and underhand – and like stabbing a man in the back. It makes me wild to think that the

---

[3] This remark was inspired by the publication in September 1914 of a report on German atrocities in Belgium. To Harper it showed the German to be a 'creature' who had refused 'the chance to become a human being' and had 'reverted to the state of a ruthless and disgusting animal'.

Hawke only an hour after she left us was simply obliterated in a few minutes without even seeing where her enemy was or being able to fire a shot. I am not the only one who is against submarine warfare – I come across people everywhere whose general opinion is 'It's not fair – I dont like it.' Of course our submarines are as much to blame as the enemy's. Anyone, of any nationality, who serves in a submarine is not playing the game.[4]

This tragedy did not prevent Harper from writing in the same passage that everyone was sick of the war's active inaction and that, if they could have their way, they would go straight into Heligoland or the Baltic and 'come to a conclusion one way or another'. But never after the *Hawke* incident did he express the desire to have a mine or torpedo sink his ship beneath him.

At the end of 1914 the *Endymion* and its fellows, worn out by their patrolling, were withdrawn from service. Harper was transferred to the battleship *Dreadnought* – the first of a famous line. He rapidly concluded that this was a good thing. The ship was splendidly comfortable compared with his last vessel – and compared also with battleships that had been built since. There were telephones, ample hot water, and sufficient space between decks to obviate regular bumping of the head. And with this transfer he was no longer involved in the interminable North Sea patrols.

But in the ensuing months Harper's contentment waned, and by the time he left the *Dreadnought*, at the beginning of March 1916, he was thoroughly sick of it. Promotion came slowly, and the best part of a year passed without leave. The personnel of the ship, when it changed, changed for the worse. And among those who remained there was a sense of 'moulding' away on 3/6d. a day, while some of their contemporaries were occupying responsible posts on destroyers at twice or three times the money. Moreover, as a vessel the *Dreadnought* was feeling its years. While its turbines were turning revolutions for 20 knots, the ship was managing only 18½. This jeopardized its place in the Grand Fleet. Then there was the experience of two winters in Scapa Flow: 'it is a certainty that the climate of the Orkneys is the worst in the world. If we are to continue having a cyclone every other day. . . .' But the most profound problem was that, in moving from the *Endymion* to the *Dreadnought*, Harper had only exchanged one form of inactivity (or 'active inaction', as he called it) for another. Instead of long hours patrolling, he was condemned to resting in harbour. Beside his diary entry for 22 February 1915 he wrote:

> I am afraid this log must be rather uninteresting – but it shows how quiet life in a battleship is compared with a cruiser. You see how we stay in harbour for weeks on end.
> Of course it is largely because it is winter.
> In summer we shall probably go to sea a lot for manoeuvres & firing etc.

As it happened Harper's one remarkable experience during his service in *Dreadnought* occurred just a few weeks after he wrote this. At sea on 18 March, he was playing a game of cards soon after midday when the double alert was sounded. He raced to his gun station and found everyone pointing forward at a small black tube in the water 'rushing along as if to avoid us':

> Gradually we closed on the periscope which seemed to be rising. Then we got it. The ship lurched & vibrated – & up came a bow with an apparently wooden upper deck. I leant over to see the number – all the ships company rushed to the side & cheered wildly. Right on the corner of the bow was a small brass plate with U29 in relief on it. There was a hole in the deck with air rushing through it & causing a spray. It passed along the starboard side & then astern tilting up more & more. Then it tilted right up on end & went under – leaving a swirl of wreckage & stuff.

---

[4] In after years Harper crossed out this last sentence and wrote 'Rot' against it.

This incident saw the demise of the U-boat captain and crew who, in another submarine, had sunk the three Cressy cruisers six months before. Oddly enough, Harper was rather sorry about it. This particular U-boat captain was one of the few Germans he excluded from his general detestation (presumably because, although he thought it cowardly to torpedo one British ship, he recognized that it required courage to remain around and torpedo two more).

'Think of it,' Harper wrote of the U29's demise, ' – 8 months war & we have just bagged *one* German submarine.' But if that was not very satisfactory, it proved to be all he was going to get. The Admiralty did not even publicize the *Dreadnought's* success. Not wishing to inform the Germans of how their submarines came to grief, it issued only a statement that it believed the U29 had been sunk. And Harper's hoped-for upsurge of activity during the summer did not materialize. Half-heartedly, he reconciled himself to the situation. 'Weather total perfection,' he wrote in August 1915. 'I went bicycling to Dingwall. The country is ripping.'

> I begin to realise now [he continued] that we are becoming more and more like guardships. We hardly ever go to Sea – we are generally at 6 hours notice – and we simply go on as if it were peace time and we lie rusting in either this place [Invergordon] or Scapa Flow. It is not very exciting is it – but perhaps we are well out of this war with its enormous casualty lists and we are quite content.

Three months later, following the slaughter at Loos of the Seaforths and Camerons whose departure to France he had once envied, he wrote:

> we are well out of this war – an enormous number of men are being killed or badly wounded and we live very safely & comfortably – so really we are the luckiest because we run even less risk of being killed tha[n] people in the streets of London at night.

But these do not read like the sentiments of a contented man. Plainly, he was making the best of a bad job. And, in the same passage as that just quoted, he said *à propos* some vessels being sent to the Dardanelles: 'Lucky dogs. . . . fancy those 3 ships just off for fine weather and scrapping.'

In March 1916 Harper was transferred to a mine sweeper, but after a few weeks his health gave way. So, ironically, when the guns boomed at Jutland he was not at sea in any capacity. Following his recovery, he spent a few months back in Scapa Flow aboard the cruiser *Devonshire*, 'a proper dud number', and then was transferred to Newcastle to form part of the crew of a quite new vessel. This was the *Courageous*, one of a type of light battle cruiser dreamed up by Jackie Fisher during his wartime spell as First Sea Lord. It had three distinctive features: speed, light armament, and long-range guns (although only in small numbers). Harper was understandably enthusiastic about his new billet.

But again his luck was out. On its initial trial on 14 November 1916 the *Courageous* achieved an excellent 31 knots but at the cost of stripping its turbines. It was not back at sea until two months later, and again calamitously. The heavy seas encountered during the journey to Scapa Flow buckled its forecastle – in dry dock at Rosyth it 'leaked out water like an old garden watering-can.' In February 1917 the ship was sent to the south of England to be fitted out as a mine layer, a function for which its special features had plainly not been designed and which indicated the Admiralty's lack of confidence in it. It served in this capacity for only a brief time.

Despite these teething troubles, by April 1917 the *Courageous* was accomplishing the high speeds hoped of it and managing to remain seaworthy. During trials at Plymouth it achieved 33½ knots: 'we *did* go,' Harper exalted, ' – and frightened everything we passed.' The ship then repaired to Scapa Flow and engaged in intensive gunnery trials.

These reduced Harper to a state of exhaustion, although he does not mention a major shortcoming of this new class of ship that these trials were making apparent: its complement of guns was too small for the fall of shot to be quickly observed and an effective hitting pattern established.

Thereafter the *Courageous* took up station at Rosyth as flagship to a squadron, and there awaited its moment of glory. The summer of 1917 passed uneventfully. Harper joined a tennis club and lived 'a peace time life of sunshine, sleep, tennis, cricket, Edinburgh etc. etc.'. 'I must say that life in a Rosyth cruiser is exceeding pleasant.' But the note of melancholy recurs. 'The navy appears to get more & more inactive as the war goes on.' 'If the present state of affairs goes on – and the Germans do not come out – we shall probably swing round this buoy till the end of the war.' Then, in the autumn of 1917, a certain liveliness intruded. The *Courageous* was sent into the North Sea hunting convoy raiders. And in mid-November Beatty used the ship to spearhead an attempted master-stroke.

Enemy mine sweepers were having to operate ever further from their home bases as the British extended the areas of their minefields. For protection the German mine sweepers were being accompanied by a force of light cruisers, destroyers, and submarines. Beatty planned to pounce on this force at daybreak with a heavy body of ships. The attack was to be led by the *Courageous* and a sister ship, and it was calculated that their speed and gun range would prove decisive. The commander of the operation was Vice-Admiral Napier, on board the *Courageous*.

On 16 November, Harper recorded, the *Courageous* and many other ships hastily raised steam and left harbour. At 6 a.m. next morning the crew took up action stations and the British force was proceeding through the minefield when ahead were sighted 4 enemy light cruisers, 12 destroyers, and 8 submarines on the surface. The *Courageous* opened fire and Harper in his gun turret was soon fully engaged.

> It was hot work in the turret but we didn't miss a single salvo although charges kept on jambing in the cages – and 2 'locks' broke. The place was full of water and cordite fumes – but we didn't have to take to respirators. We discarded most of our clothing before we had finished. The men were splendid – they thoroughly enjoyed themselves. The magazine crew simply lay down on the deck & went to sleep when it was over – they have perhaps the hardest work.

Reflecting on the matter next day he added: 'The most gratifying thing of the scrap was the behaviour of the ship's company – who simply revelled in it and worked magnificently.' It was not a case of shots being fired in anger, he wrote, but of shots 'fired with amusement and thorough delight; & pity for the poor old boshe if anything.'

But already it was becoming apparent that 'the poor old boshe' were not much in need of sympathy. The operation had failed. The enemy had made good his escape. There were many reasons, some of which Harper and his fellow participants recognized. The Germans had covered their tracks by most skilful use of smoke screens – it was difficult, Harper noted, to see the fall of shot because of the early morning mist and the excellent smoke screens made by the German destroyers. The British pursuit had been hampered by the presence of enemy submarines: Harper remarked on the great mass of submarine warnings that the *Courageous* received – messages like 'Torpedo approaching on the starboard side', 'Submarine astern', 'Two periscopes to port', and so on. Again, there was the problem of chasing a fleeing force through an unfamiliar, even if British-sown, minefield. (What Harper could not know was that the Admiralty had failed to provide all the information it possessed about the channels through the mines.) But the point that rankled more and more was the awareness that the greatest advantage of the British attackers, namely the speed attainable by the two principal vessels, had not been employed. In his first account of the action Harper wrote:

> For some unknown reason we never went more than 25 knots. I expect it was so as not to be too close for torpedo attack. As it was the sea was thick with torpedoes & submarines – the Commander N. said he spent most of his time avoiding them.

But on reflection he added:

> There is considerable surprise and indignation about our speed. It is thought that if we had gone 33 instead of 25 we could have closed enough to blow all the hun light cruisers sky high.
> I cant help thinking there was a serious mistake somewhere. If Beatty had been here it would have been different.

Harper could not know it, but he had just participated in the last big-ship engagement of the war. Even if a more dashing commander had carried it off successfully, the action could hardly have affected the naval balance of power. But it would have provided a welcome fillip to a frustrated nation – and to some of its frustrated sailors.

At the beginning of 1918 Harper was transferred from the *Courageous* to the battle cruiser *Indomitable*. This vessel had already distinguished itself in the Dogger Bank action of January 1915, and he found it a very happy and efficient ship. It was also, during Harper's spell aboard, a hard-working ship. In the previous autumn, to the great humiliation of the Admiralty, German light cruisers had twice fallen on British convoys to Scandinavia protected only by destroyers and had annihilated them. The Admiralty countered by providing big-ship support for the Scandinavian convoys. So in February 1918 Harper found himself part of a cruiser force protecting merchant ships in the most vulnerable sectors of the journey to and from Bergen.

In a North Sea winter these were exhausting operations. Here is the itinerary of one of them. At 5 p.m. on 18 February 1918 the *Indomitable* left harbour to rendezvous next morning with an outward-bound convoy. Two hours of searching were required early on the 19th before it was discovered. It consisted of 35 ships of various nationalities – British, Norwegian, Swedish, Danish, French, Dutch – with one destroyer leading and another in the rear to rally stragglers. There were also six armed trawlers in attendance to ward off submarines. Harper's squadron provided another six destroyers and four battle cruisers. It would be an ill day for any German surface raiders that sought to interfere with this aggregation.

Throughout 20 February the convoy struggled through a 'regular blizzard', which for a time forced the destroyers to retreat to base. Bergen was reached next day. There the cruisers waited while another convoy, battling the obstructions of weather, was assembled. This consisted of 50 ships, again of many nationalities, carrying foodstuffs. The weather continued atrocious. The *Indomitable* took on a lot of water; its aerials were carried away; and one of its rafts was smashed. On the 22nd:

> We sighted our convoy at daylight and spent all day sighting them every 2 hours and wandering about at about 14–16 knots. [The convoy as a whole was proceeding at 7 knots.] It blew a full gale in the dogwatches and we sent the destroyers to look after themselves. During the heavy sleet squalls it was very difficult to keep station – one could hardly see.

That night they left the convoy in the care of a southern coastal escort and repaired to Rosyth. Most of the next day was spent taking on coal from a support vessel, which, owing to the buffeting of the weather, kept parting its wires. This was followed by a good cleaning of the ship. It was, Harper observed, all 'very tiring'. As taking on coal was, at the best of times, the most hated and wearying task then experienced aboard ship, his remark constitutes a masterly understatement.

Apart from a rest period in the summer, Harper spent most of 1918 in similarly heavy activity: convoying merchant ships, accompanying mine layers, practising firing under battle conditions, and when in harbour remaining at short notice for sea. There was a lively spell in September and October 1918 when his squadron accompanied a fleet of American mine layers. The instability of American mines caused many of them to explode almost as soon as they were laid. On one occasion about 150 went off in the course of an afternoon, 'causing terrific concussions and shooting up great columns of water'. On another 300 went off during a day's sowing. 'Once 22 went up in 10 seconds. The noise & concussion was tremendous and a huge mass of water was chucked up.'

But such entertainments were no substitute for the clash of arms that Harper still longed for. All hope of this now receded. On 8 November he heard reports of a mutiny in the German navy: 'If this is true our last chance (I should say – *my* last chance) of doing anything in the war is gone – because I am certain we are at the end.' The next day brought news of the Kaiser's abdication and further details of the naval mutiny: 'there is considerable depression on the part of people who have so far taken no part in the war – because now our chance has gone – and we shall have to slink home with nothing to show for our 4¼ years waiting.' It was a dismal ending to the war, relieved a few weeks later only by the 'great performance' of the German navy's surrender. Participation in this made Harper's twenty-fourth birthday the greatest he had ever had.

What is perhaps most striking about Harper's account of his war is that he never paused to analyse what, in this situation, the real task of the navy should be. At the start of the war it seemed to him sufficient to condemn submarines and mines as unfair, and not to ponder further what must be the necessary response to them. In the same spirit he denounced the German navy as a pack of cowards for refusing to come out and do battle – a view he slightly revised in the light of Spee's fight-to-a-finish at the Falkland Islands. And he held that the appropriate answer was to sail into Heligoland or the Baltic and settle the matter 'one way or another'. The chances of success in a battle on the enemy's doorstep he did not assess. Nor did he pause to consider the momentous consequences of failure.

Continued experience of the naval struggle dulled, but did not alter, these early judgements. Mid-way through it he made a summary of 'how I have spent my time during the war'. In those two years he had served as part of the blockading force, on mine sweepers, and in the Grand Fleet. Yet the phrase that recurs in this sketch of his activities is 'nothing to do with [the] enemy'. 'So no one,' he concluded it, 'can say *I* have done much towards helping the war along – but personally I dont mind – if I am given a comfortable time & am apparently not required I am quite happy to let some one else do the work.'

Apart from witnessing the destruction of the U-29, the only war experience that brought Harper real joy was the action of 17 November 1917, which found him in his gun turret exhausted but exhilarated. The convoys of 1918, which were incomparably more important operations both potentially and actually for winning the war, provided no such satisfaction. Looking out over the merchant ships that his cruiser was accompanying to Scandinavia on 19 February he observed: 'It shows how well we look after these rotten little neutral tubs – that we send either a whole Battle Cruiser Squadron or a division of Battleships out – not counting destroyers etc.' Nowhere does he remark on the fact that the navy had allowed many 'rotten little neutral tubs' to go to the bottom before it started providing this sort of protection. Nor does he acknowledge that Britain's concern in the matter was not the safety of neutrals but its own imperilled survival.

Probably, without saying so, Harper did realize that, by eliminating the submarine threat and exercising a stranglehold on Germany's bid to dominate the seas, the Royal Navy was defeating the greatest threats that Britain faced during the war. But he could not reconcile himself to victories achieved in this way. In June 1918, with the naval war virtually won, he could still write:

> There are several references in the papers now about 'the supposed inactivity of the Grand Fleet'. It is amusing to think how little the writers realise the real inactivity of it. The Fleet spends its whole time now either at anchor or exercising in the Flow or the Firth & never goes to sea. . . . The cruisers refer to the Battleship people now as the 'carpet sailors'.
>
> We generally have a military officer from the Front living with us now. They come for 4 or 5 days, every week or so. *Why*, I don't know. I think it is rather unfortunate as they see at first hand what luxury & peace we live in – compared with themselves – and must take back a very bad impression of the Service to the Army.

Yet if Harper's attitude reflects no great calculation of the navy's proper role in this war, it does reveal something of the spirit that maintained the Grand Fleet as an unassailable force throughout the struggle. The sort of war he wanted to fight may have been only marginally related to the then naval needs of the country. But his passionate desire to fight it was part of the same urge that provided the manpower integral to Britain's maritime dominance. Harper's longing for an end to the supposed inactivity of the fleet reflected the spirit of adventure that had persuaded him, five years before the conflict began, that the navy was the only life worth living.

62

PERILS OF THE SKIES

Friday. Val gone west. . . . One of the best and a crack pilot. Bloody hell and no
mistake. . . . His old orderly cried like a child in spite of his gray hairs. . . . Everyone
getting silently blotto in mess to-night in endeavour to forget that bloody empty chair.
Diary entry of an anonymous RFC pilot, n.d. [1917]

I

After flying on the Western Front for 10 months, J. Leslie Horridge wrote home:

> Have you noticed the number of R.F.C. casualties lately? I wonder if Walter still thinks the
> R.F.C. a cushy job. Lots of people used to say it was a cushy job but they did not transfer
> all the same.

Three days later he returned to the subject:

> My flight [has] been very unlucky since I came to it. One machine was lost when I was on
> leave[,] pilot killed and observer wounded & prisoner. Three days ago another was shot
> down by a Hun and the pilot wounded, the observer escaped. Two days ago during the
> first big advance another was shot down from the ground and pilot & observer killed.[1]

Horridge was writing in mid-March 1917. 'Bloody April' lay just ahead. In these two
months Richthofen accounted for 30 out of his eventual total of 80 British aeroplanes.

By January 1918 no one imagined that the air force was a 'cushy job'. Private
Surfleet, disgusted that his army battalion was to be broken up, concluded: 'if I get
safely out of the line this next trip, I have made up my mind to apply for a commission
in the Royal Flying Corps.' It was not suspected that he was making the move for the
good of his health. 'All my pals here tell me I am a damned fool to think of joining *that*
"Suicide club" (as they call the R.F.C.) .'[2]

One who rapidly concluded that an airman's prospects of survival were small was
Lieutenant Edgar Taylor.[3] Born in the USA of English parents, he entered the US
Navy in April 1917 on the understanding that he would learn to fly. When the naval
authorities could not fulfil this undertaking they released him to the RFC. He trained
in Sussex and joined the 79th Squadron in France in April 1918. He found his
companions a cheery lot who always made a joke of their near-escapes – 'No one ever
tells a story soberly.' But Taylor soon encountered times of 'depression and weariness',
and it seemed to be during these that 'we do our most dangerous stunts.' He wrote on
14 May: 'A hundred times I have been near the end but always I have been quick
enough to cheat fate for the time being.'

---

[1] Horridge's letters are in the Imperial War Museum.

[2] A. Surfleet, 'Blue Chevrons. An Infantry Private's Great War Diary', p. 111 (26 January 1918).

[3] Typed transcripts of letters from Taylor to members of his family are in the Imperial War Museum.

'For the time being' seemed to be the operative expression. 'The fate of a pilot,' he wrote, 'is a foregone conclusion.' He instanced brilliant fliers who had shot down 'a score of huns' and then had gone home for a rest – 'only to "do it" in a training camp.' The war, he anticipated, would be 'long and deadly', and they must 'all buckle to, and do our bit until we take the "longest flight of all"'.

These were not the judgements of a congenital pessimist. Taylor generally appreciated his service in the British airforce. So on 15 May he recorded 'very good news': he had been detailed for an offensive patrol 'over hunland'. It proved no picnic. First he was buffeted by anti-aircraft fire – 'I was a little annoyed at first but soon began to enjoy it very much.' Then his engine started to give trouble, obliging him to glide back to a convenient aerodrome. None of this dismayed him. 'It was a very interesting day for me, I can tell you.' His one disappointment was that no German aircraft was encountered. 'The huns are as scary as can be.'

Taylor's ensuing weeks were spent variously. There were journeys into enemy territory, dog fights ('To be in a general melee above the clouds with our own dark colored machines and the huns brilliantly colored machines is an experience'), and the frustrations of being out of action with engine trouble ('I have had bad luck for quite a few days now and have missed some fine scraps'). In mid-June he concluded: 'There are lots of good times in the Flying Corps in France but then there are mighty blue days too. However I do not regret joining the Corps. . . . It is a sporting proposition all round.' He longed to make his first kill, writing to his brother at the end of June: 'I have not got any huns yet. They are a bunch of cowards in the air. I will drop onto one yet when he isn't ready and then I'll pot him just like shooting a coyote before he has a chance to run.' There is no record that this ambition was fulfilled. On 24 August, slightly more than four months after his arrival in France, Edgar Taylor made a forced landing behind the German lines. He was never heard of again.

II

The means by which British airmen might be at risk were various. They included hostile aircraft and ground fire, mechanical failure, 'human error' (that is, blunders by the pilot or others on his own side), adverse weather, or any combination of these. The mere fact that official policy required the RFC to dominate air space beyond the German lines greatly increased these perils. It brought British airmen within range of German aircraft and ground fire, and increased the chances that a forced landing would take place inside enemy territory. The problem was aggravated by the fact that the prevailing winds blew powerfully from the west, making the return journey for the light-weight, relatively low-powered aircraft all the more protracted. According to the historian of 60 Squadron, the prevailing wind was a 'pitiless potentate who, five days out of seven, fought with our enemies against us. . . . How many curses have been levelled at his careless head by pilots who, with trailing wires, with labouring, failing engines, and with tattered planes have tried, and often tried in vain, to reach that brown, smoky strip of battered terrain which marked the lines and safety, after a bitter fight?'[4]

The most evident danger was hostile aircraft. Private Surfleet, while still a foot soldier in the devastated Arras area in April 1917, witnessed this peril:

> Plane scraps were pretty common. I saw an old R.E.8 (those slow but persevering observation planes) calmly droning over the line one afternoon when a bosche scout dived

---

[4] A. J. L. Scott, *Sixty Squadron R.A.F.* (London: Heinemann, 1920), p. 110.

from the clouds and poured a deadly hail of bullets into the poor old bus. To our horror, the machine burst into flames and nose-dived to earth. I have never seen the boys out here more horrified: it turned me nearly sick to see those two poor fellows fling themselves out of the burning inferno and spin, top-heavily, to certain death: seemed to stop the blood in one's veins.[5]

For a British flyer on the Western Front, the most perilous time (according to the youthful pilot Cecil Lewis) was the early morning. The sun, rising in the east, blinded him; 'the Hun, attacking with this armour of light about him, was invisible even when the tracers from his machine gun were spinning through our wings.'

Lewis himself barely survived a dawn patrol in September 1917. 'It was a cloudless, perfect morning with a sun like a white eye, glaring, overpowering; a blinding arrogant sun dominating the alien heaven.' Lewis was flying in the rear of a patrol of SE5s (single-seater biplanes), guarding their tails, when his companions dived towards three German aircraft away to the east. As he followed he tested his guns and found his Vickers was jammed. (Apart from over-heating, a gun could become jammed even by a single faulty bullet. The French air ace René Fonck, who achieved the greatest number of kills of any Allied airman, 75, used to check the calibre of every bullet in his ammunition belts and eliminate any with the slightest imperfection. He was one of the aces to survive the war.)

Lewis set about trying to clear the jam. It proved no easy task. At 11,000 feet the air was frigid. Lewis was blessed with poor circulation, and when he removed the glove his hand went numb. He banged his hand on his thigh and crouched in his cockpit for warmth while still working on the gun. Unwittingly, he had become a straggler. This seemed not to matter, for the sky appeared 'utterly empty of danger'. But the appearance was deceptive. 'Then, faintly, I heard the intermittent chatter of a machine gun. I looked round. Nothing. No sign of a fight, no one in the sky – but the chatter became a jabber and then a stuttering menace – the sun ambush was down on me. I tried vainly to look up, but the glare shrivelled my eyes to sightlessness.' Tracer bullets whistled through his wings, 'and suddenly a white-hot rod was flicked along the round of my back. I jammed over stick and rudder and went flashing into a spin, then shut off the engine and collected myself to look up.' Behind him was one of the latest German Pfalz scouts, against which his own fighter was no match.

Fortunately for Lewis, his sudden spin had conveyed the appearance that he was done for, and his adversary did not follow him down. After dropping a thousand feet towards his own patrol, Lewis stopped shamming dead. The Pfalz then made move to follow, but the numbers awaiting him were too great, and he sped away.

Lewis remained unsure of his own condition: 'My back burned terribly. I tried to feel it. Was it bleeding? My shirt seemed sticky. I worked my shoulder tentatively. It ached, that was all. Nothing serious, probably; still, I had better get back to the aerodrome and see.' On landing he found the body of his aeroplane well shot up, with two big holes in a longeron and an elevator wire cut. The duplicate controls had saved him. As for himself, a long red furrow seared his back – a 6 inch graze, nothing more. 'But for the cold I should have been sitting upright, and then that bullet, instead of glancing by, would have torn its way down through the shoulder and embedded itself in the heart.' In the parlance of serving men, this brush with death constituted a 'blighty': it earned him not only a wound stripe but also a spell of leave at home. But it had amply illustrated the perils of flying towards the enemy lines and the rising sun.[6]

---

[5] Surfleet, 'Blue Chevrons', p. 78.

[6] Cecil Lewis, *Sagittarius Rising*, (Harmondsworth: Penguin Books, 1977), pp. 162–4.

In addition to hostile machines, anti-aircraft fire was an enemy device that particularly threatened British pilots. With their regular patrols and bombing raids over enemy territory, they were constantly at risk from ground fire. J. Herbert Morris, a former artillery officer who transferred to the RFC in 1917 and joined 49 Squadron at Bellevue (near Amiens) in mid-November, describes a bombing raid on 5 December.[7] During the return flight he was positioned, as he had been on a raid the previous day, in the rear of the squadron. 'I'm a bit fed up with being last man,' he concluded. He had been shelled on the ground in his time, and thought himself lucky (with the aid of cover) to survive a shell burst at 30 yards. But his experience from 'Archy' on this occasion exceeded all past experiences.

> These awful things, great black high explosive were bursting by the dozen round me and not exaggerating most of them were within twenty five yards of me. Crump, crump, they went and here was I watching them bursting all round. What could I do? Ducking was useless and there was fourteen thousand feet to fall if one hit me. One burst just in front of me and I only just managed to avoid flying into the big black ugly burst, for had I done so our height would have been given away and things would have got worse. Another one burst just under me, I didn't see it but it must have been close as the whole machine was blown up[wards] several feet and I had to be quite nippy again straightening it out. . . .

The shooting was rapid ('as fast as you could count') and accurate ('wonderful shots they were too') and went on for nearly five minutes:

> a very long time it seemed as I sat there throwing my machine about from side to side and up and down to avoid those horrid black bursts. The others in the formation said they could hardly see me for smoke and when I looked round after we had crossed our line again there seemed hundreds of little black dots filling the skies. I was glad to get home.

Not all who received the devoted attention of 'Archy' proved so fortunate; although some victims of shell fire did not even succumb to the missiles of the enemy. In September 1916 Cecil Lewis, his eyes temporarily impaired by too long observing for the artillery, had been sent home on a fortnight's sick leave. On his return he found four men in the mess where he expected nine.

> 'Where's Rudd?' I asked. Only four chaps here. Where were the others?
> 'Killed. Archie. This morning. . . .'
> 'Both of them [i.e. observer as well as pilot]?' I couldn't believe it somehow.
> 'Suppose so. Machine took fire. Couldn't recover the bodies.'
> The boy who spoke was only eighteen too. A good pilot. Brave. Rudd had been his room-mate. God, how quiet the Mess was!
> 'And Hoppy?'
> 'Wounded: gone home.'
> 'And Pip and Kidd?' I was almost frightened to ask.
> 'Done in last night. Direct hit. One of our own shells. Battery rang up to apologise. New pilots coming.'

For months Lewis and Pip had worked together daily on patrol, Lewis as pilot, Pip as observer and machine-gunner. Once, after injudiciously engaging an enemy machine, they had staggered home with a wing almost shot away. On another occasion, hit by a passing missile, they had crash-landed between the lines. There they had dodged enemy shells, wandered over 'diseased, pocked, rancid [earth], stinking of death', and chanced upon some clumps of crimson Flanders poppies, 'undaunted by the desolation, heedless of human fury and stupidity. . . basking in the sun!' Pip had been 'the darling of the Flight, for he had a sort of gentle, smiling warmth about him

---

[7] Morris's papers, consisting of a diary in letter form, are in the Imperial War Museum.

that we loved. Besides, from the old rattling piano, out of tune, with a note gone here and there, he would coax sweet music – songs of the day, scraps of old tunes, Chopin studies, the *Liebestraum, Marche Militaire.*' Lewis believed he had musical talent; anyway 'enough for us, to make us sit quietly in the evening, there in that dingy room where the oil lamp hung on a string thick with flies, and listen'. Now a British shell had stilled his hands and deprived the mess of his 'gentle, smiling warmth'.[8]

Other perils awaited the pilot. He might commit an elementary flying error that put his machine into a potentially fatal spin. The novice, of course, was at greatest risk. But even the most experienced might lapse. By mid-1918 James McCudden was a flying ace who had accounted for 57 enemy aircraft. In London early in July he received the Victoria Cross and found himself, to his amazement, a popular hero. Returning to the Continent, he set off from a French aerodrome to take up a new command. As his machine began to climb, its engine died on him. The rule in such circumstances, which McCudden had drilled into many aspirants, was straightforward. Never try to turn back. Keep on going and look for suitable ground on which to land. But for once McCudden ignored these simplicities. He attempted to regain the aerodrome. His plane went into a spin and never came out of it. The impact with the ground killed him.

A major danger to every pilot was failure of his aircraft. To the end of the war British flying machines were uncertain creatures. J. H. Morris, much engaged in bombing and photographic missions, noted on 3 January 1918 that, although eight or nine machines were detailed for every mission, only three or four usually crossed the front lines. The reason was 'rotten engines'. On 14 January he led a bombing expedition that was supposed to consist of 10 planes. Only eight managed to set out, and as they proceeded their number steadily dwindled through mechanical failure. By the time they crossed enemy lines only three were left, so that the mission had to settle for a nearer and lesser target. (Actually, the rule was that they should not have proceeded with fewer than four machines.)

Usually planes that dropped out in this way made a successful landing. Some did not. Morris relates how, on 4 December 1917, one machine that fell behind with engine trouble was later found wrecked, its engine buried 'practically out of sight in the ground'. Both crew members were dead. The propeller was found undamaged 200 yards away, looking 'as if it has been cut off beautifully square and finished off most carefully by a lathe.' 'No one knows exactly what happened but the various opinions point to the fact that something gave in the air.'

Weather was a further danger to the elementary aircraft of these days. If it was inclement ('dead weather', Morris called it), aeroplanes would be grounded. But a sudden change from fair to stormy might catch pilots in the air. Morris found himself in serious danger – exacerbated by some misjudgements on his part – on one such occasion.

On 27 February 1918 he took a machine aloft for a height test. The sky was clear when he set off, but by the time he reached 14,000 feet clouds were forming below. These he disregarded, coaxing the aircraft (which was beginning to have trouble with an exhaust valve) to 16,500 feet. Realizing that there now lay below what appeared a thin layer of cloud covering all of the ground on his side of the line, he decided to descend.

The cloud's apparent benevolence proved deceptive. When Morris sought to penetrate a hole in it, he saw not the ground but what seemed 'a black, bottomless pit . . . it looked to me as if it was raining hard and a hurricane blowing.' He went in search

---

[8] Lewis, *Sagittarius Rising*, pp. 96–8, 122–3.

of a better place for making his descent. Thinking he caught a glimpse of the earth he dived, only to find himself in deep clouds 'about ten thousand feet thick'.

> Nothing but black clouds surrounded me. It was raining in places and so bumpy that my machine seemed to quiver all over. . . .
> Down – down I went. Twelve thousand [feet], eleven, ten, nine, eight, and still in the clouds. Meanwhile my engine began to pop and bank. It was getting cold. So I opened out and flew level for a bit to warm it up again, and then down I went once more.

Morris reached 3,000 feet without finding a break in the clouds and began wondering if he would penetrate them before hitting the ground. (The altimeters of those days, Cecil Lewis tells us, were not the equivalents of modern instruments. They were set by the pilot on taking off and recorded only the aeroplane's altitude above his point of departure. If the pilot was flying over land higher than his own aerodrome, the altimeter would not register the fact. Hence in heavy cloud or darkness it was quite possible to hit the ground while this instrument was giving a height securely above it.)

Morris was down to 2,000 feet before, with his machine soaking wet and the engine missing badly, he got his first glimpse of earth. But the sight of some lines of barbed wire, 'beautifully regular and very thick', and the position of the shell holes in some buildings, convinced him that he was on the German side of the lines. Given his lack of height, he was in acute danger. So he headed back into the clouds, climbed to 8,000 feet, and set off westwards for half an hour. For some 15 minutes he was flying blind. Then he entered a sort of tunnel, with black clouds on every side but a hint of light far ahead. After another 10 minutes he saw a hole in the cloud below him and dived once more. At 2,000 feet he perceived the earth and came upon a French aerodrome.

Morris's adventure could have ended safely here. He landed and was urged to stay the night, it now being 4.20 p.m. Rashly, he declined. He believed that having got his bearings and been equipped with maps, he could reach his own base before nightfall. At 4.40 he set out. By 5 p.m. the clouds were down to 500 feet, it had started to rain, and darkness was fast approaching. 'On, on I went doing my level best to get home, but the rain got heavier and the clouds lower at every mile. Just outside Amiens I nearly ran into a hill which I couldn't see, partly owing to it almost being in the clouds and partly because my glasses were all fogged by the rain.' Morris decided that he must seek an airfield closer than his own. But events made even that impractical: 'Just then my engine started to go dud, and showed signs of cutting out at any moment. Twenty minutes flying in the rain was proving too much for it. I could by this time only just see directly below me at about fifty feet, even then sometimes losing sight of the ground.' Morris was now prepared to forget about an aerodrome. Before his engine failed or he encountered a church steeple or another hill, he must descend on any manageable piece of ground. 'All I thought of was getting down alive, and didn't care what happened to the machine.'

He caught a glimpse of a wheat field and decided on that. With visibility down to 100 yards and his machine travelling at 60 m.p.h., he could not judge the extent of the field or whether it would give way to houses or other obstacles before he managed to land. He switched off his engine so as to lessen the chance of its catching fire should he crash. 'Then bump: I had done a perfect landing on a wheat field.' All would have been well but that the field ran steadily downhill. So did the plane: into an adjoining field, which was in plough. 'The first twenty yards were all right and then, down went the nose and up went the tail. My wheels had stuck and on her nose she went. Up, up went the tail until the machine was standing practically vertical, was it going over or coming back?' Eventually it tilted back, settling at a 45° angle. For a resting place Morris could have done much worse. Three feet ahead, he soon discovered, stood a large telegraph post.

Morris was so relieved that he sat motionless in the cockpit for a few minutes. Then Frenchmen came running. So he got down and took a photograph of his observer, who was in such an elevated position that, except by damaging the aircraft, he could not descend without help. (The almost total absence from Morris's narrative of previous references to his observer is evidence of the little contact that was possible between the two men during flight.) Neither flier was injured, a fact that they had difficulty in impressing upon their rescuers. And nothing but the aeroplane's propeller was badly damaged.

By skill and some luck, Herbert Morris had survived a fairly desperate situation. Sadly, neither fortune nor flying ability would stand by him much longer. Five days later he was killed in a mishap that pre-figured the fate of McCudden. As he took off from Bellevue aerodrome his engine cut out. He endeavoured to turn back. The plane went out of control, crashed, and caught fire. His observer managed to get clear and, by rolling on the grass, to put out the flames. Morris perished in the blaze.

PART FIFTEEN

Some Social Aspects

63

WOMEN AND THE CONFLICT

I

The First World War was not, for Britain, a total war. That is, it was not a war in which the state assumed powers to commandeer, for war purposes, the lives and labour of the entire adult population. Over 50 per cent of adults were exempt, by reason of their sex, from any compulsion to contribute directly to combatant activities or war production. Such contribution as they made was voluntary, was circumscribed in the form it might take, and was considered sufficiently unusual to be received with fulsome expressions of gratitude.

No woman took a place in the British firing line during the war, even when the supply of men for the army had fallen dangerously low. No responsible individual suggested that this should happen. (Did any irresponsible individual?) Certainly, women contributed directly to the war effort in a variety of non-combatant roles. But they did so only because they chose to: under the impulse of patriotism, or money incentives, or the hope of improving the status of their sex. The conscription of women, even for industry, was never introduced. Lloyd George, among others, did on occasion argue for it. But neither as Minister of Munitions nor as Prime Minister did he attempt to implement it

Yet, in a sense, women were seen as a part of the whole range of war endeavour. Even in the activities of the battlefield – the taking of life and the making of the 'supreme sacrifice' – they were expected to participate. But they were to do so vicariously. Their role was to make straight their menfolk's path to enlistment and to ensure that concern for family did not impede husbands and sons from offering their services, and possibly their lives, to their country. A famous recruiting poster showed a group of upper-class women farewelling, wanly but stoically, a troop of departing soldiers. The caption read: 'Women of Britain Say – "*Go!*"'. A song, now difficult to take seriously, but delivered with enough intensity of feeling at the time, found females proclaiming to their menfolk:

> Oh we don't want to lose you,
> But we think you ought to go,
> For your King and your Country
> Both need you so.

By the same token, the female was expected to institute a negative sanction against any male acquaintance reluctant to 'do his duty'. She should cease having anything to do with him. This sanction was supposed to apply even against men who were prepared to join the Territorial Army, because this body existed only for home defence and so carried no obligation to serve overseas. In January 1915 the Reverend Andrew Clark of

Plate 54   *Women bus conductors taking their first lessons in their duties.*

Great Leighs, Essex, referred to three ladies of quality in his district as being 'great advocates of "the League of Honour" which binds young women not to walk out with Territorials'.

Women also participated in the public recruiting campaign, directing their appeals not only to close relatives but also to complete strangers. Here again the exhortations might come in the form of song. In the music halls and at village fêtes female entertainers enticed men to 'take the King's shilling' (that is, enlist) with such challenging ditties as:

> On Sunday I walk out with a soldier,
> On Monday I'm taken by a tar,
> On Tuesday I'm out
>   With a baby Boy Scout,
> On Wednesday with a Hussar,
> On Thursday I gang oot with a Kiltie,
> On Friday the captain of the crew,
> But on Saturday I'm willing, if you'll only take a shilling,
> To make a man of any one of you.

(Among the straitlaced this particular appeal was sometimes deemed not 'quite nice'.)

More orthodox recruiting addresses were delivered by Mrs Pankhurst, leader of the militant wing of the women's suffrage movement. Always at her most formidable when attacking Liberal rather than Conservative politicians, she had no difficulty in transferring her denunciations to those Englishmen who would not defend the womanhood of England from German brutality. Some of her followers went even further. They became active in publicly humiliating individual males who appeared to have ignored the call of duty. Such men were liable to be verbally denounced, or presented with white feathers as symbols of cowardice. These actions aroused mixed feelings, even among the patriotic. For one thing, in this new phase of their activities as in the old, the suffragettes were not always discriminating in their choice of victims. Probably most recipients of their attentions were, as intended, men eligible to enlist who had failed to do so. But there are well attested stories of occasions when this was not the case. In one instance a white feather was handed to an Essex schoolboy who happened to be rather tall for his age. (The event reduced schoolgirl onlookers to shrieks of mirth.) In another a middle-aged London surgeon of youthful appearance found himself publicly berated.

The latter incident is recorded, in his account of 'The Home Front 1914–1918', by the London ear surgeon P. M. Yearsley.[1] (He was also, ironically, much given to denouncing 'shirkers'.) While travelling by bus in December 1914, he was loudly harangued by 'an aggressive looking lady of uncertain age, evidently a suffragette, as she carried a copy of *Votes for Women*'. She demanded to know why he was not doing something for his country – 'a fine young man like you'. And she told him that he should be ashamed to travel in the same conveyance as a group of uniformed soldiers.

According to Yearsley's account (which overflows with self-satisfaction), he had much the better of the encounter. When the lady's tirade subsided he announced to her that he was a hospital surgeon, among whose duties was the care of the wounded, that he had just spent two hours drilling a Volunteer Training Corps, and that despite his appearance he was well over military age. (He was in fact 47.) Pointing to her copy of *Votes for Women* he announced: 'Before you obtain *that*, madam, you have much to learn, including how to restrain yourself and the folly of judging by appearances.' The lady muttered an apology and left the bus at the next stop.

It may be guessed that the displeasure that men like Yearsley felt towards this final phase of suffragette activity arose from more than its excesses. Yearsley admonished the 'aggressive looking lady' not only for 'judging by appearances' but also for failing to 'restrain' herself. It was the duty of women to encourage male friends and relations to enlist and even to shun the company of those who failed to do so. Haranguing them in public was another matter. Females were still expected to remember their place and to comport themselves according to the code of ladylike behaviour. For many males (and females) there remained limits to the ways in which women might tell men their business. Suffragette methods continued to be suspect even when their object was entirely acceptable.

II

At this distance it is difficult to respect the conduct of women who, themselves almost free from physical danger, were eager to exhort and even intimidate men into hazarding their lives and limbs. The activities of these non-combatant recruiters may indeed seem a grotesque form of sexual exploitation. For not only were women, while remaining exempt from danger, assigning members of the opposite sex to the risk of acute physical suffering. Further, males were being required to play out a warrior role imposed upon them by virtue of their sex, when this role did not necessarily accord with their particular natures. This point deserves more attention than, perhaps understandably, it has received in the literature of women's liberation.

Yet, if not a superficial view, then plainly this is a partial one. Events on the battlefield did involve acute suffering for many women. The enlistment of husbands often obliged married women to cope singlehandedly with problems for which they

---

[1] An unpublished account, based on his wartime diary, in the Imperial War Museum.

might be little prepared by upbringing or experience: dealing with accounts, managing a home or business, making decisions about the conduct and future welfare of children. For unmarried women, the departure of men for the front meant a deprivation of male company for the present and a distinct possibility that prospects of marriage, with all its connotations of motherhood, companionship, security, and social status, would be permanently blighted. Something of the desperation that this danger aroused in women is implicit in the notice that appeared in the Personal column of *The Times* in 1915: 'Lady, *fiancé* killed, will gladly marry officer totally blinded or incapacitated by the War.'

This notice also recalls another of the deprivations that war imposed upon women. Many lived for years on end with the daily fear that some irreplaceable member of their immediate community – husband or son or brother or fiancé – would be announced missing or dead or would return home severely mutilated. Often enough these fears were realized. The consequence for many women who lost husbands or lovers or fiancés was that all prospect of a stable married life – and sometimes even the urge for it – had vanished also. And few mothers whose adult sons fell in the war had any hope of making good their loss. Sometimes the deprivation was too great to be accepted. The post-war years saw a spate of romantic literature on the theme of the reappearance of soldiers supposedly dead but actually victims of amnesia. Such writings appealed to hopes possibly widespread. One hears of a mother in an Essex village who, right up to the time of her death more than a decade after the war, continued to affirm that one day her missing son would walk in the door, his memory suddenly restored. Perhaps she expressed the secret beliefs of many other women whose hopes of renewed motherhood lay only there.

An analogous case is provided by the wife of the writer Edward Thomas. In 1915 Thomas, then aged 37 and just beginning to find himself as a poet, volunteered for active service. (Many things contributed to this decision, but none more than love of his country. This sentiment, he wrote, was very different from that of the 'one fat patriot' about whom he felt a hatred compared with which 'my hatred of the Kaiser is love true'.) Thomas could have passed the war training soldiers in England, but he insisted on taking service in France as an artillery officer. He spent his last hours with his family on the morning of 11 January 1917 in their cottage in the Epping Forest. His wife has described how, after breakfast, he showed her his account books, responded with amused affection when she said that she too would keep accounts, gave her complete copies of his poems, and embraced her. Then he strode off into the mist and was lost to view. 'There was nothing but the mist and the snow and the silence of death.' Three months later he was killed by the blast of a German shell. When his wife received the books and papers he had been carrying at the time, 'they were all strangely creased as though subject to some terrible pressure.'

The gulf left in Helen Thomas's life was not filled. On the third anniversary of their parting she wrote to a friend about her husband:

> Tonight I think of all our life together, and I think of my life during these three years. Our life together was a restless sea, tide in, tide out, calm and glorious despair and ecstasy; never still, never easy, but always vivid and moving, wave upon wave, a wild deep glorious sea. Our life was terrible and glorious but always life.

Since then, life had also been like a sea, 'calm and cruel, happy and despairing'. But it was 'without a harbour, without an anchorage, and I have been tired to death of its tossing to and fro onto this beach and that, on to this rock and that'. So it would continue, she concluded, 'until that new life comes to me and I am gathered into my anchorage and him'. Almost twenty years later Helen Thomas rushed off a bus in a London street, convinced that she had seen her husband in the crowd.[2]

III

Nevertheless, it must still be said that, excepting those mothers and wives and brides-to-be whose loss of menfolk was never made good, the female experience of war was highly privileged compared with that of most able-bodied males. It was the latter who, by choice or (increasingly) compulsion, conformed to military direction, suffered under gunfire, saw comrades mangled, inflicted death in close combat or at remote distance, possibly sustained atrocious injuries, and sometimes died abruptly or lingeringly. For non-combatants, and this meant virtually all females, the desire to care might be present. But the gulf between experience and its absence was well-nigh unbridgeable. Siegfried Sassoon recognized, and was enraged by, it:

> You love us when we're heroes, home on leave,
> Or wounded in a mentionable place.
> You worship decorations; you believe
> That chivalry redeems the war's disgrace.
> You make us shells.[3]

and:

> I'd like to see a Tank come down the stalls,
> Lurching to ragtime tunes, or 'Home, sweet Home', –
> And there'd be no more jokes in Music-halls
> To mock the riddled corpses round Bapaume.[4]

These lines, of course, are the product of a heightened sensibility. Yet Sassoon's resentment on behalf of the mutilated against the immune found many echoes among rank-and-file soldiers: in their contempt at the outcry raised by civilians on account of the relatively trivial discomforts imposed by air raids and food shortages, and in their dismay at the sheer indifference to their own discomforts which they encountered when on leave. That wars in general, and this war in particular, soon became boring for non-participants is little cause for wonder. It went on too long, caused too many deaths, and produced the same indistinguishable episodes too many times. In April 1916 Beatrice Webb noted with surprise how callous she and others were becoming to the war's horrors. At first the conflict had been a continuous waking nightmare. But after a few months these feelings ceased and her usual activities reasserted themselves, as if colossal slaughter and devastation were part of the expected routine of life.[5] Probably few women were perceptive enough to appreciate the incongruity, and the luxury, of being able to react like this.

Even for a woman to whom the war became and remained a waking nightmare, her sex placed her in a privileged position. Vera Brittain's *Testament of Youth* is a moving account of the havoc that the war wrought in one young woman's life. In 1914 she was a university student just beginning to loosen the chains of a stifling provincial middle-class upbringing. She was also experiencing the intensity of first love. Four young men held a special – and entirely chaste – place in her affections: her brother and three of

---

[2] Quotations are from William Cooke, *Edward Thomas: A Critical Biography 1878–1917* (London: Faber & Faber, 1970), and a BBC radio programme, 'When All Roads Led to France', broadcast in 1972.

[3] Siegfried Sassoon, 'Glory of Women'.

[4] Siegfried Sassoon, 'Blighters'.

[5] Margaret Cole (ed.), *Beatrice Webb's Diaries 1912–1924* (London: Longman's, Green, 1952), pp. 57–8.

his school contemporaries, to the most brilliant of whom she became engaged. Between December 1915, when her fiancé was cut down by a machine-gun in France, and June 1918, when a sniper killed her brother in Italy, the war relentlessly extinguished each of these four men. Vera Brittain lived out these dread times, not in the comfort of home and family, but as a nurse's aid working often under fearful strain.[6] Frequently she yearned to embrace despair. But in the outcome she survived the war, and made a career, and married, and even enjoyed a measure of fame. Admittedly, it was not the career, or the marriage, to which she had looked forward in that hopeful summer of 1914. And her anguish at what had been destroyed by the war was never completely assuaged. Yet even so, compared with her brother and her fiancé and their two companions, she was lucky to have been born a woman.

IV

Apart from their roles of encouraging men to enlist and of sharing at a distance the suffering and death of the battlefield, what part did women have to play in this war? In the early stages the answer proved to be very little. Especially among the better-off, there were characteristically motherly activities to engage in, like learning First Aid, providing comforts for the troops, and seeking homes and employment for Belgian refugees. Observing some of these activities in Buxton, the Derbyshire 'mountain spa' where she lived, Vera Brittain commented:

> Few of humanity's characteristics are more disconcerting than its ability to reduce world-events to its own level, wherever this may happen to lie. By the end of August [1914]. . . the ladies of the Buxton élite had already set to work to provincialise the War.
>
> At the First Aid and Home Nursing classes they cluttered about the presiding doctor like hens round a barnyard cock, and one or two representatives of 'the set,' who never learnt any of the bandages correctly themselves, went about showing everybody else how to do them.[7]

For the rest, the immediate effect of the war was to lessen rather than increase women's range of activities. The campaign for women's suffrage was brought to a halt just when it seemed poised to succeed. ('Women get all the dreariness of war, and none of its exhilaration,' Vera Brittain wrote to her soldier-fiancé. '. . . It is strange how what we both so worked for should now seem worth so little.')[8] At the same time, an early economic consequence of the war was a sharp dislocation of the pattern of supply and demand, which particularly affected the luxury trades in which many women were employed: dressmaking, lacemaking, confectionery, and the like. A month after the outbreak of war some 40 per cent of women workers were unemployed or were on short time. A Central Committee on Women's Employment was set up to try to deal with this emergency, which it was assumed would last as long as did the war.

This proved a miscalculation. If the war had closed some avenues for women, it soon began opening others. Middle- and upper-class women in particular found increasing opportunities for service in tending war's victims: as doctors and nurses and orderlies caring for the maimed, and even as policewomen seeking to counter its social

---

[6] Her period of nursing in France was cut short in April 1918, when the Ludendorff offensive was at its height and medical services behind the British lines were stretched to breaking point, by a missive from her father. It stated that illness and lack of servants had forced her mother to go into a nursing home and that, 'As your mother and I can no longer manage without you, it is now your duty to leave France immediately': *Testament of Youth* (London: Virago, 1978), p. 421.

[7] Ibid., pp. 100–1.

[8] Ibid., p. 104.

dislocation. Women doctors had been few in number before the war, had encountered stern professional resistance, and had been restricted to caring for females and children. As for the policewoman, she was unknown in pre-war Britain. Female nurses were less of a novelty, but between 1914 and 1918 their numbers and spheres of activity expanded beyond all peacetime conception. During those four years some 23,000 served as nurses and 15,000 as orderlies of the Volunteer Aid Detachment. A handful of them went to Serbia, and in company with the beaten Serb army struggled across the Albanian mountains to the sea during the appalling retreat of 1915. Others journeyed to Russia or served in France within shell fire of the enemy lines. Most stayed closer to home, serving in base and field hospitals in France and England. But even they tended injuries on a scale and of an intensity quite beyond pre-war experience. Constantly they were having to deal with men, until recently ablebodied, whose limbs and bodies had been shattered by shells and gunfire or whose lungs and eyes had been ravaged by poison gas.

The Honourable Monica Grenfell, a daughter of the peerage and a devoted horsewoman, began training as a nurse only after the outbreak of war. Yet she was in a Red Cross hospital in France in time for the gas attack at Ypres in April 1915. She recounts how men came pouring into the hospital, choking for breath, their bodies blistered, their wounds turning septic. 'When I undressed, all my clothes, down to my chemise, reeked of pus.'[9] Another young nurse, Lesley Smith, was a characteristic product of an upper-middle-class Scottish family. She had taken no serious employment in peacetime because of her parents' opposition, and had difficulty in convincing them that she should become a nursing aid in war. The transition to a hospital in France was abrupt: 'Day after day we cut down stinking bandages and exposed wounds that destroyed the whole original plan of the body. One man had had both buttocks blown off, one arm had been amputated at the elbow, and he had a host of smaller wounds from flying metal.' In an operating theatre: 'The leg I was holding came off with a jerk and I sat down still clasping the foot. I stuffed the leg into the dressing pail beside the other arms and legs. The marquee grew hotter and hotter and the sweat ran off the surgeons' faces.'[10]

The policewomen were mainly drawn from the same strata of society as the women doctors and nurses, and their duties, if less gruesome, were even less familiar to members of their sex. They were employed particularly in areas where large numbers of troops were stationed, or where the munitions industry had drawn in a great body of migrant women workers. Somehow they had to strive to preserve order, discourage 'vice', and find shelter for those fallen by the wayside. This was no mean undertaking, given the extent of social dislocation in these areas and the limitations imposed on the policewoman's authority both by the fact of her sex and by disbelief in her capacity entertained by many police authorities. Six in number when established in August 1914, they had risen to 650 when Arthur Gleason published his study of wartime Britain in 1917.[11]

V

As the war's toll on manpower stretched Britain's reserves to the limit, even the fighting services were opened to women. There was still no suggestion of sending them

---

[9] Quoted in David Mitchell, *Women on the Warpath* (London: Jonathan Cape, 1966), p. 198.

[10] Quoted in ibid., p. 201.

[11] Arthur Gleason, *Inside the British Isles* (London: John Lane, The Bodley Head, 1917), p. 143.

to the front. But there were many fields of activity behind the lines in which women could take over the tasks of men (as typists, cooks, cleaners, mechanics, chauffeurs) and so release them for active service. In 1917 and 1918 over 100,000 women were enrolled in the various auxiliary bodies of the fighting services, the Women's Army Auxiliary Corps (WAAC), the Women's Royal Naval Service (WRNS), and the Women's Royal Air Force (WRAF). The WAACs, if not the other auxiliary services, differed from the women's organizations so far mentioned in that the rank and file–if not the higher echelons – were drawn from the working classes. (According to Robert Roberts in *The Classic Slum*: 'the Women's Auxiliary Army Corps, we soon gathered, was for the working-class females, whereas the "Wrens" and the WRAF catered for the nicer girls.')[12]

Service in these organizations, it needs to be stressed, remained entirely voluntary. One who entered the WAACs in mid-1917 and has left an account of her experiences was A. B. Baker, the daughter of a farmer, unmarried, and on enlistment only 18 years old.[13] To become accepted for service in France she had to misrepresent her age as 21, which the authorities connived at because she possessed a knowledge of colloquial French and so could be useful in translating letters. She joined up because her father was too old to fight himself, had no sons, and felt humiliated that he could contribute no one to the firing line.

She was not well versed in the facts of life. On her last visit home before going to France her father tried to explain certain matters to her. Down by the pigsties, he told her that the Tommies were heroes, but they were men too. She had only to respect herself, and they would respect her. Later she recalled this admonition while being pursued by a Tommy who did not respect her but, being out of condition, was unable to overtake her when she fled. The grunts he made during the pursuit recalled the noises emanating from the pigsties.

In France the WAACs were stationed at Etaples. During the German advance in 1918 the enemy made aerial attacks on the bridge there. Near the bridge, in the sunlight of a spring day, Baker saw 'half a company of men blown to pieces by bombs'. Some of the bombs fell on the adjoining cemetery. 'Coffins and dead men were blown from their graves. Into those graves limbs of living men and fragments of shattered dead men were flung.' Baker became somewhat hysterical. Then she was sick and wished she was home. A letter from her curate a few days later, on war as a noble discipline, lowered him severely in her estimation. For while sheltering from the bombs her only prayer had been that the war would stop.

The facts of sex presented themselves to her in various ways. She and a friend decided to go to the cinema in town and, coming upon a queue of Tommies, they joined it. This caused the soldiers some amusement, for reasons the youthful WAACs could not divine. Eventually a blushing young soldier came and told them the performance was for men only. They went away, still not understanding. 'Afterwards, when we did understand, I wondered what the curate would have said about that queue.'

Sex also occupied a place in the French correspondence she was asked to translate. Not a few of the letters concerned French girls who were pregnant by British soldiers. Sometimes the girls came in person, by turns threatening and distraught, and sometimes their relatives. There was an old grandmother, bent in back but not in spirit: 'She cursed me; she cursed the Colonel; she cursed the British Army; she cursed

---

[12] Robert Roberts, *The Classic Slum* (Harmondsworth: Penguin Books, 1973). p. 201.
[13] Her story is in C. B. Purdom (ed.), *Everyman at War* (London: J. M. Dent, 1930), pp. 380–6.

England and all the English. She went away, cursing. I sat shivering and ashamed.' Baker was shocked by these experiences, and by the blasé attitude of her superiors to this evidence of human fallibility. Later she became less so. For on one occasion she became aware that, but for the honourable nature of the man concerned, she might have proved fallible herself.

The man was a young sergeant named John. He had been in France over three years and had several times been wounded. His injuries had left him fit only for work at the base, but during the German March offensive he was recalled to action. On the day of his departure he walked with Baker in the woods and talked of his dread of going back into the line.

> He asked me if he could kiss me. I said, 'Yes.' He kissed me many times, and held me very tight. He held me so tight that he hurt me and frightened me. His whole body was shaking. I felt for him as I had never felt for any man before. . . . I might have forgotten what Daddy had told me by the pig-sties, if John had not been so decent.

Before March was out he was dead.

In April she was summoned home because her mother was ill. By the time she arrived her mother was already dead, of influenza. At the burial service the vicar preached that it was God's will, and God was good. Baker, thinking of the men blown to pieces at Arras, and the dead sergeant John, and her mother, and a French girl who had come to her distraught because there was a living child within her, wondered if the vicar knew any more about God than the curate did about war.

She was beginning to doubt the existence of God, or anyway his goodness. Strangely, what caused her to doubt her doubts, soon after her return to France, was a letter from a young man of her acquaintance who was in prison on account of his Quaker convictions. His letter seemed strangely happy. He wrote that, thinking of France and the Tommies, he had been miserable until he had been put in prison. He was so no longer, for he was sure he was doing his bit for England. Baker 'read that letter, written on blue prison paper, many times'.

As the Allies moved towards victory, she found herself involved in work with German POWs. They proved friendly men, who sang hymns to familiar tunes with great fervour. One of them reminded her of her father. She started praying again, but just the one prayer: 'O God, stop this war; stop it and set all of us poor prisoners free.' 'That seemed to cover the Tommies and me, the German prisoners and my friend in prison in England.'

On the day the war ended she drank four glasses of champagne, had a bad headache, and felt ashamed. Her return home proved unsettling.

> There they wanted to treat me as a sort of heroine. Their talk hurt me, even Daddy's. They praised me for all the wrong things. When I tried to tell them what the War had taught me, they were hurt in their turn. When I went to visit my friend not yet released from prison, they were angry. When he and I – but that is another story.

After many months the War Office sent her two medals.

64

WOMEN AND THE WORKFORCE

I do lead an extremely strenuous life nowadays. I am doing a 48 hour week at a large munition works near here to which I bicycle every morning. The buzzer goes at the, to me, unearthly hour of 8 a.m. & I am there usually till 5.45 with 1 hr off for dinner. No – I'm not making shells – but I am earning what seems to me a princely salary as a sort of works housekeeper. I have charge of all the office cleaners – all womens cloakrooms, lavatories etc – General supervision (with v. competent underlings fortunately) of the Works and the Staff kitchens & dining rooms with a little assistance to the women's employment superintendent thrown in! It is very interesting & varied, but my what a change from the lady of leisure life I have been leading!

Mabel Scott (daughter-in-law of C. P. Scott of the Manchester Guardian) *to Barbara Hammond, 29 November [1915]*

I

In any assessment of the effects of the war on women's employment, and thereby on women's status, it is necessary to set out those considerations that determined the area of 'women's work' before the war. In doing so there is a point worth bearing in mind. The attitudes that, by law or custom, debarred women from a whole range of responsible or arduous jobs were precisely those that prescribed that women were not obliged – and in major respects not allowed – to respond to the demands of war in the same ways as were men.

According to the established view, women were in an important sense special. They had unique capacities for bearing children, raising families, and moulding stable and happy homes. In another, equally important, sense they were inferior. They were regarded as lacking the mental capacity, the tenacity, the equability of temper, and the physical resources to undertake those types of work which required leadership qualities, skill, or brute force. Hence inside the home they performed an irreplaceable function. Outside it they were dependent on the opposite sex, whose members had an obligation to guard them – by legislation or physical strength or capacity to command a sufficient income.

From the male sex women, as daughters and wives, rarely enjoyed an independent existence. The novelist E. M. Delafield, looking back (in 1931) on the circumstances of middle- and upper-class young women before the war, wrote:

> We had been brought up in a tradition that a girl did not work: she was worked for, by a male relation, usually her father. Her aim in life was to find another man who would take upon himself this obligation by marrying her. In return, she became his house-keeper and the mother of his children.
>
> To some young women this ideal was satisfying: to others it was not. Only the bravest and most honest-minded failed to conform to it, for the usual alternative was to be 'the daughter at home'.[1]

---

[1] E. M. Delafield in Irene Rathbone, *We That Were Young* (London: Chatto & Windus, 1932), p. viii.

Plate 55 *Two women munitions workers decorated with the OBE for 'bravery and devotion to duty.' One lost her left hand in an explosion, the other lost two fingers.*

The manner in which these attitudes affected female employment is plain enough. Women as part of the workforce were an anomaly. Properly they belonged there only for the 'meantime': that is, during the transition from childhood to marriage, and only then if their parents lacked the wherewithal to maintain them in polite idleness. Adult women were not supposed to take paid employment, certainly not when they were married and least of all when they had children.[2] The force of this attitude is demonstrated by the fact that in 1911, the year of the last pre-war census, 90 per cent of all married women were 'unoccupied'. The vast majority of the remaining 10 per cent, where not cotton workers, were members of the lower classes whose husbands were ill, or unemployed, or on short time, or improvident of character. In such cases wives were obliged – only, it was to be hoped, for a while – to supplement their husbands' incomes. Among the middle and upper classes, where low incomes and profligacy (separately or in combination) were less common, married women hardly ever took employment. Thus a middle-class woman who continued in work after she had reached adulthood nearly always fell into a covertly pitied group, that of women who lacked both independent means and a husband.

The notion that a woman's place was not in a career, and certainly not in politics, but in the home was expressed with fervour by such varied groups as moralists, exponents of advanced thought, and tunesmiths. It was enforced by enormous social pressure from members of both sexes. Such forward-looking thinkers as the economist Alfred Marshall and the sex investigator Havelock Ellis subscribed to the view that women were different and inherently inferior. To Marshall woman was a 'subordinate being'; to Ellis she was more akin to the child. Their view was implicitly endorsed by the female social reformer Octavia Hill, who viewed the two sexes as inherently different but able to help each other because their different gifts were complementary; and by a prominent trade unionist of the late Victorian period, Henry Broadhurst. The latter saw it as the object of the trade union movement to secure for men a sufficient wage so that 'their wives should be in their proper sphere at home, instead of being dragged into competition for livelihood against the great and strong man of the world.'[3] A song writer, inspired by the concurrence of a potent musical importation from the USA and the campaign for female suffrage, penned a dire piece called 'The Ragtime Suffragette' ('she's no household pet'). It left no doubt that a woman's place was in the home and not in politics.[4]

---

[2] One region did not conform to this pattern: the cotton towns of Lancashire. This was the first region to be industrialized, and the attitude that had obtained before industrialization, that the whole family constituted the workforce, with the men doing the more arduous and responsible tasks and the women (and children) the lighter and less responsible, had been carried over into the factories. Hence what was conceived as constituting a living wage was the family's earnings and not just the husband's, and women did not generally cease working when they married or even when their first children were born. Outside Lancashire and the cotton industry, the advent of industrialization had caused married women no longer to be regarded as a proper part of the workforce.

[3] The foregoing quotations are from Sallie Heller Hogg, 'The Employment of Women in Great Britain, 1891–1921', D. Phil. thesis, Oxford, 1967, pp. 170–81. This thesis combines an extraordinary wealth of statistical and factual information with profound insight into the attitudes that moulded women's employment.

[4] The following sample of the lyrics is probably sufficient:

> While her husband's waiting home to dine
> She is ragging up and down the line
> A'shouting 'Votes! Votes! Votes! Votes!
> Votes! for Women'
> Oh the ragtime suffragette.

The author was Nat D. Ayre, an American resident in England, best remembered for his wartime hit, 'If You Were the Only Girl in the World'.

The forms of work that were considered appropriate for women largely reflected these preconceptions. Most desirable were the types of employment that most nearly approximated women's child-rearing and home-tending attributes: social work, nursing, and primary-school teaching for middle-class females; and weaving, dressmaking, and – most of all – domestic service for women from the lower orders. The last-named occupation was thought to be doubly appropriate for working-class girls. It trained them in housewifery. And it imposed on them a disciplined and supervised existence that guarded them from the temptations and dangers of unregulated employment. Outside these areas the mainstay of employment for working-class females was various sorts of factory work of an unskilled, routine kind. For middle-class girls the mainstay was light, clean work that would not detract from their femininity – secretarial work and serving in the better class of shop. It was axiomatic that women's work should not require determination, drive, ruthlessness, or a capacity for decision-making, none of which accorded with the assumed female character. And in that women workers would naturally prove inferior executants to men, and anyway were only marking time until the right man came along, it was considered inappropriate to provide them with lengthy training. Hence they never secured the qualifications for more skilled or responsible positions.

Thus the great majority of women's jobs had two things in common: they were poorly paid (at about half the rate of equivalent men's work), and they led nowhere. A single woman living alone could not support herself in conditions of adequate nutrition, cleanliness, and housing on the wages most of them received. But then the wage was not calculated to render its recipient self-sufficient. It was seen as a supplement to a family income, the bulk of which would be provided by husband or father – the 'breadwinner' as established terminology described him. How many women preferred, or were forced, to supplement their incomes not from these regularized relations but by resort to 'fancy men' or prostitution was not considered.

In addition to the low level of pay, most forms of women's employment held out no prospects for the ambitious – which was precisely what women workers were supposed not to be. For domestic servants who could never become the ladies of the houses in which they worked, for school teachers who only occasionally became the principals of the schools in which they taught, and for unskilled factory girls, the ceilings to which they could aspire were usually very low. Thus the precepts that women workers were only birds of passage on their way to domesticity and lacked the tenacity to succeed outside the home were confirmed by work conditions that sapped ambition and increased the pressure to escape into wedlock.

II

To what extent were these attitudes, and the social and economic practices produced by them, modified by the war?

As already mentioned, one immediate consequence of the war was a heavy fall in demand for the products of industries where females were concentrated: cotton, linen, silk, dressmaking, confectionery. Only after eight months of war did the number of women in the workforce regain the pre-war figure. That is, the exodus of men from industry into the army did not automatically create a demand for female labour. Most forms of industry were clearly recognized as providing either men's or women's work, or, if employing both sexes, were segregated internally as to which tasks each sex might perform. As the departure of men for the front naturally caused vacancies in men's work, there was no automatic creation of a need for women. Employers first sought alternative males: those thrown out of work by wartime dislocation, those who could be attracted from other industries by the offer of higher wages, juveniles who could be tempted to quit school earlier than intended, and older men who could be lured back into the workforce. It was only as the demands of the armed forces grew too voracious, as conscription deprived many employed men of the choice of remaining in work, and as the supply of alternative males consequently dried up that employers began resorting to female labour.

Equally, women were hesitant about availing themselves of these fresh job opportunities. Even those put out of work by wartime dislocation might be unwilling or unable to fill the growing number of vacancies. Females were not normally free to move about the country, so that those affected by unemployment in one district could not necessarily take advantage of openings elsewhere. And in that many women worked only when family finances required it, the institution of separation allowances for those whose husbands, actual or *de facto*, had joined the army removed the spur to take employment. Further, those in secure, if underpaid, positions such as domestic service hesitated to transfer to more lucrative jobs lest a speedy conclusion of hostilities should leave them high and dry.

Only as the war approached its second year did the forces making for an expansion of the female workforce overbear those of inertia. It was now clear that the war was not going to end soon. Plainly, too, the supply of alternative males was becoming exhausted. And a new force had to be reckoned with: the pressure being exerted by the government upon both employers and employees – particularly those guardians of the entrenched position of skilled males, the trade unions – to admit women into 'men's work'. The Government's immediate concern was with industries involved in munitions production. What it required was not just the substitution of women for enlisted males but a large increase in the numbers of workers engaged. And it was prepared to back up its appeal to patriotism with directives and legislation aimed at overcoming the resistance of labour and management to what was uncharitably called 'dilution' – the allocation of women ('unskilled labour' by definition) to work previously reserved for the skilled and semi-skilled. This did not necessarily mean an upgrading of female labour. Usually women did not take over the whole of the work process from skilled men. The jobs were broken down, so that the components requiring skill were performed by a skilled male or a machine and what was left by a group of females.

In industries not immediately essential to war production the Government did not intervene directly to procure the substitution of female workers. It allowed employers and trade unions to be driven to this course by the example set in the munitions industry and by the continuing depletion of the male labour force (which culminated in a measure of early 1917 forbidding non-essential industries from employing men aged between 18 and 61).

But it required more than a change of heart by male employers and employees to cause an upsurge in the female workforce. Powerful inducements to females were also necessary. The war provided several. The call of patriotism eroded the restraints on taking work that status or respectability imposed on married women of most classes, and on most middle- and upper-class women whether married or single. For once, woman's role as homemaker and childbearer was not automatically considered her highest duty.

Further, wartime conditions increased the supply of those jobs that the middle classes considered compatible with female respectability, especially posts of a secretarial, commercial, and administrative nature. For working-class women, among whom the stigma of factory work applied less forcibly, the newly established or converted munitions works were designed from the outset to accommodate female labour. It was generally recognized that women had needs peculiar to their sex in respect of the numbers of hours per shift that they could work efficiently, the heaviness of the machines that they could operate, and the welfare and refreshment facilities that they required. One of the serious obstacles to giving effect to dilution was the fact that established engineering works were geared to male labour. War-created munitions works were constructed for a predominantly female labour force.[5]

The war years provided another powerful inducement to women to enter, remain in, or return to the workforce: the changing structure of wages and prices. Inflation acted as the stick, new wage opportunities as the carrot, that induced many doubting women to take employment that was not always agreeable or even safe. Trade unions, in consenting to dilution, insisted that women taking over men's jobs must be paid at the male rate. This hardly ever happened. The fact that the tasks performed by women were rarely the direct equivalent of those previously carried out by men provided employers with a let-out. But, even so, the rates of pay for women substitutes were such a substantial improvement on what had been offered for 'women's work' in peacetime that they helped to overcome much of the unattractiveness of factory work.

This combination of patriotism, appropriate working conditions, and high wages did more than draw additional women into the workforce. It also caused females already in employment to change their jobs. In particular, women were lured from non-essential and poorly paid work, which nevertheless was indubitably 'women's work', into industries of national importance. The principal sufferer was domestic service. Overall the female workforce was greatly expanding – from under 6 million in 1914 to 7.3 million four years later – so converting women from under one-quarter to over one-third of the country's workforce. Yet the number employed in domestic service was falling by some 400,000, about one-quarter of the total. This was not on account of a falling off in demand. Wage levels and war-related activity were telling against domestic employment. So was another force much stimulated by the war: resentment among working girls themselves at the long hours and constricted independence still inherent in domestic service. This resentment increased at a time when in most other spheres the social oversight of young women was willy-nilly being relaxed.[6]

Domestic service was not the only occupation where demand for female workers outran supply. This could happen in essential industries also if other factors, like appropriateness of the work to females and especially high wages, did not apply.

This was strikingly demonstrated by the relative failure of women to make good the country's labour shortage in a vital sector, namely agriculture. (It is worth stressing that in another crucial area, underground mining, resort to the services of women was not so much as contemplated, even as a replacement for boys. So whether or not they would have answered the call was never put to the test.) Agriculture was traditionally

---

[5] Nevertheless, in that these munitions factories were rarely situated in the locality from which they drew their labour, they involved women workers in a major upheaval. Women were migrating from their homes to the munitions areas at a rate of 5,000 a month for much of the war. The lodgings available – either in private houses, where beds were often let on a rota system and were never empty, or in government-sponsored hostels, which many female workers likened to reformatories – were generally inadequate. The small children who sometimes accompanied female workers to the munitions areas must surely have been among the indirect casualties of the war.

[6] These sentiments against domestic service, although accelerated by the war, were apparent before it. So was the decline in the number of females prepared to accept this form of employment. Nevertheless, domestic service remained the largest single occupation for females (employing about one-quarter of all working women) in 1914.

regarded as heavy and dirty work, requiring long hours of labour and yielding low rates of pay. And the spread of industrialization had not only provided women with alternative forms of work but, by raising living standards, had decreased the need for females to work at all outside the home. Consequently, labour on the land had ceased to be regarded as appropriate for females. But the war and the submarine blockade revealed agriculture once again to be an industry of national importance. Correspondingly the Government became anxious to attract female labour into it. Yet despite much cajolery, including the establishment of a Women's Land Army, the response was poor. Rates of pay remained low compared with those offered in manufacturing industries. Farmers continued to resist employing females. And the stigma attaching to agriculture, that it required brute strength on the part of the labourer and so was an unfeminine pursuit, persisted.

As a result, whereas agricultural manpower fell by 260,000 during the war years, the number of females who took work on the land numbered only 48,000. In the desperate years of 1917–18 the labour of soldiers diverted from active service and of enemy prisoners of war contributed far more to bringing in the harvest than did that of women.[7]

III

Women contributed much to the country's war economy, in addition to their activities in fields directly related to the war such as nursing. But did any of this bring about a substantial change in women's position?

In an obvious sense it did. Women secured employment in areas previously closed to them and did not disgrace themselves therein. They shook off some of the restraints on their freedom of movement characterized by chaperonage. And they received tangible measures of reward. In the immediate aftermath of the war Parliament passed a Sex Disqualification Removal Act, which opened to women the Civil Service and the professions. Yet few women achieved eminence as a result of this legislation. And in the post-war sequence of boom and slump the most evident advances that women had made in the workforce disappeared.

Traditionally, one major force in depriving women's labour of status was its 'meantime' character. That is, women's work was only a resting place on the road to marriage; females were not committed to their jobs as a career. The war in no way altered this situation. Women employees were more than ever 'meantime' workers. In the most prominent instance, munitions, they were occupying male jobs only on the sufferance of trade unions and only until the soldiers were demobilized. And the commodities they were producing in such profusion would cease to be required the day the war ended.

There were other ways in which wartime conditions proved transitory. Community tolerance of married women remaining in employment was the product of the national emergency; it did not necessarily mark a permanent change. Anyway, many women who laboured longer than they had ever intended at factory benches or in hospitals did not gain thereby any desire to prolong their employment into peacetime. Further, if the war had offered proof that women were capable of performing responsible industrial tasks from which they had hitherto been excluded, it left many employers unconvinced that women workers were just as desirable as men. Indeed, women's improved wage rates had impaired one of the major reasons why employers sometimes preferred female labour – its extreme cheapness.

---

[7] Figures from Hogg, 'The Employment of Women in Great Britain, 1891–1921', pp. 393–4.

The consequence was that, even during the post-war boom of 1919–20, the wartime upsurge in female employment went into reverse. As mentioned already, it sometimes did so with the consent of the women involved. But this was not always the case. It is noteworthy that the form of female employment that had declined so markedly during the war, domestic service, made good much of its lost ground during the first eighteen months of peace. Yet this type of work was increasingly falling into disfavour. Admittedly, it was still much approved by those who believed that young women, in order that they might escape the blandishments of the devil, needed little idleness and much supervision. But, as has been suggested, among working-class girls themselves it was regarded with growing resentment. An inquiry five years after the war found that domestic service now occupied a lower status even than unskilled factory work. As one parlourmaid put it:

> I do not believe that any girl minds the work. They *do* mind being ridiculed. I have suffered untold misery by the name 'only a servant'. Invitations out state, 'Be sure and do not let it be known you are a domestic. We should not like our friends to mix with servants'. It is the snobbery of our own class.[8]

The double meaning of the word 'menial' – servant and underling – symbolized what was becoming so unattractive about domestic service. That, nevertheless, increasing numbers of females reverted to it suggested that their relinquishment of war-created employment was not always voluntary.

Yet for a while something of the advance made in war persisted into peace. This was particularly true for women working in clerical and secretarial posts and as shop assistants – forms of employment into which they had begun to penetrate before 1914 but where their advance was much accelerated by the war. However, the downturn in the economy from 1920 practically eliminated what remained of these improvements and restored the pre-war pattern. It was a clear indication that women retained a second-class position in the labour force that they were the first victims of the slump. Indeed, by 1921 a smaller proportion of the female population was in employment than had been the case ten years earlier – 32 per cent in 1911, under 31 per cent in 1921.[9]

It had, of course, been the traditional view that if one sex or the other must go without work, then women – who were supposed only to supplement a family's income, not to provide it – should make the sacrifice. What is worth stressing is that the war had reinforced, rather than altered, this attitude. Admittedly, during the conflict women had sometimes acted as adequate substitutes for men. But the men meanwhile had been enacting a yet more arduous role: that of heroes. It appeared intolerable that, as jobs became short, these returned warriors should be displaced by the women who had entered the workforce during their absence. (There were even instances where strong communal resentment was entertained towards married women who would not relinquish posts in primary schools required by unemployed ex-servicemen, even though primary teaching was more properly women's than men's work.)

These employment trends hardly support the notion that attitudes regarding women's place in the workforce were greatly changed after 1918. Certainly, there may have been more career women in England: some because they lacked male partners,

[8] Quoted in Janet McCalman, 'The Impact of the First World War on Female Employment in England', *Labour History* (journal of the Australian Society for the Study of Labour History), No. 21, November 1971, p.41.
[9] These figures are from Hogg, 'The Employment of Women in Great Britain, 1891–1921', p. 487. This writer points out that at the time of the census in 1921 the downturn in the economy had by no means reached its nadir; the proportion of females employed would almost certainly have been lower in 1922. However, she also points out that in certain areas, such as commerce, public administration, and the manufacture of chemical and leather goods, women did retain something of their wartime advances in employment.

others because they had been convinced by wartime experience that there were more interesting occupations than marriage. But there had always been a small yet revered group of women who by general agreement belonged in a career and not in a kitchen. Particularly was this true of those irreplaceables who literally occupied the centre of the stage, in theatres and music halls: Ellen Terry, Madge Titheradge, Mrs Patrick Campbell, Marie Lloyd, Vesta Tilley, and a handful of others. The post-war world could accommodate many more like these, not only on the stage but in Parliament and the professions too, without relinquishing its established view about woman's appropriate place. And unless a woman who pursued a career proved outstanding in it, she was likely to be regarded not as part of a new breed but as an indirect casualty of the war: one of those unfortunates deprived of the chance of marriage by the slaughter on the battlefield.

Anyway, far from their experiences in the war convincing women that there was more to life than marriage, it appears that they were even more attracted to wedlock after the war than before. For even though the numerical excess of females over males, which had been apparent before 1914, was increased by the war, the proportion of single to married women was lower in 1921 than it had been in 1911. In other words, women were marrying younger. Further, they do not seem to have been revising the assumption that, other than in the exceptional conditions provided by the war, females took work because they had to, not because they wanted to. As might be guessed, the number of widows in the 25–34 age group had greatly increased in 1921 as compared with 1911. But the proportion of widows in employment fell sharply: from 66 per cent to 47 per cent. Doubtless this decline had several causes. But, pretty clearly, one of them was the fact that widows of servicemen were in receipt of adequate pensions from the state and so did not need to go out to work to subsist.

65

STATUS AND THE SUFFRAGE

The position of woman as an industrial worker is and always must be of secondary importance to her position in the home. To provide the conditions which render a strong and healthy family life possible to all is the first interest of the State, since the family is the foundation stone of the social system.

While women have helped and are helping the nation splendidly, they must realise that men have not forfeited their jobs by answering their country's call, and doing work which women cannot undertake.

Resolutions of a conference on women in post-war industry, held at Penscot by a Joint Industrial Council
in 1918

I

According to a contemporary account, one unhappy social aspect of the later part of the war was 'the large measure of public approval and support' for what was described as 'the unwritten law'.[1] By this 'law', a man was 'held to be justified in killing his wife on obtaining proof, as to the sufficiency of which he is himself the judge, of her infidelity'. The first semi-formulation of this doctrine occurred when the victim was not the wife of the accused but the man who had attempted to seduce her: 'the verdict of not guilty in this case was followed by loud and general applause.' Then, at the Old Bailey, a soldier was arraigned for deliberately shooting his wife 'on receiving undoubted proof of aggravated infidelity'. The accused appeared, from his frank confession, 'to think that he had acted in the discharge of a public duty'. The Crown did not attempt to press a charge of murder, and the accused, having pleaded guilty to manslaughter, was 'bound over' and set at liberty. The judge claimed that 'he could only inflict such punishment as a reasoned and instructed public opinion would believe to be fitting.'

Further cases followed, so that (in the view of the *Manchester Guardian* history) there seemed 'every promise of the introduction of a kind of modified lynch law into English jurisprudence'. At last the judiciary insisted that it would reassert the supremacy of the law. An accused man in Manchester received a heavy sentence 'after twice asserting the right to take his own revenge' on his wife. Thereupon the public 'petitioned numerously for the exercise of the clemency of the Crown'.

The real inwardness of all this, especially in the context of the war's effect upon women, was spelled out in the *Manchester Guardian*'s account: 'we are able to perceive how essentially primeval the doctrine [of the 'unwritten law'] is from the circumstance that the supposed justification belongs to the husband only.' The 'law' did not serve, or was not generally supposed to serve, as a defence for a wife who 'might kill her husband for the same reason'.

---

[1] *The 'Manchester Guardian' History of the War* (Manchester: John Heywood, 1920), vol. 9, p. 167.

II

Too much, arguably, has been written about the effects of the war in enhancing women's status. Its effects were not clear-cut. Women had made a substantial and much praised contribution. Yet in every area this contribution was less than that of males – the 'heroes' whose names 'liveth for evermore' (if they had died) or for whom a 'fit land' must be prepared (if they had survived). In virtually every field of government, civil affairs, and the fighting services men had provided the leadership and most of the rank and file. The case of industry is not all that different. Males, in the form of boys as they reached school-leaving age (or who left school anyway) and older men who re-entered the workforce, proved a greater source of substitute labour than did females. Whatever the absolute contribution of women to winning the war, this had hardly invalidated traditional sex differentiations.

Even the long-held conviction about women's incapacity to behave responsibly outside the family circle had not been extinguished by the war. However laudatory the official comments on women's contribution to the war effort, many unofficial remarks were less appreciative. As Doris Langley Moore recalls, 'the prosperity of the domestic servant who became a munition worker had excited derision and antagonism from the first.'[2] The spendthrift habits of 'munitionettes' were a stock subject for comments and jokes. Little was made of the fact that, during the latter half of the war, sales of soap reached a record height, in part because of the increased purchasing power of working-class women ('women were always the soap makers' best customers').[3] Instead, comment was directed to the large numbers of munitions girls sporting fur coats and similar luxury items, which were presumed to be attractive simply because of their outrageous cost and unfamiliarity. It was also prophesied – in the outcome, usually accurately – that before long these items would make the journey into the pawn shop once more than they made the journey back.

A characteristic anecdote was told of two munitions girls contemplating the purchase of a pineapple. This was in an age when the pineapple was such a luxury that, for special functions, families with aspirations outrunning their means would hire a pineapple whose presence – though not taste – would add grace to the occasion. The two munitionettes, after eyeing the pineapple and learning its (exorbitant) price, informed the fruiterer: 'Well, we'll buy it if you tell us how to cook it'.

The personal conduct of females in the labour force and the service auxiliaries was also the subject of unfriendly comment. The more acerbic wondered what proportion of the factory girl's earnings was derived not from their official employment but from what was euphemistically called 'the extra shift'. As for the WAACs, tales ran rife about their want of respect for their officers and their looseness of living. According to one witness, even before any WAACs had reached France remarks against their characters were widespread in the YMCA huts. Typical comments included: 'Our poor Tommies will be ruined' and 'It is a shame to send these women to corrupt our poor lads.'

Within a year of the arrival of the first WAACs on the Continent, allegations of 'immoral conduct' and unwanted pregnancies were so rife that it became necessary to appoint a commission of inquiry.[4] This commission concluded that it could find 'no

---

[2] Doris Langley Moore, 'The Forgotten Years 1919–1924', in *The Saturday Book 28* (London: Hutchinson, 1968), p. 71.

[3] Charles Wilson, *The History of Unilever* (London: Cassell & Co., 1954), vol. 1, pp. 220–1. Total sales of soap for 1917 were 65,710 tons. Only once before (in 1905) had they exceeded 60,000 tons.

[4] Documents on this matter are in the Modern Records Centre, University of Warwick.

justification of any kind for the vague accusations of immoral conduct on a large scale which have been circulated'. Of a total WAAC personnel in France (up to 12 March 1918) of 6,023 women, '21 pregnancy cases had been reported since the arrival of the Corps in France and 12 cases of venereal disease.' (The War Office wanted all reference to venereal disease removed from the report. But its authors insisted on 'the most absolute frankness and candour' and refused to budge.) This conclusion – whether or not it was accurate – failed to set the stories to rest, for the attitudes that had given rise to them were just too strong. In fact, a powerful reason why women resisted joining the auxiliary services in the Second World War was concern about the sexual laxity they would supposedly encounter there.

One noteworthy feature of this matter is that it was the presumed sexual aspirations of WAACs towards British soldiers that aroused adverse comments, not the corresponding inclination of soldiers towards WAACs. The Great War was certainly not abolishing the double standard of morality.

III

The ambiguous effect of the war on women's status is perhaps most evident in that area where it is usually said that improvement was indubitable.

Before the war, no woman had possessed the vote. In 1918 'the Cause' triumphed. Indeed Parliament conceded what the suffrage advocates had hardly begun to demand: the right of women to sit in the House of Commons. To those who had suffered on behalf of the movement it seemed a mighty triumph.

Yet in the event it proved a somewhat muted one. Although the general election held at the end of 1918 was memorable for many things, the fact that women participated for the first time was at best one of its oddities. No woman candidate was returned (apart from an Irish revolutionary who would not take her seat), and none made much impact. Christabel Pankhurst, breathing fury against Huns and Bolsheviks, was indistinguishable – except in her failure to get elected – from any of the Government's more reactionary supporters. And if women electors cast their vote in any distinctive fashion, it was (so observers argued) only to exaggerate the stampede to the right initiated by their menfolk. Ramsay MacDonald, a pre-war suffragist who lost his seat by a large majority, considered that although he had secured the support of women in the middle artisan section, women from both the more palatial and the poorer sections had proved the most bloodlusty and credulous of voters. 'Woman as a psychological problem was in evidence; women as citizens had not appeared.'[5]

What was more, except within the ranks of the old campaigners for the female suffrage, the enactment of votes for women in 1918 did not seem like the joyous triumph of a women's crusade. Even among some feminists, it passed almost unremarked. 'With an incongruous irony seldom equalled in the history of revolutions, the spectacular pageant of the woman's movement, vital and colourful with adventure, with initiative, with sacrificial emotion, crept to its quiet, unadvertised triumph in the deepest night of wartime depression.'[6]

The anticlimactic nature of this success is illustrated by the response of the younger members of the Women's Hospital Corps to the passage of the suffrage Bill in February. The principals of the Corps were delighted. They had been active in the suffrage movement before the war, providing medical aid for suffragettes released from

---

[5] *Manchester Guardian*, 30 December 1918.
[6] Vera Brittain, *Testament of Youth* (London: Virago, 1978), p. 405.

prison (often desperately ill) after hunger-striking. So when they formed the Women's Hospital Corps in 1914 they gave it the same motto as Mrs Pankhurst's organization: 'Deeds not Words'. But in 1918 they found that most nurses in the Corps were barely interested in their great success. 'Simply topping about your bill' was how the nurses responded.[7]

There are reasons for thinking that on the eve of war the supporters of female suffrage might have been about to win anyway; that Asquith, though still hostile, was prepared to bow before their unrelenting pressure. Had the vote been accomplished in these circumstances, it would have constituted a mighty victory for the feminist cause. In any election on the morrow of such a success the fact of women's participation could hardly have failed to loom large. The war robbed the women's endeavours of this potential success, split the movement along the lines dominating 'male' politics, and submerged the suffrage cause in a far greater national emergency. Certainly, the eventual enactment of the female franchise owed something to the continuing vitality into wartime of the constitutional (as against the militant) suffragist movement. But to a considerable extent the enactment of the women's vote had the appearance of being a gift from men, not a triumph for feminist pressure. And coming as it did between the battle of Passchendaele and the Ludendorff offensive, it could hardly be more than a side issue of national affairs.

The attitude of Asquith makes it evident that not very much had changed. Publicly he proclaimed that he had been converted to the female suffrage by women's endeavours in wartime. But there is no reason to believe that he was much less hostile to it than he had been four years earlier. (In January 1920 he could still write of 'these damned women voters', 'dim, impenetrable . . . for the most part hopelessly ignorant of politics, credulous to the last degree, and flickering with gusts of sentiment like a candle in the wind'.)[8] The war had taken the sting out of suffragist demands and had provided people like him with a convenient cover behind which to retreat without loss of face. From the point of view of the woman's movement, loss of face by its opponents was hardly less important than the concessions extracted from them.

The equivocal nature of the changes wrought by the war upon the position of women is reflected in the very terms used to proclaim that their position had changed. At the end of the war the Director General of the Army Medical Services, who three years before had made a London hospital available to the Women's Hospital Corps, congratulated its members on their success. 'Let me thank you . . . not only for what you have done for the country, but for what you have done for me personally. I should have been an object of scorn and ridicule if you had failed.'[9] It was in similarly patronizing terms that Asquith announced his change of heart: he had always argued that women must work out their own salvation, and now they had done so. What in fact women had done was to show themselves capable of performing in war a variety of tasks most of which men carried out as a matter of course in peace. The equality of the sexes must continue somewhat unreal as long as men propounded, and women accepted, this other sort of double standard.

None of this detracts from the actual advances that women made during the war. Notwithstanding inflation and shortages, patronizing praise and snide criticism, they had in many instances achieved a higher standard of living, a new confidence in the range of tasks they could perform, and new expectations. Indicative of a changing

---

[7] David Mitchell, *Women on the Warpath* (London: Jonathan Cape, 1966), p. 196.

[8] H. H. A. *Letters of the Earl of Oxford and Asquith to a Friend*, First Series (London: Geoffrey Bles, 1933), pp. 120, 125.

[9] Quoted in Mitchell, *Women on the Warpath*, p. 196.

vision was the upsurge in the number of women joining trade unions in the last two years of the war. Before 1914 women workers (outside Lancashire) had proved extremely difficult to form into unions, a reflection of their lack of commitment to their work as a career. In the first half of the war they proved even more intractable, their employment now being more than usually transitional. But in 1917 and 1918 attitudes changed. Women unionists, who numbered under half a million at the start of the war, increased to 1.2 million (a rise of 160 per cent) at its end.[10]

Even industries little affected by the war revealed the change, although it was first apparent where women were substituting for men and receiving something like men's pay. The probable cause was the newly aroused consciousness among working women, and to a less extent among the community in general, of the effectiveness and worth of female labour. Doubtless the manifold shortages and discomforts and injustices of civilian life in wartime gave this consciousness a sharper edge. But it is also worth wondering whether the simple attainment of certain pay levels, and a correspondingly higher standard of nutrition, took these women past a cut-off point between docility and self-assertiveness.

Whatever the cause, a number of contemporary observers did believe that women's wartime employment was changing them. The *New Statesman*, in an oft-quoted article of June 1917, spoke of the 'amazing transformation' effected by three years of war on the average factory woman, particularly in munitions centres.

> They appear more alert, more critical of the conditions under which they work, more ready to make a stand against injustice than their prewar selves or their prototypes. . . . They have a keener appetite for experience and pleasure and a tendency quite new to their class to protest against wrongs even before they become intolerable.[11]

Yet it was only a year later that one of the nation's 'popular' newspapers, the *Daily Graphic*, relegated women workers firmly to second-class status:

> The idea that because the State called for women to help the nation, the State must continue to employ them is too absurd for sensible women to entertain. As a matter of grace, notice [of dismissal] should be at least a fortnight and if possible a month. As for young women formerly in domestic service, they at least should have no difficulty in finding vacancies.[12]

Doris Langley Moore, herself a young woman at the end of the war, recalls that

> as the men came back to 'Civvy Street', the women who had been lauded for keeping the country going were urged to get back to their homes – and lugubriously reminded how many of them were destined never to find husbands.

In her view, the period immediately after the war was 'probably the nadir of feminine social history'.[13]

If the war had raised women's aspirations, it had not overcome the most serious obstacles to the attainment of sexual equality. For one thing, few women (let alone men) believed even now that, in a situation of contracting job opportunities, women should remain in work while the traditional breadwinners, who now were also recent heroes, went without. For another, the vicious circle in which women found themselves where status was concerned had yet to be broken. The conviction remained general

---

[10] See I. O. Andrews and M. A. Hobbs, *Economic Effects of the World War Upon Women and Children in Great Britain* (New York: Oxford University Press, 1921), pp. 87–8.

[11] Quoted in ibid., pp. 200–1.

[12] Quoted in Mitchell, *Women on the Warpath*, p. 266.

[13] *The Saturday Book 28*, pp. 71–2.

that the most gratifying occupation for woman was as wife, mother, and home-maker. It existed alongside the conviction that child-rearing and home-making were inherently inferior to the career activities practically monopolized by men. That is, men's and women's tasks were separate, and they were not equal.

As long as what were regarded as the distinctively female occupations ranked below professional, commercial, and industrial occupations, then the cause of female equality was hamstrung. For it to succeed, either women would have to abandon home and children as their principal vocation and establish themselves in the predominantly male occupations, or they would have to secure a conspicuous upgrading in the respect accorded their own activities as wives and mothers. No large body of women was anxious, despite distinguished exceptions, to embrace the former alternative: the attractions of marriage and family remained great for British females. On the other hand, few advocates of feminism were eager to advocate the second alternative. Reverence for motherhood and domesticity was often the very thing from which they were trying to deliver the female sex. Whatever the changes wrought by the war, it had not resolved this impasse.

IV

Can we, then, go further in summarizing the effects of the war on women than to say that it left them second-class citizens but had improved the quality of second-class travel? That seems the conclusion to be drawn if we look at the more tangible areas from which assessment can be made. Women had been given the vote. But these years of stress had shown that they would see political matters much as their menfolk did. They had been given the right to sit in Parliament. But there was no prospect of the House of Commons being invaded by a monstrous regiment of women. They had secured new opportunities for work. But although some of them had moved into 'men's work', this was either in insignificant numbers or only for the duration. The war had accelerated those processes that were extending the range of women's work into new areas, but only by altering the boundary between men's work and women's work (to women's advantage), not by threatening to remove it.

Yet in trying to assess the changed place of women in British life, there are certain intangibles that may point to a less negative conclusion. In the first place it can be speculated that a quantitative improvement in living standards and working conditions sometimes produces a qualitative change, both in the life a woman lives and in her aspirations towards its betterment; and this may have been the case during the war. Secondly, the fact that women had temporarily occupied men's jobs may have been of more lasting importance than the heroic deeds men were performing while women were about it. After all, the Englishman as warrior was a temporary being. He had no fixed place in the nation's scheme of things. The Englishwoman as executor of tasks previously deemed beyond her was within an acceptable line of development. Thirdly, it was a probable consequence of women's experience in working alongside men, or as substitutes for menfolk fighting overseas, that females would develop a greater independence of attitude towards males, be they fathers or husbands.

Certainly, a number of observers did feel that the war had brought changes of this sort. In 1931 E. M. Delafield, after describing, in the passage quoted earlier, the confined lives of middle- and upper-class girls before the war, wrote: 'Women who were girls in 1914 will understand what that meant. Those who are girls in 1931 will not - and never can. And it is in great measure to the war-workers, as we called them . . . that these girls of to-day owe the freedom of which the large majority are making such fine and splendid use.'[14] And Robert Roberts, a marvellously literate product of a North of England slum, says something similar about working-class women. Those who had to rear families in their husbands' absence 'found in the responsibility a new freedom'. They anticipated that with the return of their menfolk they would be obliged to resume their former subservience, but this proved not to be the case: 'with surprise they discovered that husbands, home again, were far less the lords and masters of old, but more comrades to be lived with on something like level terms.'[15]

The women customers in his parents' corner shop, Roberts recalls, commented on this change time and again. And it was not only among the already established married women that a change was observed. Younger wives were to be seen drinking in pubs, round for round, with their husbands. Teenage girls were wearing dresses that their elders found highly provocative, and were refusing jobs as domestic servants because they were determined to enjoy greater independence. Furthermore, male status, according to Roberts, sometimes suffered a downgrading when unskilled female workers had a chance to observe the mysteries of the skilled tradesman at first hand. He writes of his father:

> In his cups he was wont to boast that, at the lathe, he had to manipulate a micrometer and work to limits of one thousandth of an inch. We were much impressed, until one evening in 1917 a teenage sister running a capstan in the iron works remarked indifferently that she, too, used a 'mike' to even finer limits. There was, she said, 'nothing to it'. The old man fell silent. Thus did status crumble![16]

One can draw no more than tentative conclusions from this type of evidence. For one thing such perceptive observers as Roberts are rare. For another writers like Delafield, or talkers like the customers in the corner shop, were not seeing the pre-war and post-war worlds with the same pairs of eyes. However little they realized this, it may have been themselves, rather than objective reality, that had changed with the passage of time. Even so, these indications of an altered female world deserve notice.

Moreover, they gain in weight when placed beside another consideration. If we set aside the issue of status and take account rather of power and influence, it may be that the accepted picture – that of female dependence on males caused by women's lack of economic independence and career opportunities – proves to be overdrawn from the start. The central positions that women occupy in the domestic structure as house-keepers and mothers accords some of them a substantial measure of authority *vis-à-vis* husbands and sons. We have seen already the use that, in war, some women were quick to make of dogmas like 'manliness', 'duty', and 'honour' as sticks with which to belabour males into enlisting. Such conduct has its peacetime counterparts: in the pressures sometimes exerted on sons, husbands, male relatives, and even acquaintances to strive at school, on the sports field, in a career, as parts of the workforce, lest they lose the respect of mothers, spouses, female relations, girl friends. And there are other, more beneficent, ways in which women plainly guide or direct the conduct of males upon whom, theoretically, they are dependent.

This is not to deny that in 1914 females generally occupied a second-class situation that the war did not convert into a first-class one. The point being made is that the simple dichotomy between dominant male and subservient female ignores the extent to which the family structure places women in a position to influence, and sometimes to

---

[14] E. M. Delafield in Irene Rathbone, *We That Were Young* (London: Chatto & Windus, 1932), p. viii.

[15] Robert Roberts, *The Classic Slum*, p. 215.

[16] Ibid., pp. 198–9.

determine, the conduct of seemingly independent males. Hence it may be that females' enthusiasm for marriage and home-making after the war, following on their wartime experience of a loosening of family bonds, is not evidence of how thoroughly they had been brainwashed into accepting dependence as their appropriate status. It may reflect a conviction, reinforced by the war, that the home – far more than the workplace – offered large opportunities for the exercise of creativity at the most fundamental human level, for the assumption of responsibilities, and (for those so inclined) for the use and even the abuse of power and authority.

66

BATTLE FOR THE MINDS:
THE PROPAGANDA WAR

We went to War Cinema at the Scala. There were some very interesting German propaganda ones which had been intercepted on their way to neutral countries. The sinister spiked helmets made me feel that, even yet, the Germans must win.

Lady Cynthia Asquith's diary, 29 August 1917

I

The First World War, it is generally agreed, was the first conflict in which the techniques of propaganda were widely employed. What is less generally agreed is what constitutes propaganda.

In the present context the term embraces any form of communication – be it conversation or public speech, private letter or publication, photograph or poster or moving film – that dealt with the war in such a way as to propagate the cause of one side and discredit that of its opponents. That is, propaganda in the First World War might consist of strictly factual information. Examples are a cinema film of the first tanks (which aroused much interest) and even a tank itself – one appeared to good effect at a Win-the-War Day in Birmingham in September 1918. It could, on the other hand, constitute pure invention, like the stories of a Canadian soldier crucified by enemy forces and of the existence of a German 'corpse-conversion factory'. It could be a mixture of fact and invention, like the atrocities alleged against the Germans in the Bryce Report. The tone of propaganda could vary also: from the scrupulous and sober, as with the film *Battle of the Somme*, to the base and obscene, as with many of the writings of Horatio Bottomley.

All propaganda, whether true or false, was slanted. Its intent was to give a favourable view of the deeds of one group of combatants and the cause for which they were striving, and an unfavourable view of the opposing group. This applied even to the tank that trundled through the centre of Birmingham. Its purpose was to demonstrate British ingenuity and war-winning capability; not to endorse one German view of the tank, that it was an atrocious means of waging war.

Within the context of the times – namely that there was a war to be won and a nation to be rallied – much British propaganda seems entirely legitimate. Some of it, indeed, appears quite admirable. For example the series of 'battle' films (the Somme, the Ancre, Arras, St Quentin, Allenby's entry into Jerusalem, *et al.*) have recently been described as seeming 'curiously lacking in propaganda elements' – by which is meant the sensationalist and hate-filled forms of propaganda.[1] As an indication of this, they

---

[1] Liz-Anne Bawden (ed.), *The Oxford Companion to Film* (London: Oxford University Press, 1976), p. 562.

are drawn on heavily at the present time for television documentaries that have no propaganda purpose – unless it be to prove that British commanders were incompetent. Again, the most famous British cartoon figure of the war, Bruce Bairnsfather's 'Old Bill', bears reproduction in whatever season simply because he offers no glorification of war. He is sardonic, scornful of the 'brass hats', but above all a symbol of endurance. (Characteristic is his stolid attitude even when the water level in his trench has risen so high that he can contemplate being attacked by a submarine.)

Plate 56a and 56b   *Some of the varied purposes of wartime posters and pamphlets.*

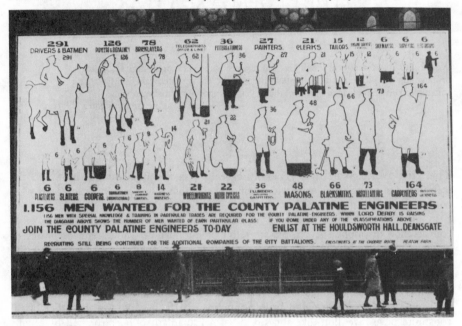

56a   *The appeal for recruits. This placard outside the Manchester Town Hall early in the war illustrates the numbers and types of men required in the Engineers. The filled-in portion at the bottom of each figure shows how many men have already come forward.*

A good deal of First World War propaganda, certainly, was not of this sort. It was founded, by omission if not commission, on falsehood. And it often bordered on the sexually pathological. In 1916 the Germans engaged in what was certainly an offence against the laws of war: they forcibly deported large numbers of civilians in occupied Belgium and France to work in other parts of their own countries or (more frequently) in Germany. This was a deliberate exploitation of its victims by the German Government to make good its shortage of labour, particularly in the mines and factories of the Ruhr and the Rhine. But British propaganda managed, as with the earlier 'atrocities' in Belgium, to convey a sense of sexual outrage. Although most of the deportees were males, a pamphlet dealing with one aspect of the subject was called *The Deportation of Women and Girls from Lille*. Again, a British poster showed a young girl of unquestionable virginity about to be led away by a hulking German soldier. And when Arthur Balfour was asked in the House of Commons in July 1917 'whether there was any official information to the effect that the German authorities were sending three thousand young Belgian girls from Antwerp to Roumania', he offered an answer that pays tribute equally to his dialectical skill and lack of scruple: 'No protest by this country to the German government is, I fear, likely to deter them from committing these atrocities' – adding that he had no official information on the subject.[2]

II

There were good reasons why propaganda was used so widely in this war. In the first place, the expansion of the media as a result of developments in technology had created the possibility of employing propaganda on a wide scale. Secondly, its use was badly needed. On the home front it was required early on to convince doubting elements of the justice of Britain's involvement in the struggle. And as the war dragged on, it was needed to keep the populace steadfast. Further, it had an important role beyond the home front. There was the necessity to convince the French and Russians that, despite Britain's limited contribution in the first two years of the struggle, the British people were not just waiting to pick up the fruits of a victory won by somebody else. They were involved in the war, heart and soul. And there was the need to counter the vast propaganda campaign launched by the Germans in neutral countries. Above all it was essential to keep the United States, even if it remained a non-combatant, sufficiently sympathetic that it would tolerate the interruption of its trade with Britain's enemies and would make its vast manufacturing resources available to the Allies.

The result of this multiplicity of needs was, in Britain as among the other combatants, a vast outpouring of propaganda. For home consumption it emanated from many semi-official sources before being placed, in 1917, under the direction of an inter-party organization called the National War Aims Committee. This had at its service a growing body of local organizations acting on a voluntary basis. For overseas purposes there was called into being, in the opening weeks of the war, a very hush-hush organization established under the direction of C. F. G. Masterman. It was situated at Wellington House in London, a venue chosen so as to help conceal its existence – for Wellington House had been the centre of Masterman's pre-war activities when he was assisting in the establishment of the National Insurance system. From this location emanated a huge quantity of officially inspired material that bore no trace of its official origin. Its publications, often written by persons of considerable eminence, were not required to follow the government line in all particulars, as long as they ended up by firmly endorsing the British cause.

In 1917, under the new-style Government of Lloyd George, this overseas branch of propaganda came a bit more into the open with the establishment of a Department of Information under John Buchan. The following year it came very positively into the open with the institution of the Ministry of Information under Lord Beaverbrook. A difference was also observable in the content of official propaganda in these years. It was geared more towards a mass than an elite appeal, making increased use of cinema films, overseas cables, and correspondents of foreign newspapers. But the contrast is easily exaggerated. Masterman (who was absorbed by first the Department and then the Ministry of Information) had early on established the essential nature of official British propaganda. The innovations of 1917 and 1918 extended and amplified what had been done and made some important modifications, not least because the state of the war was changing. (There was no longer a powerful neutral who had to be coaxed

---

[2] *The Times*, 12 July 1917, quoted in James Morgan Read, *Atrocity Propaganda 1914–1919* (New Haven: Yale University Press, 1941), p. 182.

and cajoled.) But there was no 'revolution' in wartime propaganda under Buchan and Beaverbrook.[3]

Some hard information will suggest the range and methods of official British propaganda, even if it must leave the issue of its impact as uncertain as ever. During the first year of the war no fewer than 2.5 million copies of 110 different posters were issued. This, of course, was the principal period of voluntary recruiting and so the hey-day of the poster. But as the war proceeded the poster continued to be employed. It was seen particularly as a way of combating war weariness among civilians, principally by publicizing the heroism and resolution of Britain's fighting forces and the misdeeds of the enemy. But the poster was also used to provide specific information about matters like aircraft identification, food economy, and war loans; and to rally enrolment in causes like women's war work and national service – for in such vital areas Britain remained a voluntarist nation.

Most of the same issues, with recruiting looming large in the early stages and resistance to war weariness in the later, figured in another largely employed means of contacting the populace: the public meeting. How many of these rituals took place under official aegis during the war cannot be estimated, beyond saying that they ran into many thousands. As an indication, in what seems an unexceptional fortnight in 1917 (25 September to 10 October) the number of meetings organized by the National War Aims Committee was 899. If that period was at all typical, then the total number of meetings held under official auspices during the war cannot have been much fewer than 100,000.

When it began in 1917 the War Aims Committee directed its really important meetings – those addressed by prominent public figures – simply at the largest centres of population. But as district committees capable of judging local circumstances developed, 'a certain selectivity became apparent.' When unrest in the workforce and a drop in productivity were reported from Hull (where men were said to be 'prepared to "down tools" on any trifling excuse') and from Cumberland, speaking campaigns were directed at those places. Shipyards also came to be given a good deal of attention because of the suspected prevalence there of disloyal elements. So was Wigan, reported by one informant to be '"the worst place for pacifists that I have had any experience of"', the common allegation being that the war was a capitalists' quarrel'. Other areas were deemed not to need such attentions: 'Comparatively few meetings were arranged for the general public in the Eastern counties, it being stated that the German raiders, by sea and air, provided all that was necessary to stimulate war aims.'[4]

Other types of propaganda were directed equally at the home front and at recipients overseas. Literature took the form of pamphlets and illustrated periodicals. In the course of the war Wellington House commissioned nearly a thousand different pamphlets, some written by eminent figures such as Gilbert Murray. It also reproduced in pamphlet form the speeches of individuals such as Lloyd George and Rudyard Kipling, as well as reproducing official documents on the outbreak of the war and the Bryce Report. By the beginning of 1916 pamphlets emanating from this source numbered 7 million. Great efforts were made to see that they reached suitable recipients and were not just dumped (as was said to be the case with much German

---

[3] The most satisfactory discussion of this subject is to be found in Michael Sanders, 'Official British Propaganda in Allied and Neutral Countries During the First World War with Special Reference to Organisation and Methods', M.Phil. thesis, University of London, 1972. See also M. L. Sanders and Philip M. Taylor, *British Propaganda during the First World War, 1914–18* (London: Macmillan, 1982).

[4] Quotations in this paragraph are from 'Home Publicity During the Great War: National War Aims Committee', prepared for the Ministry of Information in 1939 (INF 1/317).

material). At home distribution was carried out not only by the local branches of the War Aims Committee but also by commercial concerns – the booksellers W. H. Smith were 'good enough to undertake gratuitously a very extensive distribution through their large organisation extending all over the Kingdom'.[5] Abroad the more remote parts were attended to by the steamship companies (Cunard, P. & O.), which passed material on to their business connections. For the USA a network within Britain of voluntary organizations and private individuals sent pamphlets to contacts within America. They did not reveal that they were acting on behalf of the authorities or that the material – appearing under a commercial imprint – had a government origin.

Pamphlets, by their nature, reached only a limited readership. For a larger effect overseas Wellington House fed information to the correspondents of foreign newspapers and published its own illustrated newspapers in a variety of languages. Some of the latter were well produced, employing the format – and the presses – of the *Illustrated London News*. The most noteworthy of these, launched in 1916, was the extremely popular *War Pictorial*, which had a circulation of 500,000 a month by the end of that year and 700,000 a year later. Its various editions embraced 11 different languages.

Wellington House also commissioned war artists like C. R. W. Nevison and Muirhead Bone, giving them free reign in what they might paint, to the enormous benefit of posterity. The idea originated with a literary agent who was an active member of Wellington House and who, on learning that Muirhead Bone was about to be called up, proposed that he be employed to portray the war. (Masterman asked his wife if she had ever heard of an artist of that name, and had to be told that they owned one of his etchings.)[6] In addition, Wellington House by late in 1916 was sending out 'over four thousand propaganda photographs every week, plus maps, cartoons and lantern slides'.[7] This point deserves mention, if only because of the still often expressed view that, until Lloyd George became Prime Minister, British propaganda to neutral countries consisted only of academic tracts.

A different sort of illustration was the *Lusitania* medal. Its origin was singular. It had been struck by a private firm in Germany, and was intended to mock British hypocrisy in lamenting the loss of civilian life. One side of the medal ('No contraband') showed the sinking vessel to be carrying guns and aeroplanes. The other side ('Business above everything') showed a skeleton in the Cunard office selling tickets to prospective passengers. As a piece of satire the medal was not a success. The heavy-handed mockery of the British attitude towards the *Lusitania* was easily interpreted as a mockery of the *Lusitania* dead. Anyway it was generally assumed, and not least in the USA, that the only appropriate attitude for Germans on this matter was one of regret. The British Foreign Office, sensing the resentment that the sinking still aroused in 1916, chose to give the medal maximum publicity by itself issuing replicas. The demand, especially from the USA but also from many other countries, proved so large that a committee was formed to deal with the orders. A large firm (W. H. Selfridge) took over the manufacture on a non-profit-making basis.

The British conduct in this matter indicates the borderline between truth and falsehood occupied by much wartime propaganda. All that the authorities did was to issue, in vast quantities, a faithful reproduction of a medal originating from Germany.

---

[5] Ibid.

[6] Masterman tended to be accident-prone in such matters. On one occasion in the 1920s he suggested to the popular crime novelist Edgar Wallace that he should try writing a play. Wallace at the time had two plays running in London.

[7] D. G. Wright, 'The Great War, Government Propaganda and English "Men of Letters" 1914–1916', *Literature and History*, no.7, Spring 1978, p. 74.

The **MURDER**
of
CAPTAIN
FRYATT

2D

HODDER & STOUGHTON,
London.   New York.   Toronto.

56b   *The 'atrociousness' of the enemy. The cover of a wartime pamphlet, produced by Britain's propaganda organization but appearing under a commercial imprint, relates a German outrage: the execution of a British merchant seaman for attempting to ram a U-boat which was menacing his vessel.*

So in no sense was an attempt made to foist on the enemy something he had not done. But the wide circulation of the medal suggested that it had been created by the German Government, which was not the case. And the inept construction of the medal suggested – which may or may not have been the case generally but was not the intention in this particular – that the Germans were rejoicing in the atrocious drowning of women and children. The British authorities felt under no obligation to correct these misapprehensions.

The most novel, and one of the most powerful, forms of illustrated propaganda employed during the war was one to which the British came late: the cinema film. From the outset of the war the German high command welcomed the presence of newsreel cameramen on the battlefield. The German film editors (according to *The Oxford Companion to Film*) 'rapidly became skilled in using newsreel footage to carry a propaganda message, and their war reports became a powerful psychological tool at home and in neutral countries'. The British War Office and Admiralty, by contrast, gave cameramen short shrift, regarding film as nothing but a means of betraying military secrets to the enemy. (The French military authorities proved scarcely more amenable.) In consequence, 'the war was for a time represented almost entirely from the German point of view in neutral countries.'[8] Eventually the French and then, late in 1915, the British high command were brought to realize the huge propaganda advantage that they were handing to their enemies.

The cinema industry had been in existence long enough by 1914 for there to be a large number of picture houses. Yet it remained of sufficiently recent origin to retain much of its novelty. This made it an admirable medium for propaganda. And the war provided it with excellent copy: material that, in addition to being highly photogenic, was both exotic to most people's lives and yet, anyway in combatant countries, now an integral part of their existence. It also had the strong advantage, as far as propaganda was concerned, that it reached the masses in a way that much written material did not. For despite the benefit of having the firm of W. H. Smith distributing official literature through its nationwide chain of bookshops, the point was made that 'this did not touch the working man in Lancashire since, as it was said, he never patronised Messrs. Smith's establishments.'[9] The cinema, by contrast, was – certainly in the view of Wellington House – the Bible of the working classes. (It may be conjectured that the war helped the cinema to gain acceptance among other classes as well. For just as the conflict made it fitting for 'respectable' girls to seek employment outside the home, so it facilitated the movement of non-working-class families into the picture house by providing them with patriotic fare.)

The first noteworthy achievement of British cinema propaganda was *Britain Prepared*, launched late in 1915. With a length of 11,000 feet and a running time of around three hours, it achieved vast success and worldwide distribution on a commercial basis. (Except possibly in Russia, Wellington House insisted that it be screened commercially so as to play down its official origin.) The film was in two parts, the first dealing with the enlisting, training, and munitioning of the Kitchener armies and closing on a military review with 'regiment after regiment stretching out to the crack of doom'. (Lucy Masterman comments: 'It does not as a matter of fact take very many regiments to do this. This, however, was the most that Masterman would accept in the way of "fake". He was determined to have the films as austerely genuine as the Government documents and other matters for which Wellington House was

---

[8] Bawden (ed.), *The Oxford Companion to Film*, pp. 500,562.
[9] 'Home Publicity During the Great War: National War Aims Committee'.

responsible.')[10] The second part of *Britain Prepared* dealt with the navy, closely surveying life aboard the battleship *Queen Elizabeth*, portraying the manoeuvres of submarines and mine sweepers, and showing a large array of British naval might. It concluded with a shot of Jellicoe coming aboard his flagship and froze on him saluting a Union Jack flying in the sunset. As a finale it hardly seems novel, yet it carried sufficient impact for cinema men to suggest that Masterman, who conceived it, should join their industry.

Lucy Masterman noted a change in the response of home audiences to the two parts of the film. They reacted with enthusiasm to the military half, but 'there was a different quality in the deep roar that greeted the features of the naval section . . . . the interest in the army was the interest in individual friends who composed it. But the navy was themselves.'[11]

Britain Prepared deserves consideration for two reasons. First, it shows how a country that had so far failed to achieve any specific victory in the war could nevertheless make a powerful film about its accomplishments. This served it well among neutrals and in particular among its allies, who needed reassurance that Britain was pulling its weight. A special unit took the film to Russia and, after showing it to the royal family, toured the Russian battlefront to good effect. (Yet, like much propaganda, it proved in one respect to be a two-edged weapon. 'The underfed, inadequately armed Russian Armies saw with mixed feelings the arms and rations of the British Army.')[12]

Secondly, *Britain Prepared* helps to place in perspective the widely held notion that all British wartime propaganda was crudely sensationalist, being concerned only with fictitious enemy atrocities. The film was devoid of atrocities. And in the USA it had to overcome the handicap that it was utterly lacking in sensationalism. At its preliminary showing in New York, despite much praise, it was deemed 'too good', 'too class', 'too intellectual' to become a commercial proposition. Charles Urban, the American-born pioneer of British films, having taken the film to the USA, found that commercial rentiers were unwilling to handle it. Being 'more an astute businessman and entrepreneur than a film-maker'[13], he personally undertook its distribution. The results vindicated his initiative. *Britain Prepared* was soon playing to capacity houses. An American description conveys its extraordinary quality, so out of keeping with the popular image of First World War propaganda and so akin to the much praised British films of the Second World War:

> it is the handling of the most real and unimaginative material. It goes along without an attempt to intoxicate the emotions. It takes undecorated details that seemingly have not a thrill in them. It seems to be as uninspired as a hardware catalogue. Gradually in the mind of any perceptive person there forms the idea that this is a real nation in real trouble. The immensity of the effort begins to appal the comprehension. A thing is in the forming and it is a tremendous thing. And when out of all this grim work-a-day agony there appears on the screen such masses of trained, disciplined and willing men as American eyes have not seen since 1865, the thrill is real.[14]

This success opened a floodgate of British film propaganda. By 1918 some 700 films had been made with a total negative length of half a million feet. Special editions with captions in foreign languages enabled them to be carried to many countries. D. W. Griffith, the outstanding American director, was brought to England in 1917 to make

---

[10] Lucy Masterman, *C. F. G. Masterman* (London: Nicholson & Watson, 1939), p. 284.
[11] Ibid.
[12] Ibid., p. 285.
[13] Bawden (ed.), *The Oxford Companion to Film*, p. 720.
[14] Quoted in Masterman, *C. F. G. Masterman*, pp. 285–6.

two films financed by the British authorities. (Having failed at the box office with his 1916 film *Intolerance*, whose pacifist overtones made it singularly ill-timed, Griffith no doubt welcomed the opportunity to recoup some of his losses.) One of his films made under British auspices, *The Great Love*, dealt with the impact of war on British society. The other, *Heart of the World*, employed German newsreels, along with footage shot in France, to encompass a fictional story (mainly filmed in the USA) about an occupied French village under brutal German control. In the climax Lillian Gish barely escaped rape by a thuggish German officer

Most British-made films lacked this fictional element. A few were cartoons. But the overwhelming majority were newsreels of battles, mine sweepers, visits of King George V to the troops, food production, women's role in the war. Certainly, they were slanted, but theirs was generally an angled version of the truth. Where the truth was unpalatable no attempt was made to concoct victories. *Battle of the Somme*, for example, was no doubt intended to be a record of a great British triumph. As none occurred, it gave a fairly frank account of what had taken place. The film was censored by the military authorities (Rawlinson wrote of it in his diary for 26 July 1916: 'Some of it very good but I cut out many of the horrors in dead and wounded'), but no inventions were inserted into it. And (as Lucy Masterman observes) if 'horrors' were removed from the film, a sense of 'we who are about to die' seemed 'written all over it, over the ranks of lean, vigorous boys and the lines of guns'. Lloyd George's secretary, Frances Stevenson, whose brother Paul had been killed in action a year earlier, records in her diary for Friday 4 August 1916:

> We went on Wednesday night to a private view of the 'Somme films' i.e. the pictures taken during the recent fighting. To say that one enjoyed them would be untrue; but I am glad I went. I am glad I have seen the sort of thing our men have to go through, even to the sortie from the trench, and the falling in the barbed wire. There were pictures too of the battlefield after the fight, & of our gallant men lying all crumpled up & helpless. There were pictures of men mortally wounded being carried out of the communication trenches, with the look of agony on their faces. It reminded me of what Paul's last hours were: I have often tried to imagine to myself what he went through, but now I *know*: and I shall never forget. It was like going through a tragedy.[15]

That the Somme film, nevertheless, had considerable value as propaganda is not to be doubted. But its impact lay simply in its faithful record of the endeavours, and the courage, of Britain's soldiers.

III

Attention has been directed so far at officially inspired propaganda. Much, however, was not of this sort. A great deal emanated from the newspaper press, which, though under considerable constraints when it came to publishing military information, enjoyed a pretty free rein in the area of propaganda – as long as it was not of a sort to 'discourage recruiting'. Many of the most senseless outbursts of wartime unreason found their inspiration, or at least a willing vehicle of propagation, in this quarter.

Other forms of private-enterprise propaganda also flourished. There were meetings organized by non-governmental bodies, and privately printed circulars. And word of mouth carried items of news as well as far-fetched tales, some too obscene for publication or public utterance. Even the church service might become a propaganda exercise. According to P.M. Yearsley, in 1916 a clergyman at Wimbledon warned (with

---

[15] A. J. P. Taylor (ed.), *Lloyd George: A Diary by Frances Stevenson* (London: Hutchinson, 1971), p. 112.

scant regard for the truth) of 'the German boast that they intended, in the event of a successful invasion of England, to destroy every male child'. The Bishop of London, Winnington Ingram, became well known for his recruiting activities. It is said that at a large meeting early in the war he secured 10,000 adherents to the army. Indeed, the jingoism apparent in the established Church caused Masterman, notwithstanding his own role in propaganda activities, to undergo something of a revulsion against the Church of England, of which he was a devoted member. He felt that the Pope and the Quakers were alone in upholding the supranational message of Christianity. A service at Westminster Abbey, he complained, seemed like an activity at Wellington House.

Certainly, it was from non-official sources that the more squalid forms of propaganda emanated. The 'popular' press played the most visible and best-preserved part, giving rise to the legend that newspapers could make the public believe anything – notwithstanding the cropper which Northcliffe came when he tried to discredit Kitchener, the public's idol. What the yellow press excelled at was not creating the public mood but gauging it; and then, if economics or the proprietors' whim so required, debasing it. In wartime there existed an appetite for various forms of debasement.

A good deal of wartime propaganda belonged in the category of folk myth. People believed these myths because they yearned to do so. The sudden extreme pressures of war, giving free rein to the generally suppressed urge to hate, created a frame of mind eager to seize on tales in which the pathological and the mysterious figured prominently. Members of the respectable classes found themselves free to verbalize sexual-sadistic fantasies under the guise of patriotic warnings. We have just noted the clergyman who claimed that German invaders would kill every male child. Of the same order was a publicist who addressed well attended gatherings (not officially blessed) on the subject of the Unseen Hand. He foresaw as one consequence of a German victory that tens of thousands of British girls would be 'removed to human stud-farms in Germany'. (The account of his speech records 'Sensation' among his audience. It is unlikely that the sensation was wholly unpleasant.)

Other forms of myth, if less pernicious, indicated the irrationality that permeated the wartime mind. The craving for certainty that some force, earthly or supernatural, would always be to hand to snatch victory out of defeat probably underlay the credence attached to tales like the angels of Mons and the Russians who passed through Britain, snow on foot, to the Western Front. It may also explain the widespread belief that Kitchener had not gone down in the *Hampshire* but had been removed to a hide-out, where he was devising the master-stroke that would end the war. Again, the war provided a field day for those claiming to have access to privileged sources of information – or anyway claiming to be acquainted with individuals so privileged. Yearsley records on 15 May 1917, without apparently pausing to question the authenticity of the information: 'my bank cashier informed me that he had just heard from "a lady in the know" that Russia and Germany had signed a secret peace the week before.'[16]

In one respect anyway the war proved a comfortable time for a considerable section of people. It reduced the affairs of nations to the simplicities of a struggle between a good side and a bad side – one might fairly say 'goodies and baddies', given the juvenility of much that was said and written. Hence it became possible to interpret the world in terms of the most simple-minded type of crime story: what was then termed (and the expression seems extraordinarily apt) the 'penny dreadful'. In such a view the

---

[16] 'The Home Front 1914–1918' (an unpublished account, based on his wartime diary, in the Imperial War Museum), p. 218.

triumph of virtue over villainy could only be thwarted – for a time – by the superior devilry of the practitioners of evil.

For an example of such a thought process we may turn to a speech of Dr Ellis Powell, editor of the *Financial News*. Powell was the author of the previously quoted prediction regarding the fate worse than death awaiting English girlhood should Germany triumph. The occasion was a well attended meeting ('crowded to the very doors') on 8 February 1917. It had been arranged by the Women's Imperial Defence Council 'to protest against the influence of the "Unseen Hand"' ('the Treacherous and Devilish Influence which is at work to bring about a British Defeat and a German Victory').[17] Dr Powell had an explanation for the 'traces of pro-German malignity and treachery in every part of our national policy':

> To begin with, so vast a web of treason-treachery, woven into every department of our national life, would have been detected and destroyed long ago, if it were controlled by a group of people. The scheme could never have been kept watertight, nor could it have been manipulated with the superb and super-Satanic skill thus far displayed. But if you postulate a single dominant brain, controlling a multitude of agents, some intimate, some distant, and but few of whom knew the identity of the arch-Traitor at the centre, then you have a system which would not only be comparatively safe for the arch-Traitor himself, but would, as a hypothesis, cover all the facts. (Hear, hear.) The arch-Traitor is an individual. But he must obviously be an individual with extensive and powerful influence. He must have been preparing for years past to play the devilish role in which he is now engaged. Germany could not say to any person, no matter how clever, at the outbreak of the war, 'Go and worm yourself into every department of public life and infect them all for our advantage.' That is an impossible suggestion. (Hear, hear.) But if for many years past a magnetic and dexterous personality has been at work permeating every department of our public life, rewarding subservience, and penalising independence, he would have brought into existence just the very species of subterranean devilry which we have seen in operation since August of 1914.

If it seems open to question whether any but a handful of seriously unbalanced people would pay attention to such fantasies, it has to be said that this was not so. One well educated person, who has appeared already in these pages, was certainly prepared to take it seriously; and though a simple-minded jingo, he was far from unbalanced. P. M. Yearsley, FRCS, FZS, educated at Merchant Taylors' School and at Westminster and London hospitals, the author of several important medical books and a prominent London surgeon, attended another meeting addressed by Powell a few months later. The speaker's subject, needless to say, was the Unseen Hand, although he had a fresh batch of accusations to deliver against specific individuals. (Among them, the Tsarina had lured Kitchener to his death; Britain's Judge Advocate General was a naturalized German; German banks remained open in Britain because they threatened to reveal the names of those who had received money from them in the past; Germany had financed both political parties before the war and was now fomenting discontent and strikes in munitions works; and the Lord Chief Justice was working for Germany.) Yearsley writes of all this:

> If his statements were correct – and his speech carried conviction as a man who was sure of his facts – they revealed a disturbing state of affairs. . . . The speech was a strong indictment and one which should, if it were false, have secured the speaker's immediate prosecution. Dr. Ellis Powell was a charming personality; I met him professionally later and talked with him about this speech, when he assured me that he possessed full facts to support his accusations.[18]

---

[17] An account of the meeting appeared in the *Financial News*, 9 February 1917. It was reprinted as a pamphlet, *The 'Unseen Hand': Special Royal Commission Demanded*, which enjoyed an edition as far away as Australia.

[18] Yearsley, 'The Home Front 1914–1918', p. 213.

The people who delivered this sort of utterance, and those who embraced it, were nationalists but not seekers after national unity. The super-patriot, though ostensibly conducting a campaign against a foreign regime, was almost invariably eager to pursue vendettas against elements at home that did not conform to his stereotypes of acceptability. An example is that supremely bigoted Conservative MP Joynson-Hicks, who appeared on the same bill as Ellis Powell on 8 February 1917. He seized the opportunity to deal blows at such long-standing objects of his displeasure as Liberal politicians and aliens resident in Britain, and to demonstrate that every German who had come to reside in this country must be an object of contempt, either for severing ties with the land that gave him birth or for failing to do so.

It needs to be stressed that there remained considerable sections of the community who gave no credence, or at most but passing credence, to such extravagances. And much public speaking did not take the form of these insensate ravings. Certainly, it extolled the heroism of Britain's fighting forces and expressed the resolve to persist in the struggle against a ruthless foe until victory was attained. But it managed to do this without sinking to the level of the pathological or reducing human relations to the crudities of a conflict between good Britons and devils incarnate.

Again, there were notable churchmen even within the Anglican fold who, while arguing that there could be no peace short of victory, looked forward to the time when the warring nations would be reconciled. The Bishop of Peterborough, unveiling a temporary war memorial in June 1917, spoke of the war as a contest between the forces of autocracy and the forces of democracy and hoped that, 'once the forces of reaction are gone, there will be brought about a new fellowship among the nations, and that even our enemies, when the scales are fallen from their eyes, will share in it'.[19] Both the Church of England and the Free Churches, confronted with mounting civilian casualties from air raids, managed firmly to condemn reprisal raids against German cities for which there was a growing outcry. In May 1917 a letter of 'emphatic protest against the policy of reprisal' appeared over 92 signatures, most of them those of Christian leaders of many denominations. The Free Church Council at the same time, in a communication that *The Times* refused to publish, informed the Prime Minister of its 'grave disapproval' of a reprisals policy. And the Archbishop of Canterbury told the House of Lords: 'the Christian judgement of England . . . is that when we come out of this war . . . we mean to come out with clean hands.'[20]

To uphold such a position was no easy task. The Archbishop, in a private letter, soon after referred to being 'the recipient of a continuous shower of protest, denunciations, and often virulent abuse from every part of England, especially London'.[21] This was no unique experience. When some bishops in 1917 reminded Christians of their duty to love their enemies, one publicist raged against 'the flabby-babby babble of the Boche-defending Bishops'.[22] And the Church of England's decision to hold a National Mission of Repentance and Hope brought upon it the fury of Horatio Bottomley, who claimed that the nation needed no repentance and that the Church was undermining its morale by suggesting the opposite.

The most conspicuous victim (apart from pacifists) of the unpopularity of certain Christian tenets was the Rev. E. Lyttelton, headmaster of Eton. As the Church was

[19] F. P Armitage, *Leicester 1914–1918: The War-Story of a Midland Town* (Leicester: Edgar Backus, 1933), p. 231.

[20] See S. P. Mews, 'Religion and English Society in the First World War', Ph.D. thesis, University of Cambridge, 1973, ch. 10.

[21] Quoted in ibid.

[22] George R. Sims, quoted (with approval) in Yearsley, 'The Home Front 1914–1918', p. 224.

sounding the call to sacrifice, Lyttelton proposed in March 1915 that Englishmen should reveal the strength of their convictions by offering to make a territorial sacrifice: after the war Gibraltar should be internationalized. Lyttelton's fellow countrymen proved not to have reached this elevated condition. His suggestion was immediately distorted into a scheme to cede Gibraltar to the Germans, and caused him to become the victim of a savage campaign. Hostile crowds awaited him when he appeared to preach at Manchester Cathedral shortly after, and in the following year he was obliged to resign his headmastership.

In short, pursuit of the *via media* was not an easy matter in wartime. When Yearsley wrote that in general the clergy had not come too well out of the war, he was not echoing Masterman's criticism that they had acted as the vehicles of patriotic propaganda. He was making quite the opposite complaint: that they had failed to deliver a message of undiluted, hate-filled patriotism. The fact that such a criticism could be made is significant. It reminds us that, in the Churches as elsewhere, some voices of moderation and balance – if often still and small – were yet to be heard in the land.

IV

It is often said that in the propaganda war the British secured a clear victory over the Germans. The compliment, it should be noted, is back-handed. The assumption is that First World War propaganda was largely specious. Either it consisted of lies, or else it took the form of condemning one's opponents for reprehensible acts of which one's own side was equally guilty. Consequently, it was to the credit of the enemy that he was not sufficiently unscrupulous to win such an encounter.

This argument should be viewed with caution. Many of the writings that contain it, including some of quite recent origin, scarcely rise above the level of propaganda themselves.[23] Early on, Britain's propaganda triumph was proclaimed by at least one German commander whose concern was to explain why the war was lost in spite of his own military competence. But principally it has been put forward by Anglo-Saxons antipathetic to Britain's involvement in the war and to any notion of British moral superiority.

The claim that Britain won a propaganda victory raises several difficulties. It disregards the clear lead that the Germans established at the outset in some vital forms of propaganda activity, such as the distribution of printed matter in the USA and the use of the newsreel camera. In so far as it assumes that Britain's triumph sprang from atrocity-mongering, it fails to notice the great range in content of British propaganda, from the dishonest to the scrupulous, and so does not explain why a proportion of the most successful items fell into the latter category. And it fails to appreciate that the propaganda devices employed by all the combatants were markedly similar, including the use of manufactured atrocities. So it omits to account for the success of the British variety.

Anyway in a major respect the claim that the British won the propaganda war is plainly without substance. In terms of the appeal made to their own people and to their allies, the British achieved no superiority over the Germans. When the morale of the German people finally gave way, it was not because of a failure in their Government's publicity machine but because (in a strictly military sense) they were confronting a lost

---

[23] Nor does this apply only to some recent books. It is fair to wonder whether even so grotesque a propaganda film as *Once a Hun, Always a Hun* of 1918 offered a more slanted, tendentious view of events than the television documentary of 1972, *Who Sank the* Lusitania?.

war. The only respect in which it might sensibly be claimed that British propagandists got the better of the Germans was in the appeal to neutrals. And even here the argument about the efficacy of British propaganda usually lacks an appreciation of the state of the war as a whole and the types of society involved. Chronology reveals that the USA did not enter the war in 1915 in response to the horror stories endorsed by the Bryce Report or distorted accounts of the loss of the *Lusitania*. Indeed, it signally failed to do so. When the breach came two years later it was because the German authorities, in defiance of clear American warnings, had begun sinking US merchant ships and had sought to incite the Mexicans to hostile acts against the USA.

This is not to say that British propaganda did not help to predispose America in the Allies' favour. But to understand why, it is not necessary to assume that British propaganda was superior to German. The context is crucial. Britons and Americans, in terms of their political system, language, cultural values, and economic interests, had far more in common than did Germans and Americans. The ideals and values to which the British appealed when they denounced German conduct for such deeds as violating Belgium, sinking merchant ships, misusing civilians in occupied countries, and shooting Nurse Cavell were ideals and values widely held in America. The principles to which the German Government appealed in justifying some of these acts, the denials they issued in the case of others, and the counter-claims they made of atrocities committed against themselves (for example, that Belgian civilians had gouged out the eyes of captured German soldiers) found no such response across the Atlantic.

The case of Nurse Cavell is instructive. She was a lady of upright character who happened to be nursing in Belgium at the outbreak of the war. When that country was overrun she used her clinic to assist the escape of British soldiers who had become stranded behind the German lines. Eventually she was betrayed. The German authorities arrested, tried, and sentenced her. On 12 October 1915 she was executed by firing squad. It is a fact that the pamphlet published by Wellington House on this matter was one of its greatest successes. And it is a fact that opinion not only in Britain but also in much of the USA was revolted by Germany's action. But it would be specious to argue that American revulsion was another propaganda triumph for the British. Before Nurse Cavell's execution, the American authorities had done their utmost to secure a remission of the death sentence – at a time when many in Britain did not expect that it would be carried out. Propaganda, in short, had little to do with the American response to Nurse Cavell's death. However justified the German authorities may have felt in their conduct, they had clear warning that powerful forces in the USA took a different view, and that to shoot Nurse Cavell would be to outrage these forces (and so present the British with a propaganda weapon).

The Cavell case is of particular interest because of the ambiguity of the issues involved. From one point of view, the German action against her was plainly warranted. She was a civilian in an occupied land who had clandestinely intervened in military matters to aid the enemies of the occupying power. From another point of view, the German action against her was unpardonably excessive. In the first place, there was the question of her sex, which then, probably more than now, was deemed of great importance. In the second place, she was an honourable member of a noble profession. In the third, she had been confronted with the cruel dilemmas of living among a conquered people and having the opportunity to aid distressed members of her own country. Both lines of argument are of weight. Which of them, in 1915, would carry the greater weight among neutrals would not depend on the skill employed by the advocates of the two sides. It would depend on the ideals and values of those making the judgement. As a generalization, it may be said that those who functioned within a parliamentary democracy – especially in the more sheltered days of 1915, when the world had yet to sup full of horrors – would mostly reject the German view and be appalled by its application.

This summed up a good deal of the propaganda disadvantage under which the Germans laboured. They conducted the war by means that gave them real or hoped-for military advantages but both offended the principles of important neutrals and enabled their adversaries to embellish ruthless deeds with blood-curdling inventions. Plainly, the Germans hoped to gain significant victories by striking down a small country so as to seize a strategic advantage over France; by introducing poison gas to the battlefield; by the use of underwater attack against non-military vessels, including neutral vessels; and by the bombardment of civilian targets in Britain by warship, airship, and aeroplane. But in so doing they were undermining the notion that war was a contest between warriors, in which a clear distinction was preserved between combatants and civilians, and in which victory went to the braver and more skilful.

No doubt this notion was in good measure fanciful. Much that did not seem to fall within this heroic concept of war was deemed permissible simply because it was hallowed by time. The sinking of passenger ships was not so hallowed. The use of blockade, which in seeking to starve an enemy's army starved also his women and children, was so hallowed. The cards, in this respect, were stacked against the Germans. (The Germans were under further disadvantages in seeking to make propaganda capital out of the British blockade. At least theoretically, a blockade always leaves to the besieged army the choice of laying down its arms before the toll on women and children has become too great. Further, the Germans had themselves employed blockade against Paris with deadly effect in 1871, and so were not well placed to wax indignant at its – much less effective – use against themselves. Finally, blockade could be portrayed as an actual, as against potential, atrocity only if German women and children could really be depicted as starving. And the German authorities declined to admit that the blockade was having any significant effect.)

The heroic view of war could be subjected to a further criticism. Even if it had been valid in the past to maintain a rigid distinction between combatants and civilians, it had ceased to be so. In a major respect, waging war was a matter of converting material resources into military hardware. This was an activity of civilians. Therefore civilians were not entitled to immunity in a war to whose conduct they were making so crucial a contribution. Such a view was not confined to German militarists. It had its advocates within Britain. One of them was Maurice Low, American correspondent of the arch-Conservative *Morning Post*. As Masterman related with horror, in a pamphlet called *Freedom of the Seas* Low 'lays down as the law that in this War there is no difference between combatants and non-combatants, that every man, woman and child on both sides must be regarded as combatants'. Masterman commented: 'That, of course, is very satisfactory when he is defending the starving of Germany. It is not quite so satisfactory when we are protesting against the destruction of the Lusitania or exciting America at the death of women and children.'

For Masterman, statements by Low like 'I deny the existence of non-combatants' were 'More worthy of a mad German professor than an English "propagandist". . . . I wish the pamphlet could be suppressed! And it is written for America!!! of all places in the world.'[24] Yet, however embarrassing to Wellington House, Low's offering reveals that the shift towards a concept of total war was not confined to Britain's enemies.

Nevertheless, in 1914 and the succeeding years this view was not only novel but

---

[24] Masterman to Bryce, 21 March and 10 April 1916, Bryce papers.

frequently distressing – not least to those in neutral democracies. No country, in practice, went all the way in denying the distinction between combatants and non-combatants or in advancing the propriety of waging war upon women and children. All continued to believe that a line must be drawn somewhere. The Germans incurred disfavour by being the people, not once but on a series of occasions, who moved the line in ways that neutrals considered unwarranted.

Yet if this gave the Allies a propaganda advantage, it was probably not as great as subsequent writers have supposed. Propaganda, it has already been suggested, can prove a two-edged sword. And that is probably most true of the sort that lays stress on the ruthlessness and lust for war of an adversary. Much British propaganda, as has been evident, was based on the fact that Germany had overrun neighbouring territories where it had supposedly done frightful deeds, and had waged war by new and terrible methods. The Germans could not make similar allegations. They were doing too well in the war. Their territory was not being overrun; nor were their adversaries, at least before 1916, confronting them with fearful novelties. (In the opening weeks of the war, when the Russians invaded East Prussia, German propaganda did indeed accuse them of atrocious behaviour. One newspaper even dubbed them 'Huns'. But the Russians were so speedily ejected that this propaganda opportunity vanished.) That is, what principally gave the Allies their propaganda advantage was the superior war-waging capacity, and consequent victories, of their enemies. Ludendorff may have come to believe that the British were victors in the propaganda war. But he would hardly have welcomed the opportunity to prosper in that activity if it meant losing out on the field of battle.

From the Allied point of view, this was a poor sort of advantage. Ultimately it was so even in terms of propaganda. It was impossible to decry German conduct towards Belgium without advertising the fact that a country Britain had gone to war to defend had been thoroughly overrun, and that attempts to dislodge the invader were proving unavailing. Equally, it was impossible to denounce the atrociousness of Germany's methods of conducting war without portraying the Germans as dedicated, devoted, ruthless wagers of war. To go too far in this direction meant building up the enemy as a potential war-winner. This was not a good impression to convey to wavering neutrals.

Certainly, it was always possible that the USA might possess sufficient residual sympathy for the Allied cause that, should Britain appear on the verge of defeat, America would feel obliged to intervene. But this was too uncertain a contingency for British propagandists to gamble on. And in the absence of such certainty, they would be ill-advised to present too imposing a portrait of their enemy. For, by suggesting that Britain was seriously at risk, they might cause the wellspring of American credit, and the essential war materials it provided, to dry up.

Masterman, for one, was well aware of this problem as it affected British propaganda in the USA. His wife writes regarding it: 'By far the greatest difficulties in the early years of the war were the absence of any obvious Allied victories to set off the over-running of Belgium and the evacuation of the Dardanelles. The increasing invisible pressure of the blockade by the fleet was the kind of thing not so easy to "feature".'[25] This was one of the main reasons why Wellington House resorted to use of the cinema, which to those in governing circles remained a despised medium standing no higher than the music-hall. ('What, has the country come to that?' was the response of the secretary to the Board of Film Censors when it was suggested that films might be employed for propaganda.)[26] For Masterman the cinema was the most telling means

---

[25] Masterman, *C. F. G. Masterman*, p. 278.
[26] Ibid., p. 283.

available of representing to neutrals the might of the British navy and the vast manpower and industrial resources of the British people – the most telling means, therefore, of presenting Britain, if not yet as a battle winner, then as potentially a mighty contributor to an ultimate Allied victory. For the promise of victory, not the portrayal of the enemy as a ferocious beast, was the one indubitably effective propaganda message.

V

The Great War did indeed provide a field day for British propagandists. They could assist in calling the nation to battle, in rendering the enemy hateful, in courting the sympathy and even the aid of important neutrals. But in every one of these areas propaganda was in a dependent position. It required the enemy to act in ways that rendered it abhorrent and that propaganda could then embellish. It required the existence of a neutral of first-class importance that was responsive, on account of shared values and interests, to the presentation of the British position. And it required the base of a home country possessing the will and the resources to fight on to the bitter end.

Ultimately, British propaganda was dependent on Allied successes – in halting the Germans on the Marne, maintaining command of the sea, training huge armies, producing large quantities of munitions, inventing novel weapons (like the tank and new breeds of aeroplane), prosecuting major offensive operations. To treat propaganda as a significant element in the achievement of victories, rather than victories as the major element in the success of propaganda, is to engage in a serious reversal of cause and effect.

PART SIXTEEN

Aftermath

67

THE UNRETURNING ARMY

I am beginning to rub my eyes at the prospect of peace. I think it will require more courage than anything that has gone before . . . . one will at last fully recognise that the dead are not only dead for the duration of the war.

Lady Cynthia Asquith's diary, 7 October 1918

I

The consequences of war are immeasurable and unquantifiable. How, for example, do we project British history on the assumption that the more than 700,000 who died had remained alive? What difference can we say that it made that a further 1.6 million were injured or taken prisoner, often with the result that their subsequent lives were damaged and even shortened?

We are most conscious of deprivation when men killed at the front left behind tangible evidence of their abilities. That is one reason – and an entirely valid reason – why we feel so keenly the many deaths among the war poets, be they men whose talent had already established itself even before their experience of war, like Edward Thomas, or men who only achieved poetic expression under the impact of the conflict, like Wilfred Owen. Thomas wrote:

> Now all roads lead to France
> And heavy is the tread
> Of the living; but the dead
> Returning lightly dance. . . .[1]

Even today the journey of the living to the battlefields of France, in fact or in imagination, gives rise to a keen sense that the British nation was the poorer for the slaughter that took place there.

Yet not everyone takes this view. It is possible to regard this question of the dead and the wounded of the Great War as possessing little substance. Indeed, the temptation to do so is strong: historians are not at ease with unquantifiables and might-have-beens. Some claim that the losses on the battlefield were cancelled out by other effects of the war or by events that followed it. If the war cut short many lives, it also halted for four years the emigration to other lands of young and active Britons whose departure would equally have deprived the homeland of a proportion of its talent. And increased procreation immediately after the war rapidly made good the depletion of numbers. Again it can be argued that, in the case of at least some of the war poets, without the searing experience of war they might never have risen to such creative heights; so the war obliterated only what it had created. As for brilliant scholars trained in the classics

---

[1] Edward Thomas, 'Roads'.

like the Liberal leader's son Raymond Asquith,[2] it has been said that these were not the men whom the nation needed to make good its real shortage of talent, which lay among scientists and technicians.

These points have weight, as showing that there are two sides to this balance sheet of unquantifiables. But it may be thought that the weight is not so great as their proponents sometimes suggest. There is a qualitative difference between the chosen departure from the shores of Britain of men and women questing after a new life and the brutal and involuntary removal of young men (exclusively) to the graveyard. Nor should war be overestimated as a spur to artistic sensibility. To mention only one of the war poets who did not fall its victim: although without his experiences on the Western Front Robert Graves would scarcely have written *Goodbye to All That*, it is difficult to believe that he would not have written *I, Claudius* and a host of other distinguished works. As to the argument that Britain's deficiency after the war did not lie in the sort of distinguished men who had died in it, this is questionable on two grounds. First, it is strictly a 'Collapse of British Power' argument, concerned only with economic loss. It disregards the quality-of-life aspects that have also been a vital part of British greatness. Secondly, it fails to notice that budding men of science showed the same readiness for combatant service as budding men of letters.

Ernest Rutherford returned to England (from a visit to America and the Antipodes) in January 1915 to find his laboratory all but denuded of research staff and students. Among those who departed was the experimental physicist H. G. J. Moseley. Moseley's work on the X-ray spectra of the elements had already yielded discoveries that, though subsequently refined, remain unchallenged to the present day. He died at Gallipoli in August 1915, still only 27 years of age. Rutherford wrote of him: 'The premature death of a young man of such brilliant promise and achievement was everywhere recognised as an irreparable loss to science.'[3] All told, 35 Fellows of the Royal Society and 55 members of the Royal Institute of Chemistry were killed in combat. How many other promising scientists, yet to attain that degree of eminence, shared their fate it is impossible to calculate.

This leads to a further issue. In assessing the injurious consequences of the war's death toll, it is not only lives cut short or blemished that must be considered. There is also the effect upon those who looked out on a world where particular individuals, and whole groups of individuals, once present would be present no longer. Some students of the phenomenon of stress argue that, of all its causes, bereavement is the greatest. The war inflicted this form of stress in massive and concentrated quantities. Again, we are in the area of the unquantifiable, yet the phenomenon is apparent enough. Admittedly, it must be borne in mind that this is likely to be a short-term consequence of war, not only because of the healing properties of time but also because it is an effect limited to the lifetime of those bereaved. Yet even this is not wholly the case. The destructive aspects of the Great War, it has been powerfully argued, have not died with the generation that passed through them. They have bitten deep into 'modern memory'.[4] So it is the case that works about the war written by and for a generation that

---

[2] Killed on the Somme in September 1916. It is related that when the noted head of an Oxford college, A. D. Lindsay, was asked to nominate the most brilliant man he had ever known he replied (as if it went without saying) 'Raymond Asquith, of course.'

[3] *Dictionary of National Biography 1912–21* (London: Oxford University Press, 1927), 'Moseley'.

[4] See Paul Fussell, *The Great War and Modern Memory* (New York and London: Oxford University Press, 1975). Some of Fussell's statements about the course of events do not suggest that he is *au fait* with a good deal of recent historical writing. And it can be argued that the modern memory to which he refers is that of a section of the community rather than the community as a whole. But his possible deficiencies as an historian do not affect the central argument of his book. And the section of the community to which, at the least, his

knew neither the conflict nor its victims contain great potency – one need only mention relatively recent books like Leon Wolff's *In Flanders Fields*, films like *Paths of Glory* and *King and Country*, and plays like *Oh! What a Lovely War* to recognize this. They not only reflect great indignation on the part of their creators but also arouse it among their audiences.

Further, even so far as it is true that the deprivation caused by the war's infliction of casualties is confined to a limited time span, this remains a potent consequence of war. A week after his son's death Asquith said of his daughter-in-law: 'She lies with Raymonds two last letters in her hand, doesnt care to see the children [,is] utterly collapsed.'[5] For some this feeling of desolation, as we have seen in the case of Edward Thomas's widow, never completely vanished. One may infer it about the lady, still unmarried, who wrote in 1975, 'I lost my sweetheart at Loos,' and about Vera Brittain who, although in time she wed, did not marry the man for whom clearly she felt she had been intended. (The great popularity of *Testament of Youth* when it appeared in the 1930s, it seems reasonable to suggest, lay in its ability to evoke feelings of outrage in the community at the deprivation that the war's death toll had imposed.)

An interesting case is that of Rudyard Kipling. He received the war as a righteous struggle against brute force:

> Once more we hear the word
> That sickened earth of old:–
> 'No law except the Sword
> Unsheathed and uncontrolled.'

And he proclaimed death suffered while resisting such a doctrine as being no death:

> Who stands if Freedom fall?
> Who dies if England live?[6]

But Kipling's personal response to the war's toll in blood was not so elevated. His only son hastened to join up though no more than 17 years of age. Rider Haggard, after visiting the Kiplings in March 1915, wrote in his diary: 'Their boy John, who is not yet 18, is an officer in the Irish Guards and one can see that they are terrified lest he should be sent to the front and killed, as has happened to nearly all the young men they know.'[7]

In September, at Loos, it happened also to John Kipling. Initially he was only known to be wounded and missing, and it was some months before hope had to be abandoned. Kipling's feelings, already savage against Germans, turned also against the Pope, neutrals in general, and British politicians:

> I could not dig: I dared not rob:
> Therefore I lied to please the mob.[8]

Some of his poems came to contain a terrible poignancy:

> My son was killed while laughing at some jest. I would
> I knew
> What it was, and it might serve me in time when jests
> are few.[9]

thesis does apply happens – for better or worse – to be of considerable importance in the development of the country.

[5] Lady Scott's diary, 26 September 1916, Kennet papers.

[6] Rudyard Kipling, 'For All We Have and Are'.

[7] Quoted by Bernard Bergonzi in John Gross (editor), *The Age of Kipling* (New York: Simon & Schuster, 1972), p. 137.

[8] Rudyard Kipling, 'A Dead Statesman'.

[9] Rudyard Kipling, 'A Son'.

The life of Kipling and his wife, it has been said, was never again the same; it had lost a motive force. J. C. C. Davidson, a Conservative politician and intimate of Kipling's cousin Stanley Baldwin, recalls staying for a weekend with Kipling. (The date is not specified but seems to have been in the 1920s.) 'He read me a poem which was one of the most bitter pieces of literature that I had ever heard. It was a complaint against everybody, God and man, because his boy had been killed. I don't think, although I am not quite certain, that it was ever published.'[10] It seems permissible to suggest that Kipling – though from the parents', not the participants', standpoint – was here very close to Wilfred Owen's damning repudiation of the 'old lie' that it is sweet and becoming to die for one's country.

The war was not even-handed in the way it dealt out death and injury, although whether this made its impact more or less terrible is not apparent. Kipling lost his only son, Bonar Law two out of his four sons, Lloyd George neither of his two – though both were in uniform. (All of these men, it should be added, had at least one daughter.) This disproportion ran right through the community. Huntly Gordon recalls a school friend of his at Clifton who was killed at the battle of Loos and whose only brother (Gordon learned at the time in a letter from their mother) 'was also killed in the same attack. She was a frail little person, and her heart must have died that day; but her letter gave no sign of it.'[11] In Leicester, during the comb-out of men in 1918, a mother appealed to the tribunal for the exemption of her 18-year-old son. She had already had three sons killed, and a fourth was serving in Italy. (The tribunal, though expressing sympathy, deemed that it could not set aside its instructions.) Again, it was recorded in April 1918 by one who served under Major Kirby Ellice ('a splendid tough fellow' who had 'joined the Regiment before I was born'): 'He has lost three sons in the war – one a Grenadier, one in a Scotch regiment, and one Sailor. There is one son and two or three daughters left.'[12]

Against these may be set the case of Robert Saunders, the school headmaster in Fletching, Sussex. He and his wife were in 1914 the parents of 12 children, five of them boys. The three middle boys served throughout the war. One was in the Royal Navy at the outbreak and spent most of the next four years on a Dreadnought in the First Battle Squadron. Already by mid-September 1914: 'Poor old Bob begins to find the ceaseless watch in the North Sea very wearisome.' A second son was a trained army officer who immediately volunteered for service overseas ('but Ma doesn't know that,' wrote his father on 15 August 1914, adding optimistically, 'and I shall try to keep her ignorant in the hope that he may not have to go'). He spent the war as a captain in India, except for some months in Mesopotamia in 1918. The third son to serve, 17 years of age when the war broke out, managed to secure enlistment at his third attempt in September 1914 by advancing his age – his mother 'was of course very much upset'. By June 1915 he was in Flanders and the following month was in the trenches. He spent the next two years on active service on the Western Front, not least during the battle of the Somme. In June 1917, looking worn and thin – although generally his experience as an officer was rendering him more outgoing and self-assertive – he returned to England for a long spell. In 1918 he transferred to the RFC, receiving his wings in June.

Others among the Saunders offspring were in close proximity to the actual conflict. One daughter joined the WAACs and spent 1918 in France, and at least two others

---

[10] Quoted in Robert Rhodes James, *Memoirs of a Conservative: J. C. C. Davidson's Memoirs and Papers, 1910–37* (London: Weidenfeld & Nicolson, 1969), p. 172.

[11] Huntly Gordon, *The Unreturning Army* (London: J. M. Dent, 1967), pp. 14–15.

[12] Letter of Captain E. D. Ridley to his family, 22 April 1918, in Cambridge University Library.

who lived in London were on several occasions in danger from air raids. Yet every one of the 12 children of Robert Saunders survived the war.[13]

It should be added, however, that Saunders's correspondence reveals that he was not left unaffected by the war's death toll, even though it passed his family by. Although he had nothing but contempt for men who sought to evade military service, he was as a schoolmaster persistently being confronted with the price being demanded of his former pupils. In the particularly grim days of October 1917 he wrote: 'not many days passing without some sad tale that makes you curse all War makers.' And the coming of peace did not arouse in him an outburst of rejoicing:

> I think most people feel that some time must elapse before we can properly celebrate peace, our feelings have been too much harassed and our sympathies too often called forth, for the losses of our friends & neighbours. As I look back over the last 4½ years I can see so many tragedies in families I know well, & I can see so many of my old boys who are dead or wounded, or dying of consumption [,] & recall them as boys at school where I used to urge on them the duty of patriotism, so that at present, it doesn't seem right that those who have escaped shall give themselves up to Joy days.

These observations give rise to a further point. Perhaps we cannot assess the effect of war deaths in diminishing the quality of life or in lessening the nation's resources of human talent. But we can certainly observe ways in which the slaughter was helping to change some attitudes. For men as unlike as Wilfred Owen and Rudyard Kipling, death in battle – even when it remained a necessity – had become not the noblest fate a man might accomplish but rather a terrible (and persisting) deprivation. Similarly, for the headmaster Robert Saunders urging patriotism on schoolboys was becoming not a platitudinous exercise but a heavy responsibility, as the intimation of each new casualty among his former charges was a 'sad tale that makes you curse all War makers'. Given the scale and manner of death and injury in this conflict, war was becoming far less susceptible to the heroic delineations of conventional patriotism.

Revulsion against the war was by no means universal. Many participants looked back on their part in the conflict with real appreciation. When questioned late in their lives about their attitude towards it, the survivors of the Leeds Rifles, a force of Territorials drawn from a wide social spectrum and blessed with a remarkable *esprit de corps*, emphasized how much they had found to enjoy in their war service. Nearly all of them, including those permanently maimed, described these as 'the happiest days of my life'. They recalled their sorrow at being discharged.[14]

In part this tells us only that men, reflecting in old age on a youthful period of suffering and comradeship, remember the positive rather than the negative experiences. And the fact that they resorted to the expression so often employed by the doting and the committedly middle-aged to describe school days points to a sorry aspect of the human condition: that a great many people lose relatively early in life the capacity for intense experience of any sort.

Yet some men much closer to the event also described the war as a source of enjoyment. 'I had war in the blood, though where it came from was a mystery to all of us,' wrote John Reith in the 1930s (by which time he was Director-General of the BBC); 'certainly life at the Front suited me as no other had.' Wartime partings from his parents at the end of leave were harder for them than for him because 'I loved my job

---

[13] There had been a thirteenth child: a young girl who died before the war as the result of an accident. After the war one of the sons who had served during the conflict was, by ill-fortune, shot and killed during a hunting expedition.

[14] Information derived from an unpublished paper by Patricia M. Morris, 'The Leeds Rifles and the First World War'.

and was very happy in it.'[15] (Even the severe head wound that eventually forced him out of this agreeable employment failed to lend disenchantment to the view.) Men actually in the trenches could sound the same note. The youthful Graham Greenwell, having endured the mud months on the Somme and been hospitalized, was delighted in January 1917 to be back with his company: 'there is really no life like it.' And his conclusion on his war experiences as a whole, in December 1918, was: 'Could you ever have guessed how much I should enjoy the war?'[16]

But others who had gone to war not doubting that, anyway in these circumstances, it was a good thing came away convinced that they wanted no more of battle for themselves and hoping devoutly that there would never be another conflict to involve their offspring. Lieutenant E. C. Allfree ends his account, written two years after the Armistice, of his experiences as an artillery officer with a tribute to those with whom he served, followed by a one-sentence paragraph. It reads: 'But may there never be another War!' Many war poets, from within the conflict, said the same. They might express it sombrely:

> The unreturning army that was youth;
> The legions who have suffered and are dust.[17]

They might do so passionately:

> And hope, with furtive eyes and grappling fists,
> Flounders in mud. O Jesus, make it stop![18]

They might employ irony:

> I knew a man, he was my chum,
> but he grew blacker every day,
> and would not brush the flies away,
> nor blanch however fierce the hum
> of passing shells. . . .
>
> He stank so badly, though we were great chums
> I had to leave him; then rats ate his thumbs.[19]

But, however expressed, the point was always the same: the futility, the shocking cost, the absence of any compensating rewards. There is a tendency nowadays to discount such fine writing as a product of the highly strung and the over-sensitive. But men of sensitivity may only be expressing in compelling fashion what the less intense and less articulate also feel. One would hardly look to the *Wipers Times* to second the sentiments of Sassoon and Rickword. Yet the final issue of that notable trench journal carried an editorial whose concluding sentence possessed something of the same thrust: 'Anyway though some may be sorry it's over, there is little doubt that the line men are *not*, as most of us have been cured of any little illusions we may have had about the pomp and glory of war, and know it for the vilest disaster that can befall mankind.'

The perception of war as a vile disaster did not diminish in the following decades. It is significant that Reith's account of his war experiences, which he wrote in 1937, was not published at the time. His autocratic, highly moralistic, somewhat blinkered regime at the BBC was already under fire as a throwback to the worst aspects of the Victorian

---

[15] John Reith, *Wearing Spurs* (London: Hutchinson, 1966), pp. 132, 209.
[16] Graham Greenwell, *An Infant in Arms* (London: Allen Lane, 1972), pp. 151, 251.
[17] Siegfried Sassoon, 'Prelude: the Troops'.
[18] Siegfried Sassoon, 'Attack'.
[19] Edgell Rickword, 'Trench Poets'.

age. Nothing could better have confirmed this opinion than his expression of such seemingly antediluvian views as 'I loved my job [at the Front] and was very happy in it' or the message he records sending home to his father: 'Tell him I'm thoroughly enjoying the war.' The three friends to whom he showed his manuscript advised against publication. 'It is just what your enemies are waiting for.'[20]

In discussing the role of this conflict in rendering war unacceptable to many Englishmen, some qualifications are called for. In the first place, antipathy to war was not solely a product of the slaughter on the Western Front. If with less intensity, it existed well before 1914 as a deep-laid part of Britain's liberal consciousness. This may explain why the years 1914 to 1918 brought home to Englishmen the perception of war as 'vilest disaster' to an extent that they did not do to Germans. Germany's sufferings during those four years were by no means less than Britain's. But its liberal heritage certainly was.

In the second place, it is easy to exaggerate the extent of anti-war feeling in Britain between the wars. Too often the policy of appeasement in the 1930s is described, even by careful historians, as being one of peace at any price; or – an unhelpful qualification – as peace at almost any price. No British Government pursued such a policy. And no large section even of the declared opponents of war advocated such a policy (although they sometimes spoke as if they did). Peace at the price, say, of relinquishing France and Belgium – not to say the Channel Islands and the Isle of Wight – to German overlordship was something the rulers of Britain were not prepared even to contemplate. And the great majority of those who advocated the abolition of war took it for granted that no German Government, anyway if treated with consideration, would ever make such demands. When they learned otherwise they ceased to be opponents of at least one more war.

Yet the point remains. After 1918 revulsion against war had plainly increased among Englishmen. The lengths to which they would go in order to avoid it were greater than in the past. Eagerness to prepare against future conflicts had diminished. Most strikingly, this was not only true among those sections of the community traditionally antipathetic to the use of force. It was much in evidence too among those who in the past had railed against Britain's unpreparedness for conflict and who still lauded such concepts as patriotism, and royalty, and the glories of empire, and even the duty of sacrifice.

Discussion of the phenomenon of appeasement is usually bedevilled by the emphasis placed on such aspects as the 'Peace Pledge Union', the 'king and country' debate, and the League of Nations movement. These all belonged in the tradition of liberal internationalism to which the Great War had given powerful reinforcement and which was strong among the political parties not in office. But the men who ruled Britain in the years of appeasement were not, despite distinguished exceptions, apostles of little-Englandism or heirs of John Bright and Norman Angell. Baldwin, as became a cousin of Kipling, was an insular Conservative of no internationalist inclinations. Austen and Neville Chamberlain were sons of the man who, having contributed greatly to Britain's involvement in war with the Boer republics, had gone on to crusade for Empire Federation. Throughout all but trivial periods, the House of Commons in the inter-war years was massively dominated by the political forces that had come to power during the First World War – and had done so because, having railed against softness towards Germany (and juveniles) before 1914, they were now espousing a fight to a knock-out and condemning anyone suspected of favouring half-measures or lacking in patriotic rage.

[20] Reith, *Wearing Spurs*, pp. 11, 103, 132.

The policy that was pursued in the inter-war years was their policy. If it looked unlike the sort of policies they had advocated before the war, and during it, and in the general election that came at its close, that is not to be explained by reference to the heritage of Bright or the preachings of Angell. Rather, the explanation lies in changes in the British Conservative outlook. The causes of such a change are numerous: for example, fear of the havoc that another war might wreak upon the British economy and upon British property owners. But plainly one of the most powerful was the impact of the First World War: not only its economic cost but also its heavy toll in casualties.

II

All sections of the British community lost great numbers of their menfolk during the war. But there is no reason to doubt that the upper classes paid a disproportionately high price. They volunteered even more readily than their social inferiors. They were less likely to be engaged in reserved occupations. And, being less afflicted by malnutrition and its associated diseases, they were less prone to fail army medical examinations or be deemed fit only for service behind the lines. This does not mean that upper-class men invariably failed to avoid military service. J. C. C. Davidson, who was educated at Westminster School and Cambridge University, was 25 years of age, single, and an unpaid private secretary to Lewis Harcourt when the war broke out. According to his own account, he proposed volunteering for the army but Harcourt, Secretary of State for the Colonies, made a strong personal appeal to him to desist. He agreed. Harcourt lost office in May 1915, but Davidson seems not to have recurred to the idea of joining up. He stayed on at the Colonial Office and rendered himself even more indispensable to Harcourt's successor, Bonar Law. By the time Davidson again seriously proposed entering the army, in May 1917, Law had come to occupy a yet more important post in the Government. He threatened to resign if Davidson left him – a threat that Davidson managed to take seriously. That settled the matter. While Conscription Acts and comb-outs dragged forth the unwilling, and wounded men were returned to the front as soon as they could be regarded as recovered, Davidson spent these years performing what seems – notwithstanding the views of his political masters – to have been a less then essential service.[21]

However, exceptions like this do not invalidate the rule: the upper classes gave a larger proportion of their menfolk to the firing line than the community as a whole. And men from the upper classes stood a greater chance of becoming casualties because of the place they occupied when they got to the firing line. In their own estimation they were, by birth and upbringing, the nation's natural leaders. That estimation was endorsed by many who were not of their class. There are many instances of men from the lower orders expecting to be led into action by those with the demeanour and self-assurance of the public-school product. Haig recounts an exchange with the dockers' leader Ben Tillett – now, to Haig's surprise, 'quite converted from his anarchist views' and devoting himself to rallying 'the labour class' behind the war. As part of his effort Tillett was in France visiting dockers who were in uniform. He confessed to Haig that he was having to adjust his view of 'the British Officer'. Previously, drawing his impression from 'picture papers and society journals', he had written them off as 'fops and snobs'. He was astonished to find that dock workers in the ranks 'have unbounded

---

[21] For Davidson's account of his attempts to enlist, see James, *Memoirs of a Conservative*, pp. 22–4, 49–50. Davidson had not engaged in voluntary military training in peacetime. So at least he could not be subject to the jibe once delivered at a Prime Minister of Australia (by a political opponent) that he had had a promising military career cut short by the outbreak of the First World War.

confidence in their officers, and could not get on without them'.[22] Whether Tillett appreciated that the qualities that won these officers the confidence of working men in uniform were the same qualities as secured their inclusion in society journals, Haig does not relate.

But leadership qualities, which might bring so many rewards in civilian life, were no unmixed blessing in wartime. The life of a junior officer was certainly more comfortable than that of his subordinates. It was also more dangerous. The junior officer in battle could lead only by making himself conspicuous to his rank and file. He thereby made himself conspicuous to the enemy, who had good reason to single out leaders for his attentions. The consequence was a markedly higher rate of casualties, and particularly of dead, among junior officers than among 'other ranks'?[23]

That members of the officer class were drawn disproportionately from the upper ranks of society may be inferred from statistics comparing the death rate for mobilized men as a whole with that for men from various elite institutions. For mobilized men *in toto*, the death rate was 12 per cent. For students from Oxford and Cambridge who served in the war it was, respectively, 19 and 18 per cent. For members of the peerage it was 19 per cent. For the former scholars of 53 boarding-schools where statistics are available it was 20 per cent.[24] Other information tells the same story. Huntly Gordon, who was at school at Clifton, writes:

> Our house-group photograph of 1912 shows 40 boys. By the end of the war 13 were dead, 15 had been wounded, some more than once, and only 12 had come through physically unharmed. In later years I have often walked through the Memorial Archway, and with breaking heart read names that, in their alphabetical order, seem to re-echo the roll-call of my time. I wonder what Field-Marshal Earl Haig (O.C.) thought when he unveiled it after the war.[25]

From early in the war it was being suggested that the better-established, better-educated classes were paying a disproportionately high part of the war's death toll. To those who said this, it did not seem appropriate that those who possessed so large a part of the nation's material wealth should contribute a greater share of casualties to its defence. Rather, they felt that these were the men with whom the nation could least afford to part: because they were the bearers of its great traditions, the repositories of its finest qualities, the hope for its future.

One of the first people publicly to draw attention to this problem was Lord Bryce. And in private he sought to preserve at least one historic family from extinction. In April 1915 the war claimed the life of W. C. G. Gladstone, 'a noble young fellow', a

---

[22] Robert Blake (ed.), *The Private Papers of Douglas Haig 1914–1919* (London: Eyre & Spottiswoode, 1952), p. 95 (diary entry for 11 June 1915).

[23] Here are tables for four of the war years, taken from J. M. Winter, 'Britain's "Lost Generation" of the First World War', *Population Studies*, vol. 31, no. 3, November 1977.

	% of officers killed	% of other ranks killed
October 1914 – September 1915	14.2	5.8
October 1915 – September 1916	8.0	4.9
October 1916 – September 1917	8.5	4.7
October 1917 – September 1918	6.9	4.0
	% of officers wounded	% of other ranks wounded
October 1914 – September 1915	24.4	17.4
October 1915 – September 1916	17.4	14.0
October 1916 – September 1917	17.6	12.3
October 1917 – September 1918	17.1	13.9

[24] Statistics from ibid.

[25] Gordon, *The Unreturning Army*, p. 16. Haig, as Gordon indicates, was himself an Old Cliftonian. As a pupil at the school, according to Robert Blake, 'he made no special mark in work or games'.

Liberal MP, and the oldest grandson of the great Liberal Prime Minister. That left only three grandsons, one of them serving in France and the other two in India. Bryce wrote to Crewe, the Secretary of State for India: 'All three are unmarried, and if they are killed, the male line of our old chief will be extinguished. . . . Such an extinction would be a historic calamity'.[26] Urgency was given to his plea soon after by the news that the grandson in France had been posted missing. Through Crewe, the Commander-in-Chief in India was prevailed upon to prevent the other two from being sent abroad. But within a few months the Viceroy was finding it impossible to accord special treatment to these young men while keeping them in ignorance of what was going on. So, when the missing grandson was reported alive and a prisoner of war, the manoeuvre was abandoned.

Bryce was not alone in his concern or his efforts. In the following year H. A. L. Fisher, then Vice-Chancellor of Sheffield University and a former Oxford don, became so dismayed at the high casualty rate among university graduates that he drew up an appeal to have highly educated men employed in a non-combatant capacity. He even sent this memorandum to the War Office. 'The reply,' to quote his biographer, 'was not encouraging.'[27] The War Office advised that he and the other heads of universities should draw up a list, which 'should not be large', of 'the brainiest and most efficient fellows'. It might be possible to transfer some of them to labour battalions or garrison units – a course that, had it been acted on, would hardly have been agreeable to the men on whose behalf Fisher was trying to act.

But the most noteworthy attempt to save the young men of the British upper classes from what, in a stalemated and ever more bloody war, was threatening to become extinction was that of Lord Lansdowne. In this regard the significance of Lansdowne, as exemplar if not as executant, has been rather overlooked. As Foreign Secretary in 1904 he had laid the foundations of the entente with France. As Conservative leader in the Upper House in 1908 he had compared old-age pensions unfavourably with a great war, for the latter would at least raise, not lower, the moral fibre of the nation. On 2 August 1914 he and Bonar Law had been joint signatories, on behalf of their Conservative colleagues, of a letter urging Asquith to align Britain with France in the war against Germany. When the Conservatives joined the coalition Government in May 1915, he was the first to deal a heavy blow to its stability by indicating support for military conscription. The following year he showed himself unmoved by the tragic situation unfolding in Ireland, and by the attempt of the former adversaries Carson and Redmond to find a *modus vivendi* before time ran out. Lansdowne (a large landowner in southern Ireland) played a signal part in wrecking the arrangement that had seemed to emerge from their labours.

By every indication, therefore, Lansdowne seemed set to remain from beginning to end of the conflict an advocate of war *à outrance*. Yet by the time the battle of the Somme was done, Lansdowne had come to a painful conclusion: that the two sides had fought each other to a standstill and that, in their futile attempts to get the better of each other, the great powers of Europe were bleeding themselves to death. So Lansdowne put forward a proposal to his colleagues: not that Britain should surrender or the war be abandoned but that Britain should seek to persuade Germany to offer acceptable terms and so end the war by negotiation. The Asquith Cabinet did not agree. And when in December 1916 the advocate of 'a fight to a finish, to a knock-out' took over the premiership, Lansdowne had no place in the Government. So, in

---

[26] Correspondence in the Crewe papers.

[27] David Ogg, *Herbert Fisher 1865–1940: A Short Biography* (London: Edward Arnold, 1947), p. 59.

December 1917, he directed his appeal for negotiations between the combatants to the nation, in a letter that *The Times* refused to publish but that was accepted – though not endorsed – by the *Daily Telegraph*. His action availed him nothing. His one-time colleagues in the Conservative Party publicly deplored his conduct. And the few people who rallied to him belonged to the left-wing and pacifist sections of politics – hardly those whose welfare he was seeking to preserve.

Yet the considerations that had driven Lansdowne so to act could not be without influence on people who shared his attachment to the forces of order and privilege. In the circumstances of 1917 the threat of German domination had taken precedence in their minds over the imperilled position of the European establishment. (So it would do again in 1940.) But in the years that followed the Great War, the death toll among the elite that Lansdowne had sought to limit pressed itself upon them, not as a manifestation of the true glory but as a terrible emptiness. As for the threat to the social order illustrated by events in Ireland in 1916, it was rendered far more potent by the upheaval in Russia and its subsequent influence throughout Europe. And even Lansdowne's claim that the war could not be carried through to victory, which the events of the second half of 1918 had seemed to contradict, began to gain credence in the 1920s and 30s. For the grim fact became steadily more apparent as 1918 receded that the menace of German militarism, which the Great War was supposed to have abolished, was anything but extinct. It is little wonder that men who shared Lansdowne's concern to preserve the established social order came in the inter-war period to conclude, probably without recalling his appeals, that the British upper classes could not go on bearing the terrible human losses that the war of 1914–18 had imposed on them.

68

BETTER DAYS FOR SOME

The good health enjoyed by the civilian population throughout the country during the greater part of the war was one of the few satisfactory features of the times. . . . As the men who remained [in Birmingham] were largely those incapacitated from military service the almost consistent good health of the city was somewhat remarkable.

Reginald H. Brazier and Ernest Sandford, Birmingham and the Great War 1914–1918

I

The consequences of war that have been considered so far were negative. To an admittedly uncertain extent, they diminished the British nation. But there were ways in which the war affected the lives of sections of the community that pointed in a different direction.

Before 1914, among the working masses who constituted the large majority of the population, life expectancy was on a level that today we associate with Third World countries. Infant mortality, indeed, was a good deal higher in Britain then than it is at present among some countries deemed backward.[1] Living conditions were marked by inescapable squalor and discomfort. Working conditions, by and large, were monotonous and regimented. If the wretchedness of the trenches was a thing apart, and the manner of death and injury on the battlefield unusual in its brutality, it was still the case that squalor and premature death were no novelty for most of those who served in the war. Indeed, when out of the line many men were leading a more wholesome, better-nourished existence in the forces than in their civilian lives. A report from Bristol in 1916 referred to a number of lads, aged 15 to 17, who had entered the army by misstating their ages and then had been discharged at their parents' request. On their return home, as a rule, they 'showed great improvement in physique'. (They were also 'easy to deal with and ready to accept a reasonable wage'.)[2] Even among some of the well-to-do – namely those who came into the army from the spartan conditions of the boarding schools – the transition from civilian to military life may not have constituted all that abrupt a change.

Clearly, between 1914 and the present day there has been a marked advance in the living standards of the masses in Britain. And it is arguable that the First World War,

---

[1] These points, and much else in the discussion that follows, are derived from the writings of J. M. Winter, especially 'The Great War and the British People: the Demographic Component' (unpublished) and 'The Impact of the First World War on Civilian Health in Britain', *Economic History Review* second series, vol. XXX, no. 3, August 1977. Winter points out that infant mortality in pre-war Britain was twice as high as for Egyptians in 1972 and for black South Africans in 1975, and that the life expectancy of British males in 1914 (51.5 years) was about the same as for Ecuador in the early 1960s and Iraq in the early 1970s.

[2] George F. Stone and Charles Wells (eds), *Bristol and the Great War 1914–1919* (Bristol: J. W. Arrowsmith, 1920), p. 344.

far from impeding this process, actually contributed to it. For it is the case that British mortality statistics during the years 1914–18 do not point in only one direction. For males in the 19–45 age group, and particularly the 20–25 age group, the increase in the death rate over peacetime is evident and terrible. But against this must be set two groups among which the death rate was not rising but falling. And although the fall in these groups did not offset the losses of life occurring on the battlefield, it was at least occurring among sections whose improved life expectancy held out much hope for the future. One group was infants. The other was adult males who escaped the firing line. That is, life expectancy improved for the new-born and for males over 45. Certainly, a decline in infant mortality had been in evidence in the decade before 1914. But whereas on the continent of Europe this improvement ceased or went into reverse during the war, in Britain it not only continued but did so at an accelerated rate.

No doubt this lower death rate among infants was in part the result of fewer babies being born. For example, although the number of marriages rose in wartime Birmingham, reaching its peak in 1915 (when it still seemed possible that the married estate might preserve males from compulsory military service), nevertheless the birth rate fell steadily, from 27.3 in 1913 to 19.4 in 1918. But if fewer babies were being born, those that were stood a greater chance of survival.

In part this reflected a changing attitude towards the young. In Britain, as throughout Europe, there was a strong disposition to envisage the very young as a source of hope: they would in time fill the places left vacant by young men dying on the battlefield. So the Bishop of London, who earlier had proclaimed the Holy War, stated when opening a special Baby Week in July 1917: 'The loss of life in this war had made every baby's life doubly precious.'[3] Some commentators gave an even more war-oriented twist to this benevolence. According to the *Daily Telegraph*, with better care for child health in the past Britain would now have been able to place another half a million men on the battlefield.

This 'cult of the child' (as *The Times* referred to it), whether humanitarian or nationalistic in inspiration, helped to produce wholesome results. Measures were instituted at local and national levels for increased provision of ante-natal clinics, more rigorous training of midwives, and the establishment of infant welfare centres. In Birmingham the number of centres for counselling mothers on pre-natal and infant care rose from eight to 20, and the number of mothers with babies attending them quadrupled. In addition, 'Eighty-five per cent of all the babies born in Birmingham were visited soon after birth, and in cases where help was desired it was given by a staff of women visitors, or at the maternity and welfare centres.'[4]

Yet if these actions by the authorities aided the survival of the very young, they hardly account for improved life expectancy among non-combatant adults. The latter sector, far from having access to better medical facilities, were at a disadvantage on account of the great many doctors serving with the forces. And, especially among industrial workers (and sometimes their children), living conditions deteriorated during the war owing to the cessation of home building and the mass movement of people to munitions centres ill-prepared to house them.

No doubt, as particular actions of the authorities enhanced the life expectancy of the very young, so others of their actions prolonged the lives of adults. These included the provision of canteens in munitions factories employing, all told, 900,000 people; and

---

[3] Quoted in Winter, 'The Impact of the First World War on Civilian Health in Britain'. *Economic History Review*, vol. xxx, no. 3, p. 498.

[4] Reginald H. Brazier and Ernest Sandford, *Birmingham and the Great War 1914–1918* (Birmingham: Cornish Bros., 1921), p. 288.

measures aimed at reducing drunkenness among the workforce. The beneficial effect of the former, when set against the inadequate meals usually available to industrial workers, is apparent. The improvements wrought by the latter deserve more comment. The restrictions placed on the hours at which hotels might be open, the prohibition of 'treating', heavy financial imposts on spirits, and the markedly reduced alcoholic content of beer, all produced a decline in drunkenness. According to Robert Roberts, committals for 'drunkenness and assaults', which stood at 62,882 in 1908, fell in 1918–19 to 'a mere 1,670'.[5] From the vantage point of his slum world and the corner shop that his family ran there, Roberts could observe the wider ramifications of such statistics. 'Drunkenness was by far the commonest cause of dispute and misery in working-class homes. On account of it one saw many a decent family drift down through poverty into total want.' At his parents' corner shop, where the decision to grant or withhold credit must be judged to a nicety if custom were to be maximized yet bad debts avoided, careful note was taken of these matters. 'The man unfit for work on Monday because of week-end drinking . . . was marked and points were deducted from his social stock. The family would suffer a fall in prestige too. This could be another home on the slippery slope.'[6]

During the war, it may be surmised, enforced restraint on the consumption of alcohol did more than prolong the lives of some adults who would otherwise have killed themselves with excessive drinking. It ensured that money needed to provide nourishment for themselves and their children was not dissipated in pubs. There may (as J. M. Winter suggests) have been a further consequence: that alcohol-induced neglect of the very young, sometimes resulting in fatality, was less frequent.

However, in seeking explanations for this wartime rise in the health and life expectancy of both children and non-combatant adults it is necessary to look beyond the actions of governmental and local authorities. And in doing so it is possible to discover a force of first-rate importance (to which state action was a contributor, but only marginally so): improved nutrition. That is, the pregnant woman, the child, and the industrial worker, especially at the lower end of the social scale, were eating better. This seems hard to credit, given that Britain in the later part of the war was under a partial blockade whose impact was reflected in soaring food prices and the much discussed phenomenon of food queues. Yet the period of real shortage was not long, and it was countered by increased home production and by the institution of rationing, first on a voluntary, then on a municipal, and then, by stages, on a national basis. Rationing, it seems fair to generalize, tends to raise the consumption of the worst-fed, who will benefit crucially from any improvement, and to lower the consumption of the best-fed, who will not expire in consequence. It has even been suggested that some of the changes in diet imposed by the war were not injurious: for example, that war bread, though not so palatable and less agreeable to look upon, was more nourishing. And we have the assurance of one local history that much wartime discontent was the result less of overall shortage than of a reluctance to change eating habits. 'There was nothing like a food famine at any time.'[7]

Perhaps the existence of food queues in 1917 was not always a contradiction of this. After all, the absence of queues in poorer areas in peacetime did not usually mean that their inhabitants were getting enough to eat. It was more often evidence that they lacked the money with which to purchase sufficient. By the same token, the *New*

---

[5] Robert Roberts, *The Classic Slum* (Harmondsworth: Penguin Books, 1973), p. 218. A decline on this scale is hardly to be accounted for by the transfer of some potential drunkards and brawlers to the armed forces.

[6] Ibid., pp. 123–4.

[7] Stone and Wells, *Bristol and the Great War*, p. 360.

Statesman late in January 1918 (in an article entitled 'Short Commons') suggested that the real cause of grievance was not absolute shortage. It was the fact that there was not sufficient food to enable workers to spend the large wages they were receiving.

So food continued to be, if not necessarily so enjoyable as in the past, available in sufficient quantities. But how then do we account for the fact that those who previously had received less than they needed were now, at least marginally, doing better? To speak simply of increased money wages does not take us very far. For food prices increased at least as much. Indeed, according to one calculation wages rose 90 per cent overall during the war, while food prices rose 110 per cent.

What made the difference was that the least well-off were now gaining access to more regular sources and higher levels of income. The wives and widows of serving soldiers were in receipt of steady allowances and pensions from the state. The unskilled and the once rarely employed were now securing regular work, at higher grades than hitherto available and with the opportunity of much overtime. By these means youngsters just out of school, men whose age or incapacity had often denied them a job, and females in general could find work at a wage level beyond their peacetime expectations. In *England After War* C. F. G. Masterman gives instances of girls in wartime earning 20 to 30 shillings a week who before 1914 would have secured 5 or 6 shillings.

Certainly, whatever we make of these explanations for better nutrition among the needy, the fact that the poorer classes were getting more to eat, and also were better clothed and shod, is well supported by contemporary accounts. Masterman, once a Liberal MP and (briefly) a member of the Asquith Government, recounts visiting in wartime a region in south London ('not far different from a concentrated slum') where once he had lived for nine years. He found it looking even more forlorn than when he had resided there. Repairs had ceased; the Council had become 'indifferent to the sedulous cleansing of the streets'; and the houses 'looked as if at any moment they might collapse in ruins'. But the appearance of the inhabitants, thanks to 'the money that was pouring in', was another matter.

> The children were well fed, well dressed, well shod. The girls were adorned with cheap finery. The mothers were less careworn and could pay more attention to the children. And this same result was being obtained all over the country. 'Families that were my despair before,' said a medical officer of health, 'are now clean and well cared for.' That swamp of forlorn humanity round Dockland, Bermondsey, Wapping, South-West Ham, found itself for the first time well fed, and with good feeding came health and a new chance for the coming generations. Except for anxiety for those at the Front, many would have wished these conditions to continue for ever.[8]

The historians of Bristol during the war tell a similar story:

> A Bristol teacher in a working-class part of the city declared about the middle of the war period that his schoolboys were better fed and better clothed than before August, 1914. The destitution due to irregular employment disappeared when labour of all kinds was at a premium, and the allowances made to wives and families of men who were away, if not large, were dependable. Prior to the war the Education Committee had to supply many underfed scholars with meals; the demand for this assistance dwindled to very small proportions as the conflict with the Central Powers proceeded.[9]

During 1916 the point was made at a meeting of the Bristol City Council that whereas, on 31 March 1915, 1,445 meals were provided for needy schoolchildren, a year later the number was only 114. The chairman of the city's Health Insurance Committee also

---

[8] C. F. G. Masterman, *England After War* (London: Hodder & Stoughton, n.d. [*c.* 1922]), pp. 123–4.

[9] Stone and Wells, *Bristol and the Great War*, p. 305.

reported that fewer panel patients (that is, patients insured under the state health scheme) had been treated in 1915 and fewer prescriptions issued. By the end of 1917 the Board of Guardians was also drawing attention to the marked decline in pauperism.

Not all the social trends accompanying this process proved favourable. If Masterman found the mothers in his London district more attentive to their children, reports from Bristol disagreed. In the latter city a marked increase was noted in the number of juvenile offenders during the war, in contrast to the falling off in offences among adults. This was attributed, at least in part, to the absence of fathers abroad, the entry of mothers into the workforce, and the high earning power of juveniles. All these resulted in a breakdown of parental care for younger children and parental authority over older children. According to a school medical officer in Bristol, children at 13 and 14 were 'regrettably often' earning wages that 'tend to exempt them from parental control'. While 'on all sides those most closely in touch with the children assure me that the standard of feeding in the homes has in many cases been raised owing to the increased income earned, it is deplorably evident that lack of discipline and cleanliness and the prevalence of diseases prolonged by dirt and neglect are increasing amongst school children.'[10]

The mortality figures seem to make it clear that the ill-effects of inadequate discipline and cleanliness were more than offset, at least in the matter of life expectancy, by the improved 'standard of feeding'.

II

Did these improvements survive the war? And were they maintained after 1921, given the onset of large-scale and persistent unemployment? In a measure the answers are in the affirmative.

The post-war situation, judged absolutely, is hardly a cause for rejoicing. In the two decades following the war, it has been estimated, 'drabness was universal' and 'malnourishment common' among the lower 30 per cent of the population. As for the 'probably more than 10%' at the absolute bottom, their life experience was one of 'severe hardship and poverty'. Growing children, and particularly teenagers, were the principal victims of the incidence of malnutrition.[11]

Yet these figures, if not comfortable, constitute a marked improvement on the situation before 1914. In a study of poverty in Britain on the eve of the war, based on a close investigation of five towns, A. L. Bowley had written: 'to raise the wages of the worst-paid workers is the most pressing social task with which the country is confronted to-day.' A decade later, after a second survey of the same five towns, he was able to record that the war had done just that. (However, by 1924 the incidence of unemployment was revealing that jobs at these improved rates would not be available for all.) Bowley could also point to another factor, much accelerated by the war, that had contributed to the decline in poverty. The decrease in large families was marked in each of the five towns under study; 'and, since largeness of family was one of the principal causes of poverty in 1913, this diminution in the number of children has had a marked effect on the proportion found in poverty.'[12] Of these two forces the former

---

[10] Stone and Wells, *Bristol and the Great War*, p. 364.

[11] Sean Glynn and John Oxborrow, *Interwar Britain: A Social and Economic History* (London: Allen & Unwin, 1976), p. 37.

[12] A. L. Bowley and Margaret H. Hogg, *Has Poverty Diminished?* (London: P. S. King, 1925), ch. 1.

(that is, the rise in wages of the lowest paid) was the more powerful in combating poverty. Taken together, they had achieved a striking result. ●

Britain was not more prosperous in 1924 than it had been in 1914, so it would be no cause for surprise if the incidence of poverty was the same. Yet Bowley concluded that, even on the assumption that the effects of unemployment were at their worst (i.e. that unemployed persons had no savings to call on and were out of work persistently and not just occasionally), 'the proportion in poverty in 1924 was little more than half that in 1913.' Had there been no unemployment, he calculated, the incidence of poverty would have been down to one-third or one-quarter. In other words, although the size of the cake was not greater in 1924 than in 1913, the better-off were getting marginally less of it at the later date and the worse-off marginally more. (This redistribution of wealth did not continue after 1924. But the country's wealth did increase after that date. So, even though the shares remained the same, all sections became somewhat more prosperous.)

In addition, there were ways in which the war produced improvements in the conditions of the labour force as a whole. The state legislated to this end, not least in its introduction of a system of unemployment benefit that, if inadequate in terms of the problems ahead, had a breadth of application previously unknown in Britain. Again, actions by some powerful unions had results that benefited a large sector of the workforce: 1919 saw the almost universal adoption of the eight-hour day and the 48-hour working week. It was inaugurated by the engineering and shipbuilding unions and soon taken up by others. This, the first substantial drop in hours of work since the 1870s, marked 'a major change in the working conditions of a majority of the British working population'.[13] Its inception owed much to the particular circumstances created by the war. Trade unions were at this point in a healthy position for several reasons. The war had occasioned a great upsurge in union membership and so of union funds. There had been little call on their funds in support of strikes, if only because strikes in important industries had become illegal for the duration and so could not be supported by union finance. Regular employment and the shortage of consumer goods had caused many rank-and-file unionists to accumulate small amounts of savings, so making strike action more feasible. And the respect that the unions had gained among some of the possessing classes through their essential role in the war, together with fear of Bolshevik infection should they become too disgruntled, had further enhanced their bargaining power.

This gave trade unionists confidence as the war drew to a close. But their confidence went hand in hand with a great concern. For the fear was widespread that peace would bring an upsurge in unemployment, as war-created industries closed, war-accelerated technology displaced labour, and demobilized men sought jobs that the additional labour drawn into the workforce was striving to retain. Fear of unemployment and the desire for job security are forces that turn trade union attention to shorter working hours as a way of making jobs go further. But it is rare for such fear to find the unions in a strong bargaining position. This happened at the end of the war, and the eight-hour day was its salutary result. According to Arthur Gleason, writing in 1920: 'No movement previously recorded has equalled this "shorter week" of 1919.'[14]

The reduction in working hours is another of those consequences of war whose effects are unquantifiable. Yet it seems safe to say that the gain was considerable. Before 1914, the working man had possessed few opportunities for leisure and

---

[13] Glynn and Oxborrow, *Interwar Britain: A Social and Economic History*, p. 27.

[14] Arthur Gleason, *What the Workers Want: A Study of British Labor* (London: Allen & Unwin, 1920), p. 254.

relaxation. After it, the relentless grind of the workplace was in some measure alleviated.

In other (also unquantifiable) ways the war had affected the working class as a whole. If much deference and respect for their 'betters' persisted among labouring men, it seemed less of a force than in the past. Arthur Gleason, an American observer of the English scene, wrote in 1920: 'An old Oxford friend said sadly to me: "Ten years ago, when I came into a crowded bus, a working-man would rise and touch his cap and give me his seat. I am sorry to see that spirit dying out."' Gleason, who clearly was not sorry, commented: 'The workers are beginning to use a manner of jaunty equality in dealing with those passengers who travel through life on a first-class ticket. . . . Reverence for the gentry, for the privileged, for the idle, has withered.' This 'change in spirit', he concluded, although beginning to appear in 1910, had been 'hastened by the War'.[15]

Much about the war had caused some workmen to doubt whether they should continue through life surrendering their seats and touching their caps to those who expected such subservience. Moving about the country as soldiers or as migrant labourers, they had observed the high living standards and continued enjoyment of luxury among people prone to preach restraint. The food shortages of 1917 had driven the message home: that administrative bodies dominated by wholesalers and distributors would not ensure adequate supplies for working-class families. If equal shares were to be established at a time when equality of sacrifice was being proclaimed, then it was necessary for the working class to set up its own vigilance committees, or secure representation on the appropriate bodies, or elicit a rationing system from a reluctant Government. The fact that the application of rationing to the whole country coincided with the appointment as Food Controller of J. R. Clynes, a trade unionist and Labour MP, appeared to signify that only by asserting themselves would the less privileged classes secure tolerable travelling conditions through life. It also seemed to show that, anyway in some circumstances, such assertion did produce improvement.

In many other ways the war had helped to create both an awareness of working-class deprivation and a consciousness that workers had some power to combat it. The role that both the industrial and the political wings of organized labour had been called on to play, in the application of wartime legislation and in the government of the country, had shown that working men occupied an essential part in the nation's affairs, especially in times of crisis. It had also shown that this was recognized by members of the other classes, some of whom welcomed the fact while others, had they been able, would have preferred to overlook it. Admittedly, the authority of the state, in the form of leaving certificates, the outlawry of strikes, and the threat of military conscription for troublemakers, had in large measure replaced economic deprivation as a way of disciplining the workforce. Yet many wartime events had shown that there were limits to how far such authority could be exercised. The contentment of the workers must at some point be ensured.

The involvement of working men in the instrumentalities of government brought them closer than ever before to the centre of power. Sometimes, it should be noted, this had the effect of separating the workers' representatives from the more active elements in the labour force. One manifestation of this was the shop stewards' movement, which drew its strength from discontent among the rank and file at their distance from the trade union bureaucracy. The same thing can be seen in the political field. Several Labour MPs who entered Lloyd George's Government, such as G. N. Barnes, refused to leave it at the end of the war. They preferred to break with the Labour Party. But on the other side were noteworthy instances of a new assertiveness

---

[15] Gleason, *What the Workers Want*, pp. 250–1.

among representatives of labour, resulting from their wartime involvement in official activities. The best-known example is Arthur Henderson. Certainly, he did not so much leave the Government as receive his marching orders. But this happened because he had held out for what he considered a distinctively working-class position. And he drew from this experience the conclusion that only through an independent Labour Party making its own bid for office would that position be upheld. Others followed his lead. Clynes, who after Henderson was the most noteworthy Labour figure to hold ministerial office, was loath to break with the coalition Government at the end of the war. But he did so.

Another example may be found in the industrial field. Ernest Bevin, the dockers' leader, was engaged in many official activities as a trade union representative between 1914 and 1918. But the experience did not leave him wanting to prolong this involvement. He declined the offer of a job as labour adviser to the Government. And in February 1919 he bluntly told the National Industrial Conference:

> my experience with all this good feeling, whether on trade boards or Whitley Councils, is that the leopard has not changed his spots. It is as big an effort now to get a bob or two a week for your work-people as ever it was. . . . I have never yet convinced an employer. I will tell you what has convinced him – the economic power of the Unions we represent and no other weapon.[16]

By 1919, in short, Britain contained a working class with a greater sense of cohesion than had been the case in the past. The fragmentation, and the rigid demarcation between sectors within, had been ameliorated. For one thing, the war had helped to diminish the wide gaps in earning power within the workforce. As we have seen, the skilled workers had made no economic advances and had sometimes slipped back, while the most poorly paid had achieved at least a modest improvement. Again, for all the resistance put up by the skilled men, skill had been devalued by the demonstration that a combination of machines and semi-skilled workers could achieve the same result; as well as by the fact that, on occasions, when skilled men were called into the army to perform tasks for which their specialist abilities were required, they had failed to perform them adequately. One indication of the breaking down of the stratification within the workforce is to be found in linguistics. As Bernard Waites points out, 'The very term "artisan class" tended to disappear from the language of social observation.'[17]

It is possible to illustrate this greater cohesion within the working class from contemporary observations. In October 1917 one of the reports to the Cabinet on the labour situation, discussing events in Yorkshire and the East Midlands, referred to important meetings of railwaymen. At these it had commonly been admitted that 'the ambitious demands which have recently been put forward cannot be obtained during the war.'

> After the war however it will be a different matter and the executive of the National Union of Railwaymen is being pressed to formulate a new programme *on national as opposed to sectional lines*. The chief point is to be the eight hours day. . . . [Emphasis added]

Elsewhere in the same report is a quotation from the *Merthyr Pioneer* on the subject of a recent increase in miners' wages in the form of a flat rate advance. The Welsh journal is quoted as saying:

> There will naturally be some grumbling amongst the best paid men, but, on the whole, it is safe to say that the new principle will be recognised as a just one. . . . It will further have

---

[16] Quoted in B. A. Waites, 'The Effect of the First World War on Class and Status in England, 1910–20', *Journal of Contemporary History*, vol. 11, 1976, pp. 44–5.

[17] Ibid., p. 35.

the salutary effect of breaking down in some measure the grade barrier that has done so much to prevent that perfect unity so necessary to working class success.

Again, a long memorandum drawn up by the Ministry of Labour in February 1920, dealing with the shop stewards' movement, spoke of

> an increasing tendency for the trade unionists of one shop, works or small district, to act together, irrespective of their division into crafts or occupations. What is called 'class consciousness' is obliterating the distinctions between those who follow different occupations in the same works.

The document countered the notion that, because new machinery had 'destroyed the old distinction between the skilled and unskilled', therefore trade unionism would be weaker. It argued instead that 'this very assimilation creates a stronger bond between all workers, and an organisation based upon that bond may be much stronger than any groups of craftsmen.'

But, having drawn attention to this 'compression' within the working class and the opportunity to improve the living conditions of labourers that it offered, it is necessary again to stress that the change was relative. Many divisions concerned with status and relativities of pay remained. In addition, many working people continued ready, at any time of real or supposed national crisis, to accept the profile of the situation delineated by the upper classes. They would see themselves not as people having distinct class interests but as members of the British nation, subjects of the Crown, and followers of those born and bred to be their rulers. In general, these sectors of the workforce would not welcome being represented in Parliament by working men or being governed by a Labour ministry. (Such a ministry they would perceive, under the guidance of the *Daily Mail* and similar journals, as a 'class' Government, and consequently different in kind from the 'national' governments provided by the Conservatives.) In daily life they would be concerned more with football matches and racing fixtures and prize fights than with political gatherings or trade union activities.

These things had changed in a measure. The fact that people were now in a position to choose a Labour Government if they wanted, as they had not been heretofore, is evidence enough of that. But the change was limited. This is apparent from the restricted support that Labour secured in the seven inter-war elections. In all but two of them its showing *vis-à-vis* the Conservatives was relatively poor. And even in one of the other two (that of 1923) its performance at the polls was far from remarkable – notwithstanding the fact that in the aftermath of this contest Labour managed to form a Government for the first time in British history.

69

NOT YET ONE NATION

I

If the war had helped to produce a more coherent working class, but without abolishing divisions and differences within it, what was its effect on the class structure as a whole? The answer is of the same order. The war helped to diminish the gaps between classes, and not least the yawning gulf that separated the richest from the poorest. But class divisions remained much in evidence. And the range of wealth from top to bottom, if decreased, continued vast.

The war had subtracted from the riches of the possessing classes. It had certainly not dispossessed them. In his *Who's Who* entry before the war the Duke of Rutland had described his properties thus: 'Owns 62,000 acres; minerals in Leicestershire and Derbyshire; picture gallery at Belvoir Castle'. The post-war entry indicates diminished circumstances. The minerals in Leicestershire and Derbyshire remain, as does the picture gallery at Belvoir Castle (and the castle itself). But the total number of acres, by the mid-1920s, amounted to only 18,000. The principal alienation took place in 1920, when 28,000 acres (or about half the Belvoir estate) and an estate of 12,500 acres in Lancashire were sold.

Yet it should not be assumed that this was a family being crippled by death duties as a result of a succession of losses on the battlefield. Various forms of war-induced taxation no doubt pressed heavily, but death duties were not among them. The eighth Duke of Rutland, having succeeded his father in 1906, retained the title until his own death in 1925, when he was succeeded by his son. It is quite possible that he sold various parcels of land less because of wartime depredations (although they may have contributed) than because he had an eye for a good investment. The 28,000 acres at Belvoir realized £1.5 million, the estate in Lancashire a further £1 million. In terms of rent these properties were probably not bringing in more than 3 per cent per annum. The capital they realized, if invested in trustee securities, would have yielded 7 or 8 per cent. So it is possible, though by no means certain, that the Duke of Rutland suffered as a result of the war no greater material loss than the claims regarding landholding that he could make in his entry for *Who's Who*.

Certainly, the possessing classes had by and large paid heavily for the conflict. The war brought greatly increased income tax and super-tax and a higher incidence of death duties. It was impossible for the wealthy to fight these measures with the devoted resistance of 1909–10, for they were being imposed (in the national interest) by Governments in which the Conservatives were ever more important participants. And the measures, once conceded, tended to outlive the circumstances of their imposition. To adapt Professors Peacock and Wiseman, it is easier to keep the saddle on the horse than to get it there in the first place.[1] That is, taxes that may be resisted before

---

[1] A. T. Peacock and J. Wiseman, *The Growth of Public Expenditure in the United Kingdom* (London: Allen & Unwin, 1967), p. xxxiv.

imposition as ruinous and revolutionary cannot be so opposed once they have been in operation without producing ruin or revolution. The onus of showing that greater benefit would be gained by the removal than by the perpetuation of war-induced taxation had been transferred to the tax-paying classes. This was no easy task, given that during the war all sorts of promises had been made and commitments undertaken whose fulfilment after 1918 required the revenue that the taxes were producing.

The way in which taxation reduced living standards among some sections of the aristocracy is suggested by the figures from two landed estates for which detailed records exist.[2] In 1914 the income tax took only 4 per cent of the gross rentals that these estates brought in; by 1919 it took over 25 per cent. (The landowners could have offset some part of their reduction in income by raising rents, when wartime legislation did not prevent this, but they failed to do so.) Presumably at least some of the huge number of land sales that occurred immediately after the war were occasioned by this tax burden, although the declining social esteem attached to land-holding, combined (as already indicated) with the opportunity for more lucrative investments elsewhere, probably played a greater part. For whatever reason, acreage amounting to about one-quarter of England – some 6–8 million acres – passed out of the hands of the large landed families between 1918 and 1920.[3] As it happened, the families who sold chose their time well. By 1921 returns from agricultural products were falling catastrophically, as signalized by the Government's hasty abandonment of guaranteed prices under its Corn Production Act. Most of the land that had gone on the market had been bought at high prices by former tenants. Now, as owner-occupiers, they faced difficult circumstances burdened by heavy mortgages.

But for those great landowners who did not diversify by selling off large sectors of their holdings, this sequence of war years with heavy taxes and low rents followed by the post-war slump plainly meant a lowering of prosperity. For one thing, the owners of great houses were not again able to employ staff on the pre-war scale. The high wage levels established by the war never fell sufficiently after it to make this possible.

II

At the same time as the landed classes were undergoing a degree of economic decline they were, as members of the House of Lords, suffering the indignity of an influx of new men. Many of these interlopers had been elevated on account of 'public services' consisting of little more than handsome donations to political funds. It did not render their presence more welcome that some had acquired the wherewithal to make such gifts by decidedly questionable means, such as the transfer of capital to South America so as to escape wartime taxation.

As this creation by Lloyd George of 'dreadful knights' and upstart barons bore witness, the war had opened up many opportunities for enrichment to sectors of the business community. Some businessmen had seized upon them with more enterprise than scruple. A greater number, no doubt, had rendered good service to the nation at the same time as they were advancing their pecuniary interests. The conversion of peace-time industries to the production of war materials, as well as being profitable, was a notable achievement of British capitalism.

---

[2] See F. M. L. Thompson, *English Landed Society in the Nineteenth Century* (London: Routledge & Kegan Paul, 1963), ch. 12, for this information and for much of the material in this section.

[3] This was a resumption of a trend already evident between 1910 and 1914, again supposedly caused by new taxes on land but much more the result of the good prices to be obtained.

Other sections among the middle classes had also prospered. This was true of some professional groups, or anyway those members who had survived the war. There had been an over-supply of lawyers before 1914 and hence much stringency in the profession. By 1918, aided by the interruption of training and deaths on the battlefield, supply and demand were in equilibrium. So there was evident in the profession a self-confidence that 'replaced the dejection and apologetics of the pre-war period'.[4] Retailers also had done well in many instances. Despite shortages of many commodities, people in wartime found themselves with money to spend on goods that previously had lain outside their income range. Members of the lower ranks of the working class were eager to acquire 'status' goods that hitherto had been available only to the artisan sector and had served to mark the latter off from their less skilled brethren. The makers and retailers of such commodities as gramophones, pianos, and furniture prospered accordingly. Working people also made unaccustomed visits to professional photographers for family and individual portraits and to dentists for artificial teeth. They began buying a better class of clothes than, in the north, the shawls and clogs of old, as well as other creature comforts like soap and more interesting varieties of foodstuffs. And throughout the whole community the war and its impact at home enhanced sales of newspapers and magazines. A wide range of producers, shop-keepers, and professional people benefited from these developments.

For evidence of this we may look to the profits shown by some wholesale drapers for 1916. So John Howell & Co. returned a profit of £42,000 as against £10,500 in 1913, and Pawsons and Leafs a profit of £36,000 as against £7,500. Alliston & Co. had turned a loss of £6,500 in 1913 into a profit of £11,000 in 1916. At the meeting of shareholders of one drapery company, the Fore Street Warehouse Coy., where a net profit for 1916 of more than double that of 1914 was announced, the chairman stated: 'there were many women who for one reason or another had now more money to spend on surplus requirements than they had had at any previous time, and whose first and natural desire was to replenish their wardrobes.'[5]

While businessmen were prospering, the war was storing up a considerable long-term benefit for those sufficiently well-off to invest heavily in war loans. Many of these loans were raised in the later part of the war, when the value of money was much depleted. They were repaid in the inter-war years, by which time the cost of living had fallen markedly and the value of the pound was correspondingly enhanced. The nineteenth-century dictum of 'philanthropy plus 5 per cent' was here succeeded, albeit unintentionally, by something even more satisfying: patriotism plus a margin of profit much in excess of 5 per cent.

But for large sectors among the middle classes the war meant heavy inroads into income without compensating opportunities. It struck at those who drew their livelihood from house rents by artificially pegging their income while placing no restraints on tax levels and living costs. It damaged small businessmen by depriving them of workers who, if they escaped military service, went into essential industries. It hit particularly severely at those living on fixed incomes from investments, such as retired people, single women, and other families in which there was no 'breadwinner'. It reserved a special measure of calamity for investors in Russian loans and enterprises, who found themselves expropriated when the Bolsheviks seized power. And for any middle-class salary earner, rises in the cost of living kept ahead of advances in pay

---

[4] Avner Offer, 'The Origins of the Law of Property Acts 1910–25', *Modern Law Review*, vol. 40. no. 5, September 1977, p. 522.

[5] *The Times*, quoted in Arthur Gleason, *Inside the British Isles* (London: John Lane: The Bodley Head, 1917), pp. 331–2.

more conclusively than was the case among most wage earners. Similarly, army pay and allowances usually constituted a fall in remuneration for middle-class males who entered the services, as they were unlikely to do for men from the working class.

Faced with a reduced income, members of the middle classes often had little room for manoeuvre. Big economies could be achieved only by forgoing items whose surrender would involve a loss of caste. Choosing between such items was bound to be painful. An instance is education. Working-class children received it free from the state. The children of much of the middle class did not. The importance attached to preserving this distinction is illustrated by the early life of the film actor David Niven.[6] He was the youngest of four children. When he was 5 years old his father, who was believed to be rich, went off to the war accompanied by his valet, his under-gardener, and two grooms. At Gallipoli the father, the valet, and one groom were 'duly slaughtered'. It then transpired that his father was hugely in debt. Country residences had to be sold, and the family entered upon straitened circumstances. These were only partially relieved when, in 1917, his mother married again, to 'a second line politician' who made 'only a token subscription to the family coffers'.

Although his father's debts had still to be paid off, Niven at the earliest opportunity was sent to a boarding school; one sister was already at such a school, while his elder brother was a naval cadet at Dartmouth. (The fourth sibling, an older sister, was 'at home helping my mother'.) The 6-year-old Niven had no wish to attend such an institution. In addition to the fact that his initial experiences of public schooling were horrendous (they improved in due course), he makes this general point: 'Apart from the Chinese, the only people in the world who pack their sons off to the tender care of unknown and often homosexual schoolmasters at the exact moment when they are most in need of parental love and influence, are the British so-called upper and middle classes.'

The cost of his schooling, Niven realized only later, must have been a fearful drain on his mother at a time when, if not 'actually taking in washing', she was certainly 'sending very little out'. Soon the family had to relinquish even its 'large, damp house in Cadogan Place' and repair to 'a converted fisherman's cottage which had a reputation for unreliability' on the Isle of Wight. (As it happened, Niven was happier here than in any previous residence, except that the appearance of his address in the school list provoked sniggers among young marquesses and dukes.) But at whatever hardship to his family, his career at expensive public schools continued – apart from an interruption for expulsion – for more than a decade.

One way in which the war placed a strain on the resources of both the middle classes and the aristocracy has passed largely unnoticed. This was its constant calls on their benevolence. It was taken by these sectors to be in the nature of things that they had a duty to aid the victims of unmerited misfortune. For, as an authoritative study of one aspect of war-created charity puts it:

> Charitable activity was not only a moral duty, a form of noblesse oblige, a service performed by those with the money and leisure to work without pay. It was also a badge of class, a mark of having arrived within the upper classes, a ladder for moving higher within them, and a means of recreation. Not least, it was a means of asserting social superiority, a pedagogical device whereby the values of the philanthropic classes were inculcated in the lower orders.[7]

The problem was that the war presented the charitably disposed with so many

---

[6] See David Niven, *The Moon's a Balloon* (London: Coronet Books, 1977), pp. 13–18.

[7] Peter Cahalan, *Belgian Refugee Relief in England During the Great War* (New York: Garland Publishing, 1982), p. 503.

opportunities to exercise their largesse that the strain became intolerable.[8] At least nine main areas of charitable activity arising from the war are identified in the War Charities legislation: enemy aliens, refugees, war-devastated regions, prisoners of war, convalescent soldiers, the Red Cross, soldiers on leave, soldiers at the front and in base camps, and civilians in distress in England. Each area contained many sub-areas: 'The category for refugees alone covered Armenian, Belgian, French, Italian, Polish and Serbian refugees, and within each category there might be one, several, or many organisations.'[9] The proliferation of appeals is evidenced by the fact that at the beginning of 1916 it was possible to list 69 Belgian relief charities, while at least 24 more had at one time existed, and some of them probably still did.

Some of these groups, certainly, had only a limited appeal. Enemy aliens thrown out of employment or in other ways rendered destitute won succour from the Quakers but probably from not too many other groups. Some needy sectors, like the 200,000 Belgians who flooded into Britain during the first months of the war, attracted much private charity early on, but this dried up as it became apparent that, in terms of dimension and duration, the problem could be met only by the resources of the state. In other instances the need proved transitory (as indeed it did for many Belgians, large numbers of whom secured gainful employment in vital industries). Several millions of pounds were donated early in the war to the Prince of Wales's Fund to relieve distress at home. Initially the need was considerable. Industries closed, throwing workpeople out of employment, and separation allowances to soldiers' dependents failed to materialize. But before long these problems dwindled to vanishing point. By and large, however, the calls of charity were unrelenting, as one class of refugee or one war-devastated district was replaced by another, and as certain categories of need persisted for the duration – not least those concerned with the British soldier, be he in the trenches, or convalescing, or on leave, or a prisoner in the hands of the enemy.

The 'philanthropic community' gave generously. By the end of 1915 the Prince of Wales's Fund had raised £5 million and wartime charities overall between £20 and £30 million. Then there were the donations in other forms: hospitality, gifts of food and clothing, the provision of specialized services and organizing activities and routine work. For example, among Belgian refugees large numbers toiled in administrative and welfare activities, while doctors, chemists, dentists, and auditors provided their services free or at reduced fees, and property owners made accommodation available for no rental or a less than market rent. As the war went on, these forms of gift in cash and kind diminished, and increasingly the state was looked to as the proper supporter of the war's victims. This was evidence of the scale of the problem but also of the way in which the conflict was diminishing the incomes of the charitably inclined. Thus a large number of middle-class women began the war convinced that working without pay among refugees was an appropriate form of activity for females of their station. Before long many were obliged to forget the dictates of gentility and seek paid employment – within charitable circles, if possible, but otherwise elsewhere.

It is impossible to compute how much the war took from the middle classes in contributions to charity of one sort or another. But plainly this became another form of

---

[8] The war also provided a field day for the operator of charitable frauds, at least until August 1916 when the Government carried a measure requiring the registration of charities. Before that date numbers of worthy causes were embraced by shady individuals. For example, the Italian X-Ray Ambulance Fund provided nothing for the Italians but netted the lady who established it £1,000. And the French Relief Fund, founded by an undischarged bankrupt for the ostensible purpose of aiding French refugees, passed through a number of questionable phases. In one of them it reserved its hospitality for young Frenchwomen who (in all probability) were intended for use as prostitutes.

[9] Cahalan, *Belgian Refugee Relief in England During the Great War*, p. 452.

stress in a section of the community many of whose members felt that they were losing the struggle to preserve their class identity.

III

By the end of the war, and in the circumstances of rising prices and high taxation that continued after it, large numbers of middle-class people seemed in dismal straits. That, certainly, was how they appeared to Masterman. The author of a highly regarded survey of English society published in 1909, Masterman followed it up with a similar account four years after the end of the war.[10] In it he noted the decline that had befallen such groups as school teachers, clergymen, civil servants, clerks, and small investors: a decline in economic circumstances that was exacerbated by their heavy losses on the battlefield.

The middle classes had given their manpower generously to the firing line. Not least was this true of the clerks and bookkeepers of the lower middle class: a group who probably earned less than the best-paid workers and whose conditions of employment were usually more constricting, but who attached great price to those considerations of status that set it off from labourers and artisans. The white-collar worker had long been recognized as a particular devotee of Empire, identifying passionately with the world view of Rudyard Kipling – however remote it might be from his actual experience. The call to arms made a strong appeal to such people. J. M. Winter writes:

> The highest enlistment rates among employees in the early months of the conflict were registered by men in commercial and clerical occupations. This trend continued throughout 1915 and early 1916.... Whereas 29 per cent of industrial workers had volunteered by February 1916, over 40 per cent of the men employed in banking, finance, or commerce, in the professions – accountants, architects, solicitors, advertising agents, estate agents; and men at work in the entertainment trades – in hotels, pubs, theatres, music halls, cinemas, and restaurants, had joined up.[11]

As for the members of these sections who were not eager to enlist, it became apparent as the war proceeded that they lacked the immunity from conscription measures and comb-outs that workers in essential industries might enjoy.

The bereavements inflicted by war fell particularly heavily upon middle-class families. For this was a section of the community that had sought to raise its living standards by limiting its number of children. Masterman writes:

> The 'only child' or 'only son' which was before the war the sole luxury permitted to so many [of the middle class] . . . has perished in the ultimate and fierce demands of war. He went out – in the great majority of cases – a volunteer. Every spare farthing had been spent on his upbringing from babyhood. He was to be the pride and assistance of his parents when they attained old age. Then from all the terraces and villas which occupy the hills round great cities came the news that no blood sprinkled on lintel or doorpost had been of any avail against the Angel of Death. A house had been left henceforth for ever desolate.[12]

To this human loss sustained by many middle-class families was added, in the immediate post-war years, increasing financial stringency. The middle classes, says Masterman, had tended before 1914 to live a little beyond their incomes so as to be able to engage in what he calls 'a harmless vanity of display' (the American term is

---

[10] C. F. G. Masterman, *England After War* (London: Hodder & Stoughton, n.d. [c. 1922]), especially ch. 3.
[11] J. M. Winter, 'Britain's "Lost Generation" of the First World War', *Population Studies*, vol. 31, no. 3, November 1977, p. 454.
[12] Masterman, *England After War*, p. 79.

'conspicuous consumption'). The dweller in suburbia sent his children to 'a little too expensive school', rented 'a little too expensive house', spent a bit too much on 'little ostentations and pleasures', and anxiously avoided the 'appearance of poverty or even of strict saving'.[13] Now the 'appearance of poverty', or anyway of 'strict saving', had come upon many of them. They had regarded it as axiomatic that the doubling of the cost of living within four years lay beyond the realms of possibility. When it occurred, not even the salary-earning section of the middle classes (let alone those dependent on investments) had a ready means of redress, for they spurned the industrial militancy that might have kept their incomes within reach of price levels. (However, it should be noted that, in the later stages of the war, there was an unusual readiness among white-collar workers such as clerks and shop assistants to join trade unions. The phenomenon did not persist into the inter-war period. But while it lasted it constituted an attempt, by employing working-class methods, to keep abreast of the wages of the upper working class – a group from which, in other respects, white-collar workers usually wished to distinguish themselves.)

At the start of the 1920s a large London newspaper, the *Daily News*, in order to demonstrate the sorry straits in which many middle-class people found themselves, invited communications from the New Poor.[14] Large numbers responded – without, of course, revealing their identities. Their pseudonyms at least suggested that they were not among those who had given up the struggle: 'Resourceful', 'Optimist', 'Nil Desperandum', and even 'Art E. Fiss'. But some were plainly not far removed from despair. One oldish couple, presumably living heretofore on rents, were now selling their cottages one by one and living off the capital: 'we hope we shall die before the proceeds of the last cottage are gone.' And a secondary-school master listed the economies to which he was obliged to resort. He stuck rubber soles to his footwear. His wife went out collecting bundles of sticks to save on firewood. They had given up taking holidays, and devotedly sought bargains at department stores. He faithfully tended the vegetable garden. 'Also my wife murders her eyes with sewing, sewing, sewing. Saving is out of the question.'

This saga of petty economies ('doing without') was the universal feature of the correspondence. 'One good tailor-made garment a year for myself,' wrote a housewife; 'all other things needed I make myself, together with my husband's shirts and socks, also reversing his ties when they look worn.' One man wrote that he had halved his allocation of cigarettes and walked part of the way to work to save on tram fares. Another had taken to cycling to work, wearing old garb and keeping his 'presentable' clothes at the office. With the diminution or disappearance of servants, the housewife became a drudge. As one man put it, 'The chief factor in the management of my household is that my wife works one hundred and twelve hours a week.' Another wrote:

> The maid has gone long since. A charwoman one day a week is hired, and all the washing is done at home [without benefit, of course, of washing machines]. . . . I mend most of the boots and shoes, and cut the boy's hair. A few hens help us with eggs and an occasional pot. We are exhausting our stock of clothing, linen, china, cutlery, etc., and what renewals we make are of the cheapest possible. Holidays are confined to home and country walks. Food, always plain, is still plain; but now, sometimes, not enough – not enough milk, butter and fruit. I neither smoke nor drink intoxicants. . . . Friends have sent cast-off clothing for the children. I fell ill, and was done, but a brother gave me £50 and saved me.

Two things helped to counter this downward trend. Rents did not keep pace with

---

[13] Ibid., p. 70.
[14] Excerpts are in ibid., pp. 59–66.

the cost of living (although this contributed to the fearful shortage of available housing). And the family garden and allotment, often taken on in wartime to increase the supply of home-grown food, was now maintained assiduously to provide the vegetables that frequently replaced meat meals. In addition, people with children sought contact with families whose youngsters were older than their own, from whom to purchase clothes as they became outgrown. Another resort, especially among the childless, was to take in lodgers.

Other newspapers bore out the accounts being published in the *Daily News*. 'Appeals from decayed gentlefolk,' it has been recorded, 'multiplied in the columns of middle-class newspapers. In October, 1920, the Press reported a procession of well-dressed men and women, including a brigadier-general, two colonels and seventeen women, who carried sandwich boards up the Strand bearing the words: "High prices and the remedy – Do without." '[15]

In short, these were grim times for many salary earners. For not only had their situation deteriorated absolutely; it had done so relative to that of the working class. This was of particular moment to a body of people who needed to preserve material possessions and superior schooling not just as comforts in life but as evidence of the distinction between themselves and the masses. Of Richford, a typical middle-class London suburb (though that was not its real name), Masterman wrote:

> Richford hates and despises the working classes, as all Richfords hate and despise the working classes. Richford hates and despises them, partly because it has contempt of them, and partly because it has fear of them. It has established its standard of a civilisation, modest in demand, indeed, in face of life's possibilities, but very tenacious in its maintenance of its home and garden, its clean street, and decent clothing, and agreeable manners and ways. Just on its borders, and always prepared seemingly to engulf it, are those great masses of humanity which accept none of its standards, and maintain life on a totally different plane. . . . Labour represents for it literally the figure of the Bolshevik of the cartoons, an unwashed, ill-dressed, truculent immigrant from the neighbouring Labour cities; tearing up the tree-avenues of its streets, trampling on its flower-beds, thrusting its clumsy feet through the bow-windows and aspidistra of its front drawing-rooms.[16]

IV

Such was the condition of many middle-class folk in the immediate aftermath of the war. But it would be misleading to end the account at that date. For their downward trend did not continue. In two important respects Masterman's description, written in 1922, soon needed amending. He saw the middle classes as politically docile: they would always vote for the Conservative Party, even though the dominant forces in that party, the landed classes and the large capitalists, not only failed to give them aid but did not notice their existence. Even as he was writing, middle-class electors were starting to vote in by-elections for 'Anti-Waste' candidates, who railed against the coalition Government on account of its high taxes and big spending. Soon after, they were rewarded by a drop in the income tax and by heavy cuts in government expenditure. Again, late in 1923 the Conservative Government of Stanley Baldwin went to the country on a tariff policy that, many feared, would largely increase food prices. In significant numbers the middle classes deserted the Conservatives for the seemingly defunct Liberal Party. Baldwin, briefly, lost office. The Conservatives, for a

---

[15] Roy Lewis and Angus Maude, *The English Middle Classes* (London: Phoenix House, 1949), p. 78.
[16] Masterman, *England After War*, pp. 54–5.

longer period, abandoned tariffs. That is, the political attachment of the middle classes to Conservatism was certainly a fact, but the docility of their allegiance could not be taken for granted.

In other, more profound, respects circumstances were changing from those Masterman portrayed. He pictured the middle classes as longing for a fall in the cost of living, for new homes at cheaper prices, and for an increase in the availability of servants. These wishes, and more, were in the process of being granted. The onset of unemployment was forcing working women to accept jobs as servants, however reluctantly. As for the rise in prices, it had already passed its peak when Masterman wrote. That was attained in 1920, when the price level stood at two and a half times what it had been in 1913. (The 1920 level was not to be reached again until 1947.) Prices fell by one-third between 1920 and 1922, and even more sharply than that for some commodities. According to John Burnett, 'building costs per square foot [fell] from over £1 in early 1920 to 9s 4d by 1922, and the price of a small, three-bedroom, non-parlour house from £930 to £436.'[17] Thereafter prices generally continued on a more gradual, but steady, decline.

As money started to go further, new ranges of consumer goods were coming on the market at moderate prices. The most significant of these, as is suggested by the foregoing quotation, was the commodity that affected the comfort and status of the middle classes most nearly: housing. Between 1919 and 1939, while the state was assisting in building some 1 million houses mainly for working-class tenants, private enterprise was constructing almost 3 million houses. In the large majority of cases these were for sale, not rent. Given their moderate prices and the reasonable mortgage repayments that could be negotiated, this development opened up the opportunity of home ownership to large sections of the lower middle class for whom it had never before been available. 'Low interest rates, low material costs and low wages were combining to bring about a housing revolution which profoundly affected the lives of millions of people.'[18]

Further, as in the mid-1920s the nation recovered and then surpassed the level of prosperity of 1914, the seemingly inexorable redistribution of wealth away from the middle classes and towards the working class halted. Admittedly, this period of deflation was accompanied by general cuts in money earnings. But these fell most heavily on the wage earners, and particularly on the lowerpaid workers (as well as the unemployed). They fell least onerously on salary earners in private industry and members of the professions. 'Deflation favoured those on salaries and fixed incomes and prejudiced particularly the lower-paid worker.'[19] Unemployment, too, fell least severely on those of middle-class status. In the depths of the inter-war depression 'unemployment among male clerks amounted to less than half of that in the labour force as a whole (5.3 per cent. as compared with 12.7 per cent.). Among some groups of clerical workers there was hardly any unemployment and in general the higher ranks had the smallest proportions of dismissals.'[20] Richford would not have had it otherwise.

At the same time the power of organized labour was being weakened, first by the removal of the exceptionally favourable bargaining conditions of the war and then by the onset of mass unemployment. After 1921 there was, during the rest of the decade,

---

[17] John Burnett, *A Social History of Housing 1815–1970* (Newton Abbot: David & Charles, 1978), p. 246.
[18] Ibid., p. 247.
[19] John Burnett, *A History of the Cost of Living* (Harmondsworth: Penguin Books, 1969), p. 310.
[20] D. V. Glass in Morris Ginsberg (ed.), *Law and Opinion in England in the 20th Century* (London: Stevens & Sons, 1959), pp. 333–4.

only one industrial upheaval of note, and its outcome was entirely satisfactory to the middle classes. The coal strike of 1926 was relentlessly, even cruelly, ground to defeat. And the attempt by the Trades Union Congress to act on the miners' behalf through a general strike evaporated within days. It was defeated in part by labour's own panic at the suggestion that it might be acting illegally or even unconstitutionally. Even more, it was overwhelmed by the stern action of a right-wing Government devotedly supported by strike-breakers from outside the working class.

For almost the only time in peace, a man with the passionately aristocratic aspirations (if not income) of Evelyn Waugh was prepared not only to make common cause, but even to share living quarters, with the lower middle class whom he so thoroughly despised. On the ninth day of the general strike, he records, he thought it would be as well to find a useful way of serving the Home Secretary (Joynson-Hicks, the epitome of the middle-class morality that Waugh and his associates were determined to flout) and the constitution:

> so I went to a territorial barracks in Camden Town and joined a force called the Civil Constabulary Reserve. It was comprised . . . chiefly of what I take to be the dregs of civilisation – battered little men of middle age, debased and down at heel who grumbled all the time, refused to get up in the mornings, talked on parade, and fought for their food. In the evenings they got drunk in a canteen upstairs. The officers were solicitors' clerks in military clothes. We spent the morning drawing blankets, tin hats, field dressings, and such military necessaries. At luncheon the strike was called off unconditionally by the TUC.[21]

For the strikers, presumably, it was lunch rather than luncheon.

V

It was frequently said during the war that the common endeavours and sacrifices of all sections were eliminating class barriers. Evidence of this lay in the comradeship of the trenches and the universal experience of bereavement; in the movement around the country and abroad of men who never before had strayed beyond a particular hamlet or industrial confine; in the participation of all classes in affairs of state at local and national levels; and, above all, in the sense of national identity that the war's great crises evoked.

Yet the expectation was not securely founded. For all its comradeship in shared endeavour and suffering, the British army was not a model of a classless society. And in good measure its hierarchical divisions corresponded with, and reinforced, the divisions within peacetime Britain. On the civilian front many facets of wartime experience heightened rather than reduced class antagonisms. Middle-class people under financial stress railed against trade unions, which were 'holding the country to ransom', and felt resentment against workers who seemed to be prospering – not least when the workers happened to be munitions girls who squandered their earnings on fripperies and denied their social superiors the balm of a servant class. Equally, working folk made sweeping statements about profiteers and occupants of 'cushy' jobs, and inveighed against middle-class administrators who seemed to be ensuring that foodstuffs in short supply would not reach working-class tables.

Certainly, class divisions receded in the face of national peril. But that is saying nothing more than that, underlying the class system of Britain, is a sense of national identity. Moments of external threat make its existence particularly apparent. But it is

---

[21] Michael Davie (ed.), *The Diaries of Evelyn Waugh* (Harmondsworth: Penguin Books, 1979), p. 253.

present also in peacetime, and helps to ensure that social strife does not escalate into social disruption. The war affirmed national solidarity. It did not thereby eliminate social separation.

It is still the case that the war effected social change. As J. M. Winter has argued, it helped to accomplish a compression of classes. But bringing classes closer together, especially in economic terms, proved not to be the same thing as removing class barriers; and after the war the process of compression was in part reversed. Something much more radical than this would be required before Britain was transformed into the classless society that some contemporaries had assumed was being moulded in the fires of war. Indeed, it may be wondered if any agony the nation might undergo, however intense, would be capable of achieving so much.

70

PROFITS AND LOSSES:
THE ECONOMIC CONSEQUENCES

I

In few respects are the effects of the war more difficult to estimate than in the sphere of economics. When one highly regarded specialist concludes that 'it is not easy to say just what were the economic consequences of the war' and another reports that large areas of the subject have yet to be explored, those with no expertise in the area may be excused for approaching it with trepidation.[1]

Such is the complexity of the subject that differences exist even about whether the war played any considerable part in the altered state of Britain's post-war economy. Some would argue that, though much may have changed, the war itself was not its author. The role of war was nearer that of a beacon, revealing starkly what had long been true but hitherto little observed. If it was in any sense a cause, this was only in the matter of timing. It may have speeded up change but not in a way that was of great importance. Others take a different stance. To them the war was a force (if only one among several) that helped signally to shape the post-war economy. It initiated some things. And by accelerating already existing forces of change it warped their effect.

The position adopted here leans towards the second view. There are good grounds for questioning just how great a weight should be attributed to the economic effects of the war. But, on the most modest estimate, the weight appears altogether too considerable to be characterized as a mild acceleration of pre-ordained trends and a modest alteration of the timescale.

But the complexity of the matter does not end here. The economic consequences were not all in one direction. That is, the war was not wholly a constructive or a destructive force. Nor is it even the case that, while it acted beneficially on some sectors of the economy, its effect on others was deleterious. Sometimes the conflict in tendencies can be found in the same area.

Some illustrations will help here, if only by bringing the discussion down to earth. One example is ship-building. As will be shown later, by the beginning of the 1920s this industry was facing severe economic difficulties, aggravated (where they were not created) by the war. Yet between 1914 and 1918 shipbuilding was a major beneficiary of the technical progress that, it has been argued, 'always finds some stimulus in the distortions of war-time demand and supply' – a generalization to which 'the First War was no exception'.[2] One example was automatic welding (whose application would not

---

[1] William Ashworth, *An Economic History of England 1870–1939* (London: Methuen, 1960), p. 285; Alan S. Milward, *The Economic Effects of the Two World Wars on Britain* (London: Macmillan, 1970).

[2] R. R. Sayers, 'The Springs of Technical Progress in Britain, 1919–39', *Economic Journal*, vol. LX, June 1950, p. 278.

be confined to ship-building: it became of 'widespread importance in engineering of all kinds'). This developed from the needs of the Admiralty.

> The vibration and shock due to gunfire used to work rivets loose, so that many of the rivet-holes in the bulkheads would cease to be watertight. Welding provided a joint which would remain completely watertight. Merchant ships do not have to stand the same shocks, but they do have to suffer some, and it was inevitable that the new process, which quickly proved economical of a particularly onerous type of labour, should be applied far more widely than the original extraordinary need would have suggested.[3]

These technical developments in ship-building helped to alleviate the depression in the industry during the 1920s. By 1921 the supply of ships was outstripping need to such an extent that it might appear there would be no demand for several years. Yet, though demand proved insufficient to keep the industry fully occupied, there was always some. For technical improvements were making the purchase cost of new ships lower than the running costs of old. The war, it seemed, was giving back with one hand a part of what it had taken away with the other.

Another enterprise in which the war both retarded and fostered advance was the motor-car industry.[4] Its immediate effect was to halt the planned movement (by firms like Morris) towards a low-price, mass-produced vehicle. For it diverted most of the industry's resources into quite different areas. The legendary firm of White and Poppe, which had earlier made car engines for Morris, from the first month of the war was converted to the manufacture of fuse bodies and sockets for shells. At least three important car firms – Rolls-Royce, Sunbeam, and Napier – became so involved in the production of aeroplane engines that thereafter they devoted much of their energy to this sector and never became involved in the mass-produced motor vehicle. For those firms that returned to motor manufacture the process of retooling and re-equipping after the war proved difficult and costly, especially as they usually found themselves over-capitalized as a result of wartime expansion of plant undertaken for munitions purposes. Wolseley and Belsize were two car manufacturers that expired during the 1920s in good part on account of these war-created problems. And the Austin company survived only by the skin of its teeth.

Austin gave up making motor cars altogether during the war. With finance provided by the Ministry of Munitions, two new works (which the firm purchased at the end of the war) were added during 1916–17 to its existing plant at Longbridge. Its workforce expanded from 2,500 in 1914 to a peak of over 20,000 in 1917, for most of whom housing had to be constructed near the workplace or who were brought there by a fleet of company-operated buses. 'Between August 1914 and November 1918 the Long-bridge plant produced over 8 million shells, 650 guns, more than 2,000 aeroplanes, nearly 500 armoured cars, and vast quantities of other equipment, including generating sets, pumping equipment, aeroplane engines, ambulances and lorries'.[5] For this the company took a low margin of profit (so breaking a ring of armament firms that had been keeping up the price of shells), further reduced by excess profits duty. So it entered the post-war world with excessive plant and a shortage of liquid capital. By 1921 its problems had become so serious that the firm was in the hands of the receivers. However, late in 1922 Herbert Austin did manage to discern a way of escape from his troubles: by launching the 'baby Austin', a low-priced car reaching people hitherto able to afford only motor-cycles with sidecars.

---

[3] Ibid., pp. 278–9.

[4] See, in particular, Kenneth Richardson, *The British Motor Industry 1896–1939* (London: Macmillan, 1977), ch. 3.

[5] Roy Church, *Herbert Austin* (London: Europa, 1979), p. 43.

This is the negative side of the war's effects on the motor-car industry. There is also a positive side. The industry undoubtedly learned important technical lessons during its wartime involvement in the manufacture of engines for lorries and aircraft: in such matters as greater engine performance, air-cooling, and above all (given the small scales and excessive number of models of the pre-war industry) the mass production of a few standardized lines. Further, the industry was considerably aided by the projection into peace of the McKenna duty of 1915, which imposed a 33⅓ per cent tax on imported vehicles. This tax was in part the product of strictly wartime considerations, like the need to economize on foreign exchange, to discourage luxury (and especially conspicuous) spending, and to save shipping space. But it was also a response to the conviction that American producers were gaining an unfair advantage over British motor manufacturers who were patriotically diverting their endeavours. This 'unfair advantage' concept could be regarded as still having application after the war. Indeed, it underlay the whole particularist case for tariff protection; and tariff cover for special industries was to play a signal part in such economic growth as took place in Britain in the post-war decade.

II

The foregoing illustrations help to reveal the complexity of any attempt to assess the war's economic consequences.[6] No more is sought in what follows than to set out some principal ways in which the conflict contributed to economic changes, both creative and destructive. The account is far from exhaustive: to become so it would need to be either excessively long (and rather technical) or something of a catalogue. As for any attempt at a weighing up of the war's benefits and injuries, that must be tentative indeed.

One way in which the war clearly served Britain was by encouraging modernization where it was badly needed. The engineering industry was forced by the demand for huge quantities of standardized equipment, from ammunition to motor lorries, to move away from producing small numbers of a variety of products employing specialized craftsmen rather than machines. A particular beneficiary was the machine-tool industry. 'Limit gauges, used by non-skilled labour on mass-production processes, were introduced into British engineering firms in large numbers.'[7] In another area wartime requirements in the field of communications produced remarkable developments in radio technology: 'Although the origins of wireless telegraphy date back to the turn of the century, it was the First World War which provided the major impetus to develop the wireless transmission valve.'[8] Thus were the foundations laid for a major growth industry, serving civilian needs and enhancing everyday life, after 1918.

The war, then, caused government to make demands on British industry that stimulated developments of great long-term benefit. There was another way in which it affected the relations of government and industry: by challenging (as we have seen already in the case of the motor industry) the simplicities of free trade. The challenge went deeper than the fact that some industries, by being diverted to war production, were placed at a disadvantage on the home market against neutral competitors. Britain

---

[6] They do not, it should be added, exhaust these complexities. For example, if technical development was hastened by the war, there would almost certainly have been some without it. And though such development might have occurred at a slower pace, it would presumably have been directly linked (as some wartime innovations were not) with the demands of a civilian market.

[7] Sidney Pollard, *The Development of the British Economy 1914–1950* (London: Edward Arnold, 1962), p. 56.

[8] J. H. Dunning and C. J. Thomas, *British Industry* (London: Hutchinson, 1963), p. 23.

in 1914 found itself heavily dependent on outside countries for commodities essential in wartime – not least on the country that for some time had seemed, in the event of war, its most likely adversary.

According to free-trade theory the world was one; and in terms of economics this view may have been tenable. But events were now affirming brutally that politically the world was not unitary and that in major respects economics were subordinate to politics. An obvious case was the manufacture of dyestuffs. Germany had captured 83 per cent of the world dyestuffs trade and provided an excellent service. British manufacturers of cloth, whether for home consumption or export, much preferred German dyes to the low-quality product of the small British industry. But with the outbreak of war German supplies ceased, and Britain for a time had difficulty in providing its army with khaki uniforms and its sailors with navy blue – to say nothing of the needs of its largest export industry.

But the importance of dyestuffs went far beyond the colouring of cloth. The coal-tar used in this industry had application elsewhere: in aerial photography, in the cure of cattle disease, and in the manufacture of salicylic acid and its derivatives, principally aspirin, as well as a number of other important drugs. And, on the other side of the coin, it played a crucial role in the production of military high explosives, TNT and lyddite, as well as in the creation of poison gases. 'Thus the coal-tar technology which the Germans had chiefly developed through dyestuffs was at the very heart of the killing and curing of the war itself.'[9]

A country that neglected such an industry was placing itself in great peril if it engaged in war with an industrial power that did not. The employment of poison gas during the First World War provides an example.[10] This untried weapon carried a large and uncertain promise of harm. Clearly, it would threaten both sides should they be equally well-equipped to use it – a consideration that has played some part in its subsequent near-disappearance from warfare. There are good reasons for believing that the Germans would never have embarked on its use in 1915 had they not been aware of the industrial backwardness, in this respect, of their adversaries. Similarly, they would not have introduced mustard gas in mid-1917 but for their confidence that it would be a considerable time before the British could reply in kind. (The Germans were correct in this calculation about mustard gas. Almost a year passed before the British were able to retaliate.)

Britain devoted much effort in the war to surmounting its shortcomings in dyestuffs. As early as September 1914 Lord Moulton, who during his 70 years had managed to combine a career in politics with the attainment of eminence in law and science, was called in to organize the supply of coal-tar. And by the end of that year the decision had been taken that the Government should sponsor a British dyestuffs company to take over the existing firms, reorganize the industry, and sponsor research. This action by a British Government in itself floating a company (something that had not occurred before) has been called 'a turning-point in the relations between Government and industry in Great Britain'.[11] Certainly, the sight of two such orthodox, 'small-government' Liberals as Walter Runciman and J. M. Robertson (respectively the President of the Board of Trade and his Parliamentary Secretary) presenting the

[9] Michael Sanderson, *The Universities and British Industry 1850–1970* (London: Routledge & Kegan Paul, 1972), pp. 215–16.

[10] The matter is well explored in Stephen G. Hewitt, 'Aspects of the Social History of Chemical Warfare in World War One', M.Sc. thesis, University of Sussex, 1972.

[11] W. J. Reader, *Imperial Chemical Industries: A History* (London: Oxford University Press, 1970), vol. 1, pp. 270–1.

measure to the Commons must have seemed compelling proof that the necessities of war knew no master. (Contrastingly, it was a supporter of Lloyd George who proclaimed, 'I loathe the whole scheme, and prophesy that the Government will bitterly repent of it.')

The course of the British dye company during the war was somewhat uncertain. In part this was because it took over only one of the two main British producers, not both. But principally it was because, Lord Moulton having been speedily annexed first by the War Office and then by the Ministry of Munitions, British Dyes became mainly engaged in the manufacture of explosives and poison gas. The field of dye manufacture was consequently left to the private interests, which expanded output markedly. This was satisfactory enough as long as the question of dyes was considered as having application only to this war. But plainly it was not satisfactory if British manufacture was to continue beyond the conflict, when it would face revived German competition and also the quite new competition of an American industry. (The USA had been even more dependent on imports of German dyes in 1914 than had Britain. American businessmen took advantage of the enforced disappearance of German products to rectify the situation.) What is noteworthy is that the war had produced more than a short-term need. It had produced the conviction that Britain must not hereafter be dependent on outside, and potentially hostile, sources for such vital commodities as dyes.

So in 1918 the Government took two important steps. The first was to make it clear that the importation of dyes would be restricted after the war. The second was to initiate the establishment of the British Dyestuff Corporation, formed by the amalgamation of the existing private companies with the government industry created during the war. Life was not to prove easy for this organization in the less hospitable circumstances of the post-war world. But the Corporation managed to keep its head above water and to become one of the four major components of the merger that formed Imperial Chemical Industries in 1916.

As with dyestuffs, so with other chemicals the war 'marked the watershed in the relations between Government and industry', as revealed by the measures taken to convert chemical manufacture from a civilian to a military economy, and by the encouragement and protection granted to some sectors of the industry during and after the war.[12] It had also served to change the attitudes of the leading men in the industry. Their minds had been broadened, and they had been called on to do – on a large scale – things they had hitherto never seriously thought of doing at all. So by 1918 the major chemical firms of Britain (as of the USA), if not level with the big German groups, had gone a long way towards shortening a German lead that for years had been not only great but growing. The war had also shown British chemical firms that there was a lot of money to be made in areas they had hitherto neglected, as long as the industry, by enlarging its units through takeover or merger, was organized on a scale to counter overseas competition after the war. The strong movement towards concentration of ownership, which occurred at the end of and just after the war, was proof that the promise and the warning had not gone unnoticed.

It was not always the case, however, that the coming of peace saw the preservation of the hopeful developments of wartime. The optical glass industry is a case in point.[13] Wartime conditions revealed that Britain's backwardness in the area of optics was not

---

[12] L. F. Haber, *The Chemical Industry 1900–1930* (Oxford: Clarendon Press, 1971), p. 218.

[13] For what follows see Roy and Kay MacLeod, 'War and Economic Development: Government and the Optical Industry in Britain, 1914–18', in J. M. Winter (ed.), *War and Economic Development* (Cambridge: Cambridge University Press, 1975), pp. 165–204.

wholly, or perhaps even mainly, the result of shortcomings in technical training and scientific research. The British optical industry had languished before 1914 because it lacked a large and guaranteed market: namely an army of imposing dimensions unthreatened by government economizers. The German army, as a matter of course, placed large and ongoing orders with German instrument firms, so facilitating product specialization and the lower costs of mass production. This facilitated an industry in Germany of such quality that it then went on to secure the custom of other European armies, including that of Britain.

The severance of relations with Britain's chief source of optical goods caused the War Office severe difficulties, as witnessed by its appeals to the public to donate binoculars to the army. Not only were German supplies cut off, but the requirements of the British army were rapidly increasing. Yet this shortfall was the opportunity of the British optical industry: a large and, at least for some time, continuing market and no foreign competition. Further, there soon developed state instrumentalities – the Ministry of Munitions and the Department of Scientific and Industrial Research – that functioned as 'coupling agents', bringing together the necessary capital, the labour force, the skilled technicians, the scientists, and the manufacturers. The outcome was decidedly impressive. Major technical problems that had inhibited the industry for 25 years were overcome. Output was increased during the war by something like 20 times; and in the area where Britain had been weakest, the manufacture of prism binoculars, output grew by 500 per cent. In absolute terms optical glass had become an industry of large plant, modern machinery, the techniques of mass production, and capacity for design and innovation.

This happy situation did not continue into peacetime. Certainly, optical glass, like dyestuffs, was deemed to fall within the category of essential industries for which Britain could not afford to depend on foreign suppliers. So it qualified for tariff protection even while Britain returned to being a predominantly free-trade country. But the wartime army demobilized, and the winds of retrenchment in government spending blew through the military establishment. Hence the market for optical goods in Britain severely contracted. Even by 1920 the industry was once more at a discount – and would remain so until the rearmament of the late 1930s.

It is not difficult to enumerate other areas in which the war encouraged hopeful developments in the British economy, sometimes (although not invariably) to its permanent benefit. The output of electricity doubled during the war, principally in the service of industry and transport, which had been notably behind hand in converting to this source of energy. The steel industry underwent considerable expansion, in the process making larger use of Britain's own resources of ore. And the output of motor lorries escalated. The army possessed 100 of them when the conflict opened and 60,000 when it finished.

Particularly noteworthy, because it started from so little, was the development of the aircraft industry. The scientific base of aeronautics had certainly been established before the war. What had been lacking was any particular use (except joy-riding) for this form of activity. The war, by providing many uses, accomplished momentous change.

The output of aeroplanes, their size, their variety, and their capability grew as the uses to which they might be put became ever more apparent. Some raw statistics suggest the extent of the achievement. In the first ten months of the war 530 machines were produced; in the last ten months 26,500. Reductions of the gross weight per horse power from 23 lb. in 1914 to 7 lb. in 1918 raised bomb capacity from 20 lb. to 3,000 lb. There were equally noteworthy improvements in rate of climb – important if intruding aircraft were to be intercepted by planes not yet airborne – and in the height that could be attained. 'The war transformed the short-hopping kite-like "flying machine" of the pre-war enthusiast into a craft like the Vickers Vimy, capable and ready, had not peace intervened in 1918, of delivering bomb attacks on Berlin itself.'[14]

As with optics, the Government provided the 'coupling agents' that brought together the elements making possible these achievements. It called in the services of private firms capable (whatever they had been doing before) of manufacturing aircraft. It provided them with the designs. It managed the experimental stations at Farnborough and elsewhere that produced many of the notable advances. It tapped the capacity of university physicists such as F. A. Lindemann and Henry Tizard, who actually served as test pilots, as well as of other university men who could advise on such matters as the materials of aircraft construction, aerodynamic design (for example, the design of wings), and the mathematics of aircraft structure. The last of these was of particular importance:

> It resulted above all in [British] aeroplanes being considerably more stable than those of the Germans, an important factor in the development of aerial acrobatics and tactics. The stirring occasion on which Albert Ball, VC, flew his SK5 machine back to the lines, almost totally out of action and with the controls shot away, was a tribute not only to his own courage but to the subtlety of British mathematics and aerodynamic design.[15]

The aircraft industry was one of the clearest cases not only of advance from small-scale, highly individualistic enterprise to large-scale, standardized production but also of the application of science to industry. Yet, as in the case of optics, some of these promising developments proved of limited benefit. The end of the war deprived the aircraft industry of huge government orders and left it bereft of what, for four years, had been its *raison d'être*.

Certainly, post-war Governments recognized the importance of a strong aircraft industry for purposes of defence. Nevertheless, they were not prepared to sink large sums in military aircraft. As for civilian uses for an air service, these had definitely increased since before the war. The greater range, carrying capacity, and airworthiness of aeroplanes meant that they could offer a new variety of services. But it soon became apparent that demand was very limited. Within the British Isles air transport could not provide such benefits in time saving as to cancel out the advantages of road and rail in terms of cheaper costs and larger carrying capacity. As for transport to the Continent, the number of passengers proved too few, and too tied to particular seasons of the year, to maintain a prosperous service. Faced by subsidized foreign competitors, the private British companies established on these routes immediately after the war failed. Even the decision of the Government to provide some financial support did not save them. In 1924 the Government was itself obliged to take the initiative in establishing Imperial Airways. As the name suggests, this company was directed towards the lengthy and relatively unremunerative Empire routes in preference to traffic with the Continent. (The latter, for all its difficulties, had at the time much more potentiality for development.) The company survived only with a government subsidy.[16]

The establishment of this air service, after private enterprise had failed, is evidence that for a mixture of reasons – particularly those of defence and the strengthening of bonds within the Empire – Governments were prepared to maintain some sort of an

[14] Sanderson, *The Universities and British Industry 1850–1970*, p. 227.

[15] Ibid., pp. 229–30.

[16] A useful account of this period is to be found in Peter Fearon, 'The Formative Years of the British Aircraft Industry, 1913–1924', *Business History Review*, vol. XLIII, no. 4, 1969.

aircraft industry. But it was pretty small beer after the heroic days and dazzling technical advances of the war.

A noteworthy service rendered by the war to the British economy – already referred to with respect to chemicals and aircraft – was the growth of concentration within industries. The persistence of a multitude of small, very individualistic firms placed Britain at a disadvantage when competing against strongly centralized, semi-monopolistic rivals from Germany and the United States. In wartime it also proved a considerable headache for government instrumentalities such as the Ministry of Munitions, which were seeking to deal not with particular manufacturers but with whole industries. For this among other reasons the war proved a strong force towards industrial combination. Under government impetus trade associations were formed to allocate raw materials, stimulate common research, apportion licences for exports and imports, provide loan capital, and control prices. By 1919, according to an official report, 'Trade Associations and Combines are rapidly increasing in this country, and may, within no distant period, exercise a paramount control over all important branches of British trade.'[17] One British industrialist, looking back from the vantage point of the 1920s, saw the war years as a time of 'cooperation on a marvellous scale when . . . manufacturers for the good of their country, threw away their old prejudices and put themselves unreservedly at the disposal of one another. Patents, secret processes, special methods, goodwill, were flung into the melting pot of the common weal.'[18] 'This,' comments Leslie Hannah, 'was the authentic, exhilarated voice of a movement in business opinion which was growing in strength and which questioned the virtues of competition and championed the advantages of cooperation, merger and large-scale enterprise. Whilst many other wartime changes were abandoned, the changes in business opinion which had accompanied them were, in general, more permanent.'[19]

The establishment of the Federation of British Industries in 1916 was a clear indicator of this movement away from rugged individualism. It was one among many. 'In every direction,' write the authors of British Industry, 'collective control replaced isolated action.' Official blessing was given to unification within such industries as electrical engineering, to the modernization of equipment, and to the standardization of products. And as the Government tended to favour the more efficient firms, 'it is not surprising that they should have gradually enlarged their size and acquired a dominant share of the market.'[20]

III

Internally, then, the war served to stimulate and reshape the British economy in ways that were highly beneficial. Yet not all the stimulus proved of long-term advantage. As has been noted, wartime needs promoted a large development in the aeronautic and optical industries that did not prove to be in line with peacetime demands. At the same time the war was encouraging the hasty expansion of some of the staple industries, such as iron and steel and shipbuilding, which was unwarranted in terms of post-war markets or out of line with long-term need. In the case of the steel industry, for example, wartime expansion was undertaken in haste and with regard only to short-term requirements. This was no doubt justified in the circumstances. 'In all probability

[17] Quoted in Pollard, The Development of the British Economy 1914–1950, p. 62.
[18] Quoted in Leslie Hannah, The Rise of the Corporate Economy (London: Methuen, 1976), pp. 30–1.
[19] Ibid.
[20] Dunning and Thomas, British Industry, pp. 41–2.

only a policy of patching promised quick results.' But consequently 'the crucial fact about the war-time extensions was that they maintained with little change the chief characteristics of the pre-war distribution of plant, both within and between districts, and therefore put new obstacles in the way of radical adaptation to changed circumstances of raw-material supply, technique, and competition.'[21]

These distortions in the British economy were accompanied first by the simply destructive effects of war and, secondly, by changes in overseas markets (to Britain's disadvantage) that the war powerfully accelerated. In the short term the war consumed a great deal of Britain's wealth. It killed 700,000 healthy male adults and left the dependents of many of them for a time as unproductive responsibilities of the state. It injured another 1.2 million so severely that their productive capacity was removed or impaired and they too became recipients of state support. It destroyed a great deal of civilian property, especially shipping. It caused an inordinate amount of the nation's productive capacity to be devoted to manufacturing the means of destruction, and of its shipping capacity to be diverted from trade and commerce to the transportation of warriors and weapons. It consumed capital that would otherwise have been devoted to investment abroad or the expansion of useful industry at home. It made great inroads into the most easily accessible reserves of Britain's coal, so aggravating the problem of producing at a marketable price faced by the industry after the war. It left the British railway system in a dilapidated condition, as a result of its heavy use with a depleted labour force and inadequate maintenance. More intangibly, but still of real note, it led to promises being made and expectations being aroused of higher living standards after the war, expectations that were entirely warranted in terms of the nation's exertions but were not related to its economic circumstances. These helped to produce costly industrial stoppages.

It was not only sections of the labour force that ended the war with rising expectations. Capitalists endowed with the accumulated profits of war found themselves confronting a domestic and overseas market starved of the peacetime products of industry. And they discovered that banks were prepared to lend unguardedly for speculative activities. So at a time of mounting inflation, with goods and services at what would prove their most costly, capital running into many millions was invested heedlessly in the purchase or expansion of newer industries like aircraft and motor cars and, to a much greater extent, of older industries like engineering, shipping, shipyards, and cotton mills. So in 1919 and 1920, 238 cotton mills – approaching half the capacity of the cotton-spinning industry – with an original share capital of £11 million changed hands for £72 million. Then in the course of 1920, for complex reasons not primarily concerned with a restocked market and satiated demand, the boom collapsed. Particularly for the older industries, the consequences were disastrous. According to Derek Aldcroft:

> Their wartime profits were dissipated in a frivolous manner and once the bottom fell out of the market they were often left with virtually worthless assets together with a heavy burden of debt. . . . The cost of over-capitalization in the boom was to remain a heavy burden on some industries throughout the inter-war period. Worse still, it was in those industries whose future growth prospects were weakest that the worst excesses took place.[22]

This severe setback was a direct result of the dislocations – such as accumulated profits and pent-up demand – caused by the war.

---

[21] Duncan Burn, *The Economic History of Steelmaking 1867–1939* (Cambridge: Cambridge University Press, 1961), pp. 356–7.

[22] Derek H. Aldcroft, *From Versailles to Wall Street 1919–1929* (London: Allen Lane, 1977), pp. 76–7.

Certainly, this account of the relatively transitory damage done by the war, though substantial, looks much less so when compared with the losses of the combatants on the Continent. For Britain escaped the material destruction suffered by France as a result of the invasion and occupation of part of its territory, and the even graver economic travails sustained by Russia, Germany, and Austria-Hungary following upon defeat and political upheaval. Yet the misfortunes of continental Europe were not, by and large, the opportunities of Britain. A large sector of the British economy was concerned with financial and commercial dealings, and it had prospered from the smooth running of the world economy of which Europe had hitherto been so large a part. And a considerable proportion of Britain's exports before the war had gone to the Continent – Germany in 1914 being Britain's second largest customer. So inflation in Germany, the establishment of a succession of unstable states in Central Europe seeking economic viability behind prohibitive tariff walls, and the withdrawal of Russia from the world trading community, all served to cost Britain heavily in trade, shipping, and financial transactions.

There was another respect in which the devotion of resources to the purpose of waging war bore heavily on Britain thereafter. A large proportion of war costs were not met out of current revenue but were financed by heavy borrowing at home and overseas. After the war this obliged the Government to maintain a high level of taxation, so depriving wealthy investors of capital that might have been used to stimulate industry, while denying it to Governments for defence or social services. More important, that sector of borrowing that took place externally served to undermine Britain's secure position as an international creditor.

In the period of less than three years during which Britain was a belligerent while the United States remained neutral, their financial positions changed markedly. At the outset the USA was still heavily dependent on British capital and credit facilities to finance its development within and its trade abroad. By the time the USA entered the fray, Britain had come heavily to rely on it for foodstuffs, munitions, and the funds with which to buy them. The reversal was marked by the course of four financial missions that Britain sent to the USA during this period. The first, sent at the latter's request in the early weeks of the war to assist in financial difficulties caused by the international upheaval, 'shows Britain acting as the dominant financial power, perhaps for the last time.' The succeeding three missions were occasioned by Britain's increasingly urgent need for dollar loans to pay for the supplies it must have from America. 'In fact, the primary task of the fourth of these missions (sent out in February 1917) was, by whatever means possible, week by week to stave off ruin until the United States should become a belligerent and (it was hoped and expected) assume the major financial responsibility for the Alliance.'[23]

So strong had Britain's position as creditor been up to 1914 that it might have been able to satisfy its own wartime needs without becoming too heavily indebted to the USA. But it was obliged to employ its credit also to secure supplies for its less financially viable allies. There was, of course, nothing altruistic about this. Britain needed badly to keep the armies of France, Russia, and Italy equipped and in the field. But the double burden of securing American finance for itself and for its allies forced Britain heavily into debt with the USA, notwithstanding sales of some of its precious dollar-earning assets. (According to one calculation, these sales by government and private action caused a decline of British investments in the USA of £550 million

---

[23] K. M. Burk, 'British War Missions to the United States 1914–1918', D.Phil. thesis, Oxford University, 1976, pp. 3–4.

between July 1914 and the end of 1919.[24]) In the course of the war Britain borrowed £1,350 million all told, more than £1,000 million of which came from the United States. Certainly, it loaned even more to its allies and to Empire countries: £1,750 million. But one-third of this had gone to Russia and was probably irrecoverable, and Britain's other allies would be slow in making repayment – if they made it at all. Meanwhile Britain could not afford, even had it possessed the desire, to be less than scrupulous regarding its debts to the USA.

The movement of the USA from being a debtor to being a creditor country, and the incurring by Britain of large debts with the USA at the same time as it was relinquishing assets there, undermined Britain's position as the centre of world finance. 'After the war, and largely as its direct consequence, New York replaced London as the financial capital of the world.'[25] This reduced the large sums that Britain had traditionally earned by conducting financial and business transactions for other countries, and so further deflated 'the comfortable cushion of invisible earnings that had permitted [it] the luxury of an adverse balance of trade'.[26] This was one force that was ultimately to render vain the struggle of the post-war years to restore the pound sterling to a secure base on the pre-war gold standard. 'The consequences of Britain's international indebtedness were much more far-reaching than those of [its] domestic indebtedness' – though it was the latter that more alarmed traditionally minded economists at the time.[27]

The situation was, of course, much impaired because this decline in 'invisible earnings' was occurring at just the time when the visible export industries were encountering serious difficulties. For not only was the pattern of European trade disturbed after the war. Britain also found that it had lost crucially important markets in India, South America, and the Far East. These had been annexed by countries that, even if they were numbered among the belligerents, participated in the war to so limited a degree or for so short a time that it did not hinder their economic expansion: in particular the United States, Japan, and (especially on its home ground) India.

So by the 1920s the British coal industry, which in 1913 had contributed almost one-quarter of the world's total output of coal (287 million tons out of 1,237 million), had become an 'ailing giant'.[28] The main cause was the sharp decline in export demand. From 85 million tons per annum before the war it fell to a catastrophic 39 million in 1920 (admittedly an exceptionally bad year). Thereafter it rose to 1929 to a figure that, though decidedly better than 1920, was always below the pre-war level. Then it declined steadily in the 1930s. Certainly, the war was not the major cause of this long-term contraction. But it had seriously dislocated productivity at home by depriving the industry of much of its skilled labour, had led to concentration on the exploitation of the more accessible seams, and had interrupted the export trade at a time when competition from other countries and other forms of fuel was coming to a head.

The war had done more. It had helped to create large expectations among coal miners of an industry reorganized to their advantage. These expectations the Government, for the short-term object of keeping up productivity, had encouraged –

---

[24] See E. Victor Morgan, *Studies in British Financial Policy, 1914–25* (London: Macmillan, 1952), pp. 326–31.

[25] Gerd Hardach, *The First World War 1914–1918* (London: Allen Lane, 1977; first published in German in 1973), p. 290.

[26] Sanderson, *The Universities and British Industry 1850–1970*, p. 241.

[27] Milward, *The Economic Effects of the Two World Wars on Britain*, p. 46.

[28] Neil K. Buxton, *The Economic Development of the British Coal Industry* (London: Batsford, 1978), p. 165. While 'ailing', it should be noted, the industry was not in danger of expiry.

not least by assuming control of the industry in the later stages of the war. There was always an element of ambiguity here. Were the mines to be reorganized for the betterment of the miners or so as to establish a more competitive and efficient industry? – a question fraught with difficulty should it be discovered that the one objective clashed with the other. But neither alternative entertained as a possible outcome what in fact happened. The Government, within two years of the Armistice, abandoned the industry to its own devices and the workers to the tender mercies of their employers in most disadvantageous conditions. This sequence of raised expectations and their abrupt reversal was to have severe consequences, both economic and social, in the inter-war years.

Some of the problems confronted by coal were encountered by all the staple export industries. They found themselves facing contracted demand overseas, and in each case the war had sharply accelerated the onset of these problems. The iron and steel industry, for example, had to meet during the war a greatly enhanced home demand, which by 1917–18 was telling heavily against its export trade at a time when the USA was under no comparable inhibitions. Where United Kingdom exports of iron and steel stood at 3.9 million tons in 1914 and remained fairly high until 1916 (3.3 million), they were down to 1.6 million tons in 1918. And the dislocation of the export trade was a good deal worse than these figures suggested, in that apart from 'a few rails to South America for trade balance purposes'[29] the exports were going to Britain's comrades-in-arms, the Allied and Empire countries, who were not necessarily its regular customers.

A similar pattern applies to shipbuilding. Home demand became paramount in the war. Early on the country's shipbuilding capacity was largely annexed by the Admiralty. Thereafter it was mainly concerned with trying to make good the devastating losses of merchant ships to the U-boat. For this latter purpose the shipbuilding capacity of Britain had to be increased, yet foreign customers were being entirely neglected. The consequence was a rapid expansion of shipbuilding in foreign countries: most dramatically in the United States, but also in Japan, Holland, and Scandinavia. By the end of the war exporters of British ships found themselves (although it took a couple of years for this to become apparent) in a world where formidable rivals had arisen and where – more important – total productive capacity far exceeded the need for new ships. In addition, shipyards were at a disadvantage at home on account of the fierce contraction in government spending on defence from 1920. Before (as well as during and just after) the war the British Government had placed large orders for warships with private yards. It placed none at all in 1921–2.

The course of the cotton industry in wartime was somewhat different, although the upshot was the same. Cotton was an essential earner of revenue abroad, most of all from India; and India's balance of payments deficit with Britain – financed by surpluses with other countries – was one of the principal bases of that 'scaffolding of multilateral settlements, which before 1914 held together the structure of international trade'.[30] The course of the war did not greatly divert Lancashire's production of cotton goods to home needs, as was happening with coal, shipbuilding, and iron and steel. But it did place an intolerable strain on the resources of shipping needed to bring raw cotton to Britain and to carry cotton goods to customers abroad. And just as the shortage of shipping was reaching its height in 1917, the immediate need for those overseas revenues earned by cotton products was losing its urgency, thanks to the large credits available from Britain's new-found ally.

---

[29] J. C. Carr and W. Taplin, *History of the British Steel Industry* (Oxford: Basil Blackwell, 1962), pp. 306–7.

[30] Milward, *The Economic Effects of the Two World Wars on Britain*, p. 45.

The result was that, as the war approached its climax, the situation in the cotton industry was becoming decidedly anticlimactic. In what would prove an intriguing foreshadowing of post-war experience, cotton mills were being obliged to work short time. In consequence, the industry was allowing its markets in India and the Far East to go by default. These markets did not prove recoverable once the war was over. Exports of cotton piece goods from the United Kingdom in 1913 stood at 7,075 million linear yards. The yearly average for the period 1920–3 was only 4,072 million and for 1924–5 4,611 million.

Certainly, it may be doubted whether in the long run a serious contraction in these markets could have been avoided. Yet, but for the war, it could hardly have been so abrupt or so thoroughgoing. T. C. Barker points out that whereas in 1914 Britain's trade in the coarser cottons had reached something of a plateau, it was rapidly expanding in the better qualities.

> It seems highly improbable that the collapse of this crucial market would have occurred so quickly without the wartime curtailment of Britain's exports. If this great benefit had not been bestowed on her competitors, Britain might have been able to maintain her hegemony in India for some time longer. And if that had been the case, the move to higher qualities in the Lancashire cotton industry could well have been allowed to continue smoothly along pre-war lines, accompanied by the switch to new fibres and other products with better long-term prospects.[31]

If not all scholars would attribute such weight as this to the role of the war in Britain's decline as an exporter, many people at the time certainly did. The troubles that the economy faced in the 1920s seemed clearly the consequence of the war. This was not simply being obtuse. To all appearances, British goods had not been driven out of overseas markets but had relinquished these markets voluntarily. It seemed reasonable to hope they would in time be recovered. Similarly, many of Britain's difficulties sprang from what was seen as the temporarily unsettled state of Europe, which again it might be hoped would not continue indefinitely. So, apparently, the best course was to await recovery from the disturbances caused by the war, strive to recapture ground in former markets, maintain productive capacity (if temporarily under-employed) in traditional industries, and follow the time-honoured proceeding for bad times – a reduction in wage levels and government expenditure.

Yet whatever the warrant for these notions, they were misguided. Too many of the unfavourable trends in the export industry, whether war-accelerated or not, were incapable of being set in reverse. Too much that had gone wrong – from the point of view of Britain's financial stability – in Central and Eastern Europe, such as the turn to acute economic nationalism and the withdrawal of Russia, would not end once the world 'settled down'. Security of currency based on a fixed gold standard had gone for good. Britain lost valuable time waiting for the war's supposedly temporary distortions to ebb away. And it placed unnecessary burdens on itself by reapplying doctrines hallowed by time but positively harmful in these new conditions. One may instance the too devoted resurrection of free trade in the 1920s, despite the deviations from it embodied in the McKenna duties and the Safeguarding of Industries Act; and the grim struggle to restore the pound sterling to its pre-war gold parity, so occasioning J. M. Keynes's damning observation that economics were being sacrificed to superstition.

In sum, the war did more than occasion severe harm to the British economy. It provided a ready-to-order explanation for problems that had their origin elsewhere, and it occasioned a quite inappropriate struggle to restore an irrecoverable 'normality'.

---

[31] T. C. Barker in C. B. Cox and A. E. Dyson (eds.), *The Twentieth-Century Mind* (London: Oxford University Press, 1972), vol. 1, pp. 82–3.

IV

It can be argued that, in laying such stress on the injurious aspects of the war, one is being mesmerized by the negative side of the British economy in the 1920s: the familiar tale of unrest and disillusionment within the working class, mass unemployment, industries on short time, and savage retrenchments in government spending on desirable objects. The positive effects of war would be more apparent if due attention were given to the creative aspects of the post-war economy. For the 1920s, despite their misfortunes, were a time of considerable development in the newer industries. And these were industries which, by catering for a home rather than an export market, were directly raising living standards.

This point is worth stressing. There are good grounds for seeing the 1920s (as is becoming more usual among scholars) less as a time of unremitting decline and more as 'a sort of watershed between the old and new industrial regimes'. Correspondingly, greater stress is laid nowadays on 'the important role the war played in bringing about new developments'.[32] These can be summed up as the manufacture of products previously imported (among them magnetos, ball bearings, tungsten, ignition plugs, scientific instruments, and machine tools); the consequential rise of important new industries that expanded in the 1920s, such as dyestuffs and precision instruments; the stimulus to existing branches of industry, such as food preservation, petroleum, chemical solvents, artificial fibres, and plastics; technical developments like fuel economy techniques, alloy metallurgy, and railway electrification; and, '[p]erhaps even more important', 'the revolution which occurred in methods of production and in the attitudes of manufacturers to production problems in general'. 'Throughout industry generally there was a far greater willingness [after the war] than ever before to rationalise production methods, to economise in the use of factors of production and to replan factory lay-outs and improve management techniques.'[33]

Yet these positive aspects hardly seem to accumulate as much weight as the destructive effects wrought by war. The waste of huge quantities of resources, both human and material, the abandonment of wealth and markets overseas, the direct damage to Britain's financial position and the damage to other economies whose misfortunes also affected Britain adversely, the swift onset of a bewildering variety of problems, and the powerful encouragement to embrace false solutions constituted a heavy burden to befall a country in the aftermath of great exertions.

Certainly, in the context of war and society, it is these negative economic consequences that must attract the greater attention. For the sense of an economy in distress set the parameters within which social experimentation might take place. It inhibited legislators drawn towards, but uncertain of the viability of, benevolent social measures. It created communal misgivings about the advisability of worthy but novel courses. And it played into the hands of those conservative sections who, at the best of times, resented attempts to improve the lot of the masses, and who seized eagerly on any indication that times were not the best to thrust such aspirations out of court.

---

[32] Derek H. Aldcroft and Harry W. Richardson, *The British Economy 1870–1939* (London: Macmillan, 1969), p. 230.
[33] Ibid., pp. 231–3.

PART SEVENTEEN

Reconstruction

71

GUIDED CHANGE: MEANS AND ENDS

I

One marked effect of the First World War was to make available to the central government a much larger proportion of the community's wealth than had previously been at its disposal. That this was true for the years of combat is not surprising. More noteworthy is the fact that to some extent the change proved permanent. Certainly, after the war the Government could not call on as large a percentage of gross national product as during it. But neither did it have to retreat to pre-war levels of spending. The war, in short, was one of those 'large-scale social disturbances' that create 'a displacement effect, shifting public revenues and expenditures to new levels'.[1]

Doubtless, the 'large-scale disturbance' would not have caused this effect had not the ground been somewhat prepared. The war occurred at a time when Gladstonian orthodoxy about government spending – namely that Governments should spend as little as possible and always be on the lookout for ways in which to economize – was in retreat. Already by 1914 the view was gaining ground that the role of government, and the sums of money available to government, should be extended. Not least should this be so in order to combat the widespread poverty that social investigators were revealing, as manifested in poor nutrition and housing and insufficient protection against illness, unemployment, old age, and loss of the family breadwinner. But against the inclination to expand the activities of government stood the resistance, among those who provided the wherewithal, to contribute beyond a certain point. Strong notions existed about what levels of taxation were tolerable. The pre-war Liberal Governments took moderate action to raise these levels. They met immoderate resistance. Not only their opponents but also many of their own supporters – including some who thought that in various ways Governments should be 'doing more' – took a very restricted view of what alterations in taxation were permissible.

The war broke down many of these restrictions. The break-through, it should be stressed, was on a limited front. Much was said during the war, especially in left-wing circles, about the desirability of conscripting wealth – or anyway imposing a levy on capital – as a means of abating the growing burden of war debt. Nothing came of this proposal. The possessing classes, and their sympathizers among the non-possessors, drew the line here. All that was acceptable was a large extension of the taxes already well established, so as to strike particularly at war-created profits, plus a handful of newer measures directed particularly at what were deemed luxuries and indulgences. This much, nevertheless, removed many of the limitations inhibiting the access of Governments to the nation's wealth: not least because, in a situation where money

---

[1] A. T. Peacock and J. Wiseman, *The Growth of Public Expenditure in the United Kingdom* (London: Allen & Unwin, 1967), p. xxxiv.

incomes (though not necessarily real incomes) were increasing, progressive taxation was having a greater impact quite apart from any increase in its rates.

It may not seem surprising that government spending after the war did not return to pre-war levels. For many of the costs of the war continued into peacetime: for example, payment of interest on war loans and pensions to disabled servicemen and the families of deceased servicemen. But the Government was taking more than it needed to meet these items. And a good deal of this extra intake was being spent on enhanced social services and on the increased body of government employees needed to administer them. That is, with the aid of a larger bureaucracy it was making greater provision for housing, health, education, and the unemployed. This greater provision, as has been suggested, was in line with much pre-war thinking. But the war had affected the situation in two ways. It had lowered the resistance of the tax-paying classes (and brought new elements, including better-paid workers, within those classes). And it had enlarged the numbers of those convinced that, in matters of social distress and social need, Governments ought to be doing more.

'Wars,' it has been said, 'often force the attention of governments and peoples to problems of which they were formerly less conscious – there is an "inspection effect" which should not be underestimated.'[2] We have already noticed one consequence of this in the development of a 'cult of the child'. The war had drawn attention to the numbers of children growing up without proper nutrition and health care. At the same time it was making their well-being seem of special importance owing to the deaths and injury being inflicted on so many fit young males. Further, the experience of war, while not eliminating social distinctions and antipathies, had created much sense of community. As all sections were seen to have contributed to the nation's cause, so it seemed to follow that all sections were entitled to a tolerable level of existence. The concept of 'a fit land for heroes to live in' knew no social barriers, even though the nation to which it was being applied still did. And the ominous spectre of revolution in Europe, at a time when effective voting power was at last being extended to many of the least advantaged sections of Britain, provided powerful argument for seeking to spread minimum conditions of comfort as widely as possible. This was something that, anyway in certain areas, only the agencies of government could accomplish – as long as they had the means.

The results of this somewhat enhanced access of Governments to the wealth of the community may be indicated generally. By increasing the numbers in government employment, it opened up some places in this essentially middle-class sector to the offspring of better-placed workers. It reduced, through taxation, the wealth of the possessing classes; and though some of this returned to the same classes (if not necessarily the same members) in the form of interest payments on war loans, or government contracts, or posts in the bureaucracy, not all of it did. A proportion went to the working classes, in the form of employment on government-sponsored projects, or pensions, or health services, or unemployment benefits. It is noteworthy that up to 1914 spending on social services accounted for only 4 per cent of the gross national product, while during the inter-war years it accounted for over 8 per cent. Again, insurance against unemployment, to which government was a contributor, covered only 2.25 million workers before the war but nearly 12 million following the Act of 1920.

It is true that the techniques of taxing directly and indirectly the lower-income groups, having been developed during the war, were continued after it. Hence enhanced social services were not financed solely by 'soaking the rich'. But overall we

---

[2] Peacock and Wiseman, *The Growth of Public Expenditure in the United Kingdom*.

are witnessing a mild redistribution of wealth from those who possessed most to those who possessed least. That is, the increase in government spending facilitated by the war was serving to make an unequal society rather more equal.

II

If the war enhanced the revenue-acquiring capacity of the state, it also created powerful reasons why the Government should have access to more money. The reasons can be summed up in the already quoted expression coined by Lloyd George in the 1918 election: that Britain should become 'a fit land for heroes to live in'.

This phrase, as has been indicated, would become for the Prime Minister a liability, so far did performance fall short of expectation. Yet there is a puzzle here. Why did the expectation exist? Why was it anticipated that a better order at home should emerge from this war? The war was proving a ferociously destructive force, with no obvious capacity for amending British society. And anyway it was being fought to prevent the imposition of German autocracy upon Western Europe. That objective seemed to be about external relations, not internal reformation.

These caveats need to be borne in mind. For in part they explain why the post-war period was to provide many disappointments. The war was destroying much of the material resource, and many of the human beings, needed for the establishment of a reconstructed society. And for large numbers of British people the war was not about improving the lot of the disadvantaged at home, anyway if this could be done only at the expense of the possessing classes and the established social order. The war was about thwarting the expansion of German power at Britain's expense and asserting the superiority of British nationalism over German nationalism. In the outcome the destructive effects of the war, and the negative attitude towards social reform of many of those Britons eager to fight it, would help to impede any large-scale changes within British society.

Yet plainly the war generated many positive aspirations towards change. Certainly, Britain had gone to war initially not to alter anything but to preserve the *status quo*. Its ultimatum requiring the Germans to remove their forces from Belgian territory, and its declaration of war when that ultimatum was ignored, symbolized this fundamental aspect. But the purpose of the war could not be left there. The conflict was soon being portrayed, and not without cause, as a struggle between Teutonic autocracy and Western democracy. But emphasis on this element served to highlight the extent to which British society itself fell short of its democratic protestations: in the effective denial of the vote to about a quarter of males (in the poorer section) and all females, and in the impoverished living conditions and educational experience of a large section of the community.

Further, it seemed inappropriate to call on the masses to sacrifice so much in the war if all that would follow upon victory would be a restoration of pre-war conditions. For one thing, on a merely prudent level the appeal might stop producing the desired response. And on a less calculating plane it appeared that the lower classes, having contributed so well to the nation's cause, were deserving of some reward. Yet what gains from the war could be offered them? Even if it might be thought that the mass of the people would rejoice to see Britain acquire more territory overseas, this was not likely to be a major consequence of the war. And should Britain have a chance of picking up a few more colonies, this could hardly be advertised. Political radicals at home, whose endorsement of the war effort was important, would be swift to denounce manifestations of imperialist greed. And serious suspicions of Britain's acquisitive intentions existed already among its allies and important neutrals. It would be dangerous to demonstrate that these suspicions were well founded.

So any positive gains from the war that might be offered to the less privileged must lie within Britain. This could only mean improvements in political rights and living standards. And in one sector, particularly, there was apparent by the end of the war a strong determination to accomplish such improvements: the army. G. H. Roberts, the Minister of Labour, spent the second half of September 1918 addressing meetings of soldiers at the front and at bases in France and Flanders. Two 'general impressions' emerged from the tour.[3] The first, predictably enough, was 'intense disgust' among all ranks at recent strikes. The other is more noteworthy:

> The second point which was very clear was the excellent relations between officers and men, and the strong conviction expressed by officers of all ranks, particularly senior officers, that conditions at home must be better for their men after the war than they have been before. It was evident that the men have learned to respect their officers, and that the latter have come to know and appreciate the lives of their men at home. They have been taught to give every consideration to their comfort in the field, and many of them evidently regard it as their duty to do the same for them at home when the war is over.

Commanding officers at these gatherings, it was noted, 'showed by their remarks . . . that they were thoroughly in sympathy with the men's desire that conditions should be improved after the war'.

A main purpose of the addresses delivered on his tour by the Minister of Labour was plainly to satisfy these aspirations towards betterment. Roberts spoke of the Government's plans for demobilization, aimed at trying to ensure jobs for ex-servicemen and providing cover against unemployment. These plans 'were clearly very acceptable to the men, among whom there appeared to be a wide-spread belief that the nation was going to cast them off when they leave the army, and leave them to shift entirely for themselves'. And he outlined 'some of the steps which had already been taken towards permanent reconstruction' in areas like minimum wages, education, the franchise, and housing. 'In all these matters both officers and men were clearly deeply interested, and every audience listened intently throughout.'

But it was not only to those in the services that better times were being promised. Shortly before the outbreak of the Second World War a survey was made of 'Home Publicity During the Great War'. It brings out plainly how those in authority, especially in 1917 and 1918, helped to foster expectations of change also among civilians. Drawing on a confidential memorandum, the survey sets out the 'general aims of Home Publicity'. One of these aims was:

> To indicate, and, where possible, specifically define the advantages of an Entente Peace, especially in relation to its effect on the daily lives of the people; to dwell on the democratic development and improvement in the lot of the working classes which State control and other war changes have already secured; to suggest the prospect of further improvement and greater freedom when the war is over; generally to envisage the rewards of success.

Some of the expressions employed here are noteworthy. There are references to the beneficial effect of an 'Entente Peace' on 'the daily lives of the people'; the 'improvement in the lot of the working classes' that had already taken place and the part that 'State control and other war changes' had played in this; and the promise of 'further improvement and greater freedom when the war is over' – 'the rewards of success'. A propaganda campaign bearing such messages would no doubt help to keep the toilers resolute in prosecuting the war. It would also lead them to anticipate large improvements afterwards.

---

[3] Quotations are from the report to the Cabinet on the labour situation for the week ending 2 October 1918.

What is lacking from such propaganda, of course, and also from many other manifestations of the desire for betterment in 'the daily lives of the people', is any closely argued explanation of how improvement was to be accomplished. It was plain that much of the wartime improvement in the living standards of the poor had resulted from a massive extension of government employment, first in the armed forces, which both provided males (and, towards the end of the war, some females) with employment and caused them to vacate jobs for others, and then in war-created industries. It was unlikely that the Government would continue as a big employer or contractor, at least in the areas of the armed services and munitions, once the war was over. Into what areas would the Government move to maintain prosperous employment conditions? And, more fundamentally, on what scale did the nation desire activity by the state?

The failure to answer these questions created an ambiguity that ran right through the aspiration to create 'a fit land for heroes'. Many people, while convinced that the burdens imposed by the war could be redeemed only by the establishment of a more just society, had become certain of something else. They had had more than enough of state authority. As civilians or as members of the armed forces, they felt they had suffered an overdose of bureaucracy and form-filling and red tape. They were also convinced that they had paid too many taxes, experienced too many restrictions on their movements and drinking habits and small indulgences, and seen too many interferences with trade and commerce. Whatever they understood by a land fit for heroes, it was not a country in which there would be more bureaucrats or government enterprises or regulations. Rather, they assumed that the swelling tribe of state functionaries would now go into retreat.

But if the improved Britain was not to be developed in response to state initiative, as clearly it had been doing during the war, what alternative force was to bring it into being? Few people asked themselves this question. The omission placed the nation's leaders in an awkward position. They stood to be condemned if, out of the experience of war and reconstruction, a new Britain failed to emerge. But they would also come under fire if they tried to create the new Britain by extensive use of the only means at their disposal.

There was a further ambiguity underlying the concept of a country fit for heroes. In general, people no doubt believed that they understood what they meant by the phrase. They envisaged for the average wage earner better rates of pay and better housing, an improved educational system, freedom from unemployment, protection against the miseries imposed on families by the illness or death of its key members, and support for the aged against the loss of their earning power. But these notions failed to confront some fundamental problems. If the less advantaged sections were going to enjoy a somewhat richer life, was this to be accomplished at the expense of the more advantaged? That is, was Britain to become a more equal society and, if so, to what degree of equality? Or, on the contrary, did improvement for the less favoured depend on an increase in the nation's overall wealth, so that their advance in living standards would not threaten the living standards of the possessing classes?

These were important issues at a time when the nation was plainly facing troubled economic circumstances. If a more equal society were being aspired to, then – by the device of 'soaking the rich' – improvement could be secured for those at the bottom of the social scale even if Britain found itself declining economically. But if the same relative inequalities were to be preserved, then the notion of a country fit for heroes depended utterly on the recovery and enhancement of Britain's economic position. For only by this enhancement could improvements in the living conditions of the poor be financed. So if the intention were to give to the less advantaged not a larger share of the national cake but only their usual share though of a larger cake, then the promise being made to them was based on a gamble. It depended entirely on what would happen to the economy after the war. But when the promise was given this qualification was not expressed. Indeed, no attempt was made to explore the fundamental issue of what was being envisaged: was it a society in which inequalities were to be markedly reduced or one in which the poorest sections would secure improvement at the same rate (but only at the same rate) as the more affluent?

What emerges from this discussion is that, all along, the accomplishment of a country fit for heroes faced formidable obstacles. In the first place, there remained an important element of inflexible Conservatives who had no great wish to improve the lot of the masses, and who saw the war as having external objectives only. Secondly, the war was destroying resources and impairing Britain's position in world trade and finance, so removing some of the material supports for social betterment. Thirdly, among those who willed the end of a country fit for heroes were many people deeply antagonistic to that expansion of state authority which alone could provide the means. And, finally, a profound uncertainty existed concerning the nature of the end.

Large numbers among the possessing classes had become convinced, by the time the war was over, that the less favoured sections of Britain were deserving of a better life. But they did not understand by this that established class differentials should be undermined or that the relative apportionment of wealth between the various classes should be significantly altered. They wanted the same type of society but with the position of those at the bottom of the social scale ameliorated. Others, including a section among the wealthy and a much larger proportion of those whose possessions were modest or negligible, took a different view. They aspired to break down the barriers set up by riches and status. It was not only the disadvantages imposed on the lower classes by poverty that they were determined to eliminate. It was also the disadvantages imposed by insufficient ownership of wealth compared with those higher in the social scale. Only thus could what they understood as a just society be accomplished.

But it may be doubted whether, even among numbers of those with negligible possessions, this more radical interpretation was in the ascendant. Many relatively disadvantaged people, while welcoming the promise of improvements in their 'daily lives', did not aspire towards a marked alteration in the class system. Rather, they accepted the view that any serious challenge to the status and wealth of the upper classes was a threat to the British way of life. Yet as long as this was so, it was questionable whether any type of society very different from what had gone before was capable of attainment.

72

HOUSING: TEMPORARY EXPEDIENTS
AND GRAND DESIGNS

I

The war did not produce new ideas in the area of social policy. But it gave powerful reinforcement to ideas which, if they were ever to become established in practice, badly needed reinforcing. This was the case with both housing and education.

In 1914 much working-class housing, despite an advance since the mid-nineteenth century, was quite abysmal. Local authorities, upon whom Parliament had placed responsibility for making improvements, were loath to act because of the expense. And private investors, presented with so many attractive outlets for their money, had grown reluctant to speculate in working-class home building. The result was an 'almost total stoppage of house-building for the lower income groups between 1890 and 1918'.[1]

In consequence, working-class dwellings were distinguished by overcrowding – in 1911 over 30 per cent of the population lived in circumstances of more than three persons to two rooms – and lack of amenities. Large numbers had no running water on the premises, which meant that, in the conditions of industrial towns, the womenfolk faced a constant battle against dirt. Many gave up the struggle. Others waged it at excessive cost. Robert Roberts writes of his Salford slum: 'There were housewives who finally lost real interest in anything save dirt removing. . . . Two of these compulsives left us for the "lunatic asylum", one of them, I remember vividly, passing with a man in uniform through a group of us watching children to a van, still washing her hands like a poor Lady Macbeth.'[2]

Attempts to attack the housing problem prior to the war were bedevilled by more than the determination of the central government to pass the burden to local authorities and the reluctance of many ratepayers to accept it. There was also the passive attitude of the poor themselves. The poor already devoted a larger proportion of their earnings to housing than did other groups, low though the sum paid and the quality of residence secured might be. Any slight rise in income they might obtain went on food or similar comforts. Consequently, the agitation to improve their housing came largely from middle-class and aristocratic reformers. Enid Gauldie writes:

> among the mass of the population who were badly housed, there was at no time until the twentieth century any strong pressure for housing reform; no rioting with improved housing as its aim, no petitions, processions, secret associations or lobbying. Even the meetings held with trade union backing to discuss overcrowding were middle-class inspired. The attention of the working class was turned towards campaigns for the

---

[1] Enid Gauldie, *Cruel Habitations: A History of Working-Class Housing 1780–1918* (London: Allen & Unwin, 1974), p. 81.
[2] Robert Roberts, *The Classic Slum* (Harmondsworth: Penguin Books, 1973), p. 37.

shortening of working hours, the right to vote, the right to combine in unions. The right to live in a decent house was not clamoured for. . . . [3]

Just before the war there was evidence that this attitude of working-class quiescence about housing was breaking down in one area: that of rent increases. In a number of regions resistance to higher rents was manifesting itself. Nevertheless, it required the war to give this activity the degree of intensity, and the appropriate context, to make any impact.

The war, in important ways, affected the housing of the workers. For one thing, the 'inspection effect' of war was reinforcing awareness of the dismal conditions in which much of the population lived. It was also, at a time when fit males were urgently needed, strengthening the belief that bad habitations helped to produce unfit people. Simultaneously, what may be termed the 'consumption effect' of war was diverting labour and materials away from house building and so aggravating the existing shortage. Hence by the Armistice the pre-war shortage of 300,000 had just about doubled.

At the same time the view that the state had a duty to do something about housing was gaining strength. The individualist position, which accorded to government as small a role as possible in national life, was difficult to maintain at a time when state direction and organization were crucial to the nation's very survival. At the Trades Union Congress in September 1919 the leader of the seamen's union, Havelock Wilson, was arguing against nationalization of the mines: '"The State are not the proper people to manage industry [he asserted]. Can you point to one single thing that it has made a success of?" "The War," boomed a man, and the congress roared its delight.'[4]

If the state, with whatever shortcomings, had succeeded in organizing the conquest of German militarism, the belief was taking hold that it had a duty likewise to organize the conquest of evil habitations. This seemed the least it could offer to the masses of ordinary men who had suffered on its behalf. As the Tory squire Walter Long put it: 'To let them come home from horrible, waterlogged trenches to something little better than a pigsty here would, indeed, be criminal . . . and a negation of all we have said during the war, that we can never repay those men for what they have done for us.'[5] Nor was it only members of the political elite who were drawing this sort of conclusion. The principle of equality of sacrifice being preached so widely was rousing sections of workers to an awareness of the inequalities in basic amenities existing in the community.

As it happened, the area in which the war made its first impact on housing was also that in which, in the disturbed pre-war years, sections of the working class had been tending to act on their own behalf: rent increases. This also proved to be an area in which the Government now had a powerful incentive to act. The outcome was noteworthy. The state trampled on the rights of private property in a matter that had nothing to do with the armed services or national security.

The overwhelming proportion of working-class housing was rented. And it was inherent in the operation of the housing market that 'a slight lack of accommodation results in a rapid increase of rent.'[6] By early in the war some parts of the country, often overcrowded to begin with, were experiencing an accommodation shortage that was anything but slight. These, of course, were the areas where war commodities were

---

[3] Gauldie, *Cruel Habitations*, Introduction.

[4] Arthur Gleason, *What the Workers Want: A Study of British Labor* (London: Allen & Unwin, 1920), p. 121.

[5] Quoted in John Burnett, *A Social History of Housing 1815–1970* (Newton Abbot: David & Charles, 1978), pp. 215–16.

[6] A. L. Bowley, *Some Economic Consequences of the Great War* (London: Thornton Butterworth, 1930), p. 81.

being manufactured. At Woolwich, for example, the number of workers employed at the Arsenal rose from fewer than 11,000 in August 1914 to 44,000 in October, and it was bound to go on rising. This gave the owners of working-class residences an ideal opportunity either to raise the rents of existing tenants or to dispossess the incumbents and rent at a higher level to immigrant workers. But their actions met a hitherto unprecedented level of working-class resistance.

Tenant militancy became apparent in some London districts in the opening weeks of the war and grew during the next twelve months. In Woolwich there was a call for a rent strike in late 1914 that stimulated the authorities to undertake the construction of houses for workers in the Arsenal. Further north, in places like Luton, Manchester, and Birmingham, the same resistance to higher rents became evident. In Birmingham, in October 1915, it manifested itself even among some of 'the best class of tenants', causing one Labour councillor to speak of 'extortionate increases in rents of working class houses'.[7] At the same time the main labour organization speaking for workers on this matter, the War Emergency Workers National Committee, warned the Prime Minister that rising rents were having an adverse effect on morale, recruitment, and production.

Here indeed was the rub. The Government might prefer to leave levels of rents to be settled between landlords and tenants. But matters of morale, recruitment, and production – not least in the munitions industry – affected the Government, and the national well-being, very nearly. The outcome of this disturbance in Birmingham was noteworthy. In November 1915 the clerk of the Birmingham Assessment Committee was directed to London to seek arbitration from the Minister of Munitions. Lloyd George told him to reduce rents. Either on this account or because of popular resistance, the rent increases were dropped. This victory for the tenants was celebrated with rejoicing. 'Flags were unfurled and banners were draped across the streets from house to house.'[8]

But what happened in Birmingham and other parts of England paled before the events on the Clyde. In industrial Scotland hostility between landlord and tenant was intense; living conditions were exceptionally low; and war-induced pressure on housing was heavy. Certainly, if other parts of Britain had not also embarked on rent strikes, then the solution devised by the authorities might have been confined to this locality. But the situation on the Clyde raised the problem to crisis level and forced a solution more drastic than even the national representatives of labour were demanding. For labour's War Emergency Committee was only urging the establishment of a fair rents court. And, given the rise in prices, this would probably have accorded landlords at least a higher rent than that of August 1914.

What precipitated the government into action was the fact that, if theoretically rents were a question between landlord and tenant, a rent strike would involve the state in a most unpleasant respect. For the landlord who had secured an eviction order against a defaulting tenant could look to the police to execute it. In some circumstances this might appear a misuse of government authority. A test case in Glasgow concerned a mother of seven. Her husband was at the front and had been wounded. Two of their sons of military age had joined up. Of their younger offspring, two were seriously ill. For the police to evict her might seem not only inhumane but also injurious to the recruiting campaign. There was also a practical difficulty. A gathering of 4,000 or

---

[7] Quoted in David Englander, *Landlord and Tenant in Urban Britain 1838–1918* (Oxford: Clarendon Press, 1983), p. 208.

[8] Laurence F. Orbach, *Homes for Heroes: A Study of the Evolution of British Public Housing, 1915–1921* (London: Seeley, Service, 1977), pp. 14–15.

5,000 people, mostly women, resolved that they would resist the eviction by force. Plainly, the passivity of the poorly housed and the passivity of the female sex were both breaking down under wartime pressures. The court order was not executed.

Most of the Glasgow rent strikers, it seems probable, were not hard cases of this sort. They were workers in shipyards and engineering works. In terms of increased earnings in wartime, they were doubtless equipped to pay a higher rent. But the war had strengthened their reluctance to do so. It had done more. For the first time in their lives tenants found themselves in a position to refuse rent demands and escape the consequences. The landlord might have the rights of property on his side. But he was not highly regarded among other property owners, least of all among the owners of shipyards, who saw output being threatened by the rent issue. Indeed, he could easily be classed among that scorned body, the war profiteer. In fact, the rent increases being demanded on the Clyde so far, when set against the rise in the cost of living, hardly justified that epithet. But it was becoming convenient for others on whom the quarrel was impinging to see the landlord's conduct in this light. So Lloyd George referred in the House of Commons to 'the unpatriotic course adopted by certain landlords in taking advantage of the national need to extort increased rents in munitions areas'.[9] His choice of words showed that the landlords of Britain were on the verge of a great defeat. Their action in seeking to levy ('extort') higher rents had become 'unpatriotic'. It seemed to follow that refusing to pay them was not.

The rent crisis in Glasgow culminated on 17 November 1915, in what David Englander calls 'one of the most momentous demonstrations in modern British social history'.[10] On that day, when an important rent case was being heard, large numbers of shipyard workers instituted a 24-hour strike. A crowd, variously estimated at between 4,000 and 15,000, marched on the court. Faced with indecision by the authorities, the protestors began calling for an indefinite extension of the shipyard strike. Not a moment too soon, the landlord was persuaded to abandon the case. For the workpeople it was a notable victory and was celebrated accordingly.

Eight days later the president of the Local Government Board, Walter Long (who in June had resisted rent control as 'controversial'), introduced a Bill for restricting rents. It passed through Parliament speedily and with little controversy. The events in Glasgow on 17 November, it should be said, had not been required to convince the Government that it must act. But the upsurge on the Clyde had driven it to produce a hasty and so a far-reaching measure. Instead of trying to establish machinery to determine 'fair' rents, it took the brutal course of retrospectively pegging rents for working-class dwellings at their immediately pre-war level. It also decreed that they would remain there for the duration of the war (and for six months after it). So any decline in the value of rents as a result of wartime inflation was to be borne solely by the landlord, except in so far as he could pass it on to tenants by economizing on repairs and maintenance. To one individual much concerned in the business of housing – he was manager of a major building society and director of a property company owning 7,000 houses – this was 'the gravest act of injustice that had ever been inflicted by the British Parliament'.[11]

The principal beneficiary, obviously, was the tenant. As prices and wages rose and rents did not, the cost of housing came to occupy a steadily decreasing share of the working-class budget. But employers and consumers also benefited, for the calculation of wage rates took into account the declining expense of housing to the worker. There

---

[9] Quoted in Englander, *Landlord and Tenant in Urban Britain*, p. 224.
[10] Ibid., p. 227.
[11] Quoted in E. J. Cleary, *The Building Society Movement* (London: Elek Books, 1965), pp. 172–3.

was another respect in which the Rent Restrictions Act benefited working-class tenants. They obtained a degree of security of tenure. As long as they did not fall into arrears with their rents, they could be dispossessed only if the owner of the dwelling was able to show that he 'reasonably required' it for his own occupancy or that of an employee; and even this proviso was whittled down in the last year of the war.

The gain that this involved for the workers should not be exaggerated. So averse were members of the working class from seeking redress under the law that they sometimes preferred to tolerate infringements of the Rent Act rather than institute proceedings against landlords. For they had little expectation of securing favourable judgements from magistrates drawn from the landlords' class. And in time the rent laws came to impose a serious immobility upon workers. Workmen became reluctant to leave their established districts to take jobs at higher wages – or, during post-war unemployment, jobs at all – when this might mean moving to new residences at higher rents.

Nevertheless, in the long-standing struggle between tenant and landlord the rent legislation was a signal victory for the working class; and it occurred at a time when, with working-class housing in short supply, all the advantages had hitherto lain with the landlord. But it raises a problem. Why, although supposed to lapse soon after the end of hostilities, were rent restrictions preserved right up to the 1930s, that is, to the time when economic conditions ensured that the level of rents established by the Act would remain even without legislation? (Once that ceased to be the case, state control of rents was revived.) The answer is clear. The war had helped to establish that possessors of property did not have the right to do as they wished with their own when property took a form that involved the basic welfare of other human beings. Should property and human welfare come into conflict, the community would side with the latter. And it would continue to do so even after the national emergency had passed. This was a noteworthy development. It took the state an important stage towards involvement in responsibility for the housing, if not of the whole populace, then of those members whom private enterprise was failing adequately to serve.

II

The introduction of rent restrictions in 1915 did not deal with the actual shortage of working-class houses. In fact, rent restrictions would probably aggravate the shortfall. For in a sector where disincentives to building already abounded, this legislation could only provide further discouragement. Even when house building resumed after the war, private enterprise would hardly attend to the needs of the working classes.

It was true that the Rent Act did not determine the rents of any fresh houses. But as long as the large majority of workers paid controlled rents, these set the levels that most workers were prepared to consider. And anyway speculative builders, having seen working-class rents frozen once in a time of rising prices, could hardly feel confident that it would not happen again. They preferred not to run the risk.

At this point the case for private enterprise as the universal provider of houses simply lapsed. Correspondingly, the state, having involved itself in one aspect of working-class housing, was under great pressure to go further: from controlling rents to undertaking the provision of houses. By the time the war was over the Government had gained some experience in so doing. The Ministry of Munitions, soon after its creation, had established a housing section and during its existence had provided permanent or temporary accommodation for 20,000 of its workers. The temporary accommodation was usually of a low quality. But some of the permanent dwellings were highly satisfactory. This was true of the Well Hall Estate, constructed in response to the expansion early in the war of the workforce at Woolwich Arsenal. It was also the case with the homes constructed at Barrow after it had become apparent that the disaffection evident there in early 1917 was in no small measure attributable (as in most other parts of the country) to the housing shortage.

But the Government was confronted with the prospect of doing much more, in terms not only of organization but also of expense. The government was being called on to intervene solely in the unprofitable side of the industry. No one was proposing that it should play a part in the provision of all types of homes. Had this been so, losses on some sorts of dwellings might have been balanced by profits on others. But opinion had not become that 'socialistic'. It was still generally assumed that private enterprise would continue to deal with the profitable sector of housing. The concern of government would be only those less privileged people who could not afford an economic rent for a decent home.

Up to 1914 Governments had not been free with money for housing. They had urged local bodies to clear slums and replace them by superior dwellings. But they had offered no contribution to the cost. Similarly in 1915, with its rent-control legislation, the Government had again passed the financial buck, this time to the landlords. By the end of the war the only money devoted by the central government to this matter was £4.25 million spent by the Ministry of Munitions on housing its workers. And the Ministry, most of whose employees were well paid by the standards of the time, had striven (though not altogether successfully) to extract from them something approaching an economic rent. This had meant a rent substantially higher than that being paid by occupants of controlled dwellings. But if the state were to make a larger entry into the field of housing to meet the threefold needs of the working class – for an increased number of houses, an improved quality of houses, and houses at a rent they could afford – then it must be prepared to take on a considerable economic burden.

Deliberations proper to the adoption of a state housing programme began in 1916, proceeded during the next two years, and resulted in the Housing and Town Planning Act of 1919. This measure was the product of several important conclusions that had emerged during wartime inquiries. The first was that private enterprise was incapable of meeting the shortage of working-class housing. The second was that the shortage was very great – although the figure generally bandied about, some 300,000 houses, actually referred only to the deficiency created by the war and did not touch the pre-war shortfall. The third was that responsibility for providing these houses would rest with the local authorities but that this could no longer be left to their discretion. It was a duty that they must carry out, under the supervision of the central government. The fourth was that the expense of these houses must be borne, unequally, by three groups: the tenant, who would pay a rent deemed reasonable in terms of working-class income; the local authority, which would contribute a fixed sum ('little more than a token');[12] and the central government, which would make up the unspecified remainder. The fifth was that the standard of houses, in size and amenities, would be a marked improvement on what had hitherto been offered – and certainly on those dwellings, 'little better than a pigsty', to which Long had referred.

A measure embodying these concepts constituted a large advance towards the creation of a welfare society. Its extent should not be exaggerated. As Laurence Orbach points out, a housing programme of this sort could be pursued 'without really altering the structure of industry and society. . . . The housing program did not

---

[12] Burnett, *A Social History of Housing 1815–1970*, pp. 221–2.

threaten to destroy the building industry and did not need to lead on to further reforms.'[13] And it may be seen not as an ongoing commitment but as a response to a particular, transitory shortage and to particular, transitory challenges. There was the challenge to do the right thing by the returning heroes of the trenches. There was also the need to head off social disturbance that, according both to the inquiries into industrial unrest in 1917 and to information on subversive activities reaching the Government in 1919, owed much to the shortage of houses. Nevertheless, the Act of 1919 did embody, on the part of at least some of its sponsors and some sections of the public, a large concept: if not the belief that all citizens should have access to equally good housing, then the conviction that all should have access to housing that was decent and comfortable.

Yet as long as the war continued it was noteworthy how little solid planning was accomplished, how effectively the Local Government Board (a key body in this matter) dragged its feet, and how scanty was the support that Addison as Minister of Reconstruction received from the Cabinet in trying to expedite affairs. Housing was an area where much advance planning was needed. All schemes were based on the assumption that a great deal of house building must take place promptly upon the ending of the war so as to meet the worst of the shortage, followed by an abrupt tapering off. This called for the stern requisitioning of building materials to make the programme a reality. It also posed great problems for the building industry, which for a short period would require a huge labour force, many of whose members would then become redundant. And it promised to be very costly. Yet none of these crucial issues was taken in hand while the war lasted. When Lloyd George, at Manchester in September 1918, spoke of the urgency of the housing situation, and when during the election in November he promised homes for heroes, he was making large commitments unsupported by any concrete schemes to overcome the acknowledged problems.

III

In the immediate aftermath of the Armistice a hopeful atmosphere prevailed. The government, spurred on by a sense of good will towards returning soldiers and by dire warnings of impending social unrest, welcomed Addison's housing Bill. (Yet, according to Addison's correspondence at the time with Lloyd George, the Cabinet emasculated some of its most important proposals.) The House of Commons bordered on ecstasy in its welcome for the measure. And *The Times* likewise hailed it, only expressing doubts as to whether it went sufficiently far.

But enthusiasm was not enough. The programme possessed severe shortcomings. It did not secure control over building materials, so that at the time when the greatest construction of houses should have been occurring a large proportion of resources was going into commercial and luxury building. Local authorities were left to borrow money for housing on their own credit, which was a costly process, when the central government (which was footing the bill) could have done this borrowing more cheaply. And the scheme gave local authorities no incentive to proceed with caution, for their financial contribution was limited to a smallish fixed sum.

But the Addison programme confronted more profound problems than these. The local authorities lacked the expertise to produce housing schemes in a hurry and often were deeply antagonistic to Addison's brand of radicalism; yet it was not plain that he could have proceeded through any other agencies. The building trade was seriously

---

[13] Orbach, *Homes for Heroes*, p. 8.

depleted in manpower, and the building workers' unions were quite unco-operative about allowing their numbers to be expanded ('diluted' was the feared wartime expression) to help meet the emergency. Theirs was an industry in which seasonal and irregular employment had been endemic, and where the situation had been particularly bad at the outbreak of the war – so bad that, at the time of demobilization, trained men were refusing to return to the building trade. Those who did so had no wish, now that things were looking up, to hasten the end of the good times by admitting a mass of dilutees so as to complete jobs in a hurry.

There existed also a political threat to Addison's schemes. This threat was of great potency, notwithstanding the show of enthusiasm that had greeted the appearance of the housing programme. It lay in the attitudes and prejudices of the men who dominated Parliament, and ultimately government, as a result of the 1918 election. They might approve of homes for heroes as a safe way of rewarding the survivors of the trenches and as a bulwark against Bolshevism. But neither the obligation of gratitude nor the menace of disaffection would hold them to this course if the cost became severe or the financial stability of the country seemed under threat.

In less than two years, the housing programme had ceased to be even tolerable to the forces controlling politics. It was producing a considerable number of houses, even if not the lavish quantity expected. But it was proving excessively costly. (Ultimately Addison's measures were responsible for the construction of over 200,000 houses. But the cost to the central government exceeded £130 million.) By 1921 some of the practical difficulties that had inhibited building and had contributed to expense were coming under control. But it was too late. In an ever bleaker economic situation, social reform under radical direction had become an offence. In March 1921 Lloyd George, responding to the political forces on whom he ultimately depended, removed Addison from control of housing.

The abrupt abandonment of the housing programme was a key event in generating the disillusionment that sprang from the post-war failure to fulfil wartime promises. In a moment one signal achievement of the war years, a commitment by the Government to ensure decent housing for all its citizens, had gone. Addison's successor, Sir Alfred Mond, would before long express the hope that 'future State intervention in any form will not be required.'[14] No doubt, in the deteriorating economic climate, the lavish plans of 1919 could not be fulfilled. But that seemed hardly to explain the completeness and the display of venom with which both the programme and its architect were overthrown. To all appearances the promises had been given, not with serious intent or close consideration, but to pacify returning servicemen and secure their political support.

In time it was to transpire that not all had been lost. The rent restrictions legislation remained as token of the minimum that the state must do in housing matters to preserve industrial quiescence. And among Conservatives a residual commitment persisted to the notion that the community should do something to mitigate the mounting shortage of working-class houses. Between 1921 and 1923 private enterprise did not rise to the occasion. So under the Conservative Government of 1923 a policy of state subsidies for the construction of a limited number of houses for work people was introduced, although, unlike the Addison scheme, the state provided only a fixed amount and acted through private builders. In the following year, under the Labour Government that held office briefly, a bolder programme was undertaken, involving a larger (though still fixed) subsidy and action through local authorities. A Conservative

---

[14] Quoted in Burnett, *A Social History of Housing 1815–1970*, p. 222.

regime supplanted Labour at the end of 1924 and held office for the rest of the decade. It continued both schemes.

The significance of this should not be exaggerated. The débâcle of the Addison programme had revealed a latent hatred among the propertied classes for any bold scheme of betterment for the underprivileged, especially when presided over by self-righteous radicals like Addison and political mavericks like Lloyd George. So it was entirely appropriate that when a programme of state subsidy for working-class houses was revived it should have emanated from a man who was pre-eminently an administrator, a Conservative, and a devoted enemy of Lloyd George: Neville Chamberlain. Housing improvement for the poorer sections would proceed, where it proceeded at all, in a form that was cautious, limited, and without threat to the defenders of property.

Two things, then, remained as a legacy of the war's impact on housing policy. One was restricted rents and security of tenure for the occupants of a group of established dwellings. The other was state-subsidized construction of a limited number of houses for the working class: the council houses. The latter development, it should be stressed, was not the most noteworthy development in house building in the inter-war period. That distinction belonged to the construction by private enterprise, for purchase rather than rent, of 'suburban' dwellings for the expanding middle class (and for a section of the best-paid workers). But the council house, like rent control, did signal an improvement for those whom it served. Enid Gauldie writes: 'If council estates, brooding bleakly at the edge of our towns and swamping pretty villages, seem to have done nothing but harm to the shape and appearance of towns, they can only fairly be contrasted with what they replaced, a kind of squalor, a kind of misery even the most disparaged of council schemes has not yet achieved.'[15]

In sum, the truncated Addison programme, as well as its successors under Chamberlain and the Labour Party's John Wheatley, accomplished a measure of improvement. Within the ranks of local and central government these enactments established bodies of people with concern for, and expertise in, housing matters. In the community at large they provided a focus for the growing concern for reform in this area. And in terms of quality of dwellings (even though the later measures lessened the standards set by Addison) they instituted 'new standards for working class housing as regards size, density and amenities'.[16]

Yet what was achieved fell far short of what had been promised. Much of the workforce, not to say those out of work, continued to languish in grimly sub-standard dwellings. And nothing was done to lessen class barriers. Indeed, the council house (like the slum) affirmed class separation by giving it physical and geographical definition. In vital respects post-war reality failed to fulfil notions of not only a more comfortable but also a more equal society – notions that, for a time, had seized the imagination of some politicians and planners and had raised the hopes of people who dreamed dreams.

---

[15] Gauldie, *Cruel Habitations*, p. 310.

[16] Paul Wilding, 'The Housing and Town Planning Act 1919 – A Study in the Making of Social Policy', *Journal of Social Policy*, vol. II, no. 4, October 1973, p. 334.

73

EDUCATION: NO NEW HEAVEN OR EARTH

One area in which it was widely agreed that much needed to be done, and could be done, to establish a more just society was education. During the war great hopes were aroused. Yet in the outcome the amount achieved was decidedly limited.

In the decade or more up to 1914 some noteworthy developments had taken place in British education. These included, at the elementary school level, improved curricula with more emphasis on practical subjects, higher standards of teacher training, and a much enhanced role for schools in the health care and feeding of needy children. Yet it all took place in a context where the great mass of children would receive no education beyond the elementary level and were being trained to fulfil a role as 'followers' of their social superiors. Certainly, the beginnings of a state system of secondary education had been established. But, in addition to being slanted towards the humanities – and not least the classics – as against scientific and vocational subjects, it scarcely touched any sectors below the middle classes. So in urban areas secondary schools were situated, to a disproportionate extent, in middle-class districts, and the small number of free places in these schools generally went to middle-class children.

As a result 75 per cent of adolescents received no formal education beyond their fourteenth birthdays. Some of the consequences were stated powerfully in 1916 by an ex-Cabinet Minister who before the war had been striving for improvement, Lord Haldane. He quoted the observations of Alexander Paterson on the large number of youngsters in London who, their education ending at 13, took jobs in the categories of 'boys' work': 'beer boys' to wharf and dock labourers, van boys to railway companies and carrier firms, and newspaper boys. They earned what, for their age, were temptingly large sums of money, but within three years they were out of a job and seeking a man's wage with no qualifications. 'This,' said Haldane, 'is how we recruit our unemployables and hooligans and drain the nation of its strength. One asks oneself why the State should leave that vast majority who are least protected mentally and morally to the bare chance of getting themselves educated', while providing encouragement and assistance to those growing up 'in the calm of a well-ordered family life'.[1]

In other ways the state of education in pre-war Britain was seriously unsatisfactory. A growing, not a declining, proportion of educational expenditure was falling on local rates, penalizing poorer areas with large populations. And the level of pay for teachers, and so the status of the profession, were desperately low. The great majority of even certificated schoolteachers received under £150 a year, below what was usually considered the lowest rung of middle-class status. In consequence there was a serious under-supply of teachers. H. A. L. Fisher, as Minister of Education, was to tell the Lloyd George Cabinet in February 1917 that before the war elementary teachers were

---

[1] 'The Student and the Nation', a lecture by Haldane in the University of London in 1916, published as a pamphlet (copy in the Crewe papers).

'miserably paid', with the result that 9,000 were dropping out of the system each year as against 6,000 coming in.

On the eve of the war there were movements, particularly within the Liberal Party (which was revealing more incentive in the matter than not only the Conservative but also the Labour Party), to improve the situation. The main proposals under discussion were a firm minimum leaving age of 14, part-time continuation classes for those who left at that age, and an increase in the number of free places in secondary schools. But, apart from the fact that any attempts at educational reform were bedevilled by an on-going feud between the religious denominations, there was much apathy on this matter and a deal of downright hostility.

The war gave a powerful thrust to the forces favouring change. Perhaps in no other area did its 'inspection effect' operate more searchingly. In the first place it threw doubt upon the high standing of the great educational establishments, be they preparatory schools, public (i.e. fiercely private) schools, or universities. For the war revealed glaring inadequacies in British scientific and technical education. On 2 February 1916 *The Times* carried a communication, signed by a large number of scientists, under the heading 'Neglect of Science. A Cause of Failures in War. New Committee Formed'. The impact of these deficiencies was particularly powerful on a member of the Government who had been lukewarm on the issue of education before the war: Lloyd George. In January 1913 he had said bitter things about Haldane for trying to push education to the forefront of government priorities (if only because this might crab his own land campaign). By mid-1916, as a result of his experiences as Minister of Munitions, he was making common cause with Haldane on the matter.

But the war did more than show that British education paid insufficient attention to some important subjects. It also served to make people aware that educational opportunities were grossly unequal and, for large sections of the community, terribly inadequate. And this awareness was developing in an atmosphere conducive to change. Something of the altered expectations that were running through the community are suggested by the statistics of school attendance. The war, it is true, was circumscribing the education of some children, who were being lured by big wages to work in munitions factories or pressured by the authorities to work on the land (for inadequate wages). Nevertheless, at this same time the school life of many offspring of the working classes and lower-middle classes was being extended. So, whereas early in the war the number of children attending secondary schools fell by 1,000, in October 1915 it had risen by 3,000 and a year later by a further 9,000.[2]

Other events bear out the message of these statistics: that enhanced concern over education was not confined to particular politicians and ideologues but had a substantial base in the community. Addressing meetings on the need for greater involvement of labour in education, Haldane found in 1916 (at a time when he was not a popular figure) that he was attracting audiences of working men numbering thousands, where before the war he would have secured only hundreds. And Fisher's experiences in the year following his appointment as Minister of Education were yet more remarkable. He decided to undertake a propaganda campaign throughout Lancashire, Wales, and southern England. The response, in terms of attendance and enthusiasm, was astonishing: a packed Free Trade Hall in Manchester, a dockers' meeting at Bristol numbering 3,000 or 4,000, an audience of 2,000 at Swansea (where, on other matters, much hostility to the Government was in evidence). 'Fisher,' according to one of his aides, 'is not an exciting speaker and never plays to the gallery,

---

[2] These figures are from G. E. Sherington, 'World War One and National Educational Policy in England', Ph.D. thesis, McMaster University, 1974–5, p. 227.

but the audience jumped to its feet frequently and cheered him enthusiastically.'[3] Of the Bristol meeting of dockers ('got together at a moment's notice by E. Bevin on a Sunday morning') Fisher himself recorded: 'I have never encountered such enthusiasm. They did what I have never seen before or since, rose to their feet two or three times in the course of my speech, waved their handkerchiefs, and cheered themselves hoarse. The prospect of wider opportunities which the new plan for education might open to the disinherited filled them with enthusiasm.'[4]

These gatherings were accompanied by a notable stirring in the labour movement on the education question – in marked contrast to the situation before the war, when most Labour MPs were (according to one of them) 'rather wooden on the subject'.[5] At meetings of the TUC in 1916, soon after at a gathering of trade unionists in Bradford, and at an official Labour conference in January 1917, the labour movement began for the first time to move towards the adoption of a policy on education in advance of both the Board of Education and the Liberal Party. It included, among other things, a commitment to free and compulsory education to 16 years of age.

Many workers probably did not welcome this proposal. They were aware of few tangible benefits from education in general or from the education they had received in particular. And they expected, and probably needed, their offspring to be contributing to the family income well before this age. What is worth noting is that there were now large numbers of workmen responding to a wider vision – even to the extent of waving their handkerchiefs and cheering themselves hoarse.

Yet in important respects these expectations lacked a solid base. In his autobiography, after describing his ecstatic reception by the Bristol dockers, Fisher added: 'Alas! for these good folk. They expected from an Education Bill what no bill on education or on anything else can give, a new Heaven and a new Earth.' Perhaps they did. But perhaps they expected from it only a great deal more than a Minister with Fisher's preconceptions, and a Board of Education as then constituted, and a Government most of whose parliamentary supporters were Conservatives, were prepared to give.

The days when the officials of the Board of Education had been inspired by a driving administrator, as under Robert Morant (notwithstanding his shortcomings), had passed. His successor, Amherst Selby-Bigge, was no fire-eater. He wanted changes, but in a cautious manner and within rigidly established guidelines. The appointment of Fisher as the Minister did not endanger this situation. 'Whatever his views before entering office,' Geoffrey Sherington has noted, 'Fisher soon revealed that he was a conservative reformer in educational matters.'[6] And however much eagerness for change there may have been among individual MPs or members of the Government (including the Prime Minister), all of them were operating in the context of the sharp moves to the right that politics had taken with the formation of the new Government in December 1916 and its electoral triumph of December 1918.

What were the minister and his advisers contemplating when they envisaged educational reform? They saw change not in terms of starting afresh or applying new principles but of expanding existing undertakings and filling in gaps. There was no anxiety to make good the 'neglect of science' but rather a fear that this would imperil

---

[3] J. Herbert Lewis to Lloyd George, 17 October 1917, quoted in ibid., p. 320.
[4] H. A. L. Fisher, *An Unfinished Autobiography* (London: Oxford University Press, 1940), pp. 106–7.
[5] Quoted in Geoffrey Sherington, *English Education, Social Change and War 1911–20* (Manchester: Manchester University Press, 1981), p. 32. (This book is a reduced version of the Ph.D. thesis cited at footnote 2.)
[6] Ibid., p. 81.

humane and classical studies. There was no question of challenging the special place in the educational system, and in the structure of rule throughout the country, of the great private schools and universities – concerning which Fisher said, 'We shall still believe in private enterprise, private endowment, local initiative.' And there was no proposal to establish a system of secondary education for all – something, Fisher told Parliament in his maiden speech (as Minister and as MP) on 19 April 1917, that would raise 'very controversial questions'.

The proposals that emerged from the Ministry were circumspect and not 'controversial'. There was a firm intention to raise the salaries and status of teachers, something that could be pressed on the Cabinet (if other arguments failed) on the ground that discontented teachers were a potentially subversive body. Local authorities were to be encouraged to provide nursery schools and to spend more on school medical services. The minimum leaving age of 14 was to be applied without exception; and for children who ceased attendance at that age compulsory 'continuative education' of eight hours per week was to be provided up to 18 years. The number of free places in secondary schools was to be increased, so moving the country forward from the 3 per cent of the population who received secondary schooling in Britain towards the 10 per cent who did so in Germany. And there was to be increased state support for universities (whose financial position had been much impaired by the absence of fee-paying students at the front).

Fisher summed up the extent of, and the limits upon , his vision in a speech he made to the House of Commons in August 1919. He hoped that in the course of a generation the country would find itself equipped with 'all the types of schools which are required to give every section of the children of the people that education which is best adapted to provide them with a good start in life'. Fisher here was proposing a large improvement. Yet his references to 'types of schools', 'every section of the children', and 'a good start in life' envisaged what would remain an unequal community, in which different 'sections' of children would be segregated into different 'types' of school and in which, though all might get a 'good' start, some would get a markedly better start than others.

It was not only untutored dockers who expected something more. A widely attended conference held by the Workers Education Association in May 1917 put forward proposals for a school-leaving age rising by stages to 16, with continuation classes of 20 hours per week (as against Fisher's eight hours) to age 18, and with facilities for transfer back from part-time to full-time education. These notions would have taken the country much farther than Fisher was envisaging towards the ideal of 'secondary education for all'. And they were adopted by the education panel of the Government's Reconstruction Committee – a body set up by Lloyd George to help in 'laying the foundations of a new order': 'they had power to assist in painting a new picture of Britain.'[7]

In the outcome the views of the Reconstruction Committee went unheeded. Fisher even had to fight to preserve some – he could not save all – of his own more modest proposals. Within two years of the ending of the war the implementation of much of his programme was under threat. By 1922 even what had been accomplished up to that point was subject to retrenchment. The continuation classes, upon which Fisher had placed such stress and which were to be the Government's (inadequate) version of 'secondary education for all', never became established. The improvements in teachers' salaries, having been secured in a measure, were somewhat diminished. The

---

[7] Quoted in Paul Barton Johnson, *Land Fit for Heroes: The Planning of British Reconstruction 1916–1919* (Chicago: University of Chicago Press, 1968), pp. 37–8.

expansion in the number of free places in secondary schools and universities was not continued. The 'neglect of science' was affected only marginally: by a slight increase in attendance at technical institutions and by a modest improvement in the numbers studying science and technology at tertiary institutions.

Despite all this there were tangible accomplishments. In the long term, especially in what soon became a period of falling cost of living, the institution of national (as against local) salary scales under the Burnham Committee rendered the incomes of teachers somewhat better and more securely based. The status of the teaching profession benefited accordingly. Also, during the inter-war period state secondary schools underwent some development, with the institution of the general and then the higher school certificates providing 'precise academic targets', setting 'very high academic standards', and offering 'tangible, and relevant' rewards for success.[8] As a consequence there was a notable increase in the numbers of students proceeding from state secondary schools to universities.

But this still left Britain with an education system in which only a small minority ever went beyond the elementary level. Of young people born in the twenty years 1910–1929, less than one-fifth received secondary schooling. Of that one-fifth, only one-seventh went on to universities. The beneficiaries of the modest expansion in secondary and tertiary education that occurred after the war were largely middle-class. Had the continuation schools been established, they would have reinforced Britain's class system by providing segregated and part-time education for working-class adolescents. As they were not established (except in a very few instances), the segregation took the traditional form of the non-education of working-class adolescents. Among boys in the middle-class sector born between 1910 and 1929, 39 per cent went to secondary schools and 8.5 per cent went to universities. Among working-class boys, the corresponding figures were 10 per cent and 1.5 per cent. This was no certain reflection of where ability lay. It has been calculated that, in the decade before the Second World War, 73 per cent of children of high intelligence never got as far as secondary schools, while nearly half the children who entered those schools – because their parents were prepared to pay fees – lacked the mental equipment to benefit from the type of education being offered. This has been termed (by Michael Sanderson) 'a massive misallocation of intelligence between the resources of the educational system'.[9]

All of this seems to fall far short of the 'new picture of Britain', the 'new order', about which Lloyd George had talked to the Reconstruction Committee. In good part this is to be accounted for by the adverse economic conditions that the nation began experiencing soon after the end of the war. But that is not the whole explanation. During the war an awareness had developed that one benefit to be gained from an improved education system would be a stronger, more competitive economy. Yet the moment economic difficulties began to assert themselves the cry went up for a retreat in just this area. By those who sounded the cry education was not seen as an instrument of economic, or national, regeneration. It was at most an optional extra, in which the nation might indulge when it was in a position to afford such luxuries.

The 'inspection effect' of war had shed alarming light on the inadequacies and

---

[8] H. C. Dent, *1870–1970: Century of Growth in English Education* (London: Longman, 1970), p. 96.

[9] For the statistics in this paragraph, and their interpretation, see Jean Floud, 'The Educational Experience of the Adult Population of England and Wales as at July 1949', in D. V. Glass (ed.), *Social Mobility in Britain* (London: Routledge & Kegan Paul, 1954); D. V. Glass, 'Education', in Morris Ginsberg (ed.), *Law and Opinion in England in the 20th Century* (London: Stevens & Sons, 1959); and Michael Sanderson, *The Universities and British Industry 1850–1970* (London: Routledge & Kegan Paul, 1972), ch. 10.

imbalances of the British education system. But the war, in calling forth a vast sustained effort, had consumed much of the nation's wealth and energy and taken the lives of many of its most creative individuals. Consequently, at the same time as it was highlighting what needed to be done, the war was eliminating some of the resources with which to do it. Further, many of the schemes that Fisher put forward would come into effect only if local authorities exercised initiative and provided part of the funds. This participation at the local level was rarely forthcoming. Again, the institution of continuation classes required the co-operation of employers and employees. In the slackening mood and difficult times following the war, this was something that many in both classes failed to provide. And the general election at the end of the war further undermined the political foundations on which to construct large measures of educational reform.

Among the Conservatives, who by the end of 1918 had established an unshakeable hold on government and the House of Commons, wartime notions of change were not always welcome. In August 1916 one exceptionally titled lady, seeking to enlist the aid of the then Minister of Education, Lord Crewe, warned that the National Union of Teachers was 'a very pernicious organization & its papers and circulars are not to be commended'. What seemed to her the most hopeful course was that the Queen should become indirectly involved in educational matters: 'After all it is the mothers of England who should be allowed to say something for the education of children, and headed by the Queen so much could be done to favour a good solid religious and moral training . . . manners and discipline and respect for authority should be far more insisted on in every school than is the case at present.'[10]

The generality of Conservative MPs may not have seen royal intervention as the means of restoring 'respect for authority' to the educational system. But many would have responded to the note of distrust for developments in education sounded in this letter. The onset of economic difficulties provided the opportunity to call a halt. Early in December 1920 the Unionist Social Reconstruction Committee, which presumably was not confined to the more traditionalist elements in the Conservative Party, waited on the Prime Minister, Bonar Law, and Austen Chamberlain (Chancellor of the Exchequer). They urged the suspending of all new expenditure on education. At the time some of Fisher's most noteworthy proposals had not yet been instituted. The views of the forces now dominant in politics ensured that they would not be.

One educationist has written of the immediate post-war years: 'Many hopes were dashed, many enthusiasms chilled, many promising beginnings nipped in the bud.' The author of these words, H. C. Dent, admits that at the same time 'sound foundations were laid for a number of developments which later proved important and valuable.' But, he adds, for teachers like himself who had been looking forward to really substantial changes, 'these were years of perpetual frustration, evoking at times feelings of furious despair.'[11]

---

[10] The Duchess of Norfolk to Lady Crewe, 25 August 1916, Crewe papers. In addition to being the wife of the fifteenth Duke of Norfolk ('Premier Duke and Earl. . . .Owns about 49,900 acres') the author of the letter was in her own right Baronness Herries ('owns about 18,900 acres').

[11] Dent, *1870–1970: Century of Growth in English Education*, p. 96.

74

A WORLD NOT RENEWED

'We went where you are going, into the rain and the mud;
We fought as you will fight
With death and darkness and despair;
We gave what you will give – our brains and our blood.

'We think we gave in vain. The world was not renewed.
There was hope in the homestead and anger in the streets
But the old world was restored and we returned
To the dreary field and workshop, and the immemorial feud

'Of rich and poor. Our victory was our defeat.
Power was retained where power had been misused. . . .'

Herbert Read, 'To a Conscript of 1940', in Collected Poems *(London: Faber & Faber, 1966)*

I

For some sections of Britain, the housing and education measures instituted with hope in 1918 and 1919 were part of a larger whole. In this wider view, Britain would be transformed into a nation where harmony existed in industry, not just because one sector had been forced into quiescence but because capital and labour were acting together for the common good; and where all citizens would enjoy a decent standard of living safeguarded from the ill consequences of unemployment, sickness, and old age.

This vision, like its components in housing and education, was not fulfilled. The most obvious reason is that the economic ills of the nation after 1920 removed some of the wealth with whose aid change might have been accomplished. This caused many people, not eager for change but prepared to accept some of its instalments, to become its fierce opponents. But it should be noted that, even had economic circumstances been happier, there existed plentiful obstacles to the establishment of a new social order.

The Parliament that came into existence as a result of the 1918 election was not of the stuff to forge a more just society. On a first view, Stanley Baldwin (as quoted by Keynes) called the new House of Commons 'a lot of hard-faced men, who look as if they had done very well out of the war'. For no very evident reason, this once popular characterization has gone out of fashion. Perhaps we cannot confirm Baldwin's judgement on the parliamentarians' visages. But their contributions to debates on a range of social and international matters revealed that they possessed uncomfortably hard voices. The malevolence with which, before long, many Tory back-benchers were harrying the more evident reformers in Lloyd George's ministry – Addison and

Montagu and Fisher – made it plain that Lloyd George had secured a quite inappropriate power base from which to accomplish social amelioration.

Obstacles to a large measure of change also presented themselves in the field of industrial relations. Considerable sections of capital and labour were not eager about the proposal to establish a joint council in each industry, where issues of wages and conditions would be resolved and the whole process of decision-making perhaps be reviewed. As has already been noticed, Ernest Bevin had little faith in such a development. He bluntly told the abortive National Industrial Conference, which was supposed to inaugurate a condition of industrial harmony, that the only way labour would receive its due was by the exercise of industrial muscle. The corresponding view was widely held in the ranks of management: that the demands of the working class would be kept within bounds only by severely chastising it in industrial confrontation. And even among those, on both sides, of less obdurate view there was a disposition born of the inertia of convention to resist new methods. Established forms of haggling, which involved much give and take beneath a show of dogmatics, were seen as having served in the past and sufficing for the future.

Similarly, in the field of social reform entrenched bodies and familiar courses proved powerful obstacles to measures of change. Any attempt to break up the Poor Law system faced the established officials of the Local Government Board and the vast panoply of Poor Law authorities. As for the institution of a national health service and a general system of age benefits, this must run up against the great lobbying power and grass-roots influence of friendly societies, insurance bodies, and the medical profession. One reason, it is worth recalling, why the old-age pensions instituted in 1908 applied only to that section of the elderly who received negligible incomes was that insurance companies did not see these people as part of their clientele. Those with marginally larger incomes they did, and so these had been omitted. Similarly, widows' and orphans' benefits were absent from the National Insurance Act of 1911 to placate the private insurance companies. And, in order to overcome the resistance of the friendly societies and the industrial insurance 'combine' to the establishment of a limited health service in 1911, the Government had made these organizations the instrumentalities through which it acted. These vested interests inhibiting government action continued powerful after 1918.

There was a further problem about a large extension of social welfare. It lay in the resistance of those who would have to foot the bill, be it the workforce under an insurance scheme or the taxpayer under programmes funded out of general revenue. When in 1916 the Government extended unemployment insurance to cover workers in munitions and other war-related industries, it encountered much opposition. According to William Beveridge, in the boot and shoe trade 'the employers and work-people went into passive resistance; they refused to work the Act or to pay the contributions and were retrospectively excluded by an Amending Act in 1917. . . . None of the trades in fact made any serious attempts to frame schemes of their own; employers and work-people were content to unite in purely negative opposition to officials and the State.' As for attempts to offset inflation by raising insurance contributions so as to be able to pay higher benefits, these 'found no favour'.[1] This measure of 1916 still had the signal effect of increasing by over 1 million (something like 25 per cent) the number of people covered by unemployment insurance. But the reluctance to pay is noteworthy. The war's 'displacement effect', enabling the central government to acquire additional revenue for social purposes, was by no means unlimited.

---

[1] Quoted in Bentley B. Gilbert, *British Social Policy 1914–1939* (London: Batsford, 1970), pp. 55–6.

The resistance of vested interests and established attitudes to measures of change, powerfully reinforced from 1920 by economic adversity, ensured that no major social reordering through government instrumentalities would follow the war. The establishment of joint councils in industry (the Whitley councils) proved not to be a force to transform industrial relations. And the coming of peace was followed by no sweeping extension of old-age pensions, no wideranging health service, and no overturning of the Poor Law system. Twenty years after the end of the war, local authorities in Britain were still supporting 1 million paupers, nearly half of whom were receiving medical relief through Poor Law agencies. As Bentley Gilbert sadly observes:

> That, in a time of stable prices after three decades of experimentation with social legislation, 2½ per cent of the population of England and Wales should still be dependent upon the oldest and most despised of all welfare institutions for at least part of their needs provides perhaps the strongest indictment of social planning and political leadership in the interwar period.[2]

II

Nevertheless, in one area where the pre-war Liberal Government had engaged in social experimentation a considerable change was registered after 1918. This area was the provision of relief for the unemployed.

The major piece of post-war legislation in this area was the Unemployment Insurance Act of August 1920. One of the noteworthy things about it was the date of its enactment. For by the latter part of 1920 the winds of caution were making themselves felt in political corridors. Schemes already enacted for housing and education were struggling to survive, and all hope of their enlargement was departing. It might seem surprising that a sweeping proposal should be launched in the costly area of unemployment relief; and appear a stroke of luck for the million or more Britons soon to find themselves out of work. But that Parliament would legislate on this matter, however late the day and unpropitious the omens, had been determined by actions taken two years earlier. These actions had been intended only to cover the transition from war to peace. But they had constituted a response to powerful incentives. And they had made further measures inescapable.

As far as unemployment was concerned, the National Insurance Act of 1911 had been limited to certain industries in which employment was considered most uncertain, especially building and engineering. And even for these groups it had placed no general obligation on the state to render assistance. Although subsidized by the taxpayer and the employer, it was designed as a self-help measure by which workmen paid in so as to secure an entitlement to a limited scale of benefits. (Among the limitations, the scheme required five weeks of contributions to secure one week of relief, and benefits could be drawn for only fifteen weeks in a year.) Once an insured man who fell out of work had exhausted his entitlements he had no further call on the scheme. His position became that of any uninsured workman who lacked employment. That meant that his only recourse to community assistance was through the Poor Law. This gave relief to those utterly unable to provide for themselves, but only at the price of degrading them to the rank of paupers.

The events of the war undermined the conviction (which anyway had not been held universally) that a recipient of unemployment relief must be either an insured person with a current entitlement or a pauper. Many servicemen following demobilization might find themselves, immediately or in due course, without work. A large proportion

---

[2] Gilbert, *British Social Policy 1914–1939*, p. 235.

of these men, plainly, would not be entitled to unemployment insurance, for in November 1918 only one-quarter of the workforce (rather less than 4 million out of 14 million) were covered by it. The state could hardly express its gratitude to unemployed war veterans by asking them to choose between honourable starvation and reduction to the rank of pauper. Too strong a sense of gratitude existed for that. And there also existed a good deal of fear: that ex-servicemen who became resentful might constitute a powerful disruptive body, well trained to deal with the forces of law and order.

Considerable concern existed regarding the political reliability of ex-servicemen. As an indication of this, from early in 1918 the Special Branch of the Criminal Investigation Department, under Basil Thomson, was keeping the various organizations of ex-servicemen under surveillance. Their reports over the next three years did not reveal war veterans as eager to menace constituted authority. If anything (notwithstanding Thomson's well developed phobia about Bolshevik conspiracies) the Special Branch found it necessary to discourage the Cabinet from undue alarmism. But the reports did make it clear that ex-servicemen expected, as a right, to enjoy a decent standard of living, and that they would not endure its denial placidly. So a report to the Cabinet on 4 November 1918 warned that even one of the most respectable of the ex-servicemen's associations ('hitherto ... singularly free from extravagances') was revealing radical tendencies. Its members were 'inclining towards the Independent Labour Party for support, as they say that they must have some support to see that their pensions are not reduced, and that they are not thrown upon charity'.[3]

In order to head off such dangerous trends, and to do the right thing by returning heroes, the Government included in its plans for demobilization an out-of-work donation for ex-servicemen. Allowing for the fact that, as a transitional measure, it would terminate at a fixed date, it was in significant ways more generous than the benefit being provided by unemployment insurance – more generous, that is, to the recipient, not the taxpayer. A recipient did not need to have paid anything into a fund to qualify – he was judged to have earned entitlement by other means. And the size of the weekly pay-out was geared not to the sum of money which existed in an unemployment fund but to the actual needs of the recipient. So it took account of the cost of living and varied according to the number of the recipients' dependents.

Ex-servicemen, of course, were seen as constituting a special case. But on reflection it appeared that the case, in some of its aspects, applied also to a substantial number of civilian workers. Many toilers in factories and elsewhere had made a sacrificial contribution to the war effort. And a good many of them would be out of work once war industries closed and ex-servicemen returned to claim their former positions. Were they not also entitled to a token of the nation's gratitude? And if unemployed war veterans seemed a potent danger to civil order because of their familiarity with weapons and fighting, industrial workers deprived of financial support could also seem menacing on account of their numbers and powers of organization. Furthermore, all male workers would now have the vote in the general election that the Government was planning as the war hastened to its close, and the Labour Party was expected to pose a considerable challenge with its platform of social benefits. Here were very good reasons for extending the out-of-work donation – if for a shorter period and on less generous terms – to civilian wage earners. This decision was taken as the war ended.

Such an action established a major precedent. Certainly, it could be explained away at the time of its inception as having no permanent application. But the circumstances

---

[3] Quoted in Stephen Ward, 'Intelligence Surveillance of British Ex-Servicemen, 1918–1920', *The Historical Journal*, vol. XVI, no. 1, 1973, p. 182.

that had inspired it were by no means transitory. The sense of obligation to those who had served their country persisted, if with diminishing force and in increasingly mechanical fashion. And fear that social upheaval might result from the existence of an element that was not only unemployed but desperate continued. Hence the Government found itself committed to devising some long-term policy for those out of work.

This much, during the first year or so of peace, it came to accept. But the Cabinet's intention was to terminate the practice of a donation based simply on need and financed by the taxpayer. Its place would be taken by the insurance principle of the pre-war scheme, now given a near-general application. (In the event, the only sections of the workforce not covered by the Government's measure were agricultural labourers, domestic servants, and non-manual workers earning above £250 per annum.) This would, in good measure, move the cost of supporting the unemployed on to the workers themselves, who would draw benefits from a fund to which they had contributed.

But whether this transference could really be effected would depend on circumstances beyond the legislators' control. It required that the economy would stay buoyant, so that those who dropped out of work did so only temporarily and only after they had contributed long enough to the scheme to gain entitlement to support. Otherwise the state would be obliged to do one of two things: either leave unemployed workers who were not insured or had exhausted their insurance rights to choose between starvation and pauperisation, or begin doctoring its own scheme.

The Government produced its insurance programme only in 1920, soon after the expiry of the out-of-work donation for civilians – that for ex-servicemen had a longer life. It did so amidst evidence of considerable discontent. In his 'Report on Revolutionary Organizations' for 6 November 1919, the head of the Special Branch wrote: 'There is consternation at the announcement that unemployment doles may be discontinued this month. . . . In Liverpool they say that the Government would not dare drop it during the winter months at any rate.' A week later he recorded: 'My Liverpool correspondent even goes so far as to say that there will be serious trouble if the doles are withdrawn during the winter. . . . The discontent among ex-soldiers is not diminishing. There is a possibility of disturbances in the London district when the unemployment donation is stopped.'[4]

The scheme that eventually became law in the latter part of 1920, after an inordinately long period of gestation, was appropriate to the times only in one major respect: its near-universal application as far as wage earners were concerned. This carried it well beyond the pre-war scheme and plainly owed a lot to the impact of a war whose demands on the populace had gone far towards universality. But in most other respects the scheme and the times were sadly out of joint. Given the level of inflation since 1914, its rates were too low for a family to live on. It provided support for only a limited number of weeks each year, whereas important sectors of industry were already succumbing to long-term unemployment. And it provided benefits only for those who had been able to pay into the fund for a stipulated time, whereas by the time the scheme became operational there existed 1.5 million workers unable to make even a first payment because they were already unemployed.

The result was that, in the years that followed its enactment, the Unemployment Insurance measure of 1920 underwent a bewildering series of amendments and supplementary enactments. These were designed to accomplish what, in the economic circumstances of Britain, were contradictory objectives. The first was to preserve the

---

[4] Quoted in Gilbert, *British Social Policy 1914–1939*, p. 67.

scheme as an insurance fund, whose cost would be borne less by the taxpayer than by the workman. The second was to meet, in however grudging and inadequate a fashion, the actual needs of the unemployed at least in monetary terms. For this latter purpose the rates had to be adjusted to cover some of the family needs (in addition to the individual needs) of the recipient, even though an insurance scheme covered only the individual worker. The number of weeks during which a recipient could draw the allowance had to be extended. And those who had never paid into the insurance fund, having not been in work since its inception, had to be endowed with a fictitious eligibility to receive its benefits.

All this occurred in a halting and messy fashion and under many bogus titles. For the unemployed it entailed much hardship, anxiety, and humiliation. Even allowing for the fact that it was occurring in an economic situation whose worst features had not been foreseen, the operation of unemployment relief seemed informed by a small-mindedness and want of resolution sadly at odds with the large promises of wartime. Yet it is important not to overlook what was being accomplished. For even though the community was acting sometimes under duress and usually in no spirit of compassion, nevertheless it was moving towards implementing an important principle.

This was the principle of the national mininum, whereby all citizens, whatever their circumstances, would be prevented from falling below a tolerable level of existence. So in the area of unemployment Britain, through the out-of-work donations of the immediate post-war years and the countless amendments to the Act of 1920, was establishing a significantly new practice. Entitlement to support for the unemployed was not being confined to those who had possessed the opportunity and the will to insure against adversity. All sections of the unemployed, it was gradually being decided in practice, were entitled to adequate means of subsistence without the humiliation of pauperization.

Perhaps this summed up, in the area of government, the impact of the war upon a British society already subject in the pre-war years to strong impulses both towards change and against it. In post-war Britain all things would not be made new. Yet some things – in areas where the need for improvement was great but strong economic pressures were working the other way – would be made rather better.

III

There was another area where, during the war, great hopes had been held out not so much for innovation as for restoration. This was agriculture. There existed before the war a strong feeling, particularly among sections of Conservatives, that Britain had treated its rural sector badly. The food crisis of 1917 and 1918 gave this view powerful reinforcement, by revealing the peril of a country so largely dependent on imported food. And the conversion from pasture to arable occasioned by this crisis created an obligation to maintain grain prices at a high level for some years after the war. As long as the war lasted a guaranteed price for cereals was not needed, given the market level of prices. But the process of conversion was so onerous as to call for a high return for cereals well into the post-war period. The Corn Production Act of 1917 was intended to guard cereal producers against a fall in prices at least until 1922.

The other major provision, the guaranteed wage for rural labourers, was evidence that what was intended was a large measure of rural renewal. Yet this intention existed alongside another strong conviction: that Britons should not be required to pay a price for their wheat in excess of the world market price. The Cabinet in February 1917 was aware of the dilemma:

if they declined to give the guarantee to farmers, the country might, in view of a possible intensification of submarine warfare, find itself in a serious position owing to a decrease in home production of cereals due to the refusal of farmers to cultivate crops. If, on the contrary, the farmers were guaranteed the prices, it might result in a position after the war in which the State was paying for crops prices far in excess of what the state of the international market required.[5]

(The first point seems a trifle confused. The 'serious position' resulting from 'a possible intensification of submarine warfare' would hardly be a falling off in home production, but in imports.)

This reluctance to pay a higher price for food than was absolutely necessary, even in order to stimulate home production, was firmly founded in recent British history. High food prices would either depress the living standards of Britain's wage earners or push up wage levels and so the costs of manufactured goods. Subsidies to farmers, enabling them to compete on the home market against cheaper imported food, would burden the taxpayer and affect the competitiveness of Britain's exporters. It was on such grounds that Englishmen after 1870 had imported cheap grain and allowed the home producer to go to the wall.

The problem was that, after the war, the country could not have it both ways. Should the price of cereals overseas fall below a level at which the British farmer could produce, then a decision would have to be made. Paramountcy might be given to the rural revival, so lessening Britain's danger in any future war and redressing the balance between town and country. Or it might be decided that low taxation and viable export industries must take precedence over considerations of defence and rural revival.

The Agriculture Act of 1920 appeared to opt for the first alternative. Guaranteed minimum prices for wheat and oats, and guaranteed mimimum wages for agricultural labourers, were renewed. The Parliamentary Secretary for Agriculture, in speaking to the measure, referred to the clear intention of Parliament that the guaranteed price would not be terminated without four years' notice. But at the time he spoke world prices for cereals remained high. It was an open question whether the guarantee was a serious commitment or a gamble that the good times would continue.

Within a year Britain's farmers were to make an interesting discovery concerning the operation of the British constitution. It is a truism that no Parliament can bind its successor. What now became evident was that this Parliament had not even bound itself. Confronted with a fall in world prices beyond anyone's expectations, and so with a correspondingly high bill to assure the farmers (for the first time) of their guaranteed price, Government and Parliament abandoned the measure. The promised four years' notice was simply disregarded. A form of financial compensation at a lower level for one year was substituted, and as a further sop to the farmer the guaranteed wage to rural labourers was also abandoned. In the words of Edith Whetham: 'As the farmers began to harvest the crops of 1921, all that remained of agricultural policy was an official belief in the virtues of uncontrolled prices, at a time of disordered currencies, world-wide deflation of prices, and persistent unemployment in Britain's major industries.'[6]

This government about-turn has been termed the Great Betrayal. In an obvious sense the expression seems apt. On a more subtle level what is being observed yet again is the failure to match the noble aspirations engendered by war with hard-headed appreciation of the costs involved in fulfilling them. The Government, along with many

---

[5] Quoted in Edith H. Whetham, *The Agrarian History of England and Wales* (Cambridge: Cambridge University Press, 1978), vol. 8, p. 91.
[6] Ibid., p. 141.

citizens, willed a rural revival as they willed 'a fit land for heroes'. They did not will the economic burdens that presented themselves as the price of converting aspiration into reality. The Government beat an undignified retreat, and suffered in public standing for so doing. But the citizens – including many ex-servicemen – who berated it for falling so far short of its promises did not necessarily want it to incur the costs of fulfilling them. Very often they joined in the chants set up by disgruntled politicians and stunt journalists for 'anti-waste', cheap government, and low taxation. The consequence of such demands must be to withdraw from government the resources by which even a partial rural revival – let alone a land fit for heroes – might be accomplished.

IV

But a word more must be said about the contribution of this war to guided change in Britain. That contribution did not end in the period of the 'aftermath' or even of the 'inter-war years'. It persisted into and beyond the Second World War – even though the further one moves from 1918, the more difficult it becomes to distinguish the impact of the Great War from that of other forces.

In his poem 'To a Conscript of 1940', Herbert Read wrote concerning the outcome of the earlier conflict: 'The world was not renewed.' In that utterance he was expressing the conviction that the Great War had carried with it a promise of betterment that had yet to be fulfilled. Legislators after 1918, on account of chicane or of circumstances they had proved unequal to controlling, had left the task for another generation to complete. The low esteem in which Lloyd George was held for so long after his fall from office in 1922 sprang in good part from the conviction that he had promised a better world in return for the nation's labours and had not kept that promise.

The significant social legislation of the decade following 1940 is attributed to the impact of Hitler's war on British society. In good measure this is true. But one facet of that society was the belief that large commitments to social improvement had been entered into in the years 1914–18 and that most of these commitments remained outstanding. The idea that a great war, by calling forth the energies of a whole nation, was entitling all elements to a decent existence, and one that the state must ensure, had established a firm grip by the 1940s. It existed alongside the conviction that after the First World War the rank and file of the nation had been denied their entitlement. After the Second no such transgression must be allowed.

PART EIGHTEEN

Settling Up

75

Stern Reckoning I

But I must not go on like this [denouncing the terms of the peace settlement]. I really have nothing practical to suggest, as the dimensions of the problem are beyond me, perhaps beyond human power.

General Smuts to a friend, 14 May 1919

I

On 9 November 1918 Lloyd George spoke at the Lord Mayor's Banquet at the Guildhall in London. The event was not exceptional. By custom the Prime Minister addressed this annual gathering. Therefore the occasion should have been Lloyd George's second appearance. But, as he recalled, 12 months earlier he had been prevented from attending by the disaster that had befallen the Italian armies, requiring his presence on Italian soil.

Lloyd George delivered his first Lord Mayor's address to an audience athrob with expectation of the approaching end of hostilities. He reviewed the course of the past 12 months. The period of the Italian calamity had found the war in a dire state, with Russia out of the firing line, America not yet effectively in, and the submarine depredations continuing. But worse was yet to come. He recalled how 'in the springtime' – and, according to an observer, he used this 'phrase of tragic irony' again and again – 'the concentrated fury of the Teutonic strength burst upon our armies, and for a moment the line was broken.' His audience, even in the happier times now obtaining, was visibly moved by the recollection.

Lloyd George went on to contrast the events of the spring with what was happening in the autumn. He had recently spent a week in Versailles. In those beautiful forests the leaves were falling: but not only they. 'Empires and kingdoms, and kings and crowns, were falling like leaves before the gale.' Then, in what was deemed the most dramatic moment in his exposition, Lloyd George proclaimed: 'The potent Empire which threatened civilisation is now to-night headless and helpless. The Kaiser and the Crown Prince have abdicated.... Was there ever a more dramatic judgment – judgment, and I say again, judgment – in the history of the world?'

Germany's doom, Lloyd George told his audience, was sealed. The terms of peace must discourage arrogance and ambition from repeating this atrocity. Britain intended nothing against the liberty of the German people. But justice, divine justice, must be satisfied. There had been four and a half years of horrors, and millions had been slain: 'the country that recklessly plunged the world into that agony must expect a stern reckoning.'[1]

---

[1] This account is taken from E. C. Bentley, *Peace Year in the City 1918–1919*, printed for private circulation (London, 1920), pp. 1–23.

Two points in this utterance are worth bearing in mind when we look at the endeavours of the peace-makers. The first is the momentous political changes occurring in Europe and the magnitude of the problems that they would present to any group attempting a stable settlement: 'Empires and kingdoms, and kings and crowns, were falling like leaves before the gale.'

The second is the frame of mind of those who would be making the peace. There is no suggestion in Lloyd George's speech that the war had come about accidentally or through a failure in the diplomatic system. Nor is there any implication that what was required in the aftermath was an impartial arbitrator, seeking a settlement agreeable to all parties. The war, with its four and a half years of horrors and its millions of dead, was (according to this utterance) no dreadful accident but a deliberate criminal act: the work of 'the potent Empire which threatened civilisation', 'the country that recklessly plunged the world into that agony'. Correspondingly, what lay ahead at the peace conference was not arbitration, and certainly not forgiving and forgetting, but 'a stern reckoning', 'justice, divine justice', 'judgment, and I say again, judgment'.

II

The war ended with an armistice. So the process of peace-making began theoretically from the position that the terms of settlement must be agreed on by both sides to the quarrel. If agreement could not be reached, the fighting might be resumed. The reality was quite otherwise. The relationship of the two sides was that of victor and vanquished. Germany had sued for an end to the fighting. And the armistice terms to which it had consented were so severe that it could not possibly resume the struggle. There was no basis here for the negotiation of an agreed treaty – and no will on the part of the victors to proceed in such a manner. They would have trouble enough agreeing among themselves.

The Peace Conference was held in Paris during the first six months of 1919. (As it happened, none of the five treaties with the ex-enemy states was signed in the French capital and so none took its name.) Many countries were represented at Paris. But all along the affairs of the conference were dominated by what the treaty called 'the principal Allied and Associated Powers' – Britain, France, and Italy, which were allied, and the USA, which was associated. It was easy for these four to function among themselves because of the continued existence, in what was not yet peacetime, of the Supreme War Council. The leaders of these countries, Lloyd George, Clemenceau, Orlando, and Woodrow Wilson, could easily move from functioning as the Supreme War Council, which dealt with problems of the Armistice, to being the council of Four, which considered the terms of peace. (For a time Japan figured in this select company. But its interests were soon attended to.)

Always there were smaller countries demanding an equal voice. Always Clemenceau, as president of the peace conference, was prepared to remind them that the Big Four at the time of the Armistice had 12 million men in the field. The smaller powers might state their cases, and sometimes might hope to get their way. But they were left in no doubt that the decisions would be made by the big powers who had won the victory.

However, there was one big nation that, having contributed signally to the defeat of the Central Powers before dropping out of the fight, would not have a hand in the decision-making. The new rulers of Russia did not want to be represented at the conference table and were not wanted there. They believed that the men who sat in judgement at Paris were as doomed as the forces that had lately ruled in Germany (the extent of whose demise they probably overestimated). As for the negotiators in Paris, they devoutly trusted that the new rulers of Russia would soon be sent packing. What was more, they were prepared to give some assistance to the anti-Bolshevik forces fighting on the periphery of Russia. They did so with an uneasy conscience and in too limited a fashion to affect the course of events – except to exacerbate Bolshevik hostility towards themselves.

The course of events in Russia did not constitute a part of the peace settlement. Nevertheless, those events serve to highlight a fundamental point concerning the activities of the peace-makers. There were important regions of Europe where their writ did not run and where the major facets of the post-war settlement would be decided without regard to them. That is, the Big Four, either separately or together, did not have it within their resources to ordain the new face of all Europe – let alone the world.

For one thing, their armies of 12 million were beginning to melt away. The American forces had set out from their homeland singing, 'We won't be back 'til it's over over there.' Now they considered that it was over. Both they and the folks back home were clamouring for their return. Certainly, the shipping space that Britain and France had so eagerly made available to bring them to Europe was not being offered to take them back. But it was idle to imagine that the American forces in Europe could be employed on large-scale treaty-enforcing operations.

Similarly, by January 1919 in the British army the clamour for demobilization had reached ominous proportions. At one British port 19,000 soldiers whose leave had expired refused to re-embark for France, while in London others demonstrated with placards reading, 'We won the war. Give us our tickets.' At the end of January Churchill, who had just been appointed War Minister for the purpose of hastening demobilization, announced that the army would in short order be reduced from 3 million to 900,000. Two and a half months later some 78 per cent of rank-and-file soldiers and 55 per cent of officers had been discharged.

Of course, in the absence of adequate military forces there might have been another way of persuading refractory parts of Europe to bow to the wills of the peace-makers. This was blockade. But blockade, just because its most evident victims were likely to be women and children, could in the absence of actual conflict become a repugnant proceeding. Deep misgivings were aroused among some of the victors about the continuation of the blockade of Germany during the Armistice – an action taken in part because when the Germans stopped fighting they still possessed a formidable army and in part because the new rulers of Germany refused to turn over their merchant ships to the Allies even for the purpose of obtaining food. Anyway, as events in Russia were showing, there were crucial parts of Europe where blockade could not determine the course of events any more effectively than could (admittedly half-hearted) military intervention.

This point needs to be stressed, in that judgement on the peace settlement so often seems to spring from the assumption that the negotiators in Paris were in a position to make all things new. Certainly, this was a delusion under which the negotiators themselves seemed sometimes to be labouring. Wilson on one occasion, finding the representatives of Italy intransigent about the matter of apportioning territory between themselves and Yugoslavia, decided to appeal over the heads of the Italian delegates to the Italian people. This *démarche* was not a success. The Italian delegates indignantly absented themselves from the conference table for a fortnight. Their fellow countrymen showed no inclination to repudiate their conduct. The frame of mind that had inspired Italy to enter the war in 1915 on the terms of the highly acquisitive Treaty of London was a force with which the peace-makers must still reckon in 1919.

Even in some major areas where it appeared that the peace-makers were doing the deciding, the main course of events was not in their hands. During the war British policy-makers had spent some time considering the fate of Austria-Hungary. Should that empire continue to exist, though on a much more federal basis (so as to meet some of the aspirations of the submerged nationalities)? Or should it be disintegrated? The views of Britain's rulers tended to oscillate. Sometimes they hoped to seduce the Hapsburgs into abandoning Germany and making a separate peace, in which case they inclined towards the former view. At others they had no such hopes, in which case they encouraged the separatist movements so as to weaken the Hapsburg state. In the outcome these contemplations were of little consequence. By the time the peace conference gathered, the Austro-Hungarian Empire, like Humpty-Dumpty, had disintegrated. Nothing the Big Four might do would reassemble it. The establishment of Czechoslovakia, Poland, and Yugoslavia, the enlargement of Romania and Italy, and the separation of Hungary from Austria, were all established facts.

The most that the Big Four at Paris might do was to try to impose frontiers that would make these states economically and politically viable, apportion population in the ethnically confused areas to the most appropriate recipients, and try to provide safeguards for the various minorities. It was no simple task. Sometimes populations of different nationalities were hopelessly intermingled, as with Romanians and Hungarians. Sometimes the demands of defensibility clashed with the ethnic principle: Czechoslovakia needed the Sudetenland to become politically viable *vis-à-vis* its neighbours, but the Sudetenland was inhabited by Austrians (the so-called Sudeten Germans). In almost all these disputed areas the vanquished countries tended to come out badly, to the advantage of the victors and the succession states. But the disputes concerned areas in which, whatever the decision, some element of injustice had to be done, and it is not usually evident that a different decision would have been more just.

What does need to be stressed is that all these disputed matters dealt only with the peripheries. As far as the fate of the Austro-Hungarian Empire was concerned, the peace treaties in the main did not decide events but simply put their seal on events that were already irreversible. (The decision to forbid any merger of Austria with Germany was a different matter. But this really concerned the peace settlement with Germany. It expressed France's dismay at the possibility of confronting an enlarged rather than a reduced Germany.)

The settlement with Turkey was in some respects different. But in its final outcome, four years after the event, it also demonstrated how limited were the powers of the peace-makers in some regions. The course of the war had decided the disintegration of the Turkish Empire in Asia as thoroughly as it had put paid to the empire of Austria-Hungary. The main thing left for the victors to conclude was into which of their spheres of influence the various Arab states would fall.

But the British Government was determined to constrict the Turkish state with the utmost severity – although the Cabinet balked at Lloyd George's urge to deny it even Constantinople. The British view was embodied in the terms of the Treaty of Sèvres. However, that treaty was soon placed in jeopardy when Mustapha Kemal began raising rebellion against the Sultan and, in April 1920, set up a provisional Government. It then became evident how limited was the power of the Allies (which meant the British) to impose the terms they had decreed. On 24 March 1920 Churchill, as War Minister, presented this situation bluntly to Lloyd George: 'With military resources which the

Cabinet have cut to the most weak and slender proportions, we are leading the Allies in an attempt to enforce a peace on Turkey which would require great and powerful armies and long, costly operations and occupations.'[2]

Lloyd George was not to be deterred. But equally he was not prepared to pretend that Britain could provide the necessary forces itself. Instead he set about encouraging the Greeks to impose the Allied will (notwithstanding Churchill's warning, in the same missive: 'On this world so torn with strife I dread to see you let loose the Greek armies – for all our sakes and certainly their sakes'). As Churchill predicted, the outcome proved calamitous, especially for the Greeks. After a succession of advances that hopelessly over-stretched their lines of supply, they were routed in 1922 by the renascent Turkish forces. The Turks then proceeded to advance, from the Asian side, into the 'zone of the Straits' occupied since 1919 by the British. This zone contained the areas of Turkey that embraced the Sea of Marmora, from Constantinople in the north to Chanak, Kum Kale, and other names redolent of the Dardanelles expedition in the south. Late in September 1922 the British forces of occupation received from Lloyd George and Churchill a bellicose directive to act against the Turks. This, happily, was ignored by General Harington, Plumer's former aide and the commander on the spot. Yet more happily, the Turks were persuaded to halt. But all prospect of enforcing the original treaty had departed. In 1923 it was necessary to negotiate another and more lenient settlement. The realities of power, and the lack thereof, had firmly imposed themselves on the process of peace-making.

III

If the peace settlements in the old empires of Austria-Hungary and Turkey were decided largely without regard to the peace-makers at Paris, that did not matter too much. The main lines of those settlements – the break-up of the empires into their ethnic parts – suited the victors well. They conformed with the concept of national self-determination, and they reduced these ex-enemy states to very modest dimensions. Anyway the war against Austria-Hungary and Turkey, though involving Britain in some painful and a few rewarding episodes, had in truth consisted of sideshows. For Britain, as for France and the USA, the war had in essence been against Germany: against what they deemed to be German aggression, German expansionism, and German militarism. Two great questions confronted the peace-makers. Did they have the capacity, or even the opportunity, to make a good peace with Germany? And did they have the resources to ensure that whatever peace they made would be adhered to?

The peace settlement with Germany, the Treaty of Versailles, embodied five main aspects. The first (which appeared also in the separate treaties with Austria, with Hungary, with Bulgaria, and with Turkey) dealt with the establishment of the League of Nations. The second compelled the German state to surrender territory that Germany or its predecessors had annexed in earlier wars. The third set about inhibiting Germany's powers for waging aggressive war in the future. The fourth laid down the payment of reparations. The fifth gave legality to the transfer of Germany's former colonies to the victor powers.

The last of these went without saying. The German colonies had been of little benefit in Germany's economic life: they symbolized the desire for a place in the sun but had not provided much heat or light. Outside Germany they had aroused jealousy and anxiety. They were seen as a weapon in Germany's naval threat to Britain. And

[2] Quoted in David Walder, 'The Graeco-Turkish War', in *Purnell's History of the First World War* (London: Purnell & Sons, 1969–71), issue no. 125, p. 3484.

they were coveted by other countries that regarded them as falling within their own spheres of influence. In the course of the war, and in most instances pretty early in the war, they had been overrun: by Britain, Australia, New Zealand, South Africa, or Japan. None of these countries intended to hand them back.

To reconcile the fact of annexation with the liberal principles of self-determination and a peace without annexations, the former German colonies were not formally acquired by the occupying powers. They were deemed to be mandates under the League of Nations. The new rulers received control over these territories as a matter of trust from the League, to whom ultimate authority was regarded as belonging. Whether this meant little or much was likely to depend on whether the League itself managed to acquire any considerable authority.

Other deprivations sustained by Germany were more material. It lost territory in Europe that it had secured during distant wars and recent wars: Polish territory acquired during the partitions of the eighteenth century, north Schleswig annexed from Denmark in 1864, Alsace-Lorraine taken from France in 1871, and Russian territory occupied in accordance with the Draconian treaty of Brest-Litovsk. In the case of the more recent acquisitions (from Denmark, France, and Russia) redrawing Germany's boundaries was not difficult. But establishing the boundaries of a revived Poland caused the peace-makers untold agony – and was to prove productive of vast resentment in Germany. (There is a myth that German hostility to the terms of the treaty was directed only at clauses that varied from Wilson's 14 Points. This has little substance. The Polish aspects of the treaty, to which such exception was taken, were fully in accord with the 14 Points.)

It had been laid down that the Polish state must have access to the sea, which meant that Germany must lose Danzig, notwithstanding its predominantly German population. This port did not, however, go fully to Poland, being administered by the League. And in the important industrial region of Upper Silesia the population was terribly mixed, if only because Germany had deliberately colonized these areas – all government employment, for example, had been reserved for speakers of the German language. The population, consequently, was one in which the Poles provided the labour force and the Germans the ruling class, as land owners, mine owners, and civil servants. It is not wonderful that the 2 million Germans who found themselves included in the new Poland were deeply resentful, on grounds of class as well as of nationality.

Other territorial rearrangements that affected Germany concerned not national self-determination but reparation: that is, payment for damage done. This was the case with the Saar, which was separated from Germany and placed under League administration for 15 years as part of an attempt to make good Germany's deliberate desolation of the industrial areas of Belgium and northern France. This issue merged with that of reparations proper.

Here was the most controversial, if not necessarily the most important, aspect of the peace settlement. Should Germany be forced to make recompense for the damage and injury which it had inflicted on its adversaries? The argument against doing so was strong. To levy heavy reparations recalled, whether accurately or not, the vengeful treaties of the past and so smacked of the 'old diplomacy'. Also, it was likely to prolong the atmosphere of hostility between victor and vanquished far into the future. What was more, the economic effects of requiring one power to give away as reparations large quantities of raw materials and manufactured goods to other countries were difficult to foretell. But they might be considerable and not wholly beneficial, not only to giver and even receiver but also to third parties trying to trade in the same commodities. Finally, as far as Britain was concerned, the issue of reparations was so besmirched by its role in the 'coupon' election that it must appear not as an act of justice but as the working out of a political stunt.

Yet there were powerful grounds for asserting that Germany should make heavy payment. The war had inflicted desolation upon large areas of France and Belgium (without comparable effect upon Germany), had destroyed much British shipping, had burdened these countries with huge overseas debts, and had placed on them the responsibility of providing for the maimed and for the dependents of the fallen. Someone had to make good this destruction, pay these debts, fulfil these obligations. Should it be the countries subjected to these depredations or the country that had inflicted them?

It is not surprising that the latter view gained the ascendancy among the victors, if only in the short term. But it raised any number of problems. If Germany were to be made to pay, what was it to pay for – the whole war or only civilian damages? And how much could Germany be expected to pay? In a way the former question was academic. Admittedly, estimates of Germany's capacity to pay varied widely. Whereas the British economist J. M. Keynes put it at only £2,000 million a committee of British 'financial experts' (which included Lord Cunliffe, Governor of the Bank of England) went as high as £24,000 million – although Cunliffe halved this figure soon after. But on either estimate the figure was unlikely to cover even civilian damages, so that discussion of Germany's possible responsibility for the whole cost of the war could well have been dispensed with. (When Britain managed to have war pensions included among civilian damages it was not trying to increase the total that Germany should pay, although it might look like that. What Britain was hoping to do was to increase the share it would get vis-à-vis France and Belgium.)

In the end the peace-makers found the task of setting a reparations figure too formidable, their advisers too various, and the times too suffused with hatred. So they delegated the matter to a body of experts, who were to reach a conclusion in two years. However the treaty did demand of Germany an immediate payment of £1,000 million and interest-bearing bonds for another £4,000 million, which envisaged an ultimate figure well in excess of Keynes's estimate. (In April 1921 the figure was fixed at £6.6 thousand million, plus interest.) And they framed the demand for reparations in terms that, although compatible with moderation in practice, gave an appearance of the utmost severity.

Article 231 of the treaty required Germany to accept responsibility for all loss and damage sustained by the Western powers 'as a consequence of the war imposed upon them by Germany and her allies'. This was the famous 'war guilt' clause – in which, as it happens, the word 'guilt' does not appear. The next clause took away in practice most of the severity just bestowed in theory. It recognized that 'the resources of Germany are not adequate ... to make complete reparation for all such loss and damage.' It therefore demanded only that Germany make compensation for all damage done to civilian property by its aggression 'by land, by sea and from the air'. Such a lesser demand appears to have much warrant – as a statement of entitlement, if not as a feasible objective. Whatever qualifications may be admitted to Germany's responsibility for the outbreak of the war, its responsibility certainly seems so large as to warrant the obligation that it make good civilian damages, however defined.

The point that the 'war guilt' clause occupied so limited a place in the treaty deserves to be stressed. For the clause came to be seen, in Germany and among the critics of the treaty in the West, as the sole justification for any demand whatever for reparations – as well as for all those other sections of the treaty to which German opinion took exception. It was taken to follow that unless Germany had been wholly responsible for the war, no reparations were justified. In fact, Article 231 was employed only as warrant for a scale of reparations that the treaty then went on explicity to forgo.

However, this point should not be carried too far. Despite appearances, it is improbable that the 'war guilt' clause actually caused the repudiation of the treaty by Germany or its discredit in the West. For that one must seek profounder, and more various, causes.

IV

The manner in which the treaty set out the demand for reparations was to have another unfortunate consequence. By pitching the theoretical demand for reparations so high, the treaty-makers laid themselves open to the charge that the scale of reparations actually being demanded was out of all reason. They thereby played into the hands of one expert who was prepared to make that charge anyway – and to see a difference of opinion on this matter not as a dispute between economists but as a struggle between darkness and light, or anyway between malevolent passion and sweet reason. The expert in question was J. M. Keynes.

The role that Keynes played in discrediting the peace settlement, though often exaggerated, was of real importance. Keynes was an academic and economist of unquestioned brilliance. By the time he went to Cambridge as an undergraduate (in 1902) stories of his exceptional abilities had preceded him from Eton. After one term at university he was invited to join the group of outstanding senior students known as the Apostles. (They included Lytton Strachey and Leonard Woolf.) He rapidly established himself as a leading member of this body, which abounded with literary figures, philosophers, and mathematicians. That is, although he was to prove himself the most brilliant economist of his generation, he was a good deal more. He was a product of Cambridge rationalism with a deep distrust of religious dogma, a good European who despised nationalistic hatred, and an intimate of the Bloomsbury group and of Lady Ottoline Morrell's pacifist circle.

In the war years, it has been said,[3] Keynes was in effect a pacifist who felt that the war, once begun, must be gone through with: 'there is really no practical alternative,' he told Bertrand Russell and Lytton Strachey (who took a different view). So he brought his formidable qualities as an economist to the services of the British Government, specializing in inter-Allied loans. At the same time he did not turn his back on his pacifist friends, for whom he testified before the tribunals. It may be guessed how useful he was to the British Government that these other activities did not unseat him.

Keynes went to the peace conference as principal representative of the Treasury and as deputy for the Chancellor of the Exchequer. He did not confine himself to conferring with experts about reparations. He found time also to observe the world leaders assembled there and to notice their foibles. And he became very oppressed by the atmosphere of hatred, and the crude exaltation in victory, that pervaded the French capital. Unable to carry the day for setting reparations at the low level that he believed was alone feasible, he resigned his post and returned to England. There he wrote, in passion, a denunciation of the events he had witnessed. It was called *The Economic Consequences of the Peace* and appeared in November 1919. Within a month Keynes was

---

[3] See Leon Edel, *Bloomsbury: A House of Lions* (London: The Hogarth Press, 1979), p. 233.

informing friends that his work was being 'smothered . . . in a deluge of approval' and (tongue-in-cheek) that it might bring him 'a chit from the PM at any moment telling me how profoundly the book represents his views'.[4]

As Leon Edel remarks, Keynes in his book 'spoke not only as an economist but as one of the pacifists and humanists of Bloomsbury'. He wrote of the reparations clauses as certain to bring ruin and starvation to Germany and consequent dislocation to the whole of Europe. And he attributed this monstrous proceeding to the personal failings of the three leading peace-makers: Clemenceau, Wilson, and Lloyd George. In the case of Clemenceau an explanation of such conduct was not (for Keynes) far to seek. Athirst for revenge, Clemenceau did not hesitate to inflict economic desolation on Germany. The cases of Wilson and Lloyd George were more complex. They were men of Nonconformist and liberal backgrounds, who were expected to strive for a peace of reconciliation. But, Keynes concluded, they were liberals without substance. Wilson, a self-advertised Presbyterian, he saw as a pious humbug and (what was almost as bad) as 'slow' in intellect. So the President was easily 'bamboozled' by a cleverer man like Lloyd George into condoning a settlement that ran contrary to all his professed principles. (He proved less easy to 'debamboozle' when Lloyd George realized that they had gone too far.)

As for the British Prime Minister, Keynes judged that for all his great abilities he was, in terms of principle, 'void'. He took on the colour of his immediate surroundings: namely the group of politicians with whom he was presently conniving and the audiences he was engaged in entertaining and manipulating. He may have held good liberal notions about the peace settlement when he embarked on the election of 1918, as his speech to his Liberal supporters on 12 November revealed. But he was the ally of Conservatives engaged in smashing the Liberal Party. And he was seeking the favour of audiences thirsting for vengeance against Germany. So by the end of the election, thanks to his reckless promises and his 'hard-faced' parliamentary followers, he was bound hand and foot to adopt Clemenceau's position. Into that same position he was obliged to lure the hapless American President; a course that Wilson lacked the fixity of principle to resist. The tragedy of Paris, with its blighted hopes for a good peace, followed irresistibly.

There is much in Keynes's account that chimes with the facts. It seems, nevertheless, over-simplified and distorted. The level of reparations was certainly set too high to be economically feasible. Economics, therefore, required that France and Belgium should bear a considerable share of the cost of repairing the destruction deliberately wrought upon them by their enemy, and that the British taxpayer must largely support injured ex-servicemen and the dependents of the slain. But, with far less justification, Keynes made it appear that morality also required this, and that what had been decided upon regarding reparations was an outrage upon decency. This did not follow from his economic arguments.

Nor was Keynes's analysis of cause and effect – that is, his attribution of the reparations proposals to the personal deficiencies of the Allied leaders – without blemish. For one thing, his hostile judgements on these men did not derive solely from the peace conference. In the words of Robert Skidelsky: 'it is clear that the fury which went into *The Economic Consequences of the Peace* . . . had been building up throughout the war. The attitudes he displayed in that book – mistrust of Lloyd George, contempt for the Americans, anger that politics had ousted reason, fear of general impoverishment – had all poured out in his wartime letters.' So, back in April 1918, he had written of the British Prime Minister: 'Still and even more confidently I attribute our

---

[4] Quoted in Robert Skidelsky, *John Maynard Keynes* (London: Macmillan, 1983), vol. 1, p. 392.

misfortunes to George. We are governed by a crook and the results are natural.'[5] Moreover, it is fair to speculate that he was in a measure casting upon the Allied leaders his own burden of guilt: for having contributed so signally to the successful prosecution of a war to which he had become a conscientious objector.

Keynes's attribution of the unsatisfactory conclusion on reparations to the personal shortcomings of the three principal decision-makers deserves to be challenged. Clemenceau was not just a single-minded fanatic: he believed – and not without reason – that his country not only had been but still was in grave external danger. Wilson, in coming to see an element of truth in this attitude, was not necessarily being shallow and self-deluding. As for Lloyd George, it is not plain that his true position, from which he deviated for unworthy motives, lay with a peace of 'reconciliation'. Indeed, it is arguable that the Prime Minister was never playing to an audience more outrageously than when, as a step towards launching the election, he spoke on 12 November of such a peace. Three days earlier, as we have seen, Lloyd George in referring to a peace settlement had placed the emphasis differently. Then the precondition of a restored Europe had not been that Germany should be let off lightly. Rather, it had been that Germany should be taught the error of its ways, by passing through 'a stern reckoning' and by being brought to 'judgment, and I say again, judgment'.

Lloyd George, it may be thought, was aware that there was no self-evidently correct course to be adopted towards Germany, either of reconciliation or of punitive action. The nature of the German problem confronting the peace-makers was deeply ambiguous. Hence Lloyd George lacked Keynes's confidence that the one course was right and the other wrong. (This is not to justify Lloyd George's conduct in advocating each course separately, sometimes in the most extravagant ways, when it suited his political book. Nor can it be doubted that in so doing he marred all his best endeavours thereafter.) So, quite possibly, the actions of Lloyd George, as of Wilson, in Paris did not spring just from personal failings. They may have derived from the Prime Minister's (and the President's) recognition of the profound uncertainties in the situation and of the inherent strengths in Clemenceau's position. By the same token Keynes's failure to recognize this, and his determination to account for what occurred by *ad hominem* arguments, may be attributable to his own limitations of perception – limitations common to 'the pacifists and humanists of Bloomsbury'.

Keynes rejected Clemenceau's pessimistic view of human nature in general and of German nature in particular. Equally, he rejected Clemenceau's narrow nationalism for a wider vision of European civilization. It is proper to admire Keynes's precepts and to wish that they did constitute a vision of the truth. It is less easy to be confident that they did. And it is by no means certain that, had the sort of peace he advocated been implemented (as, in good measure, it was to be before long), the course of events would have been altogether happier: that the noble side of human nature would have triumphed over the depraved and that Europeanism would have submerged national hatred. It is here, in the end, that the judgement upon Keynes's analysis must rest. Had Germany really ceased to constitute a peril to France and to Western democracy once the Kaiser had been deposed and the fighting ended? Were punitive actions really unwarranted?

The astonishing success of Keynes's book showed that, in Britain, the assumption was present (and was growing) that the answers to these questions were in the affirmative. For traditionally minded diplomats, if they chose to reckon up the manifestations of military power rather than the possession of basic resources, it

---

[5] Skidelsky, *John Maynard Keynes*, pp. 353, 347.

seemed that the time was at hand for one of those old-fashioned diplomatic realignments. France was becoming altogether too strong. Again, for liberals and socialists who had been arguing before 1914 that the manner of conducting diplomacy was deeply flawed, the inclination was growing to regard the war as a terrible accident: Lloyd George himself would soon say that Europe had slipped and stumbled into war, a remark thereafter much quoted against the Versailles treaty. At the same time, among businessmen and financial interests and manufacturers, the conviction was taking hold that the British economy would be set to rights only when the European economy was restored to normal. Reparations came to be regarded as a major obstacle to that end. And, more generally among Britons, the past century's record of improvement rendered repugnant a view of human nature that would make a standing army and a high level of military preparedness – absent from British needs for so long – a continuing necessity.

During the 1920s, as Britain's economic problems settled in and the complexities of European relations became ever more bewildering, endorsement for Keynes's arguments mounted. Before long all belief in reparations as a viable part of the peace settlement departed. With the onset of the great economic depression at the beginning of the 1930s, the opportunity was taken to end them.

But reparations, for all the anguish they generated, were always one of the more peripheral, even expendable, parts of the treaty. The question was whether the Keynesian style of criticism, playing upon the same conjunction of attitudes, would also strike at the treaty's more fundamental aspects: those designed not to make Germany pay some part of the war's costs but to ensure that it could not wage aggressive war again.

76

STERN RECKONING II

I

In various ways the treaty set about depriving Germany of its war-waging capacity. Germany was to be quickly disarmed and to remain disarmed henceforth. It was to have no more battleships and submarines with which to threaten Britain's lifelines. Also, it was not again to have a naval or military air arm, such as had posed against British cities so potentially, if never actually, formidable a menace. Further, Germany was denied the power to conscript its menfolk, and its armed forces were to be kept severely restricted. They would be capable of repressing riot and disorder at home, and that was all.

More than this, it was deemed necessary to deprive the Germans of their jumping-off ground for a renewed invasion of France and Belgium. That jumping-off ground was the Rhineland, the region of Germany lying between the great river Rhine and the borders of France and Belgium. If Germany could not assemble forces on the borders of France, and must indeed hold them on the far side of the Rhine, this would provide France with an early-warning system of great potency. Any repetition of the strike action of August 1914 would be impossible.

The obvious way to carry this out was to separate the Rhineland from Germany and to make it an independent state ruled by what, in effect, would be a French puppet regime. That was what Foch insisted the French must demand. And General Mangin, who was in charge of the French occupying forces in the Rhineland, blatantly connived with elements there to set up a Rhineland separatist Government. Clemenceau knew that the British and the Americans would never consent to this. Their horror at the thought of creating another Alsace-Lorraine forbade it. But he used the proposal as a bargaining counter to get the next best things. These were the military occupation of the Rhineland by Allied forces for what, given his age, would certainly be his lifetime (the period set was 15 years), and its permanent demilitarization thereafter.

That was about as far as the British and American delegates would go in preventing German aggression against France by actually imposing restraints on Germany: enforced disarmament (carrying with it the promise that the Allies would also, in due course, disarm); Allied occupation of the Rhineland for a limited period; and the demilitarization of the Rhineland in perpetuity. Any further action against Germany's war-making capabilities, such as the demolition of its heavy industry, lay beyond anyone's notion of 'stern reckoning' or 'divine justice'. Anyway, it ran directly counter to the concept of reparations.

But there were things the wartime Allies might do among themselves on a much broader scale to prevent a repetition of German aggression towards France. Much had been made of the fact that Germany was encouraged to wage war in the West in 1914 because France had no major ally there. If Britain had been allied to France, it was freely suggested, Germany would have desisted. So in 1919 Lloyd George and Wilson proposed to offer France, as an item additional to the treaty, an alliance whose deterrent effect upon Germany must indeed prove formidable. This was a guarantee that, should France ever again be subject to German aggression, Britain and the USA would automatically come to France's aid.

Nor did this complete the aggression-discouraging, peace-preserving aspects of the treaty. Included within it was a provision that would not only provide France with its merited security against German attack but would also hold out a prospect of general international tranquillity. This was the League of Nations.

II

From early in the war thoughtful people in Britain were seeking a course of action which would save their country from further such calamities. The answers they proposed tended to depend on how they perceived the causes of the present conflict. The war could be seen as resulting from a breakdown in the machinery of diplomatic negotiation. What was needed, therefore, was a permanent body serving as arbitrator to which crises would automatically be referred. The mere fact of a cooling-off period would enable powers to pull back from the brink. But the war could also be seen as the product of deliberate aggression. In that case what was required was an institution which would gather together at the outset a phalanx of law-enforcing countries, such as existed by 1918. If the aggressor had known in 1914 that he would face not only his potential victims but a determined coalition of the law-abiding, he would have had good cause to desist.

Many Britons, of course, did not see the alternatives this sharply. They oscillated between the two positions, or saw the war as the product of both diplomatic malfunction and German design. They envisaged a peace-preserving body that would act as both arbitrator and law enforcer.

By the end of the war, support in Britain for an international organization fulfilling one or both of these functions was widespread, at least among the politically aware. This was especially the case with those whose politics were of the left and middle. They included churchmen and trade unionists, editors and journalists of the more responsible newspapers, academics and senior statesmen. There was much less support for such notions among right-wingers and the devotees of Empire. To them the idea of referring Britain's international affairs to a body consisting largely of foreigners was disagreeable, if not a downright affront. Yet even many of the more conservatively inclined were prepared to believe that such an organization could serve some purpose. And one committed Conservative, Robert Cecil, was to become the League's most devoted supporter in Britain.

At the peace conference, however, the most impassioned advocate of the establishment of a peace-preserving body was the President of the United States. Wilson saw it as his chief mission in coming to Europe to have such an institution not merely set up but written into the peace treaty. In this he proved successful. But his success concealed a mass of ambiguities.

Support for the concept of a League of Nations was general at the peace conference. But not everyone was envisaging the same kind of League. At least three distinct views existed as to the nature and function of the body. And although these views might exist alongside each other, anyway until the League was put to the test, fundamentally they were in conflict. In what follows they will be called the Clemenceau, Lloyd George, and Wilson views. This may seem an over-simplification. But it is not grossly misleading, and it provides a helpful piece of shorthand.

The first view, that of Clemenceau and the French, favoured a strong League, with teeth, but serving only a limited object. That object was to keep Germany in check. For this purpose the League should have a standing army capable of enforcing the treaty upon Germany. The French idea of the League, then, emphasized law enforcement and collective security, but only with regard to one potential law breaker. Clemenceau certainly did not take the view that all France's lost lives and lost treasure should be placed at the services of other possibly endangered nations that had lifted no finger on France's behalf.

Second, there was the view of Lloyd George, which was also the view of Sir Maurice Hankey and most of the more conservative League supporters in Britain. They envisaged a body whose function was conciliation and arbitration. A League country involved in a dispute would be obliged to submit the matter to arbitration and observe a cooling-off period: there would be no resort to force for three months after the judgement of the arbitrators had been handed down. But if after that the aggrieved member remained unappeased and engaged in acts of war, there would be no automatic obligation on the rest of the world body to intervene. Nations would still, on this most vital matter, consult their vital interests. That is, the League would be universal in scope but would lack teeth.

The third view was that not only of Woodrow Wilson but also of important British and Commonwealth figures like Smuts and Robert Cecil. They envisaged the League as having responsibility for both arbitration and collective security. It would not only intervene between disputants but would see that its judgements were enforced. An act of war in defiance of a League decision would constitute aggression not against one member but against all. And all would take punitive action against the law breaker. They would sever not only diplomatic but economic relations: that is, they would institute an economic blockade. They would also consider, but not necessarily act on, proposals by the League for military action. The Wilson view, it should be noted, did not envisage a permanent peace-keeping force attached to the League. In part this was because no one could anticipate the size and composition of such a force when it was not directed against any particular country. In part it stemmed from the great trust placed in the general severance of diplomatic and economic relations for halting an aggressor.

It is instructive to notice how these three concepts of the League overlap and fail to overlap. Both the first and third views place great emphasis on collective security, the law-enforcing aspect. But the advocates of the third view did not accept the necessity for a permanent peace-keeping force, and the advocates of the first view did not believe that collective security could or should be universal. For those taking the Clemenceau view, collective security was about restraining Germany, not (to suggest examples hardly chosen at random) about preventing far-off Japan from attacking even more remote China or France's good friend Italy from overrunning the backward African state of Abyssinia. In incidents such as these, advocates of the Clemenceau view were much closer to advocates of the Lloyd George view: that a nation would engage in hostile acts only if its vital interests were involved.

The overlap between the second and third views was different. They agreed that the League was not just designed to confirm the outcome of the Great War by curtailing Germany. It was intended to apply to all countries and to discourage wars wherever they might threaten to occur. So Lloyd George and Wilson agreed on universal arbitration. Where they differed, fundamentally, was on the issue of universal collective security. To the supporters of the second view this seemed impractical. It might involve Britain in action against its vital interests by requiring it to sever relations with a friendly power for the benefit of one towards which it felt no amity. This seemed an altogether too substantial intrusion on national sovereignty. But to the supporters of the third view, and above all to Wilson himself, here was the heart of the matter. Peace would be ensured only if any potential aggressor knew in advance that all other powers, including those with which it enjoyed good relations and those too far removed to feel involved, would line up beside the country threatened with attack.

There were good reasons why, in the short term, the Wilson view would triumph; that is, why it would be written into the treaty. For one thing, Lloyd George had delegated the task of acting for the British Government on this matter to Smuts and Cecil, who held to the Wilson view. By the time the Prime Minister appreciated how matters were running, it was too late. In order to reassert his own position he would have had to disavow his delegates and quite explicitly reject the President's position.[1] Further, the French, if they had to choose between the Wilson and the Lloyd George view, were bound to adopt the former. For that gave them at least part of what they wanted: collective security, if not an actual League army or exclusive attention to Germany. The Lloyd George view gave them nothing but a talking shop. And finally, if Lloyd George had to choose between an over-ambitious League of which the USA was a part and a more modest, 'realistic' League that lacked Wilson's endorsement, then he too was bound to come down on the President's side. For to him the preservation of the victory that had been won, and the abolition of future terrible blood-lettings, depended utterly on maintaining into peacetime the great coalition of Britain, France, and the USA. No course should be risked that might thoroughly alienate the American President.

Here is tragedy of a high order. Perhaps the wartime association of the great democracy of the New World with the principal democracies of the Old could not have been preserved in any circumstances. But the Treaty of Versailles in general, and the Wilson concept of a League of Nations in particular, served to bring that association abruptly to an end. The American Senate failed to adopt the treaty, principally because the League scheme that it embodied would take from America's own hands its fundamental conclusions concerning war and peace. It is indicative of the crucial part played in this decision by the League issue that the Senate, having rejected the treaty as originally presented, did give a simple majority (but not the required two-thirds majority) to a treaty containing 'reservations' concerning the authority of the League.

In consequence the USA did not enter the body whose form owed so much to the insistence of the American President. Other great powers also were absent. The Soviet Union had no wish to enter an instrument of world capitalism. Germany would not be permitted to join until it had shown that it was prepared to abide by the other provisions of the treaty of which the League Covenant was a part. So the principal members of the League became Britain and France, the countries whose leaders had resisted, respectively, its law-enforcing aspect and its universal application. It is not surprising that, during the two decades of its existence, the League was unable to fulfil the large expectations embodied in its charter.

Something else fell when the American Senate failed to ratify the treaty. As has been mentioned, the treaty was intended to be accompanied by a provision that, if seriously

---

[1] See George W. Egerton, 'The Lloyd George Government and the Creation of the League of Nations', *American Historical Review*, vol. 79, no. 2, April 1974.

meant, must serve as a telling deterrent against further German aggression towards France. This was the Anglo-American guarantee of automatic assistance to France should it be attacked. The repudiation of this provision by the Americans, and the failure of the British to replace it with at least a guarantee by themselves, is an event that deserves more attention than it usually receives. For it raises a fundamental problem. The question is often asked, and answered most variously: Why did the peace settlement fail? Given the USA's absence from the large peace-preserving body, and its rejection of this more limited aggression-deterring provision, it may well be wondered in what sense the peace settlement was ever implemented.

III

What, then, is to be the judgement passed on the Treaty of Versailles? From one viewpoint it was plainly too harsh. So it caused the Germans to rise against it as soon as they were able, and left the victor powers (particularly Britain) too conscious of its evils to spring to its defence. From a second viewpoint it was too lenient. It failed to inflict heavy punishment on the Germans for their aggression. So it encouraged them to aggress again, and left them with the power to do so successfully. A third view holds that it fell between these two stools. It went far enough in severity to create German resentment, without going far enough in severity to deprive Germany of the power with which to express that resentment. As one Frenchman summed up the treaty, it was 'too mild for the severity of its contents'.[2]

The argument that has been followed up to this point is suggestive of a rather different answer. Yet before that answer is spelled out this other issue, of the merits of the treaty, deserves to be faced.

The judgement offered here is that in most respects the treaty, though plainly a settlement imposed by victor upon vanquished (it could hardly have been anything else), was not excessively severe. The most controversial provision, concerning reparations, had some warrant, was soon modified, and before long was abandoned. The most predatory aspect, the confiscation of Germany's colonies, happened not to be a great deprivation. The mandatory separation of Austria from Germany was perhaps harsh in the case of Austria, given its now enfeebled condition. But it hardly ran contrary to the course of German history since 1848. As for other disputed proposals, like the establishment of Czechoslovakia and Poland as viable independent states, these appear actions both responsible and enlightened. The same may be said, with yet more confidence, about the redirection of the productive capacity of the Saar to France and Belgium for a set period, the demilitarization of the Rhineland, and the enforced limitations on German military power. No doubt, had European history followed a benevolent course after 1919, there might have come a time for revising some of these last aspects. But the revision that took place in the 1930s had nothing to do with a benevolent sequence of events. Nor did it spring from the ascendancy in Britain and France of statesmen more farsighted and impartial than had ruled there in 1919.

But to pass this judgement on the merits of the treaty is not to attempt an explanation as to why it failed. What is being suggested, rather, is that the treaty did not fail on account of its contents. It failed because the circumstances in which it was produced rapidly ceased to obtain. Even in 1919 the relative positions of victor and vanquished

[2] Quoted in Sir Llewellyn Woodward, *Great Britain and the War of 1914–1918* (London: Methuen, 1967), p. 585.

appeared precarious. Thereafter they were thoroughly undermined. The treaty born of the circumstances of 1919 was undermined also.

Throughout the war British spokesmen had insisted that the principal object of the war was to abolish German militarism. The manner in which this was to be accomplished they did not specify. It may be surmised that they were not very sure. Victory on the battlefield, it was taken for granted, would do much to accomplish it. And, certainly, with the ending of the war and the signing of the peace treaty many of the outward manifestations of German militarism stood abolished. The Kaiser, so often depicted as militarism's head and fount, had fled. Germany was in the process of becoming, at least as far as constitutional forms were concerned, a parliamentary democracy. Its army, navy, and air force had been abolished. Germany's wartime allies would not again rank as considerable powers. Germany itself had surrendered territory to neighbouring countries.

Yet how much had been accomplished? These changes may have left Germany a lesser power than it had been in 1914. It remained nevertheless a great power – the greatest industrial power on the Continent. So, though its instruments for waging war had been dispersed, its capacity for making war remained intact. The First World War, after all, had revealed one thing most plainly: that a country of little military tradition and an entrenched parliamentary system could in a very few years be converted into a major military (and air) power – as long as it had a great industrial base and ample manpower. In the light of Britain's wartime transformation, it was idle to imagine that a country of Germany's traditions and resources could be proclaimed demilitarized simply because its armed might had been dismantled and its system of government altered. Clearly, Germany possessed the potentiality for waging war at any time after 1919. Whether potentiality would be converted into actuality must depend on two things: whether the German people renounced such a course, and whether the victor powers possessed the will and the resources to give them no choice but to do so. The first is strictly an issue of German internal history. The second has much application to Britain.

For here is to be found the war's supreme paradox. It has just been noted that the war left Germany a lesser power than it had been in 1914. What must be stressed is that the same was true, and to an altogether greater degree, of its adversaries. There are no grounds for believing that the war was won by Britain alone, great though was its contribution. It was won by an association of four powers: Britain, France, Russia, and the USA. (The contribution of Italy and Serbia was largely against Austria-Hungary.) The role of Russia had been of great importance during the first three years: an important segment of Germany's energies had perforce been devoted to the Eastern Front. By 1919 the pre-war Franco-Russian alliance had vanished. Instead, a deep enmity existed between France and the Soviet Union. All that was left to constitute an Eastern Front against Germany in any future confrontation was the series of succession states, which even had they been capable of combining could not have filled the gap left by Russia's departure.

From 1917 to 1919 the disappearance of the Eastern Front had been compensated for by the entry into the lists of the USA. Lloyd George plainly saw in 1919 that the continuation of this alignment was crucial to the stability of Europe. But in 1920 this great and hopeful association was rudely terminated. The USA rejected the peace treaty, refused to enter the League of Nations, and withdrew into isolation. The power alignment of Europe was thrown fundamentally out of balance. Only two of the four members who together had accomplished the victory over Germany remained to uphold it.

For a time they continued to do so. But the cost proved heavy – as the French found in 1923 when they occupied the Ruhr. The will to impose the settlement proved not to be strong, particularly in Britain. Belief in the justice of doing so began to ebb away. And some forms of prudence suggested that the operation was ill-advised: that the principal business of capitalist powers must now be resistance to Communism, and that the Western democracies should not continue to thrust Germany into the arms of Bolshevik Russia.

Before long the attempt to preserve the Versailles concept of Germany as a defeated aggressor being kept under restraint, and Britain and France as the successful defenders against aggression exercising this restraint, was abandoned. The movement for restoration of equality of status gathered force. Germany entered the League of Nations as a great power; reparations were scaled down and financed by overseas loans; armaments in the West were reduced. From this point it became an open question which possessed the greater resources of power, Germany or the somewhat tattered association of France and Britain. It also became an open question whether Germany, having never lost its military potential, would seek to decide this question of power by converting potential into military actuality.

IV

In sum, the victory of 1918 and the peace settlement, certainly as they concerned Britain, were not decisive events. They were episodes in a trial of strength. In the nature of things they could not be complete. As the conjunction of forces that had accomplished the defeat of Germany did not prove permanent, neither did the victory and the settlement that followed it. This is not to say that the victory was anything less than a mighty achievement or that the settlement did not contain much that was sensible and beneficent. But high endeavours addressed to acts of war, and wise counsel directed to the making of peace, do not have it within themselves to accomplish permanent results. That will depend on other circumstances: most of all on the objective realities of power at the war's conclusion and in its aftermath.

Certainly, some wars may appear to accomplish long ends. That is because they are the manifestation and instrument of larger changes that are occurring. The Great War, as far as the victory of Britain and its associates was concerned, was not one of these. Yet failure to participate in the war, or inability to emerge on the victorious side, could for Britain have had drastic and long-lasting consequences. That is, success in avoiding defeat may for Britain have been the only major benefit that the war had to offer.

If that seemed less than satisfying after the event, and the peace settlement in its outcome therefore proved disappointing, this is not cause for wonder. Englishmen had come to take too seriously the grandiose promises that emerged during the course of the war. (Perhaps, given what the war was costing them, they were bound to do so.) So they allowed themselves to believe that this struggle would see the final overthrow of German militarism, even that this was a war that would end war. They failed to recall that these were not the reasons for which they had entered the struggle, reasons altogether more modest and hence capable of attainment. And they did not appreciate that the more grandiose results being promised could at best be fortunate by-products of victory. As it happened, the first of them (the final overthrow of German militarism) proved beyond the capabilities of this conflict. As for the second of them (that this war would end war), it might well be thought beyond the compass of any conflict.

There was a further reason why the outcome of the struggle soon came to seem disappointing. In asking what had been gained to offset the terrible costs of the war, Britons tended to look only at the condition of their country after 1918 as compared with its (rather fondly remembered) condition before 1914. They drew the reasonable conclusion that the gains were not great. What they were failing to notice was that this reckoning had no meaning. The world they recalled so nostalgically had ended abruptly the moment the first German soldier crossed into Belgian territory. Nothing could bring it back. Whatever Britain's response – to enter the war immediately, or only after France had been defeated, or not at all – the world of 1914 was gone forever.

There was only one valid comparison to be made, though it had to be speculative. That was the comparison between Britain as it was after the Allied victory and as it was likely to have been following a German triumph. Few people attempted this comparison. Some, for rhetorical purposes, appeared to be doing so. Thus Churchill wrote in the second volume of *The World Crisis* of a victory bought so dear as to be almost indistinguishable from defeat. And Siegfried Sassoon in mid-war (so he recounts in *Siegfried's Journey*) suffered anguish at the thought of 'the victory that is more terrible than defeat'. But these were not in truth statements about the nature of defeat. Rather, they were attempts, by means of hyperbole, to convey how heavy was the price of staving it off. Neither Churchill nor Sassoon was prepared to spell out the probable consequences of a British capitulation or of a French surrender consequent upon Britain's having stood aside from the struggle. Despite the potent message of Brest-Litovsk to suggest an answer, few people in Britain after 1919 were prepared to entertain that question.

77

TO WHAT PURPOSE?

I

One final question, then, remains. Had the war been for any worthwhile purpose, or was it simply a sustained exercise in futility?

A difference in attitude may be detected among historians towards the two great wars of this century. So the Second World War has been summed up by A. J. P. Taylor, in the concluding words of his book on that subject, as 'a good war'.[1] There are few historians who would say the same of the First World War. A. J. P. Taylor, for one, does not so judge it. The spirit of the Great War, to him, was epitomized by the song the British soldiers sang:

> We're here because we're here
> Because we're here
> Because we're here.

'The War,' he writes, 'in fact was fought for its own sake. . . . They fought because they fought because they·fought because they fought. The war was not a great tribute to human wisdom.'[2]

It is not surprising that the Great War excites these hostile judgements. For it was the first sustained demonstration of the monstrous powers for inflicting destruction that industrialization had bestowed upon Western man. And it was evidence that, armed with the warrant of national rivalry and ideological difference, Europeans would devotedly employ these destructive powers. The outcome was atrocious slaughter, squalid deeds contrasting with lofty promises, and an aftermath of blighted hopes culminating in another international bloodbath. In truth this hardly seems 'a great tribute to human wisdom'.

Yet although it is necessary to record this judgement, to leave it without qualification would be misleading. Admittedly, in the case of Britain no large transformation for either good or ill was set in motion. Yet some changes were accomplished that, at the time or subsequently, appeared advantageous.

We have already noticed how the war encouraged in Britain some acceleration of social reform and a rise in the living standards of the poorest sections. More agreeably for the imperially minded, it led to Britain's gaining (for a while) an enhanced position in the Middle East: former Turkish territories became the British mandates of Palestine, Trans-Jordan, and Iraq. It is difficult to believe that Britain had gone to war

---

[1] A. J. P. Taylor, *The Second World War: An Illustrated History* (London: Hamish Hamilton, 1975), p. 234.
[2] A. J. P. Taylor, 'The War in Perspective', in *Purnell's History of the First World War* (London: Purnell & Sons, 1969–71), issue no. 127, p. 3550.

to acquire these territories. But its rulers certainly willed the end of the Turkish Empire and were not averse to sharing in the spoils. Asquith had stated publicly in November 1914: 'It is the Ottoman Empire and not we who have rung the death-knell of Ottoman dominion, not only in Europe but in Asia.'[3] In private he indicated in March 1916 that as long as Turkey's imperial abdication was taking place, Britain would be in on the pickings. 'If for one reason or another . . . we were to leave the other nations to scramble for Turkey without taking anything for ourselves, we should not be doing our duty.'[4] (Duty, a word subject to much abuse in wartime, here meant the agreeable obligation to satisfy British self-interest.)

Of much greater moment than these imperial acquisitions, Britain had accomplished the elimination of the German navy. To an extent that no measure of German disarmament could do for France, the scuttling of the German fleet did provide Britain with a degree of security that even Germany's industrial strength could not speedily remove.

Less tangibly, but still of considerable note, the war had proved a striking vindication of the British way of life. Starting at a considerable disadvantage to other combatants, it had converted millions of untrained civilians into capable soldiers. It had sustained heavy losses without falling out of the struggle. It had revealed technical ingenuity, powers of scientific innovation, and a capacity for feats of productivity. Its politicians, administrative cadre, business community, and workforce had all displayed adaptability and dedication. Its community generally had summoned forth great reserves of endurance.

What was more, all this had been done without abandoning liberal precepts and the parliamentary system. Despite many lapses into beastliness, the fundamentals of a liberal community had been preserved. Conscientious objection to military service had been recognized as a valid position, even if those holding to it had been generally despised and even though particular conscientious objectors had been cruelly ill-used. The right to maintain dissenting opinions had been upheld, if only within certain limits, and Governments had never gone free of outspoken public criticism. The conviction that liberties suspended for the duration would indeed be restored at the earliest opportunity had remained firm. In its outcome the war had vindicated the liberal tenet that, when put to the test, an unregimented community would prove superior even in that undertaking which was supposed to be the special province of autocracies: the waging of war.

II

Nor can a discussion of the positive accomplishments of the war end there. For a question has many times suggested itself in these pages that can no longer be denied examination. The question can be expressed variously. If the destruction wrought by the war was great, were not the stakes also high? Was there, in fact, not much more at issue than fighting for the sake of fighting? Were not the Western Allies, notwithstanding much that was discreditable about them, upholding liberal democracy against a predatory military autocracy? These inquiries may be summed up in a single question: If the First World War, unlike the Second, could hardly be described as 'a good war', was it not also one of freedom's battles?

---

[3] Quoted in V. H. Rothwell, *British War Aims and Peace Diplomacy 1914–1918* (Oxford: Clarendon Press, 1971), p. 25.

[4] Quoted in Jukka Nevakivi, *Britain, France and the Arab Middle East 1914–20* (London: Athlone Press, 1969), p. 17.

Given the nature of the German political system and the threat that it posed from 1914 to 1918 to the parliamentary democracies of Western Europe, the onus of proof would seem to lie with those who wish to give a negative answer. Yet for those who reject such a notion, proof seems to abound. It lies in the dreadful, and to all appearances supremely futile, pitched battles, and the ferocious casualties that they exacted. It lies also in the outcome of this war not in a benevolent international climate but in a succession of crises culminating in a further holocaust.

But of what is this proof? It establishes the point, which governments in this century should not be allowed to forget, that a war even for entirely meritorious aims must carry with it a fearful risk: that not only will the cost be great, but it may threaten to become so great as to exceed the proposed benefits. It is possible, for example, to believe at the present time that falling under the sway of a communist aggressor is an unmitigated evil and yet to endorse the slogan 'Better Red than Dead'. After the Second World War the Conservative politician Lord Kennet, who as Hilton Young had fought with distinction in the Great War, made the decision that henceforth he was a pacifist. This did not mean that he repudiated his support for Britain's involvement in the wars of 1914–18 and 1939–45. Those conflicts, he judged, had resulted in the defeat of ruthless tyrannies at a cost that, although terrible, was capable of being borne. But the development of nuclear weapons had altered the nature of the transaction. No objective in a world war, however noble, could warrant the price now to be paid: wholesale annihilation. By the same token no alternative to world war, however terrible, could be as bad as the cost of waging it.

But this takes us back to the fundamental question. It goes without saying that the price of warding off defeat and achieving victory in the Great War was huge. But was the alternative, a German victory, not so repugnant as to justify the cost? In the aftermath of the First World War many Englishmen came round to the view that the game had not been worth the candle. Yet when confronted with markedly similar choices in 1939–40, and even though under no illusions about how heavy the cost might be, they nevertheless made the same decision as in 1914. For this, succeeding generations of Englishmen – even including historians not given to conformist judgements – have not seen fit to condemn them. In some circumstances, then, readiness to pay the price of 1914–18 seems to have been justified: Britons were prepared, if need be, to do it a second time in order to defeat Hitlerism. So were they simply suffering a failure in 'human wisdom' when they did it the first time, in order to defeat Kaiserism?

More than this, the issue of cost must not be allowed to blot out that other issue: the objective that pursuit of victory in the Great War was meant to accomplish, and did accomplish. The question must still be answered even by those who would argue that no goal could merit the destruction wrought by the war. To what purpose was this shedding of blood?

In what can only be offered as a piece of interpretation, the answer appears most starkly in a period of the war to which attention has already been drawn: the German successes against Britain's forces on the Western Front in March and April 1918. These events cast a terrifying illumination on what was at stake in this struggle. As is well known, in the midst of this crisis Haig issued to his troops an Order of the Day that included the passage: 'With our backs to the wall, and believing in the justice of our cause, each one of us must fight on to the end.' The concluding sentence of this appeal merits our attention: 'The safety of our homes and the freedom of mankind alike depend on the conduct of each one of us at this critical moment.' Now this might be dismissed as the empty rhetoric of an impoverished command. Yet there are grounds for not doing so. For somewhat earlier in the same crisis an identical view was being expressed in a notably different quarter. A passage in the radical periodical the *Nation*, quoted on a previous occasion, deserves repetition here. Massingham wrote:

> In the full brunt of the German assault on France, the true character of the war stands revealed. Vain projects of Imperialism obscured it, and vainer diversions of strategy. Both have disappeared. . . . The war emerges from these mists, not as a war of adventure but morally and physically as a war of defence. . . . The war was not for colonies, Imperial ambitions, or a balance of power. It was to teach militarism a lesson of restraint. . . .

What seems of particular note is the congruity between Haig's affirmation that the issue at stake was 'the safety of our homes and the freedom of mankind' and Massingham's characterization of the conflict as 'a war of defence', a war 'to teach militarism a lesson of restraint'. In short, despite their great differences in background and outlook, each was prepared to proclaim that this was in truth one of freedom's battles.

Perhaps, in so perceiving the conflict, the traditionalist Field-Marshal and the radical journalist were both deluded.

Perhaps, on the other hand, they were not.